*What They Said
in 1977*

What They Said In 1977

The Yearbook of Spoken Opinion

•

Compiled and Edited by

ALAN F. PATER

and

JASON R. PATER

MONITOR BOOK COMPANY, INC.

NINTH ANNUAL EDITION

Printed in the United States of America

Library of Congress catalogue card number 74-111080

ISBN number: 0-917734-01-7

WHAT THEY SAID is published annually by Monitor Book
Company, Inc., Beverly Hills, California. The title, "WHAT THEY
SAID," is a trademark owned exclusively by Monitor Book
Company, Inc., and has been duly registered with the United States
Patent Office. Any unauthorized use is prohibited.

To

The Newsmakers of the World . . .

May they never be at a loss for words

Preface to the First Edition (1969)

Words can be powerful or subtle, humorous or maddening. They can be vigorous or feeble, lucid or obscure, inspiring or despairing, wise or foolish, hopeful or pessimistic ... they can be fearful or confident, timid or articulate, persuasive or perverse, honest or deceitful. As tools at a speaker's command, words can be used to reason, argue, discuss, cajole, plead, debate, declaim, threaten, infuriate, or appease; they can harangue, flourish, recite, preach, discourse, stab to the quick, or gently sermonize.

When casually spoken by a stage or film star, words can go beyond the press-agentry and make-up facade and reveal the inner man or woman. When purposefully uttered in the considered phrasing of a head of state, words can determine the destiny of millions of people, resolve peace or war, or chart the course of a nation on whose direction the fate of the entire world may depend.

Until now, the *copia verborum* of well-known and renowned public figures—the doctors and diplomats, the governors and generals, the potentates and presidents, the entertainers and educators, the bishops and baseball players, the jurists and journalists, the authors and attorneys, the congress-men and chairmen-of-the-board—whether enunciated in speeches, lectures, interviews, radio and television addresses, news conferences, forums, symposiums, town meetings, committee hearings, random remarks to the press, or delivered on the floors of the United States Senate and House of Representatives or in the parliaments and palaces of the world—have been dutifully reported in the media, then filed away and, for the most part, forgotten.

The editors of *WHAT THEY SAID* believe that consigning such a wealth of thoughts, ideas, doctrines, opinions and philosophies to interment in the morgues and archives of the Fourth Estate is lamentable and unnecessary. Yet the media, in all their forms, are constantly engulfing us in a profusion of endless and increasingly voluminous news reports. One is easily disposed to disregard or forget the stimulating discussion of critical issues embodied in so many of the utterances of those who make the news and, in their respective fields, shape the events throughout the world. The conclusion is therefore a natural and compelling one: the educator, the public official, the business executive, the statesman, the philosopher—everyone who has a stake in the complex, often confusing trends of our times—should have material of this kind readily available.

These, then, are the circumstances under which *WHAT THEY SAID* was conceived. It is the culmination of a year of listening to the people in the public eye; a year of scrutinizing, monitoring, reviewing, judging, deciding—a year during which the editors resurrected from almost certain oblivion those quintessential elements of the year's *spoken* opinion which, in their judgment, demanded preservation in book form.

WHAT THEY SAID is a pioneer in its field. Its *raison d'etre* is the firm conviction that presenting, each year, the highlights of vital and interesting views from the lips of prominent people on virtually every aspect of contemporary civilization fulfills the need to give the *spoken* word the permanence and lasting value of the *written* word. For, if it is true that a picture is worth 10,000 words, it is equally true that a verbal conclusion, an apt quote or a candid comment by a person of fame or influence can have more significance and can provide more understanding than an entire page of summary in a standard work of reference.

The editors of *WHAT THEY SAID* did not, however, design their book for researchers and scholars alone. One of the failings of the conventional reference work is that it is blandly written and referred to primarily for facts and figures, lacking inherent "interest value." *WHAT THEY SAID*, on the other hand, was planned for sheer enjoyment and pleasure, for searching glimpses into the lives and thoughts of the world's celebrities, as well as for serious study, intellectual reflection and the philosophical contemplation of our multifaceted life and mores. Furthermore, those pressed for time, yet anxious to know what the newsmakers have been saying, will welcome the short excerpts which will make for quick, intermittent reading—and rereading. And, of course, the topical classifications, the speakers' index, the subject index, the place and date information—documented and authenticated and easily located—will supply a rich fund of hitherto not readily obtainable reference and statistical material.

Finally, the reader will find that the editors have eschewed trite comments and cliches, tedious and boring. The selected quotations, each standing on its own, are pertinent, significant, stimulating—above all, relevant to today's world, expressed in the speakers' own words. And they will, the editors feel, be even more relevant tomorrow. They will be re-examined and reflected upon in the future by men and women eager to learn from the past. The prophecies, the promises, the "golden dreams," the boastings and rantings, the bluster, the bravado, the pleadings and representations of those whose voices echo in these pages (and in those to come) should provide a rare and unique history lesson. The positions held by these luminaries, in their respective callings, are such that what they say today may profoundly affect the future as well as the present, and so will be of lasting importance and meaning.

ALAN F. PATER
JASON R. PATER

Beverly Hills, California

x

Table of Contents

Preface to the First Edition (1969)   *ix*

About the 1977 Edition   *xiii*

Editorial Treatment   *xvii*

Abbreviations   *xxi*

The Quote of the Year   *xxv*

PART ONE: *NATIONAL AFFAIRS*

The State of the Union Address (Gerald R. Ford)   3
Presidential Inaugural Address (Jimmy Carter)   10
The American Scene   13
Civil Rights   18
Commerce / Industry / Finance   29
Crime / Law Enforcement   52
Education   61
The Environment   75
    Energy   81
Foreign Affairs   97
    Intelligence   126
Government   129
Labor / The Economy   150
Law / The Judiciary   174
National Defense / The Military   181
Politics   201
Social Welfare   220
Transportation   228
Urban Affairs   239

PART TWO: *INTERNATIONAL AFFAIRS*

Africa   245

The Americas   263
Asia and the Pacific   285
Europe   302
The Middle East   324
The United Nations / War and Peace   345

PART THREE: GENERAL

The Arts   353
Journalism   359
Literature   373
Medicine and Health   383
The Performing Arts
    Motion Pictures   398
    Music   421
    The Stage   431
    Television and Radio   442

Personal Profiles   457
Philosophy   464
Religion   478
Space / Science / Technology   483
Sports   487
Women's Rights   512

Index to Speakers   523
Index to Subjects   539

About the 1977 Edition . . .

THE uniqueness of *WHAT THEY SAID* is that it is totally devoted to words—spoken words—by the men and women who make the news and shape the world. So it is natural that, in each annual volume, certain key words and phrases will stand out as hallmarks of the particular twelve-month period covered. The 1977 edition of *WHAT THEY SAID* is no exception.

Nineteen seventy-seven will be remembered as the year of "human rights," or at least the year when that phrase blanketed the world in connection with foreign policy. Other by-words of 1977 include "laetrile," the controversial cancer drug; "rebate," part of a tax return plan which never materialized; "saccharin," the announced ban of which led to public clamor to keep the artificial sweetener available; "Jubilee," celebrating Queen Elizabeth's 25th anniversary as Britain's monarch. "Concorde" and "Skytrain" became key words for people on the go. "Illegal aliens," "neutron bomb," "cruise missile"—all these, and more, became vernacular in 1977.

The names of 1977 include such diverse personages as Menachem Begin, Bert Lance, Morarji Desai, Freddie Laker, Tongsun Park, Andrew Young, and others for whom 1977 was the year of their debut in the world spotlight.

With no intention of being a complete news summary of 1977, following are some of the happenings reflected in many of this year's quotations . . .

Civil Rights:

The Bakke reverse-discrimination case sought to establish whether a white person could be denied entrance to a university in favor of a minority person with fewer qualifications.

Singer Anita Bryant opposed a Dade County, Fla., statute which would have banned discrimination against homosexuals in a variety of employment and housing situations.

Commerce:

Farmers demanded more government financial aid.
Business ethics remained a much-discussed topic.
Government regulation of business continued to be debated.
The U. S. steel industry was adversely affected by increased imports.

WHAT THEY SAID IN 1977

Crime:

Terrorism, and how to deal with it, became a growing concern for law-enforcement officials.

Capital punishment continued to be a contested issue.

Education:

Parents and school groups increased their calls for a return to basic reading, writing and arithmetic instruction.

Vocational education received a new impetus in many schools and colleges, as a result of a perceived need for job-related skills in the current economy.

Energy:

Imported oil continued to increase, despite government warnings of dangerous dependence and balance-of-payments deficits.

A national energy program was proposed by President Carter but was held up in Congressional debate.

Nuclear power remained the subject of widespread pro and con discussion.

Foreign Affairs:

Human rights became a criterion of President Jimmy Carter's foreign policy.

The outspokenness of new U. S. United Nations Ambassador Andrew Young stirred much controversy.

Government:

The Carter Administration took office and promised a reorganization of government operations to restore confidence and fiscal responsibility.

Continued debate centered on government influence and regulation of business and individuals.

Labor/Economy:

As a spur to an economy suffering from inflation and unemployment, President Carter suggested a $50 tax rebate to all citizens. However, this idea was withdrawn before implementation.

Law/Judiciary:

The re-introduction of lawyer advertising sparked controversy.

National Defense/The Military:

Development of the cruise missile was chosen over the B-1 bomber.

Debate was generated as to whether deployment of the neutron bomb would increase or decrease the threat of war.

President Carter fulfilled his promise to pardon U. S. Vietnam war draft resisters.

Politics:

New Federal Budget Director Bert Lance resigned amidst Congressional hearings into his past financial dealings.

A scandal involving South Korean businessman Tongsun Park over alleged payments to members of the U. S. Congress became a focal point of a government investigation.

Former President Richard Nixon talked about Watergate and other subjects in a multi-part television interview.

Transportation:

The British-French *Concorde* SST was finally granted permission to operate from New York's Kennedy Airport.

British airline operator Freddie Laker substantially cut trans-Atlantic fares with his "Skytrain" service.

The government strongly indicated its desire to scale down regulation of the airline industry.

Africa:

The controversial death of black leader Steve Biko complicated an already menacing racial situation in South Africa.

Rhodesian Prime Minister Ian Smith began negotiations to institute a one-man, one-vote policy in an attempt to smooth racial tensions in his country.

Cuba's expanding manpower and influence in Africa disturbed Western nations.

Hostilities in the Horn of Africa prompted increasing attention from Eastern and Western powers.

Americas:

U. S.-Panamanian negotiations produced treaties which would gradually turn over control of the Panama Canal to Panama. The U. S. Congress prepared to begin debate on the measures.

U. S.-Cuban relations hit a snag as a result of Cuba's increasing presence in Africa.

Asia:

Indian Prime Minister Indira Gandhi was turned out of office in an election which installed Morarji Desai.

WHAT THEY SAID IN 1977

The U. S. announced a plan to gradually withdraw its ground forces from South Korea.

Europe:

There were continuing signs of possible Communist election victories in several Western European countries.

The Soviet Union vigorously defied U. S. criticism of human rights violations inside Russia.

Britain celebrated Queen Elizabeth's Silver Jubilee.

Middle East:

Israeli Prime Minister Yitzhak Rabin lost a national election to Menachem Begin, who became the country's new leader.

Egyptian President Anwar Sadat made an unprecedented visit to Israel to talk peace with Israeli Prime Minister Begin.

Journalism:

The increasing dominance of newspaper chains, and the resultant loss of locally owned, independent papers, was a subject of concern around the country.

Medicine:

The drug laetrile remained unapproved by the Federal Food and Drug Administration, which claimed that it was ineffective in the treatment of cancer, and potentially dangerous.

Laboratory tests on animals showing a link between saccharin and cancer led to the government's announcing a ban of the artificial sweetener.

·Increasing medical and hospital costs and U. S. national health insurance continued to be debated.

Sports:

Baseball Commissioner Bowie Kuhn's judgments regarding proposed trades and sales of players initiated much heated discussion on the purpose and powers of the Commissioner's office.

Violence in sports continued as a hot issue.

Women's Rights:

The Equal Rights Amendment remained in limbo as time began running out for its passage.

Editorial Treatment

ORGANIZATION OF MATERIAL

Special attention has been given to the arrangement of the book—from the major divisions down to the individual categories and speakers—the objective being a logical progression of related material as follows:

(A)   The categories are arranged alphabetically within each of three major sections:

Part One:	"National Affairs"
Part Two:	"International Affairs"
Part Three:	"General"

In this manner, the reader can quickly locate quotations pertaining to particular fields of interest (see also *Indexing*). It should be noted that some quotations contain a number of thoughts or ideas—sometimes on different subjects—while some are vague as to exact subject matter and thus do not fit clearly into a specific topic classification. In such cases, the judgment of the Editors has determined the most appropriate category.

(B)   Within each category, the speakers are in alphabetical order by surname, following alphabetization practices used in the speaker's country of origin.

(C)   Where there are two or more quotations by one speaker within the same category, they appear chronologically by date spoken or date of source.

SPEAKER IDENTIFICATION

(A)   The occupation, profession, rank, position or title of the speaker is given as it was *at the time the statement was made* (except when the speaker's relevant identification is in the past, in which case he is shown as "former"). Thus, due to possible changes in status during the year, a speaker may be shown with different identification in various portions of the book, or even within the same category.

(B)   In the case of speakers who hold more than one position or occupation simultaneously (or who held relevant positions in the past), the judgment of the Editors has determined the most appropriate identification to use with a specific quotation.

(C)   Nationality of speakers is normally not given unless this information is of interest or relative to the quotation(s).

THE QUOTATIONS

The quoted material selected for inclusion in this book is shown as it appeared in the source, except as follows:

(A) *Ellipses* have been inserted wherever the Editors have deleted extraneous words or overly long passages within the quoted material used. In no way has the meaning or intention of any quotation been altered. *Ellipses* are also used where they appeared in the source.

(B) *Punctuation and spelling* have been altered by the Editors where they were obviously incorrect in the source, or to make the quotations more intelligible, or to conform to the general style used throughout this book. Again, meaning or intention of the quotation has not been changed.

(C) *Brackets* ([ ]) indicate material inserted by the Editors or by the source to either correct obvious errors or to explain and/or clarify what the speaker is saying.

(D) *Italics* have sometimes been added by the Editors where emphasis is clearly desirable.

Except for the above instances, the quoted material used has been printed verbatim, as reported by the source (even if the speaker made factual errors or was awkward in his choice of words).

Special care has been exercised to make certain that each quotation stands on its own merits and is not taken "out of context." The Editors, however, cannot be responsible for errors made by the original newspaper, periodical or other source, i.e., incorrect reporting, mis-quotations or errors in interpretation.

DOCUMENTATION AND SOURCES

Documentation (circumstance, place, date) of each quotation is provided as fully as could be obtained, and the sources are furnished for all quotations. In some instances no documentation details were available; in those cases only the source is given. Following are the sequence and style used for this information:

Circumstance of quotation, place, date/ Name of source, date: section (if applicable), page number.

Example: *Before the Senate, Washington, Dec. 4/ The Washington Post, 12:6:(A)13.*

The above example indicates that the quotation was delivered before the Senate in Washington on December 4. It was taken for *WHAT THEY SAID* from *The Washington Post,* issue of December 6, section A, page 13. (When a newspaper publishes more than one edition on the same date, it should be noted that page numbers may vary from edition to edition.)

(A) When the source is a television or radio broadcast, the name of the network or local station is indicated, along with the date of the broadcast (obviously, page and/or section information does not apply).

(B) One asterisk (*) before the (/) in the documentation indicates that the quoted material was written rather than spoken. Although the basic policy of *WHAT THEY SAID* is to use only *spoken* statements, there are occasions when written statements are considered by the Editors to be important enough to be included. These occasions are rare and usually involve Presidential messages, Presidential statements released to the press and other such documents attributed to a person in high government office.

(C) Two asterisks (**) after the (/) indicate the speaker supplied the quotation to *WHAT THEY SAID* directly.

INDEXING

(A)   The *Index to Speakers* is keyed to the page number. (For alphabetization practices, see *Organization of Material,* paragraph B.)

(B)   The *Index to Subjects* is keyed to both the page number and the quotation number on the page (thus, 210:3 indicates quotation number 3 on page 210); the quotation number appears at upper right-hand corner of each quotation.

(C)   To locate quotations on a particular subject, regardless of speaker, turn to the appropriate category (see *Table of Contents)* or use the detailed *Index to Subjects.*

(D)   To locate all quotations by a particular speaker, regardless of subject, use the *Index to Speakers.*

(E)   To locate quotations by a particular speaker on a particular subject, turn to the appropriate category and then to that person's quotations within that category.

(F)   The reader will find that the basic categorization format of *WHAT THEY SAID* is itself a useful subject index, inasmuch as related quotations are grouped together by their respective categories. All aspects of journalism, for example, are relevant to each other; thus, the section *Journalism* embraces all phases of the news media. Similarly, quotations pertaining to the U.S. Presidency, Congress, revenue-sharing, etc., are together in the section *Government.*

MISCELLANEOUS

(A)   Except where otherwise indicated or obviously to the contrary, all universities, colleges, organizations and business firms mentioned in this book are located in the United States; similarly, references made to "national," "Federal," "this country," "the nation," etc., refer to the United States.

(B)   In most cases, organizations whose titles end with "of the United States" are Federal government agencies.

SELECTION OF CATEGORIES

The selected categories reflect, in the Editors' opinion, the most widely discussed public-interest subjects, those which readily fall into the over-all sphere of "current events." They represent topics continuously covered by the mass media because of their inherent relevance to the changing world scene. Most of the categories are permanent; they appear in each annual edition of *WHAT THEY SAID.* However, because of the transient character of some subjects, there may be categories which appear one year and may not be repeated.

SELECTION OF SPEAKERS

The following persons are *always* considered eligible for inclusion in *WHAT THEY SAID:* top-level officials of all branches of national, state and major local governments (both U.S. and foreign), including all United States Senators and Representatives; top-echelon military officers;

college and university presidents, chancellors and professors; chairmen and presidents of major corporations; heads of national public-oriented organizations and associations; national and internationally known diplomats; recognized celebrities from the entertainment and literary spheres and the arts generally; sports figures of national stature; commentators on the world scene who are recognized as such and who command the attention of the mass media.

The determination of what and who are "major" and "recognized" must, necessarily, be made by the Editors of *WHAT THEY SAID* based on objective personal judgment.

Also, some persons, while not recognized as prominent in a particular professional area, have nevertheless attracted an unusual amount of attention in connection with a specific issue or event. These people, too, are considered for inclusion, depending upon the circumstances involved.

SELECTION OF QUOTATIONS

The quotations selected for inclusion in *WHAT THEY SAID* obviously represent a decided minority of the seemingly endless volume of quoted material appearing in the media each year. The process of selection is scrupulously objective insofar as the partisan views of the Editors are concerned (see *About Fairness,* below). However, it is clear that the Editors must decide which quotations *per se* are suitable for inclusion, and in doing so look for comments that are aptly stated, offer insight into the subject being discussed, or into the speaker, and provide—for today as well as for future reference—a thought which readers will find useful for understanding the issues and the personalities that make up a year on this planet.

ABOUT FAIRNESS

The Editors of *WHAT THEY SAID* understand the necessity of being impartial when compiling a book of this kind. As a result, there has been no bias in the selection of the quotations, the choice of speakers or the manner of editing. Relevance of the statements and the status of the speakers are the exclusive criteria for inclusion, without any regard whatsoever to the personal beliefs and views of the Editors. Furthermore, every effort has been made to include a multiplicity of opinions and ideas from a wide cross-section of speakers on each topic. Nevertheless, should there appear to be, on some controversial issues, a majority of material favoring one point of view over another, it is simply the result of there having been more of those views expressed during the year, reported by the media and objectively considered suitable by the Editors of *WHAT THEY SAID* (see *Selection of Quotations,* above). Also, since persons in politics and government account for a large percentage of the speakers in *WHAT THEY SAID,* there may exist a heavier weight of opinion favoring the political philosophy of those in office at the time, whether in the United States Congress, the Administration, or in foreign capitals. This is natural and to be expected and should not be construed as a reflection of agreement or disagreement with that philosophy on the part of the Editors of *WHAT THEY SAID.*

Abbreviations

The following are abbreviations used by the speakers in this volume. Rather than defining them each time they appear in the quotations, this list will facilitate reading and avoid unnecessary repetition.

ABA:	American Basketball Association
ABC:	American Broadcasting Companies
AFGE:	American Federation of Government Employees
AFL-CIO:	American Federation of Labor-Congress of Industrial Organizations
AMA:	American Medical Association
AP:	Associated Press
ASEAN:	Association of Southeast Asian Nations
BBC:	British Broadcasting Corporation
CAB:	Civil Aeronautics Board
CBS:	Columbia Broadcasting System (CBS, Inc.)
CENTO:	Central Treaty Organization
CEO:	chief executive officer
CIA:	Central Intelligence Agency
DOT:	Department of Transportation
EEC:	European Economic Community
EEOC:	Equal Employment Opportunity Commission
EKG:	electrocardiogram
ERA:	Equal Rights Amendment
FBI:	Federal Bureau of Investigation
FCC:	Federal Communications Commission
FDA:	Food and Drug Administration
FHA:	Federal Housing Administration
FTC:	Federal Trade Commission
GAO:	General Accounting Office
GBS:	George Bernard Shaw
GM:	General Motors Corporation
GNP:	gross national product
HEW:	Department of Health, Education and Welfare
HUD:	Department of Housing and Urban Development

ICBM:	intercontinental ballistic missile
ICC:	Interstate Commerce Commission
ILO:	International Labor Organization
INS:	Immigration and Naturalization Service
IOC:	International Olympic Committee
IQ:	intelligence quotient
IRS:	Internal Revenue Service
ITT:	International Telephone & Telegraph Corporation
JCS:	Joint Chiefs of Staff
KGB:	Soviet secret police
LSD:	Lysergic acid diethylamide (drug)
MGM:	Metro-Goldwyn-Mayer, Inc.
MIRV:	multiple independently targeted re-entry vehicles
MPAA:	Motion Picture Association of America
NAACP:	National Association for the Advancement of Colored People
NASA:	National Aeronautics and Space Administration
NATO:	North Atlantic Treaty Organization; National Association of Theatre Owners
NBA:	National Basketball Association
NBC:	National Broadcasting Company
NFC:	National Football Conference
NFL:	National Football League
OAS:	Organization of American States
OAU:	Organization of African Unity
OMB:	Office of Management and Budget
OPEC:	Organization of Petroleum Exporting Countries
OSHA:	Occupational Safety and Health Administration
PBS:	Public Broadcasting Service
PLO:	Palestine Liberation Organization
P.R.:	public relations
PTA:	Parent-Teachers Association
SALT:	strategic arms limitation talks

SAT: Scholastic Aptitude Test
SEATO: Southeast Asia Treaty Organization
SEC: Securities and Exchange Commission
SST: supersonic transport
TV: television
UAW: United Automobile Workers (of America)
UFO: unidentified flying object
UN: United Nations
UNESCO: United Nations Educational, Scientific and Cultural Organization
UPI: United Press International
U.S.:   United States
U.S.A.:   United States of America
USAC: United States Auto Club
U.S.S.R.:   Union of Soviet Socialist Republics
VISTA: Volunteers in Service to America
VOA: Voice of America
WASP: white Anglo-Saxon Protestant
WCT: World Championship Tennis
WFL: World Football League
WHL: World Hockey Association

Party affiliation of United States Senators, Representatives and Governors—

D: Democratic
R: Republican

The Quote of the Year

"Peace is not a mere endorsement of written lines. Rather, it is a rewriting of history. Peace is not a game of calling for peace to defend certain whims or hide certain admissions. Peace in its essence is a dire struggle against all and every ambition and whim. Perhaps the example taken and experienced, taken from ancient and modern history, teaches that missiles, warships and nuclear weapons cannot establish security. Instead, they destroy what peace and security build."

ANWAR EL-SADAT
President of Egypt

Before the Israeli Knesset (Parliament), Jerusalem, November 20

What They Said
in 1977

National Affairs

The State of the Union Address

Delivered by Gerald R. Ford, President of the United States, to a joint session of Congress, in the House of Representatives, Washington, January 12, 1977.

In accordance with the Constitution, I come before you once again to report on the State of the Union.

This report will be my last.

But for the Union, it is only the first of such reports in our third century of independence, the close of which none of us will see. We can be confident, however, that 100 years from now a freely elected President will come before a freely chosen Congress to renew our great republic's pledge to government of the people, by the people, for the people.

For my part, I pray the third century we are beginning will bring to all Americans, our children and their children's children, a greater measure of individual equality, opportunity and justice, a greater abundance of spiritual and material blessings, and a higher quality of life, liberty and the pursuit of happiness.

The State of the Union is a measurement of the many elements of which it is composed — a political union of diverse states, an economic union of varying interests, an intellectual union of common convictions and a moral union of immutable ideals.

Taken in sum, I can report that the State of the Union is good. There is room for improvement as always, but today we have a more perfect union than when my stewardship began.

As a people, we discovered that our Bicentennial was much more than a celebration of the past; it became a joyous reaffirmation of all that it means to be Americans, a confirmation before all the world of the vitality and durability of our free institutions.

I am proud to have been privileged to preside over the affairs of our Federal Government during these eventful years when we proved, as I said in my first words upon assuming office, that "our Constitution works; our great republic is a Government of laws and not of men; here, the people rule."

Transition of Leadership

The people have spoken; they have chosen a new President and a new Congress to work their will; I congratulate you — particularly the new members — as sincerely as I did President-elect Carter. In a few days, it will be his duty to outline for you his priorities and legislative recommendations. Tonight, I will not infringe on that responsibility, but rather wish him the very best in all that is good for our country.

During the period of my own service in this Capitol and in the White House, I can recall many orderly transitions of governmental responsibility — of problems as well as of position, of burdens as well as of power.

The genius of the American system is that we do this so naturally and normally. There are no soldiers marching in the streets except in the inaugural parade; no public demonstrations except for some of the dancers at the inaugural ball; the opposition party doesn't go underground but goes on functioning vigorously in the Congress and the country, and our vigilant press goes right on probing and publishing our faults and follies, confirming the wisdom of the framers of the First Amendment.

Because the transfer of authority in our form of government affects the state of the union, and of the world, I am happy to report to you that the current transition is proceeding very well. I was determined that it should; I wanted the new President to get off to an easier start than I had.

Past Problems

When I became President on August 9, 1974, our nation was deeply divided and tormented. In rapid succession, the Vice President and the

3

President had resigned in disgrace. We were still struggling with the after-effects of a long, unpopular and bloody war in Southeast Asia.

The economy was unstable and racing toward the worst recession in 40 years. People were losing jobs. The cost of living was soaring. The Congress and the chief executive were at loggerheads. The integrity of our constitutional process and of other institutions was being questioned.

For more than 15 years, domestic spending had soared as Federal programs multiplied and the expense escalated annually. During the same period, our national security needs were steadily shortchanged.

In the grave situation which prevailed in August, 1974, our will to maintain our international leadership was in doubt.

I asked for your prayers, and went to work.

In January, 1975, I reported to the Congress that the state of the union was not good. I proposed urgent action to improve the economy and to achieve energy independence in ten years. I reassured America's allies and sought to reduce the danger of confrontation with potential adversaries. I pledged a new direction for America.

Nineteen seventy-five was a year of difficult decisions, but Americans responded with realism, common sense and self-discipline.

By January, 1976, we were headed in a new direction, which I hold to be the right direction for a free society. I was guided by the belief that successful problem-solving requires more than Federal action alone; that it involves a full partnership among all branches and levels of government, and public policies which nurture and promote the creative energies of private enterprises, institutions and individual citizens.

A year ago, I reported that the state of the union was better — in many ways a lot better — but still not good enough.

Common sense told me to stick to the steady course we were on, to continue to restrain the inflationary growth of government, to reduce taxes as well as spending, to return local decisions to local people, to provide for long-range sufficiency in energy and national security needs.

I resisted the immense pressures of an election year to open the floodgates of Federal money and the temptation to promise more than I could deliver. I told it as it was to the American people and demonstrated to the world that, in our spirited political competition, as in this chamber, Americans can disagree without being disagreeable.

Now, after 30 months as your President, I can say that while we still have a way to go, I am proud of the long way we have come together.

I am proud of the part I have had in rebuilding confidence in the Presidency, confidence in our free system and confidence in our future. Once again, Americans believe in themselves, in their leaders, and in the promise that tomorrow holds for their children.

I am proud that today America is at peace. None of our sons are fighting and dying in battle anywhere in the world. And the chance for peace among all nations is improved by our determination to honor our vital commitments in the defense of peace and freedom.

I am proud that the United States has strong defenses, strong alliances and a sound and courageous foreign policy.

Foreign Relations

Our alliances with our major partners, the great industrial democracies of Western Europe, Japan, and Canada, have never been more solid. Consultations on mutual security, defense and East-West relations have grown closer. Collaboration has branched out into new fields, such as energy, economic policy and relations with the Third World.

We have used many avenues for cooperation, including summit meetings held among major allied countries. The friendship of the democracies is deeper, warmer and more effective than at any time in 30 years.

We are maintaining stability in the strategic nuclear balance, and pushing back the spectre of nuclear war. A decisive step forward was taken in the Vladivostok accord which I negotiated with General Secretary Brezhnev — joint recognition that an equal ceiling should be placed on the number of strategic weapons on each side.

With resolve and wisdom on the part of both nations, a good agreement is well within reach this year.

The framework for peace in the Middle East has been built. Hopes for future progress in the Middle East were stirred by the historic agreements we reached and the trust and confidence we formed.

Thanks to American leadership, the prospects for peace in the Middle East are brighter than they have been in three decades. The Arab states and Israel continue to look to us to lead them from confrontation and war to a new era of accommodation and peace. We have no alternative but to persevere. The opportunities for a final settlement are great, and the price of failure is a return to the bloodshed and hatred that for too long have brought tragedy to all the peoples of this area, and repeatedly edged the world to the brink of war.

Our relationship with the People's Republic of China is proving its importance and its durability. We are finding more and more common ground between our two countries on basic questions of international affairs.

In my two trips to Asia as President, we have reaffirmed America's continuing vital interest in the peace and security of Asia and the Pacific basin, established a new partnership with Japan, confirmed our dedication to the security of South Korea, and reinforced our ties with the free nations of Southeast Asia.

An historic dialogue has begun between industrial nations and the developing nations. Most proposals on the table are initiatives of the United States, including those on food, energy, technology, trade, investment and commodities. We are well launched on this process of shaping positive and reliable economic relations between rich nations and poor nations over the long term.

We have made progress in trade negotiations and avoided protectionism during recession. We strengthened the international monetary system. During the past two years the free world's most important economic powers have already brought about important changes that serve both developed and developing economies. The

momentum already achieved must be nurtured and strengthened, for the prosperity of rich and poor depends upon it.

In Latin America, our relations have taken on a new maturity and a sense of common enterprise.

In Africa, the quest for peace, racial justice and economic progress is at a crucial point. The United States, in close cooperation with the United Kingdom, is actively engaged in that historic process. Will change come about by warfare and chaos and foreign intervention? Or will it come about by negotiated and fair solutions, ensuring majority rule, minority rights and economic advance? America is committed to the side of peace and justice, and to the principle that Africa should shape its own future free of outside intervention.

American leadership has helped to stimulate new international efforts to stem the proliferation of nuclear weapons and to shape a comprehensive treaty governing the use of the oceans.

I am gratified by these accomplishments. They constitute a record of broad success for America, and for the peace and prosperity of all mankind. This administration leaves to its successor a world in better condition than we found. We leave, as well, a solid foundation for progress on a range of issues that are vital to the well being of America.

Foreign-Policy Formulation

What has been achieved in the field of foreign affairs, and what can be accomplished by the new administration, demonstrate the genius of Americans working together for the common good. It is this, our remarkable ability to work together, that has made us a unique nation. It is Congress, the President, and the people striving for a better world.

I know all patriotic Americans want this nation's foreign policy to succeed.

I urge members of my party in the Congress to give the new President loyal support in this area.

I express the hope that this new Congress will re-examine its constitutional role in international affairs.

5

The exclusive right to declare war, the duty to advise and consent on the part of the Senate, and the power of the purse on the part of the House, are ample authority for the legislative branch and should be jealously guarded.

But because we may have been too careless of these powers in the past does not justify Congressional intrusion into, or obstruction of, the proper exercise of Presidential responsibilities now or in the future. There can be only one commander-in-chief. In these times, crises cannot be managed and wars cannot be waged by committee. Nor can peace be pursued solely by parliamentary debate. To the ears of the world, the President speaks for the nation. While he is, of course, ultimately accountable to the Congress, the courts and the people, he and his emissaries must not be handicapped in advance in their relations with foreign governments as has sometimes happened in the past.

Economic Issues

At home, I am encouraged by the nation's recovery from the recession and our steady return to sound economic growth. It is now continuing after the recent period of uncertainty which is part of the price we pay for free elections.

Our most pressing need today and in the future is more jobs — productive and permanent jobs created by a thriving economy.

We must revise our tax system, both to ease the burden of heavy taxation and to encourage the investment necessary for the creation of productive jobs for all Americans who want to work. Earlier this month I proposed a permanent income tax reduction of $10 billion below current levels, including raising the personal exemption from $750 to $1,000.

I also recommended a series of measures to stimulate investment, such as accelerated depreciation for new plants and equipment in areas of high unemployment, a reduction in the corporate tax rate from 48 to 46 percent, and eliminating the present double taxation of dividends.

I strongly urge the Congress to pass these measures to help create the productive, permanent jobs in the private economy that are essential to our future. All of the basic trends are good; we are not on the brink of another recession or economic disaster. If we follow prudent policies that encourage productive investment and discourage destructive inflation, we will come out on top.

We have successfully cut inflation by more than half: when I took office, the consumer price index was rising at 12.2 percent a year. During 1976, the rate of inflation was five percent.

We have created more jobs. Over four million more people have jobs today than in the spring of 1975. Throughout this nation today we have over 88 million people in useful, productive work — more than at any other time in our history. But there are still too many Americans unemployed. This is my greatest regret as I leave office.

Local Issues

We brought about with the Congress, after much delay, the renewal of general revenue sharing. We expanded community development and Federal manpower programs. We began a significant urban mass-transit program. Federal programs today provide more funds for our states and local governments than ever before — $70 billion for the current fiscal year.

Through these programs, and others that provide aid directly to individuals, we have kept faith with our tradition of compassionate help for those who need it. As we begin our third century, we can be proud of the progress we have made in meeting human needs for all of our citizens.

We have cut the growth of crime by nearly 90 percent. Two years ago, crime was increasing at a rate of 18 percent annually. In the first three quarters of 1976, that growth rate had been reduced to 2 percent. But crime, and the fear of crime, remains one of the most serious problems facing our citizens.

Energy

We have had some successes. And there have been some disappointments.

Bluntly, I must remind you that we have not made satisfactory progress toward achieving energy independence.

Energy is absolutely vital to the defense of our country, to the strength of our economy and to the quality of our lives. Two years ago, I proposed to the Congress the first comprehensive national energy program: a specific and coordinated set of measures that would end our vulnerability to embargo, blockade or arbitrary price increases, and would mobilize U.S. technology and resources to supply a significant share of the free world's energy needs after 1985.

Of the major energy proposals I submitted two years ago, only half belatedly became law. In 1973, we were dependent upon foreign oil imports for 36 percent of our needs. Today we are 40 percent dependent, and we'll pay out 34 billion U.S. dollars for foreign oil this year alone. Such vulnerability at present or in the future is intolerable.

The answer to where we stand on our national energy effort today reminds me of the old argument over whether the tank is half full or half empty. The pessimist will say we have half failed to achieve our ten-year energy goals, the optimist will say that we have half succeeded. I am always an optimist, but we must make up for lost time.

We have laid a solid foundation for completing the enormous task which confronts us. I have signed into law five major energy bills which contain significant measures for conservation, resource development, stockpiling and standby authorities.

We have moved forward to develop the Naval petroleum reserves; to build a 500-million-barrel strategic petroleum stockpile; to phase-out unnecessary government allocation and price controls; to develop a lasting relationship with other oil-consuming nations; to improve the efficiency of energy use through conservation in automobiles, buildings and industry; and to expand research on new technology and renewable resources, such as wind power, geothermal and solar energy.

All these actions, significant as they are for the long term, are only the beginning. I recently submitted to the Congress my proposals to reorganize the Federal energy structure, and the hard choices which remain if we are serious about reducing our dependence upon foreign energy.

These include programs to reverse our declining production of natural gas and increase incentives for domestic crude oil production. I propose to minimize environmental uncertainties affecting coal development, expand nuclear power generation and create an energy independence authority to provide government financial assistance for vital energy programs where private capital is not available.

We must explore every reasonable prospect for meeting our energy needs when our current domestic reserves of oil and natural gas begin to dwindle in the next decade.

I urgently ask Congress and the new administration to move quickly on these issues. This nation has the resources and capability to achieve our energy goals if its government has the will to proceed.

Government Reform

I have been disappointed by inability to complete many of the meaningful organizational reforms which I contemplated for the Federal Government, although a start has been made.

For example, the Federal judicial system has long served as a model for other courts. But today it is threatened by a shortage of qualified Federal judges and an explosion of litigation claiming Federal jurisdiction.

I commend to the new administration and the Congress the recent report and recommendations of the Department of Justice, undertaken at my request, on "the needs of the Federal courts." I especially endorse its proposals for a new commission on the judicial appointment process.

While the judicial branch of our Government may require reinforcement, the budget and payrolls of the other branches remain staggering. I cannot help but observe that, while the White House staff and the Executive Office of the President have been reduced and the total number of civilians in the executive branch

7

contained during the 1970's, the legislative branch has increased substantially, although the membership of the Congress remains at 535. Congress now costs the taxpayers more than a million dollars a year per member; the whole legislative budget has passed the billion dollar mark.

I set out to reduce the growth in the size and spending of the Federal Government, but no President can accomplish this alone. The Congress sidetracked most of my requests for authority to consolidate overlapping programs and agencies, to return more decision-making and responsibility to State and local governments through block grants instead of rigid categorical programs and to eliminate unnecessary red tape and outrageously complex regulations.

We have made some progress in cutting back the expansion of government and its intrusion into individual lives — but there is much more to be done. It can only be done by tough and temporarily painful surgery by a Congress as prepared as the President to face up to this very real political problem.

Again, I wish my successor, working with a substantial majority of his own party, the best of success in reforming the costly and cumbersome machinery of the Federal Government.

The task of self-government is never finished. The problems are great; the opportunities are greater.

Defense

America's first goal is and always will be peace with honor. America must remain first in keeping peace in the world. We can remain first in peace only if we are never second in defense.

In presenting the State of the Union to the Congress and to the American people, I have a special obligation, as commander-in-chief, to report on our national defense. Our survival as a free and independent people requires, above all, strong military forces that are well-equipped and highly trained to perform their assigned mission.

I am particularly gratified to report that over the past two and a half years we have been able to reverse the dangerous decline of the previous decade in the real resources this country was devoting to national defense. This was an immediate problem I faced in 1974. The evidence was unmistakable that the Soviet Union had been steadily increasing the resources it applied to building its military strength.

During this same period the United States' real defense spending declined. In my three budgets, we not only arrested that dangerous decline, but we have established the positive trend which is essential to our ability to contribute to peace and stability in the world.

The Vietnam War both materially and psychologically affected our overall defense posture. The dangerous antimilitary sentiment discouraged defense spending and unfairly disparaged the men and women who serve in our armed forces.

The challenge that now confronts this country is whether we have the national will and determination to continue this essential defense effort over the long term, as it must be continued. We can no longer afford to oscillate from year to year in so vital a matter. Indeed, we have a duty to look beyond the immediate question of budgets, and to examine the nature of the problem we will face over the next generation.

I am the first recent President able to address long-term basic issues without the burden of Vietnam. The war in Indochina consumed enormous resources at the very time that the overwhelming strategic superiority we once enjoyed was disappearing. In past years, as a result of decisions by the United States, our strategic forces leveled off. Yet, the Soviet Union continued a steady, constant buildup of its own forces, committing a high percentage of its national economic effort to defense.

Strategic Balance

The United States can never tolerate a shift in the strategic balance against us, or even a situation where the American people or our allies believe the balance is shifting against us. The United States would risk the most serious political consequences if the world came to believe that our adversaries have a decisive margin of superiority.

To maintain a strategic balance we must look ahead to the 1980's and beyond. The sophistication of modern weapons requires that we make decisions now if we are to ensure our security 10 years from now.

Therefore, I have consistently advocated and strongly urged that we pursue three critical strategic programs: the Trident missile launching submarine; the B-1 bomber, with its superior capability to penetrate modern air defenses; and a more advanced intercontinental ballistic missile that will be better able to survive nuclear attack and deliver a devastating retaliatory strike.

Conventional Forces

In an era where the strategic nuclear forces are in rough equilibrium, the risks of conflict below the nuclear threshold may grow more perilous. A major long-term objective, therefore, is to maintain capabilities to deal with, and thereby deter, conventional challenges and crises, particularly in Europe.

We cannot rely solely on strategic forces to guarantee our security or to deter all types of aggression. We must have superior naval and marine forces to maintain freedom of the seas, strong multipurpose tactical air forces, and mobile, modern ground forces.

Accordingly: I have directed a long-term effort to improve our worldwide capabilities to deal with regional crises.

I have submitted a five-year Naval building program indispensable to the nation's maritime strategy.

Because the security of Europe and the integrity of NATO remain the cornerstone of American defense policy, I have initiated a special, long-term program to ensure the capacity of the alliance to deter or defeat aggression in Europe.

As I leave office, I can report that our national defense is effectively deterring conflict today. Our armed forces are capable of carrying out the variety of missions assigned to them.

Programs are under way which will assure we can deter war in the years ahead.

But I also must warn that it will require a sustained effort over a period of years to maintain these capabilities. We must have the wisdom, the stamina and the courage to prepare today for the perils of tomorrow.

As I look to the future — and I assure you I intend to go on doing that for a good many years — I can say with confidence that the state of the union is good, but we must go on making it better and better.

This gathering symbolizes the constitutional foundation which makes continued progress possible, synchronizing the skills of three independent branches of Government, reserving fundamental sovereignty to the people of this great land.

It is only as the temporary representatives and servants of the people that we meet here — we bring no hereditary status or gift of infallibility, and none follows us from this place. Like President Washington, like the more fortunate of his successors, I look forward to the status of private citizen with gladness and gratitude. To me, being a citizen of the United States of America is the greatest honor and privilege in this world.

Checks and Balances

From the opportunities which fate and my fellow citizens have given me, as a member of the House, as Vice President and President of the Senate, and as President of all the people, I have come to understand and to place the highest value on the checks and balances which our founders imposed on government through the separation of powers, among coequal legislative, executive and judicial branches.

This often results in difficulty and delay, as I well know, but it also places supreme authority under God, beyond any one person, any one branch, any majority great or small, or any one party. The Constitution is the bedrock of all our freedoms; guard and cherish it; keep honor and order in your own house; and the republic will endure.

GERALD R. FORD

Recalling Colleagues

It is not easy to end these remarks; in this chamber, along with some of you, I have experienced many of the highlights of my life. It was here that I stood 28 years ago with my freshman colleagues, as Speaker Sam Rayburn administered the oath — I see some of you now, Charlie Bennett, Dick Bolling, Carl Perkins, Pete Rodino, Harley Staggers, Tom Steed, Sid Yates and Clem Zablocki, and I remember those who have gone to their rest.

It was here we waged many a lively battle, won some, lost some, but always remaining friends. It was here surrounded by such friends that the distinguished Chief Justice swore me in as Vice President on Dec. 6, 1973. It was here I returned eight months later, as President, to ask you not for a honeymoon, but for a good marriage.

I will always treasure those memories. I thank you for them.

My fellow Americans, I once asked for your prayers, and now I give you mine: May God guide this wonderful country, its people, and those they have chosen to lead them. May our third century be illuminated by liberty and blessed with brotherhood, so that we and all who come after us may be the humble servants of thy peace. Amen.

Following is President Jimmy Carter's inaugural address, delivered at the Capitol, Washington, January 20, 1977.

For myself and for our nation, I want to thank my predecessor for all he has done to heal our land.

In this outward and physical ceremony, we attest once again to the inner and spiritual strength of our nation.

As my high-school teacher, Miss Julia Coleman, used to say: "We must adjust to changing times and still hold to unchanging principles."

Here before me is the Bible used in the inauguration of our first President in 1789, and I have just taken the oath of office on the Bible my mother gave me just a few years ago, opened to a timeless admonition from the ancient prophet Micah:

"He hath showed thee, O man, what is good; and what doth the Lord require of thee, but to do justly, and to love mercy, and to walk humbly with thy God."

This inauguration ceremony marks a new beginning, a new dedication within our Government, and a new spirit among us all. A President may sense and proclaim that new spirit, but only a people can provide it.

Two centuries ago, our nation's birth was a milestone in the long quest for freedom, but the bold and brilliant dream which excited the founders of this nation still awaits its consummation. I have no new dream to set forth today, but rather urge a fresh faith in the old dream.

Ours was the first society openly to define itself in terms of both spirituality and human liberty. It is that unique self-definition which has given us an exceptional appeal — but it also imposes on us a special obligation to take on those moral duties which, when assumed, seem invariably to be in our own best interests.

You have given me a great responsibility: to stay close to you, to be worthy of you, and to exemplify what you are.

Let us create together a new national spirit of unity and trust. Your strength can compensate for my weakness, and your wisdom can help to minimize my mistakes.

Let us learn together and laugh together and work together and pray together — confident that, in the end, we will triumph together in the right.

The American dream endures. We must once again have full faith in our country — and in one another. I believe America can be better. We can be even stronger than before.

Let our recent mistakes bring a resurgent commitment to the basic principles of our nation, for we know that if we despise our own Government, we have no future. We recall in special times when we have stood briefly, but magnificently, united; in those times no prize was beyond our grasp. But we cannot dwell upon remembered glory. We cannot afford to drift. We reject the prospect of failure or mediocrity or an inferior quality of life for any person.

Our Government must at the same time be both competent and compassionate.

We have already found a high degree of personal liberty, and we are now struggling to enhance equality of opportunity. Our commitment to human rights must be absolute, our laws fair, our natural beauty preserved; the powerful must not persecute the weak, and human dignity must be enhanced.

We have learned that "more" is not necessarily "better," that even our great nation has its recognized limits, and that we can neither answer all questions nor solve all problems. We cannot afford to do everything, nor can we afford to lack boldness as we meet the future. So together, in a spirit of individual sacrifice for the common good, we must simply do our best.

Our nation can be strong abroad only if it is strong at home, and we know that the best way to enhance freedom in other lands is to demonstrate here that our democratic system is worthy of emulation.

To be true to ourselves, we must be true to others. We will not behave in foreign places so as to violate our rules and standards here at home, for we know that the trust which our nation earns is essential to our strength.

The world itself is now dominated by a new spirit. Peoples more numerous and more politically aware are craving and now demanding their place in the sun — not just for the benefit of their own physical condition, but for basic human rights. The passion for freedom is on the rise. Tapping this new spirit, there can be no nobler nor more ambitious task for America to undertake on this day of a new beginning than to help shape a just and peaceful world that is truly humane.

We are a strong nation and we will maintain strength so sufficient that it need not be proven in combat — a quiet strength based not merely on the size of an arsenal, but on the nobility of ideas.

We will be ever vigilant and never vulnerable — and we will fight our wars against poverty, ignorance and injustice, for those are the enemies against which our forces can be honorably marshaled.

We are a proudly idealistic nation, but let no one confuse our idealism with weakness. Because we are free, we can never be indifferent to the fate of freedom elsewhere. Our moral sense dictates a clear-cut preference for those societies which share with us an abiding respect for individual human rights. We do not seek to intimidate, but it is clear that a world which others can dominate with impunity would be inhospitable to decency and a threat to the well-being of all people.

The world is still engaged in a massive armaments race designed to insure continuing equivalent strength among potential adversaries. We pledge perseverance and wisdom in our efforts to limit the world's armaments to those necessary for each nation's own domestic safety. And we will move this year a step toward our ultimate goal: the elimination of all nuclear weapons from this earth. We urge all other people to join us, for success can mean life instead of death.

Within us, the people of the United States, there is evident a serious and purposeful rekindling of confidence, and I join in the hope that when my time as your President has ended, people might say this about our nation:

That we had remembered the words of Micah, and renewed our search for humility, mercy and justice;

That we had torn down the barriers that separated those of different race and region and religion — and where there had been mistrust, built unity, with a respect for diversity;

That we had found productive work for those able to perform it;

That we had strengthened the American family, which is the basis of our society;

That we had insured respect for the law, and equal treatment under the law, for the weak and the powerful, for the rich and the poor;

And that we had enabled our people to be proud of their own Government once again.

11

JIMMY CARTER

I would hope that the nations of the world might say that we had built a lasting peace, based not on weapons of war but on international policies which reflect our own most precious values.

These are not just my goals, and they will not be my accomplishments, but the affirmation of our nation's continuing moral strength and our belief in an undiminished, ever-expanding American dream.

Thank you very much.

Lloyd M. Bentsen
United States Senator
D—Texas

1

An uncompromising, assertive regionalism that pits one part of the country against another in protracted competition for a larger slice of the Federal pie serves no useful purpose. To the extent our problems are distorted through the prism of regionalism, our ability to deal with them as a nation is diminished accordingly.

San Francisco Examiner & Chronicle,
6-19:(This World)2.

Edmund G. Brown, Jr.
Governor of California (D)

2

The values of hard work, of honesty, of thrift, of neighborliness, of supporting one another, self-reliance — those things are still very much a part of what makes this country strong. The challenge I see before us is to recapture and rekindle the very spirit we had in former times . . . in the face of an increasingly urban, anonymous, relentless march of progress which in many ways is very good and inevitable and necessary, but which carries with it crime and confusion and mental illness and alcoholism and dope addiction and fear.

At swearing-in of new state
agricultural director, Winters, Calif.,
March 30/Los Angeles Times, 3-31:(1)3.

3

. . . this country is on the "up" beat and . . . we are not on a declining curve but a rising curve — a curve that rises out of hard work and the imagination of people who are still willing to take risks, dream dreams that have not been dreamed before, and be able to put their money where their mouth is and be able to see that the future is as wide and as open as the human mind can conceive it.

At activation of solar water heater,
Fresno, Calif., Sept. 23/
Los Angeles Times, 9-24:(2)14.

Robert C. Byrd
United States Senator,
D—West Virginia

4

In this country and under our system, it's a matter of ambition and drive, industry, common sense and character. The highest plateau in any profession — the law, industry, the ministry, the medical profession — is not beyond the ken of any person in this country simply because he may be poor.

Interview, Washington/
The New York Times, 3-27:(1)44.

John T. Connor
Chairman, Allied Chemical Corporation

5

. . . we are becoming the world's first *over*-developed nation. I mean that in the last couple of years we have reached the point where we are consuming more goods and services than we can produce and pay for with our own resources and those readily available to us on reasonable terms from other parts of the world. We are already beginning to experience episodic shortages, like the natural-gas crisis of this past winter. The shortages are going to become increasingly more serious, and they will be shortages not only of energy and other natural resources but of financial resources — capital — as well. Because of these shortfalls, no segment of our society will be in a position to do what its members think needs to be done, much less everything we would *like* to do. How did we get in this mess? . . . The painful fact is that no one did it to us. We did it to ourselves in our quest for ever-higher standards of

WHAT THEY SAID IN 1977

(JOHN T. CONNOR)

living . . . Now we must face the consequences of our lack of foresight and our wasteful practices. It's late in the game, but not too late to start right now with a frank recognition of the rapidly changing facts of life.

At Fairleigh Dickinson University,
Teaneck, N.J., April 20/
Vital Speeches, 7-1:555,556.

Adalbert de Segonzac
Former chief North American
correspondent, "France-Soir," Paris   1

Working here (in the U.S.) has taught me — I won't say has taught me democracy, for we had the French Revolution for that — but many aspects of democracy. Freedom of speech, freedom of expression, freedom of the press — these things are applied more staunchly here than anywhere else . . . I came here with pre-conceived ideas that America was a country of ruffians with few cultural qualities, a people whose heroes were football players, rough people who drank until they went under the table. Oh, there's that side of America. In Kansas City one night, I joined some American friends who drank until 4 in the morning. But the real discovery was the depth of knowledge and moral values in this country, the flow and change in America.

Interview/U.S. News & World Report, 7-11:58.

James Dickey
Author, Poet   2

The South is the future. It's the future right now. People say it's just a fad, but it isn't a fad. It's going to have a marvelous influence on this country because it will teach people to be much kinder to each other and more forgiving and more easygoing and more neighborly and simply more forbearing and genuinely more concerned about other people . . .

Interview, New York/
The Washington Post, 10-19:(B)8.

Arthur Fiedler
Conductor, Boston Pops Orchestra   3

Some people are bothered by the fact that the United States is no longer Number 1 in every aspect of power and influence, but I'm not. It was a kind of game with some of our leaders — saying that we should be the greatest, the richest and the fastest. It's just not all that important whether we're the biggest and the best in *every* respect. I don't think we have to be first in *all* things, since I think we excel in the most important way: Our living conditions are best, and we have tried to keep the peace.

Interview/U.S. News & World Report, 3-7:44.

Gerald R. Ford
President of the United States   4

The third century of this country ought to be a century where there is a better break for the individual and less power in the hands of big labor and big business, big education, and maybe big religion. If we should ever lose the individual's right to do more for himself or more for his family, I think one of the great character builders of this country will be down the drain. And once that goes down the drain, a lot of the character in our form of government likewise will be under constant jeopardy. We didn't get to be a great country by having the government do all of that or labor do all of that or industry do all of that. We became great because of the individual. But there has been some erosion of that individual's opportunities and responsibilities. So we just better restore that kind of situation, rather than having all these institutions do everything for us.

Interview, Washington/Time, 1-10:16.

5

During the period of my own service in this Capitol and in the White House, I can recall many orderly transitions of governmental responsibility — of problems as well as of position, of burdens as well as of power. The genius of the American system is that we do this so naturally and normally. There are no soldiers marching in the streets except in the inaugural parade; no public demonstrations except for some of the dancers at the inaugural

(GERALD R. FORD)

ball; the opposition party doesn't go underground but goes on functioning vigorously in the Congress and the country; and our vigilant press goes right on probing and publishing our faults and follies . . .

State of the Union address,
Washington, Jan. 12/
The New York Times, 1-13:26.

Alex Haley
Author
1

In this country we are young, brash and technologically oriented. We are all trying to build machines so that we can push a button and get things done a millisecond faster. But, as a consequence, we are drawing away from one of the most priceless things we have — where we came from and how we got to where we are. The young are drawing away from older people.

Interview/Time, 2-14:72.

Lee A. Iacocca
President, Ford Motor Company
2

Some government regulation and control are desirable and necessary. What I am saying is that businessmen and businesswomen — in fact, everybody — in this country has got to get busy and put some controls on government or our precious, 200-year-old freedom is going to be nothing more than a collection of interesting historical documents. Growth of bureaucracy doesn't threaten just business and industry. When freedom is lost by one segment of American society, the loss extends to the nation as a whole.

Before Chamber of Commerce,
Charlotte, N.C./
Los Angeles Herald-Examiner, 1-26:(A)10.

Jesse L. Jackson
Civil-rights leader; President,
Operation PUSH (People United
to Save Humanity)
3

The same student generation that could be fighting for a full-employment economy, or marching for tax reform, or marching to reduce the military budget, or marching for more housing or health care for the elderly is now devoting its energy to fighting for the right to smoke marijuana, fighting for the right to abort babies, fighting for the right to stay together based on impulses without mutual responsibility. Students have been diverted from the grave issues they once were at the forefront of . . . They've been diverted from the great agenda that they've owned.

Interview/Los Angeles
Herald-Examiner, 9-18:(A)6.

Morris Janowitz
Professor of sociology,
University of Chicago
4

Our society is grappling with rapidly changing morals, and in many cases the problem is greater among middle-class families than on others. People are trying to cope with the increased divorces, the public parading of sexuality, what to do about drugs, how to handle homosexuality. All this contributes to the frustrations, the tensions and strains on the middle class. People had been led to believe that our economy would continually expand, that the 1950s would go on forever. Clearly, that is coming to an end. We need more production workers and fewer white-collar jobs. We've over-glamorized the consequences of a college education. All this contributes to the frustrations, the tensions and the strains on the middle class. Even affluence has its drawbacks. People have more money, so they drink more, smoke more, eat more. That in turn causes more problems: alcoholism, death from cancer, obesity. So, certainly, elements of the middle class find themselves under greater pressure today.

Interview/U.S. News & World Report, 5-2:57.

Peter Jay
British Ambassador to
the United States
5

All I would ask of Americans is that you go on being yourselves — valiant without being fanatical, individualistic without being foolhardy, skeptical without being cynical, open-minded without being indecisive, generous

15

WHAT THEY SAID IN 1977

(PETER JAY)

without being naive, patriotic without being nationalistic, and good without being perfect!

Before Pilgrims Society, Oct. 12/
The New York Times, 10-13:(C)2.

Juanita M. Kreps
Secretary of Commerce
of the United States　　　　　　　　　　*1*

Americans are spoiled. We are so accustomed to growth and expansion that we think we can find a painless solution to every problem. We pay lip service to the economic rules by which we are bound, but down deep many of us nurture the hope that we can obtain a personal waiver. The attitude that "one little exception won't hurt" amounts to a belief in free solutions. But solutions are never free; they are merely cheaper than non-solutions.

News conference, Los Angeles,
June 23/Los Angeles Times, 6-24:(3)16.

Thomas A. Murphy
Chairman, General Motors Corporation　　*2*

Maybe it's because I'm a businessman that I find the prevailing complacency about our freedoms in this country so difficult to understand and justify. I see our government reaching more and more deeply into our private lives as citizens, and into our business lives as well. Government regulation in America today is in many important respects turning into government direction, and the trend promises to continue. Freedom has sometimes been lost in history all at once, overnight, but more usually it is lost in a slow, piecemeal fashion — toe-by-toe and finger-by-finger. And it is almost always for the best of reasons — to serve national security, for example, or public safety, or protection of the environment. But, once surrendered, a precious freedom is never regained. It is gone for us and it is gone for all future generations. We must remember this whenever a well-meaning public figure, in or out of the government, tells us that we can no longer afford to act or choose in this matter or that. We must demand information on all the alternatives and guard each and every freedom

as if the whole of freedom depended on it. We know from civilization's experience that this is almost always the case.

Before Rotary Club, Champaign, Ill./
Los Angeles Herald-Examiner, 4-12:(A)10.

Jack Valenti
President, Motion Picture
Association of America　　　　　　　　　*3*

The worst thing about 1976 was the Bicentennial. The best thing is that it is finally over. For 1977, I'll just be glad I won't be around in 2076 for more of that schlock commercialism that was the hallmark of the Bicentennial.

Interview/Los Angeles Times, 1-3:(4)1.

Lowell P. Weicker, Jr.
United States Senator, R—Connecticut　　*4*

Today, while so many are watching [TV interviews with former President] Richard Nixon and savoring their warmed-over indignation, the abuses which he committed continue to be committed by our government . . . [The American people before and during Watergate failed to] disapprove of IRS abuses, wiretaps, break-ins and all the other violations of civil rights as long as those actions kept our cities quiet, our universities serene, our radicals submerged and our stock markets steady.

At Mohegan Community College commencement,
Norwich, Conn., May 15/
The Washington Post, 5-16:(A)5.

Edward Bennett Williams
Lawyer　　　　　　　　　　　　　　　　*5*

As we begin our third century as a nation, we are suffering a malaise of the national spirit. As a nation we have grown fat, indolent and apathetic, affluent and corrupt. We cannot bring ourselves to make the personal sacrifices required to have once again a national commitment to excellence. Our preoccupation with self-centered concerns and pleasures has deflected us from public obligations and necessary collective endeavors. We have lost the spirit that changed a people into a citizenry and transformed a territory into a nation. This is a time for heroes. The test at the beginning of our third century will be whether we mistake the

(EDWARD BENNETT WILLIAMS)

growth of affluence for the growth of character. The long-run challenge to our country is
nothing less than a challenge to our sense of
purpose, our vitality, our commitment and our
rededication.

Before lawyers division,
Anti-Defamation League of B'nai B'rith/
The National Observer, 3-26:12.

Civil Rights

Muhammad Ali
*Heavyweight boxing champion
of the world*
                                                    1

The whites have always had the say in
America. White people made Jesus white, angels
white, the Last Supper white. If I threaten you,
I'm blackmailing you. A black cat is bad luck.
If you're put out of a club, you're blackballed.
Angel's-food cake is white; devil's-food cake is
black. Good guys in cowboy movies wear white
hats. The bad guys always wore black hats.

The Dallas Times Herald, 7-18:(A)8.

Harry S. Ashmore
*Acting president, Center for the
Study of Democratic Institutions*
                                                    2

. . . all the people who have been discriminated against are demanding, and to some
extent receiving, the sanction of Federal law — in
some cases, state law — for affirmative action
programs. I am talking not only about blacks
and Chicanos, but about women, about homosexuals, about the American Indians. The effect
is to move more and more people into a work
force that is not expanding because the economy is not expanding. So I don't think that the
tensions that result when there are more people
than there are jobs stem directly from racism.
Most of the black leaders I know have said that
if you could cure the poverty problem in this
country, that would virtually eliminate the
minority problem insofar as blacks are
concerned.

*Discussion/
The Center Magazine, Nov.-Dec.:64.*

Frank Askin
*General counsel,
American Civil Liberties Union*
                                                    3

[Supporting quotas for admission of racial
minorities to jobs and colleges, even though

they may otherwise be unqualified]: While I
think the word "quota" is misleading, it is
absolutely essential that we devise effective
means of ending the centuries-old exclusion of
racial minorities from full participation in
American life. All things being equal, it's an
unassailable proposition that in a democratic
society people ought not use racial identification or skin color in determining entitlement to
benefits. But all things are not equal, and ours
has not been a racially democratic society for
300 years . . . The issue is whether the country
can, once and for all, move ahead toward
becoming a truly integrated and just society in
which all peoples can live in harmony — or
whether we are ready to scrap the promises of a
brief civil-rights period and doom the nation to
another era of racial strife.

Interview/U.S. News & World Report, 10-3:39,40.

James Baldwin
Author
                                                    4

[On his living in France for the past 30 years
and now returning to live in the U.S.]: I left
America because I had to. It was a personal
decision. I wanted to write, and it was the
1940s, and it was no big picnic for blacks. I
grew up on the streets of Harlem, and I
remember President [Franklin] Roosevelt, the
liberal, having a lot of trouble with an anti-
lynching bill he wanted to get through the
Congress — never mind the vote, never mind
restaurants, never mind schools, never mind a
fair-employment policy. I had to leave; I
needed to be in a place where I could breathe
and not feel someone's hand on my throat . . .
[But] history brings changes to countries and
continents. Exiles, wanderers, refugees find
different havens, from generation to generation.
I still love France; I do not want to repudiate a
former mistress. But Europe has changed. I

(JAMES BALDWIN)

went there to get away from The American Negro Problem — the everyday insults and humiliation, the continual sadness and the rage — so that I could sit down and write with a half-clear head. Now many of the former slaves of the Western colonial empires have come to Europe: blacks, Mohammedans, Pakistanis, Moluccans. A Harlem is rising in Paris.

Interview, New York/
The New York Times Book Review, 7-31:1,22.

Griffin B. Bell
Attorney General-designate
of the United States
1

[On the busing of schoolchildren for racial balance]: I think it upsets Americans to take children away from their neighborhood schools. I think neighborhood schools are preferable, all things being equal. I think in some school districts busing will be employed as a last resort.

News conference, Washington, Jan. 3/
The New York Times, 1-4:21.

Jess L. Belser
President,
Continental Forest Industries
2

It is in the area of qualifications that the next battle to define equal opportunity will be fought. While qualifications have been used in the past as discriminatory devices, setting them aside under the guise of achieving equal opportunity is in itself discriminatory. I believe that setting aside qualification requirements in the long run leads to the establishment of mediocrity as the accepted standard of performance. I realize this viewpoint is not universally accepted and is a subject of considerable discussion in academic journals. However, I would submit this for your consideration: While the marketplace may not be aware of the distinction between companies that are and are not equal-opportunity employers, it is very much aware of the difference in levels of competence on the part of the companies that compete in it.

At scholarship convocation of Tuskegee
Institute/The Wall Street Journal, 2-1:18.

Tom Bradley
Mayor of Los Angeles
3

[On the busing of schoolchildren for racial balance]: It's almost a universal thing: Most parents, whatever their color, whatever their background, wherever they live, don't want their kids transported back and forth across the city ... and I think to suggest that one group wants it and the other doesn't is an incorrect assessment of attitudes.

Before high-school students, Los Angeles,
Feb. 24/Los Angeles Times, 2-25:(2)1.

4

[On black Mayors]: I think there's no question about the fact that my election in Los Angeles has opened up opportunities for many cities to make the judgment about their candidates based upon the candidates' qualifications, programs, and their ideas — and not on the basis of race, religion or sex. In other words, one experience simply expands opportunity. Within a month after the 1973 election, there were no more references to Tom Bradley, the black Mayor. It was Tom Bradley, Mayor. That's the way it ought to be.

The Christian Science Monitor, 4-4:3.

Anita Bryant
Singer
5

[On her campaign against a proposed ordinance that would ban discrimination against homosexuals in such things as employment]: I've worked around homosexuals all my life, as you might imagine, with me being in show business. I've known many of them to be warm, sensitive people, and I'd have no hesitation in having them around my children. But when it comes to the point of the local ordinance, that we have to hire *flaunting* homosexuals to teach our children, that's where I draw the line. My basic attitude is fairly liberal — live and let live, you know. I believe that what people do in private is their own business. But this ordinance brings it out in the open, and I'm concerned about how it might influence the children. I don't mean in terms of child molestation — I know that homosexuals are no more likely to be child-molesters than anybody else. I don't even mean in terms of actually encouraging

WHAT THEY SAID IN 1977

(ANITA BRYANT)

children to be homosexuals. I mean people who are role models being able to stand up and say, "I'm homosexual and I'm proud of it," implying to our children that they have another legitimate choice open to them. It's not a civil-rights issue at all. What's happening is that, in the name of human rights, vice is becoming virtuous.

Interview/The Washington Post, 5-2:(A)23.

Joseph A. Califano, Jr.
Secretary of Health, Education and
Welfare of the United States
1

[Supporting quotas for the admission of minorities to colleges and universities]: How am I, as Secretary of HEW, ever going to find first-class black doctors, first-class black lawyers, first-class black scientists, first-class women scientists, if these people don't have the chance to get into the best [schools] in the country?

Interview, Washington, March 17/
The New York Times, 3-18:(A)1.

2

I believe that the whole college and higher-education experience will be enhanced for whites and blacks and women and other minorities if there are minorities and women in our major institutions. I also believe that, as a society, we have a Constitutional, if you will, and moral obligation to encourage and give, if necessary, some preferential treatment to minorities. Otherwise, they will never be in the power league of doctors and scientists and lawyers and nuclear physicists in this country, as they should be . . . I don't think this involves the reverse discrimination, if you will, against the white male. I think he will have his full opportunity; I think that . . . the white males and females (who) are the vast and overwhelming college population will have a more enriched experience, and I think we have to recognize, as a society, that we have got to make up for a century of brutal discrimination.

TV-radio interview,
Washington/"Meet the Press,"
National Broadcasting Company, 3-20.

Jimmy Carter
President of the United States
3

I don't see homosexuality as a threat to the family. What has caused the highly publicized confrontations on homosexuality is the desire of homosexuals for the rest of society to approve and to add its acceptance of homosexuality as a normal sexual relationship. I don't feel that it's a normal interrelationship. But, at the same time, I don't feel the society, through its laws, ought to abuse or harass the homosexual. I think it's one of those things that is not accepted by most Americans as a normal sexual relationship. In my mind, it's certainly not a substitute for . . . family life . . .

Interview, Washington/
The Dallas Times Herald, 6-19:(A)15.

William T. Coleman, Jr.
Chairman, Legal Defense Fund,
National Association for the
Advancement of Colored People
4

[Reporting after a meeting with President Carter on increasing the number of minority-group employees in high Federal jobs]: No President can commit himself to name other than the most able person. But the President certainly showed a sensitivity to this situation . . . and as a result, I expect you'll see more women and members of minorities as U.S. attorneys and judges (etc.).

Washington, May 18/
Los Angeles Times, 5-19:(1)23.

Archibald Cox
Professor of law, Harvard University
5

[On the Bakke reverse-discrimination case]: This case . . . presents a single vital question: whether a state university, which is forced by limited resources to select a relatively small number of students from a much larger number of well-qualified applicants, is free, voluntarily, to take into account the fact that a qualified applicant is black, Chicano, Asian or native American in order to increase the number of qualified members of those minority groups trained for the educated professions and participating in them, professions from which minorities were long excluded because of generations

(ARCHIBALD COX)

of pervasive racial discrimination. The answer which the Court gives will determine, perhaps for decades, whether members of those minorities are to have the kind of meaningful access to higher education in the profession which the universities have accorded them in recent years, or are to be reduced to the trivial numbers which they were prior to the adoption of minority-admissions programs.

Before Supreme Court of the United States,
Washington, Oct. 12/
The Washington Post, 10-13:(A)8.

Drew S. Days III
Assistant Attorney General, Civil
Rights Division, Department of
Justice of the United States   1

It's absurd to say a formula can be devised that says if segregation was directed toward two schools, then only two schools have to be involved in the remedy. [On the other hand,] I would hope the courts would not overreach. If there are limited violations shown, I would hope the court will not necessarily conclude that a system-wide desegregation plan is necessary. That's an abstraction, and one has to look at the specific case and the facts as they develop. It might be that 10 schools have to be involved, and not 40. Or 30 as opposed to 50 . . . In other situations, the violations may be very minor and perhaps the remedy would be somewhat restricted.

Interview, Washington, March16/
The New York Times, 3-18:(A)17.

Ronald Dworkin
Professor of jurisprudence,
Oxford University, England   2

A qualified white has no inherent right to be admitted to medical school ahead of a less-qualified minority member. Nobody has a basic right to a medical education. But the university does have a right to determine its own admissions policy based on many factors, including intelligence, reduction of racial tension and redress of historical inequities. Whites and blacks are owed respect and consideration, but

"the right to be treated as an always mean "the right to equ does always mean, however, interests will be considered making process.

Interview, Martha

Sam J. Ervin, Jr.
Former United States Senator,
D—North Carolina   3

[On quotas for minority-group admissi colleges] : I think [racial] quotas are not only unconstitutional, I think they're incompatible with liberty. And I not only think they're incompatible with liberty, I think they're incompatible with common sense. Those who advocate quotas to get people into schools and institutions are going to have to remember that they used to use quotas to keep people *out* . . . I think reverse discrimination is just as evil as the original discrimination. I don't think two wrongs make a right . . . It's more important to give minority people remedial education so that they can rise to these standards, instead of dragging [the standards] down.

At Southern Methodist University, Oct. 19/
The Dallas Times Herald 10-20:(E)1.

William C. Friday
President,
University of North Carolina   4

[Saying there is pressure from the Federal government to admit more blacks to Southern universities] : At Chapel Hill, our flagship school, the average test score for entering blacks is about 250 points below the average white score. That's why we have predominantly black schools today, not the old reason. The only way our major white schools can get more blacks without destroying our academic standards is to siphon off blacks from the traditionally black schools and then get a heck of a lot deeper into remedial education, which is something a heck of a lot of faculty don't want. All of this is getting awfully close to reverse discrimination. It threatens to change basic education concepts. It's asking us to make up for many of the shortcomings of secondary

(WILLIAM C. FRIDAY)

education, if not society as a whole. If you're black and have the grades, you can get in any school you want to in today's South, not just a historically black school.

The New York Times, 12-13:15.

Edith Green
Former United States Representative,
D—Oregon
1

I have never believed that race, sex, religion or national origin are valid criteria for either "favorable" or "unfavorable" treatment. This is one reason why I have been opposed to programs which give an advantage in job consideration and promotion to members of those groups who have suffered historic discrimination. As a woman, I am a member of one of those groups and keenly aware of the injustices which exist — and I could recite by chapter and verse personal experiences to document the case. Nevertheless, I reject the thesis that reverse discrimination is therefore justified. When Congress passed the Civil Rights Act of 1964, the purpose was to end discrimination on the basis of race, color, creed, national origin, or sex. It was not designed to replace one injustice with another. One of the most damaging things about prejudice, in my view, is that it gives primary value to a group characteristic rather than recognizing the unique individuality of each human being. It does not matter whether this discrimination works in the person's favor or against him. What he or she still loses is the irreplaceable privilege of being looked upon as an individual rather than an anonymous face in the crowd. As I see it, only genuine equal opportunity, containing neither advantage nor disadvantage, can provide this.

At Brigham Young University, Jan. 25/
Vital Speeches, 3-1:302.

Patricia Roberts Harris
Secretary-designate of Housing and
Urban Development of the United States
2

[Responding to Senator William Proxmire who expressed doubts about her ability to identify with the underprivileged]: Senator, I am one of them. You do not seem to understand who I am. I am a black woman, the daughter of a dining-car worker. I am a black woman who could not buy a house eight years ago in parts of the District of Columbia. I started, not as a lawyer in a prestigious law firm, but as a woman who needed a scholarship to go to a college. If you think I have forgotten that, you are wrong. If my life has had any meaning at all, it is that those who start out as outcasts can wind up as being part of the system. Maybe others can forget what it was like to be excluded from the dining rooms in this very building, Senator, but I shall not forget.

At hearing on her nomination before
Senate Banking, Housing and Urban Affairs
Committee, Washington, Jan. 10/
The New York Times, 1-11:1.

S. I. Hayakawa
United States Senator, R—California
3

This coalition [of blacks and liberal Democrats] is creating an impression that all blacks are intellectually, socially, culturally disadvantaged — you've got to help the poor things. Liberal whites and, I am sorry to say, a majority of black politicians, today are destroying the black people by creating a state in them of permanent dependency.

San Francisco Examiner & Chronicle,
10-9:(This World)2.

Theodore M. Hesburgh
President, University of Notre Dame
4

Racism is [still] the key problem in America. [But] during the '60s we made more progress than any civilized country in the world has ever made. Overnight we went from apartheid as unbending as South Africa's to complete equality. One day you couldn't go to the beach, eat in restaurants, go to school, even to the cemetery. The next day you could.

People, 9-26:75.

Benjamin L. Hooks
Executive director,
National Association for the
Advancement of Colored People

1

Our mission today is the same as was the NAACP goal when it was founded nearly 70 years ago — to end every vestige of racism, sexism and discrimination, whether in the Bakke [reverse discrimination] case, affirmative action and school desegregation problems of today, or the lynching and segregation of days gone by.

Boston/The Christian Science Monitor, 9-23:9.

Hubert H. Humphrey
United States Senator,
D—Minnesota

2

What I'm most proud of in my government career is the battle I waged for civil and human rights when it wasn't very popular, but I somehow had the fortitude to stick with it. And it was a very difficult time for me. I really had some pain in the Senate for several years. I was not popular. And I was not liked, and that's hard for me to take because I'm a gregarious sort of character. But, in the long run, I think that what we did with civil rights is the most important thing in my public life because it opened up opportunities for millions of people.

Interview, Washington/Parade, 10-2:11.

Jesse L. Jackson
Civil-rights leader;
President, Operation PUSH
(People United to Save Humanity)

3

[President] Carter has the message that blacks are dissatisfied with his Administration. We didn't quite put [former President Richard] Nixon in office but we did not settle for benign neglect from him, and we will not settle for callous neglect [from the Carter Administration].

San Francisco Examiner & Chronicle,
9-4:(This World)2.

Vernon E. Jordan, Jr.
Executive director, National Urban League

4

Our new President [Carter] will come to office with the trust and confidence of black citizens who, for the first time in eight years, feel they can look to the White House for constructive action to bring about full equality for all Americans ... We have to hold Mr. Carter's feet to the fire. We have to remind him that he would be a Plains (Ga.) peanut farmer who ran for the Presidency had the black vote not made the difference.

State of Black America address, Washington,
Jan. 11/Los Angeles Times, 1-12:(1)1,10.

5

What concerns me most is not the attack on the [civil-rights] reform of the 1960s by last-ditch segregationists and the radical right. Such a last gasp of venom is expected from those unwilling to admit black people's right to vote and to work. What distresses me is the failure of moderates and liberals to take pride in the accomplishments of reforms they helped institute and supported. There is a fatal flaw of compromise and timidity in conventional liberalism that today takes the form of retreat from the uncompleted battle for equality and in the overly defensive reaction to unfounded criticisms of the reforms of the '60s. It cannot be said too often — the Second Reconstruction was a success. Whatever the failings of this or that specific program, the over-all thrust to extend equality, increase community initiatives, focus attention on the real problems of our society and to mobilize national efforts to solve those problems constitute one of the few periods of our national history of which we can be proud.

At "Toward New Human Rights" conference,
University of Texas, Austin/
The Wall Street Journal, 2-7:12.

6

... just as no man is an island, separate and apart from others, so, too, no community can see itself in isolation from other towns and cities, from the nation as a whole, or from countries and peoples far from our borders. In our times especially, we have seen how racial

WHAT THEY SAID IN 1977

(VERNON E. JORDAN, JR.)

and economic dilemmas penetrate even the most self-contained affluent communities. We have seen problems of rural poverty and racism become the core problems of our urban crisis, and now we see them becoming an integral part of suburban life as well. There is no hiding place in the modern world. There can be no isolationism in regard to social problems.

At United Way of America Volunteer
Leaders Conference, Atlanta, April 25/
Vital Speeches, 6-1:494.

1

Black people, having tasted the sweetness of victory of November [last year's election of Jimmy Carter as President], resent the sour taste of disappointment in July. Black people and poor people resent the stress on balanced budgets instead of balanced lives. We resent unfulfilled promises of jobs, compromises to win conservative support and the continued accept-ance of high unemployment. We are here to file our claim, to collect on the campaign promises made in black churches and black neighbor-hoods [by President Carter].

At National Urban League convention,
Washington, July 24/
Los Angeles Times, 7-25:(1)16.

Henry A. Kissinger
Secretary of State of the United States

2

As idealists, as perfectionists, we [in the U.S.] constantly come to debate our faults; but for somebody who came to this country as a young man, I can never forget what America has meant to people who were not here born to freedom. When I came here in 1938 I was asked to write an essay at George Washington High School, here in this city, about what it meant to be an American. I wrote that, of course, I missed being separated from the people with whom I had grown up and from the places that were familiar to me. But I thought that this was a country where one could walk across the street with one's head erect, and therefore it was all worthwhile. What America means to the rest of the world is the hope for people everywhere [that] they shall be able to walk

with their heads erect, and our responsibility as Americans is always to make sure that our purposes transcend our differences.

Before Foreign Policy Association,
New York/The New York Times, 1-19:(A)3.

Juanita M. Kreps
Secretary of Commerce
of the United States

3

I don't think you have to shy away from the idea of tokenism. It's not such a bad thing. It's just a stage we have to go through, a period of "primary education" in which we can take only small steps — one woman here, one black there, or better, two. I don't think we should refuse to do that. The important thing is what we do after we are invited to join. To goof up on the job would be disastrous. And we have to keep suggesting — not just two women or two black men, but three or four or five or six. I *am* getting sort of impatient.

Interview, Durham, N.C./
The Washington Post, 2-17:(D)2.

Joseph E. Lowery
Chairman, Southern Christian
Leadership Conference

4

[On the difficulty of bringing civil-rights problems to the attention of the public today]: You've got no symbol to fight any more — except for tokenism. Today, the bank presi-dent, who is white, gets his picture in the paper with a black teller. They're both smiling. Everybody appears happy. But the truth is, the median income of blacks is less than 55 per cent of the median income of whites. And that's even less than what it was several years ago.

Los Angeles Times, 5-20:(1-A)2.

5

We're going to telephone you, [President] Carter; we're going to telegraph you and tele-vise you, and if that don't reach you [on black rights], the tramp, tramp, tramp of our feet will reach you. We may have to put on our marching shoes.

San Francisco Examiner & Chronicle,
8-28:(This World)2.

Wiley Manuel
Justice,
Supreme Court of California

1

[On his being a black in so high an office] : I hope I'm a model for all kinds of Americans — blacks, Chicanos, native Americans, Asian-Americans — who have to work their way up. A part of the problem for minorities is arriving at that point when they feel "this is my society, too. I can do as good a job as anybody else." Kids today have to have images of people who soberly go about doing their work and move along. People in the ghetto are frustrated. They see the image of the superfly who earns quick money. It's important to stress that the legitimate norms and modes of getting things are available.

Interview, San Francisco/San Francisco
Examiner & Chronicle, 10-23:(A)4.

C. Peter McColough
Chairman, Xerox Corporation

2

[On blacks and other minorities] : Progress, late in starting, has been made in industry in their behalf in the last 10 years, but there's a long way to go. We must keep on the pressure to effect more progress toward equality of opportunity, toward lessening prejudice in a society divided on [racial] lines. As it is, there's still an enormous disparity of health and longevity, as well as equality of opportunity, between whites and others. It's a white problem, created by whites way back in our history, not a black problem.

Interview, Stamford, Conn./"W":
a Fairchild publication, 10-14:19.

Wade Hampton McCree, Jr.
Solicitor General-designate
of the United States

3

I would define myself as a person who's very much concerned about the importance of preserving individual liberties in a country that continues to grow in size, complexity and interdependence. I am very much concerned to see that the social imperatives of a large country ... do not encroach any more than they necessarily must on individual rights and freedoms.

The Washington Post, 2-2:(D)2.

Wade Hampton McCree, Jr.
Solicitor General
of the United States

4

The incessant racist insinuation over the years that black people are not the intellectual peers of white people has convinced many of us [blacks] that we are defective in this respect. And the expectation that we will not measure up has become a self-fulfilling prophecy manifested by comparative college and professional-school admission test scores and by Civil Service and private-sector employment examination results ... We must not tolerate lackadaisical performance in school. We must insist upon measuring up to the highest standard ... We must reject the condescending perpetuation of second-class status that results from teaching our children "black English." Civil Service examinations and college and professional-school admission tests are given in standard English.

At Howard University commencement,
May 14/The Washington Post, 5-15:(A)2.

Russell Means
Former leader,
American Indian Movement

5

We [Indians] live in the belly of the monster, and the monster is the United States of America ... How can [President Carter] talk about human rights the world over when my people are suffering planned genocide?

At Conference on Discrimination
Against Indigenous Polulations of the
Americas, Geneva, Sept. 20/
Los Angeles Times, 6-21:(1)12.

Parren J. Mitchell
United States Representative,
D—Maryland

6

The question is, has the status of black folks substantially changed since the President [Carter] got into office, and the answer is no.

WHAT THEY SAID IN 1977

(PARREN J. MITCHELL)

Black jobless rates have gone up since January, not down. Black youth unemployment has gone up, not down. More blacks have slid back into poverty since January than before. The bottom line is, there is neglect . . .

Washington, Aug. 31/
The Washington Post, 9-1:(A)11.

1

[Saying racial minorities should get preferential treatment in admission to jobs and universities] : . . . I do not go for preferential treatment necessarily on the basis of past discrimination. I go for it on the basis of present ongoing discrimination. I think it would be ridiculous to assume that racism and prejudice and discrimination are dead in this country. I think those things are very much alive, and I think the quotas, the preferential treatments, those kinds of things, address not the past but the present . . . The second argument that I would want to raise is with reference to merit. I am not at all sure that anyone on this panel could define merit. What we see as merit is probably some measurable, objective indication of something; but whatever that measurable objective indication is, it is based upon intangibles that are very subjective, so I am not at all sure you can make out a real strong argument on merit as being a sharply defined term against which we would take action.

TV-radio interview/"Meet the Press,"
National Broadcasting Company, 9-25.

Walter F. Mondale
Vice President of the United States   2

[Supporting affirmative action, such as granting minorities special preference in college-entrance decisions] : We will not turn our backs on 200 years of discrimination against minority groups in this land. We believe in affirmative action. We think it is an essential and positive tool to overcome past denial . . . Affirmative action is the only way to overcome unequal history, and we are prepared to defend its use in the courts of this land as we have

done in the Bakke case. This much we pledge, and more.

At fund-raising dinner honoring the late
civil-rights leader Martin Luther King, New York,
· Oct. 12/The New York Times, 10-13:(B)4.

Orlando H. Patterson
Sociologist, Harvard University   3

[Calling for racial quotas leading to direct entry into the top jobs] : It really is the only way to achieve equity; the single most important factor accounting for success at the top end has to do with access. Access has little to do with things we like to talk about — the schools successful people attend, and so on . . . The effects of success work in an exponential way. And so, unfortunately, do the effects of non-access. Why are liberals prepared to accept preferential treatment of blacks when they are infants [as in the Head Start programs] but not when they are adults? . . . The best way of assuring equality of opportunity for blacks is to make sure that they go home to families that are reasonably secure. And the best way to assure this is a direct grant of access. The question isn't whether we'll have quotas. The question is whether we'll have directed quotas, or continue with non-directed, unwitting quotas that have put an effective ceiling on black aspiration.

At Howard University/
The Washington Post, 4-1:(A)27.

Wilson Riles
California State Superintendent
of Public Instruction   4

To the extent that blacks are poor and disadvantaged, they're going to get the short end of the stick on any [IQ] test — as will anyone else who is poor and disadvantaged. All tests are culturally discriminatory . . . Attempts have been made to pin everything on race without considering other variables. The worst scores in the United States on such tests are made by the isolated, disadvantaged people of the Appalachia, who are probably the purest Anglo-Saxon stock in the country. Blacks from ghetto areas score poorly on tests, but so do whites from the same type of ghetto area. And

(WILSON RILES)

black children from affluent homes in the middle class score higher, as do white children from middle-class homes.

Court testimony challenging the use of IQ tests for placement of children into educable mentally retarded classes, San Francisco, Nov. 22/ Los Angeles Times, 11-23:(1)3.

Eugene V. Rostow
Professor of law and former dean, Yale University Law School
1

[Arguing against minimum quotas for admission of racial minorities to jobs and colleges]: The quota device, to me, is the use of an immoral and illegal means to achieve a very good end. I don't think it's justified or necessary. There's a distinction between fighting for equal opportunity and fighting in ways that violate that principle . . . First, quotas threaten our basic standard of equality as a principle of constitutional law. In the second place, quotas have a dangerous impact on university practices and on the people themselves. The principle of equality is the only principle, I think, that's acceptable to us either in our constitutional law or in the administration of institutions like universities. Thirdly, it is no kindness to anyone to put him into an environment where he's under-qualified and where he will feel at a disadvantage and feel more stupid than he should feel.

Interview/U.S. News & World Report, 10-3:39.

Louis Stokes
United States Representative, D—Ohio
2

I think it is time now to recognize that there is much opposition in this nation to policies designed to gain equality in our society for minorities and for women. The opposition is largely political. It takes the form of creating in the body politic the sense and belief that minority groups have gained too much and have gone too far in their quest for equality. It takes the form of code words, such as "reverse discrimination" and movements like "anti-busing." Politicians, faced with a public

response based on misimpression of the facts, fear in larger and larger numbers to support full protection of civil rights . . . To provide an effective remedy for this situation, we are told, is somehow to discriminate against white males, who have held these positions and gained these benefits in the past. In the first place . . . when we start with an all-white male group, an increase in the number of minorities is *per se* an incursion on a domain white males have had to themselves in the past. Without an expansion in the number of opportunities, sharing of existing opportunities by including those formerly excluded will decrease some opportunity for the majority group.

July 14/The Washington Post, 8-17:(A)26.

Roy Wilkins
Executive director, National Association for the Advancement of Colored People
3

The Carter Administration is trying hard to see that it comes up to the expectations of Negroes. I can't say it has completely justified it yet, but it's trying hard. The Carter Administration has done everything that it has done with an eye on the ultimate good of the Negro.

To reporters, St. Louis, June 26/ Los Angeles Times 6-27:(1)5.

Edward Bennett Williams
Lawyer
4

If there be a cardinal sin in the litany of human evils, I believe it is racial and religious bigotry. I believe that for those who practice prejudicial discrimination against their fellow man or woman by reason of his or her color, religion, sex, national origin, or other accident of birth, there must be reserved the hottest corner of Hades. But it does not follow that we must all share equally in the rewards for the efforts, talents and enterprise of others. We are equal in the sense that we must all have equal opportunity to compete for the rewards of excellence, not share in its fruits regardless of personal effort or ability. An equal opportunity

WHAT THEY SAID IN 1977

(EDWARD BENNETT WILLIAMS)

based on merit benefits everyone. By rewarding excellence, we share in the fruits of that genius.

Before lawyers division,
Anti-Defamation League of B'nai B'rith/
The National Observer, 3-26:12.

Pete Wilson
Mayor of San Diego
1

I frankly think that any solution [to school segregation] that involves large-scale busing [of schoolchildren] is a mistake. I think it's a waste of money that should be spent on education. I think it is necessarily involved with a great deal of time that is not productively spent, and I think the alternatives are to try to encourage the kind of voluntary attendance that has been suggested through the device of magnet schools, and even those are very expensive. I think that for younger children, in particular, the idea of the neighborhood school is a very appealing idea and all of these court cases are attempting to really solve a problem that arises from housing patterns . . . The long-term solution really is probably a decision that should be made less by school boards than by city councils and by boards of supervisors.

News conference, Los Angeles, Dec. 2/
Los Angeles Times, 12-3:(1)32.

Andrew Young
United States Ambassador/Permanent
Representative to the United Nations
2

I share the total abhorrence to racism which is characteristic of two-thirds of the world. Most colored people of the world are not afraid of Communism. Maybe that's wrong, but Communism has never been a threat to me. I have no love for Communism. I could never be a Communist. I could never support that system of government. But — it's never been a threat. Racism has always been a threat. And that has been the enemy of all my life and everything I know about life.

Television interview/"Who's Who,"
Columbia Broadcasting System, 1-25.

3

[Former Presidents Richard] Nixon and [Gerald] Ford did not face it [racism in their lives], because they were, in fact, racists . . . They were racists not in the aggressive sense but in that they had no understanding of the problems of colored peoples anywhere. There's a sense in which every American, black or white, is affected by racism . . . We've got to start talking about racism without putting moral categories on it so we can understand it.

Interview/Playboy, July:70.

Fred T. Allen
Chairman and president,
Pitney Bowes, Inc.

1

The ethical standards of American business are as high now as they have ever been. They are as high as those in any profession. They are higher than business ethics standards in almost any other country. Having said that, I must add that corporate morality in this country can and should be improved. It should be beyond reproach. A small percentage of American corporations have behaved badly, and there has been a mistaken belief that other companies also have violated the rules of good corporate behavior. There has been a deterioration in the degree of respect that government and the public have for corporate executives. If this does not change, more government regulation of business will result. I hope we do not come to that . . . Ethical standards of businesses are set by chief executive officers. This has always been true. If the philosophy of chief executives is one of high ethics, and if they implement that philosophy with clearly understandable codes of company conduct, then I think the morality of our companies and the ethical standards of our employees will be improved. So, you see, the power to improve is inherently ours.

Interview, Stamford, Conn./
Nation's Business, April:41.

John J. Balles
President, Federal Reserve
Bank of San Francisco

2

There is a very serious squeeze in agriculture. On the one hand, there is the decline in the price of wheat. Alongside are rises in equipment, labor and land. It's a classic example of the double whammy. Agriculture shows the most serious decline of any area of the economy.

Interview/Los Angeles
Herald-Examiner, 12-19:(A)15.

Raymond Barre
Premier of France

3

[Addressing business leaders]: You will receive no sugar candy [from the government]. With state gifts and subsidies, increased family allocations and old-age pensions, reduced working hours and early retirement, and all the other golden gifts promised by the leftists, you can buy immediate employment and apparent growth. And then the bill must be paid and the last state will be worse than the first. Those alleged remedies would diminish exports by raising prices, thus weakening the demand for francs, reducing the value of the franc, increasing the cost of all our imports and of all our oil, and producing galloping inflation . . . Our purpose is neither to invigorate nor to inspire you as heads of your own businesses. It's your own obligation to invigorate and inspire yourselves. That's part of your duty as [business] chiefs. You are each the leader of a business. Then go ahead and lead.

At business seminar, Paris/
The Christian Science Monitor, 1-20:17.

William M. Batten
Chairman, New York Stock Exchange

4

Business may be digging a hole for itself. It isn't enough today to think in terms of making a profit. It isn't enough today for a person to be skilled in management techniques. We need the person who has those skills to have a broader understanding of the role of business and the corporation in society. Unless our citizens see the corporate form of enterprise as essentially beneficial to the quality of life, then

WHAT THEY SAID IN 1977

(WILLIAM M. BATTEN)

the corporate form of enterprise will come under increasing attack.

Flightime (Continental Airlines magazine), May:12H.

William C. Battle
President, Fieldcrest Mills, Inc.

1

Frankly, there have been transgressions by business, and much of what we businessmen say is suspect. As a result, government regulations have been instituted and the pendulum has swung, bringing us an extreme of government interference. The regulations are too costly. They increase the price of items to consumers and make business more difficult. Some environmental and health-protection measures are impractical and unachievable. Business should resist such regulations at the administrative and court levels. This would attract the attention of the public. Industry and labor should work together because some government requirements will result in putting plants out of business. Labor doesn't want that . . . One punishing side effect of the adversary relationship between government and industry is that American companies are penalized through lack of Washington cooperation at a time when foreign competitors are getting help from their governments. In many countries, industry and government are partners. Not in the United States. Here government often not only over-regulates, but it issues regulations running counter to other regulations.

Interview/Nation's Business, March:48.

Griffin B. Bell
Attorney General of the United States

2

I hope to impart a sense of mission to antitrust enforcement in this country. I believe that vigilant antitrust action serves a vital role in guaranteeing that enterprise is truly free to produce and that consumers are truly free to choose.

Before Public Citizen Forum, Washington, April 14/ The New York Times, 4-15:(D)7.

3

We are obligated to do all that we reasonably can to prosecute foreign private cartels which have the purpose and effect of causing significant economic harm in the United States in violation of antitrust laws. There is a fundamental United States interest in not having our citizens pay substantially higher prices for imports because private firms get together and rig international markets. There is also a fundamental United States interest at stake when private businesses, although foreign, get together to injure, and perhaps destroy, an American competitor.

Before American Bar Association, Chicago, Aug. 8/ The Washington Post, 8-9:(A)2.

4

[Saying he is considering giving Congress the opportunity to try some major antitrust cases that may be too complex for the courts]: Congress could hear the evidence and find the facts as to the existence of monopoly or the need for a remedy in a monopolistic situation. The process would necessarily be more political, but the questions at hand involve the basic restructuring of American industry and the shape of the American economy. These are questions that are perhaps most appropriately answered by the legislature, and not by the courts.

U.S. News & World Report, 8-15:40.

Bob Bergland
Secretary of Agriculture of the United States

5

The family farm is very strong and durable. Aside from my old-fashioned, romantic attachment to the family farm, studies show that in the Midwest the 600-acre farm is the strongest. A 600-acre diversified farm can utilize all the economies of scale and technology. From there on up, efficiency does not improve. We don't need corporate agriculture to produce efficiently . . . I regard [the 600-acre farm] as a family enterprise that is economically viable and can stand on its feet. Agriculture policy should be designed to recognize that fact. We have 150,000 farms in the U.S. which produce

(BOB BERGLAND)

maybe 60 per cent of the food and fiber. They are highly efficient and don't need any help from the government, and I'm not going to give them any.

Interview, Washington/
U.S. News & World Report, 10-31:58.

1

Any small change in the world supply-and-demand situation sends American farm prices up or down. And when you're on that price rollercoaster and it goes up, the poor suffer. When it comes down, the farmers get a pasting. Then the consumer gets hurt in the boom that follows the bust because consumer prices seem to go only one way — up.

Interview/The New York Times, 11-26:1.

2

[Saying the government will not give price parity to farmers]: We think to provide a Federal guarantee of the cost of production is about as far as the Federal government should go. If we're going to guarantee parity as some have requested for, say, hogs, we have to invent a very complicated Federal bureaucracy to displace the public market system. I don't think people are ready for that ... [But prices will probably have to go up because] the best thing the consumer has going is a strong, productive, healthy agriculture, and it's hurting — in places it's hurting bad. On some farms it's a disaster. The consumer is not going to be fed at a reasonable price if agriculture is going to be driven to bankruptcy.

TV-radio interview/"Face the Nation,"
Columbia Broadcasting System, 12-11.

C. Fred Bergsten
Assistant Secretary for International
Affairs, Department of the Treasury
of the United States

3

[Saying the U.S. should not institute tougher import restrictions]: In general ... we don't use import controls to protect jobs for two reasons. One is that import controls are not a very efficient way to preserve jobs. If we cut back on our imports, other countries will be

unable to import as much as they now do from the United States. And, under the international rules, they would frequently be authorized to retaliate against our exports. Both reactions would *reduce* U.S. jobs. We must remember that one out of every six manufacturing jobs in the United States now produces for the export market. The second thing is the cost to American consumers, retailers and the economy in general. Obviously we're concerned about jobs, but we're also concerned about prices. And import controls are inflationary ... If you ignore our large oil imports and just look at trade in manufactured goods, we're running a surplus of $10-billion or so. That means that in terms of manufacturing we have a very highly competitive position in the world economy. Some industries are more productive abroad than here, but others are less so. That's the essence of the international division of labor. Our consumers and economy benefit from importing those goods that are made abroad more efficiently, and exporting things we can produce more efficiently.

Interview/U.S. News &
World Report, 8-8:25,26.

Norborne Berkeley, Jr.
President, Chemical New York
Corporation (Chemical Bank)

4

... the revival of protectionism that has taken place in the United States and other countries in the last year or so is a reflection of impatience with the slow recovery of the world economy, high levels of unemployment, excess manufacturing capacity, and balance-of-payments deficits that are common around the world. But the orderly marketing agreements, currently so widely discussed, and other specific trade restrictions implemented in response to these pressures, have already imposed restraints on a total of $30-50 billion, or 3-5 per cent of all world trade. In my judgment, this trend toward restraint is the most significant threat to the principles of free trade in the postwar period. The very least we as a nation could expect would be retaliation in kind. What I think we need — and need soon — is a

WHAT THEY SAID IN 1977

(NORBORNE BERKELEY, JR.)

renewed dedication to free trade rather than more restrictions.

At Virginia Conference on World Trade,
Richmond, Oct. 13/Vital Speeches, 11-15:76.

John C. Biegler
Senior partner, Price
Waterhouse & Company

1

Uncertainty is the enemy of ethics. Many corporate employees have behaved improperly in the misguided belief that the front office wanted them to. If standards are not formulated systematically at the top, they will be formulated haphazardly and impulsively in the field.

At Harvard Business School
Club of Philadelphia/
The Wall Street Journal, 2-24:20.

W. Michael Blumenthal
Secretary of the Treasury
of the United States

2

If it becomes clear that we are moving in essentially a protectionist direction, that signal will be picked up by other nations, and they will no doubt do likewise. There's always the danger that if we raise barriers against products from countries that have rights of retaliation under the General Agreement on Trade and Tariffs, they will exercise those rights. So you can conceive of a situation in which precipitous action on our part would lead to counter-action and develop into a trade war ... I really don't believe that President Carter will allow that to happen. He is fully committed to the notion that world peace in the political area depends on collaboration in the economic area ... So I think the President will be very, very careful — recognizing, of course, that in particular instances some action may need to be taken if other possibilities have been exhausted and there's no other way to go.

Interview, Washington/
U.S. News & World Report, 4-11:32.

3

In our largely free-enterprise society, we cannot expect business to invest unless there is a prospect of an adequate return. In a world of increased uncertainty, and therefore increased risk, an even higher rate of return is required to induce capital expansion. Yet the trend in return on capital is in the opposite direction — the returns on investment, in real terms, have declined secularly. This should be of concern to all of us, not just to businessmen. Because of the relationship of profitability to investment, and of investment to productivity, and of productivity to real wages and living standards, it is a problem in which all of us have a stake.

Before Senate Banking Committee,
Washington, Nov. 11/
The Washington Post, 11-16:(A)26.

David Boren
Governor of Oklahoma (D); Chairman,
Southern Growth Policies Board

4

It is absolutely to no one's interest, and particularly not to the interest of the South, to begin another War Between the States or to engage the country in another economic civil war ... It certainly will not benefit the North, the Northeast, or the Midwest to blunt the economic development of the South, to halt the economic growth of the so-called Sunbelt. We're too interdependent. The Sunbelt provides markets to the Northeast. It provides an area in which capital can be invested with a good return. We need to be aggressive spokesmen not for regionalism but for a national approach to the problems that we have.

Before Southern Growth Policies
Board, Boca Raton, Fla./
The Wall Street Journal, 7-1:6.

John D. Briggs
Vice president,
Bethlehem Steel Corporation

5

... excessive dependence on foreign steel could have results not unlike our excessive dependence on foreign crude oil. The impact of steel imports as a factor in cutbacks in capacity means our country could be facing severe steel shortages, and steel users could also be facing drastic price increases .... the one thing you can be sure of is that those foreign competitors aren't going to hold their prices down any

(JOHN D. BRIGGS)

longer than they have to. Based on past experience, when the market tightens, look out! Their prices are going up . . . In the long run, the whole American economy is going to suffer unless we do something about excessive, *unfair* steel imports. That's why we're urging the [Carter] Administration to press for multinational negotiations aimed at establishing a set of rules for fair trade in steel.

Before Rotary Club,
Greensboro, N.C., Sept. 21/
Vital Speeches, 11-15:74,75.

Edmund G. Brown, Jr.
Governor of California (D)

1

If we have one risk in this society it is that we are so beset by the need to consume more and more items of personal convenience that we're losing the political and economic nerve to commit our capital, both private and public, to the full range of research and development without which we're not going to survive as a leading country of the world. We're not going to compete with those countries which are operating on a low-wage base and develop products which require people who earn a dollar an hour or a dollar a day. That is just putting our head in the sand. Where our strength is, is in our knowledge-based industries, in our scientific and technical ability and our ability to cluster large amounts of capital in untried experiments and alternatives.

At alternative energy conference,
San Francisco, Aug. 2/
Los Angeles Times, 8-2:(1)7.

Howard W. Cannon
United States Senator, D—Nevada

2

It is interesting that businessmen usually decry governmental interference and regulation of business activities except in cases where such governmental interference gives them a competitive advantage or an opportunity to be lazy and rest on their oars.

Before Aero Club, Washington, April 26/
The Washington Post, 4-27:(E)8.

Jack W. Carlson
Chief economist, Chamber of Commerce
of the United States

3

We [at the Chamber] are a spokesman for American business, and clearly in that role it is important to understand how market solutions to our public-policy issues can be the best way to achieve social objectives. So we will play such a role, and we have been invited by the Congress to advise them and other policymakers in government how to take a market approach. Also, I see my role as advising the American business community about the changing objectives of government and how the American business community can fit into those changing objectives. Businessmen are not opposed to national social policies *per se.* Usually you find that the opposition is in terms of how they go about achieving those policy objectives . . .

Interview, Washington/
The New York Times, 3-27:(3)9.

Jimmy Carter
President of the United States

4

I am very reluctant to restrict international trade in any way. For 40 years, the United States has worked for the reduction of trade barriers around the world, and we are continuing to pursue this goal because this is the surest long-range way to create jobs here and abroad.

U.S. News & World Report, 4-11:94.

5

[On the farmers' strike protesting low agricultural prices] : . . . I have deep sympathy for the farmers. I'm one of them. I understand their particular concerns at this time. They have enormous investments — capital investments. In my own county, for instance, the average farm family has a much greater investment than does the average businessman or industrialist. Their income on their investment is exceedingly low. We've made some major strides in 1977 to help ease those problems. The last time I checked, the price of wheat was up about 60 cents; the price of corn was up about 38 cents from a year ago. So the trends are in the right direction . . . Most of the farm strike impetus has been from

33

WHAT THEY SAID IN 1977

(JIMMY CARTER)

those areas of our nation who have been affected by adverse weather conditions – something over which the government has no control . . . We have passed a bill this year that will provide about $6½-billion in government payments to farmers. I've never been in favor of guaranteeing a farmer a profit. We have tried, though, to create an orderly marketing system where wild fluctuations will not devastate individual farm families, some stable price system and some adequate reserves system in an adequate way to sell our farm products overseas that we don't need on the domestic scene. We've made good progress in that respect . . . But [the farmers] are hurt very seriously financially, and a stable, healthy farm economy is very important to me.

News conference, Washington, Dec.15/
The New York Times, 12-16:(A)28.

David A. Clanton
Commissioner, Federal Trade Commission
1

I recognize . . . that advertising is a major – even a critical – component of our free-enterprise system. Its creative potential serves as a catalyst to bring producers and consumers together. Properly used, advertising can enhance product innovation and economic growth. Our job [at the FTC] is not to tell you [in advertising] how to run your business. We are not interested in creating story-boards or in stifling creativity. We have no desire to turn a 60-second spot into a video bulletin board, nor do we want to dump information on the airwaves or in print in such quantities as to make the yellow pages obsolete. The Commission's task, in my view, is one of helping to channel this creative force fairly and constructively so as to enhance economic growth and the well-being of consumers generally.

Before 3rd Annual Advertising Institute,
Orlando, Fla., Jan. 28/**

2

Consumerism is no longer a fad; it is becoming a more permanent fixture on the economic scene. That is all to the good. The millennium is not here, but neither is consumer-

ism just a passing fancy. At long last, the consumer interest is becoming more and more synonymous with the public interest. Unfortunately, in the past, that distinction has been lost on many regulators who have considered the public interest to be nothing more than a short-hand way of describing special private interests. But that is changing, and the FTC's job is to assist that process.

At University of Wisconsin, Madison, April 22/**

A. W. Clausen
President, Bankamerica Corporation
3

If we in business do not clean up our practices, the government will. We are up to our armpits with government regulations. Soon it will be over our heads. We'll be smothered by government and become a non-market economy. This is why I believe very strongly that business will disclose its practices – to reestablish credibility. Why wait for government to ask? . . . We must not invade the privacy of our customers. That is sacrosanct. But we think there are horses in the barn that it is better to let out.

Interview/People, 2-7:46

Elizabeth Hanford Dole
Commissioner,
Federal Trade Commission
4

[Calling for a Federal consumer protection agency]: I have seen, first hand, the type of "clout" which an industry can bring to bear for or against government actions which may affect it. Certainly, business' voice should be heard, but the strength and volume of that voice exceeds, by a long shot, anything I have ever seen on the consumer side . . . The truth is that on many issues, consumerists are firing popguns compared to some of the big howitzers that business rolls into Washington . . . In the past few years, the consumer movement has matured in America. It is no longer willing to accept paternalism, but wants equal representation. It says that consumers deserve an effective voice in the affairs of government. Like unions, farmers and other interest groups that have marched down this road before, the American consumer movement no longer wants to be

(ELIZABETH HANFORD DOLE)

patted on the head and shunted aside. No longer are consumers willing to scrounge for crumbs that fall to the floor. The Agency for Consumer Protection would give them their own place at the table, as equals. And that, I believe, is where they belong.

*Before American Advertising Federation/***

1

Among the marble pillars up and down Pennsylvania Avenue and along the corridors of Congress, a great controversy rages over whether the government has piled too much regulation upon our society or whether there is still too little protection by our government for those unable to protect themselves ... the business community and, more recently, several prominent members of the academic community, have launched a frontal attack on the entire regulatory framework. They claim that America is now suffocating under a deluge of Federal paperwork, that business can't even decipher, much less obey, over 60,000 pages of edicts set forth in the Code of Federal Regulations, and that government regulators are now costing the economy over $45-billion a year. The United States, they say — quoting Walter Lippmann — is badly suffering from the "sickness of an over-regulated society." On the other hand, persuasive arguments are still made that our society continues to be riddled with inequities and injustices. Unsuspecting consumers are still being gouged in the marketplace. Pollution remains a threat to our environment and may even grow apace with a renewed emphasis upon energy. Sexual and racial discrimination, while reduced, still holds people back. To those who see society in this light, the government — whether it be the Executive, the Legislative, or the Judicial Branch — remains the best vehicle for needed reform ... I can only conclude that, yes, we have indeed traveled far from the day of "caveat emptor" and the "laissez-faire" of Adam Smith. The government now regulates many areas of the marketplace where once it feared to tread, and as these regulations accumulate in one area after another, there is a significant danger that we could over-burden

our society and our economy so that things slowly grind to a halt. To protect ourselves from that end, it is essential that the government always act prudently, cautiously, and with due regard for the consequences of its acts ...

*Before American Council on Consumer Interests, Denver, April 21/***

2

Information is the oil which makes the market mechanism work. And truthful advertising is one of the best ways I know of to provide it. Advertising tells consumers that a product exists, that it has certain qualities, that it sells for a certain price, and that the seller may offer certain ancillary services. Indeed, experience teaches us that consumer ignorance about the options available in the marketplace frustrates the goals of our competitive, free-enterprise economy. Restraints on price advertising, for example, virtually force consumers to buy in the dark. As a consequence, they may end up purchasing identical or very similar products for widely varying prices, never realizing, without the help of advertised prices, that the same article could have been obtained cheaper from another retailer. A blackout on price information, then, makes life more comfortable for firms which charge higher prices, but it penalizes not only those firms which are price competitive, but consumers as well. Thus, price advertising restrictions, whether they're imposed by a state or by private codes, may seriously undermine competitive market forces and may tend to diminish incentives to lower prices.

*Before National Association of Chain Drug Stores, Palm Beach, Fla., May 1/***

William K. Eastham
*President, Johnson Wax Company;
Chairman-designate, Chamber of
Commerce of the United States*

3

The consumer is eventually in control of the markets, so there is no question that business must satisfy the consumer. The market-enterprise system in consumer goods consists of a continuous display of products the consumer may buy. Once the consumer chooses not to

WHAT THEY SAID IN 1977

(WILLIAM K. EASTHAM)

buy a product over a period of time, that product is out. In many consumer-goods markets today there are multiple choices for a consumer to make. Only the products that meet the buyer's expectations are going to survive. Manufacturers make a big mistake when they try to sell something that they have decided is good for the consumer, rather than something the consumer wants.

Interview/Nation's Business, May:54.

Lewis W. Foy
Chairman, Bethlehem Steel Corporation

1

. . . if you need steel, if you use steel, if you buy steel, you simply can't afford to rely too much on foreign suppliers. There are additional considerations. Every million tons of foreign steel imports mean about 5,000 fewer direct steel-making jobs for American workers. About 60,000 direct steel-making jobs were lost last year, when our economy sorely needed those jobs. And I've been talking about *direct* jobs. When you add in the ancillary or supporting jobs, the numbers go a lot higher. And bad as it is, this situation could get a lot worse in the years ahead. If imports ever captured 30 per cent of the market, we could be talking about another 60,000 or more lost jobs! So I think there's a very strong case for making sure it never happens. Never let our nation depend too much on unreliable foreign sources of steel products. I can assure you that every other steel-making nation in the world fiercely and jealously aids and protects its own domestic steel-making capability.

Before Executives Club of Chicago,
April 1/Vital Speeches, 5-1:435.

2

There's no question that the most critical [problem facing the U.S. steel industry] centers on the import situation. It has taken all of the integrity out of the market. Things are far worse than at any time in my experience. All of the foreign countries that built steel mills since World War II find themselves with tremendous excess capacity. The majority of these facilities are either government-owned or government-

subsidized in some way. Under pressure from this excess capacity, these countries have wanted their mills to keep producing steadily to provide jobs. And, of course, they've got to find a market for the steel they produce. The U.S. is the greatest steel market anywhere in the world. So the foreign producers have shipped steel in here and sold it at any price that they can get anyone to pay. In the case of Japan and the European Economic Community producers, we are certain steel is being dumped here at prices that don't cover their production and sales costs, and don't allow any profit.

Interview/U.S. News & World Report,
11-21:90.

Takeo Fukuda
Prime Minister of Japan

3

[Comparing the loss of free trade in the 1930s, which he says was a cause of World War II, with similar tendencies today]: I am not suggesting that we are once again on the road to a world war. Yet I feel a deep anxiety about the social and political consequences for the world if we slide once again into protectionism, or a break-up of the world economy into rival trading blocs.

Before National Press Club, Washington,
March 22/The New York Times, 3-23:(A)3.

E. J. (Jake) Garn
United States Senator, R–Utah

4

I have never heard a businessman do anything but praise and speak in support of the free-enterprise system. But many of them then turn around and support with vast financial contributions the very people who will hurt them, with the hope that a crumb or two will be thrown their way. A recently published study of contributions going from big business to various (political) candidates, both liberal and conservative, illustrates what I am saying. Of the total dollar amounts given to 117 conservative or pro-business candidates for Congress and their opponents, 50 per cent put out by the new business political-action committees went to left-leaning, anti-business candidates. A national association of lending institutions channeled two-thirds of its contributions to

(E. J. [JAKE] GARN)

liberal candidates. A leading airline gave over 60 per cent of its political contributions to anti-business candidates. Another organization of lenders was not so bad but still gave 50 per cent of its contributions to candidates on the left side of the political spectrum. And the list goes on and on. When are you people in business going to learn that you can't feed the alligators with the hope they won't eat you? Because eat you they will.

Before National Petroleum Refiners Association, San Francisco, March 28/**

Harold S. Geneen
Chairman, International Telephone & Telegraph Corporation
1

I don't believe in just ordering people to do things. You have to sort of grab an oar and row with them. My philosophy is to stay as close as possible to what's happening. If *I* can't solve something, how the hell can I expect my managers to?

Interview, New York/Los Angeles Herald Examiner, 12-27:(C)1.

Allan Grant
President, American Farm Bureau Federation
2

For some time now, American agriculture has been relatively free from government involvement. Realized net incomes have been substantially up, with only about 2 per cent coming from government programs, compared to almost 30 per cent in 1969. Thus, money earned in the open market is subject to the risks of that market, which livestock and grain farmers now understand all too well. But these risks are more predictable than political risks of Congressional appropriation actions. We recognize there is a proper role for government in agriculture, but this role should be restricted to the prevention of severe down-swings in some price cycles — to keep large numbers of farmers from going broke through no fault of their own. We ask that the market-price system have freedom to function, with emphasis placed on

building competitive opportunities in farm marketplaces of this country — and of the world.

Before American Farm Bureau Federation, Honolulu/ The Wall Street Journal, 1-12:14.

Peter Haas
President, Levi Strauss & Company
3

Businessmen can go to the Department of Commerce, farmers to Agriculture, bankers to Treasury, and workers to Labor and find government officials with expertise and responsibilities regarding their problems, needs and views. We believe that consumers should also have a separate home within the council of government.

Addressing President Carter, March/San Francisco Examiner & Chronicle, 4-17:(A)15.

Louis T. Hagopian
Chairman, N. W. Ayer International
4

... I don't subscribe to the belief that the press is generally hostile to business. But often, when controversy surrounds a corporate stance, business doesn't seem to get its full, fair shake. One mission of the press is to dig up wrong-doing, and in recent years investigative reporters have turned up some pretty hairy corporate stories. In the process, press reports have made it appear that all business is suspect. This just isn't so. Perhaps because business has been reluctant to talk about itself — to tell the whole truth about itself — for so long, it doesn't do well with the press now that it's under sharp scrutiny. And a lot of people who oppose the stands of business do a better job of communicating than business does. We are attacked from a number of sides. The aggressor is better news copy than the defender. They are quick with a jab; we may be slow with a response. The advocates of consumerism, unionism, government intervention are exciting. We are the establishment. We are often dull.

Before Advertising Club, Columbia, S.C., Oct. 11/Vital Speeches, 12-15:155.

Michel T. Halbouty
Consulting geologist
5

By any standard, America's oil and gas industry, including both majors and independ-

WHAT THEY SAID IN 1977

(MICHEL T. HALBOUTY)

ents, is the most efficient in the world. For 120 years it has provided the low-cost fuel and power that created the world's greatest industrial nation. By discovering new uses for petroleum, for plastics, for fertilizer, for other purposes, the petroleum industry has helped make America the world's greatest food producer; it has created whole new industries and hundreds of thousands of jobs. This prosperity and advanced technology benefits the entire nation. Yet it is inconceivable that there are those who would break up this industry. Also, it is incomprehensible that such indisputable facts do not deter the advocates of divestiture. They have seized on the domestic energy gap as a convenient reason for imposing an alien economic theory.

Before Gas Processors Association,
Dallas, March 22/Vital Speeches, 4-1:380.

Gary W. Hart
United States Senator, D–Colorado 1

... the question of the structure of the petroleum industry or the broader question of concentration in our private sector ... is an economic issue. It goes to the structure of our economy. It goes to the question of bigger and bigger institutions in both the private and public sectors controlling our lives, and it goes really to the kind of country we want this to be. The roots of my belief in divestiture trace back to Thomas Jefferson and all the way up through the "trust busters" and legislative divestitures in the '30s. I think it is a serious economic issue ...

TV-radio interview, Washington/
"Meet the Press,"
National Broadcasting Company, 5-15.

Robert S. Hatfield
Chairman, The Continental Group, Inc. 2

There are no precise lines regarding what companies should be regulated or how much. Some [government] regulation is necessary. The free market cannot decide everything.

However, I believe that the requirements of operations in a free market are the greatest discipline a company can have and that, in general, industries should be free of regulation in the absence of an emergency ... Americans have not become sufficiently impressed with the urgency of the problem of government interference. I don't think they perceive that their freedoms are in danger — that the loss of their economic freedom will probably be a prelude to the loss of other freedoms.

Interview, New York/
Nation's Business, September:69.

Gabriel Hauge
Chairman, Manufacturers Hanover
Trust Company, New York 3

The cost of providing banking services to consumers has been soaring in terms of people, equipment and facilities. We have to do it less expensively, and we are on the way with cash machines, electronic funds transfer, terminals in supermarkets, credit cards, and devices of that sort. The job is to put developing technologies to work to give the consumer more convenience and to help the banker save time, money and space. This must be done in the face of increasing competition from other financial intermediaries. We expect to see a very slow growth or an actual reduction in the number of full-service branches. Newer offices will be physically smaller and less spacious than some branch banks of the past. On the corporate side, the internationalization of business is compelling the banking industry to make many adjustments. Examples of services which will become increasingly important include corporate cash management, various computer-based electronic information services, and continued innovation in the term loan market. At the same time, banks must see that the financial needs of a small-businessman in America are accommodated. American banks can also be expected to establish more facilities overseas serving both corporations and consumers. It looks like good business.

Interview, New York/Nation's Business, June:33.

James H. Higgins
Chairman, Mellon Bank, Pittsburgh
1

I don't think the American businessman has lost his guts. If all things were going right in the economy and he didn't take greater investment risks and go on expanding, then I'd be worried that he has become timid. But there are so many uncertainties about the future — about energy, cash flow, regulations, taxes, the environment questions — that it makes good sense to be cautious about huge expenditures on projects that wouldn't be completed and operative for a few years ahead.

The New York Times, 7-10:(3)15.

Roderick M. Hills
Chairman, Securities and Exchange Commission of the United States
2

Frankly, I am far more concerned about the ability of our corporations to raise equity capital than I am about whether we can raise the level of management conduct. Our dramatic trend toward a debt-based industrial complex rather than the equity-based industry of 25 years ago strikes me as our most critical corporate problem. As we lean to debt, we lose the flexibility and the innovative growth critical both to capitalism and to our democratic society. I have no doubt of our capacity to raise the standards of management behavior — and I see clear progress. I am less optimistic about our ability to redress the debt-equity ratios. Surely we should be as concerned about the erosion of capitalism as we may be impatient about the slowness of our moral advancement.

Before American Enterprise Institute, Washington/The Wall Street Journal, 3-24:16.

Hubert H. Humphrey
United States Senator, D—Minnesota
3

...a handful of companies has dominated prices. Nowadays, price-fixing is not by one big company, but by a number of companies that have such a command of the marketplace that they set price. I come from a commercial family. When there is a surplus, lower prices. But what do we see? The steel industry is running at 68 per cent of capacity, so it raises prices. It creates its own inflation. When the automobile industry sees the market dropping, it doesn't cut prices, it raises them. A group of industries defies the law of supply and demand. Just raise prices!

Interview, Washington/Los Angeles Times, 3-27:(7)1.

Lee A. Iacocca
President, Ford Motor Company
4

The aspirations of the developing world include the physical needs of the people there. Food to eat and clothes to wear. Better housing. A better chance to make it in the world. The only way to provide that is by bringing money and brains together, and working with government officials to find the most effective ways of putting them to work... Productivity is the key, and that key is most accessible through the multinational corporation. You can look all around. You can study all the learned treatises on development, but you won't find a source of productivity that is more effective on an international scale, or more able to go to work right now... The multinational corporation "fights the bull." We are the ones on the line who actually produce the goods to fill the needs. We can take the labor off a man's back and make it possible for him to produce more in an hour than he ever dreamed of. We can train that man with skills that he can pass along to future generations. We can enable him to work with his mind as well as his hands. And that's just a small part of what the multinational corporation can do to make the world a better place.

Before Swiss-American Chamber of Commerce, Zurich, June 17/Vital Speeches, 9-15:721.

Neil H. Jacoby
Founding dean and professor emeritus of business economics and policy, Graduate School of Management, University of California, Los Angeles
5

The chief executive of a large American corporation is today probably the most accountable executive of any institution in American society. Competition in labor, capital and product markets compels him to account daily to his employees, stockholders, bankers

WHAT THEY SAID IN 1977

and customers. He is also accountable to society under a host of Federal, state and municipal laws.

Before Securities and Exchange Commission, Los Angeles/Los Angeles Herald-Examiner, 10-19:(A)11.

Reginald H. Jones
Chairman, General Electric Company   1

A revival of the stock market is one important element in any program to step up the nation's level of capital formation. The declining popularity of stocks as an investment has been very discouraging for anyone who sees equity as an important source of funds for corporate expansion.

Before Securities Industry Association, Boca Raton, Fla., Dec. 2/ Los Angeles Times, 12-3:(3)11.

Alfred E. Kahn
Chairman, Civil Aeronautics Board of the United States   2

In the last five or 10 years, largely because of inflation and so on, there has been this growing discontent with [government] regulation [of business] which is imposed in part for good, New Deal kinds of reasons and a recognition that regulation has come to be in very many places a means of protecting and insulating the people who were supposed to be regulated and has been extended to areas which could conceivably be more effective if competitively organized.

Interview, Washington/ The New York Times, 8-21:(4)4.

William S. Kanaga
Managing partner, Arthur Young & Company   3

. . . [there] can be little question that recent disclosures of misconduct on the part of some corporations and their executives have contributed to the low esteem of business. It is futile to argue that some of the practices which now arouse such fierce public indignation have been standard operating procedures for generations

in some areas of the world. The fact remains that the revelation of sizable payoffs to promote sales and of the diversion of corporate funds for political purposes have cast doubt upon the ethical foundation of the entire business community. Nor will it be at all persuasive to contend — though it is a valid contention — that these episodes, given the totality of our economic system, are rare departures from acceptable conduct — rarer, in the minds of most, than the instances of hanky-panky which can be found in the political realm. The public's confidence in business will not be revived by trying to make such debating points. It will be restored only by a full awareness of the constantly changing standards of behavior expected of business leaders — and by a genuine effort throughout the business community to adhere to them.

Before Executives Club of Chicago, Jan. 21/Vital Speeches, 2-15:275.

Edward M. Kennedy
United States Senator, D—Massachusetts   4

[On his bill which would prohibit major oil companies from owning or controlling coal or uranium assets]: The basic theory underlying the bill is not complicated or difficult to understand. It is that firms engaged in one line of business ought not to be able to hold or acquire firms engaged in a competing, or potentially competing, line of business. This theory does not rely on regression analyses or econometric models; it relies on common sense.

The Washington Post, 8-1:(D)10.

Lane Kirkland
Secretary-treasurer, American Federation of Labor-Congress of Industrial Organizations   5

A word needs to be said on the emerging principle of consumer sovereignty as it affects trade issues — that is, the proposition that the consumer has an inalienable, top-priority right to $4 Korean shoes, regardless of the conditions under which they are made, the human, social and economic cost of lost American jobs, and of who really gets the $4. This principle is

(LANE KIRKLAND)

mostly expounded by those who get their shoes at Gucci.

Before AFL-CIO industrial union dept., Washington, April 5/The Washington Post, 4-6:(A)12.

1

[Saying President Carter's early economic decisions, including his economic stimulus package, have been too favorable to business]: On the bottom line of that package you can read the message: "There ain't gonna be no full employment here for the next four years." Chalk up another one for business. Scratch another compromise... A central theme of [Carter's election campaign last year] was a repeated commitment to the proposition that with a new Administration would come a new spirit, governed by the needs, the problems and the aspirations of plain people, specifically including working people. Though it is yet early in the game, the recent signs and portents lead us to wonder if our support was not just another triumph of hope over experience... The process reminds us again that, in national and world affairs, whether the winds blow left or right, cold war or detente, Republican or Democratic, big business adapts and comes to winning terms. When the Republicans are in, business wins because it owns the Party. When the Democrats are in, business wins because it extracts the price of "business confidence."

Before AFL-CIO industrial union dept., Washington, April 5/The New York Times, 4-6:(A)12; The Washington Post, 4-6:(A)1.

2

[Saying the U.S. should institute tougher import restrictions]: The American market is the largest market in the world. Access to our market is a major objective of almost every country that is looking for exports, and they should think twice before endangering that access by retaliation. Besides, the word "retaliation" is inappropriate because it is we who are under attack. Other nations are targeting the American market, and in many cases they use devices that have no relevance to free-trade doctrine or classical economic theory. These

devices include dumping of goods in the U.S., pricing products by their out-of-pocket rather than real costs, enjoying subsidies from foreign governments or immunity from antitrust laws. In some countries, there is a virtual consortium between the governments and the corporations. And wages are often extremely low... This is still the freest and most open market in the world. Yet, while we cannot export a variety of commodities into Japan, the Japanese come over here and talk free-trade doctrine to us. The Common Market countries have enacted a fence — or at least a toll bridge — to keep out imports. In theory, I'm totally persuaded of the merits of free trade. I wish it really existed. But it does not exist anywhere. No country practices it, and the direction of movement is away from free trade, not toward it. That has been happening for years, and the trend is accelerating. To talk about this world in terms of free trade is self-destructive.

Interview/U.S. News & World Report, 8-8:25,26.

Paul Kolton
Chairman, American Stock Exchange

3

In the perspective of history, I'm not sure that the move to negotiated [brokerage] commission rates on May Day in 1975 will have really served a public purpose... Most of the things we thought would happen have happened. When the issue was being debated, we anticipated that it would cause institutional commission rates to drop sharply. We thought the public would pay higher rates. And we expected that negotiated rates would put a number of brokerage firms under financial pressure and make the whole network of firms smaller. We now know that all of that is true, and there's been the additional factor that the change has caused a further alienation of the public from the securities markets.

Interview, New York/ Los Angeles Herald-Examiner, 7-30:(A)11.

Juanita M. Kreps
Secretary of Commerce of the United States

4

When I was appointed by [President] Carter, I said that I thought the Commerce Department

WHAT THEY SAID IN 1977

(JUANITA M. KREPS)

ought to encourage all those business behaviors that contributed to the well-being of mankind. I think that business is perhaps our most important single instrument for doing that. The trick is, of course, to encourage business to view its contributions to the welfare of society in somewhat broader terms than profit maximization. I wanted to find a way to encourage business to go further in terms of its obligations, and I thought it would be helpful to get a dialogue going and maybe even some indices and measures that would allow the corporation to assess itself in terms other than profit maximization.

Interview, Washington/
The New York Times, 5-8:(3)1.

1

What is needed is recognition of the fact that, between government, business and the public, there is a triangular community of interest. Clearly, it is in business' interest to shape its behavior to prevailing public values; it is more efficient to do so than not to do so. It is also clear that government is the high-cost alternative through which public values are imposed on corporations that do not accurately perceive these values.

News conference, Los Angeles, June 23/
Los Angeles Times, 6-24:(3)16.

2

American businessmen claim they are in a very difficult position trying to compete with producers abroad because foreign governments — chiefly in Europe and Japan — do so much to support their industries through subsidies and tax concessions to promote exports. Businessmen interested in export trade tell me it gets harder and harder for them to compete because they're not up against private business by itself, but against business bolstered by governmental policies that go far beyond what the U.S. government does for our companies.

Interview, Washington/
U.S. News & World Report, 8-1:18.

Daniel J. Krumm
President and treasurer, Maytag Company
3

I think one reason business-endorsed economic-education programs have had such a poor track record is because, like it or not, people simply do not equate businessmen with the free-enterprise system. Rather, they see business people as self-serving individuals, trying hard to fortify their own position ... I think it's time for business to acknowledge — without apology — that we do represent a special interest, one that we believe is vitally important. We have the perfect right — in fact, the responsibility — to do what we can to correct the false impression that others have of us. But we must do this as *businessmen,* not as preservers of our great social and economic system.

Before Iowa College Foundation, Des Moines/
The Wall Street Journal, 11-2:18.

Bert Lance
Director, Federal Office of
Management and Budget
4

[On government regulation of business]: The amount of time that people in the business community — chief executive officers and on down the list — are spending on regulatory problems is almost unbelievable. We are seeing so much of our productivity directed toward something that is totally non-productive. It doesn't make any sense. It is costing too much money; it is imposing too many restrictions. Business people are not able to plan the future of their companies because they don't know what the results of regulation are going to be. Government has been terribly unpredictable ... Of course, regulation is necessary. The consumer has to be protected. There is no question about the basic over-all need for government being present. But we really ought to ask ourselves to what extent. After we have answered that, let's set a structure that enables us to carry out what we are trying to accomplish without other adverse effects.

Interview, Washington/Nation's Business, May:22.

R. Heath Larry
Vice chairman, United States Steel
Corporation; Chairman, National
Association of Manufacturers

1

The public needs to understand that a corporation has no source of wealth apart from the people who invest in it, work for it and buy from it — and thus can absorb no costs but can only pass them on to one or more groups of just plain people. But my fear is that economic education of this kind will not "take" unless people want it. And they may not want it — or believe it — unless they are more satisfied than they are now by the values business leadership appears to represent.

At economic conference, Chicago/
The Christian Science Monitor, 8-31:10.

Russell B. Long
United States Senator, D—Louisiana

2

[Saying a proposed bill to limit business airfare deductions to coach tickets would further increase the government's influence on taxpayers' lives]: If we are going to tell businessmen they cannot fly first class, then we should go the rest of the way and tell them when they get there they cannot take a taxicab, they have to take a bus; when they get to the hotel they cannot take a big room, they have to take a small room; and when they desire a restaurant, they have to go to McDonald's, and so forth. I do not have anything against McDonald's; I eat there a great deal. But the point is, once in a while a person should have freedom of choice [and this bill could lead to the elimination altogether of such things as first-class air travel].

Before the Senate, Washington/
Los Angeles Times, 5-8:(5)5.

3

So many burdens are being piled on business — on an environmental basis, on a safety basis, on the basis of the government telling business how to produce its products and to whom they can be sold. Today's businessman must have the genius of an Einstein, the memory of an elephant and the education of a lawyer, scientist and educator all wrapped in one. If we keep adding burdens on business, the system will fail. Businessmen simply cannot shoulder all of these burdens. We must reduce government interference in the operation of businesses and in the lives of our people in general.

Interview/Nation's Business, August:26.

Ben F. Love
Chairman, Texas Commerce Bancshares

4

It used to be that conversation at business luncheons centered on labor problems or productivity. Now most of the worries are over government intrusion — in ways that often border on the illegal. If [President] Carter really wanted to reassure business, he would do best to let it run in the same way he sought to run his peanut farm — with some freedom. We need to give man's creativity in the marketplace a chance to blossom.

Interview/U.S. News & World Report, 9-19:64.

Louis B. Lundborg
Former chairman, Bank of America

5

In spite of growing nationalism, the multinational corporation will play an increasing role in the world's economic stage. And because the managers of those multinational corporations will have to learn to live with and respect the differing national interests, the multinational corporation may become one of the most potent forces for world peace and order.

Before Los Angeles Area
Chamber of Commerce, Jan. 12/
Los Angeles Times, 1-13:(3)17.

Robert Lynch
Dean, Graduate School of Management,
University of Dallas

6

The chairman [of a company] should be the one to put the pressure on the management team for the sake of the board members, who are not active in the day-to-day management of the company. I don't think he can be completely separate from the management team, but he has to be far enough away to see things more as an outsider. You've got an implementing management team, headed by the CEO, that must work with the board in doing the strategic thinking for the company. The chairman's

WHAT THEY SAID IN 1977

(ROBERT LYNCH)

responsible for making sure that the board and management can take time occasionally to analyze what they're doing and where they're going. Maybe even consider whether they're even in the right business. The chairman has to have enough time, he has to be far enough removed from the day-to-day details of management, that he can see the direction and can bring everyone together on the subject.

The Dallas Times Herald, 4-3:(C)11.

Robert H. Malott
Chairman and president, FMC Corporation 1

Without question, the multinational corporation has an opportunity, indeed an obligation, to help satisfy the world's compelling needs for skills, technology and economic progress. Such firms will be essential in overcoming the growing gulf between those countries who have and those who have not. In what threatens to become an adversary economic relationship between the Northern Hemisphere countries and those of the Southern Hemisphere, multinationals can help to ease the political tension which arises from what John Steinbeck has called "the thin line between hunger and anger." No more-effective means of fulfilling these needs has been devised than the application of the private-enterprise system through the multinational corporation. To exercise their vital role in world development, multinationals must not be hamstrung — not by labor and not by government.

Before Chicago Business Publication Association, Feb. 7/Vital Speeches, 4-1:366.

John J. Matternas
President, Insurance Management of Washington, Inc. 2

For the immediate future, a company's best protection against product liability will be the strict attention it pays to quality and safety of its products and the adequacy of disclosure in its marketplace and advertising programs. Quality standards will need to be established, in writing, for all aspects of production, from raw materials through manufacture, assembly, packaging and shipping.

Nation's Business, June:28.

C. Peter McColough
Chairman, Xerox Corporation 3

Businessmen's ethics are not any worse than those of the public as a whole. It's just that the businessman is more accountable than any other level of society and is much more likely to be caught in any dereliction of duty or responsibility ... There has been a dramatic turnaround to more ethical standards in the past couple of years, not simply in words but in action. Business must continue to make sure it's running its operations with unquestionably high ethical policies and practices, that it's not involved with the price-fixing, political contributions and overseas kickbacks that have damaged its reputation in the past. Business has to be certain the quality of goods and services fully measures up to the advertising.

Interview, Stamford, Conn./"W": a Fairchild publication, 10-14:19.

George Meany
President, American Federation of Labor-Congress of Industrial Organizations 4

In all too many cases, the captains of industry and the rulers of multinational corporations have ceased to believe in the free market or in free competition or in the sacred character of work or in the duty to uphold freedom and resist tyranny.

Labor Day address, Washington, Sept. 5/The New York Times, 9-6:22.

5

Free trade today is a joke and a myth. And a government trade policy predicated on old ideas of free trade is worse than a joke. It is a prescription for disaster. The answer is fair trade — do unto others as they do to us, barrier for barrier, closed door for closed door.

At AFL–CIO convention, Los Angeles, Dec. 8/The Washington Post, 12-9:(A)3.

Melvin H. Middents
Vice president, Cargill, Inc. 6

To maintain a viable agricultural economy we must export nearly two-thirds of the wheat crop produced in the U.S. and one-quarter of

(MELVIN H. MIDDENTS)

our feedgrains. So any system of support for agriculture has to take into consideration our ability to meet the prices of other surplus producers like Canada, Australia and Argentina ... Debating what the cost of production actually is diverts attention from the fundamental reality of commercial agriculture — that products must meet customer needs at prices they are willing to pay. When we lose sight of this truth, we begin to lose marketing opportunities ...

Interview/Los Angeles Herald Examiner, 9-28:(A)15.

A. A. Milligan
President-elect, American Bankers Association
1

I see red whenever I hear anyone dismiss the allegations about [former Federal Budget Director Bert Lance's personal bank] overdrafts, and failures to disclose personal borrowings, as being typical business practice among bankers. There are 14,000 banks and a quarter of a million bank officers in this country, and I will stack up their ethical practices against those followed by any other industry in the United States any day of the week.

The New York Times, 12-20:2.

Thomas A. Murphy
Chairman, General Motors Corporation
2

Maybe it's because I'm a businessman, and business is so much a target of regulation, that I find the prevailing complacency about our freedoms so alarming and so difficult to understand. Everywhere the trend is clearly away from individual freedom. We are losing the freedom to decide for ourselves what is best for ourselves ... None of us questions the right of citizen protest [against business abuses], nor the need for some government regulation. But protest can be irresponsible and regulation can be unreasonable, and, when it is, regulation can become a usurper of freedom. When government departs from its accepted role of setting the rules of the game and, instead, decides to direct the game itself; when government goes so far as to substitute the value judgments of bureaucrats for those of the people — then

government goes too far. And goes beyond what a love for freedom should tolerate.

Before American College of Trial Lawyers, Chicago, Aug. 6/Vital Speeches, 8-6:716.

John J. Nevin
Chairman, Zenith Radio Corporation
3

I get very impatient with talk about America becoming protectionist. The Japanese, who claim we're being so protectionist, are in fact the most protectionist society in the world. In 1974, about 4.7 million television sets were sold in Japan; fewer than 16,000 of them were imported. [The same year,] 2.3 million automobiles were sold in Japan — and fewer than 50,000 were imported. Given the amount of protectionism that exists in Japan right now, there is no way that American companies are going to enter the Japanese market and achieve any kind of balance in that trade relationship. [So] the idea that someone would accuse *me* of being a protectionist is just appalling.

Interview/Newsweek, 3-28:59.

Michael Pertschuk
Chairman, Federal Trade Commission
4

I did a lot of reading getting ready for this job, and I came away more certain than ever that the antitrust laws are the strongest consumer protection we have. Competition, enforced if necessary, is the essence of consumer protection.

Interview, Washington, Sept. 23/ The New York Times, 9-25:(1)27.

5

[On ads that mention competitors]: We think they're great! Obviously, comparative advertising is subject to abuse if it is misleading or deceptive. But an ad which accurately lists performance characteristics for four or five competitors gives the consumer the kind of information he or she really needs and can act on. That's ideal. Let me make it clear that the Commission is foursquare on the side of informative advertising. It gives the consumer a lot of valuable information, letting him know the choices that are available to him and thus enhances competition. Advertising is also an aid

WHAT THEY SAID IN 1977

(MICHAEL PERTSCHUK)

to innovation because it enables a manufacturer or a new entrant to inform a mass audience about the availability of a new or significantly improved product.

Interview, Washington/
U.S. News & World Report, 10-17:71.

1

I'm greatly concerned about conglomerate mergers — mergers between firms of very substantial size which are not presently competitors ... In the first place, despite the fact that these mergers do not eliminate present competition, they may have a tendency to lessen competition substantially within the intent and meaning of the anti-merger laws, as numerous distinguished authorities have written. More broadly, large conglomerate mergers seem to contravene the basic values the antitrust laws were originally designed to preserve. These values include a strong preference for the decentralization of economic and political power and for local, independent, creative entrepreneurial enterprise which can be directly responsive to the consuming public.

Interview, Washington/
U.S. News & World Report, 10-17:72.

Robert T. Quittmeyer
President, Amstar Corporation

2

I believe the root of the regulatory impulse is often arrogance. If you scratch an advocate of regulation, you are likely to find, very close to the surface, an arrogant impulse to substitute some personal vision of order for the apparent disorder of the marketplace. Practically all of us are arrogant. Most businessmen are arrogant, particularly if, as in my case, they are chief executives. But happily, there are checks against arrogance in business. The free market and the free consumer usually dictate to business. But when arrogance is embodied in public policy — whether by legislation or administrative fiat — there are no effective checks on it. It becomes institutionalized — immortalized.

Before Swiss-American
Chamber of Commerce, Geneva/
The Wall Street Journal, 6-8:16.

Gilbert F. Richards
Chairman, The Budd Company

3

[American business] is changing. Businessmen are speaking out more. We have learned to go to Washington when we have a gripe. Businessmen are coming out of their shells. More and more companies have programs involving colleges and universities. And that's the place to start educating the public. You find that these college kids are pretty damned smart. If they have the wrong concept of what business is all about, it is because businessmen have failed to tell them what it is all about.

Interview/Nation's Business, July:45.

David Rockefeller
Chairman, Chase Manhattan Bank

4

[On press treatment of "problem banks"]: As to perspective, I think the "problem banks" episode is an example of the media's failure to provide the public with enough information to intelligently assess an issue. For example: When banks chose to stay with their borrowers during the recession rather than set off a long chain of foreclosures and bankruptcy, not to mention job losses, that would have plunged the country into a major depression — few journalists offered this perspective. When banks were caught between the Scylla of Congressional demands for credit allocation to socially responsible borrowers and Charybdis of political cries for conservative lending policies — the media offered scant perspective. Even today, with the banking system well on the road to a full recovery from as severe and deep a recession as we have had in 40 years — there is little, if any, perspective from the Cassandra commentators who told us about the "problem banks."

Before Economic Club of New York/
The Wall Street Journal, 6-22:18.

Nelson A. Rockefeller
Vice President of the United States

5

One thing I am worried about is the growing adversary [relationship] between government and the private sector. This is for the birds. This country owes much of its greatness to the combination of efforts by private citizens, private institutions and the government. The

(NELSON A. ROCKEFELLER)

government creates the framework; the private sector operates within it. We are a pragmatic people. We built the railroads because the government saw the desirability of linking the East and West coasts. We have got the greatest automobile industry because the government built the roads. We have got airlines because the government did the research on military planes.

Interview, Washington/Time, 1-17:14.

W. F. Rockwell, Jr.
Chairman, Rockwell International

1

. . . I have long maintained that what was good for America is good for American business. But I think it's time that American business took a more active role in introducing information inputs into the decision-making process that decides just what is good for America. If we look at the term Corporate Social Responsibility, we can see that this covers a broad range of areas, from pollution-control, consumer protection, industrial safety, equality of opportunity, and into countless other areas which grow in number with each year that passes. There's no doubt in my mind that American business can provide these things in the future. Because there's a basic rationale for this type of corporate responsibility. And that rationale is that a healthy and stable society is the best kind of society in which to do business. And the company which adds to that health and stability is doing itself a favor.

Before Society for Advancement of
*Management, Pittsburgh, March 23/***

Norton Simon
Industrialist; Founder, Norton Simon, Inc.

2

I am seriously concerned about the country's drift toward bureaucracy and the loss of the entrepreneurial spirit, particularly in regard to executive compensation. Rather than relating the individual's pay to his position in the bureaucracy, we must reward him in proportion to his contribution to the company. By this measure, the compensation of NSI's [Norton Simon, Inc.] executives who have produced many millions of dollars of profits over the years — and unfortunately of most other

business executives — is only modest at best and does not begin to compare with the pay in some other fields, such as baseball and football players and musicians. It is time we increased the rewards for those who contribute so much to the creation of the nation's wealth.

At NSI national meeting/
The Wall Street Journal, 6-1:16.

Nolan B. Sommer
Senior vice president,
American Cyanamid Company

3

. . . there are now some disquieting signs indicating problems with the profitability of U.S.-owned foreign subsidiaries. Business International found that last year the foreign earnings record of U.S. companies declined for the third successive year. In addition, BI reported that foreign profitability fell below U.S. levels for the first time since 1972. Although much of this is related to the relatively faster U.S. recovery from the world-wide recession, it does destroy the stereotype that foreign subsidiaries are automatically more profitable than domestic operations. Still another notion that needs updating in the face of current realities is the idea that American multinationals are able to capitalize on cheaper labor abroad. European labor is *not* cheap. And . . . the bulk of U.S. foreign investment resides in Europe. Therefore, in wholly economic terms, the mythical ability of American firms to get rich by expanding their overseas business without constraint is no longer true — if it ever was.

At Georgetown University, Sept. 21/
Vital Speeches, 11-15:86.

Jayne Spain
Senior vice president, public
affairs, Gulf Oil Corporation

4

In past years, most people were content with a corporation if it attended to business, paid a dividend, treated its employees well, and grew. Now people have all kinds of things to say to and about corporations — how they should be structured, what they should and should not do, where they should be in business, etc. Witness the large attendance of stockholders at annual meetings and all the questions asked and suggestions given. Yes, there will eventually be

(JAYNE SPAIN)

a different company structure, because nothing remains static. The only thing we can predict with certainty is change. I can't predict what the structure will be like, but I can predict that corporations must be flexible or they will cease to exist.

Interview, Pittsburgh/
Nation's Business, March: 72.

Edgar B. Speer
Chairman, United States Steel Corporation　1

The nation will need to create some 20 million new jobs in the private sector over the next eight years — just to stay even with the growth in the work population. The only way that these jobs can come into existence is to allow business to earn the level of profits necessary to attract and generate the capital that must be invested in job-producing facilities. Yet the profits of American business are not growing. They are shrinking, both as a share of gross national product ... and when measured against such other economic factors as employee compensation. Over the past quarter of a century, employee compensation has been on a steady, upward climb — and, last year, was six times greater than in 1950. During the same period of time, corporate profits declined — from 16 per cent of employee compensation in 1950 to 8 per cent last year. Moreover, an increasing share of the capital that a business attracts and generates through the profits that it earns must be spent for non-productive facilities related to the environment. Eleven per cent of U.S. Steel's total capital authorizations during the past three years have gone into air and water pollution abatement. This is not to suggest that pollution-control expenditures should be halted. Rather, I believe government and the public must recognize the good purposes served by profits. They must realize that the capital which becomes available for investment through profits must be increased, if environmental and energy goals and the building of new job-creating production facilities are to be accomplished at the same time.

At stockholders meeting/
The Christian Science Monitor, 6-22:27.

Stanley Sporkin
Director, Division of Enforcement,
Securities and Exchange Commission
of the United States　2

... the "little guy" has every reason to stay away from the [investment] marketplace. The clear fact is he has been treated unfairly. Let's look at the record. In recent times, the small investor has learned a number of unfortunate facts about the companies in which he has invested. First, he learned that his corporate managers engaged in all kinds of chicanery in order to establish off-the-book funds for the purpose of making illegal domestic political contributions. It was subsequently revealed to him that some of these same monies, and others, were used to bribe public officials throughout the world. Where he once had assurance that his corporation produced a superior product which accounted for its ever increasing sales, he now has learned that was Alice in Wonderland and his corporation was able in many instances to sustain its sales records by outright bribes. While he was told that he should not be alarmed by these revelations, because in foreign lands this was the way of life and the way all business was run, he soon learned the overseas corruption was also being practiced domestically.

Before Society of American Business
and Economic Writers, New York/
The Christian Science Monitor, 5-9:18.

Robert S. Strauss
Special Trade Representative for President
of the United States Jimmy Carter　3

As for what I think about trade, I go back to my college days. Trade brings peace. It's the opening up of the world. I expect that before this [Carter] Administration completes its eight years, before the two or three years of my own term here, we will make breakthroughs. But just as we rebuilt the Democratic Party, we have to restructure the trading posture of the United States. We don't want any home runs, any dramatic moves. We'll just have to scooch forward bit by bit.

Interview, Washington, March 14/
The New York Times, 3-15:61.

Arthur Ochs Sulzberger
Publisher, "The New York Times"

1

Is the press anti-business? That question breeds another: How can the press be anti-business when the press *is* business, and often big business at that? After all ... we, too, face boards of directors, union leaders, the EEOC, the SEC and stockholders ... My point is this: It is not so much a matter of the press being anti-business, which I have to admit it *sometimes* is. Nor is it a matter of business being anti-press, which you will have to admit it *usually* is. That tension between press and business — in a relationship not quite so adversary as that which exists between press and government — is the healthy tension in a land of separated and balancing centers of power. Is the press anti-business? The answer is no. Is the press anti-dullness, anti-stuffiness, anti-corporate secrecy? The answer is yes. Is a probing, skeptical, searching press coverage good for business? I think so. You may not agree completely. You may look at modern business news coverage the way John Wanamaker looked at advertising: Half of it is wasted, he felt, but he never knew which half. Business and journalism share certain great values: We are both pro-opportunity, we are both pro-consumer, we are both pro-profit, and we are both pro-freedom. We are looking at each other now with new eyes, in a kind of institutional mid-life crisis. And I think we're both going to come through it stronger than ever.

Before Economic Club of Detroit,
March 14/Vital Speeches, 5-1:426,427.

Robert W. Swinarton
Vice chairman, Dean Witter & Company

2

One of the greatest paradoxes of Wall Street has been its position on competition. The leaders of the investment community have been the strongest advocates of the free-enterprise system of competitive markets, which have made our economy the greatest known to man. Yet it has been the same voices that have been raised the loudest against building a national market system where the prices of security trades would be determined by full and fair competition. Open competition in public and inter-firm commission rate-setting is a revolutionary change for Wall Street and it is only one such radical change under way. Radical change is the synonym for revolution, so whether we know it or not, or like it or not, we who are directly involved in the securities business are in the middle of a revolution. Thus, at least from my perspective on Wall Street, the process of creating a new national market system essentially is revolutionary in character. However, it's not the sort of a revolution that's going to run its course in a couple of weeks or months, like a Latin American coup d'etat. More likely, judging from the complicated problems to be solved, and the tremendous opposition to change emanating from so many members and market sectors, it will be an evolutionary process continuing for many years, changing the securities markets step by step, year by year, but changing them relentlessly nonetheless.

At securities industry conference, Salt
Lake City, April 21/Vital Speeches, 6-1:508.

W. H. Tankersley
President, Council of Better Business Bureaus

3

... consumers judge the American business system primarily in terms of how they are affected personally. The shopping cart, the drug store, the service station, the clothing store, make up the arena where the public really grades the performance of business. ... the man at the top must, in today's world, give more of his time and attention to the establishment of high ethical standards — higher, I suggest, than the prevailing norms of general society ... and insist that those standards not be diluted as they are relayed layer by layer down through the corporate structure. There are corporate heads of my acquaintance whose personal conduct is in the highest tradition of ethical behavior, but who seem for some reason to disassociate the personal from the corporate and condone business behavior that would not stand the test of several of the commandments, as well as the golden rule. These good men need to obey their instincts and not be embarrassed

WHAT THEY SAID IN 1977

by charges that they are out of step with the times.

Before Economic Club of Detroit,
Oct. 11/Vital Speeches, 12-1:127.

Philippe Thomas
President, Pechiney Ugine
Kuhlmann, France   1

It is evident that we are much better piloted by market forces than are the national enterprises under the tutelage of the ministries. Thirty years of experience in industry have taught me the irreplaceable virtues of the market economy in molding men to their responsibilities. Today, those who urge the nationalization of the great enterprises clearly indicate their objective: These enterprises must become, in the hands of the state, the instrument that will permit a strict control of the economy and bring about what is called democratic planning. The result is easy to predict. The confusion of duties between supervisors and those who are supposed to be supervised will lead inevitably to a general absence of power and responsibility.

Interview/San Francisco Examiner & Chronicle,
8-7:(This World)27.

William F. Wearly
Chairman, Ingersoll-Rand Company   2

Government today sits as an invisible partner of every company, every family and every individual in the country. In business, it takes a lion's share of the earnings through taxes; regulates product content, safety, labeling, advertising and in some cases prices; sets hiring, firing and working conditions; controls relations with the environment and community; and even tells management what they can and cannot do to influence these potent factors politically ... Government regulations primarily affect business and industry's cost structure in four ways: 1) heavy expenditures for non-productive equipment to meet environmental safety and other Federal requirements; 2) interference with the operation of the free marketplace; 3) mandatory voluminous information to

various government agencies, a very expensive and time-consuming process; 4) expensive legal action to defend against government actions and charges which are sometimes frivolous.

Before Rotary Club, Syracuse, N.Y.,
Sept. 23/Vital Speeches, 11-1:44,45.

Murray L. Weidenbaum
Director, Center for the Study of American
Business, Washington University, St. Louis   3

It is a snare and a delusion to equate a more accurate knowledge of the state of business profits with a higher level of economic literacy and, therefore, with improved public policies toward business. Yes, the polls show that the public thinks profits are higher than they actually are. However, the polls also show that the public accepts the fact that profits are necessary. But the public is never going to love you because your company is showing a good profit record. At best, profit is grudgingly accepted as the price that the society has to pay for a successful economic system.

Before Pittsburgh Economic Club/
The Wall Street Journal, 7-19:14.

Harold M. Williams
Dean, Graduate School of Management,
University of California, Los Angeles;
Chairman-designate, Securities and Exchange
Commission of the United States   4

If business ethics are a luxury, or even a liability, it is only a matter of time before the system will be changed. In the long run, honesty is not only the best business policy, but the only one compatible with the free market and with open competition. Corruption — whether it involves bribes to secure overseas contracts, illegal contributions to political candidates at home, or hampering the efficient function of the marketplace — results in higher prices, lessened responsiveness to the consumer and lower quality of goods and services. Business corruption is not only inefficient, but it destroys the marketplace.

Before General Mills executives/
The New York Times, 4-3:(3)7.

Harold M. Williams
Chairman, Securities and Exchange
Commission of the United States
1

The widespread failure to understand both the function and level, in real terms, of corporate profits and cash flow is blinding many to the fact that business is simply not accumulating and retaining the resources required to meet the challenges facing it . . . [With] national objectives which are as important and diverse as full employment, energy independence and environmental protection . . . the problem of marshalling sufficient capital in order that business may discharge its role in accomplishing these goals is a serious one.

At business journalism banquet, New York/
The Washington Post, 10-24:(D)11.

William W. Winpisinger
President-elect, International
Association of Machinists
2

Maybe I was one of the last real free-traders in the American labor movement. I still basically believe in it, because I'm mindful of the lessons of history, of what happens when you start erecting barriers: You sometimes plant the seeds for the next war. But when other countries subsidize their companies so they can compete unfairly with the United States, that's not free trade; when American firms go abroad to get cheap labor to make goods to sell to American workers, that's not free trade. I say that's just giving multinationals the right to rip off workers who are put out of jobs in this country. American companies put 25 cents of every dollar they invested last year into foreign operations, and goddammit, that's not free trade.

Interview/Los Angeles Times, 5-19:(1)27.

Walter B. Wriston
Chairman, Citicorp (Citibank, New York)
3

They said floating exchange rates would dry up world trade; but they didn't. They said the Eurodollar market was a dangerous monster that would destroy us all unless tamed; but it hasn't. Now they say the developing countries will default on their debts and collapse the whole banking system — well, we here say it just won't happen.

Interview, New York/The New York Times, 3-6:(3)5.

Crime • Law Enforcement

Anthony G. Amsterdam
Professor of law, Stanford University
1

[Arguing against capital punishment] : For more than 40 years, criminologists have studied this question by a variety of means. They have compared homicide rates in countries and states that did and did not have capital punishment . . . All in all, there were dozens of studies. Without a single exception, *none* of them found that the death penalty had any statistically significant effect upon the rate of homicide or murder. Often I have heard advocates of capital punishment explain away its failures by likening it to a great lighthouse. "We count the ships that crash," they say, "but we never know how many saw the light and were saved." What these studies show, however, is that coastlines of the same shape and depth and tidal structure, with and without lighthouses, invariably have the same number of shipwrecks per year. On that evidence, would you invest your money in a lighthouse, or would you buy sonar if you really wanted to save lives?

Before Commonwealth Club, San Francisco,
July 8/Vital Speeches, 9-1:681.

Griffin B. Bell
Attorney General of the United States
2

I'm very much in favor of a charter (for the FBI). I don't think it's fair for the FBI not to know definitely — chapter and verse — what it is supposed or not supposed to do. It's no wonder that over the years the FBI is said to have done some things that perhaps were not authorized by law but may have been authorized by custom or practice or may have been ordered by some official. Right now, the FBI's authority comes from my authority. I'm the person who has to sign off on the things it does, and I don't want to be in a position where I may spend the rest of my life being sued by people who claim that I've authorized some-

thing illegal. I do not intend to have any FBI agent get in that position either. So they're entitled to a charter, and I'm entitled to a charter.

Interview, Washington/
U.S. News & World Report, 5-16:67.

3

[Proposing a uniform sentencing range for each crime] : I think that will deter, as much as anything. We're so serious about it, we're thinking of doing away with the parole board. There won't be any paroles. If you get convicted, you will get sentenced within the guidelines — unless you appeal one side or the other — and you know you're going to have to serve that sentence.

Before State Bar of Georgia, Savannah,
June 3/The New York Times, 6-4:8.

Lloyd M. Bentsen
United States Senator, D–Texas
4

[Saying promises made to terrorists are not binding] : I find no fault when authorities make promises to gun-wielding outlaws in an effort to free innocent victims. But a promise made at the point of a gun has no moral force whatsoever. You cannot negotiate in good faith at gunpoint . . . It ill becomes a great nation like our own to lecture to others about the evils of terrorism and acceding to terrorist demands if we ourselves do not practice what we preach.

Washington/
The Dallas Times Herald, 3-13:(A)31.

G. Robert Blakey
Director, Institute on Organized
Crime, Cornell University
5

In recent years, organized-crime syndicates have expanded their fencing operations to exploit the growing demand of consumers and businesses for stolen goods. This expansion has

(G. ROBERT BLAKEY)

been made possible by the ability of organized crime to marshal its tremendous resources to solve the complex financial and logistical problems that are inherent in large-scale theft and fencing activity . . . The syndicate's connections with master and professional fences, and the influence it exerts over many legitimate businesses, have enabled it to develop a redistribution system capable of funneling stolen goods through interstate commerce with great ease. Goods hijacked at 4:30 p.m. may be on retail shelves at 5:15 p.m. that same day.

U.S. News & World Report, 6-13:22.

Peter G. Bourne
Special Assistant to President of the United States Jimmy Carter for Health Issues 1

If criminal penalties were based on medical findings, we shouldn't impose penalties on marijuana, but on users of cigarettes and alcohol.

Before House Select Committee on Narcotics Abuse and Control. Washington, March 14/The National Observer, 3-15:(1)1.

Edmund G. Brown, Jr.
Governor of California (D) 2

As our neighborhoods become more anonymous, as there is more mobility in our society, we find that the social norms are not as observed as they have been in prior years. Our court system is cumbersome. Our criminal procedure is archaic. We are going to have to reform it because justice that is not swift, is not certain, is no justice at all. It is no deterrent. [Government must] ensure that the people who commit crime know there is a price to pay. And, unfortunately in our society, there are some people that have to be locked up for a long, long time.

State of the State address, Sacramento, Jan. 6/Los Angeles Times, 1-7:(1)29.

3

If I look at the death penalty over the last 20 years, very few people ever end up getting executed. There are thousands and thousands

of homicides. And by the time you go through the process — a process that has been created under liberals, conservatives, in good times and in bad times — very few people end up to the point where they get to the gas chamber. It happens many years after the fact. It seems random. It seems arbitrary. It seems irrational. Somehow in our society I think we can make people safer, we can make people more secure, if we strengthen law enforcement, if we rebuild our neighborhoods and not put our faith in a process that selects by a very arbitrary manner a very few number of people to pay the penalty for the crimes and the sufferings of thousands of other people. That's the way I see it. I realize people don't agree with me . . . [That's] because people see a society that is becoming more lawless, where the streets are not safe, where values are breaking down, where people are getting away — literally — with murder. And they don't like it, and they want to see something decisive done about it. And there's nothing more decisive than putting somebody in the gas chamber and taking his life away.

Television interview, Sacramento, May 3/ Los Angeles Times, 4-4:(1)3,24.

4

The way to deal with [crime] is not only stronger laws, not only more police, but to have citizen involvement in the neighborhoods . . . It isn't just electronic computers, walkie-talkies and paid professionals that will save this society. It is people themselves, coming together where they live and where they work. If you want to sit back and watch television and let somebody else worry about whether your neighbor's being burglarized, then don't expect your tax bill to do anything but escalate.

Before law-enforcement officials, Sacramento, April 27/Los Angeles Times, 4-28:(1)3.

Robert C. Byrd
United States Senator, D—West Virginia 5

If there are reasons to fire [FBI Director Clarence] Kelley, or depose him, or dispose of him, or replace him, certainly he should be replaced. But I'm interested in the integrity of the law. I don't believe the FBI Director should be summarily replaced just because of a new

WHAT THEY SAID IN 1977

incoming [Carter] Administration. I have heard no cause or reason for replacing Mr. Kelley immediately . . . If it were a Republican Administration and a Republican President and the circumstances were reversed, then the Democratic Senate would not stand by and watch the Director thrown out without reason. We would express our sanction against the successor. His successor would not be called up in the Senate for some time. I don't think we can blink our eyes at the law when we have a Democratic President and insist on the law when we have a Republican President.

To reporters, Feb.12/
The Dallas Times Herald, 2-16:(A)12.

Hugh L. Carey
Governor of New York (D)
1

[Arguing against capital punishment] : The death penalty would not be available to stop the rapists and the muggers, the burglar, the common thief and the violent person. It doesn't stop the hired killer. It doesn't stop the person who is too young to be tried for homicide. It's not a deterrent to the insane criminal. When you take all those classes of killers out and you take the so-called friendly killer — crimes of passion between friends and family; no one would suggest the death penalty be applied to them — so . . . the deterrent effect that people are really looking for would be better found elsewhere in a system of laws than it would be in one law that enacts the ultimate penalty.

Interview, New York/The New York Times, 12-19:19.

Norman A. Carlson
Director, Federal Bureau of Prisons
2

[On pre-trial detention] : Our first concern should be to keep as many detainees as possible out of jail. Individuals awaiting trial are presumed not guilty, incarceration is costly and jailing detainees takes them away from their jobs and families. Those who are not a threat to others should be released into the community.

Before House Judiciary subcommittee,
Washington, May 4/The New York Times, 5-5:(A)19.

If corrections have failed, it is primarily in those areas where society has expected too much. We cannot reform or rehabilitate every offender. We have neither the resources nor the knowledge to [ensure] that every person brought into our custody will give up crime and become a good citizen upon release. Until psychology and psychiatry can give us more clues as to the causes of criminal behavior, we are going to have to face the fact that we really don't know how to change offenders. The best we can do is offer offenders maximum opportunities to change themselves.

At Juvenile Justice Seminar, May 9/
The Washington Post, 5-18(A)14.

Jimmy Carter
President of the United States
4

When I was Governor [of Georgia], we organized a substantial effort to fight organized crime. And we detected the interrelationship between gambling — which a lot of people assume is just a normal part of life, prostitution — which some people think is not too bad, the distribution of drugs — which is condemned by almost everyone, and other forms of illegality. And the upshot of our analysis was that they are very closely interrelated. Profits from gambling, profits from prostitution and other more acceptable kinds of crime in some people's minds are directly used to enhance the distribution of heroin and other drugs. So I think it's a very serious problem; it's one that we ought to address from a national level. And one of the crucial elements that can be improved is to have local, state and Federal law-enforcement agencies cooperate in a much more effective fashion, in exchange of ideas and information and also in the prosecution of criminals.

News conference, Washington, March 24/
The New York Times, 3-25:(A)10.

Benjamin R. Civiletti
Assistant Attorney General,
Criminal Division, Department of
Justice of the United States
5

While white-collar criminals are selective in choosing victims, almost no class of society

(BENJAMIN R. CIVILETTI)

escapes their attention. Young and old, black and white, laborers and managers, business and government, all yield many victims. The soon-to-retire worker is a target for investment schemes; the middle-income citizen is a target for "vacation" and "resort" property; financial institutions and large businesses are targets for computer-assisted theft schemes; governments are targets for bid-rigging and procurement schemes ... White-collar crime is not new. It has been with us for years. But, more and more, it is recognized by the law-enforcement community for its far-reaching effects on our society.

The Washington Post, 10-20:(A)18.

John Conyers, Jr.
United States Representative,
D—Michigan

1

Stealing has always been a means of redistributing the wealth. Instead of taking the initiative and redistributing wealth in a fairer fashion, we arrest those who make the effort on their own and put them in prison — even though our experience of the past decade indicates that stricter law enforcement has little effect on the crime rate.

San Francisco Examiner & Chronicle,
1-16:(This World)2.

H. H. A. Cooper
Professor, American University

2

It is not simply political indoctrination or fanatical allegiance to a cause that produces terrorism. The resort to soulless violence we call terrorism requires a peculiar, personal commitment that is complex and intricate in its genesis ... Neither their politics nor ideology make terrorists; they are only rationalizations for acts of terrorism. [Biological research materials] hint at a strong connection between sex and terrorism. In plain terms, it is suggested that the politics of sex are more influential in terrorism than the politics of Mao, Trotsky or Ho Chi Minh. It is just that the latter, as a

rationalization, seems so much more respectable, and the terrorist, above all, craves respect.

Before Senate Judiciary Committee,
Washington/The Washington Post, 7-25:(A)15.

Edward M. Davis
Chief of Police of Los Angeles

3

Many police departments have abandoned intelligence activities on terrorists. Now, that is really foolish ... You can have the best team in the world, but unless you know the other team's strategy you can't win ... America has not yet learned that lesson. We're always talking about great humanism. It's nice stuff that sounds so good. Yet, unless you can anticipate the bad fellows, they're going to get you. Just a microscopic percentage can absolutely tie up the whole country. They can get the attention of the President. Some guy can come along and say, "Hey, you know, if the President calls me I'll do so and so," or "we'll get the President to call and do so and so." My God, if the President has to get involved in negotiating with every Mickey Mouse terrorist around the country, I can guarantee you that there are going to be some worse bad guys ... in the world that are going to make the nation and all humanity suffer to a great extent. We have to get back to a common-sense approach and make law-enforcement agencies realize that scouting the other team in a legal and proper ethical fashion is the only way to play ball.

Before South El Monte (Calif.) Business Council,
March 10/Los Angeles Times, 3-11:(2)2.

4

[Criticizing President Carter for urging decriminalization of possession of small amounts of marijuana]: What should happen now should be a toughening — and we could win this war against dope. Again, it is extremely unfortunate that the President should come out at this time in this battle against dope in the Western world and undermine the battle ... For the President of the United States to say that the substance should be decriminalized is tantamount to Presidential abdication of a moral responsibility to the youth of America. It wasn't too many months ago that this man was

WHAT THEY SAID IN 1977

(EDWARD M. DAVIS)

talking of a new morality in this country . . . I pray that this isn't what he was talking about.

Aug. 2/Los Angeles Times, 8-3:(1)10.

George Deukmejian
California State Senator (R)

1

[Criticizing California Governor Edmund Brown, Jr.'s veto of a bill reinstituting capital punishment in the state] : He said he wants "a society where we do not attempt to use death as a punishment." But he has ignored the fact that murderers are inflicting death as a punishment upon the innocent. I believe the majority of the people of California want a society where innocent people are not put to death.

Sacramento, May 27/Los Angeles Times, 5-28:(1)15.

John Duncan
Executive director,
Texas Civil Liberties Union

2

Tougher laws don't stop the drug traffic. Instead, they increase the risk that any particular individual who engages in the drug traffic will get caught. This increase in risk in turn increases the price for which drug dealers are willing to ply their wares. With the increase in price comes an increase in potential profitability if a person is not caught. The increase in potential profitability attracts persons who think they are smart enough to get in and make a big profit and then get out before they are caught. But someone else is always standing in line with that same American dream of making it big, so the supply does not diminish. Finally, the enormous profits which the law has made possible have made this an ideal area for organized crime to take over.

News conference, Austin, Tex., Feb. 4/
The Dallas Times Herald, 2-6:(A)34.

Robert L. DuPont
Director, National Institute on Drug Abuse

3

I have repeatedly emphasized that marijuana use should be discouraged. [But we should not threaten] the user with legal sanctions and punishments within the criminal-justice system. It is clear that the use of marijuana is no longer

an act of protest but a behavior that has for millions entered the main stream of their life-styles.

The National Observer, 3-26:3.

Peter F. Flaherty
Deputy Attorney General of
the United States

4

As a former Mayor, I know very well that the city is our first line of defense against crime. If the city government is not effective, if the city police force is not professional, if the community does not support law enforcement, then that line of defense will crumble, the city's fight against crime will become increasingly futile, and our cities will become battlegrounds. To fight crime effectively and assure urban residents the right to go about their business without fear of violence and terror is an enormous challenge. You need resources — both money and expertise.

June 30/The Washington Post, 7-8:(A)24.

Harry E. Groves
Dean, North Carolina Central
University Law School

5

I see no need for new laws as to white-collar crime. What I do see is a need for a commitment that all laws will be equally enforced, without deference to the class and status of the offender. Indeed, one might well argue that our sympathy for the white-collar offender is sadly misplaced. He does not steal from necessity. He is not one of our economy's walking wounded. He steals from greed. And he steals from a position of trust. Between the two, one might suppose that our sympathies would be with the thief who is poor. Is it not odd, the reading an affluent society gives to the Eighth Commandment: Thou shalt not steal, unless, of course, thou art already rich and well-favored.

At Rotary Club, Durham, N.C.,
May 9/Vital Speeches, 6-15:526.

Frederick J. Hacker
Psychiatrist; Authority on crime and terrorism

6

. . . I believe that the police should not be quite so confident that they can handle everything that comes up in the way of modern

56

(FREDERICK J. HACKER)

crime all by themselves. For instance, I cannot see why some of the negotiators with terrorists, whether they are crazies or criminals or crusaders, could not be qualified negotiators, such as psychologists and psychiatrists who are trained in interview techniques. Why does the police chief think he's so skilled in getting the best negotiating result with a mentally disturbed person?

Interview/U.S. News & World Report, 2-28:58.

Paul Halvonik
California State Public Defender
1

[Saying that capital punishment is no more a deterrent to murder than the health warning is to cigarette smoking]: I keep smoking cigarettes. I also drive without my seat belt. It's a long way off and I'll worry about it down the line. It's not surprising that criminals feel that way about the death penalty. The death penalty is a very vague threat of death. Who can predict who is going to get the death penalty? . . . We're just not quite prepared to kill all the people who fall within the [death penalty] statutes. We'd have to start killing people in this nation at a rate that is not going on in the entire world. If executions start again, I think we're going to see that kind of reaction from the courts again.

At symposium sponsored by California District Attorneys Association, Los Angeles, Oct. 28/Los Angeles Times, 10-29:(2)1.

John Hill
Attorney General of Texas
2

[Arguing against televising of executions]: Executions should not be made public spectacles. No enlightened person believes executions should be made public. Can anyone say what possible good it could do to watch some poor, unfortunate person go to sleep?

Before Federal appeals panel/ The Dallas Times Herald, 6-18:(B)2.

Barry Keene
California State Assemblyman (D)
3

[Arguing against capital punishment]: We kill and then we say we will not tolerate killings

or violence. The argument has been made [that] these [murderers] are not human beings, that these are animals. This kind of rationalization allowed killings of witches in Salem, hanging of blacks in the South . . . extermination of Jews in Germany.

Los Angeles Herald-Examiner, 8-12:(A)1.

Clarence M. Kelley
Director, Federal Bureau of Investigation
4

When I see the helplessness, the hopelessness, with which many Americans view crime today, I fear that they will opt for an all-too-easy but utterly dangerous answer to it. I fear that when they become completely frustrated by the lawlessness that surrounds them, they will look to the Federal government for what they might falsely believe to be the ultimate answer — the use of authoritarian measures to deal with crime. This is not the answer and should never be considered the answer. Crime can be dealt a devastating setback through total American involvement in crime resistance. That must become an American habit. We must and we can defeat crime within the law.

Interview, Washington/ Los Angeles Herald-Examiner, 4-10:(A)11.

5

While we are reaffirming the individual's right to privacy, while we are instituting, quite properly, firm measures to assure that the FBI toes the line of legality, let us also hammer out a charter spelling out what is expected of it. Never again should the FBI be handed such monumental responsibilities as it was handed in the riot-torn 1960s and early 1970s without clearly defined guidelines. Never again should other key elements of government leave the FBI to improvise its own policies and techniques when bombs are bursting and buildings are burning on campuses and in urban areas . . . when the public, the news media and public officials are clamoring for an end to it. Never again should FBI agents be placed under such tremendous pressure to act in the absence of explicit lawful authority. These things can be avoided. And a legislated charter, a modern

WHAT THEY SAID IN 1977

mandate, could go a long way in accomplishing that.

Before Los Angeles World Affairs Council,
May 18/Vital Speeches, 7-15:579.

1

Some of us in the past have been too quick to cry disaster over each new Supreme Court decision that tends to narrow our investigative prerogatives ... Maybe a few vicious fish slipped through the net as a result of Miranda, but I think effective law enforcement remains alive and well in the United States. What happened was we adapted. We updated our interview procedures ... And the net result was more precise police work, with more regard for the individual's Constitutional guarantees as they are viewed and interpreted today.

Before International Association of
Chiefs of Police, Los Angeles, Oct. 3/
Los Angeles Times, 10-4:(1)3,22.

John McLagan
Director of restitution,
Minnesota Department of Corrections ·

2

A lot of us in the field aren't so much interested in whether the punishment is "rehabilitative." The question is whether the punishment is basically fair. Too often, straight probation is a do-nothing sanction, because in so many places probation officers are bogged down with caseloads of 150 or more. The other sanction is that "big slammer" [prison], and in many cases that is too severe. A better, more fair, sanction may be making people who do wrong by harming others try to right that wrong.

Los Angeles Times, 9-2:(1)7.

Karl A. Menninger
Psychiatrist; Co-founder,
Menninger Foundation

3

... prisoners who have stolen purses, forged checks or raped people often come from homes where they didn't have any moral guidance or love. Most prisoners come from evil homes, broken homes, bad homes, cruel homes. You can almost be certain that the man who commits violent crimes has been treated violently as a child.

Interview, Topeka, Kan./Parade, 10-9:24.

Norval Morris
Dean, University of Chicago Law School

4

Rehabilitation is not a ground on which a person should be sent to prison. But when you look at any big prison, you will find people who are ill-educated, vocationally untrained, socially isolated, addicted and generally in need of help. And it seems very obvious that we should make available to them, if only in our own interests, resources to help them rectify these deficiencies *if they want to.* Rehabilitation, insofar as assisting the convicted criminal if he wishes to better conform, seems obvious good sense. But to send a person to a cage to be cured is, I think, rather silly ... Prisons exist to deter serious crime and also because, within a due respect for human rights, we do not know what else to do with certain serious offenders. We need to have punitive and deterrent processes for some criminals. People do grow out of crime. Their violence fades as the years pass. In the meantime, we have chosen to confine them.

Interview/U.S. News & World Report, 6-20:63.

5

We should get our priorities straight. I think the main business of the police, criminal courts and prisons should be the blood-and-thunder crimes that affect life in this country — homicide, forcible rape, robbery, arson, burglary — the crimes we're scared about ... The crimes we call "illicit practices" — embezzlement, white-collar crimes, trafficking in drugs — should be the business of the courts and, in appropriate cases, the prisons. But uniformed police are not very good at investigating these areas. You need an IRS auditor or investigator. He doesn't have to have 20-20 vision. He can be fat and short of breath.

Interview/People, 8-15:57.

George Moscone
Mayor of San Francisco

6

I don't ever want to minimize the problem of crime. But I don't think the people are

(GEORGE MOSCONE)

fearful to walk the streets. They'll yell at a public meeting that they are, but they probably walked to get to the meeting ... In crime, a legitimate issue is not just what the facts are but what they *appear* to be. If you beat down the spirit of a city — and you beat it down better by scaring people than anything else — you have lost.

Interview, San Francisco/
Los Angeles Times, 2-24:(1)3.

Patrick V. Murphy
President, Police Foundation
1

One of the problems has been the isolation of the average police department — there just hasn't been a good exchange of ideas and advances between the cities. One of the ways to achieve this exchange would be the consolidation of all the small departments in big cities around the country into large departments. But small-department chiefs don't want to lose their turf. They'd rather be a big fish in a small pond than a lieutenant in a large department. And unfortunately, although this is a major reform yet to be attained, the International Association of Chiefs of Police can't make headway with it because the small departments dominate the association.

Interview/Los Angeles Herald-Examiner, 9-30:)A)12.

Peter W. Rodino, Jr.
United States Representative,
D—New Jersey
2

[Advocating Federal payments to crime victims] : ... the innocent victim of violent crime has been ignored for a long time. He's been alienated from society. If we provide compensation, I think he will begin to believe that he is a part of the system and will help in the effort to reduce, deter and prevent crime ... There are people who, because of their alienation, don't report crimes — won't cooperate with law-enforcement officials. This legislation tells people that their government cares about them. Under the House bill, by the way, victims have to cooperate with law-enforcement authorities to get payment ... Government has a responsi-

bility in the first place to protect its citizens from crime. I find it hard to understand why some people will vote to help victims of a disaster like a flood, and then vote against helping the victims of a disaster like rape or murder.

Interview/U.S. News & World Report, 11-28:55.

Samuel B. Sherwin
Deputy Assistant Secretary for
Domestic Commerce, Department of
Commerce of the United States
3

Businessmen may tend to view rising crime rates as "society's problem." Unlike individuals, who take stringent measures to protect themselves from criminal acts out of fear of bodily harm, businessmen tend to think of crime as something they have no control over and from which they should be protected by others. This attitude can only lead to ever-increasing losses to crime. The real question ... is whether business wants to bear the cost of subsidizing crime by treating it with kid gloves, or wants to invest in a gloves-off strategy.

Los Angeles Times, 2-11:(3)13.

W. Raymond Wannall
Former Assistant Director, Intelligence
Division, Federal Bureau of Investigation
4

[Criticizing a bill introduced in Congress which would restrict FBI activities] : Under the proposed legislation, the FBI could not start an investigation of any person or group unless there is reasonable suspicion or a specific allegation that the person or group "has committed, is committing, or is about to commit" a Federal crime. This means, in effect, the FBI could not start gathering information until the crime had already been committed, or there was reason to believe it was about to be committed. Combatting organized crime is to a great extent gathering information to prevent the commission of the crime. Under the proposed legislation, the FBI would also be prohibited from maintaining records on a suspect unless you could prove he had committed a crime or was about to commit one. This would make preventive action virtually impossible.

Interview/Los Angeles Herald-Examiner, 4-17:(A)8.

WHAT THEY SAID IN 1977

Charles E. Wiggins
United States Representative,
R—California
1

[Arguing against Federal payments to crime victims]: Innocent victims of crimes already receive a great deal of help. Medical payments under Medicare or under Medicaid, for instance. Any number of social programs now accommodate the needs of those who are unable to take care of their own medical circumstances. But this proposal of paying victims creates a special program to provide even more for the benefit of those who suffer injuries as a result of criminal misconduct. The problem I have with the idea is that it lacks a satisfactory rationale ... If the purpose is to aid in the enforcement of criminal laws, the proposal misses the mark, because it has no application at all until after a crime has been committed. If the purpose is to encourage the reporting of a crime, then it also misses the mark. There never has been a problem of the bloody victim not reporting the crime, or participating willingly in the prosecution of that crime ... It is apt to deter them from coming forward since the plan, as debated in the House, would create another hearing — an administrative hearing — to which persons would have to go; a new burden they have to bear. Keep in mind that the problem of cooperation focuses upon witnesses who are not themselves victims, and the proposal wouldn't deal with that.

Interview/U.S. News & World Report, 11-28:55.

Evelle J. Younger
Attorney General of California
2

[Supporting capital punishment]: I don't believe the death penalty will deter all murders. It won't even deter most murders. It will deter, in my firm opinion, some murders. And when you're talking about deterring the murder of innocent people, I don't think you have to deal in thousands before you can justify what I believe to be a very realistic penalty.

Before Commonwealth Club, San Francisco,
July 15/Vital Speeches, 9-1:683.

Education

Ernest Bartell
President, Stonehill College
1

...it is always possible for independent colleges and universities to avoid some intrusion by the Federal government by refusing to accept the Federal funding through which the regulation is legitimized. But this is virtually impossible for many universities without dismantling the research capabilities, medical schools and other professional activities that have been developed with Federal funds. Nor can the smaller institutions that receive little direct aid opt for freedom more easily, since the government has extended its jurisdiction to all colleges and universities that enroll even a single student receiving Federal student aid of any kind, including guaranteed student loans. Since the inexorable rise in costs of education make all but a diminishing minority of potential students dependent upon external support, few institutions are so bold as to accept the attendant enrollment risks that would accompany ineligibility for Federal student aid at the very time that the pool of eligible candidates for higher education is expected to begin shrinking as a result of current demographic and economic pressures.

At Shell-Faculty Forum, Houston,
Jan. 18/Vital Speeches, 4-15:391.

Richard Berendzen
Provost, American University
2

The [education] reforms of the late 1960s brought both good and ill. Out went the insensitivity of universities to poor teaching. Out went some really oppressive distribution requirements. [But also,] out went the rigor that some professors had demanded of their students. Out went much of the fabric of educated civilization ... One of the cornerstones of a liberal education is that you are there to teach the whole person.

The Washington Post, 2-21:(A)1.

Dick Bestwick
Football coach, University of Virginia
3

Many scholarship players are attending college just for one purpose — to play college football and try to make the pros. They don't care about academics and neither do the coaches. Now, I'm not condoning it or condemning it, but the situation exists. That's why you see so many NFL players without degrees. I've found that more and more college athletes are getting accepted to play college football who couldn't get into school before.

Los Angeles Times, 5-5:(3)2.

Benjamin Bloom
Professor of education,
University of Chicago
4

My own research over the last decade and a half seems to indicate that most people can learn what anyone can learn. Ninety-five per cent of the population who are normal in any neurological and physiological sense can learn whatever the school or the society has to teach. If this is so, the big questions are: What is worth learning, and how can it be learned? One can list all the educational objectives that everybody should have. But I turn to the one thing that I think all of us wish for. It is the central problem in Europe and in UNESCO today: that is the notion of continuing learning. Man must adapt over and over again to social change, to changes in his own occupation, to changes in the larger society. If schools create both the desire and the capability to continue learning, then I would say they have done a very effective job. If the schools destroy interest, motivation, the ability to use the various learning materials and techniques, then they have done the most destructive of all possible things.

Panel discussion/The Center Magazine,
Nov.-Dec.:56.

WHAT THEY SAID IN 1977

Leon Botstein
President, Bard College

1

Being a college president is not a career. It has been *made* a career by some people and not to the credit of their institutions ... At best, most college presidents are running something that is somewhere between a faltering corporation and a hotel.

Interview, Santa Barbara, Calif./
The Center Magazine, March-April:23.

2

The ignorance among present college students in matters of politics, economics, history, science, technology, art and culture is appalling.

U.S. News & World Report, 5-2:49.

Ernest L. Boyer
Commissioner of Education
of the United States

3

... it's important to remember that American education is and must remain basically a state and local responsibility. At the same time, we're going to take major initiatives in those areas where the Federal government legitimately should be involved. For example, equal access to education is absolutely crucial. Economic and racial barriers must be removed, and we're determined to help the bypassed — the handicapped, poor, minorities, women — to get into the nation's schools and colleges, and the professional schools as well. We'll also be looking for ways to help the middle-income families who are so pinched when their children go to college because of the high tuition costs ... We're committed to quality as well. I'm convinced it's time to emphasize fundamental skills like reading, writing and arithmetic. I don't suggest that these subjects are ends in themselves — but without these basic tools, it's just impossible for students to be fully educated in literature, science and the arts ... Education is central to the progress of this nation. We must have schools and colleges where students not only learn about the past but are also well prepared to live successfully and joyfully in the future, too.

Interview, Washington/
U.S. News & World Report, 7-11:63,64.

4

I don't know anyone who wants to reduce schools to mere training grounds [for the job market]. But I'm convinced that not to confront the question of what the future years hold for graduates of our schools and colleges is to be not very fair to students ... The issue of the nature of work should be part of a common core experience, embodied in the general curriculum that every student would be exposed to. I would include a study of the nature of work, because it absorbs not only most of our waking hours, but determines also in large part who we are or who we think we are ... At the college level, a model that attracts me is merging the traditional degree with a complimentary field in a more concrete technical area. That way we don't say to a person, "you will be a computer programmer all your life, but you will have a job skill with an economic market when you have earned your four-year liberal-arts degree." We are asking that there be some practical training at the college level. My son, for example, has a bachelor's degree in philosophy. He loves literature, but he got a master's in library science so that he would have a marketable skill.

Interview, Washington/
Los Angeles Times, 9-9:(1-A)5,6.

5

I've always felt that assessing a teacher's performance is an appropriate goal, but I'm anxious about the use of tests as a vehicle for measuring a teacher's ability. There is a degree of correlation between good teaching and the outcome of written exams. But there is not a neat, absolute overlap. Some outcomes of good teaching don't immediately show.

U.S. News & World Report, 12-12:52.

Kingman Brewster, Jr.
President, Yale University

6

Those who are against change in society generally are going to be against change in the university ... I'm not unaware of the fact that some members of the oldest generation are full of dismay at the changes they have seen in their lifetime, and wish the world would stop spin-

(KINGMAN BREWSTER, JR.)

ning and wonder why their university can't stop it from spinning.

Interview, Yale University/
The Washington Post, 4-8:(B)3.

Joyce Brothers
Psychologist

1

. . . even in this age of television, we live in a world of the written word. Just to cross the street, we have to be able to read "Walk" and "Wait." To get a license to drive a car, to apply for a job, welfare or Medicaid, to get Social Security benefits, to get credit or a bank loan, we have to be able to read questions and write answers to them. But at least 13 per cent of our population over the age of 16 isn't literate enough to perform these simple tasks adequately, according to a survey conducted by the National Reading Council. This is good news when compared to an earlier study made at Harvard University, which found that half the adult population cannot read a variety of very ordinary reading matter. The Federal government estimates that 8 per cent of Americans are functionally illiterate. This figure represents those adults who did not finish the 5th grade and assumes that those who did are able to read . . . If you still have doubts about the downward spiral in reading and writing, as well as computational skills of American students, we should realize that, by most measures, student achievement is now below the national average of a decade ago. According to knowledgeable researchers, there are indications that the decline — reflected in a wide range of standardized test results and other evidence of academic performance — is growing much worse. It is a national problem — and a national disgrace.

At Manufacturers Hanover Trust Company,
New York, May 23/Vital Speeches, 8-1:623.

Edmund G. Brown, Jr.
Governor of California (D)

2

Never before has education been so irrelevant to so many kids in our society. The law schools and the educational schools — in many ways they are abysmal failures. And being at the top of the [academic-excellence rating] list is maybe not a sign of success but of failure. I suspect these pillars of progress and bastions of expertise have failed the society in many ways.

Before University of California Board of
Regents, San Francisco/San Francisco Examiner &
Chronicle, 1-30:(This World)5.

3

The institutions of society need revitalization if society is to maintain itself, and schools are one of the most important institutions, judging by the amount of money we put into them . . . Some of the more traditional school structures are hangovers from the Middle Ages and less-mobile times, so a lot of what's still going on in education is just a ritual without serious impact on the minds of young people. That's why in any school program I support I want to see maximum involvement of the purported beneficiaries, and not just the professional practitioners.

Interview, Sacramento/
The New York Times, 2-14:16.

Roscoe C. Brown
Professor of education, New York University

4

Education uses sports as an outlet for kids but doesn't go to the next step of using that interest as a catalyst for other learning activities. So many people think black kids can't learn, so they give them a ball to tranquilize them and keep them happy rather than confronting the real issue — make schools better. For so many youngsters, school is so unrelated to their now-life and their future life.

The Washington Post, 3-21:(D)4.

Brendan T. Byrne
Governor of New Jersey (D)

5

[On being a Princeton University alumnus]: Vocationally speaking, Princeton doesn't prepare you for anything. A degree from Princeton is not a political asset, to be sure. People resent a degree from Princeton when you are running for public office. An article in a current magazine suggests that I cannot develop the

WHAT THEY SAID IN 1977

(BRENDAN T. BYRNE)

kind of rapport with other politicians to deal with problems. One of the quotes to support this thesis is that I'm too Princeton.

Before Princeton students/
The New York Times, 4-7:38.

Joseph A. Califano, Jr.
Secretary of Health, Education
and Welfare of the United States
                                            1

[Saying he opposes Federal testing programs for schools]: One of the great virtues of our system is that, in our states, we have 50 different centers for developing ideas and programs. In its most extreme form, national control of curriculum is a form of national control of ideas.

Before College Entrance Examination
Board, San Francisco/
The Christian Science Monitor, 11-23:10.

Olin Cook
Arkansas State Director
of Higher Education
                                            2

Adult education will keep the classes filled and the bills paid.

U.S. News & World Report, 3-28:70.

Sidney B. Coulling
Professor of English,
Washington and Lee University
                                            3

Like every other college in the country, we depend for our students on an educational system that has become a national scandal, and even with highly selective admissions policies and careful screening, some students are admitted — at Washington and Lee and everywhere else — who are not fully prepared for college work, particularly in English and mathematics. The difficulty they encounter breeds discouragement; discouragement breeds frustration; and frustration often breeds a sense of defeat. At least partly because of this, the characteristic malaise among students in recent years has been the simple inability to do a job, to complete an assignment, to write a required paper. It has replaced sex and religion, the

university chaplain tells me, as the students' Number 1 problem.

Before Richmond, Va., chapter of
Washington and Lee University alumni/
The Wall Street Journal, 11-11:16.

Alonzo Crim
Superintendent of Schools of Atlanta
                                            4

The greatest fault of public schools has been in attempting to satisfy all of the requests made upon them, especially in those areas not directly related to education. The result has been a dissipation of the capabilities and the resources of school systems. We need to establish a consensus on priorities — to define just what we will do and what we cannot do. And the Number 1 priority should be a substantial improvement in the achievement of students in the area of basic skills. This goal must be presented as a systemwide objective in a community, so that every school, every principal, every classroom teacher, and every student and every parent will contribute by devising an appropriate plan that will help bring about higher student achievement. Most importantly, we must reshape our day-to-day routines and activities on a regular basis so that we know we are staying on target.

Interview/U.S. News & World Report, 9-12:33.

Melvin Dubnick
Assistant professor of political
science, Loyola University, Chicago
                                            5

More and more college students are taking courses geared for the world of work. They are taking pre-law, pre-med, pre-dental, pre-professional programs. The liberal-arts programs are feeling the effect of that. Liberal-arts teachers now look at their pre-med students and say, "Why should I teach them about Hobbes? That's going to be irrelevant to their career goals." The problem in higher education today is the emphasis on career education. In my own field — political science — our programs are not so much political science as public administration. More and more programs in chemistry and physics are going away from the experimental

(MELVIN DUBNICK)

and toward what will be useful for medical school.

Panel discussion/
The Center Magazine, Nov.-Dec.:60.

Robert Dunham
Vice president of undergraduate studies,
Pennsylvania State University
1

[On college students who have not learned writing skills]: These are not dumb students. They are bright and have come through high school with fine averages and have done fairly well on the Scholastic Aptitude Test. But somewhere along the way they have neglected to pick up those basic writing skills which are absolutely essential to making it in college. So it's not so much a remediation course [that is needed] — that suggests that the students have had a dose and failed, and have to get another dose — it's that most of them never had that done ... We are asking all faculty members to make writing more important and to give more writing assignments. When they discover students don't write as well as they used to, the faculty members have tolerated more bad writing, like going from essay exams to multiple-choice exams, and we really haven't stressed the importance of writing in our other classes.

Interview/The National Observer, 6-13:6.

David Elkind
Psychologist and psychiatrist,
University of Rochester
2

American parents were sold a bill of goods in the 1950s and early '60s. The Soviet Union had sent up their *Sputnik,* and it gave the U.S. an inferiority complex. Shortly after that, there was a big push for earlier education for our children: Teach them to read early; give them a "new math." There was a pressure for early intellectual stimulation — it's still with us — and our research shows that it has been a mistake. The average child isn't ready for formal reading instruction before the age of 6½ or 7, and forcing him into it in first grade — often even in kindergarten — is a challenge that almost guarantees failure. It turns him off reading and

sometimes promotes lifelong frustration with education ... I find most teachers are in complete agreement, that we have slipped into a system of applying too much pressure too early. But they tend to blame the parents for continuing the pressures. If parents would relax, the schools could relax. Unfortunately, in our society, with our Puritan mentality, there is a feeling that if our kids are not doing well in school, it must be because the school is too easy on them. Actually, if our kids are not doing well, I feel it is because we're being too tough. I'm sure some parents will feel I'm soft-headed when I say that. But our falling SAT scores are not, in my opinion, the result of a lax school system — which everyone assumes — but a misplaced pressure for too-early intellectual stimulation.

Los Angeles Herald-Examiner, 10-7:(C)2.

Clifton Fadiman
Author, Editor
3

My notions of an ideal education are conventional. They have to do with the liberation of the human mind. Education is a mechanism for freeing the human mind from prejudice, from parochialism, from narrowness. It is simply the best device, it seems to me, that we have yet come up with for educing whatever is best in the individual in the way of sensibility, intelligence, appreciation of the life around him, and power of growth.

Interview, Santa Barbara, Calif./
The Center Magazine, July:Aug.:54.

Robert Farrell
Dean of writing, Cornell University
4

The decline in writing skills is not only marked, but it's massive. This is not a national problem, it's an international one. My colleagues in Sweden and Germany are experiencing the same thing we are here. We get a lot of people who come to us as burnt-out cases. They're convinced they can't write. The most encouraging thing is students realize they need these skills and they want to do something about it. It's not that they're stupid or incom-

WHAT THEY SAID IN 1977

(ROBERT FARRELL)

petent. It's just they haven't been given the opportunity to write.

San Francisco Examiner & Chronicle, 10-2:(This World)33.

Joseph Featherstone
Lecturer, Graduate School of Education,
Harvard University
1

In one form or another, schools will have to figure out ways of getting parents and others in the community involved in education — not as lynch mobs demanding "back to basics" or budget cuts, but helpers in finding answers to the very real question: Can schools become more qualitative and more selective in priorities, and discard the idea that quantity must always come first? Bigness is not always better. There's no reason why a combination of centralized services and decentralized small high schools — and I'm speaking of 300 to 400 students — can't provide a good balance of human-sized scale and specialized equipment and services ... Smaller-scale schools, more attention to the needs of teachers, more respect for what parents have to say — all these fit into the broad rubric of quality, because they suggest alternatives to mass institutions that treat everybody as subservient to "the system." This means no foregoing of the old agenda: our commitment to mass education. Poor kids in ghetto schools can also benefit from not going to dungeonlike educational factories that give an assembly-line education to as many as 5,000 youngsters. The trick in this vast and muddled enterprise of American education is to recognize the urgency of the new demands without letting go of the ideal of equal access to education for all.

Interview/U.S. News & World Report, 9-12:32.

John Forbes
Deputy Director General,
United Nations Educational, Scientific
and Cultural Organization
2

Education — basic and continuing — constitutes a fundamental human right on which, moreover, many other rights depend. A world in which this right is disregarded, and thus where the development of individuals and of their communities is hampered, cannot be other than a world of frustration, incomprehension and stress.

International Literacy Day address, Sept. 8/ The Christian Science Monitor, 12:30:13.

Richard B. Freeman
Associate professor of
economics, Harvard University
3

In the last two decades, we've had a cycle of shortages of engineers followed by high enrollments in engineering, followed by a surplus of graduates — then a declining enrollment until a new shortage of engineers develops. Right now, the job market for engineers is relatively good. We're experiencing the biggest increases in freshmen enrolling in engineering programs that we've ever experienced. I am willing to bet right now that four years hence, when these large classes that are entering engineering now graduate, they will have problems.

Interview/U.S. News & World Report, 1-24:60.

Roger A. Freeman
Senior fellow emeritus, Hoover
Institution, Stanford University
4

Between 1952 and 1972, when enrollment in public schools and colleges almost doubled, the staffs in these institutions tripled and their funds multiplied eight times. Expenditures per student nearly tripled ... [Yet] mean scores on college board tests have been declining sharply and consistently for a dozen years ... Analysis of test results in the few city school systems from which detailed data are available, such as New York and Oakland, show a clearcut and strong negative relationship between expenditures per pupil and pupil achievement.

At Hillsdale College/ Los Angeles Herald-Examiner, 7-12:(A)10.

A. Bartlett Giamatti
President-designate, Yale University
5

...I happen to believe that athletics are crucial to education in that we plan to live in our bodies, and the values that are implicit in that are part of the whole educational process.

(A. BARTLETT GIAMATTI)

In a strict sense of the word, the academic is the central mission and purpose of the university. But I don't conceive of athletics as in any way ornamental or simply useful for fundraising. I conceive of athletics as an activity that engages the deepest reaches of the human spirit.

Interview/The New York Times, 12-25:(4)7.

1

The question of writing is crucial. It is the fundamental pedagogical problem in American education at all levels: How do you get people to write clearly and in an organized fashion? That means nothing other than how do you get them to think clearly. It's hard work to learn to write. But language is the medium in which we live. Whether you are going to be a clergyman or a teacher or a fireman or whatever, you've got to have control over your language. That's what helps define you.

Interview/The New York Times, 12-25:(4)7.

Donald Graves
Professor of education,
University of New Hampshire

2

[On the writing crisis in today's schools]: Today we are set up in schools and in the broad society to receive information, not to give it. That is, there is more concern about your ability to read and listen and to get someone else's message than in your ability to send one out. And to me, in a democracy it is absolutely frightening that fewer and fewer persons are doing the writing for larger and larger audiences.

Interview, Durham, N.H./
The Christian Science Monitor, 10-11:24.

S. I. Hayakawa
United States Senator, R—California;
Former professor of semantics

3

One of our ambitions as professors is to have jobs of distinction where we do not have to teach; a research institute is an ideal institution in which to get such a position . . . I have tried to become one, because it is such a nice cushy job. But I came to the Senate instead.

Los Angeles Times, 6-22:(1)2.

Douglas H. Heath
Professor of psychology,
Haverford College

4

Admissions officers and faculties, particularly of highly selective colleges, might well reconsider the types of persons that they wish to select to educate . . . If we continue to educate too narrowly, too technically, too reductively, if we continue to ignore a student's character, the skills and values of adaptability, and the contextuality of our survival problems, then our colleges do not deserve to survive as liberally educating institutions.

Los Angeles Herald-Examiner, 6-6:(A)1.

Fred M. Hechinger
Member of the editorial board,
and former education editor,
"The New York Times"

5

The massive failure in the basic skills — particularly reading and writing — is nothing short of scandalous. The strategies to reverse those failures call, not for miracle cures, but for application of common sense. The training of those teachers who are responsible for the teaching of the basic skills must be lifted bodily out of the theory-bound college campus and transplanted instead into the practicum of real classrooms with live children . . . The schools' continuing failure to teach the basic skills to so many of its clients cannot be dismissed by statistics that show — quite sincerely — that the schools did no better in the past, that they quite possibly did worse. It is only against current expectations, and against the needs of today's society, that the success and failure of contemporary institutions must be measured.

Before National School Boards
Association, Houston, March 26/
The Dallas Times Herald, 3-27:(A)34.

Terry Herndon
Executive secretary, National
Education Association

6

Teachers are under more pressure than ever, and they are more frustrated than ever. We live in a turbulent, neurotic society, and that society comes to school every day.

U.S. News & World Report, 12-12:50.

WHAT THEY SAID IN 1977

John A. Howard
President, Rockford (Ill.) College

1

The values which our schools and colleges used to teach to all their students under the headings of citizenship education and character education may very well have been the values which made it possible for our social institutions to retain their freedom in a free nation. When self-reliance, self-discipline and thrift were commended to the young as virtues, the role of government in society remained limited, and the schools and colleges and our other social institutions retained their autonomy. As modern social and psychological theory came to deride and undermine those virtues, and even challenge the very concept of virtue, the effort to train the young in self-reliance, self-discipline and thrift was phased out of the schooling process. The result has been that those qualities have greatly diminished among the populace, and the government has been called in to pick up the pieces and pay the bills through Federal aid to education and many other welfare-state programs. It is time for educational institutions to admit the truth to the American public and proclaim that the anticipated benefits of governmental aid to education have fallen short of what was expected, and the price paid for governmental aid is far greater than was anticipated. In fact, that price is altogether intolerable, for it is subservience and fast approaching captivity.

Before National Association of
Evangelicals' Commission on Higher
Education, Arlington Heights, Ill.,
Feb. 23/Vital Speeches, 5-1:431.

Harold Howe II
Vice president for education
and research, Ford Foundation

2

Further education is bound to enhance the depth and breadth of your appreciation and understanding of a whole variety of aspects of the world, be they political, scientific, artistic or whatever. By addressing oneself in an organized way to the wide-ranging field of human experience – and that's what happens in college – a person builds a bank on which to draw in the future. He or she really does have – in my

view and in the view of many people better informed than I – a more interesting life. That's the personal side of it. On what I might call the civic side of it, perhaps the best thing to say is to go back to H. G. Wells' familiar statement – that history is a race between education and catastrophe. I think there is some fundamental truth in that ... I think it's a valid argument that in a republic which depends upon the judgment, good sense and civility of its citizens, the idea of having those citizens better and better educated carries with it the idea of an improved capacity to contend with an increasingly complex world.

Interview/U.S. News & World Report, 1-24:59.

3

I think there is some threat to the important tradition of studies in the liberal arts. There is a tendency, particularly in undergraduate colleges, for youngsters to see more immediate opportunities in engineering, accounting and the like. It seems to me important to keep a solid element of liberal-arts education in the curriculum. It's quite possible to learn a vocational specialty in college and at the same time to enhance one's sense of the civilization and the country of which he is a part. The recent emphasis on the economic value of education implies that such concerns may be impractical. But without them. men and women become little more than robots trained to fit the needs of the economic system.

Interview/U.S. News & World Report, 1-24:60.

John R. Hubbard
President, University
of Southern California

4

The talk about the trend in the country of private universities and colleges becoming state institutions worries me. In 1945, there was a 50-50 public-private ratio. Now only 23 per cent of the schools are private, and in California alone there is only a 10 per cent private enrollment. There are great public universities, of course. You won't find a better university anywhere than the University of California at Berkeley, for example. But the major difference is the private university can pick and choose what it wants to do. Private universities gen-

(JOHN R. HUBBARD)

erally are the source of experimental concepts. The state university has a public mandate to meet.

Interview/Los Angeles Herald-Examiner, 7-24:(A)7.

Jesse L. Jackson
Civil-rights leader; President,
Operation PUSH (People United
to Save Humanity)
1

Parents are the foundation of the school system. The school system can do without teachers. Many of them survive with poor ones. They can do without superintendents. But no school system can get by without parents. If parents don't make kids, there won't be any schools. If parents don't pay the taxes, there won't be any teachers. If parents do not assume the primary responsibility for monitoring and disciplining their children, there won't be any results.

At Dallas School District tea, June 26/
The Dallas Times Herald, 6-27:(D)1.

John E. Jacob
Executive director,
Washington Urban League
2

Without standards to assure that grades are a true measure of educational attainment . . . not only will students lose respect for the seriousness of their educational experience, but they also will leave ill-prepared to compete for hard-to-get jobs.

Before National Association of
Personnel Workers/
The Washington Post, 3-3:(A)22.

Philip Jordan, Jr.
President, Kenyon College
3

Employers want people who know how to think effectively, who are articulate and able to reason. It does little good to know a lot about physics, or economics, or medicine if you know nothing about Socrates or Shakespeare or the Norman conquest, because you won't be able to relate your work to society at large or put it in a historical context.

U.S. News & World Report, 5-2:49.

John G. Kemeny
President, Dartmouth College
4

We should prepare our students, not for next year, but 50 years in the future for the world in which they will spend most of their lives — and a highly uncertain future that is . . . I really look with horror upon the language of financial investment being applied to college education . . . The greatest rewards . . . have always been intangible: the arousing of curiosity, the satisfaction of a thirst for knowledge, and helping our students become better human beings.

Interview, Hanover, N.H./
The Christian Science Monitor, 1-24:25.

Clark Kerr
Chairman, Carnegie Council on Policy
Studies in Higher Education; Former
president, University of California
5

While the difference between college-educated persons and others will probably never again be so great as they were in the 1950s and 1960s, that is just as well in a nation that promises justice and opportunity for all its citizens. Yet the promise of higher education and the contribution it can make, both to individuals and societies, continues to justify the decisions of those millions who choose to participate in it.

San Francisco Examiner & Chronicle,
12-4:(This World)2.

Eberhard Laemmert
President, Free University of (West) Berlin
6

This institution has had a lot of polarization, and that has damaged it. True, we have had reform. But we have also learned that bringing democracy to a university doesn't mean it can be run like a parliament. A standing opposition within an institution of learning and research harms it.

Interview, West Berlin/
The Christian Science Monitor, 5-6:24.

WHAT THEY SAID IN 1977

David F. Linowes
*Professor of political economy and
public policy, University of Illinois*
1

Basic to all public-school education is the ratio of one teacher to 25 students. This ratio is extremely critical because it determines the number of classrooms, the size of schools, the number of teachers, the number of principals, how the entire educational system is structured. I think we would have a right to assume this ratio is a relatively modern, carefully researched formula for maximum effectiveness. This is not so. This formula was established over 1,500 years ago and can be found in the Babylonian Talmud, written in the third century A.D. There it states in words to the effect that for every 25 students there shall be one teacher. If the number of students exceeds 25, but is less than 40, the teacher shall have an assistant. If there are 40 or more students, there shall be two teachers. Education is essentially communication. When we recognize the great technological strides made in communication over the past 1,500 years, as well as the tremendous body of knowledge that has accumulated during that same period of time, many intelligent persons must wonder why we have stayed with this antiquated concept. To the best of my knowledge, the answer is only inertia and adherence to archaic tradition. No research has ever established that the 1-to-25 ratio is the most effective way for education in the 20th century. Yet we continue building schools, hiring teachers, spending billions of dollars based on this outmoded approach to education. A firmly entrenched good-management policy is to constantly research and re-examine the way things are being done, always with a view toward improving the overall effectiveness of an organization. Why not education?
*At YMCA-YWCA Annual Forum, Champaign, Ill.,
Sept. 9/Vital Speeches, 10-15:17.*

Dan Lortie
Professor of education, University of Chicago
2

When teachers were thought of as underpaid, it was regarded as unfair to be critical of them. Since they have unionized and begun to strike, there is no longer a feeling of ritual pity for teachers. The feeling now is that they can look out for themselves.
U.S. News & World Report, 12-12:50.

Richard W. Lyman
President, Stanford University
3

It is very understandable that students, wishing to do something to work and act against injustice in the world . . . should see the university as their most accessible weapon with which to fight against such evils. It is also understandable that they should regard as relatively less urgent, indeed almost abstract, the argument that the price of academic freedom for our universities is our refraining from involvement, *as an institution,* in political questions beyond those most directly related to our own functioning as a teaching and learning institution. We could all ponder to advantage, however, just how long that freedom would survive in American higher education were our colleges and universities to assume a responsibility to act as institutional agents of social reform. The experience of countless other nations should stand as a warning to us: Our freedom depends, as it always has, upon our *not* becoming captives of any political movements, no matter how high-minded, and upon our being perceived by the public as educational and research institutions, first, last and always.
*At Stanford Alumni campus conference/
The Wall Street Journal, 8-10:18.*

Luis Martin
*Professor of history,
Southern Methodist University*
4

. . . any thinking person in this country should make the greatest possible effort to assure that private institutions make it. Private education is essential to a free, democratic society. Institutions that are not private have a very important role, too. But the freedom, autonomy and independence that a private institution can enjoy is something that we cannot afford to lose . . . whether university level, high school or junior high school.
*Interview/
The Dallas Times Herald, 12-4:(Sunday)24.*

Paul W. McCracken
Professor of business administration,
University of Michigan
1

[There should be] a full-dress Congressional investigation of why our educational system is turning out people so poorly trained for the labor-market opportunities that already exist. This situation is taking on the proportions of a national scandal. We have a special-interest group – the educational industry – with hardening of the arteries. They teach their traditional courses in the traditional way because the teachers feel comfortable doing that ... We have demand for auto mechanics, for instance, that we can't fill. At the high-school level, we're pressing youngsters to attend college when perhaps that isn't their aptitude. And at the college level, schools of education are pouring out people with teacher's certificates when we don't have opportunities for them to teach, and the birth statistics indicate we won't have those opportunities in the near future.

Interview/U.S. News & World Report, 2-21:56,57.

Thomas J. McIntyre
United States Senator, D–New Hampshire
2

I like to think that the litmus test of education is whether it produces arrogance or humility in those who are educated. The men and women I consider educated in the fullest sense of the word – regardless of whether that education came from cloistered halls or the streets of life – are those who are most humble before their own ignorance. They *know* how little they know. They understand how much *more* there is to be learned.

Before Phi Delta Kappa Society of
Educators, Concord, N.H./
The Christian Science Monitor, 9-2:31.

Kathleen McNally
Director of research,
Joint Council on Economic Education
3

Too often, the American history teacher fails to touch on the economic concepts and factors which influence historical events. Often, the courses are factual and descriptive and teachers lack the grasp of analytical economics

necessary to really explain the underlying economic forces at work. If the student is able to understand the economic and social implications of what has happened in the past, he will better understand the role of economics in current events. Problems change, but economic tools are as pertinent to analyzing contemporary problems as they are in analyzing prior events. For example, it's one thing to teach about the Great Depression by noting that the gross national product fell by 50 per cent and one quarter of the work force was unemployed. It's quite something else to use the tools of economics to analyze how these events could have occurred and what was necessary to correct them.

The Christian Science Monitor, 2-4:21.

Henry Miller
Author
4

I've read more than 50,000 books, but I attribute at least part of my success to never having been formally educated. Education is a hindrance, a straitjacket. I've rarely seen it work, except in Rabindranath Tagore's school under the trees, and an anarchist school in New Jersey that emphasized the spirit, the soul, sports and music. It's the closest thing I've seen to medieval training, which was a lot lustier and fuller than in our time.

Interview, Los Angeles/
Los Angeles Times, 9-9:(4)20.

Maurice B. Mitchell
Chancellor, University of Denver;
President-designate, Center for the
Study of Democratic Institutions
5

... formal institutional education, vital as it may be, necessarily meets only a part of the citizen need to improve his understanding of the world in which he lives. My own approach to life has been based on the assumption that education must be seen as a continuing process upon which the preservation of democracy depends.

Interview, Los Angeles/
The New York Times, 12-3:11.

WHAT THEY SAID IN 1977

Alfred L. Moye
Vice chancellor for student affairs,
University of Pittsburgh; Deputy
Commissioner-designate for
Higher and Continuing Education,
Federal Office of Education   1

I think our education system should prepare a person not for his first job but for his last, that we should give him the basic knowledge that can continue to grow, that will enable him to develop new skills every day. We need people with the type of education that they will be able to apply to problems we don't even yet have. If you don't educate a person to the point that he can transcend a limited skill, then there's a good chance that person will become outdated.

Interview, Pittsburgh/
The Dallas Times Herald, 9-18:(A)34.

Edwin Newman
News correspondent,
National Broadcasting Company   2

The main problem we have with the language is the bloating of it — filling it with gas. Those who are most guilty are the social scientists. The reason academics do it is that they are frequently trying to conceal the fact they have nothing to say. Students fall victim to this quite willingly. One student said her attitude was caused by "the recency of her studenthood."

Interview/"W": a Fairchild publication, 1-7:2.

Dallin H. Oaks
President, Brigham Young University   3

I reluctantly accept as inevitable the fact that many currently independent institutions must have some type of public assistance if they are to continue to perform educational functions, which, as president John Silber of Boston University has noted so persuasively, are public functions and worthy of public support. But we must find ways to make such public assistance available to independent colleges and universities with the minimum possible "strings." And the regulatory burden imposed upon those receiving such assistance must be graduated according to the magnitude of the

aid received — whether massive or *de minimus* — and adjusted according to its nature — whether direct, such as direct budgetary support or categorical assistance, or indirect, such as loans or grants to students or even tax credits for those who give contributions or pay tuitions to higher education. Private, independent institutions must have options on the amount of government regulation to which they will be subject by the receipt of different kinds and amounts of public assistance.

Before Western College Association,
San Francisco,
March 10/Vital Speeches, 4-1:373.

Angelo Picchieri
Italian sociologist   4

Our universities no longer produce culture, research or science. They exist primarily in order to mask the true extent of unemployment among our youth.

The Washington Post, 3-5:(A)10.

John Rassias
Professor, department of romance
languages, Dartmouth College   5

Language training in the country is down to a perilously low level, but I think it will rise if it is taught differently, emphasizing each person's urge to express himself. We should teach languages to communicate... I honestly believe that with the world being reduced, and the absolute necessity of people to help each other, an understanding of language is necessary. The minute you begin to speak another language, it's no longer foreign.

The New York Times, 3-23:(A)22.

Diane Ravitch
Historian, Teachers College,
Columbia University   6

Throughout history, schools have always been expected to represent and transmit values. But the public school in America today has tried to fill so many disparate needs that it is in danger of becoming a neutral institution — representing nothing, serving no particular interest well, and having no sense of direction. It's lost some of its moral center, so we're

(DIANE RAVITCH)

seeing things like classes in "value clarification." It's only when education is morally neutral that you need a special class to tell children: "Now, these are values, and here's what they are all about." What we should be doing, I think, is to teach our young people about Western civilization. At its best, it represents values which are humane, universal, liberal and democratic. By studying our history, literature and cultural heritage, a young person can learn a great deal about what's wrong and what's right. This is the kind of education that many parents want to see. What our children can learn in school are the kinds of things they'll never learn from television — the best values of our civilization.

Interview/U.S. News & World Report, 9-12:32.

Hyman G. Rickover
Admiral, United States Navy
1

Parents and students must accept the unpleasant fact that today's awards and diplomas do not necessarily imply academic achievement. Grade inflation, far from helping students, [has] robbed them of a proper education; too late they discover how little they really learned. Accepting a diploma without an education makes no more sense than getting vaccinated and not finding out if the vaccination took.

Before Senate Education Subcommittee,
Washington, July 14/
The Washington Post, 7-15:(A)17.

Wilson Riles
California State Superintendent
of Public Instruction
2

In this state we have given attention to the primary grades, and that is reflected without a doubt in higher test scores in reading and mathematics. Our third-graders are above the national average in reading. But what we didn't know and what we know now is that it's not enough to have stimulating and challenging programs at the primary grades and then cut them off [with weaker programs on the secondary level]. Youngsters don't continue to progress without that extra help and you can't just count on giving them a good start and leaving them to prosper afterward.

Interview/The New York Times, 2-6:(4)16.

John C. Sawhill
President, New York University
3

A slowed birth rate, declining Federal support, and the crunch of inflation and recession — these are the general problems besetting today's colleges and universities . . . This situation is forcing university administrators, particularly those in large, urban settings, to deal head-on with the extrinsic factors that threaten to undermine the intrinsic missions of their institutions. Unfortunately, we have seen that financial pressures create temptations to compromise traditional academic values in order to attract more students or to save on the expense in educating them. To my mind, no temptation is more to be resisted than the present trend toward over-vocationalization of undergraduate education. The tight job market has led many students and their parents to reassess the function of college. As a result, more and more students have opted to specialize in areas they feel will give them immediately marketable skills upon leaving school. Universities, facing the need to compete for a pool of students that has begun growing more slowly and will soon actually decline substantially, have too often responded by sacrificing broad-based programs in the liberal arts and sciences and emphasizing the pre-professional programs to which students have been flocking.

Before Advertising Council
board of directors, New York,
Jan. 6/Vital Speeches, 3-1:310.

David S. Saxon
President, University of California
4

[On the lack of basic skills evident in incoming university students]: Public awareness and concern are turning the situation around. There is greater concern being expressed about deficiencies in reading, composition and mathematics. What we're really talking about are the "three Rs," reading, 'riting and 'rithmetic. There is a public feeling

WHAT THEY SAID IN 1977

(DAVID S. SAXON)

that any education program which neglects them is deficient ... when students graduate after putting in 12 years of seat time and are deficient in the basic skills, that is an indictment of the system.

Interview, Los Angeles/
Los Angeles Herald-Examiner, 6-19:(A)3.

Oscar E. Shabat
Chancellor, City College of Chicago

1

... we should not write off any group or any generation and say they are incapable of learning. Those of us in the city colleges are trying to see that that does not happen. It is an extremely difficult job. We tend to blame the students. If most of our students cannot read very well, let alone write, remember that many of them are graduates of our high schools. In our massive, big-city school systems, there just is no heavy emphasis or value placed on reading. If there were that emphasis, we could change the situation. This morning's newspaper has a 17-page color section on Elvis Presley. What does that mean in our society, as compared to what we are talking about here?

Panel discussion/The Center
Magazine, Nov.-Dec.:56.

Albert Shanker
President, American Federation of Teachers

2

Police, fire and sanitation services can be traced right to the Mayor. When those services erode, the Mayor gets blamed. But when the school system erodes, the Mayor can blame the Board of Education.

Newsweek, 9-12:63.

Virginia B. Smith
President-designate, Vassar College

3

I would like to make a liberal-arts education truly meaningful in a world that is becoming more and more oriented toward vocations. I would like to make it possible for others to understand the importance of that kind of education. And I would like to see offered, in a coeducational setting, non-sexist education.

Interview/The New York Times, 4-8:(A)24.

Carolyn Warner
Arizona Superintendent
of Public Instruction

4

We now require our public schools to provide physical education, transportation, cafeterias, vaccinations, driver training and lectures on alcoholism and drug abuse. We've gotten into adult education, sex education, bilingualism, ecology and energy conservation — along with programs for the gifted, the handicapped and the children of migrant workers. There's counseling of all kinds: academic, careers, psychological and disciplinary. And we've told our schools to see to it that society becomes integrated. In short, we've loaded our schools with so many responsibilities that I view American education, as now constituted, as an endangered species. The time has come when somebody will have to stand up, with heels dug in, and say: "Look, friends, we're on a collision course with disaster. Is the public school the *only* institution for change in America? All of these programs are desirable, but when do we teach the basics: reading, writing and arithmetic — the three Rs?"

Interview/U.S. News & World Report, 9-12:34.

Robert O. Anderson
Chairman, Atlantic Richfield Company

1

I've been interested in the environment and conservation all my life and am a firm believer in sensible environmental concern. But I am not a strict preservationist. I happen to think that our social and human needs require some consideration in the order of things and that we do have to intrude on the environment at times, but that it should be done in a most intelligent, least destructive way possible.

Interview, Roswell, N.M./
The Dallas Times Herald, 4-10:(E)10.

Cecil D. Andrus
Secretary of the Interior
of the United States

2

Our President [Carter] has a deep personal commitment to end the waste and misuse of America's natural resources. He has cancelled the blank check which once went to those who would exploit resources and pollute the environment in the name of progress. Business-as-usual has been put out of business. We intend to exercise our stewardship of public lands and natural resources in a manner that will make the three Rs — rape, ruin and run — a thing of the past.

San Francisco Examiner & Chronicle,
4-3:(This World)2.

3

[Calling for more prudence in future dam-building in the West]: [In the past there has been] too much impatience for development and too little consideration of adverse consequences. Certainly, there is no question that sound reclamation projects have brought tremendous benefits to large areas of the West. But somewhere along the line we have lost sight of what reclamation is all about. It is about improving life, not destroying it. I would

suggest that perhaps we have built the best of the hydroelectric plants. Perhaps we have developed the best of the reclamation projects ... Now we have reached the point of diminishing returns, and what we do from here on should be done with the greatest of care. Streams and rivers have other values than just for electric-power generation and irrigation and transportation. We need some free-flowing water left in the nation for many reasons, including the protection of certain forms of life, for recreation, for scenic values, for maintenance of our tenuous link between modern man and his natural world.

Before National Press Club, Washington,
May 10/Los Angeles Times, 5-11:(1)8.

4

We must maintain our stewardship of water like that of fine gold. If people keep on like they're doing, wasting water, there will be two results in many areas. First, it will stop their growth right in its tracks. Second, they will flat run out of water ... Dams, reservoirs and canals do not create water. Since they take decades to plan and build, they certainly are not emergency remedies to water-short areas today ... Water is a finite resource, and what the government can do to deliver where needed is also finite. It is essential that we keep our perspective and not commit [ourselves] to long-term projects of questionable value because we have an immediate shortage of water in certain parts of the country.

Interview, St. Louis, May 24/
Los Angeles Times, 5-25:(1)14.

Carl E. Bagge
President, National Coal Association

5

I do not believe that energy and environmental concerns are necessarily in conflict, nor that energy must always win out if such a conflict occurs; but I do believe we should look

WHAT THEY SAID IN 1977

(CARL E. BAGGE)

at specific cases as well as lofty objectives. Ringing slogans, such as "non-deterioration," have a way of being translated into hard-and-fast laws that can have drastic and unforeseen results.

Before Commonwealth Club, San Francisco,
Aug. 26/Vital Speeches, 10-15:13.

Tom Bradley
Mayor of Los Angeles
1

It's a matter of human nature to consume, to live without concern at almost a luxurious level, so long as the water flows, so long as the lights burn, so long as there is gas at every gas station.

Interview/Los Angeles Times, 4-21:(1)1.

Edmund G. Brown, Jr.
Governor of California (D)
2

I see two trends in our Western society. There is the ideology of environment, ecology and preservation, which is growing stronger. Then there is the technological and scientific theology that with faith we can solve any problems with enough money. There needs to be a synthesis of these views. We must recognize that all of us have a common destiny. We must bring integration into the environmental movement. Candidly, to protect the environment we cannot neglect technology.

Before executive board of Sierra Club,
San Francisco, May 7/San Francisco
Examiner & Chronicle, 5-8:(A)5.

3

No matter what people tell you, they all want their little places in the sun, and they don't want someone to build on it. Everyone is a pro-growth advocate at the office, but when they get home at night they become environmentalists. They like the trees and the fact no one built next door.

Before AFL-CIO convention delegates, Los
Angeles/The Christian Science Monitor, 12-7:3.

Jack W. Carlson
Chief economist, Chamber of
Commerce of the United States
4

In the case of the environment, we could have taken an incentive route for environmental quality. It would have cost us far less, and we would have had more environmental quality than adopting a very heavy, burdensome, less freedom-oriented, law-and-order, haul-them-into-court-and-fine-them approach.

Interview, Washington/
The New York Times, 3-27:(3)9.

Barry Commoner
Director, Center for the Biology
of Natural Systems, Washington
University, St. Louis
5

The flashy stuff that went on in the early '70s has faded away. People who are concerned with the environment have become interested in economics. On the campuses, students want to hear about the relationship between energy and environment and economics. In a way, people have gotten trained to deal with number and scientific concepts by the environmental movement — and now they feel capable about taking on the economists, too. It's a very important development.

Interview/"W": a Fairchild publication, 6-24:2.

Douglas M. Costle
Administrator, Environmental Protection
Agency of the United States
6

Industry needs a clear signal. There should be no mistake. We intend to get the [environmental] job done. In terms of enforcement, we will be tough. We will be aggressive. But people will not be able to say that we are unfair, arbitrary or haven't done our homework . . . We are past the social debate over whether it is a good thing to protect the environment. The debate now is how to do it. We're at the difficult stage of practical problem-solving. You can't have growth without effective pollution control.

Interview/The Washington Post, 4-12:(A)4.

(DOUGLAS M. COSTLE)

1

Between 1975 and 1984, we project that industry will have to spend $260-billion to meet Federal pollution requirements and an additional $140-billion to meet non-Federal standards — state and local laws. Three quarters of that expenditure will come from six major industries: electric utilities, pulp and paper, iron and steel, petroleum refining, non-ferrous metals, and chemicals. Historically, these have been the big polluters, but some of them have become leaders in cleaning up their operations. The pulp-and-paper industry, for one, has done an exceptional job of meeting the first benchmark requirements of the Federal Water Pollution Control Act. They've done it in a fairly imaginative way. They are finding that, by cleaning up their pollution, they often can also save energy and raw materials — which ends up saving them money. Most pollution, it turns out, is the result of inefficient use of raw materials.

Interview/U.S. News & World Report, 12-19:31.

Jacques-Yves Cousteau
Explorer

2

[On the threat of over-fishing and the 200-mile fishing limit adopted by the Law of the Sea Conference]: The 200-mile limit, what does it mean? It means that the United States is going to adopt a number of rules to control foreign fishing in its waters. But other nations are going to take different rules, and everyone is going to act in their so-called waters the way they want. So instead of having one law of the sea, we are going to have 100 laws of the sea. That's wrong. The waters that are adjacent to a country . . . cannot be treated as a territory. It is just nonsense and misunderstanding. The reason it's been adopted at the Conference is that nobody there knows anything about the sea. Law-makers are lawyers, diplomats, representatives of interests; but the scientists have been carefully eliminated from the discussions . . . I think the result of the Law of the Sea Conference as it is today is to generate conflicts between nations rather than solve the problems of the fisheries.

Interview/Los Angeles Herald-Examiner, 11-28:(A)10.

George D. Davis
Director, Wilderness Society

3

[Supporting a proposed national park in Alaska]: We stand on the threshold of what could be one of mankind's most epochal conservation achievements. In the rest of the country, we see only the remnants of a once-limitless wilderness after years of settlement, resource development and growth. In Alaska we have the last opportunity to set aside great pristine, unspoiled expanses first; the opportunity to make wise choices ahead of time about where development is to occur and where conservation is to be given priority instead.

The Washington Post, 4-26:(A)3.

David E. Lilienthal
Chairman, Development and Resources Corporation; Former Chairman, Atomic Energy Commission of the United States

4

One can be deeply heartened by the recent widespread voluntary citizen movement to protect and develop our national environment; heartened, greatly heartened, by the passion and conviction of millions of our fellow citizens, expressing values and concerns which transcend the material, which appeal to the spiritual and moral impulses within us, which evoke from us something more than the "getting and spending" of our incessant daily occupations. Heartened but also perturbed, deeply perturbed, by the style and tone, these latter days, in which these vital questions are being presented and being argued. Such extremities of opinions and language! Such intolerance and abuse of those who may have a different point of view, including the men of the business world! So bold an assumption of a mandate by a few of undoubted dedication, a mandate to represent the broad public interest, in the courts and in public forums, such disregard of the mass of the people in whom the public interest resides. So many, who take extreme legal measures to protect the least of God's creatures, such as fish and fowl, somehow forget or neglect the well-being of the Lord's most remarkable creature of all, Man.

At Lawrence University/
The Wall Street Journal, 3-18:12.

WHAT THEY SAID IN 1977

Joseph T. Ling
Vice president, 3M Company

1

Resource-conservation is a simple concept, but it has profound implications. The concept is no more or less than the practical application of knowledge, methods and means to provide the most rational use of resources to improve the environment. Resource-conservation technology means eliminating the causes of pollution before spending money and resources to clean up afterward. It also means learning to create valuable resources from pollution ... like the making of nylon and other materials from the waste by-products of petroleum some years ago. It's in the over-all interest of our society to adopt this resource-conservation-oriented approach to pollution control. But this must ... by necessity ... be done in context with three environmental realities: Environmental issues are emotional; environmental decisions are political; environmental solutions are technical. No technical solution to a pollution problem can be accepted if it is not presented in harmony with the emotional and political realities.

At National Conference on Treatment and Disposal of Industrial Wastewaters and Residues, Houston, April 27/Vital Speeches, 6-15:542.

Robert S. McNamara
President, International Bank for Reconstruction and Development (World Bank)

2

Indeed, in many ways rampant population growth is an even more dangerous and subtle threat to the world than thermonuclear war, for it is intrinsically less subject to rational safeguards, and less amenable to organized control. The population growth of the planet is not in the exclusive control of a few governments, but rather in the hands of literally hundreds of millions of individual parents who will ultimately determine the outcome.

At Massachusetts Institute of Technology, April 28/The Christian Science Monitor, 4-29:1.

John R. Quarles
Acting Administrator, Environmental Protection Agency of the United States

3

[On the proliferation of environmental-impact statements issued by government agencies involved in major projects that may affect the ecology]: To protect themselves from further judicial review, the agencies have evaluated every conceivable environmental impact of their proposed action, no matter how insignificant. The result has been that the value of the final product is measured in inches rather than in the quality of its analysis ... There is a serious question if any of it is being read, much less relied upon by policy-makers.

The Washington Post, 2-13:(A)4.

4

Fish are returning to bays and rivers and waterways that had been dead. The stench of pollution has been eliminated; measurably higher levels of oxygen have been found; shellfish beds have been reopened, and [beaches for] swimming. In concrete terms of people's daily lives, as well as conversation, progress is being made in our battle against water pollution.

At press briefing, Washington/ The Christian Science Monitor, 2-22:19.

Rainier III
Head of Government of Monaco

5

Pollution of the seas is becoming more and more disquieting. Oceanography knows neither frontiers nor nationalities. The more we learn in various fields, the more knowledge of the seas becomes both important and precious ... You know, life depends on the water cycle. So life is what's in danger. And it's not something that cannot be avoided, because no unavoidable pollution exists. Pollution can be prevented. All it takes is the will and the means to fight it ... Industrial expansion and the pollution explosion have created a civilization of wastes. All of us, sooner or later, become the victims. So what we have to do is turn the pollutants around, to make them useful. Take, for example, the natural substances contained in urban sewage. This could very well contribute to the fertiliza-

(RAINIER III)

tion of a marine region if it's judiciously selected and distributed. Why, even thermal pollution, the kind created by energy plants and so harmful, could possibly be used in certain forms of aquaculture. Again, finding the answers simply takes the will and the means.

Interview, Monaco/
The Christian Science Monitor, 8-19:28.

John C. Sawhill
President, New York University;
Former Administrator,
Federal Energy Administration
1

We have to define what we mean by "damaging the environment." It's impossible to expand energy production without changing the environment, and without making some tough environmental choices. On the other hand, I don't think that these changes necessarily have to be damaging. Some of the land that has been reclaimed, after strip mining, is often in better condition than it was prior to the development of the strip mine. By the same token, some of the off-shore areas where we have drilled for oil and gas are more-productive fishing grounds than they were before drilling took place. The important thing is to anticipate and plan for these changes rather than to rush into them without proper precautions.

Interview/U.S. News & World Report, 4-18:41.

Richard M. Scammon
Public-opinion analyst
2

We are already seeing signs that people want a balance [in environmental policy]. People might like to have fresh fish in their lakes and streams, but not if it means closing down a factory that provides jobs and having that factory's workers wind up on welfare. A fresh fish isn't worth it.

Interview/Nation's Business, November:33.

James R. Schlesinger
Assistant to President of the United
States Jimmy Carter for Energy Affairs
3

I think that the American people are prepared to pay a higher price for energy to keep the air clean. There are those, of course, who would like to use the current energy crisis as an opportunity to roll back all the protections of the environmental statutes and to begin to burn raw coal again. This seems to me to be going in the wrong direction. It would mean, as we move toward the burning of a billion tons of coal a year, and ultimately two billion tons, that we would have grave problems in keeping the country a satisfactory environment. There are high costs of dirty air. We do not want to turn the country into something equivalent to Pittsburgh in the 1930s.

Interview/The Washington Post, 7-10:(B)4.

Irving S. Shapiro
Chairman, E. I. du Pont
de Nemours & Company
4

No one objects to goals such as clean water, clean air and safe industrial operations. Some of the means being used to achieve those goals, however, are quite a different matter. With the vast social and economic agenda we have in this country, it is vital we make certain that such goals are being pursued in cost-effective ways and that we are not scattering any scarce investment dollars on unneeded, premature or excessive objectives. Unfortunately, I believe that, in our zeal to better the physical quality of our lives, all due care was not taken in building the legal and regulatory structure. Preventing pollution and improving safety turned out to be far more complicated than we initially thought. Many of the basic laws and regulations were devised in haste and in at least partial technical ignorance. Energy was not then a major concern; it is now. Fortunately, the time would seem ripe for regulatory reform.

Before Atlanta Rotary Club, May 23/
Vital Speeches, 7-15:606.

Elvis J. Stahr, Jr.
President, National Audubon Society
5

There seems to be a misconception that the environmental pendulum has swung too far [toward what the ecologists want] and that some so-called balance is in order. Actually, the pendulum has only swung far enough to correct some of the severe imbalances against environ-

WHAT THEY SAID IN 1977

(ELVIS J. STAHR, JR.)

mental protection that go back a long time. I can't believe that Congress' posture reflects public feelings. The polls still show that people want a decent environment and are willing to pay for it. But Congress doesn't seem to be able to sense the mood and aspirations of the people. Polls show that Congress as an institution is held in what I think is tragically low esteem by the people. I think the Congressional mood is bound to change. But don't ask me when. At the moment, it seems to be responding mainly to special economic interests.

Interview, Estes Park, Colo./
The New York Times, 6-13:22.

Mostafa K. Tolba
Executive Director, United
Nations Environmental Program　　　*1*

There must be equitable sharing of resources. It is no use having arrogant demands by one group of countries, or refusals to share by others. Resources are not infinite. There are limits to what man is doing. We must have environmental management. There must be new life-styles both in the rich and the poor countries. People are too arrogant toward their resources, too selfish.

Interview, Geneva/Los Angeles Times, 2-6:(1)2.

Mack Wallace
Chairman, Texas Railroad Commission　　　*2*

[On those who worry about the environmental effects of energy development]: I believe there is, in fact, a feeling in this country today that the lousewort, the caribou, the black-footed ferret and the kangaroo rat are more important than national security . . . This nation did not become the nation it is without oil and gas, and without coal. We cannot maintain our position in world affairs by protecting the Tennessee snail darter, the clam larvae and the Furbish lousewort.

Before Albany (Tex.) Chamber of Commerce,
March 25/The Dallas Times Herald, 3-26:(A)11.

Charles Warren
Chairman, Federal Council on
Environmental Quality　　　*3*

We are entering a period of greater acceptance and appreciation of environmental concepts. Environmentalists are no longer regarded as posy-pluckers or bee-, bug- and bunny-watchers as they once were. Today we are concerned with environmental issues as essential to the sustenance of life — human life as well as animals.

San Francisco Examiner & Chronicle,
5-15:(This World)2.

4

I believe that environmentalism is never a case of protesting life-style amenities or assuring the presence of wildflowers. I don't want to minimize the importance of wildflowers — we still have to have them. But what this is really about is not life-style, but life-supporting necessities. There are global processes going on, including population expansion and massive industrial assaults on the environment, that are a threat to our ability to sustain life. We have to understand these problems. They have tremendous implications.

The New York Times, 5-21:19.

Robert M. White
Administrator, National Oceanic
and Atmospheric Administration　　　*5*

[On the threat to the protective ozone layer in the atmosphere from man-made chemicals]: The hazards we are concerned with are universal, and the causes widely dispersed through the world. It is clear to all that no one nation can solve the environmental problems arising from man's capability to disturb the earth's upper atmosphere. No nation has a monopoly on the production of substances which may perturb the upper and lower atmosphere, nor does any nation enjoy immunity from the possible consequences. We are involved in a problem that is truly global in scope . . .

At conference sponsored by
U.S. Environmental Program, March 1/
The Washington Post, 3-2:(A)3.

ENERGY

Morris A. Adelman
Oil economist, Massachusetts
Institute of Technology
1

The oil companies are now hired hands who supply their services. It's the OPEC governments who are running the show and taking the rest of the world to the cleaners. To blame the oil companies for it is wide of the mark.

Time, 2-28:48.

Otes Bennett, Jr.
President, North American Coal Corporation
2

From the standpoint of the energy situation, [Carter] Administration policy is headed in the wrong direction in that it provides too little incentive for the development of new energy resources. It's a mistake to keep controls on natural-gas prices, and I'm bothered by all the talk of divesting oil companies of other energy-related holdings. We desperately need big companies for new research and technology. The utilities — and in fact the entire energy industry — are simply too afraid to make big investments because they're uncertain of being able to get a proper return. Utilities, for example, are wondering whether they'll be able to pass the costs of converting to coal on to their customers.

Interview/U.S. News & World Report, 9-19:63.

Rose E. Bird
Chief Justice, Supreme Court of California
3

We have probed the earth, excavated it, burned it, ripped things from it, buried things in it, chopped down its forests, leveled its hills, muddied its waters and dirtied its air. That does not fit my definition of a good tenant. If we were here on a month-to-month basis, we would have been evicted long ago.

San Francisco Examiner & Chronicle,
12-18:(This World)2.

W. Michael Blumenthal
Secretary of the Treasury
of the United States
4

We clearly think it's better if we don't let an international cartel dictate the price for energy — but in fact the international price does play a critical role. To the extent to which we can economize on the use of energy and use more of our own resources and shift away from expensive imported oil to more coal, we will have these people dictate to us less. We may actually be able, after a while, to reduce the cost of energy.

Interview, Washington/
The New York Times, 4-11:46.

Thornton F. Bradshaw
President, Atlantic Richfield Company
5

We have always put it in terms that we would become hopelessly dependent upon foreign oil. It's true that we are almost hopelessly dependent, but it goes far beyond that. We have always looked upon foreign oil — particularly Mideastern oil — as being almost infinite. This is not true. Mideastern oil will start to decline in the early 1990s. So what we're facing is an actual world-wide shortage of oil and gas. This has to be made up in the short or intermediate run with energies that we know how to handle now — coal, nuclear and possibly synthetic fuels. These are the bridging fuels which will take us over into the new era early in the next century when, hopefully, we will have renewable energy sources, such as solar and possibly nuclear fission.

Interview/U.S. News & World Report, 4-18:43.

Bill Brock
Chairman, Republican National Committee
6

[President] Carter's energy program looks suspiciously like a back-door way of raising

(BILL BROCK)

enough taxes to pay for more government programs and still balance the budget. We will not support another tax rip-off of the middle class in America ... [A Democratic Congress is more likely] to use extra money from the taxpayers for income redistribution — with the middle class working family winding up on the short end of the stick. If the energy program is converted into an income-redistribution scheme, it will not only pit region against region but class against class. We reject the idea of income redistribution masquerading as energy conservation.

Before Republican National Committee, Chicago, April 29/Los Angeles Times, 4-30:(1)8.

Edmund G. Brown, Jr.
Governor of California (D)

1

I for one do not see the panic from the energy crisis. It is one problem among a number of others. We'll solve it. Solar energy is part of the over-all energy equation that will be met. It's a matter of time, a matter of effort ... The future is made not by going back to the dinosaur technology of the past, not by getting hung up on disputes and problems that weigh us down, but by tapping the creativity of our own intellect and our own imagination. That's the real message of solar energy ...

At activation of solar water-heater, Fresno, Calif., Sept. 23/ Los Angeles Times, 9-24:(2)14.

Harold Brown
Secretary of Defense of the United States

2

[On the energy crisis]: In amazing numbers, people refuse to see past the hood ornaments on their now-operable automobiles, beyond the four walls of their now-warm homes, beyond the easy days of the present to the harsh signs of tomorrow. Perhaps we mislead by calling the matter a crisis. A crisis is very much here today and usually gone tomorrow. The energy situation is more an impending disaster than an

intrusive crisis. It is not so visibly here today; it will be here tomorrow.

Before Council for Financial Aid to Education, New York, Oct. 26/ The New York Times, 10-27:71.

Arthur F. Burns
Chairman, Federal Reserve Board

3

Our economic future at the present time is at the mercy of a half-dozen Arab sheiks who could impose another embargo on imported oil. Our national security is in danger. We spend $100-billion a year on defense, and our defense establishment could be rendered powerless if oil is cut off.

Congressional testimony/ U.S. News & World Report, 5-2:45.

Jimmy Carter
President of the United States

4

We must face the fact that the energy shortage is permanent. There is no way we can solve it quickly. But if we all cooperate and make modest sacrifices, if we learn to live thriftily and remember the importance of helping our neighbors, then we can find ways to adjust, and to make our society more efficient and our own lives more enjoyable and productive ... There is no way that I, or anyone else in the government, can solve our energy problems if you [the public] are not willing to help. I know that we can meet this energy challenge if the burden is borne fairly among all our people — and if we realize that in order to solve our energy problems we need not sacrifice the quality of our lives.

Broadcast address to the nation, Washington, Feb. 2/ The New York Times, 2-3:22.

5

Our decision about energy will test the character of the American people and the ability of the President and the Congress to govern. This difficult effort will be the moral equivalent of war — except that we will be uniting our efforts to build and not destroy. I know that some of you may doubt that we face real energy shortages. The 1973 gasoline lines

(JIMMY CARTER)

are gone, and our homes are warm again. But our energy problem is worse tonight than it was in 1973 or a few weeks ago in the dead of winter. It is worse because more waste has occurred, and more time has passed by without our planning for the future. And it will get worse every day until we act.

Broadcast address to the
nation, Washington, April 18/
The Washington Post, 4-19:(A)14.

1

It is important that the American people be aroused to the fact that unless they are deeply involved in helping the Congress and me to come up with a substantive, comprehensive, fair and adequate energy policy, that the special-interest groups will prevail ... I have confidence in the sound judgment of the Congress and I believe that they and I are on test, and if we are not successful in coming forward with an adequate program we will be deserving of legitimate criticism by the American people for timidity and for an absence of concern about what I still consider to be the gravest domestic issue that I shall face during my own term as President.

News conference, Washington, June 13/
The New York Times, 6-14:24.

2

I am concerned that the public has not responded well [to calls for energy conservation], and I think voluntary compliance is probably not adequate at all. The public is not paying attention. And this has resulted in an enormous increase in imports [causing a] very severe [foreign-trade deficit]. I would say at this point the public has not responded well; that the absence of visibility to the impending oil shortage removes the incentive for the public to be concerned. And I am afraid that a series of crises are going to be a prerequisite to a sincere desire on the part of the American people to quit wasting so much fuel.

Interview, Washington/
The Dallas Times Herald, 7-31:(A)22.

3

The lobbying efforts of the oil and gas industry on behalf of deregulation [of natural-gas prices] show how the special interests are trying to block enactment of the entire energy program. The Congress has been lobbied continuously by the oil and gas industry to deregulate the price of new natural gas. By 1985, the industry proposal will cost the average American family that heats with natural gas an additional $150 a year. It will cost consumers almost $10-billion every year and will produce little, if any, new supplies. I call on the Senate to act responsibly in the interests of the great majority of Americans to reject narrow special-interest attacks on the national energy plan.

Washington/San Francisco Examiner
& Chronicle, 10-2:(This World)7.

William P. Clements, Jr.
Chairman, SEDCO, Inc.; Former Deputy
Secretary of Defense of the United States
4

It has been variously estimated by responsible sources that, to correct our present imbalance between energy production and requirements, it will require a capital investment of approximately $4-trillion before 1990. Without an understanding government, this will not happen. President Carter simply has not surrounded himself with experienced persons — those who really know the petroleum business. You have to take direction from flavor at the top. It just isn't there. He says there are incentives in his program for the oil and gas producers, but those included are totally inadequate. We need — and in a hurry — total understanding from our government: incentives and realistic tax laws that would encourage industry to plow back and develop the resources we have.

Dallas, Oct. 22/
The Dallas Times Herald, 10-23:(A)4.

James M. Collins
United States Representative, R—Texas
5

I want to tell you that Dallas lives under deregulation [of natural-gas prices], and we've had a 52 per cent increase in gas prices ... but industry was able to keep operating because

WHAT THEY SAID IN 1977

people paid enough to keep the gas available, and they thought it was a bargain to keep it that way and keep their paychecks coming in.

News conference, Washington, July 11/
The Washington Post, 7-12:(A)8.

John B. Connally, Jr.
Former Secretary of the Treasury
of the United States; Former
Governor of Texas (D, now R) 1

The oil industry is grossly misunderstood, frankly, because it has been grossly mistreated by people who for their own selfish reasons have demagogued the [energy] issue and created the lack of understanding. Part of the reason oil and gas companies are in trouble today is that they have been made the scapegoat — the fall-guy for politicians in Washington who haven't had nerve enough to admit it wasn't the oil companies that caused the [Arab] oil embargo [in 1973]. The embargo was the result of political decisions, namely, the increased military support for Israel.

At Society of Petroleum Engineers'
Economics and Evaluation Symposium, Dallas,
Feb. 21/The Dallas Times Herald, 2-22:(D)5.

Jacques-Yves Cousteau
Explorer 2

[Advocating development of solar energy instead of nuclear power]: The *Titanic* was unsinkable and it sank on its first voyage. So now we're building "unsinkable" nuclear power plants . . . The main source of solar energy is in the ocean. Two-thirds of all the solar energy on earth falls into the ocean . . . Solar energy, well exploited, could easily represent four-fifths of the world's energy by the year 2000 . . . The biggest danger is nuclear energy. Any other catastrophe can be repaired. A nuclear one cannot. Many scientists say there's no danger, but there is.

New York/Los Angeles Times, 2-21:(1)16.

W. Donham Crawford
President, Edison Electric Institute 3

The nuclear option is absolutely vital to the assurance of an adequate electric-power supply in the future. Although nuclear provided about 10 per cent of electric generation last year, compared to 45 per cent for coal, by the year 2000 the forecast is 50 per cent nuclear and about 40 per cent fossil, principally coal. And, at the turn of the century, electricity generation will have to be on the order of four times the 1975 level to meet the nation's needs . . . We point out that with prudent and efficient use, U.S. uranium resources are sufficient to satisfy its electric-power needs for hundreds of years, assuming that the breeder reactor is developed. In fact, the energy potential of the existing residue left from uranium-enrichment operations, which can be utilized in the breeder, is equivalent to the nation's total coal reserves.

Before New York Society of
Security Analysts, Feb. 2/
Vital Speeches, 3-1:294.

Carl T. Curtis
United States Senator, R–Nebraska 4

We should proceed full speed ahead in the search and discovery of oil in the United States. Conservation is not enough upon which to build a program for a growing America, a strong economy and expanding jobs. [The Democratic-controlled Congress] has placed every impediment imaginable in the way of oil production . . . Before the Congress embarked upon these Marxist theories of taxation and control, our oil industry was growing and expanding — it fulfilled our needs, it provided production at reasonable prices.

Before the Senate, Washington, April 21/
Los Angeles Herald-Examiner, 4-21:(A)2.

D. D. Danforth
President, Westinghouse
Industry Products Company 5

Today there are about 60 nuclear power plants in the United States accounting for around 10 per cent of the nation's production of electricity. President Carter's proposal calls

(D. D. DANFORTH)

for an increase to 125 by 1985. Our estimates are that the nation should have about 145 by then, and more than 200 by 1990, when 30 per cent of our electrical production should come from nuclear energy. Nuclear power is safe and compatible with environmental standards. It has already made a significant contribution to our requirements. For example, during last winter's crisis, nuclear reactors helped save more than a quarter of a million jobs, about $230-million in wages and $3.8-billion in goods and services by providing a steady, reliable, safe flow of electricity to factories, offices, homes, schools and hospitals.

Before National Association of Accountants, Pittsburgh, May 18/Vital Speeches, 6-15:540.

Sigvard Eklund
Director General, International Atomic Energy Agency

1

We have reached the beginning of the end of the fossil-fuel age. I don't see how mankind can satisfy his ever-increasing energy needs without the use of nuclear energy. We must be ready to accept new technology bearing in mind the finite nature of fossil fuels ... Should we continue to burn these resources when we know that they are indispensable for many products deemed necessary by society? ... Shortages of energy and rising prices of oil affect poor people and poor countries hardest. Energy growth may be marginal to us, but for a poor country it may mean an extra bowl of rice, a gallon of water, electricity and better sanitation ... I believe that today many of the fears about the safety of individual [nuclear] power stations has subsided. There has not been a single fatal accident caused by nuclear plants nor any unforeseen escape of radioactivity.

At Massachusetts Institute of Technology, March 24/The Christian Science Monitor, 3-31:13.

Gerald R. Ford
Former President of the United States

2

... we must not be fooled into thinking that creating a Cabinet-level Department of Energy [as President Carter has proposed] will solve all our energy problems. If it is a first step toward a true national energy policy ... then I am all for it. If, on the other hand, the Department of Energy is to be a substitute for an energy policy, if it is to be an expensive public-relations gimmick that does nothing more than shuffle the Federal bureaucracy from one office to another, if it gives the comforting appearance of a solution without any substance, then it is the worst possible thing we could do about the energy problem in this country.

Before All-American Wildcatters, Scottsdale, Ariz., March 19/ The Dallas Times Herald, 3-20:(A)17.

3

We do face [an energy] crisis. In meeting that crisis, there must be unselfishness, cooperation and belt-tightening. The answer to our problem does not lie with any one political party or any one source of energy, but a combination of many. The answer is not more bureaucracy but more stimulant to the free marketplace ... America has prospered in the past by depending on individual initiative, competition and the free-enterprise system. We must not abandon that approach as we face this new challenge.

At YMCA dinner, Dallas, May 4/ Los Angeles Herald-Examiner, 5-5:(A)12.

Milton Friedman
Professor of economics, University of Chicago

4

There have been winters as cold as this before, but this is the first cold snap during which the government said it would let the price of gas and oil be determined, not by the free market, but by government fiat ... How can it help a householder for the government to keep his natural gas cheap but to destroy his job, or for government to tell him that he can buy it cheap, but there is none available? Amazingly, however, the result of all this is not, as one would expect, that people wake up and say, "Boy, is this a stupid system." Instead, they say the government should have still more power. [The only reason we face an energy crisis is] because the government stuck its clumsy hands in the problem. We economists

WHAT THEY SAID IN 1977

(MILTON FRIEDMAN)

don't know much, but we do know how to create a shortage. If you want to create a shortage of tomatoes, for example, just pass a law that retailers can't sell tomatoes for more than two cents per pound. Instantly you'll have a tomato shortage. It's the same with oil or gas.

News conference, Beverly Hills, Calif., Feb. 9/Los Angeles Times, 2-10:(3)12.

Takeo Fukuda
Prime Minister of Japan

1

I believe that using such a fearful thing as nuclear weapons would be the ultimate folly of humanity. In this sense, I completely support the U.S. position that the spread of nuclear weapons must be stopped. However, when developing sources of energy for the future, nuclear energy will play a vital role.

Interview, Tokyo, March 11/ The Dallas Times Herald, 3-12:(A)5.

R. Buckminster Fuller
Engineer, Author, Designer

2

Society cannot continue to live on oil and gas. Those fossil fuels represent nature's savings account which took millions of years to form. Humanity is now burning up that savings account in a matter of generations. But with the knowledge and resources we have, it is technically feasible within 10 years to provide the highest standard of living we have ever known on the energy-income-sustaining basis while retiring fossil fuels and atomic energy. This can be done by developing such sources as solar energy, methane gas, water and wind.

Interview/U.S. News & World Report, 12-5:49.

E. J. (Jake) Garn
United States Senator, R—Utah

3

I favor permanent decontrol [of natural-gas prices]. I firmly believe that the only way we are going to solve our energy problems, as far as these limited resources are concerned, is to let the free marketplace make the decisions. It is government making arbitrary decisions about price and allocation that has added to our energy problems. At current well-head prices,

which have been mandated by the Federal government and kept artificially low for so long, producers cannot afford to drill in the places and at the depths that they must to discover new natural-gas reserves. Most of the easy, cheaper gas has been found. What Congress and the American people have got to understand is that, while we all hate to pay more for natural gas, we are going to have to pay more or do without it altogether.

Jan. 31/**

Bruce Hannon
Associate professor of energy research, University of Illinois, Urbana-Champaign

4

There are three things that Americans do to waste more energy than any other people on earth. They eat big steaks, drive big cars and live in big houses. All of that must change.

Los Angeles Herald-Examiner, 2-14:(A)5.

S. I. Hayakawa
United States Senator, R—California

5

In some ways, President Carter's energy plans are rather timid. A nickel-a-gallon tax increase is not going to change anything. A real savings in fuel can only be effected by a tax that changes people's driving habits, say 25 or 50 cents a gallon.

San Francisco Examiner & Chronicle, 5-1:(This World)7.

Denis Hayes
Senior researcher, Worldwatch Institute

6

The bad consequences that are associated with a major program of nuclear [-energy] expansion are many. My principal objections to it, I guess, are three. One is that I think that it leads to an international proliferation of weapons that is unavoidable. I don't think that we can pursue dramatically an energy source that we wish to deprive the rest of the world of, and I don't think there is any way that one can pursue even a conventional light-water-reactor nuclear strategy without bringing along with it, no matter what kinds of safeguards one attempts to supply, the proliferation of weapons among countries. Second, I think that

(DENIS HAYES)

it opens the society to a degree of vulnerability to terrorism that is necessarily a part of any high-technology, highly centralized energy source. And third, which was really a consequence of the second, I think that it implies a much more authoritarian and rigid and hierarchical type of society than the one that I would like to see. I am basically at heart a Jeffersonian Democrat, and I prefer to see energy sources that are decentralized, benign, renewable and safe. Nuclear power is none of those things.

TV-radio interview, Washington/"Meet the Press," National Broadcasting Company, 5-8.

William C. Hayes
Editor-in-chief,
"Electrical World" magazine
1

Nuclear power is less harmful and more beneficial to the country than any other energy source, but there is no way to glamorize or publicize that. Opponents of nuclear power say it will harm the environment, and the industry supports it because in an economic analysis nuclear power comes out on top. That pits purity against profit, and in the public eye purity always wins ... Everybody can marshal experts these days, and the result is a confused public.

Interview/The Christian Science Monitor, 11-3:12.

Harold J. Haynes
Chairman, Standard Oil
Company of California
2

We're concerned about the lack of balance in [President Carter's] proposed energy program. The American public is being asked to accept "painful sacrifices" in conserving energy. Yet all too little is said about the need to find and develop additional domestic oil and natural gas supplies to alleviate the severity of the required sacrifice.

At shareholders meeting, Los Angeles,
May 3/Los Angeles Times, 5-4:(3)13.

Henry M. Jackson
United States Senator, D—Washington
3

I would favor some price adjustments but not deregulation of natural gas. I think the great fallacy — as you hear it repeated over and over again — is that we will let prices be controlled by the so-called free market which we do not have, because the oil cartel controls the free market. They control 80 per cent of all oil produced in the world. And to say, then, that we will put on an excess-profits tax, that that will satisfy the problem — I am thinking of the poor people. I am thinking of the poor people who do not get enough in, say ... Social Security payments, to even meet their heating bill. And if the industry thinks they can go hog-wild as a result of a winter experience, I think they have another guess coming. There should be some sense and reason here, and that is to keep these prices within the budget of working people ... and for poor people and for retired people. It takes a very large chunk of their budget just to meet the electric and heating bills.

TV-radio interview, Washington/
"Meet the Press," National
Broadcasting Company, 2-20.

4

[On President Carter's call for tax increases on gasoline to encourage fuel conservation]: Tax will not deter consumption. There has been a 40 per cent increase in the cost of gas over the past three years with consumption growth about the same. A tax on gas at the pump, in order to be effective, would have to get up to close to $1 a gallon. That's not do-able, politically or otherwise.

TV-radio interview/"Face the
Nation," Columbia Broadcasting System, 5-1.

5

[Saying cars that get low gas mileage should be prohibited, not simply heavily taxed]: ... a person should not be able to buy his way into driving a big gas-guzzler. I think it ought to be the same for all of our people. If we are going to have a program of conservation and sacrifice, it ought to be on the basis of equality. This country, that has been able to put 12 men on

WHAT THEY SAID IN 1977

(HENRY M. JACKSON)

the moon, surely can get Detroit to move around to the point where they can produce a fuel-efficient automobile and still make a good profit. I think we can do it, and that is the route we ought to go. No less than 16 miles per gallon should be the cutoff point.

TV-radio interview/"Meet the Press," National Broadcasting Company, 10-2.

Edward M. Kennedy
United States Senator, D–Massachusetts

1

I am convinced that the U.S. energy program will remain in limbo until we decide how to deal with the reality that this country will be importing substantial amounts of oil for most, if not all, of the balance of this century. And even if, by some miracle, we could become self-sufficient in energy, our closest allies overseas will still be heavily dependent on oil imports. In this sense, the issue of energy independence is a mirage.

The Dallas Times Herald, 1-13:(A)7.

2

[Saying major oil companies should not be permitted to develop and produce coal and uranium]: . . . major oil companies, which have already effectively made competition a dead letter in the oil industry, should not have the opportunity to work their will on other industries ... [The oil companies claim] we need the leadership which only their management can provide. If this is true, then our business and financial community must surely be in a sorry state. I am confident that our country has the capital and managerial skills and technology to develop the coal and uranium industries without depending on oil companies.

Washington, July 26/The Christian Science Monitor, 7-27:2.

Harold Lever
Chief adviser to the British government on oil and international financial affairs

3

Even if we [in the West] cut down the use of oil — and there are limits to the extent it can

be cut down without affecting economic growth — we are going to be crucially dependent on OPEC oil for the next 10 years at least. We cannot escape the crucial question of our dependence upon a monopoly for vital energy supplies by saying we'll make ourselves marginally less dependent. That may have some very marginal benefit for a very marginal period of time, but it won't solve the problem facing us in the next 10 years. Nor will the efforts to develop alternative energy sources, which are not likely to have much effect before 1990 or later. What I'm talking about is the rest of the '70s and the 1980s. Our society has got to prosper during that period of time.

Interview, London, May 17/Los Angeles Herald-Examiner, 5-17:(A)3.

Henry R. Linden
President, Institute of Gas Technology

4

The biggest advantage of gas made from coal is that we have so much coal in the United States — more proved and currently recoverable reserves than any other country. In terms of energy content, they are larger than the proved oil reserves of the entire world. However, coal supplies only one-fifth of the fossil-fuel energy we consume. One reason is a lot of the coal contains too much sulfur to burn directly without some form of expensive clean-up. Coal gasification can provide an acceptable answer and, at the same time, help reduce our dependency on foreign energy sources. If we get on with it, it could contribute to our energy supply before the end of the next decade.

Interview/U.S. News & World Report, 11-21:85.

Jose Lopez (Portillo)
President of Mexico

5

Development of solar energy is an obsession with me. I maintain it is much better and safer for humanity than nuclear energy. I am convinced that safe and adequate energy for the future of mankind lies in the use of sunlight. It is something that many of the developing nations have in abundance, but they lack the technology to make use of it. If the developed

(JOSE LOPEZ [PORTILLO])

countries had a great deal of sun, they would have learned already how to make use of it.

Interview, Mexico City/Los Angeles Herald-Examiner, 10-31:(A)2.

Charles McC. Mathias, Jr.
United States Senator, R—Maryland
1

Convincing the American people that the energy crisis is real is our Number 1 national priority. If the leaders of this nation can't get that idea across, no amount of legislation is going to save us.

U.S. News & World Report, 10-10:76.

George S. McGovern
United States Senator, D—South Dakota
2

If the energy industry refuses to invest without bloated prices, then let us tax excess profits. If they hoard supplies or buy up alternative sources, then let us break their monopoly over our marketplace. The conglomerates may lobby and complain, the Executive Branch may bend to their pressure, but we must say: No gasoline taxation without anti-trust legislation.

San Francisco Examiner & Chronicle, 5-15:(This World)2.

Vincent E. McKelvey
Director, United States Geological Survey
3

Both the U.S. and the world have an immense amount of coal, many times current production, and sufficient for several decades into the future at any consumption rates we can foresee. There is enough oil and gas in the world to bridge over the next couple of decades, provided it is equitably shared and energetically explored for and developed ... The physical resources are available to carry the world through the period of transition from finite energy sources to a reliance upon those which are renewable if they are energetically sought after and developed, and if prudent use is made of them while they last. Conservation of existing resources does not add to their total supply, but it does something else just as important: It buys precious time in which to

effect the conversion to more-abundant sources; and time is the most crucial ingredient of the entire process.

At energy forum sponsored by California State University at Northridge, Los Angeles, May 6/ Los Angeles Herald-Examiner, 5-6:(A)2.

Thomas A. Murphy
Chairman, General Motors Corporation
4

[Criticizing President Carter's reported plan to impose special taxes on large cars and rebates on small cars as part of his energy-saving program]: The policy-makers in Washington haven't come right out and said to the American people, "You're not smart enough to know what's best for you and what's best for the country, so we've got to decide for you." But that's exactly what is being done ... [The energy problem will continue] until the government writes itself out of the script and lets the proven remedies of a free-market come into play over time. The law of supply and demand will not only lead to the more sensible use of the energy reserves we have left, but will make economic development of new sources of energy. It makes no more sense to dictate to a family the size of the car it must own than it does to say that everybody must live in a one-bedroom house.

Before Sales Executives Club of New York, March 31/The Washington Post, 4-2:(C)9.

Ralph Nader
Lawyer; Consumer advocate
5

There is not an energy crisis. There is an energy monopoly crisis — too many of the energy decisions are being made by a few large corporations instead of by a broader aggregate of consumer determinants. There is an energy waste crisis. We are the most wasteful country in the world. In fact, people come from all over the world to watch us and see how we waste. We are also in a crisis of choosing the best form of energy to put our program as a nation into. For example, solar energy has come a long way in the last three or four years. It is a highly practical way we can start using in our economic system, but it is not the form of energy that immediately results in profits to the energy

WHAT THEY SAID IN 1977

(RALPH NADER)

monopolies that now want to sell us more coal and oil and gas and synthetic fuels at higher and higher prices. Those are the kinds of crises we are in. We are not in an energy supply crisis, *per se*.

TV-radio interview, Washington/"Meet the Press," National Broadcasting Company, 4-17.

1

We have far more oil and gas in this country than the oil industry is officially willing to recognize. We have a waste factor of over 50 per cent in our energy consumption which means, if we were efficient, we could continue economic growth for the next 35 years without increasing the absolute amount of gas, coal and oil we are consuming now.

At Town Hall, Adrian, Mich., April 21/ The New York Times, 4-22:(B)7.

John F. O'Leary
Administrator, Federal Energy Administration

2

There will be some resistance [to President Carter's energy program announced April 20], but we have no choice. This nation needs a national energy policy that will assure our energy resources go for growth, not gluttony. There will be no free lunch in the energy cure the nation is about to undertake. It is important the American business community and the consumer understand that. We haven't scratched the surface of our potential to improve our energy efficiency. The American economy could, with known technology, operate as efficiently with 20 to 30 per cent less energy than we now use. It will require the imagination and willingness to sacrifice on the part of every segment and every sector of our economy. The American people must understand that there is no longer any choice left on conservation.

Before National Association of Manufacturers/ Los Angeles Herald-Examiner, 4-5:(A)8.

3

Is there a resource problem? The answer is no. We've got plenty of [energy] resources around for all the millenia ahead. We have carbonaceous rock to the extent we'll never touch that as a resource, and hydrogen. You can have all the hydrocarbon you want. The only thing is, it is costly. We ought to drive those costs down. We have got resources coming out of our ears; it is a matter of our mastery of the resources.

Panel discussion, Washington/ The New York Times, 7-24:(4)6.

Mohammad Reza Pahlavi
Shah of Iran

4

We increased the price of oil about four times in 1973. Since that day, [you] Americans went into much larger cars than before the price increases. And now you're importing 51 per cent of your needs in oil from outside, and a 6 to 7 per cent increase in this year's [U.S.] consumption is predicted. I told your responsible people before that I, as a friend of the U.S., allow myself to tell you that you, as representatives of the non-Communist world, don't have the right to depend on outside energy sources.

Interview, Teheran/ The Christian Science Monitor, 2-28:16.

John W. Partridge
President, World Energy Conference

5

There is tremendous reachable potential energy waiting to be exploited. Solar, wind, fusion, biomass, ocean systems, geothermal, and others are not yet thought of. Surely the civilization that put man on the moon can find and have the non-conventional energy resources available when conventional energy nears exhaustion.

At World Energy Conference, Istanbul/ The Christian Science Monitor, 9-21:8.

Charles H. Percy
United States Senator, R–Illinois

6

A lot of our [foreign] visitors will be critical of the way we squander energy resources [in the U.S.]. And their criticism will be justified ... When it comes to using resources, the United States is a pig. We have six per cent of

(CHARLES H. PERCY)

the world's population and use 30 per cent of the energy.

Before businessmen at Jonathan Club,
Los Angeles, March 7/Los Angeles
Herald-Examiner, 3-7:(A)3.

Russell W. Peterson
President, New Directions; Former
Chairman, Federal Council on
Environmental Quality

1

We in the U.S. have been the most irresponsible users of oil and maintain that dubious distinction today. We pumped it out here at home as fast as we could — selling it at prices way below its true value — leading us to waste it in a disgraceful manner. As a result, our production peaked out in 1970 and has been downhill ever since. But that didn't disturb us. We just bought other people's oil in ever greater quantities. To help hold down the use of oil and to stop wasting it, other countries have launched major conservation programs. For example, Italy has put a $1.20 tax on each gallon of gasoline, and West Germany, Sweden and Norway a tax of 70-76 cents per gallon. But good old affluent U.S.A. has a tax of 13 cents per gallon and her elected officials run for cover when someone proposes a one-cent-per-gallon increase. As a result, foreign-car fleets obtain very high mileage per gallon. By contrast, the chairman of General Motors says they can't meet the new Federal law which calls for their car fleet to be marketed in 1985 providing 27.5 miles per gallon. They *can* do it and they *will* do it — but only because it's the law. We need a tough, drastic, mandatory energy conservation program in the U.S.

Before Cleveland City Club, April 20/
Vital Speeches, 6-1:491.

Edwin R. Phelps
President, Peabody Coal Company

2

So far, our national energy policy is to talk about coal and burn more oil — and "wear a sweater." When the Arabs had us by the throat during the oil embargo, we were importing about 35 per cent of our oil. In recent months, we have imported more than 50 per cent. That is a peculiar kind of progress. If we make a national decision to lead from strength in our domestic fuels, we will burn more coal because that constitutes 80 per cent or more of our fossil-fuel supply. By a strange coincidence, the converse is true in that over 80 per cent of our energy use was not coal during 1976, and to me this does not make mathematical or economical sense . . . Every ton of coal that can be substituted for oil in an industrial furnace or an electric-generating station frees almost four barrels of oil for other purposes — such as jet fuel and aviation gas for airplanes, gasoline and diesel fuel for all types of portable equipment and asphalt for streets and highways, or the base for all types of exotic chemicals. The reserves of oil are limited and should be saved for this type of use rather than placed under boilers.

Before Economic Club of Detroit,
Feb. 28/Vital Speeches, 2-28:369.

3

[Saying coal cannot provide both high energy consumption and strict environmental standards]: The public has been hearing for years that coal is dirty and messy to handle, that mining is hazardous to the health of workers and that burning it is hazardous to the health of practically everybody. But now we' hear that coal is about to be elected messiah — the new savior of our people, the sure guide for a return to the promised land of 72-degree living-rooms, full employment and thumbing our noses at the Arabs.

The Dallas Times Herald, 4-24:(A)22.

Harvey A. Proctor
Chairman, Southern
California Gas Company

4

The energy problem in this country is not lack of available sources but lack of responsive political action to secure those sources to the marketplace . . . Systems of allocation, price control and rationing add enormously to the power of bureaucrats and politicians, at the expense of all the rest of us. No conservation program — not even the most stringent kind of program which would only be conceivable

(HARVEY A. PROCTOR)

under a totalitarian regime — could close the gap between the energy resources available to this country and our legitimate needs for economic growth and full employment.

Before Town Hall, Los Angeles, Sept. 22/
Los Angeles Herald-Examiner, 9-22:(A)1.

Dixy Lee Ray
Governor of Washington (D) 1

What distresses me is there seems to be so much emphasis upon self-flagellation and telling each other we're terribly wasteful [of energy], that we lose sight of the fact our nation is based on energy use and there is no way to live in the modern world without using large amounts of energy.

Interview/Los Angeles Herald-Examiner, 4-27:(B)2.

Ronald Reagan
Former Governor of California (R) 2

I have felt for a long time that the government is not the answer to the energy problem. Government *is* the problem. We are not troubled so much by a shortage of energy as we are by a surplus of government. The great problems in the energy field came about with government's involvement in the marketplace, regulation, price-fixing and so forth, and I think that today the answer lies in the marketplace.

TV-radio interview, Washington/"Meet the Press," National Broadcasting Company, 5-1.

John J. Rhodes
United States Representative,
R—Arizona 3

. . . if you want to get a more plentiful supply of energy, home-grown, so to speak, you had better deregulate the price, and it is very important that we do this and that we understand it because the crisis we have is more of an economic crisis, really, than it is an immediate energy crisis. The crisis is that we are importing over 51 per cent of our oil now from the OPEC nations, and it is costing us $45-billion a year, which translates itself into a balance-of-payments deficit of something like $30-billion. This kind of thing we cannot continue to

afford. This is the main reason that the dollar seems to be weakening abroad. But here we have the Carter Administration and the Democrats proposing a legislative package which will not produce one iota of energy more than we already have; in fact, it discourages it.

TV-radio interview/"Meet the Press," National Broadcasting Company, 10-23.

David M. Roderick
President, United States Steel Corporation 4

We feel very strongly that the nation needs an energy program. We'll strongly support it if it's right, but it worries me when I hear there might be a tax of $500 on large cars and rebates on small cars. I don't like to see any tinkering with something that is the strength of the whole economy at the moment. If done abruptly, it could disrupt auto sales. I hope that worries people in Washington, too.

Interview/The New York Times, 4-19:61.

John C. Sawhill
President, New York University;
Former Administrator,
Federal Energy Administration 5

The single most important thing we must do is to permit prices [of energy] to go up and send a signal to the American consumer that the days of low-cost, abundant energy are over. It's quite interesting to note what's happened since the 1973 Arab oil embargo. Fuel efficiency in automobiles has improved by 34 per cent. The thermal efficiency of American industry has improved nearly 10 per cent. We've witnessed a sharp reduction in the average annual growth rate of electricity from an annual rate of about 6 per cent in the 1960-1973 period to less than half that level in the ensuing three years. Most of these changes are the result of higher prices. The regulatory measures which were enacted last year — such as fuel-efficiency standards for new cars — have not been in effect long enough to have had any impact on the growth in consumption. The fact is that higher prices do result in more-efficient use.

Interview/U.S. News & World Report, 4-18:41.

(JOHN C. SAWHILL)

1

We can afford to depend on foreign sources for some portion of our energy supplies — particularly if we create an oil stockpile. There is no reason to be completely independent. We depend on other countries for a whole variety of important resources and raw materials that we use in our economy. And there's no reason why energy should not be in this category as well. The real problem in energy is not that we are dependent on foreign sources, but that we are dependent on foreign sources for *so much* of the energy supply, and that our dependency is increasing at such a rapid rate.

Interview/U.S. News & World Report, 4-18:42.

James R. Schlesinger
Assistant to President of the United States
Jimmy Carter for Energy Affairs

2

We must recognize that we have been burning the candle at both ends as far as energy is concerned. Present trends indicate the world will run out of oil in something like 40 years, even if we are able to obtain all of the oil that the geologists believe is out there — in their more optimistic projections. Americans have never believed in physical shortages. Many Americans today believe that these shortages somehow or other have been contrived by the industry. That is not true; they are real. Our problem as a nation till this point has been that we have had the ingredients of an energy crisis without there being an energy shortage. Once the gasoline lines disappeared after the [1973-74 oil] embargo, the American public came to believe — in fact, was informed by some political leaders — that the energy crisis was over. It is not over. It is just beginning. And if this particular episode is taken as a warning — a portent of what is to come — that would be the chief thing that this country could have learned . . . It's a problem that we have never faced before as a country. We have this short-lived legacy of oil and gas which will soon be exhausted. And we must recognize that we have enjoyed this brief [100-year] period of cheap and abundant energy through rapid mining of this geologic capital.

Interview/U.S. News & World Report, 2-14:24.

3

No comprehensive energy plan should be designed to bring about conservation at the expense of income, output and employment. So the first axiom of any comprehensive energy plan must be the maintenance of jobs, the expansion of the economy, the growth of productivity. [In coping with the crisis,] we have a hidden asset: our past prodigality, wastefulness and squandering. Given that base, we have lots of opportunities to save, and we shall be saving in the transportation market, the residential market, and to a considerable extent in the industrial market. [Still,] we face a change in American habits; that means constraint, curtailment. That is uncomfortable. Everybody will have to make some kind of sacrifice. We will not, however, be required to reduce the American standard of living. We are going to go on with suburbanized homes; we will have individualized transportation in the form of a motorcar. Both will have to be far more fuel-efficient in the future than they have been in the past.

At energy conference sponsored by Time,
Inc., Williamsburg, Va./Time, 4-25:27.

4

[On President Carter's energy program]: Many groups will find in this bill provisions which will impose burdens or sacrifice upon them. The temptation to seek exemptions from burdens and sacrifices will be very strong, but the United States will solve its energy problem only if it adopts a plan that is fair, and any fair plan will impose burdens on everyone.

Before Senate Energy and Natural
Resources Committee, Washington, May 3/
Los Angeles Herald-Examiner, 5-3:(A)2.

5

It's not that we're going to run out of oil and gas some time in the 1980s. If the world were to consume oil at our current rate of 20 billion barrels a year — and if we were able to recover all the oil that geologists think is available — we might get through another 60 to 90 years. But the problem is accommodating the voracious growth of demand. The world's present annual rate of increase is 5 per cent a

WHAT THEY SAID IN 1977

year. At that rate, we would almost double oil demand in the next decade. And it would rise to 70 billion barrels a year in the decade after that. Obviously, there is no way of accommodating this exponential growth.

Interview/Newsweek, 5-9:23.

Tom W. Sigler
Senior vice president,
Continental Oil Company
1

In a sense, we seem to be in the very early stages of a form of economic civil war over energy. This situation demands mutual understanding and compromise, not confrontation ... In the Northeast, states such as New York and Ohio still have refused to allow exploration for natural gas in the Great Lakes, though Canada has been producing gas from its side of the lakes for many years without any problems ... The fact remains that the Northeastern states have been buying natural gas at less than replacement costs while at the same time they have erected environmental and other barriers preventing development of their energy resources.

The New York Times, 4-27:44.

William E. Simon
Former Secretary of the Treasury
of the United States
2

The energy crisis should be labeled "made in Washington, D.C.," because the government has erected all the impediments, starting with the Phillips decision in 1954 for the control of natural gas, and going through the litany of environmental problems, price controls, nuclear-plant prohibitions, and all the rest. The crisis is government-caused, and now [President] Carter and the Democrats are proposing a government solution that won't work. This [Carter energy] program must make the OPEC nations extremely happy since there is nothing to promote production of domestic energy. It's an illustration of the total lack of faith in the dynamism of the free-enterprise system. The genius of the American people has been that we have always been able as a free people to produce our way out of crises. This program says we can't produce our way out of crises, only the government can.

Interview/Los Angeles Herald-Examiner, 9-4:(A)5.

Edgar B. Speer
Chairman, United States Steel
Corporation
3

There is only one reason why we have a shortage of natural gas today. The Federal Power Commission has held the well-head price of this clean-burning fuel at artificially low levels since the mid-1950s. As a result, there has been no economic incentive for energy companies to locate new reserves. Exploratory drilling for gas was actually cut in half between 1956 and 1970, so what we have been consuming is largely coming from reserves found before that time ... Since it burns cleanly, gas has been an ideal fuel for meeting government regulations on air pollution. Today, natural gas supplies about half of all the energy consumed by American industry. So when you put this whole situation in perspective, it's obvious that it isn't the cold winds of winter that we are troubled with this year, but the cold hand of government interference with the free-market system ... and the irrepressible urge of government agencies to regulate and control everything they can reach.

Before Sales-Marketing Executives of
Pittsburgh, Feb. 7/Vital Speeches, 3-1:304.

Harley O. Staggers
United States Representative,
D–West Virginia
4

For every study that shows we are going to run out of oil and gas next week, there's another saying we are not. You look for some middle ground, but all people can agree on is that supplies are finite.

The Dallas Times Herald, 5-22:(A)14.

John E. Swearingen, Jr.
Chairman, Standard Oil
Company (Indiana)
5

It isn't a question of whether we have enough nuclear power or enough electric-generating capacity, enough coal. The question

(JOHN E. SWEARINGEN, JR.)

is, do we have enough oil and gas to supply our requirements. Last year our country imported 42 per cent of the oil that we use. We buy it from other countries; most of it we buy from what we call the OPEC group, which is largely the nations of the Middle East. These nations at any time can shut off that supply if they choose to. Whether this is a result of a political policy on their part, whether it is a result of a military action that takes place in the Middle East, we are very vulnerable to our supplies of oil and gas; and, as a consequence, this nation today must do something to improve its security, both from a military and an economic standpoint . . . There is going to be no way additional supplies can come forth unless the industry, or people capable of doing so, are given the money to drill wells, and unless the output of these wells of oil and gas exceeds the cost of securing it, and the costs are continuing to rise.

TV-radio interview, Washington/"Meet the Press," National Broadcasting Company, 4-24.

1

. . . we can supply ample supplies of energy here at home if the prices of those supplies are permitted to go high enough to cover the costs of producing them and to allow a reasonable profit. This is the message that should be given to the American people, instead of the share-the-shortage, share-the-misery conversation that is so popular in Washington today. The economic aspects of our energy problem are solvable — but the political obstacles will never be overcome as long as substantial numbers of people continue to believe that they can have more energy without paying for it. Far from helping to shatter that illusion, the [Carter] Administration is proposing a reverse solution. It is asking consumers to pay more [through taxes] for energy they will not get.

Before Economic Club of New York, May 23/Vital Speeches, 7-1:572.

Edward Teller
Nuclear physicist

2

[On the just-ended massive power failure in the New York City area, believed to have been caused by lightning]: I think this repeated blackout points out again an obvious fact that too many forget: We ought not to operate our electric system on the bare edge of sufficiency, because then Jupiter sends a lightning bolt and we are in trouble.

July 15/The New York Times, 7-16:8.

Morris K. Udall
United States Representative, D–Arizona

3

We have difficulty persuading people that our energy problems are serious because a large proportion of our citizens think energy supplies and prices are manipulated by energy companies. It is imperative, therefore, that an integral part of the mandate of the new department responsible for energy policy be the promotion of competition in all portions of the energy industry.

The Dallas Times Herald, 3-29:(A)4.

Rawleigh Warner, Jr.
Chairman, Mobil Oil Corporation

4

One reason the United States energy situation is in such disarray today is that we have no rational and comprehensive national energy policy. Any realistic energy policy for this country should rest on the fact that we have within our borders the potential energy resource base to become essentially independent of other countries.

The New York Times, 1-9:(3)35.

Alvin M. Weinberg
*Director, Institute for
Energy Analysis, Oak Ridge
Associated Universities*

5

There are serious problems associated with nuclear power — proliferation, possibility of accident, and so on. But having worked with nuclear power all my life, I believe these problems can be overcome. One important way that we could proceed would be to confine our nuclear-energy enterprises to a relatively few

WHAT THEY SAID IN 1977

(ALVIN M. WEINBERG)

places in the United States. It could be controlled easier and be more acceptable if we limited the land committed to high-level radioactive operations to, let us say, 5,000 square miles. This would be a commitment into perpetuity, somewhat like our commitment of land to national parks. That's the direction we should move, rather than saying nuclear is too dangerous and let's give up on it.

Interview/U.S. News & World Report, 4-18:44.

Leonard Woodcock
*President, United Automobile
Workers of America*   *1*

We are opposing the [Carter] Administration on the so-called gas-guzzler tax and rebate parts of his energy package ... not simply because it would affect the automobile industry, but because it is absolutely unnecessary and an unwise policy. Sometimes people in Washington seem to forget what the gas-guzzling family [is]: the man and his non-working wife and five kids with a nine-passenger station wagon but no other cars, or the family of four with both father and mother working that has three efficient cars sitting in their driveway which, when they move, usually carry only one person. You have got to consider the families and not the machines that those families use.

*At UAW convention, Los Angeles, May 15/
The Dallas Times Herald, 5-16:(A)10.*

Ardeshir Zahedi
*Iranian Ambassador to
the United States*   *2*

As a major producer and exporter of oil, it is a matter of Iran's national policy never to use oil as a political weapon. As my sovereign has said, oil, like water and bread, is indispensable and no one should be denied its use. Indeed, we were opposed to the embargoes of 1967 and 1973. We did not participate in them and will not take part in any future embargoes.

*At Westminster College, May 7/
Vital Speeches, 6-15:518.*

Georgi A. Arbatov
Director, Soviet Institute of
U.S.A. and Canadian Affairs
1

[On U.S. President Jimmy Carter's criticism of human rights in the Soviet Union]: Nobody denies American citizens the right to have their opinions about what is going on in the Soviet Union, just as nobody can deny Soviet people their opinion about events in the U.S. But if we are really to base our foreign policies toward each other on our likes and dislikes, and especially on our attempts to change the other country according to our wishes, then the whole concept of detente will break up. Detente means peaceful coexistence between really different countries. We have to reckon with these differences ... There's a border line which has to be judged by the political wisdom of any statesman — where expression of support for certain ideas ends and overt interference begins. The vital rule of detente is not to trespass over this border line.
Interview, Moscow/
U.S. News & World Report, 3-14:23.

Anne Armstrong
United States Ambassador to
the United Kingdom
2

I'm more convinced than ever of the need for interdependence — the inevitability of it. It's absolutely impossible for America ever to draw inward again. For the first time in our history, we can neither dominate the world nor withdraw from it.
Interview, London/
The Christian Science Monitor, 3-3:4.

George W. Ball
Former Under Secretary of State
of the United States
3

We do ourselves a disservice when we disparage the importance of American influence and American authority in world councils. By and large, we remain the country to which practically all [in the non-Communist world] look, and we will remain in that position. The very fact that leaders in other countries shoot peashooters at us reflects the importance they attach to the United States, as well as showing that they regard the United States as a nation with a considerable degree of tolerance.
Interview/U.S. News & World Report, 6-27:46.

Douglas Bennet
Assistant Secretary for
Congressional Relations, Department
of State of the United States
4

My view is that rather than briefing Congressmen on settled policy, this Department should take a step backward and discuss with Congress what the options are ... There is expertise here [at the State Department], but that expertise ought to be made available to Congress. Congress is the greatest available source of sound, free advice around here. We'll get better policy — foreign as well as domestic — by consulting with Congress.
Interview/Los Angeles Times, 4-14:(2)5.

Christoph Bertram
Director, International Institute
for Strategic Studies, London
5

One of the striking features of the world today is the fact that the U.S. is the only real superpower. She enjoys not only military and economic power, but also has cultural influence and the influence of idealism. The Soviet

97

WHAT THEY SAID IN 1977

(CHRISTOPH BERTRAM)

Union, on the other hand, possesses little more than military power with which to pursue its global ambitions. In my view, this contrast between the United States and the Soviets defines to a large extent the security problems we will face in the 1980s and 1990s. . . . the United States does not have to follow suit automatically whenever the Soviets make a military move. It is not always necessary to fight fire with fire. The U.S. and the West have at their disposal other non-military instruments of influence which can be more effective in non-conflict situations.

Interview/U.S. News & World Report, 6-27:48.

Roelof F. Botha
Foreign Minister of South Africa 1

[Criticizing the U.S. for being selective in its human-rights foreign policy by, for example, supporting an arms embargo against his country]: If the maintenance of human rights was indeed the concern of the American government, America should be pressing for sanctions against more than half the governments in the world.

Johannesburg, Oct. 27/
The Washington Post, 10-28:(A)7.

Willy Brandt
Former Chancellor of West Germany 2

Hardly anyone among the leading statesmen of the world had the strength or the vision to prepare his country and all of us in time for the development in those countries which we have come to call the Third World. Our countries will not be able to evade [new, more just principles for the world economic order] even if they cannot bring themselves to like some of the proposed models. Justice demands — and even if we do not want to listen to justice, reason will tell us — there will never be a lasting and secure coexistence of affluence and misery.

Boston/The Christian Science Monitor, 3-22:12.

Leonid I. Brezhnev
General Secretary, Communist
Party of the Soviet Union 3

Washington's claim to teach others how to live cannot be accepted by any sovereign state . . . I will repeat again: We will not tolerate interference in our internal affairs by anyone under any pretext. A normal development of relations on such a basis is, of course, unthinkable.

At congress of trade unions, Moscow,
March 21/Los Angeles Times, 3-22:(1)1.

4

. . . the international position of the Soviet Union and the socio-political face of the world have changed dramatically. An end has been put to the capitalist encirclement of the U.S.S.R. Socialism has become a world system. A powerful socialist community has taken shape. The position of world capitalism has been seriously weakened. In place of the former colonies, many young states have sprung up which oppose imperialism. The international authority and influence of our country has grown immeasurably. As the result, the alignment of forces in the world has become completely different. There is now a real possibility to prevent a new world war.

Before Soviet Communist Party
Central Committee, Moscow, June 5/
Vital Speeches, 7-1:547.

Leonid I. Brezhnev
President of the Soviet Union; General
Secretary, Soviet Communist Party 5

[On U.S.-Soviet relations]: There is much that divides our countries, from the socio-economic system to ideology. Not everyone in the United States likes our way of doing things, and we, too, could say a great deal about what is going on in America. But if differences are accentuated, if attempts are made to lecture each other, the result will only be a build-up of distrust and hostility, useless to our two countries and dangerous to the world as a whole . . . At the very inception of the Soviet state, Lenin made it clear to the American leaders of the time that "whether they like it or not, Soviet

(LEONID I. BREZHNEV)

Russia is a great power" and "Americans have nothing to gain from the Wilsonian policy of piously refusing to deal with us on the ground that our government is distasteful to them." This was true half a century ago. It is all the more true today.

Before Communist Party Central Committee and national and Russian Supreme Soviets, Moscow, Nov. 2/The New York Times, 11-3:(A)1.

1

At times, the Communists in bourgeois countries are now promised that their "right to a place in society" will be "recognized." A mere "trifle" is demanded in exchange: that they give up fighting the power of capital, give up fighting for socialism, and abandon international class solidarity. Under no circumstances may principles be sacrificed for the sake of a tactical advantage. Otherwise, as they say, you'll keep your hair but lose your head.

Before Communist Party Central Committee and national and Russian Supreme Soviets, Moscow, Nov. 2/The New York times, 11-4:(A)9.

Harold Brown
Secretary of Defense of the United States

2

That the United States observes its commitments to other countries is nowhere shown more clearly than in the case of the Vietnam war. It is testified to by the tens of thousands of American dead and hundreds of thousands of Americans wounded in that war. It is testified to by the deep, painful and not yet healed wounds on the American body-politic from that war. So I think that as long as an American security commitment exists, no one should have any doubts about our willingness, our intention of honoring it.

News conference, Seoul, South Korea, July 26/The New York times, 7-27:(A)6.

Lester R. Brown
President, Worldwatch Institute

3

National security can no longer be regarded as merely national in scope. In a world that is not only ecologically interdependent but eco-

nomically and politically interdependent as well, the problem of "national" security requires a parallel concern for global security. The deterioration of the earth's biological systems threatens not only the security of individual nations but the survival of civilization as we know it. Anything that undermines the international monetary system jeopardizes the economic and political stability of all countries.

At luncheon, Washington, Oct. 29/ The New York Times, 10-30:(1)35.

Zbigniew Brzezinski
Assistant to President of the United States Jimmy Carter for National Security Affairs

4

It seems to me that at least since the days of Wilson and certainly since . . . World War II, the American social elite had a fairly cohesive viewpoint of what its foreign interests were and what, therefore, the foreign policy of the United States ought to be. And this social/ political elite was a fairly cohesive social formation with the WASP, Ivy-League-trained, Wall Street-based Establishment operating through such institutions as the Council on Foreign Relations, but more pervasively. And it is this elite which I think will last 10 years or so, maybe even 15 years. It's fractured, disintegrated and, most important of all, has lost its own sense of legitimacy. If you look at the societies throughout history, elites can function only when they have a sense of their own internal legitimacy. And this group has lost its legitimacy. It's disintegrated, its children have disowned it, and it's no longer very clear as to its basic values and its aspirations. So, in that sense, decision-making has become much more fragmented and dispersed in the United States.

Interview/Los Angeles Times, 1-24:(1)3.

5

We feel that detente is desirable, and we do not shrink away from the use of the word "detente." But detente to us essentially means progressive accommodation. Detente means the establishment of more cooperative relationships. And detente to us means also a process which, to be enduring and to be accepted by

WHAT THEY SAID IN 1977

(ZBIGNIEW BRZEZINSKI)

the American people, has to be both reciprocal and progressively more comprehensive... "Reciprocal" means that the rules of the game are the same for both parties. It means that one party cannot feel free to proclaim revolutionary principles or certain inevitable laws of history which give it a right to comment on the social order of other societies or even to engage in the direct abetting of revolutionary violence, and then at the same time considers it an act of intervention if the other side affirms its own beliefs, its own fundamental principles. Reciprocity also means reciprocity in more tangible relationships — access, contacts. This is what detente has to be about to be enduring.

Interview, Washington/
U.S. News & World Report, 5-30:35.

1

It is our view that we are now at a stage in history in which the United States again has to undertake a creative process of building a new world system. This must take into account the cumulative effect of all of the changes that have occurred in the past 15 to 20 years: the appearance of a massive number of new states, the extraordinary rapid decolonization, the surfacing of new social and political aspirations, the doubling of the world's population... It may be too sharp and potentially misleading to call it a new era of American leadership. But it certainly is a new era of American creativity, based this time on the need for a much greater degree of collaboration with others than was the case between '45 and '50 — when we were similarly engaged in a creative international effort.

Interview, Washington/
U.S. News & World Report, 5-30:35.

2

In my judgment, when you use a word like "Communist" we really have to ask ourselves what's hidden behind the word. I don't think that the prospect of the Third World is Communism in the first meaning of the word: namely, Soviet imperialism, Stalinism, oppression and uniformity of the '50s. I do think that for many of the developing countries undergoing

very rapid change, Marxism, Communism, offers what appears to them a relevant intellectual framework. For example, all of the Eritrean independence movements consider themselves to be Marxists. But in actual application I think we will see two things: tremendous diversity, relatively little loyalty to the Soviet Union, or none at all. And, probably more frequently, chaos rather than Communism. Indeed, if I had to put forth a proposition, I would say both the prospects and the threat in the Third World involve not Communism but chaos.

Interview/The Washington Post, 10-9:(C)5.

3

[On the U.S.' emphasis on human rights in its foreign policy]: ... the fact that even non-democratic regimes make a big show out of adopting democratic principles in itself is a demonstration of the compelling power of these principles. We are not setting out on a crusade to reproduce the American system in other parts of the world. We are very conscious of the fact that every political system is the product of its own history, psychology, social conditions, even genes. All we're saying is that it's inherent in the human spirit to desire for more individual self-expression. And we as a society, though imperfect, with many blemishes, want to stand for that. And we want to encourage others to stand for it. But what happens in individual societies, including the Soviet Union, is the affair of these countries. And we're not intruding, nor do we wish to intrude, into their domestic affairs. Nor are we making their attitude on human rights the *sine qua non* for normal state-to-state relations.

Interview/The Washington Post, 10-9:(C)5.

4

... there is a certain sense of parity in the relationship [between the U.S. and the Soviet Union] derived from the fact that we're both global powers. As a consequence of that condition, events or crises even distant from our shores or theirs tend to affect us or our relationship and this makes us more sensitive to the need to cooperate... The cooperative aspects are [indeed] on the upswing. But this should not be interpreted as meaning that the competition has been terminated. I think what

(ZBIGNIEW BRZEZINSKI)

the American people have to understand is that in the American-Soviet relationship both of these realities are present and we have to avoid and have to get into the habit of avoiding extremes of euphoria and pessimism.

Before Overseas Writers club, Washington,
Oct. 18/The New York Times, 10-19:(A)2.

1

After World War II our foreign policy, by necessity, was focused primarily on issues connected with the cold war. This gave it a sharp focus, in some cases making it easier to mobilize public opinion. A concentrated foreign policy could be supported by public opinion. Today we confront a more difficult task, one that calls for support based on reason. We must respond to a wider range of issues — some of which still involve the cold war — issues stemming from a complex process of global change. A concentrated foreign policy must give way to a complex foreign policy, no longer focused on a single, dramatic task — such as the defense of the West. Instead, we must engage ourselves on the distant and difficult goal of giving shape to a world that has suddenly become politically awakened and socially restless.

Before Trilateral Commission, Bonn, West
Germany, Oct. 25/The Washington Post, 11-1:(A)19.

Robert C. Byrd
United States Senator, D—West Virginia

2

When we look at the past experience of dealing with the Soviets we should have learned a lesson that they are hard bargainers; they are tough; and they will say "No" today and "Yes" months from today . . . They are international poker players. And, of course, if they think they are. dealing with an adversary who will buckle, knuckle under, fall back and fall back, and wring hands, they will push him to the wall.

The Washington Post, 4-13:(A)22.

Jimmy Carter
President-elect of the United States

3

[Addressing the people of the world]: I want to assure you that the relations of the United States with the other countries and peoples of the world will be guided during my Administration by our desire to shape a world order that is more responsive to human operations. The United States will meet its obligations to help create a stable, just and peaceful world order. We will not seek to dominate nor dictate to others. As we Americans have concluded one chapter in our nation's history and are beginning to work on another, we have, I believe, acquired a more mature perspective on the problems of the world. It is a perspective which recognizes the fact that we alone do not have all of the answers to the world's problems . . . The problems of the world will not easily be resolved. Yet the well-being of each and every one of us — indeed our mutual survival — depends on their resolution. As President of the United States, I can assure you that we intend to do our part. I ask you to join us in a common effort based on mutual trust and mutual respect.

Address broadcast around the world,
Jan. 19/The New York Times, 1-21:(B)2.

Jimmy Carter
President of the United States

4

We are a proudly idealistic nation, but let no one confuse our idealism with weakness. Because we are free, we can never be indifferent to the fate of freedom elsewhere. Our moral sense dictates a clear-cut preference for those societies which share with us an abiding respect for individual human rights. We do not seek to intimidate, but it is clear that a world which others can dominate with impunity would be inhospitable to decency and a threat to the well-being of all people.

Inaugural address, Washington, Jan. 20/
U.S. News & World Report, 1-31:29.

5

All the signatories of the UN Charter have pledged themselves to observe and respect basic human rights. Thus, no member of the United Nations can claim that mistreatment of its citizens is solely its own business. Equally, no member can avoid its responsibilities to review and to speak when torture or unwarranted deprivation of freedom occurs in any part of the world . . . This issue [human rights] is important by itself. It should not block progress on other important matters affecting the

WHAT THEY SAID IN 1977

(JIMMY CARTER)

security and well-being of our people and of world peace. It is obvious that the reduction of tension, the control of nuclear arms, the achievement of harmony in troubled areas of the world, and the provision of food, good health and education will independently contribute to advancing the human condition... We in the United States accept this responsibility [to foster human rights] in the fullest and most constructive sense. Ours is a commitment, not just a political posture.

At United Nations, New York, March 17/
The Dallas Times Herald, 3-18:(A)1,3.

1

In our relations with other countries, these mutual concerns will be reflected in our political, our cultural and our economic attitudes: ...We will strive for peace in the troubled areas of the world. We will aggressively seek to control the weaponry of war. We will promote a new system of international economic progress and cooperation. And we will be steadfast in our dedication to the dignity and well-being of people throughout the world. I believe this is a foreign policy that is consistent with America's historic values and commitments. I believe it is a foreign policy that is consonant with the ideals of the United Nations.

At United Nations, New York, March 17/
The New York Times, 3-18:(A)10.

2

I think the unfortunate experience that we had in Vietnam has impressed on the American people deeply, and I hope permanently, the danger of our country resorting to military means in a distant place on earth when our own security is not being threatened...

To European reporters, Washington, May 2/
The Washington Post, 5-3:(A)8.

3

We have, I think, made some progress in arousing a world interest in this subject of human rights... In the past, I think the leaders have been trying to forget about it, but now I doubt if any country who deals with us forgets

that subject very long. And I meet with foreign leaders... possibly more than anybody's ever done before. I think we have an average of about more than one foreign leader coming here every two weeks. This week I have four countries that have come. But anyway, almost invariably they bring up the subject of human rights and the progress that their own government's trying to make... to let me know they share my concern... So, I think that that concept that our nation is kind of a beacon light once again, and a decent commitment to human rights, has been fairly well accepted.

Interview, Washington/Newsweek, 5-2:37.

4

We are determined in the United States to use our economic, social, political and military strength so we can never be successfully challenged by any competitive philosophy, and we are very eager to combine with our allies and friends to make sure this resolve is clearly undisputed by all. We have an eagerness to compete in an ideological way around the world, because we know that our commitment to human freedom, human rights and democratic principles, and our compassion toward the less fortunate than we will prevail. This is a commitment we want to share with you.

Newcastle-upon-Tyne, England, May 6/
Los Angeles Times, 5-7:(1)18.

5

[On the use of human rights as a cornerstone of U.S. foreign policy]: America's concern for human rights does not reflect a desire to impose our particular political or social arrangements on any other country. It is, rather, an expression of the most deeply felt values of the American people. We want the world to know where we stand. We entertain no illusion that the concerns we express and the actions we take will bring rapid changes in the policies of other governments. But neither do we believe that world opinion is without effect. We will continue to express our beliefs — not only because we must remain true to ourselves, but also because we are convinced that the building of a better world rests on each nation's clear

(JIMMY CARTER)

expression of the values that have given meaning to its national life.

At NATO conference, London, May 10/
Vital Speeches, 6-1:483.

1

I have concluded that the United States will henceforth view arms transfers [sales to foreign countries] as an exceptional foreign-policy implement, to be used only in instances where it can be clearly demonstrated that the transfer contributes to our national security interests. We will continue to utilize arms transfers to promote our security and the security of our close friends. But in the future, the burden of persuasion will be on those who favor a particular arms sale rather than those who oppose it.

Washington, May 19/
The Washington Post, 5-20:(A)1.

2

I believe we can have a foreign policy that is democratic, that is based on our fundamental values and that uses power and influence for humane purposes. We can also have a foreign policy that the American people both support and understand. I have a quiet confidence in our own political system. Because we know democracy works, we can reject the arguments of those rulers who deny human rights to their people ... Being confident of our own future, we are now free of that inordinate fear of Communism which once led us to embrace any dictator who joined us in our fear. For too many years we have been willing to adopt the flawed principles and tactics of our adversaries, sometimes abandoning our values for theirs. We fought fire with fire, never thinking that fire is better fought with water ... This does not mean that we can conduct our foreign policy by rigid moral maxims. We live in a world that is imperfect and will always be imperfect, a world that is complex and will always be complex. I understand fully the limits of moral suasion. I have no illusion that changes will come easily or soon. But I also believe that it is a mistake to under-value the power of words and of the ideas that words embody. In our

own history that power has ranged from Thomas Paine's "Common Sense" to Martin Luther King, Jr.'s "I Have a Dream."

At University of Notre Dame commencement,
May 22/The New York Times, 5-23:12.

3

If there's one overwhelming impression that's growing on me, it's the long-range strategic need — looking 10, 15, 20 years in the future — for a close friendship and mutual trust, social and political alliance with the developing nations of the world. Our approach has been very well evoked by [U.S. UN] Ambassador [Andrew] Young, and he works very closely and intimately with me and the Secretary of State. He has a great sensitivity about the yearnings, the frustrations and, in the past, even the animosities and hatred of many developing nations' people toward our own country. I think he's made great strides in repairing that damage that had been done. And he also gives us a very clear understanding of the opportunities there. So I consider him to be a very valuable and a very compatible spokesman for us.

Interview, Washington/
U.S. News & World Report, 6-6:20.

4

We don't want to be in a position that once a country is not friendly to us, and once they are completely within the influence of the Soviet Union, they should forever be in that status. And as I've already indicated, and named several countries — Somalia, Ethiopia, Iraq, even more controversial nations like Vietnam, Cuba — I want to move as best I can to re-establish normal, friendly relations with those countries. In some instances, the obstacles are quite severe, as in the case of Cuba and perhaps Vietnam. But I think this is what our government ought to do. And I would like to have a situation when I go out of office that all the nations in the world have diplomatic relationships with us. We now have 14 who don't and I've been pursuing this aggressively ...

News conference, Washington,
June 13/The New York Times, 6-14:24.

WHAT THEY SAID IN 1977

(JIMMY CARTER)

1

Our statements concerning human rights I think have been well received around the world. We've not singled out the Soviet Union for criticism and I've never tried to inject myself into the internal affairs of the Soviet Union. I've never made the first comment that personally criticizes General Secretary [Leonid] Brezhnev. But when we pursue, aggressively and with determination, our commitment to the principle that human beings ought to be well treated by governments, that human freedom is one of the highest aspirations and commitments of our country, I think this is the right thing to do. If it hits ourselves as self-criticism, so be it. If it touches the Soviet Union, and they interpret it as intrusion, so be it. But we've tried to make this a broad-based approach. I think it's hard to assess the results of this deep commitment, which I think is compatible with the inclinations of the American people. But I don't believe that there is a single leader of a nation on earth today who doesn't have within his or her consciousness a concern about human rights — "how do we appear to our own people, how do we appear to observers from other nations?"

News conference, Washington, June 13/
The New York Times, 6-14:24.

2

We have a basic decision to make . . . about how to deal with nations who in the past have not been our friends and who in some instances have been our enemies on the war field. Should we write them off permanently as enemies and force them to be completely under the control of Communist powers, or should we start the process of giving them an option to be both our friends and the friends of others, hoping that they will come to a more democratic free society and join with us in making a better world? I am not in favor of writing those countries off.

At public meeting, Yazoo City, Miss., July 21/
The Dallas Times Herald, 7-22:(A)3.

3

It is not a question of a "hard" [foreign] policy or a "soft" policy, but of a clear-eyed recognition of how most effectively to protect our security and to create . . . a more reciprocal, realistic and an ultimately more productive basis [for superpower relationships] . What matters ultimately is whether we can create a relationship of cooperation that will be rooted in the national interests of both sides. We shape our own policies to accommodate the changing world, and we hope the Soviets will do the same . . . As we negotiate with the Soviet Union, we will be guided by the vision of a gentler, freer, more bountiful world. But we will have no illusions about the nature of the world as it really is. The basis for complete mutual trust does not yet exist.

Before Southern Legislative Conference, Charleston,
S.C., July 21/Los Angeles Times, 7-22:(1)1,15.

4

Part of the Soviet leaders' current attitude may be due to their apparent — and incorrect — belief that our concern for human rights is aimed specifically at them or is an attack on their vital interests. There are no hidden meanings in our commitment to human rights. We stand on what we have said on this subject before. Our policy is exactly what it appears to be: the positive and sincere expression of our deepest beliefs as a people. It is addressed not to any particular people or area of the world, but to all countries equally, including our own. And it is specifically not designed to heat up the arms race or bring back the cold war. On the contrary, I believe that an atmosphere of peaceful cooperation is far more conducive to an increased respect for human rights than an atmosphere of belligerence or warlike confrontation. The experience of our century has proved this over and over again. We have no illusions that the process will be quick or that change will come easily. But we are confident that if we do not abandon the struggle, the cause of personal freedom and human dignity will be enhanced.

Before Southern Legislative Conference, Charleston,
S.C., July 21/The New York Times, 7-22:(A)4.

(JIMMY CARTER)

1

. . . I respect the Soviet Union. Their technological achievements have been notable. Their influence around the world has been a matter of concern for us in the past because it has been so successful. But I think the degree to which we can properly interrelate with the non-aligned countries of the world, the developing nations of the world, and let them test the proposition that our system of government is preferable, that we want no control or domination over them — these are the kinds of things I think will ultimately prevail, and not which country is the most vigorous or which military force is most powerful.

Interview/Time, 8-8:25.

2

When I get ready to meet with the foreign minister of a country or head of state, I pretty well guarantee that I understand that country, the history of it, population, exports, imports, per-capita income, historic relationship with our country, strengths of their political leaders . . . I don't go into a negotiation session that involves the well-being of our country without being prepared. I think anybody who does come in here to tell me what went on in Helsinki or Vladivostok — what proposals we made to the Soviets — they had better know the subject, because I know it.

Interview, Washington, Sept. 28/
The Dallas Times Herald, 9-29:(A)5.

3

The authority of the Congress in helping to shape foreign decisions is greater than I had anticipated. My dealing with the Georgia Legislature [as Governor], although it taught me a great deal about the personal interrelationships with members of Congress, didn't prepare me well for the profound influence that Congress both warrants and asserts in defense and foreign matters. I have been surprised at the unexpected influence that we can have on foreign affairs, and I have realized, sometimes in an unexpected way, that actions or statements that I make here do affect the attitude of leaders in places like Malaysia, Singapore, as

well as those countries that we think about daily, like Israel or Great Britain and the Soviet Union. So, in some ways, I have more influence than I thought. In some ways, I have to share more authority than I had anticipated.

Interview, Washington/
The New York Times, 10-23:(1)36.

Leonel J. Castillo
Commissioner, Immigration and
Naturalization Service of
the United States

4

One of the biggest problems is the INS tends to look at itself only as a law-enforcement agency. INS doesn't exist just to keep out people who want to enter the country illegally. We also exist to provide a whole variety of services for immigrants who are here legally. The INS, like every police force, tends to become hardened because it sees nothing but trouble. You do get INS agents with the mentality of the immigrant as cheap soda — that goes for legal as well as illegal immigrants — and those agents become part of the problem themselves. Regardless of whether you're saying yes or no to an immigrant, I think it's necessary to realize they aren't all that different from our grandparents. My grandfather crossed over the Rio Grande at Brownsville in 1880, paid a nickel and became an American citizen. That's all it took. Now the economic condition of the United States is different, but the immigrants themselves have the same desires.

Interview/The Washington Post, 5-22:(F)5.

Nicolae Ceaucescu
President of Romania

5

[On U.S. President Carter's emphasis on human rights in foreign policy]: The way in which these matters are being approached today is in a certain respect contradictory to the very spirit of the Helsinki documents. They run counter to the established course of observing each country's independence and non-interference in the internal affairs of other nations. In Helsinki, our starting point was precisely the observance of each people's right to solve their problems as they saw fit.

Interview, Bucharest/
The Washington Post, 7-11:(A)18.

WHAT THEY SAID IN 1977

Warren M. Christopher
*Deputy Secretary of State
of the United States*
1

In some cases it is the policy of other governments that precludes normal relations [with the U.S.]. But all governments should be aware of the message sent by President Carter to the Vietnamese — that we want to put the bitterness of the past behind us and look to the future ... Right now there are scores of countries with whom we do not have normal relations. Fully aware of the difficulties involved, we are bent on shortening the list.

*At Occidental College, June 11/
The Dallas Times Herald, 6-12:(A)5.*

Frank Church
United States Senator, D—Idaho
2

I disagree with those who say that by speaking out on human rights [in foreign countries] we'll jeopardize negotiations on arms control and trade. In those negotiations, the Russians will look to their own best interests as we will look to ours. The U.S. should behave as a champion of freedom in the world. The Russians never miss a target of opportunity when it comes to attacking the Western world.

U.S. News & World Report, 3-14:21.

3

[Arguing against making the Voice of America an independent news agency without propaganda functions]: It seems to me that, when we made the decision to establish the Voice of America, we made the decision to establish a government propaganda agency, the purpose of which was to transmit our message abroad. [The Voice of America] is a government broadcasting company, and to pretend otherwise is only to fool ourselves. If the Voice of America is not going to be the expression of the American government in its foreign policy and its objectives abroad, why do we maintain it?

The New York Times, 5-29:(1)5.

Dick Clark
United States Senator, D—Iowa
4

If we're going to put our best foot forward in the world, we have to speak up for human rights. When we haven't, we have placed ourselves at the same level as countries that are not interested in human rights, and it just becomes a foreign policy of manipulation and power. We can cut off aid and even break relations, but there's a limit beyond which you don't want to go [in supporting human rights abroad]. You may encourage people to do things you're not willing to support, such as revolt in Eastern Europe.

U.S. News & World Report, 3-14:21.

Ruth C. Clusen
*President, National
League of Women Voters*
5

There are three pressure points where citizens can make their feelings on foreign policy felt: the Congress, the Executive Branch and the United Nations. It's hard to tell which to attack at any given time, for foreign affairs are like a floating crap game which changes depending on who's up and who's down at any given moment. I think if we want to be effective we have to press all three pressure points at the same time.

*Before Los Angeles World Affairs Council/
Los Angeles Herald-Examiner, 7-4:(B)3.*

John B. Connally, Jr.
*Former Secretary of the
Treasury of the United States; Former
Governor of Texas (D, now R)*
6

[On President Carter's emphasis on human rights in foreign policy]: The absolute irony of this situation, it seems to me, is the President is talking about human rights all over the world and making it a number 1 issue ... And at the very same time he is talking about normalizing relations with Cuba. This fellow [Cuban Premier Fidel] Castro, he is a great personification of commitment to human rights, isn't he! You know, I don't understand this. It seems to me in the conduct of foreign affairs the first thing you have to do is be consistent, and if I ever saw an inconsistency in the execution and the administration and articulation of foreign policy, it is in this [Carter] Administration with respect to human rights.

*TV-radio interview, Washington/"Meet the
Press," National Broadcasting Company, 6-19.*

Margaret Costanza
Assistant to President of the United
States Jimmy Carter for Public Liaison
1

We are going to work for international peace, and we are going to work for international justice. We don't see how the two can be separated, for only in a just world can peace truly be firm and lasting, and only in a peaceful world can justice and respect for the human being be nourished.

San Francisco Examiner & Chronicle,
5-8:(This World)2.

Rowan Cronje
Minister of Manpower and
Social Affairs of Rhodesia
2

I will be forgiven if one considers classifying [U.S. UN Ambassador] Andrew Young in the same category as [Ugandan President] Idi Amin. They both would have been clowns were the world's problems not so tragic. Their utterances would have been funny were they not so dangerous, pathetic, or their effect so serious.

The Washington Post, 8-25:(A)22.

Morarji R. Desai
Prime Minister of India
3

We [non-aligned nations] must persist in solving our own problems, rather than depend on the charity and benevolence of others. I do not think we need indulge in the commonplace that the rich and the strong [nations] are getting richer and stronger. I firmly believe that self-help must precede help from others. Even for making certain of help from heaven, one has to help oneself.

At conference of non-aligned nations, New
Delhi, April 7/The New York times, 4-8:(A)4.

Adalbert de Segonzac
Former chief North American
correspondent, "France-Soir," Paris
4

[On U.S. President Carter's human-rights stand in foreign policy]: As for the Russians, it's obvious they are not going to give the dissidents any more freedom than they have had. The Kremlin may even get tougher with

the dissidents. All the same, the American President has put them on the spot. I'm sure it's very uncomfortable for them and for all the other countries, like Chile, and so many more in East Europe and Africa which are run by dictatorships. Possibly Carter is going to have to ease off. The Russians can take just so much of that. But I am glad he has raised the issue of human rights. When better than now, and who better to speak out than the President of the United States? Why are we in opposition to the Russians, if not for principles of freedom, justice and human rights?

Interview/U.S. News & World Report, 7-11:56.

Milovan Djilas
Author; Former Vice
President of Yugoslavia
5

[On U.S. President Carter's emphasis on human rights in American foreign policy]: Everybody in Eastern Europe knows about what the new American Administration has been saying. It is something like the beginning of America acting once again like her traditions. Carter cannot change the situation in Eastern Europe, but maybe he can influence governments to be more careful, more respectful of laws . . . What I am afraid of, if anything, is that American pragmatism, in the form of multinational corporations, will not follow Carter's ideals. Profits are important, but in our time there is more to survival.

Interview, Belgrade/The Washington Post, 3-13:(A)18.

Abba Eban
Former Foreign Minister of Israel
6

. . . a negotiation is a process from which nobody emerges with the exact position that he took into it.

Tv-radio interview/"Meet the Press,"
National Broadcasting Company, 11-27.

Gerald R. Ford
President of the United States
7

[On the use of assassination in foreign policy]: In the atmosphere, in the circumstances we live in today, I don't think it should take place. But I can envision World War III, where the life or death of the United States

WHAT THEY SAID IN 1977

(GERALD R. FORD)

might depend upon some very strong action. I think the only one who can make that decision at that time is the person who has to look at the alternatives. All I am saying is, he might have to be that tough because, you know, moral decisions can be two-sided.

Interview, Washington/The Washington Post, 1-9:(A)6.

1

It is my feeling that in the last few years Congress has gotten into the field of foreign policy in too minute a way. I recognize they have a Constitutional responsibility, but the pendulum swings in this country. I can see that maybe in the '50s, as an outgrowth of World War II, Congress didn't perform this Constitutional role; but that doesn't justify the pendulum pointing way over.

Interview, Washington/
The New York Times, 1-12:(A)14.

2

I express the hope that this new Congress will re-examine its Constitutional role in international affairs. The exclusive right to declare war, the duty to advise and consent on the part of the Senate, and the power of the purse on the part of the House, are ample authority for the Legislative Branch and should be jealously guarded. But because we may have been too careless of these powers in the past does not justify Congressional intrusion into, or obstruction of, the proper exercise of Presidential responsibilities now or in the future. There can be only one Commander-in-Chief. In these times, crises cannot be managed and wars cannot be waged by committee. Nor can peace be pursued solely by parliamentary debate. To the ears of the world, the President speaks for the nation. While he is, of course, ultimately accountable to the Congress, the courts and the people, he and his emissaries must not be handicapped in advance in their relations with foreign governments as has sometimes happened in the past.

State of the Union address, Washington, Jan.12/
The New York Times, 1-13:26.

Donald M. Fraser
United States Representative, D—Minnesota

3

The last thing the United States needs to do is to embark on another crusade that involves our deciding for other countries how they are going to run themselves. What we need to do first of all is to quit giving help to oppressive governments. I think that is the Number 1 objective, because we are intervening, and have been, on behalf of governments who are torturing their people and putting them in jail for arbitrary reasons. Once we have done that, I think we need to approach the human-rights issue with some caution. We don't want to send troops abroad, but I do think we need to make our position clear. I think that is what Secretary [of State Cyrus] Vance is doing; that is what the President [Carter] is doing. There is no harm in our making clear where we stand on what we think is right. It is quite another matter to be deploying our resources in such a way as to attempt to force changes in another country.

TV-radio interview, Washington/"Meet the
Press," National Broadcasting Company, 7-3.

Milton Friedman
Professor of economics,
University of Chicago

4

[On whether the U.S. should do more to help under-developed countries]: Who says we've been helping them? We have been granting subsidies to underdeveloped countries, and the evidence is overwhelming that this has been hurting them, not helping them. What we have done is to strengthen the small clique which is in charge of the governments in these countries at the expense of the populace at large . . . The most effective thing we could do to help would be to drop our tariffs and thus encourage the under-developed countries to compete on fair and open terms and sell us whatever they can. That would do far more good than shoveling out bushels of money to maintain governments that do not effectively represent the public at large.

Interview/U.S. News & World Report, 3-7:22.

Takeo Fukuda
Prime Minister of Japan
1

... human rights and freedom should be promoted throughout the world. However, the important thing is to achieve desirable results toward the goal [of protecting human rights]. If, by raising one's voice, undesirable influences are created and lead to blunders, I think that would be a mistake. In some cases, it may be appropriate to raise one's voice. In others, it may be more appropriate to do it quietly, in secret ... The method should be decided on a case-by-case basis, depending upon what country you are dealing with.

TV-radio interview, Washington/"Issues and Answers," American Broadcasting Company, 3-27.

Valery Giscard d'Estaing
President of France
2

... I don't believe that [U.S.-Soviet] detente is a ruse to lull the West into a false sense of security while they [the Soviets] achieve global military supremacy and, later, world domination. In my judgment, Moscow's detente objectives are limited and specific. Firstly, a slowdown and, then, a reduction in the nuclear-arms race on the basis of parity. [Soviet leader Leonid] Brezhnev is wondering whether one of the U.S. objectives isn't to recapture a measure of military technological superiority. Secondly, the recognition that there are very real and specific areas for developing economic, political and cultural cooperation outside the ideological competition. Detente is an alternative to a senseless arms race.

Interview/Newsweek, 7-25:45.

Arthur J. Goldberg
United States Ambassador to conference on the Helsinki Agreement on European Security and Cooperation
3

The pursuit of human rights does not put detente in jeopardy. Rather, it can strengthen detente and provide a firmer basis for both security and cooperation. The issue of human rights represents the widest gap between the ideals and practices of East and West. It is a sensitive subject on the international agenda but one which can be dealt with in an understanding manner and which must be discussed in order to facilitate further progress.

At conference on the Helsinki Agreement, Belgrade, Yugoslavia, Oct. 6/Los Angeles Times, 10-7:(1)5.

Erwin C. Hargrove
Director, Institute for Public Policy Studies, Vanderbilt University
4

It's not unusual for a President to promise to concentrate on domestic issues and then find, once in office, that he's overwhelmed by the gravity of problems ahead. New Presidents also quickly discover that they can get political credit much more easily in foreign policy than they can with domestic programs, which tend by contrast to be much more sticky and difficult. Voters will support a President on foreign-policy questions if he appears to be acting decisively. But decisive actions on domestic policy are divisive. Congress plays less of a role in foreign policy, so it's less frustrating for a President. And the process is inherently fascinating — all these world figures coming to call on you at the White House, and you're on the world stage. All these facts come together.

Interview/U.S. News & World Report, 5-2:24.

W. Averell Harriman
Former United States Ambassador-at-Large
5

In 1926, I made my first trip to Russia and I made up my mind that the Revolution would be a reactionary philosophy. Man has struggled through the centuries for freedom and human dignity and not to be enslaved by the government. We [in the U.S.] are on the right track if we only recognize it. I've always called it not "peaceful coexistence," but "competitive coexistence." If we accept that competition, there is no doubt in my mind that we will win out on it.

Interview, Washington/ "W": a Fairchild publication, 2-18:21.

Robert C. Hill
Former United States Ambassador to Argentina
6

... I have serious reservations about our general human-rights [foreign] policy, born of

WHAT THEY SAID IN 1977

(ROBERT C. HILL)

the feeling that it has not been thoroughly thought through in terms of its precise objectives and possible consequences. If we are primarily concerned with halting abuses of the person, such as arbitrary arrest, indefinite imprisonment without trial, torture and similar practices, then our policy has realizable goals. There is a danger, however, that our human-rights impetus will be translated into an effort to export *democracy*. By progressively broadening the scope of the human rights that the U.S. will pressure other governments to respect, by including a wide range of civil, political and economic rights, as some advocates are wont to do, it soon becomes apparent that what we would really be asking other nations to do is make themselves over in our image. There is a well-intentioned approach without doubt, but it ignores the uniqueness of the American experience, the well-established trend toward authoritarianism in the world's emerging nations, and the lessons of our own foreign-affairs experiences. If there is anything that we should have learned since World War II, it is that democracy is not an exportable commodity.

Before Argentine-American Chamber of Commerce,
New York, June 28/Vital Speeches, 8-1:615.

Hubert H. Humphrey
United States Senator, D—Minnesota 1

[Arguing against a proposal to withhold food aid from countries that interfere with American-owned property]: I do not want to find myself having to go home and explain to [my pastor] that we cut off all the help for a particular country because somebody down there expropriated a bubble-gum factory.

Before the Senate, Washington/
The Christian Science Monitor, 9-14:9.

Donald C. Jamieson
Secretary of State for
External Affairs of Canada 2

We in countries of Western tradition too frequently assume that those standards of conduct and behavior toward our fellow men are perceived as having equal validity by other governments. But the perspective of other countries is, in fact, often different, partly because they may not be Western or democratic in background, or partly because their economic situations are vastly different from ours. Western democracies traditionally accord priority to civil and political rights, while Third World countries often place their pressing economic needs ahead of human-rights issues. . . . we are told regularly in international bodies that a majority of under-developed states are more concerned with alleviating starvation and promoting their development and, in so doing, attaching a greater priority to the duties of citizens than to their rights.

The Washington Post, 5-1:(C)6.

3

We have a responsibility . . . to exercise delicate judgments as to when to "go public" and when to continue in "quiet diplomacy." The phrase, "quiet diplomacy," may seem to some a euphemism for a lack of responsiveness. This simply is not the case. In the proper circumstances, it can accomplish far more in the long run than public appeals that may satisfy an immediate pent-up frustration but cut off prospects for a satisfactory resolution of conflicting views.

The Washington Post, 5-1:(C)6.

Peter Jay
British Ambassador to the United States 4

. . . the role of Ambassador today is clearly different. Anybody who would try to pretend it wasn't would be crazy. In the days of the lone venturer, when it would take three months to reach each country by ship, there really was one issue and that was war and peace. Now with phones and the telex, the *Concorde* [SST] and so on, an awful lot will be conducted between the specialists of various governments. So anybody from my country who wants to go to Washington has got to get guidance on the Washington scene. Washington is a special and complicated place. Knowing the place you're in is important for visiting firemen who come here — telling them how to go about things, telling them to whom they should make their pitch.

(PETER JAY)

And obviously, to make as many friends as you can for your country is certainly an objective.

Interview, London/The Washington Post, 7-7:(D)3.

Donald M. Kendall
Chairman, PepsiCo, Inc.

1

Advances in trade and economic cooperation should not be held hostage to equal advances in the human rights area. Progress in one area will significantly improve the overall climate so that the chances for progress in other, more sensitive areas will have a better chance of occurring. The two countries [the U.S. and the Soviet Union] must make every effort to strengthen their business and economic ties as the best vehicle for helping promote better political relations . . . [and] ending the arms race.

At International Trade Conference of the Southwest, Dallas/The Dallas Times Herald, 5-29:(K)2.

George F. Kennan
Former United States Ambassador to the Soviet Union

2

One of our problems overseas is the kaleidoscopic procession of [American] faces that drifts across the field of activity. We don't leave our Ambassadors long enough in foreign countries, really, for other people to get to know them, and these governments get a bit bewildered and a bit suspicious when they're constantly confronted by new people.

Interview/The New York Times, 2-11:(A)27.

Henry A. Kissinger
Secretary of State of the United States

3

[On his leaving office as a result of President Ford's loss of last year's election]: My first feeling after November 2 was one of enormous relief that I was no longer responsible for whatever might happen after January 20. Now the feeling is one of some emptiness, because I realize now that while I am not responsible, I can also not influence events, and it will be a whole change for me to select my problems. One of the attributes of being in this office is that you sometimes have the experience of a nightmare, that you see an express train come

running toward you on the railway track. You know it is coming toward you, but you have 10 other things to get done, and you just pray it doesn't hit you before you get out of the way. Now that feeling, as far as I can see, I now will lose.

Interview, Washington/The New York Times, 1-20:1.

4

I believe that it is one of our tasks . . . to make clear to the American people that they cannot permanently have a good life in a world in which they alone are perceived to have a good life. If we cannot raise hope in other parts of the world, if other people do not feel they live in an international system which is hardly theirs, we will sooner or later live under conditions of international civil war . . . I would argue that the American people can have a good life only if they assume responsibility for improving the standard of living in the developing world.

Interview/Los Angeles Herald-Examiner, 1-23:(A)9.

Henry A. Kissinger
Former Secretary of State of the United States

5

I think that, at least in the foreign-policy field, one needs above all motivation. It isn't an organizational question. If people think they're doing something important, then one has high morals and, eventually, discipline. It's more a question of inspiration than organization.

Interview/"W": a Fairchild publication, 2-4:10.

6

In the period I was in office, it became increasingly clear that the fundamental problem of the United States and the world is to form some permanent conception of the relationship between our values and possibilities. We have to avoid quixotic crusades that will sap our domestic support. But we must also avoid conducting our foreign policy on the basis of tactical considerations at the moment. To navigate between these two extremes requires an informed group of citizens. Above all, it requires experts in the field whose approach to the problem of foreign policy is not partisan but reflective, who understand that the con-

WHAT THEY SAID IN 1977

(HENRY A. KISSINGER)

cerns of our nation are not defined by a particular Administration.

At Georgetown University School of Foreign Services, March 9/The New York Times, 3-10:69.

1

Human rights is clearly a legitimate subject in international discourse, and an object of international legal standards. But our effort must be related to the full mosaic of our policy goals — to give it a place and meaning in terms of everything else we do in foreign affairs.

At Georgetown University, April 5/ The New York Times, 4-6:(A)3.

2

[Saying secrecy in diplomacy is unavoidable]: There are many ideas you try out in a negotiation that, if the other side accepts, are quite tolerable, but which, if they are publicized before they are accepted, become very difficult to handle. A foreign government must have the assurance that it can explore ideas without having the whole thing public before it is concluded. It makes compromise more possible.

Interview/Los Angeles Times, 6-20:(2)4.

3

For the first time in our history, a small group of nations controlling a scarce resource [oil] could over time be tempted to pressure us into foreign-policy decisions not dictated by our national interest . . . In another Middle East crisis the vast accumulated petrodollars could become a weapon against the world monetary and financial system . . . The consequences for the cohesion of the Western alliance are grave.

At National Conference of State Legislators, Detroit, Aug. 3/The Washington Post, 8-4:(A)2.

4

If we universalize our human-rights policy, applying it indiscriminatingly and literally to all countries, we run the risk of becoming the world's policeman — an objective the American people will not support . . . If the conservatives succeed in unraveling ties with the nations on the Left and liberals block relations with nations on the Right, we could find ourselves with no constructive foreign relations at all . . . Some of the most serious errors of our foreign policy . . . have occurred when we lost the sense of balance between our interests and our ideals.

At New York University Graduate School of Business Administration, Sept. 19/ Los Angeles Times, 9-20:(1)4.

5

For the first time in American history, we [the U.S.] can neither dominate the world nor escape from it. Henceforth, this country will be engaged in world affairs by reality and not by choice. America must now learn to conduct foreign policy as other nations have had to conduct it — with patience, subtlety, imagination and perseverance. The most fundamental challenge is thus not to our physical resources but to our constancy of purpose and our philosophical perception. Precisely because we can no longer wait for dangers to become overwhelming, they will appear ambiguous when they are still manageable . . . It is a paradox of the contemporary world that if we wait until these dangers become realities, we will lose the chance to do anything about them. At the moment when we still have great scope for creativity, the facts are likely to be unclear or ambiguous. When we know all the facts, it is often too late to act. This is the dilemma of statesmanship of a country that is irrevocably engaged in world affairs — and particularly of one that seeks to lead.

At New York University Graduate School of Business Administration, Sept. 19/ The Washington Post, 9-25:(C)3.

Edward I. Koch
United States Representative, D—New York

6

It is still legal for the United States to provide military aid to a country to help maintain its internal security. I believe that helping a regime quash an internal rebellion constitutes intervention in the internal affairs of another country. And it must be stopped.

The Christian Science Monitor, 2-10:7.

Juanita M. Kreps
*Secretary of Commerce
of the United States*

1

The American, half a century ago, was no more affected by the economic plight of another country than he was by the crabgrass in his neighbor's lawn. As long as it didn't come under the fence, it wasn't his concern. Today, it is different. Today, the crabgrass not only comes under the fence, it goes around it, climbs over it, and, if left untended, will drag the fence to the ground under its weight.

*At International Trade Conference
of the Southwest, Dallas/The
Dallas Times Herald, 5-29:(K)1.*

George W. Landau
*United States Ambassador to Paraguay;
Ambassador-designate to Chile*

2

[On the U.S. concern for human rights abroad]: We cannot tell a government what to do, but we can tell them what will happen if they do certain things. We must not be vague with the host government about our concerns for human rights.

*Before Senate Foreign Relations
Committee, Washington, Sept. 20/
The Washington Post, 9-21:(A)12.*

Mike Mansfield
United States Ambassador to Japan

3

I don't think the United States is in a position to continue to be the policeman of the world. We have neither the resources nor the manpower, and in carrying out policies embodying that factor, we have paid a pretty heavy price in blood and treasure.

*News conference, Tokyo, June 15/
Los Angeles Times, 6-16:(1)22.*

James G. Martin
*United States Representative,
R—North Carolina*

4

[On U.S. UN Ambassador Andrew Young's outspoken and controversial views]: [Young has] terrified our allies and insulted the British. [He has] misunderstood the rebellion in Zaire, incited revolution in South Africa and Rhodesia and accused the minority government in South Africa of being illegitimate, while endorsing the minority Cuban government in Angola... When he spoke [in the House as a Congressman], we listened. Now, we cringe. I had high hopes he would make us proud, but enough's enough. I think he needs to resign and go look for another line of work.

*At North Carolina Republican Party
convention, Charlotte, April 16/
Los Angeles Times, 4-18:(1)8.*

Lawrence P. McDonald
*United States Representative,
D—Georgia*

5

The U.S. recognized the Soviet Union in 1933 and gave Moscow international prestige, plus 300 million dollars in credits which it desperately needed. Since that time, Communism, subversion, terror and death have broken out of their quarantined area in Russia to take over 1 billion human beings. Today, more than one half the earth's population is either under Communist domination or threatened with Communist domination... I think we should become realistic about Communist objectives, force them to live up to past commitments and to pay their debts. Instead, we give them new credits under the guise of trade. It's not trade at all. And still they continue toward their objective of world domination through aggression, terrorism and revolution.

Interview/U.S. News & World Report, 3-7:73.

Gale W. McGee
*United States Ambassador/Permanent
Representative to the
Organization of American States*

6

Terrorism is indeed the scourge of our age. But we also know that human rights suffer when a state under attack lashes back blindly, injuring innocent and guilty alike. And here is the difference: Terrorism is a crime against the state. The suppression of human rights is a crime committed by the state against the individual.

*At OAS General Assembly meeting,
St. George's, Grenada/
The Washington Post, 6-23:(A)20.*

113

WHAT THEY SAID IN 1977

George S. McGovern
United States Senator, D–South Dakota
1

The same old rigid assumptions, based on hysteria and fear, that took us into Vietnam, into that disastrous struggle, are behind several of these amendments that have been adopted here in the Senate. One would think, listening to these deliberations, that the most powerful countries in the world are Cuba, Laos, Cambodia and Vietnam. There is almost an assumption that the United States has to cringe before these little countries, that somehow they are the basic threat. I have been trying to figure out in my own mind why it is that Senators, and I think the overwhelming majority of the American people, are willing for us to carry on relationships with [mainland] China – the most populous country in the world – [and] with the Soviet Union – the most powerful Communist country in the world – and somehow feel we cannot touch anything that approaches a relationship with a little country like Cuba, that we cannot carry on any kind of commercial contact with Vietnam or with Laos or with Cambodia. It is almost as though we were a third-rate power, fearful of dealing with these tiny little states that pose no real threat to us. I think it is fair to say that if we had not stumbled into Vietnam some 20 years ago, most Americans would never have heard of it. It would have had little or no relevance to us, and 50,000 Americans who are now dead would be alive. Why do we have to perpetuate this head-in-the-sand policy toward a little country like Cuba?

Before the Senate, Washington, June 16/
The Washington Post. 6-24:(A)20.

Robert S. McNamara
President, International Bank
for Reconstruction and Development
(World Bank)
2

Even dogs and cats in America today have a better standard of nutrition than tens of millions of children in the developing nations. But U.S. Official Development Assistance to those nations has not only not kept pace with its own growing domestic affluence. It has very substantially declined. The economies of the developed nations – already immensely productive – will become even more productive over the next few years. For them to increase their help to the poorest countries would not require them to diminish in the slightest their own high standards of living, but only to devote a tiny percentage of the additional per capita real income they will earn over the decade. If the governments of the poorest countries do not take the internal measures they must, and if the developed nations do not help them with the development assistance they so seriously need, then the outlook for three out of every four of the more than one billion human beings who live in these disadvantaged countries is unspeakably grim.

Before World Affairs Council, Boston,
Jan. 14/Vital Speeches, 5-15:451.

Margaret Mead
Anthropologist
3

People who think we can write off any part of the human race without destroying ourselves are ignoring the evolution of a global society. We have to love the whole planet. If you don't it won't do a bit of good to love your country and your flag.

Before American Association for
the Advancement of Science, Denver/
San Francisco Examiner & Chronicle, 2-27:(A)13.

Robert H. Michel
United States Representative,
R–Illinois
4

[On U.S. UN Ambassador Andrew Young's outspokenness]: We all have a high regard for Andy personally – we all like him – but we're justified in raising questions about who is speaking for the Administration – Andy or [Secretary of State Cyrus] Vance or who? Is this act pulled together? When Andy talks, is this [Carter] Administration policy or is he just blowing smoke or raising trial balloons or what?

The New York Times, 3-27:(1)3.

Walter F. Mondale
Vice President of the United States
5

[On U.S. UN Ambassador Andrew Young's outspokenness]: Ambassador Young is a mar-

(WALTER F. MONDALE)

velous person who is doing an outstanding job as our Ambassador . . . We are not a buttoned-up operation or one of those operations where everything has to be perfect, pre-planned and cleared. This is an open Administration. Andy speaks his mind. That's the way we want it.

Detroit, April 16/The Dallas
Times Herald, 4-17:(A)9.

1

[On the Carter Administration's use of human rights as a tenet of its foreign policy] : . . . we cannot teach our children to believe in human rights and democracy, we cannot honor those values in our churches and synagogues and our schools, and then betray those same ideals abroad, without betraying everything for which we stand. This Administration is not going to be strident in our defense of human rights. We're not seeking to throw down a gauntlet before any nation. Nor do we have any illusions that regimes which rule by force and terror will disappear overnight . . . our nation today is standing up in defense of human rights and human dignity throughout the world. I'm proud that no foreign leader today has any doubt that the United States condemns torture and political imprisonment and repressions by any government.

At U.S. Naval Academy commencement,
June 8/The Washington Post, 6-9:(A)10.

2

Human rights know no boundaries. We cannot protect our freedom as Americans if we ignore those parts of the world which are not free. In our relations with other nations we cannot put our democratic ideals on a shelf in the name of some higher pragmatism without denying those very ideals. Human rights must not be this year's political vogue or today's fashions . . . Let no one doubt where the American people and this [Carter] Administration stand. We are committed to advancing the cause of human rights throughout the world.

At Anti-Defamation League of
B'nai B'rith luncheon, Washington,
Nov. 20/The Washington Post, 11-21:(A)4.

Hans J. Morgenthau
Professor emeritus of political
science, City College of New York

3

[Criticizing President Carter's use of human rights as a basis of U.S. foreign policy and relations with such countries as the Soviet Union] : Interests determine nations' action, not moral principles. In the anarchistic world in which nations encounter themselves, where the quest for survival is the uppermost moral consideration, it is simply folly and useless to neglect our own interests for the effect of the rhetorical human-rights principles . . . The total-itarian system in the Soviet Union is unthink-able without the violation of human rights. And if we want to survive, not blow ourselves to kingdom come, we will have to tolerate the Soviet Union . . . [President Carter] has no experience in foreign policy or the tragedy of history. We have to wait for him to get on-the-job training.

At Brandeis Institute, Simi Valley, Calif./
Los Angeles Herald-Examiner, 5-4:(A)8.

4

[On the Carter Administration's emphasis on human rights in its foreign policy] : We must recognize that we live in a pluralistic universe. There are all kinds of cultures, some of which we don't like, some of which we detest. This is a condition of existence over which we have no control. The present Administration's attempt to exert control is futile. From time to time, we should express our allegiance to human rights. But to make this, as the Secretary of State has said, the center of our foreign policy seems to me absurd. It cannot be the center of any policy. It is not a policy. It is a moral declaration.

Panel discussion, Center for the Study
of Democratic Institutions/World Issues,
Dec.('77)-Jan.('78):13.

Daniel P. Moynihan
United States Senator, D—New York

5

In the past 30 years, there has been a high politics and a low politics in the Department of State. High politics was security politics. Those were the guys who were on the fast track, who

WHAT THEY SAID IN 1977

(DANIEL P. MOYNIHAN)

got the important jobs. They were Ambassadors by 50 or moved up to Assistant Secretary rank. You knew they were moving from the minute they got started. Hard-nosed, tough, they dealt with real things — guns, bullets, bombs, tanks, planes. Then there was low politics — what Averell Harriman would call drip. And drips would be people who deal with drip: all that ideological talk about freedom and liberty and totalitarianism, the free world and other worlds, capitalism, socialism. Well, we've found out those ideological issues are *not* drip. They are *profoundly* serious. And when you get on the losing side of them — when the symbols of progress are captured by the other side — well, you are in trouble. And you're likely to stay that way.

Interview/Playboy, March: 78.

1

I have said that democracy is beginning to look like monarchy in the 19th century. It is the place where the world was, not where it is going. This is the one thing I've been trying to say to this country. There are about three dozen democracies left. Since 1946, there have been 78 new nations formed out of former colonial possessions; 70 of them began as full-blown constitutional democracies. Of the 70, there are only 11 left. And of those 11, seven are small islands — Grenada, the Bahamas, Barbados, Mauritius, Fiji. I mean, I'm glad they're democracies, but it wouldn't make much difference if Fiji should become a small despotism. The land masses of Asia wouldn't shake! So America is not what countries are going to be like. The chaos of Lebanon may be more of a model. Now, for the rest of our natural lives, we will be in a world in which there are few of us and a great many of them.

Interview/Playboy, March: 79.

2

The President [Carter], in my view, is entirely correct in the fresh emphasis he has given to what we call North-South relations. But I wish to suggest that this must not be allowed to divert us from the reality of the military and ideological competition with the Soviet Union which continues and, if anything, escalates... If we genuinely care about the developing world, then we must look to the behavior of the Soviet Union, for with respect to the non-Communist regions of the world, be they developed or under-developed, there is one Soviet policy: the worse, the better... In nation after nation, at conference after conference, what the Soviets seek is failure, breakdown, bitterness, mistrust. They judge that they thrive on this, and history certainly does not disprove them. Our task is two-fold. First, to see this ourselves... Second, to bring the developing nations to see it as well.

*At Baruch College commencement, New York/
The Wall Street Journal, 7-8:6.*

Richard M. Nixon
Former President of the United States

3

[Saying his Secretary of State, Henry Kissinger, would sometimes express doubt about some action he took in foreign policy, such as the U.S. incursion into Cambodia during the Indochina war]: ...I said, "Henry," I said, "We've done it." I said: "Remember Lot's wife. Never look back." I don't know whether Henry had read the Old Testament or not, but I had, and he got the point. Henry and I often had a little joke between us after that. Whenever he would come in and say, "Well, I'm not sure we should have done this, or that, or the other thing," I would say, "Henry, remember Lot's wife." And that would end the conversation.

*Television interview, San Clemente, Calif./"The
Nixon Interviews," Paradine Productions, 5-12.*

4

[Lenin's doctrine was]: "Probe with bayonets; if you encounter mush, proceed; if you encounter steel, withdraw"... That's the way the Communist leaders will be all over the world. Because the Communists, they have to go forward spreading the gospel. That's what they believe. They want not just a Communist Russia or what have you; they want a Communist world.

*Television interview, San Clemente, Calif./"The
Nixon Interviews," Paradine Productions, 5-12.*

David Owen
Foreign Secretary of
the United Kingdom
1

The blunt truth is that the first and easier stage of detente is over. The issues that are today on the agenda of East-West relations are more complex, more contentious and far more intractable. We are beginning to encroach on fundamental attitudes, on human behavior, and the issues go to the heart of each side's perception of itself and its interests. Inevitably we cannot expect to maintain the momentum of the early 1970s ... The basic premise from which we in the West must start is that the Soviet Union is a world power with national interests and ambitions to match, which inevitably bring it into competition, and sometimes confrontation, with the West. To this we must add that Communist ideology invests the natural rivalry between East and West with a dynamic of unceasing struggle ... Detente is an immensely complex process, comprising innumerable strands and relationships on different levels: political dialogue, commercial and technological exchange, cultural contacts, ideological debate and military vigilance. There is no magic formula that will enable us, East or West, to strike the right balance in our relations at all times. Both sides are still feeling their way. All we can say is that balance there must be between the elements of confrontation and cooperation, whether we are talking of the detente process as a whole or of its constituent parts.

Before Diplomatic and Commonwealth
Writers Association, London, March 3/
The Washington Post, 3-10:(A)23.

Bob Packwood
United States Senator, R—Oregon
2

[On whether President Carter is overdoing his speaking out on human rights around the world]: ... if you look at the history of this country and as we were regarded, as a beacon of liberty and democracy, we didn't do it by going around the world intervening every place and trying to impose on the world what we thought was right for them. During all of those years, certainly up to World War I, when immigrants from all over the world came here, they didn't come here because we were interfering in the affairs of those countries; they came here because of what this country symbolized ... I just think it would be a better policy if we were to say, "We will recognize governments that exist." That doesn't mean we like them; it doesn't mean we pin medals on their dictators; but we don't try to make them over in our image.

TV-radio interview, Washington/"Meet the Press,"
National Broadcasting Company, 4-3.

Mark Partridge
Minister of Defense of Rhodesia
3

The major trend in the world today is the expansion of Russian Communism and the collapse of the Western world. I would go so far as to say that the psychological war between Communism and democracy has ended. Communism has won.

Salisbury, Rhodesia/The Dallas
Times Herald, 6-9:(A)4.

Claiborne Pell
United States Senator, D—Rhode Island
4

... it is foolish for the United States to refuse to recognize people because we disapprove of their regimes or things they've done. Recognition should merely be a matter of acknowledging the *de facto* regime, even if it's the devil himself ... I have long believed that it is even more important to recognize adversaries than allies because the adversaries are the ones with whom we have problems. If you want to punish your adversaries, you should do what we never do: You should withdraw aid and economic missions but keep our diplomatic missions. Instead, what we so often do is remove our political missions and leave our economic missions, which is harmful to American taxpayers.

Interview/U.S. News & World Report, 8-29:27.

Charles H. Percy
United States Senator, R—Illinois
5

I am convinced that the Voice of America must be emancipated from the interference of diplomats and bureaucrats who have limited the

(CHARLES H. PERCY)

Voice's ability to tell the whole truth in a timely manner, [depriving the Voice] of the credibility it needs to do its job as a representative voice of a free society. [The current] situation in which radio broadcasting, cultural activities and official foreign-policy articulation are concentrated for large part in the United States Information Agency has caused deep confusion, administrative chaos and conflict of purpose which serves the nation poorly.

Washington, May 3/The Washington Post, 5-4:(A)3.

Carlos Andres Perez
President of Venezuela
1

On human rights, my government fully supports [U.S.] President Carter's policy. Even before he was inaugurated, I told the United Nations that human rights are supranational and they had to be given priority value. President Carter's stand is restoring United States prestige throughout the world. It is not important how many governments criticize it. All governments — including the dictatorships — are transitory, but the human spirit is eternal. We realize how difficult it is for a great nation — for the most powerful nation in the world, from the economic and military point of view — to implement a policy on human rights. Yet that is where its value and significance lie: in the fact that a moral revolution is being led by the United States. I am certain that the spirits of [George] Washington and [Thomas] Jefferson are happy.

Interview/U.S. News & World Report, 7-25:55.

Richard E. Pipes
Professor of history, Harvard University; Senior research consultant, Stanford Research Institute's Strategic Studies Center, Arlington, Virginia
2

The Russians have become more aggressive than they had been before. Therefore, we are confronting now a more direct challenge than we did in the '60s or early '70s. For example, the Russian behavior in Angola — and now in other parts of Africa — is without precedent in its boldness ... There are two reasons. One is

that in the post-Vietnam period we [the U.S.] have become terribly discouraged with any foreign involvement — not only in terms of a willingness to send troops, but even to offer military aid. The notion is spread in the country today that if you help anybody at all, that would be the beginning of a total involvement. And secondly, the Russians are feeling militarily stronger.

Interview/U.S. News & World Report, 6-27:44.

Rainier III
Head of Government of Monaco
3

We're a small country. And the more I travel, the more I think that the small countries of this world are very useful. They have no eagerness to possess what their neighbors have ... I believe that small countries should be given more latitude. I am convinced, for example, that because of their vulnerability, small nations are the best champions of peace. Their survival depends on peace, although their voice is so feebly heard in the concert of nations.

Interview, Monaco/
The Christian Science Monitor, 8-19:28.

Ronald Reagan
Former Governor of California (R)
4

[On the Carter Administration's foreign policy]: Internationally, they don't seem to know the difference between being a diplomat and a doormat. Take, for example, our approach to the ... SALT talks, the refusal to acknowledge that the Soviet Union is building the greatest war machine known to man. Somehow, we've negotiated agreements [under which] we grow weaker and they grow stronger.

Interview, Los Angeles/
The Christian Science Monitor, 12-12:7.

John E. Reinhardt
Director, United States Information Agency
5

"Public diplomacy," meaning those efforts through which your government enters the international market of ideas, [should be governed by] a series of principles and purposes ... We must undertake these efforts in a manner consistent with the ethics, ideals and

(JOHN E. REINHARDT)

principles to which we ourselves aspire ... In all that we project to the world, we must reflect the fact that our words and actions are shaped by our view of ourselves, shaped by the American ideal. It is the best way to bring clarity and coherence to the many and bewildering images others have of us. ... we [must] present our views and policies and aspirations forthrightly to the world. Not combatively, but forthrightly. Our interests require that others know where we stand. And our great presence in the world leads others, quite spontaneously and in their *own* interests, to want to know. We should do what we can to encourage those individuals and institutions, those coalitions and "networks" – here and abroad – which are also engaged in the free flow and exchange of ideas ... They should be allowed the dignity of independence. But we can clearly *help* for the institutional links – and the exchanges between them ... We must reach beyond the ruling elites and seek out those who are the future contributors to thought, culture and leadership in their countries ... We must insist upon a dialogue. In so doing, we strike a balance between our own most fundamental beliefs and needs and recognition of the needs, perceptions and circumstances of others.

At Knoxville College/
The Washington Post, 6-5:(C)6.

1

[On whether the Voice of America will present the news straight, even if it reflects unfavorably on the U.S.]: Absolutely. It's in our interest. The radio that isn't credible is a useless radio. If a foreigner tunes into the Voice of America for news, he ought to be able to get it and be sure what he's heard is straight news ... untampered, unfiltered in any way.

Interview/The Washington Post, 7-17:(A)20.

Abraham A. Ribicoff
United States Senator, D–Connecticut

2

The United States contributed more than $1-billion in 1975 in support of international organizations. At the present time, I do not think anyone in the organizations or the U.S.

government can really tell us what all that money has achieved ... There are organizations which appear to accomplish nothing in a tangible sense. There are organizations to which the U.S. belongs without any clear idea why ... There is a disturbing tendency in many of the organizations for a majority of member countries that contribute a small proportion of the budget to want to run the organization without much attention to the views of the United States and a few other major donors ... All too often, the organizations are headquartered in extravagant and luxurious surroundings, are ineffective, over-staffed with high-paid officials, under-represented by U.S. personnel, uncertain in their purposes, and unduly repetitious of the activities of other organizations. There are 43 employees of the World Bank and 72 employees of the UN proper that are earning more than the equivalent of $60,000 a year before taxes. We must decide precisely why we have joined each organization and what the costs and benefits are in both financial and diplomatic terms.

The Christian Science Monitor, 2-9:17.

Hector Rodriguez (Llompart)
Minister of Economic
Cooperation of Cuba

3

[Criticizing the U.S., which has taken a strong stand on human rights in its foreign policy]: Those who present themselves as the paladins of human rights and of social justice are precisely those who cause the worst evils that humanity suffers and which are the result of the practice of colonialism, neo-colonialism and exploitation, to which we have been submitted.

Before United Nations Economic Commission
for Latin America, Guatemala City, May 3/
The Dallas Times Herald, 5-4:(A)4.

Dean Rusk
Professor of international
law, University of Georgia;
Former Secretary of State
of the United States

4

However deep the differences between us and the Soviet Union on human rights, at the

WHAT THEY SAID IN 1977

(DEAN RUSK)

end of the day we have to find ways to inhabit the same speck of the universe at the same time.

At University of Georgia, July 11/
The Washington Post, 7-14:(B)2.

William B. Saxbe
Former United States
Ambassador to India
1

[On what he learned as Ambassador and how that relates to U.S. UN Ambassador Andrew Young's outspokenness in criticizing some foreign countries]: Diplomacy is a different type of business, and you are dealing with the sensitivities of the country you serve. You certainly don't go around making enemies of people whose job is to make friends. If [Young] wants to do what he's doing, in going around and pointing the finger at people and saying, "You are bad," he shouldn't be in a position of a guy who is supposed to be gaining supporters for the United States.

Interview, Mechanicsburg, Ohio/
Los Angeles Herald-Examiner, 8-14:(A)6.

Robert A. Scalapino
Professor of political science
and director, Institute for
East Asian Studies, University
of California, Berkeley
2

Quite frankly, I think that the interests of the United States will be best served if, in dealing with the major Communists, we retain our flexibility and our equidistance. We should look at each issue from the standpoint of our interests and those of our allies, and remain unpredictable, avoiding any long-term tilt. Quite obviously, a *de facto* alliance with either [mainland] China or the Soviet Union would have the most profound repercussions on our relations with the other, and as a basic policy, it would be very unwise.

Interview/U.S. News & World Report, 6-27:47.

William W. Scranton
United States Ambassador/Permanent
Representative to the United Nations
3

I am very depressed, at least in the immediate future, about progress in the field of human rights. And there is a reason for this. The Communist world has a completely different concept of what a human right is — if they believe in it at all. They believe the state is pre-eminent and that the individual should be subject to the state. The Third World generally is bogged down on the question of human rights because of their tremendous need for economic improvement. Until they begin to come round to the vision of the necessity for liberties and freedoms in order to have economic betterment for people, we're bogged down over here [at the UN] on making progress over human rights.

Interview, United Nations, New York/
The Christian Science Monitor, 1-21:18.

Leopold S. Senghor
President of Senegal
4

The most pressing problem of our time is not the building up of an ordered economic system but that of a universal world culture. When the most highly developed people take advantage of the illusion of free-market economy for unequal trade at the cost of the Third World, then they do this, above all, out of a sense of cultural contempt.

At Salzburg (Austria) cultural festival,
July 24/The New York Times, 7-25:7.

Eric Sevareid
News commentator,
Columbia Broadcasting System
5

If you could by some magic lift all barriers to immigration and emigration all over the world, there'd be an enormous cavalcade of people set in motion. But they would not be heading for the Soviet Union or Africa, or China or Cuba. They'd be heading for West Europe and North America . . . Just try to imagine a world in which neither of the super nuclear powers was an open society as this one is. You know what the result would be. This world would be blown up. And I think even in

(ERIC SEVAREID)

their unconscious, most thinking people around the world know it's the existence of freedom in this country that gives the world a chance.

Interview/The Dallas Times Herald, 11-29:(B)1.

John J. Sparkman
United States Senator, D—Alabama

1

[On the current U.S. focus on human rights in its foreign policy]: On the whole, it is usually unwise — and even more usually ineffective — to attempt to reform domestic practices of either allies or adversaries. My own view is that condemnations of the internal practices of other countries should be expressed with restraint and only under unusual circumstances. But when protests are lodged, it should be in an even-handed way as between allies and adversaries. I would not have us pontificate against Communist totalitarianism while exonerating the practices of non-Communist dictatorships. But neither would I have us condemning the unquestioned deprivations in [South] Korea, Brazil or Chile without taking note of the more thoroughgoing totalitarianism of most Communist countries, to say nothing of the reported draconian cruelties of the new regimes in Cambodia and Laos.

Before the Senate, Washington, Feb. 25/ The Dallas Times Herald, 2-26:(A)4.

R. Peter Straus
Director, Voice of America

2

[On his new job as VOA Director]: I really foresee taking a highly professional group of people and trying to excite them about making the freest democracy in the world understandable to the rest of the world — not necessarily loved by, not even necessarily liked by, but understood by the rest of the world. That's an exciting enough mission.

Interview, June 29/The New York Times, 6-30:(A)3.

Philip H. Trezise
Senior fellow, Brookings Institution; Former Assistant Secretary for Economic Affairs, Department of State of the United States

3

In the early '50s — the Marshall Plan era — there was nobody else. We [the U.S.] had to take the lead, and expected other people to follow. Now we're not quite in that dominant position, but we still produce a quarter of the world's goods and services. We are still by far the biggest economy, the biggest trader, the biggest market, the biggest investor. So if we don't take the lead, there isn't anybody else to do it. The Europeans, other than Germany, are all in a state of disrepair in economic life, and Japan sees itself as much too vulnerable as a society to step out and take the lead. So if anything is to be done on our long-range problem — basically the North-South problem — or the near-term problem, the U.S.A. must be the leader. I don't see any alternative.

Interview/U.S. News & World Report, 6-27:48.

Pierre Elliott Trudeau
Prime Minister of Canada

4

Too many Ambassadors try to be popular in the country to which they are delegated. I do not think that is their job. They are there to represent the countries from which they come, not the countries to which they go.

Before House of Commons, Ottawa, Dec. 16/The New York Times, 12-18:(1)14.

Peter Ustinov
Actor, Director, Writer

5

I spend my time in America trying to explain the Russians to them to the best of my ability, and I spend my time in Russia trying to explain the Americans to them. Despite their fiscal and military collusion, they understand each other not at all.

Interview, Paris/Los Angeles Times, 9-6:(4)14.

Cyrus R. Vance
Secretary of State of the United States

6

[Saying he will delegate responsibility for foreign negotiations]: I'm going to make it

WHAT THEY SAID IN 1977

(CYRUS R. VANCE)

clear that I will not be the day-to-day negotiator. I will, of course, be involved in helping to develop and in setting the policy. I also will follow what is going on carefully, and will step in to help if problems develop. But I want the negotiating to be done as much as possible by the negotiator rather than by me.

Interview/The New York Times Magazine, 2-13:25.

1

The human-rights issue is really grounded in the fundamental values which lay at the root of the founding of this country. The dignity of the individual and the protection of those rights is a very sacred right that is of great importance to Americans, and therefore it is something which should be of importance to us in our domestic lives and in the conduct of our foreign policy. It has to be interwoven into the fabric of our foreign policy, and this we believe — it can be done. Now, insofar as speaking out on human-rights issues abroad are concerned, we will speak out when we believe it desirable to do so. We will try to do it in a non-strident, non-polemical way, and we would expect others, if they see things happening in the United States, to criticize us, because this is not a one-way street. We have not tried to single out any country. We will speak out when we believe it appropriate to do so with respect to a human-rights issue wherever it may arise throughout the world.

TV-radio interview/"Face the Nation," Columbia Broadcasting System, 2-27.

2

I think it is in the interest of both nations [the U.S. and the Soviet Union] to search for common ground and to lessen the tensions which divide [them]. In this process, I think it is necessary to try and work out a clear understanding of what the meaning of detente is ... In a sense, it is the setting down — or arriving at — a set of ground rules, which permit competition side by side with the resolution of outstanding questions.

News conference, Washington, March 4/ Los Angeles Times, 3-5:(1)10.

3

[On the Carter Administration's use of human rights as a factor in U.S. foreign policy]: Our concern for human rights is built upon ancient values. It looks with hope to a world in which liberty is not just a great cause, but the common condition ... A sure formula for defeat of our goals would be a rigid, hubristic attempt to impose our values on others. A doctrinaire plan of action would be as damaging as indifference. Our country can achieve our objectives only if we shape what we do to the case at hand ... Wherever possible, we will take positive steps of encouragement and inducement. Our strong support will go to countries that are working to improve the human condition. A decision whether and how to act in the cause of human rights is a matter for informed and careful judgment; no mechanistic formula produces an automatic answer. It is not our purpose to intervene in the internal affairs of others. But, as the President has emphasized, no member of the United Nations can claim that violation of internationally protected human rights is solely its own affair. It is our purpose to shape our policies in accord with our beliefs and to state them without stridency or apology, when we think it is desirable to do so. [The U.S.] can nourish no illusions that a call to the banner of human rights will bring sudden transformation in authoritarian societies. We are embarked on a long journey. But our faith in the dignity of the individual encourages us to believe that people in every society, according to their own traditions, will in time give their own expression to this fundamental aspiration.

At Law Day observance, University of Georgia, April 30/The New York Times, 5-1:(1)1.

4

[On what the U.S. means in referring to "human rights" abroad in its foreign policy]: The right to be free from governmental violation of the integrity of the person. Such violations include torture; cruel, inhumane or degrading treatment or punishment; and arbitrary arrest or imprisonment. And they include denial of the right to a fair trial and invasion of the home. The right to the fulfillment of such

(CYRUS R. VANCE)

3

vital needs as food, shelter, health care and education. We recognize that the fulfillment of this right will depend, in part, on the stage of a nation's economic development. But we also know that this right can be violated by a government's action or inaction — for example, through corrupt official processes which divert resources to an elite at the expense of the needy, or through indifference to the plight of the poor. The right to enjoy civil and political liberties — freedom of thought; of religion; of assembly; freedom of speech; freedom of the press; freedom of movement both within and outside one's own country; freedom to take part in the government.

At Law Day observance, University of Georgia, April 30/The Washington Post, 5-1:(A)2.

1

If terrorism and violence in the name of dissent cannot be condoned, neither can violence be officially sanctioned. Respect for the rule of law will promote justice and remove the seeds of subversion. Abandoning such respect, governments descend into the netherworld of the terrorists and lose their strongest weapon, their moral authority.

Before Organization of American States, St. George's, Grenada, June 14/ The New York Times, 6-15:(A)3.

2

We have tried to make clear from the outset that we believe it is not for us to tell any country whom they should elect in the way of their political leaders. That is their responsibility and their right. On the other hand, that does not mean that we are indifferent to who is elected and who serves in the government of any country. As we have said on a number of occasions, we would obviously prefer those who have the same kind of views with respect to fundamental values and precepts, and, therefore, we clearly prefer those who have a democratic backdrop.

Interview/The New York Times, 6-19:(1)7.

...I think it's understandable that the Congress is playing a larger part in foreign policy than it did in the past. It was clearly predictable that they intended to and would play a larger part. And as far as we're concerned, that's fine. I have said from the outset that foreign policy has to be both developed and implemented in coordination with the Congress as the representatives of the people. Unless you have a policy which has the support of the people, it's going to be hard to make progress with that policy.

Interview, Washington/ U.S. News & World Report, 11-7:30.

Paul C. Warnke
Director, Arms Control and Disarmament Agency of the United States

4

[On how he would know that the Soviets were negotiating in good faith] : I guess it's like art — I'll know it if I see it.

The Dallas Times Herald, 4-9:(B)2.

Jack H. Watson, Jr.
Secretary to the Cabinet and Assistant to President of the United States Jimmy Carter for Intergovernmental Affairs

5

The President [Carter] has made it clear that [National Security Adviser] Zbig [niew Brzezinski] doesn't make policy. He also understands, and [Secretary of State] Cy [rus Vance] understands, that Zbig is a man of wide knowledge and formidable intellect whose opinions are valuable not only to the President, but to Vance, [Defense Secretary Harold] Brown, [Treasury Secretary W. Michael] Blumenthal, and others. The fact that he's not the chief foreign-policy maker doesn't mean he shouldn't express his ideas. He should . . . When you have a strong President, and we do, the sort of multiple strong centers or sources of advice is healthy. It's encouraged. The system wouldn't work with a President not willing to exercise leadership; but with a President [who wants to] get into foreign policy, to deal even with the details, it will work.

The New York Times Magazine, 2-13:40.

WHAT THEY SAID IN 1977

Andrew Young
United States Ambassador/Permanent
Representative to the United Nations

1

[On his candid, outspoken manner of diplomacy]: When [President] Jimmy Carter said he wanted a foreign policy that was as good and decent as the American people, he was talking about a foreign policy with some open discussion of issues and not a foreign policy discussed in secret quarters of the State Department. To me, that requires a certain amount of freedom of expression . . . Maybe I have a problem with reconciling the commitment of the Carter Administration not to lie — to have government in the open — with what is a traditional reserve in the State Department. But I don't want to give in that easy . . . And because I value openness, I'm willing to take flak, to be repudiated, corrected and argued with.

Interview, Africa/
The Dallas Times Herald, 2-20:(J)5.

2

. . . don't get paranoid about a few Communists, even a few thousand Communists . . . Americans shouldn't be afraid of Communists — they just shouldn't. It offends me, really . . . We don't have to fear Communism in the area of economic competition. We do almost everything so much better than they do that the sooner the fighting stops and the trading starts, the quicker we win.

News conference, Washington, April 11/
The New York Times, 4-12:1.

3

. . . we've got to relate to the so-called Third World. I mean, of the 147 nations in the UN system, 45 of them are African; you add to that the Arab block, the Latin-American bloc, a number of the Asians — you have a majority in the world. We can't talk about nuclear proliferation, we can't talk about Law of the Sea, we can't talk about North-South dialogue, new economic order, we can't talk about a common fund for agricultural commodities unless we relate to that so-called Third-World bloc.

Television interview/"The MacNeil-Lehrer Report,"
Public Broadcasting Service, 6-9.

4

There cannot be lasting economic development without social justice. Development must be linked with liberation — from poverty, dependence and degradation. Impressive growth rates, the fulfillment of targets are not enough. This means that creating a new international economic order does not mean only equality of opportunity for all states to share in the fruits of the continued expansion of the global economy but equality of opportunity, also, for all people within those states.

San Francisco Examiner & Chronicle,
7-17:(This World)2.

5

In our pursuit of wealth and power, we [the U.S.] took for granted basic human rights, and I think we neglected them at our peril. We found that the government of which we were so proud was responsible for propping up many military dictatorships and some of the more corrupt governments in the world. The American people found that their tax dollars, which they had worked very hard to earn, were going abroad only to make the rich richer and essentially not contributing anything to help the poorest of the poor. We found our military assistance going to create military dictatorships that denied those citizens under their rule the simplest elements of due process and that engaged in savage practices of torture. [With the election of President Carter,] the American people said "No more" — that now we would use the resources at our command to help the poor, to bring freedom in the world and to extend the kind of human rights around the world that we have come to feel are the very essence of our society — the basis of our success and our aspirations for the future.

News conference, Port-au-Prince, Haiti,
Aug. 15/The Washington Post, 8-16:(A)12.

Mikhail V. Zimyanin
Secretary, Central Committee,
Communist Party of the Soviet Union

6

World socialism firmly holds the initiative in international affairs . . . Under conditions of the present balance of power, imperialism

(MIKHAIL V. ZIMYANIN)

cannot count on winning by military means. That is why the forces of reaction display unprecedented activity in the field of ideology. However hard the ideologists of the old world seek to poison man's thinking, our revolutionary ideology is in the historic offensive. The great ideas of Marxism-Leninism extend to all continents and peoples.

Lenin anniversary address, April 22/
The Christian Science Monitor, 5-4:9.

INTELLIGENCE

George Bush
*Director of Central Intelligence
of the United States*
                                                    1

[On his imminent departure as head of the CIA as the new Carter Administration takes office]: I leave the job with a sense of unfulfillment. I've been dealing with an organization that's so much better than the public perception of it that one of my frustrations has been my inability totally to get across to people how good it is. This agency has undergone a lot of changes. I'm convinced that we're living within the [Presidential] guidelines and within the law, within the spirit of the times and the spirit of change. I wish I'd been able to do more to convey to the people what a tremendous asset [the CIA] is to this country.
Interview/Time, 1-17:16.

George Bush
*Former Director of Central
Intelligence of the United States*
                                                    2

The propensity in this country to tear down and nit-pick at the CIA I think is wrong. I think we need an intelligence capability second to none. We've got it, and we ought not to always go around acting like it's illegal.
*Broadcast interview, Austin, Tex., May 21/
The Dallas Times Herald, 5-22:(A)29.*

William E. Colby
*Former Director of Central
Intelligence of the United States*
                                                    3

It is the job of intelligence to know. We must be able to tell the President what a situation is and what the results of the situation

will be. If something happens and we did not know it was going to happen, that is an intelligence gap.
Interview/The Dallas Times Herald, 2-13:(A)25.

4

One of the greatest areas of frustration and difficulty in our clandestine intelligence work abroad is the subject of cover. Intelligence officers cannot be effective in hostile areas of the world if they wear the initials "CIA" on their hatbands. It is essential that we give these officers other explanations for their presence and for their contacts with the secret intelligence sources that they must meet in other nations. They must be allowed to live and work without exposure to hostile counter-intelligence services, to disaffected ex-employees or to vicious terrorists. If you accept that intelligence work is important to the protection of our country — and both our laws and Presidential Executive órders say that it is, as does the very existence of this Committee and its Senate counterpart — then you must also give CIA the essential tools with which to do its work. The last 10 years have seen a critical erosion of the cover under which American intelligence officers must work. The Peace Corps, the Fulbright scholars, the United States Information Agency, the United States Agency for International Development, and now journalists, are off-limits, and additional groups clamor to be included in this charmed circle. But if one examines the resident American community in many countries, it is obvious that the remaining areas of cover are few and that many CIA officers are all too easy to identify. And earnest

(WILLIAM E. COLBY)

investigators and even hostile groups are today busily engaged in programs to expose them.

Before House Permanent Select Committee
on Intelligence, Washington, Dec. 27/
The New York Times, 12-28:(A)12.

Richard Helms
Former Director of Central
Intelligence of the United States
1

[On his conviction for having not testified fully and accurately to a Senate committee in 1973 about CIA activities in Chile, because he was bound by his oath of intelligence secrecy]: I don't feel disgraced at all. I think if I had done anything else, I would have been disgraced.

To reporters after his sentencing,
Washington, Nov. 4/The New York Times, 11-5:1.

Daniel K. Inouye
United States Senator, D. Hawaii
2

There is no question that a number of abuses of power, mistakes in judgment and failures by the intelligence agencies have harmed the United States. In almost every instance, the abuses that have been revealed were a result of direction from above, including Presidents and Secretaries of State. Further, in almost every instance, some members of both houses of Congress assigned the duty of oversight were knowledgeable about these activities.

Before the Senate, Washington, Dec. 1/
The Washington Post, 12-2:(A)4.

Clarence M. Kelley
Director, Federal Bureau of Investigation
3

Our experience has shown us that a substantial number of . . . Soviet-block and [mainland] Chinese officials [visiting the U.S.] are directly connected with their intelligence services. It must suffice to say that the intelligence initiatives of the Communist powers against the United States continue unabated. Their daily endeavors include the collection of military, economic, political, scientific and technical information for uses detrimental to our national defense and foreign policy. In the last

10 years, the number of Soviet-bloc officials in the United States has increased more than 100 per cent, from 806 in July, 1966, to 1,955 in December, 1976. In the last two years, the People's Republic of China also has appreciably increased its official presence in the United States.

Washington, Feb. 9/
The Christian Science Monitor, 2-10:2.

Herman Nickel
Editor, "Fortune" magazine; Former
correspondent, "Time" magazine
4

A reporter who moonlights for the CIA or any other intelligence service because of the lure of money prostitutes himself. The mighty United States government has plenty of resources of its own without having to rely on journalists to do things that simply aren't their jobs. Our patriotic duty is to keep our independence, for if we don't we can't properly fulfill our Constitutionally recognized function in a free society.

Before Oversight Subcommittee of House
Permanent Select Committee on Intelligence,
Washington, Dec. 28/
The New York Times, 12-29:(A)15.

Barrington D. Parker
Judge, United States District Court
for the District of Columbia
5

[Rebuking former CIA Director Richard Helms who was recently convicted for having not testified fully and accurately to a Senate committee in 1973 about CIA covert activities in Chile]: You dishonored your oath and you now stand before this court in disgrace and shame. If public officials embark deliberately on a course to disobey and ignore the laws of our land because of some misguided and ill-conceived notion and belief that there are earlier commitments and considerations which they must first observe [such as, in Mr. Helms' case, the oath of intelligence officials to protect sources and methods], the future of this country is in jeopardy . . . There are those employed in the intelligence security community of this country — and until recently you have been among them — who feel that they

WHAT THEY SAID IN 1977

(BARRINGTON D. PARKER)

have a license to operate freely outside of the dictates of the law and otherwise to orchestrate as they see fit. From this day forward, let there be no doubt: No one, whatever his position, in or out of government, is above the law or is relieved from complying with it.

> *At sentencing of Mr. Helms, Washington,*
> *Nov. 4/The New York Times, 11-5:1;*
> *Los Angeles Times, 11-5:(1)10.*

Otis G. Pike
United States Representative,
D—New York
1

The basic issue [in intelligence] is: are we able to predict with some degree of accuracy what is happening in the world? And the information we gather will have to be less on purely military matters and more on things like the effect of climatology on Soviet crops or the political options of developing countries, and how that might affect the availability of basic resources.

> *Interview/The Dallas*
> *Times Herald, 2-13:(A)25.*

Stansfield Turner
Director of Central Intelligence
of the United States
2

[Saying that, if Congress wishes, the overall budget of U.S. intelligence activities would be made public, but that he would object to detailed breakdowns of the budget] : There is a risk in every disclosure, but all of us feel the responsibility to be as open with the country as possible, so the need warrants the risk being taken. Accordingly, President Carter has directed that I not object to your releasing to the public the single overall budget figure of the U.S. intelligence community ... [However, a] detailed intelligence budget in the hands of our enemies would be a powerful weapon which would make our collection effort more difficult, more hazardous to life and much more costly. The way we spend our intelligence money in this country is one of our necessary secrets.

> *Before Senate Select Committee on Intelligence,*
> *Washington, April 27/Los Angeles Times, 4-28:(1)1.*

3

We are going to try to tell the American people much more than we have ever done in the past, both as to what we do in our business and what we are learning. But there clearly is a line beyond which we cannot go ... I am making a plea for balance in our view of secrecy. Everybody is not a hero because he goes out and discloses secret information.

> *News conference, Los Angeles, Aug. 12/*
> *Los Angeles Times, 8-13:(1)18.*

Cyrus R. Vance
Secretary of State of the United States
4

In the case of intelligence assistance [to foreign governments], it is given through CIA channels. There is nothing improper or illegal about that. But it cannot be done in the glare of publicity.

> *TV-radio interview/"Face the Nation,"*
> *Columbia Broadcasting System, 2-27.*

Donald C. Alexander
Commissioner, Internal Revenue
Service of the United States
1

The public deserves better government than they're getting. Part of the problem is due to the distractions that one finds in trying to do a job that is too large at best and much too large when up to four hours a day are spent running for the fire extinguisher, using it and refilling it.
Interview/Time, 1-17:21.

Cecil D. Andrus
Secretary of the Interior
of the United States
2

None of us [in government] can duck responsibility for the actions of the institutions which we serve. When institutions fail it is because people fail. Where bureaucratic red tape is being used to camouflage incompetence or arrogance, we must strip away the cover and place the blame where it belongs.
Before National Press Club, Washington,
May 10/Los Angeles Times, 5-10:(1)19.

Roy L. Ash
Former Director, Federal Office
of Management and Budget
3

Cabinet appointments are crucial. But the OMB Director is crucial in a very different way from the others. Others run their portions of the operations of government. This office doesn't have any operations except to oversee the operations of all the departments. It is the last line of review before the President, and he has to rely on it exceedingly.
Los Angeles Times, 9-9:(1)8.

Benjamin F. Bailar
Postmaster General of the United States
4

There is widespread speculation about what action the new Congress and Administration will take to cure the perceived ills of the nation's postal service. The speculation centers on the possibility of greater Congressional oversight, or a return of the postal system to full Congressional and Administration control. I believe that a re-evaluation of the future postal needs of this country is a must, but it disturbs me that in this speculation there is no recognition that the postal system today is in the best shape it has been for years ... I firmly believe that if the Postal Service is to make its way intelligently into the future, it cannot do so by gouging either the taxpayer or the mail user. We can provide any service which the public wants, and for which it is willing to pay. But we must continue to tailor our services to match the public's need and willingness to pay, and we must tie revenues more accurately to actual costs. This will protect our volume – which is essential to a universal and inexpensive postal system.
Before Comstock Club, Sacramento, Calif.,
Feb. 7/U.S. News & World Report, 2-14:81.

Peter Behr
California State Senator (R)
5

It has been my experience that, generally, persons who serve longer than eight years in the Legislature become less effective and lose much of their initiative, and a few even get so interested in staying that they forget why they were sent. So, unlike the common view, I believe that one matures in an office – and at the time you believe you are vintage wine, you may well have turned to vinegar.
San Francisco Examiner & Chronicle,
11-20:(This World)2.

WHAT THEY SAID IN 1977

Robert F. Bennett
Governor of Kansas (R)

1

If there is a hope for sanity in government, it lies with the Governors and with the individual states, and not with the Congress and certainly, under current circumstances, not with the White House. We meet at a time when states' rights are seriously questioned at the national level.

At Republican Governors Conference, Bretton Woods, N.H., Oct. 10/Los Angeles Times, 10-11:(1)16.

Bob Bergland
Secretary of Agriculture of the United States

2

Happiness is not for sale. It's a state of mind. Find it. And I bring that philosophy here to the administration of this Department. Occasionally, some greedy person will criticize something I've done because I'm not enriching them to suit them. I don't waste time quarreling with them, but I pay no attention. I mean none. Anyone whose advice is derived from greed won't get the time of day with me. I'll listen. But that's all. And I don't listen very well to those people. The people who come here with a notion that's based on a belief that there's more to this life than getting rich and that we have a responsibility, politically and morally, a responsibility to share that which we have with those who are less fortunate, will not only be given an audience but be welcomed with open arms.

Interview, Washington/ The Christian Science Monitor, 10-4:4.

Thornton F. Bradshaw
President, Atlantic Richfield Company

3

There is a basic rule: Any [government] regulation must be followed by another regulation that tries to overcome the problems raised by the first.

At energy conference sponsored by Time, Inc., Williamsburg, Va./Time, 4-25:32.

Edward W. Brooke
United States Senator, R—Massachusetts

4

[On Presidential appointments]: As I have stated many times in the past, absent a clear demonstration of incompetence or lack of integrity, I believe that the President has a right to nominate those individuals who reflect his political, legal and philosophical views.

The Dallas Times Herald, 4-24:(A)24.

Edmund G. Brown, Jr.
Governor of California (D)

5

Every group learned the lesson of the '60s, that you've got to create a propaganda campaign to get government assistance . . . Unless a lot of people scream and march around, they don't feel they're participating in democracy.

San Francisco Examiner & Chronicle, 5-1:(This World)2.

6

[On government bureaucracy]: All we can try to do is cope with it, make it work better. I've tried to eliminate some agencies, but they keep coming back. Government is going to grow, under right-wing, left-wing or middle-of-the-road Administrations. The question is at what rate and in which direction . . . Wherever you look, people are looking to government to arbitrate some dispute or another, or provide some service, and that just makes government more complicated. Our society has moved from shoveling dirt to shuffling paper. That's the fact of modern life.

Interview, Sacramento/The New York Times, 7-12:12.

Zbigniew Brzezinski
Assistant to President of the United States Jimmy Carter for National Security Affairs

7

Power is very intangible. It's nothing to be liked for its own sake. But if you can use power, and I mean this seriously, if you use power in a responsible way, in a politically and philosophically responsible way, then power is something that one can enjoy. Yes, I like to use power responsibly toward political and philosophical ends which I hope are good and morally just.

Interview, Washington/The Washington Post, 2-4:(B)3.

Dale Bumpers
United States Senator, D–Arkansas

1

All of us here [in Congress] are sort of prisoners when it comes to legislation coming from committees on which we do not sit. We almost invariably defer to the committee chairman, who is almost invariably the floor manager of the bill; and we have to do it, not only out of respect but out of ignorance of the matter. And if one raises a point on the floor, they say, "Oh, we discussed that in committee. We had so-and-so testify on that subject. He is the world's renowned expert on it, and we discarded that idea," and we have no opportunity here to know whether we want to pursue that point or not ... I am asking for a new committee assignment this year, and it is my plan not to stay on any committee more than 4 to 6 years, because I have found that you are rather limited here when you are serving on only two committees and are at the mercy of what almost anyone tells you so far as the work of the other committees is concerned.

Before the Senate, Washington, Feb. 4/
The Washington Post, 2-10:(A)14.

Robert C. Byrd
United States Senator, D–West Virginia

2

The responsibilities of leadership require that one represent an overall, middle-of-the-road philosophy. My own personal vote may be different from the position that the majority of the Senate may take, but I will not stand in the way of the Senate working its will. The Senate has to reflect the national will.

Interview, Washington/The New York Times,
3-27:(1)44.

3

The Senate has an independent role. This doesn't mean that it can't cooperate or won't cooperate with the Executive; but the role of the Senate is not to be a rubber stamp for any President.

Interview, Washington/
The New York Times, 3-27:(1)44.

Joseph A. Califano, Jr.
Secretary of Health, Education
and Welfare of the United States

4

Too many of HEW's rules impose archaic and even incomprehensible requirements – often in elaborate and excruciating detail. Our regulations today have become a Kafkaesque labyrinth that makes little sense to anyone – neither the people who write the regulations, the people who administer them, nor the people who must comply with them.

Washington, Sept. 12/The Washington Post,
9-13:(A)2.

5

My job is to run this Department, to execute the laws. To the extent that Congress legislates the way we should organize a certain way, I'll do it, but I don't think that's the right way to operate the government. I think it's imperative that we consult with Congress. But I think that the decision as to how we put the boxes together, that's something that's my responsibility, not theirs.

Interview/The New York Times, 10-24:24.

Hugh L. Carey
Governor of New York (D)

6

One of the most historic and legitimate functions of government is the undertaking of capital investment necessary for business and industry to flourish. The private sector can produce goods, but cannot rebuild and maintain the roads and bridges to bring their commerce to markets. The private sector cannot alone rescue the historic ocean and lake ports of our state. It cannot prevent the deterioration of the rail beds upon which its goods are carried. These are the legitimate functions of government, which must provide the services and facilities for the public welfare. The base for economic development, which means the present and future availability of jobs for our citizens, lies on government meeting its obligations.

State of the State address, Albany,
Jan. 5/The New York Times, 1-6:20.

WHAT THEY SAID IN 1977

Jimmy Carter
President-elect of the United States

1

In whatever way I can be open [as President], I'll do it — with frequent press conferences, fireside chats to explain complicated issues, perhaps with town-hall-type forums around the country, where I answer questions from the public. I think, on occasion, I might very well have Cabinet meetings open for a limited number of news people to come in. I would have a fairly steady stream of visitors — just average Americans whom we've met during the campaign from around the country — to come in and spend a night with us at the White House and eat supper with us, so that we could have that interrelationship.

Interview, Plains, Ga./Time, 1-3:23.

Jimmy Carter
President of the United States

2

There will never be an instance, while I am President, when the members of the White House staff dominate or actually take a superior position to members of our Cabinet. When any directive is relayed from the White House to the members of the Cabinet, it will indeed come directly from me. I believe in a Cabinet government. And although the major decisions will be made by me, as President, which is my Constitutional prerogative and responsibility, the secretaries [Cabinet officers] will run their own departments.

At swearing-in of Cabinet officials,
Washington, Jan. 23/
The Washington Post, 1-24:(A)2.

3

[On how it feels to move into the White House]: It is really awe-inspiring. I have been around just to look at and open and close the writing desk that was designed by Thomas Jefferson and built for him and used by him. To go into the Lincoln bedroom where the proclamation was signed to emancipate the slaves, and to go into the treaty room where the treaty of the Spanish-American War was signed, is a very sobering experience and a very gratifying experience for me. I can't say that I feel completely at ease with it yet. But you feel very heavily the responsibility on you and you recognize the crises through which those leaders in the past have brought our country. You see in reading history — and I have read a lot in the last three or four years — many of the mistakes and weaknesses and fallibilities of the Presidents that were compensated for by the strength of this country. That is a reassuring thought.

Interview, Washington, Jan. 23/
The New York Times, 1-25:20.

4

I have often used the phrase "competent and compassionate" to describe what our government should be. When the government must perform a function, it should do it efficiently ... Our confused and wasteful system that took so long to grow will take a long time to change. The place to start is at the top — in the White House. I am reducing the size of the White House staff by nearly one third, and have asked the members of the Cabinet to do the same at the top staff level. Soon I will put a ceiling on the number of people employed by Federal government agencies, so we can bring the growth of government under control. We are now reviewing the government's 1,250 advisory committees and commissions to see how many could be abolished without harm to the public. We have eliminated expensive and unnecessary luxuries, such as door-to-door limousine service for many top officials, including all members of the White House staff. Government officials can't be sensitive to your problems if we are living like royalty here in Washington.

Broadcast address to the nation,
Washington, Feb. 2/
The New York Times, 2-3:22.

5

[Addressing government employees]: Although many things may look to you — here in this huge building in Washington — as impersonal, the people who look to you for help have real hopes. We need to have an aggressive, constant search for a better way to deliver services. Just because there has been a policy in effect for the last five years — or 10 or

(JIMMY CARTER)

50 years — is no reason we should honor it unless it is the best policy.

At U.S. Labor Dept., Washington/
San Francisco Examiner & Chronicle,
2-13:(B)8.

1

This country has been through such an ordeal in the last five or 10 years that it is still in a healing stage — Vietnam, CIA, Watergate. It really shook the American people and their confidence in government. I don't think there will be a complete restoration of their confidence until proof is not only complete but extended over a period of time. And I am trying to do the best I can to restore that confidence. But I can't say that it has been a successful year. I think we just have got to go through a long trial period in the minds of the American people before they accept the fact they can trust the American government again.

Interview, Washington, Dec. 1/
The New York Times, 12-5:42.

David Cohen
President, Common Cause

2

The Senate's need to create a special committee to draft a new code of official conduct is tacit admission that in the past it has failed to take ethics seriously. It is a confession that the Senate as an institution has been ignoring very serious problems. . . . we want the Senate and the House to be respected institutions . . . We want to have as much respect for them as we do the flag. Don't misread the public's views. Don't let us down.

Before Senate Special Committee on
Official Conduct, Washington, Feb. 2/
The Washington Post, 2-3:(A)2.

3

[Referring to the controversy over Bert Lance's past financial dealings which led to his resignation as OMB Director]: The Lance controversy in part resulted from a confirmation process that is haphazard and leads to Senators acting and voting out of ignorance. If it had not been Bert Lance and the Committee on Govern-

mental Affairs, it would have been another committee and another nominee. If the Senate is not willing to learn the lesson of the Lance affair by improving its confirmation process, then we are sure to face the same kind of problems in the future.

Nov. 12/The Washington Post, 11-13:(A)17.

William T. Coleman, Jr.
Secretary of Transportation
of the United States

4

As T. S. Eliot said, "Between the idea and the reality falls the shadow." A Cabinet person understands that the President is operating within that shadow — educating, negotiating, compromising, transforming the idea into the reality. The Cabinet should be the cornerstone of an effective Presidency.

Interview/Time, 1-17:21.

Calvin J. Collier
Former Chairman,
Federal Trade Commission

5

Whether one favors or opposes the growth of government, one cannot dispute that agency decisions have an increasingly pervasive effect on our daily lives. With the growth of government, it seems to me, there comes naturally less accountability, less scrutiny and greater influence over decision-making by special interests.

Los Angeles Times, 5-13:(4)15.

John B. Connally, Jr.
Former Secretary of the Treasury
of the United States; Former
Governor of Texas (D, now R)

6

In the last 15 years we have had the civil-rights revolution, the youth revolution, and now it's the women's-liberation revolution. What we need in the future is a political revolution that will change the way politics operate. It is time to change things in Washington. We should limit a President to one term of six years. We should limit a Senator to one term of six or eight years and a Congressman to a total of eight years, with terms of four years per election. Once they have served their limited time in Congress, then let them go back

WHAT THEY SAID IN 1977

to their communities and live under the laws they have created.

At Pacific Coast Builders Conference,
San Francisco, June 1/Los Angeles
Herald-Examiner, 6-2:(A)10.

1

[On the difficulties of being President today] : . . . when I first went to Washington in 1939, well, Congress was in session five or six months out of the year — maximum. And President Roosevelt had six months unfettered with the Legislature. He could do what he liked. And he went to Hyde Park and Warm Springs. And he went swimming with Eisenhower in those days. They had a fairly relaxed period of time. Now it's 24 hours a day, seven days a week; Congress in session 365 days a year, adjourning for Christmas — and the whole environment of the White House has changed in the last 10 years . . . You don't dare invite your friends around. They become hot news items. You're under enormous pressure. It's unrelenting. It's a physical and mental burden of enormous proportions, so there's no great joy. Admittedly you have the prestige, the honor, the power that goes with the office. But those things are intangible. They're ego-satisfying. I've been around Washington enough to where those things don't really appeal to me.

Interview, Los Angeles/
Los Angeles Herald-Examiner, 12-18:(A)4.

Alan Cranston
United States Senator, D—California

2

[Arguing against an amendment which would prohibit anyone from serving more than 12 years in the Senate or the House] : It should be left up to the voters to decide who can best represent them. If the voters are satisfied with the performance of a Senator or a Congressman, they should not be deprived of his services and experience — nor should the country — by any arbitrary rule . . . The basic principle of representative democracy is that you elect people who are supposed to be responsive to the people they represent — not necessarily to always do what the people want, but to solicit

their views, understand their problems, stay in touch and serve their best interests. Now, if you're in your final six-year Senate term, and the law says you can run for re-election, you could become totally unresponsive to the people you serve. Also, a law-maker who is a lame duck would be less able to accomplish things. If somebody is on his way out, less attention is paid to his leadership. A Senator would be at his peak of capacity only in his first six years, and then he would lose his clout — and so would his constituents — in his second six years.

Interview/U. S. News & World Report,
11-14:71,72.

3

[Some say that] people may be losing their faith in government being able to solve their problems. The point isn't that government shouldn't try to solve all problems. But this over-intention and over-claiming the right to know exactly how every problem should be solved in infinite detail — this is driving people crazy in terms of the way that impacts on that. There is that famous remark: "Thank God we don't get all the government we pay for."

Interview/The New York times, 12-18:(4)2.

John C. Danforth
United States Senator, R—Missouri

4

[Saying there should be an amendment prohibiting anyone from serving more than 12 years in the Senate or the House] : It would accomplish two things: First, it's important for elected officials who come to Washington to think of themselves as citizens who are only on leave to their government — not permanent fixtures in Washington. A limitation on the length of service would say to a person who is elected: "Look, you are not a new resident of Washington — you are a resident of your own state or your own district. You are of the people who sent you here, and you will eventually, whether you like it or not, be returning to them." The second thing that would be gained has to do with the human tendency to want to preserve yourself in a good job by saying "yes" to everybody and "no" to

(JOHN C. DANFORTH)

nobody. That's one of the problems in government now.

Interview, Washington/
U.S. News & World Report, 11-14:71.

Morarji R. Desai
Prime Minister of India

1

Ultimately, in a democracy all must work together ... Human society must be human, not a mixture of animals, and we are 90 per cent animals today, which is not a very pleasant thought, but it is a fact. Passions belong only to animals, and if human material is superior, then we have to control passions, which should be used for proper purposes, just as steam has to be utilized for energy, not for scalding people. Government will have to set an example in its own actions. You see, to make people fearless is more a function of government than of anything else, because people are afraid of government more than any other agency. And you have to set them at rest that no honest man will ever have to suffer under that government. On the contrary, honest men will be supported and respected. Then you will create more honest men.

Interview, New Delhi/Time, 4-4:34.

Robert K. Dornan
United States Representative,
R–California

2

It's a madhouse [on the floor of the House]. It's a waste of time standing up there talking to the wind with everybody running around. Most of the time it's every man for himself.

Interview, Washington/
Los Angeles Times, 2-13:(1)4.

Stuart E. Eizenstat
Assistant to President of the
United States Jimmy Carter for
Domestic Affairs and Policy

3

I couldn't do my job if I looked at any issue with passion. I'm not a person of causes. It's my job to listen to the passionate people from both sides, to present the pros and cons, who's going to be for this and who's going to be against it,

how do we sell it, and how do we get it across. Each issue contributes like a pebble in a mosaic.

Interview, Washington/The Washington Post, 6-9:(B)1.

Millicent H. Fenwick
United States Representative,
R–New Jersey

4

Two aspects of Congress are indefensible: One is to give oneself a pay raise. If Congress decided it needs to raise its own salaries, it should discuss the matter openly on the floor, not avert our eyes, as we've done this year, slip it into law and pretend we have nothing to do with it! Secondly, we *must* get rid of office funds. Do you know that any member of Congress can accept *any* amount of money from *any*one? From a foreign government! We've got to change that. And slush funds — where a Congressman merely *pockets* any money left over from a campaign. It's shocking!

Interview, Washington/McCall's, June:36.

John J. Flynt, Jr.
United States Representative,
D–Georgia

5

Maybe I'm old-fashioned, but I never thought public service should be too rewarding. I voted against the last pay raise for Congress because it would be difficult to explain why I should get a raise that would be larger than the total incomes of most people.

U.S. News & World Report, 1-17:50.

Gerald R. Ford
President of the United States

6

I happen to think that the overwhelming majority of people I served with in the Congress, Democrat and Republican, House and Senate, are honest, hard-working people. And I believe the same about those who have been in the Executive Branch of the government. It is tragic that a few here and there created a very bad impression as far as the morals of government are concerned.

Interview, Washington/The Washington Post, 1-9:(A)6.

7

While the Judicial Branch of our government may require reinforcement, the budget and

WHAT THEY SAID IN 1977

(GERALD R. FORD)

payrolls of the other Branches remain staggering. I cannot help but observe that, while the White House staff and the Executive Office of the President have been reduced and the total number of civilians in the Executive Branch contained during the 1970s, the Legislative Branch has increased substantially, although the membership of the Congress remains at 535. Congress now costs the taxpayer more than a million dollars a year per member; the whole legislative budget has passed the billion-dollar mark ... The Congress sidetracked most of my requests for authority to consolidate overlapping programs and agencies, to return more decision-making and responsibility to state and local governments through block grants instead of rigid categorical programs, and to eliminate unnecessary red tape and outrageously complex regulations.

State of the Union address, Washington,
Jan. 12/The New York Times, 1-13:26.

1

It is only as the temporary representatives and servants of the people that we [in government] meet here. We bring no hereditary status or gift of infallibility and none follows us from this place.

State of the Union address, Washington,
Jan. 12/The Washington Post, 1-13:(A)1.

Henry Ford II
Chairman, Ford Motor Company

2

It's not just liberal do-gooders, Democrats, unions, consumerists and environmentalists who are responsible for the growth of government. It's also conservative politicians who favor increased defense programs, especially if the money is spent in their own districts. It's businessmen who want government contracts. It's bankers and transporters and retailers and manufacturers who want protection from competitors. It's insurance companies that lobby for bumper and air-bag regulations that might lower their claim costs. It's catalyst suppliers who lobby for tough emission standards. It's even, if you'll forgive me, car dealers who want

state government to protect them from the factory or from new dealers in their territory.

Before National Automobile Dealers Association,
New Orleans/The Wall Street Journal, 4-8:6.

Milton Friedman
Professor of economics,
University of Chicago

3

We have reason for hope in the inefficiency of government. I welcome government waste. Waste brings home to people the inefficiency of government and brings home the fact that more government is not the proper way to solve our problems.

At Pepperdine University 40th anniversary
dinner, Beverly Hills, Calif./
Los Angeles Herald-Examiner, 2-11:(B)3.

4

The real tax burden on the American people is the amount the government spends, not the amount that is labeled "taxes." If the Federal government spends 460 billion dollars in fiscal year 1978, which is roughly what the President [Carter] proposes, and takes in something like 400 billion in taxes, who do you suppose pays the other 60 billion? The tooth fairy? Or the Arab sheiks? The American people pay it. It's paid in the form of the hidden tax of inflation, or, if it's financed by borrowing from the public, then in the form of higher taxes that will be needed in the future to pay the interest and the principal. That means that it lowers the value of all property today to the extent that property will be subject to higher future tax burdens ... Forty per cent of our national income is spent by the Federal, state and local governments. Fifty years ago the proportion was 10 per cent. Are we getting our money's worth? I would like to see a Constitutional amendment that would say that spending for all purposes by the Federal government could not exceed 25 per cent of the income of the people. That is roughly what it is now. So the amendment would not reverse the trend, but at least it would stop it and give time for a change in attitudes and a growth in understanding to develop that would make a reversal politically feasible.

Interview/U.S. News & World Report, 3-7:20,22.

John W. Gardner
Chairman, Common Cause

1

A good constituency provides good leaders. What we've gotten is a kind of downward spiral. Citizens become disillusioned so they don't vote, they don't pay attention to public affairs; that just invites unscrupulous leaders to take advantage of the situation. So they do things that make the situation even more disillusioning, and the spiral goes down. We've got to turn it around. We have to make people more alert. We have to demand more of our leaders, get better leaders who will then inspire more confidence . . . It's like the white corpuscles in the blood system. If they decided that it wasn't worth the fight because they just licked one virus and here comes another, we'd all be dead. We're alive because the white corpuscles in the blood system just keep at it. Citizens just have to keep at it. And if citizens aren't willing to do that, they're not going to keep their freedoms. They're going to be ripped off, and they deserve it.

Interview/The National Observer, 2-26:6.

E. J. (Jake) Garn
United States Senator, R—Utah

2

During the last election, everyone, including the President [Carter], ran against Washington. They ran against big government, big bureaucracy, over-regulation, over-spending by the Federal government. Now that the election is over and the politicians are safe in the nation's capital for another two to six years, the campaign and its promises seem to have been forgotten. Government spending is increasing, the push for more regulation is on the upswing and with it will come a bigger, more cumbersome, bureaucracy.

Before National Petroleum Refiners Association,
San Francisco, March 28/**

Albert A. Gore, Jr.
United States Representative,
D—Tennessee

3

Congress' greatest strength is that it is the most representative body in government. And Congress is more representative of the people now than it has been for a long time. The House is in a period of rapid change, and even the most ardent reformers will tell you Congress is moving swiftly in the right direction. We are moving most important legislation through more quickly. It used to be that a large number of members were in Washington only on Tuesday, Wednesday and Thursday, and went home for long weekends. That's less frequent now. The biggest change of all is yet to take place. I'm convinced we will soon start television broadcasts of House action. This will enable Congress to compete effectively with the Executive Branch in forming policies. It will correct the imbalance of power that began when Presidents started taking advantage of TV.

Interview/U.S. News & World Report, 6-13:35.

Robert P. Griffin
United States Senator, R—Michigan

4

I think we would achieve reform if we required every member of the Congress to spend at least six months a year back home, earning a living like everybody else. That should mean a cut in Congressional salaries right off the bat — and where is the taxpayer who would complain about that! But, more important, it would mean less legislation — and that would be a blessing for taxpayers, too. If we had a six-month Congress — except during periods of war or national emergency — it would be necessary again for state and local governments to deal with many of the problems that now absorb the time of Congress. It would mean that Congress would have to focus its time and effort on matters of national defense, foreign policy and other issues truly national in scope. Frankly, based on my experience, I am confident that, except during periods of war or national emergency, Congress could accomplish the things that are really necessary in a six-month session.

Before American Association of the Professions and
Michigan Association of the Professions, Mackinac
Island, Mich., Aug. 27/Vital Speeches, 11-15:84.

LeRoy F. Harlow
Professor, department of business
administration, Brigham Young University

5

I believe that except for a very minimum of confidential situations, such as matters of

137

WHAT THEY SAID IN 1977

(LEROY F. HARLOW)

national or community security or when the good reputation of an individual might be adversely affected, governmental affairs should be an open book to citizens who wish to know. There should be no secrets at city hall, even if the information thus obtained might be used for the citizen's personal gain or advantage, or to the disadvantage of those in office, including the public administrator. What is more, every act of the city government and all its records should be open to the public's watchdog, the American free press. To have it otherwise is to make a mockery of our basic concept that the people are sovereign. Unless the people know the facts, how can they act intelligently on important issues, whether in a small town, a state or a nation?

At National Airports Conference, Norman,
Okla., Oct. 3/Vital Speeches, 11-15:72.

Michael J. Harrington
United States Representative,
D—Massachusetts   1

Separation of powers and responsibilities may have been an art form, with some genius attendant to it, two centuries ago. Today, I believe it breeds only frustration and ineffectiveness ... Does American government work as it is now constituted in the latter part of the 20th century? The public has said resoundingly "NO" in so many ways I find it very difficult to believe that the message has not come crashing thunderously into the chamber of the House. We have a profound problem of a constitutional and governmental nature that will not disappear in the face of narrow pieces of legislation. The situation cries for [a commission] not to study ethics, but to devise new ways of setting American public policy, a new constitutional framework. Measures short of this will be but more dressing for our windows.

Before House Rules Committee, Washington,
Feb. 23/The Washington Post, 3-15:(A)20.

Gary W. Hart
United States Senator, D—Colorado   2

We have a Constitutional process for confirmation of high-level government officials.

According to that process, the President nominates an individual for a position, and then the Senate has the obligation to review the nomination and confirm or not confirm it ... Unfortunately, what has happened too often is that once a name is suggested, even before it is presented in formal nomination to the Senate, sides begin to form both for and against that individual. The side that is against the individual begins to put items in newspapers and starts whisper campaigns about that person's qualifications. More often than not, the information that is circulated is not even accurate. So, before the Senate has an opportunity to provide that individual a platform or a forum to present his or her qualifications, the majority of Senators on the committee or in the Senate at large have already made up their minds and have stated how they intend to vote.

Before the Senate, Washington/
The Washington Post, 2-13:(C)6.

3

[On the idea that Senators should spend more time in their home states and less in Washington] : What keeps us here is the number and complexity of issues — and the desire of many people to talk about every issue. Rhetorical self-restraint would help. I'm not sure we could successfully handle oversight [of the Executive Branch] . Who is going to watch the President [while Senators are back home] ? It's a lovely Jeffersonian concept that I share, but the fact is the problems are getting more complex.

The Washington Post, 3-30:(A)5.

Orrin G. Hatch
United States Senator, R—Utah   4

Today in the United States the budget of government is larger than the value of the national income of France or Germany. It is six times the size of the GNP of Sweden and 50 per cent of the total production of the Soviet Union. In the United States, government takes from Americans in taxes a sum greater than the combined value of every marketable good and service that the total population of France can produce in one year. Does anyone really believe that the American people receive in return from

(ORRIN G. HATCH)

government services equal in value to the total production of the French nation? No one believes this. Yet it does not stop us from continually expanding the size of government. That is what shows whose interests are represented in Washington.

Before the Senate, Washington/
The Wall Street Journal, 5-24:20.

Gabriel Hauge
Chairman, Manufacturers Hanover
Trust Company, New York **1**

Congress believes, and probably correctly so, that the people still want spending but will not permit their taxes to be raised. The vaunted goal of pluralism in our democratic society retards the development of power centers that would match spending to revenue. As a result, deficit has followed deficit. There appears to be no capacity in our government to bite the bullet and stop this constant over-spending. This is one of the very few things about our country that makes me melancholy.

Interview, New York/Nation's Business, June:34.

S. I. Hayakawa
United States Senator, R—California **2**

I didn't know what to expect when I came here [to the Senate]. I had no firm, clear-cut expectations. But I wasn't shocked or startled by anything. The much-quoted statement that the Senate is a gentleman's club is something I have found very much to be so. Everyone has been very courteous and gentlemanly. It's been terribly nice. I'm having a wonderful time. The cliches in which we think about individuals — the so-called bleeding-heart liberal or cranky old reactionary — when you meet those people in person, all these characterizations disappear. Instead, you see them as very interesting, thoughtful people.

Interview, Washington/Los Angeles Times,
2-7:(4)4.

3

[Challenging the Senate's new ethics code for limiting a Senator's outside earnings from such things as honorariums]: The ethics code assumes the lecture honorarium to be a form of bribe, given by the sponsoring organization to influence the speaker. I am not capable of being bribed, and if I were I would trust the people of California to vote me out of office.

Washington, July 14/Los Angeles Times, 7-15:(1)5.

H. John Heinz III
United States Senator, R—Pennsylvania **4**

[On his being a Senator after having spent five years in the House]: You have more say, more of an input. You're more intimately involved with the Executive Branch. Your vote, you feel, counts for much more. The problems come up in the internal administration of the place. Compared to the House, the administration of the Senate is 17th century. It's badly organized, fragmented. It's absolutely medieval. My office manager is going crazy.

Interview/San Francisco Examiner & Chronicle,
3-20:(This World)26.

Hubert H. Humphrey
United States Senator, D—Minnesota **5**

There is a demand that government be more efficient. [President] Carter will do that — he will be most helpful. There is a demand for a little better response out of government. A period of tightening up on operations. That is here. That is going to be good for us. That is going to cause some trouble. When you tighten up on operations, you squeeze some vested interests, and we'll be hearing from them. Then there is a need for a new sense of directions and priorities. Many of our programs lack unified directions. Too many different agencies have their fingers in the same pie. I hope Carter will put that to rights in his government reorganization plans.

Interview, Washington/Los Angeles Times, 3-27:(7)1.

6

Congress is always trying to catch up. So is the Administration. They are playing catch-up ball. We need a planning mechanism. Not planning for a planned society, but planning for better use of the resources of the Federal government. The President should have to

WHAT THEY SAID IN 1977

(HUBERT H. HUMPHREY)

deliver a State of the Future address as well as a State of the Union. What's coming up? What ought we to look for? Not how to patch up holes in the old street, but where the *new* street should be constructed.

Interview, Washington/
Los Angeles Times, 3-27:(7)1.

1

Now, I've had some frank talks with the President [Carter] about the budget balancing. I'm going to let you in on what I said, quite honestly. I said: "Mr. President, I wish you had never put a deadline on this balancing of the budget. I'll tell you why. Look at what you started with. You started out with a budget deficit of over $70-billion. You inherited a huge deficit in international trade. You inherited 8 per cent unemployment. You inherited better than 7 per cent inflation. And you inherited a going recession. And you're going to balance the budget all in four years. If you do it, Mr. President, it will be another one of the miracles and we'll get you a brand-new chapter in the Bible" . . . He just smiled on it a little.

Interview, Washington, July 27/
Los Angeles Times, 7-28:(1)5.

2

[On the Senate]: What a wonderful place this is, where we can argue, fight, have different points of view, and still have a great respect for one another and, many times, deep affection . . . Now, my plea to us is, in the words of Isaiah, as a former President used to say — and I mean it very sincerely — "Come, let us reason together." There are no problems between the different points of view in this body that cannot be reconciled, if we are willing to give a little and to share a little and not expect it all to be our way. Who is there who has such wisdom that he knows what he says is right? I think we have to give some credence to the fact that majority rule, which requires the building of an understanding and a sharing, at times a compromising, is the best of all forms of rule.

Before the Senate, Washington/
The New York Times, 10-30:(4)17.

Eugene Jennings
Professor of management,
Michigan State University

3

[Saying business executives are becoming reluctant to work in the Federal government]: They feel it is peopled by bunglers, fools and wasters. They say it is preposterous that they, whose careers were shaped under the rules of planning, organization and efficiency, should lend their talent to a behemoth of opposite qualities . . . [Executives feel that] these bureaucrats are bunglers, stumblers, incompetents. They are becoming more convinced that government is no place for talented people.

Interview, New York/The Dallas
Times Herald, 9-6:(D)6.

Barbara Jordan
United States Representative, D–Texas

4

Whether we have a better government in the next four years will not depend on the will of the Congress; it will not depend on the determination of the President. It will depend on the outrage and concern of the citizens. This is the compelling force for precipitating change.

At Connecticut College, March 4/
The Dallas Times Herald, 3-6:(A)2.

Edward M. Kennedy
United States Senator, D–Massachusetts

5

Divided government has ended, and now there's a real chance of an important working partnership for the Administration and Congress. It's a unique opportunity to do something, to do something well. The people I respected most in the Senate . . . said you measure accomplishments not by climbing mountains, but by climbing molehills. In the Senate, sometimes the important thing is the directions which are established, which may become irreversible. Playing a role, being a link — this is important.

Interview, Washington/The New York Times, 3-5:20.

Edward I. Koch
United States Representative, D–New York

6

We must help our [government] agencies with the difficult task of reaching fair and

(EDWARD I. KOCH)

well-balanced decisions. We must provide adequate access to our Federal agencies to those whose views have been under-represented. The recent crisis of confidence in government is one that has been experienced acutely at the Federal-agency level. The repeated incidence of serious abuses of power and conflict of interest has intensified the public's perception that government regulation benefits the regulated and not the public.

Los Angeles Times, 5-13:(4)14.

Juanita M. Kreps
Secretary of Commerce
of the United States

1

The whole process of [government] appointments seems rather inefficient. In business, by the time you reach the top, you know the rules, the structure of the organization. It's a gradual, enlightened process, quite hierarchical.... in government ... one day you're a college professor and the next you're Secretary, and suddenly everybody expects you to know everything about that appointment.

Interview, Durham, N.C./
The Washington Post, 2-17:(D)2.

Bert Lance
Director, Federal Office of
Management and Budget

2

The way you measure the effectiveness of [government] reorganization is to see whether it provides the same, or even more, government services with the same or fewer people, or with the same or less money. The Carter Administration has three basic aims in this area: to make government simpler, to make it more consistent and to make it more predictable. That's been one of the big problems in this country: Business couldn't make any plans. This government order comes out today, and that order next week, and many times they conflict. Then a third order comes out the third week and conflicts with the other two. The business community — and that includes the whole range from Billy Carter's filling station to General Motors — has got to feel that they can

count on some sort of order and organization in Washington. We haven't had that for some time.

Interview, Washington/
U.S. News & World Report, 2-7:18.

Michael Maccoby
Psychologist; Director, Harvard
Project on Technology, Work and
Character

3

[President] Carter will have to resist the gamesman's natural urge to throw out everything and start all over. This is the zero-based-budgeting mentality that we have already heard him espouse. Things do not work this way. If you go in saying you intend to change everything, you create such terror that the bureaucrats hunker down until the tornado passes. People are not just pawns in a chess game, and they will resist this kind of upheaval.

Interview/People, 5-23:52.

Thurgood Marshall
Associate Justice, Supreme
Court of the United States

4

[Saying that Congress is the most powerful of the three Branches of government]: Oh, I know they are all supposed to be equal, but I was always taught that the man with the money was the man with the power. Everyone has to go to Congress for their money.

To high-school students, Washington,
Feb. 3/The Dallas Times Herald, 2-4:(A)2.

David Mathews
Secretary of Health, Education
and Welfare of the United States

5

Reality in this town [Washington] is a law passed, or budget numbers. But for people who have never been here, Washington is the way it deals with them.

Interview/Time, 1-17:16.

Spark M. Matsunaga
United States Senator, D-Hawaii

6

[Comparing the Senate with the House, where he served for 14 years]: The Senate is, how shall I say, more distinguished, and I can't get used to the place. I tend to be a friendly

WHAT THEY SAID IN 1977

(SPARK M. MATSUNAGA)

guy. I was born and raised in the spirit of aloha. Everyone in the House called me "Sparkie." Well, the Senate isn't quite like that.

Interview/San Francisco Examiner & Chronicle, 3-20:(This World)26.

Robert H. Michel
United States Representative,
R—Illinois
1

The minute a person becomes a public official, he has to be one cut above what goes on in private business or it doesn't wash.

U.S. News & World Report, 8-8:21.

Walter F. Mondale
Vice President of the United States
2

It seems to me that the Vice President's best role is to function as the only other nationally elected officer besides the President. He has no bureaucracy to defend. His political future in all likelihood is identical to that of the President. If Jimmy Carter does well, i'll do well; if he does poorly, I'll do poorly. I think I can bring him disinterested advice on broad issues, strategies and political problems. I can roam through the government on broad issues, across department lines. I can be privy to all the information, and help the President in the area where I think all Presidents have had the most difficulty — namely, having time to really think through the great strategic issues, both domestic and foreign. The President is overwhelmed and, if you're not careful, could be literally paralyzed by the minutiae of government detail. And the trick, it seems to me, is to make certain the President has time to spend on the fundamental issues that affect us at home and abroad . . .

Interview/U.S. News & World Report, 3-28:62.

3

. . . I think the role that the President [Carter] has permitted me to play is unprecedented in American history. I am privy to all of the classified and secret information; I serve on the National Security Council and all of its subcommittees; I serve on all the crucial policy committees; and I have virtually unlimited access to the President. I think that is unprecedented.

TV-radio interview/"Meet the Press," National Broadcasting Company, 11-6.

Richard B. Morris
Former president, American
Historical Association
4

It's obvious that the Constitution was constructed in a different time frame and to meet an entirely different set of problems in an era when the national purpose was conceived of quite differently from that of the present day. Now — to underscore the difference — our nation is confronted with a serious decline in popular participation in, and a pervasive distrust of, government . . . We need to find out if the Constitution can continue to function effectively against this background of corrosive distrust in government at almost every level of our society — a distrust perhaps far deeper than in any previous period. The Bicentennial in 1987 of the adoption of the Federal Constitution is only 10 years off, and that's not too much lead time to begin a really thoughtful, objective investigation of how our government functions. We should study not only the history of the Constitution and the Federal Convention of 1787, but also of the living Constitution that evolved from the application of the document to the needs of government.

Interview/U.S. News & World Report, 7-4:63.

Daniel P. Moynihan
United States Senator, D—New York
5

The Senate is, has always been, the alternative authority in government to the Presidency. The House is too large and diffuse. The Senate has always been able to produce persons, symbols of the institution, who can embody a necessary alternative to the authority of the President. That's the Constitutional role of the Senate, and it has worked extraordinarily. It has never failed to generate the tension it was intended to.

Interview/Playboy, March:65.

(DANIEL P. MOYNIHAN)

1

[Arguing against a proposed amendment which would prohibit leftover campaign funds from being used for Senators' office expenses]: I never earned more than a professor's salary or a civil servant's, and when I came to this Senate, the one source of income I have always had as a teacher – lecturing – was denied me. Now I'm told with this amendment I should bankrupt myself. There are two ways I can get money – steal it or beg it – and I'd rather beg it.

Before the Senate, Washington, Aug. 3/
The Washington Post, 8-5:(A)8.

Richard M. Nixon
Former President of the United States

2

[On whether the President, if he considers it in the best interests of the country, can take or order actions that ordinarily would be considered illegal]: Well, when the President does it, that means that it is not illegal . . . If the President, for example, approves something because of the national security, or . . . because of a threat to internal peace and order of significant magnitude, then the President's decision in that instance is one that enables those who carry it out to carry it out without violating a law. Otherwise they're in an impossible position.

Television interview, San Clemente, Calif./"The
Nixon Interviews," Paradine Productions, 5-19.

Thomas P. O'Neill, Jr.
United States Representative,
D–Massachusetts

3

I have served in the House of Representatives for 24 years. It is not an efficient institution, but it is the most democratic arm of our government. We are the people's representatives. We must act so as to justify their faith in us. I have been in politics all my life. I am proud to be a politician. No other career offers as much opportunity to help people, and there is no better political office from which to serve people than as a member of Congress.

At opening session of the House, Washington,
Jan. 4/The Washington Post, 1-7:(A)20.

4

[Defending the recent Congressional pay hike]: If you are going to continue to deny the Congressmen a pay raise, then you're going to have nothing but the rich running for Congress and representing the people of America.

TV-radio interview/"Face the Nation,"
Columbia Broadcasting System, 2-20.

5

I don't think any President can be a good President if he doesn't have the backing or the support of his party. You don't become a great President by opposing the Congress.

The New York Times Magazine, 7-24:43.

Jody Powell
Press Secretary to President of
the United States Jimmy Carter

6

[On whether the government has a right to lie]: I think that as a general rule the answer is no. But I can't say that I could not posit a hypothetical situation in which it would be a very close call at the very least. The question of whether I tell a lie involves me and what I am going to give up of my own honesty and integrity in the matter. The question is whether my integrity is more important than whatever else is at stake . . . my integrity or someone else's life. What are you going to do? . . . I can't say you could not get in a position that wasn't a damn close call. I hope I'm never faced with a situation where it ever comes to a question like that. There could be some cases where a "no comment" just wouldn't work. If I'm ever faced with one I'll just have to make the best decision I can.

Before Washington, (D.C.) chapter, Society
of Professional Journalists, Sigma Delta Chi,
March 30/Los Angeles Times, 3-31:(1)12.

Rainier III
Head of Government of Monaco

7

[On U.S. President Carter]: When the President speaks to the people it should be because he has something important to say. Too many appearances demystify the position too much. I think it would be a shame and a disgrace for blue-jeans to become the normal White House

143

(RAINIER III)

way of dressing. It's bad if there's too much contact. I don't believe in these palsy-walsy talks and appearances. I think everybody likes to think of their leader as being on a pedestal. Bringing him off that pedestal is doing harm to the position. Look at the Eastern European countries — you don't see much of the man at the top. Being democratic doesn't mean being available to everybody at every moment of the day. I get annoyed when people ask to see me and say they will be available at 4 p.m. today. They wouldn't say that to their hairdresser. It's just rude. I tell them I'm sorry, I'm busy, and I am. I don't just sit here and wait for people to knock at my door. If a person wants to see a leader and is told it will only be possible a couple of weeks from now, it gives him more pleasure than if he is told sure, come in now and have a Coke. They've got to look up to leaders — not be on the same level. They look down very quickly when you are on the same level.

Interview, Monte Carlo/
The Christian Science Monitor, 3-28:20.

Abraham A. Ribicoff
United States Senator, D—Connecticut
1

The present process of confirmation [of Presidential appointees] all too often involves very little process. There are no established standards to judge nominees; there is no regular, systematic inquiry by committees into the background and integrity of nominees; and the Senate is expected to act without having access to relevant investigative reports prepared on nominees by Executive Branch agencies.

Los Angeles Herald-Examiner, 9-15:(A)8.

Elliot L. Richardson
Secretary of Commerce
of the United States
2

[On his leaving office shortly to make way for the incoming Carter Administration] : I can imagine feeling a sense of deprivation from not being a part of things I'll be reading about in the papers. A feeling that when I get up in the morning there isn't really anything very much

facing me that day, no need to master the essence of a problem as soon as possible, no way to use accumulated experience, a sense of how to resolve problems, how to move things from here to there, how to elicit consensus and cooperation. It's like racehorses no longer brought to the track. They probably are quite comfortable in their pastures. But it's different, very different.

Interview, Washington/Los Angeles Times, 1-9:(1)2.

Herbert S. Richey
Chairman, Chamber of Commerce
of the United States
3

Inflation will be with us until most Americans realize that we are paying in three ways for all of the government services we have voted ourselves. One of these forms of payment is taxes, which everyone knows. The other two are unemployment and inflation. These last two forms of payment are much less familiar, and that's a big part of the problem. We may really want and need the additional government services, or at least some of them; that's a political question, not an economic one. But if we want them, we should be willing to face their true costs. And I believe, too, that it's time to ask ourselves if many of the things we have turned to government to do could not be done with greater efficiency by the private sector. Isn't it possible that the pendulum has swung too far? We have two bad habits when it comes to judging government projects. One of them is that we tend to be fascinated by the size and the drama of gargantuan government undertakings. The other of these bad habits is that we tend to look at the *benefits* of a government program, while forgetting first to subtract the *costs. All* the costs.

Before Ohio Chamber of Commerce,
Columbus, March 16/Vital Speeches, 4-15:388.

Lawrence K. Roos
President, Federal Reserve
Bank of St. Louis
4

Over recent years, the amount of government debt held by the Federal Reserve System has risen rapidly. Back in the 1950s, the Fed consistently held about $25-billion in govern-

(LAWRENCE K. ROOS)

ment debt. Today, that figure is nearly $100-billion and the portion of the total Federal debt held by the System has nearly doubled. Serious inflation has been the inevitable result, and further inflation is to be expected if an overly accommodative monetary policy is forced upon the Fed in the future . . . When government expenditures are financed by the indirect sale of bonds to the central bank, the costs are hidden and citizen awareness of government expenditures is diminished. When citizens are not aware of government expenditures, obviously they are being denied information they need to exercise effective control of government.

Before Federal Land Bank of St. Louis/
The Wall Street Journal, 12-14:18.

Martin O. Sabo
Minnesota State Representative (D)
1

I tend not to be a fan of most Federal programs. I find them too detailed, and consequently I think they are usually quite wasteful. Therefore, there are better ways to serve the people. There's such a great variety of differences among the 50 states. I think the combined judgments of 50 different states within some broad general guidelines will generally produce more right decisions than one very rigid and specific Federal constituent.

Interview/The Wall Street Journal, 4-13:24.

William Safire
Political columnist
2

Forty years ago, a great many people felt that individuals were getting pushed around and not getting their rights. The only way to get these people their rights was with national government action through both the courts and Washington. This was a real need and the need was filled. Then the needs began to be overfilled and we produced bureaucratic momentum which is still going on . . . In the '60s, the overfill continued and the bureaucracy continued. The result has been that most people have a sense of alienation and powerlessness as a result of too much government domination in

Washington. In other words, what started as a good idea has become an encroaching bureaucracy.

Interview/Book Digest, July:20.

James H. Sammons
Executive vice president,
American Medical Association
3

Governmental bureaucracy is a cancerous, relentless, mindless blob of a force that oozes through the cracks and seeps under the doors, and as soon as you stop it in one direction it creeps in on you from another.

San Francisco Examiner & Chronicle,
6-26:(This World)2.

Patricia Schroeder
United States Representative, D–Colorado
4

There is an image of members of Congress sitting around in overstuffed chairs, sipping tea, reading great documents, pondering what policy should be. The truth is that if you find three minutes of time like that, you're lucky.

U.S. News & World Report, 1-10:28.

John R. Silber
President, Boston University
5

The persons to be elected to office ought to be better than the average. They ought, ideally, to be the persons best qualified. They ought to be better in their moral and intellectual capacities and in their commitment to hard work. This does not mean that they should necessarily be male, college graduates, middle class, white or indeed members of any specific group. But, since law-makers really are servants of the people, it follows that for the people nothing can be too good.

At Boston University commencement,
May 22/Parade, 10-23:9.

William E. Simon
Former Secretary of the
Treasury of the United States
6

The American people today are working four months [each year] for the government. Government[s] at all levels are taxing away four months of the workers' income before they can begin working for themselves. Govern-

WHAT THEY SAID IN 1977

(WILLIAM E. SIMON)

ment regulation is costing the American consumer today $130-billion to $150-billion. Today government, at all levels, consumes 40 per cent of the national income. If the trend continues, by the year 2000 government will consume 60 per cent. At that point, our economic, and therefore our personal and political, freedoms will be lost. So will the prosperity and abundance that was America . . . I think the American people are truly fed up with over-taxation, over-regulation and deficit spending which causes inflation. Their real income is eroding. They want less government.

Interview/Los Angeles Herald-Examiner, 9-4:(A)5.

James N. Sites
Senior vice president, National Association of Manufacturers
1

. . . we've too long been making a god out of government. As a result, we've developed a gigantic Washington spending and regulating machine that's accelerated almost beyond control. The impact shows up in chronic inflation, growing economic instability, tax evasion, spreading cynicism and distrust of government and a Pandora's Box of other personal and social ills. While some Presidents have gotten out in front of Congress in pressing for new government schemes, the past few years have seen Congress taking the bit in its own teeth. Indeed, Congress has come to look more and more like a Rube Goldberg contraption, its 535 wheels propelled by a rare force — pure political power — the power to tax us, to spend our money, to coerce us, to control us. Even the most well-meaning Congressmen are eventually caught in the trap of trying to do too much for too many, all to the end of getting re-elected . . . Government is trying to do far too much for the nation and for people. Not only should our representatives *not* be expected to cover so much — they shouldn't even *try*.

At Kiwanis International convention, Dallas, June 28/Vital Speeches, 9-15:712.

Chauncey Starr
President, Electric Power Research Institute
2

[On government regulation and authority over personal decisions of individuals] : There is a substantial difference between the perception of risk by an individual and the perception of risk by overviewing bodies. Public agencies examine the statistical effect on the population as a whole of the use of seat belts or the immunization of children and determine that if the public takes certain actions, the risk of harm will be lower. But the perception of the individual is completely different. He sees about him only a few visible indications of risk, and, unless he has personal cognizance of risk, he is unlikely to do anything about it unless the problem is right in front of his nose. The individual then decides that the system is intervening for bureaucratic reasons, that it is a machine grinding him down, and he becomes paranoid about how the system is abusing him.

The New York Times, 6-12:(1)55.

David A. Stockman
United States Representative, R–Michigan
3

The greatest problem in Congress today is the tremendous pressure of parochial, narrowly defined interests. We seem unable to control the budget. Any group that can organize itself, articulate a problem and propose a solution automatically has a claim on the Treasury.

U.S. News & World Report, 2-21:21.

James R. Thompson
Governor of Illinois (R)
4

Power always scares me a little, not because I'm afraid of it, but because I think public officials to use power wisely always have to retain a sense of fear, of its consequences. You take the power of a prosecutor; this probably is the most restrained and unrestrainable power possessed by any public official in the United States. I recognized that, so I've already in my career possessed more power to affect people's lives without check than I ever will again, either as a Governor or as a President.

Interview, Washington/ The Christian Science Monitor, 4-20:6.

Pierre Elliott Trudeau
Prime Minister of Canada
1

If I asked you to lift this hotel and you couldn't do it, that wouldn't mean you were weak. It would mean the hotel was too heavy. That's the way it is with governments. We all face problems which we cannot easily solve. So there is popular disaffection.

Interview, Paris/Los Angeles Times, 5-19:(2)7.

James G. Tucker, Jr.
United States Representative,
D–Arkansas
2

The question people most frequently ask is: "Why don't you run government like a business?" Well, government is not supposed to be like a business. A business should be absolutely efficient, and there is nothing efficient about democracy or about Congress. Dictatorships are efficient. Our system makes certain that government doesn't infringe upon the liberties of individuals. The great strength of Congress is found in some of the things most often criticized. It is cumbersome, fragmented, a slow-moving process. But the energy bill is a good example — it would be dangerous to pass it without subjecting it to slow, deliberate scrutiny. Another major strength is simply the enormous diversity of individual backgrounds, of geographic regions and constituencies. In legislating, this helps Congress knock off most rough edges and minimize most unintended results.

Interview/U.S. News & World Report, 6-13:35.

Morris K. Udall
United States Representative,
D–Arizona
3

[Before writing the 1967 law which calls for the President to recommend pay increases for members of Congress, rather than the Congressmen themselves,] I discovered that in 180 years there had been nine pay raises for members of Congress. Every one of them had been controversial. In one case, 35 years elapsed and there was great controversy even after 35 years; they went from $6 a day to $8 a day. I sharply challenge this whole philosophy that the ultimate test of political courage is whether the

guys in the hot seat will vote themselves a pay raise. The answer is they won't, and 200 years of history show they won't. You've got to make up your mind whether members of Congress are going to be second- or third-class citizens and make less than judges, less than the third assistant to the fourth assistant at the Treasury Department, or less than the chairman of the board of tea-tasters and everybody else.

Los Angeles Times, 2-18:(1)16.

Jack H. Watson, Jr.
Secretary to the Cabinet and
Assistant to President of the
United States Jimmy Carter for
Intergovernmental Affairs
4

The [Carter] Cabinet is in fact independent. It's not just a show. There's such a vast amount of work to be done that if you are serious about moving the government, then you can't do it from a single fulcrum. You need lots and lots of fulcrums. That's what the Cabinet officers are.

U.S. News & World Report, 3-14:35.

Ben J. Wattenberg
Political analyst
5

All government can hope to accomplish is to bring about the elimination of specific miseries. It does that pretty well in this country. But we ask that government create jobs that workers will love to go to, and an environment in which everyone enjoys a nirvana-like happiness. Well, religion can't do that for most people. Government shouldn't be expected to.

Interview/The National Observer, 2-26:3.

Lowell P. Weicker, Jr.
United States Senator, R–Connecticut
6

[Comparing the Senate with the House]: It's really far more rewarding in the Senate for a new person. You can get something done, walk out on the floor and speak, or add an amendment. You don't have to wait around for 20 years of seniority. It's much warmer, much friendlier in the House. The terms are so short, no one knows whether they'll see each other tomorrow. There's far more aloofness in the Senate. You walk through the halls of the

WHAT THEY SAID IN 1977

(LOWELL P. WEICKER, JR.)

Senate and my door is the only one open. People have a six-year stint; they think they can afford to be aloof. In the House no doors are closed. It's a warm and personal place.

Interview/San Francisco Examiner & Chronicle, 3-20:(This World)26.

Caspar W. Weinberger
Former Secretary of Health, Education and Welfare of the United States

1

Government is a fascinating activity. The worst thing about it is the sense of frustration that you get from the knowledge that you could accomplish much more if the Congress would let you. I frequently had the feeling in government jobs that I was trying desperately to catch hold of a rapidly moving train by the last car.

San Francisco Examiner & Chronicle, 8-14:(This World)2.

James C. Wright, Jr.
United States Representative, D—Texas

2

I think if the members of this body [Congress] were to take the vows of poverty, abolish our offices, abandon our homes and pitch pup tents on the Capitol lawn, we'd still be criticized for something — maybe for walking on the grass.

Time, 3-14:12.

3

The day is ended when any committee chairman can run his domain like a feudal barony, oblivious to the wishes and sensitivities of other members. All now have been put on notice that their colleagues will hold them accountable for their stewardship. The office of committee chairman must now be regarded no longer as a right but a privilege, a gift of opportunity bestowed by one's peers. And those who give also can take away.

The New York Times, 3-20:4.

4

The White House reached its zenith of power under [former President Richard] Nixon, who was so assertive of Presidential prerogatives, many of which he assumed ... The Presidency is still a stronger office than the Constitution intended. This President [Carter] gets himself in trouble when he announces positions without consulting his troops in Congress and takes positions we can't defend. He doesn't seem to comprehend that there are people over here who have wrestled with these problems.

The New York Times, 10-9:(1)31.

Walter B. Wriston
Chairman, Citicorp (Citibank, New York)

5

The will of the people can be stifled by laws that are so numerous, so prolix, so opaque that they cannot be appraised by the public. If we have not quite reached that point, we are perilously close. The authors of the Constitution, writing in *The Federalist Papers,* clearly foresaw this danger and drove the point home again and again. Madison said [Number 62], the "facility and excess of law-making seem to be the diseases to which our governments are most liable." For all their insight, the framers of our Constitution could not foresee a day when approximately 500 legislators would employ 10,000 people to assist them in their legislative tasks ... Last year, there were 20,000 bills introduced in Congress. In a single day not less than 242 committees and subcommittees of the Congress were in session — all, under the rules, "for a legislative purpose." No wonder they produce such an indigestible mass of legislation.

Before American College of Trial Lawyers/ The Washington Post, 8-18:(A)20.

Daniel Yankelovich
Public-opinion analyst

6

All of our surveys over the last decade show that every year more and more people are coming to believe that the part of their lives that they are able to control is diminishing ... People are hanging on for dear life to the diminishing sphere of autonomy that they have ... I interpret the public's outcry over the proposal to ban saccharin as the collective response of the individual saying: "If there is a problem with saccharin I want to know about

(DANIEL YANKELOVICH)

it; but I also want to make the decision as to whether or not I use it" ... [Americans believe that] it's an arrogance that says that people don't know what's good for them and that there should be a law to protect them. They don't want to give the government a license to enter every nook and cranny of their personal lives.

The New York Times, 6-12:(1)55.

Edward Zorinsky
United States Senator, D—Nebraska
1

[On why he wanted to become a Senator]: Because as Mayor [of Omaha] I was on the receiving end of bureaucracy from Washington, D.C., telling me how to run the city, when to run it, why to run it, where to run it. The Federal revenue-sharing dollars that we received from back here — they didn't have strings attached to them, they had ropes attached to

them. And then they act like all that money is *born* in Washington; they don't give you credit for paying taxes.

Interview, Washington/
The National Observer, 3-19:6.

2

The Senate just isn't fast enough in responding to the complex issues facing the nation today. For example, I spent hours on the Senate floor during the winter energy crisis while Senator after Senator rose to express sympathy for the people back home. Well, the people back home know you're sympathetic to people going cold. Why not spend the time formulating a long-range plan to preclude any future crisis? But Senators make self-serving speeches to get into the *Congressional Record* so that somebody back home may read them. Everything here is geared to the re-election of the members.

Interview/U.S. News & World Report, 6-13:34.

Labor · The Economy

I. W. Abel
President, United
Steelworkers of America 1

When you need to use it, a strike is an effective weapon. But it is not nearly as effective as it was years ago. The impact of imports makes it less effective. The rubber workers discovered this last summer. Four and a half months into the strike, tire dealers were still holding sales.

San Francisco Examiner & Chronicle,
5-29:(B)7.

Roger E. Anderson
Chairman, Continental
Illinois Corporation 2

At the moment, capital in the U.S. is in great supply. Banks have money to lend. Businesses have funds to expand. Individuals have savings to invest. Our only problem is that the level of capital investment has not yet come up to these conditions of liquidity. The future needs of the U.S. economy seem to have lost a great deal of their urgency as businesses have concentrated upon improving their capital-to-debt ratios, rebuilding liquidity and restructuring balance sheets. Rebuilding and restructuring in many cases have been long overdue. And with the memory of recession still fresh in mind, businessmen have every right to savor and safeguard present conditions of balance-sheet strength. There is a risk, however, in postponing the commitment of capital resources to expansion of productivity. Most new capital projects to expand capacity require several years' lead time before coming on stream. In the interim, demand can easily outrun supply, shortages can quickly develop, and inflation can result.

Before Business Publications Association,
Chicago, March 7/Vital Speeches, 4-15:409.

John J. Balles
President, Federal Reserve Bank
of San Francisco 3

We hear from some quarters that we have to live with a certain amount of inflation in order to reduce the unemployment rate to respectable levels — a concept enshrined in many textbooks under the name of the Phillips curve. But our experience several years ago, when prices shot up in the middle of a recession, should have convinced us that something was wrong with that simple textbook relationship. Indeed, the economists on my staff now argue that the typical response to a high rate of inflation is more rather than less unemployment, because that inflation reduces consumer confidence, forces households to save more and spend less, and thereby reduces the level of business activity. As a policy matter, therefore, we are not faced with a choice between competing alternatives, but rather with a straightforward imperative to fight inflation if we want to conquer unemployment.

Before Town Hall, Los Angeles,
July 26/Vital Speeches, 10-1:742.

Irving Bernstein
Labor historian, University of
California, Los Angeles 4

Modern man is caught in a trap. If he wants to enjoy the fruits of advanced technology, he must subjugate himself to the clock and calendar, for industry can be run in no other way. If he wants the personal freedom and identity, he invites the grinding poverty that has been the fate of humanity over most of its history. The practical question is not how time-oriented work may be eliminated, but, rather, how it may be mitigated.

U.S. News & World Report, 4-4:81.

150

Eula Bingham
*Assistant Secretary for Occupational
Safety and Health, Department of
Labor of the United States*

1

...I feel very strongly that people in this country should expect, as a matter of right, a safe and healthy workplace ... When I hear these stories about human rights, I think, my God, workers have a right to expect they won't be killed on their jobs. If that means I should have to pay 50 cents — or $2 — more for my refrigerator, then I wouldn't want to hide it.

Interview/The Washington Post, 9-12:(A)5.

W. Michael Blumenthal
*Secretary of the Treasury-designate
of the United States*

2

I am tempted to say the best goal [for unemployment] is zero, or close to zero, and I feel strongly about that. In this great country of ours, richest in the world, there shouldn't be any people who want to work, and who are able to work, and who are looking for work, and are unable to find gainful employment. We can do so many things, we ought to be able to lick that problem as well.

*TV-radio interview/"Issues and Answers,"
American Broadcasting Company, 1-9.*

W. Michael Blumenthal
*Secretary of the Treasury
of the United States*

3

I accepted this assignment precisely because I viewed licking inflation and unemployment as linked. Because I saw in this my greatest challenge as Secretary of the Treasury; because I believe it is possible to do the job; because I believe that the time to do it is now — and above all, because we now have a President [Carter] who will fully back, and indeed insist on, sound policies to make it happen. This is not an Administration that talks about inflation but will do nothing about it.

*Before Policy Forum, New York, March 3/
Los Angeles Times, 3-4:(1)11.*

4

There is no need for inflation to become worse. As a matter of fact, we have a good opportunity to bring the rate of inflation down. We should not be mesmerized by what happens in any month or two — for example, the very cold weather that brought extraordinary increases in prices for citrus fruits and fresh vegetables in February. Over the longer run, the fact that substantial elements of the economy are under-utilized leads one to conclude that there is no reason for inflation to accelerate as a result of our stimulating the economy. If there is a major increase in the price of oil, that will have an impact, but there's not much we can do about it. But there are a lot of internal factors which we can work on to bring inflation down: inflationary and excessive government regulations, trade policies and farm programs, and uneconomic requirements that cost business a lot of money and are counter-productive. We can try to convince labor and management that the policies of the Carter Administration are going to be gradual and responsible; that there's going to be a tight rein on spending which will bring the budget into balance by 1981. If we can create confidence in that way and have a moderate program to get the economy operating more briskly and more efficiently, I think we can bring inflation down substantially.

*Interview, Washington/
U.S. News & World Report, 4-11:31.*

5

I don't believe that wage and price controls are any kind of realistic weapon, in other than war-time or an extreme emergency ... The fight against inflation is not just something that can be concentrated on wage and price decisions. It must also deal with many other structural causes of inflation. There are at least three. One is the cyclical, the internal fiscal-monetary types of things. Another is structural — regulations, impediments, actions by government. The third is external — the weather and OPEC prices and things of that kind.

Interview, Washington/The New York Times, 4-11:46.

6

We have a tax system that works — imperfectly, to be sure, but better than most. It is preferable to correct its faults and build upon our knowledge and experience than to embark

WHAT THEY SAID IN 1977

(W. MICHAEL BLUMENTHAL)

on fundamental changes with an untried system whose effect we cannot fully foresee.

The New York Times, 8-2:41.

Barry Bosworth
Chairman, Federal Council on
Wage and Price Stability
1

. . . it's wrong to name a single factor like some economists do, for example, to say if we could only do something about wages, [then] prices will take care of themselves. I don't think that's right. It's futile. Wages are simply responding to the cost of living and prices are responding to the cost of production. How many books have been written about "the" problem of inflation or "the" cure. All the one-cures are nonsense.

Interview/The Washington Post, 8-14:(L)2.

Karl Brunner
Professor of economics, Graduate
School of Management,
University of Rochester
2

The key to success is to admit to ourselves that we cannot "fine tune" the economy, much as we might want to. "Activist" responses to the weekly wiggles of interest rates, employment and economic growth lead only to destabilization and erratic fluctuations in our economy. The new Administration, the Fed and Congress must, in my view, resist the pressures of political expediency, the demands to "do something" every time some short-term problem occurs.

Before House Banking Committee, Washington/
The Wall Street Journal, 3-14:12.

Arthur F. Burns
Chairman, Federal Reserve Board
3

Now, there is a time for social reforms, but what I find so missing in much of our thinking today is that we forget there is such a thing as the middle class; that the great energies of our people are largely concentrated in that class. When we start manipulating taxes and so on, we tend to ignore that class. Perhaps that is right from a social viewpoint, but from the viewpoint

of energizing the economy, we are definitely making a mistake.

Congressional testimony/
U.S. News & World Report, 5-2:45.

4

Economists are not very helpful any longer. All they know is: spend more money or have easier credit . . . We can do a great deal in this country without spending money and without corrupting our monetary system. That is something today's economists know very little about. You members in the Senate and the House — we economists corrupt you; you corrupt the country, and that is where we are.

Congressional testimony/
U.S. News & World Report, 5-2:45.

Robert N. Butler
Director, National Institute on Aging
5

The present widespread system of mandatory retirement is based on an arbitrary, nonfunctional definition of old age. This abrupt withdrawal of the opportunity to be productive and earn what may be essential income presents a complex problem to all who work to maintain the health, dignity and well-being of older persons.

The Washington Post, 8-25:(A)26.

Robert T. Campion
Chairman, Lear Siegler, Inc.
6

I've never been one to support the idea of long-range government economic planning, as is being pushed by some Senators, but I do think the time has come for somebody to sit down and start suggesting some priorities. President Kennedy got people excited by setting a goal of reaching the moon. Now we need someone to put forth some long-range economic goals that can be achieved. There's too much shooting from the hip.

Interview/U.S. News & World Report, 9-19:62.

Jack W. Carlson
Chief economist, Chamber of
Commerce of the United States
7

Panic estimates of inflation and unemployment will likely be proven wrong when data are

(JACK W. CARLSON)

available. People find substitutes, adjust crops, change work schedules and wear sweaters.

San Francisco Examiner & Chronicle,
2-20:(This World)9.

Jimmy Carter
President of the United States
1

Inflation hurts us all. In every part of the country, whether we have a job or are looking for one, we must race just to keep up with the constant rise in prices. Inflation has hit us hardest not in the luxuries but in the essentials — food, energy, health and housing. You see it every time you go shopping. I understand that unemployment and inflation are very real and have done great harm to many American families. Nothing makes it harder to provide decent health, housing and education for our people, protect our environment or realize our goal of a balanced budget, than a stagnant economy.

Broadcast address to the nation, Washington,
Feb. 2/The New York Times, 2-3:22.

2

I announced earlier my firm commitment not to have ... wage and price authority ... I've emphasized always the word "voluntary." And to the extent that I can arrive at a common understanding with industry and labor leaders that a certain amount of cooperation and information can be exchanged [with the government] before a major proposal is made, I think that's a legitimate pursuit of mine. I can't force it. It's got to be voluntary.

News conference, Washington, Feb. 23/
The New York Times, 2-24:22.

3

There's an underlying inflation rate of 5 to 6 per cent, which is generally derived from the rate of increase in wages minus the productivity of workers. It's one of the best measurements. I think that the monthly reports that come in quite often are very misleading; they're transient in nature. We've had a drastic increase in energy costs during this winter period because of the unprecedented severity of the weather.

And we've also had a very high increase in the cost of many food items — again because of damage to crops in different regions of the country and because of coffee losses overseas. My own guess is that the inflationary pressures will continue at about the level that they have historically in the last couple of years, around 6 or a little bit better per cent.

News conference, Washington, March 24/
The New York Times, 5-25:(A)10.

4

I strongly support the autonomy and independence of the Federal Reserve. We have had a two per cent increase in interest rates this year because of action taken by the Federal Reserve. But there's a fairly good balance now, in my opinion, between the Federal Reserve on the one hand, controlling the supply of money in the marketplace to some degree, the Congress, which has direct authority to act, which indirectly controls the supply of money by changes in the tax laws, rebates and so forth, and the President, of course, who participates with the Congress in establishing budget levels, the rapidity with which programs are carried out once the money's authorized by Congress, and so forth. I wouldn't want to change that basic structure. I think it's good.

News conference, Washington, Nov. 10/
The New York Times, 11-11:(A)22.

Leonel J. Castillo
Commissioner-designate, Immigration
and Naturalization Service
of the United States
5

[Saying he doubted if mass roundups of illegal alien workers would cure high U.S. unemployment] : If you somehow miraculously rounded up several million illegal aliens, what would you have? You'd have to find U.S. workers willing to take many menial, low-paying jobs. You'd have to relocate a lot of them. Would an unemployed iron-worker in the East want to come and pick cabbages in Texas?

Houston/The New York Times, 4-18:54.

6

[On illegal alien workers in the U.S.]: I think you can say there is clearly some displace-

(LEONEL J. CASTILLO)

ment in some sectors of the economy, but there is clearly not a one-to-one displacement. By that, I mean every person who is working and undocumented is not displacing an American worker. Some are; some aren't. Some sectors, according to INS, that have most undocumented workers also have the lowest unemployment rate, like Houston. Others that have the least number have the highest unemployment rate . . . We need tougher laws on the smugglers, the coyotes, the guys who smuggle people. They smuggle people and the penalties we assess are relatively light . . . We need laws that deal with employers who knowingly participate in efforts to smuggle, and on persons who abuse and exploit the aliens. We need to be tough on those people. I think there should be amnesty for aliens in this country who have developed equity over a period of years — like those who have been here for 30 years, who have children who have served in the military.

Interview, Houston/
The Christian Science Monitor, 4-19:17.

Harold P. Coxson
Director of labor law, Chamber of
Commerce of the United States
1

[Arguing against retirement ages being raised or set by law]: This whole issue is being used as a panacea by senior-citizen groups, and it's not. Our official policy is to encourage hiring older workers, but it's also our belief that if you have fixed age retirement set by law it's going to hurt those prospects. Companies are going to be reluctant to hire a worker over 45 if they know they are going to be in violation of the law if they let him go before 70. The legislation will also impact on job opportunities for young workers, women and minorities. What's going to happen is that younger workers will be blocked and they can't move up in a company because old Joe has the job and he won't leave until he turns 70.

The Dallas Times Herald, 8-7:(A)15.

Fred G. Currey
Chairman, Continental Trailways, Inc.
2

What bothers me especially is all the talk of how tax reform will close loopholes. Yet we tend to forget that those so-called loopholes were put there originally for a purpose — whether it be for increasing efficiency in industry or spurring the building of inner-city housing. Economic incentives through the tax system have always been one of the most effective ways to address social ills.

Interview/U.S. News & World Report, 9-19:63.

John D. deButts
Chairman, American Telephone
& Telegraph Company
3

I don't think [President Carter's plan for] the $50 rebate [to all citizens] will do one thing to help the economy and the unemployment situation. We need to create the public's confidence that we can control inflation and make our dollars worth something. If we have that, the public would be willing to invest more in the big-ticket items — cars, appliances, etc. — that are costly and take a long period to pay off. I don't see the rebate helping at all to do that.

Interview, New York/The New York Times, 3-15:53.

John N. Erlenborn
United States Representative, R–Illinois
4

Too often, when Congress considers labor-management legislation, it focuses either on union rights or employer rights — either big labor or big business. Forgotten is the employee, who becomes just a pawn in these power struggles.

Nation's Business, September:22.

James H. Evans
President, Union Pacific Corporation
5

Creative tax reduction is the key to economic progress — to capital formation and the creation of permanent, productive jobs. This is not a half-baked theory; it is a fact. In 1963, to stimulate the economy and to reduce unemployment, President Kennedy, in the face of a deficit, in the teeth of conventional wisdom

(JAMES H. EVANS)

and to the consternation of some of his own advisers, actually instituted a tax cut. It worked so well that America soon took off on the longest period of sustained prosperity in its postwar history. A tax reduction today might well achieve the same thing. What is needed is the courage to try — and there are hopeful signs that that courage is beginning to appear. More and more voices are calling for fewer controls, less taxation and more realistic approaches to economic development.

Before Tax Foundation, Omaha, Neb.,
June 7/Vital Speeches, 8-1:617.

Henry Ford II
Chairman, Ford Motor Company
1

I think there'll be [economic] growth, but not big growth. But I don't think that's all bad. I think we were going high, wide and handsome, just begging for a break, and we got the break [the 1974-75 recession], and it wasn't very nice, and a lot of people suffered. We were just outliving our means, and we've got to figure out how we can get back down and live within our means. And that applies to individuals and governments as well.

Interview, Dearborn, Mich./
The New York Times, 2-13:(1)17.

Douglas A. Fraser
Vice president in charge of
the Chrysler department, United
Automobile Workers of America
2

I certainly don't think [AFL-CIO president George] Meany is senile. But he projects an image of age, and many workers, particularly young ones, feel it's ridiculous for a man of 82 to be leading the labor movement.

Interview, Los Angeles/Los Angeles Times, 5-17:(1)3.

Douglas A. Fraser
President, United
Automobile Workers of America
3

[On whether unions are less militant today]: I don't think we've lost our militancy. I think there's a difference between being a militant and being a screwball — and I think some

people confuse those things sometimes. But I think the argument can be made, and argued conclusively, that a lot of unions have gone the way of all flesh and have become conservative. You can't say that about the UAW.

Interview/U.S. News & World Report, 5-30:69.

Bill Frenzel
United States Representative,
R—Minnesota
4

[Arguing against an end to preferential tax treatment of capital gains]: ... we've come a long way in the last six months to a point where Congress wouldn't think of accepting a change in the capital-gains treatment. Maybe we will go a similar distance and actually give a lower capital-gains tax rate for assets held over a longer period. That would be my preference. Right now, many people are paying more than 50 per cent tax on capital gains when you take into account the minimum tax and state taxes — and that's confiscatory. It simply destroys the incentive to invest. We all need to keep in mind, too, that we are in a terribly inflationary period, and what is called capital gains is usually just inflation that has been pumped up mostly by reckless spending of this same Congress. We should reduce the capital-gains tax so that we are not merely taxing inflation. And we could "index" the tax rates or the capital-gains rate, and that might help some. When a person sells his house — which he bought for $15,000 — for $45,000, it's the same house he bought. All he's doing is paying a tax on some inflation. I would say we ought to keep a capital-gains preference. We ought to eliminate gains on homes from taxation entirely. And the third feature that I would be in favor of is reducing capital-gains tax for assets held over 10 years.

Interview/U.S. News & World Report, 12-19:72.

Milton Friedman
Professor of economics,
University of Chicago
5

Capitalism itself is universal. There is no society that is not at least in part capitalistic. But the real question is the future of private enterprise, or competitive capitalism. And that

155

WHAT THEY SAID IN 1977

(MILTON FRIEDMAN)

is moving in a direction that cannot long be continued.

News conference, Beverly Hills, Calif.,
Feb. 9/Los Angeles Times, 2-10:(3)21.

1

The closest approach to free enterprise we have ever had in the United States was in the 19th century. Yet you and your children will hear over and over again in their schools and in their classes the myths that that was a terrible period when the robber barons were grinding the poor, miserable people under their heels. That's a myth constructed out of whole cloth. The plain fact is that never in human history has there been a period when the ordinary man improved his condition and benefited his life as much as he did during that period of the 19th century when we had the closest approach to free enterprise that we have ever had . . . My parents came to this country in the 1890s. Like millions of others, they came with empty hands. They were able to find a place in this country, to build a life for themselves and to provide a basis on which their children and their children's children could have a better life. There is no saga in history remotely comparable to the saga of the United States during that era, welcoming millions and millions of people from all over the world and enabling them to find a place for themselves and to improve their lives. And it was possible only because there was an essentially free society. If the laws and regulations that today hamstring industry and commerce had been in effect in the 19th century, our standard of living today would be below that of the 19th century. It would have been impossible to have absorbed the millions of people who came to this country.

At Pepperdine University, Feb. 9/
Vital Speeches, 3-15:335.

2

[On President Carter's economic program]: There is nothing in the package which will stimulate anything. How can the government stimulate the economy by taking money out of one pocket of the public and putting it into another pocket? The rebate plan, for example, would distribute $50 apiece to most consumers. As a result, those consumers will tend to spend more. But where will the government get the money to send out the rebates? . . . It appears to be a stimulant because people are looking at the visible effects and paying no attention to the invisible effects. The $50 rebate checks and the extra expenditures by consumers that will result are very visible. The people who will not have employment because the government will borrow the money or cause more inflation are not very visible; nobody notices them.

Interview/U.S. News & World Report, 3-7:20.

John Kenneth Galbraith
Former professor of economics,
Harvard University

3

We all know there are only two major problems — the problem of simultaneous inflation and high unemployment; and the fact that it is easier for rich countries to get richer than for poor countries to get less poor. Whoever arranged that state of affairs should be spoken to very sternly.

Interview, New York/
The Christian Science Monitor, 5-18:26.

4

We have to recognize that the unemployment now is very structured. We can have very tight labor markets for many kinds of skills, at the same time that we have large categories of workers — minorities, teen-agers, women — with very, very high unemployment. And if we act against that unemployment by general stimulation of the economy, as with this $50 rebate, which President Carter has so wisely abandoned, we tighten the tight markets just as much as we solve unemployment in the areas where it exists, and perhaps even more. So we have to have increasingly measures which *target* our expansion action against the particular groups that are suffering. And at the same time we have to recognize that as we get at all close to full employment we have a massive inflationary problem on our hands. And part of the strategy for that must be a policy for holding onto prices and incomes.

Interview/The National Observer, 5-23:6.

(JOHN KENNETH GALBRAITH)

1

The ultimate goal of a good tax system is that everybody who is enriched by a given amount can be taxed by the same progressive amount. I emphasize the word "progressive." I'd like to see a tax system where however the money comes — earned income, unearned income, inheritance, larceny, gambling, picking it up on the floor, capital gains — the fact is that you're subject to the same progressive rate of taxation.

Interview/The National Observer, 5-23:6.

Will Geer
Actor

2

[Arguing against mandatory retirement at age 65]: It is my belief that it is criminal, absolutely criminal, that old people should be put on a shelf and told they can no longer work when they want to work and they can ... The good Lord upstairs, the "Man upstairs," your genes, your ancestors and your own life-style determine how long you are going to keep on working and living. Retirement will come from all those forces together naturally, just as it does in mother nature.

Before House Select Committee on Aging, Washington/U.S. News & World Report, 10-3:30.

Robert Gordon
Professor, Northwestern University

3

Most economists see the long-run connection between money growth, inflation and unemployment. But to wring inflation out of some economies by monetary means would mean perhaps half a decade of sky-high interest rates, massive unemployment and frequent bankruptcies. It is impossible to ask a government to do that.

The New York Times, 1-30:(12)3.

Allan Grant
President, American Farm Bureau Federation

4

Most of the professional consumer advocates reflect the aims of organized labor and serve its causes. They remain silent about worker rights stolen by union-shop compulsion; they say nothing about union featherbedding, make-work rules or excessive wage demands robbing the consumer. The consumer advocates were totally silent when cannery and freezer strikes in California at the height of the harvest left millions of dollars worth of processing fruits and vegetables to rot on the ground. The higher costs will be paid by union members and consumers everywhere. They say nothing about inflation, that greatest robber of all. Instead, they call for more government spending for Federal agencies, controls and regulations. Over the years we have allowed the voice of these so-called "consumer protectionists" to go unanswered. We have stood idly by while those who do not believe as we do, have shaped the consumer movement to their own uses.

Before American Farm Bureau Federation, Honolulu/The Christian Science Monitor, 1-12:35.

Paul Hall
President, Seafarers International Union

5

[On the Labor-Management Group, set up for cooperation between employees and employers]: I don't want to sound like a cornball, but the unique thing about this country is that in one area we can be kicking one another around and in another be working together. The Labor-Management Group is an excellent instrument even if it comes up with nothing. It couldn't exist in England, France or anywhere else in the world. Everybody in these meetings wants to see the country do well. That is why this system is the greatest.

The New York Times, 9-4:(3)14.

Sidney Harman
Under Secretary of Commerce of the United States

6

As a pragmatist, I believe absolutely in the necessity of an equilibrium between social-human concerns and technical or economic concerns. It is the only way the free-enterprise system can flourish.

Interview/The Washington Post, 2-20:(A)6.

WHAT THEY SAID IN 1977

Orrin G. Hatch
United States Senator, R–Utah
1

[Arguing against food stamps for strikers]: The Federal government is doing nothing more than unfairly subsidizing labor unions in their collective-bargaining negotiations with business. The American taxpayer is forced to help union members hold out longer for higher wages. Those higher wages are then passed on to that same tax-paying consumer in the form of higher prices in the marketplace ... The time has come for us to put a stop to this wasteful subsidy of labor-union strikes. The only possible worth of food stamps is to assist those who are in need and without the means to support themselves. Strikers don't fit that definition.

/**

2

One of the big arguments that the Keynesian economists have used in the past has been that, by deficit spending, we will increase the ability of this country to basically continue its forward momentum. In some ways, that appeared to be so during the 1940s, 1950s and even part of the 1960s. [However, during the 1970s] deficit spending has resulted not in an increase in stimulation, but in an economy that is wracked with indecision, where nobody knows what is going to happen, where the stock market fluctuates almost uncontrollably and without any definiteness, and where we have had an increase in inflation that looks like it is almost uncontrollable.

Nation's Business, November:32.

Robert S. Hatfield
Chairman, The Continental Group, Inc.
3

When I first started working in a factory in 1936, I saw long lines of forlorn men and women waiting before factory gates ... I often suspected that those who did get hired had to humble themselves in some way. And once they got in, it was no bed of roses either. The whim of the boss could make the difference, and sometimes that meant swallowing a lot of abuse, with no way to talk back. It came home to me then, as never before, that human dignity is very precious. Now when I think of the

humanity and dignity that underpins the relationships today of all working people, whether management or labor, then I know that our unions have a lot to be proud of, because it was the union movement that spearheaded the effort and made it happen.

The New York Times, 8-7:(3)5.

Gabriel Hauge
Chairman, Manufacturers Hanover
Trust Company, New York
4

When the [Carter] Administration puts its tax package together, I hope they are able to see that the real solution to the unemployment problem is removing the deterrents, and adding incentives, to investment. If it proposes a tax plan that is fully consumer-oriented, it would create some serious problems and throw the economy out of its remarkably well-balanced phase, but I don't think that will happen.

The New York Times, 7-24:(3)15.

S. I. Hayakawa
United States Senator, R–California
5

[Advocating a special youth minimum wage of $1.50 an hour to encourage hiring of under-18 workers]: Our society provides everything for youth – good high schools and luxurious facilities for high-school and junior-high-school education – but what our society does not provide is a beginning of responsibility for adulthood. The result is that we have an enormous wave of youthful crime. The young men are testing their manhood. And if they can't test them in legal ways, they'll test it by drugs, by stealing cars, by robbing liquor stores.

News conference, Los Angeles, Jan. 21/
Los Angeles Times, 1-22:(1)30.

6

[Saying he is in favor of mandatory retirement at 65]: If I hadn't been confronted with mandatory retirement, I might still have been a professor. That would have been a horrible thing. If you've been in a job 30 or 40 years, it's time you moved on and thought of something else to do.

The Dallas Times Herald, 8-7:(A)15.

Benjamin L. Hooks
Executive director, National
Association for the Advancement
of Colored People
1

I don't think anybody can accuse President Carter of breaking any speed records in moving on this unemployment thing. Inflation is a cruel enemy to the poor, but not nearly as cruel as being without a job month after month, year after year.

TV-radio interview/"Issues and Answers,"
American Broadcasting Company, 8-21.

Hubert H. Humphrey
United States Senator, D–Minnesota
2

The first thing that a young person needs is to learn how to work — to have work experience. All this business about training — important, to be sure. But the first training you need is to know how to get out, get on the job, do what you're assigned to do and understand the importance of work ... It's good for us. Work is therapy. Work is health. Work is income. Work is growing up ... We have a whole decade of youth now — a decade of them, that have never learned how to do anything, except one thing: how to get by. And they live in what I call the shadow economy ... And there is absolutely no way that man or God can figure out how to stop crime until we figure out how to put young people on constructive work.

Interview/The Christian Science Monitor, 3-2:20.

Yoshihiro Inayama
Chairman, Nippon Steel
Corporation, Japan
3

... the advanced economies have reached the point of growth where so-called prosperity has just about hit the ceiling ... Most developed countries have reached the maximum in basic human requirements and people are now turning to more non-material requirements.

The New York Times, 8-21:(3)7.

Gene F. Jankowski
Executive vice president, Columbia
Broadcasting System Broadcast Group
4

[Supporting mandatory retirement at age 65]: The retirement-at-65 policy is not ideal, but we believe its advantages outweigh the disadvantages ... Primarily, it eliminates unequal treatment stemming from individual judgments as to who should and who should not continue to work after a certain age. Employees know they are receiving treatment equal to other employees. It opens up promotional opportunities inside the company for younger people, assuring the company of fresh ideas in vital areas. It allows the employee to plan better for his or her own future, by completely removing any doubt as to the required age of retirement. It also provides the retirees with the freedom and income to pursue fulfilling goals in other areas while they are still young enough to do so. And it allows the company to plan far more efficiently for its future.

Before House Select Committee on Aging,
Washington/U.S. News & World Report, 10-3:31.

H. Roy Kaplan
Sociologist; Visiting professor,
Pitzer College
5

[On a survey he made of big-money winners in the New Jersey state lottery]: If people don't have to work, in most cases they don't ... We found that 35 of the 49 people we talked to in New Jersey who were directly affected by the winnings, and who were employed full time, quit their work. We feel that this says something about the nature of the commitment to work and of work itself in our society.

Claremont, Calif./The Washington Post, 6-17:(B)14.

Lane Kirkland
Secretary-treasurer, American
Federation of Labor-Congress
of Industrial Organizations
6

Full employment doesn't cause inflation; unemployment doesn't cure it. Putting America back to work cuts welfare and unemployment compensation costs and increases industrial efficiency. When unused plant, equipment and manpower are put back to work, unit costs go down — not up.

Interview/The New York Times, 1-9:(3)14.

WHAT THEY SAID IN 1977

Juanita M. Kreps
Secretary of Commerce
of the United States
1

It would seem to be a good time to be an economist. For the first time in history, we have a Cabinet with five Ph.D.s in economics and a sixth member who majored in the subject. One of the news magazines argued that this is a test of whether economists can run the government. Whatever our failings, it may be reassuring to note that we don't have to do much to improve on the lawyers' record.

Before National Economists Club, Washington,
March 1/The Wall Street Journal, 3-10:14.

2

. . . countries in Western Europe traditionally have had less trouble with unemployment than. we have had [because] they can offer employment subsidies to business — incentives of various kinds to keep workers on the payroll. But if our government were to offer American businessmen a partial payment of a wage so that they'd hire certain groups of people or avoid laying them off, the typical businessman here would say: "It's too much trouble, too much paper work. We want a free labor market, and we'll hire our own people." It's a fundamentally different attitude.

Interview, Washington/
U.S. News & World Report, 8-1:18.

Bert Lance
Director, Federal Office of
Management and Budget
3

The biggest perpetrator of inflationary pressure is the Federal government itself. [The] paperwork burden [and] government intervention into the private sector [are] the area[s] of greatest inflationary pressure *per se.* [Doing something in these areas is] one place where you can show the American people you mean business [in curbing inflation. But the long-term solution] lies in the area of capital investment, increased productivity and fiscal responsibility.

Before New York City Financial Writers
Association, March 31/The Washington Post,
4-1:(D)13.

R. Heath Larry
Vice chairman, United States Steel
Corporation; Chairman, National
Association of Manufacturers
4

What we should really be celebrating is the continued existence of three very basic and fundamental conditions. The first is the fact that in this 201st year of our Republic, most employees still have available to them a process by which they can vote freely to accept or to reject union representation. The second is that if union representation is voted, the union will not be a fiction, as would be the case in most socialist countries; not a creature of government — but an organization which stands free and independent, representing the interests of its members as best it knows. And the third is that when such a union sits down to bargain, the business organization with which it bargains will not be government wearing business clothing — will not be state-owned — but rather will be privately owned and required to earn its way in what is still primarily a market economy . . . Each of us — whether in union or in management — has a great stake in continuing that state of affairs.

Before National Labor Relations Board,
Washington/The Wall Street Journal, 6-24:12.

Ernest A. Lee
Director of international affairs,
American Federation of Labor-Congress
of Industrial Organizations
5

[Supporting the U.S. decision to pull out of the ILO because of that organization's increasing politization] : Now the world knows that this country does not make idle threats. The countries that want us back are going to have to make a decision now on making the rules changes needed to depoliticize the ILO. And the Soviet Union, the Arabs and the countries in the so-called Group of 77 are going to have to make a decision on whether they want to be left in sole possession of a worthless organization.

The New York Times, 11-3:(A)10.

Wassily Leontief
Professor of economics,
Harvard University
1

One reason why economists are in such disrepute is that they have pretended to understand inflation and to know how to control it, when obviously we do not.

The New York Times, 1-30:(12)3.

Sar Levitan
Director, Center for Social Policy
Studies, George Washington University
2

Public-service employment is not necessarily a bad idea. In the best of times, you will have people who can't get jobs – people who are what we call "structurally unemployed" because of certain social and educational impediments. One theory is that many of these people – many of whom are on welfare – want to work, could work and should work.

The Dallas Times Herald, 12-28:(A)21.

Russell B. Long
United States Senator, D–Louisiana
3

I would like to make the public understand something that is not apparent to everybody. We want people to contribute to charity, so we allow a [tax] deduction for charitable giving. We want manufacturers to buy new equipment, start new plants and put more people to work, so we give them tax credits and deductions for doing these things. We want those who can to give money toward education. All these things are beneficial to society. Is it not fair, then, to give a tax advantage to those who contribute in this fashion over those who don't? There must be incentives in the system if we are to continue to enjoy such contributions.

Interview/Nation's Business, August:24.

Jose Lopez (Portillo)
President of Mexico
4

[On the illegal immigration to the U.S. of Mexican nationals]: Our workers are being portrayed as criminals, and as though they are replacing North American workers. The fact is that they contribute in their own humble way to the strength of the U.S. economy ... They

pick many of your crops and do other jobs that your citizens just won't do because they are hard or pay poorly. Many Mexican women, for example, work as domestics. The problem of these workers is like the problem of drugs. As long as there is a demand in the United States, they will come – from one country or another. That is a simple law of economics. Before judging the Mexican who is looking for work, remember that their humble work has helped the U.S. economy grow, and that this work force should be protected because they are human beings with human rights. They are not criminals, but honest people who want to work.

Interview, Tijuana, Mexico/
Los Angeles Times, 4-25:(1)22.

F. Ray Marshall
Secretary of Labor of the United States
5

I think it is important to know that the composition of unemployment is different than it was, but I don't know how you can argue that joblessness of people who want to work is not a problem ... I don't take any comfort at all that the unemployed are mainly women and mainly teen-agers. If teen-agers and women want to work [but can't find work], that is a problem ... for the whole society because we lose the output of their effort and, somehow, they are being supported by other resources ... Another thing: If you look at the impact, the aggregate impact, of unemployment on other social indicators, you get the same kind of results you always got. That is, as unemployment goes up, divorce rates go up; as unemployment goes up, crime goes up; as unemployment goes up, even infant mortality rates go up and incarceration in prison. Suicides in middle-aged men tend to go up. I don't think that is entirely accidental or a random correlation ... So to argue it might be a "new" unemployment, it sure shows up in the same old way and has the same old impact when you look at it in aggregate.

Interview, Washington/The
New York Times, 2-6:(3)7.

6

I am not in favor of wage and price controls. It seems to me they haven't worked anywhere

WHAT THEY SAID IN 1977

(F. RAY MARSHALL)

in the world. The main problem, besides the problem of implementation, is that they work against the grain of the economy — you hope to restrict the money supply more than output. I favor the opposite approach. That is, you increase productivity and efficiency more than the money supply. That is an approach that works with the grain of the economy rather than against it and it does help overcome inflation. It is hard to do, but it is better.

Interview, Washington/The
New York times, 2-6:(3)7.

1

[On illegal aliens entering the U.S. to find jobs]: [There is] a serious question of identification, and I agree with the civil libertarians and others who do not want a national identification card with everyone's picture on it so that people could be stopped and checked on the streets. But if they can make a card that gives me money at the bank at night when nobody is there, and I can buy goods in the store with the card which only needs a phone call to check my card number, then I think we can make a non-counterfeitable Social Security card for workers to use when they are getting jobs. [The U.S.] also needs to make it possible for more foreign workers to acquire full legal rights as workers and residents in this country. A meaningful penalty against illegal aliens might be that after we make legal entry itself a viable right by increasing the numbers admitted to this country, workers who come in illegally could be permanently denied that right of legal entry.

Interview, Miami, Feb. 21/
The Dallas Times Herald, 2-22:(A)10.

2

I'm close to collective bargaining philosophy. I think that most people in this society, and the overwhelming majority of the business community, will accept that philosophy. Some interpret that as being close to unions. But I don't think that collective bargaining is necessarily a thing for the unions. It's a thing for society. I don't really think you can have a

democratic society without a labor movement and collective bargaining.

Interview/The Washington Post, 3-6:(G)1.

3

If there had been enough jobs on the farms during the first half of this century, millions of Americans would not have migrated to the cities looking for work. If we can do something to moderate rural problems, it will help urban problems. We have displaced millions of people from farms in our history with no preparation for urban dwelling. From 1950 to 1970, 2.7 million were displaced from farming. Eighty per cent of the black males leaving farms had less than eight years of education, 52 per cent of them had less than four years education. When a black man with less than four years of [education] in a rural Alabama school enters an urban work force, that's a labor problem.

Before National Farmers Union,
San Antonio, Tex., March 6/
The Dallas Times Herald, 3-7:(A)11.

4

[Supporting President Carter's $50 tax-rebate plan]: There is a real and persistent danger that our concern about inflation will paralyze our ability to again achieve sustained economic growth. There is a danger that every new method of stimulating a lagging economy will be ambushed by cries of "inflation is coming, inflation is coming" . . . We should not underestimate the effects on consumer confidence if they are deprived of the tax rebates they have come to anticipate . . . Our economy needs stimulus now, as well as late this year and next year. I worry about the economic outlook for the next year if we don't prevail.

At Wayne State University, April 12/
The Washington Post, 4-13:(A)4.

5

[On illegal aliens seeking U.S. jobs]: Ultimately, the only total solution to the problem of undocumented workers is the creation of jobs in the countries from which these workers flee. There is, of course, a very real limit on how much we can do by ourselves, and we cannot wait for these other countries to solve

(F. RAY MARSHALL)

their problems before we tackle ours. But I think that it is important to target some of the money which we spend on bilateral and multilateral foreign aid on the real problem of creating jobs in the source countries of the stream of undocumented workers. A second consideration is a recognition that it is important to eliminate the incentives for undocumented workers to enter this country. That means a focus on the employers who hire these workers and subject them to substandard pay and working conditions. Ultimately, illegal immigration must be seen as a labor market problem. And the only way to alleviate it is to develop some system of civil penalties for those employers who hire undocumented workers. Coupled with this must be a system that will allow the employers to determine who is an undocumented worker. If an employer can claim ignorance of the resident status of his workers, then no system of penalties will have a significant deterrent effect.

At American Immigration and Citizenship Conference, New York, May 13/Vital Speeches, 7-1:552.

1

[On OSHA safety and health regulations at workplaces]: There will be no more petty regulations like those dealing with coat hooks in bathrooms ... We're going to stop the absurd practice of printing 15 pages of regulations, in small type, on the safety of ladders ... The worst thing about wasting time and money on nitpicking regulations is that you shortchange the fight against the most serious dangers to human life and limb in high-risk workplaces.

Washington, May 19/Los Angeles Times, 5-20:(1)4.

2

... unemployment is inflationary. If you get money and are not producing, that's a lot more inflationary than getting money for producing.

Parade, 6-5:11.

3

[On the government as "employer of last resort"]: You might say we're moving toward

that day. We have not gotten there yet. Our belief is that jobs are better alternatives for unemployed people than anything else you can think of. We think the best solution to unemployment is to get the unemployed into permanent private jobs, but it is better to have public-service jobs than to have people who can work unemployed, on welfare or drawing unemployment compensation.

*Interview, Washington/
U.S. News & World Report, 6-6:56.*

4

The purposes of the ILO are very good, but the ILO hasn't been able to carry out those purposes as effectively as it should because of the violations of due process and the allowing of political matters to get mixed in with technical assistance and economic considerations.

Interview/Nation's Business, October:30.

John B. Martin
*Legislative counsel to American
Association of Retired Persons*

5

We're not arguing against early retirement. We say an employee ought to have some options. If he wants to retire early — fine. If he wants to continue working — fine. What we're dealing with essentially is the concept of freedom of choice.

The New York Times Magazine, 2-6:38.

Paul W. McCracken
*Professor of business
administration, University of
Michigan; Former Chairman,
Council of Economic Advisers to
the President of the United States
(Richard M. Nixon)*

6

I wouldn't suggest any special government public-service-type [employment] programs because I don't think they would be very successful. They tend to provide dead-end jobs. They tend to be politically popular, of course, because the people on the payroll are directly beholden to government. Politicians like to have workers know where their next paycheck comes from.

Interview/U.S. News & World Report, 2-21:56.

WHAT THEY SAID IN 1977

George Meany
President, American Federation of
Labor-Congress of Industrial Organizations

1

The nation must have an end to the mess brought about by eight years of economic mismanagement [in Washington] and the policy of creating high unemployment in order to fight inflation. The AFL-CIO firmly believes any economic stimulus program must be keyed to the nation's need for jobs, must be a large enough commitment to restore hope to the unemployed, and a sense of security to those still on the job but fearful that unemployment will once again grow and their jobs become endangered.

Before House Public Works Committee, Washington,
Feb. 1/The Dallas Times Herald, 2-1:(A)4.

2

[Criticizing the Carter Administration's idea of giving them advance notice of important wage and price increases] : If you are compelled to give the government advance notice about contract settlements and [also] give them some responsibility for a settlement, then how could you make a last-minute settlement at midnight on the day the contract expires? Actually, this is just a foot in the door. First, voluntary notification. Then the next thing is voluntary guidelines ... [then] government-imposed guidelines, and the first thing you know, wage and price controls, which do not work.

Miami Beach, Fla., Feb. 21/
Los Angeles Times, 2-22:(1)6.

3

Fifty years ago wages were very low and we were mainly battling for the right to maintain a union. We've come a long way. Collective bargaining has become quite complicated, with agreements involving 150 or 200 issues. We have people who are just as knowledgeable about business as the business people themselves. Unions are better equipped, more effective. Of course, the general attitude about striking has changed. In the old days, if you recommended that the workers go out on strike, their only loss was 50 or 60 cents an hour. But now, with workers making $15,000 a year or higher, owning a home and two cars,

and sending children to college, the penalty on the worker for striking is much higher. We used to have unions that were called strike-happy. That is no longer true. The unions are just as anxious to keep their people working as the employer is to keep his business going.

Interview/The New York Times Magazine, 9-4:42.

4

The organizations formed by wealthy white businessmen in the South to oppose civil rights in the '60s are now deep into a campaign of anti-unionism in that region. The same is true for the women's movement. Scratch an opponent of the Equal Rights Amendment, and you will find an advocate of the so-called right-to-work laws, which are clearly anti-union.

Labor Day broadcast address, Sept. 5/
Los Angeles Herald-Examiner, 9-5:(A)2.

5

Conservatives and some business leaders who kid themselves into believing they can use the extreme right wing to weaken and eventually destroy organized labor are playing a dangerous game. They would do well to remember — as we in labor remember all too well — what happened to the German industrialists who financed Hitler's Nazi movement because it was pledged to destroy the unions. After turning free unions into a huge, national compulsory company union — called a Labor Front — Hitler pounced on his industrial supporters, incorporated their plants into his totalitarian system, and reduced the former managers to mere office boys.

Labor Day broadcast address, Sept. 5/
The Washington Post, 9-6:(A)3.

6

If you remember last year's [U.S. Presidential] campaign, the Number 1 issue was jobs. My quarrel with the President [Carter] — and the quarrel of the black groups and the poor — is that he raised the expectations of these people, and they are disappointed. They have reasons to be disappointed. I don't remember that he made a great issue last year of balancing the budget, but now this seems to be the big thing.

Interview/U.S. News & World Report, 9-12:85.

Robert H. Michel
United States Representative, R—Illinois

1

Insofar as helping friends and punishing enemies is concerned, labor unions make the business community look like a bunch of kindergartners. You don't see organized labor running three ways from Sunday when one of their issues reaches Congress. Labor is organized, well-organized, untied and committed to one approach.

Before lobbyists for Chamber of Commerce of the U.S., National Association of Manufacturers and Business Roundtable, Washington, March 22/The Washington Post, 3-30:(A)2.

James A. Michener
Author

2

The legislation in Congress prohibiting forced retirement at 65 is part of a battle between old people and the productive young, and this is going to become serious. The older I get, the more convinced I am that people ought to retire from managerial positions younger than they generally do now. I think that legislation locking these positions away from young people is simply criminal. I'm at an age where you might expect me to say it's wrong to expect a man to retire. I'm almost 71, and I would think that intellectually I'm as sharp as I've ever been. My eyes aren't as good, and I tire more easily, but I could easily argue I'm entitled to sit on a Supreme Court bench or be a Senator or anything else. But I think that people ought to retire earlier. They can remain very useful, but not in the top managerial positions.

Interview/U.S. News & World Report. 9-12:60.

G. William Miller
Chairman, Textron, Inc.

3

[The private-enterprise system] has the virtue of being effective; it has produced the highest standard of living for the largest number of people. It is self-correcting; while no human endeavor can be perfect, the faults — of which there are and will be many — wither in the face of exposure and competition. Good ideas prevail; bad ideas can't survive in an open marketplace. The cumulative effect of millions of individual decisions is superior to the consequences of a few central decisions where a mistake can spell disaster. And of course, private enterprise is an inevitable link to our personal freedoms. Despite the shortcomings, despite the criticism and the cynicism, the evidence is clear that the American people believe in and are firmly committed to the private-enterprise system. Opinion research reveals two principal reasons for this abiding faith. One is pragmatic: The system works; it delivers. The other is emotional: Freedom in economic pursuits is essential to freedom in our personal lives.

Before Traffic Club of Pittsburgh, Jan. 27/Vital Speeches, 3-15:340.

George B. Morris, Jr.
Vice president,
General Motors Corporation

4

[Supporting a mandatory-retirement age]: There's one fundamental . . . aspect of having a fixed mandatory-retirement age, and that is the dignity of the individual . . . It's customary when people retire in General Motors to have a retirement party. There's reason for celebration. The man or woman has earned retirement, and they have a big, fun party . . . You're not saying poor old Joe no longer has the mental or physical power, so he's got to go. Everybody knows that [at GM], at age 68, people are going to be retired. There is no stigma attached to that, and we think that is an important psychological matter to maintain his or her own dignity.

Before House Select Committee on Aging, Washington/U.S. News & World Report, 10-3:31.

Thomas A. Murphy
Chairman, General Motors Corporation

5

A strong economy is not just our chief hope of achieving full employment in this country, it is our *only* hope. All of our public policies and efforts must be bent in that direction — to encourage the present economic recovery, to give business the incentive to invest the $100-billion a year that will probably be needed over the next decade to finance expansion, and to make necessary changes in our tax

165

WHAT THEY SAID IN 1977

policies to achieve these goals. Every time a business person calls for such action — for example, by suggesting that investment tax credits or depreciation allowances might be increased — he is invariably accused of promoting corporate interests over the public interest. This is the kind of polemical nonsense we can ill afford today. When it comes to economic growth and full employment, corporate interests are identical to the public interest — indeed, it would be a betrayal of the public interest to lead this country into another ordeal of accelerated inflation or business contraction.

Before Columbia Business School Club of New York, Feb. 9/Vital Speeches, 3-15:332.

Arthur M. Okun
Senior fellow, Brookings Institution;
Former Chairman, Council of Economic Advisers to the President of the United States (Lyndon B. Johnson)

There are enormous opportunities for reducing inflation through fairly informal government programs. A lot of our present inflation is a matter of wages chasing prices and other wages, and of prices in turn chasing costs. Past history is setting the guidelines, and they are bad guidelines, that keep inflation churning. There is no way for the individual union or company to get off that treadmill, so the situation calls out for collective action, like a gun-toting Western frontier town where everybody wants to put down his gun but nobody can afford to do so unless there's a general agreement to disarm. Meanwhile, people are getting hurt by "guns" that are being carried in self-defense, so to speak.

Interview/U.S. News & World Report, 1-24:51.

2

... the problems of those who are chronically at the back of the hiring line cannot be solved while the front of the line is swollen with experienced and skilled breadwinners on layoff. Some well-intentioned proposals to pinpoint remedies for unemployment are basically misconceived; they are like an effort to deal with a soft tire by pumping up merely the

bottom. A general infusion of pressure — or purchasing power — is the way to get the tire back in shape.

Before Senate Budget Committee, Washington, March 16/The Washington Post, 3-17:(C)1.

3

Just because my first name is Arthur, I smoke a pipe, graduated from Columbia, am from New Jersey, and am Jewish, some members of the press are convinced I should be the next Chairman of the Federal Reserve Board [replacing Arthur F. Burns]. Not me.

At National Housing Center, Washington, Nov. 17/The Washington Post, 11-18:(F)5.

Claude Pepper
United States Representative, D–Florida

4

Each day of the year, more than 4,000 Americans reach the age of 65. There is no evidence that on that day their ability to function productively in the economy vanishes. There is, in fact, ample evidence to support Shaw's observation that "some are younger at 70 than most at 17." Who would tell [anthropologist] Margaret Mead, who is 75, that her contributions to the study of sociology ended at age 65? Who would tell [conductors] Arthur Fiedler, who is 83, or Leopold Stokowski, who is 94, that those over 65 cannot contribute meaningfully to our appreciation of music? To waste the talents of the older worker is as shameful as it is to waste natural resources. Why then does mandatory retirement exist? In part, because Social Security arbitrarily set a certain age for receipt of benefits. In part, because Congress refused to protect workers over 65 in the Age Discrimination in Employment Act. And in part because we have not rid ourselves of the stereotype of the enfeebled older worker. In fact, older workers perform as well and often better than younger workers in jobs requiring experience. Mandatory retirement creates a host of additional problems. There is evidence that forced retirement accelerates the aging process, brings on physical and emotional problems, causes economic deprivation and strains an already overburdened Social Security System. Age-based mandatory retirement is discriminatory, unjust, unnecessary and

(CLAUDE PEPPER)

a waste of human talent. Depriving the person who is able and willing to continue to work of the right to work because by some arbitrary standard that person is old, is a cruel act.

Before National Council of Senior Citizens, Washington, June 6/Vital Speeches, 8-15:651.

Arthur C. Prine, Jr.
Vice president for relations services, R. R. Donnelley & Sons
1

[Supporting the mandatory-retirement age for workers in government and industry] : The concept of retirement at 65 is something of more than 40 years' standing. By now, it's deeply ingrained in our economic system. Government, employers and unions have built up a tremendous body of law, policy and practice keyed to retirement at 65. The concept reaches into Social Security, into the design of thousands of retirement plans, into funding concepts of individual plans. I simply don't think it makes sense suddenly to tear up this fundamental basis on which all these laws and benefits are based ... As soon as you say [people should have the right to stay on a job], "as long as they do it well," you raise a very big question. Today, with mandatory retirement, we don't have to discriminate among workers, telling one employee that he can continue to work while telling his co-worker that he must go. Everybody retires at the same age with dignity, with pride and with the sense that his many years of service are truly appreciated.

Interview/U.S. News & World Report, 8-22:37.

Charles B. Reeder
Chief economist, E. I. du Pont de Nemours & Company
2

[On President Carter's proposal for moderation and monitoring of wage and price increases] : The objectives may be stated in broad general terms, but in practice any program of more-active monitoring of wage and price increases will narrow down to just the pricing actions of large corporations. Price increases by small companies, no matter how much they might contribute to inflation collec-

tively, would not be deemed important enough individually to be monitored by the Council on Wage and Price Stability. On the wage side, major settlements are the end product of the collective-bargaining process, and there is no way that prior notice of the results could be given to the Council. Such a program is not needed today in view of the declining rate of inflation and, furthermore, it fails to recognize the role of the marketplace in setting prices or the true cause of inflation in this or any other country, namely, large Federal deficits financed by an excessive rise in the money supply.

The New York Times, 2-6:(3)17.

Henry S. Reuss
United States Representative, D–Wisconsin
3

At present, there is no national employment-placement system worthy of the name. The U.S. Employment Service, by operating mainly on a state-by-state basis rather than as a national service, does little to encourage inter-regional labor mobility. In any case, it functions more as a job-listing than as a job-matching service. Development of an effective national computerized service, matching job openings with the skills and interests of available and interested workers, ought not to be beyond our technological and administrative capabilities. Beyond this, the Federal government can assist by providing personalized retraining programs keyed to available jobs. It can also make available relocation aid, a device which many European countries have used with great success. An obvious starting point would be to provide a direct grant for moving expenses. The Federal government has properly focused a great deal of attention and effort on the relocation of Cuban and Vietnamese refugees. It should do as much for our own citizens.

Before Cleveland City Club, March 4/ Vital Speeches, 4-15:403.

4

What this country needs is a massive attack on unemployment, not a massive tax cut ... Direct job-making programs enable us to make jobs at a much reduced cost, and a much reduced deficit, over the trickle-down methods of a tax cut ... A direct job-making drive,

WHAT THEY SAID IN 1977

(HENRY S. REUSS)

costing around $10-billion, would provide five times as many jobs as a $20-billion general tax cut. We Democrats don't want to fight business; we want to ask business to help ... Clear and decisive action on the job front, accompanied by the announcement that there will be no major tax legislation in this Congress, will bolster business confidence and stimulate investment.

Before National Democratic Forum on Urban Policy, New York, Nov. 17/The Dallas Times Herald, 11-18:(A)19.

W. F. Rockwell, Jr.
Chairman, Rockwell International 1

What's missing in this country right now is a public appreciation and awareness of how the free-enterprise system coordinates individual plans — and the vital role played by the business community in the system's operation. In a market economy, the decisions and plans for the millions of entrepreneurs, firms, businesses, partnerships, corporations and individuals are coordinated by the prices ... and profit and loss systems. Thousands of different plans are formulated — some succeed and some fail ... They all require hundreds of thousands of hours of long-range planning — taking into account the countless details of running complex business operations in the teeth of strong competition and the constraining policies of the Federal government. ... society does not "put all its eggs in one basket." If a private plan fails, it brings losses only to the few responsible. In central planning, a mistake can drag down one whole section of the economy. We've seen this many times over in Communist and socialist economies. The market system is the most flexible and responsive system ever developed by man. And it's automatic. It does not require Congressional action. It works without fuss or fanfare every day. This is its great strength ... Unfortunately, not enough people understand the operation of the market system. Perhaps because it's such an automatic process that the average citizen, not to mention the average politician, is virtually unaware of it. Thus, the public is all too eager to listen to the siren song

of the central planners. Of course, the market system is not perfect when measured against a simplistic textbook model of perfect competition. Nothing can ever be perfect. But the market system is the best system ever devised for running an economy.

Before Tax Foundation, Denver, June 21/**

Paul A. Samuelson
Professor of economics,
Massachusetts Institute of Technology 2

"Inflation paranoia" is the modern disease. Its symptoms are an unreasoned and uninformed dread that any quickening of the pace of output growth will catapult the system back into accelerating double-digit price inflation, a temporary prelude to banana-republic hyperinflation. By contrast, careful sifting of the record suggests that for the next couple of years we can achieve real growth of about 6 per cent a year without inducing a difference in where the price level will be in 1980 of more than 1 or 2 per cent.

Interview/The New York Times, 1-9:(3)14.

3

The Federal Reserve must either be made responsible to the Executive itself or must be on a short string in its responsibility to the Congress. Not only must Congress review its operations, interrogate its officials, but in addition, at intervals of less than a year, Congress must lay down for the Federal Reserve Board the compromises and trade-offs between overall economic expansion and contraction that, willy-nilly, are involved in monetary policy.

Before House Banking Committee, Washington, Feb. 4/The Christian Science Monitor, 2-23:13.

Harland Sanders
Founder, Kentucky Fried
Chicken Corporation 4

[Arguing against mandatory retirement regulations in business and government]: I'm dead against it. I believe a man will rust out quicker than he'll wear out. Sitting in a rocker has never

(HARLAND SANDERS)

appealed to me. And golf or fishing isn't as much fun as working.

Before House Select Committee on
Aging, Washington, May 25/
Los Angeles Herald-Examiner, 5-26:(A)6.

Charles L. Schultze
*Chairman-designate, Council of
Economic Advisers to President-elect
of the United States Jimmy Carter*

1

There are any number of social costs of unemployment. There is the immediate problem of loss of income, the obvious one. Secondly, we live in a society where not only your income, but your dignity and your status and your feeling of being a full American citizen comes from what you do at work. If we can't provide jobs for people, then we are failing not just economically but as a social society. Thirdly, if you look at the problems of central cities, of crime, of delinquency, of racial discrimination, while there are any number of things which have to be done to work at those problems, I would say perhaps the most important thing is having an economy which provides jobs as much as you can, job opportunities for everybody, because without that the really difficult social problems just can't be licked in a society in which ... status, dignity, place, income come from work. And I think it is just socially disastrous to continue year after year after year at eight per cent [unemployment] ... as a means of licking inflation when it doesn't even lick inflation.

*TV-radio interview, Washington/"Meet
the Press," National Broadcasting Company, 1-16.*

Charles L. Schultze
*Chairman, Council of Economic
Advisers to President of the
United States Jimmy Carter*

2

The biggest single thing we need is a significant pickup in investment by business in plant and equipment. The Administration is trying to make that possible mainly by following an economic policy that will allow for a steady, sustained — but not inflationary — growth in

consumer and other markets. That is a central point of our economic-stimulus package. There are some other things we need to do. The last four years have increased the climate of uncertainty. We've had the worst recession in 40 years, and that raises a question of whether government is capable of developing a policy that will produce sustained and balanced growth. Businessmen are bound to be more uncertain than they were 10 years ago. We also went through a period of double-digit inflation, and inflation is still going at 5 to 6 per cent a year. That undoubtedly creates uncertainty about where prices and costs are going to be in the future. We think that one result of our strategy will be to reduce that uncertainty.

*Interview, Washington/
U.S. News & World Report, 2-28:23.*

3

We are a nation of 215 million people. Four to five million independent business firms. A long time ago we made a decision that we gain a lot more from at least a large sector of the economy left to individual decisions rather than have the government regulate everything. With direct government control of everything, you probably could avoid the fluctuations in employment that we get, and possibly even in prices. [But] what you would find in such a system is all the kinds of things you don't want, including a very poor economic performance. It is just not possible in a democratic society for the government to deploy its economic tools so that it can predetermine to a decimal point everything that occurs.

*Interview, Washington/
Los Angeles Herald-Examiner, 9-9:(A)11.*

4

The current economic recovery has been typical in many respects. The growth of real gross national product and industrial production in the past two-and-a-half years has been virtually the same as the average for other postwar recoveries. So has the decline in unemployment. But this recovery started from a much deeper recession than any of its predecessors. The unemployment rate hit a peak of 9.0 per cent in early 1975; the highest previous

WHAT THEY SAID IN 1977

(CHARLES L. SCHULTZE)

cyclical peak in the unemployment rate during the postwar period was 7.9 per cent and the average postwar recession produced a 6.9 per cent unemployment peak. And so, while the recovery has been of average magnitude, we are further from the restoration of full prosperity than at the same stage in earlier recoveries. This is one reason why the present recovery is likely to continue for some time. Ample resources are available to permit further expansion, and the recovery shows few if any signs of economic aging.

Before Economic Club of Detroit,
Oct. 4/Vital Speeches, 11-15:66.

Irving S. Shapiro
Chairman, E. I. du Pont
de Nemours & Company 1

Too often in recent years, people — particularly people in government — have pointed at labor and management and blamed the wage-price spiral as the root of inflation. That spiral is an effect of inflation, not a cause. The cause is rooted in government deficits and in the fact that the money supply has risen faster than real economic activity. Too much money chasing too few goods is the fundamental cause of inflation. It is strange that a nation that has concerned itself so deeply with the management of demand — stimulating or restraining consumption according to the needs of the moment — has assumed that adequate supplies, and adequate capital investment to meet future needs, will somehow take care of themselves. Other nations behave far differently, and Germany is the classic example. Bitter experience with inflation has created a national ethic in Germany — one that is equally needed in the United States — that permits no government to remain in power if it pursues consistently inflationary policies. That explains, I think, why close to 20 per cent of the German GNP goes into fixed business investment — twice the American rate.

At Southern Governors Conference, San Antonio,
Tex., Aug. 28/Vital Speeches, 10-1:739.

Jayne Spain
Senior vice president, public
affairs, Gulf Oil Corporation 2

There is nothing wrong with private enterprise. Many people simply don't know enough about it to appreciate it. We should stop teaching so much about what may be wrong with capitalism and teach more about what is wrong with socialism. Private enterprise has given us the highest standard of living in the world, but many Americans don't seem ready enough to acknowledge this ... Private enterprise may be facing a fight for its very life. The movement toward socialism began as a walk, then trotted, and now gallops. This is true in many parts of the world. We need more pro-private-enterprise people in Washington. They and others should explain such basics as this: When private enterprise exists and socialism enters, then workers ultimately lose the right to work where they want to work, live where they want to live, and get the kind of education they want. People don't understand that, under socialism, government takes away rights of individuals because government must have controls to maintain itself.

Interview, Pittsburgh/
Nation's Business, March : 71.

Edgar B. Speer
Chairman, United States
Steel Corporation 3

You know, you can do all the training you want to do, but if you don't have a job after you have a man trained, it isn't very productive. And until we can get expansion moving, industrial expansion moving, in this country, where we are creating jobs to take the trained people and bring them into the mainstream, we really haven't accomplished very much.

TV-radio interview/"Issues and Answers,"
American Broadcasting Company, 9-4.

Robert R. Statham
Director, tax and finance section,
Chamber of Commerce
of the United States 4

The American economy is faced with a major need for capital which we cannot con-

(ROBERT R. STATHAM)

tinue to ignore. It is important that our tax policy be remolded to encourage capital formation. We must apply those principles in our taxing system that promote the modernization and expansion of our productive facilities. The other highly industrialized nations understand these principles and are applying them. If we are to continue to improve our standard of living, reduce unemployment and solve our inflation problem, we must adjust our tax policy to favor capital formation.

Before Senate Finance subcommittee,
Washington/Nation's Business, September:46.

Herbert Stein
Professor of economics, University of
Virginia; Former Chairman, Council of
Economic Advisers to the President of
the United States (Richard M. Nixon)
1

The fundamental reason [that prices are going up so fast] is that we've had so much inflation for the past 10 years that we've built up the expectation that we will have more. We have a lot of wage agreements that are based on that expectation. And businesses don't cut prices when demand is slack, because they think the inflationary process will resume and they don't want to raise prices back up. Then, too, when inflation is going at 6 per cent a year, the Federal Reserve is faced with this terrible dilemma of whether it should try to squeeze the rate down — recognizing that this effort will restrain the growth of the economy for a while — or provide enough money to cover the inflation. There's political resistance to any steps that are taken to restrain economic growth, and to high interest rates.

Interview, Washington/
U.S. News & World Report, 8-22:20.

Clyde W. Summers
Professor of law,
University of Pennsylvania
2

[Labor-] union conventions are highly structured and controlled operations — six times as controlled as a political-party convention. You never have an opportunity to really express what you think about incumbent officers and union policies.

U.S. News & World Report, 2-21:69.

Lester C. Thurow
Professor of economics, Massachusetts
Institute of Technology
3

[Advocating an end to preferential tax treatment of capital gains]: Our tax system, by and large, is based on horizontal equity, where people who make the same income pay the same taxes. Since income from capital gains is eminently spendable — you can buy yachts, houses and lots of other things with it — it should be taxed just the same as an equal amount of income from wages and salaries ... The privilege accorded to long-term capital gains tend to attract investment into physical assets, as opposed to human capital. While no one is against investment in physical assets, we also need to invest more heavily in skills, education and the other things that build earning capacity for the future. There's no reason why the government should subsidize one form of capital investment over the other.

Interview/U.S. News & World Report, 12-19:71.

Pierre Elliott Trudeau
Prime Minister of Canada
4

Inflation has not found its Keynes. I personally think the Keynes of inflation will not be an economist. He is more apt to be a political, philosophical or moral leader inspiring people to do without the excess consumption so prominent in the developed countries.

Interview, Paris/Los Angeles Times, 5-19:(2)7.

Rexford G. Tugwell
Economist; Senior fellow,
Center for the Study of
Democratic Institutions
5

[Comparing President Carter's national economic problems with those of the late President Franklin Roosevelt]: Both succeeded Republicans who had allowed the economy to stagnate and unemployment to become a serious problem ... Carter's problem at first seems easier by comparison. The economy is operating at less than capacity, but it is not paralyzed. Unem-

WHAT THEY SAID IN 1977

(REXFORD G. TUGWELL)

ployment is 8 per cent, not 25 per cent. People are not starving or homeless. Farmers have learned how to regulate their production, and the banking system is sound. Prices are too high, not too low. Yet, in a way, Carter's problems are worse. The economy actually has been running down for some 15 years, becoming less and less productive, and the over-spending by government has created frightening deficits . . . If Roosevelt had a present disaster to overcome, Carter has a prospective one to avert. It may be harder because it lies in the future and inclinations are to meet only problems that are immediate and cannot be avoided. But if national productivity fails much longer to meet people's demands, Carter in a few years will be blamed for not seeing what was coming and showing the way to a new New Deal.

Interview, Santa Barbara, Calif./
Los Angeles Times, 4-17:(2)1.

Margaret Bush Wilson
Chairman, National Association for
the Advancement of Colored People　　　*1*

We believe people want to work. We want no workfare, welfare, foodstampfare, nor any other kind of fare. A government willing to finance welfare, unemployment insurance, poverty programs and other ideas should be willing to develop a realistic program to achieve full employment.

At NAACP convention, St. Louis/
The Christian Science Monitor, 6-29:6.

Pete Wilson
Mayor of San Diego　　　*2*

[On public-employee unions]: The public mood has changed dramatically on this issue. People are resentful of what they perceive as over-reaching by overly militant public-employee-union leaders. The question of taxes is important here, but there is another issue, too: Who will make these budget decisions — the elected representatives or the labor leaders?

The National Observer, 6-13:5.

William W. Winpisinger
President-elect, International
Association of Machinists　　　*3*

I think we in the labor movement have to quit trying to be so pragmatic all the time, and decide there are a few principles around that we stand for. Sometimes, we [the AFL-CIO] give lip service to principles, such as our stand in favor of national health insurance, which we've been pushing, for Christ's sake, since 1948 in Truman's Administration. But we're not really out there on the firing line on a consistent basis. We have to give leadership to the liberal causes we believe in.

Interview/Los Angeles Times, 5-19:(1)27.

William W. Winpisinger
President, International
Association of Machinists　　　*4*

Our members believe that [AFL-CIO president George] Meany should pack it in, and I agree. In recent years, he's given labor the public image of aging, out-of-touch leadership, and of being a selfish special interest. When you accumulate the power he has, you can intimidate a hell of a lot of people. We need a fresh start, with everyone on the starting line together, a team effort . . . I would like to see the Federation reclaim the mantle of representing the underdog and all workers. That would rekindle the spirit, and organizing opportunities would open up and people would involve themselves in the struggle. The presidency of the AFL-CIO provides a unique platform from which the spirit of the movement can be detected and portrayed. Meany hasn't used it that way.

The New York Times Magazine, 9-4:10.

W. Willard Wirtz
Chairman, National Manpower
Institute; Former Secretary of
Labor of the United States　　　*5*

. . . there are elements in the jobless picture that haven't been given enough attention — most particularly youth unemployment. That makes up somewhere between one third and one half of all the current unemployment, and almost none of the things that are being talked

172

(W. WILLARD WIRTZ)

about so far — such as a tax cut or a public-works program — would have any direct effect on putting those young people to work. Several things contribute to the problem: The young person coming into the labor market finds competition from experienced people who are out of work. The big increase in the number of women seeking jobs is a factor. So is technological change. I don't see that we've planned anything effective up to now to deal with youth unemployment.

Interview/U.S. News & World Report, 2-21:57.

Walter B. Wriston
Chairman, Citicorp
(Citibank), New York

1

There is no power on earth like the power of the free marketplace. And governments hate it, because they cannot control it.

Interview, New York/The New York Times, 3-6:(3)5.

2

There is no mystery about the definition of capital. Every economist, from Adam Smith to Karl Marx, has agreed that capital is nothing but stored-up labor, either your own or someone else's. Somebody has to work hard enough to earn a wage and then exhibit enough self-denial to save some of what he earned. There is no other way to create it. To use Marx's phrase, "As values, all commodities are only definite masses of congealed labor time." Whether the commodity is money or goods, whether it belongs to a capitalist or a Com-

munist, makes no difference. It is valuable because somebody's labor is stored up in it, and that is what you're paying for — or what you are borrowing. Or, if you're running a controlled economy, what you're trying to allocate. If you raise the price of a commodity, what you are really doing is trying to exchange the amount of labor stored in it for a larger amount of labor stored somewhere else. Neither Adam Smith nor Karl Marx would have any quarrel with that statement, but this basic fact gets lost when we fail to define terms.

At United Nations Ambassadors Dinner,
New York, May 24/Vital Speeches, 8-15:654.

Jerry Wurf
President, American Federation of State,
County and Municipal Employees

3

Organized labor's mistakes are catching up with it, and it is becoming a victim of new perceptions of its strengths and weaknesses. What happened is very simple. Organized labor displayed cynicism in staying neutral on [1972 Presidential nominee Senator] George McGovern, in its relationships with [the late] Mayor Daley in Chicago and [then-Governor Nelson] Rockefeller in New York. It displayed blindness on America's role in Vietnam. Suddenly labor made the discovery that it did not have the real clout it thought it had in Congress. Its ability to be effective electorally had lessened and so, therefore, did its influence on political leaders. The AFL-CIO treats the situs [picketing] defeat as a tactical error, but it was more — it was the voice of the United States government it helped elect.

The New York Times, 6-23:31.

Law • The Judiciary

Anthony G. Amsterdam
Professor of law, Stanford University
1

Law students can learn more from knowing how to ask good questions than from studying appellate briefs. To be able to make split-second decisions, they have to feel the law in their bones.

Time, 3-14:57.

F. Lee Bailey
Lawyer
2

It would be a service if lawyers advertise their specialties and their fees. Nothing wrong with that if done with taste.

San Francisco Examiner & Chronicle, 9-4:(B)5.

Robert Begam
*President, American
Trial Lawyers Association*
3

[On no-fault insurance laws]: I'd be less than candid if I said our [lawyers] self-interest was not involved when we lobby against these laws. No-fault is perceived by our members as an attack on the adversary system of justice. It is a threat that can take one essential freedom away.

The New York Times, 5-18:51.

Griffin B. Bell
*Attorney General-designate
of the United States*
4

People in Georgia are astounded to hear me described [now] as a conservative. I've never professed to be an activist. I've never professed to be an extreme liberal. I've always professed to be a moderate. I've always felt only moderates should be on the [judicial] bench.

*At hearing on his nomination before
Senate Judiciary Committee, Washington,
Jan. 11/Los Angeles Times, 1-12:(1)8.*

Griffin B. Bell
*Attorney General
of the United States*
5

[Addressing Justice Department employees]: Whatever your specific task may be, it is essential that all the Department's employees adhere to strict ethical standards. This means that no case – civil or criminal – is to be tried in the press. Specifically, I oppose leaks of information from pending grand-jury investigations. Not only does this violate the rule; often it denies due process ... I personally consider such legal and ethical strictures compelling. In order to tell another Cabinet official last week some information concerning a potential Presidential appointee in one department, I secured a court order permitting me to do so ... There is never any excuse for prejudicing the rights of parties to litigation. All of us in the Department should know better than anybody else that nothing so harms "justice" as the transgressions of those sworn to uphold the law. Every employee should re-read part 50:2 of Title 28 of the Code of Federal Regulations. It contains prohibitions against Department employees' saying or doing anything that might affect the outcome of a trial or prejudice a defendant's rights.

The Washington Post, 3-29:(A)14.

6

All of us have heard the term "crisis" used frequently in the past years with reference to the courts and the process of litigation. The "law explosion," with the attendant over-whelming trial and appellate caseloads, is a reality. Whatever the cause of the explosion – whether Supreme Court decision refurbishing the Constitution, the statutory expansion of jurisdiction or the natural flow from the technological revolution; the shift from a rural to an

(GRIFFIN B. BELL)

urban society or a manifestation of our litigious society, or a combination of some or all of these factors — it is here . . . The pressures from the law explosion are severe, and the courts may not be equal to the task. Important rights may be lost. Defendants charged with crime may go free on bail, some to commit other crimes. Defendants convicted of crime may be free on bail pending delayed appeals. Business controversies may go unresolved because of the lack of a forum. Hapless plaintiffs with meritorious claims may go unpaid because of delay in trial and appellate courts.

Before section of litigation,
American Bar Association, San Francisco/
The Washington Post, 11-30:(A)22.

Melvin Belli
Lawyer
1

[Applauding a recent court ruling permitting lawyers to advertise] : A hell of a good rule. It will allow lawyers to tell the public how good the law is. The law is good.

San Francisco Examiner & Chronicle, 9-4:(B)5.

Rose E. Bird
Chief Justice, Supreme
Court of California
2

The courts hold a unique position among our democratic institutions. In a sense, they represent one of our last bastions of participatory democracy, in which disputants go directly before a judge or a jury to resolve an issue. In no other governmental context does an individual have the opportunity to take a problem to a decision-maker who represents the full force and power of that particular branch of government. This direct interchange between the individual and the state is at the heart of the democratic process. As more barriers are raised between the litigant and the decision-maker, the participatory nature of the experience is diminished. We must protect this unique heritage and strive to preserve the values it represents.

Before California Women Lawyers, San Diego/
Los Angeles Times, 11-16:(2)11.

Warren E. Burger
Chief Justice of the United States
3

The administration of justice at every level has always rested to some extent upon competing philosophical attitudes concerning concepts of justice, individual liberty and the security of society; but the mechanisms of justice, the means to implement the ideals that we accept, are largely neutral concepts on which most can agree. It is heartening to see a growing realization in our profession that ideals and concepts alone are of relatively little use without the "wheels" to make delivery. We have, I think, reached the point where there is no significant acceptance of the notion that, in some strange way, efficient modern methods of administration are incompatible with the purity of concepts as to the objectives of justice. Whatever may have been the situation two centuries ago, or even a century ago, today's administration of justice is a highly complex and technical enterprise. What we must face up to is whether a process so intricate and complex can continue to be guided — if the term "guided" is the correct word — by haphazard, casual and uncoordinated approaches that have characterized the administration of justice most of our 200 years.

Before American Bar Association, Seattle,
Feb. 13/The National Observer, 2-26:13.

4

The harsh truth is that unless we devise substitutes for the courtroom processes, we may be on our way to a society overrun by hordes of lawyers hungry as locusts and brigades of judges in numbers never before contemplated . . . The role of law, in terms of formal litigation with the full panoply of time-consuming and expensive procedural niceties, can be overdone. The consumer with $300 in controversy for car repairs or a dispute on a defective roofing job or a malfunctioning home appliance prefers a reasonably satisfactory resolution to the protracted legal proceedings that are characteristic of courts. I suggest most people will prefer an effective, efficient tribunal of non-lawyers, or a mix of two non-lawyers and one lawyer, to the traditional court system to resolve his modest but irritating claim . . .

WHAT THEY SAID IN 1977

(WARREN E. BURGER)

The notion that ordinary people want black-robed judges, well-dressed lawyers and fine-paneled courtrooms as the setting to resolve their disputes is not correct. People with problems, like people with pains, want relief, and they want it as quickly and inexpensively as possible.

At American Bar Association conference,
New York, May 27/Los Angeles Times, 5-28:(1)1,4.

1

We've got to look at all of the things which are now being done in the courts and try to find out whether some of them can't be done better somewhere else. We think we are beginning to make some progress. There is movement. The first step is to get recognition among the American people that a court is not the only place or the best place to resolve disputes. No other countries draw on courts as much as we do. They have a wide range of other methods: arbitration, mediation, fact finding and, for small matters, neighborhood conciliation groups. In Europe, many disputes which would take years in our courts are disposed of briefly by other means. It can't be that the rest of the world is wrong and we are the only people who are right about this. England, from which our legal institutions sprung, has only a small fraction of the litigation per capita and only a fraction of the lawyers per 100,000 population that we do. And yet England has a highly organized, industrialized society like that in the United States.

Interview, Washington/
U.S. News & World Report, 12-19:21.

2

The [Supreme] Court's function is limited by the Constitution. It is the most limited of all three Branches, by far. It was so intended by the authors of the Constitution. My view is the traditional one: that in our system each of the three Branches of government — Executive, Legislative and Judicial — should try to keep within its own orbit. I have a strong feeling that

judges have this obligation to keep a constant focus on their proper function.

Interview, Washington/
U.S. News & World Report, 12-19:27.

Guido Calabresi
Professor of law, Yale University

3

I love teaching, and there is something particularly appealing about teaching a subject that seems to deal with the lowest kind of relationships — accidents, ambulance-chasing — because you can show students that these raise the most fundamental questions about the structure of society. And if somewhere, some time, something a law professor does hasn't a practical effect, he hasn't been a good law scholar or teacher.

Time, 3-14:57.

Jim R. Carrigan
Justice, Supreme Court of Colorado

4

[Criticizing U.S. Chief Justice Warren Burger for his emphasis on streamlining Federal courts]: I'm sick and tired of hearing about the number of cases disposed of when we discuss the judicial system. The Chief Justice should know that the job of the courts is not to dispose of cases but to decide them justly. Doesn't he know that the business of the courts is justice?

Before Association of Trial Lawyers, Washington,
Aug. 2/Los Angeles Herald-Examiner, 8-3:(A)5.

John B. Connally, Jr.
Former Secretary of the Treasury
of the United States; Former
Governor of Texas (D, now R)

5

Let's recommend the creation of citizens' courts in the judicial system, where people feel like they can go in on matters ranging up to $2,000 in value. They can go in and represent themselves; don't even let a lawyer in the courtroom. People are sick of lawyers; they are tired of their charges; they don't feel like they can afford them. Let's provide some vehicle through which people can get some objective hearing about their problems, whether it is with

(JOHN B. CONNALLY, JR.)

their neighbor or their friend down the street or somebody that they loaned $400 to.

TV-radio interview, Washington/"Meet the Press," National Broadcasting Company, 6-19.

Sandy DeMent
Executive director, National Resource Center for Consumers of Legal Services
1

(Saying that lawyers should be allowed to advertise their services): First of all, people would have a better idea of what constitutes a legal matter. Too many people swallow losses because they don't know that their problem is a legal problem, and don't know that a lawyer could help them. The second benefit would be in the area of fees. Fee information through advertising is critical because the fear of fees is one of the things that prevents people from going to see lawyers. The American Bar Foundation conducted a study recently which shows that people have a tendency to grossly overestimate the cost of simple legal services . . . We have no illusions that advertising is going to bring a sparkling new era in lawyer-client relationships. But while we expect advertising to bring some problems, on balance we think it will provide essential information to consumers . . . I believe that, within four or five years, an accommodation will be reached between consumers, the government and the bar, and a series of standards will be developed about what is and is not proper [in lawyer advertising] . . . I think if a secret poll were taken of lawyers, you would find a great deal more support for advertising than the bar-association positions would lead you to believe. I have talked to countless lawyers who say: "Privately I'm with you, but I'd be hung if I said that in an open meeting. My colleagues would have a fit."

Interview/U.S. News & World Report, 2-28:39,40.

Ronald Dworkin
Professor of jurisprudence, Oxford University, England
2

Positivism holds that there is never a single correct answer to novel, hard questions of law.

I disagree. An able judge may properly think he can find the right answer by considering written law — the Constitution, statutes and previous court decisions — plus all other considerations assumed in a society that has respect for other people's rights.

Interview, Martha's Vineyard, Mass./Time, 9-5:54.

John D. Ehrlichman
Former Assistant to the President of the United States, Richard M. Nixon, for Domestic Affairs
3

[On his conviction in the Watergate affair in relation to his having been a lawyer] : I have tried hundreds of lawsuits and many, many jury cases. And I am a — I guess you would say — a product of the system, the judicial system, our legal system. I spent 20 years practicing law. It is the first time I have ever been a litigant, or a party involved with a stake in the outcome of the case. So I've always had a kind of clinical view of lawsuits because as a lawyer you tend to be somewhat disassociated from the outcome. And if your client wins, that's good; if he loses, that's not good, but at the same time it doesn't really touch you quite the way it does when you're a party to it.

Recorded message to Watergate Judge John Sirica/The New York Times, 10-6:83.

Leroy Jeffers
Lawyer; Senior partner, Vinson & Elkins, Houston
4

[Arguing against lawyers being allowed to advertise their services] : . . . it is my personal opinion that the competent, ethical, most successful lawyers will not resort to advertising, because they will deem it unprofessional — and not only unprofessional but misleading and deceptive. You will have a situation where it's largely going to be pursued and practiced by the brazen and the incompetents who need the business . . . For many years, from the time of the end of the War Between the States up until 1908, we did have widespread lawyer advertising, and there was no prohibition against it. And it was abuses of lawyer advertising and the exploitation of the public, not only by lawyer advertising but by medical advertising, that led

WHAT THEY SAID IN 1977

in 1908, in the case of lawyers and a little later in the case of the medical profession, to the adoption of the canon prohibiting lawyer advertising and prohibiting medical advertising — not for the protection of the profession, not for the aggrandizement of the profession, but for the protection of the public. And that is still the reason for the prohibition.

Interview/U.S. News & World Report, 2-28:40.

Frank M. Johnson, Jr.
Judge, United States District Court
for the Northern District of Alabama
1

The Founding Fathers prudently and discerningly perceived that the survival of our republican form of government depended on the supremacy of the Constitution and that maintaining the supremacy of the Constitution depended, in turn, on a strong and independent judiciary, possessing the power and the authority to resolve disputes of a Constitutional nature between the states, between the states and the national government, and, most importantly, between individuals and governmental institutions. In granting to the Federal judiciary the power to decide cases arising under our Constitution and laws, the framers of the Constitution fully recognized that the exercise of such power would inevitably thrust the courts into the political arena. In fact, as the writings of the Founding Fathers illustrate, this grant of power was, in effect, a mandate to the Federal courts to check and to restrain any infringement by the Legislative and Executive Branches on the supremacy of the Constitution.

At University of Georgia School of Law/
The New York Times, 4-9:19.

Irving R. Kaufman
Chief Judge, United States Court of
Appeals for the Second Circuit
2

No other profession is subject to the public contempt and derision that sometimes befalls lawyers. This antagonism is the bitter fruit of public incomprehension of the law itself and its dynamics. The judge is forced for the most part to reach his audience through the medium of

the press — and I include television — whose reporting of judicial decisions is all too often inaccurate or superficial.

March/San Francisco Examiner & Chronicle,
4-17:(This World)39.

John F. Keenan
New York State special
anti-corruption prosecutor
3

... if we [lawyers] are unpopular, I suspect that it is because to a degree we talk in terms that sometimes are more complex than they have to be, and that we confuse ... The public sometimes sees an example of one corrupt judge or a few corrupt judges and then draws the unfair conclusion that all judges are corrupt because a few might be. I think that lawyers, like everybody else on the face of the earth, are human and we have our faults. If the public perception is indeed negative, I really don't think that's fair.

Interview/The New York Times, 4-10:(4)6.

Donald P. Kelly
President, Esmark Corporation
4

[Businessmen want lawyers'] best creative legal opinion. [Instead,] they often give business advice, which is as good as my legal opinion. We also don't appreciate their Messiah complex. They tell us "this is the law," when the truth and what they should be saying is, "this is our opinion of the law." The law is bewildering and complex to those of us without law degrees but, instead of giving clear and direct answers, the lawyers throw around buzz words and technical jargon that only they understand.

Before American Bar Association,
Chicago/San Francisco Examiner
& Chronicle, 8-14:(C)10.

David F. Linowes
Chairman, Federal Privacy
Protection Study Commission
5

The Department of Justice has always enjoyed ready access to tax-return files for civil or criminal cases. It's our judgment that for a democracy to allow any arm of government to have access in civil matters to what citizens believe to be confidential information is no

(DAVID F. LINOWES)

more than a fishing expedition. And there's no reason why the Department of Justice should not be compelled to obtain a subpoena. In criminal cases, we completely agree the Department of Justice should have ready and easy access. But when it comes to civil cases, there's no question in my mind that a subpoena should be required, because totalitarianism takes over when government decides to assert itself beyond what's reasonable in a democracy.

Interview, Washington/
U.S. News & World Report, 5-2:36.

Thurgood Marshall
Associate Justice, Supreme
Court of the United States
1

In a battle of moral authority, the allegiance of the people will lie with the courts, as long as the Judicial Branch acts responsibly under the law.

At Law of the World Conference, Manila,
Aug. 23/Los Angeles Times, 8-24:(1)13.

Stanley Mosk
Justice, Supreme Court of California
2

[U.S. Chief] Justice [Warren] Burger constantly says, "Don't expect the courts to solve your problems." But solutions to conflict by the judiciary is the best safety valve in a democracy. The encouraging thing is that disputes do get to court, and [are] not settled by force. As long as we can take the problem to the court, I suspect democracy will continue to work.

Interview/San Francisco Examiner
& Chronicle, 11-13:(A)11.

Theodore R. Newman, Jr.
Chief Judge, District of
Columbia Court of Appeals
3

We have got to recruit judges with broad backgrounds in their prime years. Lawyers in their 40s should be our prime area of recruitment. These are the years when they can work the hardest and when they will have 20 good years to give to the judiciary before they retire. The only problem is that lawyers in their 40s

are in their prime earning years and prime spending years because they have to think about sending their kids to college. We have difficulty recruiting them at present judicial salaries and, even if we could recruit them, we would have a difficult time keeping them from returning to private practice and a much higher standard of living.

The Washington Post, 6-26:(B)5.

Lester Pollace
Chairman, finance committee,
CNA Financial Corporation
4

The businessman's view of lawyers in litigation matters is not a favorable or happy one. A significant portion of litigation is unneeded and goes unchecked at great expense. Too often I hear lawyers themselves say a suit can't be settled, not because of unreconcilable differences, but because the other lawyer isn't interested in settling. His meter is running. Lawyers' own interests often cloud the time to settle and the time to fight. Lawyers assume a combative stature and want to fight to the death, with the client's interests consciously or subconsciously lost sight of. They turn litigation into a personal matter, which extends the litigation and increases the cost; and afterwards, they brag to their lawyer friends, "Did you hear what I did to old so-and-so in court the other day?"

Before American Bar Association, Chicago/
San Francisco Examiner & Chronicle, 8-14:(C)10.

William H. Rehnquist
Associate Justice, Supreme
Court of the United States
5

[Defending the Supreme Court's secret deliberations]: From public sessions of oral argument and published opinions and orders, we already know precisely what business the Supreme Court transacts, and we know a fair amount about how it transacts that business. The deliberations of the Court's conference are not public, and should not be made public, because the added information about the workings of the Court which would result would be more than offset by the probability that the usefulness of the conference as a deliberative

WHAT THEY SAID IN 1977

(WILLIAM H. REHNQUIST)

institution would be seriously impaired. The very process of reporting its deliberations could significantly change, and for the worse, the nature of those deliberations.

At Washburn University School of Law,
Jan. 27/The Washington Post, 1-28:(A)2.

Maurice Rosenberg
Professor of law,
Columbia University
1

Can it actually be good for a society to be quick to quarrel in court? Increased government involvement leads to more statutes, rules and regulations. All that creates new legal business. In the last decade, a new set of legal rights, dealing with ecology, pollution, privacy and consumer affairs, has been recognized. Critics, both in and outside the [legal] profession, contend that there is too much law and too many lawyers ...

The New York Times, 5-22:(4)7.

Garvin Shallenberger
President, State Bar of California
2

The image that many lawyers are somehow crooked, or otherwise suspect, arises in large part because we do take sides on all issues ... but rather than that being a sign that lawyers are shady, it is an expression of an extremely high duty ... The media, in part, are responsible for the unjust image that lawyers now have and therefore owe an obligation to give some coverage to some of the better things lawyers

do so the public doesn't have a crisis of confidence.

Interview, San Diego/San Francisco
Examiner & Chronicle, 10-2:(B)5.

Evelle J. Younger
Attorney General of California
3

Over the years, we've [the U.S.] built into the system an opportunity for a defendant to delay and delay and delay a criminal trial almost indefinitely. And, in many cases, delay is the best weapon a defendant has, particularly if the defendant is guilty. Sometimes it's the only weapon ... No one wants to make it so fast that the defendant doesn't get a fair trial, but we've long since passed the point where a fair trial is a problem. We're now playing games in our courts and we've become really the laughing stock of just about every other civilized nation. I used to think we had the best system of criminal justice in the world. We don't even have *one* of the best at the moment, if you measure it in terms of the results it produces. If you expect your justice system to identify the persons who commit crimes, and punish those persons with promptness and certainty, then our system is bad.

Before Anaheim (Calif.) Rotary Club,
Nov. 28/Los Angeles Times, 11-29:(2)3.

Franklin E. Zimring
Professor of law, University of Chicago
4

The law expresses aspirations that we may not be able to practically achieve. But there is nothing wrong with seeing the law exhibit aspiration.

Time, 3-14:58.

National Defense · The Military

Clifford L. Alexander, Jr.
*Secretary of the Army
of the United States*

1

[Once policy has been determined,] the professional soldier must decide whether any public discussion beyond proper articulation of the policy is in order. In almost no instance will the national interest be served by a military person voicing disagreement with established policy.

*Before U.S. Military Academy graduating
class, June 8/The New York Times, 6-9:35.*

Georgi A. Arbatov
*Director, Soviet Institute of
U.S.A. and Canadian Affairs*

2

It is understandable that the American Generals do not like the situation when parity exists [with the Soviet Union], and when they cannot attack our country, cannot blackmail us, because nuclear war would be suicide for the United States. But it is a fact the Americans will have to live with. Many serious changes have taken place for America in this respect. The country has lived for 200 years under different conditions from other countries, beyond two oceans and with feelings of complete national security. And now it has begun to live like all other countries; it is just as vulnerable in case of war as the others.

*Television broadcast, Moscow/
The Washington Post, 2-21:(A)2.*

3

In the past, it was a set American policy to have superiority in the military field. What has changed is not that the Soviets are striving for superiority but that we are effectively countering your policy. Recently the Chiefs of Staff in the United States confirmed that there is no Soviet military superiority. What was mentioned was that the Soviets "might" strive for military superiority in the future. We can suspect the United States in this respect, too. This is one very good reason to continue our negotiations, so that each side is assured that the other will not have military superiority.

*Interview, Moscow/
U.S. News & World Report, 3-14:27.*

Les Aspin
*United States Representative,
D–Wisconsin*

4

[On the controversial new neutron bomb, which destroys people but not buildings and in a relatively small area]: Basically, the neutron bomb is not really a good issue, and it points up the problems that liberals have in arms control. The real issue is whether you want to have tactical nuclear weapons or not. It's all pretty grisly. There's this relentless development of technology that's making cleaner, more discriminate weapons. Liberals haven't got any set of criteria to judge what is a good weapon, what is a necessary weapon and what is a bad weapon.

The New York Times, 7-17:(4)4.

Howard H. Baker, Jr.
United States Senator, R–Tennessee

5

I supported the all-volunteer Army. I voted time after time to eliminate the draft. I do not favor conscription in peace time. But the all-volunteer Army is contributing an extraordinary amount of these increased military costs, and I think we are going to have to give some careful national attention to that and to identify those costs and to come to terms with whether or not the country is willing to pay that price, because we dare not take that increased cost out of the muscle of the military

WHAT THEY SAID IN 1977

deterrent, whether it is strategic or whether it is conventional.

TV-radio interview, Washington/"Meet the Press," National Broadcasting Company, 1-23.

1

[On President Carter's pardon of U.S. Vietnam-war draft evaders] : I think this pardon on this broad, sweeping scale in this way is unfair. I think it is unfair to those who went [and served in Vietnam] — and not many wanted to — and those who classified themselves as conscientious objectors and non-combatants, and suffered whatever stigma might go with that. I think it is unfair in almost any way you slice it to give a broad, general, blanket pardon to such a broad class of draft evaders.

TV-radio interview, Washington/"Meet the Press," National Broadcasting Company, 1-23.

Robin Beard
United States Representative,
R—Tennessee

2

[Arguing against labor unions for military personnel] : The serious discussion of unionization of the military started when we went to the all-volunteer service. All of a sudden, the military is taking the attitude: "It's just another job." The sense of patriotism, the sense of national service is taking a back seat. So the unions are saying: "All right, if it's just a job, that's a market ripe for union organization."

Interview/U.S. News & World Report, 3-28:52.

Kenneth T. Blaylock
President, American Federation
of Government Employees

3

[Saying military personnel should be allowed to join labor unions] : History has shown us that if work forces have serious enough problems they will organize, no matter what the law says. Look at the Postal Service. The law said it couldn't strike. The postal people struck. If you want to create the crisis, we can continue to ignore the problems that people have . . . If AFGE decides not to move,

the military will organize anyway. They may turn to the Teamsters; they may turn to some of the independents; they may convert their own military professional organizations to unions — I don't know — but they will organize.

Interview/U.S. News & World Report, 3-28:52.

Leonid I. Brezhnev
General Secretary, Communist
Party of the Soviet Union

4

Not only is the planet over-saturated with means of mass destruction, but there is also a real and an annually growing danger of new kinds and new systems of weapons being created, weapons that will be many times more destructive than the old ones. Frankly speaking, our concern about the continued arms race, including the strategic-arms race, has grown because of the line taken on these questions by the new American Administration. It is patently geared to obtain unilateral advantages for the U.S.A.

Broadcast address, May 29/
The New York Times, 5-30:3.

Leonid I. Brezhnev
President of the Soviet Union; General
Secretary, Soviet Communist Party

5

We want to achieve progress in the negotiations [with the U.S. on a comprehensive nuclear test-ban] and bring them to a successful conclusion. Therefore, we state that we are prepared to reach agreement on a moratorium covering nuclear explosions for peaceful purposes, along with a ban on all nuclear-weapon tests for a definite period. We trust that this important step on the part of the U.S.S.R. is properly appreciated by our partners at the negotiations and that the road will thus be cleared to conclude a treaty long awaited by the people . . . It is our active and consistent stand that the contest between socialism and capitalism should be decided not on the field of battle, not on the munitions conveyors, but in the sphere of peaceful work. We want the frontiers dividing these two worlds to be crossed not by missiles with nuclear warheads but by the

(LEONID I. BREZHNEV)

threads of broad and diversified cooperation for the good of all mankind.

Before Party and government leaders, Moscow,
Nov. 2/Los Angeles Times, 11-3:(1)26.

1

[Criticizing the U.S.' plan to produce the neutron bomb] : . . . if such a bomb were developed in the West, developed against us, a fact which nobody tries to conceal, the latter must clearly realize that the U.S.S.R. will not remain a passive onlooker. We shall be confronted with the need to answer this challenge in order to ensure the security of the Soviet people, its allies and friends. In the final analysis, this would raise the arms race to an even more dangerous level. We do not want this to happen, and that is why we move to reach agreement on mutual renunciation of the production of the neutron bomb so as to save the world from the appearance of this new weapon of mass annihilation.

Interview/Los Angeles Times, 12-25:(1)1.

George S. Brown
General, United States Air Force;
Chairman, Joint Chiefs of Staff

2

Until now, servicemen and women have quietly accepted the judgments of the leadership of the Services and Congress. They have been silent in the process of assuring that their welfare, their rights and their compensation are established fairly. Today, however, we hear sounds of a new and different voice — that of the unions. Some unions have shown considerable interest in developing military membership. It would not be a historic "first"; several other nations have military unions. In my opinion, it is not in the best interests of our country or of our armed forces for our people in uniform to perceive that a union will provide a fairer way of life than will the American people as a whole through the Congress. Our armed forces today must be better than any we have had in peacetime. They must be ready and responsive. They are made ready by capable men and women in uniform who commit themselves to military service without a firm

contract, who place themselves at their country's service on the basis of good faith. They have faith that their services will be well used, that their reasonable economic needs will be met. They join with an understanding that what they have been promised as a way of life in the Service will be supported by their military and civilian leaders and the government. They ask fair treatment, and a sense of equity in their future. This great country — the richest in the world and the most productive in history — can afford to meet the needs and reasonable expectations of its servicemen and women. Honorably, it can do no less.

At Women's Forum on National Security,
Washington, Feb. 14/Vital Speeches, 3-15:326.

Harold Brown
Secretary of Defense-designate
of the United States

3

At present, the Soviet Union could not attack the United States without our being able to deliver a crushing retaliatory blow that would destroy the Soviet Union as a functioning society . . . If it were perceived, even mistakenly believed, by a large part of the world that the U.S. was strategically inferior in terms of nuclear arms to the Soviet Union, that might have a political effect [on U.S. foreign policy]. For that reason, I think that the so-called conservative estimates or "worst case" estimates of Soviet versus U.S. capability at this point do not do a service to American political strength throughout the world. I think that taking the opposite tack, a too optimistic appraisal of Soviet capabilities, is also very dangerous.

Before Senate Arms Services Committee,
Washington, Jan. 11/
Los Angeles Times, 1-12:(1)6.

Harold Brown
Secretary of Defense
of the United States

4

With respect to the strategic balance, I believe that we and the Soviets are in a situation of rough equivalence. We are ahead by some measures; they are ahead by other measures. We happen to have, for example, a

WHAT THEY SAID IN 1977

(HAROLD BROWN)

substantially larger intercontinental bomber force, more submarine payload — submarine missile payload. They have a very much larger land-based payload. The net effect of all this is that if the Soviets were to launch a first strike on us we could, after that, retaliate with devastating effect and essentially destroy them as a functioning modern society. The same is true in the other direction, and that, of course, is what constitutes mutual deterrence. This deterrence, I believe, is preserved over a pretty substantial range of the numbers, and modest differences in the numbers don't matter very much. If the differences get too large — and this would concern me — then I think there would start to be a political and a psychological effect, with respect to our allies, ourselves; or the Soviets themselves might think, incorrectly, that they have an advantage that they could use politically, and that would concern me. I think we have to keep working to make sure that doesn't happen. One of the things about the current strategic debate that most concerns me is that those people who undervalue our strategic force capabilities may be eroding our deterrent by giving the Soviets a mistaken idea that they in fact have an advantage.

TV-radio interview, Washington/"Meet the Press," National Broadcasting Company, 3-6.

1

National security is more than a matter of military strength. It includes economic strength; it includes, in the case of the United States, our enormous agricultural production; it includes our technological capabilities; and it includes also self-confidence, self-cohesion, political cohesion and will. I think we have to balance our response across the spectrum.

TV-radio interview, Washington/"Meet the Press," National Broadcasting Company, 3-6.

2

A comparison of United States with Soviet [military] investments during the past 20 years will show that, cumulatively, we have made as large an effort as the Soviets. However, a major part of the U.S. effort came during the first 10

184

years, while the most significant Soviet investments have been made during the past decade. We have probably lived off our earlier investments longer than we should. We have some catching up to do.

Statement to Congress/ The Washington Post, 3-15:(A)5.

3

In the past, United States arms and equipment have dominated in the NATO forces. What must evolve is a more even-handed distribution of military development and production as the United States and its allies decide on a greater measure of common procurement of weapons systems and supplies ... There certainly will have to be greater United States purchases from European sources and more licensing to produce European equipment in the United States. Wide differences in weapons systems and military equipment continue to make mutual support needlessly difficult. A common logistical support structure remains to be built. Moreover, NATO commanders, who need an effective capability to communicate up and down the chain of command in wartime, still cannot always do so, and are especially hampered in communicating with military elements drawn from different nations.

Before Atlanta Chamber of Commmerce, May 11/ The New York Times, 5-12:(A)16.

4

We have only limited experience with the all-volunteer [armed] force ... and so far I would judge that we have been able to meet our requirements for personnel, particularly in the active-duty force. [But] I don't think we use our personnel as efficiently as we might. I think we lose many of those during or at the end of their first term of service whom we would want to keep, and I think that we need to improve that situation.

Parade, 6-12:18.

5

[Agreeing with President Carter's decision not to go ahead with the B-1 bomber program, favoring, instead, development of the cruise missile]: What we have found during the last

(HAROLD BROWN)

year is that cruise missiles are harder to see even than had been expected, by radars as well as optically, and they also can fly even lower than we were sure they could. Both of these things make them more certain of penetration than a penetrating bomber, including the B-1, and more certain of penetration than we were a year ago ... The B-1 would have been a more attractive option had it been 30 per cent less expensive, but I believe that the technology of cruise-missile development played a larger part.

News conference, Washington, July 1/
Los Angeles Herald-Examiner, 7-3:(A)2.

1

All of us must recognize that the Soviets have under way a number of large, impressive and costly strategic programs to strengthen their offensive capabilities, their active defenses and their passive defense system. To give you just one indication of the effort and of the momentum behind it, the Soviets are now deploying a fourth generation of ICBMs at a rate of between 100 and 150 a year. These missiles are almost uniformly first class in terms of their accuracy and payload. At the same time that the Soviets have four new ICBMs under development, they are continuing work on the SS-16, their mobile ICBM, and they are modifying four other missiles. Exactly why the Soviets are pushing so hard to improve their strategic nuclear capabilities is uncertain ... What is certain is that we cannot ignore their efforts or assume that the Soviets are motivated by considerations of defense or even altruism.

Before National Security Industrial
Association, Washington, Sept. 15/
The Washington Post, 9-16:(A)1.

2

[On how the U.S. should respond to a military attack]: I think the strategy encompassed by the phrase "launch on warning" is not the appropriate thing for the United States to do. I think the way to describe it is "launch under attack." And the question is: would you launch land-based missiles before explosion of nuclear weapons on the United States? That is

something that should be considered only with the greatest caution. I see no reason to launch submarine-launched ballistic missiles that way, although the bombers ought to be launched on warning because that does not constitute a decision to send them to the target. Each system in the triad [of nuclear bombers, land missiles and submarine missiles] is different.

Before Defense Appropriations Subcommittee,
Washington, Sept. 15/
The Washington Post, 10-24:(A)6.

Zbigniew Brzezinski
Assistant to President of the
United States Jimmy Carter for
National Security Affairs

3

The purpose of SALT is to create conditions of mutual stability, parity. This is why the SALT negotiations are now so sensitive and so very important. One could, in the past, see the Soviet [military] build-up in some measure as a response to the real or perceived asymmetry in the American-Soviet relationship. This no longer prevails. Therefore, the question as to why the Soviets continue their build-up is a very legitimate one. If SALT results in agreements which produce both stability and parity, then I think the answer may not be very ominous. But if we cannot reach such a SALT agreement, then this question concerning the Soviet motive in continuing its build-up is bound to be raised with an increasing sense of urgency by the public and by Congress.

Interview, Washington/
U.S. News & World Report, 5-30:36.

4

I don't consider nuclear superiority to be politically meaningless. I can fully acknowledge the fact that at a certain point strategic weaponry ceases to exercise military significance in terms of marginal differences and consequences, if used. However, the *perception* by others or by oneself of someone else having − quote, unquote − strategic superiority can influence political behavior. It can induce some countries to act in a fashion that sometimes has been described as "Finlandization." And it can induce self-imposed restraint on the party that feels weaker. And, last but not least, it can

185

WHAT THEY SAID IN 1977

induce the party that feels that it enjoys strategic superiority to act politically in a more assertive fashion. In other words, it has the potential for political exploitation even if in an actual warfare situation the differences may be at best, or at worst, on the margin.

Interview/The Washington Post, 10-9:(C)5.

Georges Buis
President, French Foundation
for National Defense Studies
1

[Disagreeing with those who claim that the Soviet Union has achieved military superiority over the U.S.]: It's part of an alarmist campaign of intoxication that just does not reflect the reality of ongoing American superiority. The United States is five to 10 years ahead of the Soviets in each arms system, and that's that . . . We're watching an old operation that we've seen before. The facts don't back up the statements of alarm. They happen . . . every year when they're about to vote the U.S. military budget and right on schedule with the NATO annual general meeting.

Interview, Paris/
The Dallas Times Herald, 1-24:(A)8.

Robert C. Byrd
United States Senator, D–West Virginia
2

One of the most tragic things that could happen is that the Senate of the United States could reject an arms-control agreement [with the Soviet Union]. But it would be even more tragic if the Senate ratified an agreement that legitimized and relegated the United States to a position of inferiority rather than equality and equivalency in the area of strategic weapons.

To reporters, Washington, March 5/
The New York Times, 3-6:(1)6.

3

[Advocating caution in the development of the B-1 bomber]: By going all out on the B-1, we would drastically reduce our ability to develop and fund other weapons systems. Additionally, we would add to our budget deficit and reduce the potential for meaningful tax

reduction . . . I don't think the Soviets fear it [the B-1] very much. The cruise missile is their great fear. I'm a strong supporter of the cruise missile.

To reporters, Washington, June 25/
San Francisco Examiner & Chronicle, 6-26:(A)3.

M. Robert Carr
United States Representative,
D–Michigan
4

[Supporting development of the controversial neutron bomb]: These are weapons which will replace other weapons, other nuclear weapons which have higher blast, higher heat, higher collateral damage, which are less secure from terrorism. These weapons will result in a step back from the awful, horrible, insane kinds of things that I have been hearing out of the mouths of people who I think are misguided in their support of the Weiss amendment [which would prohibit funds for neutron-bomb development].

The New York Times, 9-30:(A)11.

Jimmy Carter
President of the United States
5

At the present time, my judgment is that we have superior nuclear capability [over the Soviet Union]. The Soviet Union has more throw weight, larger missiles, larger warheads. We have more missiles, a much higher degree of accuracy and also we have three different mechanisms which are each independently adequate to deliver atomic weapons — airplanes, submarines, intercontinental ballistic missiles. I think that we are roughly equivalent, even though I think we are superior in that either the Soviet Union or we could destroy a major part of the other nation if a major attack was made . . .

News conference, Washington, Feb. 8/
The New York Times, 2-9:(A)16.

6

At the present time, I have no intention of going back to a mandatory draft law. We do have a constant concern about the weakness of recruitment, particularly for the reserve forces. If it ever becomes obvious to me and to the

(JIMMY CARTER)

military leaders that serve with me that we could not adequately provide for the defense of our country without a draft, I would not hesitate to recommend such a change to the Congress to call for a draft law. I think if it should be considered in the future, my own inclination would be to make it much more comprehensive — not to permit exceptions for those who are wealthy or those who are college students — to make it all-inclusive and to make sure that it is fair.

Before Pentagon employees, Washington,
March 1/Los Angeles Times, 3-2:(1)10.

1

[On U.S.-Soviet negotiations to limit strategic arms, which just ended in deadlock]: I think it is important for us to take advantage of an opportunity this year to negotiate not just a superficial ratification of rules by which we can continue the arms race, but to have a freeze on deployment and development of missiles and an actual reduction in launchers ... On those terms I intend to remain very strong in my position. I don't think it is to our nation's advantage to put forward in piecemeal fashion additional proposals. Our experience in the past has been that the Soviet Union extracts from those comprehensive proposals those items that are favorable to them and wants to continue to negotiate the other parts of the proposal ...

News conference, Washington, March 30/
The Washington Post, 3-31:(A)19.

2

I think anyone recognizes that the first nation to use atomic weapons would be taking a very profound step toward the self-condemnation of the whole world. However, in areas where nuclear weapons are deployed in the Western Pacific, and also in Europe and to defend our own homeland, their very deployment implies a possibility of their use, if necessary.

Interview, Washington/
U.S. News & World Report, 6-6:19.

3

One of the disturbing failures up until this point in nuclear weaponry has been a complete absence of discussions concerning tactical or theatre nuclear weapons. The only discussions that have ever been held between ourselves and the Soviets related only to strategic weapons — those that can be fired from one continent to another or from the sea into a continent. I would hope that, as a result of the SALT II talks, we might agree with the Soviets to start addressing the question of the so-called tactical nuclear weapons, of which the enhanced-radiation, or neutron bomb, would be one. This weapon is much less destabilizing in its effect, if it should be deployed, than, for instance, some of the advanced new Soviet weapons like the SS-20 missile, which is much more destructive than any weapon held by the NATO allies and has a much greater range. . . . the whole matter must be addressed in its entirety rather than one weapon at a time. We would not deploy the neutron bomb, or neutron shells, unless there was an agreement by our NATO allies. That is where the decision will be made. But there are other new weapons, including the SS-20, much more threatening to the balance that presently exist.

News conference, Warsaw, Poland,
Dec. 30/The New York Times, 12-31:2.

John H. Chafee
United States Senator, R—Rhode Island;
Former Secretary of the Navy

4

Since the Services began to convert to an all-volunteer status, they have become more efficient in their use of manpower. The combat readiness of our forces is high; jobs and skills of those who perform them are well matched and drug problems and racial disturbances have declined.

Parade, 6-12:16.

Frank Church
United States Senator, D—Idaho

5

[On U.S. Korean forces Chief of Staff John Singlaub's warning of war with North Korea if American ground troops are withdrawn from the South, as planned by President Carter]: When I was in the Army, it was made clear to

(FRANK CHURCH)

me that the unpardonable offense was insubordination. If this holds true for enlisted men and junior officers, even more must it bind the Generals. We maintain an army, not to make national policy, but to uphold and enforce it. When a General on active duty, in command abroad, publicly criticizes or contradicts Presidential policy, then he should be disciplined or dismissed.

Washington/The Dallas Times Herald, 5-21:(A)16.

W. Graham Claytor
Secretary of the Navy of the United States 1

I would not want to see women assigned permanently to ships expected to be engaged in direct combat duties. My own experiences in the "pressure cooker" environment of long periods of combat confinement tell me that this would not work. This has nothing to do with ability but rather the mix of males and females together.

U.S. News & World Report, 7-18:84.

Robert F. Cocklin
Executive vice president,
Association of the United States Army 2

[Saying comparability should not be used as a yardstick in measuring military pay against civilian-job pay]: Military and civilian jobs are not really comparable. There's no civilian job I can think of that's comparable to that of an infantry soldier who goes where he's told to go, even to some distant land, and is subject to long separations from his family. Then there's always the element of danger — the possibility of being exposed to combat. When you enter the military, you even waive some of your Constitutional rights. You lose your freedom of action. You make a contract from which it's very difficult to back out.

Interview/U.S. News & World Report, 8-22:31.

John C. Culver
United States Senator, D—Iowa 3

[U.S. military forces] are in a shocking state of combat readiness. On any given day only about half our combat aircraft are operationally

ready to perform their missions. Only about half our ships are operationally ready at any time ... It adds little to deterrence to have exotic new weapons on the drawing boards when large numbers of our current planes, tanks and ships cannot be relied upon today ... [Increasing costs have reduced training] to the point that few soldiers, sailors and airmen actually get to fire the weapons assigned to them, or with sufficient frequency to develop proficiency.

Before Senate Armed Services Committee,
Washington, March 31 /
The Washington Post, 4-1:(A)10.

4

I am opposed to the construction of the B-1 bomber because I don't believe it is essential to the strength of our strategic deterrent, which I think is now very strong. I think at best it makes only a marginal contribution, and it certainly is not justified by its enormous cost. I think, secondly, we can carry out that same bomber mission through less-costly alternatives equally effectively. And, finally, I believe that the resources that would be dedicated to the B-1 bomber production would be much better applied in our national-security interests, properly understood, to some very real deficiencies in our conventional deterrent, as well as meeting some of the unmet domestic problems of our society, which I think go to the real question of our strength as a people.

TV-radio interview, Washington/"Meet
the Press," National Broadcasting Company, 6-19.

John E. Davis
Director, Defense Civil Preparedness
Agency of the United States 5

If deterrence fails, then we should have civil defense to try and decrease as much as possible the vulnerability of our people and give them the greatest chance of survival ... Certainly we would have to say that the Soviets have made much greater gains, given much more attention to their civil-defense preparations than we do in the States. And this has become a worrisome thing. It's as simple as that right now.

Interview, Washington/
The New York Times, 2-20:(1)35.

Ronald V. Dellums
United States Representative,
D—California

1

[Spending any Federal money on civil defense would be] a waste, ludicrous, insane. It makes me feel I'm sitting on the floor of the House in a dream. It's the height of insanity, [given the country's] other human problems.
Before the House, Washington, April 25/
The Washington Post, 5-26:(A)1.

Robert K. Dornan
United States Representative,
R—California

2

[Criticizing President Carter's decision not to go ahead with construction of the B-1 bomber]: All over the Soviet Union, the fighter pilots who would have to fly against an old, slow B-52 are breaking out the caviar and vodka. Their problem of flying against superior aircraft like the B-1, after they first-strike us, has been solved by our Commander-in-Chief.
June 30/Los Angeles Times, 7-1:(1)6.

Russell E. Dougherty
General, United States Air Force;
Commander, Strategic Air Command

3

...I can answer personally what I think would be the result if, through default on our part, the Soviets should achieve [military] superiority. We could not continue to provide the significant assurance to our policy-makers that, militarily, we are "second to none" ... as we have been throughout the past 30 years. We could not with adequate assurance continue to maintain the uncertain, uneasy and indelicate "balance of terror" that has given us 30 years of uncertain, uneasy freedom to choose our own destiny. We could not say that, as uncertain, uneasy and terrifying as it may be, we have done the best we can for the future to keep our people both alive and free. If we were to default and permit our nation to become militarily inferior — we could not say any one of those things.
At Harvard University Arms Control
Seminar, March 16/Vital Speeches, 7-15:590.

Gerald R. Ford
President of the United States

4

The Soviet Union over the last decade has had a constant program of gradually strengthening and modernizing its military capabilities. At the same time, the U.S. paid less attention to [its military strength] and permitted a narrowing of the gap with the Soviet Union. We have been able to turn it around the last two years, and we are now on the right track. If this trend continues, then the U.S. has nothing to be concerned about. However, if we again go into the posture that developed before 1974, where we were spending a smaller part of our GNP, a smaller part of our Federal budget [for defense], then we would find ourselves, ten years from now or five years from now, in a serious military national-defense posture.
Interview, Washington/Time, 1-10:15.

Gerald R. Ford
Former President of the United States

5

[On President Carter's decision not to go ahead with construction of the B-1 bomber]: I strongly disagree with the President's decision. It is a very risky gamble. He is relying on a B-52 that is 20 years old or more, an aircraft that was developed in the 1950s. He is also gambling on a cruise-missile system that is still in the research-and-development stages. In my opinion, it is too big a gamble and too much of a risk when you rely on a nearly obsolescent weapons system, the B-52, and an as yet unproven cruise missile.
To reporters, San Francisco,
June 30/Los Angeles Times, 7-1:(1)7.

E. J. (Jake) Garn
United States Senator, R—Utah

6

I am absolutely in favor of building the B-1 [bomber]. We have a system of defense in this country, strategic defense, that is based on the so-called triad of manned bombers, intercontinental ballistic missiles and, thirdly, the sea-launched or submarine-launched ballistic missiles. All three of the legs of that triad in my opinion are becoming weak. We have old *Poseidon* and *Polaris* submarines; the *Trident* will not be coming on line until mid-1980s. We

(E. J. [JAKE] GARN)

have aging *Minuteman II* missiles that are not hardened for nuclear blasts; they are becoming rather old, 25 years. The *Minuteman III,* and the replacement for that, the M-X, will not be coming on line until about 1986. Then we have the third leg of that triad, or the stool, which is the B-52, an old bomber that . . . cannot handle the job of penetration. It does not have the speed; it does not have the capability; it is not hardened. And for that reason, with all three of these legs, I believe, becoming rather weak, the B-1 is the one weapon in those three that has been tested, that is ready to start production. I think it is absolutely necessary to the strategic defense of the United States.

TV-radio interview, Washington/"Meet the Press," National Broadcasting Company, 6-19.

Barry M. Goldwater
United States Senator, R–Arizona
1

[On President Carter's decision to cancel the B-1 bomber project in favor of the cruise missile]: We are still 7 to 10 years away from a dependable cruise missile. I have followed this weapon closely. It will fly, but we still have to build in the avionics to give it a terrain-following capacity, and the target-sensing equipment, and we must know the Soviet geography over which this bird is going to fly. We need a more detailed knowledge of the ups and downs of the hills of Russia than we know today. It's quite a few years away from being a dependable weapon. What President Carter has done has been to place the country into limbo for a period of years during which we will have to modernize the B-52 and perfect the cruise missile, and I'm afraid that's going to cost as much as the B-1 would have cost.

Interview, Washington/ The Dallas Times Herald, 7-17:(A)39.

Alexander M. Haig, Jr.
General, United States Army; Supreme Allied Commander/Europe
2

[Supporting development of the neutron bomb]: . . . we have a vested interest in seeing this system provided to the [NATO] Alliance

in order to modernize our theatre nuclear capability . . . This evolutionary system, which represents an improvement in technology, provides us with additional flexibility in decision-making, with the ability to apply power in a more discriminating and flexible way, and in that context it enhances our deterrent.

News conference, Casteau, Belgium, July 12/ Los Angeles Herald-Examiner, 7-12:(A)7.

3

When both sides move toward parity in nuclear systems — which is the fact today — then credibility depends increasingly upon conventional abilities, because it drives up the force commitments. It prevents what I call "standoff conditions" in the nuclear area — nibbling erosions for which the nuclear response is not credible.

Interview, Belgium/ The Dallas Times Herald, 9-27:(A)4.

Orrin G. Hatch
United States Senator, R–Utah
4

[Arguing against labor unions for the armed forces]: Labor unions have served a great purpose in the civilian sector of our nation throughout history, but our defense system cannot survive if a "shop steward" must approve orders issued by commanding officers to enlisted people. I don't honestly believe that the unions really want to unionize the military, though it has been reported that the International Brotherhood of Teamsters is moving ahead with such plans. To me, such activity is irresponsible and not in the best interest of the nation.

/**

Mark O. Hatfield
United States Senator, D–Oregon
5

[On the controversial neutron bomb]: . . . it seems to me that deployment of these neutron warheads will lower the threshold for nuclear war — making a nuclear confrontation more likely. We are inviting the use of nuclear weaponry in conventional warfare. Their deployment also creates the illusion that we somehow can engage in a limited nuclear war

(MARK O. HATFIELD)

by using this weapon without being drawn into use of bigger atomic weapons. This is a substantive objection . . .Proponents of the bomb say it is going to provide the U.S. with some greater credibility for our defense system in Europe: A potential invading force would think twice before tempting us to unleash our neutron bomb. I think you can argue the other side of the coin just as effectively: that these weapons lower the nuclear threshold and invite use of an atomic weapon in situations that are less than disastrous.

Interview/U.S. News & World Report, 7-25:25.

Peter Hill-Norton
Admiral of the Fleet, British
Navy; Chairman, Military Committee,
North Atlantic Treaty Organization

1

[On the Soviet Union's military build-up]: We have reached a stage from which point the present adverse trend in the balance [of power] would become increasingly dangerous for the Western world unless corrected, given the indisputable evidence that we are faced with a relentless determination on the other side to achieve military superiority.

Interview, Washington, March 22/
The New York Times, 3-23:(A)7.

James L. Holloway III
Admiral and Chief of Operations,
United States Navy

2

If the Equal Rights Amendment were approved, say, and women were permitted to serve in combat units, then the U.S. Navy would certainly move quickly to abide by the law of the land. Every sailor on ship isn't engaged in pushing projectiles around. We still have yeomen and pay clerks and computer programmers and electronic repairmen and the kinds of jobs that women can perform splendidly. The transition would have to be carefully planned. Any time you have boys-girls it's a little difficult; but the problems, I guess, are no different than what's happening in college dormitories.

The New York Times, 5-1:(1)17.

3

Our single major problem is the reduced number of ships in the U.S. Navy. But naval capability means two things: number of units and the individual quality of those units. Our quality is very close to tops. Therefore, I'm able to say that the U.S. Navy is superior to the Soviet Navy, even though we have only 467 ships in the active fleet, compared to 2,000 to 3,000 in the Soviet Navy, depending on what types you count . . . We have always prided ourselves on having a two-ocean Navy, but the reduction in numbers of ships has very definitely restricted our ability to fight in more than one ocean at a time. A genuine two-ocean Navy would make me feel more comfortable.

U.S. News & World Report, 10-10:39.

Henry M. Jackson
United States Senator, D–Washington

4

[On Paul Warnke's nomination for chief U.S. arms negotiator]: . . . he has been, for many years, an articulate proponent of the notion that numbers of strategic weapons are essentially without military significance and have political significance only if we say they do. Mr. Warnke says they do not. I ask my colleagues: How can we send to negotiate at SALT a man who believes that it matters little whether the Soviets have even substantial nuclear superiority? SALT is about numbers. How can we send to Geneva a man who believes that numbers do not matter? If one is indifferent to the numbers of each side — if one believes that an imbalance is meaningless — how can he credibly insist that a SALT II treaty must be based on equality?

At Senate confirmation hearings on Paul Warnke,
Washington/The Wall Street Journal, 3-11:12.

U. Alexis Johnson
Former chief United States arms
negotiator at SALT talks (1973-77)

5

. . . to my mind, SALT is a continuing process. The dialogue we have had over thousands of hours, from the President down to subcommittees of the Geneva delegations:

191

WHAT THEY SAID IN 1977

(U. ALEXIS JOHNSON)

These are in part an educative process. I have a feeling that this dialogue must continue in some form, or some place along the line we are going to blow each other up — commit suicide. Agreements reached as the dialogue moves along will be limited, like the Vladivostok agreement that there would be a ceiling of 2,400 delivery vehicles and 1,320 MIRVed missiles. As we reach such agreements on limited areas, we can recognize that this isn't the be-all and end-all — that you're not going to reach a definitive agreement to resolve for all time the whole strategic problem between ourselves and the Soviet Union.

Interview, Washington/
U.S. News & World Report,
4-4:26.

David C. Jones
General and Chief of Staff,
United States Air Force   *1*

This is the smallest Air Force we have had since Korea, but I wouldn't trade it for any air force in the world. But you can go only so far in quality in a trade-off for quantity. Quantity is one thing we're worried about. We probably got down a little too low, but we're working our way back up in numbers . . . Sustainability is a major issue: How long can we fight a war? Our greatest shortage is in air-to-air munitions to be able to fight for a sustained period of time. We have been short of spare parts and the ability to repair broken parts. But appropriations for '77 and what's proposed for '78 are a step in the right direction . . . We have the best airlift capability in the world, a very impressive capability. But we are far short of what's needed if we are to move U.S. forces around the world, particularly the Army with its heavy equipment. On manpower, we are in good shape. We can put a crew in every cockpit in very short order. We can mobilize everyone within three days, including the reserve components. We are not "week-end warriors," even in the Reserves.

U.S. News & World Report,
10-10:39.

George J. Keegan
Major General (Ret.) and former
Assistant Chief of Staff,
Intelligence, United States Air Force   *2*

American strategy is premised on the principle of war avoidance, while that of the Soviet Union is premised on war winning.

Interview, Washington/
Los Angeles Herald-Examiner, 1-3:(A)6.

3

By every criterion used to measure strategic balance — that is, damage expectancy, throw-weight, equivalent megatonnage, or technology — I am unaware of a single important category in which the Soviets have not established a significant lead over the United States.

Interview, Washington/
Los Angeles Herald-Examiner, 1-3:(A)6.

4

The pursuit of another SALT agreement, based upon what we have heard from [U.S. arms negotiator] Paul Warnke and President Carter, and on what has been alluded to in the press, would be the height of folly and national irresponsibility. If the United States means to maintain its stability, in the light of what has transpired between the Soviets and us in arms accords over the last six or seven years, I cannot conceive the present guidelines as serving other than exciting the Soviets to realize the possibilities of a decisive shift of the balance in their favor and in their forthcoming ability to take increasing advantage of our growing weakness.

At conference on the Soviet Union,
Santa Barbara, Calif./World Issues, Oct.-Nov.:29.

George F. Kennan
Former United States Ambassador
to the Soviet Union   *5*

[On the recent U.S.-Soviet negotiations to limit strategic arms, which ended in deadlock]: . . . I think the new [Carter] Administration has made just about every mistake it could make in these Moscow talks, and has defied all the lessons we have learned in dealing with the Soviets since the last world war . . . Our proposals should not have been broadcast to the

(GEORGE F. KENNAN)

whole world before the talks began. This was not a good idea. In Moscow's way of thinking about things, this was propaganda and not policy, not even polite . . . and it put them on the spot . . . The questions involved in the strategic-arms talks should not, in my opinion, have been taken up in isolation. We should have been talking about wider things . . . and wider political relations, too, because it's all one package . . . The Secretary of State [Cyrus Vance] should not have been involved in all this unless there was a pretty good prospect that something helpful was going to come out of it. And finally — this is a wider question I feel very strongly about — these SALT talks have very poor chances of success unless they are accompanied by certain unilateral military measures of restraint by both sides, which of course have to be understood privately and informally.

Interview/The New York Times, 4-3:(4)17.

Henry A. Kissinger
Secretary of State of the United States
1

I do not believe that the Soviet Union is achieving military supremacy over the United States. I do not believe that any American Administration would permit a situation to arise in which the Soviet Union could achieve strategic superiority over the United States. But the essence of the contemporary problem in the military field is that the term "supremacy," when casualties will be in the tens of millions, has practically no operational significance, as long as we do what is necessary to maintain a balance.

Before National Press Club, Washington, Jan. 10/The New York Times, 1-11:6.

Henry A. Kissinger
Former Secretary of State of the United States
2

[On U.S.-Soviet negotiations to limit strategic arms]: The problem is as difficult as the technology which spawned it, and its solution is bound to be complicated and therefore time-consuming. Negotiations must proceed in a calm, non-confrontational way without self-imposed deadlines or rhetorical battles that publicly stake the prestige of both sides. The limitation of arms is not a favor one side does for the other. It is a fundamental necessity. A reasonable, balanced agreement taking into account the security concerns of both sides is achievable.

At Georgetown University, April 5/ The New York Times, 4-6:(A)3.

3

Though we cannot surpass the Soviet Union in all categories of military power, the free nations cannot fall behind in every significant category without suffering profound political consequences. Diplomacy, no matter how imaginative, cannot operate from impotence. Matching Soviet power in realistic ways that remove the incentive for oppression is the precondition of all effective policy.

At Georgetown University, April 5/ The Washington Post, 4-6:(A)4.

Edward I. Koch
United States Representative, D–New York
4

[Approving President-elect Carter's plan to pardon U.S. Vietnam-war draft evaders]: Whether one was for the war or opposed to the war — and I fall into the latter category — I believe it's time that we ended a period in the life of this country which is very divisive. And the only way that we can end that divisiveness is to pardon or amnesty these people . . . It is not in any way an attack upon those who responded to our country's call. And I must say candidly — and I served in World War II — that if I had been called to serve during Vietnam, my makeup is such that I would have gone in and fought, because that's the way I would respond even though I was opposed to the war. But that doesn't mean that those who refused to serve should not receive a compassionate response from this country. We are now four years past the point where the war was ended, and most people looking back would say: "We never should have been in that war in the first place."

Interview/U.S. News & World Report, 1-10:37.

WHAT THEY SAID IN 1977

George H. Mahon
United States Representative,
D–Texas
1

[Saying he opposes the B-1 bomber project because time has passed it by]: The only purpose of the B-1 bomber is as a clean-up weapon, and there won't be much to clean up if a war comes. You could use an ox-cart.

Before the House, Washington, Oct. 20/
The New York times, 10-21:(A)1.

George S. McGovern
United States Senator, D–South Dakota
2

[Opposing new nuclear weapons, such as the neutron bomb]: Our nuclear arsenal now is strong enough . . . If we don't have enough weapons now, when both sides are capable of utterly destroying the world, then there is no hope for the human race.

News conference, Las Vegas, Nev./
The Christian Science Monitor, 7-26:5.

Walter F. Mondale
Vice President of the United States
3

. . . I think the problem with SALT is that we're trying to go into a different generation of agreements that go beyond these policies of simply agreeing to outer limits. I consider the Vladivostok agreement, although I supported it, to be a situation in which our country simply took the two lists of everything they planned to do, stapled them together and called it an agreement, a breakthrough. Well, what we're trying to do is go beyond, from just putting outer limits on things both countries are planning to do, to a next-generation pact of actually reducing our armaments levels. I mean, that will bring real stability. And that's what's taking the time.

Interview, Washington/
The Christian Science Monitor, 6-22:6.

G. V. (Sonny) Montgomery
United States Representative,
D–Mississippi
4

[Arguing against President-elect Carter's plan to pardon U.S. Vietnam-war draft evaders]: These persons broke a Federal law. Unless the

law is changed retroactively, I think they should have to come back and face the music like everyone else who breaks a Federal law. We would be setting a bad precedent by giving a pardon to draft evaders. I think President-elect Carter is really opening up a can of worms that goes further than the precedent that he will set. The hard feelings that he will cause among the families whose sons have lost their lives, or husbands whose lives have been lost in Vietnam, or the millions of other Americans who went to Vietnam — I think he's going to have to face all that if he goes ahead and gives his pardon.

Interview/U.S. News & World Report, 1-10:37.

Thomas H. Moorer
Admiral (Ret.), United States Navy;
Former Chairman, Joint Chiefs of Staff
5

With modern intelligence, it is not possible to make a surprise attack from a world situation that is perfectly calm. We are not going to look up suddenly and see all those weapons falling on Washington.

U.S. News & World Report, 9-5:18.

Paul H. Nitze
Chairman, advisory council, Johns Hopkins
School of Advanced International Studies;
Former Deputy Secretary of Defense
of the United States
6

Nowhere am I saying that the Soviet Union wants a war or will make a war. All I'm saying is that we can have a situation where their superiority is clear. We know it and they know it. That kind of situation carries its own message before it.

The Washington Post, 2-20:(A)17.

Sam Nunn
United States Senator, D–Georgia
7

I do not think our young people have ever realized that the volunteer [armed] force could not possibly work in a war. I don't think any knowledgeable person would claim that we would be able to go back to even the Vietnam level of manpower with a volunteer force. What we now have is a peacetime volunteer force, with the inevitability that if we had a war —

(SAM NUNN)

even a limited war — we'd have to go back to the draft. Now, evidence that the volunteer force is in trouble is visible in severe discipline problems, particularly in the Marines. Also, the reserve forces are not able to meet their quotas ... The Army itself is experiencing recruiting difficulties. The Army is about 6 per cent under their quota so far in fiscal year '77. They also are experiencing more and more difficulty in getting high-school graduates. These are problems that are happening during a period of time when we have the most favorable possible circumstances for the volunteer force ... In my opinion, the volunteer force came about not on the basis of good analysis but on the basis of a political decision that was made by the Executive Branch — and, I must say, endorsed by Congress — that would buy time for Vietnam, cool the campuses, take the political heat off. I think it has been a real national mistake.

interview/
U.S. News & World Report,
2-14:59.

1

In the neutron bomb, NATO would have a weapon at its disposal that could be used on its own territory without devastating its own population. The neutron bomb would thus raise the nuclear threshold when compared to present-day nuclear weapons, increase the deterrent effect of our current tactical nuclear force, and lessen any temptation the Soviet Union and Warsaw Pact might have in the future to launch an invasion of Western Europe. It does these things, but I want to add what it does not do. It does not replace the need for strong conventional forces. If NATO's conventional forces are strong, we reduce even further the possibility of using any nuclear weapon. It does not totally redress the military balance in Europe. It does not cure the two main problems with our present tactical nuclear weapons: lack of range and poor survivability if hit by a surprise attack.

Interview/U.S. News & World Report,
7-25:26.

Michael O'Kennedy
Foreign Minister of Ireland

2

... the waste of resources in the widening and increasing build-up of armaments has become a scandal which is crying out for change. Today, 25 per cent of the world's scientific manpower is engaged in military-related pursuits, and 40 per cent of all research-and-development spending is earmarked for military purposes. For the past several years, world military expenditure has been about $300-billion each year. This sum is spent in a poverty-stricken world which urgently needs a new, more equitable international economic order. It is a chilling fact that the resources devoted to the arms race since the end of World War II are roughly the equivalent of the total 1976 gross national product for the entire world. Think for a moment what a difference it would mean to the developing world if even a proportion of these funds could be used to help the countless millions living in poverty, those still without clean water, the sick, the uneducated, the deprived. How much longer can the community of nations accept this scandal — that we direct so large a part of our resources to weapons with which to destroy one another?

At United Nations, New York/
The Christian Science Monitor, 11-30:31.

Richard E. Pipes
Professor of history, Harvard University;
Senior research consultant, Stanford
Research Institute's Strategic
Studies Center, Arlington, Virginia

3

[On whether "overkill" has made the arms race a fantasy]: No. If, for example, the Russians were to knock out a good part of our missile force in a massive preemptive strike, they would hold our cities hostage. They then would be able to tell us that the price of firing the weapons we had left for a second strike would be the destruction of our major cities. Who would dare it? "Overkill" assumes that the aim of strategic nuclear weapons is mass destruction of people, whereas their real purpose is to destroy the enemy's capacity to resist ... The notion that all we do is press the button

(RICHARD E. PIPES)

and the U.S.S.R. will blow up is unrealistic. The issue is whether you have the ability and the will under wartime conditions to launch missiles, if the cost is possible destruction of one-half your people. You can lay waste to Moscow and Leningrad, but at what price? In 1962, because of our vast superiority, we forced the Russians to back down in the Cuban missile crisis. Some day they might be able to do the same thing to us.

Interview/People, 4-11:46.

William Proxmire
United States Senator, D—Wisconsin
1

[On reports of Soviet military superiority over the U.S.]: [I question whether those reports take into consideration] our lead in [nuclear] warheads over the Soviet Union — 9,000 to 3,600 — or our five-year lead in MIRV technology; or the increased capabilities of the *Trident* submarine program; or the improved command, control and communications procedures; or the greatly enhanced re-targeting capability of the U.S. missile forces; or the U.S. development of cruise missiles; or our early-warning devices in space and at sea and on the ground; or many other areas where the U.S. has a significant lead over the Soviets.

Jan. 5/The Washington Post, 1-6:(A)4.

2

[Saying he approves of the all-volunteer armed forces]: I think we have to consider the unfortunate effects of the draft. After all, the draft is one thing in a wartime, when you induct most of the draft-age people. But during peacetime we would conscript a relatively small proportion of those who would be eligible. And that would mean that those who are not drafted would have an enormous advantage over those who are drafted. It would be a real injustice. [Universal national service] would be a nightmare. The idea of requiring conscripts to go into the Peace Corps, VISTA or something of that kind if they don't go into the military would be extremely bad. It would throw away the great virtue of the Peace Corps and VISTA — that is, volunteers that come in because they

want to be there. That volunteering makes for great morale and real motivation. And you'd lose all that. And you'd lose it also in the military. The fundamental argument for the volunteer Army is that it's just, it's fair. People are in the Army now because they want to be there. They're not in the Army because they're forced to be there. And in a society which is at peace, that's the way it ought to be.

Interview/U.S. News & World Report, 2-14:59.

3

I've felt right along that we should and can reduce certain military forces. There are many areas of waste. There's a waste not only of military manpower but of civilian manpower. We have a million civilians employed by the Department of Defense all over the world. More people are employed by the Department of Defense than all of the other agencies of government combined, if you leave the Post Office aside. There can be a great savings in that area. Furthermore, there are ways to save money on military manpower without decreasing our capability.

Interview/U.S. News & World Report, 2-14:60.

4

Myths about a Soviet civil-defense "gap" should not stampede Americans into the bomb-shelter mentality of the 1950s. Massive industrial and civil-defense efforts against nuclear attack are neither militarily effective nor cost effective. Soviet defenses have not kept pace with advances in U.S. strategic weapons and can easily be overcome by retargeting the U.S. inventory of more than 8,900 nuclear warheads.

The Christian Science Monitor, 5-17:1.

Thomas C. Reed
Secretary of the Air Force
of the United States
5

[On the incoming Carter Administration and how they will handle national defense]: They assume their responsibilities at a major crossroads. One road will cost money; it is paved with expenditures for the B-1 [bomber] and the M-X [missile]. The other road is not so costly now, in dollars. It bypasses these major

(THOMAS C. REED)

strategic programs in the name of economy and diverts the funds to other purposes. The first road, as I see it, is the road to stability and peace. The second road — well, let me quote from Somerset Maugham: "If a nation values anything more than freedom, it will lose its freedom; and the irony of it is, that if it is comfort or money that it values more, it will lose that too." We are now at a historic crossroads. The man who will next exercise authority over our national choices [President-elect Jimmy Carter] will assume office Thursday. He will be responsible for facing our adversaries, for meeting their challenges in the 1980s. The question is, will he face them with adequate strategic forces to back him up, or will he face the 1980s alone, like Willy Loman — with a shoeshine and a smile?

Before Houston Committee on Foreign Relations, Jan. 17/Vital Speeches, 2-15:271.

Hyman G. Rickover
Admiral, United States Navy

1

We have now chosen not to challenge [the Soviets] with numbers of ships. It is, therefore, essential that the ships we do build are the most powerful and effective weapons we know how to build. This means nuclear propulsion and the best anti-air, anti-submarine and surface-to-surface weapons we have for major warships.

U.S. News & World Report, 3-14:61.

2

[Saying there are too many Admirals in the Navy]: [If the Navy still had a carrier-pigeon service,] the senior pigeon in the pecking order would, I suppose, be a line Admiral. What we must recognize is that the purpose of our military is to defend the country, not to provide a place for comfortable careers.

Before Senate Armed Services Subcommittee on Manpower and Personnel, Washington, April 4/The Washington Post, 4-5:(A)8.

Thomas B. Ross
Assistant Secretary for Public Affairs, Department of Defense of the United States

3

[On recent incidents of military officers speaking out against government policy]: The right lesson [to be learned from the incidents] is that military men should not speak out against established policy. The wrong lesson is that military men should refrain from speaking to the press.

The New York Times, 6-17:(A)3.

Donald H. Rumsfeld
Secretary of Defense of the United States

4

When I came to Defense [in 1975], I spent time studying what the Soviet Union had been doing, and the facts then remain the facts today. We are looking at about 15 years of steady, purposeful effort on the part of the Soviet Union [to build up military capability], and 10 to 15 years of the U.S., for a variety of reasons, reducing its level of effort. My conclusion was that there was no doubt that were those trends to continue, then inevitably the lines would cross, and we would be injecting a fundamental instability into the world. Further, you didn't have to wait until we were in an inferior position for that instability to occur. Anyone can attack the [defense] budget; a trained ape could cut the budget by five, 10, 20 or 30 billion dollars. But the cumulative effect is that we would end up where we were last year: paying the penalty for successive reductions in real terms in the defense effort.

Interview/U.S. News & World Report, 1-17:15.

Dean Rusk
Professor of international law, University of Georgia; Former Secretary of State of the United States

5

... I'm very strongly opposed to unilateral disarmament. We demobilized after World War II, and have been picking up the pieces ever since. We didn't have a division in our Army ready for combat in 1946 or a group in our Air Force. [Then-Soviet-leader] Josef Stalin tried to take the northwest province of Iran. He demanded the two eastern provinces of Turkey. He supported the guerrillas going after Greece.

WHAT THEY SAID IN 1977

(DEAN RUSK)

He ignored the wartime agreements for the countries of Eastern Europe with regard to free elections. He organized the coup in Czechoslovakia, blockaded Berlin and gave the green light to the North Koreans to go after the South Koreans. Now, that's the kind of harvest you reap from unilateral disarmament. But on the other hand, in order to keep this arms race from just going through the ceiling, I'm very strongly in favor of verifiable and trustworthy agreements to limit these arms races.

Interview/U.S. News & World Report, 6-27:44.

Richard G. Stilwell
General, United States Army (Ret.);
Former Commander, U.S. forces in Korea
1

The *sine qua non* of a military establishment is discipline. If your superior has enunciated a policy, you may take public issue with that policy only if you are prepared to accept the consequences . . . Assuming that you know what the policy is, and if you feel strongly that it is wrong, then you can deliberately take your case to the public and retire from the service. That's professionalism.

Interview, Tokyo/Newsweek, 6-6:51.

John Taylor
Editor, "Jane's All the World's Aircraft"
2

[On the Soviet *Backfire* bomber] : You [the U.S.) have nothing really to counter it. Look at your North American Aerospace Defense Command. You have 325 *Delta Darts;* that's a 20-year-old aircraft. You have no surface-to-air missiles; you disbanded the lot. Your home defenses have been run right down. Just imagine 50 *Backfires,* each with one of these missiles attacking 50 American cities . . . On the other hand, the Russians have 2,600 fighters defending their country and 12,000 missiles on 10,000 launchers.

London/Los Angeles Herald-Examiner, 7-11:(A)10.

Stansfield Turner
Director of Central Intelligence
of the United States
3

While virtually all of the Soviet inventory of weapons falls within U.S. production technology, the Soviets simply do not have the technology required to produce many of the U.S. weapons, nor could they produce close substitutes.

Before Congressional Joint Economic subcommittee,
Washington, June/The New York Times, 8-23:10.

Cyrus R. Vance
Secretary of State of the United States
4

There are several things that should benefit [the Soviets in a comprehensive SALT agreement with the U.S.]. I believe they are seeking greater stability in the long run, and the comprehensive U.S. proposal will lead to that end. Our proposal also begins for the first time to get a handle on the problem of qualitative improvements. Rather than letting the cruise missile run free, our proposal would put a limit on the range, and that's something that should interest the Soviets. I think the Soviets recognize that we really have to make real cuts. How deep they are prepared to go I don't know. We will have to wait and see.

Interview, Washington/Time, 4-18:27.

William R. Van Cleave
Director, strategic and security
studies program, University
of Southern California
5

[On President Carter's expressed desire to rid the world of nuclear weapons] : [That is] such a silly platitude that one has to wonder why on earth it is worth uttering in an inaugural address . . . If that simplistic approach is a fair reflection or description of the attitude of the new President toward strategic and military matters, then I have a good measure of despair in me.

Panel discussion, Jan. 21/
The Christian Science Monitor, 1-27:9.

Lewis W. Walt
General (Ret.) and former Assistant
Commandant, United States Marine Corps

1

... we're not getting the kind of people in the armed forces we need. At the time when we got to the all-volunteer forces, weapons sophistication increased and sophistication of personnel went down ... I have been to [the] bases and have been measuring the troops and talking to them, seeing what their jobs are, for four years. They don't have the capabilities. We're putting 60 cents on a dollar into recruiting, bonuses, nice barracks and conveniences. And discipline is going down. They're not training them the way they used to. I'm telling you what the Generals are telling me — the people who know. . . . if you had a draft, what would it amount to? With the President's amnesty [for Vietnam draft resisters] they would say, "If they got away with it, why can't I?" The country has to talk up the military to our young people instead of talking it down. This is what killed the all-volunteer concept, the attitude of the American people since Vietnam. The only way it will work is to turn the people around.

Interview/The Dallas Times Herald, 5-19:(E)1.

Paul C. Warnke
Director-designate, Arms Control and
Disarmament Agency of the United States

2

I think we have to recognize that any arms-control agreement [with the Soviets] is going to have to be fair to both sides because, otherwise, there is no way in which it can endure. If, for example, we were to end up with an imbalance on one side or the other, the side that found itself at a disadvantage would have to repudiate the treaty in its national interest. Rough equivalence will have to do.

Before Senate Armed Services Committee,
Washington/The Washington Post, 2-27:(A)2.

3

... effective [arms-control] agreements would save us a hell of a lot of money. But more important, if you have effective arms control, you know you are going to have stability. If you have unregulated competition on arms, how do you know you are building the right weapons? You would end up with a continued competition and I would say at least moments of instability during the competition. If these moments coincide with times of grave international crisis, then you have significantly increased the chance of nuclear war. Arms control is a cheaper and safer alternative.

Interview, Washington/Time, 3-21:28.

James D. Watkins
Vice Admiral and Deputy Chief of
Operations (Manpower), United States Navy

4

[On the problem of illiteracy of naval recruits]: Attrition of personnel in the 19-to-24-year-old bracket is not a problem unique to the Navy. It is a problem for all branches of military service ... We have looked at the effects [on attrition] of such things as education levels, race, sex, age of recruits, marital status and intelligence and have found that, while all these factors play a part, the Number 1 descriptive predictor of attrition is the educational background of recruits.

Before San Diego Chamber of Commerce,
July/The Dallas Times Herald, 8-17:(I)1.

Lowell P. Weicker, Jr.
United States Senator, R—Connecticut

5

[Criticizing President Carter's blanket pardon of U.S. Vietnam war draft evaders]: [The late civil-rights leader] Martin Luther King broke the law but he changed the conscience of the country ... and he didn't run to Canada to get a pardon. He went to jail. Civil disobedience is fine. But you must also pay the consequences. I don't want the idealists of this nation to use the excuse that something is all right if everybody does it. I don't want to compromise so we can all feel better.

Before U.S. Senate Youth Program delegates,
Washington/Los Angeles Herald-Examiner, 2-4:(A)9.

Ted Weiss
United States Representative, D—New York

6

[Arguing against development of the controversial neutron bomb]: Since the atomic bomb was dropped on Hiroshima, the use of nuclear weapons has been regarded as a last resort. The

WHAT THEY SAID IN 1977

(TED WEISS)

neutron bomb changes all this. It is ballyhooed as a weapon that can be used in a limited war. This kind of thinking drops the threshold point for nuclear weapons from a last-resort situation to a tactical, field situation.

The New York Times, 9-30:(A)11.

Louis H. Wilson
General and Commandant,
United States Marine Corps

1

The readiness of the Marine Corps is unprecedentedly high everywhere. We are at full strength — 192,000 — and 78 per cent of our personnel are high-school graduates. We don't want to get bigger — just better ... The basic concept of the Marines hasn't changed, but the days of slow, ponderous movement across beaches are gone. We can achieve our objectives now in a more efficient manner, using modern technology such as helicopters ... The Marines' stock in trade is readiness.

We could get a division to Europe as fast as aircraft are available to move them. We expect to be the first to fight. We are ready to go.

U.S. News & World Report, 10-10:39.

Andrew Young
United States Ambassador/Permanent
Representative to the United Nations

2

[On the proposed neutron bomb]: Were I still a member of Congress, I would have certainly strongly opposed and worked against that weapon. It doesn't make sense to spend all that money killing folks. The problem in the world today is learning to understand people, not to destroy people. I would hope that maybe the meaning behind the vote in the Senate [to give President Carter funds to produce the bomb if he so decided] would be that it would strengthen the hand of our disarmament negotiators and that it would be mainly a bargaining point but never developed.

To reporters, Geneva, July 15/
The Washington Post, 7-16:(A)13.

James Abourezk
United States Senator, D—South Dakota
1

[Saying he will retire after only one term in the Senate]: I would like to return to a normal private life. I mean, something happens to you here [in Washington]. Most people come here with pretty high ideals. Then the day comes when you become convinced that you have to stay here in order to finish the work you have started. Then, suddenly, you're not being as hard-hitting. You lose your cutting edge. You start thinking that getting elected is more important than doing things.
Interview/The Dallas Times Herald, 11-27:(H)3.

Spiro T. Agnew
Former Vice President of the United States
2

[On the scandal that forced his resignation from office in 1973]: I don't think my name needs rehabilitation. I did nothing morally wrong in my eyes. I never accepted payments for my own personal use ... I made some errors in the way political money was collected and used. The error was drifted into because of the way the system worked.
Interview, Cairo, Egypt, May 1/
The Washington Post, 5-2:(A)18.

John B. Anderson
United States Representative, R—Illinois
3

That is a sort of general commentary on what has gone wrong with the first year of this [Carter] Administration: the tendency to pop out ideas, be it welfare reform, tax reform or energy plan; and then there hasn't been the sustained follow-through that would enable the President to take one thing, achieve it, and then build on that success. We are sort of practicing government on the deferred installment, and welfare reform gets put off until '78 or '79, tax

reform is kind of brushed aside now in a desire to pass an individual and business tax cut. As the President has gradually lowered some of the expectation that he had created for himself, he suffered a corresponding loss of credibility ... given the fact that we are at peace, given the fact that the recession did reach its low point more than two and a half years ago ... the President really had a golden opportunity. He did have his huge [Democratic] majorities, particularly in the House. Yet, for some curious reason, he somehow has not been able to perform the role of bringing together the forces in this country that want to see solutions. And I think that an opportunity lost is an opportunity seldom regained.
Interview/The New York Times, 12-18:(4)2.

Peter L. Berger
Professor of sociology, Rutgers University
4

[On whether President Jimmy Carter's being a Baptist affected his election last year]: I haven't seen any convincing evidence that the religious factor was very important in how people voted. My hunch is we don't learn very much from this about American religion, except perhaps the same kind of thing we learned from John F. Kennedy's election: that it's possible for a Roman Catholic to be elected. Fine. We've learned now that it's possible for this kind of a Baptist to be elected.
Interview/U.S. News & World Report, 4-11:71.

Alexander M. Bickel
Professor of law, Yale University
5

The monopoly of power enjoyed by the two major parties would not likely survive the demise of the Electoral College. Now the dominance of two major parties enables us to achieve a politics of coalition and accommodation

WHAT THEY SAID IN 1977

(ALEXANDER M. BICKEL)

rather than of ideological and charismatic fragmentation, governments that are moderate, and a regime that is stable.

Newsweek, 4-4:96.

Julian Bond
Georgia State Senator (D)
1

[On President Carter]: He promised no raise in Social Security taxes when he was candidate Carter, but President Carter says they must go up. He promised parity for blacks in his Administration, but the record shows few dark faces in Washington's high places, and many who make headlines, not policy. He promised to cut the defense by $15-billion, but his budget cuts totaled $2.8-billion. He promised to let us know when the CIA and the FBI abused our trust, but he tried to stop the American press from telling the story of CIA payoffs to foreign heads of state. He said that if winning jobs conflicted with fighting inflation, then inflation would have to continue, but now we hear that a balanced budget comes first. While New York smolders and burns, he visits Yazoo City. He has told poor women that life is unfair, and now tells us that the best way to help the poor is not to talk about them at all. In short, he is not evil, but he is President, not candidate, now; and like all those [who] preceded him in the Oval Office, is giving the squeaky wheel the most grease.

At National Student Association Congress, Houston, Aug. 15/The New York Times, 8-16:16.

Edward W. Brooke
United States Senator, R—Massachusetts
2

When you go to the [Carter] White House, the place looks physically dirty, people running around in jeans. It just doesn't look right.

Time, 11-28:121.

Robert F. Burns
Secretary of State of Rhode Island
3

[Arguing against a proposal to permit voter registration at the polls on the day of the election]: The problem in Rhode Island has never been low voter turnout ... [but] pre-

venting a return to the days when a voter turnout of 110 per cent was considered commonplace ... We have already identified and removed the names of over 6,000 people who were registered on voting rolls twice ... Those rolls are 99 per cent pure right now, and we want to keep them that way ... If the sponsors of this legislation don't believe that the registration of voters on the day of an election will open up new opportunities for vote fraud, they don't know the history of elections in the state of Rhode Island. If they don't believe that virtually eliminating the fundamental right of one voter to challenge the veracity of another ... will not result in assault and battery at the polls, then they have never heard of the Fourth Ward in the city of Providence. And if [they] believe that the mere threat of perjury for signing an affidavit at the polls will scare some of the over-zealous supporters of candidates ... then they are mistaking the kind of elections we have in Rhode Island for those peaceful caucuses that may be held in the farm-belt areas of America.

Before Senate committee, Washington/ The Washington Post, 5-20:(A)26.

Jimmy Carter
President-elect of the United States
4

I hope I have a chance to exemplify accurately what the American people are and what they would like to be. If I can stay close to the people of this country and not disappoint them, I think I have a chance to be a great President. It still remains to be seen. I'm determined to do the best I can and I think I have it within me, to the extent I can represent the American people well, [the ability] to achieve greatness. I hope that achievement doesn't come through unanticipated crisis or the prospect of war or some catastrophe that I might help to resolve, but through steady but exciting progress to the future.

Plains, Ga., Jan. 19/ The Washington Post, 1-20:(A)24.

Jimmy Carter
President of the United States
5

[Saying a Presidential candidate has an advantage over those running for Congress]:

(JIMMY CARTER)

You have a much broader range of issues to be fuzzy on.

Before press club, Washington/
The New York Times, 1-30:(4)1.

1

... all of the country has learned a great lesson from Watergate — to have a maximum amount of openness; to have much stricter standards of conduct required by public officials, those appointed and those elected; to scrutinize very closely the appointment procedure so that if someone does have a concealed conflict of interest financially it might be revealed. And I think the new election laws have brought us through the 1976 Presidential elections, and others, with a minimum of obligation on my part to anyone. I was elected without ever having promised anyone to be appointed to a major position.

News conference, Washington, Feb. 8/
The New York Times, 2-9:(A)16.

2

... I do favor at least an automatic vote by Presidential electors once the general election is completed. I think the Electoral College, for instance, should be eliminated. Whether the ratio among states of votes ought to be changed I'm not prepared to comment on now. As far as the financing of Congressional elections by public funds — it has proved to be successful, I believe, in the Presidential election. I strongly favor that, yes. And the other element of the overall package would be a simple way for American people who are citizens and 18 years old to register to vote. I am committed to that proposition.

News conference, Washington, Feb. 23/
The New York Times, 2-24:22.

3

[On former President Richard Nixon's recent broadcast interview about Watergate]: I think he was guilty of impeachable offenses [during Watergate]. But I believe that he doesn't think he was. I think he's rationalized in his own mind that he did all these things for the benefit of his staff members and so forth, and that he didn't have any criminal intent. I think he's mistaken, but I'm sure it's possible for any human being to rationalize [his] own actions.

News conference, Washington, May 12/
Los Angeles Times, 5-13:(1)7.

4

I think one of the characteristics of some liberals is that they are very difficult to please. And when some of the groups make a list of things that they want, if they get 95 per cent of what they want, they can only remember the other 5 per cent. And this is something which I don't particularly deplore but which I do recognize.

News conference, Washington, May 12/
U.S. News & World Report, 5-23:22.

5

It's a strange thing that you can go through your [election] campaign for President, and you have a basic theme that you express in a 15- or 20-minute standard speech that you give over and over, and the traveling press — sometimes exceeding 100 people — will never report that speech to the public. The peripheral aspects become the headlines, but the basic essence of what you are and what you stand for and what you hope to accomplish is never reported.

Interview, Washington/The New York Times,
6-19:(Book Review)34.

6

[On the controversy regarding Federal Budget Director Bert Lance's past financial dealings]: I don't know of anything illegal that Bert Lance has done. I don't know of any unethical conduct on his behalf. And I am keeping an open mind about this entire subject until the Senate goes through its present procedure ... [He is] now being given a fair chance to say, "These are all of the charges; this is my answer to them." And, of course, I will certainly have an eagerness to learn of any reason for me to change the assessment that I have just made. But I want to be fair about it ... There is a general sense at home [in

WHAT THEY SAID IN 1977

Georgia, where both he and Mr. Lance come from], not because it is in the South but because I live in a small town, that if you have several [bank] accounts and a substantial balance in all those accounts, but then you become overdrawn in one of those accounts, then that is not considered to be an illegal or unethical act ... I can't say that it is an acceptable thing. But I still don't believe that it is an unethical or illegal thing in the banking circles in which I have had to operate.

To editors and news directors, Washington, Sept. 16/The Washington Post, 9-18:(A)1,6.

1

[On the resignation of Federal Budget Director Bert Lance because of the controversy regarding his past financial dealings]: I accept Bert's resignation with the greatest sense of regret and sorrow. He is a good man. Even those who have made other statements about Bert have never alleged on any occasion that he did not do a good job as the Director of the Office of Management and Budget. He is close to me and always will be, and I think he has made the right decision, because it would be difficult for him to devote full time to his responsibilities in the future ... I have always trusted Bert Lance to do the proper and the unselfish thing. And my guess is that he was much more concerned about me and my Administration and the reputation of the government and the diversion of our attention to his case away from things that were important for the people. I think that was by far the most important factor in his decision.

News conference, Washington, Sept. 21/ The Washington Post, 9-22:(A)16.

Fidel Castro
Premier of Cuba

2

I observe American politicians and see them become corrupted in order to achieve power. In one state they make one statement, and in another a different one. There is no one speech for the entire American people. And once they are elected, they have to deal with a whole set of pressures and forces which prevent them from doing what should be done.

Interview/People, 3-21:67.

Clark M. Clifford
Former Secretary of Defense of the United States; Former chief defense attorney for then-Federal Budget Director Bert Lance

3

[On Bert Lance's resignation as OMB Director as a result of the controversy involving his past financial dealings]: I know Bert Lance to be an honest man and an able, devoted public servant. I was impressed that not one word of criticism concerned his administration of the office of OMB. I thought there was a good deal of justification for Senator [Thomas] Eagleton's comment that, whereas in the days of Senator Joseph McCarthy the slogan was "guilt by association," now apparently it's "guilt by accumulation." If you present enough charges over a sufficient period of time, perhaps you can ultimately drum a man out of government.

Interview/People, 11-14:97.

John B. Connally, Jr.
Former Secretary of the Treasury of the United States; Former Governor of Texas [D, now R]

4

[President Carter] promised that he was going to do something about unemployment; he over-promised on unemployment, and he hasn't been able to do anything about it. He over-promised on taxes, and he hasn't been able to do anything about that. He over-promised all across the board, including his own staff, the size of his staff; he hasn't been able to do anything about that ... He did this largely as a campaign strategy, partially, I think, from a lack of understanding of how difficult it was to deal with this national government.

TV-radio interview, Washington/"Meet the Press," National Broadcasting Company, 6-19.

5

[On why he switched from the Democratic to the Republican Party]: I felt that the Democrats were committed to more and more government, bigger and bigger bureaucracy, more and more spending; and, frankly, I think

(JOHN B. CONNALLY, JR.)

that is the worst thing that could happen to the country. I thought that the only hope among the viable political parties lay with the Republican Party, and so I switched and became a Republican. That essentially is the reason, and I have no regrets about it at all. I think subsequent events have certainly borne out my fears that the Democrats were committed to more and more spending, more and more government, greater and greater and bigger and bigger bureaucracy.

TV-radio interview, Washington/"Meet the Press," National Broadcasting Company, 6-19.

Alan Cranston
United States Senator, D–California
1

[On criticism of President Carter's first year in office]: In the context of the turmoil our country has been through in recent years, the fact is no President has been able to lead to the degree that we expect a President to lead, for 16 years now. We have had disasters, division, destroyed Presidencies; and meanwhile all sorts of problems have been unattended, festering, getting worse and worse. Whoever became President on January 20, 1977, could not have been expected to resolve them all at once or all with success. President Carter, with a conscientious concern, with a good deal of courage, and with perhaps a lack of total wisdom in terms of tackling them all at once, felt it necessary to do so.

Interview/The New York Times, 12-18:(4)2.

John C. Danforth
United States Senator, R–Missouri
2

[Addressing Federal Budget Director Bert Lance on the controversy involving his past financial dealings]: The Senate has a role in . . . confirming Presidential nominees and overseeing the performance of the Executive Branch. [But] I do not believe that the Senate has a continuing role to review the past personal life or business life of a person serving in the Executive Branch after the confirmation process has been completed. Therefore, my view is that while it might be of interest to

other agencies of government what you did with respect to overdrafts and what you did with respect to airplanes while you were living in Georgia, that is not of special interest to me as a Senator.

At Senate Governmental Affairs Committee hearing on the Lance controversy, Washington, Sept. 15/Los Angeles Times, 9-22:(2)7.

Pete V. Domenici
United States Senator, R–New Mexico
3

[On President Carter's support of former Budget Director Bert Lance, who resigned amid controversy over his past financial dealings]: I believe that Carter did what he had to do under the circumstances. I disagree with those who think that people in high places cannot afford a real friend. These jobs are lonely, difficult, and a real friend is important. I'm not critical of the President at all. This was a sad, hard, personal decision for Carter, and it will not hurt him with Congress.

Interview/U.S. News & World Report, 10-3:19.

Abba Eban
Former Foreign Minister of Israel
4

Voluntary abdication from the political arena seems to be a rarity. Somehow, politics is a kind of addiction and, like many addictions, sometimes you know it's not very good for you, and yet you go on with it.

Interview, New York/ The New York Times, 8-21:(1)34.

John D. Ehrlichman
Former Assistant to the President of the United States (Richard M. Nixon) for Domestic Affairs
5

[On his involvement in the Watergate affair]: When I went into government, it was the first time that I worked for anyone in a principal-and-agent or a boss-and-employee relationship [in over 20 years]. And I took that relationship very seriously. For one thing, my boss was the President of the United States. For another, it was my first experience in government. He [then-President Nixon] had experience in government of 25 or 26 years as a man of government. And I had a — what I now

WHAT THEY SAID IN 1977

(JOHN D. EHRLICHMAN)

realize to have been — an exaggerated sense of my obligation to do as I was bidden, without exercising independent judgment in the way I might have if it had been an attorney-client relationship. In looking back on it, there were all kinds of red flags. And had I been wiser, I certainly would have crept out when my instincts told me that this was a moral dilemma in which I was finding myself. I went and lied; and I'm paying the price for that lack of will-power. I, in effect, I abdicated my moral judgments and turned them over to somebody else. And if I had any advice for my kids, it would be never, to never ever defer your moral judgments to anybody — your parents, your wife, anybody. That's something that's very personal. And it's what a man has to hang onto.

Recorded message to Watergate Judge John
Sirica/The New York Times, 10-6:83.

Millicent H. Fenwick
United States Representative,
R—New Jersey 1

We've got to get a standard that is an acknowledged shame to break. I know there can be an exaggeration of strict morality, the blue laws and the puritanical impulses; but there's a happy medium between that and what we've got now . . . We've come a long way from Pericles, and Washington's no Athens, but questions about accepted standards of ethical conduct are certainly not academic in the capital these days. They are, in the truest sense, the most unhappy talk of this town.

Interview, Washington/The Washington Post, 7-17:(A)3.

Gerald R. Ford
Former President of the United States 2

[The U.S. is] a moderate nation of moderate people to whom ideology is far less important than practicality . . . A contest within our [Republican Party] ranks to prove who is the purer of ideology will not attract the American people . . . They prefer common sense to conservatism and/or liberalism, and if we are to earn the support of the American people we must prove ourselves to be the party of common sense and results.

At conference of Republican state legislative
leaders, Los Angeles/The Washington Post, 4-18:(A)5.

3

[Saying he will continue to speak out on public issues]: I'm not running for anything. But I'm not ready for the rocking-chair and I will not be muzzled by any partisan, Democratic, self-annointed censors. The quiet role of elder statesman, so comfortable for some of my predecessors, holds very, very little appeal for me.

At Republican fund-raiser, Milwaukee/
The Dallas Times Herald, 6-13:(A)2.

4

[President Carter has done] a superior job of convincing the American people by very skillful use of the media that he's on top of the job . . . that he was the right choice for the Presidency . . . But my impression is that the public now wants to see how the President and his Administration will deal with substance and the tough decisions that have to be made.

Interview/Los Angeles Times, 6-27:(1)4.

5

[On the achievements of his Administration]: The most difficult problem we inherited was the total division within the country, the angry mood, the turmoil, plus a number of very serious international problems. Over a period of time, by keeping cool and getting good people to do the job in each and every department, we dissipated the angry attitude that people had toward the government and toward one another. If I were to write my own summary, that would be what I am most proud of — and what I would want history to record as an achievement of the Administration.

At panel discussion sponsored by American
Enterprise Institute for Public Policy
Research/The Christian Science Monitor, 7-15:31.

Alexander George
Political scientist, Stanford University 6

[President] Jimmy Carter appears to be still trying to figure out how to get a handle on the

(ALEXANDER GEORGE)

established political system in Washington — how to make it work for him. I think he realizes that he doesn't yet have a good strategy for getting results out of his Presidency . . . The biggest disappointment is that a Democratic President has been unable to develop better working relations with a heavily Democratic Congress. There are many reasons for this, including Carter's own inexperience and the fact that Congress itself has undergone major changes recently because of Watergate and the infusion of a lot of new faces. Carter has not yet used the strategy that worked so well for him with the Georgia Legislature — developing well-considered reforms and pushing them against opposition. He hasn't taken this bold approach yet with Congress, but sooner or later he will have to face a showdown.

Interview/U.S. News & World Report, 11-7:23.

Barry M. Goldwater
United States Senator, R—Arizona

1

[On former President Richard Nixon's recent televised interview on the subject of Watergate]: He's as dead as he can be. I have no sympathy for him at all. I don't know any Republican in his right mind who would want him back.

The Dallas Times Herald, 5-5:(A)1.

2

[On President Carter]: His problem is getting Jimmy Carter across. He had the bad habit of taking both sides of a problem every day. The man I admired the most was Harry Truman. I disagreed with him on most things, but you knew where he stood.

To reporters, Washington, Oct. 11/
Los Angeles Times, 10-13:(1)6.

Robert P. Griffin
United States Senator, R—Michigan

3

There is nothing new about the observation that P.R. imagery is important in politics. But with the emergence of TV and TV advertising, it becomes all but crucial. The higher the office, the more important P.R. imagery becomes. The

smile, the catchy slogan, the choice of a campaign jingle often decide elections. It is necessary and valuable, of course, for a candidate to take his stand on issues and to formulate and articulate his program. But there is no assurance whatever that the election will be decided on that basis. When talking to a small group of potential Senate candidates recently, I had to advise them that the most critical decision they might make in setting up a campaign is likely to be the selection of the advertising agency. In a closely divided state, if your TV ads are better — if they carry more wallop — than your opponents', you'll probably win.

Before American Association of the Professions and Michigan Association of the Professions, Mackinac Island, Mich., Aug. 27/Vital Speeches, 11-15:83.

Paul R. Haerle
Chairman, California Republican Party

4

With all due respect for our old heroes, I think it's time for new people to come forward and lead us in battle. I believe that within the next couple of years the [Republican] Party will be inherited by new faces . . . people never photographed with [former President Richard] Nixon in the '50s.

San Francisco Examiner & Chronicle,
2-20:(This World)2.

H. R. Haldeman
Former Assistant to the President of the United States (Richard M. Nixon)

5

[On his role in the Watergate affair]: I have strong feelings of responsibility that whatever wrong was done will never be done again by me. I have a feeling I have an obligation to make amends . . . I have no bitterness. I have no personal animosity toward anyone. I have the deepest personal regret for everything I have done. I realize the damage it has done to the nation, and I will carry for the rest of my life the burden of knowing how greatly my acts contributed to this tragedy.

Recorded message to Watergate Judge John Sirica/Los Angeles Times, 10-5:(1)22.

WHAT THEY SAID IN 1977

Erwin C. Hargrove
Director, Institute for Public Policy
Studies, Vanderbilt University
1

[On President Carter]: I never felt I had a grasp of what makes him tick ... Here's a guy who's a moralist with high standards and all that stuff, and yet, when the chips are down, a complete blind spot for his friend [former Budget Director Bert Lance who resigned amid a controversy about his financial dealings]. So which is stronger here? The more human qualities are kind of appealing, but what does that say for the preachy part of him? I suppose that's the thing that puzzles people. Carter is a many-sided man. There was a kind of moral absolutism which has given way to pragmatism — and now, what next?

U.S. News & World Report, 10-17:26.

Gary W. Hart
United States Senator, D–Colorado
2

There's no Southern bloc for [President] Carter — there's not even a Georgia bloc for Carter that he can go back to, time after time, for support. He has no ideology, so there's no ideological bloc. He ran against the Democratic Party in the election [last year] and beat it, but he did not form any Carter coalition. Blacks voted for him. So did labor. But he did not really form a coalition that he can turn to. So there's no natural Carter base in Congress.

The New York Times, 6-18:7.

Hubert H. Humphrey
United States Senator, D–Minnesota
3

Every time I've been with him [President Carter], I come back with greater respect for him. I come back feeling that he knows a lot more than his critics give him credit for. This is no country boy. This is no naive fellow ... He understands how you appeal to the public. Now he's also going to have to understand that, public or no public, he's got to work with Congress ... He's a man who wears a velvet glove and has a very strong fist. He's a persevering man and he's tenacious. I don't say he's stubborn ... But he knows that when you deal with the Congress, if you give in too soon, they get used to that. I think he has sized us up

and he is not ready to back off right at the beginning on one thing after another, because there's no limit to what the Congress will ask of a President ...

Interview, Washington/
The Dallas Times Herald, 5-1:(A)9.

4

What I want more in life than anything else now is respect, which I think I'm beginning to earn and get. I don't want to be President. I don't want to be Vice President. I don't want to be Secretary of State or Majority Leader. I know that these things are not to be mine, and I have put them very neatly aside, without remorse. But what I do want is to be known in the history books — and I am interested in that as an effective man in government: that I was a decent man, that I knew my job, that I knew how to get things done and that I did important things in government.

Interview, Washington/The Washington Post, 6-23:(A)3.

5

[Saying President Carter has been guided by public-opinion polls]: I think that's a very dangerous thing to do. I think that a man who is President has to lead and has to be willing to take some risks and do things that at times, at the beginning, may not seem very popular.

Interview, Washington, July 27/
Los Angeles Times, 7-28:(1)5.

E. Howard Hunt
Convicted Watergate conspirator
6

[On the time he spent in prison for Watergate crimes]: Yes, I would say that I entertain a pretty good amount of bitterness. I'm bitter, I would say, against [Judge] John Sirica for the absolutely unprecedented sentence that was handed me, but also [toward] those White House elements who remained in power after I was in prison and were too busy seeking their own salvation to pay any attention to the plight of those of us who were already broken and in custody ... Because I've paid my price for Watergate — in sorrow ... wasted years; in tragedy, ridicule and humiliation — I feel no public act of contrition can be required of me.

Brookline, Mass./The Dallas Times Herald, 2-25:(A)5.

Jacob K. Javits
United States Senator, R—New York
1

. . . I think people should rally to the Republican Party and make it what they want to make it, precisely because the two-party system is essential to American freedom and the Republican Party is in jeopardy. It is having an appeal to so small a part of the electorate as to jeopardize its very existence. It needs a broader base. It needs really to espouse essentially an economic policy which will be attractive to this country, because we are a business country and the Republican Party is a business party. But business today includes millions upon millions of professionals and semi-quasi-professionals and small businessmen and blue-collar workers who are making $15,000, $18,000 and $20,000 a year. So the field is enormous, and we should be able to rally.

TV-radio interview/"Meet the Press,"
National Broadcasting Company, 11-13.

Leon Jaworski
Lawyer; Special Counsel,
House Ethics Committee
2

[On his investigating the scandal involving South Korean businessman Tongsun Park's payments to U.S. Congressmen] : It is my firm conviction that the pertinent facts will ultimately come to light. I would advise those who may believe that the investigation will blow over or prove fruitless to take a closer look. It will not go away until the American people are satisfied that all of the significant facts have been laid bare . . . The American people . . . can forgive wrongful conduct freely admitted far more easily than wrongful conduct covered up.

Before House Ethics Committee, Washington,
Aug. 24/Los Angeles Times, 8-25:(1)1.

Hamilton Jordan
Assistant to President of the
United States Jimmy Carter
3

[On President Carter's popularity drop in public-opinion polls] : Why have the polls dropped? Because people don't like us. We've done a lot of things simultaneously. We're right smack dab in the middle of it all. Of course, the best way to be a popular Governor or Mayor or

President is not to do a hell of a lot. If you do a lot — and he found this out when he was Governor of Georgia — you bounce up and down in the polls . . . We're not reacting; we're leading. Welfare reform. Social Security. We're showing leadership and guts. Previous Presidents, some of them, have not wanted to tackle any of the rough problems. We do.

The Dallas Times Herald, 12-4:(A)25.

Marvin Kalb
Diplomatic correspondent, Columbia
Broadcasting System News
4

[President Carter] tends to say things perhaps prematurely. He'll say that we're a couple of weeks away from a strategic-arms agreement. Then his people back at the State Department and the White House will say, "Well, the President didn't quite mean that. It's not that we're quite a few weeks away but probably quite a few months away if we're lucky." The only thing we're a couple of weeks away from is some guidelines on one aspect of the problem. So that the impression in Washington is that the President tends to . . . "over-speak" himself. He goes beyond whatever he himself knows to be the case. He leaves the impression of trying to win an audience for momentary advantage. Then he'll pull back and realize what he said, and at the next news conference go back and explain it.

Interview/Parade, 12-11:4.

Bert Lance
Director, Federal Bureau of
Management and Budget
5

[On the controversy involving his past financial dealings] : The rights that I thought I had as an American have been treated in the most irresponsible and destructive manner. The basic American principle of justice and fair play has been pointedly ignored by certain members of this committee. Certain persons have publicly, in effect, brought in a verdict of "guilty" before I had been given the opportunity to present my side of the case. It has been a saddening and disillusioning experience . . . I have worked hard these past eight months in Washington, and I am proud of the job I have

(BERT LANCE)

done in OMB. But is it part of our American system that a man can be drummed out of government by a series of false charges, half-truths, misrepresentations, innuendos and the like? I have long felt that businessmen should be willing to take positions in our government. They can bring new ideas, new attitudes, new philosophies and, as a result, our government can be more responsive to the views of all our people. I speak, more in sorrow than in anger, when I suggest that it won't be any easier to get these men and women to volunteer for public service after my experience of these past weeks. Abraham Lincoln had a rare facility for putting into words what many men have felt through the ages. Let me close with this famous quotation from President Lincoln: "If I were to try to read, much less answer, all the attacks made on me, this shop might as well be closed for any other business. I do the very best I know how — the very best I can; and I mean to keep doing so until the end. If the end brings me out all right, what is said against me won't amount to anything. If the end brings me out wrong, ten angels swearing I was right would make no difference."

Before Senate Governmental Affairs Committee, Washington, Sept. 15/Los Angeles Times, 9-16:(1)28.

Arthur A. Link
Governor of South Dakota (D)　　　　　*1*

[On the "instant, election-day registration" system for voters in his state]: Voting should present the fewest obstacles for the greatest numbers of people. Our system helps bring to the polls people who would find it a burden to pre-register — young people who haven't voted before, the elderly who can't travel easily, people who hold jobs with inflexible hours, and those who can't afford a car and find it difficult to use public transportation.

U.S. News & World Report, 5-30:51.

Russell B. Long
United States Senator, D—Louisiana　　*2*

I am a populist in some respects, and I would like to think I am a conservative in other respects. I think some of the best Senators and best Presidents are both conservative and liberal by the best definition of those words. If you mean conservative because they favor keeping the good things about the existing order, I would call them conservatives. And if you mean liberal because they favor aggressive, constructive change, I favor that. In some respects I even regard myself as a reactionary because there were some very good things in our lives that we let get away and should try to regain. Some of the old values had much more to be said for them than some of these new values we hear so much about. Whatever it was that gave us our inner strength as a nation, we should try to recapture it.

Interview/Nation's Business, August:23.

Alice Roosevelt Longworth
Daughter of the late President of the United States Theodore Roosevelt　　*3*

[On the new Southern influence in Washington now that Georgian Jimmy Carter will be President]: I don't see any excitement about anything — there's nothing new about these people at all. What's so special about these Georgians? — they don't wear queer clothes; they don't wear masks; they're not hermaphrodites. Administrations come and go, and this one will behave like the others, behave just like ordinary people with extraordinary power. It's tiresome. I'm not in the least excited about these people. I've looked on it all too long and I can only be mean about it. I'm interested, but only as an ancient observer. Just say I'm old and half-witted; just say I'm a tottering old thing who remembers nothing at all; say that I've lost my senses. You see, I don't think nobly about politicians. I think ignobly about them.

Interview/The New York Times, 1-19:(B)4.

Lester G. Maddox
Former Governor of Georgia (D)　　　*4*

If I had become part of the Establishment, I would have come out of office without owing a penny. Politics is ugly, brutal, mean; yessir, it's been a disaster for me. It's interrupted my

(LESTER G. MADDOX)

family life. It's destroyed me financially. I've paid my price. I'll never go back to politics.

Interview, Atlanta,
The Washington Post, 6-23:(B)15.

Charles McC. Mathias, Jr.
United States Senator, R—Maryland
1

There are really three possibilities for the Republican Party to come back: One is on the heels of a national disaster, and no patriotic Republican wants that. Another is the kind of gradual disintegration that always overcomes an incumbent party, like the Democratic ascendancy that ran from Franklin Roosevelt's election in 1932 to the Eisenhower victory a generation later. Then there is what I call the high-road approach through the development of solid, intellectual programs. I think that's the best way — and a great national party can't come back without it.

Interview/
U.S. News & World Report,
8-29:24.

John L. McClellan
United States Senator, D—Arkansas
2

[Saying he will not seek re-election next year, after 35 years in the Senate]: There is a proper time to aspire, a time to achieve, and a time to retire.

The Dallas Times Herald,
11-26:(B)2.

George S. McGovern
United States Senator, D—South Dakota
3

The present economic and social policies of this [Carter] Administration are out of step with the [Democratic] platform of 1976, the platform of 1972 and the platform of 1968. These are the kinds of things that mainstream Democrats have deplored when advocated by Republicans, and I don't see why we should be silent when they are advocated by a Democrat.

To reporters, Washington, May 13/
The Washington Post, 5-14:(A)2.

Marshall McLuhan
Professor of English and director,
Center for Culture and Technology,
University of Toronto
4

[California Governor Edmund Brown, Jr., has] a very charismatic image and otherwise he wouldn't be here. That is, he resembles an awful lot of other very pleasant people. [Former President] Richard Nixon only looked like himself [on television], not like a lot of other people. [The late President] Jack Kennedy looked like the all-American boy. [President] Jimmy Carter looks like the all-American Southern boy — Huck Finn in the White House.

To reporters, Sacramento, Calif., July 12/
The Dallas Times Herald, 7-13:(A)2.

Lee Metcalf
United States Senator, D—Montana
5

[On a lawsuit brought by Common Cause, which challenges Congressmen's franking privileges as being used for political purposes]: This is a very grave issue. The Senate and the House are being challenged in their right to communicate with constituents. All of us are political. We are members of a political institution. A member of Congress is part of the political process. But to make the political process work, it's essential that our people at home know what we're doing. It's a question of accountability.

The New York Times, 6-12:(1)27.

William G. Milliken
Governor of Michigan (R)
6

We have tried very hard in Michigan to broaden the base of the [Republican] Party to include groups within our society that are not normally, at least currently in the present day, associated with the Republican Party. We, for example, believe very strongly in this state and, I believe, strongly across the country, that there has to be representation of black citizens. I think any policy of the Republican Party, or for that matter of the Democratic Party, which attempts to write off blacks is not only morally wrong but it is politically stupid. We have to set out deliberately, in my judgment, to broaden

211

WHAT THEY SAID IN 1977

(WILLIAM G. MILLIKEN)

this base ... First of all, to enlist competent blacks as candidates for office at all levels. That is Number 1. Secondly, to be sure that the positions that our Party takes and articulates are reflective of the problems that blacks have in this country.

TV-radio interview, Detroit/"Meet the Press," National Broadcasting Company, 9-11.

Walter F. Mondale
Vice President of the United States 1

[On whether he would seek the Presidency in 1984 if President Carter is re-elected in 1980]: You're not going to believe this, but I don't have any thoughts about 1984. I have always tried to do my job well on the theory that's the best politics and on the theory that it may be the last public job you're going to have and that it is important that you do it properly. I have one goal right now — to the extent I can, I want to help President Carter be the best President we can possibly have. If he succeeds, that's my success. I have no plans; I've given no thoughts to what happens after that.

Interview, Washington/ The Christian Science Monitor, 4-25:14.

2

[On the Carter Administration's accomplishment in its first year]: I think this first year in office and in cooperative relationship that has been established with the Congress has brought about one of the most significant periods of accomplishment in American history. If you just look at what has happened already: perhaps the most pervasive economic stimulation package in American history, public-service employment, accelerated public works, counter-cyclical revenue-sharing, the first Youth Employment Act in American history, strip-mine legislation, a major new reorganization act, the creation of a Department of Energy in less than five months, a major farm bill — many, many other programs that have already been adopted. We are going to have, before this Congress is over, I am sure, a long overdue and absolutely crucial restructuring of the Social Security fund so that fund will be

restored to integrity. And we will, at long last, have a major, profound energy program in place with a good department to run it. And all of that has occurred in the first year. I don't think there have been many periods in American history where more has been accomplished than this.

TV-radio interview/"Meet the Press," National Broadcasting Company, 11-6.

Daniel P. Moynihan
United States Senator, D–New York 3

There's a certain insensitivity to untruth that politicians acquire. Even to genuinely villainous distortion. They start saying, "Well, it's part of the game," and it should *never* be part of the game. You shouldn't become, as some do, amiable about it. It's wrong, because your capacity for indignation atrophies. If you become tolerant of distortion when it is done by other people, you become tolerant about doing it yourself. I really do think that happens.

Interview/Playboy, March:66.

4

I think Gerald Ford will be remembered as the President who bumped his head, had a wonderful wife and left Americans more at peace with themselves and the rest of the world than at any time since the United States became a world power. He got us out of the Watergate nightmare and got us back some pride and self-reliance. Ford's Cabinet table-talk was perhaps the best I've ever heard in Washington. When you had Ed Levi and John Dunlop and Bill Coleman triangulating a complex Constitutional issue — "What does the Federalist Paper number 59 have to say about this?" — and you had Jim Schlesinger participating and Henry Kissinger listening — when he was there, which wasn't often — well, you had pretty high-quality conversation. And Ford was very good, presiding but not interfering. Not a bad Administration.

Interview/Playboy, March:78.

Ron Nessen
Press Secretary to President of
the United States Gerald R. Ford

1

[On President Ford's loss in last November's Presidential election] : None of us who hasn't experienced it can ever come close to understanding that feeling. You work hard; you campaign hard. On November 2 you seek the ultimate judgment of your peers, 215 million people, and it comes back, thumbs down.

Interview, Washington/Los Angeles Times, 1-9:(1)2.

Richard M. Nixon
Former President of the United States

2

[On statements he made about Watergate after April 30, 1973, until he resigned in August of 1974] : I would say that the statements that I made afterwards were, on the big issues, true: that I was not involved in the matters that I have spoken to, about — not involved in the break-in [at Democratic headquarters] ; that I did not engage in the, and participate in, or approve the payment of money or the authorization of clemency, which were, of course, the essential elements of the cover-up. That was true. But the statements were misleading in exaggerating, in that enormous political attack I was under. It was a five-front war with a fifth column. I had a partisan Senate committee staff. We had a partisan special-prosecutor staff. We had a partisan media. We had a partisan Judiciary Committee staff in the fifth column. Now, under all these circumstances, my reactions in some of the statements and press conferences and so forth after that, I want to say right here and now, I said things that were not true. Most of them were fundamentally true on the big issues, but without going as far as I should have gone, and saying perhaps that I had considered other things, but had not done them. And for all those things I have a very deep regret.

Television interview, San Clemente, Calif./"The Nixon Interviews," Paradine Productions, 5-4.

3

[On the Watergate cover-up] : If a cover-up is for the purpose of covering up criminal activities, it is illegal. If, however, a cover-up . . . is for a motive that is not criminal, that is something else again. I didn't believe that we were covering up any criminal activities. I didn't believe that [then-Attorney General] John Mitchell was involved. I didn't believe that, for that matter, anybody else was. I was trying to contain it politically. And that's a very different motive from the motive of attempting to cover up criminal activities of an individual. And so there was no cover-up of any criminal activities. That was not my motive.

Television interview, San Clemente, Calif./
"The Nixon Interviews," Paradine Productions, 5-4.

4

[On the Watergate affair] : I let down my friends. I let down the country. I let down our system of government and the dreams of all those young people that ought to get into government but think it's all too corrupt and the rest. Most of all, I let down an opportunity that I would have had for 2½ years to proceed on great projects and programs for building a lasting peace, which has been my dream . . . I let the American people down, and I have to carry that burden with me for the rest of my life . . . As far as the handling of this matter is concerned, it was so botched up. I made so many bad judgments. The worst ones, mistakes of the heart, rather than the head . . . But let me say, a man in that top job, he's got to have a heart — but his head must always rule his heart.

Television interview, San Clemente, Calif./
"The Nixon Interviews," Paradine Productions, 5-4.

5

I can only say that no one in the world, and no one in our history, could know how I felt [when resigning the Presidency in 1974]. No one can know how it feels to resign the Presidency of the United States. Is that punishment enough [for Watergate]? Oh, probably not. But whether it is or isn't . . . we have to live with not only the past but for the future, and I don't know what the future brings; but whatever it brings, I'll still be fighting.

Television broadcast, San Clemente, Calif./
"The Nixon Interviews," Paradine Productions, 5-25.

WHAT THEY SAID IN 1977

Thomas P. O'Neill, Jr.
United States Representative,
D–Massachusetts

1

They [President Carter and his aides] came up here and they didn't understand us Irish politicians or Italian politicians or Jewish politicians from the urban areas. The average Southerner is a sweet-talker and a charmer and charismatic, a smooth type that can skin you alive with sweetness and kindness.

San Francisco Examiner & Chronicle,
4-10:(This World)2.

2

I sat down with the President [Carter] and I said, "Let me tell you something: Franklin Roosevelt in 1933 came in with a mess of legislation, the country was in the throes of a revolution – economic and every other way. The question was, does democracy work? He had a rubber-stamp Congress. Of the elected Presidents along the way, Eisenhower, Kennedy and Nixon, not one of those Presidents in the first 100 days passed a major piece of legislation. You have passed an economic stimulus package. You have seen the House pass an ethics bill, which you asked for and which would be the core of your ethics legislation. We have passed your reorganization bill. We have passed your bill creating the Energy Department. You have done more in the first 120 days or so than any President since Roosevelt in 1933."

Interview, Washington/Los Angeles Times, 6-21:(1)10.

Bob Packwood
United States Senator, R–Oregon

3

[Opposing a bill which would provide public financing of Senate election campaigns]: There is nothing to stop a rich man or a wealthy special-interest group from spending a million dollars buying up huge blocks of television time or buying massive amounts of newspaper ads, radio spots, bumper stickers or billboards for the election or defeat of a candidate, provided he does it on his own and not in coordination with a candidate. What we are talking about with public financing is transferring the power of the individual choice from the average individual to the wealthy and the powerful . . . We are talking about giving up control to organizations and individuals unaccountable to anybody but their own special interests and momentary passions.

The Wall Street Journal, 7-19:14.

Tongsun Park
South Korean businessman

4

[On the scandal involving alleged payments he made to U.S. Congressmen]: Whatever I have done in Washington has been done on my personal account as a private businessman; it has nothing to do with the Korean government. It is important to realize, once and for all, that it is strictly for my own private business, and that's my gospel truth. It seems to me that many people are trying to create certain allegations, that I must be a lobbyist working for the Korean government, and I came to Washington with sacks full of money and started to distribute. That sort of allegation is not simply true. As I have always maintained, I would always cooperate, and that's the reason why I submitted myself to officials of the [U.S.] Justice Department. But whatever we discussed, in absolute confidence, that as you know, not only what I said came out but in gross exaggeration and innuendos, and all kinds of allegations came out, and I really don't think that I should subject myself to that kind of situation again. And unless I get an absolute guarantee of some sort that is written, or something else, I would not even consider going to Washington at this time.

News conference, Seoul, Aug. 24/
The New York Times, 8-25:(A)12.

Charles H. Percy
United States Senator, R–Illinois

5

We have to get the [Republican] Party out of the country clubs, out of a Caucasian atmosphere, away from the Anglo-Saxon approach. As long as the Republican Party takes a Neanderthal point of view, I don't see why it deserves to win.

Time, 12-12:93.

Jody Powell
*Press Secretary to President of
the United States Jimmy Carter*

1

. . . we came into the Administration after a campaign in which the fact that Jimmy Carter was new on the political scene was a major basis for attack by our political opposition. They saw it as an opportunity to exploit, and they did a fairly successful job of it. We have, to some extent, been in the process of repairing the damage done from that campaign. But I don't think there's any magic solution to it. You are dealing with a man who is not particularly easy to put into a box. And over the course of this first year, we have irritated just about every interest group and area of the political spectrum from one end to the other. We are taking a pragmatic approach to problems. Look at two of the major things we've proposed so far — welfare and energy, for example. They are a combination of proposals that could be traditionally considered conservative or liberal.

*Interview, Washington/
U.S. News & World Report, 10-10:27.*

Ronald Reagan
Former Governor of California (R)

2

The time has come to start acting to bring about the great conservative majority party we know is waiting to be created . . . I believe the political success of the principles we believe in can best be achieved in the Republican Party. I believe the Republican Party can and should provide the political mechanism through which the goals of the majority of Americans can be achieved. For one thing, the biggest single grouping of conservatives is to be found in that party. It makes more sense to build on that grouping than to break it up and start over. Rather than start a third party, we can have a new first party made up of people who share our principles . . . The New Republican Party I envision will not, and cannot, be limited to the country-club/big-business image that it is burdened with today. The New Republican Party I am speaking about is going to have room for the man and woman in the factories, for the farmer, for the cop on the beat and the millions of Americans who may never have thought of

joining our Party before but whose interests coincide with those represented by principled Republicans.

*At Conservative Political Action
Conference, Washington/San Francisco
Examiner & Chronicle, 2-6:(A)16.*

3

[On whether the Electoral College system should be abolished]: Conveniently forgotten . . . is the fact that our Constitution binds us together as a federal union, not a national state with state capitals serving simply as administrative subdivisions. We vote as citizens of separate states. Elimination of the Electoral College would almost certainly result in Presidential elections being decided by swing votes in a handful of the largest cities. It doesn't take much imagination to see the potential linkage between this and doing away with registration.

The Christian Science Monitor, 4-26:12.

4

If you analyze it, a [political] party is not a social club; it is not an organization that says, "Let's have an organization." It is a group of people brought together because they share a common belief in what government should be like, and the party is only a mechanism to further that belief. It isn't the mechanism that brings the people together. It is the belief, and the cause, and this is why I am asking the Republican Party to take that platform which, for the first time in either party, explicitly states what is the belief of Republicanism, so that we are able to say to the independents and Democrats who are looking for a home because they are disenchanted with their own party, "Here is what we stand for; here is what you can count on."

*TV-radio interview, Washington/"Meet
the Press," National Broadcasting Company, 5-1.*

John J. Rhodes
United States Representative, R—Arizona

5

[On President Carter's open support for resigned Budget Director Bert Lance, who left because of the controversy about his past financial dealings]: This Administration has in a very short time appeared to lose its moral

WHAT THEY SAID IN 1977

nerve ... A President who declared that obeying the law would not be sufficient for officials in his Administration now publicly declares his pride in his closest and most powerful aide simply because a highly critical government report declared that *there were no apparent violations of the law* in that official's conduct. A President who received his party's nomination with the words that the American people are tired of seeing big shots evade the consequences of their actions now appears to millions of his fellow citizens to be singing a very different song ... If there is one strand of behavior discernible through the fabric of the Carter Administration's policy, it is the strand of duplicity ... If the White House is to be perceived as a place of moral leadership, then its occupant, particularly when he has made such leadership his principal rallying cry, must call the shots as he sees them, and if he is to see them as they are, he must take the moral mote from his eye.

Before Commonwealth Club, San Francisco, Sept. 23/U.S. News & World Report, 10-3:18.

1

I think that the [Carter] Administration's performance thus far has been inept. Nothing really has been accomplished, and one of the reasons it hasn't been accomplished, I think, is because the Administration started out not knowing a thing about Congress, not knowing very much about the government — and apparently proudly so — with the idea that "anything that happened prior to January 20 just had to be wrong, so we have to do everything differently." You know, a brand new ballgame. I think it has been a terrible failure and that the country has eight months of churning and chaos without any great amount of results.

TV-radio interview/"Meet the Press," National Broadcasting Company, 10-23.

Nelson A. Rockefeller
Vice President of the United States

2

I rate [Watergate] as evidence that the Constitution is a brilliant document that had the flexibility and strength to cope with a situation that the Founding Fathers antici-

pated, which was weakness of human nature. If we'd just go back to that and not think we could legislate morality and not keep thinking about this business of everybody being superhuman. The country stood strong, the people stood calm, and he [former President Richard Nixon] is out. We are now back to normal. This is the thing ... this mystical thing that is democracy.

Interview, Washington/ U.S. News & World Report, 1-17:15.

Peter W. Rodino, Jr.
United States Representative, D—New Jersey

3

[On former President Richard Nixon's recent televised interview on the subject of Watergate]: It made me sad to see a President of the United States trying one way or the other to explain away the facts. You can't rewrite history.

The Dallas Times Herald, 5-5:(A)1.

Fernand J. St. Germain
United States Representative, D—Rhode Island

4

[On the controversy involving Budget Director Bert Lance's past financial dealings]: Banks are not the personal toys of bankers — at least they are not supposed to be. While I do not want to prejudge, the evidence I have seen to date leads me to believe that Bert Lance, his family and friends regarded the Calhoun First National Bank [of Georgia] as their playpen — to be used as they pleased.

Los Angeles Herald-Examiner, 9-6:(A)1.

Richard M. Scammon
Public-opinion analyst

5

Labor is strongest politically in the cities that have traditionally sent most of the liberal Democrats to Congress. The newer Democratic members are coming from suburban areas and small towns where labor has relatively little clout. As a result, each new increment of Democratic Party members in Congress tends to be less responsive to the labor-liberal philosophy.

Interview/Nation's Business, November:31.

Harrison H. Schmitt
United States Senator, R—New Mexico

1

Am I a Reagan conservative? No, I'm some-what different. That's why I say "younger Western conservative," with a somewhat different approach, although the principles are basic-ally the same ... The key to understanding the new Western Senators [is] they're generally going to be conservative and always be quite imaginative in how they search for solutions to problems based on conservative principles ... They have broader breadth of experience than those 20 to 30 years older. Breadth of experi-ence forces you to look at alternatives.

Interview, Washington/
The Christian Science Monitor, 3-10:8.

B. F. Sisk
United States Representative,
D—California

2

[On some of those involved in Watergate who wrote books, articles, and sold film and TV rights to their stories resulting from the scandal]: With the people of the nation fed up with the "Watergate syndrome," the recent spate of books, movies and TV programs making rich men out of convicted criminals, such as John Dean and John Ehrlichman, is repugnant to the law-abiding citizen.

Washington, Sept. 27/Los Angeles Times, 9-28:(1)5.

Mary Louise Smith
Former chairman, Republican
National Committee

3

Although every two years we [Republicans] suffer additional losses at the polls, we continue on the same course, secure in the smug knowl-edge that no voter can resist the allure of the Republican Party. We continue to lose, but we do not take the initiative to change our ways ... We are more concerned at times with a balanced budget than a balanced society. In our zeal, we must not overlook the human element. The Republican Party's apparent lack of concern for the needs of people has fre-quently left the impression that ours is a party without soul.

At Republican Party fundraiser, Grand Junction, Iowa,
Sept. 19/The New York Times, 9-20-32.

James R. Thompson
Governor of Illinois (R)

4

It's a curious thing — I sometimes get criticized by the press for harboring Presidential ambitions, as though that were some sort of national crime ... I grew up in the generation that told every American boy in 1947 it was not a crime to want to be President. That was part of our culture. There was something wrong with you if you didn't. Once you decided you didn't want to be a fireman and fastened onto the Presidency, you were all right.

Interview, Washington/
The Christian Science Monitor, 4-20:6.

5

Politicians take themselves entirely too seri-ously. Self-deprecating humor is one of the politician's best offensive weapons. It is better to make fun of yourself than let your opponent do it for you.

At Republican Governors Association
convention, Bretton Woods, N.H., Oct. 10/San
Francisco Examiner & Chronicle, 10-16:(This World)2.

John V. Tunney
Former United States Senator, D—California

6

[On his losing re-election last year]: The climate of opinion now ... is one that people want detachment, because they are detached. They don't want to make passionate commit-ments because they're afraid of getting hurt. They don't like father figures because they were disappointed with [the late President Lyndon] Johnson and [former President Rich-ard] Nixon. They are uncommitted, particu-larly in interpersonal relations, but uncommit-ted to ideologies [too]. They want a politician who is cool ... I was very passionate when I took on the Vietnam war, when I took on Richard Nixon, Richard Kleindienst, ITT, Pat Gray, and helped to get the special [Watergate] prosecutor ... I was passionate about that. I was passionate about my Angola amendment, passionate when I got my toxic-substances bill through after fighting for it for four years. I was passionate about the voting-rights act. I mean those things; I am a passionate person ...

WHAT THEY SAID IN 1977

(JOHN V. TUNNEY)

and I'm not detached and I'm not uncommitted and I'm not cool . . .

Interview, Los Angeles/
Los Angeles Times, 6-29:(1)29.

Morris K. Udall
United States Representative,
D–Arizona

1

[Calling for public financing of election campaigns]: We have to respond to evolving conditions. When Abraham Lincoln was in the House of Representatives, he had a constituency small enough so that he could shake hands with every voter. My constituency is a half-million people. I can't shake everyone's hand. So you resort to television, to radio, to direct mail, to newspaper ads – and all of these things cost money. If we had stayed a small, rural country, or if we had stayed a nation in which life wasn't so complex that the Federal government didn't have to maintain a large role, I don't think we would have needed public financing of elections. But the decisions made in Washington affect everybody's life, and with so much at stake in who wins elections, bigger and bigger money has gotten into it . . . You have got to have access to substantial amounts of money, or you're not going to get elected. It's just that simple. So the question is: Who is going to put up the money? Those of us who support public financing say: "Let's let everybody have a piece of the action. Let the ordinary citizen give a dollar for clean politics. Let him have some say, too."

Interview/U.S. News & World Report, 4-25:63.

2

[On the recent controversy over Bert Lance's past financial dealings which resulted in his resignation as Federal Budget Director]: [President] Carter went to bat for an old friend and stood by him too long. In an implicit, hard-to-quantify way, it took a little of the gloss off the Carter image of morality and high standards, and that will have a lingering effect even on people who don't remember the Lance affair six months from now.

Los Angeles Times, 9-24:(1)4.

Jesse M. Unruh
California State Treasurer

3

I think the two-party system is an absolute necessity. I simply do not believe we can afford in this country today the luxury of allowing either one of our parties, major parties, to become unable to offer the proper competition. And I'm of the great belief that landslide victories and top-heavy majorities are extremely bad both for the majority party and the country in general, to say nothing of the minority party.

At Republican legislators' conference, Los Angeles, April 17/Los Angeles Times, 4-18:(1)3.

Peter Ustinov
Actor, Director, Writer

4

What is interesting about politicians in a democratic society is that, whereas they are motivated by power as they are in all societies, everything is done constitutionally to make that power an obligation instead of a source of enjoyment.

Interview, Paris/Los Angeles Times, 9-6:(4)14.

Lowell P. Weicker, Jr.
United States Senator, R–Connecticut

5

I think the whole idea of public financing [of election campaigns] stinks. What you'd be doing is subsidizing mediocrity. You'd be taking away from the people of this country one of the checks which they have on their government: specifically, the power to politically utilize their resources. What particularly nettles me is that I've heard Federal financing of campaigns referred to as a Watergate reform. This is absolutely wrong. The Senate Watergate Committee explicitly opposed public financing in its final report. I can only say that if there is to be "Watergate reform" of our election process, more power should be put in the hands of the people – not less . . . It is a raid on taxpayers' money for the support of failing politicians. Politicians should get out and earn their votes, earn support. A time of declining faith in politicians is no time to reward them financially. In essence, you are eliminating competition in our election process; you're saying that a warm body is enough to get

(LOWELL P. WEICKER, JR.)

money . . . I can't accept any part of public financing. I intend to fight tooth and nail to block passage of this political meadow muffin.

Interview/U.S. News & World Report, 4-25:63,64.

Samuel W. Yorty
Former Mayor of Los Angeles
1
. . . gradually the Democratic Party is becoming the enemy of the middle class. And the middle class is not too aware of it. They think Republicans are for "big business." But Republicans aren't for "big business"; they're for free enterprise. "Big business" is very fickle; they give money to anyone. So the middle class really needs a Republican philosophy today to protect the free-enterprise system. Because guys like [California Democratic] Governor [Jerry] Brown keep wanting to take from the middle class and give to the poor. Instead of pulling the poor up, they want to pull the middle class down; and instead of creating more wealth, [they] want to take what we have and divide it. They're killing all the incentive for people to go out and build the free-enterprise system.

Interview/Los Angeles Herald-Examiner,
12-18:(California Living)8.

Andrew Young
United States Ambassador/Permanent
Representative to the United Nations
2
[On criticism, especially by Republicans, of the way he has conducted himself since becoming Ambassador]: The Republicans have really had so little to criticize in this [Carter] Administration that if I didn't do what I'm doing I think they'd have to invent me. In a way, I think that's what you guys [in the press] are doing — trying to invent me.

News conference, Washington, June 7/
The New York Times, 6-8:(A)6.

Social Welfare

Clifford R. Allen
United States Representative,
D—Tennessee

1

[Arguing against a proposed amendment which would deny food stamps to families of strikers]: What is actually proposed in this amendment is for the government to take sides in all management-labor disputes. What this amendment talks about are mothers and children and the elderly who do not have money to put food on the table simply because a member of the household is on strike.

Before the House, Washington/
The New York Times, 7-28:(D)18.

John B. Anderson
United States Representative,
R—Illinois

2

If you give the average American taxpayer a word-association test and mention the word "welfare," he will come right back at you with the word "mess." Those two words seem to go together in the American vocabulary. Obviously the people on welfare rolls aren't happy about being locked into that system. Government officials, the administrators, aren't happy. Goodness knows the taxpayers aren't happy. We do have to change. We do have to radically restructure and reform the welfare system.

TV-radio interview/"Meet the Press,"
National Broadcasting Company, 8-7.

3

[On the imminent increase in Social Security taxes]: This Social Security thing isn't going to go down very well. People are going to blame this Congress when they see the additional deduction coming out of their paycheck in January. If I were to give advice to the President [Carter] — if I ever were to be

ushered into his presence — I would suggest he better get on with his first priority of a [general] tax cut in 1978.

Interview/San Francisco
Examiner & Chronicle, 12-25:(This World)7.

Bill Archer
United States Representative, R—Texas

4

[Criticizing the Carter Administration's proposal to use $14-billion of general Federal tax revenues to bolster the Social Security System]: This may well be the most brazen demonstration of fiscal legerdemain ever given in this room. It boggles the mind. [The] proposal means one of two things: either you're planning to take $14-billion away from other programs, or the Treasury Secretary is going to borrow that amount. I suspect it's the latter case, which will increase the public debt, build up inflationary pressures and ultimately add to the already oppressive burden on the American taxpayer.

At House Social Security Subcommittee
hearing, Washington, May 10/
Los Angeles Times, 5-11:(1)11.

Howard H. Baker, Jr.
United States Senator, R—Tennessee

5

[On the looting during the recent power blackout in New York]: The blackout in this city last summer demonstrated with awesome destructive power how desperate some of our citizens have become, how isolated they have become from the mainstream of our society, how much they have become strangers in their own land, how profoundly and consistently our system has failed to provide the initiative and the skills they need to live successfully in America ... The simple fact is that those individuals are bewildered, frustrated and

(HOWARD H. BAKER, JR.)

angered by the image of the good life as advertised in living color on the nation's television screens. That image has nothing to do with the aimless lives they live on the streets of our large cities, and they have little reason to believe that it will be more than a television picture to them or to their children . . . What we must avoid above all else is the creation in the United States of what Disraeli called, more than a century ago, "two Englands," the rich and the poor. In our time and in this land, there is no room for two Americas. . . In 1977, we cannot permit the untrammeled growth of an American underclass.

Before Institute for Socioeconomic Studies, New York, Dec. 13/Los Angeles Times, 12-16:(8)4.

Urie Bronfenbrenner
Professor of human development and family studies, Cornell University
1

Family is the primary institution we have. It certainly is the most effective and most economic system we have for making human beings more human. Family is important for nurturing not only the next generation, but everybody. They care for physical and emotional well-being, especially when an individual is young, old, sick, tired or lonely.

Interview, Ithaca, N.Y./Los Angeles Times, 9-4:(1)2.

Edmund G. Brown, Jr.
Governor of California (D)
2

If you'll remember after the Second World War people had homes of 7-8-900 square feet. Now they're talking about double that. And there's a basic incompatibility between a lower-priced house and low density. If you take a look at Japan and the land costs and the housing costs — I'm not saying we're going there, but we're moving in that direction. I think density is going to have to increase if you want the cost of housing to go down . . . Unless more people can live in the same amount of space, costs are going to keep going up.

Television interview, Sacramento, May 3/ Los Angeles Times, 5-4:(1)24.

Robert N. Butler
Director, National Institute on Aging
3

Americans suffer from a personal and institutionalized prejudice against older people. Although this may be a primitive, universal dread of aging true in all cultures, it is reinforced and thus more striking in our own. This is a cultural sensibility that could be changed through study and education. When the medical student or the doctor shares in that negative attitude, it is all the more disturbing.

Before Senate Special Committee on Aging, Washington/The Washington Post, 3-9:(A)10.

4

Ways must be found to better distribute education work, retirement and leisure over the course of the life cycle. From early childhood, the life of the modern American is rigidly programmed. First comes a block of education extending at least into late adolescence and, increasingly, often into his 20s. He then faces a massive block of work for 40 years, followed by retirement and leisure. This fixed design is stultifying not only to the individual but to his society . . . We must free ourselves from seeing education, work and leisure-retirement as three separate periods of life. We must begin thinking of these activities as running concurrently and continuously . . . Existing financial supports — private and public funds for education, unemployment insurance, in-service training funds, Social Security, pensions, etc. — would, of course, have to be reallocated to support such a basic reshuffling of life-cycle activities. Youth could then feel free to work or loaf as well as to attend college. The 35-year-old would be encouraged to take time off to study, change directions or relax. The 70-year-old, in part because he would have had these constantly refreshing experiences through life, would be as prepared for work and study as he would be for a true enjoyment of leisure.

The Washington Post, 8-25:(A)26.

Joseph A. Califano, Jr.
Secretary of Health, Education and Welfare of the United States
5

There are no perfect solutions to the welfare program. But it is clear that there is support in

WHAT THEY SAID IN 1977

(JOSEPH A. CALIFANO, JR.)

our nation for an income-security system for those who are unable to earn an adequate income. It is also true that the American taxpayer is impatient with the inability of our government to remove from the welfare [rolls] those persons improperly on them ... I want, I hope for, I welcome, a serious national debate [on welfare reform].

The Christian Science Monitor, 2-23:2.

1

The most pernicious and widespread myth is that people are poor because they don't work and don't want to work and that the welfare rolls are replete with loafers. The facts are quite different. Nearly 71 per cent of the 26 million poor individuals in the nation represent people that we do not normally ask to work: children and young people under 16; the aged; the severely disabled; students; or mothers with children under 16 ... Thus, 90 per cent of poor Americans either work full- or part-time, or are people no civilized society would force to work.

The New York Times, 5-8:(4)19.

2

I'd like to have people look back and say that our social programs are good, that they are an important part of our society. I'd like to get people to recognize the reality of poverty. It's there, and no civilization in history has been able to eliminate it. But the better civilizations have had the compassion and the decency to provide for people. There is nothing special about you and me, you know. We could have a heart attack or something, and be there, too. We could all be there.

Interview, Washington/Los Angeles Times, 5-16:(1)9.

3

[On President Carter's proposed welfare-reform system]: Under this program, everyone who works will make more money than anyone who is receiving cash benefits alone, and everyone who works in the private sector will make more money than someone in one of the public-service-employment jobs. Those mothers

who work, whether they're working now or whether they take jobs under the new program, will have increases in their earnings of from 21 to 41 per cent when the program is in full effect. And I think that it will help in another very significant way by helping hold families together, instead of destroying them the way the present welfare system does.

TV-radio interview/"Face the Nation," Columbia Broadcasting System, 8-7.

4

I think there is a limit to the extent to which we are able to redistribute wealth. The biggest difference between today and the '60s is that then we had more and more money to spend because real income was still rising. Today there isn't any money coming from some kind of economic surplus or bonus. When you want to do something new, you have to take from something — whether it is more taxes from people or money from other programs. But we should have fewer poor people in this country. There is no question about that.

Interview/Time, 8-15:7.

James B. Cardwell
*Commissioner, Social Security
Administration of the United States*

5

No other agency has enjoyed a better reputation for general efficiency, sensitivity to the public interest, than Social Security. The image always has been it was an agency that had a considerable *esprit*, a good feeling about itself, a healthy self-respect. I don't think that's any longer true. I don't want to be pessimistic about it, but I doubt that it's healthy today. I think what is occurring is the result of a multiplicity of very complex developments in and around the agency. One of them is Watergate, and the general public disillusionment with and cynicism toward government in general. Others involve such things as the rapidity with which new assignments have been given Social Security; the complexity of those assignments, the failure to appreciate the complexity of those assignments by the agency itself and by the people who made those assignments in the Legislative and Executive Branches. But also there's the theoretical — and to me it's not

(JAMES B. CARDWELL)

theoretical, it's real — change in the attitude of the American work force toward what they want out of and from work.

Interview/The Washington Post, 3-28:(A)8.

Jimmy Carter
President of the United States

1

[On the new Social Security legislation]: This puts the Social Security System on a sound financial basis at least for the next 25 years, throughout the rest of this country. It's a little more costly than I had hoped it would be, but we were able to stop some of the very costly proposals that either the House or Senate had proposed. I think it's a good resolution of a very serious problem that did exist when I took office; that is, that the Social Security System was on the road toward bankruptcy. Now, it's sound. The American people will pay more taxes into the Social Security System, but in return they'll know that it will be there permanently and in a sound condition.

News conference, Washington, Dec. 15/
The New York Times, 12-16:(A)28.

Wilbur J. Cohen
Professor of public welfare administration, University of Michigan; Former Secretary of Health, Education and Welfare of the United States

2

[On the use of general tax funds for the financing of Social Security]: Under no circumstances should the general revenue be used for more than one third of the total cost. I can see a system in which the employers pay a third, the employees a third and government pays a third. Employers and employees would still have a major role to play in the political process of setting contributions and benefits, which, I think, is there whether you have general revenues or not. Let me add this: Using general revenues should be justified by a very specific rationale — a rationale widely accepted by business, labor and government, so that it does not invalidate the earned-right insurance concept of the program.

Interview/U.S. News & World Report, 7-4:38.

Alex Comfort
Author, Biologist

3

Although nobody is putting the old in concentration camps, nobody is killing off the old, nobody is overtly expressing hatred against the old, it is possible to have the same effects that are similar in the long term to those of overt persecution by putting them, for instance, in atrocious nursing homes where they are treated in a far less than humane way. The alternatives are in properly conducted in-home care of the sort that doesn't depend on semi-gangster contractors, as it often does in the United States, who have been paying minimum wages and receiving subsidy and providing very poor services. What I'm saying is, although only four per cent of older Americans are in nursing homes, it's generally agreed, and it's documented, that many of them are quite disgraceful.

The Dallas Times Herald, 7-6:(A)26.

Ronald V. Dellums
United States Representative, D–California

4

[Criticizing a proposed amendment that would limit food-stamp purchases to nutritious products]: Any human being in America, irrespective of income, should be afforded the dignity of freedom of choice. If they choose to buy Twinkies or Coca-Colas, so be it.

The New York Times, 7-28:(D)18.

Pierre S. du Pont
Governor of Delaware (R)

5

The welfare system in America today is a disaster. It encourages the break-up of the home; it is laced with fraud and opportunities for fraud; the benefits are uneven; the administration is cumbersome; and there are dozens of different small programs that make for an awful lot of confusion. I have long supported welfare reform and voted for the Family Assistance Program when I was in the Congress before becoming Governor, and I believe that we ought to give reform a try. I think the President's [Carter] concept of folding the program together into a single welfare program is a good one, but costs have been going up so

WHAT THEY SAID IN 1977

rapidly in the welfare program . . . and I don't see anything in the Carter program that is going to reduce those costs for the states. That is why I am skeptical.

TV-radio interview, Detroit/"Meet the Press," National Broadcasting Company, 9-11.

Gerald R. Ford
Former President of the United States
1

Propping up the [Social Security] fund with general revenues may bring some short-term gains, but these will be far outweighed by long-term pains, both economic and social. We simply cannot go on this way. Budgetary sleight-of-hand can conceal the problems only so long — and then we will see them clearly enough in the prices we pay, in the strength of the dollar and in the deterioration of the American standard of living.

At "Invest in America" luncheon, Washington, May 24/The Washington Post, 5-25:(A)2.

E. J. (Jake) Garn
United States Senator, R–Utah
2

. . . the welfare system must be reformed because there are thousands of families that desperately need help and the government is not meeting its obligations to them. The truly needy can be directly benefited in the following ways: limit benefits to only the most needy families, generally those meeting official poverty limits; tighten eligibility requirements and improve incentive payments to eliminate loafers and crooks so that money is freed for the legitimately needy; eliminate eligibility of persons voluntarily unemployed such as strikers and students; eliminate loopholes such as those relating to lump-sum income; and continue the effort to reduce paperwork and simplify the bureaucracy, so long as such efforts are consistent with necessary reporting requirements to operate a "tight" program.

At welfare reform hearing, Salt Lake City, April 1/Vital Speeches, 6-1:485.

Peter C. Goldmark, Jr.
Director of the Budget of New York State
3

Welfare is hated by those who administer it, mistrusted by those who pay for it and held in contempt by those who receive it. Welfare reform and a Federal take-over of welfare are two completely different things. Reform is aimed at the recipient, and take-over is aimed at helping those who pay for it.

Interview/The New York Times, 5-24:25.

Carl Holman
President, National Urban Coalition
4

Politicians, including this [Carter] Administration, are so preoccupied first with building business confidence. But, just once, I wish somebody would talk about establishing the confidence of the nation's poor.

Interview/The New York Times, 2-16:63.

Vernon E. Jordan, Jr.
Executive director, National Urban League
5

We ask tonight that President Carter signal to the nation his concern for the cities and for the poor who live in them by going to New York and by speaking with the looters and the looted [in the recent power blackout] in the south Bronx, Harlem and Bedford-Stuyvesant. A nation of cities is adrift in confusion and the President of all the people has to show his concern. He has to show he understands the despair and anger, the hopes and the needs of the urban poor.

At National Urban League convention, Washington, July 24/Los Angeles Times, 7-25:(1)16.

Edward M. Kennedy
United States Senator, D–Massachusetts
6

Over six million elderly persons live in dilapidated, deteriorating and substandard housing. They are already spending a third or more of their income for housing. Their choice is not between paying more for rent and less of luxury items. It is between rent and bread.

The Dallas Times Herald, 10-3:(B)3.

Juanita M. Kreps
Secretary of Commerce of the United States

1

If you were to extend work life to 68 and not start Social Security benefits until age 68, you would reduce enormously the Social Security burden. I now see in the press frequent references to the fact that the only way to solve the Social Security problem is to spread the work life out a little longer. I never saw reference to that except in my own writings until the last several months. It could gain some momentum; it could happen. We would do it gradually. But I think within eight years it's possible that could become a policy.

Interview, Washington, July 30/
The Dallas Times Herald, 7-31:(A)1.

Russell B. Long
United States Senator, D–Louisiana

2

Some people criticize the Social Security tax as being regressive, but keep in mind that we have an earned-income credit which is paid out of general revenues to reimburse the working poor for the Social Security taxes they pay. In view of the fact that the Social Security benefits are weighed heavily in favor of people at the lower end of the economic ladder and against people at the upper end, it seems to me there should be no complaints that an income tax is more progressive than a Social Security tax.

Interview/Nation's Business, August:25.

3

[On President Carter's proposed new welfare plan]: The same types of problems that exist in the present welfare program will exist in the new one, for the simple reason that we are dealing with human beings. Congress would be foolhardy to jump into such a vast undertaking without exploring some of the problems that will develop by field-testing the system long enough to know what we can expect.

Aug. 15/The Washington Post, 8-16:(A)7.

Ashley Montagu
Anthropologist

4

Most people don't know how to be parents today. The family has become an institution

geared to the systematic reproduction of mental illness in each other. I mean, do you realize that a human being is the only 150-pound, non-linear servo-mechanism that can be wholly produced by unskilled labor?

Interview, Princeton, N.J./
"W": a Fairchild publication, 1-21:5.

George Moscone
Mayor of San Francisco

5

I think the issue is the needs of the people, and I don't think anybody who is without decent housing or health care or an ability to earn a dignified living for their family or having decent education is the least bit concerned about balancing the [Federal] budget.

TV-radio interview, Tucson, Ariz./"Meet
the Press," National Broadcasting Company, 6-12.

Daniel P. Moynihan
United States Senator, D–New York

6

If welfare reform meant putting arsenic in children's milk, there would be local officials who would settle for that — as long as it meant full Federal funding.

San Francisco Examiner & Chronicle,
1-30:(This World)2.

7

[On President Carter's welfare program, which includes a ceiling on Federal spending for welfare]: What animates the Administration? An indomitable innocence or a profound cynicism? Are they sending us a welfare program that will do such injury to welfare recipients that we will not enact it? Are they sending us a program that provides no relief to state and local governments — relief that has been solemnly pledged by the President — such that state and local governments will urge us not to enact it?

Before Westchester County Association,
Rye, N.Y., May 26/The New York Times, 5-27:(A)11.

8

[On Administration objections to his plan to provide $1-billion in Federal welfare aid to states with high welfare costs]: Yes, it would go in largest measure to New York and California and Illinois and Ohio, because those

WHAT THEY SAID IN 1977

(DANIEL P. MOYNIHAN)

states have chosen to be responsible about their poor, and have more of them, and have had more people come to them. If this [Carter] Administration is going to take the position that if you have tried to do a respectable job, a compassionate job, and in consequence you have got yourself in trouble, then it's your tough luck . . . well, I think they ought to say it pretty openly. I don't like hearing that those states which have tried to deal fairly with their poor have made a mistake, and it's just tough luck. You never hear the President or Secretary of Defense say we cannot build this bomber because most of the money would go to state X. You never hear the legislators from New York say we will not support this water project because it isn't in our state. We are one nation. It's not a question of what state will get the money — it's a question of what poor people need.

At Senate hearing, Washington, July 12/
The Dallas Times Herald, 7-13:(A)13.

Bob Packwood
United States Senator, R—Oregon

1

The average Democrat in politics prefers that the Federal government deliver social services. When given the choice, most Republicans prefer that the services be provided by the private sector. A good example of this difference is in the area of health insurance. The majority of Democrats in Congress prefer a national health-insurance system run from Washington. Most Republicans prefer an expansion of the present system by which business covers its employees through private health insurance. Let me emphasize that the issue is NOT whether social services will be provided at all. That battle is over. The issue is whether they will be provided by government or business. If people want help in educating their children, if they want day care, health insurance, or legal services to feel secure, they will find a way to get it.

At Dorchester Conference, Seaside, Ore.,
March 5/Vital Speeches, 5-15:455.

Charles B. Rangel
United States Representative,
D—New York

2

[On the looting that took place in the poor, black areas of New York City during the recent power blackout]: I wish [President] Carter would go there. I wish he would see for himself the powder keg and see how little it takes to set if off. It's not a question of justification; those people were breaking the law. But the government is breaking the law letting them live in those places. There comes a breaking point. This wasn't racial — it was economic. Sixty per cent of my constituents are unemployed.

Washington/Los Angeles Times, 7-21:(2)7.

Carlos Romero (Barcelo)
Governor of Puerto Rico

3

Poverty has been and still is our most profound preoccupation. Poverty demoralizes the poor who suffer from it as well as the society which tolerates it. We cannot accept poverty and ignorance.

San Francisco Examiner & Chronicle,
1-9:(This World)2.

John G. Tower
United States Senator, R—Texas

4

There are short-range possibilities of averting the initial crisis in the Social Security System without having to increase the employer's tax or resorting to general revenue funds. We could adjust the tax rate and the wage base slightly and eliminate the double indexing for inflation. But it is the long-range solution that we must now debate openly and in the clear air of candor about the way the program currently operates. Depending on the increase in wage rates and the cost of living, young people entering the Social Security System today may find that they can buy a comparable annuity for less on the private market. If the tax burden becomes too heavy, they may lobby for doing precisely that . . . We must find some means of making both saving and investment more attractive to younger people so that they will not be inclined to live only for the moment and rely on Social Security as their sole means of

(JOHN G. TOWER)

support in their old age. Social Security was meant as a supplement, not an income.

*Before Kiwanis International, Dallas,
June 27/The Dallas Times Herald, 6-28:(C)20.*

John E. Tropman
*Professor, department of social
work, University of Michigan*

1

[Saying his studies have shown that poor people are disliked in the U.S.]: If the poor were not to blame for their own predicament — through laziness, lack of ambition or the like — it would have to follow that the non-poor are not responsible for their success. This conflicts with an important American value. Most people assume that status is determined by personal effort, not by external conditions or chance. Poverty is linked to moral failure; wealth is associated with virtue.

The Washington Post, 2-18:(A)31.

Al Ullman
United States Representative, D—Oregon

2

[Arguing against using general tax revenues for the financing of Social Security]: I am very reluctant to go to any device that would use general revenues to correct the short-term imbalance in the funds . . . Because the concept of separate taxing and funding for Social Security gives it fiscal integrity. In other words, whenever you add a benefit, you have to add a tax to pay for it. If you start using general revenues, that discipline is lost. Going to general tax revenues would be a real fiasco — if you wanted to increase benefits, you could just increase the contribution from the general fund from zero today to 33 per cent to 40 to 50 and on up. The discipline is gone.

Interview/U.S. News & World Report, 7-4:37.

3

[Saying he disagrees with President Carter's program of assistance to the working poor based on both family income and number of children]: I believe it's proper to pay them some supplement, at least for a time, not based on a welfare concept — on the size of the family — but based on a job concept. When you go to work, you don't get paid according to the size of your family; you get paid because you're working.

*To reporters, Washington, Aug. 2/
Los Angeles Times, 8-3:(1)9.*

William W. Winpisinger
*President, Institute of
Collective Bargaining*

4

In an economy where we are taking out $200-billion to build guns and bombs and all that kind of nonsense, I am appalled to hear people say we can't take out $5-billion or $6-billion to cure poverty and unemployment. I agree with [President] Carter that the defense budget can be cut.

*Interview, Washington/
The New York Times, 2-9:(D)7.*

Transportation

Brock Adams
*Secretary of Transportation
of the United States*
1

You have got to put the whole transportation net together. We have got to have multimodal terminals; and you have to be able to shift from truck to rail to water, back to truck, in the most fuel-efficient manner; not because it is some theory I have, but . . . we are running out of petroleum products, and their availability and their cost is going up, so we have to use more cost-efficient modes. This means, also, the government has to be working on its regulatory system to encourage the shifting from one transport mode to another.

*TV-radio interview, Washington/"Meet
the Press," National Broadcasting Company, 2-6.*

2

[Mass transit] should not be considered a service to commerce but part of urban development — a public service needed to restore life to our cities. The farebox will clearly never pay the capital or operating costs of mass transit, and private enterprise does not want to be involved unless subsidized.

*Interview, Washington, March 20/
Los Angeles Herald-Examiner, 3-20:(A)5.*

3

[On why he doesn't favor a Federal no-fault auto-insurance system]: Because I don't think the Federal government should regulate insurance and set rates. There's too much disparity among individual states. Driving conditions are far different in Rhode Island or Massachusetts, for instance, than in Nebraska or Texas. Cost-of-living factors vary considerably. And neither the President nor I want to create any more Federal bureaucracy. What we are telling the states is this: The present insurance system is a national problem. People are mobile; they drive from one state to another. They get involved in accidents, and our tort-liability system is not working. Accident victims may not get paid for years, and then they often get back only a small portion of the premium dollars they paid in. Let's set up some minimum standards, have them adopted by the states and run by the states.

*Interview, Washington/
U.S. News & World Report, 8-15:45.*

4

[Endorsing mandatory passive restraint systems, such as air bags, in automobiles]: We could cut losses — save lives, reduce the severity of injuries and lower the incidence of personal grief and human misery — by the simple expedient of requiring passive restraint systems in our motor cars. Yet we have procrastinated in coping with motor-vehicle deaths, counting the speculative dollar costs of prevention rather than the whole-life benefits mandatory passive restraint systems can deliver.

*Before Congressional committee/
The New York Times, 9-29:(A)21.*

5

I firmly believe that rail transit does have a future . . . Freeways do not cure urban congestion, air pollution remains a problem, land values make parking increasingly expensive, and the prospects of rising fuel prices and declining supplies make the inefficient use of the private car unwise and costly . . . We cannot realistically expect to reverse the pattern overnight, but our goal must be to achieve a better balance to our transportation system.

*To reporters, Atlanta, Oct. 12/
The Dallas Times Herald, 10-13:(A)7.*

Edward Ball
Chairman, Florida
East Coast Railway

1

. . . rail management is impotent to deal effectively with the vast power of the labor unions. And Congress permits this situation to continue to the detriment of the whole country. It is unconscionable for Congress to use taxpayer dollars to subsidize the railroads while perpetuating make-work union rules — particularly when those very rules are the reason for the crisis facing the industry.

Nation's Business, July:61.

Raymond Barre
Premier of France

2

[On opposition in the New York area to allowing the British-French *Concorde* SST to use Kennedy Airport because of environmental reasons]: It will be a very serious attack if the New York Port Authority blocks *Concorde* flights. I cannot really appreciate the U.S. attitude. People here are shocked to see a plane, furnished with the proper navigation certificate, excluded from an airport — the most important airport in the world. They cannot help believing this is an act of bad faith. They feel that a technologically advanced carrier is being eliminated from access to New York, and maybe the entire United States, when all other countries, including France, have willingly accepted U.S. aeronautical equipment. We are especially shocked to see this occur in an industry where all Europe has accepted American supremacy, although naturally our own aircraft factories must keep their potential. It is difficult under existing circumstances to envision the desirable long-term cooperation between Europe and the United States on future development of aircraft. Beyond that, I am genuinely concerned about Franco-American cooperation on other bilateral and multilateral projects.

Interview, Paris/The New York Times, 3-12:23.

Frank Borman
Chairman and president, Eastern Airlines

3

[Arguing against loosening government regulation of the airline industry]: [Deregulation legislation now before Congress] would, in one fell swoop, destroy a system that has produced the finest airline-transportation network in the world, with fares in the U.S. being about half what they are in foreign countries. If carried to extremes, it could lead to concentration in the industry and to a decline in the quality of passenger service . . . Airlines possessing the largest financial resources could clearly dominate any market they set out to, simply by adding more flights. The resulting excess capacity could force other carriers to abandon the same markets. Revenues would go down, because there would be either fewer passengers per flight or lower fares designed to attract more passengers. With fewer airlines in the market, quality service would suffer and the cost would likely increase.

Interview/U.S. News & World Report, 5-9:75.

Howard W. Cannon
United States Senator, D–Nevada

4

[Calling for less government regulation of the airline industry]: The industry needed protection when it was getting started in 1938. But as time has gone on, we have just piled regulation on top of regulation to the point that the airlines are a completely protected industry. Fares are the same, and airlines can't raise or lower them without the Civil Aeronautics Board's approval. The only competition is in service . . . I do not want to get rid of all regulation. If the bill I introduced in the Senate is passed, there will be regulation in the future — but, hopefully, it will be regulation that serves the public better. Fares right now are not unreasonably high. But, for many routes, they could be substantially reduced if there was less regulation and we gave the airlines an opportunity to try innovative fares. My bill would permit the airlines to adjust prices up or down without CAB approval . . . I can understand why labor opposes my bill. Labor would probably be in a stronger position with total regulation, complete route protection and controlled fares — because then the extra cost of doing business that way is simply passed on to the customers. That's one of the reasons we have such high fares today. If labor has to bargain in a less-regulated, more-efficient and

WHAT THEY SAID IN 1977

(HOWARD W. CANNON)

competitive environment, they may have to sharpen their pencils somewhat.

Interview/U.S. News & World Report, 5-9:75,76.

Jimmy Carter
President of the United States   *1*

[On the banning of the British-French *Concorde* SST from New York's Kennedy Airport]: My own statement to [French] President [Valery] Giscard [d'Estaing] is that we are not concerned about the SST flights because of commercial competition — about six years ago our own Congress decided not to go into the SST-building business — and the whole problem in our country is noise and environmental-quality maintenance . . . I think that the noise standards in our country are going to be stricter and stricter in the future and not more lenient; and the same noise standards ought to apply to an airplane, whether it's a *Concorde* or a Lockheed or some other kind or any sort of American commercial plane. So I think we can establish strict environmental laws. I think they ought to apply to the SST flying a course at subsonic speeds and our own commercial planes the same. But it's the environmental question that will exclude the *Concorde,* if it is excluded, and not any sort of animosity toward the French people, nor is it any commercial competition between us and France on SST flights.

National call-in radio program, Washington,
March 5/The New York Times, 3-6:(1)33.

     2

[Calling for less government regulation of the airline industry]: There is a potential market among Americans for airline service use that hasn't yet been tapped. I believe that more competition, lower rates, high use of airplanes, more entry into new markets, better protection for smaller communities, all tie together in a very worthwhile pursuit.

Before airline-union officials, Washington,
June 20/Los Angeles Herald-Examiner, 6-21:(A)6.

Joan Claybrook
Administrator, National Highway
Traffic Safety Administration   *3*

[Saying passive restraints, such as air bags, should be required equipment on automobiles]: . . . the auto companies will not make air bags available as optional equipment. You cannot today go into a dealership and buy a car with an air bag in it. Just as important is the fact that because most people do not wear seat belts, will not wear seat belts or, in some cases, cannot wear seat belts, we're losing many lives and having many injuries that would not occur were the cars equipped with some kind of passive restraint — either an air bag or passive belt. The overriding benefits that would come from passive restraints prompt the government now to insist that these be made available to purchasers of new cars. They would be phased in over three years: 1982-model large cars would have to meet the standards first, followed by medium and smaller cars in 1983 and 1984 models.

Interview/U.S. News & World Report, 9-26:33.

Glenn A. Cramer
Chairman, Trans International Airlines   *4*

Despite the eased restrictions, our present air-transport system continues to be inadequate for a number of reasons. It still deprives a large part of the public of the right to convenient and readily accessible low-cost air transportation, and therefore is discriminatory. It has resulted in a complex fare structure that no one can fully understand. It has invited wholesale violations on the part of the public, who apparently have no intention of abiding by restrictions on their right to buy air transportation at the lowest possible cost. And it has given birth to an ever larger CAB policing machinery to enforce regulations that are difficult, if not impossible, to understand — and less possible to enforce.

Before International Aviation Club, Washington/
The Wall Street Journal, 4-27:20.

Fred G. Currey
Chairman, Continental
Trailways (bus lines), Inc.

1

[Criticizing the Federal subsidy for the Amtrak railway system]: What we should ask ourselves is whether we should subsidize people to force them out of one mode of transportation into another. Our position is that Amtrak is a political animal and basically a political problem. Looking at it realistically, we have legislators voting to provide rail transportation to particular communities peculiar to their own interests without looking at the economics. Amtrak has no master — either political or economic — but hundreds of masters. [We at Trailways] don't expect Amtrak to disappear, but realistically we expect it should be brought under some kind of control. At the least, it should be prohibited from predatory pricing — charging non-economic fares that are lower than the economic fares of others.

The National Observer, 4-16:3.

2

[Saying intercity bus lines need a Federal subsidy]: Amtrak receives direct rail subsidies totaling almost $500-million annually. Airlines receive $73-million in direct subsidies and are also subsidized by municipal financing and construction of airports. In contrast, the bus industry now finances and builds its own terminals and pays more than $100-million annually in taxes ... In a climate of heavy regulation and competition, the bus industry has been forced to price its passenger service below realistic levels. Measured in 1967 dollars, bus fares have not increased over the past decade. Unprofitable passenger service is subsidized by profitable segments of the industry, such as package express ... We've got to have some Federal help or we'll be in trouble like the railroads, and the public will lose.

Interview, Los Angeles/
Los Angeles Times, 8-15:(3)10.

E. M. "Pete" Estes
President, General Motors Corporation

3

[On his company's program of decreasing the size of its cars]: With the energy situation, economy regulations and other factors, unless we are faced with a total disaster, it will be absolutely impossible for us to ever increase the size of our cars again ... I felt all along that this was the right formula for this period. A lot of people said we took a big chance, a big gamble, but as far as I am concerned that just isn't true. This was the lowest-risk program we have undertaken in years. It was something we had to do for our customers and we did it two years ahead of our competitors. And at the same time [we] did something for the country.

Interview, Dallas, Jan. 6/
The Dallas Times Herald, 1-7:(D)5.

Henry Ford II
Chairman, Ford Motor Company

4

Everything is working against us [in the auto industry] at the moment. I don't care whether it's on emissions or air bags or fuel economy, it's more severe and drastic as far as the industry is concerned than we expected it to be at the turn of this year. I think the thing the [Carter] Administration, and the Congress as well, forgets is the fact that the automobile is a system, and you can't look at the system by looking at the parts individually and forgetting others. Therefore, when you talk about emissions, you've got to think about fuel economy. And when you think about safety, you've got to think about both fuel economy and emissions.

Interview/Newsweek, 4-25:66.

5

I've always maintained that automobiles change in an evolutionary manner, not revolutionary. We'll be driving smaller cars, and they are going to be a lot different under the hood but won't look an awful lot different. I think Americans will keep their cars longer. But what's really changing is in the marketplace. People are giving up cars for other kinds of transportation — four-wheel-drive Jeeps or Blazers. They're giving up station wagons for pickup trucks and putting tops on them. Or big vans where they install an icebox, AM-FM radio, waterbeds and carpet up to the ceiling.

WHAT THEY SAID IN 1977

(HENRY FORD II)

They're going into something they can personalize.

Interview/People, 5-2:80.

Douglas A. Fraser
Vice president in charge of the
Chrysler department, United
Automobile Workers of America   *1*

The automobile is something special for the American worker. In most cases, he has a confining job. The job runs him, not he the job. His car is the only outlet for his individuality. That is why it is so difficult to get him interested in share-the-ride arrangements. When it comes to changing life-styles to advance national objectives, we ought to concentrate on changing those of the wealthy. It is an elitist attitude for those who load their families into jet planes for vacations in Bermuda or on the Riviera to say that the American worker should not have a car big enough to load his family into for a camping trip to the Grand Canyon . . .

Interview, Detroit/The New York Times, 5-11:55.

Valery Giscard d'Estaing
President of France   *2*

[On the current ban by New York City airports of the British-French *Concorde* SST] : The *Concorde* affair has seriously tarnished [the U.S.] image, for two reasons. First, this fierce resistance against a limited European technological breakthrough appears to be quite out of proportion with the event. Secondly, the flight of governmental responsibility — with the Federal authority saying yes, then a local authority saying no, and so forth — which may strike some as the expression of democratic institutions, hits others as a structural weakness. It is utterly incomprehensible that the *Concorde* can land every day at Dulles Airport outside Washington without anyone talking about it, while it is prevented from landing at Kennedy [Airport in New York] on the edge of the Atlantic Ocean because it will allegedly upset the ecology.

Interview, Paris/Newsweek, 7-25:48.

Knut Hammarskjold
Director general, International
Air Transport Association   *3*

. . . politics have gotten into air transport. What is essentially a public service has become a plaything for politicians, and now we are at a crossroads. A number of elements will determine in which direction we go. One is the fact that the United States is the most important aviation nation. It is no exaggeration to say that everybody is respecting this fact and eagerly looking to you for guidance . . . Unfortunately, for the last few years there has been no U.S. airline policy — or rather, the United States officially has been speaking with many tongues. Different U.S. agencies have been talking and acting at cross purposes. There has been no consistent guidance for the international airlines . . . The U.S. has a very strong self-interest which goes far beyond the U.S. airlines because the U.S. is the world's most important manufacturer of civil aircraft, and those suffering from the present state of affairs include very much the manufacturing industry and its workers. Not knowing what the future regulatory system will be has produced a sort of deadlock. If this deadlock is not broken through positive policies, it could very well happen that the ones who are able to buy new aircraft will not be U.S. airlines but foreign airlines which have other sources of revenue. They may be state-owned or state-supported, or they may carry the flag of a very rich country. It would be strange if the only ones able to buy new aircraft are foreigners — and why should they buy them in the States?

Interview, Montreal/
U.S. News & World Report, 3-21:56.

Alfred E. Kahn
Chairman-designate, Civil Aeronautics
Board of the United States   *4*

I know less than I plan to know about the airline industry before I make any pronouncements about the things I'm going to do. But I do begin with a clear philosophical economic conviction that in regulated industries generally, more competition is desirable where it's feasible. If I'm confirmed, I aim to see — with

(ALFRED E. KAHN)

caution and care — to what extent the market-place can take over the functions that are now performed by very imperfect regulators like me.

At his confirmation hearing before Senate Commerce subcommittee, Washington, June 6/The Washington Post, 6-7:(D)6.

Alfred E. Kahn
Chairman, Civil Aeronautics
Board of the United States

1

[On the practice of airlines overbooking flights and then having to "bump" passengers with a confirmed reservation]: An economist looks for ways of minimizing social damage. There are obvious things an economist thinks about overbooking that everyone in the industry thinks is impossible. Well, I damn well want to be convinced that it's impossible to get to a system in which you have some rational way of choosing who gets bumped and who does not ... It does not make sense that somebody to whom ... being bumped or not being bumped is a matter practically of indifference should automatically stay on a flight while somebody to whom it may be a matter of life and death is bumped from a flight.

News conference, Washington/
Los Angeles Times, 7-6:(3)20.

2

... I'm not really interested in temporary and possibly evanescent benefits from sporadic [airline-fare] price wars, but in seeing what you can do to have a permanent change in the structure of the industry that promises a continuation of low prices. That's why I'm willing to limit the price competition, if [for instance] I see it eliminating a group of carriers ... whose operation is such to give you reason to believe that they will continuously exert price pressure. That really is the kind of competition we don't need.

Interview, Washington/
The Dallas Times Herald, 10-16:(E)5.

Arthur F. Kelly
President, Western Airlines

3

The promise of lower fares in an era of continuing inflation is a cruel hoax and a delusion. I feel it [deregulation of the U.S. airline industry] will do irreversible damage to the best transportation system in the world.

At public hearing, Los Angeles, Aug. 23/
Los Angeles Herald-Examiner, 8-23:(A)1.

James S. Kemper, Jr.
Chairman, Kemper Corporation, insurance

4

There is good and bad news for the insurance industry and the car owner in the energy program. The good is that no matter in what form the program emerges from Congress, the public is going to drive less. There is a very direct correlation between the number of miles driven and the number of accidents. As the public voluntarily heeds the plea for conservation and as penalties take effect, accidents will decrease and so will insurance claims. However, the push to sub-compacts and smaller cars is bad news, even as it may reduce gasoline consumption. It has been amply demonstrated that in an accident involving a sub-compact the risk of death and serious injury is higher. Don't hold me to the figures, but the generalization is true that when a medium-sized car is hit from the side by a car going 30 miles per hour, the occupants may escape being killed. But the very same accident may kill everyone in the car if the auto is a sub-compact. Unfortunately, we're probably going to see more serious injuries and deaths per accident in the years ahead and that, unfortunately again, is going to raise the cost of insurance for everybody.

The Dallas Times Herald, 4-25:(D)7.

Edward M. Kennedy
United States Senator, D—Massachusetts

5

The relative competitive freedom given to intrastate airlines led those companies to try different types of air service at different prices. These airlines lower their fares, compete with the automobile, the bus and the train for passengers who would travel anyway, attract many other people who would not have traveled but for the lower fare, put more people in

233

their planes than the CAB carriers and spread the operating costs over a much greater number of passengers. The companies stay profitable, and that pleases stockholders. The fares stay low, and that pleases travelers.

Los Angeles Times, 5-31:(1)17.

James L. Kerrigan
President, Greyhound (bus) Lines
1

[Arguing against the Federal subsidy for Amtrak]: The public is getting robbed; Amtrak is getting away with murder. And if something isn't done about it, Congress will wake up in the 1980s and discover it's got another Vietnam on its hands. They'll ask: How did we get into this? ... The bus is the national transportation system for the least affluent Americans. We serve 15,000 communities, most of which don't have any other public transportation. But we won't be able to continue to operate the way we have unless we have legitimate competition in the marketplace. We're turning Amtrak into part of our welfare system. They're spending hundreds of millions of dollars without being accountable to anyone. A lot of people who complain about welfare — aid to dependent children and so forth — well, when they ride Amtrak, it is just as much of a public-welfare program.

The New York Times, 1-2:(3)7.

Freddie Laker
Chairman, Laker Airways
2

[On his new low-fare "Skytrain" service between New York and London]: The people who are running national airlines today don't understand the interdependence of the whole tourist industry. There are 10 million people in the United Kingdom and another 50-odd million in the United States who are potential Skytrain users and who, without such a facility, would never cross the Atlantic. And there are — and this is not a separate, but a connected, issue — umpteen thousand hotel beds on both sides of the Atlantic that remain empty half the year. All the national airlines can think of, to deal with their disastrous economic problems, is to

demand ever-increasing subsidies from government or to reduce services. But there is no record anywhere of any business expansion by contraction. What air tourism needs is a new dimension. The only way to achieve this is by deregulating the ridiculously regimented air-transport structure, allowing competition between operators — which will improve standards — and by lowering air fares.

The New York Times Magazine, 9-4:14.

Warren G. Magnuson
United States Senator, D—Washington
3

[Advocating national no-fault automobile insurance]: On the basis of the extensive hearing record and two DOT studies, I am convinced that the concept of no-fault is sound. I am convinced that the economics of no-fault are cost-efficient. I am convinced that accident victims deserve more than a lottery ticket. A no-fault system creates incentives for rehabilitation and recovery, not retribution. It shifts the emphasis to getting well, not getting back at the other accident victim. I am convinced of the wisdom of a basic-standards approach to implement a no-fault system nationwide. The progression of enactments of state no-fault laws has been halted in the state legislatures by a small group of dedicated opponents. Under a basic-standards approach, a balance can be struck to improve the hodgepodge non-system of conflicting statutes which exists today, while at the same time responding to individual state needs.

Before Senate Commerce Committee,
*Washington, July 13/***

L. B. Maytag
Chairman, National Airlines
4

[Criticizing proposals aimed at increasing competition among airlines]: After looking at what is proposed, I've fallen in love with the CAB and its regulations ... Low air fares by legislation has become an American dream. But it is that — a dream. And it is an illusion from which we must open our eyes to examine fares in the harsh daylight of reality ... Permanent price reductions in air fares cannot be legislated any more than can yesterday's $1,500 car or its

(L. B. MAYTAG)

18-cent gallon of gas . . . [Government sanction of increased fare competition would cause several carriers to be] swept into oblivion. Only giants could survive in this land of milk-and-competition . . . who could then set whatever fares they choose once the monopolistic dust has settled.

Before Town Hall, Los Angeles, April 26/
Los Angeles Times, 4-27:(1)32.

Louis W. Menk
Chairman, Burlington Northern (Railroad)
1

My personal view is that, except in a few heavy-traffic corridors such as Washington-New York-Boston, it's not worth it [to continue Amtrak rail passenger service]. I'll stand by the comment I made before a Congressional committee some years ago: that, like the stagecoach and the paddle-wheel steamer, the long-distance passenger train ought to be allowed to die an honorable death. Of course, it's hard for a politician to say to a constituent in a small town, "We can't any longer afford to run a train through here." But I think the day of reckoning is coming, and that Congress will get more sensitive to how much it's costing taxpayers to maintain rail passenger service on routes that are obviously uneconomic.

Interview/U.S. News & World Report, 2-21:73.

Dale Milford
United States Representative,
D–Texas
2

Some day there will be an advanced supersonic transport flying people around the world that has solved the environmental and economic problems [of current SSTs]. I want that airplane to be made in America . . . What we must do is not allow our own aeronautical industry to fall behind their foreign competitors. We cannot continue to lead the world in the field of aviation if we don't increase the pool of knowledge.

The Dallas Times Herald, 3-18:(A)7.

E. Spencer Miller
Chairman and president,
Maine Central Railroad
3

I don't favor mergers of railroads, because every single one of them has been a disappointment in that they resulted either in bankruptcy, or the combined earnings subsequent to merger were less than the combined roads prior to merger, or the high-drawn prognostications of efficiency and savings never, never materialized. My feeling is that the concept of a merger of a few lines to compete with other lines just aggravates the situation. It does nothing to solve the car-service problems or the standardization of engineering or the labor problems of the industry. I think if we're going to avoid Uncle Sam eventually controlling all the railroads [through nationalization] as has been done by France, Italy, Germany and Great Britain, then we have to have a private corporation controlling all of them — an amalgamation of all the United States' railroads into one national corporation, like the Bell Telephone System.

Interview/The New York Times, 10-9:(3)3.

Ralph Nader
Lawyer; Consumer advocate
4

[On whether there must be a trade-off between automobile safety and efficiency]: I am bothered by the fact that some people in the [Carter] Administration and, of course, the auto industry, want us to believe that there must be a trade-off. The important crash-protection feature of a car is its size more than its weight, and cars can be made lighter but still without a drastic [decrease] of the size, to protect the occupants in a crash and absorb the energy. Secondly, cars can remain the size they are and still have lower horsepower and more-efficient engines, and that, of course, will improve gasoline efficiency. The Administration, I think, is getting itself boxed in by a gasoline tax and a high-horsepower tax or a gas-guzzler tax, without taking into account that if it doesn't also hold firm and advance the auto-safety frontiers and deal with the problem of imports, it may result in bad economic and safety consequences. So there has to be a

235

(RALPH NADER)

program going on all three of those fronts if we are going to achieve our goals.

TV-radio interview, Washington/"Meet the Press," National Broadcasting Company, 4-17.

1

[On the British-French *Concorde* SST]: I think it is an atrocious economic venture. I think the small taxpayers in England and France are paying the bill for millionaires and government officials from those countries to travel on the SST. And on this side of the continent, the people who live around New York or Washington or elsewhere are suffering from the sonic abuses, and perhaps, if there are more SSTs, more serious environmental abuses. It can't be justified from either an economic or environmental point of view.

TV-radio interview, Washington/"Meet the Press," National Broadcasting Company, 4-17.

2

[Expressing criticism that the government's new automobile air-bag requirement will be introduced gradually, with larger cars the first to be required to comply]: This is the first time the Federal government has phased in an auto safety standard. This is a very bad precedent. This says to the public, if you can't afford a large luxury car, you're going to have to wait for safety protection. While we have one government agency telling us to buy small cars to save fuel, we have another telling us we cannot yet have safety devices in those cars.

News conference, Washington, June 30/ Los Angeles Times, 7-1:(1)13.

John J. O'Donnell
President, United States
Air Line Pilots Association   3

[Saying the UN should adopt a convention against airliner hijacking]: As long as there are nations which harbor hijackers and terrorists, or fail to prosecute or extradite them, international aviation will remain a prime target for these criminals... The convention should clearly define a terrorist or hijacker, make punishment swift and inevitable and provide economic, political and social sanctions against these countries which fail to comply.

Washington, Oct. 18/ The Dallas Times Herald, 10-19:(A)4.

A. Daniel O'Neal
Chairman, Interstate
Commerce Commission   4

[Saying one must be cautious about deregulating the trucking industry]: You can't complain about the overall general performance of the motor-carrier industry. Service has been generally good, but at the same time there are a lot of specific areas that need study... Truckers play the game of business under the rules that are laid down. They have a right to expect that those rules aren't changed precipitously. Lots of money is invested, and a lot of families depend on those businesses that have developed under this system. We have to be concerned with disrupting an entire industry.

Interview/The Washington Post, 12-13:(D)7.

John E. Robson
Chairman, Civil Aeronautics
Board of the United States   5

[Saying the airline industry should have less regulation by the CAB]: Looking backwards, 40 years of regulation hasn't produced an economically strong industry in pretty good circumstances, so I don't know any reason to feel that 40 more years in not-so-good circumstances are going to make them stronger. [Without change,] my own belief is that, in the long run, the industry will gradually become weaker, that there will be continuing and growing incentives for the Board to get further and further into the airlines' activities as a means of controlling costs in order to keep fares down. The long denouement of that, I think, is to increase the responsibility that the agency assumes for the carriers, and when things go bad — when economic forces create problems — the likelihood of ending up with them in your lap is a heck of a lot greater.

Interview/The Washington Post, 5-1:(G)3.

John H. Shenefield
Assistant Attorney General
of the United States

1

The case for regulatory reform in trucking is not theoretical. It is based on hard, indisputable fact: Interstate Commerce Commission-regulated carriers are allowed to agree on and fix the rates charged to shippers. What would be a felony in most American industries is not only condoned but affirmatively encouraged in the trucking business ... The minimum rates enforced by the ICC are higher than those that would be determined in a competitive market. Put in plain English, shippers, and ultimately you and I, pay more for truck transportation than it costs — much more. Because of this loaded regulatory scheme, trying to lower rates in the trucking industry is not merely a business decision; it is a decision to go to war, to litigate — for those who would lower rates will inevitably face vigorous protests from rate-bureau members ... Trucking rates would be lower if there was substantial regulatory reform. The experience with agricultural commodities is instructive: When transportation of poultry and fruits and vegetables was "deregulated" in the mid-1950s, rates dropped by 33 per cent on poultry and 19 per cent on fruits and vegetables.

Senate testimony/
The Washington Post, 11-4:(A)18.

Robert H. Shertz
Chairman, American
Trucking Associations

2

The fact is that Federal regulation of transportation holds down the cost of trucking while ensuring adequate service. During the 1972 to 1974 period, when inflation was at its most rapid upward pace, the price of most commodities and services rose in the range of 25 to 30 per cent. Regulated, for-hire trucking, by contrast, rose only 15 per cent ... That there may be some flaws in our regulated trucking system I won't deny. It is not perfect and I get naturally suspicious of things that do work perfectly. But if I had to sum it all up for you

concisely, I would simply say: "It works." The fact is ... it works extremely well.

Before Economic Club of Detroit,
Sept. 26/Vital Speeches, 11-1:42.

E. G. (Bud) Shuster
United States Representative,
R—Pennsylvania

3

[Saying passive restraints, such as air bags, should not be made required equipment on automobiles, and that people should rely on seat belts]: I am very much in favor of seat belts. I make speeches about wearing seat belts. It's foolish not to wear them. But my position is that free people have a right to do foolish things. Instead of ramming air-bag regulations and laws down people's throats, we can do better. If we have the ingenuity in America to sell cereal and all the other fine American products, then I say that we have the ingenuity to educate the American people on the importance of using seat belts.

Interview/U.S. News & World Report, 9-26:34.

B. R. Stokes
Executive director, American
Public Transit Association

4

Simply put, there has been no [Presidential] leadership [on mass transit]. It is not enough to say that performance to date has not been satisfactory; there has been no performance ... We must conclude that President Carter does not yet understand what public transit means to our citizens. He seems to confuse all transit with subways, and he says, "Underground railways are anathema to me" ... What is needed now is Executive action to carry out campaign rhetoric — a recognition that the energy crisis, inevitably and inexorably, will demand that public transit carry a greater and greater proportion of urban trips in the years ahead, and that we must do everything possible now to prepare for that time.

Before public works officials, Chicago,
Sept. 14/The New York Times, 9-15:(A)24.

WHAT THEY SAID IN 1977

Winfred L. Thornton
President, Florida East Coast Railway
1

If the railroads are to be competitive and provide more economical transportation costs to the consumer, they must have efficient operations. Mergers of the rail lines are not the answer. We must have better, not bigger, railroads. Elimination of the featherbedding rules will require political courage, but it will be in the best interest of every working person, union member or not. Without a strong and viable rail system throughout the nation, all industry will be crippled and jobs will be lost.

Nation's Business, July:63.

Wesley C. Uhlman
Mayor of Seattle
2

[On his city's free bus service in the downtown area]: Public transportation is as vital a service as putting out fires or catching criminals. A city doesn't charge you if you've suffered a burglary. We take for granted that government is supposed to provide such service. I see no difference.

Interview, Los Angeles/
Los Angeles Times, 5-23:(4)4.

Archie L. Wilson
President, Dixie Carriers, Inc.
3

Is the transportation system going to have the capacity to handle the business as the economy grows? Will the most efficient means of transportation be available to you? It's no use saying to an industry that needs a pipeline that there are plenty of trucks, or to a man who needs a railroad that there are plenty of pipelines, or to a man who needs a barge line that there are plenty of railroads. All modes are needed, particularly modes that compete with each other, because competition is the most effective way of assuring maximum efficiency on the part of everyone.

Before Rotary Club, Beaumont, Tex.,
Jan. 12/Vital Speeches, 3-15:338.

George R. Ariyoshi
Governor of Hawaii (D)

1

Many Hawaiians agree with me that, unless we change our ways, Hawaii will become unrecognizable. Take a hard look at our problems and you find one central irritant straight through — too many people are moving in. Too many people means too few jobs, too little land for agriculture, too much crime, too much pressure for government help, too many taxes, too much of a combination of negative conditions that spell out disaster for a very fragile kind of paradise.

Interview, Honolulu/Los Angeles Times,
4-17:(Home)36.

Les AuCoin
United States Representative,
D–Oregon

2

Until the Federal government, working in cooperation with state governments and local governments, can stop the rot that is eating away at every major urban center in this country, this nation is going to be picking up the pieces for years to come. The problems of energy consumption that stem from transportation patterns caused by suburban sprawl, the loss of agricultural land . . . the incredible financial loss to taxpayers when they have to subsidize and pay for new municipal services resulting from the exodus from the decaying center city — these problems have to be stopped.

Before the House, Washington, May 6/
The Washington Post, 5-10:(A)18.

Abraham D. Beame
Mayor of New York

3

The banks and unions both have indicated the Federal government should be involved [in helping New York out of its fiscal problems]. It is fundamental that all local government must be relieved from the burden of matching Federal public and medical assistance to the indigent. There is a pressing need for a Federal program which provides a financing mechanism for municipalities recovering from financial difficulties which are unable to sell securities in the public market.

Before Senate Banking Committee, Washington/
The Christian Science Monitor, 1-3:12.

4

The Federal government has in fact made a profit on New York. They borrowed money at 5 per cent, but charged us 6 per cent. . . . they don't do that when they make a loan to Zaire.

News conference, Tucson, Ariz./
The Dallas Times Herald, 6-13:(A)8.

5

[At the launching of a new submarine named after his city] : Some people are always negative, and, for a while, these people were saying that New York City was going under. Only in Groton, I'm happy to say, only in Groton! I'm delighted to be here for this historic launching of the nuclear submarine *New York City.* The submarine is supposed to go under. The city never will.

Groton, Conn., June 18/
The New York Times, 6-19:(1)29.

W. Michael Blumenthal
Secretary of the Treasury
of the United States

6

Why are places like New York, Detroit, Cincinnati and similar old urban centers in financial trouble? Are there some common factors? To what extent can these factors be eliminated by more intelligent local govern-

WHAT THEY SAID IN 1977

(W. MICHAEL BLUMENTHAL)

ment? If in New York the pension system is abused, you can correct that. If there is padding of payrolls with a lot of people that don't do any work in a particular city, you can correct that. If you have improper budget procedures or controls over expenditures, you can correct that. So assuming, therefore, you take these cities and you make them more efficient, you still have some inherent problems. One of them may be the load of welfare, and with that we'll see what comes out of welfare reform. Let's assume that you have some changes in the welfare system such as you would be able to get through Congress, and let's assume that you would have a relatively efficient administration — are the cards simply stacked against large cities? [The critical problem is that the] political boundaries of cities and the fiscal [tax] boundaries [do not match].

Interview, Washington, April 7/
The New York Times, 4-8:(A)24.

1

The Federal government cannot take over the responsibility for maintaining the financial health of the cities. Cities have to do that themselves. The Federal government cannot manage cities efficiently. Cities have to do that themselves. So nothing the Federal government will do can be a substitute for local responsibility and efficient local management. At the same time, there may be some peculiar elements in urban finance that are beyond the capacity of cities to cope with by themselves. The great burdens of welfare are one example. We see lack of confidence; the vicious circle of tax-payers moving out of the cities into the suburbs; shrinking tax payments leading to higher tax rates which cause more people to move out. Then you get to the cutting of services — police and fire protection — which then makes the city less secure, so that more people move out. That process has to be stopped at some point. We're attempting to isolate the problems that cities really have to solve locally, and see if there is a residual

problem that some Federal mechanism can help to solve.

Interview, Washington/
U.S. News & World Report, 4-11:33.

William A. Donaldson
City Manager of Cincinnati

2

You have to break down the institutions that isolate people from accountability for what they're doing. What's happened in city government is that you have 18 or 20 different governments — the water department feuds with the sewer department, and the sewer department feuds with public works. They become isolated little kingdoms. We end up changing the problem to fit it into a department. So the question is, what can we do to wreck that system?

Interview, Cincinnati/
The Dallas Times Herald, 12-7:(G)2.

Dianne Feinstein
San Francisco City and
County Supervisor

3

You can build skyscrapers and a perfect art center, but if you don't have beauty shops, groceries and life on the streets, the city will disintegrate. The key to urban survival is keeping the working middle class.

San Francisco Examiner & Chronicle, 4-10:(A)5.

Patricia Roberts Harris
Secretary of Housing and Urban
Development of the United States

4

I think that the Federal government in past years was a party to discrimination against the city. In the late 1940s and in the early 1950s, the Federal Housing Administration was the culprit. Its insurance standards, in my judgment, had racist overtones and encouraged development in the suburbs rather than in the cities. We have a great deal of past misbehavior to set right. The new HUD is in the process of changing that policy drastically. There's nothing wrong with FHA insuring homes in suburban subdivisions — as long as it also insures center-city homes, too. The key is to provide freedom of choice. I don't intend to discriminate between the suburbs and the city, except

(PATRICIA ROBERTS HARRIS)

to provide incentives to live in the cities, because in the past we have provided so many disincentives against living in the city.

Interview/U.S. News & World Report, 12-12:64.

Janet Gray Hayes
Mayor of San Jose, California
1

The President [Carter] cannot understand the problems of cities from Plains or the Georgia statehouse or from a walk through New York City. We [at home] face the brickbats of the taxpayers. Who's the President listening to? There's not one Mayor in the Administration . . .

At National League of Cities'
Congress of Cities, San Francisco/
Los Angeles Times, 12-12:(1)28.

Hubert H. Humphrey
United States Senator, D—Minnesota
2

I think the problem with the [Carter] Administration on the cities is that there's been no focus. There's been lots of little pieces. It's like building blocks — they are spread all over the table and nobody has built them into any kind of system.

Interview, Washington, July 27/
Los Angeles Times, 7-28:(1)5.

Juanita M. Kreps
Secretary of Commerce of the United States
3

Each of us might have a different definition of what it is that a city is and does. But certainly we would all agree that the city ought to be a focus of cultural, political and economic activity which serves the interests of its people by generating jobs and creating a certain kind of infrastructure . . .

Before National League of Cities/
The Washington Post, 3-26:(B)1.

Phyllis Lamphere
President, National League of Cities
4

It's ridiculous . . . for the Congress to decide on a so-called safe drinking-water standard and, without so much as a by-your-leave, drop the expense on city governments of building and operating the facilities . . . Too often we [the cities] are hypnotized by the prospect of a grant of several millions and oblivious to economic policy decisions that may cost us billions . . . The time is upon us . . . when we must monitor Federal revenue-sharing, a time when we will realize that adverse Federal policy and administration can cost us more than Federal grants or payments will ever bring.

Before National League of Cities, Washington,
March 7/The Dallas Times Herald, 3-8:(A)5.

Ralph Lazarus
Chairman, Federated Department Stores
5

Having affirmed my belief in the future of our cities, I want now to make it clear that, in my judgment, we can get where you and I want America to go only if we are willing to face up to some unpleasant truths. One such unpleasant truth is the existence of the myth that business, by itself, can rebuild the vitality of our cities. . . We have all learned by now, I think, that government, at whatever level, cannot — by itself — solve our problems. Well, business can't, either. A successful community is the product of effort, dedication and intelligence on the part of all segments of society.

Before International Downtown Executives
Association, Atlanta/The Wall Street Journal,
11-8:22.

George Moscone
Mayor of San Francisco
6

I happen not to believe in the view that Mayors are beggars, that all we stand for is for hat-in-hand, and doling out of money. This is a country of people, and we break ourselves down, for better or worse, into three levels of government. The important issue is that Mayors are charged with the responsibility of taking care of the problems of people. They are the ones at the firing line. When we go to Washington, we don't go there to say we want something to which we might otherwise not be entitled, but for political influence or something else. We go there because we think we can direct the resources of this country, which are paid just by the people of our city as the people

WHAT THEY SAID IN 1977

(GEORGE MOSCONE)

of our state to the Federal Treasury. We want to be able to help the President to be able to come forward and put the monies, our monies, into programs that really work.

TV-radio interview. Tucson, Ariz./"Meet the Press," National Broadcasting Company, 6-12.

Henry S. Reuss
United States Representative,
D-Wisconsin
1

With the neighborhoods as the new focus of attention, low-income groups should be encouraged to develop their own economic institutions, such as neighborhood credit unions, consumer cooperatives and development corporations. And local financial institutions, always so fearful of "credit allocation," must themselves do a better job to see that a reasonable share of the nation's capital is available to those neighborhood institutions. The cities themselves must provide the level of services — police, street lighting, trash collection, and so on — needed to sustain the neighborhood as a viable community. They also ought to re-examine their property-tax burden and its deadlining effect on rehabilitation. For example, raising the tax on vacant central-city land, and lowering the tax on improvements could make rehabilitation of homes and commercial establishments more attractive to owners and investors, and reduce the misuse of scarce land . . . Too often in the past, Federal programs, particularly urban renewal and construction of the interstate-highway system, have destroyed existing neighborhoods. Other Federal programs — FHA and water and sewer grants — have in effect encouraged movements out of viable existing urban neighborhoods to the suburbs. Washington must change its emphasis to neighborhood conservation and rehabilitation.

Before National Women's Democratic Club,
Jan. 6/The Washington Post, 2-17:(A)18.

Felix G. Rohatyn
Chairman, Municipal Assistance
Corporation of New York
2

A balanced Federal budget is not a moral imperative, but a livable urban civilization is. Basically, only the President of this country can light the candle that will lead the cities of this country out of the darkness they are in . . . Although the rhetoric has changed, the message is essentially the same [as that during the Administration of former President Gerald Ford], and our hopes of getting some relief for the city are very long-shot hopes. [President Carter's emphasis on] human rights [in foreign countries] is a terrific thing, but it really should begin at home. Human rights in Bedford-Stuyvesant and Watts are something we have to begin paying attention to.

Before Association for a Better New York/
Los Angeles Times, 7-25:(1)13.

Wesley C. Uhlman
Mayor of Seattle
3

[On the decrease in families residing in the city]: I am not wringing my hands. If Seattle is more desirable to singles and older people, or smaller households, or gays, that's not necessarily bad. Most Mayors wring their hands about the loss of the white middle class, but a city is like a living organism that changes every 20 or 30 years.

Interview/The New York Times, 3-28:32.

Coleman A. Young
Mayor of Detroit

Downtown is an anchor and a radiator. Literally everything radiates from here. And if we have a rotten center, then we have a rotting city.

Los Angeles Times, 10-31:(1)1.

PART TWO

International Affairs

Idi Amin
President of Uganda

1

What I want is for blacks and whites to stay together. The whites could have good jobs. We need them because they have technical ability; we need their brains, because the Africans have so much to learn. We want them to stay in Africa, but they must accept that we [blacks] are the majority.

San Francisco Examiner & Chronicle,
7-24:(This World)2.

Christiaan Barnard
South African heart surgeon

2

South Africa has become the scum of the world community [because of its apartheid policies]. Nobody wants to have anything to do with us. We rarely get invited to functions by other countries and, if we do, we are avoided like the plague by other members of the diplomatic corps.

Before South African Freedom Foundation,
Johannesburg, Aug. 12/
The Dallas Times Herald, 8-13:(A)2.

Steve Biko
South African black leader

3

The [white] Afrikaner is suffering from the seeds of his own racial prejudice that he has sown in the community. To maintain the system, he had to sow very deep-seated prejudices against the black man. A grand scheme that now cuts across that type of prejudice will require the defeat of the Afrikaners' own right wing. That is why they fight with their backs to the wall, why their responses are not always the most logical . . . Also, any concessions to blacks will generate more violence. [But] people here are going to have to think seriously in terms of living together, permanently, not just for the

next 10 or 20 years, which is the calendar the current politicians are working on. But they are old — 65, 66 — and they don't really think they'll be around more than 20 years, and so they are just holding the fort. In the next few years, you will get leaders who are planning not so much for themselves but for their children and their children's children. If they do that realistically, they'll realize it's better to weld the population inside than to try to block the rest of Africa coming down.

Interview, King William's Town, South
Africa/Los Angeles Times, 10-27:(1)7.

Roelof F. Botha
South African Ambassador to the
United States; Foreign Minister-
designate of South Africa

4

Anybody who still doubts that the Russians are bent on establishing all-out influence [in Africa], just take one look at the map of Africa. Mombassa [Kenya] is the only deep-water port still open to the free world on the east coast of the continent.

News conference, Washington, March 17/
Los Angeles Herald-Examiner, 3-17:(A)8.

Roelof F. Botha
Foreign Minister of South Africa

5

[On U.S. UN Ambassador Andrew Young's statement that the minority white government of South Africa is illegitimate]: If Mr. Young's criterion of majority rule forms the basis of his recognition of other governments, then he must consider as illegitimate half the governments of the world.

Interview/Los Angeles Herald-Examiner, 4-18:(A)4.

WHAT THEY SAID IN 1977

(ROELOF F. BOTHA)

1

[On U.S. criticism of apartheid in his country]: ... thousands of black Africans are in jail without trial in many independent African countries. Why are we singled out? Are our blacks the only ones worth paying attention to? Are the rest of Africa's imprisoned blacks worthless? Why do you claim a benevolence from us while you seem prepared to accept its violation as typical elsewhere in Africa? You are telling us, in effect, that because you succeeded in integrating some Southern states, we must do exactly the same in our country. We have moved a long way but, while we have done so, you have radicalized your demands to the point of threatening our destruction. It is *our* country, yet you tell us *your* morality requires full and equal participation, which [U.S. Vice President Walter] Mondale said means the same as one-man, one-vote. In the end, we are not going to agree voluntarily to let others impose our ruin. Don't forget that unlike the French, unlike the British and unlike the Portuguese, we Afrikaners have no other place to go. When the chips are down, those who fight to defend South Africa will not only be whites. They will include thousands of blacks, Asians and coloreds who are receiving arms and training from us. A new unity is growing, based on the determination not to have our problems settled from outside. Make no mistake. We are not afraid. This is a question of resolution. Do not underestimate the severity of our resistance because, if it should come to that point, our survival is at stake.

Interview, Vienna/The New York Times, 5-25:35.

2

[On U.S. demands for one-man, one-vote in his country]: As the Americans say, there is no way, baby, in which we are going to accept this. Forget it. We are not going to do this after 300 years ... We fear black domination. That is a fact, and that is the basis of our policy. An unqualified one-man, one-vote cannot be allowed ... I believe the average American will side with us on our right to survival. He won't side with us militarily, but he will support our right to survive.

Before Cape Town Press Club, June 4/
The Washington Post, 6-6:(A)21.

3

[On those members of the UN who voted for an arms embargo against his country because of its racial policies]: ... now that they have so cynically discarded principles in favor of selfish political motives, one might well ask whether they have considered the implications of their action, and whether they are prepared to accept full responsibility for what can only be termed an incitement to violence. The UN can no longer claim to be an instrument of peace now that it has condoned the use of violence to settle international disputes, in direct contradiction of its very *raison d'etre*, the maintenance of international peace and security. No state can accept the prescriptions of an international body as to how it should deal with its own affairs. No state can accept that its capacity to act in a given domestic situation is qualified by what an outside body may later have to say. No state can afford to cede its future right to act decisively and in good faith within its borders as it deems appropriate in order to solve a problem, to avoid a potentially explosive situation or to establish order.

Pretoria, Nov. 4/The New York Times, 11-5:7.

Zbigniew Brzezinski
Assistant to President of the
United States Jimmy Carter for
National Security Affairs

4

We recognize that in the kind of world we live in, the principle of [black] majority rule has to be the basis for international order in Africa. Secondly, we recognize that precisely because implementation of majority rule was so long delayed, its quest today has become much more urgent, potentially much more destructive. Thirdly, it is our intention to try to avoid transforming the black-white conflict in southern Africa into a Red-white conflict — which it can easily become if violence escalates and if foreign aggressive powers are drawn into it. Given all of that, it is our intention to try to

(ZBIGNIEW BRZEZINSKI)

use the leverage we have to obtain rapid movement toward majority rule in Rhodesia and Namibia. At the same time, we intend to use our leverage to encourage the South Africans to start the process of the progressive transformation of some of their internal arrangements, lest otherwise they become the target of a massive conflict in which we will not — I repeat — we will not support them.

Interview, Washington/
U.S. News & World Report, 5-30:38.

1

I would say what is at stake [in the racial situation in South Africa] is of really major importance, both in international and human terms. What is at stake is how to avoid a transcontinental war, a war which will merge the racial conflict into an ideological conflict. What is at stake is the livelihood of some millions of people, black and white. What is at stake here is how to avoid historical tragedy. There's no doubt that there are compelling reasons why the South African society has to undergo a progressive process of transformation. Its values, its social arrangements are out of keeping with the spirit and moral imperatives of our time. At the same time, what is involved here is a deep legacy of history: 300 years of white society, some of whose people fought for their own independence only 70-some years ago. They have deeply ingrained national feelings, reinforced by history and the Bible. These are not circumstances which are amenable to easy change. These are circumstances which have to be dealt with with compassion and with a sense of historical perspective. What we're trying to do is to encourage a process of change which will outpace what otherwise looks like a rather apocalyptical alternative.

Interview/The Washington Post, 10-9:(C)5.

Gatsha Buthelezi
Political leader of South
Africa's Zulu people.

2

[On the possibility of racial war in South Africa]: My position is that violence has already started. Some blacks are now training

for war. Our aim is no longer to prevent violence from starting. Our aim is to prevent its escalation . . . We have never muted our feelings that we reject apartheid. The Zulus and all blacks reject apartheid and the homelands idea. I think we're part of South Africa. It seems ridiculous that we should be divided.

News conference, Beverly Hills, Calif.,
Feb. 17/Los Angeles Times, 2-18:(1)28.

Hodding Carter III
Assistant Secretary for Public
Affairs and Spokesman, Department
of State of the United States

3

The idea that we are either aloof from Africa, withdrawing from Africa, or in some way abandoning interest in Africa is erroneous . . . The fact that we forcefully recommend African solutions to African problems and elimination of great-power rivalry in Africa cannot be taken in any way as a signal of disengagement or disinterest. If anything, our interests in Africa have increased, but we wish it to be a common interest with Africans.

Washington, April 14/The New York Times, 4-15:(A)3.

Jimmy Carter
President of the United States

4

[Upon signing a bill banning U.S. imports of Rhodesian chrome]: Our country is committed to the concept of rapid transition to [black] majority rule in Rhodesia under non-violent conditions. I view this measure today as an appropriate and positive step toward that goal. We have consistently stated our belief that a peaceful solution in Rhodesia depends upon negotiations that involve a full spectrum of opinion among its leaders, both black and white. This legislation probably has as high a symbolic importance in international affairs as anything I'll do this year . . .

Washington, March 18/Los Angeles Times, 3-19:(1)3.

5

Obviously it would be better for the peace of Africa if other nations would not send troops and military forces. Cuba still has almost 15,000 troops in Angola. They have recently sent about 50 military advisers into Ethiopia,

WHAT THEY SAID IN 1977

(JIMMY CARTER)

and they have . . . people in Mozambique and in eight or 10 other countries. Sometimes it's three or four, sometimes it's a larger number. We would like very much for Cuba to refrain from this intrusion into African affairs in a military way. Obviously this is one of the problems that Cuba creates.

To reporters, Brunswick, Ga., May 30/
Los Angeles Times, 5-31:(1)6.

1

[In South Africa,] we are not trying to overthrow their government, but we do feel that there ought to be some equality of hiring practices, equality of pay . . . promotion opportunities for black citizens . . . an end to the highly discriminatory pass system that exists . . . Just some demonstration of good faith on the part of the South African officials is what we would like to see.

Interview/The Washington Post, 6-12:(A)11.

Fidel Castro
Premier of Cuba

2

They speak a lot in the U.S. about Cuban aid to the Angolan people, but no American leader has spoken publicly about the invasion of Angola by South African troops, which I am sure was instigated by the U.S. government. The government of Angola asked us for help and we decided to send it. It is a completely temporary situation.

Interview/People, 3-21:67.

3

Those of us who have visited Africa and seen the traces of colonialism, capitalism, imperialism and racism well understand what "human rights" the imperialists are defending. [The nations there] are making a final choice of the road toward socialism. . . . that struggle is backed by our complete solidarity.

At banquet in his honor, Moscow, April 5/
The Washington Post, 4-6:(A)8.

4

[On his country's presence in Africa]: We are not only a Latin American nation. We are a Latin African nation.

Los Angeles Times, 5-27:(1)6.

5

[On the Cuban military presence in Angola]: Our duty is to maintain military collaboration while the Angolan armed forces are organized, trained and equipped. The day will come when Angola has sufficient military units, tanks, cannons, airplanes and soldiers to confront all imperialist aggression. How many years? How many [Cuban] soldiers will stay in Angola? We don't have to discuss that with the Yankee imperialists.

At rally, Angola/San Francisco Examiner &
Chronicle, 12-4:(This World)20.

Dick Clark
United States Senator, D–Iowa

6

If South Africa wishes to go in the direction of a totally segregated society at the same time that we [the U.S.] are integrating our society, then it should be pointed out that the inevitable result is going to be their becoming increasingly isolated . . . If they expect to continue to have the relationship with us they have now, then they must reform their own system as well as take steps to put the necessary pressure on Rhodesia to accept [black] majority rule.

Interview, Feb. 3/Los Angeles
Herald-Examiner, 2-4:(A)4.

7

What we're seeing [in U.S.-Africa relations] is a shift of alliances and friendships. In the Horn, our traditional ally was Ethiopia. Now we're beginning to look in a broader sense to the other countries in the Horn — first and foremost to Sudan and Egypt — who have a common enemy — [Libyan Chief of State Muammar] Qadaffi. The Saudis are trying to get Somalia weaned away from the Soviets, through money and talk. In southern Africa, we are developing reliance on the "frontline states" — Tanzania, Zambia, Botswana, for whatever it can do, and, to the degree that we can do it, Mozambique. I hope this is the beginning of a shift away from Mobutu [President of Zaire] as the central African ally, and increasing identification with the frontline states and with the people of South Africa.

The Washington Post, 5-15:(E)10.

Reg Cowper
Former Minister of Defense of Rhodesia
1

[On the UN sanctions against his country]: We have perfected, over the years, ways and means of procuring our basic requirements, and from overseas we have friends willing to cooperate with us. I think we have proved that sanctions are really a rather futile and wasteful means of bringing people around.

Los Angeles Times, 2-20:(1)1.

Cas de Villiers
Director, Foreign Policy Association
of South Africa
2

The U.S. could play a very useful role by concentrating on fields in which large numbers of people, both in South Africa and abroad, want to see change: racial discrimination, the unfulfilled aspirations for equality of the urban black community and the coloreds and Indians, and the need for more imaginative means of consolidating the tribal homelands. The wrong way would be to opt for economic sanctions [against South Africa] and other draconic measures, because that would play into the hands of the forces which are resisting change. I think a positive approach by the U.S. would be one that achieves the right balance between pressure on the one hand and recognition of significant changes on the other — the carrot-and-stick approach.

Interview/U.S. News & World Report, 8-29:47.

Colin Eglin
Leader, Progressive Reform Party
of South Africa
3

For the U.S. to make any meaningful impact on [racial] attitudes in southern Africa, it must demonstrate clearly its willingness to live up to the nation's original concept of fundamental liberty in both its internal and external policies. The response from whites will be negative if it appears that the U.S. call for the abolition of racial discrimination is merely a form of big-power politics used in a competitive struggle for influence in Third World countries. I feel it is perfectly proper for the U.S. to spell out the consequences of a continuation of apartheid policies in terms of its relations with South Africa. But America should not appear to threaten or coerce. Coercive pressures are generally counter-productive. South African whites, like citizens of any sovereign independent country, resent dictation from outside.

Interview/U.S. News & World Report, 8-29:47.

Valery Giscard d'Estaing
President of France
4

[On the Cuban presence in Africa]: If the Cubans left their shores to read *Playboy* [magazine], that would certainly not be a threat. But I don't think they traveled thousands of miles in uniform on such an innocent errand. The presence of large non-African military contingents in Africa is a destabilizing factor because neighboring countries feel the need to arm themselves against them. I can assure you that there isn't a single African leader, regardless of his political outlook, who would not tell you in private that he ardently wishes the Cubans would go home.

Interview, Paris/Newsweek, 7-25:46.

5

There is an armaments race in Africa today because there is no common security code as exists, for example, in Europe with detente between the Atlantic Alliance and the Warsaw Pact nations. In Africa, the only common security ground was respect for the old colonial frontiers, but even that principle is now being challenged — for example, between Ethiopia and Eritrea and Somalia, or in the Shaba affair in Zaire. So we must urgently think through new security arrangements that African countries would agree to abide by in a solemn declaration, such as the one Western and Eastern nations subscribed to at the European Security Conference in Helsinki in 1975. This would have to include respect of borders and non-recourse to force to settle disputes.

Interview, Paris/Newsweek, 7-25:47.

Elliott Gabellah
Vice president,
African National Council
6

[On Rhodesian Prime Minister Ian Smith's acceptance of the principle of one-man, one-

WHAT THEY SAID IN 1977

(ELLIOTT GABELLAH)

vote in his country] : We have always said that the war that is going on [for black rights] is not a racial war but a franchise war. Now [that] the Prime Minister has agreed to universal adult suffrage, we think we got what we have been fighting for. If we achieve that, there will be nothing left to fight for.

Los Angeles Times, 11-26:(1)1.

Hassan Gouled
President of Djibouti
1

[On his country's new independence]: At last our people are free and upright. We are a nation of shepherds and we are proud of it. Let us return to our roots. Independence is only a step. We must now work and build and share together.

Upon taking the oath of office, Djibouti,
June 27/Los Angeles Herald-Examiner, 6-27:(A)4.

Roger Hawkins
Minister of Combined Military
Operations of Rhodesia
2

[On U.S. UN Ambassador Andrew Young's outspokenness against white minority governments in Rhodesia and South Africa]: Rhodesians initially read the various dramatic statements made by Mr. Young with mild amusement, until it was realized that he is no clown but a black-power fanatic who has been given open license to operate on behalf of the United States of America in the world forum. America's use of Mr. Young as an official mouthpiece is a threat to white people throughout the world, as black power surgery can only result in a terminal prognosis for the white man.

At opening of new dam, Rhodesia, May 20/
The Dallas Times Herald, 5-21:(A)4.

Donald C. Jamieson
Secretary of State for
External Affairs of Canada
3

South Africa . . . is the only country which as a basic part of its government structure — whether it is constitutional in a legal sense is beside the point — has a declared and unequiv-

ocal policy [of apartheid]. It stands apart as a country which makes decisions affecting human beings on the basis of race and color. Therefore, over time it is not surprising that the attitude of the vast majority of the countries of the world has become harder, particularly during these past months when we have seen an increase in the amount of repression, rioting and especially in the disturbances which followed the still unexplained death of a respectable and respected black leader of South Africa, Steve Biko . . . We strongly believe that what must come in South Africa is the destruction of that kind of system, the introduction of the principle of one-man, one-vote, and of the normal democratic process which all of us in this part of the world take for granted. I am, therefore, announcing today that Canada is phasing out all its government-sponsored, commercially supported activities in South Africa.

Dec. 19/The Washington Post, 12-27:(A)18.

Paulo Jorge
Foreign Minister of Angola
4

[On U.S. criticism of Cuban troops in his country]: I think there is a kind of nightmare about Cubans in the United States and among some Western powers; they see Cubans everywhere . . . I don't know if there is a principle, a law or a treaty on which the United States can base its demand for the removal of Cuban troops from Angola. If there is such a law, we can also demand the withdrawal of American troops from West Germany, from Italy, or even from [the American base at Guantanamo] Cuba.

Interview, United Nations, New York/
The Christian Science Monitor, 10-19:9.

Kenneth Kaunda
President of Zambia
5

We [African and Arab countries] lack confidence in one another. Zambia still buys Ghanian cocoa from London and Saudi Arabian oil from New York. Arab states still buy African tobacco, tin and copper products from European markets. African countries depend on

(KENNETH KAUNDA)

European and American money markets for loans to finance their developments.

At Afro-Arab summit conference, Cairo, Egypt, March 8/Los Angeles Times, 3-9:(1)9.

1

[On attempts to establish black majority rule in Rhodesia]: There have been all sorts of negotiations — on battleships, on railroad bridges, everywhere. We have followed the Organization of African Unity *Manifesto on Southern Africa,* which says that we must do everything possible to negotiate for a transfer of power from the minority [whites] to the majority [blacks], and only when this fails should we decide to fight. But everything has failed, all due to the intransigence of [Rhodesian Prime Minister Ian] Smith. Up to about a year ago, we thought there was a possibility of change. Then we realized that this man was just playing with words. So we have taken up arms to fight for freedom and justice for all, regardless of color ... I can see no peaceful settlement at all. It is finished.

Interview, Lusaka, Zambia/Time, 8-8:35.

2

Long ago I told the Americans that if the West was not careful, it would find itself fighting against black people in southern Africa because, according to the West, the blacks were supporting Communism. Western civilization is based on Christian love. The racists, the Fascists in southern Africa are the opposite, but they do what they do in your [the West's] name, and the black masses begin to consider Western civilization as racist and Fascist. Africans have turned to the only people who support their case voluntarily, the Eastern countries, the Chinese and the Soviets. And because the guns come from the Eastern countries, they'll need training, and so, of course, some people who are so trained will become Marxists.

Interview, Lusaka, Zambia/Time, 8-8:36.

3

If by next year all the five million Zambians choose to be as lazy as they are now, I would willingly step down as President because I don't want votes from lazy people during next year's Presidential and Parliamentary elections. If you are one of the lazy ones, do not vote for me. I don't want to be voted for by lazy people.

San Francisco Examiner & Chronicle, 9-11:(This World)2.

Henry A. Kissinger
*Former Secretary of State
of the United States*

4

[On the invasion of Zaire by troops based in Angola]: [The invasion] could not have taken place — and it could not continue — without the material support or acquiescence of the Soviet Union. Such irresponsible acts set a dangerous precedent. If all African problems are to be settled hereafter by radical means, with weapons brought in from the outside, a catastrophic race war in southern Africa will become more and more likely with profound implications for us [the U.S.] both at home and around the world. If attacks across sovereign borders are supinely accepted by the international community, sooner or later events will get out of control.

*At Georgetown University, April 5/
The Washington Post, 4-6:(A)4.*

James Kruger
Minister of Justice of South Africa

5

[On whether there will be martial law in his country to deal with black uprisings]: If such should happen, it will be for a very short period. I think that [our] security measures are adequate. But it is an old Roman-law maxim that the security of the state is the highest law. The state is entitled to take exceptional measures to preserve its own security in exceptional circumstances. I think that anybody who says my country is not under exceptional circumstances must have his head examined. We have no option; I must keep this country safe. If [the blacks] were not stimulated from the outside, then I think they would change their minds. I sincerely believe we can show our black people the good fruits of our policy of separate development.

Interview, Pretoria/Time, 10-17:38.

WHAT THEY SAID IN 1977

Felix Malloum
President of Chad

1

In the last decade, Africa has become a savage battlefield for the superpowers, seeking to avoid direct confrontation among themselves. We think it is about time the superpowers have an ideological disarmament in Africa so they can do their share in peacekeeping and providing economic and social development.

Interview/The Washington Post, 12-18:(K)2.

James R. Mancham
President of the Seychelles

2

We are trying to play it like Switzerland. We're only a small nation, so we say, "Sure, come and watch the world here and send your spies through. But for God's sake, don't interfere with us."

*Interview, Seychelles, May/
Los Angeles Times, 6-6:(1)8.*

James R. Mancham
Former President of the Seychelles

3

[Upon learning that he has been overthrown by a coup]: I am personally convinced that the actions taken have been done with the active agreement and connivance of the Soviet government and is part and parcel of the Soviet policy of controlling the Indian Ocean ... I am a victim of the fact that I have been a friend of the West. It's a question of Western resolution. The support one gets is rather half-hearted.

*News conference, London, June 5/
The New York Times, 6-6:11.*

Michael Manley
Prime Minister of Jamaica

4

[Criticizing Ugandan President Idi Amin]: We of the Third World rightfully unite to fight racist tyranny in southern Africa and to denounce it in its various forms. We should not hesitate, therefore, to denounce tyranny, whether of the tribal, military or Fascist kind, when it is found in our own ranks.

*Before Royal Commonwealth Society, London,
June 9/Los Angeles Herald-Examiner, 6-10:(A)2.*

Mengistu Haile Mariam
*Head of the Revolutionary
Council of Ethiopia*

5

The broad masses of Ethiopia will, by struggling, sacrificing, wrestling and overcoming, destroy all their enemies. Just as revolutionary Russia was encircled 60 years ago, revolutionary Ethiopia, too, is encircled by forces that are anti-people and anti-revolutionary. This is a force organized to completely crush once and for all those elements like the Ethiopian Democratic Union, the Ethiopian People's Revolutionary Party and the reactionary Eritrean secessionist groups who are making a frantic attempt to throw the Ethiopian broad masses back into that repugnant system.

*Upon reviewing his troops, Addis Ababa,
June 25/The Washington Post, 6-26:(A)1.*

Mobutu Sese Seko
President of Zaire

6

[On the invasion of his country from Angola]: I must confess we are bitterly disappointed by America's attitude. [Angolan President Agostinho] Neto is a pawn of the Cubans and Russians, but you [the U.S.] won't face up to the threat. It is your weakness versus their will-power and strength. If you have decided to surrender piecemeal to the Soviet-Cuban grand design in Africa, I think you owe it to us and to your other friends to have the frankness to admit it. [U.S. UN Ambassador] Andrew Young says it does not matter if African states go Marxist, because they want to go on trading with America. Is that the position of the Carter Administration? If it is, we should be told about it and we will then be in a position to arrange for our own surrender on better terms today than tomorrow. The OAU has backed our position. Yet Angola, Cuba and Russia have the gall to warn you [the U.S.] not to interfere, and you seem to be acquiescing.

Interview/Newsweek, 4-18:50.

Walter F. Mondale
Vice President of the United States

7

We hope the South Africans will not rely on any illusions that the U.S. will in the end

(WALTER F. MONDALE)

intervene to save South Africa from the [racial] policies it is pursuing, for we will not do so . . . I think the message is now clear to the South African government. They know that we believe that perpetuating an unjust [racial] system is the surest incentive to increase Soviet influence and even racial war; but quite apart from that, it is unjustified on its own grounds . . . I cannot rule out the possibility that the South African government will not change, that our paths will diverge and our policies come into conflict should the South African government so decide. In that event, we would take steps true to our beliefs and values.

News conference, Vienna, May 20/
Los Angeles Herald-Examiner, 5-20:(A)7.

Robert Mugabe
Rhodesian black nationalist leader

1

[On how to obtain black majority rule in Rhodesia]: Experience past and present has shown that negotiations cannot induce reason in racist heads. Immediate intensification of the armed struggle is required before we reach our long-cherished goal, and many of us will have to be prepared to die . . . before our battle can be over.

At funeral of a black nationalist official, Lusaka,
Zambia, Jan. 29/The New York Times, 1-30:(1)8.

2

Only through the instrument of war is peace possible in Zimbabwe [Rhodesia]. We will hunt [Prime Minister Ian] Smith down. His empire must go and the emperor with it.

At conference on Rhodesia and Namibia,
Maputo, Mozambique, May 16/
Los Angeles Times, 5-17:(1)10.

Abel Muzorewa
Rhodesian black nationalist leader;
President, African National Council

3

The only proof of [Rhodesian Prime Minister Ian] Smith's sincerity about [black] majority rule is that he hand over power to the majority through the exercise of one-man, one-vote . . . [There should be] a national

referendum to elect a leader to whom Mr. Smith must hand over power. Following the precedent set by the Pearce commission in 1972, Britain must organize the exercise and ensure that there is free political activity throughout the country. All persons in political detention, and in so-called "protected villages," must be released and allowed to participate in the referendum. Facilities must be provided for nationalist guerrillas, wherever they may be, to enable them to take part. As soon as possible thereafter, the British government convenes a full constitutional conference to work out and finalize the details of the independence constitution. Failure to carry out this plan will result in continued and unabating bloodshed.

Before African National Council National
Consultative Assembly, Salisbury, March 27/
The Christian Science Monitor, 3-28:6.

Joshua Nkomo
Leader, Zimbabwe (Rhodesian)
African People's Union

4

The only relevant thing to be discussed is what machinery will be used after we throw out [Rhodesian Prime Minister Ian] Smith. He will have to be thrown out. He will not walk out of power.

At United Nations, New York, Aug. 12/
The New York Times, 8-13:3.

Julius K. Nyerere
President of Tanzania

5

The U.S. can do three things [to help bring about a peaceful change to black majority rule in Rhodesia]: First, it can discourage [Rhodesian Prime Minister Ian] Smith from believing that eventually the Western world must regard him as an ally against Communist penetration of southern Africa. Second, it must follow up with action to discourage Smith. It encourages him that you now buy his chrome openly and break sanctions. Third, you must realize that South Africa is a strong supporter of Smith. Rather than pursue past policy and use South Africa as your ally against Smith, you should realize that the politics of South Africa simply do not allow this. Instead, the U.S. and the West should say to [South African Prime

WHAT THEY SAID IN 1977

(JULIUS K. NYERERE)

Minister John] Vorster, "Look, we don't expect you to help bring about majority rule in Rhodesia. All we ask is that you don't stop it."

Interview, Dar es Salaam/Time, 3-14:25.

1

[On Cuban involvement in Africa] : Cuba, Cuba, Cuba! The question is always Cuba, not the military might of the West behind South Africa. No African country or combination of African countries could be a military threat to South Africa. Yet France and others continue to arm South Africa. Why is the U.S. so worried about tiny Cuba? Or is Cuba being used as a cover-up to arm South Africa? I tell you, brother, if South Africa uses its army to prevent Rhodesia from becoming free, then we have the right to ask for support from anywhere else — and from much bigger powers than Cuba.

Interview, Dar es Salaam/Time, 3-14:25.

2

I discovered that [U.S. President Carter] is not making a show about [black] majority rule. He is not trying to please us about majority rule. He is committed to the achievement of majority rule in southern Africa. Secondly, I found that he is willing — I can't say what pressures, what actual pressures he is going to use to bring about majority rule in southern Africa — but I found that he is willing, together with his allies in Western Europe, to put on whatever pressures are needed in order to bring about majority rule, so I feel very encouraged ... This is the first time a voice from the White House is hinting that, unless there is cooperation to bring about change in southern Africa, sanctions may be considered against South Africa itself. I don't want to misinterpret this. I want to interpret it as encouragement to us.

TV-radio interview, Washington, Aug. 7/
The New York Times, 8-8:3.

3

[Saying the U.S. should boycott South Africa] : The United States has lots of money

to invest. I need some of that money and I don't get it. Your country's investments in South Africa pay for and reap the benefits of racism. I propose a total American boycott of South Africa. If you believe in your own edict of equality, trading with South Africa must be an embarrassment to you. Reaping the benefits of racism must be an embarrassment.

News conference, Los Angeles, Aug. 7/
The Dallas Times Herald, 8-8:(A)9.

David Owen
Foreign Secretary of
the United Kingdom

4

I am convinced that many of the Africans who currently believe that the armed struggle is the only way forward [to obtain black majority rule in Rhodesia] are essentially men of peace ... Much as we all wish violence to stop, we cannot immediately expect it to stop while the wall of skepticism and disbelief — which I met all over Africa — remains about the intentions of the [Ian] Smith Administration [in Rhodesia].

Before British Parliament, London, April 19/
The Washington Post, 4-20:(A)14.

5

If it was in my power, I would have removed [Rhodesian Prime Minister Ian] Smith the day I took office ... I do not believe Smith has a contribution to make to black majority rule and to peace in that country, but we have to deal with Smith, and the only thing we can do is to remove him from office through negotiation.

Before Parliament, London, July 25/
The Christian Science Monitor, 7-27:5.

Ilkka Olavi Pastinen
Finnish Ambassador/Permanent
Representative to the United Nations

6

[On human-rights violations in Uganda] : As far as the situation in Uganda is concerned, the evidence is so massive and it has been known for such a long time that it is high time that the international community also officially takes cognizance of this situation and expresses its concern over it. To continue to observe in

(ILKKA OLAVI PASTINEN)

silence, whatever the reasons for such a silence, would be beyond comprehension to public opinion everywhere.

At United Nations, New York, Dec. 6/
The New York Times, 12-7:(A)2.

Alan Paton
South African author

1

South Africa can experience an evolutionary revolution or a revolutionary revolution [in its racial affairs]. What I fear is a revolutionary revolution, because the government is unwilling to make meaningful changes . . . The Afrikaaner could be forced into a corner, where he would fight like an animal, destroying himself and a lot of us — and disrupting the entire well-being of a country. Sometimes you think of apartheid as a fort. Often it is seen as a prison. But it is really a grave the Afrikaaner has dug for himself.

Interview, Seattle, Oct. 28/Seattle
Post-Intelligencer, 10-29:(A)10.

2

If I believe the future lies in out-and-out confrontation between black and white South Africans, I think I would rather come to a country like this [the U.S.] which has become my spiritual home . . . I don't want to be corny. It is because of your Constitution, and because of the fact you live under the rule of law. I regard the rule of law the most fundamental of human rights. And we [in South Africa] do not live under the rule of law.

News conference, Washington, Nov. 22/
The Dallas Times Herald, 11-24:(A)46.

Nikolai V. Podgorny
President of the Soviet Union

3

Nowadays, when the ideals and principles of equality and freedom become universally recognized rule of law, the maintenance in southern Africa of pockets of racism arouses the wrath and anger of all the peoples throughout the world . . .

At luncheon in his honor, Livingstone, Zambia,
March 27/Los Angeles Times, 3-28:(1)13.

Muammar el-Qaddafi
Chief of State of Libya

4

We are against terrorism. We stand with those who urge its complete elimination by international law. But having liberated ourselves through revolution, we are concerned with promoting freedom everywhere. We also feel that with the creation of a system headed by the People's Congress we have attained the ultimate form of democracy — neither capitalism nor Communism. We look upon this system as one that contains lessons for others striving for ways to establish the authority of the people. If our activities in support of democracy and freedom did harm to other people, they would have an excuse to condemn us. But our government is inspired by the right of all people to move toward justice, equality and non-alignment. That makes us welcome to the masses everywhere — if not to all governments.

Interview, July/U.S. News & World Report, 8-8:37.

Albert Rene
President of the Seychelles

5

[On the coup which recently installed him as President] : One reporter sent a beautiful message yesterday saying that the interesting thing about the Seychelles [coup] is that the [mainland] Chinese and the Russians have not yet contacted the new government purely because they don't know whether it's the other one which was responsible for it. I thought that was beautiful.

News conference, Seychelles, June 8/
The Dallas Times Herald, 6-9:(A)5.

Anwar el-Sadat
President of Egypt

6

I am very, very worried about the way events are shaping in Africa, particularly in Zaire. The Soviets are dabbling in sinister plots from one end of the continent to the other. In Sudan, they have tried to overthrow the regime of General [Jaafar] Nimeiry, who has had to put up with an uprising fomented by thousands of guerrillas armed by [Libyan leader] Colonel [Muammar] Qaddafi . . . Ethiopia, which has become a major center of Soviet plotting, is one of the recipients of lavish Libyan money and

WHAT THEY SAID IN 1977

Russian arms. As regards the civil war in Zaire, this evidently is not an internal matter. The Katangese are armed with modern Soviet tanks, namely T-54 and T-55, which are as effective as the American M-60 tanks ... The situation is critical. I wonder where they will strike next. ... the Soviets have already begun creating troubles in our country. But I am thinking especially of Sudan, where any upheaval is likely to have repercussions in Egypt. We would be directly involved, since we are linked with a common defense pact.

Interview/Los Angeles Times, 4-5:(1)10.

Denis SassouNguesso
Minister of Defense of the Congo
1

Everyone must understand that imperialism is the sole cause of our improverishment and that it is determined to continue dominating and exploiting us forever. The aggressions and assassinations on our continent are the ultimate weapon of those who want to dominate the world.

Los Angeles Herald-Examiner, 6-24:(C)3.

Mohammed Siad Barre
President of Somalia
2

We prefer direct state-to-state assistance with no strings attached. We must avoid dollar corruption. America lost its global prestige by defending individuals at the expense of the masses ... Russia has given us billions and never bragged about it. You won't even find propaganda about it on the billboard in front of their embassy. I am not anti-American — just giving you friendly advice on how to get good relations back on track.

Interview/Newsweek, 6-27:45.

3

[Asking for aid in his country's conflict with Ethiopia]: It seems that the United States and some other Western countries have adopted a wait-and-see attitude on what is happening in Africa and the Indian Ocean. We, Iran and other countries in the area don't think this is a wise attitude. We are seeking arms to defend ourselves. How can you stop missiles? Not with prayers, certainly. Is the United States being responsible by adopting a wait-and-see position? We denounce this.

News conference, Teheran, Iran, Dec. 28/
The New York Times, 12-29:(A)3.

Ndabaningi Sithole
Rhodesian black nationalist leader
4

Whatever settlement [Rhodesian Prime Minister Ian] Smith has in mind [for the racial conflict in his country] ... it must be based on one-man, one-vote and the effective transfer of political power to the [black] majority. Nothing else will do ... We're our own liberators. We cannot wait for the United States, Britain and the Organization of African Unity to decide what is good for us. If we reached an agreement that had the support of the people of Zimbabwe [Rhodesia], it would be irretrievably immoral for Britain, the United States, the Organization of African Unity or the international community to refuse to recognize it.

Interview, Los Angeles, Nov. 21/
Los Angeles Times, 11-22:(1)14.

Ian Smith
Prime Minister of Rhodesia
5

[The British plan for Rhodesia would] entail immediate black rule, which would be imposed from outside and would in no way represent the views of the majority of black Rhodesians. It would come into being not in two years' time, or when the agreed constitutional and electoral processes have been completed, but immediately. It would in no sense be an elected government. To put it in a nutshell, the British government wishes to impose upon us an interim government, recommended to them by the front-line Presidents [of Botswana, Tanzania, Angola, Mozambique and Zambia] working in collusion with the terrorist-oriented Patriotic Front. We were absolutely clear in our minds that if we accepted these, this would lead almost certainly to a stampede as far as white Rhodesians were concerned ... In such a country not only would there be no place for the white Rhodesians, moderate black Rhodesians would find themselves an enslaved and perse-

(IAN SMITH)

cuted people ... My government is committed to creating a non-racial society in Rhodesia. I have also urged the British government to change their approach — which has clearly been a failure — and to deal with the Africans in Rhodesia rather than the terrorists and their hosts and sponsors in neighboring countries. Why should a few thousand terrorists, the majority of them mere schoolboys, call the tune to 6 million basically peaceful and peace-loving Africans?

Broadcast address to the nation, Salisbury,
Jan. 24/The Washington Post, 1-25:(A)1,9.

1

[On his country's declaration of independence from Britain in 1965]: There are no regrets. We have had twelve of the best years of our lives — great years, stimulating years, in which we have created a small nation with great national pride. We have had economic development such as we never had before. Whatever happens in the future, Rhodesia will benefit from the years we have been through.

Interview, Salisbury/Time, 3-7:31.

2

I believe that if the rest of the world would only leave us alone, give us a fair chance, then we would solve our problems quickly, and I believe we would establish a country and a society where you would find blacks and whites working together to their mutual benefit. I think we have a chance of creating something unique on the African continent.

Interview, Salisbury/Time, 3-7:31.

3

[On his dissolving Parliament and setting elections for August]: It was clear to me, and to our other representatives who participated in [last week's discussions with a British-American diplomatic team on the racial situation in the country], that the British believe they are dealing with a divided and weak Rhodesia and that they have us on the run ... Certainly, on the surface one can understand people coming to such a conclusion. And therefore I believe it is imperative that we should take positive and decisive action in order to remove any such illusion. Accordingly, in terms of the Constitution, I have advised the President to dissolve Parliament ... I envisage the creation of a broad-based government incorporating those black Rhodesians who are prepared to work peacefully and constitutionally with the present government in order to establish a base from which we would be able to draw up our future Constitution.

Broadcast address to the nation, Salisbury,
July 18/Los Angeles Times, 7-19:(1)8.

4

My aim is to keep the confidence of the white man by producing the type of constitution which will guarantee him such things as impartiality of the courts, maintenance of law and order, and a continuation of decent, civilized standards — the sort of things that are essential to a highly sophisticated nation such as ours. Rhodesia vitally needs the white man with all of his skills and knowledge and capital. Our objective is to maintain the conditions under which he will want to stay, and I am reasonably confident that we can succeed.

Interview, Salisbury/
U.S News & World Report, 8-8:35.

5

[Accepting the principle of one-man, one-vote in his country]: [Black leaders said that] the only way of successfully launching the negotiations [to settle the racial conflict in Rhodesia] would be for the government to make a firm commitment to the principle of majority rule based on adult suffrage ... It's not the kind of problem we can solve in weeks, but I would hope that within months we would be able to see results ... Much time has been given to contacts with the parties concerned. Now that I have made this offer, I think I can safely say we can get this one off the ground.

To reporters, Bulawayo, Rhodesia, Nov. 24/
The Washington Post, 11-25:(A)1.

Helen Suzman
Member of South African Parliament

6

[Applauding U.S. pressure on South Africa for racial change]: While it is certainly desirable

WHAT THEY SAID IN 1977

(HELEN SUZMAN)

that South Africa's problems in the last resort be solved by black and white South Africans, I welcome such powerful allies to the cause of non-discrimination, allies who will keep the pressures up for change on our intransigent government. It is when America and the West write us off as a hopeless case that we should start worrying.

Report to her constituents, Johannesburg,
July 14/Los Angeles Times, 7-16:(1)11.

1

[Calling for a vote against the government's apartheid policies] : It's time every voter let his conscience speak. Let it speak against bannings and against interference with our free press . . . against inferior education for blacks . . . against a government that has failed on all counts.

At Progressive Party rally on eve of
national election, Johannesburg, Nov. 29/
The Washington Post, 11-30:(A)15.

Desmond Tutu
Anglican Bishop of Lesotho
2

The only thing surprising about the uprising of blacks in South Africa is that it has been so long in coming. What is more surprising is that blacks genuinely still want to speak to whites and still long for a peaceful, but just, solution. But this cannot go on forever. In the face of white arrogance and intransigence, blacks are growing even more hate-filled . . . They have, as they see it, no other option left open to them but to resort to violence.

At symposium on southern Africa
sponsored by U.S. Catholic Conference and
National Council of Churches, Marcy, N.Y.,
March 7/The New York Times, 3-13:(1)3.

Cyrus R. Vance
Secretary of State of the United States
3

The Rhodesian authorities should understand clearly that under no circumstances can they count on any form of American assistance in their effort to prevent[black] majority rule

258

in Rhodesia or to enter into negotiations which exclude leaders of nationalist movements.

News Conference, Washington, Jan. 31/
The Washington Post, 2-1:(A)1.

4

I have heard some suggest that we must support the white governments in southern Africa — come what may — since they are anti-Communist. In fact, the continued denial of racial justice in southern Africa encourages the possibilities for outside intervention.

Before National Association for the Advancement
of Colored People, St. Louis, July 1/
Los Angeles Herald-Examiner, 7-1:(A)3.

5

We have said to South Africa that we feel they must deal with the problems of discrimination and, ultimately, the problems of permitting all of the South African people to participate fully in the political processes of the country. We have indicated to them that we have no specific timetable or blueprint as to how this is to be done; we have said that this is up to them to determine. But we have indicated to them that progress — or lack of progress — cannot but have an effect on the relations between our two countries. I think this is a straightforward position which will not mislead the South Africans in any way, and I think we ought to be honest and straightforward with them.

Interview, Washington/
U.S. News & World Report, 11-7:29.

Pieter van der Byl
Foreign Minister of Rhodesia
6

We have made an irrevocable commitment to [black] majority rule within two years, and we are also irrevocably committed to elimination of the remaining forms of discrimination. If discrimination is done away with and majority rule comes along and we make an agreement on that basis within the terms of the Kissinger plan with the representatives of the 6 million Africans in Rhodesia, what else could anybody possibly want?

The Washington Post, 1-26:(A)14.

(PIETER VAN DER BYL)

1

[On the future of Africa if the black nationalist Patriotic Front had its way in Rhodesia]: Once Rhodesia's gone, you'll have a belt of Marxist states running across southern Africa — Angola, Rhodesia, Mozambique. From there, they'll move north — Zambia first, then Zaire, then, one by one, farther north, until they have the bulk of sub-Saharan Africa.

Interview, Salisbury, March 9/
The New York Times, 3-10:4.

2

[On his country's policy if the guerrilla race war goes against it]: We will contest every hill, every village and every town, every crossroad and every bridge. Inevitably and unavoidably, the land will suffer. Indescribable chaos and irreparable destruction will follow but, come what may, we will uphold the ideals for which these men fought. We cannot let them down.

At opening of memorial to Rhodesia's
armed-forces dead, Inyanga,Rhodesia, June 26/
The Dallas Times Herald, 6-27:(A)7.

John Vorster
Prime Minister of South Africa

3

[On U.S. criticism of his country's racial policies]: It is fast reaching the stage where we feel that the U.S.A. wants to prescribe to us how we should run our country in total, and that, of course, is unacceptable to us. It's a fool who doesn't listen to advice, but nobody can allow outsiders, however well-intentioned, whatever their motives are, to meddle in their internal affairs. Therefore, my attitude has always been that I am prepared to discuss my policies with whomsoever wishes to discuss it with me, but I am definitely not going to let anybody tell me how to do it and to prescribe to me what I should do and what I should not do.

Interview, Pretoria, Sept. 16/
The New York Times, 9-17:4.

4

[U.S. Vice President Walter] Mondale used the expression, talking to me, that all that the U.S. wanted from me was full participation by everybody, regardless of color, in the political process [in South Africa]. I said that this was precisely the policy of my government ... It was my government, the National Party government, which brought all the blacks into the political process. He [Mondale] then went to his press conference and [said], "Every citizen should have the right to vote, and every vote should be equally weighted" — in other words, [that] the U.S. wants black majority rule. I explained that if that is what they want, that's out. We believe in self-government for the blacks, and they have that at the moment [in the "homelands"]. And as far as [homeland] viability is concerned, the fact is [that] the standard of living of the South African black is from two to five times higher than that of the rest of Africa.

Interview, Pretoria/Newsweek, 11-7:32.

5

[On criticism of his country's apartheid policy]: It suits people to use that word [apartheid] because it carries a certain connotation, even though my policy is not apartheid but separate development. Let me give you a few examples: Under previous governments, a black policeman could only graduate as far as a sergeant. This government lifted the ceiling, and today you will find black lieutenants and captains. We have created three black universities, and today there are ever so many black professors. This wasn't possible under the old regime. And we are closing the wage gap. We can't do it overnight, but it will be closed. Or take sports. We have made it possible for black athletes to compete with whites in South Africa as well as internationally; yet we were kicked out of the Olympics. There is the double standard again.

Interview, Pretoria/
U.S. News & World Report, 11-21:40.

6

You cannot equate the situation of the American black with that of the South African black. The way that his forebears came to be in America shows you the initial difference. The American black was divested of his African

WHAT THEY SAID IN 1977

(JOHN VORSTER)

personality, his original language, his culture, his tradition and his way of life. He is, in fact, a black American in every sense of the word. And I accept him as such. The South African black, on the other hand, has always been a member of a nation with its own language, its own culture, its own traditions, its own way of life. And the mistake — that is how I found it, discussing these matters with American politicians — they make is that they argue that because all South African blacks have a black skin, they are all one. They look upon them as tribes of the same nation. They are, in fact, not tribes of the same nation. They are different nations. A Xhosa is as different to the Venda as the Italian is to the Swede. And the Zulu is as different to the Tswana as the Turk is to the German. All that they have in common is a black skin. But that does not make them one people. The same as we whites are not one people because we have a white skin in common. The misunderstanding arises from the fact that the outside world, including the United States, refuses to accept the fact that South Africa is a multinational country. We are not a multi*racial* country but a multi*national* country.

Before American Society of Johannesburg/
The Washington Post, 12-18:(C)6.

Franklin H. Williams
Former United States Ambassador
to Ghana; Former Director,
U.S. Peace Corps in Africa
1

[U.S. policy in Africa] has been one of accommodating to the white and to the European regimes; of hypocritically, if you will, emphasizing a peaceful change while war is taking place; of avoiding confrontation and of carrying on business as usual . . . I believe we ought to be supporting the liberation forces. At a minimum, we ought to be supplying a variety of all kinds of health and food and medical supplies — and, if necessary in a confrontation with a government that illegally continues to

occupy a territory and by force of arms keeps itself in office, yes, with weapons.

Television interview/
The Christian Science Monitor, 3-16:22.

Marcel Yondo
Finance Minister of Cameroon
2

[African nations] must endeavor to establish and strengthen our own institutions in order to transform the present economic order which keeps our economies under the domination of those of the powerful countries, which do not take our problems into account when they make decisions that affect our future. [Yet], one may justly ask whether the international community finds it in its interest to remain heedless of these ills that beset the African economy. It is to everyone's advantage that the chain of solidarity that binds the nations remains unbroken, so that misery will not be joined by despair, the wellspring of frustration.

At meeting of International Monetary
Fund and World Bank, Washington/
The Christian Science Monitor, 11-1:12.

Andrew Young
United States Ambassador/Permanent
Representative to the United Nations
3

[On the presence of Cuban troops in Angola]: There's a sense in which Cubans bring a certain stability and order to Angola. The enemy all over the world is chaos. When there's a nation with a military unit that is disciplined it can be ordered in; it can be ordered out. I have no question in my mind but that we could negotiate very successfully a withdrawal of Cuban troops from southern Africa.

Television interview/"Who's Who,"
Columbia Broadcasting System, 1-25.

4

[Saying he does not consider the prospect of Marxist governments in Africa a threat to the U.S.]: What is a Marxist government? If Angola is a Marxist state and its major trading partner is the United States, that does not worry me. For all its ideology, Angola has never broken relations with Gulf Oil . . . One of the most

(ANDREW YOUNG)

wholesome things about our [Carter] Administration is that . . . it won't be paranoid about Communism.

To reporters, Zanzibar, Tanzania, Feb. 5/
The Washington Post, 2-6:(A)14.

1

[On those who criticize the presence of Cuban troops in Angola] : . . . when people began to get knee-jerk reactions to Cuba as though the presence of twenty Cubans anywhere in the world is a threat to the peace, I said that's stupid. It *is* stupid, and if the American people stop to think they'll realize it's stupid.

Interview/Newsweek, 3-28:30.

2

[On whether the U.S. should send military aid to President Mobutu Sese Seko of Zaire to defend against the current invasion of his country from Angola by Katanga rebels] : If he can't stop a couple of thousand Katanga gendarmes, we shouldn't send the Marines to help him do it . . . [If Mobutu] has not been able to consolidate that nation, and I think he has made a valiant attempt, I just question the extent to which America needs to get involved with anybody as a personal leader. I think our dedication is to the territorial integrity of Zaire, to the people of Zaire . . . The days when you send the 82nd Airborne every time there is something you don't like, or don't understand, I think are over. The American people want them to be over.

To reporters, Chicago, April 13/
Los Angeles Times, 4-14:(1)7.

3

I condemn the Cuban military presence in Angola. But in terms of its technical assistance, the Cuban presence can also be a force for stability. Look: When the Portuguese decolonized Angola, they simply picked up and left. They had 19,000 trucks in the country and took 18,000 with them. They left a phone system without operators, hospitals without doctors. They weren't honorable in their decol-

onization, not compared with the British or even the French. They were more like the Belgians. They took home everything that wasn't nailed down. When the Cubans arrived, they filled a gap. They provided order where there was essentially an undisciplined guerrilla army that wasn't ready to govern. So I'm not trying to defend the Cuban presence. I'm just trying to get people to be rational about it.

Interview/Playboy, July:68.

4

. . . I was asked if I thought the South African government was illegitimate and I was quoted as saying, "Yeah." Actually, it was more of a grunt. But it didn't just slip out. You can define legitimacy in a variety of ways. I wouldn't question the legality of the South African government; but in terms of its being a moral or legitimate representative of the nation as a whole — I mean, it's ridiculous to argue that it's an expression of the will of the 20,000,000 inhabitants of South Africa . . . I feel a great deal of sympathy for the white position. The last thing I want to see is the white community destroyed or pushed into the sea. And I don't think there's any independent African nation or liberation movement that advocates that. Nor do any of the Presidents of the front-line countries immediately surrounding South Africa. . . . the whites can survive if they allow their economic system to serve the needs of all their people. Capitalism has got to separate itself from racism and demonstrate that it's not dependent on racism. I think we demonstrated that to some measure in the [U.S.] South. The enfranchisement of blacks did not hurt the economy. In fact, it created an economic boom. The only way the whites [in South Africa] can survive is if they are willing and able to modify their system to involve blacks in the decision-making and in economic participation.

Interview/Playboy, July:78.

5

African leaders are getting very concerned about [the presence of Cuban military forces in African countries] and so are we . . . I think what disturbs me is that the continued Cuban

WHAT THEY SAID IN 1977

(ANDREW YOUNG

military presence is not bringing the degree of progress and development that's needed. And what we see are a continuation of death and destruction almost everywhere there is a Cuban military presence. It's [a] kind of new colonialism, and they have tended to back up totalitarian regimes whose main contribution is to wipe out the intellectual elite. That is not a contribution for development.

TV-radio interview/"Face the Nation,"
Columbia Broadcasting System, 12-4.

[Criticizing Cuban and Soviet involvement in Africa]: The presence in Africa of nearly a quarter of Cuba's armed forces and the interjection of Cuban military advisers in troubled areas throughout the continent can only lead to more deaths and suffering — both Cuban and African. The injection of arms to areas with turbulent regimes like the Horn of Africa or turbulent societies like Uganda can only step up tension, spread conflict and lead to unnecessary loss of life.

Before UN General Assembly's political committee,
New York, Dec. 6/Los Angeles Times, 12-7:(1)11.

Tom Adams
Prime Minister of Barbados
1

Traditional U.S. policy toward the [Caribbean] region has been predicated on the "sphere of influence" concept reflecting the prevalent "power" approach to international relations. [Such an approach is] no longer appropriate in an increasingly interdependent world in which all the countries of the region, in spite of their small size, seek to be active and independent participants.

At Caribbean trade and development conference, Tampa, Fla./The Dallas Times Herald, 7-6:(C)18.

Jaime Benitez
Former Resident Commissioner of Puerto Rico
2

[Saying Puerto Rico should remain a Commonwealth instead of become the 51st state of the United States]: The Commonwealth form of government is one that has been developed by the people of Puerto Rico and the United States after a long period of trial and error — mostly errors at first. . . . the United States came to recognize the basic fact that Puerto Rico is a distinct cultural community with its own style, language, traditions and personality, with special problems and relationships with the mainland, and that it should be dealt with on its own, not necessarily subject to the uniformities applicable to states or to incorporated territories destined for inclusion into the union.

Interview/U.S. News & World Report, 4-11:47.

Jonathan B. Bingham
United States Representative, D–New York
3

[Saying the U.S. should lift its economic embargo against Cuba]: Basically, the barrier to

normalization [of relations] is the trade embargo that we have imposed. And I don't see why we should impose an embargo on Cuba because of our quarrel with the Communism that they practice, when we don't impose an embargo on the Soviet Union, China or Communist countries of Eastern Europe with which we trade. Also, the maintenance of this artificial barrier creates a bad image for the U.S. It's kind of an up-to-date version of the day when we used to send in the Marines to small Caribbean and Central American countries when we thought they were getting out of line. Nowadays, we don't send in the Marines; we just impose an embargo . . . Let me emphasize that lifting the embargo would not constitute endorsement of the Cuban government any more than our re-establishing of trade relations with [mainland] China involved endorsement of the Peking government. I can think of no situation under which we would endorse the government of Cuba.

Interview/U.S. News & World Report, 3-7:74.

Ellsworth Bunker
United States negotiator at Panama Canal treaty talks
4

Contrary to the belief of many Americans, the U.S. did not purchase the Canal Zone for $10-million in 1903. Rather, the money we gave Panama then was in return for the rights which Panama granted us by treaty. We bought Louisiana; we bought Alaska. In Panama, we bought not territory, but rights. It is clear that under the law we do not have sovereignty in Panama.

San Francisco Examiner & Chronicle, 8-21:(This World)14.

5

[Supporting the proposed new treaties which would gradually turn over control of the

WHAT THEY SAID IN 1977

(ELLSWORTH BUNKER)

Panama Canal to Panama]: The claim by those who oppose the treaties that the Panamanians will close the Canal to spite the U.S. is incorrect. The Canal benefits Panama, and the U.S. will remain a big user. Another point is that the Canal is needed for transshipments of Alaskan oil to Atlantic ports. If there is guerrilla warfare in Panama over non-ratification of the treaties, this waterway could be threatened.... the greatest threat to the operation and security of the Canal would be to try to insist on the retention of the present outmoded treaty in the face of increasing Panamanian discontent. The Canal issue involves much more than the relationship between the U.S. and Panama. It is an issue which affects all Latin American-U.S. relations. The problem also significantly affects the relationship between our country and the entire Third World. To the developing countries, the present status of the Canal Zone is an outmoded relic of a bygone imperialist age. If we can reach a fair and mutually satisfactory solution with Panama, we will therefore significantly enhance our position in the Western Hemisphere and in the world at large. In negotiating the new treaties, the U.S. proceeded on the basis that its national interests lie in assuring that the Canal continues to be efficiently operated, secure, neutral and open to all nations on a non-discriminatory basis.

Nation's Business, October:60.

Jimmy Carter
President of the United States　　*1*

I'm familiar ... with the problems in Quebec and the inclinations of some of the French Canadians to have an independent status from the rest of Canadian provinces. I don't know what's going to be the ultimate outcome. But I believe that we are so closely tied together with Canada on a mutually beneficial basis – sharing problems, sharing opportunities, sharing trade, sharing manufacturing companies that have joint ownership, our exchange of energy sources, our sharing of the St. Lawrence Seaway, the Great Lakes as far as water pollution is concerned, the bringing of Alaskan oil and natural gas down to us – that we have got to have a continuing relationship with Canada. My own personal preference would be that the commonwealth stay as it is and that there not be a separate Quebec Province.

News conference, Washington, Feb. 23/
The New York Times, 2-24:22.

2

Before any full normalization of relations [between the U.S. and Cuba] can take place ... Cuba would have to make some fairly substantial changes in their attitude. I would like to insist, for instance, that they not interfere in the internal affairs of countries in this hemisphere and that they decrease their military involvement in Africa and that they reinforce a commitment to human rights by releasing political prisoners that have been in jail now in Cuba for 17 or 18 years – things of that kind. But I think before we can reach that point we'll have to have discussions with them, and I do intend to see discussions initiated with Cuba quite early on re-establishing the anti-hijacking agreement, arriving at a fishing agreement between us and Cuba, since our 200-mile limits do overlap between Florida and Cuba. And I would not be averse in the future to seeing visitation rights permitted as well.

National call-in radio program, Washington,
March 5/The New York Times, 3-6:(1)30.

3

As nations of the "New World," we [in the Americas] once believed that we would prosper in isolation from the "Old World." But, since the Second World War, all of us have taken such vital roles in the world community that isolation would now be harmful to our best interests. The International Monetary Fund, the World Bank, and the General Agreement on Tariffs and Trade are signs that we understand this. So is the United Nations Conference on Trade and Development, which Raul Perbisch of Argentina made into an important forum of the developing world. Venezuela is now co-chairing the Paris Conference on International Economic Cooperation. The United Nations Economic Commission for Latin America is the source of many creative ideas on development throughout the world. The leaders

(JIMMY CARTER)

of many Latin American nations have been the driving force behind the North-South negotiations. In all these ways, the nations of Latin America were among the first in our changing world to see the importance of adapting global institutions to new realities.

Before Permanent Council of Organization of American States, Washington, April 14/ The New York Times, 4-15:(A)10.

1

[On negotiations with Panama over control of the Canal]: . . . the common purpose is to have the Panama Canal protected and open for free use by world shipping interests. And I think there is a potential threat to the Canal if we don't act in good faith concerning the demands for increased control over the Canal Zone by the Panamanians. We have had obviously no threat from the Panamanian government of attacks on the Canal if we don't work out an agreement. But I would really hate to see sabotage result from any lack of sensitivity on our part in the desire to work out this question in a peaceful way. We're going to protect the rights of our own country, of the world shipping needs, and of the maintenance and the security of the Canal itself. Those are the overriding questions for us . . .

Interview, Washington/ U.S. News & World Report, 6-6:20.

2

[On the proposed new treaties — which he is today signing, but which still need to be ratified by the Senate — that would gradually turn over control of the Panama Canal to Panama]: This agreement . . . forms a new partnership to insure that this vital waterway, so important to all of us, will continue to be well operated, safe and open to shipping by all nations now and in the future. Under these accords, Panama will play an increasingly important role in the operation and defense of the Canal during the next 23 years, and after that the United States will still be able to counter any threat to the Canal's neutrality and openness for us . . . The accords also give Panama an important eco-

nomic stake in the continual safe and efficient operation of the Canal and make Panama a strong and interested party in the future success of the waterway . . . This opens a new chapter in our relations with all nations of this hemisphere, and it testifies to the maturity and the good judgment and the decency of our people. This agreement is a symbol for the world of the mutual respect and cooperation among all our nations.

At signing of the treaties, Washington, Sept. 7/The New York Times, 9-8:(A)10.

3

[Supporting the proposed new treaties which would gradually turn over control of the Panama Canal to Panama]: The philosophical point is *use,* not ownership. This has been recognized for a long time now. Since Eisenhower's Presidency, there has been agreement by successive Administrations that the existing Canal accord must be modified. We still see the Panama Canal as vital and we must remain capable of defending it with our forces if necessary. But our main objective is to be able to keep it open without violence, as the treaties provide. And we want Panama to be our partner, not our potential adversary. The Panamanians have negotiated with Washington under four United States Presidents during 14 years. The new treaty drafts are fair to the United States and protect our national interests, our security and our trade, while at the same time being fair to Panama. Furthermore, the issue is important to our whole international position. This new agreement will not only demonstrate to everyone our good faith as a nation and our intention to refute any charges of vestigial colonialism. These treaties erase whatever is left of colonialism. They show the world that the United States, as a superpower, is prepared to act fairly with a small country like Panama.

Interview, Washington/ The New York Times, 11-20:(4)15.

Leonel J. Castillo
Commissioner, Immigration and Naturalization Service of the United States

4

. . . full employment in Mexico would not stop the flow [of illegal Mexican workers into

WHAT THEY SAID IN 1977

(LEONEL J. CASTILLO)

the U.S.]. A lot of people think that it's because unemployment in Mexico is roughly 30 per cent, and in the border towns much higher — that if you had full employment in Mexico, or at least high levels of employment, you would stop the flow. But high-level officials in the Mexican government say that that's not so, because the reason people come is that they make more money in the United States for doing the same work, and if people are working and doing a job in Mexico — a machinist, for $1 an hour — and they could do the same job in the U.S. for the same company at $7 an hour, they'll come.

Interview, Washington/Los Angeles Times, 7-24:(7)3.

Fidel Castro
Premier of Cuba

1

There is no personality cult in Cuba. There are no official photographs and no street, no farm bears the name of any leader. I consider myself a neighbor, and I travel to all parts of the island without announcing my arrival. There is no protocol, no ceremony, no motorcades, no police. I bear in mind the thought of [19th-century Cuban revolutionary] Jose Marti who said all the glory in the world can be contained in a kernel of corn.

Interview/People, 3-21:62.

2

We fight against the tendency of leaders to live a soft life, and to my knowledge we don't have a single one who has taken more than his due. Man doesn't need very much to live. We have some diversions here — fishing, hunting, going to the movies. But, in general, the people know nothing but work. And there is no need to change suits all day, even when we go out. After all, we are all in uniform.

Interview/People, 3-21:67.

3

To create a favorable climate for improving our relations with the United States, it is indispensable that the discredited and intolerable economic blockade should be lifted . . . This remains our position today and for this fundamental reason: We did not impose an economic blockade against the United States. We do not have a naval base in the United States. We do not practice subversion or espionage against the United States. That is why we cannot accept a policy that is a one-way street. That is why we consider that the condition for negotiations is the disappearance of the economic blockade. This is a fair position from our point of view because otherwise we will get nowhere. We accept the possibility of contacts [with the U.S.] to clarify this position. Contacts, yes, but discussions, no.

Interview, Havana/
Los Angeles Herald-Examiner, 5-7:(A)4.

4

[On the U.S. Carter Administration] : This is the first U.S. government in 18 years which has not committed itself to a policy of hostility with Cuba. I think that [former U.S. President Richard] Nixon was a humbug, an individual without any ethics at all. I do not think the same of Carter. I believe he has ethics based principally on his religious formation. And, by his statements, he gives me the impression of being a sincere man. [But] the end of the [U.S. economic] embargo [against Cuba] must be total. If they relax the embargo only insofar as they can sell to us and we can only buy, we will buy absolutely nothing from the United States. This would create an irritating situation which to our people would sound like something unworthy and discriminatory. Only the total suppression of the embargo would create conditions which would justify talking about an improvement in U.S.-Cuban relations.

Interview/The New York Times, 7-12:3.

5

We are satisfied with our efforts and our revolution, but we do not wish to impose our system on any country, and this is a very important matter. [For instance,] Jamaica is our closest neighbor. We have never interfered in Jamaica's internal affairs. We shall never interfere in the internal affairs of Jamaica.

At national heroes day rally, Montego Bay,
Jamaica/Los Angeles Times, 10-18:(1)19.

(FIDEL CASTRO)

1

The United States does not have anything to show us [in the field of human rights]. We have no prostitution, no gambling, no racial discrimination. The cultural level and the health level of our people are the highest of all Latin America. And I think, in the field of human rights, actually we are better off than the United States.

Television interview/Los Angeles Times, 12-13:(1)2.

Frank Church
United States Senator, D–Idaho

2

If, in order to trade with the United States, anyone expects [Cuban Premier] Fidel Castro to change colors, to empty his jails, to abandon his role in Africa, to sever his close ties with the Soviet Union, and to pay in full for our expropriated property, that person has simply exchanged one delusion for another.

The Christian Science Monitor, 10-12:12.

Philip M. Crane
United States Representative,
R–Illinois

3

[Arguing against a proposed new treaty which would gradually turn over control of the Panama Canal to Panama]: The United States has spent $163.7-million to acquire rights and title to the Canal and Canal Zone, to say nothing of the $366-million in construction costs and the $6.35-billion over the years that went for operation, administration and defense. And now it is proposed that we not only give this investment away but that we pay Panama almost $2-billion more between now and the year 2000 for taking it. The very thought of such an incredible arrangement boggles the mind.

Los Angeles Times, 10-23:(1)1.

Roberto de la Madrid
Governor of Baja California, Mexico

4

[On the problem of illegal Mexican aliens taking jobs in the U.S.]: Unemployment is a malignant tree planted in Mexican soil, but the roots have extended deeply into American territory. Thus the problem pertains to both countries. If for the United States, with its vast wealth and resources, this is a grave problem, for Mexico, with many shortcomings, this matter is a wound in our flesh. But whatever the magnitude of this problem, nothing legitimizes the inhuman treatment of those whose only crime has been to procure an honest occupation in a foreign land.

Inauguration address, Mexicali, Mexico,
Nov. 1/Los Angeles Herald-Examiner, 11-2:(A)3.

Jean-Claude Duvalier
President of Haiti

5

We will have our own form of democracy one day. But we do not wish to imitate the U.S. The Haitian mentality is that your democracy lets people take advantage of weakness to get rid of leaders. If I were to announce a democracy now, it would be considered a sign of weakness on my part.

People, 11-14:39.

Elizabeth II
Queen of England

6

A generation of Canadians has been born and grown to maturity during my reign. I know you will understand me when I say that I have a special interest in these young men and women, contemporaries of my own children. They are people made strong by the achievements of their parents and grandparents, but not imprisoned by the prejudices of the past. In their sensitivity toward other people, in their sense of justice, their generosity and good-will, lie not only lessons for us all, but also the best and surest hope for unity and understanding among Canadians everywhere.

Before Canadian Parliament, Ottawa,
Oct. 18/The Dallas Times Herald, 10-19:(A)5.

Romulo Escobar (Bethancourt)
Chief Panamanian negotiator
at Panama Canal treaty talks
with the United States

7

[On the recent agreement between U.S. and Panamanian negotiators on a treaty that would gradually turn over control of the Canal to

267

WHAT THEY SAID IN 1977

(ROMULO ESCOBAR [BETHANCOURT])

Panama]: There are people here who criticize [the agreement] on this treaty. But there is more opposition in the United States than here. We don't even know if the U.S. Congress will approve this treaty. If the United States doesn't, we are going to take a road of violence ... There were many roads we could have taken in order to get the Canal. Sabotage is one. But the responsible ruler ... looks around for alternatives so that his country is not massacred. There are people who criticize this treaty, although we arrived at this pact without sacrificing 50,000 young Panamanians. Nonetheless, wherever you go, people respect you when they know you are a Panamanian because they know you have been struggling against imperialism.

Before local government officials, Panama City, Aug. 19/Los Angeles Herald-Examiner, 8-20:(A)2.

1

Getting control of the Canal Zone and the Canal is one of Panama's oldest national desires. To generation after generation of Panamanians, the Canal has symbolized the country's national patrimony — in the hands of foreigners. We developed a kind of national religion over the Canal.

Time, 8-22:8.

2

We have repeated time and again that [under the provisions of the proposed new Canal treaty] the United States will not have the right to intervene in the internal affairs of Panama. Nowhere does it appear that there is a special right for the United States to intervene in the internal affairs of our country. But Panama and the United States have the responsibility to keep the Canal open, secure and accessible. And each one has the right to defend the Canal.

Broadcast address to lawyers, Oct. 7/
Los Angeles Times, 10-10:(1)1.

Marcelo Fernandez (Font)
Minister of Foreign Trade of Cuba
3

[Encouraging U.S. trade with his country]: I think that for any country, even the United

States, $20-billion worth of business a year is worth having. And this is a growing market. In the last five years our economic growth has averaged about 9 per cent a year. It has slowed down now, suffering from some of the problems that have plagued the world's economy ... We know just how far we can go in incurring foreign debt. We have always carried out our promises and Cuba has a record that can be compared favorably with any underdeveloped country in the world. When a country lends Cuba money, it knows it will be paid. It is the only way we can retain our credit ... The sensible thing for our two countries is free trade. We impose no political conditions. It is the United States that imposes them. Why does the United States take this position with Cuba, especially when it sometimes works against the interests of the United States itself? A blockade is an act of war, to be used only against an enemy with which you are at war. But we do not feel we are at war with the United States.

Interview, Havana/Los Angeles Times, 7-4:(1)14.

Bernard J. Finestone
President, Montreal Board of Trade
4

[Arguing against separatism for Canada's Quebec Province, and French as Quebec's only official language]: It requires an incurable optimism, or a total disregard for the economic facts of life, to conclude that Quebec as a separate entity is not going to regress. And the language bill will not work. Their theory is that if you squash an Anglo out of a job, you can put a Frenchman in it. The reality is that you will be able to put no one in it. You will simply drive the job out of the province.

The Dallas Times Herald, 6-15:(E)12.

Gerald R. Ford
Former President of the United States
5

As long as Cuba continues to have substantial military forces in Angola — the latest estimates are around 15,000 troops — as long as Cuba continues its policy of moving from Angola to other African nations such as Ethiopia, I believe the United States ought to keep Cuba at arm's length. I think it would be rewarding the wrong nation to grant diplomatic relations as long as Cuba is cooperating with the

(GERALD R. FORD)

Soviet Union in undertaking an expansionist foreign policy in all of Africa. I can see reasons for negotiating with Cuba on airplane-hijacking and fishing agreements. Those are practical things.

Interview/U.S. News & World Report, 7-4:22.

Ernesto Geisel
President of Brazil

1

I say we live in a democracy. We live in liberty. And I repeat what I have said many times before — that there is no liberty only for those who want to use it to destroy our nation.

Before military officers on 13th anniversary of coup that brought them to power, March 31/The New York Times, 4-1:5.

Barry M. Goldwater
United States Senator, R—Arizona

2

[On the proposed new treaties which would gradually turn over control of the Panama Canal to Panama]: [The Canal] is both symbolically and practically the key to hemispheric defense. If we [the U.S.] were, as proposed in the new treaties, to create a power vacuum by giving up our right to maintain a military presence in Panama after 1999 — or before that time, in my opinion — it seems inevitable that the Soviets, not directly but probably through Cuban surrogates, would move in quickly to fill it . . . Even if it were quite clear that the United States had the right to send forces into Panama to defend the Canal — and the proposed new treaties are wholly unclear on that point — the cries of "imperialist aggression" and "imperialist intervention" would be so orchestrated internationally as to effectively deter any such action on the part of the United States.

Before State Bar of Georgia, Atlanta, Dec. 2/ Los Angeles Herald-Examiner, 12-4:(A)2.

Ulysses Guimaraes
President, Brazilian Democratic Movement

3

Despite the precarious situation we are in, it is still worth it to continue fighting for democracy. The reason is simple: Democracy is the best form of government for Brazil. History proves it. The most advanced countries in the world today are democracies — with congresses or parliaments.

The Washington Post, 4-23:(A)17.

W. Averell Harriman
Former United States Ambassador-at-Large

4

[Supporting the proposed new treaties which would gradually turn over control of the Panama Canal to Panama]: It's unthinkable that these treaties won't be ratified once the American people understand what's involved. I'm absolutely convinced that the treaties are clear; they don't need clarification . . . Now, the treaties don't write out in plain English that we have the right to intervene [in the Canal during an emergency], but I went over them with [U.S. treaty negotiator] Sol Linowitz and he convinced me that the language gives us the full right to move in a military way if we had to — and that the Panamanians agreed to this. There are going to be things said in Panama about these treaties that we don't like — to get them through down there — and we have to live with it.

Interview, Washington/ The New York Times, 10-9:(1)19.

S. I. Hayakawa
United States Senator, R—California

5

[Supporting the proposed treaty which would gradually give control over the Panama Canal to Panama]: In gradually relinquishing management responsibilities for the Canal to the Republic of Panama, we [the U.S.] are not "giving away" anything. We are, if I read the memo correctly, guaranteeing rights and privileges we must indeed retain — the permanent rights of access and the "permanent right to defend the neutrality of the Canal from any threat."

San Francisco, Aug. 17/The Dallas Times Herald, 8-19:(A)4.

WHAT THEY SAID IN 1977

Jesse A. Helms
United States Senator, R—North Carolina 1

[Criticizing the proposed new treaties which would gradually turn over control of the Panama Canal to Panama]: First of all, we give up our sovereign rights. Everybody agrees that would happen. There's a great deal of talk about sovereignty. Nobody knows exactly how to define sovereignty, but it's absolutely clear that we do have full sovereign rights now. It's there in black and white in the 1903 treaty. The question is this: If we give up ownership and full sovereign rights, how can we be certain that we will continue to have use of the Canal? In my opinion, which I believe is shared by the majority of the American people, it is far less likely that we can continue to have the use of the Canal if these treaties are ratified. I am opposed to any treaty in which we would give up our sovereign rights.

Interview/U.S. News & World Report, 12-12:33.

Hubert H. Humphrey
United States Senator, D—Minnesota 2

[Supporting the proposed new treaty which would gradually turn over control of the Panama Canal to Panama]: The United States has lost nothing through these treaties. No international relationship negotiated more than 70 years ago can be expected to last forever, without adjustment. Senate approval will add substance and character to the Good Neighbor policy first enunciated by President Franklin Roosevelt.

U.S. News & World Report, 9-19:19.

Rashleigh E. Jackson
Ambassador/Permanent Representative to the United Nations from Guyana 3

We [in Guyana] will not permit the establishment of any foreign military bases on our soil. We have never been aggressive and we do not have aggressive intentions. We have neither the capacity, nor the will, nor the desire to be a threat to anyone. We are non-aligned. As a small state, we see in non-alignment, through cooperative efforts with like-minded states, the opportunity to work for the construction of a regime of secure peace resting on the creation of an international economic order based on justice and equity and on the eradication of colonialism.

At symposium, New York/ The Christian Science Monitor, 4-11:27.

Henry A. Kissinger
Former Secretary of State of the United States 4

[Supporting the proposed new treaty which would gradually turn over control of the Panama Canal to Panama]: The new treaty marks an improvement over the present situation in that it assures continuing, efficient, non-discriminatory and secure access to the Panama Canal with the support of the countries of the Western Hemisphere, instead of against their opposition and eventually their harassment.

Washington, Aug. 17/The New York Times, 8-18:(A)3.

Robert C. Krueger
United States Representative, D—Texas 5

[On a proposed new Panama Canal treaty which would gradually turn over control of the Canal to Panama]: First, the United States will need, over the foreseeable future, to maintain some kind of military protection over the Canal. Second, we need to realize that although it is an emotional issue with certain parts of the American voting public, it is equally an emotional issue with Latin America. To break off negotiations, or to refuse to negotiate, would be contrary to our national interests. If there were a 15-mile strip between Dallas and Fort Worth that people had to show passports to pass through and was under the control of a foreign power, that would be a source of irritation to the citizens of the [Dallas-Fort Worth] Metroplex. That is basically the circumstances in which the Panamanians find themselves.

Interview/The Dallas Times Herald, 8-17:(C)2.

Camille Laurin
Minister of Cultural Development of Quebec, Canada 6

[On his proposal to make French the official language of Quebec]: The Anglophones have

(CAMILLE LAURIN)

listened too much to the media . . . They have not taken account of changes in the Francophone attitude. There is a refusal to see the legitimacy of the other's point of view. They are afraid, perhaps, that they are going to lose the gilded life they have led. There is too much of the old philosophy, "What I have, I hold." It has been a tremendous shock to the Anglophones to realize they are losing their dominant role in Quebec. When they read the [proposed] law they will find that what we demand is not enormous. We simply insist that the use of French must be institutionalized. They will recover when they take another look at the situation and realize they can still speak English, work in English, obtain their services in English. I count on this second reaction, which will be a return to realism. We are not extremists. But we have our pride, our dignity. There were injustices to correct and that is all we are trying to do.

Interview, Quebec City/
The Dallas Times Herald, 8-15:(D)6.

Rene Levesque
Premier of Quebec, Canada

1

In my opinion, the important question – the question everyone interested in Quebec and Canada should be asking – is not *whether* Quebec will become independent, nor indeed *when* it will happen, but rather *how,* in due time, Quebecers can be expected to take full charge of their own political affairs. In this respect, I believe the past augurs well for the future. For one thing, Quebec citizens are determined that change, especially great change when required, can and must be brought about strictly through the democratic process. This is rather well illustrated by our recent election, and the orderly way in which, after patient and solid preparation, a whole new perspective came out of it as confirmed. All our history shows that our people dislike upsetting things in a panic just as much as they dislike being upset themselves. There's nothing we like more in our affairs than a sense of continuity. We have managed to survive, to grow and make progress despite great obstacles, by being stead-

fast as well as cautious, proceeding not in spurts but in careful transition. We may want change, but not through disorder, since any kind of extremism goes against the very grain of our society. Such is the way in which Quebec, since 1960, has gone through greatly accelerated change, in fact a complete restructuring of its social fabric, without suffering the traumatic shocks or disruptions that so often afflict other countries in similar circumstances. In our case, this period is generally referred to as the "quiet revolution." And now, for the last seven or eight years, Quebec has been going through a similar, and in fact logically related, reassessment and transition in constitutional matters. And once again, if you consider how delicate such matters can be, the evolution is going on in an atmosphere of remarkable serenity. Initially there were a few tense moments, but now there is nothing but patient democratic work, so that after the "quiet revolution," we are entitled to expect "quiet independence" in the near future.

Before Economic Club of New York,
Jan. 25/Vital Speeches, 2-15:284.

2

[On whether an independent Quebec would turn to the Left and become an anchor for Soviet or other foreign interests in North America]: Good Lord! We're North Americans, we're part of North America and we're very aware . . . that that kind of intervention would be a serious thing. It is a God-given right to be hostile to the evolution of Quebec. But some of the crappy – there's no other word – the crappy scare propaganda which is being spread around, some reaching the United States, about the future of Quebec, to me is one of the gratuitous insults that you can see. Anyone with a head on his shoulders that has followed the evolution of the Parti Quebecois [Levesque's political party] . . . knows damn well it is basically a democratic party. It has, let's say, leftist leanings, very moderate in the same sense maybe as the New Democratic Party, which is a party well known in Canada and has never worried anyone. In fact, we're trying to be in the sort of mainstream . . . When you look at the requirements, the needs, that are foreseeable in any society, any modern

WHAT THEY SAID IN 1977

(RENE LEVESQUE)

society, it's obvious that you can't go back to the 19th century. We'd be dodos. But, on the other hand, we're certainly not prophetic in the sense that we want to change the world from a modest base like Quebec. We're, I think, a center-left party and a center-left government which is more or less attuned to what I think is the drift of civilization right now.

Interview, Montreal/Los Angeles Times, 5-26:(1)17.

1

[On the possibility of French-speaking Quebec separating from Canada]: Canada is on record, in Helsinki and elsewhere, as respecting the right of peoples to self-determination — and the Quebec people are a national entity. Americans find it hard to grasp the way we are moving because they have nothing like Quebec. You [the U.S.] have been collectively, officially English-speaking since the Revolution, with a national identity tied to a Constitution and a flag and other elements of nation-building. Not even the color bar stops most blacks from saying, "We are American." Here, for 300 years, there has been a different population with a different language and a different culture and, in many ways, a different outlook. An Asian friend once told me Quebec has one of the most complicated color bars in the world because it's based on language and doesn't show as much.

Interview, Montreal/
U.S. News & World Report, 9-26:70.

2

[On the separatist movement in his province]: Canada is two nations, two societies, two identities, whether you like it or not . . . What we're doing is no different from what the nine European Common Market [members] are striving to achieve — a confederation while retaining their sovereign identities and prerogatives.

Interview, Quebec City/Newsweek, 12-5:55.

Sol M. Linowitz
United States negotiator at
Panama Canal treaty talks
3

[Supporting the proposed new treaty which would gradually turn over control of the Panama Canal to Panama]: . . . we believe that the American people have been either uninformed or, in some cases, kept ignorant about what is really involved in these negotiations and in the new treaty. We think that when the American people understand what we have negotiated, recognize why it is in our highest national interest, they will indeed re-examine their previous convictions and their previous point of view, and see why the treaty ought to be approved. On the issue of "We own it; we bought it" and so forth, that is simply not the fact. We have never had sovereignty over the Canal, over the territory. In the original 1903 agreement, we said that we had certain rights, power and authority "as if" the United States "were sovereign," which indicated clearly that sovereignty had not passed. Unlike the case of Alaska and Louisiana, we did not purchase territory; we got certain rights with reference to territory. So the situation is not one where we have actually owned and have sovereignty over a piece of property which we are transferring. We are merely, pursuant to the recognized sovereignty of Panama, making a new arrangement.

TV-radio interview/"Meet the Press,"
National Broadcasting Company, 8-14.

4

[Supporting the proposed new treaty which would gradually transfer control of the Panama Canal to Panama]: All the countries of the Hemisphere have made common cause in looking upon our position in the Canal as the last vestige of a colonial past which evokes bitter memories and deep animosities. The greatest threat to the operation and security of the Canal would be to try to insist upon retention of the present outmoded treaty and its anachronistic provisions — provisions which have in the past, and can so easily again in the future, trigger hostility and violence. The simple fact is that if we do not agree upon treaties which are mutually agreeable and acceptable, the time

(SOL M. LINOWITZ)

may come when we may find ourselves in the position of having to defend the Canal by force against a hostile population and in the face of widespread condemnation by the countries of Latin America and even the rest of the world.

Before Senate Foreign Relations Committee, Washington, Sept. 26/Los Angeles Times, 9-27:(1)6.

Jose Lopez (Portillo)
President of Mexico

1

[On the dispute between the U.S. and Panama about sovereignty over the Panama Canal]: This is a cloud in relations of the United States with Latin America that should be dispelled. It's simply a question of whether the most powerful country on earth can restore to a sister Latin American country the dignity and honor it deserves.

Before National Press Club, Washington, Feb. 15/Los Angeles Times, 2-16:(1)8.

2

You [the U.S.] constitute a powerful political unit and it is difficult to be powerful. We [Mexico] are a long way from being powerful. It is also difficult to be the neighbor of someone as powerful as you. There are two grave risks: arrogance, which is easy but sterile, and submission, which is easy but abject. We have chosen the difficult road of dignity, based on the liberty that we want to sustain and the responsibility we wish to assume . . . In order of importance, you are our first client and we are your fourth. The balance of trade is very unfavorable for us and, at times, you restrict imports that might improve it, aggravating our economic problems by causing unemployment. It is understandable that many of our men want to work in your country in order to improve their standard of living, as has been the case in other times and places. Due to these and other known and reprehensible reasons, some of our people and some of yours cultivate and deal in drugs. Thus, many of the problems that bother you the most are closely related to our economic problems. Mexico must solve its own problems and you must examine those of your

decisions which may adversely affect or undermine our development effort and, above all, the spirit of the political ideal of international coexistence.

Before U.S. Congress, Washington, Feb. 17/ The New York Times, 2-18:(A)14.

3

[On illegal Mexican immigration into the U.S.]: We have told American officials that illegal migration is related directly to our country's economic situation. We have pointed out to them that illegal migration to the U.S. will end when we solve Mexico's economic problems, when we create enough jobs here at home. The United States should help us solve this problem. We aren't asking for gifts, but we do recognize the need for a balanced relationship between the United States and Mexico on trade, financing and currency values. Mexico suffers from a major negative balance of trade with the U.S. But if America would buy more from us than it does now — and we do have a lot more to sell — that would create jobs in Mexico. Then my people wouldn't have to cross the border to seek jobs in the United States.

Interview, Mexico City/ U.S. News & World Report, 7-4:28.

Jose Maria Machin
Venezuelan Ambassador to the
Organization of American States

4

[Addressing a Chilean representative at an OAS meeting]: We said it yesterday, we say it today and you may be sure, sir, that we will continue to say it in the future: You can achieve development and the happiness of all men . . . only within a democratic system.

At OAS General Assembly meeting, St. George's, Grenada/The Dallas Times Herald, 6-23:(A)4.

Michael Manley
Prime Minister of Jamaica

5

[Saying his country must free itself from dependency on foreign investment]: This government on behalf of our people will not accept anybody anywhere in the world telling us what we are to do in our country. We are the master in this house; and in our house there shall be no

273

WHAT THEY SAID IN 1977

(MICHAEL MANLEY)

other master but ourselves. Above all, we are not for sale.

Address to the nation/
The Christian Science Monitor, 1-24:10.

1

[On his country's "democratic socialism"]: In Western terms, we are completely committed to pluralistic democracy, but we also believe in participatory democracy at the grass-roots level. In Eastern terms, we honestly believe that in trying to achieve a socially responsive economy, we will not have to eliminate the private sector. A more important question than how much of the economy should be taken over by the state is industrial democracy — worker participation in ownership, collective responsibility and so forth.

Interview, Kingston/Newsweek, 2-28:38.

2

I don't need to tell you, brothers and sisters, that Jamaica has been through three of the roughest years in our history — years that will go down as the worst of the 20th century. We've been battered by world inflation, battered by oil prices, battered by a slowdown in tourism. [A] minority clique [inside Jamaica] is talking you down and saying your government was no good, and they blame you and me for all these problems.

To farmers, Jamaica/
The New York Times, 12-15:(A)3.

Lawrence P. McDonald
United States Representative,
D–Georgia

3

[Saying the U.S. should not lift its economic embargo against Cuba]: "Normalizing" relations with [Cuban Premier] Fidel Castro would free the Cuban economy and release the Soviet Union from the burden it now carries. It would bring financial benefits to a hard-pressed regime and allow Cuba to step up its terrorism and subversion throughout the Western Hemisphere. In all likelihood, we would see a continuance of Cuban troops acting as proxy fighters for Soviet world conequest . . . If Castro were to renounce

terrorism, dismantle his terrorist training centers, restore human rights in Cuba and release his political prisoners, that might persuade me to take a different attitude. But that would be asking Communism to reverse itself, and that is not in the cards. The Communists have never altered their objective of world domination. Cuba is just the Western outpost in that drive.

Interview/U.S. News & World Report, 3-7:73.

George S. McGovern
United States Senator, D–South Dakota

4

I recommend that the [U.S. trade embargo against Cuba] be lifted now without delay. It never made any sense. It hurts everyone but our competitors. We trade with Peking, Moscow, why not Cuba? There may be some objections in the Cuban community in Miami, but we can't let a small group determine U.S. foreign policy.

To reporters, Havana, April 8/
Los Angeles Herald-Examiner, 4-8:(A)4.

George Meany
President, American Federation of
Labor-Congress of Industrial Organizations

5

[Supporting the proposed new treaty which would gradually turn over control of the Panama Canal to Panama]: My general attitude is that there is no particular reason for us [the U.S.] holding onto territory 6,000 miles away just because we built the Canal on somebody else's land back in 1904.

The Dallas Times Herald, 9-3:(B)2.

Thomas H. Moorer
Admiral (Ret.), United States Navy;
Former Chairman, Joint Chiefs of Staff

6

[On the proposed new treaty which would gradually turn over control of the Panama Canal to Panama]: I am very much concerned about the proposals to surrender the Panama Canal to a leftist-oriented government allied with Cuba. There exists the potential danger for giving this U.S. advantage to a man [Panamanian leader Omar Torrijos] who might allow — or might be persuaded — that it was in his best interest to permit Soviet power and influence to prevail by proxy over the Canal, in much the

274

(THOMAS H. MOORER)

same manner as happened in Cuba. I was convinced as Chairman of the JCS — and I remain convinced today — that if the Soviet Union ever gained even proxy sovereignty and control over the U.S. Canal Zone and Canal through Cuba, U.S. security as well as U.S. prosperity would be placed in serious jeopardy. The United States would be placed in jeopardy because interocean mobility would be threatened. The mobility of Allied commercial shipping and naval forces would face the same threat. The economic lifelines of the entire Western Hemisphere would be needlessly jeopardized.

Before Senate Foreign Relations Committee, Washington, Oct. 10/ U.S. News & World Report, 10-24:27.

Francisco Morales (Bermudez)
President of Peru

1

Without any question, there will be general elections [in Peru] in 1980. We call on all sectors of the nation to create a climate of peace and mutual respect to make possible the transfer of power in 1980.

Broadcast address to the nation, Lima, July 28/The New York Times, 7-29:(A)5.

Claude Morin
Minister of Intergovernmental Affairs of Quebec, Canada

2

[On the Parti Quebecois, which governs the province, and which advocates independence from Canada]: We want to avoid a negative image. . . . we are not revolutionaries, sponsored by the KGB, to create political turmoil in North America . . . We seek political sovereignty for Quebec with continued economic association with the rest of Canada and the world . . . We seek to change the relationship between Ottawa and Quebec — not to secede.

Interview, Los Angeles/ Los Angeles Herald-Examiner, 11-25:(A)15.

John M. Murphy
United States Representative, D—New York

3

[Criticizing the U.S. Carter Administration's proposed new Panama Canal treaty which

would gradually turn over control of the Canal to Panama]: To any who might doubt this member's intentions, I shall state that not a centimeter of the Canal Zone, not one piece of United States property, not the fate of a single Zone employee, or another nickel beyond that which has already been appropriated, will be turned over to the Republic of Panama's dictator without the prior approval of the House of Representatives, as provided by the Constitution.

Los Angeles Herald-Examiner, 8-28:(B)7.

Richard M. Nixon
Former President of the United States

4

[Comparing the current government in Chile with that of the late President Salvador Allende, which was overthrown in 1973]: I am not here to defend, and will not defend, repression by any government, be it a friend of the United States or one that is opposed to the United States. But in terms of national security, in terms of our own self-interest, the right-wing dictatorship [such as that now in Chile], if it is not exporting its revolution, if it is not interfering with its neighbors, if it is not taking action against the United States, it is therefore of no security concern to us. It is of a human-rights concern. A left-wing dictatorship, on the other hand, we find that they do engage in trying to export their subversion to other countries, and that does involve our security interests. As far as the situation in Chile was concerned [when Allende was in power], he was engaging in dictatorial actions which eventually would have allowed him to impose a [left-wing] dictatorship. That was his goal : . . . Allende lost eventually. Allende was overthrown eventually, not because of anything that was done from the outside, but because his system didn't work in Chile and Chile decided to throw him out.

Television broadcast, San Clemente, Calif./ "The Nixon Interviews," Paradine Productions, 5-25.

Alejandro Orfila
Secretary General, Organization of American States

5

"Interest" is the key word here. What Latin Americans appreciate more than rhetorical

(ALEJANDRO ORFILA)

visions or grandiose plans from the United States is a clear and convincing demonstration of "interest." We saw this "interest" at work in such policies as the "Good Neighbor" attitudes of President Franklin D. Roosevelt and the Alliance for Progress of President John F. Kennedy. These and similar U.S. policies were perhaps too ambitious in scope and, in consequence, their goals were not fully realized in practice. But they did possess the central element without which inter-American cooperation is bound to run aground on the shoals of mutual suspicion; that is, they were motivated, first and foremost, by a high degree of U.S. interest in the fortunes of the Western Hemisphere.

At National Sister Cities Conference,
Palm Springs, Calif., Aug. 19/Vital Speeches, 10-15:22.

Harold R. Parfitt
Governor of the Canal Zone　　　1

When the Americans built [the Panama] Canal, they took on a job many people said was impossible. Remember, Count Ferdinand de Lesseps, the great French engineer, had failed. We cleared the jungle, eradicated yellow fever and built it. We've run it efficiently and cheaply. It just wasn't the Army Corps of Engineers; it was also the laborers who toiled in awful conditions. Many employees today, American and Panamanian, are grandchildren and great grandchildren of those men. To people from outside, it's an unreal world. But to them it is, in a sense, the only world. Now this world is about to change [as a result of negotiations which may turn over control of the Canal to Panama]. They find that hard to accept. They know that some day they no longer will be living in a small part of the United States but in a foreign country with foreign police, foreign laws, foreign courts. They worry about the explosiveness of feelings of the Panamanians. They wonder if they will have a job, where their kids will go to school ... Being here is like living in a fishbowl with a strong light shining on you. You live, eat and talk Canal. When times are good, that's fine. But when times are bad, it's awful bad.

The United States and Panama have to come soon to an accommodation acceptable to the skilled people needed to run the Canal.

Interview, Canal Zone/Los Angeles Times,
4-24:(1)16.

Carlos Andres Perez
President of Venezuela　　　2

Economic instability is the reason so many of our [Latin American] nations have dictatorships. In general, our misery, our lack of education, our malnutrition diminish our creative capacity. This stirs up conflicts and tensions which, in turn, lead to dictatorships being created in order to restore order. The only solution to this tragic cycle is to establish just and equitable international economic relations, and this directly involves the industrialized nations — and especially the United States. Let's not talk about oil, but about another product — coffee — which right now costs consumers a lot. Take Colombia, whose economy is based on coffee. In one year, they may earn as much as $500-million from coffee exports. On the basis of that income, they start planning their economic development. But the next year, they earn only 300 million because the price of coffee has gone down. What kind of investment can you count on when your earnings are so unstable? If we want democracy to survive, we must establish a stable economic relationship.

Interview/U.S. News & World Report, 7-25:54.

　　　3

[Supporting a proposed new treaty which would gradually turn over control of the Panama Canal from the U.S. to Panama] : The world would be scandalized, in the 1970s, if the United States should try to keep a colonial enclave in the Western Hemisphere. It would destroy all the democratic foreign policies of the American government, because it would force the United States to occupy the Republic of Panama militarily. It's not necessary to comment how America's leadership would suffer if it should occupy one of our allies ... One does not have to be a strategist, or to sit in the

(CARLOS ANDRES PEREZ)

Pentagon, to know that without Panamanian cooperation the Canal is indefensible.

Interview/Caracas/
The Dallas Times Herald, 9-27:(A)5.

Augusto Pinochet (Ugarte)
President·of Chile
1

Chile does not beg the applause or international favor of anyone. Chile has not modified, nor will it modify, the course it has planned, neither to ingratiate itself with certain countries nor much less to yield to foreign pressures.

Broadcast address to the nation, Santiago,
Sept. 11/The Washington Post, 9-12:(A)17.

Ronald Reagan
Former Governor of California (R)
2

It should never surprise us that whenever the United States withdraws its presence or its strong interest from any area, the Soviets are ready, willing and often able to exploit the situation. Can we believe that the Panama Canal is any exception?

Before Senate Separation of Powers
Subcommittee, Washington, Sept. 8/
Los Angeles Herald-Examiner, 9-8:(A)3.

3

[Arguing against the proposed new treaty which would gradually turn over control of the Panama Canal to Panama]: We're [the U.S.] turning one of the world's most important waterways over to a country no one can believe. How can a country of 1.7 million [people] guarantee it will remain open? ... Who knows how hostile [the Panamanian] administration will be? We know their relationship to Cuba. We know the Russians were there in July, offering to buy 50 million tons of sugar at double the world price. If they decide to throw in their lot with the Soviet Union, [then Russia will be] the influential power over this strategic waterway. Isn't confrontation with the Soviet Union what we've been trying to avoid? ... For 60 years we've made the Canal available for all the shipping of the world. Never for profit. Never amortized the original cost of the Canal. Why is that such a bad thing? What have we done that is so wrong?

Interview/Newsweek, 9-19:50.

Luis Reque
Former Executive Secretary, Inter-
American Commission on Human Rights
4

[On the OAS' including in its forthcoming agenda a topic dealing with human rights in Cuba]: The placing of this topic in the agenda of the forthcoming General Assembly ... is nothing but a cover-up for the grim brutality and savage repression that exist in the majority of the Latin-American countries. But what can we expect from an organization that has become a debating society, and from its General Secretariat that has degenerated into a social club where receptions and social gatherings have taken priority over the sufferings of thousands of political prisoners in the hemisphere?

Before American Ethical Union/
The Washington Post, 5-3:(A)18.

John J. Rhodes
United States Representative,
R–Arizona
5

I recognize the desire of Panama to control that [Panama] Canal. If I were a Panamanian, I probably would feel the same way. On the other hand, I don't think the people of the United States are unreasonable in feeling that, Number 1, this is a very important asset, not only to us, but to the world; and Number 2, some doubt, some fear that Panama cannot operate the Canal properly; and, Number 3, some fear that they can't defend it properly, that there might not only be incursions from without, but also subversion from within. It is not an easy situation to analyze or to evolve, but I would hope that, if the [proposed] treaty [which would gradually turn over control of the Canal to Panama] does not succeed, that the [U.S. Carter] Administration might look toward an initiative that would bring in the nations of the hemisphere in a combined effort to do something about this strife which we seem to have over the Canal.

TV-radio interview/"Meet the Press,"
National Broadcasting Company, 10-23.

WHAT THEY SAID IN 1977

Gordon Robertson
Secretary to the Canadian Cabinet
for Federal-Provincial Relations

1

Our country today is in grave peril; the secession of Quebec would shatter our dream and the reality of Canada stretching from sea to sea. At this time of crisis we must try to see our history through the eyes of French Canadians, or we cannot hope to understand their bitterness. If the United States was dedicated to the proposition that all men were created equal, French Canadians believe with equal fervor that Canada was founded on the understanding that two linguistic communities could live together with each respecting the rights, dignity and full existence of the other. A major part of our problem is that, while many French Canadians lived up to the underlying proposition in Quebec, where they had the majority, few English-speaking Canadians lived up to it where we had the majority . . . We also should remember that our challenge is not ours alone. It is the challenge of a diverse humanity crowded onto a small planet. Our two peoples in Canada are among the most fortunate in the world in wealth, education, cultural enrichment and traditions of personal freedom. French philosophical humanism and British Parliamentary democracy are among the great accomplishments of civilized man. If we fail — after 110 years of free self-government as one country — who can hope to succeed in solving this basic problem of the human condition?

At Dalhousie University, Halifax,
Nova Scotia/Los Angeles Times, 7-3:(6)6.

Bernard W. Rogers
General and Chief of Staff,
United States Army

2

[Supporting the proposed new treaties which would gradually turn over control of the Panama Canal to Panama]: I and the other Joint Chiefs of Staff believe the ratification of these treaties is in the best interests of our nation. We so recommended to our Commander-in-Chief . . . It is the use of the Canal which is important, not its ownership nor the control of the land through which it flows. That use, in my opinion, is best safeguarded by

a cooperative effort with a Panama which has a stake in the efficient and continuous operation of the Canal. As we debate the issue of ratification, we must start from where we are today, not where we were in 1903 or 1914, and we must deal with the realities of today's world, to include our current and future relationships with all Latin American countries. When the delusive myths and emotional non-issues are stripped away from this subject and the matter is reduced to the hard facts, I believe that most persons will tend to agree that ratification of the treaties is in our best interests.

Before Association of the United States Army,
Washington, Oct. 18/Vital Speeches, 12-15:138.

Carlos Romero (Barcelo)
Governor of Puerto Rico

3

[Saying his Commonwealth should become the 51st U.S. state]: We [Puerto Ricans] are disenfranchised American citizens. Our situation is an affront to the principles of American democracy and is a source of embarrassment in the United Nations as the United States is perennially accused of colonialism. Only by statehood will the United States prove that the great principles of democracy are still vibrant.

Before editors and publishers, Dorado, P.R.,
Oct. 10/The New York Times, 10-11:27.

4

In 1952, only 12.9 per cent of the Puerto Rican electorate voted for the statehood party. In the intervening quarter-century, however, the situation has been reversed dramatically. The statehood party consistently has increased its support with each election, and triumphed with 48 per cent of the vote in 1976. There should be no doubt in anyone's mind as to our residents' love for the ideals of American democratic government.

Before Los Angeles World Affairs Council,
Dec. 6/Los Angeles Herald-Examiner, 12-7:(A)9.

Dean Rusk
Professor of international law,
University of Georgia; Former
Secretary of State of the United States 1

[Defending the proposed new treaties which would gradually turn over control of the Panama Canal to Panama]: In the modern world, one nation cannot maintain a presence within another nation without the consent of the second nation. If the situation in Eastern Europe is different, the contrast merely emphasizes the general rule and provides no precedent for the United States. An attempt to maintain our position in the Panama Canal Zone on the basis of the 1903 treaty would be an act of force . . . If, God forbid, it should ever become necessary for a President and a Congress to take strong measures to keep the Canal functioning and safe, they would be in a far stronger position to do so under the treaties of 1977 than under the anachronistic treaty of 1903.

Before House International Relations
Committee, Washington, Sept. 14/
The New York Times, 9-15:(A)13.

Ramon Sanchez (Parodi)
Chief of Cuban diplomatic
mission in Washington 2

[On the reopening of U.S.-Cuban relations after 16 years]: These ideas [integrity, independence and sovereignty of all nations] have been gaining strength over the last centuries. They were expressed through their deeds by the American revolutionaries who, under the leadership of George Washington, fought the independence war of the United States of America . . . In our time, within a new historical, political and social context, Cuban revolutionaries led by [Premier] Fidel Castro, with the full support of the Cuban people, wage a struggle to place our country among the most advanced philosophical, political, economic and social trends in the world today . . .

Washington, Sept. 1/Los Angeles Times, 9-2:(1)10.

L. Ronald Scheman
Assistant Secretary for Management,
Organization of American States 3

The [U.S. trade] embargo [against Cuba] for all practical purposes is nonexistent . . . If anyone did any research, he would find that Cuba gets whatever it needs from U.S. companies operating abroad. [The boycott is] nonfunctional, unpractical and costing the American taxpayer money. We're not embargoing anything.

Interview/Los Angeles Herald-Examiner, 1-12:(A)3.

Howard K. Smith
News commentator,
American Broadcasting Company 4

After 18 years, [Cuban Premier Fidel] Castro's revolution is still an economic failure. Worker productivity is lower than it was when he took over. Cubans live on a bare, basic level – and even that Cuba can't pay for; Russia pays for it. Cuba can make it on her own only by ending her economic slavery to selling sugar, by diversifying and industrializing her economy. A trade partnership with the U.S. could meet that basic need faster and better . . . Removing Communism from Cuba by war is impossible – it would take years; we would lose every friend; the American people have no stomach for it. On the other hand, leaving things as they· are would only mean an increasing disbalance of power in this hemisphere against us. Only slow, prosaic, normal trade with Cuba, a Cuba we acknowledge as independent and equal, holds any promise of gradual lessening of frictions and avoiding the perils of some possible future warlike crisis between us.

Television broadcast/"ABC News Closeup:
Cuba – the Castro Generation,"
American Broadcasting Company, 3-4.

Adlai E. Stevenson
United States Senator, D–Illinois 5

[On the proposed new treaty which would gradually turn over control of the Panama Canal to Panama]: I support the treaty. Its purpose is not to relinquish [U.S.] control but to preserve access and guarantee Panamanian neutrality in perpetuity. Without it, the Canal

WHAT THEY SAID IN 1977

Zone would be an object of violence. Soviet and Cuban influence in the region would be increased and ours diminished.

U.S. News & World Report, 9-19:19.

Maxwell D. Taylor
General, United States Army (Ret.);
Former Chairman, Joint Chiefs of Staff   1

[Supporting proposed new treaties which would gradually turn over control of the Panama Canal to Panama]: Under the terms of these treaties, the U.S. and Panama would be bound in a partnership based on reciprocal self-interest, jointly committed to an efficient and unimpeded operation of the Canal. The local government would have an equal interest with us to restrain outbreaks of violence and lawlessness. A peaceful settlement of past differences should moderate the present anti-American bias, which has often made the country a recruiting base for perpetrators of violence and a sympathetic environment in which they may find shelter . . . In supporting these treaties, I am aware of certain risks which their adoption may entail . . . After weighing the pros and cons, I am convinced that the advantages of approval definitely outweigh the disadvantages.

Before Senate Foreign Relations
Committee, Washington, Oct. 10/
U.S. News & World Report, 10-24:27.

Strom Thurmond
United States Senator, R—South Carolina   2

[Criticizing the proposed new treaty which would gradually turn over control of the Panama Canal to Panama]: We cannot hope to deal effectively with other nations if we yield to blackmail. That is the only way to describe the threats of violence in Panama and in the Canal Zone and threats of sabotage to the Canal which treaty proponents are using as their chief argument for ratification.

U.S. News & World Report, 9-19:19.

3

[On the proposed new treaty which would gradually turn over control of the Panama

Canal to Panama]: If the Canal is given away, the entire economic and political structure of Panama, as an independent country, would be undermined. Rival factions within the Panamanian government would be tempted to take over the government by coup in order to control the Canal and its revenue. Moreover, Communists and leftists would seek to control the present government in order to make the Canal an instrument of Communist policy. Instead of stabilizing the situation in Panama, the new treaty would almost certainly destabilize it.

Nation's Business, October:62.

Omar Torrijos (Herrera)
Head of Government of Panama   4

[On Guatemala's breaking of relations with his country because of his support for the independence of the British colony of Belize, which Guatemala claims]: Yes, I have my hands in Belize. Someone has to help those people to free themselves. I know that [Guatemalan President Kjell] Laugerud is mad at me since he knows about this. But colonialism knows no frontiers. It is the same in Belize as it is in Panama.

To reporters/The Washington Post, 5-20:(A)20.

5

[On a proposed treaty which would gradually turn over control of the Panama Canal to his country]: Proof of my sincerity and honesty and political maturity is that as Head of State I have accepted the U.S. presence and control for 23 more years. I have never in my life dealt with people as hard as [U.S. negotiators Sol] Linowitz and [Ellsworth] Bunker. They fought for 1,440 square kilometers of the Zone like the Russians fought at Leningrad. Literally, we fought over every house in the Zone. I have great admiration for people who fight for things with dignity. Probably with other [U.S.] negotiators we [Panamanians] could have obtained more, but we would have fallen into the danger of obtaining illusory conquests that wouldn't have been backed by the American people. I know that the [Panamanian] leftists will be on me like a pack of dogs over the treaty. They are against it

(OMAR TORRIJOS [HERRERA])

because their goals were total liberation now, or death. In the U.S., those who are against the treaty simply lack knowledge of the situation. The fundamental part of the treaty is that we didn't have to lose 50,000 young Panamanians in a fight.

Interview, Panama City/Newsweek, 8-22:35.

1

[The Panama Canal] is as indefensible as a newborn baby. It cannot be defended against a large power, nor can it be defended against a single saboteur. The Canal was designed for peaceful transit of the world's merchant fleets, and it is militarily impossible to prevent a group of men — if they are ready to go — from damaging it. [U.S. Joint Chiefs of Staff Chairman] General [George] Brown told me that 100,000 troops could not guarantee its safety. Definitely the Canal cannot be defended. The only thing that would guarantee its safety is to tell all the countries of the world that they can transit freely and without discrimination 24 hours a day, 365 days a year. Then no power would want to attack.

Interview/U.S. News & World Report, 9-19:20.

2

[Supporting the proposed new treaty which would gradually turn over control of the Panama Canal from the U.S. to Panama]: Study the treaty for yourself; see that the Isthmus of Panama will remain under the protective umbrella of the Pentagon. Learn to know my people, and you will have more confidence in us. Study your geography and you will see that Panama is not just an isthmus; it's a nation. If the Americans are educated on these matters, their fears about Cuba and the Soviet Union [increasing their influence in the Canal area] will vanish. And another thing: Do you think that we are going to bring down the U.S. flag just in order to hoist another foreign flag? No, that would be the triumph of hope over experience — and our experience has been harsh.

Interview/U.S. News & World Report, 9-19:21.

3

The [Panama Canal] Zonians haven't realized they live without human rights now. They are a hybrid product and have developed their attitude from the colonial enclave. They are owned by the [U.S.-administered] Canal Company. I felt profound pity when I met several leaders of the Zone. We talked about many things, and I asked their opinion. One was honest and said, "General, we aren't used to being asked our opinion. Everything is decided for us." The Canal Zone system turns people into robots. All that will change, and I've told them so, but they don't want to believe me. The first thing which comes to their mind is that they are looking at a Communist in flesh and blood. I am a little less Communist than Franklin Roosevelt and John Kennedy and a lot less Communist than Abraham Lincoln. I am conservative in some things, progressive in others. I won't give the people a TV set, because they would all watch the soap operas and start living and acting just like them. I don't build roads all the time either, because then they would move and migrate to the cities . . . This is a revolutionary government in the sense that it is a government of change; but there is no blood, no revolution. I've never really agreed to the term "revolutionary" as part of our name, the revolutionary government. That is something history must qualify, not us . . . I like [Cuban Premier] Fidel [Castro] because he is able to say each night that all Cuban children got enough to eat. That is my wish for Panama — that every future chief of state can say the same thing. Many world leaders who criticize Fidel cannot say that.

Interview, Farallon, Panama/
Los Angeles Times, 9-28:(1)24.

4

[Advising the U.S. to ratify the proposed new treaty that would gradually turn over control of the Panama Canal to his country]: I have watched the American people move away from the ideas of Vietnam, the Bay of Pigs invasion of Cuba, intervention in the Dominican Republic. But if they now do an about-face on Panama, it should be remembered that, to

(OMAR TORRIJOS [HERRERA])

have a Vietnam situation, you don't need
Vietnamese.

U.S. News & World Report, 11-7:61.

Pierre Elliott Trudeau
Prime Minister of Canada

1

I'm afraid that the national will to exist as a
country is not very strong in Canada, that there
are all kinds of centrifugal forces, economic
discontents, regional discontents, social discontents which have caused the national will to
weaken over the past, I'd say, few decades . . . I
think Canadians were growing soft in their
desire to exist as a country. You know, in
historical terms we were on the way to becoming one of the freest, one of the most prosperous democracies in the world. But look
around. Talk to the people. Read the media.
Listen to the grumblings. Canadians aren't
happy with their fate . . . There's not a great
feeling of content in Canada, of achievement.

Interview/The Washington Post, 1-6:(A)10.

2

We have not yet . . . created a condition in
which French-speaking Canadians have felt they
were fully equal or could fully develop the
richness of the culture they had inherited. And
therein is the source of our central problem
today. That is why a small minority of the
people of Quebec feel they should leave Canada
and strike out in a country of their own. The
newly elected government of that province
asserts a policy that reflects that minority view
despite the fact that during the election campaign it sought a mandate for good government,
and not a mandate for the separation from
Canada. The accommodation of two vigorous
language groups has been, in varying fashion,
the policy of every Canadian government since
Confederation. The reason is clear. Within
Quebec, over 80 per cent of the population
speak French as their first or only language. In
Canada as a whole, nearly one-fifth of the
people speak no language but French. Thus,
from generation to generation, there has been
handed down the belief that a country could be
built in freedom and equality with two lan-

guages and a multitude of cultures. I am
confident it can be done. I say to you with all
the certainty I can command that Canada's
unity will not be fractured. Revisions will take
place. Accommodations will be made. We shall
succeed.

*Before U.S. Congress, Washington,
Feb. 22/Vital Speeches, 3-15:323.*

3

. . . the separatist movement of various
forms of ultra-nationalism have been existing in
Quebec for at least a couple of generations. The
separatist party itself was created as a political
party around 1968. It had two general elections
in the province where it tried to get elected on
a separatist plank . . . and it was very, very
roundly defeated. The election of '73 brought
the greatest majority to the Liberal Party in the
history of the province, because the separatist
party was campaigning on separatism. This time
[in the last election] they said, "We are not
going to campaign on separatism; we are going
to campaign on good government. We want to
provide an alternative to the tired government,"
and they insisted that separatism was not the
issue. And because of our two-party system,
people threw the government out and threw the
separatists in. So that is the explanation of the
assurances that we have that the people don't
want separatism. Whenever separatism was put
to them as a question, "Do you want a
separatist government?" they said no, and they
said no very roundly. But when the separatist
party said, "Well, we are not talking about
separatism; we won't have separatism 'unless
you have a referendum and you consent to it as
a special operation; elect us as an alternate
government," they were elected. It is based on
that. I have repeated the assurance, which I
think is confirmed by the election, that the
people don't want separatism. When given a
choice they rejected it.

*Tv-radio interview, Washington/"Meet the
Press," National Broadcasting Company, 2-27.*

4

[On why his country was among the first to
deal with mainland China, Communist Cuba
and North Vietnam]: Foreign policy requires

(PIERRE ELLIOTT TRUDEAU)

facing facts. Over one-fifth of the human race lives in the People's Republic of China. That goes for dealing with the Soviet Union, Rhodesia, Cuba and South Africa as well. By facing facts, you don't necessarily put your stamp of approval on another country's system or its injustices. We've expressed ourselves where it was appropriate. Canada supported UN sanctions against Rhodesia and helped get South Africa kicked out of the [British] Commonwealth.

Interview, Ottawa/People, 2-28:59.

1

We in Canada and you in the United States have learned through experience that diversity brings richness beyond measure in artistic achievement, in cultural accomplishment, in social enlightenment. Neither country has escaped the tensions which accompany social variety; but this fact, I think, makes us more understanding of difficulties elsewhere, and [makes] outsiders more willing to accept our experience as a credible model for their own social progress.

San Francisco Examiner & Chronicle,
4-17:(This World)2.

2

[On the separatist movement in Quebec Province] : Any political theory that says ethnic groups should be sovereign can only be regressive and destructive. The separatist philosophy is an untenable proposition in the modern world. If Quebec separated, a horrendous unraveling process would be under way. The one million English-speaking Canadians who live and work in Quebec province would then separate from the separatists. This cannot work in any other nation, either. Think of Yugoslavia with four ethnic groups, Czechoslovakia with two, African countries with two or three major ethnic tribal groups ... If Canada, with two principal ethnic groups can't hack it, imagine what could happen in the U.S.

Interview, Ottawa/Newsweek, 12-5:53.

3

There are many countries in the world with which Canada and Canadians engage in trade. We disagree with the ideology of many of them. Many of them have non-democratic systems, indeed probably many of them practice murder, terror and torture. [But] I do not think even the Tory opposition is suggesting that we should cut off trade with all the countries with which we disagree.

Before Parliament, Ottawa, Dec. 20/
The Dallas Times Herald, 12-21:(A)7.

Brady Tyson
Deputy leader of the United States
delegation to the United Nations
Human Rights Commission, Geneva

4

Our delegation would be less than candid and untrue to ourselves and our people if we did not express our profoundest regrets for the role some [U.S.] government officials, agencies and private groups played in the subversion of the previous, democratically elected Chilean government that was overthrown by the coup of September 11, 1973 ... The expression of regrets, however profound, cannot contribute significantly to the reduction of the suffering and terror that the people of Chile have experienced in the past two years.

Supporting a draft resolution condemning the
current Chilean government for human-rights violations,
Geneva, March 8/The Washington Post, 3-9:(A)1,9.

Cyrus R. Vance
Secretary of State of the United States

5

[Supporting the proposed new treaties which would gradually turn over control of the Panama Canal to Panama] : Panama is a small country. It would be all too easy for us to lash out, in impatience and frustration, to tell Panama and Latin America — and other countries around the world — that we intended to speak loudly and carry a big stick and to turn away from the treaties four [U.S.] Presidents have sought over so long a time. [But] I believe the American people want to live in peace with their neighbors ... want to be strong, but to use their strength with restraint ... want all peoples, everywhere. to have their own chance

WHAT THEY SAID IN 1977

to better themselves and to live in self-respect. And that is why I am convinced that, after the national debate they deserve, these treaties will be approved without reservations by the Senate, with the strong support of the American people.

Before Senate Foreign Relations Committee, Washington, Sept. 26/ The Washington Post, 9-27:(A)10.

Jorge Rafael Videla
President of Argentina

1

The paramount role which the armed forces have assumed at this historic moment consists of making precise — with the contributions of everyone — those basic common principles which will allow us to build a solid and stable democratic system. In this order of ideas, to the classical values of liberty, equality and justice which make up the essence of democracy, we must add a principle of vital importance in the modern world: security.

Clarin, Argentina, Jan. 30/ Nation's Business, December:57.

Lowell P. Weicker, Jr.
United States Senator, R—Connecticut

2

[Supporting the proposed new treaties which would gradually turn over control of the Panama Canal to Panama]: The United States is not meant to be a democratic rerun of the colonialism of European monarchs or the totalitarianism of Communist central committees. We are a free people in a free land. To wish for,

never mind negotiate, something less with other people and other lands, compromises America's greatest strength — its idealistic commitment to human freedom and national self-determination. Militarily, the treaties pass muster in that for an indefinite period the United States has the permanent right to defend the neutrality of the Canal from any threat — with U.S. warships having the permanent right to transit the Canal without conditions.

News conference, New York, Aug. 29/ The New York Times, 8-30:3.

Andrew Young
United States Ambassador/Permanent Representative to the United Nations

3

We [the U.S.] have learned that we cannot solve world problems or those of the [Western] Hemisphere, and that "made in U.S.A." does not mean it will necessarily work in Latin America.

Before Economic Commission for Latin America, Guatemala City, May 3/ The New York Times, 5-4:(A)4.

4

Because the United States dealt with Panama [in negotiating a new Canal treaty], this giant of a nation showed the world that it is not throwing its weight around like it did in Vietnam, but is willing to search for the paths of justice.

San Francisco Examiner & Chronicle, 9-18:(This World)2.

Zulfikar Ali Bhutto
Prime Minister of Pakistan
1

The United States presence in Asia — and do not think I mean military presence — could be of a positive nature. Withdrawal of the U.S. economic, technological, political, scientific and cultural presence would not be good for the equilibrium of Asia. Let us not forget the fact, which sometimes is overlooked in America, that the United States is partially an Asian power because of the Pacific Ocean. Your own west coast is ever increasing in importance. The same waters that wash San Francisco wash the coast of China and Japan. So, in that sense, you are a Pacific power and have an Asian responsibility.

Interview, Rawalpindi/
U.S. News & World Report, 3-14:71.

2

[The U.S. and Pakistan] are allies in the sense that Pakistan has been a friend and an ally of the United States for almost a generation. But the alliance has been one-sided. We are not treated as well as many countries which are not allies, or sometimes not even friendly to the United States. We are members of CENTO, and we have two bilateral military agreements under which we are supposed to get military assistance from the U.S. without payment, the same as other allies. But we have to buy every little thing, even a screw driver, cash down. Not only that, the United States objects to certain armaments being supplied to us because they might antagonize India. That's an unlikely story, because India's military position is well known, as is the support and assistance India gets from the Soviet Union. We have taken on commitments on the side of the United States; we have made military commitments which still exist. But the military assistance which we were supposed to receive is now being given to states which are not America's allies, which are even non-aligned. They are getting military equipment on credit terms which we are denied.

Interview, Rawalpindi/
U.S. News & World Report, 3-14:72.

Shirley Temple Black
Former United States Ambassador to Ghana; Former U.S. delegate to the United Nations
3

I need not remind Washington that it faces formidable unfinished business in the People's Republic of [mainland] China. New developments and old ... enmities magnify the situation. Preoccupation with the rigidities of the past often obscures both problems and opportunities of the present ... If non-secrecy and public participation are indeed the new spirit of Washington, I detect less than a unified approach on matters clearly related to China.... We seem to be losing U.S. initiatives ... In effect, the conditions for our action have been stipulated by China. This is a poor way to play international chess ... U.S. diplomatic recognition of China today is ill-timed. It sets the stage for miscalculations by the Soviet Union, produces only marginal incremental values for the U.S., and leaves unanswered ... the old hostilities of the Korean Peninsula.

Before Commonwealth Club, San Francisco,
May 13/The Christian Science Monitor, 9-14:13.

Harold Brown
Secretary of Defense of the United States
4

[On the planned withdrawal of U.S. ground troops from South Korea]: I assure you that this carefully planned action definitely will not diminish our commitment to South Korea's

WHAT THEY SAID IN 1977

(HAROLD BROWN)

security ... I believe that withdrawals of U.S. ground combat forces from Korea can be safely accomplished over the period of four to five years under the conditions we have publicly declared, namely, the maintenance of U.S. air and logistic support, continued strengthening of South Korean military forces and the full commitment of the United States to the security of Korea.

Before National Press Club, Washington,
May 25/Los Angeles Times, 5-26:(1)22.

1

[On the planned withdrawal of U.S. troops from South Korea] : The experience always has been that if you ask the people in Korea whether they think American ground forces, which have been there more than 25 years, should remain there indefinitely, the answer by and large is, "No, but they shouldn't be withdrawn now." Then if you ask when the troops should be withdrawn, the answer is, "Five years from now." It's five years from now whenever you ask the question. Therefore, it seemed to the Administration — and it seems to me — that you have to make plans for the withdrawal of ground-combat forces, and ask what has to be done to fill in. I think the Korean economy is such, and the Korean military capability is such, that over this period of four to five years the military structure can be built up in such a way as to continue to provide deterrence and defense. And, once we do that, the big advantage of having done it is that you're more stable then than you are now.

Interview, Washington/
U.S. News & World Report, 9-5:23.

Zbigniew Brzezinski
Assistant to President of
the United States Jimmy Carter
for National Security Affairs

2

[On the U.S. plan to withdraw its ground forces from South Korea] : I think it is noteworthy ... that South Korea has a population twice that of North Korea and a remarkably successful economy, a military establishment which is very impressive, troops which have performed well — most recently in the Vietnam

war. So one can certainly take another look at the situation in Korea today in contrast to that which prevailed in the 1950s when the present military arrangements were shaped. South Korea then was impoverished, devastated, recently overrun, and so forth. It seems to me that responsible statesmanship entails the requisite of periodically looking at a situation and asking ourselves: "What has changed? If so, what adjustments do you make?" It doesn't mean making snap decisions, altering arrangements capriciously. But it does mean making judgments as to what is possible which was not possible in the past.

Interview, Washington/
U.S. News & World Report, 5-30:36.

3

Insofar as the Chinese-Soviet relationship is concerned, predictions pertaining to relationships between states that are controlled by highly centralized leaderships tend to be very dangerous. But it does appear that the cumulative effect of historical forces, of geographical propinquity, of ideological disagreement, indicates that the conflict will continue — and that China and the Soviet Union will not return to the kind of relationship they had in the past ...

Interview, Washington/
U.S. News & World Report, 5-30:36.

4

No architecture for a more stable and just world order would be complete without taking into account the proper role of the People's Republic of [mainland] China. We recognize not only that peace in East and Southeast Asia depends upon a constructive Sino-American relationship, but also that China can help immensely in maintaining a global equilibrium as well. Mutual interest, not sentiment, brought our two countries closer together. We must continue working to make our relationship closer still. Normalization of that relationship is necessary, but, even short of it, both sides should find it useful to develop a closer consultative relationship, so that each side adequately understands and takes into account the legitimate global concerns of the other.

Before Trilateral Commission, Bonn, West Germany,
Oct. 25/The Washington Post, 11-1:(A)19.

William F. Buckley, Jr.
American political columnist;
Editor, "National Review" 1

[On the possibility of the U.S. severing ties with Taiwan in order to improve relations with mainland China]: Who put the fox in the American bosom to give up Taiwan? . . . You would think that American leaders have been baptizied with a pledge to Chinese irredentism . . . Let us reaffirm our determination to keep Taiwan free and show the wretched people on the other side of the strait that it is possible to remain free and prosperous without the degradation of the human soul.

At conference on U.S.-China relations,
Washington/The Christian Science Monitor, 1-17:16.

George Bush
Former Chief, United States Liaison
Office in Peking; Former Director of
Central Intelligence of the United States 2

My own view is that it's in our national interest to have normalized relations with [mainland] China as soon as possible. Our systems are enormously different — and every time I go back there, I come back respectful in many ways for the job they've done, but grateful for the freedoms we have in this country. I also come back impressed that we have many things in common with China, not the least of which is our strategic interests vis-a-vis the Soviet Union. So I think we should do whatever we can through quiet diplomacy to seek improved relations with China. China should never be slighted in our foreign policy. However, I don't think it is in the interest of the United States to abrogate our mutual-defense treaty with Taiwan without plenty of assurances and safeguards that the eventual solution to the Taiwan problem will be a peaceful one.

Interview/U.S. News & World Report, 11-14:34.

Robert C. Byrd
United States Senator, D–West Virginia 3

[Saying the U.S. should not cut off military aid to South Korea if that country refuses to cooperate in the investigation of industrialist Tongsun Park, who is implicated in a Washington political scandal]: The stability of South Korea is important to that whole area and important to ourselves, and that stability can be best enhanced by continuing cooperation and mutual understanding between the United States government and the South Korean government. You cut off military aid to South Korea — and we still don't get Tongsun Park — what have we done? I don't think we should let one situation get in the way of the other.

News conference, Washington, Oct. 29/
The Washington Post, 10-30:(A)3.

Jimmy Carter
President of the United States 4

I can't say what my position would be now in future economic relationships with Vietnam. I think that could only be concluded after we continue with negotiations to see what their attitude might be toward us. My own natural inclination is to have normal diplomatic relationships with all countries in the world . . . I don't know what the motivations of the Vietnamese might be. I think part of the motivation might be to be treated along with other nations in the economic assistance from our country and in trade and development of their fairly substantial natural resources, including oil. Other considerations might be political in nature. They might very well want to balance their friendship with us with their friendship for the Soviet Union and not be completely dependent upon the Soviet Union. That's just a guess on my part. But I'm willing to negotiate in good faith. But as far as describing what our economic relationship might be with Vietnam in the future, after the relationships are established, I just couldn't do that now. . . . we went to Vietnam without any desire to capture territory or to impose American will on other people. We went there to defend the freedom of the South Vietnamese, and I don't feel that we ought to apologize or to castigate ourselves or to assume the status of culpability. Now, I'm willing to face the future without reference to the past. And that's what the Vietnamese leaders have proposed. And if normalization of relationships there evolves trade, normal aid processes, then I would respond well. But I don't feel that we have, that we owe, a debt nor

WHAT THEY SAID IN 1977

(JIMMY CARTER)

that we should be forced to pay reparations . . .

News conference, Washington, March 24/
The New York Times, 5-25:(A)10.

1

Whatever our [U.S.] goals might be . . . throughout the world, we will never again bypass the tremendous, sound judgment of the Japanese people before we make a decision that is of importance to our people.

Los Angeles Times, 4-3:(7)2.

2

We have espoused, and I have renewed my commitment to, the . . . [U.S.-mainland Chinese] Shanghai Communique, which says that there's just one China — we didn't say which one, and neither did anyone else — and we have moved, I think, to strengthen our ties with the People's Republic of China . . . The one obstacle — major obstacle — is the relationship we've always had with Taiwan. We don't want to see the Taiwanese people punished or attacked. And if we can resolve that major difficulty I would move expeditiously to normalizing relationships with [mainland] China. But I can't put a time limit on it.

News conference, Washington, May 12/
The New York Times, 5-13:(A)12.

3

[On his plan for withdrawal of U.S. ground forces from South Korea]: The essence of the question is, is our country committed on a permanent basis to keep troops in South Korea, even if they are not needed, to maintain the stability of that peninsula. I think it's accurate to say that the time has come for a very careful, very orderly withdrawal, over a period of four or five years, of ground troops, leaving intact an adequate degree of strength in the Republic of [South] Korea to withstand any foreseeable attack; and making it clear to the North Koreans, the Chinese, the Soviets, that our commitment to South Korea is undeviating and is staunch. We will leave there adequate intelligence forces, observation forces, air forces, naval forces, and a firm, open commitment to our defense treaty so there need be no doubt about potential adversaries concerning our support of South Korea . . . South Korea, because of their own incentive and deep dedication to progress, now has one of the most strong economies in the world. Their growth rate last year in real terms was 15 per cent. They have massive, very healthy industry in steel, ship-building, electronics, chemical industries, to make it possible for them to go into a position of defending themselves.

News conference, Washington, May 26/
The New York Times, 5-27:(A)10.

Frederick Chen
Vice Minister of Foreign Affairs of the Republic of (Nationalist) China

4

[On U.S.-Taiwan relations]: Basically, we have a fine substantial relationship, but there are some aspects which are absent. I cannot describe our relationship as a warm or intimate one. There are few consultations at a high level following the U.S. intention to improve its relationship with Peking.

The Christian Science Monitor, 8-9:(B)10.

John C. Culver
United States Senator, D—Iowa

5

We have had United States ground forces in Korea now for some 25 years. There never has been a determination to leave them there in perpetuity. U.S. policy always has been to assist in the development of an indigenous South Korean military capability that would insure their own security and maintain a credible deterrent and balance in the area. So I believe now is an appropriate time to phase out the redundant American ground presence there. Of course, any planned withdrawals would be carried out prudently, with appropriate consultation, over four to five years, and give us more global troop flexibility. I might add that this is not a new policy — we withdrew one division in 1970-71.

Interview/U.S. News & World Report, 6-20:27.

Morarji R. Desai
Prime Minister of India

6

[On his recent election victory defeating Indira Gandhi as Prime Minister]: I am more

288

(MORARJI R. DESAI)

humble than before, because it is a tremendous task which has to be fulfilled and it is only God who can enable us to fulfill it. What has taken place must convince the world that democracy is basic to the culture of this country. It was always thought that democracy was foreign to us and given only by the British. That is wrong; we had democracy in this country before Greece. It is so ingrained that it asserts itself in time of crisis and it has asserted itself now.

Interview, New Delhi/Time, 4-4:34.

1

The foreign policy of India has always been non-alignment. We [the new government] also believe in non-alignment, but it must be done without fear and we must not lean to one side or another. There is a feeling amongst the people that we are leaning toward Soviet Russia. This sort of thing should not happen. For example, I believe that [mainland] China and Russia are irreconcilable, yet we would like to have equal relations with both of them. The same applies to the United States.

Interview, New Delhi/Newsweek, 4-4:36.

2

Our relations will be the same with all. We will have no special relations with one country. If Russia objects to that, it is free to remove [its treaty with India]. We look forward to better relations with our neighbors such as Pakistan, not by pampering them, but by equality. We have no intention of annoying our neighbors, and we will try to avoid hurting their feelings; but we will not do anything at the point of a gun or blackmail.

Interview, New Delhi/Time, 4-4:34.

3

Population by itself is not a problem [for India]. If means of production are supplied to every person, then population will be an asset because man produces much more than he requires. And, therefore, population would be no problem. England is far more densely populated and so is Japan. And yet they are prosperous. Most of the countries except the United States and Soviet Russia, which have a very large area, are populated far more densely.

But for us it is a problem because prosperity and means of production are not available for everybody.

San Francisco Examiner & Chronicle,
7-24:(This World)2.

Pham Van Dong
Premier of Vietnam

4

We fought for 30 years to obtain our independence. That is what we understand as the rights of man ... the right of every man to a dignified, free life, and to participate with all his strength in the common task.

News conference, Paris, April 28/
Los Angeles Herald-Examiner, 4-29:(A)4.

Billy Lee Evans
United States Representative,
D–Georgia

5

[On charges of human-rights suppression in South Korea]: I believe that a country could not develop [as South Korea has] if there was a great deprivation of human rights. I see a free people here. While there may be some problems of human rights, they're not different from the problems of civil rights that we have had in the United States.

News conference, Seoul/
Los Angeles Times, 5-8:(5)3.

John K. Fairbank
Professor emeritus of Chinese
history, Harvard University

6

I think it's very desirable that we [the U.S.] move toward normalization of relations with Peking ... The State Department has made it perfectly plain that normalization is the only feasible approach and the question is how to work it out. I would be dismayed if [U.S. President] Carter departed from the normalization aim. If it is left on the back burner too long we might see a shift in Chinese-Soviet relations. We can't count on their always being enemies. The Russian-Chinese record is one of considerable peace. They have very seldom fought each other.

At Center for the Study of
Democratic Institutions, Santa Barbara,
Calif./World Issues, April-May:4.

WHAT THEY SAID IN 1977

(JOHN K. FAIRBANK)

1

Taiwan, despite appearances, is not seeking the "independence" that [U.S.] President Carter once offhandedly ascribed to it. It is not a country separate from [mainland] China. Its government claims to be the rightful government of *all* China. Americans who respond to Taipei's pleas for support seem not to recognize what they are asked to do — namely, back one side in an ongoing Chinese civil war.

San Francisco Examiner & Chronicle,
7-31:(This World)2.

Hiram L. Fong
Former United States Senator, R—Hawaii

2

[Saying the U.S. should improve relations with mainland China but should not rush into recognition yet]: The problem which we have to understand and consider is: What has America to gain at this time to change the status quo? I have said when I first came back from China to leave everything alone. Let time solve it. Maybe there will be a lessening of the totalitarian rule in China. Maybe there'll be a little more of a compromise from Taiwan. Who knows? But let time make that change.

Interview, Honolulu/Los Angeles Times, 10-23:(1)4.

Gerald R. Ford
Former President of the United States

3

In the case of Vietnam, duplicity has been carried out since January of 1973, when that country's leadership said they had no more information about our missing-in-action. Then, over a period of months, they dribble out names. They're just lying to us. They had that information a long time ago. They're offering that kind of information as bait for us to give them recognition, economic aid and assistance. I just think it would be dead wrong to give them diplomatic recognition now.

Interview/U.S. News & World Report, 7-4:22.

Takeo Fukuda
Prime Minister of Japan

4

When the United States withdrew from Vietnam, all the people of Asia feared there might be a domino phenomenon of instability.

Fortunately, this did not happen, and we now have a certain degree of stability. But there could be a new worry in Asia about instability if the U.S. Administration were suddenly to start on a completely new policy. All the Asian nations — collectively and individually — are very deeply concerned about what attitudes the United States will take toward Asia . . . Many Asian nations have commitments or agreements with the United States. The Philippines and Republic of [South] Korea are the only countries where military troops are physically present. But the United States has defense or other agreements with many other countries. I think the key thing will be the U.S. to give assurances to all the Asian countries that America will honor these commitments. At the same time, Asians want very much for the United States to show interest in promoting the economic dimension.

Interview, Tokyo/
U.S. News & World Report, 3-28:76,77.

5

Always before in history, economic giants have become military powers. Japan, however, has resolved not to select the path toward military power. Even though Japan has the ability to create its own nuclear weapons, it has refused to do so . . . Japan's existence threatens no other country either militarily or in any other way. Our power will be used to build peace and prosperity.

Manila, Philippines, Aug. 18/
Los Angeles Times, 8-19:(1)10.

Indira Gandhi
Prime Minister of India

6

[On the restrictions she imposed during the current state of emergency in her country]: We did not want to cause hardship to anyone. But no government would have tolerated the threats, the violence, the assault on democracy that we faced . . . The opposition parties have taken a path of disintegration and disunity. What do they have in common except that they are personally against me and my government? . . . During its 90 years, the Congress Party first helped India achieve independence, and then progress. India has become strong —

economically, militarily and otherwise. Now we want to make this a beautiful nation . . . Democracy has been, is and will remain in India. Even after the [forthcoming] elections, people will have the freedom to talk and act in a democratic manner, though not to assault democracy itself.

Re-election campaign address, New Delhi, Feb. 5/The New York Times, 2-6:(1)1,8.

1

[Announcing her resignation after the defeat of her party in the recent national election]: The collective judgment of the people must be respected. My colleagues and I accept their verdict unreservedly and in a spirit of humility. Elections are part of the democratic process to which we are deeply committed. I have always said, and I do believe, that the winning or losing of an election is less important than the strengthening of our country and insuring a better life for our people. I give my good wishes to the new government that will be formed. I hope that the secular, socialist and democratic foundations of India will be reinforced. The Congress Party and I are ready to give constructive cooperation in the common tasks that face our nation. We are proud of our great country. As I take leave of you as Prime Minister, I should like to express my deep gratitude to my colleagues, to my party and to the millions of men, women and children who have given me their trust, cooperation and even affection over the years. My love and concern for the welfare of every section of the people remain unchanged. Since childhood, my aim has been to serve the people to the limit of my endurance. This I shall continue to do. My good wishes to you now and always.

Address to the nation, New Delhi, March 22/ The New York Times, 3-23:(A)12.

Indira Gandhi
Former Prime Minister of India

2

After the central government [declared the state of emergency in 1975], it was the states that [enforced it], and maybe they did some things that weren't right. They did arrest people

whom they shouldn't have. It was an exceptional situation. People did suffer, and we've said we're sorry that they suffered. Maybe it could have been better managed. But something had to be done to stop this kind of agitation at the time of very great economic crisis and shortages. It was like a wartime situation. Maybe it went on too long, but during that time we pulled the nation up so that India was never stronger politically or economically than it was in these last few years, whether it's foreign exchange, production, exports, food or general discipline. And this [current, recently elected] government wouldn't have lasted a month if we hadn't left the country in such a good situation. Out of 30 years [of independence], for only a year and a half we didn't have open debate. And we had more of it than necessary all the other years.

Interview/Time, 9-12:30.

E. J. (Jake) Garn
United States Senator, R–Utah

3

We've got to get away from the fallacy that either the People's Republic of China on the mainland or the Republic of China on Taiwan is the only government of China. Both ultimately will have to recognize the existence of two Chinas. I think that is going to have to come. We will have to be tougher to make both sides accept the facts of life — that they must mutually coexist and that we are not going to pick one over the other as the only legitimate government of all of China. If we stimulate that idea and if we are tougher about supporting it, maybe we ultimately can solve the China problem that way.

Interview/U.S. News & World Report, 8-29:28.

Muhammad Ghazali
Minister of Home Affairs of Malaysia

4

What do we [in Southeast Asia] really want [from the U.S.]? We don't expect nor want another SEATO military alliance, a major American military presence, because we do not expect an invasion. Our struggles are small ones, internal ones. What is needed to fight this is to build our economies, develop our countries.

WHAT THEY SAID IN 1977

(MUHAMMAD GHAZALI)

That's what we need your help for. Our insurgencies we can handle with cooperative arrangements among ourselves.

Denpasar, Indonesia/
The New York Times, 6-22:(A)4.

Robert F. Goheen
United States Ambassador to India   *1*

Whether you look at it in geographical terms, in military terms or in economic terms, India and Pakistan really aren't competitors any more, so that the game we played for many years of trying to balance one off against the other, greatly influenced by concern about Russia — that's a dead game.

Interview, New Delhi, Sept. 26/
The New York Times, 9-27:13.

Barry M. Goldwater
United States Senator, R—Arizona   *2*

The [U.S. Carter] Administration's obvious desire to normalize relations with Communist China at the earliest possible moment is what sustains Peking in the belief that we will ultimately sacrifice the Republic of [Nationalist] China and abrogate our long-held commitments to the government on Taiwan ... This is perhaps the first area in the world where the Administration should put on the brakes and curb its feverish haste.

Before the Senate, Washington, July 29/
The Washington Post, 7-30:(A)5.

Richard Holbrooke
Assistant Secretary for East Asia
and Pacific Affairs, Department
of State of the United States   *3*

Based on all the evidence available to us, we have concluded that Cambodian authorities have flagrantly and systematically violated the most basic human rights. They have ordered or permitted extensive killings; forcibly relocated the urban population; brutally treated supporters of the previous government; and suppressed personal and political freedoms.

Before House International Relations
subcommittee, Washington, July 26/
The New York Times, 7-27:(A)3.

Hong Sung Chick
Professor of sociology,
Korea University   *4*

Religion prospers when life is uncertain, and Koreans for centuries have led an uncertain life. There was the Yi dynasty collapse in 1910, Japanese colonization, the collapse of colonization in 1945, and then the Korean war showed again how power could easily collapse. The student uprising in 1960 toppled the government of Syngman Rhee, the coup of 1961 brought Park [Chung Hee] to power, and there were all sorts of economic difficulties and threats of another war from the North. Now there is the withdrawal of U.S. ground forces. All of these elements make Koreans feel the future is precarious and naturally they look for security somewhere.

Los Angeles Times, 8-19:(7)1.

Hua Kuo-feng
Chairman, Communist Party of China   *5*

We are determined to liberate.Taiwan. When and how is entirely China's internal affair, which brooks no foreign interference whatsoever.

At Communist Party Congress/
Los Angeles Herald-Examiner, 8-23:(A)2.

6

All attempts by class enemies at home and abroad to make our Party change its Marxist-Leninist line, which was formulated by [the late] Chairman Mao, are no more than reactionary daydreaming.

San Francisco Examiner & Chronicle,
9-18:(This World)2.

7

A new leap forward in China's national economy is taking shape ... The national economic plan for 1977 will be fulfilled successfully or over-fulfilled ... There will still be difficulties of one kind or another on our road of advance, but we are convinced that no difficulties can block us Chinese people from marching toward our set goal, for we have a correct line, we have a great Party, a great army and a great people fighting in unity, and we enjoy extensive international support.

At banquet, Peking, Sept. 30/
Los Angeles Times, 10-1:(1)12.

Huang Hua
Foreign Minister of the People's
Republic of (mainland) China

1

The U.S. does not have the strength to deter the resolution of the Chinese people to liberate Taiwan. This does not mean that American atomic bombs cannot be dropped on Peking, or that American airplanes, guns and tanks are all useless scrap. It is rather that the U.S. government cannot manipulate such a crisis that might lead to war, and the American people will not allow it to do so . . . We dare say that, in fact, to the United States, although the [U.S.-Taiwan defense] treaty is an obligation, the United States does not regard it as a responsibility. Why is it that the U.S. would not assume the responsibility? When the Chinese people deem the time to be ripe to liberate Taiwan by force, would the American people really have the resolve to live or perish with the Chiang dynasty and share the fate of the island of Taiwan? Go read American history: We have not seen an instance in which the United States has had such resolve and courage to sacrifice for others. This has been determined by the intrinsic character of the bourgeoisie. That is why we dare to conclude that the United States is a paper tiger.

Address in preparation for Chinese
Communist Party Congress, Peking, July 30/
Los Angeles Herald-Examiner, 1-11('78):(A)16.

Edward M. Kennedy
United States Senator, D—Massachusetts

2

We must end our diplomatic presence [in Taiwan], our defense treaty and our formal diplomatic relations with the island . . . We should continue to ensure that Taiwan has access to supplies needed for self-defense. [And] we should encourage the [mainland] Chinese to indicate unilaterally that they will be patient and will continue to prefer peaceful means of reunification with Taiwan. The Chinese, in turn, should be expected to be sensitive to our interests and concerns. [This means that mainland China would] not . . . oppose reasonable steps by the United States to provide for a prosperous and peaceful Taiwan.

Before Boston World Affairs Council,
Aug. 15/The WAshington Post, 8-16:(A)1,13.

Khieu Samphan
President of Cambodia

3

[Saying Cambodians now have enough to eat and that agricultural production is up]: Have these achievements been made possible by machines? No. We have no machines. We do everything by mainly relying on the strength of our people. Though barehanded, they can do everything . . . The cattle and buffalo are our closest comrades-in-arms in the nation-building campaign. If our cattle work hard, we can build our country rapidly . . . Our children do not play with toy cars, toy boats or toy guns. They are happy with driving sparrows away from the crops, tending cattle and buffalo, collecting natural fertilizer and helping to build dams and embankments and dig reservoirs and ditches.

On second anniversary of Communist
victory in Cambodia, April 15/
The New York Times, 4-19:10.

Henry A. Kissinger
Former Secretary of State
of the United States

4

[On Vietnam's demands for U.S. aid]: Among the many claims on American resources, I would put those of Vietnam in alphabetical order.

Before Chamber of Commerce of the
United States, May 3/Newsweek, 5-16:47.

Nguyen Cao Ky
Exiled former Premier and
former Vice President
of South Vietnam

5

[Arguing against U.S. aid to now-Communist Vietnam]: Aid to underdeveloped countries is good, but aid to Communists — that's something to watch carefully. Giving them aid will help them build a new strength, and once they are strong they will go after other Asian countries.

Newsweek, 4-11:14A

Lee Kuan Yew
Prime Minister of Singapore

6

We must hope that in the process of rehabilitation, the Vietnamese will discover — as indeed there are signs that they are discovering — how much easier it is to destroy than to build. And the more they rebuild, the more they become linked with sources of development capital like the World Bank and the Asian Development Bank, which must require minimum standards of peaceful and cooperative conduct. Therefore, if a cycle is established in which Vietnam gets more credits, more help from Western sources for her reconstruction, the desire to rebuild and develop could make her behave in a more rational and peaceful way than if she were making little progress in peaceful reconstruction of the economies both in the North and South.

Interview, Washington/
U.S. News & World Report, 10-31:44.

Li Hsien-nien
Vice Premier of the People's
Republic of (mainland) China 1

To realize the normalization of relations between China and the United States, the U.S. government must fulfill the following: severance of diplomatic relations with the [Nationalist Chinese Premier] Chiang clique in Taiwan; withdrawal of all U.S. forces and military installations from Taiwan and the Taiwan Strait; and abrogation of its mutual security treaty with the Chiang clique – and none of the three can be dispensed with.

To former U.S. Naval Operations
Chief Elmo Zumwalt, Peking, July 4/
The Dallas Times Herald, 8-21:(E)1.

Mike Mansfield
United States Ambassador to Japan 2

[U.S.-Japanese relations] must be based upon equality, mutual understanding and mutual tolerance. There is no junior partner in the relationship between our two countries. We meet as equals and we will continue to meet as equals.

News conference, Tokyo, June 15/
Los Angeles Times, 6-16:(1)22.

3

[On the U.S. plan to withdraw its ground troops from South Korea]: It was not a sudden reduction. It was started by [then-U.S.

President Richard] Nixon in 1969 when he withdrew the 7th Division and reduced the forces in Korea from 60,000 to 40,000. The Koreans were told that this reduction would be continued in the years ahead ... South Korea, with a population more than twice that of North Korea, with a booming economy, with a self-sufficiency one has to see to believe, is in a position to make up for the reduction through revving up of its own armaments industry, plus sales and transfers by us over the four-to-five-year period involved.

Interview, Tokyo/Los Angeles Times, 12-17:(3)16.

Ferdinand E. Marcos
President of the Philippines 4

[Saying an end to martial law in his country depends on U.S. policies]: [U.S. President Carter] can assure us that we will be defended if we are attacked and that we don't need to spend too much money on the self-reliance defense project, that we can spend it on economic development, that we will be helped in our efforts to rectify the injustices committed by the American government against our products like mahogany and coconut oil ... The [U.S.] government has of course not taken any position [on the martial law issue], although we presume that in view of the continued good relations between our two countries they understand that this is a phase, a transition, that the basic idea of democracy has been maintained.

Interview, Manila, Feb. 12/
The New York Times, 2-13:(1)11.

5

[On U.S. policies in Asia]: ... the United States has after Vietnam, of course, wanted to forget all about Southeast Asia, a bad dream. And you remember detente, which practically dismembered the Southeast Asia Treaty Organization. And then you pulled out of Thailand. Now all of these, plus your changing relations with Japan. I say changing because you have also been reassessing and reviewing your military arrangements with Japan, Okinawa and the rest of your other bases, including bases on the mainland itself.

Interview/The New York Times, 2-24:10.

(FERDINAND E. MARCOS)

1

The nature of the American presence in Asia is something for the Americans to decide. But our situation here in Asia is dependent upon the balance, both psychologically and militarily. This recognizes the presence of the U.S. in the Western Pacific.

Interview, Manila/
U.S. News & World Report, 7-18:53.

Chalid Mawardi
Deputy secretary general, United
Development Party of Indonesia

2

There is no longer any rule of law in this country for the people. There is only law for the rich man or the government or official. This is what we are fighting for — not for an Islamic state but for a state where the people come first.

The New York Times, 6-19:(1)9.

George S. McGovern
United States Senator, D—South Dakota

3

I believe it is time for a complete reappraisal of the U.S. diplomatic policy toward Korea. U.S. policy has been based on the premise that there is no serious possibility for negotiations with North Korea and that the military confrontation between North and South Korea, along with some U.S. military presence, must remain for the foreseeable future. In an era of detente, in which the U.S. carries on negotiations on a wide range of issues with the Soviet Union, [mainland] China, Cuba and Vietnam, it is a strange anomaly that, 23 years after the abortive Geneva Conference on Korea, there have been negotiations between the U.S. and North Korea for a resolution of the Korean conflict.

At Conference of Japanese and
U.S. Parliamentarians, Washington, September/
The Christian Science Monitor, 10-12:35.

Takeo Miki
Former Prime Minister of Japan

4

... Japan's remarkable economic growth in the postwar years has broadened the base of effective participation in, and support for, the democratic process. Widely shared prosperity has created an electorate that is overwhelmingly middle class in its interests and values. According to one public-opinion poll, over 90 per cent of all Japanese consider themselves members of the middle class, and 60 per cent place themselves in the middle stratum of the middle class. It is inconceivable to me that totalitarianism, whether from the extreme left or the extreme right, could again capture the minds of a people who now have great stakes in the rights and freedoms — and the affluence — democracy has brought them.

Before Commonwealth Club, San Francisco,
June 10/Vital Speeches, 8-15:660.

Daniel P. Moynihan
United States Senator, D—New York

5

While the second most populous nation in the world [India] was a democracy, the United States had an enormous ideological interest in the prosperity and the success of that country. We want the world to know that democracies do well. So they've given up the one claim they had on us. When India ceased to be a democracy, our actual interest there just plummeted. I mean, what does it export but communicable disease?

Interview/Playboy, March:78.

6

[On the defeat of Indian Prime Minister Indira Gandhi, and her emergency powers, in the recent national election]: Nothing that will happen in Washington this year will be as important to America as what happened in New Delhi in the last few days. Political democracy has reasserted its claim on the future of the world. Civil liberties were on their way to becoming a curious regional custom of the peoples of the North Atlantic. Now, once again, these liberties can claim to be a belief of world-wide validity and strength.

Before the Senate, Washington, March 22/
The New York Times, 3-23:(A)12.

Robert Muldoon
Prime Minister of New Zealand

7

Economically, our ties with Britain and Europe are still important. But we are now

295

(ROBERT MULDOON)

primarily a Pacific country — no longer a transplanted England, but a hybrid. Increasingly we look to the Pacific and to America, rather than to Britain and Europe.

Honolulu, Hawaii/The
Christian Science Monitor, 12-7:28.

Jayaprakash Narayan
Indian political leader
1

The conditions of the poor [in India] have deteriorated [under Prime Minister Indira Gandhi's government]. Corruption has increased because there is no check on the arbitrary powers exercised by those in office, from ministers to petty officials. Nothing has been done to remodel the educational system in keeping with the country's needs. Administrative powers and decision-making are increasingly monopolized by a small ruling group ... The ruling Congress Party, which has been guilty of murdering democracy, of putting thousands of innocent citizens behind bars, and of other undemocratic acts, should never be elected to power again.

News conference, New Delhi/
The New York Times, 1-30:(4)5.

Ne Win
President of Burma
2

As [mainland] China and Burma are close neighbors, it would be best if no problems arise at all between them. If and when differences unavoidably arise at times, both sides should try to resolve them in a spirit of frankness and with patience. If we both adopt this way we shall be able to contain the problems and to prevent any deterioration in our friendship, even if the problems do not submit themselves to an immediate solution. The amicable settlement of the boundary between our two countries is an outstanding case in point.

At banquet in his honor, Peking, April 27/
The Dallas Times Herald, 4-28:(A)7.

Richard M. Nixon
Former President of the United States
3

... the actions I took with great reluctance, but recognizing I had to do what was right, the actions that I took in Vietnam: one, to try to win an honorable peace abroad; and two, to keep the peace at home, because keeping the peace at home and keeping support for the war was essential in order to get the enemy to negotiate. And that was, of course, not easy to do in view of the dissent and so forth that we had. And so it could be said that I was ... one of the casualties, or maybe the last casualty, in Vietnam. If so, I'm glad I'm the last one.

Television interview, San Clemente, Calif./
"The Nixon Interviews," Paradine Productions, 5-19.

Richard E. Pipes
Professor of history, Harvard University;
Senior research consultant, Stanford
Research Institute's Strategic Studies
Center, Arlington, Virginia
4

We [the U.S.] have so far failed to exploit our mutual interest with [mainland] China — to the great anguish and anger of the Chinese. They thought when they opened up the relationship with us six years ago that we would know how to play our cards. But we have not done so — largely because we've been so terribly obsessed with the notion of detente with the Soviet Union. This triangular relationship-could be a powerful stabilizing factor, in the sense that a Soviet Union, confronted with the possibility of having rivalries with both the United States and China, would behave more soberly than if she felt she could take on China and the United States separately ... We can normalize relations with China, and I would not be averse to informing the Russians that, unless they stop behaving so aggressively, we would be ready to help the Chinese to defend themselves.

Interview/U.S. News & World Report, 6-27:44.

Pol Pot
Prime Minister of Cambodia
5

Social blemishes and the depraved culture, debauchery, brigandage, crimes and other decadent phenomena in the age of imperialism, colonialism and other exploiting classes have been basically abolished by the great mass movement in our country.

At banquet in his honor, Peking, Sept. 28/
The New York Times, 9-30:(A)4.

Muammar el-Qaddafi
Chief of State of Libya
1

[Saying the Philippines should get rid of U.S. bases on its territory]: The presence of alien troops in any country will only encourage or draw interest from the Communists. I do not see the need for these American bases in your country [the Philippines]. I am not sure if the Americans are willing to die for your country. History does not recall any precedent to this effect. The lesson in Vietnam is good enough ... Continue to fight for your true independence from the United States, and we will help you.

Interview/Los Angeles Herald-Examiner, 1-8:(A)4.

Brahmananda Reddy
President, Congress Party of India
2

The Indian National Congress has been a party of the Indian masses, a party of the people, a party which played a great role in the political history of the nation for 60 years, preparing and leading the nation in its successful struggle for independence; and, for 30 years after independence, in building a democratic political structure and in laying the foundation for a modern, progressive and egalitarian society. [But] certain things have been done [the limitations on freedom during the emergency declared by recently defeated Prime Minister Indira Gandhi], or purported to be done in the name of the Congress government, that deeply hurt the people's feelings. The Congress deeply regrets the misuse of power at various levels and wishes to assure the people that never again would such a situation be allowed to arise.

Radio broadcast/The New York Times, 6-6:11.

Edwin O. Reischauer
Professor of Far Eastern languages, Harvard University; Former United States Ambassador to Japan
3

[Japan has a] history of isolation from the rest of the world that has left a strong sense of separateness from other peoples. [The Japanese] have assiduously studied the rest of the world for their own benefit but have paid less attention to the need for two-way communica-tion ... Japanese need to have a stronger sense of being sharers in a common human fate.

Nagoya, Japan, May 15/
Los Angeles Times, 5-16:(1)12.

Toshio Sakaki
Member, presidium, Communist Party of Japan
4

[On the security treaty between the United States and Japan]: We think of the security treaty from the Japanese viewpoint. And, from that viewpoint, the treaty is a means of helping the United States to keep bases here and to keep Japanese forces subordinate to the United States Asian policy. This is why we consider it our historic task to get rid of the security treaty. Once we have done so, we certainly will not get involved in an alliance with [mainland] China, nor with the Soviet Union. We are an island nation, and we consider neutrality and non-alignment to be the best posture for us.

Interview, Tokyo/
The Christian Science Monitor, 1-3:6.

William B. Saxbe
Former United States Ambassador to India
5

You never read anything good about the United States in the Indian papers, and you never read anything bad about Russia. But I feel that that honeymoon is about over, simply because the Indians are beginning to realize they are being used. The Russians sell them tremendous amounts of military equipment at high prices — and without concessionary terms. They are unable to supply India with the thing it needs most — food — in a bad crop year. Russia won't or can't take the things that India wants to sell — sugar, jute, shrimp, cashews and heavy equipment. And finally, the Russians keep demanding things from India that they never get but still think they should.

Interview, Washington/
U.S. News & World Report, 1-24:41.

James C. H. Shen
Ambassador to the United States from the Republic of (Nationalist) China
6

[Saying U.S. President Carter's human-rights campaign should include criticism of mainland

WHAT THEY SAID IN 1977

(JAMES C. H. SHEN)

China]: [The Communist Chinese are the] worst offenders of human rights in the world and yet we have yet to hear anything about them. . . . on the Chinese mainland you don't hear about dissidents. No one dares to air his grievances. That shows the degree of control the government has over the populace. The United States stands to gain little or nothing from normalization [of relations with mainland China]. But it could inflict irreparable harm on Taiwan, whose only wish is to remain a friend and ally of the U.S.

News conference, Los Angeles, June 24/
Los Angeles Herald-Examiner, 6-25:(A)3.

Charan Singh
Home Minister of India
1

[Defending the arrest of Indira Gandhi the day before]: The wrongs she committed [when she was Prime Minister] and the indignities she heaped on the nation — the Constitution perverted, the fundamental freedoms forfeited, the press muzzled, the judiciary robbed of its independence — called for a trial on the Nuremburg model. [But] we have rested content with a trial for offenses under the ordinary law of the land.

News conference, Oct. 4/
The New York Times, 10-5:(A)1.

John K. Singlaub
Major General, United States Army;
Chief of Staff, U.S. forces in Korea
2

[On President Carter's plan to gradually withdraw U.S. land forces from South Korea]: If we withdraw our ground forces on the schedule suggested, it will lead to war [with North Korea] ... An intensive intelligence effort over the last 12 months has discovered North Korea to be much, much stronger than we thought. My deep concern is that people making the decisions are basing them on information that's two or three years old ... The questions asked after U.S. setbacks in China and Vietnam was, "Did the military people in the know express themselves loudly and clearly enough that the decision-makers understood?" We want to make sure. If the decision is made,

298

we will execute it with enthusiasm and a high level of professional skill.

Interview/The Washington Post, 5-19:(A)1,14.

Richard L. Sneider
United States Ambassador
to South Korea
3

[On the planned withdrawal of U.S. ground troops from South Korea]: Staying would have been anachronistic in terms of not only the American sense but also in terms of the Korean sense. We're not pulling out of this place and we're not foolhardy and we're not about to commit *hara-kiri* here. It's obviously as much in our interest as it is in the Korean interest to do the job the right way, and I'm convinced that we are going to do it the right way.

Seoul, July 26/
The New York Times, 7-27:(A)6.

Donn A. Starry
Lieutenant General, United States
Army; Commander, U.S. V Corps,
West Germany
4

In your lifetime, the Soviets will fight the Chinese, probably in a major war. Difficult as it may be to see the United States becoming involved in such a war, it is likely we would do so once it became apparent that one or the other of the antagonists was about to win and gain absolute control over the bulk of the Eurasian land mass.

At American High School graduation,
Frankfurt, West Germany, June 10/
The New York Times, 6-16:(A)9.

Richard G. Stilwell
General, United States Army (Ret.);
Former Commander of U.S. forces in Korea
5

I don't want to give the impression that the U.S. ground forces should stay in Korea forever. We have a responsibility to work to ameliorate the tensions which dictate our deployments around the world. The basic source of tension on the Korean peninsula is North Korea's refusal to accept the existence of two Koreas. So I believe that withdrawal of U.S. [ground] forces from Korea should be predicated on some forward political steps that would provide a logical basis for withdrawal —

(RICHARD G. STILWELL)

to wit, efforts to achieve a non-aggression pact, the entry of both nations into the United Nations, and big-power actions to somehow lend their prestige to guarantee the security of that area. The one really important lever we have is the presence of our troops. That is the controlling factor in determining how long our troops have to be on the Korean peninsula.

Interview/U.S. News & World Report, 6-20:28.

Ross Terrill
Associate professor of government,
Harvard University; Authority on China
1

U.S.-[mainland] China relations have reached a state, like seeds when broadcast on the soil in changing weather, that must lead now either to growth or to a withering.

At conference on U.S.-China relations,
Washington/The Christian Science Monitor, 1-17:16.

Nguyen Co Thach
Deputy Foreign Minister of Vietnam
2

Our policy is peace, and I stress this because our neighbors fear our strong army. I am 56 years old, and have spent 30 years in war and 26 years under French colonial rule. This has taught me how precious peace is. If we ask people to fight again they'll revolt, unless of course Vietnam is invaded again. We do not demobilize, because peace is essential to our economic plans.

San Francisco Examiner & Chronicle,
5-29:(This World)24.

Fumihiko Togo
Japanese Ambassador
to the United States
3

... the free nations of Asia, such as Japan, are surrounded by the big three powers: the United States, China and the Soviet Union. The current stability and well-being of these peoples of Asia are dependent on the equilibrium of power among those big three. That is why the free nations of Asia place such importance on their relations with the United States. It is in this vein that the sole purpose of the Japanese-American security arrangement lies in

maintaining peace and stability in the Far East. The presence of American military bases in Japan, and the regular consultations between our professional defense establishments, are a provocation or threat to no other country. On the contrary, our alliance is a form of reassurance to our Asian neighbors that the present power balance in the Northwestern Pacific will remain stable. The countries of Southeast Asia, jointly grouping as ASEAN, call for neutrality, national resilience and non-intervention from outside. In my experience of talking with the high officials of these countries, they welcome the United States' continuing participation in the Asian affairs, as it will make their avowed policies realistic.

Before Executives Club of Chicago,
Feb. 4/Vital Speeches, 3-15:328.

Upadit Pachariyangkun
Foreign Minister of Thailand
4

The U.S. as a superpower cannot lose sight of the fact that somehow the American presence here in this part of the world is still necessary ... We cannot accept any other ideology, especially Communism. And I hope that our American friends will support our desire to remain free people as we are now.

Interview, Bangkok/
U.S. News & World Report, 7-18:51,52.

Cyrus R. Vance
Secretary of state-designate
of the United States
5

[On his being Deputy Secretary of Defense during much of the Vietnam war]: Let me say, in light of hindsight, it was a mistake [for the U.S.] to intervene in Vietnam. The motivations and initial involvement were not based on evil motives but were based on misjudgments and mistakes as we went along. I knew I made more than my share of mistakes. We learned a number of lessons in Vietnam and I'm wiser for that.

At his confirmation hearing before Senate
Foreign Relations Committee, Washington,
Jan. 11/The New York Times, 1-12:(A)8.

WHAT THEY SAID IN 1977

Cyrus R. Vance
Secretary of State of the United States
1

We consider friendly relations with [mainland] China to be a central part of our foreign policy. China's role in maintaining world peace is vital. A constructive relationship with China is important, not only religiously, but also for global equilibrium. Such a relationship will threaten no one. It will serve only peace . . . We recognize and respect China's strong commitments to independence, unity and self-reliance.

Before Asia Society, New York, June 29/
Los Angeles Herald-Examiner, 6-30:(A)4.

2

I cannot stress too strongly that the relationship of the United States and Japan is the pillar of our foreign policy in the Pacific and is a major feature of our foreign policy in the world. Ours is a special relationship of paramount importance to us.

At dinner in his honor, Tokyo,
Aug. 26/Los Angeles Times, 8-27:(1)5.

John W. Vessey, Jr.
General, United States Army;
Commander, U.S. forces in Korea
3

In my view, the withdrawal of all American ground troops [from South Korea] would raise the probability of war in Korea. We are here to prevent a war, not to fight one. The presence here of two well-armed, highly trained American divisions is more of a psychological deterrent on the North Koreans than either nuclear weapons or Air Force contingents.

April/Los Angeles Times, 5-26:(1)22.

4

[On U.S. President Carter's plan to withdraw American ground forces from South Korea]: There is concern [in South Korea] about the solidness of the U.S. commitment. It is characterized by those who hear us say we're going to remain a Pacific power, but look at what we're doing. Our actions seem to say we're moving the power we have out of the Pacific . . . President Carter's decision is based on a vision of the future, a Korea four or five years from now in which United States ground troops won't be required. That's not the situation now. Ground forces are required. Our job is to help President Carter's vision of the future come through. But none of us can control all the wires of the assembled props of the stage five years from now. We don't know what five years will bring. Hopefully, it will bring just exactly what President Carter is looking for — a more stable situation on the Korean peninsula, a situation where our ground troops won't be required.

Interview, Seoul, Aug. 2/
The New York Times, 8-3:(A)3.

James N. Wallace
Tokyo bureau chief,
"U.S. News & World Report"
5

Japanese policy-makers are in a terrible dilemma. They think they have to balance Russia and China off against one another and maintain acceptable relations with both of them. One element looks at China and says: "Ah! Look at these millions and millions of potential customers for our refrigerators, our cassette recorders, our radios, maybe even our automobiles some day." Then another group says: "Ah! But can China supply us with energy? Russia has natural gas and coal we need badly. So we'd better forget about selling to China because that will annoy the Russians. We'd better invest in energy-development programs in Siberia." I don't know how this argument will come out. But Japan wants to trade with everybody.

Interview/U.S. News & World Report, 9-26:46.

Leonard Woodcock
Head of U.S. White House
mission to Vietnam
6

[Addressing Vietnamese Foreign Minister Nguyen Duy Trinh]: There are many problems between our two countries, but we believe that with patience and perseverance and creation of understanding these problems can be cleared away. We will approach our talks with good will. We bring the best wishes of our new President, Jimmy Carter.

Hanoi, Vietnam, March 16/
The New York Times, 3-17:(A)17.

Yeh Chien-ying
Minister of Defense of the People's
Republic of (mainland) China
1

[The U.S. and Soviet Union] are locked in an increasingly fierce struggle for hegemony, [and] a war will break out some day. We [China] must be clearly aware of this situation, keep war in mind and get prepared for it, for a big war that will break out at an early date . . . We must build the interior . . . as fast as possible so that it can make greater contributions to the development of our national economy and our preparedness against war in peacetime and operate as our strategic rear base area in time of war.

At industrial conference, Peking, May 9/
Los Angeles Herald-Examiner, 5-13:(A)4.

Yun Po Sun
Former President of South Korea
2

I believe the importance of the American military presence [in South Korea] is not when they should be withdrawn, such as by 1980, as [current South Korean President] Park has said, or any other deadline proposed by either government. It is important that American troops remain until it is reasonably certain that war [with North Korea] can be avoided. Mr. Park has said that American troops should stay until 1980, but I believe it isn't wise. It is premature to say 1980 or another date . . . I don't think America should give up South Korea because the political system here doesn't endear itself to many Americans. To give up South Korea would challenge America's own liberal values of human rights and democracy. We are struggling to restore many of the values Americans champion.

Interview, Seoul/The New York Times, 3-7:5.

Mohammad Ziaul Haq
Head of Government of Pakistan
3

[On the recent coup installing him in power]: I want to make it abundantly clear that I have not assumed responsibility because of political ambitions. Nor does the army want to be distracted from its profession of soldiering. My chief mission is to hold free and fair general elections . . . in October this year. After the completion of elections, I shall hand over the government to the elected representatives of the people. I genuinely feel that the survival of this country lies in democracy and democracy alone.

Broadcast address to the nation,
July 5/Los Angeles Times, 7-6:(1)1.

Europe

Andrei A. Amalrik
Exiled Soviet historian
1

[On U.S. President Carter's criticism of the human-rights situation in the Soviet Union] : I think the Carter Administration must be patient, consistent and firm. It must not let itself be swayed either by the current reactions of the Soviet regime or by the discomfiture and alarm of its West European allies or, indeed, by public opinion, which fails to understand that the Soviet regime is not going to change its policies, mildly or drastically, overnight. Besides, why all this talk about "pressure"? As far as I can see, the U.S. government has not applied any pressure whatsoever. It has simply voiced its concern, and has made it known to Moscow that its oppressive policies will not go unnoticed. For the Soviet government, whose press, radio and television never cease to portray the West in the most reprehensible terms, now to complain about being criticized by the West is simply absurd. What Carter is saying now is long overdue. His policy is both morally just and, in addition, politically sagacious.

Interview/The Wall Street Journal, 8-11:14.

Giulio Andreotti
Premier of Italy
2

I believe that the so-called historic compromise [between his Christian Democrats and the Communists] would be a great mistake. A coalition of the two major parties would strike a serious blow at political pluralism in Italy by virtually eliminating the historic parliamentary function of the other parties. I believe that these parties must continue to play their role to assure the proper working of Italian democracy. Equally serious: The formation of a Big-Two government would create such a political vacuum in the opposition as to lead to a dangerous counter-reaction from both the

extreme right and the extreme left. These are the forces that already are making such trouble in Italy through their terrorism. The consequences of an escalation of tension are easily imaginable. So I repeat that a coalition of the Christian Democrats and Communists would be a great mistake.

Interview, Rome/
U.S. News & World Report, 8-1:31.

Yuri V. Andropov
Chief of KGB (Soviet security police)
3

[On dissidents in his country] : We have such people in a miniscule number. We still have them. Unfortunately, they exist — like thieves, bribe-takers, speculators and other criminals exist. Both are inflicting harm to our society and that is why they should bear punishment in complete accordance with the demands of Soviet law.

At commemoration of 100th birthday
anniversary of Soviet secret-police founder
Felix Dzerzhinsky, Moscow, Sept. 9/
Los Angeles Herald-Examiner, 9-11:(A)2.

Georgi A. Arbatov
Director, Soviet Institute of U.S.A. and Canadian Affairs
4

In Moscow, American human-rights rhetoric is perceived not as simply a matter of expressing opinions; in our view, it has become an organized political campaign against us. The participation of private American organizations as well as the government centered on the so-called dissidents [in the Soviet Union] . This is a rather small group, but it has become very much involved with foreigners, mainly Americans — journalists, diplomats and some people who come as tourists. The so-called dissidents get financial help, are prompted in their

(GEORGI A. ARBATOV)

statements, and every word is picked up not only by the mass media but by [U.S.] governmental agencies like the Voice of America, and then the President and other agencies get involved. So it all acquires a quality of massive interference in our internal affairs and raises questions whether the Americans are returning to cold-war practices.

Interview/The Washington Post, 7-20:(A)22.

Giulio Carlo Argan
Mayor of Rome
1

The city council is aware of the worry of the Bishop of Rome about the suffering of this great city, dilapidated and laid waste in contempt of the laws of the state, of the sacrilegious outrages of Rome — which is not only the supreme custodian of the ancient and revered Christian faith of which it is the symbol and the center, but of the evils of real-estate and building speculation that all deplore and which strikes the population, especially the poor and defenseless.

Jan. 3/Los Angeles Times, 1-4:(1)14.

Raymond Barre
Premier of France
2

The French temperament naturally tends to resist any established order, whatever it is. It tends to seek extreme solutions, and intellectually perfect plans rather than practical ones adapted to things as they are. It was to preserve France from the dangerous results of this tendency that the present system was devised by [the late President Charles] de Gaulle. It is a regime of authority, durability, ensuring institutional stability while resting solidly on popular approval. It is the present government structure that justified the hope that the series of changes of regime is now at an end. The President holds the supreme authority and he appoints the government. Yet the government itself is responsible to Parliament for all that it does. And the Parliament is elected by the people of France.

Interview, Paris/
The Christian Science Monitor, 5-25:24.

Leonid I. Brezhnev
General Secretary, Communist Party
of the Soviet Union
3

What is detente or relaxation of tensions? What meaning do we invest in this term? Detente means, first of all, the overcoming of the cold war and the transition to normal, stable relations among nations. Detente means willingness to resolve differences and disputes not by force, not by threats and "saberrattling," but by peaceful means at a conference table. Detente means a certain trust and ability to take into consideration each other's legitimate interests. Life has shown that the atmosphere of international relations can be noticeably changed within a short period of time. Contacts between countries in the political, economic, cultural and in other fields have expanded. And what is most important, comrades, is that the danger of a new big war has been pushed back. People now draw an easier breath and [begin] to look to the future with greater hope. That is what detente or relaxation of tensions means, and these are its inevitable results.

At celebration meeting, Tula, U.S.S.R.,
Jan. 18/Vital Speeches, 2-15:263.

4

... the allegations that the Soviet Union is going beyond what is suitable for defense, that it is striving for superiority in armaments with the aim of delivering "the first strike" are absurd and totally unfounded. Not so long ago, at a meeting with prominent representatives of the American business community, I said — and I want to emphasize it again — that the Soviet Union always was and continues to be a convinced opponent of any such concepts. Our efforts are directed precisely at avoiding either the first or the second strikes and at avoiding nuclear war in general. Our approach to these questions can be formulated as follows: The Soviet Union's defense potential must be sufficient to deter anyone from taking a chance at violating our peaceful life. Not a course toward superiority in armaments, but a course toward reducing them, at lessening military confrontation — such is our policy. On behalf of the

WHAT THEY SAID IN 1977

(LEONID I. BREZHNEV)

people, I declare that our country will never embark on the road of aggression and will never raise the sword against other nations.

At celebration meeting, Tula, U.S.S.R., Jan. 18/Vital Speeches, 2-15:263.

1

[Saying that Soviet workers have not met the demands of the technological age]: Losses entailed by every violation of technological discipline are growing incredibly ... Everyone must work so that he does not have to be ashamed before himself, so that he can look with a quiet conscience into the eyes of his comrades ... Discipline has not become any worse, but we apparently are unable to heed the requirements of modern technology ... and to conform with the new aspect of our economy.

At congress of trade unions, Moscow, March 21/The Christian Science Monitor, 4-12:6.

2

Some sort of ersatz is being invented and the semblance of an "internal opposition" in socialist countries is being created by means of false publicity. That is the reason why the clamor about the so-called "dissidents" is organized, why a hullabaloo is raised about "violations of human rights" in the countries of socialism. In our country it is not forbidden to "think differently" from the majority, to critically appraise various aspects of public life. It is another matter when some people who have broken away from our society come out actively against the socialist system, embark on the road of anti-Soviet activity, violate laws, and, having no support inside the country, turn for support abroad ... Quite naturally we have taken and will take against them measures envisaged by law.

At congress of trade unions, Moscow, March 21/ Los Angeles Herald-Examiner, 3-21:(A)5.

3

There exist circumstances directly opposing a further improvement and development of Soviet-American relations. One of them is the ballooning of the slanderous campaign about

the mythical "military menace" posed by the U.S.S.R. ... The other circumstance is constituted by outright attempts by official American bodies to interfere in the internal affairs of the Soviet Union [by criticizing human-rights conditions in Russia]. But Washington's claim to teach others how to live, I believe, cannot be accepted by any sovereign state, not to mention the fact that neither the situation in the United States nor U.S. actions and policies in the world at large give justification to such claims. I will repeat again: We will not tolerate interference in our internal affairs by anyone and under any pretext. A normal development of relations on such a basis is, of course, unthinkable ... We would like these [Soviet-American] relations to be good-neighborly ones. But these require a definite level of mutual understanding and at least a minimum of mutual tact.

At congress of trade unions, Moscow, March 21/U.S. News & World Report, 4-4:24.

4

... some years after the adoption of the current [Soviet] Constitution [in 1936] were darkened by illegal repressions, violations of the principles of socialist democracy, Leninist norms of Party and state life. This was done in contravention of the Constitutional provisions. The Party has resolutely condemned this practice and it should never repeat ... [But] the rights and freedoms of citizens cannot and must not be used against our social system and to damage the interests of the Soviet people ... Political freedoms are granted in accordance with the interests of the people and with the aim of strengthening the socialist system.

Before Soviet Communist Party Central Committee, Moscow, May/ The Washington Post, 6-6:(A)1,24.

5

The capitalist encirclement of the U.S.S.R. exists no more. Socialism has turned into a world system and a mighty socialist community has formed. The position of world capitalism has been substantially weakened. Dozens of young states, former colonies, are coming out against Western imperialism.

Before Soviet Communist Party Central Committee, Moscow, May/ Los Angeles Times, 6-19:(6)2.

(LEONID I. BREZHNEV)

1

[On his country's new Constitution] : The political rights and freedoms of U.S.S.R. citizens have been formulated more fully in the draft. The right of every Soviet citizen to take part in running state and public affairs is proclaimed, and concrete forms of such participation are indicated. The freedom of expression, the press, assembly and meetings and street marches and demonstrations recorded in the current Constitution have been fully reaffirmed. A substantial addition to the Constitutional guarantees of the rights of the individual will be the right of citizens to introduce proposals to government and public bodies, criticize shortcomings in their work, file legal complaints against actions of officials, and also the right to legal defense from encroachments on their life, health, property and individual freedom, honor and dignity. Of course, comrades, the draft Constitution proceeds from the assumption that the rights and freedoms of citizens cannot and must not be used against our social system or to damage the interests of the Soviet people. That is why the draft says directly, for example, that the exercise of the rights and freedoms by citizens should not damage the interests of society and state and the rights of other citizens, and that political freedoms are granted in accordance with the interests of the people and with the aim of strengthening the socialist system. It is necessary for every Soviet citizen to understand clearly that the main guarantee of his rights in the final analysis is the might and prosperity of our homeland.

Before Soviet Communist Party Central Committee, Moscow, June 5/Vital Speeches, 7-1:548.

Leonid I. Brezhnev
President of the Soviet Union;
General Secretary,
Soviet Communist Party

2

[On his being made President of the Soviet Union in addition to his remaining Party Secretary] : The discharge of the lofty and responsible state functions connected with this, parallel with the duties of General Secretary of our Party's Central Committee, is, of course, no easy matter. But the will of the Party, the will of the Soviet people, the interests of our socialist homeland have always been for me the supreme law to which I subordinated and subordinate my entire life.

Accepting the Presidency, Moscow, June 16/The New York Times, 6-17:(A)1.

3

[On foreign criticism of his country's arms build-up] : The Soviet Union is simply placing itself in a defensive position. The Soviet Union wants to be so strong that no one will deal it the burning wounds it received in the last war and from which it is still suffering. The Soviet Union will never raise the sword against anyone.

Rambouillet, France, June 21/ The Dallas Times Herald, 6-21:(A)4.

4

Imperialist propaganda is blind to the achievements of our great country, with its heroic history, a vital and many-sided culture, one of the world's best educational standards, the vigorous joint creative activity of its numerous nations and peoples. "Psychological warfare" experts take very little interest in this. Their only goal is to obstruct the growth of the influence of socialism on human minds, to induce distrust and hostility toward it by whatever means. Hence the stereotyped inventions, shameless fabrications and blatant lies about the Soviet Union, intended for misinformed audiences, gullible readers, listeners and viewers.

Before Supreme Soviet, Moscow, Oct. 4/ The New York Times, 10-5:(A)3.

Claude-Pierre Brossolette
Director general, Credit
Lyonnais (France)

5

[Comparing Britain with the rest of the West] : In a way, they're more civilized than we are. After the Second World War, they decided to enjoy themselves more than the rest of us. They are less efficient, but maybe they are happier.

The New York Times, 1-30:(12)7.

WHAT THEY SAID IN 1977

Harold Brown
Secretary of Defense of the United States 1

The strength or vulnerability of Western Europe involves a complex of economic, political and military factors. We don't want any of those to get too adverse. The military one, for example, could by itself under some circumstances get so adverse as to allow Soviet blackmail of Western Europe — if not a Soviet overrunning of Western Europe. The same thing, however, is true politically. If the Western Europeans were all to decide to vote for Communist parties which identified with Moscow, that would finish it right there, even if the military balance were in great shape. Economically, the Soviets have rather little leverage directly on Europe. When you look at all of these together — the military, political and economic areas — Western Europe does not seem very vulnerable to me. If I were asked, "Which of these areas is the weakest and which needs to be built up the most?" I would have to say it's a combination of military and political.

Interview, Washington/
U.S. News & World Report, 9-5:22.

Zbigniew Brzezinski
Assistant to President of the
United States Jimmy Carter
for National Security Affairs 2

... first of all, we do not wish the Communist parties to come to power in Western Europe. Secondly, we have confidence that the West European electorates will use their best judgment to preserve democratic systems and will therefore opt for democratic parties. Thirdly, we have to deal with the world as it is. Fourthly, the existence of Eurocommunist parties, as of themselves, does encourage change in the nature of Communism, and it is unwise for the United States to engage in direct interference in domestic affairs of other countries, of the sort that could make the Eurocommunist parties symbols of national independence. Lastly, Eurocommunism is a highly differentiated phenomenon. All it is really is a catchword for West European Communist parties.

Interview/The Washington Post, 10-9:(C)5.

Ihsan Sabri Caglayangil
Foreign Minister of Turkey 3

The [Greek-Turk] Cyprus problem can only be solved by a package deal, including the boundaries and all other issues involved. Turkey is ready to withdraw from the island all the troops outside the figure to be established by a final agreement. A total of 12,000 men have been pulled back already and the latest withdrawal of the Turkish Air Force units from the island has a special significance. Further troop withdrawals will be possible to the extent that conditions permit them ... This is an opportunity to restore mutual confidence and cooperation, and this appeal should not be left unanswered.

The Christian Science Monitor, 11-25:11.

James Callaghan
Prime Minister of the United Kingdom 4

A 10 per cent increase in national [wages] means a lower rate of inflation in 1978 than we have enjoyed for several years. More than 10 per cent means inflation will go up once again. To those who tell me no way will the country accept 10 per cent, I reply, then no way will you stop prices or unemployment going up again. Every negotiator knows that if the first wage settlements in the current round start well above 10 per cent, that will set the pattern for the whole year. It's as plain as a pikestaff that the level of wages enters into export prices, and if one goes up the other will follow almost automatically. And the end of that road is that Britain becomes uncompetitive once more — export orders are lost to other countries and unemployment will grow even more. I shall do all I can to prevent us following that road. Either back us or sack us.

At Labor Party convention, Brighton, England,
Oct. 4/The Christian Science Monitor, 10-5:4.

5

The next 20 years will be unlike anything that this country has seen since it first moved to become an industrial power 200 years ago. The oil riches beneath the North Sea, properly used,

(JAMES CALLAGHAN)

can transform our economic future in a way inconceivable even 10 years ago.

At Labor Party convention, Brighton, England, Oct. 4/The Dallas Times Herald, 10-5:(A)16.

Constantine Caramanlis
Premier of Greece

1

It seems that in Greece we must fear success and not disaster. Disaster unites us, while success, with the envy it produces, divides us.

The New York Times, 1-30:(1)10.

2

There are three kinds of democracy in Europe: Anglo-Saxon, Scandinavian and Mediterranean. Of the three, the Mediterranean is the least disciplined and the most difficult to manage, largely because of the passionate nature of the Mediterranean personality. I detest passion in politics. Passion obscures issues and blinds citizens to the truth.

The New York Times, 3-13:(4)7.

Jimmy Carter
President-elect of the United States

3

[On the possibility of Communists joining the government in Italy and France] : It matters a great deal. And concerns me very much, depending on the degree of Communist participation in the government, and the loss of the respect and confidence of the citizens of those nations in the democratic processes that we prefer over Communism. Another factor is the degree of allegiance that might be shown by Communist leaders toward the Soviet Union and away from our own nation and from NATO. I think the best way to minimize the Communist influence in Italy and France is to make the democratic processes work, and to restore the confidence of the citizens in the government.

Interview, Plains, Ga./Time, 1-3:25.

Jimmy Carter
President of the United States

4

[On Soviet leader Leonid Brezhnev's outspoken displeasure at U.S. criticism of the human-rights situation in the U.S.S.R.] : We're not trying to overthrow the Soviet government nor to intrude ourselves into their affairs in a military way. I think it has been a well-recognized international political principle that interference in a government is not a verbal thing ... Mr. Brezhnev and his predecessors have never refrained from expressing their view when they disagreed with some aspect of social or political life in the free world. And I think we have a right to speak out openly when we have a concern about human rights wherever those abuses occur.

News conference, March 24/ U.S. News & World Report, 4-4:24.

5

[There] must be strong ties between Europe and North America. In maintaining and strengthening these ties, my Administration will be guided by certain principles. Simply stated: We will continue to make the [Atlantic] Alliance the heart of our foreign policy. We will remain a reliable and faithful ally. We will join with you to strengthen the Alliance — politically, economically and militarily. We will ask for and listen to the advice of our allies; and we will give our views in return, candidly and as friends. This effort rests on a strong foundation. The state of the Alliance is good. Its strategy and doctrine are solid. We derive added strength and new pride from the fact that all 15 of our member countries are now democracies. Our Alliance is a pact for peace — and a pact for freedom. The Alliance is even stronger because of solid progress toward Western European unification and the expanding role of the European Community in world affairs. The United States welcomes this development and will work closely with the Community.

At North Atlantic Treaty Organization conference, London, May 10/The New York Times, 5-11:(A)14.

6

I believe that the best way we can prevent the enhancement of Communist political strength in Europe is to show that democratically controlled governments can function effectively and openly, and with humaneness

WHAT THEY SAID IN 1977

(JIMMY CARTER)

and a genuine and continuing comprehension of what people need and expect from a government.

Interview/U.S. News & World Report, 5-16:22.

1

I think that our concept of human rights is preserved in Poland . . . much better than other European nations with which I am familiar. There is a substantial degree of freedom of the press exhibited by this [news] conference this afternoon, a substantial degree of freedom of religion demonstrated by the fact that approximately 90 per cent of the Polish people profess faith in Christ, and an open relationship between Poland and our country and Poland and Western European countries in trade, technology, cultural exchange, student exchange, tourism. So I don't think there is any doubt that the will of the Polish people for complete preservation and enhancement of human rights is the same as our own.

News conference, Warsaw, Dec. 30/
The New York Times, 12-31:2.

Frederick Donald Coggan
Archbishop of Canterbury, England

2

[On Queen Elizabeth II, now celebrating her Silver Jubilee on the throne] : Our nation and Commonwealth have been blessed beyond measure by having at their heart an example of service untiringly done, of duty faithfully fulfilled, and of a home life stable and wonderfully happy. For this we thank God. From this we take courage.

Sermon at celebration of the Silver Jubilee,
St. Paul's Cathedral, London, June 7/
The New York Times, 6-8:(A)14.

Anthony Crosland
Foreign Secretary of the United
Kingdom; President, Council of Ministers,
European Economic Community

3

In the field of foreign policy, there is growing cooperation between the nine [members of the EEC]. At the meetings of foreign ministers on political cooperation, I have been impressed by the ability of member-states to reach an agreed view and take up common positions on important issues. As an illustration, I note that at the 31st session of the United Nations General Assembly the nine have voted together on 82 per cent of all resolutions, and the country holding the Presidency has spoken on behalf of all the nine on no fewer than 50 occasions. There is no doubt room for further improvement in developing the Community's collective voice at New York. But what a contrast to the *petit-bourgeois* nationalism, as it has been called, which wrecked the League of Nations in the '20s and '30s. Increasingly, this habit of cooperation is enabling the Community to take fuller advantage of the influence in world affairs which it derives from its commercial and economic importance. The Community's growing influence in the world constitutes . . . a historic change, and for me it validates the reasons why first I welcomed the formation of the Community and then desired Britain to join it.

At European Parliament, Luxembourg,
Jan. 12/Vital Speeches, 2-1:234.

Alvaro Cunhal
Secretary general,
Communist Party of Portugal

4

They say my Party is the last Stalinist party in Europe, but those who say so must justify their claim. If by the word "Stalinist" they mean administration by violence and force, an undemocratic life in the Party, decisions controlled by the leaders, the superimposition of the opinion of the chief over the collectivity, then my Party is not "Stalinist" . . . We are not interested in the fall of this government, if it is to be substituted by a more reactionary one. What we favor is a democratic alternative with the participation of the workers — which means with the Communists — and with all those who agree on a common platform, including the military.

Interview, Lisbon/
The New York Times, 4-17:(1)11.

308

Etienne Davignon
Commissioner, European
Economic Community

1

The disappointments [of the Common Market] come from the expectations. We all expected we would become a United States of Europe from one day to the next. That didn't happen. But people do sense that they belong to something big, something that helps create stability. Let's not forget that one big achievement: War among the traditional enemies of Europe is now impossible, and that's something we have not known in centuries. The Market has become complicated and technical, but the change in the mood of Europe has been significant.

The New York Times, 3-25:(A)2.

William Davis
Editor, "Punch" magazine

2

The people [in Britain] who have the least humor are the middle classes, because they're insecure. They're the ones who resent mockery of the monarchy or the Prime Minister or anyone in authority . . . A middle-class Englishman will assume arrogantly that the English have a monopoly on humor, but he doesn't have the ability to laugh at himself. There are just a few tolerated subjects — he will laugh at foreigners and blacks and the lower orders.

Interview, New York/
The New York Times, 10-12:(B)1.

Adalbert de Segonzac
Former chief North American
correspondent, "France-Soir," Paris

3

Europe always looks to America for leadership. It doesn't want to say it too much and it rather has a tendency to think that American leadership is sometimes a bit too obvious, the pressures are too considerable. There is a view that the United States has a tendency to mix up leadership and partnership, a tendency to impose its own opinions on its neighbors. But definitely the Europeans need American leadership. They recognize the power is here, the facilities, the wealth are here, and, therefore, they expect a great deal from the United States. On the other hand, they also have a great deal

to bring and they are quite conscious of it. Europe was badly battered during the war and, thanks to the generosity of the United States and the Marshall Plan, it has picked up. It has picked up to the point of being independent, which has created a certain amount of friction between the United States and Europe. Being independent means that it's looking after its own problems with much more freedom than it did early on when it was very much in need of American help. But this being said, the majority of Europeans still look toward America and expect that America will bring some leadership in all domains.

Interview, Washington/
The National Observer, 5-23:13.

4

. . . my own theory is that there is no real love for France here [in the U.S.] nor for America in France. Actually, there may be more sympathy for France here than there is for America in my country. The Americans are, of course, weaned on Lafayette and on our role in your Revolution. From that point on, we were not so close. Even your soldiers in two world wars went to Europe to find the French living all closed up in their little worlds — closed even to other Frenchmen — while in Germany the people open their doors to strangers. You have a small number of Americans who have a passionate love for France, a larger number of Americans who hate France, and a great mass of Americans who are rather indifferent but think the French are a difficult people, hard to understand. As we are. But, as you do, we believe passionately in democracy and freedom.

Interview/U.S. News & World Report, 7-11:58.

Elizabeth II
Queen of England

5

During the last 25 years I have traveled widely throughout the Commonwealth as its head. And during those years I have seen from a unique position of advantage the last great phase of transformation of the Empire into Commonwealth and the transformation of the Crown from an emblem of dominion into a symbol of free and voluntary association. In all

WHAT THEY SAID IN 1977

(ELIZABETH II)

history this has no precedent. It is easy enough to define what the Commonwealth is not. Indeed this is quite a popular pastime. But from my own experience I know something of what it is. It is like an iceberg, except that it is not cold. The tip is represented by the occasional meeting of the heads of government and by the Commonwealth Secretariat. But nine-tenths of Commonwealth activity takes place continuously beneath the surface and unseen. Cultural activities, professional, scientific, educational and economic bodies have between them created a network of contact within the Commonwealth which are full of life and much valued. And right at the base of the iceberg, the part which keeps the rest afloat, is friendship and communication, largely in the English language, between people who were originally brought together by the events of history and who now understand that they share a common humanity. I have also no doubt that, politically, the Commonwealth has something rare and valuable to offer — a capacity for enlightened tolerance; the ability to see things in the long-term perspective; and the willingness to concede that there just may be another point of view. It has the strength to endure difference for the sake of basic identity, and the courage to prefer compromise to conflict.

On her Silver Jubilee as Queen, London, June 7/
The Washington Post, 7-10:(A)26.

Amintore Fanfani
President, Italian Senate;
Former Premier of Italy
1

I can make no prediction about what will happen in Italy in 1977. I can only say I hope that the government will take necessary economic measures and that all parties will show a sense of responsibility. The labor unions and all Italian people have to show this sense. Italy must reduce waste, increase productivity and make the prices of its products competitive on the world market. The realization of these hopes will make it easier for our NATO allies to help sustain our efforts ... If our hopes come true, Italy can make a modest but necessary contribution to the solution of the world's economic problems and thus help maintain the economic equilibrium of the world.

Interview, Rome/
Los Angeles Herald-Examiner, 2-7:(A)3.

Gerald R. Ford
Former President of the United States
2

Today, a shadow hangs heavy over the future of Europe. This time it is the threat of Communist parliamentary takeover in some Western European nations that shrouds the fate of democracy. In Italy, the Communists, by winning 34 per cent in last year's election, have already won a virtual veto over government policies in the Italian Parliament. In France, a coalition of the Communists and Socialists in the Presidential election of 1974 came within two percentage points of victory. A victory for such a coalition next March would bring Communists in key ministerial positions. And in the Iberian Peninsula, where democracy, after an era of autocracy, is having its fragile beginning, Communist leaders in Portugal have brutally fought to increase their anti-democratic influence to dominance. From the shores of the Adriatic to those of the Atlantic, a new specter of Communist control hovers over the countries of Western Europe. Lisbon, Paris, Rome — all of the parliaments in those capitals — now confirm the clutch of Communist power. Yet, I do not find such Communist domination to be inevitable ... If we can strip from the so-called Eurocommunists their deceit of democratic pretensions, the forces of freedom will win. If we can be as ruthless in telling the truth about the Eurocommunists as they would supress it, the cause of democracy will live. For Eurocommunism is not, like their propagandists say, "Communism with a human face"; it is Stalinism in a mask and tyranny in disguise, and of that let there be no doubt.

At Westminister College, Fulton, Mo.,
Oct. 29/Vital Speeches, 12-15:130.

Felipe Gonzalez
Secretary general,
Socialist Workers Party of Spain
3

[On what a Socialist Spain would be like]: We would confront the economic crisis with

(FELIPE GONZALEZ)

different nuances than the present government. What the Socialists would not do would be to subject society to a traumatic change [that might make it] lose confidence. For example, a Socialist government would not fall into the temptation of nationalizing the economy. We would try to reorient foreign investment and to control it. But we would not fall into the trap of saying no to foreign investments — that's perfectly stupid — [or of] nationalizing foreign-owned industry. For us Socialists, it's better to create jobs in our country than to export workers to European countries. As long as they create jobs, foreign investments will be welcome — but knowing that there are rules of the game that they will have to respect.

Interview, Madrid/
The Christian Science Monitor, 12-14:19.

Andrei A. Gromyko
Foreign Minister of the Soviet Union

1

[On criticism by the U.S. Carter Administration of human-rights conditions in the U.S.S.R.]: Despite critical remarks, our wish is to see relations with the U.S.A. as good, still better — as friendly relations — political, economic and commercial. We ourselves have no claim to teach others. But we shall not permit others to take the stance of tutors and teach us how to conduct our internal affairs. By the way, back at the time of the establishment of diplomatic relations betweem the U.S.S.R. and the U.S.A., the American side put forth the thesis of non-interference in the two countries' internal affairs. This thesis is all the more correct today. No kind of noise, squeal or screech addressed from abroad to the Soviet Union will detract us from this road.

News conference, Moscow, March 31/
The New York Times, 4-1:(A)9.

Alexander M. Haig, Jr.
General, United States Army;
Supreme Allied Commander/Europe

2

I think it is clear, regardless of the perspective you choose, that Soviet military capabilities have been growing at a relentless pace. To understand what that implies for the West requires that we recognize several critical aspects of their development: First, what we are observing today is not the result of a sudden, recent or precipitous shift in Soviet priorities. Rather, the threat confronting us now is the product of sustained and determined Soviet defense spending, dating back to at least the Cuban Missile crisis [1962], and perhaps earlier. Second, these defense efforts have radically altered the nature of Soviet military capabilities, transforming what was once an essentially continental military force to one of global dimensions capable of supporting an imperialistic phase in their foreign policy. Finally, it is clear the Soviets have pursued a balanced-force effort, allocating resources across the entire spectrum of their capabilities — indeed cannot afford to speculate — about Soviet intentions. My concern is with Soviet capabilities. And by any objective criteria, the totality of those capabilities exceeds what is required for purely defense purposes.

Interview, Brussels/
U.S. News & World Report, 1-17:35.

3

In the purely military field, the balance of forces is very perceptively shifting to [the Soviets'] favor, [and] unless the West acts quickly, the Soviet bloc will have military superiority. Our deterrent forces currently concern me, but I do not expect in the short term a classic Soviet attack on the Western frontiers of Europe. I fear much more the development of an ambiguous and dangerous situation on our flanks and periphery. I fear particularly the dangers which could result in the evolution in the Third World.

Interview/The Dallas Times Herald, 7-15:(A)7.

Lady Harlech
Wife of the former British Ambassador
to the United States

4

In America, excellence is something that is appreciated. In England, generally it is considered ungentlemanly, not quite nice to be at the top of your profession. It has slightly got to the point where people disapprove of success.

Interview/The Wall Street Journal, 3-3:12.

WHAT THEY SAID IN 1977

Hassan II
King of Morocco

1

I agree with those who say [Soviet strategy] is to encircle, weaken and neutralize West Europe by controlling its sources of key minerals in Africa. If the Shaba operation had succeeded and if the Middle East were allowed to continue to drift, not one moderate regime would survive. They would all be radicalized either from within or from without. It wouldn't only be Europe's oil route — but the oil itself. Add to the mix the threat of popular fronts in Italy and France and you don't have to be a geopolitical genius to grasp the consequences for world peace. I happen to know that it was Russia that encouraged [Libyan leader] Muammar Qaddafi to buy 10 per cent of Fiat in order to undermine the last great private enterprise in Italy; our intelligence on this is unimpeachable. Russia says it stands for non-interference in internal affairs — non-interference by non-Communist powers, that is. Because when they intervene — either directly as in Hungary or Czechoslovakia, or through proxies, as in Angola — it suddenly becomes a sacred, international revolutionary duty.

Interview/Newsweek, 5-16:58.

Pierre Hassner
*Senior research associate, National
Foundation of Political Science, Paris;
Professor of political science, Johns
Hopkins University's Bologna (Italy) branch*

2

Contrary to what most people believe, my own view is that Eurocommunism will be more troubling for France than for Italy. In Italy, the Communists cannot come into power in any other way than a grand national coalition with the Christian Democrats. While, in international politics, Italy with this grand coalition is going to be a pain in the neck, I think in domestic Italian policies — economics, law, and order — it is the only solution. Neither of the two halves of the country can govern the country alone, so it's worth the price to have some trouble for NATO to improve the chance of stability in Italy. With the French it's different. What will come into power is one half of France against the other — not a national

coalition. Hence, there will be a very tense situation with reactions from the right. Also, the French Communist Party has remained very, very, anti-American — very, very tough. They have their own troubles with the Soviet Union, but if you look closely at their recent pronouncements, they make no attempt at all, unlike the Italian Communists, to placate business, the Germans, the Americans. Still, it won't be the end of the world. They won't go over to the Soviets, but they will be every bit as difficult partners as [the late French President Charles] de Gaulle was, and the relative improvement which one has seen with [current President Valery] Giscard d'Estaing will disappear.

Interview/U.S. News & World Report, 6-27:49.

Hubert H. Humphrey
United States Senator, D—Minnesota

3

We've been going around worrying how are we going to accommodate ourselves to the Russians. It's a two-way street. Let them figure out how to accommodate with us; they've got more problems then we've got. Their economy is in a shambles. [Soviet President Leonid] Brezhnev is in serious difficulty, there isn't any doubt about it. We know that from our intelligence reports. We hear it from Western countries and Eastern European countries. I don't want any break with the Soviet Union, and the Soviet Union doesn't want any break with us; I don't think there's going to be any nuclear war, but this [Soviet] crowd has been going hell-bent on military build-up. They've got a military-industrial complex that's in charge pretty much in their country. And I think they ought to be given reason — without our being arrogant or bellicose — for them to wonder, well, how are the Americans going to react. You know, we're not going to roll over and play dead.

*Interview, Washington, July 27/
Los Angeles Times, 7-28:(1)5.*

Henry M. Jackson
United States Senator, D-Washington

4

[On U.S. President Carter's criticism of the human-rights situation in the Soviet Union]: I

(HENRY M. JACKSON)

commend the President for what he has done. He is simply, of course, asking the Soviet Union, in effect, to honor international law. The right to leave a country, the right to return freely, is guaranteed under two agreements. One is the International Convention on Human Rights; the Soviet signed that in 1969. And the Helsinki Agreement. I am glad the President is speaking out. The Russians know that these positions have strong underpinning based on international law. The element of interference [in the Soviets' internal affairs] is nonsense . . . It is high time that the Russians honor these commitments. If they will not honor a commitment on human rights, what are they going to honor on a SALT agreement?

TV-radio interview, Washington/"Meet the Press,"
National Broadcasting Company, 2-20.

Andre Jacomet
Chairman, Foundation Europeene
Pour L'Economie
1

One point can be made with reasonable certainty — the [European Economic] Community has an excellent chance of preserving what it has already acquired. It has upset enough old habits, proved its usefulness to its members, and acquired sufficient prestige in the eyes of the world to be assured that its existence will not be threatened. A return to the savage protectionism and deep inter-country rivalries of the past is not likely. Common customs and common trade and agricultural policies have undeniably borne fruit . . . What has been built will not be torn down despite the forces of change that now weaken, now strengthen the bonds that bind its members together. The recent deep recession disrupted the economic, monetary and political unity to a halt. But it has had its salutary aspects as well. Continuing economic stagnation and the changes it brought about confront the member countries with new challenges. They cannot solve these problems alone. Only through joint efforts within the Community's organizations can they achieve full employment and at the same time respond to their citizens'

desires for less dramatic growth and a better quality of life.

At International Trade Conference of the Southwest,
Dallas, May 25/Vital Speeches, 7-15:582

Peter Jay
British Ambassador to the United States
2

[On his new post as Ambassador] : I love my country and I love the U.S.A. It is going to be an exciting assignment to go and tell what I believe is a very exciting story about our country. I think Britain is now a land of hope and opportunity. And I think the strength of our political institutions and enormous reserves of good sense among our people are enabling us to overcome our economic problems.

London, July 21/The New York Times, 7-22:(A)3.

Roy Jenkins
President, European Commission
3

If our community cannot be made to work, what can? If we, among the richest and certainly among the most favored and talented of the populations of the globe, cannot learn to work together, what prospect is there for humanity, or for a decent, civilized life for ordinary men and women? These are the stakes and these are the issues. Let us approach them with an awesome sense of responsibility, but also with a courageous and determined optimism.

Before European Parliament, Luxembourg, Jan.11/
The Christian Science Monitor, 1-14:5.

Juan Carlos I
King of Spain
4

[On the increased freedom in his country since he became King] : The path covered up to today has not been easy or simple. But it has been possible because of the sensible maturity of the Spanish people, its desire for harmony, because of the realism and the capacity for evolution of the leaders who are today seated in this session, and because of the favorable attitude of the high organs of the state to rise to the demands of society.

Before the Cortes (Parliament), Madrid, July 22/
The New York Times, 7-23:5.

WHAT THEY SAID IN 1977

George F. Kennan
*Former United States Ambassador
to the Soviet Union*
1

The danger that would be presented for the Soviet leadership by the loss of importance as the center of the Communist world is not just a political and psychological one. It also has military strategic implications of the gravest nature. [The Soviet Union] would fall between two chairs: between a Communist world that had rejected it, and a capitalist world that would not accept it.

U.S. News & World Report, 8-1:28.

Henry A. Kissinger
Secretary of State of the United States
2

I believe that, of course, the Soviet Union is a superpower and as such impinges on us [the U.S.] in many parts of the world. It is a growing military power that in many respects has the capacity to threaten our survival. I believe, however, that the military problem is soluble. I believe the Soviet Union as a system is beset by tremendous weaknesses. There is no Communist state in the world that has managed to achieve spontaneous support of its population. The states of Eastern Europe have to appeal to a sort of bourgeois nationalism to maintain a modicum of legitimacy. And to imagine that societies that are doing well in certain high-priority areas of military technical knowledge but that have never solved effectively the problem of distribution and of even simple administration — that those societies can launch themselves on an indeterminate course of world domination without grave hesitation, seems to me unrealistic.

*Interview, Washington/
The New York Times, 1-20:16.*

Henry A. Kissinger
*Former Secretary of State
of the United States*
3

We must frankly recognize the problem that we will face if the Communists come to power [in Europe]. We must avoid giving the impression that we consider Communist success a foregone conclusion by ostentatious association or consultation with Communist leaders or by ambiguous declarations. We do our friends in Europe no favor if we encourage the notion that the advent of Communists and their allies into power will make little or no difference to our own attitudes and policies. If the United States has a responsibility to encourage political freedom throughout the world, we surely have a duty to leave no doubt about our convictions on an issue that is so central to the future of the Western alliance and therefore to the future of democracy.

*At conference sponsored by American Enterprise
Institute for Public Policy Research and Hoover
Institution on War, Revolution and Peace,
Washington, June 9/The New York Times, 6-10:(A)6.*

Panayotis Lambrias
*Undersecretary to Premier Constantine
Caramanlis of Greece*
4

I think the greatest threat to democracy [in Greece] will be if a trend develops to negate Caramanlis' policy of removing passion from politics and exercising restraint. If, for reasons of demagogic pressure or political animosity, the present stability is reversed, it would be catastrophic. But this time, as opposed to 1967, it would be very difficult for the military to intervene — primarily because by then we hope to be integrated into the Common Market. Isolated countries are much more easily threatened than a country belonging to a larger European order, such as the EEC.

The Washington Post, 7-17:(A)18.

Joseph Luns
*Secretary General, North Atlantic
Treaty Organization*
5

There is no doubt that, without economic strength and without healthy economic development, the NATO nations could maintain neither their military posture nor their cohesion. Weaknesses in the economic position of countries of the Alliance might, as a by-product, lead to countries trying to take independent measures against one another. Certainly, the recession of recent years has shown how interrelated economic strengths and military posture are. Compared with the Eastern bloc, of course, our economic strengths are

314

(JOSEPH LUNS)

immense. But the priorities given to the military posture are not often those the present times demand. That is not so much the fault of the economic establishment as it is the fault of the political establishment.

Interview, Brussels/
The Christian Science Monitor, 12-15:10.

Jack Lynch
Prime Minister of Ireland

1

[Supporting the unification of Ireland and Northern Ireland]: I remain strong in my belief that it would take nothing from the honor of Britain, or from the rights of the [Protestant] majority in Northern Ireland, if the British government were to acknowledge this aspiration and positively to encourage the people of this island to progress together as a nation of many traditions — each entitled to its own value and entitled to its own respect in harmony with the people of the United Kingdom with whom we have such close ties.

Before Dail (Parliament), Dublin, Oct. 12/
The Dallas Times Herald, 10-13:(A)4.

Georges Marchais
Secretary general,
Communist Party of France

2

A lot of water has flowed under the bridge since 1917. We think that the conditions exist today for using a democratic way to achieve a socialist society. Socialist democracy in our country will not be of the same kind as social democracy in countries where it already exists. If all that is Eurocommunism, we are in agreement on its meaning.

News conference, Madrid, March 3/
The Washington Post, 3-4:(A)8.

Dom Mintoff
Prime Minister of Malta

3

Throughout this [Mediterranean] area, Communism has grown with little Soviet help. The Italian, French, Greek and Spanish parties found there are as many minuses as plusses in Moscow's approach. They feel — and are — internally independent. They don't believe in

Soviet dictatorship. They favor pluralism. They are getting nearer to the brand of humanistic socialism we want. We don't wish to be hostile to the Soviets; simply to coexist. We are more likely to change the Russians than they are to change us. We want both superpowers to help this region. After all, U.S. interests here — like access to oil — are the same as Europe's.

Interview, Valletta, Malta/
The New York Times, 1-9:(4)21.

4

Being a foreign base brings us into trouble with our neighbors. So, since we became a republic in 1974 — 10 years after Malta received its initial independence but still acknowledged England's Queen — we decided to become a center for peace. We must make sure that our neighbors in both Europe and North Africa accept us as such. Luckily, there is more cohesion between these areas than appears at first sight. They can't advance if they move separately, and we want to help them work together. That is our conception of non-alignment.

Interview, Valletta, Malta/
The New York Times, 1-9:(4)21.

Walter F. Mondale
Vice President of the United States

5

I am here [in West Berlin] . . . to assure you that United States policy is based on our full support for your city — a policy that guarantees, with our allies, your freedom and security . . . . the United States will not only fulfill its promise to see that Berlin survives, but also to go further to help this city and its residents flourish as an important part of the Western world.

West Berlin, Jan. 26/
Los Angeles Herald-Examiner, 1-26:(A)1.

6

One cannot celebrate the independence of my nation without once again being profoundly grateful to the spirit and contributions of the people of France who helped bring about our [U.S.] independence. We can be successful in shaping a better world but we cannot do it alone. It is especially important in the mind of

WHAT THEY SAID IN 1977

(WALTER F. MONDALE)

our government that we have the best possible relationship with France . . . our oldest ally and friend.

Paris, Jan. 28/
Los Angeles Times, 1-29:(1)3.

1

[On the forthcoming Spanish Parliamentary elections, the first free elections in Spain in 40 years]: Both of our countries now share a common love and support of democracy and human liberty. I wish to say on behalf of my President, on behalf of the people of my country, that we are thrilled and excited by the developments toward a democratic society here in your country.

Madrid, May 17/
Los Angeles Times, 5-18:(1)11.

Richard M. Nixon
Former President of the United States

2

[The late Soviet leader Nikita] Khrushchev was boorish, crude, brilliant, ruthless, potentially rash, terrible inferiority complex. I'll never forget one time at Camp David when we were up there with [the late U.S. President Dwight] Eisenhower, that we were trying to make pleasant conversation at lunch and Eisenhower asked Khrushchev where he went for his vacations. He says he went to the Crimea, and . . . Eisenhower said, well, he didn't like the seashore so well, he liked to go to the desert. And Eisenhower said: "The only trouble with vacations is that you . . . can't get away from the telephone. You've always got the telephone." The translation was made and Khrushchev blew up, angry. He says: "We've got telephones in the Soviet Union, too! We've got more telephones than you have!" Well, in any event, that's typical of what we ran into . . . [Current Soviet leader Leonid Brezhnev is] intellectually not as quick as Khrushchev, but smart. As far as his temperament is concerned, not as rash as Khrushchev, more cautious, one who consults with people before acting, rather moving off impulsively on his own; not as volatile as Khrushchev, and in that way, a much

safer man to have sitting there with his finger on the button than Khrushchev.

Television interview, San Clemente, Calif./
"The Nixon Interviews," Paradine Productions, 5-12.

David Owen
Foreign Secretary of the United Kingdom

3

It is deliberate that I have not once mentioned the term "Eurocommunism." I am deeply skeptical that any such a unified phenomenon exists. It is a dangerous term. It confers a respectability of an ill-defined, disparate and as yet unidentifiable phenomenon . . . I reject the term because it can easily mean lowering the guard of democratic socialists. It will not be long before we will be asked to link the British Communist Party with Eurocommunism. An attempt is already being made to persuade the Labor Party to confer on British Communists the same credibility we are in danger of giving to their Italian, French and Spanish counterparts. The danger is that the Labor Party will be slowly turned away from its present outright opposition and traditional hostility to the Communist Party in Britain. We will be asked, first, to tolerate, then to associate and then to combine with the Communists under the broad banner of the left and embraced within the heady froths of Eurocommunism. We must resist, for it could spell electoral death for the Labor Party. In working with our fellow socialists, we are bound to pay due regard to their own national political circumstances and their own national involvement with the Communist parties. But it is not part of our philosophy to work independently with their Communist parties. We should deliberately fragment so-called Eurocommunism so as to deal with it country by country, recognizing that vigilance should be our watchword and that it is not in the interest of democratic socialism to promote Communism at the expense of our fellow socialists anywhere in Europe.

Nov. 18/The Washington Post, 11-23:(A)16.

Giancarlo Pajetta
Member, politburo, Italian Communist Party

4

It's not obligatory today to be a Marxist. You can still be a Communist if you want to

(GIANCARLO PAJETTA)

participate in the realization of our program, if you seek social justice in society. It's not different from being able to be an Episcopalian or a Mormon or a Catholic and still be a Democrat or a Republican. We are not an ideological party. We want to emphasize our lay character. The culture and philosophy of Marx and Lenin and Gransci [the first Italian Communist ideologist] taught us to understand historical developments, but a revolutionary thought cannot be frozen in dogma. We don't want to reduce Marx to a catechism. The Communist Manifesto is useful in some ways, but there are parts which may have nothing to do with today, that are about another epoch altogether.

The New York Times, 12-1:(A)10.

Andreas Papandreou
Greek politician
1

[On the left's capturing 38 per cent of the vote in the recent national election]: It is very clear that whatever plans [Premier Constantine] . Caramanlis has concerning his foreign policy will have to be revised ... On Cyprus and the Aegean, Washington has supported Turkish expansionism and pressured the Caramanlis government to behave "responsibly" – in other words, not to react. I can assure you that, through our voice in Parliament, the voice of Greece will be heard ... We are a genuine opposition this time ... NATO has meant for Greece a seven-year dictatorship ... It is therefore not surprising that in Greece, where American policy has had a greater impact than in other European countries, the majority of the people are not pro-NATO. We want Greece out of the Alliance, and the American bases must go.... there can no longer be a client-state relationship between Athens and Washington.
Interview, Athens/The Washington Post, 11-27:(A)15.

Sotiris Papapolitis
Member of Greek Parliament
2

[Lamenting the domination of Greek politics by small elite groups]: There is an irreversi-

ble demand to eliminate these dynasties. An increase in literacy and education, immigration, urbanization – they're all involved. As we say in Greek, they're all cooking, and cooking means pressure. Consider it in the context of the historical process. For sociologists, historians, political scientists studying revolution, these are the characteristic signs. And if there is not an outlet, a political discipline and apparatus, the process will not be peaceful, I'm afraid. It is unbearable, it's crazy, in 1977 – the 20th century – to still have a feudal political and social system, a geronocracy ordering arbitrarily, from the top.
The Washington Post, 5-2:(A)10.

Ion Patan
Deputy Prime Minister and Minister of Foreign Trade of Romania
3

[On his government's large investment in an American coal mine]: I did have to do a lot of explaining here why a developing socialist country, which has a per capita income of $1,000, should invest in the United States. I explained that it was a good investment for a resource we need, and that it was part of a process of increasing the understanding between the peoples of our countries ... We do intend to diversify. You can't go only on one side in the world today. We have economic relations with every country except South Africa, Rhodesia and South Korea. We have even had problems of [Arab] boycott because of our trade with Israel.
*Interview, Bucharest/
The Washington Post, 7-12:(A)12.*

Claiborne Pell
United States Senator, D–Rhode Island
4

[Saying the U.S. should not interfere if Communists are allowed into the Italian government]: Continued appeals to anti-Communism are likely to fall on deaf ears if the economy continues to deteriorate and feelings of social injustice grow. We should also make it equally clear that we have no intention of interfering in Italy's internal affairs or threatening to punish the Italian people if their leaders choose to run

WHAT THEY SAID IN 1977

(CLAIBORNE PELL)

the great risks involved in bringing the Communists into the government.

Washington, Jan. 29/
The Dallas Times Herald, 1-30:(A)4.

Prince Philip
Duke of Edinburgh
1

[On Britain's growing bureaucracy in government] : Once a determined government begins the process of eroding human rights and liberties — always with the best possible intentions — it is very difficult for individuals or for individual groups to stand against it. If the experience of other countries is anything to go by, this [increasing bureaucracy] will mean a gradual reduction in the freedom of choice and individual responsibility, particularly in such things as housing, the education of children, health care, the ability to acquire or inherit personal property, to hand on commercial enterprises, and the ability to provide for old age through personal savings, and, perhaps the most important of all, the freedom of the individual to exploit his skills or talents as suits him best . . . Some of the things I have said may strike you as unthinkable in this country, with its tradition of freedom and tolerance. I can only say that there were people to be found in many other countries who felt the same way, but the unthinkable happened to them.

Radio interview, Oct. 27/
The Dallas Times Herald, 10-27:(A)5.

Richard E. Pipes
Professor of history, Harvard University;
Senior research consultant, Stanford Research
Institute's Strategic Studies Center,
Arlington, Virginia
2

The Soviet government lacks a mandate to rule; it rules by coercion. Yet it claims to be the world's most democratic and egalitarian society, [and] its greatest fear is that the Soviet people will call upon it to make good this claim. Democracy and equality would entail, for the elite, the loss of all the privileges it now enjoys. Hence [the regime] will fight ruthlessly for the status quo — and react violently to any

pressure on behalf of human rights. This means constantly improving internal security and military power.

Interview/Newsweek, 11-14:60.

J. H. Plumb
British historian
3

[On the monarchy as an institution] : You know, intellectually, it has a sense of the dinosaur about it. Emotionally and socially, it works. All heads of state are expensive to staff, and [the British monarchy is] probably less expensive than many, oddly enough. You get an enormous amount of dedication to the task to be done because people are trained from birth to do it. I've fought for many things in England — certainly to remove the hereditary aristocracy I wouldn't hesitate. But to remove the monarchy? I should feel very concerned about that.

Interview, New York/
"W": a Fairchild publication, 1-7:10.

Andrei D. Sakharov
Soviet physicist
4

. . . in order to achieve the good life here [in the Soviet Union] , one necessarily develops a certain conformist mentality. For most people, there is no opportunity to compare the system here with systems outside. The material side of life has improved here and people know it. So humans work, live and exist here, not knowing of any other kind of life. On the surface, this might appear to be harmonious, but this life has many tragedies . . . Everyone wants to have a job, be married, have children, be happy; but dissidents must be prepared to see their lives destroyed and those dear to them hurt. When I look at my situation and my family's situation and that of my country, I realize that things are getting steadily worse. But for myself, I cannot consider emigration or even leaving this country provisionally. When people who are very close to me are persecuted, it creates an almost unbearable situation for me personally.

Time, 2-21:29.

(ANDREI D. SAKHAROV)

1

The activities against dissidents [in the Soviet Union] in recent times have always been cruel. We only know what they [the authorities] do; we can't know what they are thinking. They began to see there was support of a wide group of the population, and the regime cracked down because they didn't want any worse trouble. I believe that the point is that the dissident movement grows out of the conditions of our lives. So when one layer of ice is removed from the surface of the water, a new crust forms, and then another ... It is a continuous process.

Interview, Moscow/
The Washington Post, 11-28:(A)12.

Helmut Schmidt
Chancellor of West Germany

2

[On terrorist violence in his country] : The murderers want to create a general feeling of official powerlessness. They hope that their violence will bring about an emotionally charged, indiscriminate, uncontrolled reaction so that they can then denounce our country as a Fascist dictatorship. Their expectations will not be fulfilled. Our free way of government could be sacrificed only by us ourselves. Our moral condemnation of the perpetrators and anger and shock will not lead us to act out of emotion.

At funeral for assassinated Federal prosecutor,
Karlsruhe, West Germany, April 13/
The New York Times, 4-14:(A)3.

3

I have been hearing about the so-called "NATO crisis" for the last 20 years and I expect to hear about it for some time to come. Facts and figures must of course be taken seriously, but not the general pessimism of the newspaper headlines. Generally speaking, the West has been able to maintain an equilibrium of military capabilities that has deterred adventurism, and will, I think, continue to do so in the future. I don't see any drama there.

Interview/Newsweek, 6-13:50.

Klaus Schutz
Mayor of West Berlin

4

Our people are the same as the people in any other large German city, yet they are asked to think in international terms. This is easy to do in time of crisis when there appear to be only two choices – freedom or the Soviets. But with the pressure off, local considerations loom larger and, of course, political differences are greater ... When I travel, I feel interest in and support for Berlin. But overall it is not the same as before, because if one is not attacked, no one needs to defend you. I'm urged on all sides to give the citizens new goals – but believe me, that isn't as easy as it used to be.

Interview, West Berlin/
The Christian Science Monitor, 1-14:7.

Harold E. Shear
Admiral, United States Navy;
Commander-in-Chief, Allied Forces/
Southern Europe

5

It's the Greece-Turkey [rift] situation that's the most difficult, the most unhealthy now. We simply can't afford to have these two nations as less than fully viable members of NATO ... There's tremendous dependence by the Alliance on Greece and Turkey. The loss, political or military, of any of these nations would mean a tremendous degradation of the Alliance across the board, a big hole as far as the effectiveness and cohesiveness of the Alliance across Europe.

Interview, Naples, Italy/
The New York Times, 10-16:(1)5.

Dimitri K. Simes
Director of Soviet policy studies,
Center for Strategic and International
Studies, Georgetown University

6

Planned economies of the Eastern European states have failed to cope with technological progress and growing consumer expectations. Highly centralized bureaucratic planning, subject to political influences from the Communist Party apparatus, is incapable of providing the degree of flexibility vital for advanced industrial societies.

Nation's Business, August:51.

WHAT THEY SAID IN 1977

Marshall D. Shulman
Senior adviser on Soviet affairs
to Secretary of State of the
United States Cyrus R. Vance
1

The Soviet Union is on the threshold of a wholesale generational turnover at the upper levels of its power structure. Not necessarily in the next succession, but within the foreseeable future, it is clear that an ascendant generation will be holding the levers of power, and one of the most intriguing questions before us concerns the character of that generation, men now in their 40s and early 50s . . . Whether they will tend to move toward nationalism and orthodoxy, or toward Western-style modernization, we cannot now predict. All that we can say, perhaps, is that to the extent they see their interest in a responsible involvement of their country in the world economy and the world community, they should not feel from what we do or say that this option is closed to them.

Before House International Relations
Subcommittee on Europe and the Middle East,
Washington, Oct. 26/The New York Times,
10-27:(A)3.

Mario Soares
Prime Minister of Portugal
2

The Communists are a force [in Portugal] and we cannot ignore them, nor can we ignore the extreme right. The Socialist Party is the only force which can keep the balance, the only democratic option.

The New York Times, 5-15:(1)5.

3

Democracy is pluralism, and when you've emerged from a dictatorship as we did . . . you have no trouble recognizing where it exists and where it does not.

At symposium on the future of democracy,
Athens/San Francisco Examiner & Chronicle,
10-16:(This World)2.

Adolfo Suarez (Gonzalez)
Premier of Spain
4

[On terrorism]: If you are prepared not to allow yourself to be intimidated by these criminal acts; if you, people of Spain, ladies and gentlemen, continue to want elections so that our country can be governed by authentic representatives in the near future . . . then I assure you that terrorism will be defeated, Spain will continue its way to a future of order and liberty, though at times with pain, and the government will go forward with its program, which is *your* program.

Broadcast address to the nation/
Los Angeles Times, 2-13:(1)17.

5

To the right of us are parties and coalitions with programs that we consider absolutely insufficient and with political characteristics unpropitious for dialogue. To our left, the most important parties offer programs that are moderate in the short term, but they themselves do not hide that their programs have goals inspired and dominated by the Marxist ideology . . . The Union of the Democratic Center offers the middle way, without risks, improvisations or inexperience.

Broadcast election campaign address, Madrid,
June 13/The New York Times, 6-14:16.

Margaret Thatcher
Member of British Parliament;
Leader, British Conservative Party
6

. . . as far as the Helsinki Pact was concerned, the Communists themselves put their signatures to the clauses about safeguarding human rights. So it's not only a question of individual rights as a universal concept. In this case, they are part of an international agreement to which the Communists committed themselves in return for other things which they got from that agreement. I think that is very important. The Russians signed up for human rights because, by doing so, they were able to bargain for something else they wanted: trade credits and so on. So they can't therefore just ignore them. They must not expect to take advantage of those parts of Helsinki which suit them, while turning their backs on the parts they find embarrassing. They said they would do something to improve human rights in return for other things they wanted. The West . . . cannot and must not forget that.

Interview, London/U.S. News & World Report, 9-12:71.

(MARGARET THATCHER)

1

In our system, the government can choose when it calls an election at any time within five years. Therefore, the present government can go on as long as the Liberals or one of the other minor parties will support it. But I take the view that some of the things this government has done are such that their own people have lost confidence in them. So whenever there is an election, we [Conservatives] shall win, and I hope with a good majority. Inflation, a drop in the real standard of living, no increase in our manufacturing output in three years, a taxation system so heavy that many ordinary people say there's no incentive to work — those sources of resentment [will not] disappear.

Interview, New York/Time, 9-19:44.

2

[The British Labor Party] wants the people to believe that it's a gentle, well-behaved, social democratic pussycat. But from one election to the next, Labor's programs get meaner, more narrow, more Marxist. Destroying freedoms we have cherished and defended down the centuries won't worry the far left. They like everything about Eastern Europe, except, alas, going to live there, because, after all, the living standards are very low.

At Conservative Party conference, Blackpool,
England, Oct. 14/The New York Times, 10-15:9.

Penelope Hartland Thunberg
Economic research director, Center for
Strategic and International Studies,
Georgetown University

3

The claim of the centrally controlled economies of Eastern Europe that they have solved the problems of unemployment which plague industrial democracies had a somewhat hollow ring when one observed employed workers in Poland revolt against what they correctly perceived as their government's attempt to lower further their standard of living. Similarly, the claim of these countries to having solved problems of growth and the business cycle are not persuasive when one notes the wave of borrowing by these countries from the indus-

trial democracies in order to finance imports of Western technology. All regimes in Eastern Europe unequivocally state these imports are essential to reverse the decline in their own growth rates.

Nation's Business, August:54.

Leo Tindemans
Prime Minister of Belgium

4

Three points of friction with the United States worry Europe — the growing energy crisis, the low value of the dollar and the rising threat of protectionism. Economics are involved with politics, and the prolonged world economic crisis is threatening stable U.S.-European relations.

Interview, Brussels/The Washington Post, 10-17:(D)13.

Fumihiko Togo
Japanese Ambassador to the United States

5

Japan and other free nations of Asia, having these two great powers [China and the Soviet Union] with different social systems as neighbors, realize that the participation of the United States in Asian affairs is very important for maintenance of an equilibrium of power in that part of the world.

Before mid-Atlantic regional organization of
Association of Asian Studies, Princeton University,
Oct. 29/The New York Times, 10-31:3.

Aldo Tortorella
Member, executive committee,
Communist Party of Italy

6

What does it mean to be a socialist [i.e., a Communist] in Italy? It means to be for a process we frankly call gradualist, designed to resolve the practical questions facing our country, with full understanding both of the faults committed in socialist [i.e., Communist] states and of the inadequacy of pure capitalism as a system ... To us, the welfare state is not of itself an answer. We want to go beyond the welfare state. We want to modify, to change the state so that we have a democracy of the masses — the full participation of citizens in all aspects of society. It is up to the trade unions to defend the economic interests of workers. A political party should have other preoccupa-

WHAT THEY SAID IN 1977

(ALDO TORTORELLA)

tions. You cannot talk of defending the interests of workers without opening up the question of the country as a whole. If you have high wages in the north and miserable pittances in the south, that is not just an economic anomaly. It is a political question.

Interview, Rome/
The Christian Science Monitor, 4-14:30.

Stansfield Turner
Director of Central Intelligence
of the United States
1

The Soviets have their strengths and they have their own weaknesses. Their weaknesses are in economics and politics. I don't see the Soviet economy climbing to outdistance us. Our lead is so great that they cannot hope to overtake us unless our percentage of growth every year were to be a lot smaller than theirs. And that is not happening . . . As for ideology, the Russians may think it is a strength for them, but I am sure we would all agree that their ideology is hamstringing them in many ways. After all, what's left of pure Marxism? Where is it practiced or believed in? You have a different brand of Communism in every country in Europe — and a different brand in Yugoslavia, a different brand in China. Even in the Soviet Union, they don't hold to it very carefully. So, no, I don't think the Soviets are on the ascendancy ideologically . . . They have a strong military position. One of the reasons they are putting such emphasis on their military strength is that they are trying to convert military power into political advantage. They have no other strengths that they can exploit in Africa and elsewhere. Military is all that they have.

Interview/U.S. News & World Report, 5-16:24.

Dmitri F. Ustinov
Minister of Defense of the Soviet Union
2

Our country's economy, science and technology are now at such a high level that we are capable, within the shortest period, of matching any type of weapon that the enemies of peace create . . . The Soviet Union spends for military purposes as much as is necessary to ensure a reliable defense.

San Francisco Examiner & Chronicle,
2-27:(This World)2.

Peter Ustinov
Actor, Director, Writer
3

Of all nations, the French seem to me the most vindictive, and most able to carry their quarrels into the beyond, after death has put an end to their tumultuous eloquence. Ancient hatreds are nurtured like precious flowers in a garden, and diatribes about half-forgotten and even historical contentions have all the freshness of a burning topicality.

Interview, Paris/Los Angeles Times, 9-6:(4)14.

John A. Volpe
United States Ambassador to Italy
4

I like to believe that [Italian Communist Party leader Enrico] Berlinguer, in good faith, believes they could enter the government and be a democratic and pluralistic party. But history has not yet indicated that has been the case with the Communist Party. So it is up to the Italian people to determine whether they want to look at what history has to show, or whether perhaps there is a definite change in the position of the Communist Party and leaders.

To reporters, Rome, Jan. 21/
Los Angeles Times, 1-22:(1)3.

Yuli Vorontsov
Chief Soviet delegate to conference
on the Helsinki Agreement on
European Security and Cooperation
5

[Human rights and fundamental freedoms in the Soviet Union are] more than just proclaimed and laid down in laws; they are guaranteed by our socio-economic system itself. It is a fact that unemployment is non-existent in the Soviet Union and Soviet citizens enjoy free medical care and free education . . .

At conference on the Helsinki Agreement,
Belgrade, Yugoslavia, Oct. 6/
The Washington Post, 10-7:(A)23.

Lewis W. Walt
*General (Ret.) and former Assistant
Commandant, United States Marine Corps*

1

... the Soviet Union has the military capability to take Western Europe in 14 days. I don't think they will now, because of China. But with the lack of vehicles and the lack of tanks we have there, our capabilities to defend are extremely limited. We are terribly outnumbered and, in fact, we don't have enough trucks over there to carry the ammunition up to the guns ... People think that when the time comes we'll be alerted and be able to build up in Europe. Well, we won't have time to get built up. The world is too small now. The advantage the Soviets have is that they maneuver on the western border all the time with 135 divisions. They could mass on one front and break right through. Furthermore, they control the seas. We couldn't resupply or reinforce.

Interview/The Dallas Times Herald, 5-19:(E)1.

Harold Wilson
*Former Prime Minister
of the United Kingdom*

2

Two world wars took all our investments. And the lend-lease agreement with the Americans not only took all our markets — which was justified as we didn't want shipping going to Latin America — but we had to give them all our inventions [such as hovercraft, penicillin, radar, nuclear inventions]. All these things were handed over without a penny back. [If Britain received 100 sterling royalties for every jet engine produced in the U.S.,] we would have the biggest balance-of-payments surplus in the world. We have to sell it all as part of sacrifice in the war.

*On British TV talk show, Jan. 22/
The Washington Post, 1-24:(A)14.*

The Middle East

James Abourezk
United States Senator, D–South Dakota   1

[Criticizing the so-called "Israeli lobby" in Washington] : Its ability to accomplish virtually any legislative feat involving military or economic assistance to Israel is legend . . . I gave an oath to support the United States, but I am not willing to swear my allegiance to Israel or any foreign government . . . Just as we have seen U.S. Presidents wrap themselves in the American flag in efforts to stifle criticism of their policies, so do we see a foreign country wrapping itself in its state religion, so that criticism of the state or its policies is perceived as a form of racism.

At Jefferson-Jackson Day dinner, Denver,
March 26/The New York Times, 3-28:12.

Farouk al-Akhdar
Chairman, royal commission supervising
industrial, port and pipeline
projects in Saudi Arabia   2

[On possible U.S. legislation outlawing cooperation by American firms with the Arab economic boycott of Israel] : We are sorry if the boycott issue excludes U.S. firms from Saudi Arabia. They are good companies. They make fast decisions and work well. We empathize with them. If they go, we will be sorry, because we prefer them. But others — Japanese, West Germans, French — can and will take their place . . . These ridiculous actions by the U.S. Congress are opposed more to the American interest than ours. They make us certain that this is an Israeli effort aimed at ruining American business with the Arab world, which is growing steadily despite everything.

The Christian Science Monitor, 2-17:5.

Mouaffak el-Allaf
Syrian Ambassador/Permanent
Representative to the United Nations   3

[Criticizing Egyptian President Anwar Sadat's recent unprecedented trip to Israel] : Could this hero of the July 23 revolution, the successor of Gamal Abdel Nasser, be the same man who shook the hand of terrorist [Israeli Prime Minister] Menachem Begin, the one who shook the hand of the war criminal [Israeli Foreign Minister] Moshe Dayan, who planted a kiss on the cheek of the racist [former Israeli Prime Minister] Golda Meir? What has happened? . . .

At United Nations, New York, Nov. 22/
The New York Times, 11-23:(A)3;
Los Angeles Times, 11-23:(1)12.

4

Why does this President of Egypt go to visit officially the occupied [Arab] lands in a ceremonious visit which is greeted by 21 shots, a red carpet and fluttering banners? Did Israel withdraw from any inch of occupied territory? Did Israel suddenly announce it welcomed the convening of the Geneva conference without conditions or obstacles? That it no longer refuses to speak to the Palestinians? No. Not one iota of this took place.

At United Nations, New York, Nov. 22/
The New York Times, 11-23:(A)3;
Los Angeles Times, 11-23:(1)12.

Yasir Arafat
Chairman, Palestine Liberation Organization   5

The question is whether the U.S. is willing to put pressure on Israel. Everybody in this area believes that the U.S. can make Israel change its position; but in the American position I see only a continuous pursuit of how many more concessions the Arabs can give.

Interview, Beirut, Lebanon/Time, 3-21:33.

(YASIR ARAFAT)

1

[I am] not a man for settlements or concessions. I will carry on the struggle until every inch of Palestinian soil will be retrieved [from Israel] ... Our revolution is a revolution of liberation, not a revolution of concessions. We will not give up one inch of our lands, nor will we relinquish a single one of our rights.

Interview/Los Angeles Herald-Examiner, 8-24:(A)8.

2

[Condemning Egyptian President Anwar Sadat's unprecedented trip to Israel] : ... I say to our masses in [Israeli-] occupied Jerusalem that occupied Jerusalem will only be regained through blood and struggle and not through capitulation and kneeling.

At rally, Beirut, Nov. 20/
The New York Times, 11-21:18.

Hafez al-Assad
President of Syria

3

A just solution [to the Arab-Israeli conflict] is a solution under which all grievances and injustices are removed so that there will be no territory occupied by others. Such a solution can be embodied in these three terms: (1) withdrawal by Israel from territories occupied since 1967; (2) ensuring the rights of the Arab people of Palestine; (3) ending the state of war ... We may agree to discuss certain kinds of guarantees, provided that such guarantees are equal on the Arab side and the Israeli side. All this must be within the framework of a just and peaceful solution. For example, if [that] solution requires the presence of a United Nations observer force or a UN emergency force on the line that divides the two parties, then we are willing to discuss this, provided that the presence is on both sides of the line. Again, it is possible to discuss the idea of a demilitarized zone, provided it is of narrow limits and on both sides.

Interview, Damascus/Time, 1-24:32.

4

We have no doubt that the role of the U.S. with regard to what is happening in this area [the Middle East] is a major role. However, our constant criticism of this role is that it does not conform to the special responsibilities of the U.S. and its huge interests in this region. It also does not conform to the lofty principles for which the American people have fought and struggled. If the American role should develop in such a way as to conform to the special responsibilities of the U.S. as a superpower, to the interests of the American people and to the principles for which they stand, then the American role will be more effective in achieving a just peace in this area.

Interview, Damascus/Time, 1-24:38.

5

[Rejecting the idea that, to be meaningful, a peace agreement with Israel would have to be followed by normalization of diplomatic, trade, cultural and other relations): There is no precedent in history for such a thing, except when a victor imposes such relationships on a defeated state. For instance, could any state in the world force the United States to establish trade or economic cooperation when the United States is not desirous of that or thinks it is not in her interest? Or could the United States impose such a requirement on anyone else? Ending the state of war in accordance with a peace agreement is one thing; the imposition of the will of Israel with regard to diplomatic relations, cultural and economic cooperations is another thing.

Interview, Latakia, Syria, Aug. 26/
The New York Times, 8-29:1.

6

There's no third choice; it's either peace or war [between the Arabs and Israel]. I don't mean today or tomorrow. But eventually, Israel will not be able to continue challenging us. Arabs have a population many times that of Israel; we have many times the area; we have many times the resources; we're going to have many times more technicians. The qualitative gap is closing. The future cannot be in favor of Israel.

Interview, Latakia, Syria, Aug. 26/
The New York Times, 8-29:10.

WHAT THEY SAID IN 1977

(HAFEZ AL-ASSAD)

1

[On Egyptian President Anwar Sadat's decision to go to Jerusalem in search of an end to the Arab-Israeli conflict]: We disagree on this issue. Peace is an objective for both Syria and Egypt, but I don't see that there was a need for Sadat to visit Israel for the sake of peace. I am convinced that this trip will not achieve the aims of the Arab nation. But, of course, President Sadat had a different view on this matter. [Sadat's surprise decision] deeply hurt me because I was unable to convince him of the dangers and far-reaching repercussions for the Arab cause and nation.

Damascus, Syria, Nov. 17/
Los Angeles Times, 11-18:(1)1.

George W. Ball
Former Under Secretary of State
of the United States

2

The Middle East is top priority — a challenge that requires this country [the U.S.] to pursue an extremely assertive policy. We must lay out the terms of an Arab-Israeli settlement that seems fair and reasonable, and make it clear that we're not going to continue to pour $2-billion of public money into Israel to sustain a state of affairs that can have only a disastrous outcome ... [A new Arab-Israeli war] would be different in character from earlier Middle East wars. Civilian populations in cities would be targets, as both sides now have surface-to-surface missiles. And it would be a war involving great danger of a superpower confrontation. So I regard the Arab-Israeli problem as the most serious and urgent problem that we face.

Interview/U.S. News & World Report, 6-27:46.

Menachem Begin
Prime Minister-elect of Israel

3

[On his being called a terrorist]: I don't give a damn what I'm called. I'm used to it. Let me explain. In the '40s, the Germans were killing our brethren. No Jews were allowed to come into this country. We begged the British, "Open the gates; let them come in." What did we do? We started to fight, to open the gates and allow our people to be saved from destruction. We started to fight to save our people. Now, take [PLO leader Yasir] Arafat. What is his aim? He said in the so-called Palestinian charter that it was the destruction of the Jewish state. Israel must disappear. He wants to destroy a nation. Our aim is to save a people. When I am called a terrorist and Arafat is called a guerrilla, I think it is the apex of injustice.

Interview, Tel Aviv/Time, 5-30:31.

4

[On his country's settlement of the West Bank]: We are ready to give the people of Samaria and Judea free option of citizenship. If they want Israeli citizenship, they will get it. If they prefer to keep their previous citizenship, they may. We are not going to force ours on them. They can have complete cultural autonomy and social and economic advancement, living in their homes. This is their homeland — living together with us. What is wrong with a Jewish majority living together with an Arab minority in peace, in human dignity, in equality of rights? I believe that we can live together. It is not an "occupied" country as people understand that horrible term. We let them live in their homeland.

Interview, Tel Aviv/Time, 5-30:31.

5

The Americans give us aid because we fulfill a very serious role in the vital interests of the U.S. For example ... in 1970, Syrian tanks were poised to invade Jordan, and the U.S. Sixth Fleet was in no position to do much. So they asked us to move. We concentrated a certain number of troops, and three days later the Syrians withdrew. We prevented a conflagration in the Middle East. And then there is the very large issue of Communism. If we should give up Judea and Samaria, there would be a Palestinian state there which would become a Soviet base. We prevent Communism from taking over this part of the world, which links three continents.

Interview, Tel Aviv/Newsweek, 5-30:37.

Menachem Begin
Prime Minister of Israel

1

Israel will not ask any nations to recognize its right to exist. Israel's very existence is its right to exist, paid for in its blood, such as no nation has ever paid . . .

Upon being sworn in as Prime Minister, Jerusalem,
June 20/Los Angeles Times, 6-21:(1)6.

2

[Saying his country cannot allow the PLO to participate in any Arab-Israeli peace negotiations]: We cannot accept participation of that organization. They declared in their covenant or charter — in Article 19 of their charter — that the state of Israel is null and void fundamentally. They also declare that only those Jews who were born or lived in Palestine until the beginning of the Zionist invasion, as they put it — in other words, until the proclamation of the Balfour Declaration — will be regarded Palestinians. And all the others, as assumption goes, will have to leave the country. And other articles whose contents are quite known. So we do know what is their design, what they strive for. To put it bluntly and simply, their design is to destroy our country and to destroy our people. Therefore, they cannot be a partner to any negotiations with Israel.

News conference, Washington, July 20/
The New York Times, 7-21:(A)14.

3

The Arabs living in our country have a perfect right, always, forever, to live in our country, and they have a perfect right to have equality of rights. The Jewish majority and the Arab minority should live in equality of rights, in human dignity, in economic advancement. This is our attitude, and therefore this is their absolute right. As far as sovereignty is concerned, this is the only country which as a right belongs to the Jewish people. May I explain to you that now the Arab people, the great Arab people whom we respect, have 21 sovereign states, stretching from the Atlantic Ocean to the Persian Gulf, with an area of more than 12 million square kilometers. I think this is the most far-reaching expression of the right of

national self-determination. We have our little country to live in and want to keep it for our people.

TV-radio interview, New York/"Meet the
Press," National Broadcasting Company, 7-24.

4

[Addressing the people of Egypt]: Your President [Anwar Sadat] said, two days ago, that he will be ready to come to Jerusalem, to our Parliament — the Knesset — in order to prevent one Egyptian soldier from being wounded. It is a good statement. . . . it will be a pleasure to welcome and receive your President with the traditional hospitality you and we have inherited· from our common father, Abraham. And I, for my part, will, of course, be ready to come to your capital, Cairo, for the same purpose: no more wars — peace, a real peace, and forever . . . Let us not only make peace, let us also start on the road of friendship, sincere and productive cooperation. We can help each other. We can make the lives of our nations better, easier and happier . . . I say to you with all my heart: Shalom. It means sulh [peace]. And vice-versa: Sulh means shalom.
Jerusalem, Nov. 11/The Washington Post, 11-12:(A)9.

5

[On his invitation to Egyptian President Anwar Sadat to visit Israel]: This invitation does not constitute any attempt to drive a wedge between the Arab states. We are prepared to conduct negotiations for the achievement of peace in the Middle East and the signature of peace treaties with all our neighbors. With each and every one of them. I think it was only natural that I invited the President of Egypt. It is the largest of the Arab states. In our conviction, there is no basis for the conflict between Egypt and ourselves. The conflict has been tragic. Superfluous. Prolonged. And this is our appeal.

Before the Knesset (Parliament), Jerusalem,
Nov. 15/The Washington Post, 11-16:(A)18.

6

[On Egyptian President Anwar Sadat's unprecedented trip to Israel]: The reaction was positive, in the government and Parliament, but

WHAT THEY SAID IN 1977

(MENACHEM BEGIN)

first and foremost among our people. We drove, President Sadat and I, several times together. We have seen our people on the streets in the thousands, men and women and little children, and all of them greeting the President, taking him to their hearts. Our children waved both flags, the Egyptian flag and the Israeli flag. I wish, with your permission, Mr. President, to express my sincere hope that the day is not too far when Egyptian children will wave the Israeli flag and the Egyptian flag. This visit is a real success for both countries and for the cause of peace. And as we both, the President and I, believe in divine Providence, we pray, before the departure of the President and his party, we pray that the Almighty, that He give all of us the wisdom to continue in our efforts to bring peace to our nation, real peace, and so make sure that this region and all the nations dwelling here achieve peace, advance, and live in liberty, in justice and in happiness.

News conference, Jerusalem,
Nov. 21/
The New York Times,
11-22:16.

1

We have never asked for [security] guarantees ... We try to prove to people that we do not suggest to have guarantees for the state of Israel ... In the whole world there is no guarantee that can guarantee an international guarantee. That was proven after Czechoslovakia. When the test comes, guarantees do not stand the test. Therefore we ask for borders, for permanent boundaries for security. But not through guarantees. Guarantees do not give you any security whatsoever. We are experienced people. We have survived ... We can sustain our independence without anybody to fight for us, should the necessity arise to wage our battles, and shed his blood for us. We can sustain ourselves. We don't believe in guarantees.

Interview, Jerusalem/
The New York Times,
12-14:(A)20.

Leonid I. Brezhnev
General Secretary, Communist
Party of the Soviet Union

2

The Soviet Union ... has its own opinion about the main principles and directions of the future [Arab-Israeli] peace settlement. We hold, in particular, that the final documents should be based on the principle of the impermissibility of acquisition of territory by war, of the right of all states of the area to independent existence and security. It goes without saying that the inalienable rights of the Palestinian Arab people should be insured, including its right to self-determination, to the creation of its own state. We regard as unquestionable that the documents on peace should provide for the withdrawal of Israeli troops from all Arab territories occupied in 1967. Such a withdrawal could be carried out not at once, but in stages, in the course, say, of several months, within strictly defined datelines. The appropriate border lines between Israel and its Arab neighbors, participants in the conflict, should be clearly defined. We proceed from the premise that from the moment of the completion of the withdrawal of Israeli troops, the state of war between the Arab states participating in the conflict and Israel will be ended and relations of peace established.

At congress of trade unions, Moscow,
March 21/The New York Times, 3-22:14.

Zbigniew Brzezinski
Assistant to President of the
United States Jimmy Carter
for National Security Affairs

3

I think the point to bear in mind is that the United States is not just an interested bystander, not even just a benevolent mediator. The United States has a direct interest in the outcome of the Middle East conflict. The United States has a direct interest in obtaining a resolution of the conflict. And, therefore, the United States has a legitimate right to exercise its own leverage, peaceful and constructive, to obtain a settlement. And that's exactly what we will be doing.

Interview, Washington, Oct. 1/
The Washington Post, 10-3:(A)21.

(ZBIGNIEW BRZEZINSKI)

1

A Geneva settlement [to the Arab-Israeli conflict] is like a tall mountain, full of crevices and sharp rocks. Therefore, you don't go to it in a straight line. You go through zigs and zags. You even go down a little bit, then you keep moving. As long as you know where you're going, that's what's important. And we know where we're going. We know we've got to make zigs and zags.

Time, 10-17:25.

2

[On Egyptian President Anwar Sadat's decision to journey to Israel to seek peace]: This trip is an affirmative recognition by an Arab leader of the existence of Israel. This is a gesture for peace probably without parallel in contemporary history.

To reporters, Nov. 18/
Los Angeles Times, 11-20:(1)1.

Jimmy Carter
President of the United States

3

I think that what Israel would like to have is what we would like to have — a termination of belligerence toward Israel by her neighbors, a recognition of Israel's right to exist, the right to exist in peace, the opening up of borders with free trade, tourist travel, cultural exchange between Israel and her neighbors. In other words, a stabilization of the situation in the Middle East without a constant threat to Israel's existence by her neighbors. And this would involve substantial withdrawal of Israel's present control over [occupied Arab] territories. Now, where that withdrawal might end, I don't know. I would guess there would be some minor adjustments in the 1967 borders, but that still remains to be negotiated. But I think this is going to be a long, tedious process. We're going to mount a major effort in our own government in 1977 to bring the parties to Geneva. Obviously, any agreement has to be between the parties concerned. We will act as an intermediary when our good offices will serve well. But I'm not trying to predispose our own nation's attitudes toward what might be

the ultimate details of the agreement that can mean so much to world peace.

News conference, Washington, March 9/
The New York Times, 3-10:26.

4

We have a special relationship with Israel. It's absolutely crucial that no one in our country or around the world ever doubt that our Number 1 commitment in the Middle East is to protect the right of Israel to exist, to exist permanently, and to exist in peace. It's a special relationship. Although I've met with the leaders of Egypt, Syria, Jordan, and had long hours of discussion, I've never found any of those Arab leaders who objected to that special commitment of ours to the protection of the integrity of Israel. And obviously, part of that is to make sure that Israel has adequate means to protect themselves without military involvement of the United States. I have no objection about this arrangement — I'm proud of it — and it will be permanent as long as I'm in office.

News conference, Washington, May 12/
The New York Times, 5-13:(A)12.

5

I don't think that there can be any reasonable hope for a settlement of the Middle Eastern question, which has been extant now on a continuing basis for more than 29 years, without a homeland for the Palestinians. The exact definition of what that homeland might be, the degree of independence of the Palestinian entity, its relationship with Jordan or perhaps Syria and others, the geographical boundaries of it, all have to be worked out by the parties involved. But for the Palestinians to have a homeland and for the refugee question to be resolved is obviously of crucial importance.

News conference, Washington, May 12/
The New York Times, 5-13:(A)12.

6

The historic friendship between the United States and Israel is not dependent on the domestic politics of either nation. It is derived from our common respect for human freedom and from our common search for permanent

WHAT THEY SAID IN 1977

(JIMMY CARTER)

peace. We will continue to promote a settlement which all of us need. Our own policy will not be affected by changes in leadership in any of the countries in the Middle East. Therefore, we expect Israel and her neighbors to continue to be bound by UN Resolutions 242 and 338, which they have previously accepted. This is the most propitious time for a genuine settlement since the beginning of the Arab-Israel conflict. To let this opportunity pass could mean disaster, not only for the Middle East, but perhaps for the international political and economic order as well.

At University of Notre Dame commencement,
May 22/Vital Speeches, 6-15:516.

1

Some would say that peace cannot be achieved because of the accumulated mistrust and the deep emotions dividing Israelis and Arabs. Some would say that we must realistically resign ourselves to the prospect of unending struggle and conflict in the Middle East. With such an attitude of resignation, Israel would never have been created, and with such an attitude peace would not be achieved. What is needed is both vision and realism, so that strong leadership can transform the hostility of the past into a peaceful and constructive future.

Before World Jewish Congress, Washington,
Nov. 2/The Washington Post, 11-3:(A)20.

2

... I have talked to all of the leaders in the Middle East — both the Presidents, the Kings, the Prime Ministers and the Foreign Ministers — and I know from personal experience that they genuinely want peace. Some of them, I think, have underestimated the willingness of their own people to accept strong moves toward a new understanding. And I think that [Egyptian President Anwar] Sadat and [Israeli Prime Minister Menachem] Begin will show today [by Mr. Sadat's unprecedented trip to Israel] that the two nations that have continuously been at war, with tremendous suffering, whose leaders have only been separated by a 30-minute plane ride, have responded well. I think this is proof

in itself that had we leaders of the world been more aggressive in taking bold steps, that the people would have responded well.

Interview, Washington, Nov. 20/
The New York Times, 11-21:18.

Frank Church
United States Senator, D—Idaho

3

[On Egyptian President Anwar Sadat's unprecedented trip to Israel]: I would say that the curtain has gone up on a new stage in the Middle East on which the scenery has been arranged by Sadat and [Israeli Prime Minister Menachem] Begin. I don't think anyone can predict what kind of a play will unfold on that stage, but the United States suddenly finds itself a spectator, or, at most, relegated to a supporting cast — which may be the best role for us at this time.

Washington, Dec. 6/
The Washington Post, 12-7:(A)22.

Moshe Dayan
Foreign Minister-designate of Israel

4

There is nothing wrong with pushing for an agreement [between Israel and the Arabs]. The danger is if we are told that in order to get an agreement we have to accept Arab dictation — that the Arabs' terms are a, b, c, and you have to take it not because it is good or it's right but because they're the only terms under which they are ready to make peace. I say, gentlemen, we haven't lost a war that we have to accept an unconditional surrender. The danger is not pushing for a peace agreement; the danger is pushing us to accept the Arab terms.

Interview, Zahala, Israel/
The New York Times, 6-5:(4)3.

5

I personally don't think we can reach agreement [with the Arabs] by excluding the Russians altogether from the agreement. I'm not talking about the start of negotiations — that maybe can be done without the Russians. But because some of the Arab countries, like Syria, have close ties with Russia and also because we cannot pass any resolution in the [UN] Security Council without Russia. If we

(MOSHE DAYAN)

want Sharm el Sheikh as an international waterway and not territorial water, you have to have international acceptance of the agreement. I think we have to enlist Russian good-will.

Interview, Zahala, Israel/
The New York Times, 6-5:(4)3.

1

[On the Arab-Israeli conflict]: Maybe we will have to live without a solution because we have been trying for 30 years ... and I cannot see any solution that would be acceptable to the two parties. What we want, the Arabs reject; what they suggest, we do not want to accept. So it is as simple as this: It is not [Prime Minister Menachem] Begin or [former Prime Ministers] Golda [Meir] or [Levi] Eshkol or [Yitzhak] Rabin — it's everybody ... saying we shall not go back to the old [frontier] line and that we shall not have a Palestinian state. While the other party [the Arabs] say go back to the old line ... cut Jerusalem in two and have a Palestinian state on the West Bank and Gaza. Except for the Communists, there is no [Israeli] party that will accept this.

At forum organized by Hebrew University,
Jerusalem, June 7/The Washington Post, 6-9:(A)19.

Moshe Dayan
Foreign Minister of Israel

2

[On his country's refusal to deal with the PLO]: ... if you want to make peace, you don't talk to your friends. You talk to your enemies. But the question is whom do we want to make peace with — not just who are our enemies. Now, we want to make peace with all our neighbors — Egypt and Syria and Jordan. And when we say Jordan, that includes Palestinian Arabs who are living on the West Bank ... and in the Gaza Strip, with whom we have to live together ... But the PLO organization, which is headquartered in Beirut, is a very specific organization — terrorists — and, in their covenant, it's clearly put that their aim and target is to destroy Israel.

Interview/Newsweek, 10-17:33.

Simcha Dinitz
Israeli Ambassador to the United States

3

It would be the greatest mistake for Israel, for America and for American Jews if Israel were to depend on United States guarantees for her continued existence. I don't want a single American mother to mourn for the death of a son defending the state of Israel. The day we win the war [against the Arabs] with American help will be the day we lose the war.

Before American Jewish Committee, New York,
May 15/The New York Times, 5-16:30.

4

We want to make Israel not only a country worth dying for, but a society worth living for. We want for her a place where she will be threatened by no enemy, and saved by no friend.

At Israeli Independence Ball, Washington,
June 5/The Washington Post, 6-7:(B)12.

Abba Eban
Former Foreign Minister of Israel

5

[Criticizing "open diplomacy" as advocated by the U.S. as a method of dealing with the Arab-Israeli conflict]: If the Arabs can get their main demands through open diplomacy, it is hard to see what Israel would have to offer at a peace conference. Thus, we reach the conclusion that excessive zeal in support of the open-diplomacy methods — excessive zeal by a great power in defining parameters of a settlement publicly and in advance — could well disrupt the balance of incentives which is the key to all successful negotiations.

At conference on the press and political conflicts,
Jerusalem, June 13/The New York Times, 6-14:5.

Fahd (ibn Abdel Aziz)
First Deputy Premier of Saudi Arabia

6

[Addressing U.S. President Carter and saying he is optimistic about the Middle East situation]: This optimism stems from your own views, the wise views that the issue of Palestine is the core of the problem and that it is necessary to create a homeland for the Palestinian people ... At the same time, we share with you, Mr. President, the belief that unless

WHAT THEY SAID IN 1977

(FAHD [IBN ABDEL AZIZ])

there is a comprehensive and just solution to this problem, it will remain a source of great danger, not only to the area, but to the whole world.

Washington, May 24/Los Angeles Times, 5-25:(1)6.

1

Israel cannot have both [Arab] territories and peace at the same time, and I don't believe that there is any people or nation in the world that accepts such an illogical claim. Occupation of land by force does not confer any right recognized by civilized law. We Arabs want peace for its own intrinsic value and to enable us to concentrate our energies to develop our own countries, both economically and socially. We have expressed our own readiness for peace, while it appears that Israel is the one who doesn't want it. As for the recognition of Israel, let's have peace first.

Interview, Washington/Newsweek, 6-6:54.

Ismail Fahmy
Foreign Minister of Egypt

2

What's new in the situation is that the Arab countries are ready for the first time to accept Israel as a Middle Eastern country to live in peace in this area, in secure borders, and these borders must be [the] international borders from 1967 . . . So it is a must that Israel should really become convinced that it is in their best interest to live in peace and relinquish completely their dependence only on military might. Time is not working in favor of Israel, but if they are wise they should grab the hands extended by the Arab countries to have a permanent and just peace — and [for] peace to be permanent it must be just.

News conference, Washington, Sept. 22/
The New York Times, 9-23:(A)4.

3

[Saying the PLO must take part in a renewed Geneva conference on the Middle East despite Israeli objections]: We have the PLO representing the Palestinians in the Arab League; we don't have any other. Again, in the Organization of African Unity, it's the PLO. In the non-aligned group [of nations], it's the PLO. In the (UN) Security Council, when Palestinian issues have been discussed, the representatives have been the PLO. You may report that at the very beginning, when debate was instituted here [at the UN], the Israelis chose to absent themselves. They are out and the PLO is in. I can't see what kind of justification there can be that at Geneva, a conference created by the United Nations, that there we have somebody else. Take it from me, if the PLO is not represented in Geneva, the conference will serve no useful purpose.

To reporters, United Nations, New York,
Sept. 26/Los Angeles Times, 9-27:(1)5.

Valery Giscard d'Estaing
President of France

4

[There is a] need to establish a Palestinian homeland on the West Bank, to restore the [Arab] territories occupied [by Israel] in 1967 and, for the Arabs, to establish real peace and normal relations with Israel. What is difficult to understand is why Israeli opinion does not comprehend that if real peace is achieved, the entire Mideast situation would be transformed. Instead, they seem to believe that even with real peace, as was achieved between France and Germany after World War II, the situation would be the same as today — only worse. Real peace, on the contrary, would give Israel more security than its present beleaguered-state status.

Interview, Paris/Newsweek, 7-25:47.

Andrei A. Gromyko
Foreign Minister of the Soviet Union

5

[Criticizing Egyptian President Anwar Sadat's unprecedented trip to Israel]: We ourselves are systematically working to promote the solution of these [Middle East] problems. But if one country demonstratively departs from the common Arab front and sacrifices the interests of the Arab states as a whole, first of all those who have suffered from Israeli aggression, this then is quite another matter. How can one approve such actions? One cannot.

At reception for the Syrian Foreign Minister,
Moscow, Nov. 29/The Washington Post, 11-30:(A)14.

George Habash
*Leader, Popular Front for
the Liberation of Palestine*
1

[Criticizing Egyptian President Anwar Sadat's unprecedented trip to Israel]: The obstinacy of Israel will not make any solution possible. Sadat's strategy will naturally lead to disaster. It is the strategy of a desperate man. His strategy after the 1973 war led to concessions, such as Sinai II. And he is 100 per cent wrong. I don't believe Sadat can last. His days are numbered. Outside Egypt, he is finished as an Arab leader... Sadat is facing special hardships within Egypt. His economy is facing almost imminent collapse. But Egypt is only strong as long as it is linked to other Arab countries. By going to Israel, Sadat has isolated himself, and his policy will end in ruination.

Interview, Tripoli, Libya/Time, 12-19:33.

2

If one thinks in terms of 1967 and 1973, no one could make the decision to fight. Israel is too powerful for that kind of war, and Israel would win. But there is another way of fighting. One can fight inside Israel. We can fight from the borders of Lebanon, Syria and Jordan, and we can cross into Israel. This is the long struggle. In 20 years I can see us fighting in Haifa, Jerusalem, in all the occupied towns, and I don't see any reason why we shouldn't win that war.

Interview, Tripoli, Libya/Time, 12-19:33.

Yehoshafat Harkabi
*Adviser to the Prime Minister
of Israel on Intelligence*
3

In [the late Egyptian President] Nasser's time, the tendency was to see the destruction of Israel by one all-out war. The attitude nowadays is incremental ... reaching your purpose slowly and not necessarily by your own forces. Before, they tended to see our strengths. Now they tend to see our weaknesses ... to see our society disintegrating. They feel now, "We don't have to destroy Israel but make it unviable, produce the conditions by which Israel will destroy itself" ... They speak of the withering away of Israel ... Egyptian intellectuals speak of dissolution.

*Interview, Jerusalem/
The Christian Science Monitor, 3-8:3.*

Hassan II
King of Morocco
4

With the material possibilities now at the disposal of the Arab world and the particular genius of the Israeli people, imagine what this region could be like in the intellectual, scientific, artistic and economic fields [if the Arabs and Israel could combine their resources]. It is the dream that I have and I hope that one day it will come about ... We are presented with an undeniable fact: It is impossible to dream of pushing Israel into the sea.

Interview/Los Angeles Times, 11-18:(1)7.

Mohammed Hassanein Heikal
Former editor, "Al Ahram," Cairo
5

Since 1974, all attempts to solve the Middle East crisis have come up against what the Arabs call a "dialogue of the deaf." Thus, we have two views of the situation: the Arabs insisting on regaining all their occupied territories in exchange for less than complete peace with Israel, and Israel insisting on complete peace for itself in exchange for less than the return of all the Arab territories it now occupies. Israel was able to maintain the *fait accompli*, its continued occupation of Arab territories, because its qualitative superiority canceled the enormous [numerical] superiority of the Arabs. But there came a time when this quality/quantity balance began to tilt. Several factors contributed to this, starting with the Arabs' political refusal to give in to Israel's military victory in 1967 and followed, in succession, by the October war, the oil embargo, the power of petrodollars and, finally, the emergence of the Palestinian factor as an essential component of the conflict ... The course of history is bound to give Arab quantity — with its vast human, oil and financial resources – a qualitative factor.

Interview/Newsweek, 5-30:43.

WHAT THEY SAID IN 1977

Chaim Herzog
Israeli Ambassador/Permanent
Representative to the United Nations

1

[Defending the Jewish settlements on the West Bank]: It is historically inaccurate and misleading to characterize the settlement of a few thousand Jewish settlers in areas inhabited by over one million Arabs as an obstacle to peace. Furthermore, I ask you why should Jews not live among Arabs when no Arabs are being thereby dispossessed? It is not wrong for Arabs to live among Jews in Israel. Why is the reverse forbidden?

New York, Aug. 21/The New York Times, 8-22:7.

Saddam Husayn
Head of Government of Iraq

2

The attempt at [an Arab] reconciliation with Israel may succeed under the cover of a settlement. But it will be only a respite — and a short-lived one at that. If the goal is for a constant and permanent formula for peace in the region, then it is being approached in the wrong way. First, let me say that the impression in Western circles that Iraq is determined to throw the Jews into the sea is incorrect. This is not part of our ideology or policy. The Arabs historically have never been bigoted or fanatic, and never denied people the right to their own way of life and religious practice. But we feel that the questions raised in the search for a settlement are the wrong ones, and they will not lead to peace. What is being discussed now is not how the Jews can ultimately live in the area peacefully, but rather how Zionism and expansionism can be protected and guaranteed. Also, the Palestinian question is being posed wrongly ... What should be asked is how everyone in the region can live with dignity and in peace. When viewed this way, it will be possible to find a correct solution for all parties to live with dignity and in freedom. I think you will find that, when addressed in this light, the Arabs will be the first to seek a humanitarian solution. But we will never recognize the right of Israel to live as a separate Zionist state.

Interview, Baghdad/
U.S. News & World Report, 5-16:96.

Hussein I
King of Jordan

3

The realities are that Israel still occupies Arab territory and it is still unclear whether Israel has made a definite choice between peace or continued occupation. Both are impossible. Militarily, Israel is stronger than it has ever been, whereas the same cannot be said of her neighbors, even compared with 1973. Israel must evolve a new courage to break away from the fortress mentality to a willingness to take a gamble on peace. I believe this is the only hope for Israel and all of us. Otherwise, prospects remain dismal and if this year passes without definite signs of progress, the fact that hopes have been raised so high will result in despair. We will face a rise of extremist attitudes and turbulence.

Interview, Amman/Time, 2-14:34.

4

I feel very strongly that Jerusalem must be the symbol of peace, the city of believers in God, and I don't believe it can be an Israeli city. It must be a city for both sides, and a return of sovereignty over the east side to the Arabs is a necessity. But it can belong to both, the capital of the Arabs of Palestine as well as of the Israelis.

Interview, Amman/Time, 2-14:34.

5

[On the disclosure in the U.S. press that he had taken secret CIA payments over the years]: ... the report that payments were made directly to the King and for his benefit and with political conditions and obligations — this is a complete fabrication. The assistance was designed only to enhance our intelligence and security capabilities, period. To us, the CIA is a part of the U.S. government. We have sought to acquire know-how, equipment and new capabilities to defend ourselves in the face of a world-wide battle, be it hot or cold, which is still with us ... My duty is to develop my country, its human resources, armed forces and security and intelligence services, to face the tremendous threats that lie ahead. The road is strewn with mines to sabotage the peace process. One has just exploded in Washington

(HUSSEIN I)

[disclosure of the payments]. There will be others. But bear in mind that Jordan is not unique in receiving such help. Israel falls into the same category and is a far greater example of all kinds of assistance. As far as I am concerned, these will be my first and very last words on that matter. My personal pride is a very touchy subject. And my main concern is to preserve Jordan in freedom. Finally, regarding your [U.S.] media attacks against a branch of your government [the CIA], if you choose to denude a vital arm that is there to protect you, that is your affair, not Jordan's.

Interview, Amman/Newsweek, 3-7:17,18.

1

[On the recent election victory in Israel of the right-wing Likud Party]: Before the Israeli election, the chances of war were rather remote, but now I think there is ground for serious concern . . . The United States has always supported a strong Israel in the past with the view that a strong Israel would be moderate and reasonable. Now Israel is the strongest force in the area, with American help. However, this has not brought a moderate government to power but an extremist one, and for this reason we are deeply concerned . . . If [Likud leader Menachem] Begin persists in saying the West Bank is Israeli-liberated territory and not to be evacuated, we wonder what he considers as the complete map of Israel. What is the Israeli vision of the shape and size of Israel?

Interview, May 31/The New York Times, 6-1:(A)3.

2

If [Arab-Israeli] peace moves fail, not only is war inevitable, but I believe, prior to that, upheavals in the entire area are likely to occur and the effects might be far-reaching in terms of the danger to world peace . . . I can see no solution without the return of the West Bank and Gaza, the Arab territories and Palestinian territories occupied [by Israel] in 1967, and recognition of the rights of the Palestinians — their right to self-determination, to indicate their opinion regarding their future, regarding a

link with Jordan, regarding their leadership — rights they have been denied throughout the many tragic years that have passed.

Interview, Amman/The
Dallas Times Herald, 7-27:(A)13.

3

[On Egyptian President Anwar Sadat's recent unprecedented trip to Israel]: . . . he's gambled the Arab world's last card — a unilateral offer of total peace — without consulting anyone and without any assurance from Israel that it will lead to the overall settlement we had discussed with Sadat just a few days before. And I remain highly skeptical that Israel will now deliver its part of the peace package. Look at their government's settlement policy on the West Bank. Nothing has changed. There are now 31 Israeli settlements on the West Bank, with 49 new ones planned. They have gone ahead with six of them since Sadat's visit.

Interview, Hashemiah, Jordan/Newsweek, 12-12:59.

4

[On Egyptian President Anwar Sadat's attempts to improve relations with Israel, such as his recent unprecedented trip to Jerusalem]: I believe that this is an opportunity that will never occur again. . . . it is a final gesture made with sincerity and the greatest proof that we could offer the world of our good-will. If we were to fail, I can't begin to think of the disasters that could befall this area and maybe the world. This is a moment not to be lost . . .

News conference, Amman, Dec. 12/
The Washington Post, 12-13:(A)18.

Ahmad Iskander
Minister of Information of Syria

5

Taking into consideration Israel's daily statements indicating its refusal to withdraw from [occupied] Arab lands, we do not think there is one glimmer of hope that the Geneva conference will convene . . . With Israel announcing in advance its refusal to withdraw and its rejection of Palestinian rights, to what purpose are we to hold a Geneva peace conference? . . . When the fighting is imposed, we are ready to defend our rights and our lands, and we are fully equipped to fight with the same courage which we

WHAT THEY SAID IN 1977

exhibited in the October war of 1973 ... The Arabs will take any initiative, any measure which might help them regain their lands and their rights. When all peace efforts are blocked, when the political attempts currently being made on various levels to achieve a lasting and just peace fail ... the Arabs must use all means at their disposal to ... liberate the lands taken from them in 1967 and restore the rights of the Palestinians.

Interview/Los Angeles Times, 8-29:(1)10.

Abdel Halim Khaddam
Foreign Minister of Syria   *1*

[Lamenting the improved relations between Israel and Egypt as a result of Egyptian President Anwar Sadat's trip to Israel]: The Israelis realize that only by establishing normal relations can they liquidate the Palestinian cause and achieve the Israeli concept of security ... [With normal relations, Israel would establish] complete control over the Arab homeland, economically, culturally and politically ... Lands in Syria, Lebanon, Jordan and Egypt will be inhabited by Jewish immigrants and become a base for a new Israeli expansion within the framework of establishing the Jewish state from the Nile to the Euphrates.

*Before Syrian Parliament, Damascus/
The New York Times, 12-1:(A)3.*

Henry A. Kissinger
*Former Secretary of State
of the United States*   *2*

[Israel] must maintain its faith in itself and its confidence that it is a master of its own destiny and not just the protectorate of some other country, however well-intentioned that country may be. The present situation is one that must fill all Jews with a sense of responsibility and a sense of concern. All Jews know that peace cannot rest only on professions and on verbal statements because they have seen too much of the transitory nature of human intentions. All Jews know that in time of crisis and of frustration they can easily become the target of popular emotions and that they

therefore feel it in their deepest being that they must not be seen as the cause of international difficulties. And yet all Jews have seen too much suffering and too many people killed to be able to abandon their own judgment as to what is necessary for peace and for survival. As I see them, one cannot separate the destiny of Israel and the destiny of the Jewish people from the destiny of mankind.

*Before World Jewish Congress, Washington,
Nov. 3/The New York Times, 11-4:(A)1.*

Abdel Rahman al-Mansouri
Deputy Foreign Minister of Saudi Arabia   *3*

For Saudi Arabia, the central and most pressing issue [in the Arab-Israeli dispute] is that the Palestinians must attend whatever peace conference takes place — at Geneva or elsewhere — from the beginning of the talks. The opportunity for a settlement is unique this year, but it must be started quickly. Moderate governments are now in power in the key states confronting Israel — Egypt, Jordan and Syria. We want the future independent Palestinian state to be a moderate one, too. This state should be established through U.S. influence, not Soviet influence, because Soviet influence would mean a danger of Communism in this area. We don't want it and you [the U.S.] don't want it. The present PLO leadership, too, is moderate. But extremists might take over if the whole Mideast question is allowed to stagnate much longer.

*Interview, Jiddah/
The Christian Science Monitor, 2-7:4.*

Golda Meir
Former Prime Minister of Israel   *4*

The boundaries of this country have always been drawn — not by declarations, talk, lofty speeches and rhetoric — but by people willing to settle the land and work.

Time, 9-5:13.

5

[Addressing Egyptian President Anwar Sadat during his unprecedented visit to Israel]: When I was asked many years ago when I thought peace would come [between the Arabs and

(GOLDA MEIR)

Israel], I said the date I do not know. But I know under what conditions it will come — when there will be a great leader of an Arab country. He will wake up one morning and feel sorry for his own people, for his sons that have fallen in battle. That day will be the beginning of peace between us and them ... I congratulate you, Mr. President, that you have this privilege of being the first great Arab leader of the greatest of our neighboring countries, that with courage and determination ... [you] have come to us and bring us the message for the sake of your sons as well as for the sake of ours, of all mothers who mourn their sons that fell in battle.

Jerusalem, Nov. 21/
Los Angeles Times, 11-22:(1)17.

Walter F. Mondale
Vice President of the United States
1

[Saying the U.S. will not use military aid to pressure Israel in negotiations with the Arabs]: If we have differences over military aid — and we may have some — it will be on military or economic grounds, but not political grounds. If we have differences over diplomatic strategy — and that could happen — we will work this out on a political level. We will not alter our commitment to Israel's military security. America has a "special responsibility" to the defense of Israel. There must be no question in anyone's mind that the United States will do what is necessary to ensure the adequacy of Israel's military posture and its capacity for self-defense.

Before World Affairs Council of Northern California,
San Francisco, June 17/Los Angeles Times, 6-18:(1)3.

2

We realize that peace cannot be imposed from the outside and we do not intend to present the [Middle East] parties with a plan or a timetable or a map. Peace can only come from a genuine recognition by all parties that their interests are served by reconciliation and not by war, by faith in the future rather than bitterness over the past.

San Francisco Examiner & Chronicle,
6-26:(This World)2.

Hisham Nazzer
Minister of Planning of Saudi Arabia
3

[On the controversy in the U.S. over cooperating with the Arab economic boycott of Israel]: The U.S. must stop allowing a few well-organized people there to try to make its Arab friends into enemies. The boycott is a negative issue. Constant focus on such negative issues makes it tougher to keep our friendship. Anyway, the boycott is just one of many secondary issues arising from the Arab-Israeli conflict. Stop focusing on secondary issues and go after the central one. Once a peace settlement is under way, the boycott and other such problems will disappear by themselves.

The Christian Science Monitor, 2-17:5.

Mohammad Reza Pahlavi
Shah of Iran
4

Some people might [think] that maybe a safety device for a small country is to have atomic weapons, as the best guarantee not to be attacked. But I have adopted just the opposite [position]. If you want to defend your country, defend it by conventional means. If there is somebody wishing you ill, he will have to use atomic weapons, and it won't be so easy in this world ... I don't consider myself so weak as only to depend on a few silly atomic bombs, but on the contrary, on a strong, modern, hard-fighting conventional force.

Interview, Teheran/Newsweek, 1-24:48.

Shimon Peres
Minister of Defense of Israel
5

I firmly believe that we should negotiate with [Jordan's] King Hussein, and that we should neither annex the West Bank nor permit the introduction there of a Palestinian state. It is my view that we should avoid talking about territorial arrangements, which are likely to prove very difficult, and that we should aim for political arrangements instead. My proposal is to create either a federation of Israel and the West Bank, or a confederation of Jordan, the West Bank and Israel. In other words, instead of dividing the land, I would prefer to divide the government.

Interview, Tel Aviv/Newsweek, 1-17:36.

WHAT THEY SAID IN 1977

(SHIMON PERES)

1

[Arguing against Israeli recognition of the PLO]: Stroking a tiger will not make it a pussycat.

Time, 4-18:24.

2

We cannot return to boundaries so vulnerable that Israel could not defend herself. I am talking about the coast where two-thirds of us live. I am afraid that if we were pushed into a strip of land 10 to 12 miles wide we would have to become a satellite of another nation that could guarantee our security. That means we cannot return to the 1967 borders — not for the sake of geography, but for the sake of independence.

Interview/Newsweek, 4-18:39.

3

The truth is that only Israel is ready for territorial compromise. There is no one Arab I know who is prepared to accept territorial compromises in order to put an end to war and bring about peace. [No Arab leader] has expressed himself fully and unconditionally in favor of true peace with Israel. When the Arab leaders talk of peace, their words are accompanied by a wink, nebulous phraseology or political doubletalk such as "termination of belligerency" or "normalization." Actual peace — this is something they still find hard to pronounce . . . [The] true beginning of Arab readiness for peace will be their willingness to meet with us face to face, not only to announce their definite dictates but also to listen to our conditions.

Jerusalem, April 25/
The New York Times, 4-27:(A)8.

Muammar el-Qaddafi
Chief of State of Libya

4

[Advocating renewed Arab commando attacks against Israel, instead of negotiations]: We do not accept a single foreign soldier on Arab territory. Nor do we agree to stop fighting or negotiate with him. We are a nation that goes to war just as if it were going to a celebration.

The problem of the Palestinian people is not [a] Geneva [conference]. It is the problem of the enemy who planted the spear in its chest. The Palestinians are . . . being stabbed by an Arab spear from behind and stabbed in the chest by the enemy.

At rally, Tarhouna, Libya, Oct. 7/
The Washington Post, 10-9:(A)30.

Ghazi al-Qusaibi
Minister of Industry of Saudi Arabia

5

The foreign press used to complain that the Saudi people were sleeping, that they never moved and they were living in the 13th or 14th century. Now all of a sudden the press is complaining that we are moving too fast, that we are spending too much money. They say we are changing our own traditions, destroying our own society. I really don't know what we are expected to do. "Look what they are doing to their way of life. The government is so greedy. It keeps all the money and the people suffer." But when we spend it, they say, "Look at the inflation. They are crazy. They are spending every penny they have." So really, I am glad that we are not dying to please you. Because if we were, we would get nowhere.

Interview, Jiddah/The New York Times, 7-10:(3)6.

Yitzhak Rabin
Prime Minister of Israel

6

. . . with all our friendship and appreciation of United States' support for Israel, when it comes to our defense we consider ourselves to be the ones that will decide these issues . . . What we need for the purpose of the advancement of peace, on the part of the United States, is the readiness to offer good offices, not to be involved in the details of the agreements that have to be negotiated between the parties to the conflict. I think this is the most important role that the United States should play. And if the United States should try to impose a solution . . . then I think many things might go wrong.

TV-radio interview, Washington/"Issues and Answers," American Broadcasting Company, 3-13.

Yitzhak Rabin
Former Prime Minister of Israel

1

I think that under [U.S.] President Carter, there has been a positive change in the definition of a desirable [Arab-Israeli] peace, which is now much closer to our position than it has been in the past. On the shape of future boundaries, the present U.S. position seems about the same as always, although there has been some recognition of our defensive needs in the proposal for separate security lines. But I can't recall any other President who used President Carter's language about the Palestinian "homeland." This is a real setback for Israel, because it hints at the need to create a Palestinian state, which we all oppose ... I hope that [Carter will] come up with a fall-back position in case the gap between the Arabs and us proves unbridgeable. The possibility of a limited agreement was part of our understanding with [former U.S. President Gerald] Ford, and I hope that the Carter Administration is thinking in similar terms, even if it doesn't talk about it.

Interview, Jerusalem/Newsweek, 7-4:51.

Abraham A. Ribicoff
United States Senator, D–Connecticut

2

[U.S. President Carter] has been doubted, questioned and pressured to prove his commitment to Israel — and he has repeatedly done so ... He is talking frankly about final, recognized and secure borders, about full normalization of relations among the countries of the region, and he is talking about the Palestinian question. Simply raising these basic issues raises the level of anxiety. But it is the only honorable course for a President of principle and courage ... Let us support an American President who is doing exactly what he should be doing.

Before the Senate, Washington, Nov. 3/
The Washington Post, 11-4:(A)12.

Ali al-Khalifa al-Sabah
Undersecretary of Finance of Kuwait

3

[Saying the Persian Gulf's influx of money from oil exports has not been used in the most beneficial and practical manner]: Treasure brought back from the New World created a prosperity [in Spain] which discouraged the pursuit of previously productive employment. Spaniards abandoned their traditional skills and started importing many of their needs. This in turn led to the decline of Spain once the treasures of the New World were exhausted or were no longer its monopoly. We have learned the historical lesson. The oil-based boom we have experienced was not paralleled by an increase in production and led to loss of traditional skills. From now on we will only encourage productive investment and pursuits.

Interview/Los Angeles Times, 11-24:(7)7.

Anwar el-Sadat
President of Egypt

4

Permanent [Arab-Israeli] peace comes when both sides are faithful to a peace agreement. The end of belligerency can be accomplished when Israel withdraws to the June 4, 1967, borders and a Palestinian Arab state is created. I won't oppose any guarantees Israel asks for. By ending belligerency everything will again become normal. But then we'll need a breathing space after almost 30 years of belligerency and four wars. If both Prophet Mohammed and Jesus were to come back and try to convince Moslems and Christians among the Arabs to open borders right now with Israel, they would refuse. Let's drop such matters as diplomatic relations, open frontiers and so forth for the moment. Israel seeks to impose conditions like diplomatic recognition; but these things take time. Look how long it took Washington to recognize the Soviet Union and Communist China. A transition period doesn't mean we don't have peace. We should be very careful and concentrate on the main issue, which is permanent peace in this area. I am ready to go to Geneva and sign a peace agreement with Israel. If I sit next to the Israelis and sign the same paper they sign, doesn't that mean I actually recognize them? I am not signing with a ghost.

Interview, Cairo/The New York Times, 1-19:(A)23.

5

I defy the Israelis to state what they are willing to do as I have stated my plan. They will not do it. [Israeli Prime Minister Yitzhak]

WHAT THEY SAID IN 1977

(ANWAR EL-SADAT)

Rabin's government has been very weak, and they are afraid of peace. I tell you frankly, I would have preferred it if I were dealing with [Rabin's predecessor] Golda Meir. Even though she is a "hawk," she at least has guts; she has *all* the guts in Israel. As it is, the Israelis have nobody in power telling them the facts, telling them what must be done. Meanwhile, we are ready here. I have the confidence of my people, and I am putting my plans quite clearly for everyone to see ... Believe me, I am sincere when I say I am ready to end the state of war with Israel; and, goodness knows, they must be ready, too. We in Egypt do not wish to go on like this, spending money and losing our people in war. My country needs peace. We have many domestic problems, and we need peace so that we can grow and develop normally.

Interview, Cairo/Parade, 2-6:9,12.

1

Quite frankly, my relations with the Soviet Union are still very highly strained. They are not sending us military equipment, not even spare parts, and they refuse to reschedule our debts to them. I would prefer to normalize my situation with them, though I have told them I am willing to do so only if they accept me as I am and don't try to make me into what they want. But, for their part, they don't like how I have dealt with [former U.S. Secretary of State Henry] Kissinger and how I have made such an understanding with the United States.

Interview, Cairo/Parade, 2-6:10.

2

No Arab leader could, even if he wanted, cede even a centimeter of territory to Israel. It's simply impossible, especially for Sinai and the Golan. As for west Jordan [the West Bank], where the frontier with the Jewish state was not definitively established, minor rectifications could be negotiated, for example to reunite villages which were divided by the armistice line ... It's ridiculous to suppose a few kilometers of land are indispensable to the security of Israel. We have ground-to-ground missiles that can reach Israeli cities from the west bank of the Suez Canal. On the other hand, we are prepared to discuss an entirely different arrangement, including the creation of demilitarized zones on both sides of the border, capable of guaranteeing the security of all the belligerents.

Interview, Paris/The New York Times, 4-5:11.

3

I told him [U.S. President Carter] that if we resurrected Jesus Christ and the Prophet Mohammed together, that they would not be able to persuade Moslem and Christian Arabs to open the borders with Israel after 29 years of hatred, four wars, rivers of blood and massacres. I told President Carter that the creation of a Palestinian state is imperative, because this is the backbone of peace. We all, as Arabs, struggle for the Palestinian cause, rather than for the Sinai or the Golan Heights ... America is 100 per cent responsible for Israel's existence and survival. So America is 100 per cent responsible for peace. We reject the concept that the U.S. can only be a catalyst.

Interview/San Francisco
Examiner & Chronicle, 7-10:(This World)19.

4

[Addressing the Israeli Knesset during his unprecedented trip to Israel]: If I said that I wanted to avert from all the Arab people the horrors of shocking and destructive wars, I must sincerely declare before you that I have the same feelings and bear the same responsibility toward all and every man on earth, and certainly toward the Israeli people. Any life that is lost in war is a human life, be it that of an Arab or an Israeli. Innocent children who are deprived of the care and compassion of their parents are ours. They are ours, be they living on Arab or Israeli land. They command our full responsibility to afford them a comfortable life today and tomorrow. For the sake of them all, for the sake of the lives of our sons and brothers, for the sake of affording our communities the opportunity to work for the progress and happiness of man, feeling secure and with the right to a dignified life, for the generations to come, for a smile on the face of every child born in our land — for all that, I

(ANWAR EL-SADAT)

have taken my decision to come to you, despite the hazards, to deliver my address. . . . the Arab nation, in its drive for permanent peace based on justice, does not proceed from a position of weakness. On the contrary, it has the power and stability for a sincere will for peace. The Arab declared intention stems from an awareness prompted by a heritage of civilization that, to avoid an inevitable disaster that will befall us, you and the whole world, there is no alternative to the establishment of permanent peace based on justice, peace that is not swayed by suspicion or jeopardized by ill intentions.

Before the Knesset (Parliament), Jerusalem,
Nov. 20/The New York Times, 11-21:13.

1

[Addressing the Israeli Knesset during his unprecedented trip to Israel] : . . . peace cannot be worth its name unless it is based on justice and not on the occupation of the land of others. It would not be right for you to demand for yourselves what you deny to others. With all frankness and in the spirit that has prompted me to come to you today, I will tell you you have to give up once and for all the dreams of conquest and give up the belief that force is the best method for dealing with the Arabs. You should clearly understand the lesson of confrontation between you and us. Expansion does not pay. To speak frankly, our land does not yield itself to bargaining. To us, the nation's soil is equal to the holy valley where God Almighty spoke to Moses — peace be upon him. We cannot accept any attempt to take away or accept to seek one inch of it, nor can we accept the principle of debating or bargaining over it . . . What is peace for Israel? It means that Israel lives in the region with her Arab neighbors in security and safety. Is that logical? I say yes. It means that Israel lives within its borders, secure against any aggression. Is that logical? And I say yes. It means that Israel obtains all kinds of guarantees that will ensure these two factors. To this demand, I say yes . . . I declare clearly and unequivocally that we agree to any guarantees you accept, because in return we shall receive the same guarantees. In short,

then, when we ask what is peace for Israel, the answer would be that Israel lives within her borders, among her Arab neighbors, in safety and security, within the framework of all the guarantees she accepts and which are offered to her.

Before the Knesset (Parliament), Jerusalem,
Nov. 20/The New York Times, 11-21:14.

2

[Addressing the Israeli Knesset during his unprecedented trip to Israel] : As for the Palestinian cause — nobody could deny that it is the crux of the entire [Arab-Israeli] problem. Nobody in the world could accept today slogans propagated here in Israel, ignoring the existence of a Palestinian people and questioning even their whereabouts. Because the Palestine people and their legitimate rights are no longer denied today by anybody, that is, nobody who has the ability of judgment can deny or ignore it. . . . even [Israel's ally] the United States has opted to face up to reality and admit that the Palestinian people are entitled to legitimate rights and that the Palestine problem is the cause and essence of the conflict and that so long as it continues to be unresolved, the conflict will continue to aggravate, reaching new dimension. In all sincerity, I tell you that there can be no peace without the Palestinians. It is a grave error of unpredictable consequences to overlook or brush aside this cause.

Before the Knesset (Parliament), Jerusalem,
Nov. 20/The New York Times, 11-21:14.

3

[On the Soviet attitude against Egypt's new peace initiative with Israel which included his recent unprecedented trip to Jerusalem] : Moscow hasn't liked me or my government for years now. The Russians do not like anybody who rejects their control. They are on record as wanting peace in the Middle East, having acted with the U.S. as cochairmen of the first Geneva Conference. But they obviously wish the peace initiative had come from somewhere else than Cairo . . . Moscow still has leverage in some other Arab nations to which it is a heavy arms supplier — Syria, Libya, Algeria, Iraq and South

WHAT THEY SAID IN 1977

(ANWAR EL-SADAT)

Yemen ... As things stand, Syria does what Russia wants, and the Palestine Liberation Organization — heavily dependent upon both — does what Syria wants. That makes it difficult for our peace initiative to obtain support — and especially the support of the very Arab Palestinians for whom I am determined to obtain legitimate rights as the core of the peace initiative.

Interview, Cairo/
U.S. News & World Report, 12-19:13.

Ariel Sharon
Minister of Agriculture of Israel

1

[On his plan to settle two million Jews in Israeli occupied Arab lands in the next two decades]: You're wrong if you think that [Arab-Israeli] peace will come if Israel remains a nation of three million Jews. Peace will come, but our first problem is to assure that Israel will exist forever. To that end, we have to have a population of six to eight million Jews within the next 20 to 50 years, and we have to settle them. I don't believe that my plan blocks any diplomatic solutions, because we've made it perfectly clear that we'll never leave the West Bank. I believe that if we establish these settlements, we will feel sufficiently secure to accept risks for the sake of peace.

Interview/Newsweek, 9-19:65.

Edward R. F. Sheehan
Research fellow, Center for International
Affairs, Harvard University;
Former U.S. Middle East diplomat

2

The victory of the Likud [Party in Israel] is exactly what the U.S. deserves. For 10 years, we have been fatuously maneuvering to buy time in the Middle East, manipulating the Arab-Israeli conflict for votes in American elections, making Israel so militarily strong that she can wield that power almost independently of U.S. constraint. We had the chance to impose a fair settlement [of the Arab-Israeli conflict] following the October war, but we let it pass. Since then, we had diddled with Band-Aid peripheral solutions and too much

talk. [U.S.] President Carter's pronouncements on full peace, the 1967 frontiers and a Palestinian "homeland" were promising, but they may have been too late. Conceivably, [new Israeli Prime Minister Menachem] Begin will become a Zionist de Gaulle who in common sense will render up the [occupied] Arab territories, but he is a zealot and I doubt it. Another hope is that a Likud government, impotent internally and isolated internationally, will fall flat on its face and be replaced by a more moderate government that will negotiate sensibly.

Interview/Newsweek, 5-30:38.

Joseph J. Sisco
President, American University; Former
Assistant Secretary for Near Eastern and
South Asian Affairs, Department
of State of the United States

3

The "time for a change" psychology dominated last week's Israeli elections. It was less a Likud [Party] victory, more a self-inflicted Labor Party defeat. Israelis are sick and tired of economic difficulties and indecisive government. But it would be a mistake to conclude that Israelis seek a tougher stance on peace negotiations [with the Arabs]. The overwhelming majority favors a negotiated peace settlement, [new Prime Minister] Menachem Begin notwithstanding. The turn for the worse in Israel need not be irreparable. If the period ahead is not dealt with carefully by all concerned, it could in time lead to heightened tensions, if not a needless resumption of hostilities. Begin will have to demonstrate he can make the transition from fiery, hard-nosed politician to responsible statesman. The Arabs will have to keep their powder dry until the situation in Israel takes on direction. The role of the U.S. becomes even more crucial as a moderating influence. President Carter's strategy to get Arab-Israeli talks started will be more difficult to achieve, but it is essential that the U.S. not be diverted by the change in leadership in Israel.

Interview/Newsweek, 5-30:43.

Nicholas G. W. Thorne
Director, Sinai Field Mission
1

We have been the only American Foreign Service officers able to move freely back and forth — often on the same day — between the two sides [Egypt and Israel], and perhaps that's given us a unique insight. We think neither side wants war; and in our opinion both will act responsibly. It is not new to hear them following a tough rhetorical pattern. But you can't escape the feeling from the many people we have met — government officials, military officers, academics, businessmen, farmers or whatever — that there must be a Geneva meeting this year, and that there must be progress, even if it is only toward an expanded and more sophisticated cease-fire. They are convinced on both sides that there has to be at least one tiny step toward peace and away from renewed war this year ... After gaining the confidence of many people on the Israeli side and the Egyptian side during the last year and a half, we've been amazed at how similar their attitudes really are toward the fundamental questions of security and peace.

Interview, Cairo, July 5/
Los Angeles Times, 7-6:(1)5.

Cyrus R. Vance
Secretary of State of the United States
2

The United States would not do anything which would jeopardize Israeli security by trying to exercise pressure through the withholding of military or economic assistance. We shall continue to give Israel strong support in international bodies against those who would isolate her. We have served notice, for instance, that the United States will not participate in any United Nations conference on racism if any item on its agenda seeks to equate Zionism with racism. This is the way I see our relations with Israel. The United States and Israel will approach their shared goals together, not through the distortions of distrust and difference, but from the perspective of proved friendship and mutual respect.

Before Council of Jewish Federations, Dallas,
Nov. 10/The Dallas Times Herald, 11-11:(A)3.

3

[On Egyptian President Anwar Sadat's unprecedented trip to Israel]: President Sadat has taken a courageous and imaginative step to which [Israeli] Prime Minister [Menachem] Begin has responded with statesmanship and vision. President Sadat's visit to Jerusalem can transform fundamentally the psychological atmosphere for Arab-Israel peace negotiations. It can dispel the mutual suspicions and mistrust that have been the principal barrier to fruitful negotiations.

Nov. 19/The Washington Post, 11-20:(A)15.

Ezer Weizman
Former Chief of Staff, Israeli Air Force;
Former chief political adviser to
Prime Minister Menachem Begin
4

[On whether Prime Minister Begin's Likud Party is stable]: I don't understand what all the fuss is about. We have a new government headed by a party elected in a democratic way. Why can't Washington just listen to us and understand our position? Just after the election, things got out of control. We were like a man who has spent years in the desert finding champaign instead of water! We were drunk with the elation of victory. But I assure you that the first thing Begin told me the day after the election was that we have a historic opportunity and mandate to build the state of Israel — and to avoid a war. He stressed that. Believe me, we are soldiers, and we know what it is like to fight a war. We hope that, with imagination and new ideas, we can avoid a confrontation [with the Arabs]. We will play with ideas and seek a way out of the impasse.

Interview, Jerusalem/
U.S. News & World Report, 7-4:61.

Geoffrey Wigoder
Director, Institute of Contemporary
Jewry, Hebrew University, Jerusalem
5

Every Jew carries the Holocaust in his subconscious. Every Israeli has at least a subconscious fear that what happened before could happen again. There is a general fear of the destruction of Israel, especially since the Yom Kippur war. ... any retreat [from the support of Israel] on the part of America once again

WHAT THEY SAID IN 1977

brings back the sense of isolation that Jews knew at the time of Hitler, the same feeling they had in the late '30s and '40s when they were on their own.

Time, 10-17:30.

Andrew Young
*United States Ambassador/Permanent
Representative to the United Nations*　　1

I would contend that there is, and has been for the last year, a climate in which Israel was more secure militarily than at any time in Israel's existence. There has been an absence of the kind of aggressive terrorism of three or four years ago. That is because the United States has entered into that situation as an honest broker. This usually means you are hated by both sides... The goals and objectives of this [Carter] Administration are identical with the goals and objectives of [the late U.S. President] Harry Truman, when he recognized Israel in 1948. But this is not 1948. Peace in 1978 may require more understanding and more risks. But one should be willing to accept risks for peace, rather than the risks of war.

*Before World Jewish Congress, Washington,
Nov. 1/The New York Times, 11-2:(A)5.*

2

[On Egyptian President Anwar Sadat's recent unprecedented trip to Israel] : The politics of the region will never be the same as they were before President Sadat visited Israel. President Sadat came in peace, was welcomed in peace by Prime Minister [Menachem] Begin and the Israeli people. By that simple yet dramatic act, the prospects for a just and durable peace have been significantly advanced if all concerned have the vision and the will to recognize and build upon the psychological transformation it has made possible. My government urges all of the parties to maintain the momentum toward peace.

*At United Nations, New York/
Los Angeles Times, 11-25:(1)6.*

Ardeshir Zahedi
Iranian Ambassador to the United States　　3

The foreign policy of Iran can be stated quite simply. We believe in an independent national foreign policy which permits us to deal with any nation, no matter what its ideology, as long as there is true respect for the rights and sovereignty of other nations. The cornerstone of our policy is the desire for peace and stability which will permit us to achieve our national goals. In this spirit, we have contributed to the maintenance of international peace and stability, in the world in general and in the Middle East in particular.

*At Westminster College, May 7/
Vital Speeches, 6-15:518.*

Leonid I. Brezhnev
President of the Soviet Union;
General Secretary, Soviet Communist Party
1

It is our belief, our firm belief, that realism in politics and the will for detente and progress will ultimately triumph and mankind will be able to step into the 21st century in the conditions of peace stable as never before — and we shall do all in our power to see it come true.

At reception for foreign Ambassadors,
Moscow, July 8/The Washington Post, 7-9:(A)8.

Edmund G. Brown, Jr.
Governor of California (D)
2

The earth map is drenched in the blood of a thousand, a million conflicts in recorded history. But when we look at earth and the human species from a few hundred miles up [in space], we can't help but sense the oneness of the human race.

At Space Day conference, Los Angeles, Aug. 11/
Los Angeles Times, 8-12:(1)30.

Harold Brown
Secretary of Defense of the United States
3

Each nation [the U.S. and Soviet Union] is capable of destroying the other — but not without being destroyed itself. In the light of this, I believe that a major nuclear conflict is unlikely to occur. But I also believe that this rough strategic balance requires the United States and its allies to be especially able to deter conventional non-nuclear wars.

To American troops, Grafenwoehr, West Germany,
March 24/Los Angeles Herald-Examiner, 3-25:(A)4

Zbigniew Brzezinski
Assistant to President of the
United States Jimmy Carter
for National Security Affairs
4

... I do emphasize the importance of the deterrent effect; namely, that no one should ever calculate that they can launch a nuclear attack on someone without suffering the consequences. That's essentially important. As far as [nuclear war's effect on] human society is concerned, it sounds great in a rally. The fact of the matter is — and I don't want this to be understood as justifying the use of nuclear weapons, because we don't want to use them and we're not going to use them first in an attack — the fact of the matter is that if we used all our nuclear weapons and the Russians used all of their nuclear weapons, about 10 per cent of humanity would be killed. Now, this is a disaster beyond the range of human comprehension. It's a disaster which is not morally justifiable in whatever fashion. But, descriptively and analytically, it's not the end of humanity. It's not the destruction of humanity. People like to use slogans and, therefore, one of the most frequently used slogans is that the United States and the Soviet Union have in their power to decimate, to destroy humanity.

Interview/The Washington Post, 10-9:(C)5.

Jimmy Carter
President of the United States
5

The United Nations is the global forum dedicated to the peace and well-being of every individual — no matter how weak or how poor. But we have allowed its human-rights machinery to be ignored and sometimes politicized. There is much that can be done to strengthen it.

At United Nations, New York, March 17/
San Francisco Examiner & Chronicle,
3-27:(This World)17.

WHAT THEY SAID IN 1977

(JIMMY CARTER)

1

I am absolutely certain that the people of the Soviet Union, who have suffered so grievously in war, feel this yearning [for peace]. And in this they are at one with the people of the United States. It is up to all of us to help make that unspoken passion into something more than a dream — and that responsibility falls most heavily on those, like [Soviet] President [Leonid] Brezhnev and myself, who hold in our hands the terrible power conferred by modern engines of war... With all the difficulties, all the conflicts, I believe that our planet must finally obey the Biblical injunction to "follow after the things which make for peace."

At Southern Legislative Conference, Charleston, S.C./The Christian Science Monitor, 8-12:32.

2

Peace will not be assured until the weapons of war are finally put away. While we work toward that goal, nations will want sufficient arms to preserve their security. The United States' purpose is to insure peace. It is for that reason that our military posture and our alliances will remain as strong as necessary to deter attack. However, the security of the global community cannot forever rest on a balance of terror. In the past, war has been accepted as the ultimate arbiter of disputes among nations. But, in the nuclear era, we can no longer think of war as merely a continuation of diplomacy by other means. Nuclear war cannot be measured by the archaic standards of "victory" or "defeat." The stark reality imposes on the United States and the Soviet Union an awesome and special responsibility.

At United Nations, New York, Oct. 4/ Vital Speeches, 10-15:3.

3

I know in more vivid terms than before that nations like your own [Poland] and like the Soviet Union, which have suffered so deeply, will never commence a war unless there is the most profound provocation or misunderstanding brought about by lack of communication.

We also want peace and would never start a war except by mistake, when we didn't understand the motives and attitudes and desire for peace on the part of our potential adversaries.

At dinner in his honor, Warsaw, Dec. 30/ Los Angeles Herald-Examiner, 12-31:(A)1.

S. T. Cohen
Nuclear physicist

4

All military weapons, more correctly their employment, are immoral. The recipient of their effects in the main have been ordinary human beings who have had the misfortune to be on the other side. Regarding the choice of weapons to be used in a possible war, the immoralities having to do with differences in kill mechanisms logically must be assessed in the context of a vastly different immorality — the great obscenity of war itself. Most Americans feel that the greatest obscenity would be nuclear war. If fighting such a war would be humanly immoral to an extreme, then taking the necessary means to deter its outbreak can only be construed as a moral imperative. It is in this context that the development of any nuclear weapon must be judged.

The New York Times, 7-17:(4)4.

Morarji R. Desai
Prime Minister of India

5

What must be done is to have the atomic bomb disappear from the world. The scientists who first of all showed us the use of this bomb were the greatest enemies of man. The discovery was all right, but to put it to that use ... the poisons will always be there.

Interview, New Delhi/Time, 4-4:34.

R. Buckminster Fuller
Engineer, Author, Designer

6

If there's another shooting war, it's all over for us. We're in the middle of a final examination on this planet. Whether we pass that examination depends on whether we run things with our minds instead of our muscle.

Interview/U.S. News & World Report, 12-5:49.

U. Alexis Johnson
Former chief United States arms
negotiator at SALT talks (1973-77)
1

We've got to be *prepared* to fight a nuclear war — horrible though it may be — in order really to prevent a nuclear war. If you're really not *prepared* to do so, then your deterrent is not persuasive.

Interview, Washington/
U.S. News & World Report, 4-4:25.

George J. Keegan
Major General (Ret.) and former
Assistant Chief of Staff, Intelligence,
United States Air Force
2

As long as the Soviets seem fervently bent upon what they are now doing in Africa, in the Middle East, in the Indian Ocean littoral, in Latin America, I think there is high likelihood of some perceived important interest · being transgressed in which we will react as we did in Korea, or the Soviets will react to something we are doing or responding to, and the process lends itself to global conflict.

At conference on the Soviet Union, Santa Barbara,
Calif./World Issues, Oct.-Nov.:28.

Henry A. Kissinger
Secretary of State of the United States
3

I believe that to achieve a usable military superiority in the field of strategic nuclear weapons is extremely unlikely and relatively easy to prevent, and the obsession with it detracts us. I would say that if there is a conflict between the Soviet Union and us, it is much less likely to occur as a result of a Soviet ·attack, [a] deliberate attack on a vital interest of the United States, than as a result of a conflict that maybe neither of us saw, into which we are drawn through a series of escalating moves. In other words, I think World War I is a better guide to our dangers than World War II.

Interview, Washington/
The New York Times, 1-20:16.

George B. Kistiakowsky
Professor of chemistry, Harvard University
4

There are no cases in history of absolutely insane arms races ending peacefully by simply laying down arms. Arms races usually end up in wars.

The Washington Post, 2-20:(A)17.

Henry Cabot Lodge
Former United States Ambassador/
Permanent Representative
to the United Nations
5

[On controversial U.S. UN Ambassador Andrew Young]: I think he's doing fine. That doesn't mean you agree with everything he says. He says what he thinks. And the UN General Assembly is a forum — and a forum is a place where you don't agree; that's why you have a forum. You certainly can't criticize a man for saying things people disagree with. At least I can't.

Radio program/The New York Times, 8-24:22.

Imelda Marcos
Special envoy to the United Nations
from the Philippines; Wife of
Philippine President Ferdinand Marcos
6

[Suggesting that the UN General Assembly could hold its next session some place other than New York]: Who knows what subtle influence might be exercised on our deliberations if the General Assembly were to consider the question of nuclear proliferation in Hiroshima ... the Palestinian problem in Gaza ... famine and food resources in the Sahel ... or apartheid in Soweto.

At United Nations, New York/
Los Angeles Times, 10-3:(1)2.

Daniel P. Moynihan
United States Senator, D–New York;
Former United States Ambassador/Permanent
Representative to the United Nations
7

[On whether there was animosity toward him at the UN when he was Ambassador because of his outspokenness]: You're damn right there was — from those people who had been having a free ride. They'd vote against the

WHAT THEY SAID IN 1977

(DANIEL P. MOYNIHAN)

United States 100 per cent and nobody ever said a word to them, and suddenly I was saying, "You're sitting here, asking us for bread; you're sitting here, asking us for food; you're sitting here, asking us to help you against your traditional and mortal enemies, the mugwumps on the other side of the border; and there's your guy back there voting against us. How can we help you if you're not going to help us out?" And suddenly, these Ambassadors were getting cables from home saying, "What in the hell are you doing? We need help against those mugwumps." Damn right they were standing around the bar in the diplomatic lounge, asking, "What the hell is this guy [Moynihan] doing?" That is exactly what I intended them to be asking.

Interview/Playboy: March:138.

Fred Warner Neal
*Professor of international relations
and government, Graduate School,
Claremont (Calif.) College* 1

... it seems to me that Soviet ideology provides a very strong rationale for the Soviet Union to go to considerable lengths to avoid thermonuclear war at almost any cost, on the grounds that the most important objective, the first priority of Soviet ideology, is to defend the Soviet Union and to maintain a soil on which it and Communism can develop. The ideology here is very clear, i.e., that this cannot be done if the Soviets have a thermonuclear war. So I am not sure what the rationale is as to why the Soviet Union should risk such a war. Unless we can say what that rationale is, we are asserting that unknown motives impel the Soviet Union either to make war or to take exceptional risks which might endanger us. That is not an adequate analysis of the situation.

*At conference on the Soviet Union,
Santa Barbara, Calif./World Issues, Oct.-Nov.:30.*

Richard M. Nixon
Former President of the United States 2

[On his 1976 meeting with then-Chinese Communist Party Chairman Mao Tse-tung]: He talked fatalistically. He said, "How long will peace last? One generation?" He held his finger up like that, and I said, "No, I think longer." And then he, without saying, held up another. I said, "No, longer than that." And then he smiled rather ironically, skeptically. "No, I think maybe a hundred years." And then he [said] it would be very difficult, and I said, I quoted one of his poems to him, I said, "Nothing is hard if one dares to scale the heights." And I said, "Of course, it is difficult, but the stakes are so great here." And he reached over and grasped his cup at that point ... and we raised our hands in a toast. And ... he seemed to be quite moved by that thought.

*Television interview, San Clemente, Calif./
"The Nixon Interviews," Paradine Productions, 5-12.*

Yoshio Okawa
*Director General, Japanese
Mission to the United Nations* 3

Our impact in the United Nations has perhaps been less than we had hoped for. Our entry in the United Nations had meant to the Japanese people a readmission to the international community as a peace-loving nation. We used to feel like an international orphan in the years before our admission. We thought that the United Nations would be the solution to all the world's ills. But perhaps we were a bit starry-eyed ... We feel that the responsibilities and privileges of member states should correspond to their contributions. Japan's contributions are a reflection of her economic standing in the present-day world, and she accepts this with good grace. However, Japan feels she can and should be allowed to play a more prominent role in the political field as well ... is it right that the present five permanent members [of the Security Council] are all nuclear powers? Won't it correspond to the reality of the world if non-nuclear members also have an important role to play in the Council? We could be very useful in the Council.

Interview/The New York Times, 10-2:(1)10.

Paul VI
Pope

1

Episodes, symptoms and rumblings of war still rise up today in the life of the world and paralyze progress toward peaceful coexistence, arousing hatred and greed and causing terrible harm to precarious peace.

Palm Sunday mass, Vatican City, April 3/
The Dallas Times Herald, 4-4:(A)3.

2

We desire above all that the UN be the expression *par excellence* and the bulwark of those human rights which it so solemnly proclaimed 30 years ago. There must be an increase of conscience to make of these rights the criterion of a truly human civilization.

To UN Secretary General Kurt Waldheim,
Vatican City, July 9/San Francisco
Examiner & Chronicle, 7-10:(A)20.

Thomas C. Reed
Secretary of the Air Force
of the United States

3

Clearly, the Soviets do not view nuclear war as unthinkable. With adequate evacuation of their cities, the Soviets believe they can limit casualties to four-to-six per cent of their population in a nuclear exchange. Whether that is true or not is beside the point. If they believe it, if they believe their losses would be far fewer than those suffered in World War II and even less than their self-inflicted losses during the purges of the '30s, they might be tempted to gamble, to push, to conduct themselves differently in another Cuban missile crisis. If nuclear coercion becomes the issue, they do not plan to be the first to blink.

Before Houston Committee on Foreign Relations,
Jan. 17/Vital Speeches, 2-15:269.

Donald H. Rumsfeld
Former Secretary of Defense
of the United States

4

The Soviets, by their activities, indicate that they are not interested in mutually assured destruction. Accordingly, they must be accepted for what they are, not for what we want them to be. Their actions indicate that they take

nuclear war seriously; the United States must do no less.

The Washington Post, 2-20:(A)17.

Anwar el-Sadat
President of Egypt

5

...peace is not a mere endorsement of written lines. Rather it is a rewriting of history. Peace is not a game of calling for peace to defend certain whims or hide certain admissions. Peace in its essence is a dire struggle against all and every ambition and whim. Perhaps the example taken and experienced, taken from ancient and modern history, teaches that missiles, warships and nuclear weapons cannot establish security. Instead, they destroy what peace and security build.... for the sake of the civilization made by man, we have to defend man everywhere against rule by the force of arms, so that we may endow the rule of humanity with all the power of the values and principles that further the sublime position of mankind.

Before the Israeli Knesset [Parliament], Jerusalem,
Nov. 20/The New York Times, 11-21:14.

William W. Scranton
United States Ambassador/Permanent
Representative to the United Nations

6

I think there are two things [regarding the UN] which are very important. One is the work of the specialized agencies which most Americans ... probably know very little about ... The other is that if you're going to do the three things that the UN was primarily set up to do — peacemaking and peace-keeping, economic development, and human-rights improvement — it is extremely important to have a body where everyone is represented — I happen to believe in universality despite my vote on Vietnam — and where they have a chance to bring to such an organization all their international problems. That has been achieved. Practically every country in the world that has an international problem now brings it here. However, you can't solve it here with 147 nations trying to work together. But you certainly can bring the problems here. Then, it seems to me, it's got to break down into areas and organizations that

(WILLIAM W. SCRANTON)

can work on them independently. . .and bring them back here for approval and so they can be implemented.

Interview, United Nations, New York/
The Christian Science Monitor, 1-21:18.

Donn A. Starry
Lieutenant General, United States Army;
Commander, U.S. V Corps, West Germany

1

Peace is an illusion. Conflict of some kind is a natural state of man.

At American High School graduation,
Frankfurt, West Germany, June 10/
The New York Times, 6-16:(A)9.

Andrew Young
United States Ambassador/
Permanent Representative-designate
to the United Nations

2

I have never been one to feel that I was the only one who knew the answers. I think if I do participate in the decision-making process I am willing to be enlightened by other members of the Cabinet and certainly by the President [of the U.S.] any time, and I am sure that the opinions that I do represent at the United Nations will be opinions that I can believe in. If it ever comes to the point where I can't passionately believe in them, I might resort to the measure used by Mr. Gross when he was Ambassador there. He introduced his statement saying, "Mr. President [of the UN], I would like to share with you some of the views of my country on this matter," and it was very clear

where he stood: that this was his country's policy and perhaps not necessarily his own.

TV-radio interview, Washington/"Meet the Press,"
National Broadcasting Company, 1-2.

Andrew Young
United States Ambassador/Permanent
Representative to the United Nations

3

I love this job [of UN Ambassador], this challenge of working with people. You know, I never had any patience. Still don't. My wife puts together jigsaw puzzles; I never had the patience to sit down with a jigsaw. But people-puzzles fascinate me. How do you get the right combination of people working together so they make sense? We did it in the civil-rights movement. We did it in Congress. And we're doing it now. I love people-problems, and the UN is filled with people and problems.

Interview, New York/
The New York Times, 3-27:(1)3.

4

[On his outspokenness as UN Ambassador]: The fact that I've been able to say things that everyone thinks and feels has given me a little more attention. I don't expect any dramatic victories or successes here, but I would like to stay here long enough to develop a pattern of operation that would make the United Nations a relevant part of United States policy. My job is to get something done. I don't get frustrated. It's like a football game. You know, three yards on this play, two yards on that play, and you get thrown for a six-yard loss the next time. But then you get another chance to get the ball.

Interview, New York/The New York Times, 3-27:(1)3.

PART THREE

General

The Arts

Amyas Ames
Chairman, Lincoln Center for the
Performing Arts, New York; Chairman,
Concerned Citizens for the
Arts of New York State

1

. . . the arts are as important as hospitals, universities, welfare, the police. Millions of people coming to museums or to special performances bring life, security and pleasure to communities and increase the economic activity and employment in the state, a service worth many times the state aid coming to these institutions.

The New York Times, 2-6:(1)45.

Gunnar Birkerts
Architect

2

I have been working, not on a form of building, but on a form of thinking. Our buildings should draw on, and identify with, the resources that our own time gives us. They should also relate to human nature, emotions and needs in an informative, inviting way. Architecture may indeed be an art of accommodation, but it is also an art of *communication.* It is not unlike folklore — the passing along of messages and images, the sharing of emotions and feelings.

Interview/The Christian Science Monitor,
12-15:31.

John Brademas
United States Representative, D–Indiana

3

. . . I think it's important that in wanting to support the performing arts that we don't lose sight of individual artists in our desire to keep theatre companies and symphonies alive. That's always a preoccupation of mine: that we're not doing enough to help the individual creative artist, whether painter, writer, dancer or poet.

Second . . . it's important to encourage quality while at the same time trying to insure as much accessibility as possible. You always have these twin objectives when you get into areas like the arts and humanities and education.

Interview/The Washington Post, 5-8:(E)6.

4

Today, the arts are politically saleable. Now a Congressman could get into more difficulty voting against the arts than for. All the evidence points to the fact that Federal support has become not only acceptable but popular.

The New York Times, 9-4:(2)18.

Elizabeth Catlett
Sculptor

5

Part of my acceptance [as a black] in the art world now is because of my maturity. In the '30s and '40s, tokenism was practiced by the exhibitors and only Jacob Lawrence or Horace Pippin would have a show. Now the art world is slightly more broad-minded. It's both a response to the political demands of the '60s and the economic realities. Black art is marketable.

Washington/The Washington Post, 3-4:(B)11.

Marc Chagall
Painter

6

[Saying his opposition to Realism has diminished over the years]: It was during the war, when I was in a ship to America after the occupation of France. I thought about quality when everything was being destroyed, when the world was being turned upside down. Before, when I saw a picture whose subject was real, I said it was not for me. But when everything was being turned upside down, I thought of quality. Now I seek out quality like a bride seeks out

353

(MARC CHAGALL)

love. Quality and love are the same thing, and for love I am very strong.

Interview, St. Paul de Vence, France/
The New York Times, 1-5:(C)15.

Joseph D. Duffey
Chairman-designate, National Endowment
for the Humanities of the United States 1

People feel intensely about it [the National Endowment], and the government has to play its part with sensitivity. In the learned community there is the ever-present fear of a cultural czar. I know; I had that feeling myself. It is right to worry about the possible politicization of the arts and humanities. It is also right to worry about elitism, though there are those who confuse elitism with snobbery. Snobbery is repulsive anywhere you find it. We have to recognize, too, that there is a certain amount of elitism in many parts of American life. But here we get into definitions of excellence. Of course, excellence must be rewarded. We want a society that rewards and encourages achievement. But we also have to *initiate* excellence. Fortunately we've accepted the point that it is important to preserve our cultural and intellectual organizations. That battle has been won.

Interview, Washington/.he New York Times, 8-3:18.

Eliot Feld
Dancer, Choreographer

The thing we need most in the arts is more money — mainly more money from the Federal government. It would be nice not to live so much from hand to mouth, as so many artists do now. It's not that government support should be automatic for any company; we all have to earn our way by merit alone. Even with all the troubles in New York, the state government is very generous in its support of the arts. It's time that the Federal government did much more.

Interview/U.S. News & World Report, 10-10:68.

John Fowles
Author 3

I think art is genetic, patterned. I think you can't learn art. Which is why I think courses in creative writing and water-color painting are useless. I'm not against them in that you get pleasure; but I think if you are being a serious artist, you have no choice — it is decided for you: one, genetically; and two, I suspect by an area we know very little about — probably in the traumas of extreme infancy, and I think the key trauma is the separation trauma. Psychiatrists are doing very interesting work on the nature of the artist, why some people are artists. But I think their theories are really based on how the infant gets through the first identity crisis, separation trauma. The more I go back in my own writings, the more I'm convinced they are right. You know, bound up with all artists is this irrevocable need to go back, this need to go back and recover what is lost.

Interview, New York/
The Christian Science Monitor, 10-3:16.

Francoise Giroud
Secretary of State
for Culture of France 4

[On the opening of a new modern-art center in Paris] : The new is never sure, never accepted until it is no longer new. People have the right to come and say, "It's awful," "What's it for?" "What is it supposed to mean?" The criticism won't be sparing, but when an ambition is noble, isn't it a superior act to support it rather than to clip its wings?

Paris, Jan. 31/The New York Times, 2-1:21.

Nancy Hanks
Chairman, National Endowment for
the Arts of the United States 5

Cultural and economic activities ricochet off each other all the time. It's like a ballet dancer having to be a very good athlete. Grace and strength become each other. You put one of the touring dance companies that we sponsor

(NANCY HANKS)

on a downtown square and, I'll tell you, the shopkeepers won't be tapping their feet to just the music.

Interview/The Christian Science Monitor,
3-24:17.

Barry Jagoda
Special Assistant to President of
the United States Jimmy Carter
for Media and Public Affairs
1

Cultural affairs are receiving more responsible attention in the Carter White House than at any time since the Thomas Jefferson Administration. The number of people on the staff and the personal attention of the President, Mrs. Carter and Mrs. [Joan] Mondale should assure the public that cultural affairs are receiving more attention than ever before. I am surprised that those citizens concerned with cultural affairs have not recognized that leap forward in attention from the White House.

Interview/The Christian Science Monitor,
8-29:23.

Garson Kanin
Author, Playwright
2

All arts are mysteriously connected one with the other. There is a great deal of poetry in architecture, a great deal of dance in drama. All of the arts, in one way or the other, are related. I cannot imagine any writer not being interested in music. All of the arts have rhythm, form. Arts are what brings some kind of form into the chaos of our daily life. Life is, of course, nonsense; it has no meaning, is mostly silly, largely unjust, ludicrous, chaotic, whimsical. If we didn't have the arts to give it some form, we'd go nuts. It is only the arts that give us feeling.

Interview, Beverly Hills, Calif./
Los Angeles Herald-Examiner, 4-7:(B)3.

Rouben Mamoulian
Motion-picture director
3

Bear in mind what is the purpose of art. Science is amoral; it has nothing to do with morality. Science is interested only in facts.

Where is our hope? Religion is failing. The economy is failing. The ultimate last hope is art. Art unites people. It makes life more beautiful.

Interview, San Francisco/San Francisco
Examiner & Chronicle, 1-23:(Datebook)13.

Arthur Miller
Playwright
4

[On the artist in society]: His nature and, I could almost say, his function, is to be the party of the opposition. Power is the most dread disease of mankind and always has been. It disfigures everything . . . and the people who possess it. And I think the artist is that fool who takes on the task of correcting power and defending the truth against it. It's the old failure of speaking truth to power. That's why they're hounded in places where there is not a legal hedge around power. One of the first things they do is attempt to use the artist as a voice of power, to co-opt him.

Interview, Washington/
The Christian Science Monitor, 8-8:30.

Joan Mondale
Wife of Vice President of the
United States Walter F. Mondale
5

Every museum teaches the lesson that there is no substitute for the real thing . . . In a world where so much is artificial, museums have the authority of the genuine. Museums are a major and irreplaceable national resource. They play a role that no other institution in our society can play. They enrich the mind and challenge the imagination. They conserve knowledge and they give pleasure.

Before museum professionals, Washington,
March 9/The Washington Post, 3-11:(B)3.

6

. . . it occurs to me that many great things indeed have been achieved by those who chose not to leap into the mainstream. Things like novels and symphonies and paintings, for example — works achieved by people who stood aside, for a while or for a lifetime, from the practical, problem-solving world. One of my abiding preoccupations is art in America — art

WHAT THEY SAID IN 1977

(JOAN MONDALE)

in all its unpredictable richness and diversity. I spend some of my time going about encouraging artists — and encouraging our citizens to support and enjoy the arts. Again and again I am struck by how much we owe to those who enrich our lives without "solving problems." These people work in quiet isolation, in lofts and studios; they pay little attention to headlines or clocks or schedules. We are infinitely the richer for their non-involvement — and I will defend to the last barricade their right . . . to let the world go by.

At Macalester College commencement/
The New York Times, 5-29:(4)15.

1

The private sector must continue to invest in the arts because it is good for us, it is good for business, it is good for education and, ultimately, because the life of the arts in America happens at the local level. It is at the local level where artists are bred, audiences are formed and organizations receive their mandate. Long-range financial planning and marketing studies are necessary in the business of art, as in the business of business. [But] the business of art organizations is not business, but art.

At symposium on the arts, Washington,
June 18/The New York Times, 6-19:(1)43.

Walter F. Mondale
Vice President of the United States

2

Those who say that politics and culture do not mix have missed an important point about both disciplines. No serious student of these issues has ever suggested that esthetic or academic questions should be decided by politicians or bureaucrats. Our social and political system has always demanded — and provided — a vigorous private cultural system. And it is the role of the Federal government, through our two Endowments [Humanities and Arts], to strengthen that private system without imposing any ideology upon it other than openness.

This delicate role implies a commitment to two principles: quality and access.

At swearing-in of Joseph Duffey as
Chairman of the National Endowment for
the Humanities, Washington, Oct. 18/
The Washington Post, 10-20:(D)13.

Vincent Price
Actor; Art patron

3

All the emphasis [in art] is in the money. And this doesn't interest me at all. The minute a picture becomes too expensive, I get rid of it. Suddenly it is like a dollar bill hanging on the wall. I don't want to be bowled over with monuments in my living-room.

San Francisco Examiner & Chronicle,
8-28:(This World)2.

Frederick W. Richmond
United States Representative,
D—New York

4

[Advocating a checkoff box on tax returns to aid the arts and humanities]: Take an Oldsmobile factory worker in Lansing, Michigan. He makes more money than most of us do. And a poll by Lou Harris has shown that he's willing to give $15 or $20 more, each year, to arts and education. He's probably got a daughter going to ballet school, and a son heading toward college some day — if the college is still there. But he doesn't know how to give. And we don't know how to reach him, without colossal fund-raising costs. This bill is made for him. And us.

Interview, New York/
The Christian Science Monitor, 3-22:7.

Artur Rubinstein
Pianist

5

[On those who say he is the greatest pianist of the century]: Not only do I not believe them but I get very angry . . . There isn't such a thing as the greatest pianist . . . Nothing in art can be the best . . . It is only different . . . An artist in any way must be alone . . . Mozart is alone. Titian is alone.

Television interview/
Los Angeles Herald-Examiner, 1-23:(F)2.

W. Eugene Smith
Photographer
1

When I started to take photographs, I was 14 and I was looking for excitement. But as I went along, I realized that photographs can cause people to look and to take action and to change their attitudes. And I still haven't found the limits of the photographic potential. But I am always on the threshold . . .

Interview, Dallas/
The Dallas Times Herald, 2-13:(F)1.

Isaac Stern
Violinist
2

The United States is the center of the cultural world as far as performance and presentation is concerned. All the major orchestras, opera companies, theatre companies and performers want to come here for two reasons: This is where their accomplishments are most recognized and recompensed. This country is without doubt the center of the Western world.

U.S. News & World Report, 2-14:47.

3

My Russian friends tell me it's not the ministry of culture that you worry about. It's the culture of the minister.

Time, 12-12:93.

Edward Durell Stone
Architect
4

It is the desire of every good architect, I believe, to imbue a building which he designs with beauty. The basic reason for this is a moral one: Beauty is righteous, and ugliness is sinful. Ugliness, like sin, usually reflects a grossness of mind and a poverty of spirit. It would be silly, however, to deny that economic limitations often impede the desired objective. The traditional role of the architect has been to try to create beauty within the budgetary capability of his client. In almost every project, there are a number of compromises between the architect and the owner. The architect's role is to assist the owner in making determinations which are economically feasible but which minimize the negative impact on a truly creative design.

Interview/U.S. News & World Report, 8-15:55.

Michael W. Straight
Acting Chairman, National Endowment for the Arts of the United States
5

No one expects President Carter, beleaguered as he is by the SALT talks, the Middle East crisis and everything else, to spend more than five minutes a month on the arts. But there isn't a qualified senior staff member, such as Leonard Garment in the Nixon Administration, to make decisions in his name. What you have are some 28-year-olds out of their depth. The reason is that the Carter Administration doesn't want senior people interfering with Mrs. [Walter] Mondale. That's unfortunate, because by the fact of her being the Vice President's wife, she's political. She's a public figure saying all the right things, but she cannot watch over the integrity of the Endowments day by day . . . The problem now is the reassertion of the non-political, non-partisan nature of the Endowment. It has had unparalleled success with both artists and citizens for two reasons: It was created in response to a need, and it's grown along the right lines — non-partisan, non-political and completely professional in everything it's done. The difficulty is, we were once a small, $7-million operation, and everyone left us alone. Now we're a $200-million affair, and everyone wants in.

Interview, New York/
The New York Times, 10-12:(C)19.

Alfred Wallenstein
Former musical director,
Los Angeles Philharmonic Orchestra
6

The arts all over this country [the U.S.] function haphazardly. Music is a way of life in Europe and needs no extra boost. Here sports are of paramount importance. Still, if the tax laws were changed to stimulate corporation writeoffs for cultural expenditure, instead of encouraging all those billions to be spent on TV — this nation's wretched soporific — our cultural institutions might not be an endangered species.

Interview, Los Angeles/
Los Angeles Herald-Examiner, 3-11:(A)1.

WHAT THEY SAID IN 1977

Andy Warhol
Artist
1

I don't really understand why everybody is so art-conscious all of a sudden, except that there are so many great artists around now. There are so many galleries. There's a gallery for everybody. I guess somebody turned art into a business, and it just caught on. Most of the artists make money — some a lot and some a little. The man on the street is pretty knowledgeable about art, even in smaller cities like Chattanooga, where some very good smaller museums have been opened.

Interview/U.S. News & World Report, 6-27:57.

Tom Wolfe
Author, Journalist
2

[Saying the current cultural explosion is due in part to snobbery]: Now that the plumber makes as much or more than a museum assistant, they both have the same clothes and the same kind of car. The only thing that separates them is "culture."

U.S. News & World Report, 8-8:53.

Jamie Wyeth
Painter
3

I've taken a few trips abroad recently . . . and it's fascinating to discover that so many foreigners are intrigued about what's going on in American arts. They almost overwhelm you with questions about painting, dance, movies and literature. It strikes me that the arts are an ideal instrument for foreign policy that we haven't used much. We've sent nothing overseas on the scale of the Egyptian exhibit on Tutankhamen or the huge show the Chinese put on display here. I guess it's because there's still so much of an attitude in this country that our arts are the stepchildren of foreign culture. But that's not true any more. We've got a splendid array of artistic endeavors in this country that we should be showing off all around the world.

Interview/U.S. News & World Report, 5-16:90.

Shana Alexander
Author, Journalist

1

I don't believe in objectivity. I'm a writer, not a photographer, and even they do interpretive things with a camera. [News commentator] Walter Cronkite makes editorial comments with his eyebrows.

Interview/
"W": a Fairchild publication, 1-7:2.

Roone Arledge
President, American
Broadcasting Company News

2

One of the things that I think we have a great opportunity to do is to extend the usage of the technology of this industry the way it currently exists. We have reached the level of technology where we can, utilizing mini-cameras and satellites and all the various things that have been developed over the years, literally be on top of a story any place in the world. I think the old concept of the anchor position is outdated and outmoded and it can be changed. This doesn't mean we are going to eliminate anchor people and it doesn't mean that people are going to tune away from Walter Cronkite right away . . . But we can offer an alternative and I think we will. I think we will offer more coverage and better coverage and more lively and more interesting coverage. And I don't think you have to equate, as the press seems eager to do, entertainment with making something interesting. The mere fact that you make it more interesting does not mean you are trying to add show-biz techniques or anything else that we are undoubtedly going to be accused of.

Before ABC-TV affiliates, Los Angeles,
May 10/The Washington Post, 5-11:(B)1.

John D. Backe
President, CBS, Inc.

3

[On critics of bigness in media]: [What] many so-called media critics — both in and out of government — really want is not diversity. What a lot of them really want is to remove a thorn from their sides — a strong, independent and outspoken communications industry. And they are trying to do it with economic pressure, because they know political pressure won't work. They know that only big communications companies with extensive resources can properly report on, and investigate, and stand up to, the powers of big government, big business and big labor.

Before International Radio and Television Society,
New York, Nov. 15/
The Washington Post, 11-16:(D)9.

Clive Barnes
Drama critic, "New York Post"

4

[On his leaving *The New York Times* to join the *Post*]: Anyone attached to *The New York Times* has a kind of instant credibility and instant glamour. One wonders how much of that is a cloak bestowed by the paper and how much it is one's own. I felt it was more challenging to be without *The Times* rather than with *The Times.*

Time, 12-5:67.

Joseph Benti
Television news commentator,
KNXT, Los Angeles

5

When [a TV newscaster] has a negative effect on viewers, management dumps us, whoever we may be. It's a terrible way to have our information measured. But so much of television news these days is not news. It's NEWZAK, like the music heard in elevators and

359

WHAT THEY SAID IN 1977

(JOSEPH BENTI)

airports, and it's all over the country. The greatest danger is that inexperienced people who are good performers can be presented to the public as serious, professional broadcast journalists. It degrades what we do, and the public is the loser. The job of journalist in a free society is like a doctor's. If there is a cancer, a doctor should not hide it with a pleasing personality. But when a pseudo-journalist is chosen for his personality, he is not going to tell people they have cancer. He is more concerned with making people feel comfortable and relaxed. The result is the quality of news and information is degraded.

TV Guide, 3-26:10.

Roscoe C. Born
Associate editor,
"The National Observer"

1

We all know of newspapers whose achievements earned them a place in the annual listings of the nation's "10 greatest newspapers." Once a newspaper makes that list, it appears there year after year, usually long after the newspaper has ceased to be great. But even while long-distance observers are continuing to rate a newspaper as great — because they really don't read it — the younger staffers and editors know it has begun to decay, that it no longer nourishes creativity and no longer stokes the journalistic fires . . . I think it's a malady we're all vulnerable to, and for which there is no immunization. I hope all of us can manage to fend it off.

At William Allen White School of Journalism,
University of Kansas/The National Observer, 1-15:13.

Benjamin C. Bradlee
Executive editor,
"The Washington Post"

2

[On government suggestions to the press not to print certain stories]: In almost 20 years in a decision-making seat, I've heard lots of claims about the serious harm our stories would do, but not one panned out. People are always trying to get me to be a statesman instead of a journalist. It's fine work, but not what I chose.

Time, 3-14:80.

Art Buchwald
Newspaper columnist

3

[Upon acceptance of the Jefferson Award for public service performed by a private citizen]: It is truly a humbling experience to be standing in this impressive Supreme Court building and to accept an award from a jury of distinguished Americans. In 80 per cent of the countries around the world the only time their writers and artists are brought to a supreme court is to be sentenced to a prison or mental institution for a "crime against the state." In America, for some reason, which I believe has to do with the nine men who preside in this building, the tougher you are on the state, the more honors your fellow citizens bestow on you . . . Under our system, we have discovered that when the writer, or anyone else, speaks his mind, the walls of this building, as well as those of the Capitol and the White House, won't come tumbling down. The continual questioning of our institutions is actually the mortar that keeps the walls from crumbling. Not everyone in this country understands this. But fortunately the majority of the people instinctively do — and it is for this reason that writers like myself are not only permitted to walk around as free citizens, but are paid vast sums of money to point out . . . that the Emperor has no clothes on. I don't know whether it's a good idea to accept this award or not. On the one hand, I'm terribly flattered. But there is a tiny voice in me that says when the establishment drags you kicking and screaming up to the Supreme Court and gives you a medal and a large check for attacking it, it means you must be doing something wrong.

At award ceremony sponsored by American Institute
for Public Service, Washington/
The Washington Post, 7-12:(A)18.

Al Capp
Cartoonist

4

[On his terminating the *L'il Abner* comic strip after 43 years]: If you have any sense of humor about your strip, and I had a sense of humor about Abner, you knew that for three or four years Abner was wrong. But I didn't turn it over to any kids to do. I own the strip and I

(AL CAPP)

could do what I chose to end it. Oh, hell, it's like a fighter retiring. I think I stayed on longer than I should have. There's no goodbye strip on November 13 — it seems to me cheap to say something maudlin. Whatever you say is a strip too much, so I just broke off. There's a story and it cuts without any farewell, without any goodbye.

Interview, Cambridge, Mass./
The New York Times, 11-11:(B)8.

1

"Satirist" is a dangerous word for a cartoonist. As soon as you think of yourself as a satirist, you're sunk. You're pompous. You think your words have great and enduring meaning. I was a cartoonist. Of course, anybody that does comedy does satire. Even if a cartoonist draws a dog and a pole, the way he draws dogs and poles is a comment on dogs in that society, and on poles.

San Francisco Examiner & Chronicle,
11-20:(This World)2.

Jimmy Carter
President of the United States

2

There is in the press, as there is in politics, some degree of complete irresponsibility and some absence of integrity, some deliberate distortion; but I have said many times, truthfully, that my over-all relationship with the press is good and my respect for the press is high. What sometimes impresses us on a day-by-day transient basis is the aberration and the misreporting of something about which we know the facts. I think some of this may stem from an overemphasis in reporting on the mechanics and politics of policy-making, as opposed to the substance of the policy. In my experience, so-called inside stories on policy-making are usually more wrong than right. But I would say, in general, the press has treated the Administration fairly. They and I are trying our best, but we all make mistakes, not because of evil intent but because we're human.

Interview, Washington, Dec. 1/
The New York Times, 12-5:42.

John Chancellor
News commentator, National
Broadcasting Company

3

[Saying he will be leaving his job as anchorman on the "NBC Nightly News"]: I've done every kind of news job in my 25 years at NBC — covering foreign affairs, politics, even the police stories. After seven years as anchorman, I missed the travel and missed the feeling of being purely responsible for my own material. Being an anchorman is 75 per cent rewrite and 25 per cent reporting. It may be the top job and pay the most money, but it's not very satisfying to a journalist. I decided that I don't want to measure out my life in 30-second introductions to other people who do the reporting.

Interview, Dec. 1/The New York Times, 12-2:(C)28.

Otis Chandler
Publisher, "Los Angeles Times"

4

In terms of impediments, intimidation and exclusion of Western correspondents, a few Africans, Arab and Asian states have gone even further than the Soviet Union did under Josef Stalin to isolate their societies from outside scrutiny. To cite a few examples, it is virtually impossible to report anything meaningful on a sustained basis about Guinea, Nigeria, the Congo, Mozambique or Angola in Africa; about Cambodia, Laos or Burma in Asia; or about Iraq, South Yemen or Saudi Arabia in the Middle East.

Before Senate Foreign Relations Committee,
Washington, June 9/
The Washington Post, 6-10:(A)8.

5

[On concentrated news-media ownership]: On the one hand, I can, if I'm asked . . . make a persuasive argument . . . about the advantages of group ownership. I can also be persuaded to make an argument on the other side for independence, that loss of independent newspapers and voices around the country is a bad thing; and so I guess I'm kind of on the fence . . . I just don't know, but I'm not convinced that this is a major new serious threat to the press. I think politicians have

(OTIS CHANDLER)

always disliked us; they wish they could control us; they wish we wouldn't print things about them that they do, except for the good things ... [But] all they [the people] really care about is who's got the best paper; and if you've got a good paper, I'll read it and buy it, rather than necessarily how many papers there are, or, if two or three disappear, isn't it terrible. I just don't think they care.

The Washington Post, 7-24:(G)3.

Alvah H. Chapman, Jr.
President, Knight-Ridder Newspapers 1

Today, many newspaper companies can boast a new breed of professional editors, managers, sales and marketing executives, circulators and financial executives. Without modern management procedures and the new technology [of production], many newspapers today would be drowning in a sea of red ink.

Interview, Miami/The Washington Post, 7-29:(D)9.

John B. Connally, Jr.
Former Secretary of the Treasury of the United States; Former Governor of Texas (D, now R) 2

We've now reached the point where the press has become such an incredibly powerful force in itself that it has more influence even than government. The truth is that our nation's institution of "the press" in 1977 is a giant financial and influential power center equivalent to the Presidency, the Congress or the Supreme Court. We recognize the ageless value of freedom of the press. We should also conclude that this freedom carries with it the dangerous freedom to oppress. So it seems to me that in this age of accountability we must ask the press, like other institutions, to undergo a re-examination of itself ... When you talk about concentration of power, I think the news media ought to be subject to the same standards and guidelines that are applicable to others, because I think, frankly, the purveyors of thought, the product of thought, the product of information, is far more important

than the manufacture of automobiles or any other consumer items we use on a daily basis.

Before Press Club of Houston, March 22/ The Dallas Times Herald, 5-23:(A)21.

Walter Cronkite
News commentator, Columbia Broadcasting System 3

I still get great pleasure out of what I'm doing. The greatest pleasure I get is from what seems the routine: going out to the [news] desk every day to decide what goes in and how much to give each piece of news. You know — the managing-editor aspect. I enjoy the extended nights, too, the ad lib nights. On a good night, when it's just been smooth, and I haven't had to back and fill, and I've told a coherent story from beginning to end — I know it.

Interview/Los Angeles Times, 1-30:(1)20.

4

[On the scramble for ratings on news broadcasts] : ... it is *how* we get those ratings, what we do to make us competitive, that bothers me. For just as it is no good to put out a superior product if you can't sell it, it is far worse to peddle an inferior product solely through the razzle-dazzle of a promotion campaign. And aren't we guilty of that when we put the emphasis in our news broadcasts on performance and performers rather than context? Isn't that really what we are looking for when we examine ourselves to see whether we are indulging in show business rather than journalism?

Before CBS-TV affiliates/ Los Angeles Herald-Examiner, 8-24:(B)2.

Robert J. Donovan
Associate editor, "Los Angeles Times" 5

In one word, the biggest change [in journalism] has been "television." It has made journalism into an agony because we have to perform a different function. Reporters used to be the purveyors of yesterday's news. Now TV is the purveyor of today's news. Newspapers have had to go to a whole new dimension. This used to be a rather mild business — but no

(ROBERT J. DONOVAN)

longer. And there are a lot of broken bodies along the way in the transformation.

Interview, Washington/
The Washington Post, 8-24:(B)2.

Allen Drury
Author; Former journalist

1

There is a very bad tendency among the media to censor opposing points of view — not telling both sides. Opinion is no longer confined to where I think it should be — editorial columns. Opinion is now evident not only in the news pages, but in the way newspapers are made up and in the photographs. It is the function of the press to present news as fairly, completely and as objectively as possible. The opposing viewpoint shouldn't be relegated to page 22.

Interview, Dallas/
The Dallas Times Herald, 9-20:(B)5.

Oriana Fallaci
Journalist

2

[Politicians] need journalists for publicity. It's their life. And they're right. I am a marvelous instrument of publicity whether you like me or no. If you are the Shah of Iran and you want to say a few things about your oil, you give me four or five hours, as he did, [and] you do not lose your time because it goes everywhere in the world. And I understand them, and I listen to them. In their place I would do it. In their place, if Fallaci comes to interview me, I wouldn't reject her because she would be useful to me.

Interview, Washington/The Washington Post, 3-5:(B)2.

Keith Fuller
President and general manager,
Associated Press

3

As you watch acquisitions [of newspapers by chains], you are aware that obviously some are quite good for the reader. Some groups improve the product. Where they have capital to automate and where they take those automated savings and plow them back into the editorial product, it's all to the good. But if it is

a bottom-line acquisition, and they go in and start cutting the staff and just squeezing the product, that is a very different proposition.

Los Angeles Times, 1-9:(6)5.

Frank Grad
Professor of law, Columbia University

4

It's very dangerous to restrain First Amendment liberties. The chance of occasional excesses [by the press] is not too heavy a price to pay for assurance of liberty.

Time, 3-28:57.

Katharine Graham
Publisher, "The Washington Post"

5

The effects of Watergate have not been entirely constructive; it troubles me that reporting, particularly investigative reporting, has become so glamorous, and that so many young people have developed such an unrealistic impression of the nature of the news business — and of the number of jobs available.

Before International Newspaper Promotion
Association, Washington/
The Wall Street Journal, 1-5:10.

6

I think that newspapers do have personalities and souls [that] they derive from people who make it . . . I inherited it as tradition and I can build on and augment it, and the tradition was established not only by my family but by previous editors . . . I think that personality was probably most imprinted on the paper by my father, who said he viewed newspapering as a public service, and he wanted it to be independent of his particular beliefs. On the other hand, he had a view of the decency of society . . . the almost sacredness of the democratic system and a newspaper's role in it in general and in Washington in particular.

Interview/The Washington Post, 7-31:(F)3.

George J. Green
President, "The New Yorker" magazine

7

[On his magazine's criticizing newspapers]: The unwritten rule is not to criticize your media associates. It's like doctors and lawyers not talking about other doctors and lawyers.

WHAT THEY SAID IN 1977

(GEORGE J. GREEN)

But I think if you have a responsible press, you have a requirement — an obligation — to speak up if you think there is something awry. And I think that is exactly what we have done.

Interview, Los Angeles/
Los Angeles Times, 9-26:(3)14.

Frederick J. Hacker
Psychiatrist; Authority on
crime and terrorism
1

It strikes one as peculiar that while even Nobel Prize winners have some difficulty getting across to the media, the news organizations give totally free prime time to disorganized criminals or the crazy ramblings of this, that or the other offender simply because he has a gun in his hand. We pay a high price in violence for our entertainment by violence. The media publicize these events, they say, to inform the public. But it is, in fact, done to entertain and to titillate the public . . . There is no Constitutional or other justification to guaranteeing that every criminal should have the right to be publicized for some sensational act. On the contrary, what I call the "showification" of an event prevents sensible, long-term handling of the situation and promotes short-range escalation of violence.

Interview/U.S. News & World Report, 2-28:57.

Lee Hills
Chairman, Knight-Ridder Newspapers
2

[Comparing print with other types of media] : Print is referable; it is there to reread at your convenience. Print is preservable; you can clip, save and file it. Print is convenient, so you may read what you want, at the speed you want, and when you want to. Print is portable . . . With print, the reader is in control. He can skip. He can go back. He can observe; he can turn the page or section. It is intimate communication.

U.S. News & World Report, 8-15:33.

Norman Isaacs
Chairman, National News Council
3

If journalists catch some Congressman on a weekend retreat paid for by special interests, everybody gets excited. Yards are written about conflict of interest. But what if a journalist, or the owner of a paper, has a conflict of interest?

U.S. News & World Report, 10-10:29.

Stuart H. Loory
Managing editor, "Chicago Sun-Times"
4

The press must start thinking more about the ways people, like terrorists, are using us. We have become part of the story.

Time, 3-28:57.

Elmer W. Lower
Vice president, corporate affairs,
American Broadcasting Companies;
Former president, ABC News
5

The American media are unsurpassed in their coverage of catastrophes, the details of a disaster, a plane crash, an assassination, a flood, famine, a riot, an earthquake. This is, of course, reactive journalism. The American press, radio and television are the greatest reactors in the world. We're good at it because we've had a lot of experience working under a free press to develop this talent. I often wonder if the greatest fault of American journalism isn't that we're too reactive. We are good at wars but slow at finding out *now* what the major events are going to be two, five, 10 or 25 years from now. The media need to put aside some time to think. If we must hire professional thinkers, so be it. If the public has a right to know what happened hours .ago, it has the same right to know what's in the future. At first blush, concern with future crime, future food, future population, future energy, future water, future environmental problems and the rest doesn't seem to warrant the same worry as a deadline story because it is presumed the audience isn't interested right now. So the duty then becomes to get them interested.

At Madison College/
The Christian Science Monitor, 5-19:31.

Clare Boothe Luce
Former American diplomat
and playwright

1

[The press] is the strongest "branch of government," but it leaves much to be desired. The press is terribly biased on the liberal Democratic side, and everybody knows it. On the other hand, the same bias existed in favor of the Republicans in the 1920s, 1930s and 1950s. So it's turn and turn about. It's exasperating, but . . . objective journalism is totally impossible. What you've got to do is find the side of the angels and stay on it.

Interview, Washington/People, 7-25:29.

Mary McGrory
Political columnist

2

You can always excuse a bad column one day by saying you were pressed in writing it. If you don't do a good job one day you can make up for it the next. It's like always being born again.

Interview, Washington/
"W": a Fairchild publication, 10-28:20.

Rupert Murdoch
Newspaper/magazine publisher

3

Too often we [in journalism] have accepted the proposition that we must be soporific to be significant and colorless to be credible. Too often we appear oblivious to changes in life-styles and buying habits . . . [Newspapers should not] fall for the temptation of retreating to the minority quality audience at the top of the market. This would be an abdication of our role — I would say of our responsibility — of communicating via the written word with the great mass of the public. We must recapture the essentiality of the daily newspaper in the life of the ordinary person . . . I am not suggesting that human interest — sometimes derisively called sensationalism — is the only legitimate standard of news judgment. Far from it. I am saying that without first gaining the attention of our readers, the rest is so much waste of time . . . The TV soap opera has often been ridiculed and reviled. Yet in its more expert presentations it often touches more authentic nerves among harassed housewives and alien-ated young people than thousands of the abstract, ponderous words that are printed.

Before American Newspaper Publishers
Association, San Francisco/
Los Angeles Times, 5-2:(3)12.

4

[On journalism] : I cannot avoid the temptation of wondering whether there is any other industry in this country which seeks to presume so completely to give the customer what he does not want.

Before American Newspaper Publishers
Association, San Francisco/Time, 5-30:49.

Ron Nessen
Former Press Secretary to the
President of the United States
(Gerald R. Ford)

5

[The popular view is that the Press Secretary and his staff are there to] withhold, censor and cover up information. The fact of the matter is — as any press secretary will tell you in the White House or any other government department or agency — that there is far more information available to put out than is ever asked about [by the press] . That's the frustration. I would come to my briefing room after having spent 4½ or 5 hours every morning gathering information in anticipation of questions. I would get asked about 40 per cent of that information and often it was the more trivial element. I would walk back to the office, with Ford, after news conferences almost all of the time and he invariably would say, "Why didn't they ask me about this; why weren't the questions tougher on that; why didn't they follow up on this?" . . . You have reporters basically who are generalists — they have to know a little about a lot of things because they cover everything that comes out of the White House. Their questions are necessarily shallow; they just don't have the depth of expertise. The Press Secretary's knowledge also is necessarily shallow; he doesn't know as much as that assistant secretary at one of the agencies who deals with it every day.

Interview, Washington/
Los Angeles Times, 8-15:(1)15.

WHAT THEY SAID IN 1977

Allen H. Neuharth
President, Gannett Company
1

Everything in the newspaper business starts with the reader product, and unless you're on target in terms of what you're giving the reader, then you can't make it. If you are on target with that, everything else — advertising, circulation — will follow.
U.S. News & World Report, 1-24:56.

Edwin Newman
News correspondent, National Broadcasting Company
2

I believe some silence is helpful to thought, and I believe to some extent radio and television discourage thought and reflection. I'm talking about something everybody in this business [broadcast journalism] comes to at one time or another. You're on the air and you want to show you're more amusing and more trenchant than the people you're working with, or against. We ought in some sense encourage thought. I'm saying we ought to make an effort to shut up.
Interview, New York/
Los Angeles Herald-Examiner, 12-12:(A)17.

Richard M. Nixon
Former President of the United States
3

Let's just not have all this sanctimonious business about the poor repressed press. I went through it through all the years I've been in public life, and ... they never have been repressed as far as I am concerned. I don't want them repressed, but believe me, when they take me on, or when they take any public figure on, Democrat or Republican, liberal or conservative, I think the public [figure] ought to come back and crack 'em right in the puss.
Television interview, San Clemente, Calif./
"The Nixon Interviews," Paradine Productions, 5-25.

David R. Obey
United States Representative,
D–Wisconsin
4

There are not many stories written about the amount of taxpayers' money spent to support the Washington press. Let's look at some of

those costs: 24 employees of the House and Senate press galleries, plus special doorkeepers and messengers, at a total cost during 1977 of $529,517; 181 free, reserved parking spaces in choice locations on the Capitol grounds at a cost, based on comparable parking downtown, of $130,000; about 180 free telephones, adding up to approximately $23,000 a year in phone bills; desks, chairs, typewriters and other equipment worth about $40,000; exclusive press tables in the House and Senate dining-room ... Some of these privileges are hard to measure, but the cost to the taxpayers comes to way over $1-million a year ... [which is] a small price to pay to enable the press to do its Constitutionally protected job of reporting to the American public of the activities of their elected public servants ... But the same is true of Congress. I don't mind serious stories about Congressional waste; I welcome them, because with a $60-billion deficit we cannot afford waste anywhere. What I do mind is the misplaced sanctimony of some of the reporters who have populated the House and Senate galleries in increasing numbers the last few years. What I do mind is the national TV reporter who does a three-minute network clip on Congressional "perks," such as free parking, without ever getting around to telling his viewers that he himself has a free space on that same Capitol Hill.
Before Western Wisconsin Press Association,
Eau Claire, May 27/The Washington Post, 6-7:(A)16.

Michael J. O'Neill
Editor, "New York Daily News"
5

We [in journalism] must weigh one value, of a fully informed public, against another, the risk of some madman imitating what he has seen or read. The first enormously outweighs the second.
Time, 3-28:57.

Walter Porges
Chief writer, "ABC (TV) Evening News"
6

I personally hate listening to formal broadcast journalism. "Prime interest rate," "three-point-five-billion-dollar tax cut" — it just doesn't relate to the viewer. We should be able

(WALTER PORGES)

to present the news in a *comfortable* way. I think the viewer is saying to us, "Talk to me and tell me what happened today — don't *read* to me."

The New York Times Magazine, 2-13:33.

John R. Purcell
President, CBS/Publishing Group
1

[Supporting the growth of chain-newspaper companies]: Fragmentation of the media plays into the hands of big government. As long as there is a centralized big government, there is a need for a powerful and financially able free press.

U.S. News & World Report, 8-15:29.

Dan Rather
News commentator,
Columbia Broadcasting System
2

All other things being equal, in broadcast journalism the person with the best appearance is likely to do best [with viewers]. I would hate to anchor the news opposite Paul Newman.

Interview/People, 9-5:61.

George E. Reedy
Professor of journalism, Marquette
University; Former Press Secretary
to the President of the United States
(Lyndon B. Johnson)
3

The purpose of [news] papers is to carry on a dialogue, not to perform an educational function. Too many in the press forget that.

U.S. News & World Report, 8-15:30.

James Reston
Political columnist
4

[The capacity of] any group to circulate its ideas or report news of any type is greater today than it has ever been in the history of this country.... economically, we're at the point that the old printer was, when he had a sack of type ... swung it over his shoulder. Anybody, whether he's a lover of roses, a homosexual, a nut on changing the Constitution, can get himself a little ... machine and, if

he can type, he can paste up paper and go down to a corner printer and get that thing printed up, really quite cheaply.

Interview, Washington/
The Washington Post, 7-24:(G)3,4.

Abraham A. Ribicoff
United States Senator, D–Connecticut
5

The investigative reporters have become the king of the press. "Get everybody" — that's the name of the game in America today.

At Senate Governmental Affairs Committee
hearing, Washington, July 25/
Los Angeles Times, 7-26:(1)1.

Carlos P. Romulo
Foreign Minister of the Philippines
6

While you [journalists] think governments are trying to run the press, governments think the press is trying to run their countries.

Before Hong Kong Foreign Correspondents Club/
The New York Times, 4-7:29.

Richard S. Salant
President, Columbia Broadcasting
System News
7

The professional issue facing journalism — both print and broadcast — is whether or not to give the people what they want to know or what they need to know ... In a democracy, the public cannot exercise its power unless it is informed. It's the job of the press to provide for an informed citizenry.

Before National Academy of Television Arts
and Sciences, New York, Sept. 29/
The Hollywood Reporter, 9-20:4.

Herbert S. Schlosser
President, National Broadcasting Company
8

[Criticizing the equal-time rule]: [The rule] still artificially restricts the form and variety of programs that can feature candidates' appearances. It still interferes with journalistic enterprise ... Last year, however, [the FCC] broadened its previous interpretation and ruled that candidates' news conferences and debates could be treated as exempt on-the-spot coverage of news on one condition — that they happen

WHAT THEY SAID IN 1977

(HERBERT S. SCHLOSSER)

independently of broadcasting, without any broadcasting pre-arrangement. The League of Women Voters stepped into the breach and organized the 1976 [Presidential candidates'] debates so that they could be regarded as independently occurring news events. To my mind, and to millions of others, the debates were the most important use of television in the Presidential election. But their importance does not disguise the fact that they were arranged to meet a legal situation. In order to preserve their appearance as independent news events, they could not serve the electorate as well as they might have ... Responsible journalistic judgment should determine news coverage of the candidates. With the present [equal-time] restrictions removed, broadcast journalism would be better equipped to fulfill its responsibility for covering all newsworthy candidates, not only those of the major parties ... It is time for television to have full freedom to meet the needs of the public in understanding the candidates and the issues.

At Georgia Association of Broadcasters
Annual Institute, Athens, Ga., Jan. 26/
Daily Variety, 1-27:4.

Daniel Schorr
Former news correspondent,
Columbia Broadcasting System

1

One of the functions of objective journalism is not simply to give undigested facts but to give the meaning of facts. Between the editorial and the totally flat repetition of what someone else said is a large area of middle ground — the information in perspective. That, I find, is a very important role for journalists. Otherwise ... politicians feel they can go on the air and say things over the heads of people.

Interview, Beverly Hills, Calif./
Los Angeles Times, 11-17:(4)33.

Eric Sevareid
News commentator,
Columbia Broadcasting System

2

I could never understand the court's argument that the Fairness Doctrine for broadcast-

ing enhances the First Amendment. The First Amendment is a prohibition. How do you enhance a negative? No means no ... The censorious instinct is always present and it shifts its operating base from time to time. The Federal government under [former President Richard] Nixon tried prior restraint, which not even the Alien and Sedition Acts permitted. The Federal government went through a spasm of subpoenas against news people but has since tried to restrain itself. Courts have increased their gag rules on journalists, and both prosecuting and defense attorneys increasingly try to compel journalists' disclosure, sometimes just to make their own work easier.

Before National Association of Broadcasters,
Washington/Variety, 3-30:35.

3

If people like me [journalists] were literally elected, it would mean a majority would hear what they wanted, and that isn't the idea of a free press. In one sense, we're elected every day — or thrown out: Tune me in or tune me out; read you or pass over you. I don't know what the "power of the press" really is. I read the phrase all the time, but I don't know how you measure it. The press doesn't have any power to arrest anybody or tax anybody or declare war. I've always thought the government was growing in power. How do you measure influence? I haven't the faintest idea.

Interview/Los Angeles Times, 11-13:(6)3.

4

We've been awfully privileged people in our business. To have been an American journalist in this generation is the luckiest thing that could happen to anybody. You're taken seriously; you're well paid; you sit above the salt. That isn't true in many countries. Why Washington now? There's never been a news center like it since ancient Rome. It's fabulous. And now it's beginning to be kind of a glamour center. Isn't that interesting?

Interview/Los Angeles Times, 11-13:(6)3.

5

I have tried to remain objective, always aware, however, that objectivity and neutrality

(ERIC SEVAREID)

are not the same thing. Objectivity is a *way* of thinking *about* an issue, not the summation of the thought.

The Christian Science Monitor, 11-29:48.

1

Mine has been, here [as a broadcast journalist], an unelected, unlicensed, uncodified office and function. The rules are self-imposed. These were a few: Not to underestimate the intelligence of the audience and not to overestimate its information. To elucidate when one can, more than to advocate. To remember always that the public is only people, and people only persons, no two alike. To retain the courage of one's doubts as well as one's convictions, in this world of dangerously passionate certainties. To comfort oneself, in times of error, with the knowledge that the saving grace of the press, print or broadcast, is its self-correcting nature. And to remember that ignorant and biased reporting has its counterpart in ignorant and biased reading and listening. We do not speak into an intellectual and emotional void. One's influence cannot be measured. History provides, for the journalist, no markers or milestones. But he is allowed to take his memories. And one can understand, as he looks back, the purpose of the effort and why it must be done.

Farewell remarks upon retiring after 38 years
with CBS News/"Evening News,"
Columbia Broadcasting System Television, 11/30.

2

[On criticism of broadcast journalism]: I don't worry about criticism of me. I expect to be criticized. This industry has to be criticized. It is big and very pervasive. More pervasive than persuasive, I think. But I don't want criticism to come from the government. They've got a club over us. This is a licensed press. We act as though we're free, but the Fairness Doctrine, equal time — they are over us. I don't think it's healthy.

Interview/People, 12-12:66.

William Sheehan
Senior vice president for news,
American Broadcasting Company

3

The concept of a free flow of news is so foreign to many governments that they have a pathological fear of any reporting which they do not directly control.

Before Senate Foreign Relations Committee,
Washington, June 9/
The Washington Post, 6-10:(A)8.

Howard Simons
Managing editor, "The Washington Post"

4

One of the myths about our business is that a daily newspaper is a total, objective and accurate account of events everywhere on a given day. Nothing could be further from reality. What we do, rather, is to write a first rough draft of history. Indeed, I often wonder why we don't confess to our readers by carrying a box on the front page of our newspaper, a warning to the consumer that the product is incomplete, sometimes inaccurate, and is put together by editors and reporters who have differing metabolism, skills, inculcations and educations; not to mention whether they slept well the night before ... Some persons would like to believe that each day's paper has been plotted by a small group of persons who make deliberate determinations on critical issues and personalities. This is simply not true. Though I am intimately and directly involved in what *The Post's* front page will contain and will look like each day, more often than not I practice more staff psychiatry, law without a license, office management, budget control and labor relations than news editing ... What *The Washington Post* is, is a collection of bright, aggressive, hard-working humans reporting as best they can what is new and profound and different and significant and funny and sad and telling. More often than not, what is printed has more to do with what's wrong than with what's right; more to do with keeping persons honest than with honest people; more to do with illuminating dark places than reflecting sunlight; most to do with seeking the truth. Not all newspapers are good newspapers. Not any one newspaper is totally

WHAT THEY SAID IN 1977

(HOWARD SIMONS)

good or bad, fair or unfair. We have our warts and our biases — just as do our readers. But — and it is a terribly significant but — if we do not do the digging and the reporting, the investigating and the commenting, the probing and the exposition, then who will?

At inauguration of a new president
of Northeastern Illinois University, May 12/
Vital Speeches, 9-1:689,692.

Joe D. Smith, Jr.
President, American Newspaper
Publishers Association 1

An expressed concern of some elected officials and others is the growing number of newspapers which have been acquired by multiple or group owners. One proposal is for a study of newspaper operations with the inference that our business and its ownership might be regulated by the government if the government decides we are not serving our communities in a manner that the same government decides is fair and proper. If any idea was ever in conflict with the letter and spirit of a Constitutionally mandated free press, this one takes first prize. Just remember that a government which can tell you that you can own nine [newspapers], and not 10, can also deem you unqualified to own even one.

Before American Newspaper Publishers Association,
San Francisco, April 25/
The Dallas Times Herald, 4-26:(A)12.

Tom Snyder
Host, "Tomorrow" show, National
Broadcasting Company Television 2

There are two kinds of [TV] news: local and national. If the local news doesn't get ratings in a hurry, a consultant is called in and — boom! boom! — there's a quick changeover in personnel and format. Network news is straight-ahead; it's not show-biz; I don't think it's ever going to be show-biz. But the local news is different. It emphasizes the most sensational aspect of the news — child pornography, violence in the streets, wife-beating, things like that. That's wrong. People are decrying violence on televi-

sion and there has been talk of programming for the family. The audience will soon be saying, "What the hell is going on in the news?"

Interview, Los Angeles/
Los Angeles Herald-Examiner, 6-14:(B)1.

I. F. Stone
Former editor and publisher,
"I. F. Stone's Weekly" 3

In our humble way, [we journalists are] under some of the compulsions that imprison the historian, and that is the necessity to find meaning in events. Everybody wants to know, "What's it mean? What's it mean? What's it mean?" And half the time, it doesn't mean anything ... It's very easy to create plausible patterns from the little we know, put them together, make them look very interesting, very meaningful, and feel like a very bright and very good journalist and say to yourself, "Well, it sounds good, but is it true?" And very often, one missing fact, one missing fact can destroy the whole fabric of a plausible pattern. And you know, in the sciences, and in true scholarship, the great advances are made by a patient willingness to re-examine what other people regard as obvious ... But we, under the compulsions of the deadline and our necessary and inevitable superficiality, find it very easy to grab whatever bit of news, whatever speech, whatever gossip that fits our preconceptions and the preconceptions of our readers or our own political following, and create a pleasing and satisfactory pattern that sounds good and may be a lot of nonsense.

At "Journalism and Social Change" conference,
Princeton University/The Wall Street Journal, 3-4:10.

Arthur Ochs Sulzberger
Publisher, "The New York Times" 4

I like little, independent papers. I think it's a strength of America ... If somebody were to blow the whistle on newspaper acquisitions and say that it's enough, I, for one, would applaud it. But if those are not going to be the rules of the game, I'm going to keep *The New York Times* in the newspaper-acquisition business.

U.S. News & World Report, 8-15:28.

Morris K. Udall
United States Representative,
D–Arizona
1

Of the 1,500 cities with daily papers, 97.5 per cent have no local daily newspaper competition. This trend signifies a very real loss to American society, the publisher with roots in the community ... [The *Tucson Daily Citizen,*] a good, solid, conservative daily owned for years by the Small family, was sold a few months ago to the Gannett chain. I've nothing against Gannett ... but still I'm going to miss that local ownership at the *Citizen.* I do not condemn Gannett for adding to their long list of acquisitions, What does bother me is that there is an increasingly prevalent pattern here that has disturbing social implications ... I am not asking that newspaper chains be outlawed, or publishers prosecuted, or even that coercive Federal legislation be enacted. [But] editors and journalists should be thinking and speaking out on this issue. Today, what the titans of the chains want is profits — not power, just money. I fear that the quest for profits and higher dividends for their growing lists of [stockholders] will transcend their responsibility to maintain an independent and dedicated influence in the community.

Before National Press Club, Washington, April 5/
The Dallas Times Herald, 4-5:(A)6.

Richard C. Wald
President, National
Broadcasting Company News
2

In television, the personality [of the newscaster] — the impact of one person on the viewer — is as important as style is to the written word.

The New York Times Magazine, 2-13:33.

Barbara Walters
News commentator,
American Broadcasting Company
3

I was amazed at the kind of anger when I became the first [TV network news] anchorwoman. One of the things that bothered me about network news was the treatment that it's a holy organization, that you have to be somehow endowed to even set foot in it. That was part of the controversy ... I didn't fit the mold. I learned news by running around with a microphone and working in TV. I wasn't trained by AP or UPI the way most of the commentators were. But just the fact that there is a woman in network news now is important. I've said that I may not last, but I know that I won't be the last. I think within the next year or two, each of the networks will have an "anchorhuman," which is the way we're referring to it.

Before Hollywood Radio and Television Society,
Los Angeles, May 10/Los Angeles Times, 5-12:(4)17.

Walter E. Washington
Mayor of Washington
4

[Criticizing newspaper attacks on officials in his Administration by articles using unnamed sources] : Attack me where my programs are or if you have something. But to create a situation in this town, or in any town, where you can't face someone who raises the question and we must work in the background of "reliable sources" — what kind of democracy are we creating? [When there is continued use of unnamed sources,] then you've got a democratic process that's going to erode before your eyes. That erosion will eventually pull not just the government and the city but all other institutions down.

At testimonial in his support, Washington,
Jan. 5/The Washington Post, 1-6:(A)1.

Av Westin
Former president, American
Broadcasting Company News
5

[On the pressure to be Number 1 in TV news] : Sure, you want to be Number 1. Your stock goes up. You are beholden to the stockholders in a business. Because, as chairman of the board, you are beholden to your stockholders in any corporation. [In local news operations] the pressure is on to do something different that is going to get the people to look at you, which would get the ratings to go up, which would look very good on the bottom line, which would make the guys in the home office happy, which would make their stock-

WHAT THEY SAID IN 1977

holders happy ... Unfortunately, news has become big business.

Interview/Los Angeles Times, 6-6:(1)14.

Tom Wicker
Political columnist   *1*

I think [the press is] impartial in the broadest general sense. I think that many of the same people who wrote exposure stories, for example, about the Nixon Administration, are now writing exposures about [former Budget Director] Bert Lance. So I suggest that it is not a case of partisanship — either pro-Republican or pro-Democrat. Now, I have no doubt whatever that someone could point to an instance where a particular publication or journalist or broadcaster has not been impartial. I think a better ·word than impartial is "dispassionate," because nobody in his heart of hearts is impartial. The question is whether journalists can be dispassionate despite their personal views ... Objectivity has always been the god to which journalists appeal. But I think that it is an impossible god, because everyone has opinions. I state to you that there is no more subjective profession in the world than journalism. You make a speech and I go to cover that speech. The very first thing I decide is whether to cover it or not. That is a subjective decision. Secondly, what points did you make that I'm going to report? Third, among those points, which of them am I going to emphasize? All those are subjective decisions. I think that is one of the great strengths of the press because it means *The New York Times* will treat a story differently from *The Washington Post* or from the *L.A. Times.* There is diversity, and I think it tends to serve the purposes of truth. People get different versions of the same thing, and they tend to bring their own intelligence into it.

Interview/Book Digest, December:22,28.

Literature

Eric Ambler
Author

1

I just don't see how one would go about doing a screenplay of one's own novel. You've written your story the one way, and doing it over again another way seems awfully difficult, far more difficult than writing an original or adapting someone else's book. Actually, I was only asked to do a novel of my own once as a film, and when I was done the producer read it and told me I'd completely missed the point of the book!

Interview, Los Angeles/
Los Angeles Times, 8-28:(Book Review)3.

Richard Armour
Author, Poet

2

. . . many people could be writers, but they receive a rejection slip or two and they give up. I was incredibly lucky. The first two poems I ever sent out were accepted by *The New Yorker* and *The Saturday Evening Post.* Had they come back, I might have quit writing immediately. But, since they sold, I decided I could do it. Afterward, I discovered volume is the major secret of making it. Just to send out manuscripts I spend more than $400 a year on postage. Counting poems and articles, I average 200 published pieces a year, plus two or three books. It means I keep my typewriter smoking hot, morning and night, week in and week out.

Interview, Claremont, Calif./
Los Angeles Times, 7-10:(Home)35.

Isaac Asimov
Author

3

Thinking is the activity I love best, and writing is simply thinking through my fingers.

Interview/Reader's Digest, August:123.

Robert L. Bernstein
Chairman, Random House, Inc., publishers

4

Freedom of expression is, of course, intimately connected with the fate of the publishing industry. When freedom of expression is curtailed — and this means the freedom to express unpopular, inconvenient, even outrageous thoughts, for what government or society has ever censored the expression of views echoing the official line? — then publishing becomes merely propaganda. John Steinbeck once gave John O'Hara a silver cigarette case with this inscription: "The lonely mind of one man is the only creative organ in the world, and any force that interferes with its free function is treason." Treason, I believe Steinbeck meant, against our inalienable human rights. Freedom of expression is not a luxury reserved for prosperous states or selected individuals; it is not a privilege to be granted or withheld by governments or parties. Freedom of expression is the *inalienable* right of every man and every woman. And, as a citizen and publisher, I urge that the United States government make plain that it does not condone the denial of this right anywhere, or at any time.

Before Helsinki Commission, May 25/
Los Angeles Times, 9-4:(4)2.

John Cheever
Author

5

Writing is for me a means of communication. It is for me my ultimate — as far as I know — usefulness. It is talking with people whose company I think I would enjoy if I knew them. And it's speaking to them about my most intimate and acute feelings and apprehensions about my life, about our lives. The point of this communication is that it is a *useful* performance. The force of reality in fiction and the

WHAT THEY SAID IN 1977

(JOHN CHEEVER)

force of reality in a dream are very much the same. You find yourself on a sailing boat that you do not know — don't know the rig — going along a coast that is totally strange to you, but you're wearing an old suit, and the person beside you is your wife. This is in the nature of a dream. The experience of fiction is similar: One builds as if at random. But whereas the usefulness of the dream, in a rudimentary sense, is only for your own analyst to interpret, fiction builds toward an illumination — toward a larger usefulness.

Interview, Ossining, N.Y./
The New York Times, 3-6:(Book Review)27.

1

I used to detest being interviewed. I used to detest giving readings. I used to dislike meeting people, especially people who'd say, "How can I thank you for all the hours of reading pleasure you've given me!" My stores of contempt were much higher then. Now it's clear to me that I count on this audience of strangers to whom I speak my most intimate thoughts. I'm dependent emotionally upon their response . . . If there were no response, I would have to think my emotions were so eccentric as to have no universality at all.

Interview/Newsweek, 3-14:73.

2

Writing is not at all a competitive sport. I don't think of myself as being less than Saul Bellow or better than Herbert Gold. The essence of literature is always the singularity of the writer.

Interview/Newsweek, 3-14:73.

James Dickey
Author, Poet

3

For too long, poetry was obscure and weighed down with symbolism. Writers like T. S. Eliot and Ezra Pound — much as I revere those two masters — took poetry too far into the library and graduate schools. Poetry had too much heavy literary apparatus and required too much analysis. But now a beautiful new kind of poetry, clear and meaningful, is emerg-

ing. People really need poets now because language has been so abused by advertisers, journalists and newscasters, who are always making designs on us through the use of words. Poetry doesn't make you want to buy razor blades or vote for a candidate. It makes you want to be as you wish to be of your own volition, and expresses feelings you weren't able to articulate before. It's the last place left that supplies the magic of language for communication between one person and another — and in depth.

Interview/U.S. News & World Report, 4-18:67.

4

I really do think the South tends to produce better writers. There's no mystery about it. We're all Southerners, and we belong to a rural tradition. It's an oral tradition . . . We like words. We like to tell stories . . . That's where great literature comes from.

At Texas Christian University/
The National Observer, 5-16:4.

Joan Didion
Author

5

There's a point in a novel where it shifts, or the narrative won't carry. That point has to come before a third of the way through. It goes into overdrive. There are some novels you pick up and start reading, and they're wonderful. Maybe you have to go to lunch or something and you get to page 70 and never pick them up again. You're not moved to keep turning pages. That's the narrative curve you've got to allow, around page 70 or 80, to give it enough thrust to send it out. Imagine a rocket taking off. There's a point at which it drops its glitter or glamour and starts floating free.

Interview, Malibu, Calif./
The New York Times Book Review, 4-3:36.

6

Our best friends are writers but they don't talk about it. If you're a writer, you're always afraid it isn't going to work out. So you don't want to be asked about what you're doing, and you don't ask. And there aren't many who aren't writers who care. So you can operate without other people's opinions. You don't

(JOAN DIDION)

have to worry about how what they're doing might conflict with what you're doing — how much was your advance compared to their advance.

Interview, Washington/The Washington Post, 4-4:(D)3.

E. L. Doctorow
Author
1

Certainly I like my books to be accessible. I don't believe literature should be an elitist taste. I love the thought of books in paperback, with cheap prices and available to many, many people. I'd like to see reading restored in this country so that there's little self-consciousness about it, so that people won't have the feeling about opening a book and saying, "Well, I will now do this thing that is good for me." I'd like to see reading become as pleasurable as going to a film.

Interview, Dallas/The Dallas Times Herald, 11-14:(B)1.

Dorothy Eden
Author
2

I wouldn't ever want to write about squalor, or poor people. I love glamorous backgrounds — they give me vicarious pleasure, and I think that's what readers want to enjoy, too. I don't mean I want to write only about millionaires — just people who are comfortably off.

Interview, New York/Publishers Weekly, 3-28:9.

John Fowles
British Author
3

I find lots of moral anger in American novels, but not moral seriousness.

*Interview, New York/
The New York Times, 9-30:(C)23.*

Romain Gary
Author
4

Why is it assumed that the central character of a [novel] must be the author? In fact, I've never published a book in France where I was not construed with the hero. I reminded my friends that it was Raskolnikov and not

Dostoyevsky who killed the old woman in *Crime and Punishment.*

Interview/"W": a Fairchild publication, 4-1:2.

Barry M. Goldwater
United States Senator, R–Arizona
5

[Arguing against abandoning the special reduced postal rates for books, magazines and newspapers]: A book should not be charged the same rate for mailing as a brick.

*Before Commission on Postal Service,
Washington/The New York Times, 1-20:(4)16.*

Gerald Green
Author
6

. . . I hate to sound like a sociologist, but I want to write about important issues. I'm not happy with a book unless it has some sort of spine. I wouldn't want to do anything based purely on character, or fortuitous incident — which means, I guess, that I'm out of touch with most contemporary fiction.

Interview/Publishers Weekly, 3-7:11.

Arthur Hailey
Author
7

I'm human and if it's between a good review and a bad review, I'll take the good one. But one learns a few things about reviews. To the best of my knowledge, I have never had a good review in *The New York Times.* And they seem to get more acerbic as time goes on. And one tends to be a little amused by that. For some reason I've had consistently good reviews in Chicago. You can't be in this occupation without expecting to get some blood on your head. And everyone who expects to be favorably reviewed is foolish. A little cold water is probably a deterrent to vanity.

Interview, Bahamas/Book Digest, April:29.

Alex Haley
Author
8

[On the effect on his life of the success of his book, *Roots*]: Got to get away. Phone never stops ringing. Talk shows. Interviews. Socializing . . . I've got a new book all worked out in my head. I'm high as a kite about it, but

WHAT THEY SAID IN 1977

(ALEX HALEY)

I can't get time to write. Got to get out to sea, ship out on a freighter; don't care where it's headed, long as it's a long, slow voyage. Out on the water, you get back to primal conditions; you're one with creation. Just sea and sky. You can take the time to think. That's where I can write . . .

Interview/Los Angeles Times, 1-2:(Book Review)3.

1

[Saying the success of his book, *Roots,* is not due just to the subject matter] : Beyond that, I would soberly and somberly ascribe it to God himself. There is no man, no committee of men or women, who could sit down with whatever media expertise, and predictably create a program or an event of any kind of comparable spontaneous national response. It obviously transcends us.

The National Observer, 2-12:6.

2

[On his dissatisfaction in dealing with publishers] : We writers work to produce the crop, deliver it to someone else, and they give us what they decide is right. They run the land; they own the cotton gin and the company store . . . I am just asking to be treated fairly and equitably. Corporations do not write books. Authors do.

Interview, Los Angeles/The New York Times, 3-30:27.

Mark Jaffe
Senior vice president and
editorial director, Bantam Books

3

[Saying the Western cowboy novel will always be around] : I think it's basically a cyclical thing. Of course, we have to find new writers — that's all important to survival of the genre. But I have faith that a new generation of reader — the kid 16, 17 years old — is going to discover Westerns and keep them alive. We all went through this tremendous social upheaval a few years back. Now we're looking for a return to values. The cowboy has always offered love and courage and . . . well, accomplishment. Just think of those epic cattle drives. I mean, you could dream of those for the rest of your life and probably never get tired. That's what the Western myth offers, and that's why it'll always be around.

The Washington Post, 9-27:(B)4.

Robert Kirsch
Literary critic, "Los Angeles Times"

4

[On the difference between reviewing and criticism] : My favorite analogy is that the book *reviewer* is like a handicapper — he tells you what to bet on tomorrow; and a literary *critic* is like a writer for *Thoroughbred* magazine — he tells you which bloodline is likely to win the Derby 50 years from now.

Interview/Publishers Weekly, 12-12:10.

Irving Lazar
Literary and theatrical agent

5

The book-selling business and all its subsidiary rights has mushroomed into a giant. In many cases non-fiction outsells fiction. U.S. Presidents, once out of office, have almost all written their memoirs — but until recently for very small markets. Now it's coming to the point probably where U.S. Presidents are going to sign up with an agent before they leave office — not only for themselves but for their families as well. . . . what's involved is money — millions, not peanuts, but millions. Why do you think [President] Jimmy Carter's mother, Miz Lillian, put together a book? Why do you think his sister, or sisters, are doing more books? Because they want to explain the peanut plantations of Plains [Ga.] ? I think that, with the Nixon deal, I started the million-dollar trend for ex-Presidents. And now it's spread to other people of prominence. But for big money, the personality who writes a book can't afford to be shy or timid. The book's got to be revealing or shocking or startling. It's got to tell some truths, some information the book-buying public was unaware of.

Interview/Parade, 8-14:5.

William P. McGivern
Author

6

[On freelance writing] : Security is just an illusion. A writer makes a huge mistake if he ties his fate and fortune to one publication.

376

(WILLIAM P. McGIVERN)

Just think of the people who had secure jobs with *Collier's, The Saturday Evening Post, Liberty, Life, Look* and a couple of dozen other fine magazines. I've written for many of them, and I know the only security is found in having a good story to tell. Magazines may go out of style, fall from public taste, but a good story endures.

Interview, Palm Desert, Calif./
Los Angeles Times, 3-20:(Home)36.

1

Generally, a writer has only two ways to go. He can break new ground, like Milton, Shakespeare or Dante. Or he can take a familiar tale and look for a new way to tell the story ... I make no claim to newness. I look at the people around me, choose someone I know really well and place the person in a crisis situation. Then I ask myself, "How does the person react and deal with the crisis? Is my attention grabbed by the problems involved? Can I pour those problems into the tight-fitting cloak of an attention-riveting story?" Graham Greene once observed that writers are constantly trying to explain the adult world to the small child within them. He certainly spoke for me, because that's the way I've been all my life.

Interview, Palm Desert, Calif./
Los Angeles Times, 3-20:(Home)43.

James A. Michener
Author

2

American writers are enjoying an expanding reputation around the world. This is a marked change from a few years ago when the Europeans, by and large, depreciated the reputation of American writers. Then came Hemingway, who spoke with an authentic American voice. One reason why our writers are recognized so widely now is that, as we become a major nation, outsiders are hungry to know about us. We don't have anybody like Gunter Grass, who is supposed to speak for the entire German people. Saul Bellow and Joan Didion don't speak for the American people, and neither do I. What we have is a group of very brilliant performers — people who use language with exquisite ability — and this is valued, and it is read. I'm sometimes surprised to find that my books have done almost as well overseas as they have at home. It must be because I'm dealing with American themes that have an emotional or sentimental value to people of varied backgrounds in all parts of the world. It's part of the process of trying to understand each other better.

Interview/U.S. News & World Report, 9-12:61.

3

I divide writers into two groups. There are those with one idea, and they spend their lives on it; sometimes they produce only one book, an excellent one. Then there are writers like Zola, Dostoyevsky and Tolstoy; they wrote every week. I fall into their category. I've got enough replenishment of ideas for the rest of the century.

Interview, Los Angeles/
Los Angeles Herald-Examiner, 12-9:(C)1.

4

A great French philosopher once said that a work of art is never finished — it's released. And I suppose this is true ... that if one kept it a decade or more one could improve upon it slightly ... it would be better. But unfortunately most of us can't keep our work for a decade or so. We're professionals; we live off our writing. I have no other income, and, after you've spent three or four years on a work, that's about all you can do. It isn't all you *ought* to do, but it's all you *can* do. So that I would say that everything I've done could have been improved upon. On the other hand, if you look at my output and its variety and its cleanliness, and going into new fields and the relative seriousness of it, it's not a *bad* body of work.

Interview, St. Michaels, Md./
The Christian Science Monitor, 12-16:16.

Henry Miller
Author

5

I don't have any regular hours for writing. I don't have any regular hours for anything. I don't ponder over things, wrestle with ideas. I don't follow any program. You write when

WHAT THEY SAID IN 1977

(HENRY MILLER)

you're hot and you stop when it gives out, or maybe you hold some for the next day. And now that I really have come to the end of the line, everything I do is gratuitous, something to be accepted as a gift. I'm not a Hemingway methodical writer. He made quite a to-do over how he turned it out. I am one who does not believe in work, which is what Hemingway did. People consider him so highly. Well, I don't consider him highly. He was slave-driving himself.

Interview, Los Angeles/
The Washington Post, 10-23:(H)6.

Alberto Moravia
Author
1

It is impossible today [for writers] to live like Joyce or Proust — outside of politics and cultural happenings. They lived in bourgeois society. But today, it's not possible for writers to take this position. The people expect much more. They expect from a writer what they once expected from a priest. They want spiritual and moral guidance — one of the greatest needs in our modern world.

Interview, Rome/"W":
a Fairchild publication, 10-28:51.

Dan Rather
News commentator,
Columbia Broadcasting System
2

... I find writing such a valuable safety valve. You can give much more of yourself than when you're in front of the camera for a few minutes. And there's always the thrilling, if unlikely, thought that 100 years from now someone could pick up your book and read it and remember you by it. They're much more likely to do that than to pick up a tape cassette of a TV broadcast.

Interview, New York/Publishers Weekly, 5-9:9.

Harold Robbins
Author
3

I'm a people's writer. I write about the contemporary world and identifiable themes. That's why the books translate well and are

sold in 54 countries. I don't imitate — I initiate. My books have to be entertaining. The story's got to move, and fast. People no longer have time to spend three weeks reading a beautifully written novel. Now everything is competing for your time — sports, TV, movies, hobbies. A Harold Robbins book is something you can read in a few evenings. Romantic, picaresque novels, which deal with basic emotion so the reader can identify part of himself and live the book vicariously. People like to read about sex. So I write about sex. And violence ... you sometimes need it to keep interest heightened and the plot moving. Who could deny we live in a violent society? Finally, a Harold Robbins book never gets bogged down in wordy descriptions. I allow the reader to bring his own contribution to the story.

Interview/San Francisco Examiner & Chronicle,
11-27:(Datebook)25.

4

... every writer, artist or otherwise has what we call creative conceit. Each of us, whether we admit it or not, thinks he is the best. I know it hurts some of the others to admit that I am the best, but I couldn't care less about their feelings. I'll make it very simple. I've been writing books now for 30 years, and my books have lasted. There's not an author being published today whose every book, every book he's ever written, is always on sale everywhere. You can find my books anywhere in the world in any language. That's got to mean something ... Like anybody else in business, I do it to earn money. And these days my name is worth a lot of money. Who cares about the critics? I could publish the Los Angeles telephone directory with the byline "Harold Robbins," and it would sell.

Interview, Cannes, France/
Los Angeles Herald-Examiner, 12-11:(E)9.

Judith Rossner
Author
5

Really, the most interesting thing about novelists is what goes into our books. Everything else is the same as other people. A novel, almost by definition, should say what it has to say and get out.

Interview, Los Angeles/Los Angeles Times, 10-11:(4)1.

Philip Roth
Author

1

I've largely lost touch with what's said about my work in print. I haven't read the reviews of my books since 1972, and I usually make it my business to be out of the country when a book appears. I find the best place to be when a book comes out — at least for a Western writer — is behind the Iron Curtain. I've celebrated the publication of several recent books of mine in Prague, dining out with my writer friends there — upon whom the ironies of the situation are wasted, by the way. I spent some 10 or 12 years paying attention to criticism and charges made in the press, and that seems to me to be enough. I think I've gotten the idea by now.

Interview, New York/
The New York Times Book Review, 9-18:52.

2

My own way seems to be to write six months of trash . . . and then to give up in despair, filing away 100 pages or so that I can't stand, to find 10 pages or so that are actually alive, and then to try to figure out what it is that's going on there that *makes* for the life— and then to run with that. Often, in the first few months after finishing one book, I find that whatever I begin is really only my old departed pal returned in a sheet from the grave. It's awfully hard to cut loose from a way of perceiving things and a way of presenting things that has taken so much work to establish in the first place. But I find that, if I just keep going, some six or eight months later I will somehow have laid the ghost to rest and be ready to write something new.

Interview, New York/
The New York Times Book Review, 9-18:53.

Charles Schulz
Cartoonist

3

As a kid, I adored *Popeye, Buck Rogers,* all those Big Little Books, and *Dick Tracy.* When I got older, I found myself studying *Terry and the Pirates,* and comic strips that only real aficionados would remember such as J. R. Williams' *Out Our Way* and Roy Crane's *Wash Tubbs.* They had a strong influence on me.

Today I feel about cartoons the way many people feel about films. But then, how many films can reach 100 million people per day? . . . Cartoons are thought of as fillers. Cartoons just plod along from day to day. Cartoons are not looked upon as serious work. *Peanuts Jubilee* got good reviews. It was extremely well received in both hard cover and in paperback. But a best-seller? I will never be able to reconcile the fact that writers are more important than cartoonists.

Interview, Santa Rosa, Calif./
The Christian Science Monitor, 7-20:24.

Erich Segal
Author

4

The reason people cried over [his best-selling novel] *Love Story* is because I did. I was innocent. I believed every word I wrote.

Interview/People, 3-28:85.

Irwin Shaw
Author

5

"Famous" doesn't mean anything to me, because it means nothing about your work. So many people are famous that you wouldn't want to have in your living-room. I just consider myself an artist who works, and anything else that goes good is just fine.

Interview, New York/
"W": a Fairchild publication, 6-10:8.

6

No writer has ever come out of the world full-fledged. Anything a young writer does is good experience, even if it's awful! A writer has to learn to speak in a lot of different voices . . . television, the printed page, radio. That's what I told my classes when I was teaching. Read everything you can, read the best writers — Chekhov, Joyce, Hemingway, Faulkner — and see how they do it. A good writer hides the skeleton, and an astute student will see it and realize how to construct what he wants.

Interview/The Hollywood Reporter, 11-25:12.

WHAT THEY SAID IN 1977

Robert Shaw
Actor

1

Writing, although I don't love it, is more important than acting. One can make a personal statement as a writer which you can't as an actor. How can you compare Robert Redford and Shakespeare?

Interview, New York/
The Dallas Times Herald, 7-24:(F)5.

Andrei Sinyavsky
Author

2

All genuine artistic activity varies from the established patterns, and thus it dissents. The true literary language is the language of direct confrontation with reality on ultimate issues, an attempt to converse with readers about things which are vital and therefore menacing.

Interview, Fontenay aux Roses, France/
The New York Times Book Review, 10-30:51.

Wallace Stegner
Author

3

[On writing]: You're never confident. You go in fear and trembling every day. It would be awfully nice to think that you know how to write a novel. But what you know is the novel you just wrote. You don't have the slightest notion how to write the one you're going to do next.

Interview, Los Altos Hills, Calif./
Los Angeles Times, 12-25:(Book Review)3.

David Storey
Author, Playwright

4

My view of art has always been the posthumous view. If you get somebody to publish your book, it's miraculous. If you have two people reading it, you're lucky. If you get somebody to put on your play, it's a bizarre stroke of fortune. If you start from a position of negligible hopes, anything you get in terms of recognition is a huge bonus.

Interview, London/
The New York Times Book Review, 8-28:11.

John Updike
Author, Poet

5

I'm into books and the pocket of silence that surrounds books. And the curious permanence of books. Books don't fail the way plays do. There's always a chance with the next generation, as with *Moby Dick.* But a failed play sinks without a trace.

Interview, San Diego, Calif./
Los Angeles Times, 3-27:(Calendar)54.

6

. . . I feel more at sea writing a novel than a poem, and often re-read my poetry and almost never look at my old novels. Also, poetry, especially since we have purged it of all that is comfortingly mechanical, is a sporadic activity. Lightning can't strike every day. It is always at the back of my mind to be a poet. Lately I had the occasion to get out the collected poems of my fellow Pennsylvanian, Wallace Stevens. He didn't publish his first collection until he was almost my present age and didn't publish another for 12 years more. Yet the total production, in the end, weighs like a bible, a beautiful book as published by Knopf, with big print on big white pages, all this verbal fun and glory and serene love — what a good use of a life, to leave behind one beautiful book.

Interview/The New York Times Book Review, 4-10:28.

Leon Uris
Author

7

. . . it's always your first book that they [critics] say is the best-written . . . because three or four successes is a little much for the critics to handle . . . They like old, asthmatic female poets who threw themselves off the roof and left a volume 30 years ago. There is a little establishment of ten who think they are guarding literary taste, and they're so out in orbit, they don't know what the rest of the world is thinking or reading . . . I don't know the name of a single reviewer. I think they live under rocks in New York. It's part of the New York intelligentsia. I don't have a great deal of respect for them.

Interview/Book Digest, October:27.

Peter Ustinov
Actor, Director, Writer
1

I write longhand with a felt-tipped pen . . . I don't know how dictating is done. I can't share my secrets with someone else at the first moment. I've always thought one of the great unknown heroines of history was Dostoyevsky's secretary. He dictated his books to her, and I think once you know that, his style becomes quite understandable. There must have been evenings when he said, "and then old Karamazov staggered to the fireplace, took the axe, lifted it high over his head," and then said, "I'm tired, Miss; I'll think we'll continue this tomorrow."

Interview, New York/
The Christian Science Monitor, 12-7:24.

Mario Vargas (Llosa)
Peruvian writer
2

Literature in Latin America has been at the same time an artistic creation and [an] instrument to describe and fight social injustice. Literature did and still does what press and universities could not do because of dictatorships, censorship and repression. Therefore, literature has always had a very important social and political role . . . I think literature is a very non-conformist institution. I don't think literature has ever existed as a testimony of happiness. I think literature has always been a testimony of unhappiness. I think you write because you have problems.

Interview, Norman, Okla./
The Christian Science Monitor, 4-22:26.

Gore Vidal
Author
3

[Author Norman] Mailer said he would be a better writer if his contemporaries had been better writers, and, pitiful statement that it is, one knows what he means. If there were a half dozen good literary critics around, all writing would be better. As it is, an act of publication is almost for its own sake — there are so few critics writing whose opinion one would care to read. It's better to publish in England because the level of criticism is a bit higher [than in the U.S.]. At least they know how to describe books. And there is some continuity. Critics themselves have careers, develop, change and modify their views. Having careers themselves, they feel obliged to deal with the careers of the writers they discuss. Here [in the U.S.] it's hit and run. There's no accountability. A critic whom no one knows strikes out at a writer whose other work he doesn't know . . . It was [composer] Virgil Thomson who advised a young music critic not to evaluate the music he heard but to describe it. The description would *be* the evaluation. But that requires that the critic, the describer, is an informed and evolving sensibility, not a camera. The biggest problem with our contemporary bookchat critics is that they are incapable of describing, or apprehending, or comprehending what they see. Is it the Taj Mahal? Is it a pavilion? A coliseum?

Interview/
The New York Times Book Review, 4-17:47.

Irving Wallace
Author
4

I think that you're always going to have two kinds of novels: one based on imagination, observation, feelings, and the other based on those things overlaid with reporting and investigative work. When I'm on a book tour, people may say that I got the idea for *The Fan Club* from Patty Hearst. You are always getting books out of the headlines, they say. If I took books out of the headlines, it would be three years by the time I wrote them and they were published. Who would want that? I seem to unconsciously anticipate what the events may be — what people will get involved in which I can make happen for the reader . . . [I'm put down] by the unthinking who claim that I have a best-selling formula, and every time I sit down, I follow the formula. Even when one of my books has no sex in it, they say it has sex. They haven't read it, and of course there's no formula. If there were a formula, publishers wouldn't need us, would they? What I write is what interests *me*.

Interview, Brentwood, Calif./
Book Digest, November:27.

WHAT THEY SAID IN 1977

Robert Penn Warren
Author, Poet

1

You don't write poems sitting at a type-writer; you write them swimming or climbing a mountain or walking. And I must confess that I've found a slight hangover — not a real one; I've never had a real one; I've got inborn resistance — but a creative languor useful for writing poems. I might say that it requires a high-quality whisky.

Interview, Baltimore/
The Washington Post, 2-25:(B)7.

2

In America they have to know just what you are — novelist, poet, playwright. You can't be all of them, because that resists categorization. Well, I've been all of them. I started out at Vanderbilt as a poet, influenced by John Crowe Ransom and the others. I thought the novel was just beneath contempt. Then I began meeting some novelists — Katherine Anne Porter, Ford Madox Ford — and I got a different feeling for it. I think poems and novels and stories spring from the same seed. It's not like, say, playing polo and knitting. Why, I might start something as a poem and finish it years later as a novel.

Interview, Fairfield, Conn./
The National Observer, 3-12:20.

Robert Wedgeworth
Executive director,
American Library Association

3

Millions of unemployed Americans, or Americans subsisting on fixed or inflation-ravaged incomes, have come to depend on the library to fill such basic needs as free recreation and education as well as to help in job-hunting, resume-writing, filling out tax returns. When funding cuts require that [library] services be cut off or cut back, people suffer.

The Christian Science Monitor, 4-19:1.

Medicine and Health

Paavo Airola
Nutritionist

1

The United States is the sickest nation in the world. We consume too much protein. And it's not necessary. The less protein you eat, the better you will feel. . . . there are as many diet fads as there are religious fads. The nutrition "gurus" say, "just try it and you'll feel better," and everyone tries it and they say they feel better. The validity of a diet must be determined over the period of a lifetime, sometimes over generations, but not in a faddish three weeks. Protein is the magic word today. It's in your hair spray, your shampoo and deodorants. But you've been brainwashed about protein.

Los Angeles/
Los Angeles Herald-Examiner, 11-6:(A)8.

William J. Barclay
Editor, "Journal of the American
Medical Association"

2

I see major changes ahead [in medical care] — more nurse practitioners treating patients, computers running tests, therapists doing the laying on of hands. In my darkest thoughts, I think doctors are becoming systems managers. Practicing medicine is no longer any fun. I'm not convinced that the best way to improve medicine is to remove physicians from the decison-making process.

U.S. News & World Report, 10-17:57.

Bob Bergland
Secretary of Agriculture
of the United States

3

Should we allow tobacco to be consumed in the United States? It should be dealt with from a health standpoint . . . There is political resistance to banishing tobacco because it is an important economic crop — about 600,000

producers; it's a $6-billion tax earner; it generates about a billion dollars in overseas income from trade. And so it is a very important crop economically. But I try very hard not to confuse economics with the health aspects.

Interview, Washington/
U.S. News & World Report, 10-31:59,60.

Edgar Berman
Physician; Former research associate
and teacher, Johns Hopkins
University School of Medicine

4

The doctor-patient relationship is dead. We have a great profession going down the drain. It could come back, but now we can't get house calls, the phone is off the hook on Wednesdays, weekends and nights, and doctors have become so involved with lavish equipment for their offices that they have to take an EKG when a patient comes in with a pimple.

Interview, Los Angeles/
Los Angeles Herald-Examiner, 3-27:(A)10.

Henry B. Betts
Medical director, Rehabilitation
Institute of Chicago

5

Historically, we relate on obvious physical disability with evil. In fairy stories, for instance, the guy with a hook for a hand is always a bad guy; the hunchback is a bad guy; the person with one eye is a bad guy. We learn this from early childhood. Then all you need to do is read the ads, and everybody is bouncy and young and beautiful. Even our Presidents try to be young and beautiful. It makes it very hard on people who don't fit that mold. The reality is that some of the greatest contributors to society can be people who don't fit that mold — including our ancestors, many of whom came to this country because they were essentially

WHAT THEY SAID IN 1977

misfits somewhere else. So at this point, if you don't fit the mold, you've very often got a rough deal in this country. You can look at the physically handicapped and see that they don't conform because they don't look like everybody else. And that should not be the way to judge them. I wouldn't ever go around and say, "All of you must hire all the handicapped." I don't know what jobs you have open, and I don't know what every handicapped person can do. All I can say is that they should be judged on an individual basis without a preconceived idea — just the way everybody else should be judged. And in that, they have not gotten a fair shake.

Interview, Washington/
U.S. News & World Report, 1-31:63.

Peter G. Bourne
Special Assistant to President
of the United States Jimmy Carter
for Health Issues
1

More persons die from barbiturates than all other drugs put together — suicides, accidental deaths of children who get them in medicine cabinets, inadvertent overdoses. We've decided to look at whether we really need barbiturates now that there are many other drugs on the market that are much safer. We're going to be doing an extensive study to look at the possibility of taking barbiturates off the market on an out-patient basis.

Interview/The Washington Post, 3-30:(A)1.

Irwin D. J. Bross
Director of biostatistics,
Roswell Park Memorial Institute,
Buffalo, New York
2

Cancer is a multi-billion-dollar industry, but if patients know that treatment can do no lasting good, they may not be willing to submit to mutilation, disability and prolonged suffering for the sake of a few extra days of life. If the public realizes the futility of trying to control cancer through treatment after the disease has generalized, the public would demand prevention of cancer as the most sensible way to eliminate the disease.

Before House Government Operations Subcommittee,
Washington/The Dallas Times Herald, 6-15:(A)16.

Edmund G. Brown, Jr.
Governor of California (D)
3

[Praising those who volunteer their services to help the mentally retarded] : Volunteerism is not a luxury. It is a necessity for a civilized society that wants to truly meet its human needs. Volunteerism is a bridge. A bridge for the community into something that for many people is something they don't talk about, don't want to hear about — just out of sight, out of mind. These people [the mentally retarded] look different, talk different, are unpredictable, but in the big scheme of things are just as human, same species. They're us in a slightly different form. And as you go there and volunteer, you provide human contact that to me is an obligation to being part of this community. And as you do that, they [the patients] themselves become part of it. And instead of just a stereotype of the all-American on television, you understand that this is a very rich and diverse culture . . . It's all us and we're all part of it.

At Junior League volunteer recognition
luncheon, San Jose, Calif./
Los Angeles Times, 4-27:(1)3.

4

[Calling for government regulation of hospital costs] : What we find now is a gross irresponsibility because the doctor has an incentive to provide every conceivable service. The patient has an incentive to get all those conceivable services. And a third, invisible, anonymous, impersonal party pays the bill — namely, the United States government, the state of California or an insurance company. And that is a formula for runaway inflation. If we took away all insurance, and the doctor could only do or charge what he thought the patient could pay, then this entire [proposed regulatory] system might not be necessary. But given the fact we have socialized the payment of medical costs through insurance or through government payment programs, we now have to have a govern-

(EDMUND G. BROWN, JR.)

ment mechanism to control those runaway costs. And there's no other way to do it.

News conference, Sacramento, May 9/
Los Angeles Times, 5-10:(1)3.

John Budd
President, American
Medical Association
1

Most doctors agree in principle to a health-insurance plan that would cover all people. We don't know exactly what plan the [Carter] Administration would offer but we suspect it would be similar to the Kennedy-Corman plan, and we would oppose that very vigorously because of its cost. The big issue, we feel, is the government financing of this, and the cost of a Kennedy plan to taxpayers would be staggering. The assumption is made that a national health-insurance plan would contain the costs of health care; but it won't, it can't. The Administration is going to have to wrestle with cost containment first because, until they get an insurance plan that isn't going to go through the roof, they aren't going to push one because Congress would never buy it.

Interview, San Francisco/
Los Angeles Herald-Examiner, 6-21:(A)12.

2

[On the controversy over whether laetrile, a drug some say is effective against cancer but which the AMA says is worthless, should be legalized]: I can't imagine anyone would believe that a doctor who had a drug available to cure cancer would withhold that drug from a patient. Using an unproven drug such as laetrile is not in the patient's interest and its legalization makes patients susceptible to being exploited. We don't oppose people using laetrile as a last resort. But it's very hard to get people to believe what they don't want to believe and that is that laetrile is no good. The public can get just about anything it wants. Public opinion can do anything, whether it's good or evil, if it is strong enough.

Interview, San Francisco/
Los Angeles Herald-Examiner, 6-21:(A)12.

Robert N. Butler
Director, National Institute on Aging
3

In this country [the U.S.] today we have some 330,000 practicing physicians, many of whom are not equipped to meet the needs of today's 23 million old people — a situation which is likely to grow worse as the number of older people increases by almost 50 per cent in the next three decades . . . The question is how can we expose every physician to the procedures of primary care which are necessary to deal with older patients . . . Perhaps at the root of our failure to adequately provide for our older people is an attitudinal problem . . . One study of University of California medical students showed that their attitude toward old people actually deteriorated over the course of their four years in medical school. Medical students are not exposed to healthy older people in the same fashion that they are exposed to healthy babies in sunny, well-baby nurseries and clinics. In fact, there isn't a medical school in the country which routinely and systematically rotates students through community senior centers. One wonders whether medical students would choose [pediatrics] if they only saw babies suffering from irreversible conditions.

Before Senate Special Committee on Aging,
Washington/The Washington Post, 3-9:(A)10.

Joseph A. Califano, Jr.
Secretary of Health, Education and
Welfare of the United States
4

I have a point of view on cigarette smoking. As an ex-smoker, I realize how difficult it is to quit. It is obviously one of the major causes of bad health, heart attacks, lung cancer and other circulatory and respiratory diseases in this country. Cigarette smoking is a killing habit. Whether or not this country is prepared to make a judgment that cigarette smoking is illegal is a major issue, and I would doubt that that would make any sense. Perhaps it should be made more expensive, but I don't see any point in making cigarette smoking illegal.

TV-radio interview, Washington/"Meet the Press,"
National Broadcasting Company, 3-20.

WHAT THEY SAID IN 1977

(JOSEPH A. CALIFANO, JR.)

1

The overarching problem of the health-care industry in America [is] the problem of runaway costs . . . This rapid inflation imperils the ability of uninsured people to get health care at all. It gobbles tax dollars at such a rate that they are not available for other public priorities. The Federal government spends 12 cents of every taxpayer dollar on health care. The average American worker works one month each year to pay health-care costs. Clearly the health-care industry as presently structured has become a problem for all of us: patients, physicians, providers of care and public officials. Certainly we can understand why the American consumers and taxpayers — and more and more top executives of large corporations — are demanding that something be done.

Before American Medical Association,
San Francisco/U.S. News & World Report, 10-17:58.

2

[On the swelling health-care industry and its penchant for buying all the latest medical equipment]: The hallowed, sacred symbol of medical care has been the doctor with the little black bag, treating his patients . . . Doctor and patient are still central to health care in America — and always will be. But they are surrounded in today's world by something new: a vast health-care industry — the third largest industry in the United States after construction and agriculture . . . Keeping up with the Joneses is understandable, even excusable, for neighbors spending their own money on lawnmowers or sprinkler systems, but we can no longer afford to indulge this wasteful medical arms race. In health care we are driving the ultimate gas guzzler: heavy, expensive, laden with optional accessories.

At Lyndon Baines Johnson Foundation
award luncheon, New York, Oct. 27/
Los Angeles Times, 10-28:(1)12.

Truman Capote
Author

3

I am an alcoholic. Now, you can say this and this about alcohol and an alcoholic, but people don't understand what an alcoholic is. An alcoholic is a person who has absolutely no control whatsoever. No matter how much they want not to do this thing [drink], they will do it. They will do it because they are under a fantastic compulsion . . . I-am-an-alcoholic. I can go three weeks, I can go four months, I can do anything that I try, and in the end, I will do it [drink]. And I don't know why. And no analyst, no therapist, no psychiatrist, nobody, has ever been able to figure out why.

Interview, Baltimore/
Los Angeles Herald-Examiner, 11-20:(A)6.

David T. Carr
Associate director for cancer control,
Mayo Comprehensive Cancer Center

4

[Saying the controversial drug laetrile should not be legalized because it is ineffective]: . . . there are many documented cases all across the country of patients who, when faced with the choice between laetrile and orthodox treatment, turned to laetrile. Then, when the cancer progressed, they returned to their physician with much less chance of recovery. Admittedly, laetrile is easy to take while orthodox treatment is sometimes difficult, whether it involves radiation or surgery or chemotherapy or some combination of these. But even if no patient ever took laetrile for an early and curable cancer, I still believe it is dishonest to sell the American public a worthless drug that is touted as being a cure for cancer — or as the proponents are now saying, "Laetrile really won't cure cancer, but if you take it every day, you'll never get cancer."

Interview/U.S. News & World Report, 6-13:52.

Jimmy Carter
President of the United States

5

We are committed to guaranteeing the civil rights of the disabled. For too long, the handicapped have been denied opportunities for education and employment. For too long, they have been stymied by buildings, streets and transportation facilities which could not accommodate them, shut out by a world that thrives on communication but makes little

(JIMMY CARTER)

allowance for those who cannot see or hear, and denied services that they desperately need.

At White House Conference on Handicapped
Individuals, Washington, May 23/
Los Angeles Times, 5-24:(1)6.

1

I do not think that the Federal government should finance abortions except when the woman's life is threatened or when the pregnancy was a result of rape or incest. I think it ought to be interpreted very strictly. In my opinion, the Federal government being willing to finance abortions, as it has been in recent months, is an encouragement to abortion and its acceptance as a routine contraceptive means; and I think within that strict definition that I've given to you I would like to prevent the Federal government financing abortions.

News conference, Washington, July 12/
The New York Times, 7-13:(A)10.

2

It's too early yet to lay down specifics for the national health-insurance program. This was a concept that was endorsed by all the candidates for President last year. And it's a need in our country that this entire health-care system be improved. One of them is to cut down the exorbitant increases in national health care. Take the hospital cost – and we've already initiated a major effort on the hospital-cost containment bill. These costs have been doubled every five years, which makes it almost impossible to give better health care because the costs have grown up so rapidly there.

News conference, Washington, Nov. 10/
The New York Times, 11-11:(A)22.

Eric J. Cassell
Clinical professor of public health,
Cornell University Medical College

3

Apparently medical care alone, no matter how well delivered or technically complete, cannot be expected to lift the burden of sickness. Even if present surgical techniques were perfected, the value of a new or repaired heart in the body of a patient whose life-style remained otherwise unchanged would not be very high.

U.S. News & World Report, 10-17:52.

Hale Champion
Under Secretary of Health, Education
and Welfare of the United States

4

Until we reduce the enormous glut of excess hospital beds in this country, physicians and surgeons will continue to fill them with patients who could be treated on an outpatient basis. We have to recognize that there are many thousands more surgeons than we need, and cut back significantly on the number trained at public expense. Surgeons, as you might expect, favor a surgical approach to medical problems. And the result is that excess surgeons lead to excess surgery.

Before House Commerce subcommittee, Washington,
Nov. 1/The Dallas Times Herald, 11-2:(A)14.

Theodore Cooper
Former Assistant Secretary for Health,
Department of Health, Education and
Welfare of the United States

5

It's the fashion these days to talk about what is wrong with medicine, to characterize its practitioners as avaricious, insensitive and even incompetent. That is a paradox, indeed almost schizophrenic, when measured against the great success of the past decade of American medicine. One could rightly say of American medicine today: "Never has anything sounded so bad that has actually been so good."

U.S. News & World Report, 10-17:51.

Michael De Bakey
Surgeon

6

It's time to place the spotlight of public scrutiny on the way FDA regulations virtually rewrite the law. We're constantly being told that the regulations are simply a means of implementing measures by Congress, but the fact is that the regulations are becoming increasingly more stringent and limiting than the law ... The patient in the United States is the only American without a constituency.

San Francisco Examiner & Chronicle, 6-26:(A)15.

WHAT THEY SAID IN 1977

Robert L. DuPont
Director, National Institute
on Drug Abuse

1

Marijuana is not safe. The idea that it is safe, although accepted by some of the public, is clearly not endorsed by the research community. Considering the widespread use of marijuana in our society, particularly our youth, it is critical that we continue to study the long-term effects of the drug.

Washington, March 10/
Los Angeles Herald-Examiner, 3-13:(A)11.

2

Some of the most striking facts to emerge from [a new survey on drug use] are an apparent stabilization in drug use and the attitudes toward drugs in general. The public, including youth, clearly recognizes the addictive effects of tobacco and alcohol and has very negative attitudes toward the use of all illicit drugs. Although drug abuse continues to be widespread in every region of the country, we are seeing some slight downward trends for amphetamines, LSD and barbiturates. Marijuana is the only drug showing a definite upward trend.

Los Angeles Times, 3-16:(1-A)6.

Milton Friedman
Professor of economics,
University of Chicago

3

The drug industry is an example of an industry that has been seriously hampered by government intervention and regulation. I believe that the [U.S.] Food and Drug Administration has, on the whole, done a great deal more harm than good. The reason is very simple: No drug administrator has ever been pilloried for not approving a drug which was potentially capable of saving many lives. The administrator is bound to be pilloried for making the other mistake, namely, approving a drug which turned out to be harmful. As a result, the Food and Drug people have a bias in favor of holding up good drugs in order to avoid the possibility of a mistake in approving a bad one. The result is that there are many effective drugs which are available in Canada, in

Britain and elsewhere which cannot be purchased [in the U.S.], which might very well save lives.

San Francisco Examiner & Chronicle, 6-26:(A)15.

E. J. (Jake) Garn
United States Senator, R—Utah

4

[Calling for lower taxes for low tar and nicotine cigarettes]: Health problems now facing the country, as a consequence of cigarette smoking, are of crisis proportions. Approximately one out of every three Americans smokes, and those who don't are often forced to breath air laden with tobacco smoke. Eight per cent of our annual 84,000 lung-cancer deaths are caused by cigarette smoking, and smoking costs our health-care system between $11.5-billion and $30-billion each year. It is clear that smoking-related diseases are exacting an intolerable price from the American public, both in terms of human suffering and in terms of an unnecessary financial drain on our economy. Since smoking cannot be banned, we should provide an incentive for smokers to reduce their consumption of toxic substances. Any reduction in the amount of toxic substances inhaled or put into the air by cigarette smokers will ultimately result in a reduction of smoking-related deaths and disease.

*April 23/***

Kenneth A. Gibson
Mayor of Newark, New Jersey

5

A national health program is in my opinion a top priority. If it has to be to sacrifice the people of this country to inadequate health care, then I would say we have to put aside the balancing of the budget, and this is most important.

TV-radio interview, Tucson, Ariz./"Meet the Press,"
National Broadcasting Company, 6-12.

Robert A. Good
Director, Memorial Sloan-Kettering
Cancer Center, New York

6

Sixty-five per cent of Americans say that the thing they fear the most is cancer — not war, not economic destruction, not famine, not even

(ROBERT A. GOOD)

death. Scientists are not prepared to deal with that kind of force, that emotionalism.

Newsweek, 6-27:49.

John W. Hanley
Chairman and president,
Monsanto Company
1

[On the controversy about the safety of saccharin]: American industry has produced so many innovative products that it's become, in effect, a victim of its own success. The public thinks the chemical industry could develop another saccharin if it only wanted to ... the auto industry could produce the perfect car if it only wanted to ... utilities could provide cheaper power if they only wanted to. The fact is that the chemical industry has been trying to improve upon saccharin now for some 80 years — and hasn't succeeded yet! So my advice is: Don't let your coffee get cold while you wait for that eventuality. The judgment called for transcends the saccharin dispute. What's needed on the food-additive issue must be applied to all consumer-safety issues: a reasonable weighing of benefits against costs or risks. An emotional charge against any detectable risk should not replace a balanced consideration of both the level of the risk and the scope of the benefits.

Before Economic Club of Detroit,
Oct. 17/Vital Speeches, 11-15:94.

Jesse A. Helms
United States Senator, R–North Carolina
2

[Pro-abortion advocates] do not want to confront the inevitable basic question, the only one that really matters. And that ... is the deliberate termination of an innocent human life ... Let every woman control her body, including the time that she conceives, or prior thereto ... But after that, there is another life, another body, that has some rights too — including the right to live.

Before the Senate, Washington/
The Washington Post, 7-3:(A)3.

Victor Herbert
Professor of medicine,
State University of New York
3

There is nothing magic about being a physician. Physicians can lie just like non-physicians can lie. And physicians can be deceived just like non-physicians can be deceived. Physicians are not a special breed. They are good, bad and indifferent, just like everybody else. They range from brilliant to stupid, just like everybody else.

At Dairy Council Annual Press Conference,
Carmel, Calif./Los Angeles Herald-Examiner,
4-27:(C).

Robert Hogan
Professor of psychology,
Johns Hopkins University
4

The conventional wisdom is that heroin addicts are sick. Compared to neurotics, they are not sick at all. Rather, they are comparable to you and me. There is nothing wrong with their self-confidence and self-esteem. There is not one shred of evidence they are sick, that they are living a dark night of the soul. They are just hedonists; they are just having a good time. They are immoral. Heroin addiction is not a medical problem. It's a moral problem.

Interview, Baltimore/
The National Observer, 1-8:1.

Hubert H. Humphrey
United States Senator, D–Minnesota
5

We don't have any health-protection program in this country. We have a sickness program. You have to get sick before you get anything. Humphrey wants to have a program on how to *prevent* disease. Otherwise, there will be no end to the costs of health care.

Interview, Washington/
Los Angeles Times, 3-27:(7)1.

6

I try not to think about my illness because it doesn't bother me much. But I do have to recognize that cancer is, like my friend, a cancer specialist out at Rochester, said, "Hubert, cancer is like a thief in the middle of the night. It can stab you in the back any time.

WHAT THEY SAID IN 1977

(HUBERT H. HUMPHREY)

You never know it." So what is my theory, my philosophy? Live each day, do what you want to with whatever strength you have. Get the most out of it. Look ahead as far as you can. Don't worry. There's not much I can do about it. As I told those doctors the other day, "Listen, if you let me die, it's going to cost you millions of dollars 'cause I can get you more for your cancer-research projects than you'd ever believe possible. Keep me alive." So I joke with them about it.

Interview, Washington/
The Washington Post, 6-23:(A)3.

Hardin Jones
Professor of medical physics and physiology,
University of California, Berkeley 1

[Saying marijuana has caused brain damage to many of its users]: There are millions of them. After all, the leading cause of admissions to Federally funded mental hospitals is heroin addiction; the second leading cause is marijuana. I believe that the lower half of the population on the intelligence scale has already been severely affected by marijuana. Are those in the upper distribution of mental capacity also affected? In my opinion, yes. Middle-class children in the millions are a dreg to their parents. They haven't been able to make the transition from childhood to independent adult status — and marijuana is the reason.

Interview, New York/San Francisco Examiner &
Chronicle, 6-5:(This World)33.

Donald Kennedy
Commissioner of Food and Drugs
of the United States 2

The exposure of test animals to high doses is the most valid way we know to predict whether a chemical may cause cancer in people. Such tests are essential to predict rare occurrences, for example to seek out and identify a substance that can cause cancer in only one out of every 20,000 Americans. That may be a rare occurrence statistically, but it's more than 10,000 people in the U.S. population.

News Conference, Rockville, Md.,
April 14/The New York Times, 4-15:(A)16.

3

[On the controversial cancer drug, laetrile]: [Laetrile is] of unproven safety and of no effectiveness whatsoever ... I think it is a deplorable suggestion that this government should, on the falsely applied issue of freedom of choice, stand aside and allow [patients and family] to be exploited by the purveyors of a therapy that is of unproven merit and even of uncertain identity.

Before Senate Health and Scientific Research
Subcommittee, Washington, July 12/
Los Angeles Herald-Examiner, 7-12:(A)2.

4

... the actual number of health hazards linked to compounds in foods, drugs and cosmetics has gone up considerably in recent years because of all the new chemicals entering the environment. Of course, it's also true that our ability to detect the *presence* of hazardous elements also is much higher. What troubles many of us, from a regulatory point of view, is this: As we learn to detect substances in amounts at the pre-trillion level, are we picking up such infinitesimally small amounts of a hazardous substance that it can be considered insignificant from a toxicological viewpoint? Maybe we have to define more closely what makes a product acceptable or unacceptable in terms of safety.

Interview, Washington/
U.S. News & World Report, 11-21:66.

Edward M. Kennedy
United States Senator, D—Massachusetts 5

[Criticizing members of Congress who look with disfavor on national health insurance]: They take to the floor of Congress to lash out against the role that government would play under national health insurance. Then they drive out to Walter Reed Army Hospital or Bethesda Naval Hospital for the free medical and dental care the government provides. If it's good enough for the President and the House and Senate, it's good enough for . . . all the other taxpayers who already pay the bill.

Before United Automobile Workers of America,
Los Angeles/Los Angeles Herald-Examiner, 5-17:(A)3.

(EDWARD M. KENNEDY)

1

We should be spending more, not less, money to fight cancer. Cancer is the disease that most Americans are most frightened of. It's the most agonizing of all diseases. It causes the most suffering. It's the disease that has the most devastating effect on the family as well as on the patient.

Parade, 9-11:5.

Irving I. Kessler
Professor of epidemiology,
Johns Hopkins University

2

There is a rigid law on the books — the Delaney law — that the FDA must follow, even if it is illogical. The Delaney law requires that the FDA ban any food that causes cancer growths in animals. But just because a food causes cancer in animals does not mean it will cause cancer in humans . . . The FDA always makes a technical decision to ban a food first, and then calls in a team of experts to come up with an evaluation [of its effects on humans]. That's the cart before the horse.

Interview, March 12/
The Dallas Times Herald, 3-13:(A)18.

C. Everett Koop
Surgeon-in-chief, Children's Hospital,
Philadelphia; Professor of pediatric
surgery, University of Pennsylvania

3

It both saddens and frightens me when I see the trends in our society and recognize the acquiescence, if not the leadership, of the medical profession on a path that I think leads to destruction. I am speaking of the growing disregard for life itself of what was called, in a more moral, or perhaps a more religious, generation, the sanctity of human life. In January, 1973, the Supreme Court declared that a new right existed in the Constitution — the right of a woman to have an abortion on demand. At the time, I expressed concern that the abortion of between one million and two million unborn babies a year would lead to such cheapening of human life that infanticide would not be far behind. Infanticide is being practiced in this country, and what saddens me the most is that it is being practiced by that segment of our profession that has always had the role of advocate for the life of children — pediatricians and pediatric surgeons . . . Medical-school graduates of my time believed they had been trained to save lives and alleviate the suffering of their patients. Now this thought has become distorted in the semantics of the euthanasia movement: You are to save lives; that is part of your profession. If the life you are trying to save, however, is producing suffering on the part of the family, then you are to alleviate that suffering by disposing of your patient. So in a strange way you can still say that you are saving lives and alleviating suffering, but the practice of infanticide for the well-being of the family is a far cry from the traditional role of the pediatrician or pediatric surgeon — who in earlier days responded with love and compassion to a helpless child. I am a proponent of the sanctity of life, of all life, born and unborn. I hate the term "death with dignity," because there is no dignity in death.

Before American Academy of Pediatrics/
The National Observer, 1-29:13.

Leslie Libow
Chief of geriatric medicine, Jewish
Institute for Geriatric Care, New
Hyde Park, New York

4

Senility is one of the most serious medical diagnoses that can be given to a patient, because the prognosis is so serious and the effectiveness of treatment is not clear. If we value our older people, how can anyone seriously argue that every physician should not do the tests to make sure a treatable cause has not been overlooked?

The New York Times, 5-8:(4)9.

William Lilley III
Acting Director, Federal Council on
Wage and Price Stability

5

. . . here's a segment of our economy [medicine] — almost 10 per cent of our gross national product — where the normal checks and balances don't apply. Instead of producing cars for different pocketbooks, the medical-care industry produces an endless number of

391

(WILLIAM LILLEY III)

Cadillacs . . . Everybody gets all the options. If you're a hospital administrator, you want the best and the biggest hospital and the most modern equipment. Everyone, including the patient, wants the best — it's human nature, and that's all to the good. But these things are bought without regard to the cost, or without regard to the relationship between the cost and the benefits derived from them.

Interview/The National Observer, 1-22:10.

James J. Lynch
Professor of psychology and scientific director of the psychosomatic clinics, University of Maryland School of Medicine
1

Like the air we breathe, human companionship is taken for granted until we are deprived of it. The fact is that social isolation, sudden loss of love and chronic loneliness are significant contributors to illness and premature death. Loneliness is not only pushing our culture to the breaking point, it is pushing our physical health to the breaking point . . . We have to realize that human relationships are literally another form of life insurance, and that we *are* our brother's keeper. Society must act to reaffirm the importance of the family. If we do not live together, we will die — prematurely — alone.

Interview/People, 8-22:30,31.

Warren G. Magnuson
United States Senator, D—Washington
2

It's the toughest job in the world to get Congress to vote the money for pure [medical] research. Congressmen are apt to say, "What have you got to show for it?" Well, sometimes we don't have much to show for it. We just know that it has to be done if we are to make headway in applied research. It's easy to excite people about a prospective cure for heart disease or a lung disorder, but it's hard to explain what the results of preventive medicine are. It's too iffy. When we say that we've prevented something, the taxpayer can't quite understand it. He knows that something bad didn't happen, but he isn't the least bit sure that what we did helped.

Parade, 9-11:6.

James G. Martin
United States Representative, R—North Carolina
3

[On why he opposes the government's ban of the sale of saccharin because of alleged links to cancer] : The principal reason is the hardship that it would impose on many millions of people who depend on saccharin as an artificial sweetener—a sugar substitute. I'm talking about some 10 million people who suffer from diabetes, millions of heart patients, some 40 million or so overweight people who must control their weight to decrease their chances of becoming heart patients. I'm talking about people who have hypoglycemia. I'm talking about elderly invalids who have only limited exercise and therefore must strictly control their diet. For these people saccharin is a necessary part of preventive medicine.

Interview/U.S. News & World Report, 4-4:59.

Rene C. Mastrovito
Psychiatrist, Memorial Sloan-Kettering Cancer Institute, New York
4

[On cancer] : There is no other illness with this mystique, no other with less social value. Attitudes are changing but, traditionally, a man who had a heart attack had something socially redeeming about him . . . he was considered a hard worker . . . Even influenza could suggest you worked too hard. People with ulcers are regarded as worriers in a culture where worrying has an honorable connotation. With cancer, you get none of that feeling.

Interview/The New York Times, 5-4:(B)1.

Bruce Mazlish
Professor of history and head of the humanities department, Massachusetts Institute of Technology
5

What I find attractive about psychoanalysis, which I take with large grains of salt, is that it is dealing with something called unconscious mental processes, and you either believe these exist or you don't. If you think they don't exist,

(BRUCE MAZLISH)

then psychoanalysis is going to be junk. I happen to think that psychoanalysis is accurate in this: It is a subtle and special effort at a science, a type of psychology. It is not verifiable in the accepted sense of the word "science." But it gives us a greater knowledge of the way human beings think and feel. If you wish to close yourself off from that knowledge, that is one thing. I just happen to think that closing oneself off from it is itself a bad scientific approach.

Panel discussion, Center for the Study of Democratic Institutions, Santa Barbara, Calif./ The Center Magazine, Sept.-Oct.:9.

Robert S. McNamara
President, International Bank for Reconstruction and Development (World Bank)
1

In most developing countries, health expenditures have been excessively devoted to supplying a small urban elite with expensive curative health-care systems — highly skilled doctors and elaborate hospitals — that fail to reach 90 per cent of the people. What are required are less-sophisticated, but more-effective, preventive health-delivery systems that reach the mass of the population.

At Massachusetts Institute of Technology/ The Christian Science Monitor, 5-2:11.

Walter J. McNerney
President, National Blue Cross Association
2

The health field needs government not only to make medical care available to people who can't afford it but also to enforce regulations to keep the system reasonably on track. If the government does what it can do well and stops at that point, we're in good shape. What government does well is such things as setting objectives, setting standards, introducing various forms of regulations, insuring social justice, assuming certain exceptional risks — while the private sector is perfectly capable, under good leadership, of managing its financing and delivering programs effectively . . . I realize that in these matters there's a tendency to be drawn

irresistibly toward extremes — either no government or all government. That's a challenge we must accept. I think we've [the U.S.] gotten over the tendency to say: "Let's simply go the way Britain went, or France, or Canada." There is a resurgence of interest in finding more pragmatic, uniquely American ways to deal with the problem at the community level.

Interview, Washington/ U.S. News & World Report, 3-28:40,45.

3

Now that communicable diseases have been largely eradicated, the evidence is overwhelming that there is less and less relationship between morbidity and mortality, on the one hand, and medical services on the other. In short, more doctors and more hospitals don't necessarily add up to better health. We are discovering that health depends less on medicine than on lifestyle, environment and cultural factors. For example, when the Canadians investigated the five leading causes of man-years lost, they discovered that three were not affected by the health services; they were related to the environment, driving speeds, alcoholism and so forth.

Interview, Washington/ U.S. News & World Report, 3-28:45.

Karl A. Menninger
Psychiatrist; Co-founder, Menninger Foundation
4

People repeat in adult life emotions they experienced in childhood. Many of the people whom I spent the last 30 to 40 years treating at so much per minute wouldn't have needed any treatment if they'd had the right kind of care as children.

Interview, Topeka,Kan./Parade, 10-9:24.

Andrew W. Miller
President-elect, Federation of American Hospitals
5

[Arguing against proposed government-imposed hospital-cost ceilings]: [If Congress approves the ceiling, it] will be voting to establish itself as the moral judge of the dollar value of increased life spans, fewer fatal heart

WHAT THEY SAID IN 1977

attacks, reduced infant mortality, significant survival rates for cancer patients and every life-saving device or technique.

At House committee hearing, Washington,
May 11/Los Angeles Times, 5-12:(1)5.

John M. Morris
Professor and chief of gynecology,
Yale University School of Medicine

1

If we want to eliminate unwarranted surgery, we have to control malpractice-insurance rates. Some surgeons now pay $100 a day for malpractice insurance. That can't help but affect some surgeons' judgment when they're considering an operation.

Before House Commerce Oversight and
Investigations Subcommittee, Washington,
May 9/The Dallas Times Herald, 5-10:(A)8.

Gaylord Nelson
United States Senator, D–Wisconsin

2

[Approving the government's ban on the sale of saccharin]: The law requires the removal from the food supply of any agent that has been proven to cause cancer in animals or man. Tests indicate that saccharin is such an agent. Scientists now believe that anywhere from 80 to 90 per cent of cancer is, in large part, caused by agents introduced into the environment by man. Why add another potentially dangerous agent? The question constantly to be kept in mind is this: Should the public be massively exposed to cancer-causing agents through the food supply? The answer to that is no . . . [Furthermore,] it's not clear that saccharin has had much beneficial effect as a weight-controlling aid. The FDA stated in 1969 that scientific studies had not "established a useful role for non-nutritive sweeteners as weight-reducing aids except under the most carefully controlled conditions." However, a compelling point in this whole discussion is that the industry has low-calorie sugar substitutes. We should move to the substitutes.

Interview/U.S. News & World Report, 4-4:59.

Richard E. Palmer
President, American
Medical Association

3

[Arguing against government control of medicine]: Historically, the tremendous advances in medicine took place under the system of free professionals. This system does work. It has produced great benefits to many people . . . regulation by government is the very opposite of freedom. There must be a free interchange between patient and doctor. Otherwise, we have lost the very heart and essence of the practice of medicine . . . In the past several years I've been to the People's Republic of [mainland] China. I've been to countries in South America, and Scandinavia, to Belgium, Germany, Switzerland, England, Bulgaria. And I just got back from the Soviet Union. In all these countries, with the possible exception of West Germany and Belgium, there is government control of medicine. The most disheartening example, I think, is Great Britain, where they have long queues of people waiting for simple operations. There's not enough money to run the system. The doctors are totally frustrated. They have said to me time and again in many of these countries: "For heaven's sake, can't your politicians see what has happened in our country? Can't they see that you [in the U.S.] have the best system for the practice of medicine and that you're doing the best job in the world? Can't they leave you alone?"

Interview/The National Observer, 4-23:12.

Paul VI
Pope

4

[Criticizing abortion]: What drug, what legal gilding can ever deaden the remorse of a woman who has freely and consciously murdered the fruit of her womb? Is the life that at its very conception springs up in the mother's womb not really and truly a human life? Does it not need every care, every love, seeing that this embryonic life is innocent, defenseless but already inscribed in the divine book of the

(PAUL VI)

destiny of humanity? Who could suppose that a mother would kill her offspring or let it be killed?

At mass, Vatican City, Jan. 1/
San Francisco Examiner & Chronicle, 1-2:(A)16.

Christopher A. Rodowskas, Jr.
Executive director, American
Association of Colleges of Pharmacy

1

Back in the dark ages of 1961, when I graduated from a college of pharmacy, we were instructed to function solely in a support role and to keep quiet. As I look upon the curriculum of that day, it was designed to teach you to develop and analyze drug products and to dispense. The new look in pharmacy education calls for graduates to be more independent, communicative, and to take the initiative in responding to patient needs. It also faces up to the all-too-often hidden side of the pharmacy profession. We have seldom spoken openly of the fact that, in millions of patient encounters, the pharmacists, without the direction of a physician, have recommended treatment, performed triage and offered a long array of patient services. We now admit that this takes place, and the colleges and profession are attempting to upgrade that service. This will lead to an expansion of the pharmacist-client relationship with new independence in professional judgment. We are now in an era of product selection, and we will be moving into one of limited prescribing with the emergence of a third class of drugs to be dispensed on the order of a pharmacist.

At University of Utah, June 11/
Vital Speeches, 7-15:597.

E. Kash Rose
President, California
Medical Association

2

I think that part of the future of medicine must include a more humanistic approach. We must treat our patients as friends, not as "cases" or as "diseases." And we are beginning to return to this philosophy. Look at the increase in family practitioners. The growing popularity of hospices is another example. Medicine has a high cost not because of the mistakes we have made, but because of the advances we have made. But those advances, because they have made medical care less personal, translate into more angry patients, more demanding patients, patients more likely to sue, patients less willing to pay for our services and patients who would just as soon have the government give them everything free, and guarantee their care to boot . . . I believe that one of the great needs in the coming years will be for doctors to take the "coldness" out of medicine, and, in its place, put a more human response. This could solve one hell of a lot of problems, for with patients on our side, how can we lose?

At Anaheim Memorial Hospital, Santa Barbara,
Calif., Oct. 13/Vital Speeches, 12-1:117.

Richard S. Ross
Dean, Johns Hopkins
University Medical School

3

Hospitals have come to see cardiac-surgery programs as status symbols. They compete with each other to have the latest equipment and the biggest case loads. Cardiac-surgical programs are developing in suburban hospitals which 10 years ago would never have considered such a program to be an economic feasibility, and in most of these hospitals the bypass procedure is the only heart operation being done. The administrators see the new program as a way to fill beds and increase revenue. The diagnostic and therapeutic equipment required for such a program is expensive and once purchased it must be used, to amortize the purchase cost. The need to generate a case load to justify the program undoubtedly results in overuse.

Before Senate Human Resources
Health Subcommittee, Washington, July 25/
The Washington Post, 7-26:(A)6.

James H. Sammons
Executive vice president,
American Medical Association

4

[On the Carter Administration's criticism of the rising cost of medical services]: Health is not the top priority in the new Administration.

WHAT THEY SAID IN 1977

(JAMES H. SAMMONS)

Cost-control is. When cost becomes the overriding factor in medical decisions ... you get rationing of care to patients. Next, you get second-rate medical equipment ... Finally, you wake up one day to find you have a second-rate medical-care system instead of a first-rate system.

Before American Medical Association House
of Delegates, San Francisco, June 19/
Los Angeles Times, 6-20:(1)20.

Alexander M. Schmidt
Former Commissioner of Food and Drugs
of the United States
1

I once analyzed about a year's worth of what I considered major criticisms of FDA gleaned from newspapers, from letters written by consumer advocates, from GAO reports and Congressional hearings. I discovered that the root cause of a surprisingly large amount of what I thought valid criticism stemmed, not so much from what the agency did or didn't do, but from the slowness — sometimes really incredible slowness — with which we appeared to act. Sometimes we were doing it, whatever it was; sometimes we were about to do it; but if only we had done it, we wouldn't have been vulnerable. Why is the agency so slow sometimes? The answer is interesting. First, the agency has a rapidly growing job to do — increasing both in size and complexity. To plan what to do, to line up the scientific support, to satisfy the general-counsel's office, and then to write it down well, in regulations that will hold up in court, takes time, and a surprisingly large number of skilled people at headquarters. The FDA is a highly people-intensive organization, and it is only as good as its staff. If someone wants to create beneficial change in FDA, I think the single most important thing to do is to improve the ability of the agency to recruit and retain professional staff. FDA is blessed by having on its staff highly competent, hard-working, long-suffering professionals, but in totally inadequate numbers for the jobs given the agency to do. So, give FDA the people it

needs, help FDA keep them, or else don't expect so much to be done so fast.

The Washington Post, 1-27:(A)22.

Hans Selye
Endocrinologist
2

Stress is the non-specific response of the body to any demand placed upon it. [Some people are] stress seekers. They need it to live and be happy. This is good, and they should seek it. They are like race horses. [Other people are] stress avoiders. They want to be placid and easygoing. This is what they need to live, and they should avoid stress. We call them turtles ... If a person is a stress seeker, and his body is falling apart, the last thing I would ever diagnose is that he be imprisoned on a beach for three months. He will do nothing but run up and down the beach and think about Wall Street. He might as well be on Wall Street and learn to accept the type of person he is and develop the disciplines that will help him live in harmony with the stresses of his life. If a person is a turtle and he is forced to run like a race horse every day, he will have trouble. If he should want to be a beachcomber, then he should do that. Whatever he does, a person must simply strive to live with his nature and be useful. Usefulness can simply be that a man has good-will toward others.

San Francisco/The New York Times, 10-16:(1)15.

Gus Speth
Member, Federal Council on
Environmental Quality
3

By comparing various cancer rates, scientists now estimate that as much as 60 to 90 per cent of cancer is related to environmental, as opposed to heredity, factors. Examples of such environmental factors include smoking habits, alcohol consumption, dietary habits, exposure to various forms of radiation ... and to a wide range of industrial chemicals and minerals ... How do we know which ones are harmful? Of all the chemicals that have been released into the human environment, we *know* that a small number cause cancer in man. We know this for the best and most tragic of reasons: They *have* caused cancer in man, and we have taken steps

(GUS SPETH)

to prevent or reduce their further introduction into our environment. But we cannot patiently wait for other carcinogens to make themselves known in this manner. Cancer has a typical latency period of 15 to 40 years; by the time a carcinogen has been positively identified, many thousands of our population may already have contracted cancer. Hence we have to figure out some way to spot a cancer-causing agent before we expose humans to it.

The Washington Post, 10-23:(C)6.

Steven D. Symms
United States Representative,
R—Idaho
1

[Saying the requirement for effectiveness before the FDA approves a drug should be removed]: I think that law should be changed so that the Food and Drug Administration must return to judging drugs solely on their safety. Once safety is proven, the product should be allowed to be marketed, because everyone is a unique person, and what's good for one person is not necessarily good for another. Right now we're denying physicians and trained people in the medical profession the opportunity to try innovative procedures on patients and improve medical care.

Interview/U.S. News & World Report, 6-13:51.

Arthur C. Upton
Director, National Cancer Institute
2

[On whether saccharin should be banned because of evidence that, in large quantities, it causes cancer in rats]: The animal research indicates conclusively that saccharin administered to rats in high doses can lead to the development of tumors in the bladder. The question then involves two kinds of extrapolation. If we lower the dose, even in the rat, will we find a dose ultimately that is small enough so that it carries no risk whatever? The second question involves the question of extrapolation across species. If saccharin causes cancer in the rat, can we infer it will cause cancer in the mouse, the dog, or in man? The answer to both of these questions has to remain tentative at the present time. It would appear from the bulk of animal research that as one lowers the dose,

although the risk may go down, we cannot be sure that it ever goes to zero, at least in many instances, saccharin included. The extrapolation across species likewise involves uncertainties, but in general there is a close correlation between carcinogenic activity in animals and carcinogenic risk in the human. So I think the problem really involves a public judgment. Given the uncertainties we have, what is the most acceptable course of action for society? Would society choose to use saccharin, perhaps in a limited way, in the expectation that its use will provide a social benefit and willingly accept the level of risk, or would society prefer to play it absolutely safe, as it were, and not utilize this substance at all, on the ground that it may involve risk, and also on the ground that we cannot estimate the risk precisely?

TV-radio interview/"Meet the Press,"
National Broadcasting Company, 8-28.

Sidney M. Wolfe
Director, Public Citizen Health
Research Group
3

[On the Delaney clause which prohibits the use of food additives that cause cancer in animals or man]: There have been several situations in the recent past where the Food and Drug Administration should have invoked it and didn't. FDA has more discretion than it should have; saccharin is a good example. In 1973, there were several studies that showed quite clearly that saccharin caused cancer in animals. FDA should have banned it then. If they had, we might have another artificial sweetener on the market — perhaps one which doesn't cause cancer ... Animal tests are as good a predictor, before the fact, that one can have. After the fact, one can always say that the best evidence of human cancer is human cancer. Unfortunately, it was after the fact that we learned about a number of workplace chemicals which cause cancer. After the human bodies piled up, we were able to say, "Well, it looks like this chemical causes cancer." Not paying attention to animal evidence is too big a risk. In the past few years, we have found out that a number of chemicals that were shown in earlier tests to cause cancer in animals fed high doses, cause cancer in humans.

Interview/U.S. News & World Report, 5-30:25.

The Performing Arts

MOTION PICTURES

Robert Aldrich
Producer, Director
1

Unless you're really retarded, you determine that the seat of power is in the hands of the director — then, now, next year, always.
Interview, Washington/The Washington Post, 2-9:(B)1.

Irwin Allen
Producer, Director
2

If the picture is bad, then stars won't help. But if it's pretty good, then it has a much greater chance of being enormously successful with name stars. That's a giant plus. But the bottom line is always audience interest in the characters in the film. If the audience cares about the people, then the bigger the disaster that befalls them, the bigger the success of the film.
Interview, Burbank, Calif./
Los Angeles Times, 12-18:(Calendar)66.

Woody Allen
Actor, Director, Writer
3

When you conceive of something, you have idealized, grandiose ideas. Then you write it, and it's a little less funny than you had imagined. Then you film it, and it's a *lot* less funny. By the time it ends up on the screen, you're down to 50 per cent of that brilliant idea. So you always think, "If only you could have seen it as it appeared in my mind."
Interview, New York/
The Christian Science Monitor, 5-4:18.

Robert Altman
Director
4

... I *never* have a finished screenplay when I begin [filming]. I write as I go along. That doesn't mean I literally have never started

filming with a finished screenplay, only that whatever is written I consider nothing more than a guide, an outline which is subject to change as we move along. For instance, when I begin to shoot, not only do I welcome suggestions from the actors, I insist on it.
Interview/The Hollywood Reporter, 5-10:(C)10.

5

I think people try too hard to get a single comprehensible meaning out of a film. You don't have to approach it that way. It can be more like a painting. I also think film-makers try to explain what they're doing too precisely. The worst thing [director Federico] Fellini did was talk about what he intended *Casanova* to mean in advance. He prepared the way for his own bad reviews.
Interview, New York/
The Washington Post, 5-8:(E)4.

Alan Arkin
Actor
6

The admission that acting is a business seems to be annoying to a lot of people. You can be as creative as you can be — until there's nothing left in the icebox. Then you do what you can get away with, sacrificing the purity of your vision — or you can go work in a store somewhere. You have van Gogh on the one hand, who never sold a painting, and on the other hand you have Eleanora Duse, who always made it her business to do very popular things between the things she really wanted to do ... There are about eight people in the business who have their choice of what they want to do. Maybe not even eight. As for the rest of us, it's kind of arrogant to put us down

THE PERFORMING ARTS — MOTION PICTURES

(ALAN ARKIN)

for the kind of material we're in. An actor does the best of the parts he's allowed to see.

Interview, London/San Francisco Examiner
& Chronicle, 1-2:(Datebook)20.

Samuel Z. Arkoff
Chairman and president,
American International Pictures

1

The whole movie business has changed, which makes it thrilling and interesting. Making pictures is tougher today than ever. And it will get tougher. Costs have risen fantastically, and proceeds can't keep up. You can't charge $20 for an admission ticket. Management has defaulted by letting the stars, agents and unions take charge. The flies have taken over the fly paper. We are in a carnival business today because of television. The networks are capable of turning out good movies. The quiet movie without big names has no chance to break through because it can't be kept in theatres long enough to earn money. The more movies TV makes, the more carnival atmosphere is needed for theatres. You've got to give them something they can't see for free on the tube ... Movies get in trouble when they call themselves art instead of carnival. Any successful picture today has to have carnival excitement. It's a matter of appealing to the young people who want to get out of the house. Boys taking girls to movies is all that keeps theatres open. The rest is gravy, but the fundamental reason for theatrical pictures is making films for young adults.

Interview/The Dallas Times Herald, 1-5:(G)6.

Edward Asner
Actor

2

[On acting]: With all its drawbacks, this is still a marvelous kind of career. When I first blundered into acting, I had serious doubts about my ability to make the grade. I figured an actor had to look like Tyrone Power, Errol Flynn, Gary Cooper, Ronald Colman. So what chance did I have? But there's room for all kinds, and I can point to myself as proof. Not only did I find room but, as I began to grow, I discovered a special power inside me. Just as a musician learns to play notes, I learned to play dialog, to take words off paper and breathe new life into the experience. Maybe it won't last long. Maybe, as Edwin Booth said, an actor is a sculptor who carves in snow. But for someone like me, who began without great expectations, it's the most fulfilling kind of life I can imagine.

Interview, Los Angeles/
Los Angeles Times, 11-20:(Home)41.

Fred Astaire
Actor, Dancer

3

People believe show business is so beautiful. Somebody said to me, "Oh! You're going to make a movie in Ireland! What fun!" But I never have any of those Gee! Hooray! feelings. Acting isn't fun. It's a job ... I can't think about anything other than the job and making good in it. I'm always pretty tense till I get a job done. The fun comes when the job's over, if it's a success. And even if it isn't a success, at least it's over.

Interview, Dublin/San Francisco Examiner
& Chronicle, 5-1:(Datebook)32.

4

My dancing is done; it's in the past. I'm not that much interested in it any more. When they tell that to people, they seem horrified. But I'm not trying to be snobbish. I mean it. People tell me how much they liked what I did. Well, good. I'm glad. They ask me, "Weren't you thrilled?" No. I wasn't thrilled. Each time, I did the best I could. I more or less took it for granted. I had a job to do. Am I expected to jump up and down and yell, "Goody! Goody! I'm a success!"? I'm not impressed. I'm pleased that I can or have done it. But people go overboard. They think I do a dance every day somewhere.

Interview/Los Angeles Herald-Examiner,
11-25:(C)6.

Richard Attenborough
Director

5

The thing I enjoy most is working with actors. There are sequences that don't have any relation to actors at all — scenes that are

399

WHAT THEY SAID IN 1977

literally mechanical operations that have to be worked out like a military operation. One works as a boss or commander or general. And as with a general, the buck stops with you. You have total command, and it's frightening — dealing with vast sums of money not your own, and gambling with other people's reputations and careers. When you tell an actor to say a line differently, you pray you're right — for the sake of the movie and for him.

Interview, Nijmegen, Netherlands/
The Christian Science Monitor, 6-6:34.

Ingmar Bergman
Director
1

I am obsessive about films. I feel a lust while I'm directing, a definite sexual feeling; but I must always struggle to keep my obsession in control.

Interview, Munich/Time, 2-14:78.

Pandro S. Berman
Producer
2

The average producer today is a business-man, someone who is good at packaging things and then running away. In my time, we were as creative as the director or anyone else. I used to bring the director onto a movie 10 days before we began shooting. The producer's function was to a property, persuade the company to buy it, collaborate with the writer he himself had chosen, select a director and stay with that movie right down through the final editing. That was the era of Thalberg, Zanuck, Selznick and Goldwyn, men who were *responsible* for their films. The producer is a kind of nonentity in the present market. Today, the directors are doing the job.

Interview, The New York Times, 3-11:(C)6.

Bernardo Bertolucci
Director
3

. . . when I make a film, all of me goes into it. Otherwise there is no other reason to feel alive, to live. It is also communication, being in touch with a lot of people. Don't you think it is probably a great need of affection? See my movie. Look my movie. Touch my movie. It's always indirect but the movie is an extension of me, the extension of my dreams. To me, dreams are very important. I use my dreams. I interpret them. It's hard work. It's discipline.

Interview/The Washington Post, 10-16:(G)5.

Tony Bill
Producer
4

The key to success [in motion pictures] is not fooling around with a script. Good ones are hard to find and they are the key to any movie. When you get one, trust it.

Interview, Venice, Calif./
Los Angeles Times, 5-28:(2)6.

Karen Black
Actress
5

The movies have come to such a point that what makes you watch is that you're afraid the man you are looking at is not going to stay alive for the next five minutes.

Interview/Los Angeles Times, 4-25:(4)8.

Robert Blake
Actor
6

. . . I've got to tell you that the buck stops in front of the box, the camera. That's where it all stops and I'm out there alone. There are no excuses and no subtleties on the screen. If the props don't work or the story isn't there or the lines aren't right, the actor's out there with a lot of egg on his face. But, man, I tell you, when it's working right, when you're in front of the camera and soaring, there's nothing like it, not mountain-climbing, nothing.

Interview, Los Angeles/
Los Angeles Times, 4-24:(Calendar)31.

Peter Bogdanovich
Director
7

There's no such thing as making the "first" movie any more. I'm living now, so I am aware of what came before me, just as a novelist is aware of Dickens and Joyce. There's nothing new, it's just how you do it. Even the ancient Greeks used the same plots over and over, and the awards were for how the story was told, not

(PETER BOGDANOVICH)

for the story. The story is the least important thing, in a movie or anything else.

Interview, New York/
The Christian Science Monitor, 1-14:31.

1

In movies you're creating a world. At your best, you're creating your own world — populated with your own people who walk on streets you made for them, saying things you meant them to say . . . For me, it's still like a magic trick. You take two pieces of film that don't mean anything by themselves, and put them together, and wow! Look at that! How did that happen?

Interview, New York/
The Christian Science Monitor, 1-14:31.

Richard Boone
Actor

2

I have never wanted to act. Paint, yes. Write, yes. Direct, yes. Produce, yes. But act? Acting is one of the dumbest things of all time. If you can act like Gielgud or Paul Scofield or Sir Ralph Richardson or Marlon Brando or Bobby Blake, then act.

Interview, Beverly Hills, Calif./
San Francisco Examiner & Chronicle,
2-13:(Datebook)27.

James Brolin
Actor

3

Until you've got a major hit under your belt, you get nothing but scripts with Redford, McQueen, Eastwood, Bronson and Newman's fingerprints all over them. Without a hit you've got no control over your professional life. That's what I'm after. The people who run this town [Hollywood] respond to box-office smashes like they respond to nothing else. For some of them, it's all that life offers.

Interview, Los Angeles/
Los Angeles Herald-Examiner, 5-15:(B)1.

Mel Brooks
Actor, Director, Writer

4

A comedy should never run more than 90 minutes. By then, the audience's Raisinettes are all used up. In editing a comedy, one usually starts with a finely honed scalpel and ends up in the last week using a blunt ax — hacking out whole scenes that were your babies.

Interview, Los Angeles/
Los Angeles Times, 9-4:(Calendar)26.

5

[On his being named director of the year by the National Association of Theatre Owners] : I was a little surprised that NATO would have the good sense. I was surprised that a comedy director was chosen as the director of the year, because normally we are not. Normally, we are overlooked as directors, and we are considered funny-men or comic personalities, but we are not considered film directors . . . If we go back in time and talk about great motion pictures, the great golden era of silent pictures, what do you see? We talk about *Greed* and *Birth of a Nation,* [but] they are not with us. They are in museums. But *The Gold Rush* and *The Navigator* — they are with us today. The great silent comedies are making money for us in our theatres, and people are going to see them. The great silent dramas are not. They're in museums. They're dusty and they're dead . . . I feel that, in recognizing me as the director of the year, NATO is in a sense not only saluting me, but saluting such directors as Charles Chaplin, Buster Keaton, Paul Mazursky, Woody Allen, Stan Laurel and great, great film directors like Ernst Lubitsch and Billy Wilder, who have worked for many years in the fields of comedy, harvesting a very important and prized possession — humor.

Interview/Daily Variety, 12-20:6.

Genevieve Bujold
Actress

6

I come from the stage, where it is like having a religious experience each night for a period of three hours, and then you go about your normal business. But in films, you don't go shopping during the day and then put on a

401

WHAT THEY SAID IN 1977

(GENEVIEVE BUJOLD)

costume at night and become somebody else for a while. You are the character you play for the duration of the shooting. That's why I try to bring life-affirming qualities to my movies. I don't think I could ever play a killer.

Interview/
Los Angeles Herald-Examiner, 11-16:(B)6.

Carol Burnett
Entertainer
1

I'm most comfortable when I'm playing to a live audience. We tape our television show that way, and I'm always so surprised when movie people come on the show and say they don't think they can do it, because the audience scares them. With me, it's just the opposite. I'm scared on a movie set playing to that camera. I'd like to be loose and adventurous in front of the movie camera, and not play it so close to the vest. After all, I go into my television show without knowing what the heck I'm doing.

Interview/The New York Times, 4-8:(C)8.

Ellen Burstyn
Actress
2

[On acting]: If you just learn to speak like a person instead of a kangaroo, and learn to turn your head this way and that and smile, of course it's a silly profession, and of course you're over-paid. But if you get involved in the whole craft and its history — and if you delve into the human psyche — which is what acting is really about — it's a life-long study.

Interview, New York/
The Christian Science Monitor, 3-17:17.

Frank Capra
Director
3

I was short, born in a foreign land [Italy], and son of poor and illiterate peasants. But in the cinema there is no formula for success except, perhaps, for creativity.

Interview, Palermo, Sicily/
The Dallas Times Herald, 6-6:(D)5.

Leslie Caron
Actress
4

I'd rather do a small film which has quality than a commercial film. I'm at war against corporate film-making. I think corporate dread-and-disaster films and their sequels are sick and unimaginative and undermine our profession. I want to be a part of the new Italian cinema which, I think, is currently the best in the world. Take Nanni Loy, Ettore Scola or Francesco Rosi — for them the bottom line is not "let's make money"; it's "let's redress a social or political wrong." And, as the Italians tend to be gifted story-tellers anyway, their films are also entertaining. I think it's fair to say that they are carrying on the great cinematic traditions of von Stroheim and Renoir. Their movies deal with important themes. My movies will, too.

Interview, Norfolk, Va./
The New York Times, 8-28:(2)31.

5

I think women in the film industry are entering a different phase surreptitiously. A lot of good writers are women and recognition of women's intelligence is growing. Actresses used to be considered a race of dummies — no one ever forgave Katharine Hepburn for being intelligent.

Interview, London/
Los Angeles Herald-Examiner, 11-9:(B)6.

Jimmy Carter
President of the United States
6

Movies have tied our highly diverse American society together because those who were rich could learn what poverty was and those who were poor could see a vision of a better life; those who were happy could learn about hunger and sorrow and those who were stricken could learn about happiness.

At 10th anniversary celebration of American
Film Institute, Washington, Nov. 17/
The Hollywood Reporter, 11-21:4.

Tom Courtenay
Actor

1

I prefer low-budget films, but [they] don't seem to make them any more. There just doesn't seem to be a market for anything with any aspiration any more. There is less nonsense in that kind of film. The more money is involved, the more nonsense. I've had two big-money offers before . . . but I didn't want them. I didn't want to be paid a lot of money to make a fool of myself, and I didn't want to get into the film business wholeheartedly.

Interview, Washington/
The New York Times, 1-30:(2)7.

Broderick Crawford
Actor

2

[On acting] : Do *not* use the word "method" in my presence! I act by having led *multiple* lives. I've lived in the streets, in cold-water flats without the cold water, in big Hollywood spreads; I act by having let every second of it all go in here [the right ear] and never letting any of it go out here [the left ear].

Interview, New York/
The New York Times, 1-16:(2)11.

George Cukor
Director

3

It's an ever-present danger that you will make a picture too long. There's always a lot of heartache; if you shoot something you like very much, it's hard to cut it out. You always have to arrive at the agony of editing.

The New York Times, 2-27:(2)17.

Tony Curtis
Actor

4

The "Oscars" have been turned into a big business, and they can be bought. You tell me, what the hell was [football player] O. J. Simpson doing up there on that [Academy Award] stage? Or [boxer] Muhammad Ali? What do they have to do with movies? Where was Barbara Stanwyck, baby?

Interview/Los Angeles Herald-Examiner, 6-5:(B)2.

Bette Davis
Actress

5

Those of us who chose this profession are not fond of ourselves. We're delighted to become other characters. I've never been terribly fond of me. I always disliked enormously the way I looked. I was ordered out of watching rushes; I would be so depressed for days . . . Actually, I always thought that male stars are much vainer than women. Acting is sort of an uncomfortable profession for a male. There's a French saying: An actor is less than a man and an actress is more than a woman. Men weather better. But women owned Hollywood for 20 years, and we must not be bitter.

Interview, Weston, Conn./
The New York Times, 1-19:(C)17.

6

They now call them [the 1930s] the Golden Years [of films]. From the standpoint of those of us who worked, they weren't really. It was such hard work. But what was golden is that you were really given a chance to do a performance. That was the focus and that was why it was great . . . Then there was the contract system and all the blood, sweat and tears that meant. We made some terrible movies. We learned that a great script is *it*. The crime of the '30s was to the writers. They went through absolute hell. Without the writers nobody has a job. It's that simple. The lack of knowledge of what goes into a great play or screenplay boggles the mind . . . The point is that acting is a secondary art. We're not the originators. But hopefully we can add something.

Interview, Los Angeles/
Los Angeles Times, 2-27:(Calendar)84.

7

[On the diminishing of women's roles in films] : It just happened, and no one has devised a system to compensate for the changes. Perhaps we shouldn't complain. We had wonderful opportunities for more than 20 years. Maybe it's just the actors' turn to dominate for a generation. The themes and problems seem so much more formidable and violent now. They overshadow the content of

WHAT THEY SAID IN 1977

most of our pictures, which usually had a romantic conflict at their core and were designed to appeal to a large, faithful audience of women. Those forms don't seem adequate now, but I'm not sure what can replace them. They certainly can't have the impact of the conflicts one sees in the men's vehicles.

Interview, Washington/
The Washington Post, 2-27:(E)3.

Robert De Niro
Actor

1

Some of the old movie stars were terrific, but they romanticized. People chase illusions and these illusions are created by movies. I want to make things concrete and real and to break down the illusion. There's nothing more ironic or strange or contradictory than life itself. What I try to do is to make things as clear and authentic as possible.

Newsweek, 5-16:83.

Robert Duvall
Actor

2

[On why he has played so many villains in his career]: You have to pay the rent. So you repeat yourself a little. But looking back I can't be too sad about what I've played as far as versatility goes. There are different kinds of villains. Tom Hagen in *The Godfather* was really a good guy. Jesse James in *The Great Northfield Minnesota Raid* — I played him as a bad-ass neurotic. Alec Guinness — he's still somewhat in touch with himself when he plays all these characters. If it's not you, you'll put me to sleep, I'll tell you. If you try to emulate imagined emotions, you can't do it. I'll argue with anybody over it. If you're here and the character's there, you're in trouble. Every now and then, someone runs a 9-flat 100-yard dash. I've given some 9-flat performances, on a good night. You come to see me — I'll show you real people.

Interview, London/San Francisco Examiner &
Chronicle, 4-10:(Datebook)18.

Robert Evans
Producer

3

I don't think it's true a movie has to be louder than the decibel level of the society. I think that good movies have to have good writing. The biggest stars of a film are the writers.

Interview, Los Angeles/
"W": a Fairchild publication, 1-7:20.

4

I've lived with [the films] *Chinatown, Marathon Man* and now *Black Sunday* from the very beginning. Maybe I can get away for a while after *Black Sunday* opens. I'd like to take a three-week vacation, but I'm not sure my metabolism could stand it . . . I'm not certain film-making would survive without people who became obsessed with the process. One of the things wrong with the business right now is that more people are involved in making deals than making pictures. You can get rich just making deals, but that's bull----. I'd rather be remembered than rich.

Interview, Washington/
The Washington Post, 3-28:(B)9.

Peter Finch
Actor

5

. . . I think you have to teach yourself absolute concentration. By that, I mean you've got to concentrate totally on the scene and the character you're playing, without becoming so intense that it loses reality. Very young actors have to break through a dreadful barrier — the barrier of intensity. And, the poor darlings, they have such a desperate ambition to be actors they close themselves up in a huge mass of anxiety. They have to learn to relax a little.

Interview/The Miami Herald, 1-23:(Tropic)25.

Albert Finney
Actor

6

I've always envied and admired writers and painters. An actor is an interpretive artist. We're motivated by somebody else's work. We read a text, and hopefully juices start to flow, and we get our ideas and thrills from digging into it. As an actor, I don't have any blanks; except for

(ALBERT FINNEY)

fleshing out, it's a question of finding things that are there on the page and being fed by them. But a writer sits down with something blank in front of him, and has to decide where to make the first mark, and what kind of mark it will be.

Interview, New York/
The Christian Science Monitor, 8-22:26.

John Frankenheimer
Director

1

I don't know any American directors who are *auteurs* in the French sense — and not many French directors either. Film is not a director's medium; it's a collaborative medium.

Interview/Los Angeles Times,
4-10:(Calendar)31.

2

For years I've had the reputation of being a wild character, who got into fights often and gave other people trouble . . . But in fairness to me, my fights have always been with my bosses. I never gave an actor a bad time, because I see myself clearly as a failed actor, and I sympathize with anyone working that lonely, treacherous road.

Interview/Los Angeles Times, 5-1:(Home)40.

Eva Gabor
Actress

3

. . . actors are rotten. I'm one, and we're rotten. When we're up, when we're popular, the phone is ringing all the time, and when we're down there's silence. I know how it is because I've been up and I've been down. In show business it's the way you find out what the rest of the world thinks of you. Actors are rotten, but because I'm one, I can relax among them.

Interview, Los Angeles/
Los Angeles Times, 4-24:(Home)64.

James Garner
Actor

4

I get a kick out of this business every day. Because I get to do something different, meet somebody new. Through my work, I have met some of the most influential men of our time, and been to places I'd otherwise not have visited. My God, I've played golf with kings, dined with queens and princesses! Me — this little ol' boy from Oklahoma! If *they* only knew who *they* were having dinner with!

Interview, Los Angeles/San Francisco Examiner &
Chronicle, 5-29:(Datebook)35.

Marvin Goldman
President, National Association
of Theatre Owners

5

In effect, you have an industry that is making movies only for people in the 18-to-32 age group — it's a rare picture that goes past these boundaries. They [the studios] say this is where the audience is, so they give them violence, strong language and gratuitous sex. We're saying there is a whole segment of the population we don't want in our theatres . . . Well, I say there is a mass audience out there still, but you're not going to get it with violence, dirty language and sexual depictions.

The New York Times, 1-27:42.

Jerry Goldsmith
Composer

6

[On writing music for films]: No, you can't save a scene with music, but you can sure help. I've said many times, great pictures have saved some bad scores, but great scores never save bad pictures. I can write a brilliant score, but, if the film flops, I'm going down the tubes with everybody else.

Interview, Los Angeles/
The Washington Post, 5-15:(H)4.

Richard Harris
Actor

7

You can't understand the pressure that producers, directors and studio publicity people put on an actor. They play on your ego and your guilt. I would never live in Hollywood because there are no friends there. You've got to be a ruthless, tough person, like Barbra Streisand, to survive the acting business. That old expression is quite true: "Nice guys just don't come in first."

New York/San Francisco Examiner & Chronicle,
2-13:(Datebook)35.

405

WHAT THEY SAID IN 1977

Goldie Hawn
Actress
1

I feel the essence of what God gave me will bleed through anything I do, and what He gave me is a feeling for comedy. Why should I try to extend myself when it's not necessarily what the public wants me to do? This is a business, after all, and our job is to please the people, to get them to come and buy tickets. It's funny, but your peers all seem to want you to do something other than what you do best. "Come on, Goldie, it's time to show them what a serious actress you are." Well, that's fine, but not in 1977. This is an enormous year for "up" pictures.

Interview/The New York Times, 8-26:(C)8.

Edith Head
Motion-picture fashion designer
2

In film-making, color is both the best friend and worst enemy of the costume designer. Every time I dress a star for a picture, I am changing her into someone else, and color helps bring this out. For instance, if the character an actress portrays is fragile, appealing and helpless, I go for soft pastels. If she plays a lady of easy morals, I use "catch-'em" colors — flamboyant, badly matched colors like orange, purple and red. But if she were to play a *femme fatale,* I would choose the non-color colors like black and soft crimson and avoid anything bright or harsh. Color can be very dangerous. Alfred Hitchcock would only use bright colors if they were a story point. He contends that color steals the scene from actors and prefers muted or non-colors.

Interview/
"W": a Fairchild publication, 8-5:14.

Charlton Heston
Actor
3

I never put down the stuff I'm in. I do my best and I try to persuade myself it's a worthwhile enterprise — especially in film. I do the best of what I'm offered and I keep working. There are all kinds of pleasures: the pleasure of a great commercial success, the pleasure of a critical success, the pleasure of a very good part in an unsuccessful film or play. There are lots of satisfactions.

Interview, Los Angeles/Los Angeles Times,
2-6:(Calendar)52.

Alfred Hitchcock
Director
4

[On film schools] : What's missing in these classrooms is the purity of cinema, the idea of pieces of film joined together and run through a machine. Each piece is an idea, just like a sentence in a book. There has been too much emphasis on the verbal and not enough on the visual. I design a picture on paper and then give it to a writer to fill in the dialogue.

Interview, Los Angeles/
Los Angeles Times, 2-21:(4)8.

5

I don't believe in throwing money away. I wouldn't be able to sleep nights if I thought I had to spend even 10 million on a picture. I'm still the humble little film-maker. I'm of a lowly order. I'm not in a position to make multi-million-dollar epics. Apparently there is a breed of directors who makes at least one of those obnoxiously expensive films during their careers. I've managed to ignore the temptation.

Interview, Los Angeles/
The Dallas Times Herald, 12-20:(B)6.

William Holden
Actor
6

For anyone who has had some success in this business . . . it's really remarkable. The experience itself is so all-encompassing. You meet such talented and creative people. And before you've done your work, a writer has written your part. After you're finished, a composer comes in to score the picture. That composer might be Aaron Copland or some very talented new fellow. The writers over the years have been men like Faulkner and other great talents. Jim Michener wrote the book, *The Bridges at Toko-Ri,* and I made the picture. Getting to know him was such a pleasure. Taking advantage of the locations where films are shot. It's foolish to spend eight months in Ceylon and feel you have to get up in the morning and just

(WILLIAM HOLDEN)

go to work. That's terrible. There's so much to see and do. The whole thing is a marvelous springboard for enriching your life.

Interview, Beverly Hills, Calif./
Los Angeles Times, 2-20:(Calendar)38.

1

It's really an undeniable thrill to be nominated for an "Oscar." It's the only thrill for a film actor. On stage, you get that immediate response from an audience, and you do get an audience reaction to movies; but, by the time a film is out, you're so removed from the doing of it you've lost that identification of the moment when you perform.

Interview/The Hollywood Reporter, 3-14:22.

Rock Hudson
Actor

2

Time is the enemy in this business. I'm 51 now. I should have taken on challenging parts a long time ago, but I was too busy being Charlie Moviestar.

The Dallas Times Herald, 6-22:(D)2.

Glenda Jackson
Actress

3

Acting is extremely difficult, and anybody who tells you different is a liar. It requires a great deal of concentration and a great deal of sweat. I don't know who said genius was 90 per cent perspiration and 10 per cent inspiration. I'm not saying all actors are geniuses — or indeed that I am — but you don't arrive at a performance by a magical process. You arrive at it by sheer day-after-day slogging. It can often be an extremely boring business, at least in theatre. If there is any pleasure in it, which I think is doubtful, it's like when you stop beating your head against the wall.

Interview, New York/
The Dallas Times Herald, 3-1:(B)4.

4

The only roles that women seem to get concern their functioning or non-functioning within the realm of their own emotions. They are characters who bemoan their lack of love. It's not just because most of the writing is done by men. Even women writers deal with women and their emotions. I'm bored with it.

Interview, Beverly Hills, Calif./
The Washington Post, 8-26:(B)6.

Charles Jarrott
Director

5

There was a time when the motion-picture business was based on women. Actresses were the big stars on every lot. Leading ladies were the ones who filled theatres. Now it's a different and sadder story. [George] Cukor is a fine director of women-oriented films. But writers aren't coming up with the right scripts and producers aren't building pictures around women. Ernst Lubitsch was a magnificent director of women. He and Cukor treated women like actors, not just sex commodities, which has been the trend for too many years ... The situation is a strange circumstance in view of this decade's women's-liberation movement.

Interview, Los Angeles/
The Washington Post, 5-29:(E)7.

Norman Jewison
Director

6

I don't want to make a dull film. God, there's nothing worse than a dull, boring film. And I don't want to make a film small groups are going to screen for each other. Spending two years of my life on a film which nobody comes to see would be a disaster, the worst thing in my life. I don't give a f--- what critics say. I don't care if they say, "Don't worry, Norman, it's brilliant," the Cinematheque Francaise says it's brilliant, [critic] Pauline Kael says, "The last vestiges of film art are in your hands." I can't stand that elitist approach to film. It's a popular art, and, unless that audience is there, film is a dead thing, just a lot of cans on the shelf.

Interview, Culver City, Calif./
The Washington Post, 9-7:(C)13.

407

WHAT THEY SAID IN 1977

Marthe Keller
Actress
1

[On her current film, directed by Billy Wilder]: I was used to working with directors who discussed motivation before each scene. Wilder just says, "Do this," and doesn't believe in pre-analysis. I found it very difficult at first. I fought him for the first two weeks, but then I realized there was no point. He is the director. He could just cut me out if I didn't do it the way he wanted. Now I do what he says and think about what it means afterward.

Interview, Munich/
Los Angeles Herald-Examiner, 7-25:(B)1.

Henry King
Director
2

The culture of the world has been deeply influenced by motion pictures. And we did a great job with them until they dropped the Code. And now anything goes. I don't believe for one minute the public will go to see violence for violence's sake, or vulgarity for the sake of vulgarity. If a story is worth telling, it has something to say. If it has any importance at all, the audience stays with it. And it rubs off. There must be resistance to violence and language, because the excess use of it indicates a lack of thinking, a lack of control. That's wrong. After all, we have an obligation.

Interview, Los Angeles/
Los Angeles Times, 5-8:(Calendar)20.

Stanley Kramer
Producer, Director
3

Film students talk about the *auteur* theory — the director as total boss — but I disagree. A project works only when there's collaboration between writers, actors, photographers, musicians and everybody else. A director has to be, above all, sensitive to others. For example, working with Spencer Tracy I knew he didn't like to experiment, he didn't care for surprises. He was comfortable acting only when all the details were laid out carefully before him and he knew precisely what he was supposed to do. Gene Hackman, by way of contrast, wants to have plenty of freedom to work out an improvisation. So, as a director, it would be a mistake for me to give too much freedom to a Tracy or to be overly restrictive with a Hackman. I always come to the set totally prepared to give an actor the range he requires. If an actor needs a friend, I'll even be his friend.

Interview/Los Angeles Times, 4-3:(Home)35.

Arthur Laurents
Playwright, Screenwriter
4

I just don't believe you can predict the success or failure of a film; and I don't believe in all their studies, the demographics. Studio heads listen to secretaries, cleaning ladies, viewers in test markets. And obviously I'm right, otherwise they wouldn't be making so many bombs. Why not do something, instead, that you hope will be good? ... Because the careers of the moguls, shareholders — the entire studio — are at stake. They have to make money. And it's rare that you come up with a film that is both good and commercial.

Interview, New York/
Los Angeles Times, 11-29:(4)13.

Cloris Leachman
Actress
5

I don't ever get a good script handed to me bound in leather. A script should only be a blueprint. If you think it's really complete in the script, you won't do any more to help it. A script is not a book, enacted and fleshed out. A script should make you think visually and dramatically. It's like the commercial: You get a plumber that's had 10,000 hours. I'm a plumber that's had 10,000 hours. Where can I find a clogged drain?

Interview/Los Angeles Herald-Examiner, 2-8:(B)6.

Ernest Lehman
Screenwriter
6

No matter how easygoing and unfailingly cheerful he might be ... a writer becomes at some point the antagonist in the process of making a movie. The producer, director, actors, set decorators, carpenters, electricians all take it for granted they are experts on writing. It would be outrageous for a writer to tell them how to do their jobs, but everyone tells a writer how to write. That kind of presumption is

(ERNEST LEHMAN)

infuriating to me, and to every writer I know. The maddening difficulty is: who's to say whether a scene is written in the best possible way? Writing can't be reduced to a measuring rule. One man's opinion is simply one man's opinion. Maybe the writer is wrong and everybody else is right.

Interview, Los Angeles/
Los Angeles Times, 2-13:(Home)29.

Jack Lemmon
Actor

1

In general, the American movie-going public does not exist any more. People don't "go to the movies"; they go to *a movie,* and the producer hopes that word-of-mouth advertising will suddenly hit like lightning as it did for *Star Wars.* But attracting lightning isn't just a matter of making a movie twice as good as *Citizen Kane.* You have to have the right combination of ingredients — in addition to quality — that suddenly seems to appeal to enormous numbers of people. And it's very, very difficult to figure this out in advance. After you think you know what will hit, a year may have gone by, and what might have been a dandy idea is no longer that.

Interview/U.S. News & World Report, 8-22:44.

Mervyn LeRoy
Director

2

It's hard to get pictures started these days, very hard. We don't have the oustanding creators that we used to have. There are too many committees making pictures now.

Interview, Los Angeles/
Los Angeles Times, 5-8:(Calendar)20.

Joseph E. Levine
Producer

3

People in the [film] business think I'm nuts. That's okay, because this is not a logical business. If I was logical, I wouldn't be in this business. It's not a business, and it's not an industry either. Don't bother asking me what it

is. I still can't tell after 40 years. As much as anything else, it's a gut feeling about people or stories.

Interview, New York/
The Washington Post, 6-15:(B)3.

4

These authors who act like their [books] are carved in marble give me a pain. A producer would have to be insane to let a writer have final script approval.

Los Angeles Herald-Examiner, 12-15:(A)10.

Sidney Lumet
Director

5

[On film pornography]: There are the exploiters who could make Shirley Temple's first kiss with John Agar seem dirty. And there are the non-exploiters. Simple as that. Exploiting means it wasn't necessary to the story, or was put there for shock effect or to get attention or pick up the pace ... When you have a work of art, it has the responsibility of being so well-done and generic to its thematic line that there's no possibility of being too violent or pornographic. Otherwise it's not art. The only germane question is, is he an honest movie-maker? This leads to anarchy in terms of opinion, because my idea of an honest movie-maker might not be somebody else's. But over the long run there's not much doubt about where creative people migrate to.

Interview, New York/
The Christian Science Monitor, 2-23:18.

Rouben Mamoulian
Director

6

Film is a powerful instrument. Blue jeans are worn all over the world because of American movies. Everyone in the world says, "Okay" — that comes from American movies. Film-makers carry a responsibility. And films have failed. They don't live up to their artistic and humanistic responsibility. The film-makers have so much freedom now, a total absence of censorship. They can do what they want. You'd think they would have tremendous concepts. But what happens? Films have gone back to the beginning of time, to primitive sex and brutal-

WHAT THEY SAID IN 1977

(ROUBEN MAMOULIAN)

ity. After a million years, you'd think we'd take sex for granted, but now it's back to raw sex. Erotic sex belongs in art, but not raw mechanics. There is no love on the screen, just raw sex. Freedom became a license for brutality. And I'm sick of it.

Interview, San Francisco/San Francisco Examiner & Chronicle, 1-23:(Datebook)13.

Ed McMahon
Television personality

1

[Comparing his co-host job on TV's *Tonight* show with acting in motion pictures]: When I first began in this business, I realized the only way I was going to make it was by being natural. In that respect, I modeled myself after Arthur Godfrey and Dave Garroway and my idol, Paul Douglas. Doing the *Tonight* show for 14 years, 90 minutes a night, I've had to be myself; that camera is like a telescope, and if you do something phony, it shows up right away. The problem with doing a movie is that I have to be the character I'm portraying and do it well enough so that the viewer forgets he's watching Ed McMahon up there on the screen. One of the dangers is that people will say, "Hey, why is *he* doing this movie? Why didn't they give the role to some *actor?*"

Interview/The New York Times, 2-4(C)6.

Burgess Meredith
Actor

2

... in terms of judgment, you can't pay much attention to critics, because they disagree — they'll say opposite things. You can't be wrapped around by that diversity of opinion. You have to listen to that still, small voice of your own. And I'll tell you . . . lots of performers, from Katharine Cornell to the Lunts, didn't read reviewers at all. And I more or less do that, too.

Interview, New York/ The Christian Science Monitor, 3-23:22.

Ann Miller
Actress

3

... Hollywood is giving the public dope, sex and nudity — with everybody stripped down like a turkey with no feathers, which is very ugly and unattractive. Who wants to see a turkey without feathers? Who wants to see a human body without black lace around it? . . . The whole thing is sick, sick. We've moved into something that's like the devil walking the earth. Hollywood sits here making and selling pornography, trash, garbage. What the world needs right now is films by Frank Capra. If Cecil B. DeMille could come back again, he would give the world something worthwhile to see . . . If Greta Garbo were young again, if Clark Gable were only here, and Mr. [Louis B.] Mayer alive to guide the stars. But it's all gone. What we have now is a *nouveau riche* copy — no, it isn't even *nouveau riche* — what we have is a kitsch copy of everything good made ugly. Ugly is in; beautiful is out. Everything now is tacky.

Los Angeles Herald-Examiner, 8-5:(C)1.

Arthur Miller
Playwright

4

In the movie, the words don't mean much. They really don't. The words simply provide a very primitive connective tissue . . . You don't hear much, watching. It's a bit like a dream. . . . dreams are the art of the deaf, and I think movies are like that.

Interview, Washington/ The Christian Science Monitor, 8-8:30.

Liza Minnelli
Actress

5

In the new Hollywood, there's a great deal of treachery. You must be very careful. When you're doing well, they start waiting for you to do something wrong. Which is one reason I don't like to stay in any area too long. Chances are you'll end up doing something that doesn't work; then producers will start looking at you funny. When you're swimming with people who have sharp teeth, you have to learn to swim fast. And the money you make? I think it's ludicrous. Often I can't believe they're giving me so much for so little. But other times it

(LIZA MINNELLI)

seems . . . nothing would be enough. It's fun to get awards, too. They're like funny little trophies. You've got to see humor in all this. If you don't, you're dead. I am serious about my work, but I wouldn't miss all the surrounding stuff.

Interview, Los Angeles/
The Dallas Times Herald, 7-10:(D)6.

1

Hollywood in the '50s was dead. My father [director Vincente Minnelli] kept the musicals going with things like *Gigi.* But it was a very dull town. There was nothing to do. Now it's a working town again. Not a swinging town, like most people think. You go to the studio, work, and go home. And these new directors have made Hollywood exciting again. They're wonderful. They're imaginative, questioning. They're like the wave of new directors that hit Europe years ago.

Interview, Chicago/San Francisco Examiner &
Chronicle, 7-17:(Datebook)17.

Jeanne Moreau
Actress

2

As long as men directors and screenwriters don't want to relate intimately with nature, there won't be strong, valuable women's parts. Even when there are big women's parts they are hysterical characters, or they drink, they are off-balance. *That's* the only adventure that can be imagined for a woman? Change is the way of the world. It's human nature, and even landscapes change; rocks are erased and washed away. With cinema, it's the same thing. There has been dominance by the strong drives of men, who perhaps have felt a need to escape the powerful influence of women in their lives, and lately they have decided to speak about themselves. But nothing lasts. Fashions don't last. Let's compare the noises made by human beings to a symphony. One has to admit that among the bass, male instruments, the music is not always full of harmony. So why not imagine that suddenly there will be female

instruments that will change the rhythm and the melody. That could be a good thing!

Interview, New York/
The Christian Science Monitor, 1-31:22.

Al Pacino
Actor

3

I like anything that gives me routine. Acting gives an organization to the chaos that I have in my life . . . Acting makes me feel as if I'm functioning, as if I'm working. Part of it is being a craftsman, as if I'm making chairs or rugs — or playing baseball. Part of it has to do with giving, with sharing — something I'm learning about. Acting is more than just an anodyne. It is closest to what I want to do.

Interview/The New York Times Magazine, 6-5:66.

Alan J. Pakula
Director

4

The reason I became a director was that I've always loved actors. The very first time I worked with actors on a stage, while I was still at Yale, I got this very exulted feeling that I was finally a part of the universe, in the adolescent Thomas Wolfean sense. I remember leaving the theatre that night and leaping, goat-like, all the way home, full of the arrogant belief that those actors had done something they could never have done without me. Now I'm not so sure.

Interview/The New York Times, 6-3:(C)8.

S. J. Perelman
Author, Playwright

5

I used to watch people leaving a Marx Brothers film, their cheeks stained from tears of laughter. Then they would say, "Wasn't that silly?" If they had been equally churned up by a Garbo movie, they wouldn't say that. They'd think they had been purged — you know, catharsis. But with comedy, people do not trust their reactions. The trouble is, people do not have the courage of their laughter.

Interview, Washington/
The Washington Post, 10-1:(A)1.

WHAT THEY SAID IN 1977

Sidney Poitier
Actor
1

I believe that my principal responsibility is to entertain, and that takes the better part of my energy when I'm trying to figure out what I'm going to make a film about. The structure of the film has to first be an entertaining structure. Then I can balance within that structure various and sundry things that I would figure are important. I can even make a speech on behalf of something that's very dear to my heart, as long as that speech is within the context of good entertainment. Ofttimes people make pictures where the principal energy is directed toward what they want to say, at the expense of entertainment. I hope I don't do that.

Interview, New York/San Francisco Examiner & Chronicle, 10-16:(Datebook)17.

Sydney Pollack
Director
2

There's no way I can like a critic — or take them seriously. Most critics try to sit clean on the sidelines while they pick at the bones of a director who's spent perhaps two years of work on a film. So I don't feel there's any way that a person who makes a film is going to think very much of a critic. I would love it if all the critics loved me, but I can't worry about it if they don't.

At San Francisco Film Festival/ Variety, 10-12:22.

Carlo Ponti
Italian producer
3

[On the renewed popularity of U.S. films and the decline of the Italian film industry] : I always said that when American film-makers discovered America, we would be ruined. The truth is that they have discovered America [as a subject] and they have lots to say. As for us [Italians], our films no longer cost any less than in America. We have reached the point that an Italian producer cannot worry too much about quality, but must make "commercial" films because of the cost factor.

The Dallas Times Herald, 7-19:(B)5.

Vincent Price
Actor
4

I love playing villains; they're such wonderful parts. I do a lecture on villains, and I'm writing a book called *Man and the Monster Image*. And, really, the villain is the hero; he's the person who keeps you guessing. Without him you can't have conflict, you can't have drama.

Interview, Washington/ The Washington Post, 10-9:(H)9.

Anthony Quinn
Actor
5

To me, acting is like a fight. I spend all my time preparing for that three or four minutes of battle. Acting involves struggling to tell the character you're playing as truthfully as possible.

Interview, Washington/ The Hollywood Reporter, 9-15:18.

Lynn Redgrave
Actress
6

It's a great myth that actors are so emotional and unreliable. There are always stories about the ones who fell apart, of course. But actors are probably second only to dancers in discipline. In the theatre, you have to be ready with a performance every night at five past eight. In a film, you don't just emote, you emote when the director says "action," and at the precise moment when the sun comes out from behind a cloud. If you were this great unstable person, you couldn't do it. You have to be stable, actually, to survive the insecurity of our business. It's a rollercoaster.

Interview, New York/ The New York Times, 3-17:(C)29.

Vanessa Redgrave
Actress
7

As far as an actor's skill is concerned, in the fullest and most complete sense, it can only be developed in the theatre. To be able to shape, each night, the flow of a performance is possible only in the theatre. Movies are a different medium and are able to say in a

(VANESSA REDGRAVE)

different way all sorts of things that the theatre can't. Without any words at all, in about 20 seconds, you can express character, an event, and an analysis of that event, in a most powerful way. To express a whole character in a few seconds and without words is still acting. The basis of being able to do it isn't any different.

Interview, New York/
The New York Times, 10-2:(2)30.

Robert Reed
Actor

1

I love the life of an actor — as much as anybody could actually love their life, I mean. I like the people in the arts; I think they are more interesting, know themselves better. The time I'm happiest to be an actor is at the start of a new job. There's nothing to deal with but beginnings, acceptance. You haven't fluffed a line; you haven't argued with the director; you haven't had a chance to fail — everything is ahead of you.

Interview, Beverly Hills, Calif./San Francisco
Examiner & Chronicle, 4-10:(Datebook)37.

Carl Reiner
Director; Humorist

2

It sounds pretentious and pompous, but I'm interested in how people relate to each other in a comic sense. Life has so much fun in it, and you have to see this. When I see heavy drama with no comic relief, I don't think they're honest. I don't think people go through life miserable all the time. In fact, if you're very miserable, you giggle a lot at the oddest things. You can't stay miserable for too long — it's not the human condition.

Interview, New York/
The Christian Science Monitor, 12-16:27.

Burt Reynolds
Actor

3

I hope films are going to become more romantic. My God, when *Casablanca* plays on television it has the highest rating of any show on the air. That's the kind of picture I'd like to do. But when you go to borrow a few million dollars from the Bank of America, and you say it's a love story between two people who meet in a foreign country, they say — after looking at you strangely — "Who's in it?" And unless it's Barbra Streisand and [Robert] Redford, they're not going to let you take that kind of chance . . . Because the motion-picture industry is run by shoe salesmen and manufacturers and businessmen, not by artists, and they go by what makes money.

Interview/San Francisco Examiner &
Chronicle, 11-27:(Datebook)17.

Ginger Rogers
Actress, Entertainer

4

I haven't made a movie in years, and I never go to them. The only way you can get me to see a movie is on an airplane. Today's films have no happiness or hope. A child going to a movie learns the answer to an argument is to kill somebody.

Interview, San Francisco/San Francisco Examiner
& Chronicle, 9-25:(Scene)2.

Herbert Ross
Director

5

What makes directing hard is the endless chain of decisions. First and most importantly, there's the script. You want to be sure it's the best and most eloquent possible arrangement of words, so you worry and fuss and torture it to death. Then comes a gigantic array of decisions about casting actors, choosing locations, art direction, costumes, cameramen, hairdresser. Then, because my background's in the theatre, I rehearse the entire production like a play. My objective is to achieve an ensemble where all the parts come together . . . I try to convey to actors a sense of not mere limited participation but an overall concept and total involvement. A film is a collection of minute details, and preparation is the biggest detail of all. My film work has gone smoothly up to now, not because I'm particularly blessed or enormously talented, but rather because . . . [of] an enormous amount of preparation and homework. A romantic version of a busy director's life would have him rushing around breathlessly, barking

413

(HERBERT ROSS)

orders, screaming complaints, creating scenes for the camera out of marvelously intuitive inspirational moments. The plain truth is I'm very quiet and methodical. I walk away from hysteria and pressure. It didn't happen easily. It's taken most of my life to learn how to do it.

Interview, Beverly Hills, Calif./
Los Angeles Times, 10-30:(Home)24.

Mort Sahl
Political humorist
1

... [film mogul] Jack Warner facilitated the decapitation of the intellectual community in Hollywood when he let in the House Un-American Activities Committee. And you know what Mayer's politics was and [Harry] Cohn's and Sam Goldwyn's. Tyrants all. But how is it such wonderful movies came out from under them? Boy, do I miss those tyrants!

Interview, Beverly Hills, Calif./
Los Angeles Times, 8-8:(4)1.

Roy Scheider
Actor
2

My job is to act — period. I believe that the actor is important to society, that he mirrors his times, that he's no more than a fool — we're the king's jesters, we're the chroniclers. We're all those things that Shakespeare said we are. But that's *all* we are — we're not supposed to have any particular wit or wisdom or philosophy or *politics* ... I don't care what Warren Beatty or Paul Newman or Robert Redford preach; you cannot be a movie star and do social work, too.

Interview, New York/
The New York Times, 7-31:(2)16.

Maria Schell
Actress
3

It's not difficult to be someone else when you're acting. You do it all the time anyway. In your room at 6 a.m., you're no beauty; but at a ball, you're beautiful. Who is the President when he's looking in the mirror or washing his face? Maybe I'm more a queen when I'm playing the role than the [real] queen, when

she's just getting the mail in the morning; she can't be the queen all the time — she'd be sick.

Interview, New York/San Francisco Examiner &
Chronicle, 3-20:(Datebook)24.

Maximilian Schell
Actor, Director
4

At a certain point, I was very selective [in choosing roles], with the effect that I didn't work for years. Then I felt like a soccer player who only practices but never faces a real match. An actor has to face a challenge all the time. In Europe, I'm offered a variety of roles; but in this country [the U.S.] I only portray Germans, and most American films that deal with Germans are World War II pictures. It's ironic that I, who hate war and anything to do with an army, should play all these Germans. On the other hand, if I didn't do them I would not work in America. You see, an actor is like a lady waiting in a ballroom to be asked to dance. If there are many people who ask her, that's fine. If there are not so many who ask, she cannot be so selective.

Interview, Los Angeles/
Los Angeles Times, 6-10:(4)14.

5

I'm used to working at lots of things at the same time. I'm an actor, director, dramatist, pianist. I even paint. It isn't as impossible as everyone seems to think to cram so much into one day. When you're at school, no one tells you that you're doing too much. You're studying English, geography, history, math, languages, art, science ... My secret is that I just concentrate. Right now, I have at least 10 pictures in my head that I'd like to direct. I'm wearing a lot of hats ... and one inspires the other.

Interview, Vienna/San Francisco Examiner &
Chronicle, 7-17:(Datebook)16.

George C. Scott
Actor
6

There's no question you get pumped up by the recognition [you get as an actor]. And then a kind of self-loathing sets in, when you realize that you are enjoying it. But what is ultimately

(GEORGE C. SCOTT)

so harmful is that you are being recognized not for the thing that you worked so hard for, but for other reasons — that you're a movie star, for instance, which is a category that doesn't mean anything in terms of acting and that you're not especially proud to share; there are a lot of bums in that category. After a while, the pleasure stops, but the self-contempt stays . . . You can't go through life parceling out emotionality, parceling out nerve fibers, which is what actors do. You sell your nerve fibers for money. That's just as bad as hooking on Eighth Avenue; it's the same principle. What you're doing is, you're hustling for money. Now, there are high-class hustlers and there are $4 hustlers.

Interview, New York/ The Miami Herald, 1-23:(H)3.

1

I've been interested in the subject of porno movies for some time. I find them an abhorrent form of exhibitionism, a cop-out in which the performers are the victims of unscrupulous people who will do anything to turn a dollar.

Interview/The New York Times, 9-23:(C)6.

Robert Shaw
Actor

2

Can you imagine being a movie star and having to take it seriously without a drink? I agree with Richard Burton that drink gives poetry to life. Drink for actors is an occupational hazard born largely out of fear.

Interview, Ireland/People, 4-25:50.

Sidney J. Sheinberg
*President, MCA, Inc.
(Universal Pictures)*

3

What happens is that the audience is usually ahead of the film-makers or the programmers. It's a form of elitism that makes people who are in the business believe that they are somehow ahead of an audience. The audience is usually ahead of the people who are making the product; and the people who are making the product simply have not perceived that fact. We are not leaders in that sense.

Los Angeles/The Washington Post, 3-2:(B)8.

O. J. Simpson
*Actor; Football player,
Buffalo "Bills"*

4

[On reviews]: In football, I don't care about them. There's one writer in Buffalo who gets on me all the time, but I don't honestly mind it because I know what I can do on the field, and what I've done. But in acting, I'm dependent on critics in the long run. All actors are. They're on pins and needles waiting for the reviews, whether they want to admit it or not.

Interview/Los Angeles Herald-Examiner, 5-10:(C)8.

Steven Spielberg
Director

5

I feel that most people only see one motion picture every two years. And when they pick that picture to see, it's second only to the Oklahoma land rush in terms of box-office. They see *The Godfather,* they see *Jaws,* they see *Star Wars* — and then they go back to the TV for another two years of *Charlie's Angels.* Nobody in the movie industry has ever been able to figure out exactly what attracts people to one picture and not to the next. Personally, I think it takes a good concept, identifiable characters and lots of action. But, ultimately, it's the audience who decides what pictures are going to be powerfully popular and which pictures are going to be forgotten in three months.

Interview/U.S. News & World Report, 11-21:62.

Robert Stack
Actor

6

Acting is a super turn-on when a scene works. It's the greatest high in the world. The problem is that so much depends on the material. When a script is lousy, you can't help feeling embarrassed; it's like bending over at a formal dinner and splitting your pants. Actually, it's worse, because that's over and done with in a few minutes; it's not being filmed for posterity.

Interview/TV Guide, 1-22:24.

WHAT THEY SAID IN 1977

Sylvester Stallone
Actor

1

I really believe that the primary responsibility of the entertainer is to entertain. Nobody is asking you to win a Nobel Peace Prize or split the atom, to enlighten them or alter their philosophy.

Interview, New York/
The Christian Science Monitor, 3-21:31.

2

I am at the beginning of a new cycle of actors. Hollywood had the stage types in the '30s. Then it developed its own bigger, broad-shouldered type of acting — Kirk Douglas and Vic Mature and Burt Lancaster. Then it kind of went into the woodwork and started coming out with the cerebral types. But the world is bicycle wheels, and now again we are going to see the communicative actor, the actor who will be a hero, the actor who will inspire confidence and imitativeness in his viewers. Positiveness!

Newsweek, 4-11:72.

Rod Steiger
Actor

3

An actor is insecure, for openers, because he has no way of proving himself unless there's an audience. Without someone to watch and listen, an actor is just a raving maniac, shouting into the wind. Just as an audience is a vital part of the experience, so is the basic material. An actor can go out of his blazing mind waiting for the right part to come along. But if he waits long enough, he begins to feel like an athlete playing tennis without a ball, just swinging a racquet at thin air. So one day, in quiet desperation, he decides the time of his life is rushing by and he signs up for some dreadful movie.

Interview, Malibu, Calif./
Los Angeles Times, 1-23:(Home)20.

George Stevens, Jr.
Director, American Film Institute

4

There's nothing like seeing films on a big screen . . . I love the big canvas, seeing pictures "properly hung." Running [your] movie before 2,000 spectators is like a fiesta — people applauding, laughing, moved . . . Feelings come across in the movies, more than on the small TV tube with all the distractions . . . Movies are a special and even profound experience.

Interview, New York/
The Christian Science Monitor, 1-13:22.

James Stewart
Actor

5

The most important thing about acting is to approach it as a craft, not as art and not as some mysterious type of religion. You don't have to meditate to be an actor. And for heaven's sake, stay away from acting schools. The only way to learn is to act.

Interview, Beverly Hills, Calif./
"W": a Fairchild publication, 4-29:21.

Andrew Stone
Producer, Director

6

All I ever did was to keep my plots uncomplicated as possible. A complicated plot is exposition; and face it, exposition was dull a hundred years ago on the stage — and in film it's a disaster. I always worked my suspense films around the same logic: Get the leads in jeopardy before the titles are over, and you keep them in jeopardy for the whole picture, until the end titles come on. Underlining the whole thing are the Greek unities of time, place and action. *The Last Voyage* was 90 minutes long, and audiences knew the entire plot before the titles were finished. After that, we had no more exposition.

Interview/Los Angeles Herald-Examiner, 10-15:(B)6.

Peter Stone
Screenwriter

7

Directing a movie badly is the easiest task ever given to man — it's easier than falling down and breaking a tooth — but directing *well* is the hardest task of all. There's no question but that movies are a director's medium. If actors get phenomenal salaries, it's because *directors* — who make all the important choices — have decided they are worth it.

Interview, New York/The New York Times,
8-19:(C)8.

Susan Strasberg
Actress
1

There is something about a live audience that charges the adrenalin. You plug into the audience. In films, it's the camera. My mother told me that if I felt out of touch, and sometimes one does, to go up and touch the camera. It's like a good plumber relating to machinery. He accuses, "What are you doing to the garbage disposal?"

Interview, Los Angeles/
Los Angeles Herald-Examiner, 3-18:(B)1.

Ned Tanen
President, Universal Theatrical
Motion Pictures
2

Nobody sets out to make a bad picture; everything looks good when you start. Then there's that terrible moment when you look at the film and say, "What happened? What happened to the picture we started to make?" You ask yourself at 4:30 in the morning: "How could I pass that?" It's amazing so many good movies do get made. And boy, it sure is a cold slap in the face to make a picture that you love and then nobody cares to see. But the public is right — it picks it — and it's always right.

Interview, Los Angeles/
The New York Times, 8-7:18.

Marlo Thomas
Actress
3

We need women writing films and women directing and producing. It has been almost impossible for a woman to find a good role to play in films for years and years. The great roles have been for men, because men were writing them. No one can blame men for writing about their own experience, but we need the fullness of a woman's insight, a woman's voice, to say what we mean ... It is important that we encourage each other, welcome each other into the business, fight for each other's rights in the business. For half the world's joy, half its laughter, fully half the beauty and intelligence and insight available to the human race is in the minds and hearts of women. And, so far, only a tiny bit of it has been expressed.

At American Film Institute, Beverly Hills, Calif./
The Hollywood Reporter, 2-28:4.

Francois Truffaut
Director
4

The period of decadence [in films] began with James Bond. Before that, there were no parodies. Movie-makers had the ambition of telling you a story — to make you laugh or cry. Before the Bond pictures, parody was elitist, something for snobs. After the Bond pictures, parody became a popular form. After Bond, even Hitchcock had to be half self-parody. Parody came from the British, who were always ashamed of the cinema. The Americans were more pure. They were never ashamed. But now the Americans have taken over parody — all the films seem to be false film musicals, false science fiction. It's stupid to imitate the cinema of innocence — you can't imitate innocence. It sounds very cynical to say, but I think American movies were better when they were in the hands of the studios. In Europe we always admired Americans for the vitality of their films. Now I think we see less a vitality than a desire for vitality.

Interview, New York/
"W": a Fairchild publication, 10-28:5.

Liv Ullmann
Actress
5

I'm fond of half of Hollywood. There is generosity and warmth in Hollywood which is never talked about. There are people who will call you even when you are not on [the cover of] *TV Guide.* Of course the film-making there is much different from what I was used to with [Swedish director Ingmar] Bergman. They [in Hollywood] have this crazy star thing. You sit in your trailer and be "special," and that is a lonely and ridiculous thing. In Sweden, you're ashamed to drive around the streets in anything else than a Volkswagen; and that is healthier, I think — a shame of having too much — than Hollywood, where the shame is in having too little privilege, too small a car.

Interview, Washington/
The Washington Post, 3-8:(B)9.

Gore Vidal
Author
6

I don't think there is much of anything to directing. I've worked on about 15 movies, I

(GORE VIDAL)

suppose. I've done perhaps 100 live TV plays. I've done five plays on Broadway. I've never seen a director yet who contributed much of anything.

Interview/The Hollywood Reporter, 4-29:8.

King Vidor
Director 1

We [who made films during the silent era] believed in the articulate powers of pantomime; we felt the things we were doing were bigger than words. Words reduced the action, the emotions, the story we were trying to tell. It was like using words at the ballet. It made specific what we wanted to keep general. [With the advent of sound,] we could no longer appeal simultaneously to all audiences, to the various levels of age and intelligence and sophistication. People were no longer free to fill in their own words.

Interview, Paso Robles, Calif./ The New York Times, 1-14:(C)6.

2

Going to [film] festivals and looking back over your films, sometimes skipping 10 years or so from one to another, you begin to see a continuity. You see that your own life has rubbed off on your films. It couldn't help but do that. That is why the *auteur* theory developed, the discovery there is a certain way people make films. I began to see this about myself as I learned more about myself. My belief always was very strong in the individual, in the divinity of the individual. To me, that is what is interesting, to see now what was happening. You don't look consciously at those things when you are making a film. The realization comes later.

Interview, Dallas/ The Dallas Times Herald, 3-20:(K)3.

3

There's something magical and mystical in this profession that has smiled upon us ... We influence the world greatly ... a bunch of rugged individualists having to say what they want to say. It can't be taught in film schools;

you have to be born with the determination. I wouldn't have missed being a director for anything.

At luncheon sponsored by Motion Picture Academy, Beverly Hills, Calif./ Los Angeles Times, 4-8:(4)1.

Eli Wallach
Actor 4

Actors are insecure, and it's hard for me. When I was a kid in Brooklyn, for me to buy a suit was a family decision. Even now I walk in to buy a suit and, when a salesman comes toward me, I get scared and start to run away. You hear of actors wanting to keep the shirt or the shoes they wore in a picture. They're afraid they might need them.

Interview/ Los Angeles Herald-Examiner, 3-18:(B)2.

5

[On the kind of movies that were made when he was first starting out as an actor]: They played a lot of foreign films then. I'd sit and watch some of the greatest actors, in films that harnessed the human dilemma and tried to illuminate it — films by Bergman, Fellini and others. In America, now, they rarely do this. You have pictures like *The Deep*, which I'm in, and *Black Sunday*, which I saw recently. We're reaching the outer limit of thrill exploitation. One reason is that there's much more drama going on day in and day out, and depicted in the news with its murders, fires and all. The actual raid on Entebbe was much more exciting than any dramatization of it. The old films and plays used to point a moral. It was an educational entertainment as opposed to a visual thrill. But this emphatic response is what audiences want nowadays.

Interview, New York/ The Christian Science Monitor, 4-8:24.

Oskar Werner
Actor 6

I think the responsibility of an actor in a mass medium is very great. What influence we have! And I say violently that I rebel against the spirit of our time. With the bad taste of today's pictures, I would not like to be in 99

(OSKAR WERNER)

per cent of them. I'm a pacifist. I hate war. And I hate all the brutality and blood and pistols and pornography you see. I am not a voyeur; why should I look at this? Some works are so destructive that you don't know if you should have dinner afterward or commit suicide. I find it offensive. And we have such a great influence on youngsters. It's no wonder crime is going up. We advertise it all the time!

Interview, New York/
The Christian Science Monitor, 2-24:30.

Richard Widmark
Actor

1

[On being an actor] : I hate to say this, but I don't like that life. Early on, I decided the kind of life I wanted, and that's what I got, right or wrong. I was never so crazy about acting that I wanted to dedicate my life to it. I'm very lucky to be living the kind of dumb life I like to live. I hate cities, and I love farming and a million other things that have nothing to do with the theatre.... at this stage I just go along if someone wants me and [the part] looks enjoyable. Just say that I'm not a true artist. Hell — look at my age; I'm grateful if I wake up in the morning and I'm still breathing.

Interview/The New York Times, 3-4:(C)8.

2

The whole thing fell apart when they started calling movies "films" and began attaching social importance to them. Now they've become pompous, arrogant and boring, thanks to the critics. Movies aren't art. They're a collaborative craft. That's all they'll ever be. I worked for one of the greatest directors of them all, John Ford. He used to say, "I'm not an artist. I make movies." And sometimes his movies were art, but only because of the craft he put into them. Today's young actors and directors concentrate on the mechanics of the business. When you are aware of the camera movements or the director instead of the story, it's all over.

Interview, Los Angeles/
The Dallas Times Herald, 11-6:(F)2.

Gene Wilder
Actor

3

It's been my experience that a movie producer gets more money than anyone else for what is essentially a $6.50-an-hour job.

Interview/
"W": a Fairchild publication, 7-22:13.

Michael Winner
Director

4

Film audiences are people who are seeking light relief in a dark room for an hour and a half. There's nothing wrong with making popular entertainment. You have to say something about society at the same time. Some people see it, others don't. If 15 per cent see it, I'm happy. That proves it was there, because it was seen. People come up to me and say, "I like your work," as if they were saying something they had to keep secret. Whatever "serious" critics may say, I do approach my work very seriously. Of course, I work within the limits of only being able to make pictures others think will make money. It's unfortunate, but you must do it to remain an active director.

Interview, London/San Francisco Examiner &
Chronicle, 11-27:(Datebook)26.

Natalie Wood
Actress

5

I suppose it's not necessary to be neurotic to be an actor, but it helps. Most performers have some sort of neurosis or they wouldn't be actors in the first place. It's not normal for people to enjoy baring their feelings ... In a peculiar way, acting in a movie relieves you of making decisions, because everything is decided for you. You're told what time to get up, what clothes to put on, what you're going to say and do, what time you eat and what time you go home. You're even told who you are going to be and how you are going to feel. A performer's private life is easier to contend with in those circumstances because there are no decisions to make. The structure of the day can become so regimented that it eliminates a normal life altogether.

Interview, Los Angeles/
The Dallas Times Herald, 12-13:(B)6.

WHAT THEY SAID IN 1977

Joanne Woodward
Actress
1

Acting is making a fool of yourself; but it's wonderful to be able to do it on stage instead of everywhere else.

Interview/"W": a Fairchild publication, 1-7:2.

Frank Yablans
Producer
2

[On the trend toward more expensive pictures]: It's disastrous. If you bomb out with one picture you've blown it for the year. Paying an actor $2-million or $3-million for a picture is obscene. An actor can't have any respect for a picture if he's getting paid $2-million. Who's going to bother reading a script if you are going to get the $2-million anyway? . . . I'd love to have good reviews. I'd love to win an Academy Award. I'd like to be loved by everybody. But mostly I'd like to pay my bills.

*Interview,New York/
The New York Times, 7-15:(C)6.*

Robert Young
Actor
3

People are always coming up to me and talking to me about the good old days when I was at MGM. They weren't so hot. Those days were just as tough for people as these days are. I was scratching around trying to keep my head above water . . . Some really fine things were done in the way of movies then. But there was a lot of junk, too. The junk isn't shown on television now. They say we don't make films the way we used to. Ten, 25 years from now, they'll be saying how we don't make films the way they did in the '70s.

*Interview/Los Angeles
Herald-Examiner, 5-15:(TV Weekly)5.*

Richard D. Zanuck
Producer
4

This is a guts business, filled with dreams, disappointments and sadness. There's a lot of happiness and glory, too, for the winners . . . It's all kind of a giant guessing-game with gigantic stakes. You put in as much artistry and experience as you can, and you hope you guessed right.

*Interview/Flying-Colors (Braniff
International travel magazine), Vol.6,No.2.*

Efrem Zimbalist, Jr.
Actor
5

. . . I have no illusion about being one of the great ones. I became an actor for all the wrong reasons. I wasn't much good at anything else, and acting looked like a glamorous and easy career. I was reinforced by the discovery of a characteristic in common with other actors. Down beneath the layers of showmanship there's a terribly reclusive nature. Instead of outgoing relationships with the rest of the world, many actors find a sense of release only when they're acting.

*Interview, Los Angeles/
Los Angeles Times, 4-10:(Home)44.*

Fred Zinnemann
Director
6

[Commenting on what some say is the high moral tone of his films]: That stuff about morality — I don't know where that came from. I'm an old-line Hollywood director and my generation believes in entertaining the public. When people come out, I don't want them to feel they wasted their money. If they find a moral, too, okay.

*Interview, Schirmeck, France/
"W": a Fairchild publication, 1-7:19.*

7

I feel I'd be personally embarrassed to direct an excessive sexual scene. I'd rather let the audience imagine what it wants to, without getting too overt about it. I also hate showing violence as a means in itself. I'd hate to exploit or enjoy showing it. If I use violence, it's in a negative sense, not to tickle the audience. This is purely a personal feeling of embarrassment.

*Interview, New York/
The Christian Science Monitor, 12-9:28.*

MUSIC

Janet Baker
Art-song singer

1

A [musical] program must be of super quality and it has to be planned like a good meal with the right balance and contrast. People do like to hear fireworks, but these pieces are relatively easy. The difficult thing is to sing a work that is simple but deeply felt. If your audience understands you then, you have really succeeded. In this respect I like to think of myself as a door through which something much more important is coming. The real message is the great music which I have the privilege of singing — I only make the connection between the composer and whoever is listening to me . . . When I am up on the stage singing, all those people in the audience seem to be saying, "We want you to tell us something we want to hear." It's a marvelous process. It's magic, really.

Interview, New York/
The New York Times, 1-28:(C)8.

Tony Bennett
Singer

2

It gets to the point where one decides what comes first — the bucks or the people. Quality takes precedence. And to bring quality to an audience means not only the right material, but the right room, sound system and, most of all, mood. You've got to musically say something to people . . . If I can, I want to make my music a work of art — something that can be enjoyed and remembered forever. Nat [Cole] used to do that. When he recorded, he used a lot of care so that those recordings, going back years, sound like they were made just yesterday. He had the touch.

Interview, Los Angeles/
Los Angeles Herald-Examiner, 6-6:(B)1.

Leonard Bernstein
Composer, Conductor

3

In my case, I suppose I am a problem for critics trying to be objective; I haven't opted for one school or style or cult. I am very hard to pinpoint as either a performer or a composer. But they have to find a label for me, so a word like "flamboyant" attaches itself to me and becomes a sort of slogan. I'm so sick of that word, I can't tell you. Another reason I think I cause trouble is that the critic has one function he thinks important — to be the great interpreter, the middle-man between the artist and the audience. He interprets for the readers of his paper what happened the night before on the grounds that the audience couldn't possibly understand it deeply without him. He thinks of himself as John the Baptist telling the great unwashed masses what they could not know, or so the critic thinks, by themselves. And if I tend to go over the critics' heads directly to an audience, which apparently I do, the critics feel left out; their function has been voided. Now, if I err, which I do, on the side of stressing, underlining or overstating, it is in the interest of an educational, direct approach to the hearer. I feel everything I do is teaching, whether it is conducting a Beethoven symphony or lecturing at a university. But I do tend to eliminate the middle-man, and this is something he doesn't like.

Interview/The New York Times, 12-11:(2)38.

Anthony Bliss
Executive director,
Metropolitan Opera, New York

4

[On how the Met got into financial trouble] : The attitude used to be that we would announce, "We are Culture," and as soon as we opened our doors, we expected people to flock

421

WHAT THEY SAID IN 1977

(ANTHONY BLISS)

to us. We forgot the fact that the U.S. was built on aggressive salesmanship.

Interview/
"W": a Fairchild publication, 3-18:2.

Julius Bloom
Vice chairman and director of corporate
planning, Carnegie Hall, New York 1

The cost of putting on concerts keeps increasing. It means only the most successful performers can appear in the large halls. The others have to shift from large halls to medium ones to small ones to churches to the graveyard. We're living in a period where we've come to realize there's no one audience for good music. There are audiences. There are also different kinds of good music. They don't have to be presented in an orthodox way.

Interview/
"W": a Fairchild publication, 12-23:9.

Richard Bonynge
Music director, Australian
National Opera 2

To me, the voice is not only another instrument, but it is the greatest of all instruments. It not only communicates from within a person, but if that person's got a big heart *and* a big voice, no other instrument can begin to touch it, because it has such an emotional communication. And when people sitting in an audience can identify with the person and the voice on stage, then, of course, this is when all the magic starts to happen.

Interview, New York/
The Christian Science Monitor, 1-21:26.

Stan Cornyn
Executive vice president,
Warner Bros. Records 3

It seems to me, sitting in the same record company for 20 years, that I've seen a marked change in the nature of records that are being sold. They seem to be less widespread in terms of that awful word "demographics." There was a time, years ago, when you would find *The Sound of Music* as a prime record seller. I [do]

not want to be saddled with the impression that I [am] saying we should go out and all sign Steve Lawrence and Eydie Gorme to record contracts today and try to make them saleable to the public. What I really [am] saying is that we have narrowed the sort of material that you choose to record to what we might broadly call rock-and-roll. That has left not the fringes of our society but the majority of our society alienated from recorded music. Radio has become dominantly rock-and-roll, and that has restricted the exposure of other elements of our music. We've gotten into the rock-and-roll business rather than the music business.

At symposium, Los Angeles/
The New York Times, 5-22:(2)1.

Jimmy Dean
Singer 4

[On country music]: In my opinion, it is surging because of today's youth. When I started in country music, there were a lot of "closet" country listeners who would never admit it. If you listened to country, it was considered a reflection on your intelligence. But the kids of today are pretty darned honest. They do not listen to things because it's the "correct" thing to do. There's a lot less pseudosophistication in the children of today. If they like something, they say so — and it don't matter if it has steel guitars or fiddles or banjos.

Interview, New York/
The Christian Science Monitor, 4-29:27.

Neil Diamond
Singer, Songwriter 5

When I'm onstage, it's me. I'm not acting; I'm not trying to portray someone I'm not. I don't put on any airs; I'm straight. My music doesn't focus on any one group — it just talks about people, about love and life and loneliness. It's just me, and I think that audiences relate to that. What they see is what they get.
Interview/The Dallas Times Herald, 2-21:(C)7.

Placido Domingo
Opera singer

1

. . . there is a different element in my voice, and it is a quality of Spanish singers in general. In Italian tenors the predominant sound is that of metal — bright, pinging resonance that can cut through the orchestra like a knife. My voice has more of a cover to it, and the best Spanish voices, if they are well produced, have more velvet than metal. But velvety voices have a tendency to diminish in projection when they are tired, so I have to work very hard to build up my velvet to penetrate thicker orchestral sonorities. The secret is to keep the smooth texture, the flexibility, while you develop the power, and I have tried to do this so that my range of roles can be as wide as possible. In Italy, they call my voice "brown." I like that. If I compare it to a liquid I would say it resembles nothing alcoholic but, rather, dark chocolate. I also like to think of my voice as a long-lined lyrical instrument such as the cello — in fact, in rehearsal I often catch myself bowing to an imaginary cello as I sing.

Interview/The New York Times, 3-13:(2)17.

Arthur Fiedler
Conductor, Boston Pops Orchestra

2

There's really no borderline in music. I find that the "classical" listeners in our audiences enjoy the pops, and vice versa. I've never objected to young people listening to rock and roll — if they have any intelligence, they eventually go on to other music. I don't mean rock isn't good, but you tire of it. As a matter of fact, I find some classical nuts are more narrow-minded than young rock fans, who at least are willing to explore new things.

Interview, Boston/Parade, 2-27:16.

3

There are quite a few musicians who believe that the era of the great symphony orchestra is ending. They are very expensive to maintain, and I'm afraid some of them may not make it much further — although I hope I'm wrong. If that happens, the best we can hope for is that even though there will be fewer orchestras, they will be better ones.

Interview/U.S. News & World Report, 3-7:44.

Rudolf Firkusny
Pianist

4

The greatest difficulty in piano playing, of course, is to overcome the fact that the piano is a percussive instrument. I mean, you hit a note and it dies. With the violin or the voice you can make a crescendo, you can prolong a note, you can do all kinds of things; but in piano, the moment you hit a note — no matter how hard — it's dying. So I think one of the most difficult things in piano playing is to make it a kind of singing instrument. It's a question of pedaling, it's a question of phrasing, it's a question of all kinds of things. In a way, you have to fake — you can't do these different things you would like to do, so you have to fake in a way with all these helps, like phrasing especially, to make it not only a percussive instrument.

Interview, Dallas/
The Dallas Times Herald, 1-9:(H)6.

Carlisle Floyd
Opera composer-librettist

5

Opera in this country [the U.S.] has always been something of a hothouse flower; certainly not the girl next door, it carries some kind of a stigma. There is a very large American audience of rather well-to-do upper-middle-class people who are very disaffected from opera. They like the symphony, art, film, but they're simply turned off to opera.

Interview/The Washington Post, 6-19:(E)1.

Joseph Fuchs
Violinist

6

[On the training he received from violinist Franz Kneisel]: He said, "There's so much I taught you. Remember — if you keep 25 per cent, it's enough. If you keep 50 per cent, it's not as good as 25. If you keep 75, you're in danger. And if you keep 100, then God help you." That's gorgeous. Because what is the hallmark of a great player? Individuality. Today, the greatest compliment I can get is when somebody plays a record of mine and says, "You know, I knew from the first moment it was you."

Interview/The New York Times, 11-11:(C)9.

WHAT THEY SAID IN 1977

Carlo Maria Giulini
Musical director-designate,
Los Angeles Philharmonic Orchestra
1

I do not want to conduct too much. I need time to think. It is necessary. I always want to be a little hungry for music ... In Italy, football coaches make the players go for two, sometimes three, days without touching a ball. Then, when it is given back to them, it is a special event. A rehearsal must be a special event. Music is a secret, a mystery. How do vibrations produce a tone? Every concert is a miracle. The worst thing that could happen would be for music to become routine. I am an enemy of routine ...

Interview/Los Angeles Times, 5-1:(Calendar)68.

Benny Goodman
Bandleader, Clarinetist
2

[Saying the clarinet has all but disappeared]: They can't play it. It's a difficult instrument. And when they're making all that noise, you can't hear a clarinet. You can't just honk and make noises like you can with a sax. It goes back to basics. They've gotten away from basics, playing all these crazy sounds.

San Diego, Calif./
Los Angeles Times, 7-21:(1)2.

Marvin Hamlisch
Composer
3

Composing is a tough life. People think you have a hit and the money comes rolling in, but that's not the problem. That creates the problem. Now I have to think, "How can I beat *Chorus Line;* what can I do now to satisfy my need to write something as good?" And that is a much bigger problem than worrying, "Where am I gonna get the dollar-fifty for the hamburger tomorrow?" You cannot sit down and write it and say, "If it doesn't come today, I'm gonna kill myself. " No, you can't do it. I just wish I weren't so tough on me in terms of what my expectations are of me. I wish I could just sit back and relax and let it happen.

Interview, New York/
The Washington Post, 6-14:(B)2.

E. Y. (Yip) Harburg
Lyricist
4

When songs are convulsions or paroxysms, when the words are ragged and tough and demeaning — *light my fire, baby* — they lessen the person who hears them. Plato said that when the modes of music change, the laws of the state have to change. Music is the alarm. The songs of the kids today are not joyous. They're grim. Most of them are shrieks, cries in the wilderness, cries of fright at a world of bombs, missiles, Vietnam. The acid-rock-and-rollers, the shrieks you hear on the air, are a form of exorcism, a way of consoling themselves. I'm not bitter. In a way, I welcome their revolution, making things even uglier than the ugliness we gave them. But I deplore their lack of craftsmanship, their imitative music and poor rhymes.

Interview, Los Angeles/
The New York Times, 3-16:(C)15.

Vladimir Horowitz
Pianist
5

I don't play for politicians. I was asked many times to play at the White House. I turned down Eisenhower. I turned down Kennedy. I turned down Johnson. I turned down Nixon ... I don't play for politicians. They have dinner, then they have a few drinks, then they sit down half drunk, and they fidget and look at their watches while you play for 15 minutes. They don't understand what they are hearing.

News conference, Dallas/
The Dallas Times Herald, 2-21:(C)1.

Tom Jones
Singer
6

[On his show]: It's very sexual and it's aimed at women. If you sing a song that is sexy, you sure as hell can't sing it to men. I couldn't sing a song and not be sexual, unless I was in church singing a hymn or something. When I'm on stage I'm aware of sex most of the time. There is always a sex thing when any man is on stage. I don't know whether other singers realize it, but I do and I take advantage of it. I realize that I'm a man and that there are

(TOM JONES)

women in the audience and I should appeal to them. If I didn't, then I'm lacking something as a man. On stage I'm a different person. I have a wife and a son. My wife understands what's happening with me on stage. I get rid of a lot of tension and energy on stage. I'm expressing myself on stage. Being married or single doesn't matter when you're on stage. It doesn't matter whether you have 10 wives or one or none at all. I really get into the songs. On stage I become the person in the songs.

Interview, Los Angeles/
Los Angeles Times, 7-27:(4)14.

Garson Kanin
Author, Playwright

1

Opera is perhaps the single greatest art — for music, dance, poetry, story and graphics are combined.

Interview, Beverly Hills, Calif./
Los Angeles Herald-Examiner, 4-7:(B)3.

Herbert von Karajan
Music director and conductor,
Berlin Philharmonic Orchestra

2

We [conductors] don't actually fight an orchestra but there is a natural resistance toward the interpretation of any conductor, because pitting the creative mind against the recreative mind is always a struggle. Don't forget that we musicians have very little to go by. Dots on paper, that's all. That's the music. The tempi are indicated, the dynamics, too. But who can tell for sure what the composer intended? All we know is: A good thought well expressed will live forever.

News conference, Salzburg, Austria/
Daily Variety, 8-25:10.

3

I don't think the body is important. It is the spirit that never dies. The more you concentrate on a score, the more you realize the great masters never really died. Their spirit lives on.

Interview, Tokyo/
Los Angeles Herald-Examiner, 12-28:(B)5.

Peggy Lee
Singer

4

I have been accused of having an obsession with perfection. I get the impression that what that means to the general public is that everything I do has to be perfect. That's not so. It's striving to be better, striving for perfection — but there is no perfection.

Interview, San Francisco/San Francisco
Examiner & Chronicle, 1-30:(Datebook)14.

Eric Leinsdorf
Conductor

5

To know a work on purely musical grounds is insufficient, because it doesn't stick in the mind. As a conductor, you have to come up with something that is colorful, explicit and which, at the same time, fires the imagination. For example, at the sunrise of the second "Daphnis and Chloe" Suite, the conductor has to know exactly when the climax is reached; and, as I always say to the orchestra, there must be a sonority that is "blinding." I remind them: I didn't say "deafening." I had for many years been frightened to make these extra-territorial marks. But I'm no longer. Even if sometimes I know certain players will go out snickering and saying, "What the hell is he talking about?" I know what I'm talking about. This is all I'm studying today — the meaning of music.

Interview, New York/The New York Times,
1-2:(2)17.

Alan Jay Lerner
Lyricist

6

It's nothing for me to go three days to get that one line I want. Then I find the one key and suddenly it all opens up. Suddenly you reach out and catch it in the air. I get a line, or a few lines of lyric, or a page of dialogue, and, at that one moment, I get an exhilaration with that line, or those few verses, like no time else. At that moment, I'm probably as jubilant, as close to the real joy of living as I ever get. And, somehow, that makes it all seem worthwhile. It's maddening. But that's what's mysterious about it.

Interview, New York/
Los Angeles Times, 1-30:(1)3.

WHAT THEY SAID IN 1977

Loretta Lynn
Country-music singer

1

Country music is nothing but life. Every song that the country singer is singing is a true story to thousands and thousands of people. It just lays it out there, and sometimes the story ain't pretty — but sometimes life just ain't pretty. I think country-music fans like straight talk because not everybody can appreciate classical music or poetry. They don't like words that say one thing and mean another. Country music is real.

Interview/U.S. News & World Report, 10-24:71.

Yehudi Menuhin
Violinist

2

The whole beauty of the violin is you make your sound in your own image — your strengths, weaknesses, flexibilities, the way your blood flows, your temperament — that is you. I always wanted the music to speak. I wanted the listener to say, "Ah, yes, that is true." I didn't just want to play the violin — I wanted to say something.

*Interview, New York/
"W": a Fairchild publication, 4-29:13.*

Robert Merrill
Opera singer

3

Opera singers are a different breed from musical civilians. Basically, they are more sexy — or sex-oriented. Even before sex became the preoccupation of the general public, it was the preoccupation of opera singers . . . It is because we're in a very tough business. Grand opera produces the most hypochondriacal people in the world. So much depends on that one very delicate instrument called the throat, and the throat is always the first to give way — if you develop a cold, if you develop fright, even if you develop a strong emotion. The result of this constant concern for the throat is a preoccupation with sex — when it is permissible to make love and when it can destroy you. It leads to confusion, and a feast-or-famine situation.

*Interview/Los Angeles Herald-Examiner,
4-4:(B)2.*

Claus Moser
*Chairman, Royal Opera House,
Covent Garden, London*

4

I know my friends at the Metropolitan [Opera] in New York say they envy my secure government support; and, indeed, it is very good to have this solid foundation. But for it, we pay two prices. When we go after private money for special projects such as new productions — and we must raise 200,000 to 300,000 pounds a year for these purposes — the private people say: "Why do you need this? You're supported by the government anyway." The second price is the tendency of the public to complain that taxpayers' money is used to support a theatre that has high ticket prices and thus is directed to an audience that is better off financially than most.

*Interview, Chicago/
Los Angeles Times, 1-2:(Calendar)54.*

Magda Olivero
Opera singer

5

The voice is only 40 per cent of an operatic performance. The other 60 per cent is made up of innumerable intangibles. When I sing I do not think of singing, but of acting the character. Of course, to do this you need a great deal of vocal technique, otherwise it is impossible. But you must never think, oh dear, now I have to get myself ready for this high note. No, the voice has to be there automatically before you can travel beyond to what the composer is really asking for. One's technique should always be in service of the character until the technique itself disappears in front of the dramatic image.

Interview/The New York Times, 12-4:(2)32.

Eugene Ormandy
*Musical director,
Philadelphia Orchestra*

6

This new crop of conductors is marvelously talented, and so eager to make a success in two minutes. There is a very famous one who wants one leg in Berlin, one in London, one hand in Florence, the other in Paris. It can be done, of

(EUGENE ORMANDY)

course, but you must, in the end, belong to one orchestra.

Interview, Los Angeles/
Los Angeles Herald-Examiner, 7-20:(B)1.

Leontyne Price
Opera singer

1

In the last decade or two, serious music has become an integral part of our life — although unfortunately not as much as I'd like it. But, over all, the growth has been astounding. People are finally getting over the idea that opera is a luxury item that appeals only to a few. More and more people are coming to realize that opera is something very beautiful that nearly everyone can appreciate. If the old attitudes hadn't changed, I wouldn't be in opera.

Interview/U.S. News & World Report, 3-28:56.

Richard Rodgers
Composer

2

When I studied music, we were taught that there were three components — melody, harmony and rhythm. With some of the more recent developments, they seem to have left out the melody, most of the harmony, and you've only got a third left.

Interview, New York/
The New York Times, 6-22:34.

Linda Ronstadt
Singer

3

Success does mean you get to work with the best musicians, have the best sound equipment and have the best people handling your tours. That's a big help. But it doesn't get rid of your personal problems. I don't think any amount of applause or gold records can convince you about your singing. What does convince me is when I have a good night on stage; when I know I sang okay. That's the only thing that works and it just lasts for a little while. There are periods when I begin to think, "Jesus Christ, my nerves aren't going to stand this." Then, things get better for a while and I say, "Hey, this is great. I've got it all figured out.

I'm never giving up." I go back and forth like a Ping-Pong ball.

Interview, Cleveland/
The Los Angeles Times, 9-18:(Calendar)1.

Mstislav Rostropovich
Cellist; Musical director,
National Symphony Orchestra, Washington

4

The cello is like an imperfect woman whom you love for her imperfections. Through the cello I can speak with my own personal voice, without intermediaries between me and the audience.

Newsweek, 10-17:75.

Artur Rubinstein
Pianist

5

They [the audience] come after a good dinner. The women look at each other or . . . at other women's dresses. Men think mostly about business or some games or some sports or God knows what. And there I have this crowd not entirely quite musical, not really knowers of music, but who like music, who love music. And that is a very difficult proposition. I have to hold them, you know, in attention, by my emotion — nothing else. I can't look at them. I can't make faces. I can't tell them . . . now comes a great moment, now you listen, now is a great thing for you — nothing of the kind. I have to play. Look here, straight in front of me. But there is a certain antenna. There is a certain secret thing. There is a thing which goes out, emanates from me, from my emotion — not from me — from my emotion, from the feeling — you like to call it "soul" . . . It suddenly puts the audience into my hands. There is a moment where I feel them all here. I can do anything. I can hold them as one little note in the air. . . . they will not breathe because they wait what happens next, you know, what will come in the music. That is a great, great moment. Not always does it happen, but, when it does happen, it is a great moment in our lives.

Television interview/"Rubinstein at 90,"
Public Broadcasting Service, 1-26.

6

[On contemporary music]: Sometimes I fear it might really become the music of the

427

WHAT THEY SAID IN 1977

(ARTUR RUBINSTEIN)

future ... When [conductor Igor] Stravinsky spoke at Harvard University, he uttered this very bad sentence that "music does not need any emotion." Now, this is something absolutely, utterly, completely false. For me, this is treason of music. The existence of music is solely due to emotion. Of course, Stravinsky pretended, because he was never able to write any music without emotion. You would never get me to listen to music which has no emotion. Most people who go to such concerts do it because they are snobs who fear being called dated ... [But] the music of today is out of reach for me ... I have no right to judge what I do not understand.

Interview, Geneva/
The Dallas Times Herald, 12-16:(C)13.

Andres Segovia
Guitarist
1

An artist knows very well when acoustics are not good. When the people in the last rows do not hear, they do not applaud.

Interview, New York/
The New York Times, 2-15:20.

Beverly Sills
Opera singer
2

I sing for sheer pleasure. I only hope to God the audience enjoys it as much as I do. It's a great advantage to be a late bloomer. All the pressures are off. I feel I don't have to prove myself any more. I feel the public senses that. I'm relaxed, it's relaxed and not nervous, and it comes along with me for the ride. I'm just out there enjoying myself and the people realize this. They stop me in restaurants and call me by my first name. They say they always feel so friendly to me. I'm not by nature a machine. I'm not by nature a perfectionist. I do the best I can. If it's not good — so please come back and hear me the next time.

Interview/Los Angeles Times, 1-30:(1)3.

Leonard Slatkin
Conductor
3

[His advice for young conductors]: You've got to know the literature; you've got to go to all the concerts you can. There are certain things about conducting that can be taught — score reading, ear training, some rehearsal techniques — but there are also things that cannot be taught. How can you teach someone what to say to an orchestra, for instance? How do you teach communication? I think of it very much as a partnership. I am just another musician who happens to be a conductor. I can't play the clarinet; what right do I have to make a dictatorial decision about the clarinet? I don't see any reason to be unpleasant — actually, I don't think there ever was any reason for a conductor to be unpleasant, but that used to be the style.

Interview, Dallas/
The Dallas Times Herald, 1-16:(F)6.

Isaac Stern
Violinist
4

A prodigy is a kid who picks up a violin at 3 and can't live without it ... A prodigy should be encouraged, but he has to be handled with great care. What must be controlled is the greed of parents and teachers. The biggest problem is to encourage the child while letting him develop normally as well. A prodigy is a phenomenally talented child who can progress maybe four times faster than the normal child — but this still may be four times slower than his parents and teachers want. I've known prodigies who were burned out by the time they reached adulthood, because they were pushed too hard.

Interview, Dallas/
The Dallas Times Herald, 9-12:(B)4.

Rise Stevens
President, Mannes College of Music,
New York; Former opera singer
5

I loved the [opera] stage, and this is what I tell our young performers. They must feel love; the stage must be a friend. It becomes a question of security and confidence and, of

(RISE STEVENS)

course, can be gained only by regular opportunity to perform, suffer, enjoy and grow.

Interview, New York/
Los Angeles Times, 7-3:(Calendar)64.

Leopold Stokowski
Conductor
1

[On why he is still conducting at age 95] : It is the music, the music. Brahms, he has been in the grave a very long time. But his music lives. That is why I am here today.

Interview, London/
Los Angeles Times, 4-12:(1)4.

Jule Styne
Composer
2

With [lyricist] Steve Sondheim on *Gypsy,* I wrote all the music first. That's the healthy way. That way, you get the most out of the composer and you give the lyricist new rhythmic ideas. All lyric writers, except Oscar Hammerstein, have preconceived rhythmic patterns. When the music is written first, the lyricist will do his best job because he is not writing to his own preconceived rhythmic notions.

Interview, New York/
The New York Times, 1-16:(2)22.

Joan Sutherland
Opera singer
3

I think today there is a danger [for new singers] in listening too much to records and aiming for an effect and not knowing how the effect is reached. What is part of one voice is foreign to another voice and to try and imitate the end product without knowing how it is accomplished, or why, is very dangerous. I mean, someone said to me the other day, "I noticed when you go for your high notes that your chin is sort of flat and drops backward." And I said, "I do that because when I go for my high notes, I open my mouth very wide and I have the sort of face that's shaped that way . . . Don't *you* try and sing your high notes by

putting your chin back! That's terribly wrong!" It amazes me that people would think like that!

Interview, New York/
The Christian Science Monitor, 1-21:26.

Peter Ustinov
Actor, Director, Writer
4

[On his experiences directing opera] : [There are] among the younger singers, singers who are eager to act well, and there are some of the older ones who can't act at all; there are some who can act very well, but can't sing any more very well; and there are others, if you are unlucky, who can't do either very brilliantly and you have to — more than in the theatre — be a psychologist and try and drag some cohesion out of all this. And there are those who do exactly what you say during rehearsal and then, when the first act comes, they do what they did in some other previous production because it made them sing more easily . . . And then, just when you are most depressed, considering the enthusiasm of your beginnings, suddenly Mozart or Verdi or Puccini gallops to the rescue. And when the music is added, you wonder why you've taken such trouble, because that's what people want in any case. And they are absolutely right!

Interview, New York/
The Christian Science Monitor, 12-7:25.

Frederica von Stade
Opera singer
5

The opera- and theatre-going public is very different from what it used to be a few years ago. People are entertained to death by television, and it is necessary to give them something really exciting. It isn't enough any more just to provide live entertainment. Opera's growing popularity is the product of that search for something different. It combines the voice, instrumental music, drama and ballet in a way no other form of entertainment does. Audiences also are getting the benefit of up-to-date direction by some fine people in this country and Europe. All this is making new demands on singers, who have to act as well as sing with more vitality than was often the case before.

Interview/U.S. News & World Report, 11-7:52.

WHAT THEY SAID IN 1977

William Warfield
Singer

1

I think the general level of musicianship among singers these days, particularly among Americans, is on a very high level. The old days, when major singers could not even read music, are gone forever — I hope. [Ezio] Pinza, you know, never learned to read a score.

San Francisco Examiner & Chronicle,
3-27:(This World)2.

Andre Watts
Pianist

2

Music is a difficult, very competitive, field, and I suppose that's why there are so many mean musicians around today. They're often at each other's throats. But it wasn't always that way. The older musicians were much kinder to each other, and, even when they weren't, they were open about their feelings and not underhanded. I love the story about one famous pianist, just after a war broke out, who was told that another pianist was exempted from the draft. "What can you expect?" the first pianist said. "He has no fingers!"

Interview/U.S. News & World Report, 6-6:69.

Lawrence Welk
Musician; Orchestra leader

3

The kind of music that will last in America is sensible music — songs that have a melody and harmony that everybody understands. Rock and roll already has tamed down somewhat, and the type of music we play on my television program is attracting more and more young people. America doesn't like extremes for very long, and our music reflects this.

Interview/U.S. News & World Report, 1-24:69.

THE STAGE

Edward Albee
Playwright
1

A playwright is often at odds with the theatre, particularly one who tells the audience what it doesn't want to hear. I've had to go through a whole set of barriers. Not just the audience and critics, but actors and directors who don't seem to understand that their function is to deliver the script intact and not get in the way of the author's work. But it's nice being a playwright. I feel at home and comfortable with plays. There's an extraordinary immediacy, since everything's in the present tense and it's exciting to hold up a metaphoric mirror to reality.

At University of California,
Davis/San Francisco Examiner & Chronicle,
5-1:(Scene)10.

Jane Alexander
Actress
2

A good play distills the consciousness of the times and is a purveyor of things to come.

Interview, Dallas/
The Dallas Times Herald, 11-1:(B)1.

Craig Anderson
Producer
3

[On his being an Off-Broadway producer]: The commercial theatre is just not very good. It's star-tripping. The fact that *Fiddler [On the Roof]* is back with Zero Mostel, or that Yul Brynner comes in with *The King and I,* is a sign of bankruptcy. New York produces so much that's not serious — black musicals and white nonsense. We did our season at the Hudson Guild to 98 per cent capacity houses. We had to turn away 7,000 people in the last seven months. Our budget for the season is only

$40,000. For $600,000 I could mount a full repertory company.

Interview/The New York Times, 4-8:(C)2.

George Balanchine
Director, New York City Ballet
4

We dancers are more like horses, not like athletes, runners, baseball players. We have a different desire. An athlete is a man who runs hard and fast because he wants to win the race. We don't win anything — we are just beautiful things.

Before National Press Club, Washington,
March 3/The Washington Post, 3-4:(B)2.

5

[On whether he would take his company on another tour of the Soviet Union]: I will not return there. Younger people from the company may represent us there, but it's too defeating an environment and too uncomfortable a place for me. When we toured in '62, the authorities tried to censor my work. They objected to Stravinsky and Webern ballets and asked me to present Tchaikovsky instead. Of course I refused. The real audience was wildly enthusiastic. But those who attended, along with government officials, went through their routine of deadly, dutiful clapping. Too frightened to clap not at all, too frightened to stop before anyone else had, lest their insubordinate behavior be observed.

Interview/
Los Angeles Herald-Examiner, 3-4:(B)5.

Mikhail Baryshnikov
Ballet dancer
6

Celebrity is like having an extra lump of sugar in your coffee. It really doesn't mean very much to me. In fact, I think it's stupid to be

WHAT THEY SAID IN 1977

(MIKHAIL BARYSHNIKOV)

placed in such a position. To tell you the truth, my life hasn't basically changed all that much. I just do what I want to do and what I have to do. You know, I recently read an interview in *The [New York] Times* with Judith Jamison. At one point she says, "Don't call me a star. Just call me a dancer!" Well, that's exactly how *I* feel. Being a star has no meaning for me. Being a dancer is all I care about.

Interview/The New York Times, 11-13:(2)20.

Leonard Bernstein
Composer, Conductor
1

[On Broadway] people get scared of experiments. I mean, with *West Side Story* 20 years ago we took a very dangerous and experimental step. You see, I've always thought that the American musical would eventually spawn a kind of American opera — would grow into it — and *West Side* was certainly a step in that direction. Then I thought a lot of young composers would come along and take the next step, and the next one, and so I . . . sort of retired from Broadway for 10 to 12 years. And, to my amazement, that did not happen. It went backwards. It retrogressed. And I've been very disappointed in the course of the American musical ever since, with some exceptions . . . I had thought that American musical theatre would become a kind of natural native opera — not based on the European operatic style, but growing out of our own Broadway musical.

Interview, New York/
The Dallas Times Herald, 11-20:(H)7.

Theodore Bikel
Actor
2

Theatre is conceived as a huge money-maker by the public because they only see Broadway, not regional or workshop theatre. We haven't really got our feet wet yet. The U.S.A. is a Johnny-come-lately in terms of government interaction with the arts. The entire budget of the National Endowment [for the Arts] doesn't amount to the cost of one super nuclear sub. The Endowment's budget of $117-million

works out to 50 cents per person. It's not enough. Austria has an arts endowment equivalent to $2.40 per capita.

Interview, Beverly Hills, Calif./
Los Angeles Herald-Examiner, 10-6:(B)6.

Victor Borge
Entertainer, Musician
3

Actually, I feel most relaxed on the stage. I am my own master. I decide the tempo. I don't have to do anything that's given. I do whatever I feel at the moment. Nobody interrupts me, and all that I ever hear is civilized laughter. How can I ever tire doing this? Even when I go on with a heavy cold, when I'm not feeling well, it takes over. It is relaxing. The opposite of this was concertizing. I would live a year in a half hour. A mistake could ruin your career. I was scared. I was frightened. Around my 20th year, I knew that if I had to go through this for the rest of my life, I wouldn't last very long. So I stopped.

Interview/The New York Times, 9-30:(C)2.

Erik Bruhn
Ballet dancer
4

In America, there is so much emphasis on youth, some dancers think that's all they need — to be young forever. But in Europe, in Denmark where I was raised, there is a long tradition of respect for maturity. I remember seeing Youskevitch dance for the first time. He was in his mid-thirties, which nowadays is considered advanced for a dancer, and I remember thinking, when I get to be 35, that's when things will really start for me. But the world's attitudes changed so much, so suddenly, that by the time I reached 35, you couldn't afford to admit it — it felt wrong to be mature. The sad thing is that it takes maturity in a dancer to know what to do with the great classic roles; but just when you get there, the body is ready to depart from such roles.

Interview, Washington/
The Washington Post, 4-7:(C)17.

Ellen Burstyn
Actress

1

Ever since the Appollonian cults, there has been theatre wherein the mysteries of life have been enacted by priests and priestesses — who later became actors and actresses — who stand up before a gathering and perform certain designed rituals that talk about the human condition. The people looking respond in prayers and laughter and tears, and a feeling of understanding themselves better for having seen this. That was the birth of theatre. And it continues to the present day, when the most popular form is film. It's still basically that centuries-old ritual . . . People are still looking at their own lives through a reflection.

Interview, New York/
The Christian Science Monitor, 3-17:17.

Carol Channing
Actress

2

Opera is not an outgrowth of our [America's] mores. Neither is ballet. They're perfectly beautiful things from an era that is not our own. But the only contribution that the United States of America has made to the arts is musical comedy, and no other country in the world can do that. Years from now, they will be saying that this is the United States of America's art form. And I notice that even when the British do one of our musicals, it's really strange. You know, it's like an operetta. They just don't get it. They are well-schooled, but they just don't grow Jimmy Durantes there or Ethel Mermans or Mary Martins or people like that.

Interview, Houston, June 23/
The Dallas Times Herald, 6-27:(B)2.

Harold Clurman
Director

3

Directing is not staging. I can stage a play in six hours — where the actors should stand, how they should move, where the furniture should be, etc. — but the real job is conceiving the production, which may take months of thinking and reading and analyzing. So the real work is coming up with the conception of the play, and then somehow transmitting that to the actors — not always explicitly — and to the audience as well, without making them aware of your hand in it. The primary job of the director is to make his direction useless, in the sense of not sticking out, not robbing the production of its inner value.

San Francisco Examiner & Chronicle,
8-21:(Datebook)19.

Alexander H. Cohen
Producer

4

When all is said and done, the theatre is a "Hey, rube!" business. "Hey, rube!" is a circus expression. When anybody in the circus gets into trouble, he simply yells, "Hey, rube!," and everyone else drops what he's doing and rushes to his or her defense. That's what happens in the legitimate theatre. We're allowed to backbite and fight and disagree about the Tony [Award] nominations among ourselves. It's in the family, so to speak. But let any civilian come around and start criticizing, and we yell, "Hey, rube!" Basically, theatre people are lunatic and irreplaceable and full of impossible dreams. Put them in front of a live audience and you know what happens — it's magic.

The New York Times, 6-5:(2)7.

Tom Courtenay
Actor

5

[Broadway is] such a lottery, because success is so dependent on the reviews. You know, I have a rather good idea: People shouldn't go to the theatre at all. Instead, they should just buy leather-bound copies of the reviews. The actors would give the play for a week to allow the critics to see it, and then the actors would go off and do television while the critics wrote their reviews for the leatherbound books, which would be quite expensive, by the way. Say, I do think that's a rather clever idea . . . I [as an actor] don't want to [read reviews] . I have my feelings about a play and the people I'm working with, and I know more about what's going on than some critic, and I don't want to read his version — something he's written in 10 minutes. I just saw a play that got tremendous reviews, and it was a disgraceful play, it was impossible to follow. A lot of what happens in

WHAT THEY SAID IN 1977

(TOM COURTENAY)

the theatre is the emperor's clothes. Sometimes the very best things pass the critics by, and the most ornate, silly things draw them in.

Interview, Washington/
The New York Times, 1-30:(2)7.

Alfred de Liagre, Jr.
Producer

1

I got so discouraged, about five years ago, with the direction that theatre was taking — such a preoccupation with sexual deviation and obscenity. Seven or eight years ago I was at Yale, and a student asked me where the theatre was going. I said I wouldn't be surprised if someone didn't do a play called "The Toilet." Not long after, someone did.

Interview/The New York Times, 11-11:(C)2.

Agnes de Mille
Choreographer

2

Dances are the most fundamental castings of a civilization that we have, except for folk music. They tell you what a people is about. If you want to understand a nation, look at its dances and listen to its folk songs — don't pay any attention to its politicians.

Interview, New York/
"W": a Fairchild publication, 12-9:24.

Eliot Feld
Dancer, Choreographer

3

When I'm working, I'm either manic with elation or depressed with disappointment. And when I've finished a ballet, I'm lost, fearful that I'll never be able to do another. I'm always under the compulsion to begin a new work because the dancers need me to energize them, to keep them employed. I just hope that deep down something is going on, that I'm feeling something subliminally. The more I try to control the process, the more trouble I get into. I just start listening to music wildly, to all kinds, desperately, until I suddenly find music that crystallizes something inside me.

Interview/Newsweek, 3-21:61.

4

Dance brings to an audience something very different from the other fine arts — beautiful bodies. It also brings grace. That is what we are basically doing: presenting beautiful bodies that are capable of expression in a way that no other art form provides.

Interview/U.S. News & World Report, 10-10:68.

Burry Fredrik
Producer

5

People sometimes ask why produce a drama rather than a musical or a comedy. But in many respects, musicals or comedies are more difficult to do than dramas. Musicals are so complex and comedies generally don't have the depth of writing, while dramas have a filled-in plot line and delve psychologically into characters that are recognizable to the audience.

Interview/The New York Times, 9-18:(2)9.

Martha Graham
Dancer, Choreographer

6

Young dancers are much more facile than I've ever seen. I mean just that. Very little depth. My feeling — and I worry about it — is *what* are they dancing about. Why are they dancing, except physically, which is the language of dance and very important. The language of the human being, the inner language, is being neglected. They don't have to look deeply *because* they can do so much physically. They don't go into the cave. They are well-trained bodies but not well-trained in their adjustment to life, or in recognition of their mission. Dancers today don't go into the meaning of things. I don't mean you have to dance a message. But people must feel your completeness and not just physical virtuosity. Civilization is at its height when you see a great dancer. Then you see the human race in its potential. You see a person willing to work and to dare. [Young dancers today] are willing to work — but not to dare.

Interview/The New York Times, 5-15:(2)15.

George Grizzard
Actor

7

When I was little, I wanted to be a cowboy movie star — a Tom Mix or Hoot Gibson. But,

434

(GEORGE GRIZZARD)

when I started seeing theatre and reading about the reigning stars of the theatre, like Helen Hayes and the Lunts, I knew that's what I wanted to be. They were not the same in every play, whereas actors in movies were always basically the same. Most successful movie stars play themselves. They're personalities. I figured that the art of acting was in playing somebody else and making people believe you.

Interview, New York/
After Dark, February:50.

Charlton Heston
Actor

1

Anyone involved with a play finds the last week of rehearsal very demanding and draining. Anyone, period. Especially the playwright. He has worries right up to the last moment that he might have done something better. And if he doesn't get the reception he hoped for, he's worried even more. Even if you're a Neil Simon.

Los Angeles/
Los Angeles Herald-Examiner, 10-3:(B)3.

Arthur Hill
Actor

2

...I've never won a popularity contest among my fellow actors. Not that I'm intentionally rude. But I've never been known as Mr. Congeniality. Working on the stage, for example, many actors are inclined to hang around together doing a post-mortem after the evening performance. But during many years in the theatre I was always a sort of Mr. Seldom Seen. Every night, seconds after the curtain rang down, you could hear them say, "There goes Arthur. He's out the door already." I'm sure my haste has often been interpreted as a self-centered refusal to be sociable; but when a play's over I just want to get the hell out of there.

Interview, Los Angeles/
Los Angeles Times, 7-24:(Home)30.

Robin Howard
Director, London Contemporary
Dance Theatre

3

We've been trying to build a logical and verbal world, and we have forgotten the body and the spirit. Dance can bring this back into the correct relationship with the mind. Youngsters from every political regime and religion can meet naturally, because they are prepared to hold hands and dance in the park together. I have an obsession with this lopsided area of the world and that is why I am in dance. That's why our organization teaches in youth programs. Dance is one of the areas where people can meet as themselves.

Interview/The New York Times, 6-26:(2)22.

Garson Kanin
Author, Playwright

4

The difference between literature and writing plays is that the playwright draws prints and specifications of parts that actors and actresses are eventually going to have to collaborate with, acting as a spokesperson between you and the audience. With a novel, each reader is the collaborator.

Interview, Beverly Hills, Calif./
Los Angeles Herald-Examiner, 4-7:(B)1.

Gene Kelly
Actor, Dancer

5

Being a dancer is closely allied to being an athlete, on which my whole style is based. Dancing is a very tough job; it's like playing football. You have to extend yourself if you want to be good. You can dance till you're old and gray if you want to do just what you can do. But if you want to be very good ... you have to go to the outer limits; you don't want to stay within the limits of your abilities.

Interview, Washington/
The Christian Science Monitor, 12-5:46.

Deborah Kerr
Actress

6

[On performing on stage]: It's like a drug — although it's a nice drug. I think it has something to do with the power — and I say

WHAT THEY SAID IN 1977

(DEBORAH KERR)

this most humbly — of controlling an audience. In movies you have no control except that you know what you can give. But there's not that immediate challenge of facing a noisy group and quieting them down and making them listen to you. One of the largest rewards in the theatre is feeling you are touching people with some kind of emotion and getting it back. Except on those days when you get nothing back. Then you want to cut your throat . . . As an audience member, I love the moment when all the lights go down and the curtain comes up; but as a participant, I'm throwing up in the wings. But I really love the theatre, even though before one goes on one thinks, "Why am I doing this to myself?" But it's all part and parcel of the business, and it's like a bullfighter overcoming his fear. That's why I like bullfights. They're so much like the theatre.

Interview, Los Angeles/
The Hollywood Reporter, 2-17:8.

1

I think it must be frightfully difficult [for an actor] to cope with success without an apprenticeship, as can happen. All of it is necessary: the working, being turned down, getting parts, flogging around to the agents' offices with your photographs and lying your head off about how many things that you've done when you haven't. It's a good bedrock to have, really. I did all of that. I also managed to get myself in a couple of seasons at the Oxford Repertory Company, which is invaluable to anyone who wants to act. One week you're the lead; the next you're the maid; the week after that, you are the assistant stage manager; and the week after that, you're painting the scenery.

Interview/Los Angeles
Herald-Examiner, 3-3:(B)1.

Richard Kiley
Actor

2

There's a curious line of demarcation with the footlights. If you are shy, it's almost an internal Maginot Line. I think that the prosce-

nium — that protective arch — has a kind of magic about it, a removal factor.

Interview, Washington/
The Washington Post, 8-20:(B)1.

Burt Lancaster
Actor

3

I don't know why most playwrights [in the American theatre] seem to be coming from England. There's enough to write about in America. But then, we [in the U.S.] don't even have a national theatre. Mediocrity seems to be our norm.

Interview/
"W": a Fairchild publication, 3-18:2.

Eva Le Gallienne
Actress

4

It's the unions, really, that have raised the prices [of theatre] so enormously, and I don't know what one can do about that. It does cost an awful lot to put on a play. It's just dreadful — even a play with one set and not a lot of costumes; it costs a terrible lot, people don't realize it. Managers think they've got to charge so much. But I don't see how people can afford to go to the theatre. And the funny part is I feel that the people who really love the theatre are those who don't have a great deal of money. They don't go to the theatre because it's the thing to do or because they can put it on their expense accounts as entertainment; they go because they love the theatre and acting.

Interview, Los Angeles/Los Angeles
Herald-Examiner, 1-18:(B)1.

Murray Lewis
Modern-dance choreographer

5

To be frank about it, I don't know how much the character of modern dance can withstand the refinement that the ballet insists upon. And I don't know how long ballet can withstand the audacity that modern dance is bringing to it — the sass, the weight . . . The fact is, if modern dance and ballet are going to submit to each other, both forms will lose their identity. I'm not holding out, really, but I think there is always the weakness of dilution, before

(MURRAY LEWIS)

the next strength can be developed, and I believe both modern dance and ballet will suffer during this period of transition.

Interview/The New York Times, 2-6:(2)28.

Joshua Logan
Director, Playwright

1

The whole of entertainment cannot exist without theatre. If the stage dies, then so do the rest. Nothing mechanical can match what happens when a live cast faces a live audience. You get more creativity in those moments than anywhere else.

Interview, London/San Francisco Examiner & Chronicle, 6-19:(Datebook)14.

Marcel Marceau
Mime

2

A real artist should not care about what a producer says to him; he should do what he feels is right, as long as he keeps his style. If he feels he has to experience new dimensions, even if he is in advance of his time, he should experience them. We should be ahead of our time, even when we are witnesses and we reflect our time. An artist has to live a total life; he is not only an entertainer. I like the public to laugh and to cry, but I like also to disturb them, to create a consciousness in their minds. I am a silent witness of my time . . . An artist has to experience in his traumatism, in his world, in his subconscious; he has to fix on the stage the world we live in. Not only the world, but all the ideas he gets from imagining a world. All that he senses the public does not sense, like a seeing brother. He has to show them the light. He has to care about style, perfection and touching the public, but in no way has he only to want to please the public. Life is very exciting; often it is bigger than reality: What is real to us can suddenly be overthrown by something we don't expect.

Interview, Los Angeles/
The Christian Science Monitor, 2-2:26.

3

There are more than 400 young mime groups in this country [the U.S.] now. There is a mime craze. They are just in awe over this art form. They want to know everything of the history of mime. They have become aware of the silent movie stars — Chaplin, Keaton . . . Mime transcends national barriers; the spoken word cannot.

At press luncheon in his honor, Washington/
The Dallas Times Herald, 6-21:(B)5.

Alec McCowen
Actor

4

It's strange being an actor. We lead a kind of heightened existence when we're performing, but our lives are also full of frustration and ambivalence. Maybe that's why we usually huddle together for protection. To survive, an actor needs extraordinary quotients of the active and the passive in his makeup. Passive in that you have to wait for the phone to ring; passive in that you have to please a great many people — agent, producer, director, playwright, even the secretary who may get you to that producer or director. You have to take so much nonsense from so many people, maybe for years. And in spite of the bad breaks, the disappointments, you must hold on to your innocence, you must remain open and receptive no matter how much you get hurt. And then comes that moment, if you're lucky, when you step out in front of an audience — and suddenly you can't be passive any more. You have to be aggressive. You have to deliver, take the stage, be the boss.

Interview, New York/
The New York Times, 2-27:(2)6.

David Merrick
Producer

5

Some people think Broadway is dying, but it's not. They're selling an awful lot of tickets to largely meretricious plays. Business is very good. Sadly, there are many, many revivals and not enough new plays. I object to most revivals because we ought to be trying new things and advancing . . . The highest-quality drama being produced in this country today is in films. The reason is that Hollywood pays good money, and some of the best actors and writers are now in California. Even the character actors can earn

437

WHAT THEY SAID IN 1977

(DAVID MERRICK)

a good living there — in films and a commercial or two — and they can't do it on Broadway. They have to wait too long between jobs. It's difficult to cast a play in New York. You can get some stars, but there aren't enough of the good character actors around.

Interview/U.S. News & World Report, 7-18:61.

Anthony Newley
Actor, Singer, Composer 1

There is no such thing as a musical any more. What is there? A show like *A Chorus Line*, which is really a stripped-down version of what we used to call a musical. Rock musicals? I hate rock musicals.

Interview, Beverly Hills, Calif./
The Dallas Times Herald, 4-10:(F)6.

Mike Nichols
Director 2

... one of the many pleasures of directing is that I don't have to experience that baby feeling that comes with acting. You know ... "I don't like my dressing-room" and "Who stole my mascara?" I feel more adult as a director. It's like being a father in real life.

Interview/People, 1-10:79.

3

All my life I've wanted to be a producer. To me, a producer is the guy who comes in once every three weeks or so and says the shoes are wrong. It's the ideal job.

Time, 3-14:33.

4

Some plays are just blah, nothing. I hate theatre like that. I believe that when the audience gathers, it's full of great expectations. Otherwise, it wouldn't have come. They're there. It's an event before it starts, and *that's* where the challenge is. It must continue throughout to be an event. The way things have gotten, economics, tickets for $15 and up, it's hard to get at that feeling. So, with it getting out of hand in New York, theatres like Long Wharf [in New Haven] and Arena [in Washing-

ton] are where the action is. It's not a great crisis, nerve-jangling kind of thing. Only in that way can work be done. The need has resulted in smaller theatres, smaller plays.

Interview, Washington/
The Washington Post, 3-2:(B)2.

Stuart Ostrow
Producer 5

[On the good response to a newspaper ad he ran soliciting the public to invest in shows]: When the big Broadway angels disappeared, investors became more traditional in their tastes, played it closer to their vests. But theatre isn't a business. It never has been and never will [be]. The response to the ad says to me there are people out there who want to be patrons of the arts. Boy, oh boy! Think of the kind of theatre that could be produced with them!

The New York Times, 12-30:(C)2.

Joseph Papp
Producer, New York
Shakespeare Festival 6

[On the theatre world's "Tony" awards]: I feel better when I lose "Tonys" than when I win them. When I win, I become part of that Broadway thing. When I lose, it makes me feel clean. It defines me again.

Interview/Newsweek, 6-27:57.

7

The most popular, democratic way to fund non-profit theatre is through government. After all, the government represents the public's tax money. I hate subsidy. I love the free market. Ideally, it would be fine if we could live off the productions that we do, with the public supporting us by buying tickets. But it is impossible in an institutional setup. You have an obligation to keep producing, break certain barriers, provide a forum for new ideas, new writers. A Broadway producer doesn't have to do that — he just has to make money.

Interview/
The Christian Science Monitor, 8-31:22.

Stephen Porter
Director

1

People are always talking about style in relation to my work. Actually, the more I do and the older I get, the more it seems to me that style simply is the realism of another time. Of course, no one ever really talked the way people talk in [Oscar] Wilde's plays. Or talked ceaselessly in rhyme, like the people in Moliere. But you try to think yourself into a state of mind where people can do that.

Interview, New York/
The New York Times, 6-12:(2)3.

Robert Preston
Actor

2

I've been asked to revive *[The Music Man]*. *My Fair Lady* came back. Zero [Mostel] came back. Yul [Brynner] is coming back. But I don't want to be the one who makes the theatre people say, "Not another revival." I did it *[Music Man]* 18 years ago and ran a four-minute mile. Now I feel fine vocally, but I'd probably run a six-minute mile. Also, what the hell would I do it for? I'd only make a lot of money.

Interview/The New York Times, 4-1:(C)2.

John Reardon
Singer, Actor

3

Musical theatre has been in a slump for a long time, and strangely enough it wasn't rock that did it. It was *My Fair Lady* which dealt almost a death blow to singing leading men. When you think of the musicals that came along after that, like *The Music Man,* singing wasn't what they wanted. They wanted a song-speech kind of thing . . . It's a symptom of our times, this new kind of longing for beautiful melody and sentimental story and that sort of thing. I think people are kind of tired, really, of the slick, cynical musical. I mean, all you do is go and hear, in rhymes, how unpalatable marriage is, and how working is no fun either, and living isn't much, you know, but you say it in slick rhymes and some sort of music which you don't remember when you get out of the theatre. I think we're really going to go into a more healthy period.

Interview, Los Angeles/San Francisco Examiner
& Chronicle, 10-30:(Datebook)17.

Herbert Ross
Director

4

When you work with an actor in a movie, you get him to do a moment well just once. In theatre, you get to that place and then discover you have to go on and develop such a foundation that he can recreate that moment eight times a week.

Interview, New York/
Los Angeles Herald-Examiner, 12-27:(B)3.

Alan Schneider
Director

5

I don't believe in a National Theatre to be housed in one building. When we have 200 major theatres in this country — when every city has at least one major theatre as part of its cultural life — then we'll have a genuine national theatre. I support institutionalized theatres, subsidized companies that don't have to worry about the hits-and-flops syndrome to stay alive. The English theatre does so many awful plays, but they do so many good ones as well. Here [in the U.S.] everything has to be a smash-hit all the time, with the result being that producers are afraid to try anything new. Theatre is like air: You have to breathe it all the time, not occasionally. Theatre is special because it's necessary; it's not an accidental thing, like a trip to Disneyland.

Interview, San Francisco/San Francisco
Examiner & Chronicle, 5-1:(Datebook)25.

6

I bled internally at certain reviews, especially those of Clive Barnes. But critics can help and hurt; I never minded getting clobbered by Brooks Atkinson, for example, because he really cared about the theatre, whereas the present generation of New York critics have hardly any respect for it. They're like scramblers around a ring. It's unfortunate that critics have this power, especially since they hardly ever really get into the theatre enough, as

WHAT THEY SAID IN 1977

observers and practitioners. Soviet critics, for example, have to study and work in the theatre before they can begin writing.

Interview, San Francisco/San Francisco Examiner & Chronicle, 5-1:(Datebook)25.

George C. Scott
Actor
1

In stage acting, the fulfillment comes in your relationship with the audience. When it works, when the audience is with you, there's nothing more rewarding; it's like riding a terrific roller-coaster. And when you don't have that relationship, you're disgusted and revolted and hurt and confused.

*Interview, New York/
The Miami Herald, 1-23:(H)3.*

Andrei Serban
Director
2

I make theatre because I don't know what it is and because I feel the need to. It's a certain joy. It's a certain inner sexual pleasure. But it's more than that. I am aware that in true theatre something is available that can lead us to discoveries as important as nuclear energy. None of us has really found it. The fact that the theatre is still a word on our lips today, even though it's almost entirely dead — there are a few maniacs still doing it — there's still a hope it's alive because it's connected with an ancient source which isn't lost.

*Interview, New York/
The New York Times, 2-13:50.*

Neil Simon
Playwright, Screenwriter
3

It's hard to explain when things are going well. Sometimes when I write something I like, I ask, "Who wrote that?" And I tell myself, "I didn't. I don't know where it came from" . . . And yet, I do know this: I think a writer's sensitive antenna picks up things he's not aware of. Like a sponge picks up water. And it just lays there until it's ready to be used.

*Beverly Hills, Calif./
Los Angeles Times, 1-30:(1)3.*

4

[Saying he prefers to write plays rather than films]: I like the confinement of the stage. I can see in my mind what the audience is going to see. I can control the rhythm of the piece. The dialogue goes at a certain pace. I write rhythmically. How many words here, how many words there. I say them aloud. But I can't control the rhythm of a movie. I never know where the camera is going to be. The camera breaks the rhythm.

*Interview, Culver City, Calif./
The New York Times, 3-30:24.*

Roger L. Stevens
Chairman, Kennedy Center for the Performing Arts, Washington
5

Maybe there is a need for some [government] subsidy of certain theatre groups. But if people are left alone to work out their own problems instead of depending upon "Big Brother," they're better off, even if they obviously need some money from government for certain things. The Metropolitan Opera had a $12-million deficit and they managed to raise the money. If they had not had to, they wouldn't have. I like the pressure of efficient operations. I'm all for subsidizing young artists. But if you're going to be a professional producer, part of the job is raising money. I believe that total subsidy in the case of institutional theatre — as well as any other institutional cultural form — can be very wasteful . . . and in the long run harmful.

*Interview/
The Christian Science Monitor, 8-31:22.*

Lee Strasberg
Artistic director, Actors Studio
6

Acting on screen can be as great as on stage, but on-stage the high quality is obligatory; it can't be faked. That's why stage work is still the primary training. Our people go easily from stage to screen or TV, but you can't automatically go the other way. And, of course, you don't have that basic difficulty in the movies — the need to repeat. So the stage gives a truer image of your capacity.

*Interview, New York/
The Christian Science Monitor, 3-10:26.*

Jule Styne
Composer

1

[On where the musical theatre is going]: I sat back for three years doing a couple of movies, but mostly watching and waiting. *A Chorus Line* was fresh, new, and we all said, "This is different." Then along comes *Annie* — the flag, orphans, a dog; it's *Oliver* in drag. Who knows what will work now in a musical? The rock sound doesn't work. It's not dramatic. All the characters sound alike. But what do I know? Here I am sitting here, but what do I know?

*Interview, New York/
The New York Times, 5-27:(C)2.*

Edward Villella
Ballet dancer

2

To me, the ultimate idea is total concentration, to eliminate all impeding outside ideas and thoughts. So the moment I step on stage, I have a straight line of concentration. From then on, everything is spontaneous, a conditioned reflex. You can't think your way through a performance. When I have those fantastic moments, when all is happening right, it's so easy. I say to myself, "My God, it's so easy."

Interview/Los Angeles Times, 1-30:(1)3.

Eli Wallach
Actor

3

[On the future of the theatre]: The fabulous invalid is quite healthy, because nothing yet devised by man has been able to replace theatre. Neither movies nor TV can equal that experience of going in and having the lights come down and seeing a play. It's like watching a football game: On TV you can see it *better*, but it's not like really being there.

*Interview, New York/
The Christian Science Monitor, 4-8:24.*

Andy Warhol
Artist

4

Unfortunately, drama critics ruin plays, and that's too bad. Often I go to a play before a critic has reviewed it, and I love it. Then his review comes out, and it sounds terrible — just like it was two different plays! And people who trust that critic won't go to the play or movie, and it's ruined. I prefer reporters who simply say what the movie or play was all about, and let the audience decide for itself whether it likes it.

*Interview/
U.S. News & World Report,
6-27:57.*

Oskar Werner
Actor

5

[Comparing stage and screen]: The two media are completely opposite and different . . . I would compare the theatre to music. The score might be *Hamlet*. You have to cast it as if you had a flute, a fiddle, a trumpet. If one plays off-key, the whole thing is off-key. And with the last word or the last beat, communication with the public is over. You might reproduce it the next day, but it will be different . . . Film, on the other hand, is close to the fine arts. It only becomes a piece of art when there is an observer. It is like a canvas on a wall — only when the roll of celluloid is running can it be a Charlie Chaplin masterpiece or a piece of phony porn.

*Interview, New York/
The Christian Science Monitor,
2-24:30.*

TELEVISION AND RADIO

Lucille Ball
Actress, Comedienne

1

They change presidents at CBS so fast nowadays that I can't keep up with them. No sooner do I know what the new president looks like, than he has been fired and there's another one. People who don't know showbiz make the decisions about showbiz. But then the question is, who does know showbiz?

Interview, Los Angeles/Los Angeles Herald-Examiner, 11-21:(B)1.

2

It's a wild medium, television. The closeness of it! It was apparent from the first two years we were on the air [in the 1950s]. At the time, it was a great surprise because we had no idea that people would run up and want to touch you. We had to get used to it, because they had never done that before. But they felt so close to you because you had been in their living-rooms. Now, of course, it's old hat. Everybody knows it. Television is the quickest form of recognition in the world.

Interview, Los Angeles/ The Dallas Times Herald, 11-27:(D)12.

Robert Blake
Actor

3

Once a [TV] series is sold, the profit comes from making it as quickly and as cheaply and as efficiently as possible, with the cheapest writers and directors. You [the star] have a personal incentive for doing the best you can, but there's no corporate incentive to back you up. A series is really the opposite of a movie-for-television in that way. In the movie, you're always trying to do the best you can for the money because you've only got that one shot at it. But there's

always tomorrow on a series, and if somebody starts screaming too loud you can fix it up.

Interview, Los Angeles/ Los Angeles Times, 4-24:(Calendar)31.

Richard Boone
Actor

4

Television is capable of doing some great things. We're not even touching its potential. It aggravates me more than I can say. Now they've "discovered" the anthology. What did they think I was trying to do 10 years ago? That goes on my tombstone: "Ten years ahead of his time."

Interview, Beverly Hills, Calif./San Francisco Examiner & Chronicle, 2-13:(Datebook)27.

Daniel J. Boorstin
Librarian of Congress of the United States; Historian

5

I think the fact that mankind has survived television is an encouraging sign.

Discussion/"Today" show, National Broadcasting Company Television, 1-14.

6

The act, or rather the non-act, of television viewing now constitutes more of our citizens' and our children's waking hours than is spent reading or eating, and almost as many hours as are spent sleeping. This is revolution. This has revised our American vocabulary and now governs our times of rising and of eating and of retiring, the hours set for public events, the schedule of our daily lives. Television has become the authenticating experience. We can no longer say, with Oscar Wilde, that life imitates art, for now life imitates television.

At dedication of National Humanities Center at Research Triangle Park, North Carolina/ The Washington Post, 4-24(H)3.

Allan Burns
Producer

1

There was a time, perhaps 15 or 20 years ago, when the areas of television to which the networks pointed with the most pride, I think, were the drama shows — human dramas, dramas about important topical subject matter. I think those types of shows have almost disappeared in favor of the action shows, euphemistically called action shows, which are substitutions for violence.

Los Angeles Times, 6-27:(1)3.

Red Buttons
Actor

2

Look what's happening in the television business. Shows are being canceled right and left. When you finally get into one, you don't have any idea how long it's going to last. There are so many trapdoors for the actor. Where are the guys in a network who can look at something and say, "That's good" or, "That's bad"? Where are such people? They don't seem to have anybody. They all try to lay the decision off on somebody or something else. This wild way of doing things is here to stay.

*Interview/Los Angeles Herald-Examiner,
6-5:(TV Weekly)6.*

Johnny Carson
TV talk-show host

3

Basically, our show *[The Tonight Show]* puts the accent on comedy. And when we get criticized for being superficial, we don't really have to defend ourselves — just as Ed Sullivan didn't have to defend his show, or Dean Martin or Jack Benny or Red Skelton or anybody else. I don't know why people always call us a talk show. I don't particularly like that label. To me, *The David Susskind Show* is a talk show, where you sit down and discuss socially relevant issues. Our show is basically entertainment. You know, it's very easy to sit down and say, "Well, tonight we'll discuss recidivism in prison." Hell, you bring somebody on and get yourself a clipboard and say, "Now, tell me — what do you think of capital punishment?" And you sit back and let the guy talk for 20 minutes. That's much easier than what I do every night.

*Interview, Burbank, Calif./
The Dallas Times Herald, 1-17:(C)6.*

Dick Cavett
TV talk-show host

4

Being on TV every night is something you don't think you could ever miss while you are doing it. But later, you can. When the pressure's gone, it's like being over a headache. It's like remembering a day when you had a terrific headache and you went to the circus. But you only remember the circus, and so it seems like it was fun.

*Interview, New York/
The Washington Post, 7-6:(B)11.*

5

I could maybe make a case that the sitcom would disappear, along with those crappy TV-movies. But the talk show? It's one of the few things television does well. It will last forever.

TV Guide, 7-30:6.

Dick Clark
Television personality

6

The faultless formulas of television, the ones that last, are so simple. I guess that's the reason they last ... I am absolutely convinced it was more fun then [in the early years of TV]. It was more earthy; it had an essence. Today, it's very sterile. We've got to the point of perfection where you can watch, and the damn thing has no heart.

*Interview, New York/
The Dallas Times Herald, 2-4:(C)8.*

James E. Duffy
*President, American Broadcasting Company
Television Network*

7

Broadly speaking, there are only three directions in which we [in TV] can go in the years ahead. We can continue the system largely as it has evolved and as it is today, constantly striving to improve its quality and responsiveness. Or we can take a turn to the right toward

WHAT THEY SAID IN 1977

(JAMES E. DUFFY)

a system which is tightly controlled. Or we can take a turn to the left, in an egalitarian direction, toward a fragmented system which might go totally out of control. I say let's go straight ahead. I don't think that either of the other two alternatives is imminent. But the pressures are there, and nothing in the world is immutable, certainly not in an industry that's only 30 years old.

Before Oregon State Broadcasters
Association, Mount Hood, Ore./
The Hollywood Reporter, 6-28:14.

Charles Ferris
Chairman, Federal Communications
Commission 1

The First Amendment is something, as a lawyer, I cherish ... I am very hesitant for government to be prescribing actual [TV] program content. The end doesn't justify the means, even though it probably would seem best that we could say that "this shall not occur on television." If we have the capacity to do that, I fear the implications of the abuse of that type of government involvement.

Interview/
The Christian Science Monitor, 12-8:1.

John Fowles
Author 2

I was watching the Emmy Awards the other night and it was [appalling] — all the narcissism and self-adulation of it. And when they go sincere, you can see it trickling off the edge of the screen. The boosterism of television is sickening. You know, there's an old English saying, "Good wine needs no bush." If you've got something good, you don't have to spend your life telling everyone how good it is.

Interview, New York/
"W": a Fairchild publication, 10-14:12.

James Franciscus
Actor 3

An actor is restricted in his interpretation of dramatic roles in a [TV] series. I've relied on the basic Jim Franciscus elements for each of my parts and pick up a few peripheral characteristics for the individual man I play. Sure, the wardrobes are different and the nuances differ to a degree. But a leading man in a dramatic series has to fit some preconceived outlines ... I've done comedy in television movies. But I wouldn't want to spend all that time in a situation comedy just getting laughs without communicating something more to an audience. Even in the worst dramatic scripts there are worthwhile elements to bring to the audience. At least the characters are put in situations and confronted by experiences that provoke some thought from viewers.

Interview, Los Angeles/
The Washington Post, 4-7:(C)17.

Fred W. Friendly
Professor of journalism, Columbia
University; Former president,
Columbia Broadcasting System News 4

There's no doubt in my mind that when the Carnegie Commission Report and Public Broadcasting Act were written — and I lived through all that — it was never intended that the Corporation [for Public Broadcasting] would be [involved] in programming. The Corporation has a big job to do, if they'll do it. But their job is not to duplicate what PBS does. It's to defend the system, to get funds for it, to put a buffer around it, to articulate the goals and purposes of it and to make policy. But there's a territorial imperative that is tugging away at public broadcasting — everybody defending his turf. They've got to stop all this infighting. The territory is the public's and that's why it's called public broadcasting.

TV Guide, 7-23:5.

John Kenneth Galbraith
Former professor of economics,
Harvard University 5

[On doing his TV series, *The Age of Uncertainty*]: I've always thought of myself as a succinct writer, but I've never had such an exercise in that craft as television compels. The most characteristic feature of the three years I spent on this was first to find some idea or some episode which I could tell admirably in

(JOHN KENNETH GALBRAITH)

some 5,000 words and then being asked to compress it into 2,000 words. Trying it out before the camera, I would be told it couldn't be more than 1,000 words. Trying it a second time, I would discover that it really needed to be about 500.

Interview/
"W": a Fairchild publication, 8-19:2.

James Garner
Actor

1

Most everyone watching TV has bifocal vision. They say they don't want violence and then go home and watch it. If we followed the TV code literally, *Bugs Bunny* wouldn't be on . . . There is a difference between "action" and violence. Driving a car down the street and skidding is action; shooting a guy in the head, that's violence.

Interview/Daily Variety, 8-1:7.

David Gerber
Producer

2

[On pressure groups and TV]: You're talking about an industry that is vulnerable to criticism. To this day, two or four letters complaining about a show would disturb sponsors and even networks, even though maybe 30 million people are watching it. This system is based upon fear and the making of profits. These groups come along and exert pressures on the networks, who have affiliates with licenses that periodically come up for renewal. So as not to get themselves in trouble with Congressional investigations, they then accede to the pressure groups. They then force us to come up with the kind of programming that is against our very nature as responsible producers. We're talking about creative integrity being stifled. Police shows are dying without the pressure groups. The Western died that way, too. I'm suggesting that the cure is worse than the disease. So we're not just talking about violence and sex; we're talking about a climate of repression. It's already around us; it's already stifling us. Where does it go from there?

Panel discussion, Los Angeles/TV Guide, 8-27:15.

George Gerbner
Dean, Annenberg School of
Communications, University of Pennsylvania

3

To say an increase in street crime is connected to an increase in violence on television over-simplifies the problem. It is not that clear-cut. A lot of things are learned from television . . . honesty, heroism, patriotism. But television also shows the rules of society's game, the transgressions and the consequences. Persons with little chance to succeed in other ways are exposed to the ways of the criminal and adopt that as their way to success.

Los Angeles Herald-Examiner, 9-30:(A)13.

Julian Goodman
Chairman, National Broadcasting
Company

4

[Criticizing major film companies for going to the FCC to try to lessen the networks' program control]: I must admit that it does not make me sleep any better to know that [MPAA president] Jack Valenti is there in Washington, poised astride the motion-picture industry's enormous war chest, using profits they made from us to attack the few foundations of our business that remain to us — the right to operate the broadcast network itself. Neither does it aid my sleep to note that Jack has hired a lobbyist for those studios, who has registered his major activity as the rewrite of the Broadcast Section of the Communications Act. I would like to think that Jack's acknowledged powers of persuasion . . . could be used for purposes other than to undermine the system of free American television.

Before South Carolina Broadcasters Association/
Los Angeles Herald-Examiner, 7-14:(A)15.

Trevor Griffiths
Playwright

5

The big plays to be written will be television; that's where the news will be made for people in our society. I don't believe in the telly-glued masses — that's the tired copy of frightened minds. I've got files, cupboards full of letters from people arguing, disagreeing with what I wrote in *Through the Night* [a TV play], all contentious, wanting to involve themselves in

WHAT THEY SAID IN 1977

the debate. That's thrilling, like somebody coming up to you at the end of a class and saying, "You know that book you mentioned — where can I get it?" Terrific.

Interview, London/Los Angeles Times, 10-30:(Calendar)56.

Lawrence K. Grossman
President, Public Broadcasting Service

1

I think the obligation that PBS has is to take the resources we have and put out the most useful, informative, educational and culturally enriching and uncorrupting programs that we possibly can. You know, one of the main reasons we don't have a tradition for high quality TV in this country [the U.S.] is that we have not had a first-class public-broadcasting system. Our function is not only to put on good programs for their own sake, watched by a small minority most of the time, but it is also to set a standard, a sort of jewel, a thing that people can look up to and say: why isn't there more like that? Instead, there has been no such example stressing the best in our society, so television viewers have nothing with which to compare what they are getting on commercial TV. In England, where the BBC is so strong, the commercial guys have a standard of excellence to look up to and they don't dare put out [only] garbage ... The television environment is not only air waves. It is a tidal wave which we must use to reflect the best and most constructive quality of our lives rather than the most destructive.

The Christian Science Monitor, 5-6:19.

Alex Haley
Author

2

TV has contributed to killing off the old form of entertainment where the family sat around listening to older people. TV has alienated youth from its elders, and this has cost us culturally and socially.

Interview/Time, 2-14:72.

Earl Holliman
Actor

3

[On TV violence] : I firmly believe we would be doing a disservice to our children if we did not show them how ugly violence really is. You *should* see the blood and the gore. It shouldn't be made to look pretty, or easy, with a dab of red. The world is a violent place, and it should be shown as such.

Interview/San Francisco Examiner & Chronicle, 8-14:(Datebook)30.

Rock Hudson
Actor

4

Television is the monster of all time. It's a monster that eats everything and everybody ... The villain in all this is time. There's not enough time. A movie, for instance, is treated with some care. When I made *Seconds* with John Frankenheimer, it was shot in four months. A *McMillan and Wife* [TV] segment is shot in three weeks, for the same amount of screen time as *Seconds*. They're made back-to-back, one after another, with no development of character, always the same. It's grounds for alcoholism. For five years I had to remain an all-knowing super-human son of a bitch who never went to the bathroom.

Interview, London/San Francisco Examiner & Chronicle, 2-13:(Datebook)34.

Jesse L. Jackson
Civil-rights leader; President,
Operation PUSH (People United
to Save Humanity)

5

Twenty years ago, life revolved around three centers — the home, the church and the school. The home gave discipline, the church gave moral values — whether you followed them or not, they were there — and the school gave information. Now television and radio are the primary conveyors of both information and ethos. But television has the power without the responsibility. That's where the parents come in. They must see to it that the set is turned off so the children can do their work and their reading. That's where the competition for the mind is coming.

Interview/Parade, 2-13:20.

Barry Jagoda
Special Assistant to President of
the United States Jimmy Carter
for Media and Public Affairs
1

[Appearing on] television has become a regular part of [President Carter's] life, as natural as anything else in his life. It's not a big deal. That's what we set out to do — to make television neutral ... There's no such thing as overexposure on television. You're overexposed when you run out of good ideas on how to use television ... If a picture is worth a thousand words, a television show is worth millions.

The New York Times Magazine, 5-15:17.

Nicholas Johnson
Chairman, National Citizens Committee
for Broadcasting; Former Commissioner,
Federal Communications Commission
2

[On the networks' position that citizens' urging corporations not to support violent TV programming is a form of censorship] : The gall of them — the utter gall! To argue that the public, which is the recipient of this violent abuse of their sense, is engaging in some improper action in rising up in defense, but that it is appropriate for them [the networks] to decide what is on — because they have the advantage of being a commercial enterprise out to make a profit — is appalling. Why can't a citizen say what he wants to see on television just like a programming or advertising executive?

Los Angeles Times, 2-28:(4)12.

3

Television is narcotic and addictive. It alters consciousness and it blots out reality. Doctors who work with drug addicts say that television addicts have the same behavior; television watching is compulsive, addictive behavior. If it were wired to the brain like an electro-encephalogram, then people would realize exactly what it is.

San Francisco Examiner & Chronicle,
12-11:(This World)2.

Robert L. Joseph
Screenwriter, Playwright
4

In the theatre you don't get paid to write a play. You write a play because you want to. Then you hope it is good, you hope your agent options it to Hal Prince and you hope it makes some money. Under the Writer's Guild contract you have total approval of casting; they can't change a line, hire a director or rewrite a scene without your permission, because it's your play. In TV and films you are paid up front. That's the difference between an author and a writer. The writers out here [in Hollywood] want to be called authors, but they want that money; they don't want the risks. In television, you try to get it down the best you can and you hope like hell that once in a while someone good will do it, someone will watch it and it will have some meaning and illumination. In one sense everything fails ultimately. What matters is how well you fail.

Interview, Los Angeles/
Los Angeles Times, 10-2:(8)25.

Brian Keith
Actor
5

The executives who run television aren't the wisest or the greatest people. What do they do? They bring in a bunch of bums off the street [as the test audience to view proposed programs]. Your whole life and $20-million are dependent on how they press buttons. What a wino says is going to decide everything for you ... It's all pretty well fouled up between the ratings race and the egos of the top executives. [To determine ratings,] they hook up 1,200 sets, and that's supposed to be a cross-section of the United States. Everybody in our business lives in isolation from the real world and they assume they know everything ... You can't take it seriously; you'd shoot yourself if you did. You do the best you can. At least you get some personal satisfaction from that. When all is said and done, and the flowers are gone, you have to go to bed with yourself, and you have to look at yourself in the mirror when you're shaving. You have to have a sense of your own worth.

Interview/Los Angeles Herald-Examiner, 11-27:(D)1.

447

WHAT THEY SAID IN 1977

Spencer W. Kimball
President, Church of Jesus Christ
of Latter-day Saints (Mormon)
1

[On declining standards of morality] : Television may have something to do with it. Certainly it reflects the prevailing permissiveness and encourages it. Children sit in front of television for hours and hours and see violence and immorality. This is the way America is shaping the ideals and values of much of its youth.

Interview/U.S. News & World Report,
12-19:60.

Richard L. Kirschner
Former vice president in charge of
program practices, Columbia
Broadcasting System Television
2

Let's face it. When we've tried to do cultural stuff, it's been toilet time. People still want the hard-boiled cop. The softer cop shows like *The Blue Knight* have been canceled. It's a strange animal out there [the audience]. They talk out of both sides of their mouths, saying they don't want violence. But they're not buying the shows without it.

TV Guide, 6-4:8.

Paul Klein
Vice president, National Broadcasting
Company Television
3

I don't believe there is such a thing as TV addiction. I believe there is a human condition called irresponsibility. Somehow people cannot go through their life being responsible — so when they break down it takes the form of smoking, drinking, drug-taking, not working, not living up to potential, watching TV. It happens to be the easiest form of irresponsibility to watch TV. That's why so many people are hooked. Media are very easy to become addicted to, but anybody who becomes addicted to TV would become addicted to any other medium — radio, movies, press.

The Christian Science Monitor, 5-5:15.

Jack Klugman
Actor
4

[As a TV actor,] you compromise a little piece at a time. There's no more theatre. There's no place else to go. I go on the road with a play every year — back to the well. You do the best you can. But there's a limit. I think that's what [screenwriter] Paddy Chayefsky was getting at in the movie *Network.* There's got to be a limit. Otherwise, you're swallowed. Otherwise, it's all for the buck. I don't know. If a network is going to make $150-million profit, would it hurt if it only made $125-million and spent the other $25-million on doing entertainment of value?

Interview, Los Angeles/
Los Angeles Times, 2-20:(TV Times)4.

Harvey Korman
Actor
5

. . . I want a television show of my own [after 10 years of being second banana in TV comedy sketches]. I want to call the shots on the content of a show and express my point of view. If you work as long as I have doing sketch material, you begin living a sketch life. Offstage you begin to believe you have a sketch wife, sketch children and a sketch doctor.

Interview, Los Angeles/
The Washington Post, 8-14:(E)11.

Carol Lawrence
Entertainer
6

To survive in show business today, especially television, you have to be a multi-talented person. You have to be able to sing and dance and act — yes, even do comedy routines. Television is such a monster that if you only do one thing well, it eats you up and spits you out very quickly. So many shows are relatively the same. So many tired ideas are constantly being warmed over that no wonder the networks always seem to be announcing a second season. I'd rather watch a documentary than almost anything. Too often on regular shows the quality isn't there because things have to be done so quickly and because costs are such a factor. If a scene is close to what a director wants, he feels obliged to print it, rather than

(CAROL LAWRENCE)

shoot that one more take. Everybody in the industry knows the problems, but nobody seems to have the answers.

Interview, Beverly Hills, Calif./
The Christian Science Monitor, 1-6:18.

Norman Lear
Writer, Producer
1

There is no sex on television. That is a red herring. Where the hell is the sex on television? . . . Maude and Walter alluding to the fact that they are going to bed? . . . I mean, married people and unmarried people do bed each other. . . . that is not sex in the context of "sex and violence." That's life!

Los Angeles Times, 6-27:(1)3.

2

Why are they always talking about television as the worst offender? . . . I don't think that it serves the public interest as well as it could but, by the same token, I haven't noticed that the three largest motor companies in this country have been serving the public interest as well as they could — or we wouldn't have 7,000 of this model and 4,000 of that model recalled . . . Same thing is true for the three top oil companies, and the last three national Administrations. How have the last three national Administrations served the public interest better than the three networks?

Los Angeles Times, 6-27:(1)12.

Jack Lemmon
Actor
3

Television has taken over the entertainment business to an incredible extent because it's far and away the most-used medium of entertainment. It has affected the theatre, and films have been suffering since the beginning of TV's rise a few years after the Second World War. American movies are still very popular abroad because they don't get anywhere near the TV saturation that we do. Movies shown on television in a sense have a captive audience. People do want to see movies, but by watching one on TV they don't have to pay money out of pocket. It's

one reason for the violence and sex in today's films: a competitive desire in the movie industry to present in films what you can't get on The Box.

Interview/U.S. News & World Report, 8-22:44.

Sidney Lumet
Director
4

Whatever crimes the movies have been guilty of — and heaven knows they have been — movies are still voluntary; the audience pays to get in. And nobody ever sat a screaming 2½-year-old in the first row of a theatre to quiet him. TV is used as a babysitter and a pacifier. It is in the home, unrestricted. And this is where it begins to dovetail with American behavior. It is a perfect excuse for the lack of personal responsibility.

Interview, New York/
The Christian Science Monitor, 2-23:18.

Marshall McLuhan
Professor of English and director,
Center for Culture and Technology,
University of Toronto
5

Television has peculiar dimensions that are ignored. For example, it's not a visual medium. It is audible-tactile. It's something that uses the eye as if it were an ear. Television uses the eye as an ear literally because the characteristic mode of the image is discontinuous, whereas the movie image is visual, shutters and still shots with frames and so on. The TV camera has no shutter and is a continuous pickup just like the sound pickup. The image enhanced to you for participation is mostly acoustic and very little visual. The effect is that it's an inner trip. TV is addictive; it's a drug. Tests have been run, you know — they paid people to stop watching it and then tested them to see what happened to them. They show all the withdrawal symptoms of drug addicts. And so, for people who have goals in life the inner trip is fatal. Goals and objectives disappear on the inner trip, and one becomes involved in role-playing.

Interview, New York/The Washington Post, 5-15:(H)1.

449

WHAT THEY SAID IN 1977

Henry Miller
Author
1

Recently, a writer I know wanted me to go on the *Saturday Night Live* show for two minutes. But I told him, "TV is the slaughterhouse of culture," remembering Victor Hugo's line that "The whorehouse is the slaughterhouse of love." I couldn't think of one good thing to say about it. It offers no reality to feed on.

Interview, Los Angeles/
Los Angeles Times, 9-9:(4)20.

Mary Tyler Moore
Actress
2

[On why she is voluntarily ending her TV series after a seven-year run]: Creative people need challenges, and when they get comfortable, that's the time to say "Enough." It's not right to sit back and say, okay, I know all the tricks now, it's just a matter of shuffling them around. I miss losing sleep over struggling with a new project. It's nice to be successful, but nice isn't the essence of living. Struggle is.

Interview/The Dallas Times Herald,
3-16:(F)1.

William S. Paley
Chairman, CBS, Inc.
3

I think everything is in its infancy. This is an evolving world and things don't stand still — they change. Newspapers won't be the same 20 or 30 years from today and they're not the same today as they were 30 years before. So, always in life, there are changes taking place. But to predict now as to what forms television will take 20, 30, 40 years from now is very difficult. We respond very quickly and very effectively to what the public wants and what it needs. There are certain limits, of course, because we have to maintain certain standards. So the public will be the determining factor in what kind of television we'll be giving the public.

The Christian Science Monitor, 5-9:15.

4

The inhibitions placed on radio in the early days were to provide "public service, interest and communion," that was the phrase. The Communications Act clearly states that no government body shall dictate the content of programs. The Fairness Doctrine was developed much later and enunciated by the FCC and upheld by the courts. That is where I think we had our first important departure from the liberties that are given to the press. Right from the beginning I used to preach the need for broadcasters to be very responsible. We did have a great responsibility. It would be a cinch to run a broadcasting network if the government tells you exactly what you could and could not do. You'd simply live by the book. But here you have to live by your conscience and by your sense of responsibility.

Interview, New York/
The Christian Science Monitor, 5-11:27.

Richard E. Palmer
President, American
Medical Association
5

Television violence is a mental-health problem and an environmental issue ... Television has been quick to raise questions of social responsibility with industries which pollute the air. In my opinion, television, through its access to air waves, may be creating a more serious problem than air pollution.

The Wall Street Journal, 2-23:18.

Frederick Pierce
President, American Broadcasting
Company Television
6

[Arguing against government censorship of violence on TV]: TV is not only for children. It's a meeting place for the family. Everything on TV cannot be bland. We have less shows on our schedule which fall into the action category, but there are those viewers who want to see them, and they have that right. Who is to dictate and tell them they cannot see it?

Before ABC-TV affiliates, Los Angeles,
May 11/Daily Variety, 5-12:10.

Frank Price
President, Universal Television
7

[On pressure groups and TV]: You don't realize what has happened. Last year it was

(FRANK PRICE)

"family hour." Now we're talking about 9-11 [p.m.] sex and violence. Next year they'll be saying they don't like fantasy because some report says it makes kids fantasize. And three years from now we'll be talking about something else. Step by step, the pressure groups are eroding television. And the networks don't give a damn because they're going to sell the advertising time, anyway.

Panel discussion, Los Angeles/
TV Guide, 8-27:11.

David Rintels
President, Writers Guild
of America-West
1

One thing unites us [TV writers]. There is not a man or woman, dramatic writer or comedy writer among us, who is allowed to do his or her best, or who feels he or she couldn't write better without the programming and censorship restrictions which dominate our lives and our art. There's not a woman or man among us who couldn't better serve the public interest if the censors and numbers specialists and lowest-common-denominator programmers were not forever clinging to our backs, slowing our uphill climb toward the truth. There is not one among us who has not felt the bitter humiliation of Berthold Brecht when he said, "Each day I journey to the marketplace where lies are bought; hopefully, I take my place among the sellers." Between us, we must find ways to effect change — in our interests . . . and in the country's.

Los Angeles Times, 6-27:(1)12.

Rachel Roberts
Actress
2

I adore doing [TV] comedy . . . but I don't think the craft or subtleties of acting are called for; there isn't the time. A lot of TV people couldn't really take the lead in a dramatic Broadway show. They get by on personality, the way they look instead of skills.

Interview/Los Angeles, 2-2:(4)9.

Telly Savalas
Actor
3

The truth is that I made more than 60 major motion pictures — and was nominated for an Academy Award in 1963 for *Birdman of Alcatraz*. And people said there goes what's-his-name. But one major shot on television in *Kojak,* and the next day they knew my name. TV gives you more exposure than anything you could possibly do.

San Diego, Calif./
Los Angeles Times, 3-27:(5)22.

4

I abhor [TV] violence when we paint it as a two-fisted, macho, good guy who goes in there and cleans them up. I hate that. I hate it whenever violence is painted attractively or excitingly without showing the after-effects. The *Kojak* show doesn't do that. I insist on it. No heroes on *Kojak;* no such thing as "job well done" when there's been death on the show. Kojak [a police detective] takes time to cry. You find that dimension of pathos in the man, the sadness of the man when something violent does happen, whether it's the bad or the good guy.

Interview, Los Angeles/
Los Angeles Times, 10-20:(4)25.

Herbert S. Schlosser
President, National Broadcasting
Company
5

We are on the verge of the greatest technological change in communication since the introduction of color [TV]. Optical fibers that can transmit enormous amounts of audio and video data; satellites; videodisk and videotape players; tiny microprocessors that can store and retrieve masses of video information. Our mini-cameras will become even smaller and more versatile, and they will be joined by miniaturized tape and transmitting equipment. All these applications will change our industry in years to come in ways we cannot accurately predict.

Before NBC-TV affiliates, Los Angeles,
May 16/Daily Variety, 5-17:6.

WHAT THEY SAID IN 1977

Eric Sevareid
News commentator,
Columbia Broadcasting System　　　*1*

Intellectual critics of academia do not love me very much because I try to puncture the mythology they foster. The silliest myth of all is that TV is making mental zombies out of us, that our minds are turning to mush. Such nonsense. They said the same thing about radio and movies. Millions of people are out hunting and fishing and going to concerts and museums. And children − they watch a lot of trash, but the children today are much better informed and much more knowledgeable than we ever were. They tell me television has destroyed the art of conversation. Do they think that before TV and radio families sat around in the evenings and had meaningful dialogues? Like hell they did. No, our people are much too tough and resilient to be put down by a machine . . .
Interview, Los Angeles, May 25/
Los Angeles Times, 5-27:(4)36.

2

I have never understood the reasoning of those critics who seem to be saying that broadcasting will enjoy full rights under the First Amendment when it is worthy of them. Constitutional rights do not have to be earned; we were all born with them.
Before National Association of Broadcasters/
TV Guide, 10-29:5.

Fred Silverman
President, American Broadcasting
Company Entertainment　　　*3*

It isn't fun any more [being a TV programmer]. It used to be. When I joined CBS, it was terrific. You made a couple of changes in midseason and put on a couple of summer shows, and that was all there was to it. Now it is just like a Turkish bath. Every morning you wake up and they're scheduling this and we're changing that. There are 15 seasons and 180 specials, and it is a totally different business − the most competitive, I would imagine, in the entire world.
Interview/Time, 9-5:52.

4

[Criticizing those who look down at U.S. television]: We [at ABC] are synchronized, we are in harmony with the contemporary preferences of an overwhelming majority of the American television viewing public. We not only reflect those preferences, we respect those preferences. And often, in our programming decisions, we anticipate those preferences . . . I believe television is providing quality across the board. Tune in any of the three commercial networks any day and you'll find quality. You'll find expertly produced program schedules responsibly meeting today's entertainment and informational needs in a contemporary, meaningful and human way . . . Certainly everyone's entitled to his own opinion, but I hope those who sometimes think condescendingly or disdainfully about television will keep in mind how eminently popular and widely appreciated are so many of its programs . . . If we were programming for England, I dare say we'd have more felicitous speaking characters and more subtle dialogue. But we're programming for Des Moines, Boise and Newark, not Hereford, Hertford and Hampshire. . . . the public, by exercising its free choice in selecting what it wants to watch, will ultimately determine what stays on the air. And that's the way it should be.
Before Hollywood Radio and Television
Society, Beverly Hills, Calif., Nov. 8/
Los Angeles Times, 11-10:(4)29.

5

[On pressure groups who try to get off the air programming they don't like]: Now, some may resent comparing today's modern pressure group circulating lists of advertisers associated with a particular program or type of program with what went on back in the '50s. But I ask you if there isn't an insidiously dangerous parallel. I ask you: Aren't blacklists, *per se,* anti-democratic? Aren't threats of economic reprisals, aren't ultimatums to advertisers to pull their commercials out of a show, or else − aren't these things ominously similar to those tactics of the '50s? . . . What about free speech? Isn't it someone's right to criticize a program and urge others not to watch it? Of course it is. No one is saying that's not their right. But is it

(FRED SILVERMAN)

someone's First Amendment right to conspire to boycott a company for advertising on a program one doesn't happen to like? I don't think so. I don't think anyone has the right to coerce and punish. I think everyone's right to extend their arms, as a Supreme Court Justice once observed, stops at the tip of someone else's nose. Your [advertising agencies'] clients have noses and First Amendment rights, too. But pressure groups, with their proposed ban on Saturday morning commercials and with other encroachments, are close to abridging the advertiser's First Amendment rights to communicate with his customers. . . . there seems to be a growing unwillingness today to trust broadcasters with the responsibility for program content, but more than that there seems to be a growing unwillingness to trust the intelligence, the taste and the judgment of the general public to which that content is aimed. Today . . . pressure groups are trying to muscle their way into decision-making concerning what goes on television because they don't trust the judgment of the general public. They want to pre-screen, then either prejudice or pre-empt the public's judgment.

Before American Association of
Advertising Agencies central regional meeting,
Chicago, Nov. 9/Variety, 11-16:54.

Aaron Spelling
Producer

1

I agree there's too much violence [on TV], but I just hope to God this doesn't mean we're going to turn all of television into pap, that we're going to be stampeded by the pressure groups into making all of television for children. We don't want television to become some kind of candyland, some kind of fairyland. That's terribly dangerous. You simply can't say we will have no more violence on television. *Roots* was a very violent show; does that mean we shouldn't have done *Roots?*

Interview, Los Angeles/
The Washington Post, 2-23:(B)7.

Robert Stack
Actor

2

TV is weird, and you have to accept that going in. There are so many factors that go into making a show a hit that you can't sit around worrying about it. Most of it is luck. If you have a strong lead-in and weak competition, you're going to go through the roof. If, on the other hand, they stick you up against Carol Burnett and a bunch of Clint Eastwood and John Wayne movies, you're obviously not going to have the ratings of *Charlie's Angels.*

Interview/TV Guide, 1-22:22.

Arthur R. Taylor
Former president, CBS, Inc.

3

This medium [TV] shapes the nation's social agenda, and yet there is a great sameness in the schedules of all three networks, dominated by excessive brutality and shallowness. Television needs more experimentation, more untried talent, new directions and more fulfilling drama. Sadly, too few of these things have yet come to pass.

U.S. News & World Report, 2-7:30.

Toni Tennille
Singer

4

Television is a great garbage disposal. It keeps grinding up artists like us and throwing them away. People think of me as the rah-rah All-American-girl cheerleader type. And All-American girls don't have any insight, and they don't have a brain in their heads. On TV, I was one-dimensional.

San Francisco Examiner & Chronicle,
12-18:(This World)2.

Richard Thomas
Actor

5

[Disagreeing with actors who lament their identification with a role they have played in a TV series]: You spend five years coming into people's living-rooms every week, teaching them to love you, trying to make them like you. You train them to feel a certain way. I never understand all of this overreaction by people about a character. I mean, that's what

453

WHAT THEY SAID IN 1977

(RICHARD THOMAS)

you do [as an actor]. You make money at it. You teach people to love you in that role, then you turn around and say, "Hey, that's not me! I don't want you to call me by that name." That doesn't make sense. Isn't it the most natural thing in the world for people to think of you that way? In my mind [some actors' attitude toward this] seems to be ungrateful. I don't think people, at least subconsciously, like that sort of thing. It's a put-down of what made you famous. You shouldn't fight that too hard — having people associate you with a particular role or character. Especially one they have liked. That's a negative process. Just because I don't do that show *[The Waltons]* any more doesn't mean it is a thorn in my side. If anything, it is a jewel in my crown. How could you not be proud and happy over something that has been so good to you? Besides, people are understanding. They are not totally dumb. You can show them you are something else beside that one character that is so familiar to them.

Interview, Los Angeles/
The Dallas Times Herald, 12-4:(F)1.

Peter Ustinov
Actor, Director, Writer   *1*

TV makes it impossible to have any more great men. It brings people too close. It eliminates the distance needed for greatness.

Los Angeles Herald-Examiner, 9-29:(B)2.

Jack Valenti
President, Motion Picture
Association of America   *2*

What the members [of the MPAA] seek is emancipation from self-serving controls that enable ABC, CBS and NBC to decide arbitrarily what the millions of American viewers may see on their home sets. This tight oligopoly domination stifles artistic creativity and slams the door to independent productions that could bring refreshed vitality, greater diversity and new excellence to the TV screens.

News conference, Washington, June 1/
Los Angeles Herald-Examiner, 6-2:(A)11.

Andy Warhol
Artist   *3*

Television is by far the most popular kind of entertainment around. The number of people who watch it every day — including me — is amazing. But most people don't take it all that seriously. It's just fun to watch. TV has replaced movies in keeping everybody entertained, in making us laugh when we are lonely. But the real power isn't exercised by TV. Most people still turn to newspapers and magazines for serious information. I know there was a lot of talk that television would put the press out of business, but that hasn't happened — and it won't.

Interview/U.S. News & World Report, 6-27:57.

Vincent T. Wasilewski
President,
National Association of Broadcasters   *4*

[Saying the TV industry must develop and maintain a program of self-regulation in order to discourage government regulation]: My invitation and my challenge to each of you [broadcasters] is to devote your time, your energy and the utmost of your resources to the job of getting them [First Amendment rights] and, once gotten, of keeping them for all time. For, if the most important of the news and information media — broadcasting — continues to be restricted, eventually all First Amendment rights of all the media will suffer, and the public will be the inevitable loser. We are being challenged more frequently, more insistently and more stridently than ever about sex and violence on television. A right acquired means a duty assumed. If we are to acquire and then maintain those rights, we must have a program of self-regulation. It is the only answer to those who call for governmental regulation of advertising and program content.

At National Association of Broadcasters
annual meeting, Washington, March 28/
The Washington Post, 3-29:(B)12.

Sylvester L. (Pat) Weaver
Former president,
National Broadcasting Company   *5*

What's lacking in television today, mainly, is that network managements have no real design,

(SYLVESTER L. [PAT] WEAVER)

no real plan. I had a grand design — a system of programs to reach and influence and enlighten and entertain the people at home. You've got to care. The great communications entities of the world were always made by people who cared. If they cared, they made them great; and when you ran a great anything, you made money.

At party celebrating the 25th anniversary of the "Today" show, New York, Jan. 14/ The Washington Post, 1-25:(C)4.

Margita White
Commissioner, Federal Communications Commission

1

[I am] a regulator for less, rather than more, regulation, especially in the sensitive area of broadcasting. And I firmly believe that the future of broadcasting should not, and hopefully will not, be determined by Federal laws and regulations but by the performance of radio and television as judged by the American people.

At American Women in Radio and Television convention, Minneapolis/Daily Variety, 5-2:3.

John Wicklein
Dean, School of Public Communications, Boston University

2

Although, ultimately, we would like to convince [TV] station owners and network managers to provide access to minorities and women because it is *right,* it is more likely that we are going to have to rely on the law and FCC rulings to open up the air to its rightful owners, the people ... I think it would be better to require stations to provide "open time" daily — even in prime time, if you could accept that heresy — for community groups to present information that they believe is in the public interest. That way, you eliminate government control over program content, and you provide time on air for material that is not specifically shaped to meet the station's primary concern of making a buck.

At Institute for Democratic Communication conference/The Christian Science Monitor, 11-23:43.

Richard E. Wiley
Chairman, Federal Communications Commission

3

My view that government involvement in specific programming, and advertising, content is neither desirable nor Constitutionally appropriate extends beyond the field of TV violence and sex. In any number of areas — whether it be children's programming and advertising, network reruns, ethnic, racial and sexual stereotyping, counter-advertising or over-the-counter advertising, to name only a few — the FCC has been asked by well-motivated people to step in and to adopt corrective regulations. [It is] clear that the FCC cannot regulate programming in any significant degree of detail or specificity. We can do very little to affect the quality of service. [What the FCC can do is] ensure that competition has a real chance to operate and to produce diversity, choice and innovation in the public interest.

Before National Association of Television Program Executives, Miami Beach, Feb. 14/ Daily Variety, 2-15:1.

Flip Wilson
Comedian

4

I don't want to get the whole Hollywood community down on me, but I think TV is *it.* I could spend six months or a year working on a movie and hope it gets to 20 million people; or I could spend a week doing a TV show and get to 40 or 50 million ... Comedy has an immediate magic. If something's funny, it's funny right then; you can't keep doing it over and over like you have to do in a movie.

Interview/Los Angeles Times, 9-2:(4)18.

David L. Wolper
Producer

5

[On pressure groups and TV]: Start with one group criticizing violence, and soon they're going to be criticizing thing after thing, and in two years we're going to be wondering why TV is full of nothing. The answer will be because two years ago we let a bunch of people who knew nothing get control of what we were doing ... You ask what can be done. Somebody should attack the PTA. Is its job to

(DAVID L. WOLPER)

monitor television with a bunch of inexperienced people? ... certain television programs
that a year ago you [the audience] thought
were terrific can't be done today. Certain
television shows that *TV Guide* said represented
the best in television can't be done today. That
is the point we want made.

Panel discussion, Los Angeles/
TV Guide, 8-27:18.

Robert Wussler
President, Columbia Broadcasting
System Television   *1*

Something has taken place that, in my
opinion, has changed television for all time.
This transformation has been brought by a
public which has become more demanding.
Viewers are bored with the familiar. They are
impatient with imitation. They hunger for
innovation. They have become more sophisticated. More discriminating. Everyone is a critic,
making snap judgments, quick to turn to
something else. To keep pace with this restless
public, television has abandoned life-long patterns, forms which the medium took over from
network radio so many years ago — that basic
pattern of presenting the same program at the
same time, week after week, year after year.
For years, once a schedule went on after Labor
Day, it was set in stone for the entire season.

Before CBS-TV affiliates, Los Angeles/
Los Angeles Herald-Examiner, 5-27:(C)5.

2

[Television] should be about a half or
three-quarters of a step behind where society
is ... I don't think that we want to be two
steps ahead of society ... I don't want one
couple in America to get a divorce as a result of
something he saw because we were ahead of the
times where we should be.

Before TV editors and critics, Los Angeles,
June 23/Daily Variety, 6-27:1.

Ansel Adams
Photographer

1

Most people who accomplish anything have a hell of a lot of drive. I don't know if I'm combative, but as far back as I can remember I had the urge to do *something*. A vacation bores me to death.

Interview/Los Angeles Times, 1-30:(1)20.

Muhammad Ali
*Heavyweight boxing
champion of the world*

2

The [championship] title doesn't really matter, because I'm bigger than boxing. And if I lose all my wealth that's all right, too, because I'm just a trustee. I don't worship money; I worship Allah. The important thing is I'm the first black man in this country that can do anything he wants. See how free I am? See how calm I am? Do you see any bosses? We could all take off right now to Mexico if I wanted.

*Interview, Berrien Springs, Mich./
The New York Times, 4-6:22.*

Woody Allen
Actor, Director, Writer

3

I don't care about money at all. I get a moderate salary to do my job, and I get a percentage of the movies after they make a substantial profit — but I rarely see that because they rarely make a substantial profit. What money I get, I spend as soon as I get it — on junk, on books, records, eating out — you know, anything I want. The only value of money is to spend it on what you want. Otherwise, what's the point in it?

*Interview/Los Angeles Herald-Examiner,
4-8:(B)2.*

Gene Autry
Former actor

4

I was the first of the singing cowboys. I'm not sure I was the best, but when you're first it doesn't matter. Even if everybody else is better, no one can ever be first again.

The Dallas Times Herald, 6-1:(E)7.

Edmund G. Brown, Jr.
Governor of California (D)

5

I'm eclectic. There's a wide range of ideas that I've been able to synthesize in my own philosophy and that's what people find unpredictable . . . You can't just have a self-enclosed, impersonal, hermetically sealed idea machine.

*San Francisco Examiner & Chronicle,
3-6:(This World)2.*

Richard Burton
Actor

6

I've been in trouble all my life. I've done the most unutterable rubbish, all because of money. I didn't *need* it — I've never needed money, not even as a child, though I came from a very poor family. But there have been times when the lure of the zeros was simply too great.

*Interview, New York/
The New York Times, 10-5:25.*

Michael Caine
Actor

7

I'm a peaceable sort of bloke . . . and I don't go looking for trouble. I don't have that hell-raiser tough-guy image that could mean trouble, and people know it. No one sees me as a challenge. I look on life like a man wearing tight shoes: You don't want to get your feet

457

WHAT THEY SAID IN 1977

(MICHAEL CAINE)

wet, so you don't step in any puddles. I don't make waves, you see.

Interview, Beverly Hills, Calif./
San Francisco Examiner & Chronicle,
12-18:(Datebook)15.

Johnny Carson
Television talk-show host
1

They call me a loner. It's like you're damned if you do and damned if you don't. If you go out to parties, you're a bum and a rounder; if you stay home and live a quiet life, you're a loner, a snob. There's a strange fetish people have of rooting for the underdog on his way up, but once he gets there they want to knock him off, they want to throw rocks at him. It goes with the territory.

Interview, Los Angeles/San Francisco
Examiner & Chronicle, 10-9:(Datebook)28.

Jimmy Carter
President of the United States
2

I'm still a farmer at heart, and I miss the planting season and the crops being pro-duced.... it's just a basic part of my life.... the community, the attitudes, the closeness, the sharing of a common life in a small group of people ... I feel at home when I'm here.

News conference, Plains, Ga., May 31/
The Washington Post, 6-1:(A)2.

3

Our whole family has always been remark-ably individualistic. My mother has a life of her own. She doesn't permit any interference in it, nor is any attempted. My sister, Gloria, has a life of her own, and prides herself on making her own decisions. The same is true with my sister Ruth, with [brother] Billy and with me. Billy is a good man. I think he has remarkable characteristics which have attracted the interest of the nation. He has never embarrassed me.

Interview, Washington/People, 12-26:30.

Richard Chamberlain
Actor
4

I'm just one of these people who plods along. I have no idea what the long-range possibilities are. There will always be some place to act. And if there isn't, I'll just go make stained-glass windows somewhere. I'd just as soon do that, anyway!

Interview, New York/
The Christian Science Monitor, 1-3:22.

James Dickey
Author, Poet
5

My wife can't understand why I'm always getting up so early and getting to doing stuff — writing and pacing around and thinking and answering letters, and God knows what else, playing the guitar or something that I want to do. She wants to sleep ... but me, I want to get to doing things. What is it that the philosopher Heraclitus said about the sun — "The sun's new every day." And it is.

Interview, New York/
The Christian Science Monitor, 10-5:23.

Joan Didion
Author
6

... I think of myself as really happy. Cheer-ful. I'm always amazed at what simple things can make me happy. I'm really happy every night when I walk past the windows and the evening star comes out. A star of course is not a simple thing, but it makes me happy. I look at it for a long time. I'm always happy, really.

Interview, Malibu, Calif./
The New York Times Book Review, 4-3:38.

Robert Evans
Motion-picture producer
7

My priorities are totally out of balance. The only thing that matters with me is a driving obsession to do the best work I can. When I finish a film and see it on the screen and experience the audience reaction, it's the great-est "come" of my life. It's the criteria I live by. I don't know if it's necessarily good. My obsession to do well broke up my marital life. This driving obsession, it's really a striving for

(ROBERT EVANS)

perfection in myself. But in striving for perfection, I become imperfect. In my way of life, I pay for what I do. Ah, but what I do is a complete joy. The completeness of it is a joy.

Interview/Los Angeles Times, 1-30:(1)20.

Clifton Fadiman
Author, Editor
1

George Bernard Shaw said he wanted to live so that when he was ready to die he would be fit only for the scrap heap. He wanted all his faculties to be used up, so there would be nothing left at the end. I feel the same way. I can't do very many things, and I can't do any of them terribly well, but I want to do them as well as I can, and as many of them as I can, so that when I die I can say to myself, well, I have used up everything inside me. That seems to me the only end of life.

Interview, Santa Barbara, Calif./
The Center Magazine, July-Aug.:51.

Jackie Gleason
Entertainer
2

Yeah, I guess I'm flamboyant, one of the last. If you work at it, you ain't got it. Anyone in show business who plays "humble" is full of crap. Forty-50 million people don't get riveted by "humble." It would be commercial naivete to think so. You've got to have a pretty good opinion of yourself going in, and I always had that, always.

Interview, Miami/
Los Angeles Times, 11-8:(4)14.

Merv Griffin
Television talk-show host
3

If there's one thing I fear, it's that day I'm going to wake up and not want to do the show any more, not want to talk to those people on that show. That day has got to come . . . I'll say, "I'll be right back after this message," and I won't be.

Interview, Los Angeles/
Los Angeles Times, 5-26:(4)16.

Gene Hackman
Actor
4

Success had more of an effect on me than I realized. Things started happening and I thought I was handling them. Now I realize they handled me. It was wonderful, before. I would get a job and we'd go out to supper to celebrate. Now I feel I've got to go out and buy a new Mercedes.

Interview/The Dallas Times Herald, 9-5:(B)4.

Hugh M. Hefner
Publisher, "Playboy" magazine
5

I am by nature a romantic. Sure, I enjoy my bachelor freedom. But I need a one-on-one relationship. The possibility of finding the right woman, of falling in love with her, and having her fall in love with me, is what motivates me today more than anything . . . It is true that I would rather meet the right girl than make another hundred-million dollars.

Interview, Los Angeles/San Francisco
Examiner & Chronicle, 3-20:(This World)24.

Charlton Heston
Actor
6

I'm too dull, square and protestant – in the philosophical, not the religious, sense – to be a big popular public figure, a beloved figure. I'm not a public drunk. I've only had one wife. My kids aren't runaways. It's not what people expect. I go schlepping along in a square way and it's not very interesting. People don't find a big public flaw in me and they seem to need it – not just from me, but from anyone who's had success and attention . . . I'm addicted to peanut butter. Only Americans know how to make it. Before I go on a location outside the country, I check out the local lines of supply. If they can't get it, I bring my own peanut butter. For me, joy is peanut butter spread on an English muffin.

Interview, Los Angeles/Los Angeles Times,
2-6:(Calendar)52.

WHAT THEY SAID IN 1977

Hamilton Jordan
*Assistant to President of the
United States Jimmy Carter*　　　　*1*

[On himself]: Loyal, yeah; iconoclastic, maybe. Disorganized? Not in the head, but from all exterior appearances — yes, my car, my desk, you'd say yes. In my head I have a sense of what needs to be done and priorities, but from the outside it looks bad, I'm sure. Anti-intellectual? I admire intelligence and ability; I don't know what anti-intellectual means ... Machiavellian? I don't think that's true. I have a good political sense; I think I'm probably shrewd politically, and I understand what motivates people. I don't think that the ends justify the means always, and I don't enjoy personal confrontation. Let's say I don't relish personal confrontations; you can be successful in politics without being Machiavellian.

*Interview, Washington/
The Christian Science Monitor, 8-9:22.*

Ray A. Kroc
Chairman, McDonald's Corporation　　　*2*

... you know my attitude when they say to me, "Why do you work?" I don't work. Work is doing something you don't like to do. I like the smell of success. I like the challenge, the pride of accomplishment. Why does Bob Hope work, so to speak? Well, it's not for him. He loves that applause. Sinatra loves the applause. Jack Benny loved the applause. I like the applause.

*Interview, San Diego/
Los Angeles Times, 2-13:(3)10.*

Bert Lance
*Director, Federal Office of
Management and Budget*　　　　*3*

Maybe my philosophy is not what it ought to be, but I don't worry about things I can't do anything about. Once I've made a decision about something, I don't think about it any more. I have confidence in my ability to get things done. There's no sense in feeling inadequate if everything doesn't turn out right. I guess a lot of people have got a better basis than I have; they have a lot more educational background. But I've been out in the real world

26 years, seeing people be successful, seeing people fail, and in between. I've always been able to learn from people who are older than I am, to listen to what they say so I don't have to relive the bad experience they've had.

Interview/The Washington Post, 2-27:(H)6.

Irving Lazar
Literary and theatrical agent　　　　*4*

My drive for success is insatiable. It's true of anybody who is really good. It is true of Beverly Sills, who happens to be a friend of mine. It is true of Jerry Robbins [the choreographer]. Of Vladimir Nabokov. It was true of Hemingway, Joyce and GBS. But I'm not an artist; I'm a trader. If I were not a trader, I would be a Fuller Brush man, and I would sell more Fuller Brushes than anybody else in the world. Or more computers. Or pianos.

Interview/Los Angeles Times, 1-30:(1)20.

Alistair MacLean
Author　　　　*5*

... I'm not really a modest man. Modesty can be subjective and objective. I know that I am competent at my job. But I know that I am no genius. And I think it is the fact that a great amount of modesty is the obverse side of the coin of total immodesty. And one must be very careful.

Interview, London/Book Digest, January:27.

Margaret Mead
Anthropologist　　　　*6*

When I was 30, I decided that I had paid back — in field work and new ways of doing anthropology — everything that had been invested in my education, the money spent and all the hours my parents and teachers had devoted to me. From that day on, having paid for the past, I was free. Whatever else I did, whatever else I could contribute to the world, would be for the future. And so it has been.

Interview, New York/Redbook, June:168.

James A. Michener
Author　　　　*7*

One time in Marrakesh, I went into a cafe and a young girl back in a corner suddenly

(JAMES A. MICHENER)

cried: "James Michener. Oh, wow!" A lot of things have happened to me — honors, prizes, the Pulitzer. But nothing ever meant as much as that girl in Morocco crying, "Oh, wow!" Of course, it turned out that was about her total vocabulary. She said it about everything — tomato soup, oh, wow! Chevrolet truck, oh, wow! But it didn't matter. I have never forgotten it . . .

Interview, Los Angeles/
Los Angeles Times, 6-8:(4)1.

Robert Mitchum
Actor
1

I worry about everything. The only thing constant in my life is fear. But I actually enjoy it. Thrills of fear go up and down my spine. I have nightmares every night. The best ones come from exhaustion and not sleeping. Those produce a really malevolent presence.

Interview, Amsterdam/
Los Angeles Times, 2-27:(Calendar)35.

Anthony Newley
Actor, Singer, Composer
2

People ask me why I don't try something new, create and experiment; but that takes a great deal of time and money. I've gotten to the point where I don't have the drive nor the ambition that I used to have. I think to be really creative you have to be a little hungry. You have to take a chance and work for almost nothing. I'm lazy. I'm not forced to work any more and I refuse to do anything any more unless I get paid.

Interview, Beverly Hills, Calif./
The Dallas Times Herald, 4-10:(F)6.

Rudolf Nureyev
Ballet dancer
3

I don't appreciate any kind of sentimentality. When you believe in sentimentality you are masking a more fundamental truth. To be perfectly honest, I don't even like the publicity that follows me wherever I go. I enjoy pushing myself to the limits of my endurance because that is the only way I know how to dance. I

must dance that way. The publicity? All of that means nothing. Many people are very surprised when I tell them that I don't even have a publicity agent. Hollywood stars must have publicity agents. I'm a dancer; I must dance. I don't even like to look at myself or pictures of myself. They say I am narcissistic. But you know, you would be hard pressed to find many mirrors in my home.

Interview, London/
The Christian Science Monitor, 2-9:27.

Dolly Parton
Singer
4

I have always wanted to shine and glitter. I always thought when I got rich I would have lots of loud colors, flashy clothes and fancy jewelry because I didn't have any of that when I was growing up. When I was just getting started I decided that I would dress in gaudy, outrageous clothes because that fit my outgoing personality. Since I already had other parts of my body that were extreme, I figured I might as well be totally extreme. Now if I want to wear two wigs at a time piled 40 feet high on my head, I feel free to.

Interview, New York/
The Dallas Times Herald, 6-3:(G)7.

Sidney Poitier
Actor
5

When I was a kid, my mother, who was a very inarticulate and very gentle woman, would call for me and sometimes I'd answer by saying "What?" She would fire a slap across my mouth. Very early I learned to say "Yes," "Yes, Momma," "Yes, ma'am." I learned it all. All those years in New York — from the time I was 15 on — I was saved time and time again by that lesson. I was completely alone, without friends or family. All those years I was really hanging on and struggling to learn about life. I was saved many times by the simple lessons I learned from my mother. I was considered a youngster who respected his elders, and that simple respect did a lot for me.

Interview, Beverly Hills, Calif./
Los Angeles Times, 10-30:(Calendar)40.

461

WHAT THEY SAID IN 1977

Anthony Quinn
Actor

1

I have no idea — no idea at all — what Anthony Quinn looks like. It changes, depending on what I do . . . I have no faith at all in my face. I never know what is behind this face of mine. So I have to hide behind the characters I play.

Interview, Washington/
The Washington Post, 9-9:(B)2.

Artur Rubinstein
Pianist

2

I never met in my whole life anyone who is as happy as I am, and at 90 that is a very big declaration. I'm wildly interested in everything. For me, everything is eternally different, eternally new — when I play a composition for the 150th time it is new again. Maybe that's what keeps me alive.

Interview, New York/
The Dallas Times Herald, 1-29:(A)2.

3

I go to the piano like other people go to a bar for a drink.

New York/San Francisco Examiner &
Chronicle, 2-6:(This World)4.

Telly Savalas
Actor

4

The bubble could easily burst in show business. But while I adjust to luxury very well, I can also adjust to poverty. If they say the merry-go-round is over and they say, "Go home, Telly," I'll take my press clippings and go back to what I was doing before — teaching psychology in schools. And, no matter what I do, I'll have a ball.

San Diego, Calif./
Los Angeles Times, 3-27:(5)22.

5

The talent I do have is to represent the average guy's taste, even though I may be mingling as a participant in the clever world of Cannes and Hollywood. A year ago, someone said to me, "Why not sing at the Academy Awards?" And I said, "Why not?" Now, some

would say, "Gee, what gall. What arrogance." But to tell you the truth, I did pretty good. I'm everyone's Uncle Harry. And when I get on stage and sing, they say, "There but for the grace of God go I." Now, Sinatra's not out there worrying. It's just ol' Telly doing his thing. And that's the ballpark. I just keep blowing bubbles.

Interview, Cannes, France/
The Washington Post, 5-26:(D)3.

Eric Sevareid
News commentator,
Columbia Broadcasting System

6

[On his impending retirement]: Someone asked me what I'd do after 45 years of daily deadlines. I have two contrasting temptations. One is to sit in a rocking-chair for two weeks, after which I will slowly begin rocking. The other is to go fishing. Charlie Brown may say that happiness is a warm puppy, but I can tell you that happiness is a cold trout.

Before CBS-TV affiliates, Los Angeles, May 26/
The Dallas Morning News, 5-27:(A)3.

Rod Steiger
Actor

7

During the years of growing up, there was nobody for me to depend on. I had to rely entirely on myself. This builds an admirable kind of self-reliance, but it also produces what psychiatrists call an autocratic personality, a person who tries to make the whole world out of himself. I went into analysis for five years to cope with a number of personal problems, and I found I'm very definitely an autocratic personality. It's a special asset to someone in the creative arts. It helps me to be a convincing actor. I can invent and believe in the imaginery world around me. But while it's a professional blessing, it's a personal curse. It puts a suit of armor around me.

Interview, Malibu, Calif./
Los Angeles Times, 1-23:(Home)20.

Elizabeth Taylor
Actress

8

My life has been what it has been and I have no regrets. I've been up and down so many

(ELIZABETH TAYLOR)

times in my career. I've been spat upon; I've been cheered; I've been photographed; I've been accepted; I've been rejected. Being in films and leading the kind of extraordinary life I have led, has had deep purple moments and bright yellow ones.

Interview, Vienna/
Good Housekeeping, February:167.

Leon Uris
Author

1

... I don't put labels on myself. But obviously I have a loyal and very large following who seem to like what I do and who have really covered me with a very quiet sort of adulation. I am totally content to live within that. The seeking of prizes and doctorates is something I just don't give a damn about. I never have.

Interview/Book Digest, October:28.

Peter Ustinov
Actor, Director, Writer

2

I have neither the temperament nor the build for screams of horror. I am resigned to the fact that anything profoundly felt by me takes on the mantle of lighthearted mischief because it emanates from the heart of a jocular rotundity ... Maybe I should like to be taken

more seriously, but I don't want to be more serious.

Interview, Paris/
Los Angeles Times, 9-6:(4)14.

Robert Penn Warren
Author, Poet

3

I've been a lot of places and done a lot of things, but writing was always first. It's a kind of pain I can't do without. It's not a particularly fun way to live. It's just scratching where you itch. But it's my life.

Interview, Fairfield, Conn./
The National Observer, 3-12:20.

Andrew Young
United States Ambassador/Permanent Representative to the United Nations

4

[Saying he will pursue "impossible dreams" despite criticism of his being too outspoken and naive]: It's those impossible dreams that have made my life worth living, and I wouldn't trade them for any amount of realism and protocol in the world ... [The hope of charting new areas of cooperation among conflicting groups is] terribly naive ... terribly optimistic. [But] I really like it that way. Anything I've ever done has been both controversial and naive.

Before United Nations Association, United Nations,
New York, April 19/Los Angeles Times, 4-20:(1)5.

Mortimer J. Adler
Author, Philosopher
1

If you want to know the single most important insight I've learned in living my own life, it is the right understanding of happiness. The modern understanding of happiness is confused with pleasure or satisfaction, having a good time. Aristotle used the Greek word *eudaimonia,* and that translates into "good life." He meant the good life as a whole. But how can you experience a whole good life? What you can have is the moral aim of leading a whole good life — by building it the way one builds part of a play.

Interview, New York/
"W": a Fairchild publication, 4-15:13.

2

This notion of tapering off is just crazy. That's the way you die. Retire and die. I'll never forget an article I read by a heart specialist. "We Don't Wear Out, We Rust Out," it was called. Put a car up on the block for six months and it's no good. Put a *man* up on the block for six months, *he's* no good. It's as simple as that.

Interview, New York/
"W": a Fairchild publication, 4-15:13.

Lew Ayres
Actor
3

It's been said that true culture in a person is the capacity to know one's subject thoroughly. But I'm not sure I entirely believe that, because I've found that almost every discipline is limitless. There's no philosopher, no man of religion, no artist who would honestly say, "I am in command here of all that is accessible." You finally say, like Socrates, "I know that I know nothing."

Interview, Los Angeles/Los Angeles Times, 5-16:(4)1.

Simone de Beauvoir
French author
4

... freedom of speech in the West is greater than in the East. There's no doubt that in the Soviet Union freedom of speech is choked, totally cut off. In the United States the freedom of speech is great, but it is also insignificant, because intellectuals can say whatever they want — people don't listen. I was told American television broadcast frightening programs about Vietnam, but the horrors went on. You have people who are totally gagged in the East; and you have people who can speak freely in the West, but nobody cares.

Interview, Paris/Book Digest, February:24.

Peter L. Berger
Professor of sociology,
Rutgers University
5

Through most of human history, if the individual asked himself, "Who am I?," around him arose a chorus of firm replies: "You are such and such." The answers might not be very pleasing to him. It could be he was a serf, but at least his identity was clear and defined. A person growing up in our kind of society, especially in the upper middle class, has very weak and contradictory answers when he asks, "Who am I?" of parents, schools, peer groups and mass communications. I think there is in human beings a very profound desire for a clear answer to the question of "Who am I?" This means that anybody who comes around with a seemingly authoritative and firm answer is almost guaranteed a following. My general hypothesis would be that whether a person follows a religious leader of some sort, or goes into some psychological therapeutic cult, or — as happened particularly in the 1960s — follows political direction, what he is responding to is a

(PETER L. BERGER)

movement which tells him what he is. Whichever he bumps into first, he responds to.

Interview/U.S. News & World Report, 4-11:71.

Leonid I. Brezhnev
President of the Soviet Union;
Chairman, Soviet Communist Party
1

What real rights and freedoms are guaranteed to the masses in present-day imperialist society? The "right" of tens of millions to unemployment? Or the "right" of sick people to do without medical aid, which costs a vast sum of money? Or else the "right" of ethnic minorities to humiliating discrimination in employment and education, in politics and everyday life? Or is it the "right" to live in perpetual fear of the omnipotent underworld of organized crime and to see how the press, movies, television and radio go out of their way to educate the younger generation in a spirit of selfishness, cruelty and violence? Propagandists and ideologists of capitalism cannot deny the fact that socialism has long cured these social sores.

Before Supreme Soviet, Moscow, Oct. 4/
The New York Times, 10-5:(A)3.

Robert C. Byrd
United States Senator, D—West Virginia
2

One's family is the most important thing [in life]. I look at it this way: One of these days I'll be over in a hospital somewhere with four walls around me. And the only people who'll be with me will be my family. The rest will be busy with their responsibilities. It's pretty easy to be fast forgotten.

Interview, Washington/
The New York Times, 3-27:(1)44.

Sarah Caldwell
Director, Opera Company of Boston
3

The secret of living is to find people who will pay you money to do what you would pay to do if you had the money.

Los Angeles Times, 1-30:(1)20.

Richard Chamberlain
Actor
4

I grew up thinking life meant getting someplace — to a certain amount of money, a certain family situation, etc.; or to a certain enlightenment situation. But I don't think you ever get there. Or anywhere. If you're moving, that's the most you can ask for. That's what's always excited me about acting. People ask why I didn't stay in a [TV] series. I didn't want to stay anywhere. I want to keep moving!

Interview, New York/
The Christian Science Monitor, 1-3:22.

Prince Charles
Prince of Wales
5

A sense of humor is what keeps me sane. I would probably have been committed to an institution long ago were it not for the ability to see the funny side of life. If only more politicians were capable of laughing at themselves occasionally, the world would be a happier and sensible place.

San Francisco Examiner & Chronicle,
1-9:(This World)2.

Bertram J. Cohler
Psychologist, University of Chicago
6

We parents are not nearly as responsible for our children as we've come to believe. Kids are really independent creatures who create their own lives for themselves. Sure it's good to have nice, warm parents, but where's the hard evidence that it makes much difference in child development?

San Francisco Examiner & Chronicle,
11-27:(This World)2.

James P. Comer
Professor of psychiatry, Yale University
7

We ought to discard the notion that, if you work hard, you'll make it to the top. We should continue to promote the idea that you should work hard. But people ought to realize that, even if they do, they may not make it to the top. The anticipation that we're bound to be affluent and influential and have control over things is unrealistic. Yet many people have that

WHAT THEY SAID IN 1977

(JAMES P. COMER)

feeling and are disillusioned, frustrated and angry when reality crowds in. In my view, we're no longer an expanding society, and we may never be again. We should readjust our values to reality — recognizing that a good, decent, hard-working cleaning woman may be just as successful a human being as a millionaire. When we reach that point, we will be a much happier society — and a lot less frustrated and angry.

Interview/U.S. News & World Report, 10-10:54.

Norman Cousins
Editor, "Saturday Review"
1

What gives man uniqueness in the animal kingdom is his ability to do things for the first time.

At "Future of the West" conference,
University of Southern California/
Los Angeles Times, 3-28:(1)17.

Bette Davis
Actress
2

Nuts to growing old. Don't you ever believe that life begins at 40 or that it's wonderful to be 70. I'd give anything to be 30 again.

Interview, Weston, Conn./
The New York Times, 9-4:(2)21.

John Denver
Singer, Songwriter
3

My music is a celebration of life, all aspects of life. Everybody is calling out about how crappy life is, how hard it is; they're talking about drudgery, murders, muggings ... Yes, all that's out there, but it's only a slice of the cake. Now, look around you. The sun is shining. There are trees, rivers, lakes, mountains. And down the road two boys are helping their dad paint the house. I want to tell people how great the world is, tap their spirit so they might feel a oneness with God, with the universe.

Interview, Lake Tahoe, Nev./San Francisco
Examiner & Chronicle, 9-25:(Datebook)21.

Morarji R. Desai
Prime Minister of India
4

A poor man has more virtues than a rich man. Domestic servants, for instance, rarely steal. Yet the rich live by felony. How else but by felony does a man become rich?

The Washington Post, 3-25:(A)25.

Joan Didion
Author
5

Behavior is right or wrong. I was once having dinner with a psychiatrist who told me that I had monocular vision, and there was no need for everything to be right or wrong. Well, that way lies madness. In order to maintain a semblance of purposeful behavior on this earth, you have to believe that things are right or wrong.

Interview, Malibu, Calif./
The New York Times Book Review, 4-3:38.

6

As a writer, I used to think that I was outside politics, that I was, by definition, an outsider, an observer. But I have come to see that every time we put two words together, it is a political act. Politicians may think they are planning things, but it is the unheard masses, the powerless people, who will bring great changes in history.

At National Town Meeting, Washington/
The New York Times, 9-6:50.

Will Durant
Author, Historian
7

... I believe that there is as much love as hostility in the world. Even in the small circle of my acquaintances I have found ... so much incidental kindness that I have almost lost my faith in the wickedness of mankind.

At dinner in his honor,
Beverly Hills, Calif., Nov. 8/
Los Angeles Herald-Examiner, 11-10:(C)3.

Robert Evans
Motion-picture producer
8

Success has to have a natural talent, a natural sense, a natural something. It could be a

(ROBERT EVANS)

smell, a feeling, an instinct — something unique that makes you different from others.

Interview/Los Angeles Times, 1-30:(1)22.

Clifton Fadiman
Author, Editor

1

How dull life would be if we were constantly "adjusted" to our environment, from beginning to end! How poverty-stricken our minds and hearts would be if we did not occasionally fail! How dreadful it would be if we did not have to suffer the loss of loved ones!

Interview, Santa Barbara, Calif./
The Center Magazine, July-Aug.:51.

2

What is a sense of humor? Surely not the ability to understand a joke. It comes, rather, from a residual feeling of one's own absurdity. It *is* the ability to understand a joke — and that the joke is oneself.

Interview, Santa Barbara, Calif./
The Center Magazine, July-Aug.:53.

Marty Feldman
Actor, Comedian

3

All comedy seems to come from the same mainspring; the engine-room is the same, no matter what the superstructure is like. It's the need to make people laugh, the need for instant demonstrable approval. All clowns have a fellow feeling. We're all deeply insecure whatever we may claim, because if we were not, why the hell would we want to present ourselves as figures of fun?

Interview/San Francisco Examiner &
Chronicle, 8-14:(Datebook)15.

Paul A. Freund
Professor of law,
Harvard University

4

We see the effect of bigness — where individual responsibility becomes fuzzy in a large enterprise; of modern psychology, which tends to minimize the element of blame; and of insurance, which has become a convenient way of papering over irresponsible management or professional conduct.

U.S. News & World Report, 9-26:84.

J. William Fulbright
Former United States Senator,
D–Arkansas

5

Man isn't inherently destructive. That is, he isn't inherently destructive in his genes. He isn't inherently trying to destroy his own kind. And we're capable of learning and acting differently from the way we've acted for 10,000 years . . . The destruction comes from the culture. We have engaged in these self-destructive things, but, being limited in our capacity for destruction, so far we've survived. But now, with nuclear weapons, if our destructiveness is in our genes there certainly isn't any hope. There's a hell of a difference between that belief and the idea that we can learn to be different. Now, when I say that to most people, I'm sure they say, "Good God, how presumptuous. How could that damn stupid fellow ever think he could do anything about human nature?" But there's got to be something new; there's got to be a better approach.

Interview/The Washington Post, 11-13:(A)3.

John Kenneth Galbraith
Former professor of economics,
Harvard University

6

I come from a family of tall men, and I have always believed that the discrimination in favor of tallness is one of the most blatant and forgiven prejudices in our society. There was a day when my height gave me a range of opportunity that I would never have had otherwise, because people always remember the guy whose head stands high above the others when they are trying to think of somebody for a job. Once I had a long conversation with General Charles de Gaulle, whose head I saw across a crowded room at a party in Washington. "Professor," he said, "what is your philosophy about our vast height?" "We tall men," I said, "being higher than anybody else, are much more visible and thus more closely watched. Therefore it follows that our behavior is

WHAT THEY SAID IN 1977

naturally superior. So the world instinctively and rightfully trusts tall men." "Magnifique!" the General exclaimed. "But there is one thing you have forgotten: The small men must be treated without mercy." Then he laughed at his little joke. At least I hope it was a joke.

Interview, New York/
The Christian Science Monitor, 5-18:26.

Will Geer
Actor
1

Young people keep people young. Keeping up with young people is important. Don't lay down and die and give up, or roll over and say, "What's the use?" You'll lose in some departments as you get older, but the main thing is, don't lose in all the departments at once! Get rid of that quiet frustration; don't resign yourself to the slough of despond. Everyone has to love and be wanted and desired. You won't be wanted if you go around complaining all the time, even though there are little aches and pains. Don't criticize the way a young person does something; let them do it their way, and then show them by example how you do it. Growing old gracefully comes from not being too concerned with yourself. People get old and fall apart at 65 because they have nothing to do. They need hobbies. Be interested in other people; meet new people and learn their views. Don't pretend you're God or mother; don't be nosy, just sincerely interested. That's enough to keep you young.

Interview, Burbank, Calif./
Los Angeles Herald-Examiner, 2-28:(B)1.

Ruth Gordon
Actress
2

Work is life, and life is work. I do not know what people do who are born rich, because I was not. I do not think they enjoy life as much as I do. Yesterday, I went out speaking; today, I am speaking; and Sunday, Canada wants me, and I am going up there ... Well, that is a lovely set of engagements, and where would I

be without that? I would be dead ... I would not know how to fill my time if I did not work.

Before House Select Committee on Aging,
Washington/U.S. News & World Report, 10-3:30.

Theodore J. Gordon
President, The Futures Group
3

Values are a particularly difficult topic because new values inevitably challenge our familiar values, and to agree that change may be desirable is tantamount to admitting that our present values are less than ideal and that, in fact, living by another standard might have been better. But values of one generation inevitably challenge values of another. Technology, the media, economic necessity and political expediency add their own opportunities and distortions, and values change, not toward an optimum, but toward a difference. And that difference makes the life-styles of the future.

Before The Conference Board, New York,
May 19/Vital Speeches, 7-1:563.

Arlo Guthrie
Folk singer; Composer
4

There are not many circumstances that allow me to be me. I think everybody feels that. I'm limited by life, by the work I have to do, by mothers, fathers, sisters, brothers. The world is a restrictive place — except for those who go at it with pride or lust or envy. Spirit is, however, not burdened by such things.

Interview/The Washington Post, 7-29:(B)1.

Alex Haley
Author
5

There's just no question that to know one's own history is a very valuable thing. The greatest strength the Jewish people have, for instance, is their sense of history. And it's a beautiful thing — to have survived. It's enough to make one fall on one's knees that it was possible to weather all these trials. Look at England. By almost all the material measures, England is in dire straits. But England has a fantastically preserved historical image of itself, and others have it as well. I think, as a human race, one of the greatest dangers we're [the

(ALEX HALEY)

U.S.] in is that of moving too fast, too far, from a sense of our past, and how we got to where we are. We are becoming very much a rootless people.

Interview, Cheviot Hills, Calif./
TWA Ambassador, January:16.

Rex Harrison
Actor

1

Charm is nebulous. It may be a mannerism; it may be a voice; it may be the movement of a hand. But whatever it is that makes a person charming, it needs to remain a mystery, particularly to the charmer, herself or himself. Because once the charmer is aware of a mannerism or characteristic that others find charming, it ceases to be a mannerism and becomes an affectation. And good Lord, there is nothing less charming than affectations!

Interview/
Los Angeles Herald-Examiner, 6-24:(C)2.

Theodore M. Hesburgh
President, University of Notre Dame

2

[On happiness]: It can only come from giving at least a corner of yourself to others. People today are so egocentric. God help the person who goes through life doing nothing for someone else. He's doomed.

Interview/Time, 5-2:74.

Robert Hogan
Professor of psychology,
Johns Hopkins University

3

You can give a philosophical, religious, ethical or moral justification for living the life you do. You become a good Catholic, a Marxist, a Fascist, a member of Kennedy's Peace Corps, a flaming liberal or a Young Republican. Ideologies are usually philosophical world views. From your parents, you learned specific rules; and from your peers, specific expectations. It's like a laundry list: The ideology puts it all together and gives it a defensible structure. It rationalizes all those

rules. People need that. My favorite quote on this is from Malcolm X: "Doing good is a hustle, too."

Interview, Baltimore/
The National Observer, 1-8:6.

Hubert H. Humphrey
United States Senator, D–Minnesota

4

What I've learned from living is that there are some things over which a man has no control. You are buffeted by events that are unknown, uncharted, unpredictable. And one has to learn to live with the uncertainties of life. That's really what you have to do, what I think you learn. When you're young, you feel that you can conquer almost anything. You've got the answers. You're sure, if only the old folks would get out of the way, then you could really set everything straight. But what you learn from life is that there are unknowns and problems for which there are as yet no answers. There are still forces and powers that move the universe in your life, and these are not always subject to your personal control. Therefore, you've got to have an awful lot of faith that somehow things are going to work out and that you're running with a destiny that's maybe not fully in your hands. I'm philosophizing and as usual talking maybe a little more about it than I should. But I've also learned from life to be tolerant, forgiving, understanding. You cannot go around and keep score. If you keep score on the good things and the bad things, you'll find out that you're a very miserable person. God gave man the ability to forget, which is one of the greatest attributes you have. Because if you remember everything that's happened to you, you generally remember that which is the most unfortunate.

Interview,Washington/Parade, 10-2:10.

5

. . . a society needs tension and dissatisfaction. Also restlessness. You've got to have restlessness in order to have progress. Stagnant waters stay stagnant. They become polluted. They've got to move. They may at times tear out the embankment. They may at times rip up

WHAT THEY SAID IN 1977

the landscape. But they're fresh, and they cut new streams, new channels.

Interview, Washington/Parade, 10-2:11.

Jesse L. Jackson
Civil-rights leader; President,
Operation PUSH (People United
to Save Humanity)
1

When I was a child in Greenville, we never were poor — we just didn't have any money. We didn't have a poverty complex. We had limited options — but we had options. Even in the worst of situations, you still have the choice between the high road and the low road. It didn't take money to buy character, integrity and decency.

Interview/Parade, 2-13:20.

Spencer W. Kimball
President, Church of Jesus Christ
of Latter-day Saints (Mormon)
2

It's distressing, very distressing — all this discussion we are getting about morality and the new permissiveness in reports dealing with such matters as homosexuality, abortions and pornography. It's bound to have an effect on people's thinking, and the evidence points to a great deterioration in their standards of morality . . . For instance, you see this permissiveness all over the country in coeducational colleges and universities where they allow men and women to use the same dormitories. Like so many things today, it has very quickly become the fashion — even if it goes against all the things people have been taught.

Interview/U.S. News & World Report, 12-19:60.

Henry A. Kissinger
Former Secretary of State
of the United States
3

I never harass somebody I think is working at his capacity. A mediocre person I never harass. I believe most people don't know what they can do. Look, what's the difference between [the legendary late pro football coach] Vince Lombardi and a high-school

football coach? They both know the same plays. It's a question of getting a little more precision.

Interview, Washington/
"W": a Fairchild publication, 2-4:10.

Alfred A. Knopf
Book publisher
4

The state of the Western world is so bad that I think we are living through the beginning of the end of a great civilization. You can sum up the reason in a five-letter word: greed.

Interview/The New York Times, 9-12:42.

Chuck Knox
Football coach, Los Angeles "Rams"
5

Some people think experience is a synonym for a term of years on a job, but it isn't. In any profession you'll find some 20-year men who learned rapidly for three years and have been coasting for 17. Experience is not what happens to a man. It's what a man *does* with what happens to him.

Interview/Los Angeles Times, 12-23:(3)1.

Bert Lance
Director, Federal Office of
Management and Budget
6

Success is a journey and not a destination. I don't see I'll ever arrive at the point where I'll say, "Lance, old boy, you've arrived at success." There's no question about it. Once you get to the point where you've arrived at a station called success, you get complacent and lethargic.

Interview, Washington/
Los Angeles Times, 4-17:(4)22.

Anne Morrow Lindbergh
Author; Widow of the late aviator,
Charles Lindbergh
7

Some would say there can't be heroes any more, that my husband was the last one. Some say we have witnessed too much suffering and treachery to believe in heroes. I think there still are and always will be heroes, but they only arise of troubled times — wars, riots, tragedies, great changes. Right now, we are not an

(ANNE MORROW LINDBERGH)

especially troubled people in the context of history. Our attention isn't focused on any one crisis. There are heroes today; we just call them something else. They are the ones who have endured and won through great difficulties.

Interview/Good Housekeeping, June:80.

John D. MacDonald
Author
1

The only thing I got out of Harvard Business School was that I learned how to think. I found out that a decision is never made absolutely coldly; it is never reached with 100 per cent logic. I learned that, whatever course of action you take, the decision is going to be affected by our inner feelings, emotions, prejudices and self-deceit. God deliver me from the man who says, "I'm doing this out of pure logic." This is the deification of the computer.

Interview/
"W": a Fairchild publication, 5-27:2.

Shirley MacLaine
Actress
2

When you look back on your life and try to figure out where you've been and where you are going, when you look at your work, your love affairs, your marriages, your children, your pain, your happiness — when you examine all that closely, what you really find out is that the only person you really go to bed with is yourself. The only person you really dress is yourself. The only person you really eat with is yourself. So, in the end, life must be what you do with yourself. And all the wonderful surroundings, like people you live with, your friends, your co-workers, are all extensions but they're not you. The only thing you have is working to the consummation of your own identity.

Interview, Washington/
The Washington Post, 11-14:(C)3.

Paul W. McCracken
Professor of business administration,
University of Michigan; Former
Chairman, Council of Economic Advisers
to the President of the United States
(Richard M. Nixon)
3

The long history of mankind clearly establishes that it is the liberal and open society that generates progress. The burst of creativity in Athens, the Great Age in England following limitations placed on the powers of the Crown, the explosive development of Japan after the Meiji Restoration a century ago, what free men and free institutions wrought here [in the U.S.] in bringing this land from an empty wilderness to the world's most productive economy — these are but a few of history's illustrations. These results are what we would expect. Only if people are free to do their thing can we have an aggregate of knowledge and innovativeness and creativity that does not exist in its totality any place, and cannot be managed from any one place. Only with free and open markets — whether for new products or new art forms or new ideas generally — does the new have a chance to out-compete and disestablish the old. This is why state-organized systems, however *avant garde* their rhetoric, are so disappointing in their results. The "new" which those at the top can manage and implement is so restricted.

Before Economic Club of Detroit,
Feb. 7/Vital Speeches, 3-1:313.

Margaret Mead
Anthropologist
4

People who think we can write off any part of the human race without destroying ourselves are ignoring the evolution of a global society. We have to love the whole planet. If you don't, it won't do you a bit of good to love your country and your flag.

San Francisco Examiner & Chronicle,
3-6:(This World)2.

5

I have been studying many kinds of primitive peoples for 50 years, and I am finding that as a civilization gets more complex, maturity — in the sense of being able to handle the whole

(MARGARET MEAD)

repertoire of society — gets postponed. Eskimo children learn almost everything they need to know before they are 6. In rural societies, young people learn everything they need to know by the teens. But as a society gets more complex there's more and more room for people to keep on learning new things all their lives. If you value wisdom, you also value people continuing to develop. You don't have much wisdom if you close your mind and don't learn anything new. The wise people in society are the people who can deal with change. The people I admire most are those who have open minds and are learning new things when they're quite old.

Interview/The National Observer, 5-9:7.

Takeo Miki
Former Prime Minister of Japan
1

Democracy has never been an answer to problems. It is a process for solving problems, by reconciling and protecting the interests, and rights, of diverse groups in the society. Democracy cannot be imposed. It must be learned — and earned — by the people who choose it. Once learned, democracy is not given up lightly, as the recent events in India demonstrate. The future of democracy . . . rests on the historical fact that no other system, however "efficient" or tidy, can guarantee individual initiative, and personal freedom and fulfillment, as effectively as democracy.

Before Commonwealth Club, San Francisco,
June 10/Vital Speeches, 8-15:661.

Henry Miller
Author
2

We don't have anything in the way of culture here [in the U.S.] any more. We're too deodorized and mechanized. Somebody once asked me what the difference between civilization and culture was, and I remembered Spengler's line that civilization is the arteriosclerotic phase of culture. The only people who have culture now are the primitives. My favorite people are the pygmies. They live a total life. Their forest is their god. They have no need for

refrigerators or screw drivers. Where else could we find men who are happy with what they've got?

Interview, Los Angeles/
Los Angeles Times, 9-9:(4)20.

3

[On death] : I don't fear it; sometimes I feel it's time I ought to be there. Life must be just as good on the other side. Life goes on, I'm sure; my intuition, feeling, lead me to believe these things exist. Otherwise, it's a waste of time to exist. You live a few years, you're snuffed out — it doesn't make sense.

Interview, Los Angeles/
The Washington Post, 10-23:(H)8.

Robert Moses
Government planner and builder
4

Youth is increasingly contemptuous of second- and third-rate administrators, tired of drugs, disorder, murder, rape, unreliable safety at home and in the streets. The voters want an end of political shenanigans. They are sick of junkyard statuary at the crossroads. They are bored with ads of in- and outdoor spas where nude ladies with protruding bellies are reduced and males have their spare ribs covered. Youth is beginning to ask why the lowest common denominator must rule, and why we must go straight from Watergate to Billingsgate. I speak for the middle road. I am for the radius which unites the suburbs as against the roundabout, circumferential routes advocated by fanatical environmentalists. I am against all extremists, all social snobbery, all exclusiveness, all catering to a disappearing aristocracy, all prolonged hearings and futile, expensive delays.

At Fordham University/
The New York Times, 5-19:35.

Malcolm Muggeridge
Author; Former editor,
"Punch" magazine
5

[The media are] a Frankenstein monster which we as yet have no means of controlling . . . the single greatest influence of our age, exerted arbitrarily and without reference to moral guidelines, carrying out a mighty brain-

(MALCOLM MUGGERIDGE)

washing operation denigrating moral and spiritual values and leaving a vacuum.

Dallas, April 13/
The Dallas Times Herald, 4-14:(F)1.

1

I always think that the best jobs are the jobs that are completely useless, because they're the only ones that teach you anything. I've had a number of useless jobs myself, notably military intelligence. To be occupied with something that has absolutely no point is, in terms of one's spiritual growth, a very valuable experience, because it delivers you from the idea that the purpose of being in this world is to operate in this world's terms. Doing something, say, military intelligence, which is completely futile and absurd makes you realize that about 99 per cent of all human activities are, as Pascal says, diversions.

Interview, Dallas/
The Dallas Times Herald, 5-9:(C)3.

Louise Nevelson
Sculptor

2

I am very careful with language. When you use words like "perfection" it can kill you. Or "happiness." These are vague words, cliches people use, that cannot be fulfilled.

Interview, San Francisco/San Francisco
Examiner & Chronicle, 3-6:(Scene)3.

Richard M. Nixon
Former President of the United States

3

[People say,] "Well, gee, isn't it just great to . . . have enough money to afford to live in a very nice house and to be able to play golf and to have nice parties, and to wear good clothes and shoes and suits, et cetera, et cetera, et cetera, or travel if you want to." They don't know life; because what makes life mean something is purpose; a goal; the battle; the struggle — even if you don't win it.

Television broadcast, San Clemente, Calif./
"The Nixon Interviews," Paradine Productions, 5-25.

Vance Packard
Author

4

Genes, instincts and environment do play a role in shaping our lives. But it is also a fact that with effort we can still influence our destinies. Man is many things, admirable and unadmirable, but he has the potential for self-mastery and social direction, and he is at his best when he is achieving these ends. To a very great extent, each of us can be his own shaper.

Interview, Martha's Vineyard, Mass./
People, 9-26:41.

Irene Papas
Actress

5

. . . everyone can attain the asset of individuality. Some people get in a rut and fail to discover their assets. So much can be achieved if you never let the fire of self-improvement be extinguished. Maybe you begin with only a little spark, but if you make the effort to fan it you'll have a flame. If you are pessimistic or procrastinate, you can fan the ashes forever, but it will be too late.

Interview/Los Angeles Times, 11-20:(5)5.

S. J. Perelman
Author, Playwright

6

I think there's a scarcity of humor because these last two or three generations have been joyless people. Modern youth is remarkably solemn. It could be argued that they have reason to be solemn. But they don't laugh very much and, consequently, there's not very much output.

Interview/
"W": a Fairchild publication, 3-18:2.

Prince Philip
Duke of Edinburgh

7

Measured in terms of the incidence of such community diseases as alcoholism, vandalism, mugging and social, racial and religious friction, there are a good many communities which can only be described as sick. The age of the social conscience, social justice and concern seems to have coincided with the age of crime, pornog-

WHAT THEY SAID IN 1977

(PRINCE PHILIP)

raphy, mugging and international terrorism. What started out as a liberalization of restrictive social conventions seems to have developed into a dictatorship of license. It is becoming only too apparent that it is possible for communities to achieve quite high standards of material development with, at the same time, the moral and behavioral standards of a colony of monkeys.

Before Men's Canadian Club, Ottawa,
Oct. 17/The New York Times, 10-18:20.

Carl Reiner
Motion-picture director; Humorist
1

Comedians come when the time needs commenting on. The more inflation, recession, oppression, wars or whatever, the more comedians will come. When everything is perfect, there won't be any more comedians. Or they'll be laughing at something else — behavior, or how funny we look when we trip. There will always be wit.

Interview, New York/
The Christian Science Monitor, 12-16:27.

Ginger Rogers
Actress, Entertainer
2

I. think that one's trek through life is limited only by oneself, and one's unwillingness to work. I'll try anything new and I think that working is where you find success . . . If I was a painter, I'd be up painting all night. My hours would be just as rigorous [as being a performer], because I love doing. Doing — I adore it.

Interview/After Dark, February:30.

Telly Savalas
Actor
3

Money can do a lot of beautiful things for you, baby, but not if you put money in a safe place in the closet. It has no value at all then. Use it. Spend it. Spread it around. All that money hoarded up won't make you feel secure. How dull life would be if you knew tomorrow exactly what's going to happen. I may be poor tomorrow. I may be infamous. I may be

scandalous and no one would want to interview me. Now, wouldn't that be a lot of fun?

San Diego, Calif./
Los Angeles Times, 3-27:(5)22.

Maria Schell
Actress
4

I think that mistakes are very creative if you can try to come to understand that they were mistakes. One should trust one's mistakes as well as one's achievements, because the mistakes may even better show you the way than the achievements. The failures and the discontentments can be very creative if you use them right.

Interview, New York/
The Christian Science Monitor, 1-5:26.

Helmut Schmidt
Chancellor of West Germany
5

We cannot act as if we were free from the burden of the past. History cannot be shaken off. The only chance of overcoming the burden of past history is to write better contemporary history.

At Social Democratic Party convention,
Hamburg, Nov. 16/
The Washington Post, 11-17:(A)34.

Neil Simon
Playwright, Screenwriter
6

Success takes you to some very strange places. It isolates you and it affects people around you — your family and friends. They begin to view you differently, as though you were some sort of extraordinary person — you have been to a place they haven't seen, a place they don't know at all. For example, I had relatives who used to call and who stopped calling. Finally, when they did call they would say, "I hate to disturb you." In other words, they were saying that you are now a separate person. Also, it was very difficult for me as a writer to walk along the street and be recognized. One of the joys of being a writer is one's anonymity. I've never enjoyed being stared at or mumbled about. You begin to wonder about being a celebrity. You realize you need not have done anything wonderful. You can assas-

(NEIL SIMON)

sinate the President and be a celebrity. People will say, "Oh, there goes Lee Harvey Oswald" [assassin of President John Kennedy]. You begin to wonder what it is people are thinking about you.

Interview, Beverly Hills, Calif./
Los Angeles Times, 4-22:(4)6.

Red Skelton
Comedian
1

I sat through 15 minutes of *Dog Day Afternoon* and counted 71 four-letter words and got up and left. I turned down the movie, *The Sunshine Boys,* because I refused to call Jack Benny a son of a bitch and to look up under a nurse's dress. Humor is truth. Wit is an exaggeration on that truth. I don't think you have to talk about personal parts of the body or bodily functions. I always put myself below the audience. People using off-color material put themselves above the audience. It's a shortcut for thinking. The audience may laugh, but their laughter is out of embarrassment.

Interview, Palm Springs, Calif./
The New York Times, 3-9:19.

Henryk Skolimowski
Professor of philosophy, University
of Michigan College of Engineering
2

We often resort to the knowledge stored in the layers of our evolution, and on occasion we have an awareness of it, too. Take the language of the body, the language of the skin, the language of the eyes — the eyes in particular. What would our life have been without those languages? When my eyes meet your eyes, after three seconds I know who you are, even if I cannot express it, either to you or to myself. I walk through life avoiding those against whom my eyes have warned me; and spreading an invisible net on those whom my eyes have approved. I have knowledge in my eyes, and I know it. When I look into your eyes, you are an open quarry to me, in which I can see all the shapes chiseled out by life. I can understand you through my skin. I can grasp the quivering of your biology through the sparks of your

eyes. I can submerge myself into your being, because my being and your being have been molded by the same evolutionary forces and they share the same heritage of life. Through my skin and my tissues, through my senses and my mind acting in unison, I can tune in to listen to you and to myself as the music of evolution. My body, my skin, my eyes are the tentacles through which life rolls in, through which we tune in to the music of evolution, of which we are a part. To be rational is to understand the music of the universe in the Pythagorean sense.

Lecture/The Wall Street Journal, 1-28:12.

Paul Taylor
Choreographer
3

I look at people in the streets and in the country, and I come to the conclusion that the most beautiful things to see are not in the art galleries. They are all around. You just have to open your eyes.

Interview/Time, 7-18:78.

Margaret Thatcher
Member of British Parliament;
Leader, British Conservative Party
4

All Communism worries me. Fundamentally, it's not very different wherever it occurs, because it is a creed which allows only one political view. Wherever the Communists get into power, they prevent anyone else from having any other kind of politics but their own. Then, too, it is a creed that's based on economics — controlled economics at that. There's no thought for the dignity of the individual or for his place in society. So, of course, Communism worries me.

Interview, London/
U.S. News & World Report, 9-12:70.

Gus Turbeville
President, Emerson College
5

Too often we attempt to get turned on by *things:* a new automobile, a pretty home, a fine job, a trip around the world. We fail to realize, however, that these are ephemeral, and that a permanent turning on can only be found in eternal values such as service to mankind,

WHAT THEY SAID IN 1977

(GUS TURBEVILLE)

compassion for one's neighbors, and love of all of God's creations. Where can you get tuned in and turned on? Many people report that they get this kind of sensation whenever they enter a church or other holy building. Some obtain it at home while quietly meditating and listening for the inner voice. Others find that being near a body of water — a lake or the ocean — helps induce this feeling of tranquility. I find that a walk along the Charles River [in Boston] or a ride on a lonesome farm road on a motorcycle does it for me. But the important thing is that you don't have to be *somewhere* to attain it. Rather, when you become the right kind of person, the strength and beauty of this inner presence will manifest itself in you. And you won't have to tell people you have it; your facial expression and the kind of life you lead will point unerringly to your real character.

At Emerson College, Sept. 15/
Vital Speeches, 10-1:748.

Cicely Tyson
Actress
1

Challenges make you discover things about yourself you really never knew. I love challenges. They're what make the instrument stretch, what make you go beyond the norm.

Interview/Los Angeles Times, 1-30(1)20.

Liv Ullmann
Actress
2

[The film] *Scenes [from a Marriage]* taught me what success is. And what it is, really, is nothing to strive for. Suddenly I was being photographed with all these famous people; I was talking and dancing and drinking and sharing with them — but inside nothing really changes. It's still you there in the middle of it. It's not so fantastic.

Interview, New York/TV Guide, 5-5:28.

Peter Ustinov
Actor, Director, Writer
3

There has never been an anthem which sets my foot tapping, never an occasion which

brings a lump to my throat. I can take no allegiance to a flag if I don't know who's holding it.

Interview, Paris/
Los Angeles Times, 9-6:(4)14.

4

"Image" is an awful thing. You say to somebody, "I'm going to write about this, that and the other," and they say, "Oh! I hope you'll be careful about your image!" I just don't know what my image is and I don't want to know. If you arrive at the point where the man looking back at you in the mirror is more important than the man who is looking into the mirror, then you might as well pack up . . .

Interview, New York/
The Christian Science Monitor, 12-7:25.

Ralph Waite
Actor
5

I'm not any more moral than my neighbors. I have vanity and greed enough for one person. But at the same time I feel in my bones you lose a lot of life's value if you don't see yourself as a member of the family of man. The beauty of life is in people who feel some obligation to enhance life. Without that, we're only half alive.

Interview/People, 2-14:85.

Eli Wallach
Actor
6

[On marriage] : You assume that only *you* grow and change, that the other person will stay arrested at the point when you met them. But time takes its toll; the other person develops intellectually or doesn't develop. You have to share it. Nature is so involved. Different parts of us mature at different times. Yet today everything is so disposable, we're such a mobile country. Nobody makes an investment in a relationship any more.

Interview, New York/
The Christian Science Monitor, 4-8:24.

Ben J. Wattenberg
Political analyst

1

[On what happened to the visions of new life-styles by dropouts of the 1960s]: They had to make a very basic decision: whether to let their own daughters grow up with buck teeth. So they went to work for the same reason the rest of us do — to assure for themselves and their children the things they had learned to appreciate when they were growing up: a decent home, a college education, and, yes, orthodontics. No doubt, when they reach age 40, they will [ask], "What is the meaning of life?" They will find no satisfactory answer and go out and buy a cabin cruiser or find a lover and smile indulgently at their own rebellious children and plod onward. Progress? What can I tell you? Life is a tough racket. But it gets even tougher if you have to buy your kid braces at the same time you're trying to resurrect an abandoned farm.

Television program/"In Search of the Real America,"
Public Broadcasting Service, 3-29.

Edward Bennett Williams
Lawyer

2

. . . we must remember that our kind of free society is still the exception in the world — still unattainable to most people, for most of the world lives under government that has no interest in fostering and nurturing the concept of freedom. The world is full of people who think men need masters.

Before lawyers division,
Anti-Defamation League of B'nai B'rith/
The National Observer, 3-26:12.

Andrew Young
United States Ambassador/Permanent
Representative to the United Nations

3

If we ever believe things are impossible, then we've got nothing to live for at all. These impossible dreams make life worthwhile, and I wouldn't trade them for any amount of realism, caution or protocol in the world.

Before United Nations Association of the U.S.,
New York, April 19/The New York Times, 4-20:(A)3.

Ardeshir Zahedi
Iranian Ambassador to the United States

4

We cannot continue to live in a society where a few are rich and the rest are poor. Surely, we can leave no more brilliant heritage than the knowledge that we saw the need of our fellow man and worked to save him from disease, poverty and starvation. Saadi, the great Persian poet, said, "To serve humanity is the ultimate goal of worship." Like the human organism, if one part of mankind is in want, or diseased, all of humanity is affected and thereby suffers.

At Westminster College, Fulton, Mo., May 7/
The Washington Post, 5-31:(A)16.

Efrem Zimbalist, Jr.
Actor

5

When I was a young man, I suffered from day to day with what seemed like momentous decisions. Should I make this or that choice? Like so many young people, I looked upon each new event as a crisis situation, a turning point in the road, a place where I had to take a stand on some monumental problem. But over the years I've found life has a way of writing its own story. Maybe it's just the viewpoint of my maturing years, but it seems to me most crises and problems do get smaller and even disappear as the weeks and months go by. The perspective of time is nature's own sweet song.

Interview, Los Angeles/
Los Angeles Times, 4-10:(Home)45.

Religion

Lew Ayres
Actor

1

What we take to be the meaning of life is only a hypothesis, a hypothesis in which we must have enough faith to give a reasonable share of our time and effort. I've found that the various religions give you a hypothesis: This is the meaning of life, or that is the course you must follow. You take elements from each of the religions and test them against the facts of life as you encounter them ... For me, [religion is] an area of ultimate concern. It's that thing in your life to which you give the best of yourself, your greatest measure of devotion. I believe there is a mind and spirit in the universe, that there is meaning in the universe and that life is not a tale told by an idiot. There is a plan, I think; and, since we live in a climate of free will, we may reject that plan. I think we've been given the opportunity to find our way toward better fulfillment, but we may reject that possibility and accept a life that is limited, frustrating and without any meaning whatsoever.

Interview, Los Angeles/
Los Angeles Times, 5-16:(4)4.

Peter L. Berger
Professor of sociology,
Rutgers University

2

We already have in this country [the U.S.] probably the most diverse religious life of any society in human history. It's hard to imagine how it could be any more diverse. On Saturday, the religious pages of any large-city newspaper in this country [are] like an introductory course in comparative religion ... I think there's more religious vitality in this country than [in] any other Western country. Look how many Americans go to church and how many of them give money to religion. If you're asking whether they care on a deep level or on a shallow level, I see absolutely no reason to say it's on a shallow level. People are more committed, more interested — even intellectually interested — than Europeans are. Over and over again, what strikes Europeans who are interested in religion is the incredible vitality of religion they see in America.

Interview/U.S. News & World Report, 4-11:72.

Daniel Berrigan
Clergyman

3

Churchgoers are used to lukewarm yogurt, but the Bible is about sin, scandal, violence, about lousy authorities, sex, money — what life is about today. A lot of people think the church ought to be some sort of haven to protect the self, turning their backs on human degradation and suffering. But that's not the Bible. If faith does anything, as shown by the prophets and Jesus, it leads us into the injustice and suffering in the world. It means entering the public arena, speaking up.

Interview, New York/
Los Angeles Herald-Examiner, 10-29:(A)7.

Zbigniew Brzezinski
Assistant to President of the
United States Jimmy Carter
for National Security Affairs

4

I think we do not understand fully what we are, why we're here. This is the ultimate mystery of human experience and, therefore, some search by man for meaning beyond himself is a necessary condition of life. I'm religious in a searching way. I would like to know why we are here. I would like to relate to

(ZBIGNIEW BRZEZINSKI)

something transcendental which can be called God and to religion as a search for God.

Interview, Washington/
The Washington Post, 2-4:(B)3.

Jimmy Carter
President of the United States 1

We believe in separation of church and state, that there should be no unwarranted influence on the church or religion by the state, and vice versa. My own religious convictions are deep and personal. I seek divine guidance when I make a difficult decision as President and also am supported, of course, by the common purpose which binds Christians together, and a belief in the human dignity of mankind and also in the search for worldwide peace, recognizing, of course, that those who don't share my faith quite often have the same desires and hopes. My own constant hope is that all nations would give maximum freedom of religion and freedom of expression to their people, and I will do all I can within the bounds of propriety to bring that hope into realization.

News conference, Warsaw, Poland,
Dec. 30/The New York Times, 12-31:2.

Julie Nixon Eisenhower
Author; Daughter of former
President of the United States
Richard M. Nixon 2

I think that one thing that has helped me is my faith. I really am quite reluctant to talk about faith in God, because I think it is a very personal thing and, in a way, it cheapens it to go into it in great depth. But I think if you really study the Bible, you really learn more all the time; it is such a rich source. And a lot of these things you worry over don't seem that important when you are focusing on the spiritual side of life.

Interview, New York/
The Christian Science Monitor, 6-23:21.

Clifton Fadiman
Author, Editor 3

I have never been afflicted by the idea of God. I have never awakened in the middle of the night and said, without the idea of God my life is useless and meaningless. I read with reverence the outpourings of religious men. I acknowledge the validity of the visions of the saints. I do not mean by validity that these visions are real, but that these visions are generative, interesting, beautiful. But I find no need for them in my own life ... I believe in nothing but the necessity of all human beings to exhaust the capacities that are in them, if those capacities are such that their exercise will not harm others. I believe in the normal morality that I was brought up in. I believe, on the whole, that the Judeo-Christian tradition, putting aside the transcendental element, has much to commend it, and I try to follow it in my small way as well as I can. But I have never found it necessary to set down my beliefs as if they were an inflexible system. I do not believe in absolutely permanent truths. It seems inconceivable to me that men and women a million years from now should be at all like what you and I are at this moment. So I cannot believe in any unchanging, permanently true system of beliefs, beyond the simple one I have just expressed.

Interview, Santa Barbara, Calif./
The Center Magazine, July-Aug.:55.

R. Buckminster Fuller
Engineer, Author, Designer 4

What of our own experience provides experimental evidence of a greater intellect operating on our universe than the human one? Personally, I am overwhelmed by the spiritual evidence of a greater intellect. Call it God, but a word is just a direction and so utterly inadequate to capture the meaning of this 100-percent efficient, eternally unlimited integrity. I refuse to believe that we were put here on earth to be amused or displeased. The evolution of the universe was not intended for such small things. The universe and man are utterly metaphysical.

Interview, Cambridge, Mass./
The Christian Science Monitor, 3-9:17.

WHAT THEY SAID IN 1977

Jackie Gleason
Entertainer

1

I've been searching for God all my life, but just never found Him. Organized religion treats people exactly like television executives treat actors: They use threats to your security and offer appeals to your vanity. Oh, I think there's a divine being, but we haven't the slightest idea who he is, what he does, or what his intentions may be.

Interview, Fort Lauderdale, Fla./
San Francisco Examiner & Chronicle, 7-31:(Scene)6.

Jesse L. Jackson
Civil-rights leader; President, Operation
PUSH (People United to Save Humanity)

2

The church is by far the strongest black institution. Some left the church a few years ago to join other movements. But, in fact, most of those movements have gone, and the church remains. The church addresses needs, not fads, and invariably it is the institution most likely to act.

At conference sponsored by
Black Theological Project, Atlanta/
The New York Times, 8-6:6.

Spencer W. Kimball
President, Church of Jesus Christ
of Latter-day Saints (Mormon)

3

If one's life is built around a commitment to worthy beliefs and ideals, it becomes a practical way of dealing with one's problems. When people live by their faith, they don't go out and commit crimes, take something without working for it or neglect their families. Religious faith should encourage believers to work hard — not just for themselves but for their families and for others. Self-help and helping others — they go together.

Interview/U.S. News & World Report, 12-19:61.

Marcel Lefebvre
Roman Catholic Archbishop

4

[On his campaign against church reforms and his ordination of 14 priests against Pope Paul's orders]: The Pope said that what we are doing today will be a rupture. But who is the Pope? What is the Vatican? The Vatican is only a residence for the successor of St. Peter. The Holy Church is the center ... Priests being turned out these days no longer know what their role is. But our future is our past. Jesus Christ reigns yesterday, today and forever. We must be the Jesus Christ of yesterday in order to be the Jesus Christ of tomorrow.

Sermon, Econe, Switzerland, June 29/
Los Angeles Times, 6-30:(1)16.

5

[Pope Paul VI] is weak as a Pope and is being misled by enemies of the church who surround him. I have sent my seminarians to Rome so that they can become Romans and in the hope that the Pope will become Catholic.

Rio de Janeiro, Brazil/
Los Angeles Times, 8-1:(1)2.

Nikodem
Russian Orthodox Archibishop
of Leningrad and Novgorod

6

The mere idea of the existence of the church [in the Soviet Union] is in opposition to atheism [which is promoted by the government]. In our country, atheistic propaganda is very strong which maintains that church life is not important. [But] if church life here was weak, it would not be necessary to spend so much [government] money to campaign for atheism.

Interview, Leningrad/
Los Angeles Times, 5-22:(1)4.

Paul VI
Pope

7

[On the Church's prohibition against women becoming priests]: Christ chose His apostles from men. The Church has imitated Christ in choosing only men. We cannot change our Lord's actions or His call to women to follow Christ as beloved disciples and co-workers ...

Interview, Vatican City/
The New York Times Magazine, 4-10:52.

8

People today are abandoning religion and do not give a ready hearing to our message because

(PAUL VI)

they are convinced, wrongly, that the immense progress of rational civilization, the result of technology and science, removes the need for religion.

At synod of Roman Catholic bishops,
Vatican City, Sept. 30/
The New York Times, 10-1:7

Charles P. Price
Theologian, Virginia Theological Seminary
1

... it's human nature to resist change, most of all when it comes to change in one's church. Church and liturgies are supposed to be comfortable, reliable places in people's lives — not threats. I always like to think of new liturgies in terms of new shoes: Until you wear them in, they're awful.

The Washington Post, 11-1:(B)3.

James V. Schall
Associate professor, department of government,
University of San Francisco
2

Our recent era has been dominated by a pessimism as profound as any ever conceived, one at almost every point contrary to the essential dogmas of the faith, a pessimism that has pitted the earth against man and caused him to doubt the riches and even existence of providence. It is ironic, today, that the God of creation is a much vaster God than that of many of our pessimistic scientists. And yet we really understand something of the immensity of our universe. For this reason, I suspect, one of the major functions of religion, and particularly Christianity which is the one religion that has confronted science and out of which science arose, will be to save science from and for itself. The need for a scientifically educated clergy has never been greater, exceeded perhaps only by the need of scientists to cease being so ignorant of religion. We are in an era almost the opposite of the Galileo crisis. This time, it is more often science that needs religion to see the stars and the cosmos in their ultimate meaning and order.

Before Sierra Club, Modesto, Calif.,
Jan. 7/Vital Speeches, 2-15:273.

Andrei Sinyavsky
Exiled Soviet author
3

I know very little about church affairs, but religiosity is another matter. I witnessed it firsthand, in [Soviet labor] camp. Its intensity and many-sidedness are remarkable. So many shades of Orthodoxy, such a variety of sects! I have met people who were ready to give their lives for their faith, who were almost saints... There are people in camps today serving terms for their religious convictions who, through their suffering, attain the highest degree of spirituality.

Interview, Fontenay aux Roses, France/
The New York Times Book Review, 10-30:50.

David Tracy
Associate professor of theology,
School of Divinity,
University of Chicago
4

[Religion has] survived the materialism of the '50s, the romantic rebellion of the '60s. Now we're having to survive the narcissism, and it could be the most deadly of the three because it's the most seductive — it tempts one to believe that one is searching for authenticity in searching for personal experience, and it removes a serious social consciousness... We've moved one step beyond the 1960s and we're in a new phase. But we might have to go through more phases before we finally begin to find the nature of religion's mission in this country — what we are supposed to be doing and how to do it.

U.S. News & World Report, 4-11:55.

Peter Ustinov
Actor, Director, Writer
5

I believe that the Jews have made a contribution to the human condition out of all proportion to their numbers. I believe them to be an immense people. Not only have they supplied the world with two leaders of the stature of Jesus Christ and Karl Marx, but they have even indulged in the luxury of following neither one nor the other.

Interview, Paris/
Los Angeles Times, 9-6:(4)14.

WHAT THEY SAID IN 1977

Theo C. van Boven
Director-designate, United Nations
Commission on Human Rights

1

When conducting a survey of religious liberty in the world, many people have in mind violations of religious freedom in cases where certain forms of worship and religious teaching are curtailed, the observance of prescribed rituals and customary practices is impeded, the property of churches is affected, the distribution of religious literature is hindered or prohibited. It is obvious that these violations of religious liberty, which often occur in countries where atheism is the official philosophy, are inadmissible. But I want to add that the correct identification of these violations of religious liberty does not give the full picture of the state of religious freedom in the world. I regret to say that in many countries with so-called Christian traditions and with rulers who profess the Christian faith, religious liberty in its political and social implications is also in jeopardy. I refer to countries in Latin America, to southern Africa, to countries in East Asia with a large Christian population. Priests, pastors, laymen and laywomen who, as part of their Christian witness, work for social justice, who act as advocates of the oppressed, who provide relief to the persecuted, often get crushed. They risk their lives and liberty. Many of them are arrested and tortured; they may be expelled, or they may even disappear and get killed. In those situations, the ruling powers accept or support the church as a protector of the status quo; but the same ruling powers take action against men and women of the church, and others who are not associated with the church, when they voice criticism and when they come out in favor of social justice on behalf of the dispossessed and the victims of discrimination.

Liberty, May/June:5.

Space · Science · Technology

Edmund G. Brown, Jr.
Governor of California (D)

1

[On current U.S. space efforts]: For a country that wants to think of itself as a leader [in space], I find it rather disquieting that its aerospace budget is only slightly larger than the budget surplus of California and slightly larger than the aerospace budget of Japan. For a country that has pioneered so much in the field, I say the time is right for much greater investment.

At alternative energy conference, San Francisco, Aug. 2/Los Angeles Times, 8-3:(1)7.

2

. Instead of fighting or ignoring space exploration, we ought to be developing, celebrating and encouraging it ... We have to be struck with the fact that we live in a closed system with finite limits to what is possible. But, as we look into space, we can see immense possibilities ... As our frontiers on earth close down, people turn on themselves and jeopardize the future of society. Space, however, is a safety valve.

At space symposium, Los Angeles, Aug. 11/ Los Angeles Herald-Examiner, 8-11:(A)3.

Michael S. Dukakis
Governor of Massachusetts (D)

3

Genetic manipulation to create new forms of life places biologists at a threshold similar to that which physicists reached when they first split the atom.

Before Senate health subcommittee, Washington, April 6/ Los Angeles Herald-Examiner, 4-7:(A)16.

Robert A. Frosch
Administrator, National Aeronautics and Space Administration of the United States

4

I am often asked how I justify the NASA budget when we have so many problems back home ... The question is really backward. Is it really possible for the richest country in the world to say the entire thrust of intellectual effort to look outward [over the centuries] was wrong?

San Francisco Examiner & Chronicle, 8-21:(This World)2.

R. Buckminster Fuller
Engineer, Author, Designer

5

Many people ask me these days where I live, and I don't mean to be facetious. But I say I live on a planet that is making 60,000 miles per hour around the sun. We are all astronauts aboard Spaceship Earth, you know, and, with the movement of the galaxies, it becomes nonsensical to ask where we live.

Interview, Cambridge, Mass./ The Christian Science Monitor, 3-9:16.

Robert Jastrow
Director, Goddard Institute for Space Studies, National Aeronautics and Space Administration of the United States

6

One thing people don't understand about science is that it does not have the full story to tell, and there's a great big world out there with a lot more in it than physicists and astronomers know about. One of the biggest questions of both religion and science has been the origin of the universe. There was a time when scientists disputed the biblical view that there was a precise beginning to the universe. But now the almost universal consensus is that what astrono-

WHAT THEY SAID IN 1977

(ROBERT JASTROW)

mers call the "Big Bang" really did occur about 20 billion years ago. They trivialize this, in my view, by talking about it as if it were a firecracker when in fact what they're saying is that the universe began at a definite moment in time under circumstances of great heat and pressure that have wiped out all evidence of any pre-Creation world that might have existed. Because of that, it is impossible to ever find by scientific reasoning what the creative force or the prime mover or the energy was that brought this universe of ours into being. So the scientists have painted themselves into a corner by proving by their own methods that there are forces in the world — and you can call them God or the forces of physics — that are forever beyond the reach of scientific inquiry. And that's just mind-blowing to me. This is a point of contact between science and religious thinking that goes beyond the superficial resemblance of the flash of light to a few passages in the Bible. The important thing is the fact that there was a beginning not within the power of science to investigate. It has proven to me that one has to keep an open mind about what scientists call the body of science. It has defects in it, as it had in the 19th century, and it has what looks like permanent limitations on it, which means, in a way, that anybody can believe what he wishes.

Interview/Los Angeles Times, 11-9:(4)8.

Edward M. Kennedy
United States Senator, D—Massachusetts 1

The greatest potential threat to science is the lack of public understanding and public participation. We cannot afford irrational, unthinking, unknowing intrusions into sensitive and highly emotional areas like scientific policy. The best safeguard against future error is a more informed and participating public.

San Francisco Examiner & Chronicle,
11-20:(This World)2.

A. M. McMahon
Vice president, Bell Canada 2

One of the key factors in the success of the telephone system is the availability of a univer-

sal, cheap, reliable device to access the network — the telephone instrument itself. It doesn't take too much imagination to visualize the next generation . . . son-of-telephone, a more sophisticated instrument evolving from the simple telephone, with the ability to handle both voice and data. It will be able to signal the network, connect to a data base, input into the computer and receive the output, either in audible form, or by means of a simple digital display, much like an electronic calculator. Throw in small chips and microprocessors, and you could add automatic dialing, maybe a credit-card reader, as well as some memory and information storage capability. The result: a relatively simple low-cost device, giving ease of access, that could change the economic structure of communicating with computers, and change the whole marketplace . . . Can it be done? A few years ago, the answer would have been "no," because the technology simply wasn't there. Today, the answer is "yes."

Before Financial Analysts Federation,
Montreal, May 3/Vital Speeches, 6-15:530.

Margaret Mead
Anthropologist 3

[Saying the government should fund a project to make film records of disappearing ways of life]: We will never have another chance to do this. Modernization is quickly extending into the last remote corners of the world . . . To whatever degree we allow such data to vanish, we diminish our ability to understand our own species. We need better understanding of how man fits into and copes with the world and its transformations, including those he himself generates.

Before Senate appropriations subcommittee,
Washington, April 19/The Washington Post,
4-20:(B)7.

Thomas Moffett
Astrophysicist, Purdue University. 4

Obviously, none can say for certain that there is or isn't intelligent life outside the earth. All you can do is discuss the possibilities. One would expect about 100,000 technically developed civilizations, at least on a par with

(THOMAS MOFFETT)

our own, to have developed in each galaxy since the beginning of the universe. But while I'm convinced there is intellect in other parts of the universe, it's very improbable we'll ever know it for certain, much less communicate with it.. The very immensity of the universe lengthens the odds against our detecting other intelligent life in it ... What if our radio signals did reach an outer-space civilization that had developed a more advanced means of communication to whom radio was an antique? How often do we walk around looking for smoke signals or other such outmoded means of communication?

West Lafayette, Ind./
Los Angeles Times, 9-4:(1)17.

George E. Mueller
Chairman, System
Development Corporation
1

We are in a completely new era of technology ... I think we are on the threshold of completely changing our way of life. Whether this is good or bad, I don't know. For example, take those little electronic games you can now play on your TV set — you can use the same technology to provide home instruction for your children. We are just beginning to understand the full implications, in terms of how we live, of the computer's entry into the home. I don't think the impact of technology is going to be diminished. My concern is that we aren't doing the basic and applied research to take full advantage of this next revolution. What is going to take the place of the solid-state circuit developments, which are now 30 years old?

Interview/Nation's Business, August:47.

Lord Ritchie-Calder
Member of British Parliament; Associate,
Center for the Study of Democratic
Institutions, Santa Barbara, California
2

[Scientific] knowledge is available to anyone who wants access to it, who knows how to go about getting it, and who understands what it is all about. That is the difficulty. The members of the commonwealth of science — the scientists — are truly international in the peripatetic sense, but they are like the craft guildsmen of the Middle Ages: They have their "mysteries," their rituals and their sign language. Qualifications for entry come from academic training and increasing specialization. So science is an open book — but only for those who know how to read it.

At "Pacem in Maribus" conference, Algiers/
The Center Magazine, March-April:5.

Trent C. Root, Jr.
Vice president, Texas Utilities Company
3

Visible scientists are not very popular in the scientific community. They speak out from personal conscience rather than from popular consensus. When Linus Pauling came out in favor of Vitamin C as a sound treatment for the common cold, he invited the wrath of the entire medical community, which had opposed megavitamin treatment for generations. He got the expected reaction, including the accusation that, being over 70, he was senile. The visible scientist looks for new approaches and, finding them, advocates change. His position is usually interesting and debatable — not frightening and absurd.

At International Conference on Energy Use
Management, Tucson, Ariz., Oct. 25/
Vital Speeches, 12-15:134.

Alice S. Rossi
Psychologist, University of Chicago
4

Campaigns to encourage women to enter the sciences can only effectively help the young woman who already is interested and prepared by a background in science and mathematics. Such women are a tiny minority ... If we want more women to enter science ... some quite basic changes must take place in the ways girls are reared. A childhood model of the quiet, good, sweet girl will not produce many women scientists.

San Francisco Examiner & Chronicle,
8-7:(This World)30.

Carl Sagan
Director, Laboratory for Planetary
Studies, Cornell University
5

Probably owing largely to our educational system, there is a general perception of science

WHAT THEY SAID IN 1977

as being too difficult to understand; and, since it is all-important, this means many people see society as controlled by forces they cannot understand. There's no way to back off from science and technology, so the answer has to be a better understanding of what science is and how it operates.

Interview/Publishers Weekly, 5-2:8.

Robert L. Sinsheimer
Chairman, division of biology,
California Institute of Technology   1

When there's a science story in the newspaper that I know something about, it almost invariably will lack perspective and be a very distorted account. Most people writing about science in the press just don't know enough about science to write intelligently or responsibly. I was invited to speak to a group of science writers four or five years ago, and, frankly, I was shocked at their ignorance and ineptitude.

Los Angeles Times, 1-13:(1)26.

George Wald
Biologist   2

The information explosion is so great that the individual scientist has been forced to follow a narrower and narrower path. And what science is about, and whom it's for, has gotten lost.

San Francisco Examiner & Chronicle,
6-26:(This World)2.

Ben J. Wattenberg
Political analyst   3

Man has always been able to meet ... challenges by his intelligence and by his imagination. We took coal, we took uranium. They were rocks, useless. We made them into great energy sources. Why won't this process of creativity continue in the years to come? In the 20th century the technological optimists have been the realists.

Television program/"In Search of the Real America,"
Public Broadcasting Service, 3-8.

David Williamson, Jr.
Assistant Administrator for Special
Projects, National Aeronautics and Space
Administration of the United States   4

[On whether NASA should probe the field of unidentified flying objects] : We're not anxious to do it because we're not sure what we can do. It's my personal opinion that it's not wise to do research on something that is not a measurable phenomena. Spending public money for such research is questionable. There is no measurable UFO evidence such as a piece of metal, flesh or cloth. We don't even have any radio signals. A photograph is not a measurement ... Give me one little green man — not a theory or memory of one — and we can have a multimillion-dollar program. It's a scientific dilemma. How do you prove something that doesn't exist? It's like the Loch Ness monster revisited. Everyone sees it, but there is no physical evidence.

Los Angeles Herald-Examiner, 11-27:(A)11.

Henry Aaron
Former baseball player

1

Girls excel at basketball, golf and tennis, and there is no logical reason why they shouldn't play baseball. It's not that tough. Not as tough as radio and TV announcers make it out to be ... Some can play better than a lot of guys who've been on that field ... Baseball is not a game of strength; hitting is not strength.

San Francisco Examiner & Chronicle,
7-17:(This World)2.

Muhammad Ali
Heavyweight boxing champion
of the world

2

I just *said* I was the greatest. I never thought I was. A long time ago, I saw Gorgeous George promote a wrestling match he had coming up. He promised blood and guts. He promised to kill his opponent. He said anything to sell tickets. And he sold out. I saw an opportunity to do the same thing. So I started the "I am the Greatest" thing. I began with the poetry and predicting rounds. And it worked. They started coming in with their ten- and twenty-dollar bills to see the braggin' nigger. How do I know who the greatest fighter was? How can you compare fighters from different eras? I was probably the best of my time, but how do I know what would have happened if I fought Louis, Dempsey or Jack Johnson? I've been looking at some old boxing films and some of those guys were tremendous.

Interview/Los Angeles Times, 5-11:(3)2.

Sparky Anderson
Baseball manager, Cincinnati "Reds"

3

Long contracts can do one of two things to players. They can hurt them by causing a complacency. Or they can help them by reliev-
ing pressure. It's all kind of crazy, and it all started with a fellow named Catfish Hunter. He showed the world how foolish some owners can be. Catfish went home to Ahoskie, North Carolina, and did nothing but sit there, holding court. The owners came to him with fortunes. This is how the madness began. If a guy wants to get drunk and wrap his car around a pole, that's his business; but when he hurts others, you've got another story. Everyone got drawn into the spending, and that's why all you hear in spring camps today are arguments over money.

Interview, Tampa, Fla./Los Angeles
Herald-Examiner, 3-10:(C)2.

Arthur Ashe
Tennis player

4

I strongly believe the black culture expends too much time, energy and effort raising, praising and teasing our black children about the dubious glories of professional sport ... Your son has less than one chance in 1,000 of becoming a pro. Would you bet your son's future on something with odds of 99-to-1 against you? I wouldn't.

San Francisco Examiner & Chronicle,
2-20:(This World)2.

George Atkinson
Football player, Oakland "Raiders"

5

Football has always been a rough, tough game, from back in the Doak Walker days. You can call it violence if you like. But this game is a contact sport. It would be different if we had flags in our pockets. Hitting people is something I've been doing a long time. If you're not a person who can hit or be hit, you shouldn't be in this game.

Interview/The Washington Post, 7-21:(C)2.

487

WHAT THEY SAID IN 1977

Red Auerbach
President and general manager,
Boston "Celtics" basketball team
1

The [player] salaries today are astronomical, but then again they're not. It's a matter of supply and demand. It's what the public wants... The public demands to see great performers, like entertainers. Athletes are destroying their bodies, so to speak, and on that basis they have a valid point for demanding these contracts. The public determines salaries. In sports, very few people have what I call charisma, but people pay to see the ones that do. And that's how they get the money, because people pay to see them... Some players have it if they're part of a team that wins. Sometimes you think a player has charisma, but it turns out he doesn't. That's how you get stuck with certain [contract] deals. All players want charisma, but most can never have it.

Interview, Boston/
Los Angeles Times, 11-27:(3)11.

2

You can't tell [players] you want them to play specific roles any more and get them to listen. They all want to be stars, score 20 points a game and become very visible, because that's where the money is. There are agents now who tell them: "Hey, you don't like it here; play out your option and I'll get you an even bigger contract somewhere else." And the sad thing is that those agents aren't kidding; they can do it. The way pro basketball is set up today, the leverage is all with the players. Years ago when I coached, I was like a dictator. When I told my players something, I never wanted to hear the word "why," or anything like that. I just wanted a reaction. But you tell a guy something today and he says he'll bring it up to Players Association.

Interview, Los Angeles/
The Christian Science Monitor, 12-22:17.

Nick Auf de Maur
Member, Montreal City Council
3

Last year the Shah of Iran decided to shuck the 1984 Olympics. He decided he couldn't

afford it. If the Shah didn't think he could swing it, how in bloody hell does New York think it can? ... My advice [as a councilor of the city that hosted the 1976 Games] to New York, and any other city attempting to host the Olympics, is stay away unless you can get the international sports federations and the IOC to reduce its demands and settle for a make-do Olympics. But I doubt that can happen. The IOC is composed of aristocrats and princes, sporting gentlemen who see the Games as a hobby. They think they're the most important people in the world. They make all sorts of demands and don't pay a penny. It would be like the U.S. moon program being paid for by Canada. They just won't accept a modified Olympics. The international sports federations keep making these insane demands. They want absolute perfection. In Montreal, we had to build a $24-million kayak and canoeing course. The bottom had to be uniform for 1½ miles. It was a bloody swimming pool. Then they wanted to build 25,000 permanent seats along the course. We negotiated it down to 16,000 seats. So what do we have? Probably the best course in the world that nobody uses, along with 16,000 useless seats. If the Olympics can hold its rowing events in the East River [in New York in 1984], then it would be fine. But based on my experience, that won't sit with the federation. It would mess up their standardized records and timing. We had a bloody river in Montreal, but they demanded a 1½-mile swimming pool ... Everything in the Olympics is done on that basis. Money is no object for these princes of sport.

Interview, Montreal/
Los Angeles Times, 8-4:(3)1.

Rick Barry
Basketball player,
Golden State "Warriors"
4

[On what it takes to win a division title over an 82-game season]: I think you have to get players who are less concerned with their own statistics and more concerned with what the team needs to function best as a unit. You can call it unselfishness, an awareness of the situation or anything you want, but you've got to have it to win. A lot of it also stems from how

(RICK BARRY)

well the coach deals with the super egos of his team. Once a player becomes successful, and knows it, he sometimes begins to think differently. Instead of asking people around him the best way to do things, the way he used to, he stops being an Indian and becomes a chief. That's when the trouble starts, when players think they don't have to listen any more.

Interview, Los Angeles/
The Christian Science Monitor, 4-11:14.

Richard Barthol
Professor of psychology, University
of California, Los Angeles
1

Sports reflects the subculture of which it is a part. For example, in rural areas you find certain kinds of sports that allow for open areas and small numbers of participants. In the ghetto, you find stickball and rows of basketball hoops. In this part of the country, there's a lot of tennis and swimming. In these cases, socio-economic conditions and local weather determine the extent of sports. But sports also reflects society as a whole. Sports changes as society's interests change. You can pretty well trace what's happened in the history of our country by examining changes in sports.

Interview, Los Angeles/
Los Angeles Herald-Examiner, 5-15:(A)1.

Elgin Baylor
Basketball coach, New Orleans
"Jazz"; Former player
2

The majority of today's players are better than most of the guys I competed against. They are bigger, stronger, faster and better shooters than we were. But I don't think they have the drive we did, or the fun, or the dedication. Most of today's high draft picks start out with huge salaries and no-cut contracts. Basically they don't have to worry. But for some of them motivation becomes a problem and they never do reach their potential. You can blame the coach for that if you want to, but the real problem obviously lies somewhere else.

Interview, Los Angeles/
The Christian Science Monitor, 11-21:38.

Johnny Bench
Baseball player, Cincinnati "Reds"
3

After [Oakland owner] Charles Finley revealed, a couple of weeks ago, what all of his players got in the free-agent draft, everybody is going to put himself in the same shoes. They will say to themselves, "If that guy is worth $1-million, I must be worth $2-million" ... I have said that I would not want to play any place but Cincinnati. But with all this money around, I have to think of myself, too ... [The owners] are as greedy as we are. They want to win the pennant. They want recognition. They want to put people in the ballpark.

The Dallas Times Herald, 1-6:(B)2.

Sid Borgia
Former referee,
National Basketball Association
4

Years ago, the owners were basketball guys. But now the owners just think about the players without realizing that the two referees are the most important people on the floor. The two referees can't help a game, but they can ruin it ... Everybody says it's harder than ever to referee pro basketball. But it should be easier. The shooting is better than ever. And the better the shooting, the easier it should be to officiate – if you know what you're doing. And that's the idea – help officials know what they're doing. If you took the major corporations in our country, if their owners knew as little about their product as the NBA owners know about theirs, all the major corporations would be bankrupt. What the NBA needs is what I call roast-beef guys, the guys who know the game. There aren't many roast-beef guys around, and it's starting to show.

Interview/The New York Times, 12-15:(D)15.

Jim Bouton
Former baseball pitcher
5

The trouble with throwing knuckleballs is that 95 out of 100 pitches have to be right. If you get only 85 out of 100, the 15 that miss are going to turn into eight triples, five doubles and a home run or two.

Los Angeles Times, 6-2:(3)4.

489

WHAT THEY SAID IN 1977

Lou Brock
Baseball player,
St. Louis "Cardinals"

1

At this point, baseball is pretty much a year-to-year thing with me. The one thing I would never want to do is embarrass myself by staying around too long. I've seen it happen with other players, and no record or big paycheck is worth it. I think once a ballplayer has proved that he can make it in the big leagues, he also creates a level of achievement for himself in relation to his ability. If, when he gets into his thirties, his decline is gradual and he doesn't start worrying about whether he can perform in the clutch any more, there is no reason for him not to stay in uniform. But if there were to be a sudden decline in my ability, I wouldn't stay around and let it demoralize me. I'd quit immediately. I'd be grateful for all the good years I've had, and I'd try to find something else that would satisfy me.

Interview/
The Christian Science Monitor, 6-30:17.

2

Normally, when people think of entertainers, they think of actors, singers, comedians and dancers. [But] athletes, too, are very much in the entertainment business. They are performers who play to live audiences of anywhere from 20,000 to 50,000 people per game. They're under the same kleig-light pressure as actors. At least I am, when I'm out there on the field listening to a standing crowd shout "Go, go, go!" So ballplayers really are performers, too. I try not to let the crowd influence my actions on the field, just as a Broadway actor tries not to let his audience affect his performance.

Interview/The Dallas Times Herald, 8-7:(D)13.

3

[On the possibility of his breaking Ty Cobb's record of 892 stolen bases]: I sometimes have second thoughts about breaking this record. I feel like getting to 892 and stopping, so when somebody asks who was the best base-stealer, people will say, "Brock and Cobb."

"Brock" probably wouldn't mean very much but "Cobb" would mean a lot.

Los Angeles Times, 8-27:(3)1.

Jim Brown
Sports commentator, Columbia Broadcasting System; Former football player

4

The true superstars now are not O. J. [Simpson] and [Joe] Namath and people like that. They're the [TV] people, because television has taken over . . . I mean, the game has now been geared to the television industry. So, consequently, my respect for the game is not on the same level. That's not to put down; it's an observation, see. You see, Lynn Swann is a friend of mine, for example. Lynn has become a tremendous television personality. He's a great football player, one of the greatest in history. But yet, I can see him in the middle of a game, making faces at the camera, talking to the guys in the [broadcast] booth, and I cannot understand his concentration.

Interview/The Washington Post, 10-23:(D)4.

5

Men who played football are the people I like best in life. What I have found is they have an ability to deal with friendship in a truthful way. I meet players now and talk about the most mellow things. There's a lot of love between individual players; it's a strange kind of relationship. You put yourself on the line in pro football. You deal with a challenge. Real life just isn't made up of that kind of excitement. But the only way to deal with certain things is to put yourself on the line.

Interview/The Washington Post, 12-18:(D)10.

John Y. Brown
Owner, Buffalo "Braves"
basketball team

6

I find everything about professional basketball to be thoroughly distasteful — except the game itself. The greed, the way people throw money around with no regard for reality or common sense, the whole business end of the sport — I hate all of it. But the game itself is

(JOHN Y. BROWN)

something I love. I could not stand to be apart from it.

Interview, Coronado, Calif./
Los Angeles Times, 6-26:(3)1.

Larry Brown
Basketball coach, Denver "Nuggets"

1

[On the substitute referees being used during the current strike by NBA officials]: The NBA should be more concerned with the welfare of the game than just trying to stop a few referees from getting what they deserve. I've gotten tired of . . . coaches saying the officiating by these new guys is great. It's not. It reminds me of the early days of the ABA when they just picked guys off the street.

Los Angeles Times, 4-20:(3)2.

Rod Carew
Baseball player, Minnesota "Twins"

2

I'm not on any ego trip to be the highest-paid player. Being happy and healthy means more to me. Before all this free agency came into being, a lot of fellows playing ball said we were "slaves." Well, what are you doing when you go through free agency? You're selling yourself as if you were a slave. That doesn't interest me at all.

Los Angeles Times, 12-16:(3)2.

Ron Cey
Baseball player, Los Angeles "Dodgers"

3

There are a lot of egotistical people in baseball, and I understand and totally accept and tolerate them. But that doesn't mean I have to like them. If I had to do it over again and say I was the best, I couldn't. That's not me. It would be a waste of my time. I have never solicited publicity . . . Oh, sure, I'm courteous to reporters. I usually tell them what they want to hear. But when you hear a player saying, "The reason I'm doing well is because I'm great," it's nothing but BS. Individual success is created by your teammates, and don't let anybody tell you any differently.

Interview/Los Angeles Times, 7-19:(3)1.

A. B. (Happy) Chandler
Former Commissioner of Baseball

4

Under the circumstances, I wouldn't have the job [of commissioner today]. It's impossible to do it. Every time the commissioner makes a decision, he's in court. Every player has an agent; every club owner has a lawyer. The game has left the field and gone to court.

Interview, Versailles, Ky./
The Dallas Times Herald, 5-15:(C)14.

Don Chaney
Basketball player, Los Angeles "Lakers"

5

[On being a highly paid, rarely used substitute player]: People have a tendency to say, "You guys are making all that money; it must be easy to sit on the bench." Well, it isn't easy. No one wants to *not* earn their money. A lot of players will tell you, "I don't care what they do to me, as long as I make my money." But they're just talking. This bothers me. It hurts your pride. It hurts very much.

Interview/Los Angeles Times, 11-11:(3)1.

Don Cherry
Hockey coach, Boston "Bruins"

6

[On his regular routine after a game]: I get in the car, go home as fast as I can, take my dog for a walk for about three minutes, and then have about five beers. Since I've taken over coaching, antacid sales have gone up 10 per cent.

Los Angeles Times, 5-16:(3)2.

Jimmy Connors
Tennis player

7

[On being top-seeded in the U.S. Clay Court championship]: What are seedings? Just one time, I'd like to float around, without being seeded, and just play whoever I get in the draw. So what if I drew Manuel Orantes in the first round? I'd have to play him later, anyway, to win.

Los Angeles Times, 8-11:(3)2.

491

WHAT THEY SAID IN 1977

Fred Cox
Football player, Minnesota "Vikings"
1

[On the Super Bowl] : It really has become a spectacle, but that's what the league wants and what the people want. When you come right down to it, we are in the entertainment business. But I think you'd see a better game if you just brought the teams in to play.

Los Angeles Times, 1-26:(3)5.

2

[On being a placekicker] : There is pressure. I never tried to dramatize that, because it comes with the job. A lot of people's money and futures ride on field goals — mostly the kickers'. But that's really subconscious stuff when the clock is winding down. I just go through my check list. "Keep your head down. Lock the foot. Kick through the ball. Don't stand too far away or too close."

Interview, Bloomington, Minn./
The Washington Post, 11-23:(D)5.

Ben Crenshaw
Golfer
3

. . . if you can't putt, you're in a hell of a lot of trouble out here. A lot of guys hit it super but can't stick it in the hole. Arnold Palmer, for instance, and Ben Hogan and Sam Snead near the end of their careers. Maybe that seems unfair, but that's the way it is.

Interview, Augusta, Ga., April 8/
The Dallas Times Herald, 4-9:(C)3.

Harry Dalton
General manager, California "Angels"
baseball club
4

[On the non-productivity of many highly paid free agents obtained by major-league teams when the reserve system was changed] : If we saw a way to fill a need, I don't feel that what's happened this year would prevent us from going back to the free-agent market. I also think that other clubs will determine the extent of their participation on the basis of their own financial situation rather than on the history of

some other club or clubs. Trades are always backfiring and yet that doesn't stop anyone from trading.

Los Angeles Times, 7-20:(3)6.

Mike Davies
Executive director,
World Championship Tennis
5

I think tennis is suffering because nobody really knows what the structure of the professional game is. The public sees so many tournaments going on, with the same players in WCT events one week, Grand Prix events another week, "special events" the next. It is absolutely confusing. I think we have got to have one major tournament per week, like golf. That way, the average person can understand what is going on. That's what we're aiming for.

The Washington Post, 3-26:(C)6.

Glenn Davis
Former football player,
United States Military Academy
6

[Criticizing the antics of today's football players when they score] : I don't know anything that irritates me more than seeing guys hot-dog. I just want to get up and go through the TV. Today I think it is an absolute farce and stupidity the way guys act. If they don't spike, they do a dance or hold the ball overhead like, "Look, God, how great I am." I think it takes away from the game and shows the immodesty of the athlete. It seems like so many athletes today have to tell you how great they are rather than letting their record show it. They've taken all the class out of it. I think it's a coaching problem. Coaches are afraid to do anything to dampen the spirit of the team. They should say, "Let's not look like jerks. Let's forget about showboating." [In the old days,] you felt elated but you didn't go berserk. You realized you were just the one carrying the ball and the others helped you get there.

Los Angeles Times, 12-26:(3)4.

Joe DiMaggio
Former baseball player

1

[On baseball's new free-agent status for players]: I was around at a time when the club owners said, "Buddy, you sign that contract or else." We either signed or we didn't play. It didn't do much good to say, "Hey, trade me." I asked to be traded early in my career and they told me to forget it. They said I was with the *Yankees* and I was going to stay with the *Yankees.* They didn't raise their price, either. I was a holdout for two weeks and they didn't raise my price, either. I only make that point because now the shoe's on the other foot. It's hard to sympathize with some of these owners that wouldn't modify the reserve clause at that time.

Interview/Los Angeles Times, 2-13:(3)6.

2

[On the $100,000 salary he received as a player]: ... it doesn't seem like much when you compare it to today's salaries. And I guess that's one of the most significant changes in the game today. Baseball today is big business. You know, I never had a contract for longer than one year at a time. There was no such thing as a multi-year deal. One year. Players were at the mercy of the club owners. Now the pendulum has swung. It's the players who call the shots. It was one extreme, now it's another. And I'm not necessarily convinced it's for the better. I still have a great love for baseball and I'd hate to see it suffer. I'd hate to see big business ruin baseball.

Interview, San Francisco/
The Christian Science Monitor, 5-25:27.

Larry Doby
Baseball coach, Chicago "White Sox"

3

[On his being in major-league baseball for 30 years]: If you're black and you're working in a white man's world and you survive that long, you are strong. The disappointment in the 30 years is in the percentage of black ballplayers — a lot — and you're talking about no black managers now that Frank Robinson is gone; you're talking about one or two blacks in the

front offices. It's heartbreaking not to have that representation.

Interview, Chicago/Los Angeles Times, 7-6:(3)1.

Jean Drapeau
Mayor of Montreal

4

[On the recent Olympic Games in his city]: The Games were obtained, were held and proved successful. That is enough for me. Whatever the moral and financial costs, regardless of all the incidents and handicaps, the putting of questions and the raising of questions, it was worth it. No matter the difficulties, I would do it again ... We have created a new world where amateur sports is a reality. Before, our [Canada's] radio and television never found time to present amateur sports, only the professionals. Now amateur sports are present on television, in magazines. There is pressure on municipalities, colleges and even private corporations in favor of amateur sports. Parents have discovered sports who never realized they could be so attractive and significant.

Interview, Montreal/
The Washington Post, 1-24:(D)5.

Julius Erving
Basketball player, Philadelphia "76ers"

5

I watch players, all players. I watch them on television, at college games, in the playground — you can learn from anybody. Even now I'll be watching a game somewhere, and I'll see somebody do something that'll remind me of something I've forgotten — some little move, maybe. I'll practice it a little, and I've got it back; and when the right situation comes along, against some player, maybe I've got a little edge I didn't have before.

The New York Times Magazine, 2-13:59.

Chris Evert
Tennis player

6

The more I play, the harder it is to get inspired on the court. I either have to set goals for myself or go out there because I hate to lose. Ever since I was nine years old I've been at the top of my age group. I'm used to being on top

493

(CHRIS EVERT)

and I don't know how I could handle being number 5 or 6.

Los Angeles Times, 2-4:(3)2.

Chuck Fairbanks
Football coach, New England "Patriots";
Former coach, University of Oklahoma

1

[Comparing pro and college football] : Personally, I have found that pros work as hard and are as amenable to discipline as college players. There's more closeness in college ball. The pro game is a cold, cutthroat business. One of the most difficult things for me to accept is the pointed criticism leveled at the pro. Because he is playing for money, people are less sympathetic toward his failures.

Interview/Los Angeles Times, 12-16:(3)9.

Charles O. Finley
Owner, Oakland "Athletics"
baseball club

2

I don't blame the athletes for all these astronomical, unjustified [player] salaries. If I was an athlete working for such stupid owners, I would take all they handed out. I'm concerned about the future of all sports. I was the only person I know to own teams in three different sports. I had the California *Golden Seals* in the National Hockey League and the Memphis *Tams* in the American Basketball Association, and I sold them because I saw the handwriting on the wall. When I see the World Football League fold, the American Basketball Association go out of business, teams in the World Hockey Association folding, and other teams in baseball, basketball and hockey in trouble financially, I don't have to be any genius to know what the score is today and what it's likely to be tomorrow. It amounts to this: Play hog and you wind up eating corn cobs. There are many owners playing hog today. Joe Fan is paying the freight right now but won't continue to pay it much longer the way things are going. Everybody has a point where he says that's it, and gets off. I don't think your average Joe Fan is far from that

point, only some owners still can't see it. The reason they can't is because they're stupid.

San Francisco Examiner & Chronicle, 1-23:(C)8.

3

[Comparing baseball commissioner Bowie Kuhn's allowing the New York *Mets* to trade pitcher Tom Seaver to the Cincinnati *Reds* with the commissioner's disallowance of his sale of several players last year] : Kuhn's irresponsible and selective use of his office is a dishonor to the game of baseball, insulting to the millions of baseball fans and a total betrayal to the once-respected office of the commissioner. It is tragic the great game is burdened with such an irrational and vindictive person. The similarities between the Seaver deal and my assignment of Vida Blue to the New York *Yankees* are striking. Both deals were made on June 15, the trading deadline. Both involved Cy Young Award-winning pitchers. Kuhn disapproved Oakland's assignment, waving the banner of competitive balance. Yet Seaver has gone to the strongest team in baseball, who has won two consecutive world championships and allows them to virtually cinch their third.

Interview, Chicago/
Los Angeles Herald-Examiner, 6-17:(D)2.

4

[On how he operates the team] : We run our club like a pawn shop — we buy, we trade, we sell.

Los Angeles Times, 6-23:(3)2.

Emerson Fittipaldi
Auto-racing driver

5

I regard a car very much like a woman, and I treat them both the same. When I'm at the wheel, I start by showing I'm the boss. Then, instead of caressing the flesh of a woman, I am caressing the controls. When I've tamed her, when I've had my way, it is time to be oh, so gentle. Over the last 10 laps, I treat her as though she were very, very frail . . . very, very tired. It would be a disaster if my lady let me down. So this is why I start with the grand

(EMERSON FITTIPALDI)

seduction, and change my style when I know I am in command. We must remain friends until the end.

Interview, Los Angeles, April 1/
Los Angeles Times, 4-2:(3)1.

George Foster
Baseball player, Cincinnati "Reds"

1

The idea isn't to swing for the home run, but to hit the ball hard every time up and hope it goes where nobody can catch it. I'm a .300 hitter because I'm consistent and a home-run hitter because I have power. That's the difference between me and other long-ball hitters. They don't make good contact every time up the way I do, and it kills their over-all average. That's what I mean by being consistent.

Interview/
The Christian Science Monitor, 8-12:26.

Joe Garagiola
Sports announcer,
National Broadcasting Company

2

[On the state of baseball today, with its lawyers, agents, options, special clauses, etc.]: Maybe one day [attorney] F. Lee Bailey will be the most valuable player in the American League. And the things players are asking — guaranteed playing time, so many starts for pitchers... Where will it end? Eventually you'll have a batter file a grievance if he gets a curveball on a 3-and-2 count.

The New York Times, 3-27:(5)11.

Steve Garvey
Baseball player, Los Angeles "Dodgers"

3

The secret of good hitting is to be able to adjust against every pitcher and sometimes with every pitch. Most new players who make the majors come in as good fastball hitters. But the only ones who stay are those who become good curveball hitters, because after a while they don't see the fastball any more. I don't think a hitter can say he's attained the kind of success he wants until the defense is forced to play him

straight-away, and pitchers realize they can't get him out the same way all the time.

Interview, Scottsdale, Ariz./
The Christian Science Monitor, 2-11:10.

4

The home run is the most shocking thing in baseball. A man can turn a game around with one swing. And that takes some of the anxiety out for the manager. He doesn't have to worry about the hit-and-run, and nursing people around the bases. For that reason, I like home runs...

Interview/Los Angeles Times, 2-15:(3)1.

Lefty Gomez
Former baseball pitcher

5

The secret of my success was clean living and a fast-moving outfield.

The Christian Science Monitor, 2-4:6.

Lou Gorman
General manager, Seattle
"Mariners" baseball club

6

[On the big salaries paid by major-league teams to obtain many of the new free agents as a result of changes in the reserve system]: I have to wonder now if all those owners would do it over again. Two or three of the free agents have been highly productive, but there are more minuses than plusses. Some of the owners have to be taking a second look. I would predict that there will be less activity in next year's draft and a hell of a lot less money spent.

Los Angeles Times, 7-20:(3)1.

Calvin Griffith
Owner, Minnesota "Twins" baseball club

7

... we're one of the few clubs that still feels a player is worth what he earns, not what other players are getting. If I think a player is worthy of it, I'll pay it. If I think he's a parasite, I won't. A player has to show he's worth it before I pay him. I don't give a damn what other players are making. I'll pay what I think is justifiable to my organization.

Interview, Orlando, Fla./
The New York Times, 2-25:(A)14.

495

WHAT THEY SAID IN 1977

Ray Guy
Football player, Oakland "Raiders"

1

A punter is the only player on a football team who is completely on his own. And it's hard to concentrate when you're standing back there 15 yards away from everybody else in the stadium and there are 70,000 people looking down at you. In a spot like that you feel all those eyes. You feel the solitude, the loneliness. You want to hide and there's no place to hide — as there is, at times, for the other players. You're all alone, and if you don't ignore the rush and everything else and concentrate 100 per cent on what you've got to do, you're in trouble.

Interview, Oakland, Calif./
Los Angeles Times, 12-2:(3)17.

Pat Haden
Football player, Los Angeles "Rams"

2

When you think of the fellows in the steel mills, you have to feel uncomfortable with the money I'm making. It sometimes seems to me that athletes' [high] salaries are immoral. You can't really say our profession is as socially redeeming as the other professions. But I guess my whole feeling on this is ambivalent. I strongly believe in a free-market economy, and athletes are in that, too ... You have to keep several things in mind. Our careers are brief, we take a lot of chances on injuries, we lead a transient life — here today, Green Bay tomorrow — and the pressure on us is enormous. All in all, I suppose if someone is willing to pay us, we rate it. My problem is not so much with what athletes make as with what others don't make. Teachers' salaries, for instance, are a scandal. It's what teachers don't make that makes me feel queasy about my salary.

Interview/Los Angeles Times, 8-12:(3)6.

Marv Harshman
Basketball coach,
University of Washington

3

I'm kind of a ham, an actor. All coaches are. But more, I think coaching is the greatest opportunity a man can have if he wants to be a teacher — a teacher who gets to see the progress of what he's teaching happening right before him.

Interview/Los Angeles Times, 2-2:(3)6.

Whitey Herzog
Baseball manager, Kansas City "Royals"

4

I think the most significant aspect of the 1977 season will be how all the players now under multi-year contracts will perform. I don't think there's a manager or general manager anywhere who can say for sure what the reaction will be ... I don't say it critically because, given a five-year contract that includes 20 years of deferred payments, we all might be tempted to slack off some. Virtually our whole team will be on multi-years, and I'm just certain that a few of the players will have to be handled differently than they've ever been handled before. What form that handling will take, I can't say. We're going to have to operate on a day-to-day basis because in many ways baseball has become a whole new ballgame. Every manager's job will be tougher. Not only are we faced with the prospect of getting through to players who may not be giving out as much, but the entire manager-player relationship might be changed by the fact that we're now giving orders to players who can tell us to forget it. I mean, I expect to hear some players say, "I know I'm going to be here five years from now, how about you?"

Interview, Kansas City/
Los Angeles Times, 2-11:(3)1.

Ben Hogan
Golfer

5

I am often asked if I'm not a bit envious of these young [golfers] making all that money [today]. I think I got $1,500 for winning my first U.S. Open in 1948. But a man must wind up with self-satisfaction. It's the game, the performance that counts. The big thing is the thrill of competition. I would have played as hard for an orange as a big purse. Money isn't everything. I have no bitterness. I made out very well when I played and I don't envy the present crop. It's just that when I played I was

(BEN HOGAN)

a perfectionist. I had to do what I did well or it wasn't worth doing.

Interview, Fort Worth, Tex./
The Washington Post, 4-28:(E)4.

Red Holtzman
Basketball coach,
New York "Knickerbockers"
1

If coaching was just a matter of X's and O's, I'd be great. I can make X's score every time. Lock me up in a room with a blackboard and I'll win every game.

The Dallas Times Herald, 4-3:(C)4.

Charlie Hough
Baseball pitcher, Los Angeles "Dodgers"
2

[On being a relief pitcher]: A hitter can go 0-for-4 in three straight games and it's forgotten if his team wins all three. If the relief pitcher has three bad days in a row, there is probably no way his team will win. The game is on the line. There is no room for mistakes. You learn to live with it. You have to. I get mad when I lose, but I never feel I'm the only one responsible for that loss, though for us to be successful I know I have to pitch well.

Interview, Philadelphia/
Los Angeles Times, 8-8:(3)5.

Deacon Jones
Former football player
3

[Time] has made me miserable. If it weren't for time, I'd still be playing football. And I'd be a happy man if I were still playing football. Believe me, I'd be happy. Man, I'll tell you, I wish I never got old. In other jobs you get old, big deal. In football you get old, you're fired. That's what happened to me. Time got me. Damned time.

Interview, Scottsdale, Ariz./
Los Angeles Herald-Examiner, 1-30:(C)11.

Robert J. Kane
President, United States Olympic Committee
4

You'll never be able to get away from political interference while the whole world is involved in the Olympic Games. There will always be someone who seizes the Games for propaganda and political purposes. But those people should not go·unpunished. I would favor sanctions against countries which made a point to come to the scene of the Olympics and then left. It just isn't fair to the Olympic organizations and the athletes.

Interview, Colorado Springs, Colo./
Los Angeles Times, 5-8:(3)3.

John Kasyola
Kenyan representative to the
Supreme Council for Sport in Africa
5

[Supporting the OAU's policy of boycotting sports competition with countries whose teams play South African teams]: The OAU decision is binding on all of us and it would be a mockery of our stand if we let the United States get away with a Davis Cup match against South Africa. We shall have to boycott them and any other country without fear or favor.

The New York Times, 3-8:37.

Ewing Kauffman
Owner, Kansas City "Royals"
baseball club
6

[Supporting a strong Commissioner of Baseball]: Baseball has 24 teams and the owners have inherited wealth, or become wealthy themselves. They are self-confident, egotistical, even egocentric, and need a broad, strong hand in order to keep baseball running smoothly.

In Federal court, Chicago, Jan. 7/
The Washington Post, 1-8:(B)5.

Jim Kensil
Executive director,
National Football League
7

The Super Bowl is now an institution, but it is still just a football game, nothing more, nothing less. It's simply a game, the last game in a long season, and people want to see who wins and loses. We don't call it Super Sunday or the American pinnacle or a sociological event. It's entertainment.

The New York Times, 1-9:(5)29.

497

WHAT THEY SAID IN 1977

Billie Jean King
Tennis player

1

Amateur athletics — I've lived a big part of my life in that system and it stinks . . . As far as I'm concerned, a college scholarship is nothing but a scholastic contract. The athlete says he or she will perform this many services for this amount of money. Football players are entertainers, and when you consider that the Ohio State [University] athletic department budget is $6-million, then you know you're talking not about sports but big business.

Los Angeles Times, 1-14:(3)2.

2

Tennis is a business today and as a business it has to be sold. It's important to get the public emotionally involved in what we're doing and the only way we can do that is to promote. The trouble is, a lot of these new girls don't know what a promoter's problems are, how to work with the media, or even how to sign autographs or meet the public. They just can't play their matches and walk away. They've got to learn the importance of talking off the tennis court too.

*Interview, Palm Springs, Calif./Los Angeles
Herald-Examiner, 1-16:(California Living)4.*

Don King
Boxing promoter

3

Rival promoters are out to get me because I pay my fighters more than they do; I'm pushing their prices up. That's because I consider fighters as human beings, not slaves, and paid them more money than they ever made before. It became a burden for my rivals.

*Interview, Landover, Md., May 7/
The New York Times, 5-8:(5)5.*

David Klatell
*Director, Institute in Broadcast
Sports, Boston University*

4

TV sports involve massive amounts of money, billions of dollars; and the consumer pays for it when costs double like this because he buys the advertised products . . . [Football player] O. J. Simpson has a contract to broadcast for ABC, which covers the games he plays in. The same for NBC and Fran Tarkenton. Is there a conflict of interest? . . . The networks say sports is entertainment and there is nothing more to it. But they said there was nothing more to violence and sex and questions about TV news and the content of ads. But there was always something more to these things.

*Interview, Boston/
The Christian Science Monitor, 11-4:2.*

Chuck Knox
Football coach, Los Angeles "Rams"

5

In professional football, a consistent winning team is one that does the little things well. I mean basics, like hanging onto the football, avoiding the needless penalty, avoiding blocked kicks, covering kickoffs properly, emphasizing the proper foot to step with, knowing when to utilize the fair catch. Everybody talks about well-designed plays and whether to pass on second-and-one, and such irrelevant things as the Super Bowl. But consistent winners think about other things. They want to make sure nobody jumps offside on a crucial down.

*Interview, Long Beach, Calif., Dec. 15/
The Washington Post, 12-16:(E)3.*

Jerry Korab
Hockey player, Buffalo "Sabres"

6

My role is to be aggressive . . . I don't mean we have to go out and be goons. Just good, hard-hitting hockey is what we need . . . When you hit extra hard, keep on hitting, it can make the other guy shy, make him think about being hit. That little bit of intimidation can be so important.

*Interview, New York/
Los Angeles Times, 10-9:(3)16.*

Ray A. Kroc
Owner, San Diego "Padres" baseball club

7

[Criticizing the control TV now has over baseball]: Baseball has prostituted itself. Pretty soon we'll be starting games at midnight so the people in outer space can watch on prime-time television. We're making a mistake by always going for more money.

The New York Times, 2-6:(5)4.

498

(RAY A. KROC)

1

[On baseball's free-agent draft being held in New York's Plaza Hotel]: This is the most inefficient society I've ever been in. They call a meeting at the Plaza — at Plaza prices — that they could have held in Omaha, or even on the telephone. Later this month the general managers are meeting in Phoenix, and next month everybody's meeting in Honolulu. I never knew baseball was so profitable. If so, I'd have got into it sooner.

New York/The New York Times, 11-8:27.

Bowie Kuhn
Commissioner of Baseball

2

[Arguing against a "troika" to govern baseball, composed of the commissioner and the two league presidents]: A troika would not be good for baseball. It would stall the decision-making process. It just wouldn't work. The commissioner should be able to move without hindrance, to make those determinations he feels are necessary for the integrity of the game. That's what the owners had in mind when they created the commissioner's office in 1920 . . . The club owners, as men, are very individual, very successful and very strong. Outside, in their own industries, they are the top people. The commissioner needs very great powers to keep such ownership going on an even keel.

Interview, New York, March 30/
Los Angeles Herald-Examiner, 4-3:(C)12.

Bill Lee
Baseball player, Boston "Red Sox"

3

There's the designated hitter in baseball and artificial turf, a petroleum-oriented plastic. We're using all that energy to make something to play on when all you have to do is throw out a handful of seeds and let the sun do it. But you can't put a tax on the sun. Also, you'd have 20 groundskeepers — give them work — instead of just five . . . [I'd] change policy, bring back natural grass and nickel beer. Baseball is the belly-button of our society.

Straighten out baseball, and you'll straighten out the rest of the world.

Interview/Los Angeles Times, 2-3:(3)5.

Jim Lefebvre
Baseball coach, Lotte "Orions,"
Pacific League of Japan; Former
player, Los Angeles "Dodgers"

4

[Comparing Japanese baseball with U.S. major-league clubs]: I look on Japanese baseball as kind of a glorified industrial league. The Yumiuri club is owned by a newspaper chain; the Taiyo *Whales* by a shipbuilding firm; the Nankai *Hawks* by a railroad. My club is owned by a chewing-gum firm. The overall depth isn't major-league caliber but it's better than Triple-A. Consolidate all the teams, and you could come up with one that wouldn't embarrass itself here [in the U.S.], that would be competitive. Many individual players could play in our major leagues . . . The fielding is good. The pitchers specialize in control. The hitters generally don't strike out. They hit for average and handle the hit-and-run well. They have to go to the States, however, to get their power. The real difference is in the farm system. Our club, for example, had only 12 players in the minors.

Interview, Los Angeles/Los Angeles Times, 1-22:(3)7.

Bob Lemon
Baseball manager, Chicago "White Sox"

5

It's not the total job of a manager to motivate the 25 individuals on a big-league roster. Self-motivation is a key to success on any team . . . The high-priced contracts players are being offered should be motivation enough for each individual to do the best possible job. Too much emphasis is being placed on the word "motivation." Each individual should strive to excel himself. If a fellow doesn't want to give 100 per cent, there's nothing a manager can do. Motivation and communication are blown out of proportion. Why should you have to motivate a man to make $200,000 a year? I think that a fellow who walks out across the white lines knows, if he performs up to his abilities,

499

(BOB LEMON)

he can be a wealthy man. Why should a manager have to motivate him to get success for his wife and family?

Interview, Cleveland/
The Washington Post, 5-8:(D)13.

Bruce Lietzke
Golfer

1

I love competition so much that when I'm alone I compete with myself. Shooting baskets or playing golf or whatever I do, I pretend I'm someone else. I take my shots, then take the opposition's shots. I've always been that way. I play hard against myself.

Interview, Palm Desert, Calif., Feb. 9/
Los Angeles Times, 2-10:(3)6.

Davey Lopes
Baseball player, Los Angeles "Dodgers"

2

How many bases can I steal this year? If I stay healthy I think I can get 120. But you have to be greedy to steal that many — you're going to have to steal when your team is way ahead or way behind; you're going to have to steal almost every time you're on base no matter what the circumstances. I plan to be greedy this season. I know this may sound cocky, but you have to be cocky to be a good player. Cocky with humility. I think cocky with arrogance is bad.

Interview, Los Angeles/Los Angeles
Herald-Examiner, 2-20:(D)7.

Frank Lucchesi
Baseball manager, Texas "Rangers"

3

I'm getting sick and tired of [players] making $80,000 a year and moaning and groaning about their jobs. I think about players in the minors, just begging for a chance. Baseball has been good to me. I'm sick and tired of these punks saying "play me or trade me." Let 'em go find a job ... You give me $80,000 a year for the next 10 years and I'll play utility man for 162 games and love it.

Pompano Beach, Fla./
Los Angeles Herald-Examiner, 3-25:(D)2.

Ron Lyle
Boxer

4

America wasn't built on going to church; it was built on violence. I express America in the ring.

The New York Times, 5-29:(5)2.

John Madden
Football coach, Oakland "Raiders"

5

The first quality that makes a player a winner is simple pride. He has such a desire to excel that he will take enormous pains. He will work out beyond what is demanded, build his body during the off-season, guard his weight and study the problems of his position. The second quality is toughness — doing what the job requires without worrying about the physical consequences. A wide receiver will make the catch, untroubled by the possibility of getting blindsided. A quarterback will hold the ball until the final instant, knowing the rushers will flatten him. The winning player has no fear of doing what must be done in order to be great.

Interview/TV Guide, 9-17:48.

6

I wish somebody would explain "motivation" to me some time, because I don't know what it is. I sure don't teach it and I've never given a pro football team a pep talk in my life. I wouldn't know how to do that and I doubt if anybody would listen. If you want to do something, whether it's play football for a living or something else, the drive has to come from within. I can't make another man jump into a pile of players in the hope of grabbing a loose football. He's got to want to do that himself, which is why I think one person trying to motivate another is so overrated.

Interview, Oakland, Calif./
The Christian Science Monitor, 9-23:6.

7

Everyone's goal is to get to the Super Bowl. When the season starts, you don't hear people say, "We want to *win* in the Super Bowl"; they say, "We want to *go* to the Super Bowl." It may be just semantics, but I think it reveals something about how they really feel. In the playoffs, or the championship game, when you

500

(JOHN MADDEN)

lose you are out of it, suddenly. There's no chance to bounce back as in the regular season. In the Super Bowl, the season is going to be over, win or lose. That doesn't mean there's any less desire to win, or any less disappointment about losing — but there's no looking ahead, either. It's a sort of completion, if you know what I mean.

Interview, Oakland, Calif., Dec. 27/
The New York Times, 12-28:54.

Garry Maddox
Baseball player, Philadelphia "Phillies"
1

Hitting a home run is a great feeling — it gives you a big charge. You know that's what the people like to see. It's what you guys [reporters] like to see, too. Just stop and think how you rush up to the home-run hitters after every game. With all that glamor attached to hitting the ball out of the park, it takes a lot of discipline to go up there and just try to get a base hit.

Interview/The Christian Science Monitor, 4-25:24.

Pete Maravich
Basketball player, New Orleans "Jazz"
2

We live in an unbalanced world, and sports should be one dimension that leaves people happy and carefree.

San Francisco Examiner & Chronicle, 2-13:(C)4.

Billy Martin
Baseball manager, New York "Yankees"
3

As a manager, I ask only one thing of a player — hustle. If a player doesn't hustle, it shows the club up and I show the player up. Hustle is the only thing I really demand. It doesn't take any ability to hustle.

Boston, June 18/
Los Angeles Times, 6-19:(3)1.

Gene Mauch
Baseball manager, Minnesota "Twins"
4

There are 25 players on a big-league team, and every one of them has a preconceived idea of what kind of player he wants to be. Now,

some guys are pretty good at evaluating their own skills, and some are dead wrong, and some are halfway in-between. If you're any kind of a manager, you leave the first group alone. For example, I wouldn't change a thing about the way Rod Carew hits, even if he is constantly changing his stance. For him, it's okay. The guys you have to reach are the players who are trying to be something they're obviously not. First you have to believe that what you're going to ask them to do is absolutely right for them, and then you have to sell them on the idea. After that, you have to hope that they have some immediate success with what you've suggested. Otherwise, they'll go right back to what they were doing before. I've succeeded with some players and missed with others, but I know that you'll never get anywhere if you don't try.

Interview, Anaheim, Calif./
The Christian Science Monitor, 6-6:33.

Al McGuire
Basketball coach, Marquette University
5

Statistics are the cancer of basketball. Everyone is so aware of shots taken, time played. They think, "If I can get six points in five minutes, what could I do in 40 minutes?" So everyone wants to play more. I tried to stop making our statistics public about six years ago ... So now I've got mothers calling me and telling me Johnny should score more. Maybe we should start keeping statistics for warmups. You know, Johnny made five or six before the game. That way, everyone has numbers and all the parents are happy.

Interview, Virginia/
The Washington Post, 3-1:(D)4.

Joe Morgan
Baseball player, Cincinnati "Reds"
6

Those years, chasing and catching the *Dodgers*, were the most fun I've ever had in baseball. When you're out front, you're always looking back. But when you're behind, there's no way to look but up. Being behind makes you play harder and better. That is the big thing.

Interview, Cincinnati/
Los Angeles Herald-Examiner, 5-4:(D)15.

WHAT THEY SAID IN 1977

Stan Morrison
Basketball coach,
University of the Pacific

1

I'll tell you what keeps me in coaching. And unless you've ever gone through the process of selling kids on your school and your program and worked with them for four years, you might not understand. Eventually, you'll beat a team that's better than you. After that, you're hooked. You'll put a game-plan together and work on it for a week. You feel yourself and your players becoming prepared. Then you go on the floor against that team that should beat you . . . and you win! No one outside the coaching profession can understand what that feels like. You hug each other in the locker room and you shout and yell but nothing makes much sense because it's a feeling not meant for words.

Interview/Los Angeles Times, 4-5:(3)6.

George Moscone
Mayor of San Francisco

2

. . . I never believed a city had to have a [winning baseball club] in the sense they must win most of their games, but only that they be a representative ball club, reasonably colorful and one the fans could identify with as their ball club.

Interview/San Francisco
Examiner & Chronicle, 4-10:(C)1.

Dick Motta
Basketball coach, Washington "Bullets"

3

The [NBA] is incredibly more sophisticated than it was when I broke in [in 1968]. There's more stability now. I think the only time you'll see big trades is when someone of top value is right at the end of his contract. The players are looking at this as a career. They ought to — the

average salary is over $100,000 a year. They used to look for off-season jobs; now they read *The Wall Street Journal.* There weren't even assistant coaches when I broke in. If you had anybody helping you, he usually went out and scouted. Now good organizations have two men on the bench and a third out on the road.

Interview/The Dallas Times Herald, 2-17:(F)8.

Ilie Nastase
Tennis player

4

I think the most enjoyable time for me in tennis was when I was very young. I didn't make any money, I just enjoyed to play. I played for hours and hours every day, and I loved it. When there was no money around, I didn't feel any pressure. When you start to win lots of money, is different story. Before, I was content with little things — little food, little money, little anything. I was very happy. Now, not so much. I'm not tired physically, but in the mind. I don't feel like practicing today, but everybody else does it, so I have to practice.

Interview, Paris/
The Washington Post, 3-31:(D)3.

5

[On his behavior on the courts]: People wonder why I am acting crazy. Is because no one will give me one hundred per cent chance. I am villain; so is okay for them to make noises when I try to hit a first serve; is okay for them to call me bum and yell "foot fault." But is difficult to play when there are 15,000 people against you on every point. Sure, I am no angel, but the people provoke me so much. If I am insulted, why cannot I insult back?

Los Angeles Times, 5-5:(3)2.

Harry Neale
Hockey coach, New England "Whalers"

6

It's a fact that a number of teams in our league [the WHL] are struggling like a sonofagun, and probably the same number in the NHL are. Unless the two leagues get together, there

(HARRY NEALE)

are going to be more franchise failures. Everybody in the industry has got to take a hard look at why it's happening. Ticket prices are too high, and they have to be because we have two drafts and a kid who has never passed a puck in either league is making $100,000. Then it's pretty tough to tell the 15-year veteran he can't make that, and your payroll goes out of sight. It's not worth the $12 or $13 the crack teams are asking to watch anybody play hockey. It's just too much money. It's a $50 evening at best, and there are a lot of places you can go for 50 bucks. And we're asking people to do it 40 times a year . . . The pendulum has got to swing back. The players will still be a hell of a lot better off than they were, but the ones who have played the last five years will just have to look at that period as a bonanza. Just like the stock market was great for a while, and now it's not bad. The salaries in hockey have to get back to the "not bad" level.

The Washington Post, 3-8:(D)3.

Jack Nicklaus
Golfer
1

I keep playing golf because I feel there are still a lot of things I want to accomplish. I want to be a part of history . . . My desire and determination are still there, and I think I still know how to play my shots. And I still look upon golf as a game. I don't feel [my] ability will deteriorate for awhile and I'm anxious to finish leaving no question as to who was the best.

Interview, Carlsbad, Calif./
Los Angeles Herald-Examiner, 4-15:(C)2.

Lawrence F. O'Brien
Commissioner, National
Basketball Association
2

Sports is not isolated from society. We are not an island unto ourselves. Sports at all levels is an integral part of American society. It's a rare young person, boy or girl, that hasn't had some exposure to participation in sports. Certainly, these people become fans. It's a healthy situation. It adds a dimension to a free society.

There's been a great emphasis in the past 15 or 20 years on physical fitness, and certainly sports has played a major role. Look at the growth of tennis, or of skiing. I think that's progress. Of course, there can be an excess, when a small group of people allow a sport to become so involving for them that it becomes their life. There has to be a rule of normality in a healthy society.

Interview, New York/
Los Angeles Times, 3-6:(3)4.

3

[On player violence in games] : As a statistic, last season we had possibly 10 or 12 incidents that could be described as violent in nature involving punching. We are now closing out the first third of our season, and approximately 300 games have been played. We have had two serious incidents. It's obvious that the degree of violence inherent in these incidents and the end result of the acts are of an extremely serious nature. So, while the statistic might indicate a lessening, clearly the intervening of the two occurrences to date this season extend beyond past experience. We are not only concerned [with] containing violence in our sport by direct and strong action by way of penalty, coupled with continuing, repeated urging, pleading and demanding that everyone in this league avoid violence, but we are also concerned to extend every effort to determine, if possible, the root causes of these occurrences. Currently, we have a committee compiled of representatives of the Players Association, general managers, coaches, along with NBA staff, endeavoring to determine why these acts occur. Why they occur eludes me in specific terms at this point.

Interview, New York, Dec. 14/
The New York Times, 12-15:(D)15.

Peter O'Malley
President, Los Angeles
"Dodgers" baseball club
4

[On the use of TV in calling plays] : When you think of all the cameras you'd need to do a perfect job, the complications are enormous. One complication alone — the delays you'd

WHAT THEY SAID IN 1977

(PETER O'MALLEY)

have while the umpires consulted their TV sets — probably outweighs the problems caused by an umpire's occasional mistake. A ballgame isn't like a horse race, in which one camera can determine who won after they raise the inquiry sign. Baseball's answer is to pay the umpires well and train them well. I believe the integrity of the game is safe in their hands.

Los Angeles Times, 2-7:(3)4.

Arnold Palmer
Golfer
1

I always enjoy meeting someone I know [in the crowd]. Through the years I've become good friends with these people, and at tournaments we have a lot of fun. I've got a warm spot in my heart for anyone who would take his vacation and fly to a tournament to watch me play. Besides, the biggest mistake any athlete can make is to think he can exist without the crowd. Galleries are the one essential. They're more important to professional sports than the athlete.

Palm Springs, Calif./Los Angeles Times, 2-16:(3)8.

Ara Parseghian
Former football coach,
University of Notre Dame
2

I think one of the great things about participating in athletics is that you learn from winning and from losing, and you learn to live with those things. Every day is not a bright, sunshiny day. Not everything is good, and that is what happens in athletics, and I think it is a great learning process ... We learn a lesson as we move through life: Sometimes you lose a game.

On "The Way It Was" TV program, Los Angeles/
Los Angeles Times, 3-15:(3)3.

Floyd Patterson
Former heavyweight boxing
champion of the world
3

No matter how much chicanery goes on outside the ring, I still say that inside the rings those fights [during the days when he was active] were genuine. Maybe this boy was badly

overmatched and maybe that record was faked. But when they got in the ring it was real. In the ring there's no room for anything but truth.

Interview, May 28/The New York Times, 5-29:(5)3.

Richard Petty
Auto-racing driver
4

In my career, I never challenged what someone else did. My philosophy is to do better today than I did yesterday. So I've never been afraid once I'm in a race car. Because, by the time I'm supposed to be afraid, I'm too busy doing something about it; and, by the time I'm through doing something about it, it's all over anyway.

Interview/Los Angeles Times, 1-30:(1)3.

5

Racing is the last thing I would recommend a person go into to make a living. There's eight years of experience you've got to get, and that costs money. And then it takes that long to find out whether you're going to be able to do the job or not. And then the cat is 30 years old before he can be considered a consistent winner. A lot of people don't want to spend eight years and a bunch of money to find out they're not good enough to begin with. In football there's a lot of money invested in you, but it's not your own. In racing you've got to dish the cash out, or find some cat who will. The money aspect of what you've got to spend and what your chances are of getting it back are very slim. There's not but six-eight people that make a super good living driving stock cars.

Interview/Los Angeles Times, 11-15:(3)7.

Chester M. Pierce
Psychiatrist, Harvard University
6

In football, the contract is either you hurt the opponent or he hurts you. The coach must have his men feeling that they not only can kill, but that they should kill.

The New York Times, 5-29:(5)2.

Willis Reed
Basketball coach,
New York "Knickerbockers"

1

Players have to know that when they sign a contract, it means they are saying that "for this amount, I will give 100 percent of my body." My job [as coach] will be to tell them when they are giving 85 per cent and that they owe me 15.

The Dallas Times Herald, 10-23:(C)8.

Joe Robbie
Owner, Miami "Dolphins"
football team

2

[Criticizing an NFL Player-Club Relations Committee ruling that two of his players, who he had put on suspension pending their trial on drug possession, be either reinstated, traded or put on waivers]: The action of the PCRC establishes a dangerous precedent and could rise to haunt the NFL in the future in protecting the integrity of professional football. What will happen if two players are arrested for fixing a football game? Will their owner be prohibited from suspending them until they are tried in court so that they can play again while under indictment? The fundamental question here is protecting the integrity of professional football and the public confidence in the game.

Miami/The Dallas Times Herald, 8-3:(D)8.

Pete Rozelle
Commissioner, National Football League

3

Entertainment is all we [in football] are. Until [the broadcast of the motion picture *Gone With the Wind*,] our Super Bowl last year had the highest [TV] rating ever. Eighty million viewers. What we do object to is constant psychoanalysis: "Football is warlike. Football is violent." The game has nothing to do with war. Our league provides action entertainment, nothing less and nothing more.

Interview, New York/Time, 1-10:34.

4

Sports has had too much of internal strife. It turns off the fans. In the last few years, my mail has reflected a growing disenchantment. We were getting increasing complaints about the fighting between owners and players. The public doesn't like to see that as a part of sports. People can read that kind of news in the rest of the paper. They turn to sports for entertainment and escape.

U.S. News & World Report, 5-16:54.

Joe Rudi
Baseball player, California "Angels"

5

Let me tell you something about hitting. When you're going good, it doesn't make any difference who the pitcher is, whether it's a night game or a day game, or where the ballpark is located. I don't take a lot of theories up to the plate with me. I look for what I think is a good pitch and then I swing at it. If there is more to hitting than I just told you, I don't know about it.

Interview, Anaheim, Calif./
The Christian Science Monitor, 5-9:23.

Adolph Rupp
Former college basketball coach

6

When someone asks me to assess myself as a coach, I just say, "Look at my record." I say that about the other coaches, too. Look at the man's record. That will tell you if he can coach or not. Winning is the reason for everything. All this stuff that they say about getting by on building character, that's fine. But you can build it better if you win. Success is the best builder of character there is. Failure isn't.

Interview, New York/
Los Angeles Herald-Examiner, 3-13:(D)6.

Nolan Ryan
Baseball pitcher, California "Angels"

7

I can't think of anything more humiliating than losing a ballgame to a guy who steals home on you. It happened to me one time against Kansas City. I had a 2-and-2 count on the hitter — and Amos Otis broke from third. The pitch was a ball and he slid in safe. I felt like a nickel.

Interview/Los Angeles Herald-Examiner, 7-13:(D)2.

WHAT THEY SAID IN 1977

Bo Schembechler
Football coach,
University of Michigan　　　　　　　　　　1

The thing that makes college football what it is is that those who watch it and those who play it are so enthusiastic about it. And what holds their interest is the complexity of the positions — by comparison with other sports. Football is the epitome of team games because there are some 22 or 24 positions, all different and all difficult. But most boys will never put on another hip pad after they leave school. It is hogwash to say college football is a farm system for the pros. Some 90 to 95 per cent of the young men who play football at Michigan and other colleges never turn pro. So I say we better make sure they have something to show for all the time they put in learning this difficult game. At the very least, they should come out with a college degree.

At college-football symposium, Kansas City/
Los Angeles Times, 3-22:(3)1.

Mike Schmidt
Baseball player,
Philadelphia "Phillies"　　　　　　　　　2

Aside from the fact that there's better pitching now, the uniform ballparks have had a lot to do with the decrease in home runs. The fences are farther away than in the old parks and in most of the new stadiums the ball just doesn't carry as well. Which brings up another point: The balls are different today. They're mass-produced and just thrown together. You can tell almost by looking at them they're poorly made. I once hit one last year that had the cover flapping right after I made contact. What chance has a ball like that got of going out of the ballpark?

Los Angeles Times, 4-17:(3)10.

Tex Schramm
President, Dallas "Cowboys"
football team　　　　　　　　　　　　　3

[On electronic officiating, such as TV instant replays]: Fans go to football games to see people, not robots. It would be possible to have not only computerized officiating but also mechanical men playing football at the direc-

tion of a computer center — but I don't see that as a great improvement . . . The trouble with relying on television part of the time is when do you decide to do it? When do you decide not to do it? There are an awful lot of marginal cases. Where do you draw the line? Using TV part time would be bound to raise as many questions as it answered, and probably more. The rational way to go is to strengthen the officiating.

Los Angeles Times, 2-7:(3)4.

　　　　　　　　　　　　　　　　　4

The whole damn business [of football] is scary. I mean, your whole season may rest on some guy kicking a field goal in the last three seconds of a game. You can go into the red ink real fast. If you don't win on the field, you can become a loser, financially, very easy. Winning is the name of the game.

Interview, Dallas/Los Angeles Times, 2-13:(3)4.

Norm Sherry
Baseball manager, California "Angels"　　5

[On his job as manager]: When you go out there, you have 25 people you've got to regard almost as you would your own children. And that's exactly what I believe, because you're going to have to talk to them, want to be able to relate to them; and yet, as your own flesh and blood, they have to know when you say something . . . that you mean it, and they have to respond. I talk to and with my players. I don't want to be up on one level and they're down on another. I want them to be on the same wave length of communication. I'm the manager and they're the players. I'm responsible for certain things, and they're responsible for certain other things. And I expect them to be done!

Los Angeles Herald-Examiner,
4-17:(California Living)6.

O. J. Simpson
Football player, Buffalo "Bills"　　　　6

[On his game-winning, 64-yard, Pacific-8 championship run in 1968]: Ah man, I just took off and ran. When it was over, I felt good. But somehow I knew it was going to happen,

(O. J. SIMPSON)

even though it was a spontaneous thing. I knew it was time, time in the fourth quarter of the biggest game of the year, time for O. J. to do something. . . . sometimes when your legs feel hollow, you just shift into overdrive. Nothing goes through your mind. You just react when you get the ball. In a game, you've got to clear your head, so you can see certain things without thinking. Improvise. But I'd made that run a million times before in my mind. All the runs I've ever made on the field, I've made a million times in my mind. Cats come up to me afterward and say, "How'd you know how to do that? How'd you know to make them feint?" I tell them, "I've run that play so many times in my mind, I just *knew* it. It blows the way it does in my head."

Interview/Los Angeles Times, 1-30:(1)3.

1

Fear of losing is what helps make competitors great. Show me a guy who is a gracious loser and I'll show you a perennial loser. I'll show class, but I take losing hard.

Interview/Los Angeles Times, 1-30:(1)3.

Enos Slaughter
Former baseball player
2

One year I hit .291 and had to take a salary cut. If you hit .291 today, you'd own the franchise.

The New York Times, 5-15:(5)11.

Reggie Smith
Baseball player, Los Angeles "Dodgers"
3

I came into baseball trying to emulate Henry Aaron and Willie Mays. I wanted to be a power hitter. That's where the money, the fame and the excitement were. Well, I soon found out, as a lot of others did, that power hitting on a consistent basis is becoming a thing of the past. The pitchers today are too smart. They aren't going to give you the fat one as often as pitchers did before.

Interview, Vero Beach, Fla./
Los Angeles Herald-Examiner, 3-6:(D)2.

Stan Smith
Tennis player
4

In the past, if you were an established player, you could usually breeze through the first round of most tournaments. But the way it is today there are no more easy matches. You have to beat everybody, including the kids who just came up . . . No new kid gets to hide anything once he's on the pro tour. But if I've never seen him before I'll feel him out in the first couple of games, just like a boxer would. Then I'll go to work on his weaknesses.

Interview, Palm Springs, Calif./
The Christian Science Monitor, 3-4:22.

Tom Sneva
Auto-racing driver
5

[On his winning the USAC national championship]: To put it into perspective, winning the national championship is like winning the National or American Football Conference title and then losing the Super Bowl. Winning the NFC title is a tremendous accomplishment because it's something you have to do over the course of a season; but the Super Bowl is such a big event that people tend to remember who won it and not who won the NFC. It's the same way with the USAC national championship and Indy. People tend to remember the Indy winner and not the driver who won the national title. But it's still important because you have to put it together all year to win. You have to have consistently high finishes in all the races.

Interview/The New York Times, 9-18:(5)11.

George Steinbrenner
Owner, New York
"Yankees" baseball club
6

When people ask me whether [player] Reggie Jackson was worth all that money [an estimated $2.9-million for five years] and what it was we expected in return, I tell them we would have liked him to hit 30 homers, and he hit 32; we wanted him to drive in 100 runs, and he drove in 110; and we would have liked him to have 20 game-winning hits, and he had 21. Most of all, we would have wished him to be one of our biggest contributors when we

507

WHAT THEY SAID IN 1977

needed it most. It was during August and September that we needed it most, and he was.

Los Angeles Times, 11-9:(3)2.

Jose Sulaiman (Chagnon)
President, World Boxing Council   1

[Current heavyweight champion Muhammad] Ali has said that he is bigger than boxing. Well, I don't know the height of boxing, I know that he's about 6 feet and something... Muhammad Ali is wrong. Definitely. He is not bigger than boxing... There is nobody, absolutely nobody in the boxing business bigger than boxing itself... In the past, we had Jack Dempsey, and the same question always came up: "What is going to happen to boxing when Jack Dempsey leaves? ... What is going to happen to boxing when Joe Louis leaves?" I don't ever foresee a time when boxing will not exist. There is a lot of hunger in the world, and, when you see hunger, you've got to see people striving to eat. Some have the natural abilities to get money and feed themselves. As long as there is hunger in the world, boxing will exist.

Interview, Las Vegas, Nev./
Los Angeles Times, 1-17:(3)8.

Frank Tanana
Baseball pitcher, California "Angels"   2

[On pitching]: It requires a lot of skill and a lot of effort to throw a baseball to a certain location with something on it. That's the damn good thing about baseball: There's so much effort and skill involved. The hardest thing to do, they say, is to hit a baseball. The reason it's so hard is the people who throw it.

Interview/Los Angeles Times, 10-7:(3)13.

Fran Tarkenton
Football player, Minnesota "Vikings"   3

[On the Super Bowl]: That's the greatness of our game: What other part of life can you get in, and in three hours of an afternoon have a chance to be the best in the world at what you do? It's not anybody's opinion — you have a chance to be that. You as a writer may think you're the greatest in the world, but you have

no way of proving that. I haven't in my other jobs. But in this job [football] I have a chance in three hours to show it one way or another. That's exhilarating in itself. That's a trip. There's nothing like it in sports right now. Everything else is three-of-five or four-of-seven or four rounds of golf. But this one is sudden death, one day, three hours, and either you got it or you don't.

Interview, Los Angeles/
The Dallas Times Herald, 1-6:(B)12.

Dan Thomas
Baseball player, Milwaukee "Brewers"   4

[On batters being hit by pitched balls]: I think they ought to make a rule that if a guy gets hit and is able to get up, they should tie the pitcher's hands behind his back and let the hitter smack him in the face.

The New York Times, 5-15:(5)11.

Thomas Tutko
Professor of psychology, San Jose
(Calif.) State University   5

[On the antics of football players when they score]: There's so much intensity and threat and insecurity in the game that when you finally do something that gives you temporary security, there's a real desire to make it known, that you finally made it to the top ... People who make the rules [who are critical of the antics] are ordinarily from successful, upper-middle-class, conservative backgrounds. Most of them have some sort of psychosomatic illness now, and most will probably die of heart attacks. Instead of spiking, they would rather we ulcerate, have migraines, asthma, lower-back pains — all of which are mental illnesses, although we have never recognized them as such. I, for one, would say why not let them spike it? It's legitimate to have feelings.

Los Angeles Times, 12-26:(3)5,6.

Bill Veeck
Owner, Chicago "White Sox" baseball club   6

I think there will be a lot of free agents [players] after this year, and as a result the prices players are asking will go down. You can't pay a player twice as much as you did a

(BILL VEECK)

year ago if he had the same statistics he had the previous year, just because of the free-agent business. You cannot continue running up deficits. It's not realistic. Look what happened to the ABA and WFL.

Los Angeles Herald-Examiner, 2-6:(C)5.

1

In the 1960s there was a period of unrest, speed and violence in this country. There was the war in Vietnam. There was mugging, meanness and violence. In this spirit, football and basketball were natural sports . . . [But then], suddenly, people were tired of violence. They were seeking stability and escape. They were tired of concrete, steel and artificiality. They found baseball again, a sport to be savored. The game is perfect for the time right now and that's one of the reasons attendance is up all over the country . . . Where else but at a ballpark can you stand up and yell and holler your head off without landing in the pokey?

Interview, Chicago/The Dallas Times Herald, 7-19:(D)3.

Guillermo Vilas
Tennis player

2

Some people play [tennis] because it is the only thing they can do and they die if they don't win. For them, that is everything and it is destructive because they fight and don't have any friends. You don't have to be a killer to be a good competitor. Your opponent can also be your friend. You are having fun together; you are first a sportsman, then a professional athlete.

Interview, Palm Springs, Calif./
Los Angeles Times, 2-23:(3)6.

3

The worst part of a person who becomes an important person is, they call him a celebrity. It's not the person who changes, but the persons who surround him. My parents have become so conditioned to reacting for the benefit of local newsmen and television cameras

that they smile when the light goes on in the refrigerator at home.

San Francisco Examiner & Chronicle,
9-18:(This World)2.

Virginia Wade
Tennis player

4

I've always thought that you sort of peak at two ages in tennis: at 18 or 19, when you haven't had a chance to explore all the possibilities in your life or your tennis, including the possibility of failure — or else much older, when you're more mature as a person.

Interview/The Washington Post, 1-9:(D)8.

Kermit Washington
Basketball player, Boston "Celtics"

5

Frustration causes the [player] fights [during games]. It leads to aggression. In football, where contact is the whole purpose, a player can take out his frustration and aggression on the very next play. He just hits somebody a little harder, and it's legal. But you can't do that in basketball. If you want to find out how to stop violence in sports, you'd have to find out how to stop violence in the world outside sports.

Interview, Palos Verdes, Calif., Dec. 29/
The New York Times, 12-30:(A)21.

Tom Watson
Golfer

6

Confidence in golf means being able to concentrate on the problem at hand. It's really having no outside interference on what you know you can do. Sometimes, by thinking too much, you can destroy your momentum and instinct. A lot of times, when you're under the gun, you have to make the best judgment you can, and instinct takes over. Sam Snead was the best at it, I think. He never used yardage. He had a great hand-eye coordination and sense of distance. His instincts for this game were tremendous.

Interview, Turnberry, Scotland/
The Washington Post, 7-8:(D)4.

WHAT THEY SAID IN 1977

Jerry West
Basketball coach,
Los Angeles "Lakers"
1

I don't buy the fact I'm a good coach. The players have done the winning. They're the ones who have scored the points, grabbed the rebounds, played tough defense. The coaches can prepare them, but it's still the players who decide whether you win or lose.

Interview, Los Angeles/
Los Angeles Herald-Examiner, 4-17:(C)9.

Dick Williams
Baseball manager, Montreal "Expos"
2

I've always demanded 100 per cent from my players, and when I don't get it I get mad. Everybody is going to boot a ball once in a while in the field, but the one thing I can't stand is mental mistakes. If a man isn't willing to pay the price, he can play for somebody else. It's fun to watch a team grow and it's fun to win, but anything less is miserable.

Interview/The Christian Science Monitor, 8-3:12.

Maury Wills
Sports announcer,
National Broadcasting Company;
Former baseball player
3

It used to be very prestigious, managing in the major [baseball] leagues. That was when it was up to the player to make the manager like him. The manager was the boss, a real authority figure. But all that has changed. Now it's the manager who has to make the players happy. He's the one who's always walking on thin ice.

Los Angeles Herald-Examiner, 6-24:(D)2.

John Wooden
Former basketball coach,
University of California,
Los Angeles
4

I made every effort to keep my players from ever becoming excessively jubilant or excessively dejected. That helped prevent peaks and valleys over the course of a season. I really never tried to get a team "up" for a game. I always felt the importance of the game would do that in itself. Fortunately, in each cham-

pionship game we were usually ahead enough right near the end so I could call a time-out in the last few minutes. During these time-outs, I reaffirmed to everyone that when the game was over we shouldn't act like fools. I told them it was a basketball game, and nothing more.

Interview/The Christian Science Monitor, 5-31:29.

Cale Yarborough
Auto-racing driver
5

I think racing is the greatest sport in the world. I had an opportunity to try to play football but I chose racing instead and I'm glad I did. You haven't seen the top of this sport yet. It's going to continue to climb. I started driving for the enjoyment of it, but later on it became a profession and then the dollar marks became the name of the game. I know there's no way I could have made two million bucks playing football. And I could never have made it in basketball, either.

Interview/Los Angeles Times, 11-15:(3)7.

Jack Youngblood
Football player, Los Angeles "Rams"
6

[On the provision in the new player-owner agreement which enables a team to keep a player who wants to change teams by matching the other team's salary offer]: The agreement isn't in the best interests of the [National Football] League's best players. A veteran playing out his option to become a free agent really isn't free any more. Theoretically, he is free to bargain with other clubs — but in practice he can't get away. He is restricted by the right of first refusal. If he can't stand the head coach or the owner — or the town he has to play in — he's stuck anyway. The new compensation rule is another thing designed to hinder the movement of free agents. Most are worse off than they were under the old Rozelle Rule.

Interview/Los Angeles Times, 4-22:(3)1.

John A. Ziegler
President, National Hockey League

1

The viewpoint that says fighting [in hockey games] should not be permitted, that you should go to the other sports' position of automatic suspension for [player] "fisticuffs" — I personally don't agree with. I think the fighting aspect provides an outlet for the frustrations, the need to retaliate sometimes. When you think of the speed of the game, the demand on reaction and competitive drive, it's almost a natural function for some people to have that kind of outlet.

The Christian Science Monitor, 12-7:10.

Women's Rights

Bella S. Abzug
*Chairman, National Commission on the
Observance of International Women's Year;
Former United States Representative,
D–New York*
                                                    1

There is a place for women in the power
structure. We don't want so much to see a
female Einstein become an assistant professor.
We want a woman *schlemiel* to get promoted as
quickly as a male *schlemiel*.

U.S. News & World Report, 4-25:61.

                                                    2

The women's movement isn't any one organization or set of ideas or particular life-style. It
is the homemaker deciding that raising children,
cleaning, cooking and all the other things she
does for her family, is work that should be
accorded respect and value. It is the young
woman student asserting she wants to play
baseball, major in physics or become a brain
surgeon. It's the working woman who demands
she gets the same promotion opportunities as a
man. It is the divorcee fighting for Social
Security benefits in her own right, a widow
embarking on a new career, a mother organizing
a day-care center, a battered wife seeking help,
a woman running for public office. It is all
kinds of getting together to make their needs
known and to get action.

At National Women's Conference,
Houston, Nov. 19/San Francisco Examiner &
Chronicle, 11-20:(A)22.

Judith Bardwick
Psychologist, University of Michigan
                                                    3

If you define dominance as who occupies
formal roles of responsibility, then there is no
society where males are not dominant. When
something is so universal, the probability is — as

reluctant as I am to say it — that there is some
quality of the organism that leads to this
condition. So women may achieve greater
parity, but will they achieve full parity? I don't
know.

The New York Times, 11-30:24.

Candice Bergen
Actress
                                                    4

I think the women's movement was crucial
and valid in all the basics. But it ignored some
emotional and biological realities. And that part
of it was dangerous and destructive. After all,
there are only certain times in your life when
you can have children and build a family. So
I'm now wondering if all this liberation
shouldn't be re-evaluated. I mean, five years ago
I thought the most courageous thing was not to
get married, not to have children. That all
seemed so predictable and safe. Now I think the
most courageous thing is to get married and
have children, because that seems the most
worthwhile — if not the most impossible thing
— to try for. There are certain age-old realities
you can't refute. You can modify them and try
to make them more intelligent, which is what
the women's lib movement basically did. But,
in the process, a lot of people got dehumanized.

Los Angeles Times, 7-24:(5)8.

Jimmy Carter
President of the United States
                                                    5

When I ran for President, I made it clear that
I was in favor of the Equal Rights Amendment
passing and still am in favor of it and hope it
does pass. But I respect very well and very
consistently the right of individual state legislatures to vote the way they choose. But I think
it's good to point out to the legislators individually, and to the people of the country as I am

(JIMMY CARTER)

doing at this moment, that we do need to give women equal rights. They've been cheated too long. They don't have equal pay for equal jobs and I think that this Equal Rights Amendment, which is very simple and very clear, would be a good thing for our country.

National call-in radio program, Washington, March 5/The New York Times, 3-6:(1)31.

Rosalynn Carter
Wife of President of the
United States Jimmy Carter
1

I really believe that once the Equal Rights Amendment is passed, the opposition will go away and people will see that it's not what some [critics] have made it out to be. And I think that ERA is going to be around forever if we don't go on and pass it. If they don't vote for it this year, it's going to come back next year. If they don't pass it next year, it's going to come back the following year. I want to go ahead and get it passed and be done with it.

Interview/U.S. News & World Report, 3-21:33.

Shirley Chisholm
United States Representative,
D—New York
2

The programming begins the moment the doctor says, "Mr. Jones, you have a beautiful baby girl." From that time on, she is wrapped in a pink blanket because that is the color for her sex and she is conditioned to follow specified patterns of behavior. Women must become revolutionaries; we must refuse to accept the old stereotypes ... Sometimes I don't know if I am being discriminated against because I am black or because I am a woman. I know I have met more prejudice in politics because I'm female. In 1972, when I dared to say I wanted to be President, I knew there would be laughter, snickers and racial slurs, and as many of these came from black men as from white men. All men, no matter what their color or background, have some basic feelings about women. And discrimination of any form is

anti-human. We need the collective ability and genius of all our people.

Interview, Dallas/The Dallas Times Herald, 1-28:(B)3.

Karen DeCrow
President,
National Organization for Women
3

Beware a woman's culture. ... separatism is not the way to go. We are struggling because we live in a male separatist world. We don't want to replicate that mistake ... It may be an unpopular view, but history will prove me right.

At NOW's annual national meeting, Detroit, April 23/San Francisco Examiner & Chronicle, 4-24:(A)17.

Morarji R. Desai
Prime Minister of India
4

I have been the greatest champion of women and have put more women in the legislatures than anyone else. But I have changed my views after the experience of history and three women Prime Ministers — Sri Lanka, India and Israel. And [Margaret] Thatcher will be the same if she becomes Prime Minister of Britain — let me tell you that! You see, women on the whole have better, softer qualities than men, and on the whole they don't go as devilish as men. But when a woman becomes devilish, she beats all records.

Interview, New Delhi/Time, 4-4:34.

India Edwards
Former vice chairman,
Democratic National Committee
5

Today's women are going about it [equal rights] in all the wrong ways. They should not make men feel they are rivals. The women are defeating themselves. They approach men as if they were their enemies. They make men afraid of them. They're too aggressive. You win more in this world with honey and sweet words than with anything else.

Interview, Washington/ The Washington Post, 6-16:(C)3.

WHAT THEY SAID IN 1977

Nora Ephron
Writer
1

There's really no use pretending the women's movement is this vibrant, wonderful thing that's out there doing something. For a while, I was Pollyannish about it. I believed the movement was an Idea, and there was nothing you could do to stop it. But I was wrong. The movement was not just an idea but a group of people, and I don't know who those people are today ... Because the movement aimed at being a monolith, it was accused of falling short of the ridiculous goals it set for itself. The big issues of the movement were never what they should have been — not divorce or motherhood or jobs or abortion. They were things like, "Are we gonna let lesbians in?" — you know, who cares?; okay, let's do it and get it over with because it's *boring* — and "Who is gonna have more power, Betty or Gloria?" ... In a period when the movement should have looked vibrant and quarrelsome and alive, it tried to look like a monolith, and a lot of women were turned off by that. They always tried to say it was a middle-class movement. I wish it *were* more of a middle-class movement.

At Richland College, Dallas/
The Dallas Times Herald, 3-2:(G)1.

Sam J. Ervin, Jr.
Former United States Senator,
D—North Carolina
2

The ERA is not necessary because the Supreme Court now holds that every law in the land — Federal or state — which makes any distinction between the rights of men and women is un-Constitutional, unless the law is based on reasonable grounds for the protection of women.

At University of Missouri, Kansas City, Oct. 12/
The Dallas Times Herald, 10-14:(A)2.

Oriana Fallaci
Italian journalist
3

The feminist movement is very strong in Italy, much stronger than in America where I'm afraid many ladies, they talk very well and they write very well about certain things and I don't know how much they apply these in their daily lives. I would say that one of the strongest feminist movements is now in Italy. The reason is obvious. Where the oppression is heavier, the rebellion is heavier. Don't forget we have something called the Vatican in Italy, with the Pope saying what he says about women. The movement is very strong there in number — when you see a rally you get scared, honestly, you get scared. The police get scared because, you know, you can see rallies with 50,000 women, and it's continuous because the rally begins and then you see people leaving their houses and coming — old women, young women, it's very strong. Do not forget that Italy is the only country in the world where the feminist movement has been capable to cause the fall of a government on one of their issues. Do not forget that the last government fell on the issue of abortion, which was brought up by the feminists. God knows how furious, how angry I am with my country, and how things are going wrong. But the feminist movement I think is going all right; I'm very happy with it.

Interview/Los Angeles Times, 6-19:(4)14.

Jane Fonda
Actress
4

The [women's] movement to me is not as the media tend to portray it. It's not a bra-burning, down-with-men kind of movement. Even more important, I don't think it's "We want a piece of the pie." Putting a woman in the White House or replacing the president of Exxon with a woman isn't going to change anything. Sometimes one has the impression that the women's movement is saying, "Move over. We want in," and that when women get power, the problems will be over. I don't think that's true. I think if you just kept the current structure and put women in it, the problems would still exist. Upper-middle-class and intellectual women would be in positions of power, but the mass of women would be in just the same situation as they're in now. I think you need a whole restructuring of who has power and what it is being used for. In order to achieve that, women have to work with men.

Interview, Los Angeles/Time, 10-3:91.

John Fowles
Author

1

My respect for the feminine principle long predates "women's lib." And for me it comes because I know I have a large feminine component of my own. I think most of us do. I say this is almost altruism — all male novelists I know have a large female component and all females a large male component, and I would suspect [that if] psychiatrists discover why one is a novelist and not a hotdog seller, then this might be one of the reasons. Also, I was very much under the influence of Jung — you can't really read Jung and not get hooked on the feminine principle. And I think culturally the periods when woman was being, if not equal, at least treated better, are periods I like: the Renaissance, the 18th century. In the 19th century they were pushed down.

Interview, New York/
The Christian Science Monitor, 10-3:16.

Barry M. Goldwater
United States Senator, R—Arizona

2

[Arguing against proposed legislation that would relax restrictions against military combat roles for women]: I don't object to a woman doing anything in combat a man can do as long as she gets home in time to cook dinner.

Before the Senate, Washington/
Los Angeles Times, 5-19:(1)2.

Erwin N. Griswold
Lawyer; Former Solicitor General
of the United States

3

[Criticizing a proposal to extend the deadline for ratification of the ERA]: To change the time now is clearly a change in the announced rules governing a substantial matter in our Constitutional structure. It is a little like extending the time of a football game after 14 minutes in the final quarter, with the score tied and one team on the other's one-yard line.

Before House Civil and Constitutional
Rights Subcommittee, Washington, Nov. 8/
The Dallas Times Herald, 11-9:(A)22.

Erica Jong
Author

4

We simply have no way of dealing with the ideal of the successful woman in America. We have to cast her in some stereotype, and it doesn't work. Either she's got to be cold and calculating and emotionally stunted, or she's got to be like Emily Dickinson and can't get a man. The Erica Jong I read about is a circus. She has nothing to do with the person I really am. It's like anti-matter universe: It's almost as if somebody out there has my name and is pretending to be me.

Interview, New York/The National Observer, 4-16:26.

Barbara Jordan
United States Representative,
D—Texas

5

Human rights apply equally to Soviet dissidents, Chilean peasants and American women. Women are human, and when our rights are limited or violated, we need a domestic human-rights program.

At National Women's Conference, Houston,
Nov. 19/San Francisco Examiner & Chronicle,
11-20:(A)1.

Juanita M. Kreps
Secretary of Commerce
of the United States

6

While it is generally recognized that women play a vital role in the social and economic growth of our nation and are essential participants in our labor force, few efforts have been made to encourage them to enter the business world as owners, co-owners and managers of viable businesses. . . . the prospective businesswoman faces barriers generated by decades of societal attitudes and by the overt and covert sex discrimination which continues to persist in our society . . . We are now, in the late 1970s, as poorly informed about the dimensions of discrimination against women in business as we were a decade ago.

Before House Subcommittee on Minority
Enterprise, Washington, June 7/
The Washington Post, 6-8:(D)10.

Loretta Lynn
Singer
1

Lots of people see me out there making a living and say that means I'm for "women's lib." Well, I can tell you I'm out there working because I have to, and our family's no different from lots of others where both the man and the woman have to work just to keep up with prices and taxes. If they want to make that into something about women's lib, okay. But maybe what we ought to do is fire all the women so they can go home — and then raise the man's pay so families can get by on one paycheck. Millions of women are out there working because they've got no choice. Nothing to do with liberation — it's inflation!
Interview/U.S. News & World Report, 10-24:71.

C. Peter McColough
Chairman, Xerox Corporation
2

I'm all in favor [of the women's movement]. It's a positive force. Traditional discrimination over the centuries unfairly deprived women of equal opportunity and equal pay. This has been a tremendous waste of the great asset of a large number of intelligent, educated women. The extreme fringe elements are sometimes annoying but, in any movement, there has to be smoke and yelling to gain the attention of society.
Interview, Stamford, Conn./
"W": a Fairchild publication, 10-14:19.

Jane McMichael
Executive director, National
Women's Political Caucus
3

We women have had so little power that we're uncomfortable with it, embarrassed by it; we want to step back from it. But once you're a feminist, you're always a feminist. There is no going back. It was difficult for a lot of women to be comfortable with men for a while. The initial break caused a lot of disruptions. But we've worked out the kinks, worked out our marriages. We certainly don't hate men. If anything, we like them more. They don't make me cower any more.
Interview, Houston/
The New York Times Magazine, 12-25:13.

Margaret Mead
Anthropologist
4

We have left the women at home and the men in the marketplace, each isolated. If the future is to be at all, it must be done by all. The day is past when women's talents should be left to smother in the isolation of the suburbs and men should kill themselves with heart attacks in jungles of the cities . . . We need to rid ourselves of the stereotypes that either men or women have exclusive ability to perform some roles. Women may be a little better at rearing children; men may be a little better physicists — but we don't know that because we haven't let either sex try these many different roles. All we now have is historic occupations. We must give both sexes the training and the chance to do all things. We can't possibly lose by giving every person a chance to be what they are.
At "Dallas Times Herald" Women's Forum, Dallas,
Dec. 5/The Dallas Times Herald, 12-6:(B)1.

Ashley Montagu
Anthropologist
5

I think the goals and aims of the women's movement are totally desirable. In fact, I made the point long ago that for women to get anywhere they'd have to become a political force. Of course, women should do anything they want, but if they're going to have children they must realize that having and raising children are the most important things anyone could ever undertake. The mother-child relationship is the basic pattern deciding how a human being becomes. Therefore, it is absolutely idiotic for feminists to say a woman's career is more important than raising a child . . .
Interview, Princeton, N.J./
"W": a Fairchild publication, 1-21:5.

Eleanor Holmes Norton
Chairman, Equal Employment Opportunity
Commission of the United States
6

Am I treated as an equal by my male peers? I think that question is naive. Women in high-level posts are more likely to be treated as exceptions to whatever chauvinist rules apply. What would really tell you something is how many men deal with women who do not rank.

(ELEANOR HOLMES NORTON)

There is a pool of women who qualify for top jobs, but enlarging that pool can't be done overnight. Women have been trapped into a narrow range of occupations. If a man has an elementary-school certificate, he can still go out and become a salesman, while women with the same education are supposed to go on until they qualify for a teaching job.

Interview/U.S. News & World Report, 9-5:39.

Paul VI
Pope

1

I know some feminist groups suspect we want to confine women to austere, limited tasks within the family, blocking their talents in other fields . . . yet they are overreacting against the woman in the home. Is it realistic, is it wise to fall from one excess to another? Going their way, you risk masculinizing or depersonalizing women . . . [My mother] gave me the example of the completely dedicated life. In my father, this was translated into action, and in my mother into silence. We all live from what woman has taught us of the sublime.

Interview, Vatican City/
The New York Times Magazine, 4-10:52.

Charles H. Percy
United States Senator, R—Illinois

2

Any society that stifles the potential of more than one-half of its population [women] is more than prejudiced and discriminatory. It is foolish and wasteful as well.

At "Good Housekeeping" magazine's
Congress of Presidents, Washington, April 28/
Los Angeles Herald-Examiner, 4-28:(A)4.

Alan Pifer
President, Carnegie Foundation

3

While some strong rearguard actions are being fought, more and more Americans are beginning to see the full employment of women's abilities as a social and political imperative.

San Francisco Examiner & Chronicle,
4-10:(This World)2.

Helen Reddy
Singer

4

It's the women who are traditionally concerned with family and family values. But today they're throwing out a lot of traditional female strengths, along with the weaknesses. That bothers me. In the '50s, the women's magazines said you could be a career woman or a wife and mother, but it was better to be a wife and mother. Today they say it's better to be a career woman. Nonsense! Women can do them both and do them both well . . . The family can still be a woman's strength.

Interview, New York/
The Christian Science Monitor, 12-19:26.

Maria Schell
Actress

5

Many think [women's] liberation is not to clean your room, or to have affairs when you want them. But the actual power a woman has is to make a group of people happy and make them grow in the right way and contribute to the world. Knowing that you release your family in the morning into the day with your love and with your warmth is the richness of life. To be a powerful businesswoman — I really don't think this brings the richness. *This* we can do when they are gone! But let the family go happy out of the house, and happy let them come back. I think that is very important. And it is fulfillment, also, for us women.

Interview, New York/
The Christian Science Monitor, 1-9:26.

Phyllis Schlafly
National chairman, Stop ERA
(Equal Rights Amendment)

6

[On why her campaign against ratification of the ERA has worked well so far]: I think there's no way to explain it except to say that we do represent the majority of women. That has to be the answer when you consider the odds we've been fighting, in terms of White House pressure, Federal money, prominent politicians, media support, organizational support, and money that the other side has put into it. I think there's no way we could have done what we have done if we just simply

WHAT THEY SAID IN 1977

(PHYLLIS SCHLAFLY)

didn't have the grass roots with us . . . I think the issues raised by ERA are vital and personal to people. The trouble with ERA is that you've got to take everything that goes with it. It's rigid. It's absolute. You've got to conform, and everything else falls by the wayside . . . I am a good example of how women have every type of option available to them now. They can live a fulfilling life any way they choose to make it. You can be a housewife all the time. You can have a career all the time. You can do both at the same time. You can do both at different times. I think the American woman is the luckiest person who ever lived. She can make her life any way she wants to.

Interview, Washington/
Los Angeles Times, 11-11:(4)10,11.

Hans Selye
Endocrinologist   1

. . . the more the women's-liberation movement permits women to take what have usually been considered male jobs, the more women are subject to so-called male diseases, such as cardiac infarctions, gastric ulcers and hypertension. They get the same satisfactions, too, of course, but at a price.

Interview, Montreal/
U.S. News & World Report, 3-21:51.

Omar Sharif
Actor   2

What I dislike most about women's lib is that it has made so many women in the Western world less romantic, particularly in America. A great many of them just don't go for the romantic type of man any more — they go for the straight-to-bed scene. And while it may save a lot of time to be so direct, it takes away a lot of pleasure, too.

Interview, London/San Francisco Examiner
& Chronicle, 5-22:(Datebook)22.

Eleanor Cutri Smeal
President, National Organization for Women   3

If you will look at the people who oppose the Equal Rights Amendment, you will find they are the same people who opposed the civil-rights movement, freedom of choice in controlling our reproduction, those who oppose the labor-right movement, those who oppose sex education in the schools, those who oppose ratifying the Panama Canal treaty. They are the people who never wanted a better social system of any kind. Their opposition to the women's movement is a ploy to get people involved in their right-wing philosophies. They are using it as a vehicle just as they wrapped themselves around super patriotism in the '50s. Our leading opponents are the very, very wealthy tho have always opposed equal rights for humanity. They represent the vested interests who want to contain the benefits of society for a small privileged group.

Dallas, Sept. 29/
The Dallas Times Herald, 9-30:(E)3.

Jayne Spain
Senior vice president, public
affairs, Gulf Oil Corporation   4

I went on the Litton Industries board of directors in 1970, and I was among the first two women ever to sit on such a large company's board. Today, there is hardly a company among the largest 100 or 200 that does not have a woman on the board. Now I have a senior management position here at Gulf. Gulf is the only corporation among the seven largest in the country with a woman ranked this high. What I am getting around to is that in a short time women in senior management positions will be as commonplace in the largest corporations as women now are on big companies' boards. Make no mistake. Women are climbing the ladder. The emphasis now in business is less on what and who you are and more on what you can do.

Interview, Pittsburgh/
Nation's Business, March:73.

Bette Ann Stead
Professor, department of marketing,
University of Houston

1

We need ERA because the Supreme Court has never decided whether the 14th Amendment prohibits discrimination based on sex. Women are not now, nor have they ever been, a part of the United States Constitution. The Constitution granted what we today consider to be fundamental rights only to white men. The 14th Amendment extended those rights to black men. With the exception of the suffrage amendment, women have never been included. The ERA says nothing about drafting women — Congress already has the power to do that. The ERA says nothing about sharing restrooms — we are Constitutionally guaranteed a right of privacy. The ERA says nothing about removing child support. What would ERA do? Today there are some 250 Federal laws and numerous state laws that discriminate against women. ERA would make it possible, in all states, for women to serve on juries, start a business, get a mortgage, control their own property and paychecks, meet the same qualifications for military service as men, be meter-readers, receive the same prison sentences for the same offenses and be eligible for parole at the same time as men, hold state office, and be subject to the same inheritance tax laws as men.

At Executive Development Program, Houston,
Oct. 11/Vital Speeches, 12-15:159.

Rosalyn Yalow
Radio-physiologist; Winner, 1977
Nobel Prize in medicine

2

[Among students in the Western world,] women are represented in reasonable proportion to their numbers in the community. Yet, among the scientists, scholars and leaders of our world, they are not. No objective testing has revealed such substantial differences in talent as to account for this discrepancy. The failure of women to have reached positions of leadership has been due in large part to social and professional discrimination . . . We still live in a world in which a significant fraction of people, including women, believe that a woman belongs and wants to belong exclusively in the home, that a woman should not aspire to achieve more than her male counterparts and, particularly, not more than her husband. We cannot expect in the immediate future that all women who seek it will achieve full equality of opportunity. But if women are to start moving toward that goal, we must believe in ourselves, or no one else will believe in us; we must match our aspirations with the competence, courage and determination to succeed; and we must feel a personal responsibility to ease the path for those who come afterward. The world cannot afford the loss of the talents of half its people if we are to solve the many problems which beset us.

At Nobel banquet, Stockholm, Dec. 10/
San Francisco Examiner & Chronicle, 12-11:(A)27.

The Indexes

Index to Speakers

A

Aaron, Henry, 487
Abel, I. W., 150
Abourezk, James, 201, 324
Abzug, Bella S., 512
Adams, Ansel, 457
Adams, Brock, 228
Adams, Tom, 263
Adelman, Morris A., 81
Adler, Mortimer J., 464
Agnew, Spiro T., 201
Airola, Paavo, 383
Akhdar, Farouk al-, 324
Albee, Edward, 431
Aldrich, Robert, 398
Alexander, Clifford L., Jr., 181
Alexander, Donald C., 129
Alexander, Jane, 431
Alexander, Shana, 359
Ali, Muhammad, 18, 457, 487
Allaf, Mouaffak el-, 324
Allen, Clifford R., 220
Allen, Fred T., 29
Allen, Irwin, 398
Allen, Woody, 398, 457
Altman, Robert, 398
Amalrik, Andrei A., 302
Ambler, Eric, 373
Ames, Amyas, 353
Amin, Idi, 245
Amsterdam, Anthony G., 52, 174
Anderson, Craig, 431
Anderson, John B., 201, 220
Anderson, Robert O., 75
Anderson, Roger E., 150
Anderson, Sparky, 487
Andreotti, Giulio, 302
Andropov, Yuri V., 302
Andrus, Cecil D., 75, 129
Arafat, Yasir, 324-325
Arbatov, Georgi A., 97, 181, 302
Archer, Bill, 220
Argan, Giulio Carlo, 303
Ariyoshi, George R., 239
Arkin, Alan, 398
Arkoff, Samuel Z., 399

Arledge, Roone, 359
Armour, Richard, 373
Armstrong, Anne, 97
Ash, Roy L., 129
Ashe, Arthur, 487
Ashmore, Harry S., 18
Asimov, Isaac, 373
Askin, Frank, 18
Asner, Edward, 399
Aspin, Les, 181
Assad, Hafez al-, 325-366
Astaire, Fred, 399
Atkinson, George, 487
Attenborough, Richard, 399
AuCoin, Les, 239
Auerbach, Red, 488
Auf de Maur, Nick, 488
Autry, Gene, 457
Ayres, Lew, 464, 478

B

Backe, John D., 359
Bagge, Carl E., 75
Bailar, Benjamin F., 129
Bailey, F. Lee, 174
Baker, Howard H., Jr., 181-182, 220
Baker, Janet, 421
Balanchine, George, 431
Baldwin, James, 18
Ball, Edward, 229
Ball, George W., 97, 326
Ball, Lucille, 442
Balles, John J., 29, 150
Barclay, William J., 383
Bardwick, Judith, 512
Barnard, Christiaan, 245
Barnes, Clive, 359
Barre, Raymond, 29, 229, 303
Barry, Rick, 488
Bartell, Ernest, 61
Barthol, Richard, 489
Baryshnikov, Mikhail, 431
Batten, William M., 29
Battle, William C., 30

WHAT THEY SAID IN 1977

Baylor, Elgin, 489
Beame, Abraham D., 239
Beard, Robin, 182
Beauvoir, Simone de, 464
Begam, Robert, 174
Begin, Menachem, 326-328
Behr, Peter, 129
Bell, Griffin B., 19, 30, 52, 174
Belli, Melvin, 175
Belser, Jess L., 19
Bench, Johnny, 489
Benitez, Jaime, 263
Bennet, Douglas, 97
Bennett, Otes, Jr., 81
Bennett, Robert F., 130
Bennett, Tony, 421
Benti, Joseph, 359
Bentsen, Lloyd M., 13, 52
Berendzen, Richard, 61
Bergen, Candice, 512
Berger, Peter L., 201, 464, 478
Bergland, Bob, 30-31, 130, 383
Bergman, Ingmar, 400
Bergsten, C. Fred, 31
Berkeley, Norborne, Jr., 31
Berman, Edgar, 383
Berman, Pandro S., 400
Bernstein, Irving, 150
Bernstein, Leonard, 421, 432
Bernstein, Robert L., 373
Berrigan, Daniel, 478
Bertolucci, Bernardo, 400
Bertram, Christoph, 97
Bestwick, Dick, 61
Betts, Henry B., 383
Bhutto, Zulfikar Ali, 285
Bickel, Alexander M., 201
Biegler, John C., 32
Bikel, Theodore, 432
Biko, Steve, 245
Bill, Tony, 400
Bingham, Eula, 151
Bingham, Jonathan B., 263
Bird, Rose E., 81, 175
Birkerts, Gunnar, 353
Black, Karen, 400
Black, Shirley Temple, 285
Blake, Robert, 400, 442
Blakey, G. Robert, 52
Blaylock, Kenneth T., 182
Bliss, Anthony, 421
Bloom, Benjamin, 61
Bloom, Julius, 422
Blumenthal, W. Michael, 32, 81, 151, 239-240
Bogdanovich, Peter, 400-401

Bond, Julian, 202
Bonynge, Richard, 422
Boone, Richard, 401, 442
Boorstin, Daniel J., 442
Boren, David, 32
Borge, Victor, 432
Borgia, Sid, 489
Borman, Frank, 229
Born, Roscoe C., 360
Bosworth, Barry, 152
Botha, Roelof F., 98, 245-246
Botstein, Leon, 62
Bourne, Peter G., 53, 384
Bouton, Jim, 489
Boyer, Ernest L., 62
Brademas, John, 353
Bradlee, Benjamin C., 360
Bradley, Tom, 19, 76
Bradshaw, Thornton F., 81, 130
Brandt, Willy, 98
Brewster, Kingman, Jr., 62
Brezhnev, Leonid I., 98-99, 182-183, 303-305, 328, 345, 465
Briggs, John D., 32
Brock, Bill, 81
Brock, Lou, 490
Brolin, James, 401
Bronfenbrenner, Urie, 221
Brooke, Edward W., 130, 202
Brooks, Mel, 401
Bross, Irwin D. J., 384
Brossolette, Claude-Pierre, 305
Brothers, Joyce, 63
Brown, Edmund G., Jr., 13, 33, 53, 63, 76, 82, 130, 221, 345, 384, 457, 483
Brown, George S., 183
Brown, Harold, 82, 99, 183-185, 285-286, 306, 345
Brown, Jim, 490
Brown, John Y., 490
Brown, Larry, 491
Brown, Lester R., 99
Brown, Roscoe C., 63
Bruhn, Erik, 432
Brunner, Karl, 152
Bryant, Anita, 19
Brzezinski, Zbigniew, 99-101, 130, 185, 246-247, 286, 306, 328-329, 345, 478
Buchwald, Art, 360
Buckley, William F., Jr., 287
Budd, John, 385
Buis, Georges, 186
Bujold, Genevieve, 401
Bumpers, Dale, 131
Bunker, Ellsworth, 263
Burger, Warren E., 175-176

Burnett, Carol, 402
Burns, Allan, 443
Burns, Arthur F., 82, 152
Burns, Robert F., 202
Burstyn, Ellen, 402, 433
Burton, Richard, 457
Bush, George, 126, 287
Buthelezi, Gatsha, 247
Butler, Robert N., 152, 221, 385
Buttons, Red, 443
Byrd, Robert C., 13, 53, 101, 131, 186, 287, 465
Byrne, Brendan T., 63

C

Caglayangil, Ihsan Sabri, 306
Caine, Michael, 457
Calabresi, Guido, 176
Caldwell, Sarah, 465
Califano, Joseph A., Jr., 20, 64, 131, 221-222, 385-386
Callaghan, James, 306
Campion, Robert T., 152
Cannon, Howard W., 33, 229
Capote, Truman, 386
Capp, Al, 360-361
Capra, Frank, 402
Caramanlis, Constantine, 307
Cardwell, James B., 222
Carew, Rod, 491
Carey, Hugh L., 54, 131
Carlson, Jack W., 33, 76, 152
Carlson, Norman A., 54
Caron, Leslie, 402
Carr, David T., 386
Carr, M. Robert, 186
Carrigan, Jim R., 176
Carson, Johnny, 443, 458
Carter, Hodding, III, 247
Carter, Jimmy, 10-12, 20, 33, 54, 82-83, 101-105, 132-133, 153, 186-187, 202-204, 223, 230, 247-248, 264-265, 287-288, 307-308, 329-330, 345-346, 361, 386-387, 402, 458, 479, 512
Carter, Rosalynn, 513
Cassell, Eric J., 387
Castillo, Leonel J., 105, 153, 265
Castro, Fidel, 204, 248, 266-267
Catlett, Elizabeth, 353
Cavett, Dick, 443
Ceaucescu, Nicolae, 105
Cey, Ron, 491
Chafee, John H., 187

Chagall, Marc, 353
Chamberlain, Richard, 458, 465
Champion, Hale, 387
Chancellor, John, 361
Chandler, A. B. (Happy), 491
Chandler, Otis, 361
Chaney, Don, 491
Channing, Carol, 433
Chapman, Alvah H., Jr., 362
Charles, Prince, 465
Cheever, John, 373
Chen, Frederick, 288
Cherry, Don, 491
Chisholm, Shirley, 513
Christopher, Warren M., 106
Church, Frank, 106, 187, 267, 330
Civiletti, Benjamin R., 54
Clanton, David A., 34
Clark, Dick, 106, 248
Clark, Dick, 443
Clausen, A. W., 34
Claybrook, Joan, 230
Claytor, W. Graham, 188
Clements, William P., Jr., 83
Clifford, Clark M., 204
Clurman, Harold, 433
Clusen, Ruth C., 106
Cocklin, Robert F., 188
Coggan, Frederick Donald, 308
Cohen, Alexander H., 433
Cohen, David, 133
Cohen, S. T., 346
Cohen, Wilbur J., 223
Cohler, Bertram J., 465
Colby, William E., 126
Coleman, William T., Jr., 20, 133
Collier, Calvin J., 133
Collins, James M., 83
Comer, James P., 465
Comfort, Alex, 223
Commoner, Barry, 76
Connally, John B., Jr., 84, 106, 133-134, 176, 204, 362
Connor, John T., 13
Connors, Jimmy, 491
Conyers, John, Jr., 55
Cook, Olin, 64
Cooper, H. H. A., 55
Cooper, Theodore, 387
Cornyn, Stan, 422
Costanza, Margaret, 107
Costle, Douglas M., 76-77
Coulling, Sidney B., 64
Courtenay, Tom, 403, 433
Cousins, Norman, 466

Cousteau, Jacques-Yves, 77, 84
Cowper, Reg, 249
Cox, Archibald, 20
Cox, Fred, 492
Coxson, Harold P., 154
Cramer, Glenn A., 230
Crane, Philip M., 267
Cranston, Alan, 134, 205
Crawford, Broderick, 403
Crawford, W. Donham, 84
Crenshaw, Ben, 492
Crim, Alonzo, 64
Cronje, Rowan, 107
Cronkite, Walter, 362
Crosland, Anthony, 308
Cukor, George, 403
Culver, John C., 188, 288
Cunhal, Alvaro, 308
Currey, Fred G., 154, 231
Curtis, Carl T., 84
Curtis, Tony, 403

D

Dalton, Harry, 492
Danforth, D. D., 84
Danforth, John C., 134, 205
Davignon, Etienne, 309
Davies, Mike, 492
Davis, Bette, 403, 466
Davis, Edward M., 55
Davis, George D., 77
Davis, Glenn, 492
Davis, John E., 188
Davis, William, 309
Dayan, Moshe, 330-331
Days, Drew S., III, 21
Dean, Jimmy, 422
De Bakey, Michael, 387
deButts, John D., 154
DeCrow, Karen, 513
de la Madrid, Roberto, 267
de Liagre, Alfred, Jr., 434
Dellums, Ronald V., 189, 223
DeMent, Sandy, 177
de Mille, Agnes, 434
De Niro, Robert, 404
Denver, John, 466
Desai, Morarji R., 107, 135, 288-289, 346, 466, 513
de Segonzac, Adalbert, 14, 107, 309
Deukmejian, George, 56
de Villiers, Cas, 249

Diamond, Neil, 422
Dickey, James, 14, 374, 458
Didion, Joan, 374, 458, 466
DiMaggio, Joe, 493
Dinitz, Simcha, 331
Djilas, Milovan, 107
Doby, Larry, 493
Doctorow, E. L., 375
Dole, Elizabeth Hanford, 34-35
Domenici, Pete V., 205
Domingo, Placido, 423
Donaldson, William A., 240
Dong, Pham Van, 289
Donovan, Robert J., 362
Dornan, Robert K., 135, 189
Dougherty, Russell E., 189
Drapeau, Jean, 493
Drury, Allen, 363
Dubnick, Melvin, 64
Duffey, Joseph D., 354
Duffy, James E., 443
Dukakis, Michael S., 483
Duncan, John, 56
Dunham, Robert, 65
du Pont, Pierre S., 223
DuPont, Robert L., 56, 388
Durant, Will, 466
Duvalier, Jean-Claude, 267
Duvall, Robert, 404
Dworkin, Ronald, 21, 177

E

Eastham, William K., 35
Eban, Abba, 107, 205, 331
Eden, Dorothy, 375
Edwards, India, 513
Eglin, Colin, 249
Ehrlichman, John D., 177, 205
Eisenhower, Julie Nixon, 479
Eizenstat, Stuart E., 135
Eklund, Sigvard, 85
Elizabeth II, 267, 309
Elkind, David, 65
Ephron, Nora, 514
Erlenborn, John N., 154
Ervin, Sam J., Jr., 21, 514
Erving, Julius, 493
Escobar (Bethancourt), Romulo, 267-268
Estes, E. M. "Pete," 231
Evans, Billy Lee, 289
Evans, James H., 154

Evans, Robert, 404, 458, 466
Evert, Chris, 493

F

Fadiman, Clifton, 65, 459, 467, 479
Fahd (ibn Abdel Aziz), 331-332
Fahmy, Ismail, 332
Fairbank, John K., 289-290
Fairbanks, Chuck, 494
Fallaci, Oriana, 363, 514
Fanfani, Amintore, 310
Farrell, Robert, 65
Featherstone, Joseph, 66
Feinstein, Dianne, 240
Feld, Eliot, 354, 434
Feldman, Marty, 467
Fenwick, Millicent H., 135, 206
Fernandez (Font), Marcelo, 268
Ferris, Charles, 444
Fiedler, Arthur, 14, 423
Finch, Peter, 404
Finestone, Bernard J., 268
Finley, Charles O., 494
Finney, Albert, 404
Firkusny, Rudolf, 423
Fittipaldi, Emerson, 494
Flaherty, Peter F., 56
Floyd, Carlisle, 423
Flynt, John J., Jr., 135
Fonda, Jane, 514
Fong, Hiram L., 290
Forbes, John, 66
Ford, Gerald R., 3-10, 14, 85, 107-108, 135-136,
    189, 206, 224, 268, 290, 310
Ford, Henry, II, 136, 155, 231
Foster, George, 495
Fowles, John, 354, 375, 444, 515
Foy, Lewis W., 36
Franciscus, James, 444
Frankenheimer, John, 405
Fraser, Donald M., 108
Fraser, Douglas A., 155, 232
Fredrik, Burry, 434
Freeman, Richard B., 66
Freeman, Roger A., 66
Frenzel, Bill, 155
Freund, Paul A., 467
Friday, William C., 21
Friedman, Milton, 85, 108, 136, 155-156, 388
Friendly, Fred W., 444
Frosch, Robert A., 483

Fuchs, Joseph, 423
Fukuda, Takeo, 36, 86, 109, 290
Fulbright, J. William, 467
Fuller, Keith, 363
Fuller, R. Buckminster, 86, 346, 479, 483

G

Gabellah, Elliott, 249
Gabor, Eva, 405
Galbraith, John Kenneth, 156-157, 444, 467
Gandhi, Indira, 290-291
Garagiola, Joe, 495
Gardner, John W., 137
Garn, E. J. (Jake), 36, 86, 137, 189, 224, 291, 388
Garner, James, 405, 445
Garvey, Steve, 495
Gary, Romain, 375
Geer, Will, 157, 468
Geisel, Ernesto, 269
Geneen, Harold S., 37
George, Alexander, 206
Gerber, David, 445
Gerbner, George, 445
Ghazali, Muhammad, 291
Giamatti, A. Bartlett, 66-67
Gibson, Kenneth A., 388
Giroud, Francoise, 354
Giscard d'Estaing, Valery, 109, 232, 249, 332
Giulini, Carlo Maria, 424
Gleason, Jackie, 459, 480
Goheen, Robert F., 292
Goldberg, Arthur J., 109
Goldman, Marvin, 405
Goldmark, Peter C., Jr., 224
Goldsmith, Jerry, 405
Goldwater, Barry M., 190, 207, 269, 292, 375, 515
Gomez, Lefty, 495
Gonzalez, Felipe, 310
Good, Robert A., 388
Goodman, Benny, 424
Goodman, Julian, 445
Gordon, Robert, 157
Gordon, Ruth, 468
Gordon, Theodore J., 468
Gore, Albert A., Jr., 137
Gorman, Lou, 495
Gouled, Hassan, 250
Grad, Frank, 363
Graham, Katharine, 363
Graham, Martha, 434
Grant, Allan, 37, 157

Graves, Donald, 67
Green, Edith, 22
Green, George J., 363
Green, Gerald, 375
Griffin, Merv, 459
Griffin, Robert P., 137, 207
Griffith, Calvin, 495
Griffiths, Trevor, 445
Griswold, Erwin N., 515
Grizzard, George, 434
Gromyko, Andrei A., 311, 332
Grossman, Lawrence K., 446
Groves, Harry E., 56
Guimaraes, Ulysses, 269
Guthrie, Arlo, 468
Guy, Ray, 496

H

Haas, Peter, 37
Habash, George, 333
Hacker, Frederick J., 56, 364
Hackman, Gene, 459
Haden, Pat, 496
Haerle, Paul R., 207
Hagopian, Louis T., 37
Haig, Alexander M., Jr., 190, 311
Hailey, Arthur, 375
Halbouty, Michel T., 37
Haldeman, H. R., 207
Haley, Alex, 15, 375-376, 446, 468
Hall, Paul, 157
Halvonik, Paul, 57
Hamlisch, Marvin, 424
Hammarskjold, Knut, 232
Hanks, Nancy, 354
Hanley, John W., 389
Hannon, Bruce, 86
Harburg, E. Y. (Yip), 424
Hargrove, Erwin C., 109, 208
Harkabi, Yehoshafat, 333
Harlech, Lady, 311
Harlow, LeRoy F., 137
Harman, Sidney, 157
Harriman, W. Averell, 109, 269
Harrington, Michael J., 138
Harris, Patricia Roberts, 22, 240
Harris, Richard, 405
Harrison, Rex, 469
Harshman, Marv, 496
Hart, Gary W., 38, 138, 208
Hassan II, 312, 333

Hassner, Pierre, 312
Hatch, Orrin G., 138, 158, 190
Hatfield, Mark O., 190
Hatfield, Robert S., 38, 158
Hauge, Gabriel, 38, 139, 158
Hawkins, Roger, 250
Hawn, Goldie, 406
Hayakawa, S. I., 22, 67, 86, 139, 158, 269
Hayes, Denis, 86
Hayes, Janet Gray, 241
Hayes, William C., 87
Haynes, Harold J., 87
Head, Edith, 406
Heath, Douglas H., 67
Hechinger, Fred M., 67
Hefner, Hugh M., 459
Heikal, Mohammed Hassanein, 333
Heinz, H. John, III, 139
Helms, Jesse A., 270, 389
Helms, Richard, 127
Herbert, Victor, 389
Herndon, Terry, 67
Herzog, Chaim, 334
Herzog, Whitey, 496
Hesburgh, Theodore M., 22, 469
Heston, Charlton, 406, 435, 459
Higgins, James H., 39
Hill, Arthur, 435
Hill, John, 57
Hill, Robert C., 109
Hill-Norton, Peter, 191
Hills, Lee, 364
Hills, Roderick M., 39
Hitchcock, Alfred, 406
Hogan, Ben, 496
Hogan, Robert, 389, 469
Holbrooke, Richard, 292
Holden, William, 406-407
Holliman, Earl, 446
Holloway, James L., III, 191
Holman, Carl, 224
Holtzman, Red, 497
Hong Sung Chick, 292
Hooks, Benjamin L., 23, 159
Horowitz, Vladimir, 424
Hough, Charlie, 497
Howard, John A., 68
Howard, Robin, 435
Howe, Harold, II, 68
Hua Kuo-feng, 292
Huang Hua, 293
Hubbard, John R., 68
Hudson, Rock, 407, 446
Humphrey, Hubert H., 23, 39, 110, 139-140, 159, 208, 241, 270, 312, 389, 469

Hunt, E. Howard, 208
Husayn, Haddam, 334
Hussein I, 334-335

Joseph, Robert L., 447
Juan Carlos I, 313

I

Iacocca, Lee A., 15, 39
Inayama, Yoshihiro, 159
Inouye, Daniel K., 127
Isaacs, Norman, 364
Iskander, Ahmad, 335

J

Jackson, Glenda, 407
Jackson, Henry M., 87, 191, 312
Jackson, Jesse L., 15, 23, 69, 446, 470, 480
Jackson, Rashleigh E., 270
Jacob, John E., 69
Jacoby, Neil H., 39
Jacomet, Andre, 313
Jaffe, Mark, 376
Jagoda, Barry, 355, 447
Jamieson, Donald C., 110, 250
Jankowski, Gene F., 159
Janowitz, Morris, 15
Jarrott, Charles, 407
Jastrow, Robert, 483
Javits, Jacob K., 209
Jaworski, Leon, 209
Jay, Peter, 15, 110, 313
Jeffers, Leroy, 177
Jenkins, Roy, 313
Jennings, Eugene, 140
Jewison, Norman, 407
Johnson, Frank M., Jr., 178
Johnson, Nicholas, 447
Johnson, U. Alexis, 191, 347
Jones, David C., 192
Jones, Deacon, 497
Jones, Hardin, 390
Jones, Reginald H., 40
Jones, Tom, 424
Jong, Erica, 515
Jordan, Barbara, 140, 515
Jordan, Hamilton, 209, 460
Jordan, Philip, Jr., 69
Jordan, Vernon E., Jr., 23-24, 224
Jorge, Paulo, 250

K

Kahn, Alfred E., 40, 232-233
Kalb, Marvin, 209
Kanaga, William S., 40
Kane, Robert J., 497
Kanin, Garson, 355, 425, 435
Kaplan, H. Roy, 159
Karajan, Herbert von, 425
Kasyola, John, 497
Kauffman, Ewing, 497
Kaufman, Irving R., 178
Kaunda, Kenneth, 250-251
Keegan, George J., 192, 347
Keenan, John F., 178
Keene, Barry, 57
Keith, Brian, 447
Keller, Marthe, 408
Kelley, Clarence M., 57-58, 127
Kelly, Arthur F., 233
Kelly, Donald P., 178
Kelly, Gene, 435
Kemeny, John G., 69
Kemper, James S., Jr., 233
Kendall, Donald M., 111
Kennan, George F., 111, 192, 314
Kennedy, Donald, 390
Kennedy, Edward M., 40, 88, 140, 224, 233, 293, 390-391, 484
Kensil, Jim, 497
Kerr, Clark, 69
Kerr, Deborah, 435-436
Kerrigan, James L., 234
Kessler, Irving I., 391
Khaddam, Abdel Halim, 336
Khieu Samphan, 293
Kiley, Richard, 436
Kimball, Spencer W., 448, 470, 480
King, Billie Jean, 498
King, Don, 498
King, Henry, 408
Kirkland, Lane, 40-41, 159
Kirsch, Robert, 376
Kirschner, Richard L., 448
Kissinger, Henry A., 24, 111-112, 193, 251, 270, 293, 314, 336, 347, 470
Kistiakowsky, George B., 347
Klatell, David, 498
Klein, Paul, 448

Klugman, Jack, 448
Knopf, Alfred A., 470
Knox, Chuck, 470, 498
Koch, Edward I., 112, 140, 193
Kolton, Paul, 41
Koop, C. Everett, 391
Korab, Jerry, 498
Korman, Harvey, 448
Kramer, Stanley, 408
Kreps, Juanita M., 16, 24, 41-42, 113, 141, 160, 225,
    241, 515
Kreuger, Robert C., 270
Kroc, Ray A., 460, 498-499
Kruger, James, 251
Krumm, Daniel J., 42
Kuhn, Bowie, 499
Ky, Nguyen Cao, 293

L

Laemmert, Eberhard, 69
Laker, Freddie, 234
Lambrias, Panayotis, 314
Lamphere, Phyllis, 241
Lancaster, Burt, 436
Lance, Bert, 42, 141, 160, 209, 460, 470
Landau, George W., 113
Larry, R. Heath, 43, 160
Laurents, Arthur, 408
Laurin, Camille, 270
Lawrence, Carol, 448
Lazar, Irving, 376, 460
Lazarus, Ralph, 241
Leachman, Cloris, 408
Lear, Norman, 449
Lee, Bill, 499
Lee, Ernest A., 160
Lee Kuan Yew, 293
Lee, Peggy, 425
Lefebvre, Jim, 499
Lefebvre, Marcel, 480
Le Gallienne, Eva, 436
Lehman, Ernest, 408
Leinsdorf, Eric, 425
Lemmon, Jack, 409, 449
Lemon, Bob, 499
Leontief, Wassily, 161
Lerner, Alan Jay, 425
LeRoy, Mervyn, 409
Lever, Harold, 88
Levesque, Rene, 271-272
Levine, Joseph E., 409

Levitan, Sar, 161
Lewis, Murray, 436
Li Hsien-nien, 294
Libow, Leslie, 391
Lietzke, Bruce, 500
Lilienthal, David E., 77
Lilley, William, III, 391
Lindbergh, Anne Morrow, 470
Linden, Henry R., 88
Ling, Joseph T., 78
Link, Arthur A., 210
Linowes, David F., 70, 178
Linowitz, Sol M., 272
Lodge, Henry Cabot, 347
Logan, Joshua, 437
Long, Russell B., 43, 161, 210, 225
Longworth, Alice Roosevelt, 210
Loory, Stuart H., 364
Lopes, Davey, 500
Lopez (Portillo), Jose, 88, 161, 273
Lortie, Dan, 70
Love, Ben F., 43
Lower, Elmer W., 364
Lowery, Joseph E., 24
Lucchesi, Frank, 500
Luce, Clare Boothe, 365
Lumet, Sidney, 409, 449
Lundborg, Louis B., 43
Luns, Joseph, 314
Lyle, Ron, 500
Lyman, Richard W., 70
Lynch, Jack, 315
Lynch, James J., 392
Lynch, Robert, 43
Lynn, Loretta, 426, 516

M

Maccoby, Michael, 141
MacDonald, John D., 471
Machin, Jose Maria, 273
MacLaine, Shirley, 471
MacLean, Alistair, 460
Madden, John, 500
Maddox, Gary, 501
Maddox, Lester G., 210
Magnuson, Warren G., 234, 392
Mahon, George H., 194
Malloum, Felix, 252
Malott, Robert H., 44
Mamoulian, Rouben, 355, 409
Mancham, James R., 252

Manley, Michael, 252, 273-274
Mansfield, Mike, 113, 294
Mansouri, Abdel Rahman al-, 336
Manuel, Wiley, 25
Maravich, Pete, 501
Marceau, Marcel, 437
Marchais, Georges, 315
Marcos, Ferdinand E., 294
Marcos, Imelda, 347
Marshall, F. Ray, 161-163
Marshall, Thurgood, 141, 179
Martin, Billy, 501
Martin, James G., 113, 392
Martin, John B., 163
Martin, Luis, 70
Mastrovito, Rene C., 392
Mathews, David, 141
Mathias, Charles McC., Jr., 89, 211
Matsunaga, Spark M., 141
Matternas, John J., 44
Mauch, Gene, 501
Mawardi, Chalid, 295
Maytag, L. B., 234
Mazlish, Bruce, 392
McClellan, John L., 211
McColough, C. Peter, 25, 44, 516
McCowen, Alec, 437
McCracken, Paul W., 71, 163, 471
McCree, Wade Hampton, Jr., 25
McDonald, Lawrence P., 113, 274
McGee, Gale W., 113
McGivern, William P., 376-377
McGovern, George S., 89, 114, 194, 211, 274, 295
McGrory, Mary, 365
McGuire, Al, 501
McIntyre, Thomas J., 71
McKelvey, Vincent E., 89
McLagan, John, 58
McLuhan, Marshall, 211, 449
McMahon, A. M., 484
McMahon, Ed, 410
McMichael, Jane, 516
McNally, Kathleen, 71
McNamara, Robert S., 78, 114, 393
McNerney, Walter J., 393
Mead, Margaret, 114, 460, 471, 484, 516
Means, Russell, 25
Meany, George, 44, 164, 274
Meir, Golda, 336
Mengistu Haile Mariam, 252
Menk, Louis W., 235
Menninger, Karl A., 58, 393
Menuhin, Yehudi, 426
Meredith, Burgess, 410
Merrick, David, 437

Merrill, Robert, 426
Metcalf, Lee, 211
Michel, Robert H., 114, 142, 165
Michener, James A., 165, 377; 460
Middents, Melvin H., 44
Miki, Takeo, 295, 472
Milford, Dale, 235
Miller, Andrew W., 393
Miller, Ann, 410
Miller, Arthur, 355, 410
Miller, E. Spencer, 235
Miller, G. William, 165
Miller, Henry, 71, 377, 450, 472
Milligan, A. A., 45
Milliken, William J., 211
Minnelli, Liza, 410-411
Mintoff, Dom, 315
Mitchell, Maurice B., 71
Mitchell, Parren J., 25-26
Mitchum, Robert, 461
Mobutu Sese Seko, 252
Moffett, Thomas, 484
Mondale, Joan, 355-356
Mondale, Walter F., 26, 114-115, 142, 194, 212, 252, 315-316, 337, 356
Montagu, Ashley, 225, 516
Montgomery, G. V. (Sonny), 194
Moore, Mary Tyler, 450
Moorer, Thomas H., 194, 274
Morales (Bermudez), Francisco, 275
Moravia, Alberto, 378
Moreau, Jeanne, 411
Morgan, Joe, 502
Morgenthau, Hans J., 115
Morin, Claude, 275
Morris, George B., Jr., 165
Morris, John M., 394
Morris, Norval, 58
Morris, Richard B., 142
Morrison, Stan, 502
Moscone, George, 58, 225, 241, 502
Moser, Claus, 426
Moses, Robert, 472
Mosk, Stanley, 179
Motta, Dick, 502
Moye, Alfred L., 72
Moynihan, Daniel P., 115-116, 142-143, 212, 225, 295, 347
Mueller, George E., 485
Mugabe, Robert, 253
Muggeridge, Malcolm, 472-473
Muldoon, Robert, 295
Murdoch, Rupert, 365
Murphy, John M., 275
Murphy, Patrick V., 59

Murphy, Thomas A., 16, 45, 89, 165
Muzorewa, Abel, 253

Ormandy, Eugene, 426
Ostrow, Stuart, 438
Owen, David, 117, 254, 316

N

Nader, Ralph, 89-90, 235-236
Narayan, Jayaprakash, 296
Nastase, Ilie, 502
Nazzer, Hisham, 337
Ne Win, 296
Neal, Fred Warner, 348
Neale, Harry, 502
Nelson, Gaylord, 394
Nessen, Ron, 213, 365
Neuharth, Allen H., 366
Nevelson, Louise, 473
Nevin, John J., 45
Newley, Anthony, 438, 461
Newman, Edwin, 72, 366
Newman, Theodore R., Jr., 179
Nickel, Herman, 127
Nichols, Mike, 438
Nicklaus, Jack, 503
Nikodem, 480
Nitze, Paul H., 194
Nixon, Richard M., 116, 143, 213, 275, 296, 316,
    348, 366, 473
Nkomo, Joshua, 253
Norton, Eleanor Holmes, 516
Nunn, Sam, 194-195
Nureyev, Rudolf, 461
Nyerere, Julius K., 253-254

O

Oaks, Dallin H., 72
Obey, David R., 366
O'Brien, Lawrence F., 503
O'Donnell, John J., 236
Okawa, Yoshio, 348
O'Kennedy, Michael, 195
Okun, Arthur M., 166
O'Leary, John F., 90
Olivero, Magda, 426
O'Malley, Peter, 503
O'Neal, A. Daniel, 236
O'Neill, Michael J., 366
O'Neill, Thomas P., Jr., 143, 214
Orfila, Alejandro, 275

P

Pacino, Al, 411
Packard, Vance, 473
Packwood, Bob, 117, 214, 226
Pahlavi, Mohammad Reza, 90, 337
Pajetta, Giancarlo, 316
Pakula, Alan J., 411
Paley, William S., 450
Palmer, Arnold, 504
Palmer, Richard E., 394, 450
Papandreou, Andreas, 317
Papapolitis, Sotiris, 317
Papas, Irene, 473
Papp, Joseph, 438
Parfitt, Harold R., 276
Park, Tongsun, 214
Parker, Barrington D., 127
Parseghian, Ara, 504
Parton, Dolly, 461
Partridge, John W., 90
Partridge, Mark, 117
Pastinen, Ilkka Olavi, 254
Patan, Ion, 317
Paton, Alan, 255
Patterson, Floyd, 504
Patterson, Orlando H., 26
Paul VI, 349, 394, 480, 517
Pell, Claiborne, 117, 317
Pepper, Claude, 166
Percy, Charles H., 90, 117, 214, 517
Perelman, S. J., 411, 473
Peres, Shimon, 337-338
Perez, Carlos Andres, 118, 276
Pertschuk, Michael, 45-46
Peterson, Russell W., 91
Petty, Richard, 504
Phelps, Edwin R., 91
Philip, Prince, 318, 473
Picchieri, Angelo, 72
Pierce, Chester M., 504
Pierce, Frederick, 450
Pifer, Alan, 517
Pike, Otis G., 128
Pinochet (Ugarte), Augusto, 277
Pipes, Richard E., 118, 195, 296, 318
Plumb, J. H., 318
Podgorny, Nikolai V., 255

Poitier, Sidney, 412, 461
Pol Pot, 296
Pollace, Lester, 179
Pollack, Sydney, 412
Ponti, Carlo, 412
Porges, Walter, 366
Porter, Stephen, 439
Powell, Jody, 143, 215
Preston, Robert, 439
Price, Charles P., 481
Price, Frank, 450
Price, Leontyne, 427
Price, Vincent, 356, 412
Prine, Arthur C., Jr., 167
Proctor, Harvey A., 91
Proxmire, William, 196
Purcell, John R., 367

Q

Qaddafi, Muammar el-, 255, 297, 338
Quarles, John R., 78
Quinn, Anthony, 412, 462
Quittmeyer, Robert T., 46
Qusaibi, Ghazi al-, 338

R

Rabin, Yitzhak, 338-339
Rainier III, 78, 118, 143
Rangel, Charles B., 226
Rassias, John, 72
Rather, Dan, 367, 378
Ravitch, Diane, 72
Ray, Dixy Lee, 92
Reagan, Ronald, 92, 118, 215, 277
Reardon, John, 439
Reddy, Brahmananda, 297
Reddy, Helen, 517
Redgrave, Lynn, 412
Redgrave, Vanessa, 412
Reed, Robert, 413
Reed, Thomas C., 196, 349
Reed, Willis, 505
Reeder, Charles B., 167
Reedy, George E., 367
Rehnquist, William H., 179
Reiner, Carl, 413, 474

Reinhardt, John E., 118-119
Reischauer, Edwin O., 297
Rene, Albert, 255
Reque, Luis, 277
Reston, James, 367
Reuss, Henry S., 167, 242
Reynolds, Burt, 413
Rhodes, John J., 92, 215-216, 277
Ribicoff, Abraham A., 119, 144, 339, 367
Richards, Gilbert F., 46
Richardson, Elliot L., 144
Richey, Herbert S., 144
Richmond, Frederick W., 356
Rickover, Hyman G., 73, 197
Riles, Wilson, 26, 73
Rintels, David, 451
Ritchie-Calder, Lord, 485
Robbie, Joe, 505
Robbins, Harold, 378
Roberts, Rachel, 451
Robertson, Gordon, 278
Robson, John E., 236
Rockefeller, David, 46
Rockefeller, Nelson A., 46, 216
Rockwell, W. F., Jr., 47, 168
Roderick, David M., 92
Rodgers, Richard, 427
Rodino, Peter W., Jr., 59, 216
Rodowskas, Christopher A., Jr., 395
Rodriguez (Llompart), Hector, 119
Rogers, Bernard W., 278
Rogers, Ginger, 413, 474
Rohatyn, Felix G., 242
Romero (Barcelo), Carlos, 226, 278
Romulo, Carlos P., 367
Ronstadt, Linda, 427
Roos, Lawrence K., 144
Root, Trent C., Jr., 485
Rose, E. Kash, 395
Rosenberg, Maurice, 180
Ross, Herbert, 413, 439
Ross, Richard S., 395
Ross, Thomas B., 197
Rossi, Alice S., 485
Rossner, Judith, 378
Rostow, Eugene V., 27
Rostropovich, Mstislav, 427
Roth, Philip, 379
Rozelle, Pete, 505
Rubinstein, Artur, 356, 427, 462
Rudi, Joe, 505
Rumsfeld, Donald H., 197, 349
Rupp, Adolph, 505
Rusk, Dean, 119, 197, 279
Ryan, Nolan, 505

S

Sabah, Ali al-Khalifa al-, 339
Sabo, Martin O., 145
Sadat, Anwar el-, 255, 339-341, 349
Safire, William, 145
Sagan, Carl, 485
Sahl, Mort, 414
St. Germain, Fernand J., 216
Sakaki, Toshio, 297
Sakharov, Andrei D., 318-319
Salant, Richard S., 367
Sammons, James H., 145, 395
Samuelson, Paul A., 168
Sanchez (Parodi), Ramon, 279
Sanders, Harland, 168
SassouNguesso, Denis, 256
Savalas, Telly, 451, 462, 474
Sawhill, John C., 73, 79, 92-93
Saxbe, William B., 120, 297
Saxon, David S., 73
Scalapino, Robert A., 120
Scammon, Richard M., 79, 216
Schall, James V., 481
Scheider, Roy, 414
Schell, Maria, 414, 474, 517
Schell, Maximilian, 414
Scheman, L. Ronald, 279
Schembechler, Bo, 506
Schlafly, Phyllis, 517
Schlesinger, James R., 79, 93
Schlosser, Herbert S., 367, 451
Schmidt, Alexander M., 396
Schmidt, Helmut, 319, 474
Schmidt, Mike, 506
Schmitt, Harrison H., 217
Schneider, Alan, 439
Schorr, Daniel, 368
Schramm, Tex, 506
Schroeder, Patricia, 145
Schultze, Charles L., 169
Schulz, Charles, 379
Schutz, Klaus, 319
Scott, George C., 414-415, 440
Scranton, William W., 120, 349
Segal, Erich, 379
Segovia, Andres, 428
Selye, Hans, 396, 518
Senghor, Leopold S., 120
Serban, Andrei, 440
Sevareid, Eric, 120, 368-369, 452, 462
Shabat, Oscar E., 74
Shallenberger, Garvin, 180
Shanker, Albert, 74

Shapiro, Irving S., 79, 170
Sharif, Omar, 518
Sharon, Ariel, 342
Shaw, Irwin, 379
Shaw, Robert, 380, 415
Shear, Harold E., 319
Sheehan, Edward R. F., 342
Sheehan, William, 369
Sheinberg, Sidney J., 415
Shen, James C. H., 297
Shenefield, John H., 237
Sherry, Norm, 506
Shertz, Robert H., 237
Sherwin, Samuel B., 59
Shulman, Marshall D., 319
Shuster, E. G. (Bud), 237
Siad Barre, Mohammed, 256
Sigler, Tom W., 94
Silber, John R., 145
Sills, Beverly, 428
Silverman, Fred, 452
Simes, Dimitri K., 320
Simon, Neil, 440, 474
Simon, Norton, 47
Simon, William E., 94, 145
Simons, Howard, 369
Simpson, O. J., 415, 506-507
Singh, Charan, 298
Singlaub, John K., 298
Sinsheimer, Robert L., 486
Sinyavsky, Andrei, 380, 481
Sisco, Joseph J., 342
Sisk, B. F., 217
Sites, James N., 146
Sithole, Ndabaningi, 256
Skelton, Red, 475
Skolimowski, Henryk, 475
Slatkin, Leonard, 428
Slaughter, Enos, 507
Smeal, Eleanor Cutri, 518
Smith, Howard K., 279
Smith, Ian, 256-257
Smith, Joe D., Jr., 370
Smith, Mary Louise, 217
Smith, Reggie, 507
Smith, Stan, 507
Smith, Virginia B., 74
Smith, W. Eugene, 357
Sneider, Richard L., 298
Sneva, Tom, 507
Snyder, Tom, 370
Soares, Mario, 320
Sommer, Nolan B., 47
Spain, Jayne, 47, 170, 518
Sparkman, John J., 121

Speer, Edgar B., 48, 94, 170
Spelling, Aaron, 453
Speth, Gus, 396
Spielberg, Steven, 415
Sporkin, Stanley, 48
Stack, Robert, 415, 453
Staggers, Harley O., 94
Stahr, Elvis J., Jr., 79
Stallone, Sylvester, 416
Starr, Chauncey, 146
Starry, Donn A., 298, 350
Statham, Robert R., 170
Stead, Bette Ann, 519
Stegner, Wallace, 380
Steiger, Rod, 416, 462
Stein, Herbert, 171
Steinbrenner, George, 507
Stern, Isaac, 357, 428
Stevens, George, Jr., 416
Stevens, Rise, 428
Stevens, Roger L., 440
Stevenson, Adlai E., 279
Stewart, James, 416
Stilwell, Richard G., 198, 298
Stockman, David A., 146
Stokes, B. R., 237
Stokes, Louis, 27
Stokowski, Leopold, 429
Stone, Andrew, 416
Stone, Edward Durell, 357
Stone, I. F., 370
Stone, Peter, 416
Storey, David, 380
Straight, Michael W., 357
Strasberg, Lee, 440
Strasberg, Susan, 417
Straus, R. Peter, 121
Strauss, Robert S., 48
Styne, Jule, 429, 441
Suarez (Gonzalez), Adolfo, 320
Sulaiman (Chagnon), Jose, 508
Sulzberger, Arthur Ochs, 49, 370
Summers, Clyde W., 171
Sutherland, Joan, 429
Suzman, Helen, 257-258
Swearingen, John E., Jr., 94-95
Swinarton, Robert W., 49
Symms, Steven D., 397

T

Tanana, Frank, 508
Tanen, Ned, 417

Tankersley, W. H., 49
Tarkenton, Fran, 508
Taylor, Arthur R., 453
Taylor, Elizabeth, 462
Taylor, John, 198
Taylor, Maxwell D., 280
Taylor, Paul, 475
Teller, Edward, 95
Tennille, Toni, 453
Terrill, Ross, 299
Thach, Nguyen Co, 299
Thatcher, Margaret, 320-321, 475
Thomas, Dan, 508
Thomas, Marlo, 417
Thomas, Philippe, 50
Thomas, Richard, 453
Thompson, James R., 146, 217
Thorne, Nicholas G. W., 343
Thornton, Winfred L., 238
Thunberg, Penelope Hartland, 321
Thurmond, Strom, 280
Thurow, Lester C., 171
Tindemans, Leo, 321
Togo, Fumihiko, 299, 321
Tolba, Mostafa K., 80
Torrijos (Herrera), Omar, 280-281
Tortorella, Aldo, 321
Tower, John G., 226
Tracy, David, 481
Trezise, Philip H., 121
Tropman, John E., 227
Trudeau, Pierre Elliott, 121, 147, 171, 282-283
Truffaut, Francois, 417
Tucker, James G., Jr., 147
Tugwell, Rexford G., 171
Tunney, John V., 217
Turbeville, Gus, 475
Turner, Stansfield, 128, 198, 322
Tutko, Thomas, 508
Tutu, Desmond, 258
Tyson, Brady, 283
Tyson, Cicely, 476

U

Udall, Morris K., 95, 147, 218, 371
Uhlman, Wesley C., 238, 242
Ullman, Al, 227
Ullmann, Liv, 417, 476
Unruh, Jesse M., 218
Upadit Pachariyangkun, 299
Updike, John, 380

Upton, Arthur C., 397
Uris, Leon, 380, 463
Ustinov, Dmitri F., 322
Ustinov, Peter, 121, 218, 322, 381, 429, 454, 463, 476, 481

V

Valenti, Jack, 16, 454
van Boven, Theo C., 482
Vance, Cyrus R., 121-123, 128, 198, 258, 283, 299-300, 343
Van Cleave, William R., 198
van der Byl, Pieter, 258-259
Vargas (Llosa), Mario, 381
Veeck, Bill, 508-509
Vessey, John W., Jr., 300
Vidal, Gore, 381, 417
Videla, Jorge Rafael, 284
Vidor, King, 418
Vilas, Guillermo, 509
Villella, Edward, 441
Volpe, John A., 322
von Stade, Frederica, 429
Vorontsov, Yuli, 322
Vorster, John, 259

W

Wade, Virginia, 509
Waite, Ralph, 476
Wald, George, 486
Wald, Richard C., 371
Wallace, Irving, 381
Wallace, James N., 300
Wallace, Mack, 80
Wallach, Eli, 418, 441, 476
Wallenstein, Alfred, 357
Walt, Lewis W., 199, 323
Walters, Barbara, 371
Wannall, W. Raymond, 59
Warfield, William, 430
Warhol, Andy, 358, 441, 454
Warner, Carolyn, 74
Warner, Rawleigh, Jr., 95
Warnke, Paul C., 123, 199
Warren, Charles, 80
Warren, Robert Penn, 382, 463
Washington, Kermit, 509

Washington, Walter E., 371
Wasilewski, Vincent T., 454
Watkins, James D., 199
Watson, Jack H., Jr., 123, 147
Watson, Tom, 509
Wattenberg, Ben J., 147, 477, 486
Watts, Andre, 430
Wearly, William L., 50
Weaver, Sylvester L. (Pat), 454
Wedgeworth, Robert, 382
Weicker, Lowell P., Jr., 16, 147, 199, 218, 284
Weidenbaum, Murray L., 50
Weinberg, Alvin M., 95
Weinberger, Caspar W., 148
Weiss, Ted, 199
Weisman, Ezer, 343
Welk, Lawrence, 430
Werner, Oskar, 418, 441
West, Jerry, 510
Westin, Av, 371
White, Margita, 455
White, Robert M., 80
Wicker, Tom, 372
Wicklein, John, 455
Widmark, Richard, 419
Wiggins, Charles E., 60
Wigoder, Geoffrey, 343
Wilder, Gene, 419
Wiley, Richard E., 455
Wilkins, Roy, 27
Williams, Dick, 510
Williams, Edward Bennett, 16, 27, 477
Williams, Franklin H., 260
Williams, Harold M., 50-51
Williamson, David, Jr., 486
Wills, Maury, 510
Wilson, Archie L., 238
Wilson, Flip, 455
Wilson, Harold, 323
Wilson, Louis H., 200
Wilson, Margaret Bush, 172
Wilson, Pete, 28, 172
Winner, Michael, 419
Winpisinger, William W., 51, 172, 227
Wirtz, W. Willard, 172
Wolfe, Sidney M., 397
Wolfe, Tom, 358
Wolper, David L., 455
Wood, Natalie, 419
Woodcock, Leonard, 96, 300
Wooden, John, 510
Woodward, Joanne, 420
Wright, James C., Jr., 148
Wriston, Walter B., 51, 148, 173
Wurf, Jerry, 173

Wussler, Robert, 456
Wyeth, Jamie, 358

Youngblood, Jack, 510
Younger, Evelle J., 60, 180
Yun Po Sun, 301

Y

Yablans, Frank, 420
Yalow, Rosalyn, 519
Yankelovich, Daniel, 148
Yarborough, Cale, 510
Yeh Chien-ying, 301
Yondo, Marcel, 260
Yorty, Samuel W., 219
Young, Andrew, 28, 124, 200, 219, 260-262, 284, 344, 350, 463, 477
Young, Coleman A., 242
Young, Robert, 420

Z

Zahedi, Ardeshir, 96, 344, 477
Zanuck, Richard D., 420
Ziaul Haq, Mohammad, 301
Ziegler, John A., 511
Zimbalist, Efrem, Jr., 420, 477
Zimring, Franklin E., 180
Zimyanin, Mikhail V., 124
Zinnemann, Fred, 420
Zorinsky, Edward, 149

Index to Subjects

A

Aaron, Henry, 507:3
Abortion—*see* Medicine
Acting/actors, 398:4, 399:2, 399:5, 400:6, 401:2,
    401:3, 402:2, 403:6, 405:2, 405:3, 405:7, 406:6,
    407:3, 408:3, 411:3, 411:4, 412:5, 413:5, 414:3,
    415:2, 415:4, 415:6, 416:2, 419:1, 420:1, 420:5,
    431:1, 433:1, 435:2, 435:4, 435:6, 437:4, 440:1,
    462:1, 465:4, 490:2
    baby feeling, 438:2
    a business/job, 398:6, 399:3, 399:4
    importance of, 414:2
    influence of, 418:6
    insecurity of, 416:3, 418:4, 467:3
    intensity aspect, 404:5
    interpretive aspect, 404:6
    "method"/experience aspect, 403:2
    neurotic aspect, 419:5
    recognition, 414:6
    reliability of, 412:6
    salaries, 416:7, 420:2
    satisfactions of, 405:4, 406:3, 406:6, 413:1
    schools, 416:5
    selectivity aspect, 414:4, 416:3
    stage and film compared, 401:6, 407:1, 412:6,
        412:7, 417:1, 434:7, 435:6, 437:5, 439:4,
        440:6
    stars, 398:2, 407:2, 414:6, 417:5
    success aspect, 436:1
    television aspect, 402:1, 410:1, 443:2, 444:3,
        448:4, 451:2, 451:3, 453:5, 480:1
    time aspect, 407:2
    villains, 404:2, 412:4
    women, 402:5, 403:5, 403:7, 407:4, 407:5,
        411:2, 417:3
    writing books compared with, 380:1
Advertising—*see* Commerce
Africa, 124:3, pp. 245-262
    Communist/Marxist/socialist aspect, 246:4, 248:3,
        251:2, 252:6, 253:5, 258:4, 259:1, 260:4
    defense/military aspect, 249:5
    economic aspect, 260:2
    foreign affairs/policy:
        China (mainland), 251:2
        Cuba, 247:5, 248:4, 249:4, 254:1, 261:5,
            262:1, 264:2, 267:2, 268:5

Africa *(continued)*
    foreign affairs/policy *(continued)*
        Europe, 250:5, 254:2
            Belgium, 261:3
            Britain, 246:1, 261:3
            France, 246:1, 261:3
            Malta, 315:4
            Portugal, 246:1
            Soviet Union, 118:2, 245:4, 251:2, 252:6,
                252:7, 255:6, 262:1, 268:5, 312:1,
                322:1, 347:2
        immigration, 120:5
        imperialism/colonialism, 248:3, 256:1
        Middle East/Arabs, 250:5
            Iran, 256:3
        superpowers aspect, 252:1
        U.S., 247:3, 248:7, 249:3, 250:5, 254:2,
            256:3, 258:4, 260:1, 321:5
            Young, Andrew, 252:6
    human-rights aspect, 107.4
    Organization of African Unity (OAU), 251:1,
        252:6, 256:4, 497:5
    racial aspect, 245:1, 246:4, 248:3, 251:4, 252:4,
        254:2, 255:3, 258:4
    religious aspect, 482:1
    security aspect, 249:5
    tribes, 283:2
    See also specific countries
Agar, John, 409:5
Age/youth, 15:1, 221:4, 466:2, 468:1, 469:4, 472:4,
    473:6, 477:5
    See also Social welfare—elderly
Agnew, Spiro T., 201:2
Agriculture/farming, 44:6, 171:5, 458:2
    costs/prices, 29:2, 31:1
        parity/profits, 31:2, 33:5
        strike, 33:5
    family farm, 30:5
    government aspect, 37:2
    jobs, 162:3
Air Force, U.S.—*see* Defense
Air transportation—*see* Transportation
Alaska:
    oil, 263:5, 264:1
    park, national, 77:3
Alcohol—*see* Medicine
Algeria, 341:3
Ali, Muhammad, 403:4, 508:1

Aliens, illegal—*see* Labor
Allen, Woody, 401:5
Allende (Gossens), Salvador, 275:4
America/U.S.:
  Bicentennial, 16:3
  democracy in, 14:1
  freedom in, 14:1, 15:2, 16:2, 24:2, 120:5
  growth/expansion, 16:1
  history, sense of, 468:5
  the individual in, 14:4
  morals, 15:4
  Number 1, 14:3
  opportunity in, 13:4
  over-developed, 13:5
  progress, 13:2
  regionalism, 13:1, 32:4
  shortages, 13:5
  spirit, malaise of, 16:5
  standard of living, 13:5
  technologically oriented, 15:1
  traits, national, 15:6
  "up" beat, 13:3
  values, 13:2
American scene, the, pp. 13-17
Americas/Latin America, 124:3, pp. 263-284
  Caribbean, 263:1, 263:3
  coffee aspect, 276:2
  dictatorships, 276:2
  economic aspect, 276:2
  foreign affairs/policy:
    Soviet Union, 347:2
    U.S., 263:1, 263:3, 263:5, 270:2, 272:4,
      273:1, 275:5, 278:2, 284:3
  literature, 381:2
  medicine/health aspect, 394:3
  Organization of American States (OAS), 277:4
  religious aspect, 482:1
  repression, 277:4
  See also specific countries
Amin, Idi, 107:2, 252:4
Angola:
  Communist/Marxist aspect, 259:1, 260:4
  foreign affairs/policy:
    Cuba, 113:4, 247:5, 248:2, 248:5, 250:4,
      252:6, 260:3, 261:1, 261:3, 268:5
    Portugal, 261:3
    Rhodesia, 256:5
    South Africa, 248:2
    Soviet Union, 118:2, 251:4, 252:6, 312:1
    U.S., 113:4, 248:2, 250:4, 252:6, 260:4
    Zaire, 251:4, 252:6, 261:2
  press aspect, 361:4
Architecture—*see* Arts
Argentina, 264:3, 284:1
Aristotle, 464:1

Army, U.S.—*see* Defense
Arts/culture, pp. 353-358, 464:3
  architecture, 353:2, 355:2, 357:4
  Austria, 432:2
  best, being the, 356:5
  black aspect, 353:5
  business aspect, 356:1, 357:6
  dissent aspect, 380:2
  economic aspect, 354:5
  elitism/snobbery, 354:1, 358:2
  explosion, cultural, 358:2
  foreign-policy aspect, 358:3
  genetic aspect, 354:3
  government support/involvement, 353:3, 353:4,
    354:2
    National Endowment for Arts/Humanities,
      354:1, 356:2, 357:5, 432:2
    tax aspect, 356:4
    White House aspect, 355:1, 357:5
  importance of, 353:1
  individual artist, 353:3
  money aspect, 356:3
  museums, 355:5, 358:1
  never finished, 377:4
  non-involvement aspect, 355:6
  opposition, party of, 355:4
  painting/painters, 353:6, 356:3, 358:1
  Paris center, new, 354:4
  photography, 357:1
  politicization of, 354:1
  purpose, 355:3
  Soviet Union, 357:3
  U.S., 357:2, 357:6, 358:3, 472:2
  See also Performing arts
Asia/Pacific, 124:3, pp. 285-301
  Asian Development Bank, 293:6
  domino principle, 290:4
  foreign affairs/policy:
    Association of Southeast Asian Nations
      (ASEAN), 299:3
    China (mainland), 299:3
    Southeast Asia Treaty Organization (SEATO),
      291:4, 294:5
    Soviet Union, 299:3
    U.S., 285:1, 290:4, 291:4, 294:5, 295:1,
      299:3, 299:4
    Vietnam, 293:5
  religious aspect, 482:1
  See also specific countries
Atkinson, Brooks, 439:6
Austria, 432:2
Auto racing, 494:5, 504:4, 504:5, 507:5, 510:5
Automobiles—*see* Transportation

B

Bahamas, 116:1
Bailey, F. Lee, 495:2
Bakke case—*see* Civil rights—affirmative action
Ballet—*see* Dance
Banking—*see* Commerce
Barbados, 116:1
Barnes, Clive, 439:6
Baseball, 494:4, 499:1
  agents, player, 491:4
  American League, 495:2
  black aspect, 493:3
  commissioner, 491:4, 494:3, 497:6, 499:2
  consistency, 495:1
  contracts, player, 487:3, 493:2, 496:4, 499:5
  entertainers, players as, 490:2
  fans, 494:2, 509:1
  hitting, 495:3, 505:5, 507:3, 508:2
    designated hitter, 499:3
    home runs, 495:1, 495:4, 501:1
    strength aspect, 487:1
  hustle, player, 501:3
  Japan, 499:4
  legal aspect, 491:4, 495:2
  longevity, player, 490:1
  managing/managers, 496:4, 499:5, 501:3, 501:4,
    506:5, 510:3
    black, 493:3
  mistakes, mental, 510:2
  motivation, player, 499:5
  owners, 487:3, 489:3, 493:1, 494:2, 495:6, 499:2
  parks, 506:2
  pitching/pitchers, 495:5, 505:7, 506:2, 507:3,
    508:2
    hitting batters, 508:4
    knuckleball, 489:5
    relief pitchers, 497:2
  player ego/independence, 491:3, 495:2, 496:4
  player sale, 494:3
  player skills, 501:4
  reserve system/free agents, 491:2, 492:4, 493:1,
    495:6, 508:6
  salaries, player, 487:3, 489:3, 491:2, 493:2,
    494:2, 495:6, 495:7, 499:5, 500:3, 507:2,
    507:6, 508:6
  savored, sport to be, 509:1
  stolen bases, 490:3, 500:2, 505:7
  television aspect, 498:7
    umpiring, 503:4
  turf, artificial, 499:3
  umpiring/umpires, 503:4
  winning/losing, 501:6, 502:2, 510:2
  women, 487:1

Baseball *(continued)*
  clubs:
    Cincinnati *Reds,* 494:3
    Kansas City *Royals,* 505:7
    Los Angeles *Dodgers,* 501:6
    Lotte *Orions,* 499:4
    Nankai *Hawks,* 499:4
    New York *Mets,* 494:3
    New York *Yankees,* 493:1, 494:3
    Oakland *Athletics,* 494:3
    Taiyo *Whales,* 499:4
Basketball:
  agents, player, 488:2
  American Basketball Association (ABA), 491:1,
    494:2, 508:6
  coaching/coaches, 488:2, 488:4, 489:2, 496:3,
    497:1, 502:1, 505:1, 505:6, 510:1
  contracts, player, 505:1
  fans, 494:2
  greed aspect, 490:6
  Memphis *Tams,* 494:2
  motivation, player, 489:2
  National Basketball Association (NBA), 489:4,
    491:1, 502:3, 503:3
  owners, 489:4, 494:2
  player ego/independence, 488:2, 488:4
  referees, 489:4, 491:1
  salaries, player, 489:2, 491:5, 494:2, 502:3, 510:5
  stability/sophistication, 502:3
  statistics, 501:5
  substitute players, 491:5
  ups/downs, player, 510:4
  violence, 503:3, 509:1, 509:5
  watching games, 493:5
  winning/losing, 488:4, 502:1, 505:6, 510:1
  women, 487:1
Beatty, Warren, 414:2
Beauty, 475:3
Beethoven, Ludwig van, 421:3
Begin, Menachem, 324:3, 330:2, 330:3, 331:1, 335:1,
  342:2, 342:3, 343:3, 344:2
Belgium, 261:3, 394:3
Belize, 280:4
Bellow, Saul, 374:2, 377:2
Benny, Jack, 443:3, 460:2, 475:1
Bergman, Ingmar, 417:5, 418:5
Berlin (Germany), 315:5, 319:4
Berlinguer, Enrico, 322:4
Bible, the—*see* Religion
Bigness, 467:4
Biko, Steve, 250:3
Blacks—*see* Civil rights
Blake, Robert, 401:2
Blue, Vida, 494:3
Blumenthal, W. Michael, 123:5

Books—*see* Literature
Booth, Edwin, 399:2
Botswana, 248:7, 256:5
Boxing, 457:2, 498:3
   greatest fighter, 487:2, 508:1
   honesty, 504:3
   violence, 500:4
Brahms, Johannes, 429:1
Brando, Marlon, 401:2
Brazil, 269:1, 269:3
   human-rights aspect, 121:1
Brecht, Berthold, 451:1
Brezhnev, Leonid I., 104:1, 109:2, 307:4, 312:3, 346:1
Britain—*see* United Kingdom
Bronson, Charles, 401:3
Brown, Edmund G., Jr., 56:1, 211:4, 219:1
Brown, George, 281:1
Brown, Harold, 123:5
Brynner, Yul, 439:2
Brzezinski, Zbigniew, 123:5
Bulgaria, 394:3
Bunker, Ellsworth, 280:5
Burger, Warren E., 176:4, 179:2
Burma, 296:2, 361:4
Burnett, Carol, 453:2
Burns, Arthur F., 166:3
Burton, Richard, 415:2
Business—*see* Commerce
Busing—*see* Civil rights—education

C

Cambodia, 292:3, 293:3, 296:5
   human-rights aspect, 212:1
   press aspect, 361:4
   U.S. aspect, 114:1, 116:3
Canada:
   contentment, 282:1
   diversity, 283:1
   foreign affairs/policy, 282:4, 283:3
      China (mainland), 282:4
      Cuba, 282:4
      Rhodesia, 282:4
      South Africa, 250:3, 282:4
      Soviet Union, 271:2, 282:4
      U.S., 264:1, 272:1
      Vietnam, 282:4
   Liberal Party, 282:3
   medicine/health aspect, 388:3, 393:2, 393:3
   New Democratic Party, 271:2
   new generation, 267:6

Canada *(continued)*
   Quebec/French aspect, 264:1, 268:4, 270:6, 271:1, 271:2, 272:1, 272:2, 275:2, 278:1, 282:2, 282:3, 283:2
   sports, 488:3, 493:4
Cancer—*see* Medicine
Capital punishment—*see* Crime
Capitalism, 39:2, 98:4, 155:5, 170:2, 182:5, 248:3, 261:4, 304:5, 321:6, 465:1
   See also Economy—free enterprise
Capra, Frank, 410:3
Caramanlis, Constantine, 314:4, 317:1
Carew, Rod, 501:4
Caribbean—*see* Americas
Carter, Billy, 458:3
Carter, Jimmy:
   charisma, 211:4
   Congressional aspect, 206:6, 208:2, 208:3, 214:2, 216:1
   environmental aspect, 75:2
   ethics, 266:4
   Lance, Bert, affair, 205:3, 208:1, 215:5, 218:2
   many-sided, 208:1
   marijuana, 55:4
   "over-speak," 209:4
   performance/Administration, 201:3, 202:1, 202:2, 204:4, 205:1, 206:4, 206:6, 207:2, 209:3, 209:4, 212:2, 214:1, 214:2, 215:1, 216:1
   political base, 208:2
   popularity/public-opinion aspect, 208:5, 209:3
Carter, Lillian, 376:5
Carter, Rosalynn, 355:1
Cartoons—*see* Journalism; Literature
Castro, Fidel, 106:6, 267:2, 274:3, 279:2, 279:4, 281:3
Catholicism—*see* Religion
Central Intelligence Agency (CIA), U.S.—*see* Foreign affairs—intelligence
Challenges, 476:1
Change, 471:5
Chaplin, Charles, 401:5, 437:3, 441:5
Charm, 469:1
Chayefsky, Paddy, 448:4
Chekhov, Anton, 379:6
Chiang Ching-kuo, 293:1, 294:1
Chile:
   democracy in, 273:4
   foreign pressure, 277:1
   human rights/repression, 107:4, 121:1, 283:4, 515:5
   U.S. aspect, 275:4, 283:4
      CIA aspect, 127:1, 127:5
China (mainland/Communist):
   Communism, 322:1
      Communist Party, 292:6

China (mainland/Communist) *(continued)*
  economic aspect, 292:7, 301:1
  foreign affairs/policy:
    Africa, 251:2
      Seychelles, 255:5
    Asia, 299:3
      Burma, 296:2
      China (Nationalist)/Taiwan, 290:1, 290:2,
        291:3, 292:5, 293:1, 293:2, 294:1
      India, 289:1
      Japan, 297:4, 299:3, 300:5, 321:5
      Korea, 285:3, 288:3
    Canada, 282:4
    immigration, 120:5
    intelligence/spying, 127:3
    Soviet Union, 285:3, 286:3, 287:2, 289:1,
      289:6, 296:4, 298:4, 300:5, 301:1, 323:1
    U.S., 114:1, 120:2, 285:3, 286:4, 287:1,
      287:2, 288:4, 289:6, 290:2, 291:3, 292:2,
      293:1, 293:2, 294:1, 295:3, 296:4, 297:6,
      298:2, 298:4, 299:1, 300:1, 301:1, 339:4
      Shanghai Communique, 288:2
      trade aspect, 263:3
  human-rights aspect, 297:6
  medicine/health aspect, 394:3
China (Nationalist)/Taiwan:
  Chinese (mainland) aspect, 290:1, 290:2, 291:3,
    292:5, 293:1, 293:2, 294:1
  U.S. aspect, 287:1, 287:2, 288:2, 288:4, 290:1,
    291:3, 292:2, 293:1, 293:2, 294:1, 297:6
Christ, Jesus—*see* Religion—Christianity
Christianity—*see* Religion
Cincinnati (Ohio), 239:6
Cinema—*see* Motion pictures
Cities—*see* Urban affairs
Civil rights/racism, 16:4, pp. 18-28, 35:1, 164:4,
  465:1
  affirmative action/quotas/reverse discrimination,
    18:2, 18:3, 19:2, 20:1, 20:2, 22:1, 26:1, 26:3,
    27:1
    Bakke case, 20:5, 23:1, 26:2
  blacks/Negroes, 18:2, 18:4, 21:4, 23:3, 23:4,
    23:5, 24:1, 24:5, 25:2, 25:6, 26:3, 27:3,
    164:6, 202:1, 259:6, 261:4, 272:1
    arts aspect, 353:5
    Democratic Party, 211:6
    income aspect, 24:4
    intellect/IQ, 22:3, 25:4, 26:4
    Mayors, 19:4
    religious aspect, 480:2
    Republican Party, 211:6
    sports aspect, 487:4
      baseball, 493:3
    women, 513:2
  Carter, Jimmy, aspect, 20:4, 23:3, 23:4, 24:1,

Civil rights/racism *(continued)*
  Carter, Jimmy, aspect *(continued)*
    24:5, 25:6, 27:3, 164:6, 202:1
  chicanos, 18:2
  Civil Rights Act of 1964, 22:1
  education aspect, 18:3, 20:1, 20:2, 20:5, 21:1,
    21:2, 21:3, 21:4, 23:1, 26:1, 26:2, 27:1, 62:3
    busing, 19:1, 19:3, 27:2, 28:1
  employment/jobs, 18:2, 18:3, 19:2, 20:4, 22:1,
    25:6, 26:1, 26:3, 27:1
  equal opportunity, 27:4
  Ford, Gerald R., aspect, 28:3
  homosexuality, 18:2, 19:5, 20:3, 470:2
  Indians, American, 18:2, 25:5
  liberalism aspect, 23:5
  National Association for the Advancement of
    Colored People (NAACP), 23:1
  Nixon, Richard M., aspect, 23:3, 28:3
  opposition, 27:2
  poverty aspect, 18:2
  progress, 22:4, 23:5, 25:2
  public attention, 24:4
  segregation/integration, 21:1, 23:1, 28:1, 246:1
  Southern (U.S.) aspect, 21:4, 164:4, 246:1
  tokenism, 24:3, 24:4
  See also specific countries and areas
Coal—*see* Energy
Cobb, Ty, 490:3
Coffee, 276:2
Cohn, Harry, 414:1
Coleman, William T., Jr., 212:4
College—*see* Education
Colman, Ronald, 399:2
Colombia, 276:2
Commerce/business/industry/finance, pp. 29-51,
  168:1
  advertising, 44:3
    comparative, 45:5
    FTC aspect, 34:1
    half wasted, 49:1
    language, abuse of, 374:3
    lawyers—*see* Judiciary—lawyers
    medical, 177:4
    political campaigns, 207:3
    price advertising, 35:2
  antitrust/monopolies/mergers, 30:2, 45:4, 46:1
    Congressional aspect, 30:4
    divestiture, 38:1
  arts aspect, 356:1, 357:6
  banking, 38:3, 51:3, 171:5, 203:6, 216:4
    ethics, 45:1
    press aspect, 46:4
  big business, 14:4
  capital—*see* investment, below
  Carter, Jimmy, aspect, 41:1

Commerce/business/industry/finance *(continued)*
  Chamber of Commerce of the U.S., 33:3
  change, 47:4, 49:2
  college aspect, 46:3
  competition, 45:4
    foreign, 30:1, 30:3, 32:5, 33:1, 42:2
  consumerism, 34:2, 34:4, 35:3, 37:3, 40:5, 45:4,
    157:4
  crime aspect, 59:3
  debt/equity aspect, 39:2
  employment subsidies, 160:2
  environmental aspect, 77:1, 80:4
  ethics/behavior/corruption, 29:1, 32:1, 39:2, 40:3,
    45:1, 48:2, 49:3, 50:4
    price-fixing, 39:3, 44:3
  Europe, 42:2
    France, 29:3
  government aspect/regulations, 15:2, 29:1, 29:3,
    30:1, 33:2, 33:3, 34:3, 35:1, 38:2, 40:2, 41:1,
    42:1, 42:2, 42:4, 43:3, 43:4, 44:1, 45:2, 46:2,
    46:5, 50:2, 131:6, 136:2, 141:2, 142:1, 147:2,
    156:1
    nationalization, 50:1
  government, businessmen in, 140:3, 209:5
  interest rates—*see* monetary system, below
  investment/capital, 32:3, 33:1, 39:1, 39:2, 40:1,
    48:1, 51:1, 150:2, 154:5, 158:4, 160:3, 169:2,
    170:1, 170:4, 171:3, 173:2
  Japan, 42:2
  lawyers aspect, 178:4, 179:4
  management/executives, 29:1, 29:3, 37:1, 39:5,
    40:3, 43:6, 49:3
    compensation, 47:2
  monetary system, 152:4
    Congressional aspect, 153:4, 168:3
    exchange rates, 51:3
    Federal Reserve System, 144:4, 153:4, 166:3,
      168:3, 171:1
    interest rates, 153:4, 157:3, 171:1
  multinational corporations, 43:5, 44:4, 51:2,
    107:5
    developing countries aspect, 39:4, 44:1
    foreign earnings, 47:3
  political contributions, 36:4
  press aspect, 37:4, 46:4, 49:1
  profits, 29:4, 32:3, 41:4, 48:1, 50:3, 51:1, 107:5
  public attitude toward, 40:3, 42:3, 43:1, 48:2,
    50:3
  quality standards, 44:2, 44:3
  regionalism, 32:4
  Republican Party aspect, 209:1, 219:1
  social responsibility, 29:4, 41:4, 47:1
  stock market/securities industry, 40:1, 158:2
    brokerage rates, 41:3, 49:2
    "little guy," 48:2

Commerce/business/industry/finance *(continued)*
  tax deductions, 43:2
  urban/cities aspect, 241:5
  women, 515:6, 517:5, 518:4
  See also specific industries; Economy; Trade,
    foreign
Common Cause, 211:5
Common Market—*see* Europe— economic aspect
Communism, 28:2, 99:1, 100:2, 103:2, 113:5, 116:4,
  117:1, 117:3, 120:2, 120:3, 121:1, 124:2, 168:1,
  260:4, 274:3, 284:2, 295:3, 297:1, 314:2, 475:4
  See also specific countries and areas; Lenin,
    Vladimir I.; Marx, Karl; Socialism
Congo, 361:4
Congress/Senate/House, U.S., 130:1, 131:5, 140:4,
  148:1
  antitrust aspect, 30:4
  appointments, confirmation of, 133:3, 138:2,
    205:2
    See also Government—appointments
  catching up, 139:6
  committees, 131:1, 148:3, 148:5
  Congressional Record, 149:2
  defense/military aspect, 105:3, 137:4
  efficiency, 143:3, 147:2
  environmental aspect, 79:5
  ethics, 133:2, 135:6, 139:3
  foreign-policy aspect, 97:4, 105:3, 106:5, 108:1,
    108:2, 109:4, 123:3, 137:4
  franking privilege, 211:5
  gentlemen's club, 139:2
  Goldberg, Rube, aspect, 146:1
  home, time at, 137:4, 138:3
  honorariums, 139:3
  House and Senate compared, 139:4, 141:6, 142:5,
    147:6
  labor aspect, 173:3
  a madhouse, 135:2
  monetary-system aspect, 153:4
    Federal Reserve System aspect, 168:3
  money aspect, 141:4
  national will, reflection of, 131:2
  office funds, 135:4, 143:1
  people, representative of the, 137:3, 143:3
  Postal Service aspect, 129:4
  Presidential aspect, 131:3, 134:1, 137:3, 138:3,
    139:4, 140:5, 142:5, 143:5, 148:4, 205:2,
    206:6, 208:2, 208:3, 214:2, 216:1
  pressure on, 146:3
  public attitude toward, 79:5, 133:2, 148:2
  reasoning together, 140:2
  responsiveness, 149:2
  rich running for, 143:4
  salaries, 135:4, 135:5, 137:4, 143:1, 143:4, 147:3
  slush funds, 135:4

Congress/Senate/House *(continued)*
    staff size, 137:5, 148:5
    television coverage of, 137:3
    term, length of, 133:6, 134:2, 134:4
    time available, 145:4
Conservatism—*see* Politics
Constitution, U.S., 142:4, 216:2
    First Amendment, 363:4, 368:2, 441:1, 452:2,
        452:5, 454:4
    14th Amendment, 519:1
    Supreme Court interpreting of, 178:1
Consumerism — *see* Commerce
Cooper, Gary, 399:2
Copland, Aaron, 406:6
Cornell, Katharine, 410:2
Courts — *see* Judiciary
Crane, Roy, 379:3
Crime/law enforcement, pp. 52-60
    authoritarian measures against, 57:4
    business aspect, 59:3
    capital punishment/death penalty, 52:1, 53:3,
        54:1, 56:1, 57:1, 57:3, 60:2
        televising of, 57:2
    causes, 58:3
        social aspect, 473:7
        unemployment, 159:2, 161:5, 169:1, 226:2
    citizen involvement in dealing with, 53:4
    detention, pre-trial, 54:2
    drugs (criminal aspect), 58:5
        heroin, 54:4
        marijuana, 53:1, 55:4, 56:3
        tough laws, 56:2
        See also Medicine — drug abuse
    fear of, 58:6
    Federal Bureau of Investigation (FBI):
        abuses, 202:1
        charter, 52:2, 57:5
        Director, replacement of, 53:5
        intelligence activities, 59:4
    gambling, 54:4
    "illicit practices," 58:5
    intelligence activities, 55:3, 59:4
        See also Foreign affairs — intelligence
    looting, 220:5, 224:5, 226:2
    motion-pictures aspect, 418:6
    organized crime, 52:5, 54:4, 56:2, 59:4, 465:1
    police, 55:3, 56:6, 58:5, 59:1
    press coverage of, 364:1, 364:4, 366:5
    prisons:
        parole, 52:3
        pre-trial detention, 54:2
        rehabilitation aspect, 54:3, 58:2, 58:4
    probation, 58:2
    rate, 55:1
    sentencing, uniform, 52:3

Crime/law enforcement *(continued)*
    strict enforcement, 55:1
    Supreme Court rulings, 58:1
    television aspect, 57:2, 445:3
    terrorism, 52:4, 55:2, 55:3, 56:6, 113:6, 123:1,
        255:4, 319:2, 320:4, 473:7
    urban/cities aspect, 56:4, 58:6
    victim, compensation for, 59:2, 60:1
    white-collar crime, 54:5, 56:5, 58:5
    youth aspect, 158:5
Cronkite, Walter, 359:1, 359:2
Cuba:
    Communism, 263:3, 274:3, 279:4
    economic aspect, 279:4
    foreign affairs/policy:
        Africa, 247:5, 248:4, 249:4, 254:1, 261:5,
            262:1, 264:2, 267:2, 268:5
            Angola, 113:4, 247:5, 248:2, 248:5, 250:4,
                252:6, 260:3, 261:1, 261:3, 268:5
            Ethiopia, 247:5, 268:5
            Mozambique, 247:5
            South Africa, 254:1
        Canada, 282:4
        immigration, 120:5
        intervention/subversion, 266:5, 274:3
        Jamaica, 266:5
        Panama, 269:2, 274:6, 277:3, 279:5, 281:2,
            281:3
        Soviet Union, 267:2, 268:5, 274:3, 274:6
        U.S., 103:4, 106:6, 114:1, 250:4, 252:6,
            254:1, 263:3, 264:2, 266:3, 266:4, 267:1,
            267:2, 268:3, 268:5, 274:3, 274:4, 279:2,
            279:3, 279:4, 295:3
    human-rights aspect, 264:2, 267:1, 274:3, 277:4
    personality cult, 266:1
    soft life, 266:2
Cukor, George, 407:5
Cyprus, 306:3, 317:1
Czechoslovakia, 283:2, 312:1

D

Daley, Richard J., 173:3
Dance/ballet, 354:5, 355:2, 434:3, 434:4, 435:3
    athletes compared with, 431:4, 435:5
    celebrity aspect, 431:6, 461:3
    civilization at its height, 434:6
    concentration aspect, 441:2
    European aspect, 432:4
    modern, 436:5
    Soviet aspect, 431:5
    understanding a nation through, 434:2

Dance/ballet *(continued)*
U.S. aspect, 432:4
youth aspect, 432:4, 434:6
Dante (Alighieri), 377:1
Dayan, Moshe, 324:3
Dean, John W., III, 217:2
Death, 459:1, 472:3
Defense/military, 82:3, 127:3, pp. 181-200
aid, foreign military, 112:6, 118:2, 124:5
Air Force, U.S.:
bombers, 183:4, 185:2, 198:2
B-1, 184:5, 186:3, 188:4, 189:2, 189:5,
189:6, 190:1, 194:1, 196:5
B-52, 189:2, 189:6
Delta Dart, 198:2
size, 192:1
arms control/disarmament/SALT, 106:2, 118:4,
182:5, 185:3, 186:2, 187:1, 187:3, 191:4,
192:4, 192:5, 193:2, 197:5, 198:4, 198:5,
199:2, 199:3, 312:4
Vladivostok agreement, 105:2, 191:5, 194:3
arms race, 109:2, 111:1, 182:4, 183:1, 197:5,
347:4
arms sales, foreign, 103:1
Army, U.S., 194:7
atomic bomb, 346:5
balance/superiority/parity, 181:2, 181:3, 183:3,
183:4, 185:3, 185:4, 186:1, 186:2, 186:5,
189:3, 190:3, 191:1, 191:4, 192:3, 193:1,
194:6, 196:1, 199:2, 303:4, 311:3, 347:3
Carter, Jimmy, aspect, 198:5
civil defense, 188:5, 189:1, 196:4
Congressional aspect, 105:3, 137:4
conventional forces, 190:3, 195:1, 337:4
Defense, U.S. Dept. of, 196:3
deterrence, 181:5, 183:4, 188:3, 188:4, 188:5,
190:2, 311:3, 345:4, 346:2, 347:1
discipline aspect, 198:1
dissent/criticism of policy, 181:1, 187:5, 197:3,
198:1
foreign-policy aspect, 102:2, 183:3, 193:3
good/bad weapons, 181:4
immorality of weapons, 346:4
intelligence aspect, 194:5
as a job, 188:2
Marine Corps, U.S., 194:7, 200:1
missiles, 185:2, 187:1, 198:2
cruise missile, 184:5, 186:3, 189:5, 190:1,
196:1, 198:4
ICBM, 185:1, 186:5, 189:6
Minuteman, 189:6
MIRV, 191:5, 196:1
M-X, 189:6, 196:5
SS-16, 185:1
SS-20, 187:3

Defense/military *(continued)*
national security, definition of, 184:1
Navy, U.S.:
Admirals, too many, 197:2
fleet size, 191:3, 197:1
recruits, illiteracy of, 199:4
submarines, 183:4, 185:2, 186:5
Polaris, 189:6
Poseidon, 189:6
Trident, 189:6, 196:1
two-ocean aspect, 191:3
women in, 188:1, 191:2
neutron bomb, 181:4, 183:1, 186:4, 187:3, 190:2,
190:5, 194:2, 195:1, 199:6, 200:2
nuclear weapons, 86:1, 86:6
number of weapons, 191:4
overkill, 195:3
pardon/amnesty of Vietnam resisters, 182:1,
193:4, 194:4, 199:1, 199:5
patriotism aspect, 182:2
quality vs. quantity, 192:1
readiness, 188:3
response to attack, 185:2
spending/budget, 136:2, 184:2, 186:1, 189:4,
195:2, 197:4, 202:1, 227:4
triad, 189:6
unions, labor, 182:2, 182:3, 183:2, 190:4
volunteer forces/draft, 181:5, 184:4, 186:6,
187:4, 194:7, 196:2, 199:1
vulnerability, 181:2
war avoidance, 192:2
waste aspect, 195:2, 196:3
women in, 188:1, 191:2, 515:2
See also specific countries
de Gaulle, Charles, 303:2, 312:2, 467:6
de Lesseps, Ferdinand, 276:1
DeMille, Cecil B., 410:3
Democracy, 14:1, 109:6, 116:1, 147:2, 175:2, 179:2,
269:3, 284:1, 295:5, 295:6, 367:7, 472:1
See also specific countries and areas
Democratic Party (U.S.), 204:5, 206:6, 208:2, 211:1,
211:3
blacks in, 211:6
constituency, 216:5
middle class, enemy of, 219:1
social-welfare aspect, 226:1
Dempsey, Jack, 508:1
Denmark, 432:4
Destiny, 473:4
Detente—*see* Foreign affairs
Detroit (Mich.), 239:6
Developing countries—*see* Third World
Dickens, Charles, 400:7
Dickinson, Emily, 515:4
Didion, Joan, 377:2

Disraeli, Benjamin, 220:5
Djibouti, 250:1
Doctors—*see* Medicine
Dostoyevsky, Feodor, 375:4, 377:3, 381:1
Douglas, Kirk, 416:2
Douglas, Paul, 410:1
Dreams, impossible, 463:4, 477:3
Dropouts, 477:1
Drugs—*see* Crime; Medicine
Dunlop, John, 212:4
Durante, Jimmy, 433:2
Duse, Eleanora, 398:6

E

Eagleton, Thomas F., 204:3
Eastwood, Clint, 401:3, 453:2
Economy, pp. 150-173, 212:2
    balance of payments—*see* Trade, foreign
    controls, wage/price, 151:5, 153:2, 161:6, 164:2
    economists, 152:4, 160:1, 161:1, 171:4
    "fine tuning" of, 152:2
    free/private enterprise/market system, 30:2, 34:1, 35:2, 35:3, 36:4, 37:2, 38:2, 42:3, 44:1, 44:4, 46:2, 49:2, 50:1, 50:4, 155:5, 156:1, 157:6, 160:4, 165:3, 168:1, 169:3, 170:2, 173:1, 219:1, 471:3
        See also Energy
    government regulations/involvement, 151:4, 151:5, 152:6, 157:4, 160:3, 169:3
    gross national product (GNP), 169:4, 170:1
    growth/expansion of, 15:4, 155:1
    inflation, 29:3, 30:1, 31:1, 31:3, 136:4, 140:1, 144:3, 144:4, 145:6, 146:1, 150:2, 150:3, 151:3, 151:4, 151:5, 152:1, 152:7, 153:1, 153:3, 154:3, 155:4, 156:2, 156:3, 156:4, 157:3, 157:4, 158:2, 159:1, 159:6, 160:3, 161:1, 161:6, 162:4, 163:2, 164:1, 165:5, 166:1, 167:2, 168:2, 169:1, 169:2, 170:1, 170:4, 171:1, 171:4, 202:1, 220:4, 306:4
    Keynesian, 158:2, 171:4
    middle class, 15:4, 81:6, 152:3, 219:1, 240:3, 242:3, 295:4
    outliving means, 155:1
    productivity, 32:3, 39:4, 150:2, 160:3, 161:6, 171:5
    prosperity, maximum, 159:3
    rebate, $50, 154:3, 156:2, 162:4
    recession, 140:1, 155:1, 169:2, 164:4
    shadow economy, 159:2
    standard of living, 13:5, 32:3, 86:2, 93:3, 156:1, 165:3, 170:2, 170:4, 224:1

Economy *(continued)*
    teaching of economics, 71:3
    See also specific countries; Commerce; Labor; Taxes; Trade, foreign
Education/schools, pp. 61-74, 225:5
    achievement, pupil, 66:4
    adult, 64:2
    arrogance/humility aspect, 71:2
    athletics/sports aspect, 61:3, 63:4, 66:5, 498:1
        See also Football, college
    basics/reading/writing, 62:3, 64:4, 65:1, 65:4, 67:1, 67:2, 67:5, 73:4, 74:1, 74:4
        literacy, 63:1
    bigness, 14:4, 66:1
    business/industry aspect, 46:3
    change, 62:6
    college/university:
        admissions, 67:4
        business/industry aspect, 46:3
        football—*see* Football, college
        glamorization of, 15:4
        preparation for, 64:3
        president, 62:1
        Princeton, 63:5
        unemployment, masking of, 72:4
        value, 69:5
    as communication, 70:1
    continuing, 61:4, 71:5
    democracy in, 69:6
    diploma, meaning of, 73:1
    early start, 65:2
    economics, teaching of, 71:3
    engineering, 66:3
    equal access to, 62:3
    financing/funding of, 61:1, 68:1, 72:3
        expenditures per pupil, 66:4
    grades, 69:2, 73:1
    a hindrance, 71:4
    history, teaching of, 71:3
    ignorance, student, 62:2
    language aspect, 72:2, 72:5
    law, teaching/students of, 174:1, 176:3
    learning ability, 61:4
    length of, 221:4
    liberal arts, 61:2, 64:5, 68:3, 69:3, 73:3, 74:3
    liberation of mind, 65:3
    luxurious facilities, 158:5
    malaise, student, 64:3
    medical schools, 385:3
    parents aspect, 69:1
    priorities/responsibility, 64:4, 66:1, 74:4
    private/public, 68:4, 70:4, 72:3
    reforms of 1960s, 61:2
    relevancy, 63:2, 63:3, 63:4
    as a right, 66:2

Education/schools *(continued)*
science aspect, 485:5
social-reform aspect, 70:3
standards, 69:2
state/local responsibility, 62:3
Mayors, 74:2
teaching/teachers/professors, 69:1, 71:1
jobs of distinction, 67:3
performance, 62:5
pressures, 67:6
ratio to students, 70:1
training, 67:5
unions, 70:2
television aspect, 485:1
testing programs, Federal, 64:1
value/purpose of, 68:2, 69:4, 69:5, 73:3
values, teaching of, 68:1, 72:6
vocational/career/job aspect, 62:4, 64:5, 68:3, 69:3, 71:1, 72:1, 73:3, 74:3
See also Civil rights—education
Ego, 459:2, 469:2
Egypt, 336:3
Israeli aspect, 329:4, 331:2, 333:3, 339:4, 339:5
Sadat visit—*see* Middle East—Sadat
Libyan aspect, 248:7
Soviet aspect, 255:6, 340:1, 341:3
Sudanese aspect, 255:6
U.S. aspect, 248:7, 340:1
Ehrlichman, John D., 217:2
Eisenhower, Dwight D., 134:1, 211:1, 214:2, 265:3, 316:2, 424:5
Elders, respect for, 461:5
Elections—*see* Politics
Eliot, T. S., 133:4, 374:3
Elizabeth II, 308:2
Energy, 35:1, pp. 81-96
blackout, New York, 95:2, 220:5, 224:5, 226:2
coal, 79:3, 80:2, 81:2, 81:4, 81:5, 84:3, 88:2, 88:4, 89:3, 89:5, 90:1, 91:2, 91:3, 94:5
conservation/consumption/waste, 84:4, 86:4, 87:2, 87:4, 87:5, 89:3, 89:5, 90:1, 90:2, 90:6, 91:1, 91:4, 92:1, 92:5, 93:3, 93:5
costs, 153:3
crisis/shortage, 81:5, 82:2, 82:4, 82:5, 83:2, 85:1, 85:3, 85:4, 89:1, 89:5, 92:3, 93:2
environmental aspect, 75:5, 76:5, 77:1, 79:1, 79:3, 79:4, 80:2, 91:3, 94:2, 94:3
free enterprise/market aspect, 85:3, 86:3, 87:3, 89:4, 91:4, 92:2, 94:2, 94:3
government aspect, 83:4, 84:4, 85:4, 86:3, 92:2, 94:2
Dept. of Energy, U.S., 85:2, 212:2, 214:2
Federal Power Commission, 94:3
incentives, 83:4
independence, 88:1, 93:1, 95:4

Energy *(continued)*
natural gas, 81:2, 83:3, 83:5, 85:4, 86:3, 87:2, 87:3, 94:1, 94:2, 94:3
nuclear power, 81:5, 84:2, 84:3, 84:5, 85:1, 86:1, 86:6, 87:1, 88:5, 94:2, 94:5, 95:5
oil/gasoline/fuel, 83:4, 84:4, 86:2, 87:2, 90:4, 91:1, 96:2, 235:4
Alaskan, 263:5, 264:1
embargo, 82:3, 84:1, 91:2, 92:5, 93:2, 94:5, 96:2
foreign-policy aspect, 112:3
imported/foreign, 81:4, 81:5, 83:2, 88:1, 88:3, 90:4, 91:2, 92:3, 93:1, 94:5
North Sea, 306:5
off-shore drilling, 79:1
OPEC/cartel, 81:1, 87:3, 88:3, 92:3, 94:2, 94:5, 151:5
prices/costs, 81:2, 81:4, 83:3, 83:5, 85:1, 85:4, 86:3, 87:3, 87:4, 92:3, 92:5, 94:2, 94:3, 95:1, 228:1, 228:5
reserves/supplies, 89:3, 90:1, 90:3, 90:5, 93:2, 93:5, 94:3, 94:4
transportation aspect, 228:1, 237:4, 239:2
automobiles, 86:4, 87:5, 89:4, 92:4, 92:5, 93:3, 96:1, 228:5, 231:3, 231:4, 233:4, 235:4
as weapon, 96:2, 112:3
See also specific countries and areas; tax aspect, below; Oil industry
political aspect, 95:1
program/policy, 81:6, 82:1, 83:1, 85:2, 87:2, 88:1, 89:4, 90:2, 91:2, 92:3, 92:4, 93:3, 93:4, 94:2, 95:4, 212:2
regionalism, 94:1
solar power, 81:5, 82:1, 84:2, 86:2, 88:5, 89:5, 90:5
tax aspect, 81:6, 84:4, 86:5, 87:3, 87:4, 87:5, 89:2, 89:4, 91:1, 92:4, 95:1, 96:1, 235:4
England—*see* United Kingdom
Environment/ecology, pp. 75-96
Carter, Jimmy, aspect, 75:2
coal aspect, 79:3, 80:2, 91:3
Congressional aspect, 79:5
dams/reclamation, 75:3
energy aspect—*see* Energy—environmental aspect
enforcement aspect, 76:6
fishing rights, 77:2
growth aspect, 76:3, 76:6
impact statements, 78:3
incentives, 76:4
industry aspect, 77:1, 80:4
interest in/acceptance of, 76:5, 80:3
life, threat to, 80:4
oil drilling, off-shore, 79:1
parks, 77:3

Environment/ecology *(continued)*
　pollution, 35:1, 76:6, 78:1
　　air, 79:3, 79:4, 94:3, 228:5
　　ozone layer, 80:5
　　water, 78:4, 78:5, 79:4
　　　Water Pollution Control Act, 77:1
　population, 78:2, 80:4, 289:3
　priorities/balance, 75:1, 79:2, 79:5
　resources/raw materials, 77:1, 78:1, 80:1
　strip mining, 79:1
　style/tone of movement, 77:4
　technological aspect, 76:2
　transportation aspect, 228:5
　　SST/*Concorde,* 229:2, 230:1, 232:2, 236:1
　water conservation, 75:3, 75:4
　See also Energy

Equal Rights Amendment (ERA)—*see* Women
Eritrea, 100:2, 249:5, 252:5
Eshkol, Levi, 331:1
Eskimos, 471:5
Ethiopia:
　Cuban aspect, 247:5, 268:5
　Eritrean aspect, 249:5, 252:5
　Libyan aspect, 255:6
　Somalian aspect, 249:5, 256:3
　Soviet aspect, 255:6
　U.S. aspect, 103:4, 248:7

Europe, pp. 302-323
　business aspect, 42:2
　civil-rights aspect, 18:4
　Communism, 306:1, 306:2, 307:6, 310:2, 312:2,
　　314:3, 315:3, 316:3, 322:1
　dance aspect, 432:4
　defense/military aspect, 187:2, 190:5, 195:1,
　　306:1, 314:5, 319:3
　　North Atlantic Treaty Organization
　　　(NATO)/Atlantic Alliance, 184:3, 186:1,
　　　187:3, 190:2, 195:1, 307:5, 310:1, 312:2,
　　　314:5, 317:1, 319:3, 319:5
　democracy in, 307:2
　Eastern Europe, 279:1
　　British aspect, 321:2
　　government aspect, 143:7
　　human-rights aspect, 107:4, 107:5
　　legitimacy, 314:2
　　U.S. aspect, 106:4, 107:5, 263:3
　economic aspect, 121:3, 313:1, 314:5, 321:3
　　Common Market/EEC, 272:2, 307:5, 308:3,
　　　309:1, 313:1, 313:3, 314:4
　　employment, 160:2
　　trade, foreign, 41:2
　　steel, 36:2
　foreign affairs/policy, 121:3
　　Africa, 250:5, 254:2

Europe *(continued)*
　foreign affairs/policy *(continued)*
　　Helsinki conference, 105:2, 105:5, 249:5,
　　　312:4, 320:6
　　immigration, 120:5
　　Malta, 315:4
　　Middle East, 312:1
　　New Zealand, 295:7
　　Soviet Union, 195:1, 306:1, 311:3, 312:1,
　　　323:1
　　United Nations, 308:3
　　U.S., 47:3, 229:2, 307:5, 309:3, 314:3, 315:3,
　　　321:4
　　　See also Eastern Europe, above
　judiciary courts, 176:1
　literature/books aspect, 377:2
　music aspect, 357:6
　oil aspect, 312:1, 315:3
　political aspect, 321:4
　religious aspect, 478:2
　unification/United States of, 307:5, 309:1
　See also specific countries
Evolution, 475:2
Experience, 470:5

F

Failure, 467:1, 474:4, 505:6
Family, the, 221:1, 222:3, 225:4, 242:3, 512:4,
　516:5, 517:1, 517:4, 517:5
Farming—*see* Agriculture
Fascism, 251:2, 252:4
Fashion, 406:2
Faulkner, William, 379:6, 406:6
Fear, 461:1
Federal Bureau of Investigation (FBI)—*see* Crime
Federal Reserve System—*see* Commerce—monetary
　system
Federalist Papers, The, 148:5
Fellini, Federico, 398:5, 418:5
Fiedler, Arthur, 166:4
Fiji, 116:1
Films—*see* Motion pictures
Finley, Charles O., 489:3
First, being, 457:4
Firsts, 466:1
Flynn, Errol, 399:2
Football, 415:4, 504:5, 506:6
　American Football Conference (AFC), 507:5
　coaching/coaches, 470:3, 492:6, 504:6
　college aspect, 494:1, 506:1
　entertainers, players as, 492:1, 497:7, 498:1, 505:3

Football *(continued)*
    fans, 494:2, 506:3
    free agents, 510:6
    infractions, player, 505:2
    kicking, 492:2, 496:1
    motivation, player, 500:6
    National Football Conference (NFC), 507:5
    National Football League (NFL), 61:3, 505:2, 510:6
    officiating, 506:3
    owners, 494:2
    player relationships, 490:5
    players, effect of time on, 497:3
    pride, player, 500:5
    Rozelle Rule, 510:6
    salaries, player, 494:2, 496:2, 510:5
    spiking/player antics, 492:6, 508:5
    Super Bowl, 492:1, 497:7, 498:5, 500:7, 505:3, 507:5, 508:3
    television aspect, 490:4, 505:3
        instant replays, 506:3
    violence, 487:5, 504:6, 505:3, 509:1, 509:5
    winning/losing, 498:5, 500:5, 504:2, 506:4, 507:1
    World Football League (WFL), 494:2, 508:6
Ford, Ford Madox, 382:2
Ford, Gerald R., 28:3, 206:5, 212:4, 213:1, 339:1, 365:5
Ford, John, 419:2
Foreign affairs/policy, pp. 97-128
    Agency for International Development, U.S., 126:4
    aid, foreign, 110:1, 117:4, 162:5
        military, 112:6, 118:2, 124:5
    alliances/commitments, 99:2, 346:2
    Ambassadors, 110:4, 111:2, 121:4
    arts aspect, 358:3
    assassinations, 107:7
    coexistence/confrontation, 97:1, 104:4, 109:5, 117:1
    cold war, 101:1, 303:3
    colonialism—*see* imperialism, below
    complexity, 101:1
    Congressional aspect (U.S.), 97:4, 105:3, 106:5, 108:1, 108:2, 109:4, 123:3, 137:4
    consistency/permanence aspect, 106:6, 111:6
    Council on Foreign Relations, 99:4
    defense/military aspect, 102:2, 183:3, 193:3
        arms sales, 103:1
    democracy, export of, 109:6
    detente, 97:1, 99:5, 109:2, 109:3, 117:1, 249:5, 294:5, 295:3, 296:4, 303:3, 345:1
    diplomacy, 110:3, 118:5, 120:1
    elections, foreign, 123:2
    elitism in, 99:4
    "Finlandization," 185:4

Foreign affairs/policy *(continued)*
    "hard"/"soft" aspect, 104:3
    high/low politics aspect, 115:5
    human-rights aspect, 97:1, 98:1, 100:3, 102:3, 102:4, 102:5, 103:2, 104:1, 104:4, 105:5, 106:2, 106:4, 106:6, 107:1, 107:4, 107:5, 108:3, 109:1, 109:3, 109:6, 110:2, 111:1, 112:1, 112:4, 113:2, 113:6, 115:1, 115:2, 115:3, 115:4, 117:2, 118:1, 119:3, 119:4, 120:3, 121:1, 122:1, 122:3, 122:4, 124:5, 242:2, 267:1, 297:6
    idealism, 101:4, 112:4
    immigration, 120:5
        Immigration and Naturalization Service, U.S., 105:4
        See also Labor—aliens, illegal
    imperialism/colonialism, 98:4, 100:2, 119:3, 124:6, 248:3, 265:3, 272:4, 284:2, 304:5, 465:1
    influence, U.S., 97:3, 97:5, 100:1, 101:3, 112:5, 121:3
    Information Agency, U.S., 117:5, 126:4
        Voice of America, 106:3, 119:1, 121:2, 302:4
    intelligence/spying, 127:3, 194:5, 473:1
        abuses, 127:2, 202:1
        budget, 128:2
        Central Intelligence Agency (CIA), U.S., 126:1, 126:2, 126:4, 127:4, 128:4, 133:1
            abuses, 202:1
            Chilean aspect, 127:1, 127:5
            Jordanian aspect, 334:5
        cover, 126:4
        foreign assistance, 128:4
        importance/necessity of, 126:2, 126:4
        job is to know, 126:3, 128:1
        journalists, use of, 126:4, 127:4
        military aspect, 194:5
        secrecy aspect, 127:1, 127:5, 128:3, 128:4
        Soviet/Chinese aspect, 127:3
        See also Crime—intelligence
    interdependence, 97:2, 99:3, 113:1, 263:1, 471:4
    intervention/involvement, foreign, 112:6, 118:2
    motivation in, 111:5
    negotiations, 101:2, 105:2, 107:6, 112:2, 121:6, 123:4
    non-alignment, 107:3, 315:4
    North-South aspect, 116:2, 121:3, 124:3
    oil aspect, 112:3
    organizations, international, 119:2
    paper tiger, 293:1
    Peace Corps, U.S., 126:4, 196:2
    policeman of world, 112:4, 113:3
    Presidential aspect (U.S.), 108:2, 109:4, 123:5
    prestige aspect, 118:1
    reciprocity, 99:5

Foreign affairs/policy *(continued)*
  recognition of governments, 117:2, 117:4
  secrecy aspect, 110:3, 112:2, 124:1
  security, national, 99:3
  self-help aspect, 107:3
  small countries, 118:3
  sphere of influence, 263:1
  State, U.S. Dept. of, 97:4, 115:5, 124:1
  State, U.S. Secretary of, 111:3
  terrorism—*see* Crime
  unfriendly nations, relations with, 103:4, 104:2,
    106:1, 114:1
  See also specific countries; Third World; United
    Nations
France:
  arts center, Paris, 354:4
  characteristics, personal, 322:3
  civil-rights aspect, 18:4
  commerce/business aspect, 29:3
  Communism/socialism, 307:3, 310:2, 312:1,
    312:2, 315:2, 315:3, 316:3
  Concorde SST, 110:4, 229:2, 230:1, 232:2, 236:1
  democracy, 309:4
  foreign affairs/policy:
    Africa, 246:1, 261:3
      South Africa, 254:1
    Saudi Arabia, 324:2
    Soviet Union, 307:3, 312:2, 315:3
    U.S., 309:4, 315:6
      Concorde SST aspect, 229:2, 230:1, 232:2,
        236:1
    Vietnam, 299:2
  government, 303:2
  medicine/health aspect, 393:2
  motion-pictures aspect, 405:1
  railroads, 235:3
Frankenheimer, John, 446:4
Freedom/liberty, 14:1, 15:2, 16:2, 24:2, 38:2, 45:2,
  101:4, 101:5, 120:5, 165:3, 196:5, 471:3, 477:2
  See also Democracy; Foreign affairs— human rights
Friedan, Betty, 514:1
Fuel—*see* Energy—oil

G

Gable, Clark, 410:3
Galileo Galilei, 481:2
Gandhi, Indira, 288:6, 295:6, 296:1, 297:2, 298:1
Garbo, Greta, 410:3, 411:5
Garment, Leonard, 357:5
Garroway, Dave, 410:1
Gasoline—*see* Energy—oil

General Motors Corp. (GM), 165:4
George, Gorgeous, 487:2
Germany, Nazi, 164:5
Germany, West, 309:4
  Berlin, 315:5, 319:4
  economic aspect, 170:1
  foreign affairs/policy, 121:3
    Saudi Arabia, 324:2
    Soviet Union, 319:4
    U.S., 250:4, 315:5
  gasoline aspect, 91:1
  medicine/health aspect, 394:3
  railroads, 235:3
  terrorism, 319:2
Gibson, Hoot, 434:7
Gielgud, John, 401:2
Giscard d'Estaing, Valery, 312:2
God—*see* Religion
Godfrey, Arthur, 410:1
Gold, Herbert, 374:2
Goldberg, Rube, 146:1
Goldwyn, Samuel, 400:2, 414:1
Golf, 492:5, 500:1, 503:1
  concentration, 509:6
  fans, 504:1
  money aspect, 496:5
  putting, 492:3
  women, 487:1
Gorme, Eydie, 422:3
Government, pp. 129-149
  abuses, 16:4
  accountability/responsibility, 129:2, 133:5
  appointments/confirmation, 130:4, 133:3, 138:2,
    141:1, 144:1, 203:1, 205:2
  attention of, getting, 130:5
  businessmen in, 140:3, 209:5
  competent/compassionate, 132:4
  distractions, 129:1
  divided, 140:5
  domination/power/doing too much, 14:4, 130:7,
    134:3, 144:3, 145:2, 146:1, 146:4, 147:5,
    148:6
  efficiency, 136:3, 139:5
  employees, number of, 132:4
  ethics/honesty, 133:2, 135:1, 135:6, 137:1,
    139:3, 206:1
    lying, 143:6
  greed aspect, 130:2
  idealism, 201:1
  leadership, 131:2
  leaving office, 111:3, 144:2
  length of service in, 129:5
  limousines, 132:4
  Management and Budget (OMB), Federal Office of,
    129:3

Government *(continued)*
  Management and Budget, Office of *(continued)*
    See also Politics—Lance, Bert, affair
  openness, 137:5, 203:1
  passion aspect, 135:3
  planning, 139:6
  press coverage—*see* Journalism
  public attitude toward, 133:1, 133:2, 134:3, 135:1, 137:1, 140:4, 140:6, 141:5, 142:4, 145:2, 146:1, 147:1, 148:2, 148:6, 222:5
  regulations, 15:2, 16:2, 130:3, 131:4, 137:2, 140:6, 145:6, 146:1, 146:2
    See also Commerce—government
  reorganization of, 139:5, 141:2, 141:3
  revenue-sharing, 149:1, 212:2, 241:4
  royalty aspect, 132:4
  separation of powers, 138:1, 176:2
  servants of the people, 132:5, 145:5
  size/growth/bureaucracy, 130:6, 133:5, 136:2, 137:2, 138:4, 145:3, 145:6
  spending/budget/costs, 136:4, 137:2, 138:4, 139:1, 140:1, 144:3, 144:4, 145:6, 146:1, 146:3, 151:4, 153:1, 157:4, 164:6, 171:5, 202:1, 225:5, 242:2
    debt, 144:4
    deficit spending, 158:2
    Presidential aspect (U.S.), 153:4
    zero-based budgeting, 141:3
  staff size, 135:7
  State of Future address, 139:6
  state/local, 137:4, 137:5, 145:1, 149:1, 225:7, 239:2, 239:3, 239:6, 240:1, 240:2
    Governors, 130:1, 209:3
    Mayors—*see* Urban affairs
  temporarily in office, 136:1
  transition, 14:5
  See also specific countries; Congress, U.S.; Politics; Presidency, U.S.; Vice-Presidency, U.S.
Governors—*see* Government—state/local
Grass, Gunter, 377:2
Gray, L. Patrick, 217:6
Great Britain—*see* United Kingdom
Greece, 307:1
  ancient Athens, 471:3
  Communism, 315:3
  democracy in, 314:4
  foreign affairs/policy, 317:1
    Common Market/EEC, 314:4
    Cyprus, 306:3, 317:1
    NATO, 317:1, 319:5
    Soviet Union, 315:3
    Turkey, 306:3, 319:5
    U.S., 317:1
  politics, elitism in, 317:2
    left, 317:1

Greed, 130:2, 470:4
Greene, Graham, 377:1
Grenada, 116:1
Guatemala, 280:4
Guinea, 361:4
Guinness, Alec, 404:2
Gulf Oil Corp., 518:4
Guyana, 270:3

H

Hackman, Gene, 408:3
Haiti, 267:5
Hammerstein, Oscar, II, 429:2
Happiness, 458:6, 462:2, 462:6, 464:1, 465:7, 469:2, 472:2, 473:2
Harriman, W. Averell, 115:5
Hawaii, 239:1
Hayes, Helen, 434:7
Health—*see* Medicine
Hearst, Patty, 381:4
Height, 467:6
Helms, Richard, 127:5
Hemingway, Ernest, 377:2, 377:5, 379:6, 460:4
Hepburn, Katharine, 402:5
Heraclitus, 458:5
Heroes, 470:7
History, 71:3, 468:5, 474:5
Hitchcock, Alfred, 406:2, 417:4
Hitler, Adolf, 164:5, 343:5
Ho Chi Minh, 55:2
Hockey:
  California *Golden Seals,* 494:2
  coaching/coaches, 491:6
  fans, 494:2
  National Hockey League (NHL), 494:2
  owners, 494:2
  salaries, player, 494:2, 502:6
  ticket prices, 502:6
  violence, 498:6, 511:1
  World Hockey League (WHL), 502:6
Hogan, Ben, 492:3
Hollywood—*see* Motion pictures
Homosexuality, 18:2, 19:5, 20:3, 470:2
Hope, Bob, 460:2
House of Representatives, U.S.—*see* Congress, U.S.
Housing—*see* Social welfare
Houston (Texas), 153:6
Human nature, 467:5
Human rights—*see specific countries;* Foreign affairs
Humor, 309:2, 318:1, 465:5, 467:2, 467:3, 473:6, 474:1, 475:1

Humor *(continued)*
　　See also Motion pictures—comedy; Television—
　　　　comedies
Hungary, 312:1
Hunter, Catfish, 487:3
Hussein I, 337:5

I

Identity, 464:5, 468:4, 471:2
Ideology, 469:3
Image, 476:4
Imports/exports—*see* Trade, foreign
India:
　　conditions in, 291:2, 296:1
　　Congress Party, 290:6, 291:1, 296:1, 297:2
　　democracy in, 288:6, 290:6, 291:1, 295:5, 295:6,
　　　　296:1, 298:1
　　economic aspect, 290:6, 291:2
　　elections, 290:6, 291:1, 295:6
　　emergency, state of, 290:6, 291:2, 295:6, 297:2,
　　　　298:1
　　foreign affairs/policy, 289:1, 289:2
　　　　Britain, 288:6
　　　　China (mainland), 289:1
　　　　Pakistan, 285:2, 289:2, 292:1
　　　　Soviet Union, 285:2, 289:1, 289:2, 292:1,
　　　　　　297:5
　　　　U.S., 285:2, 289:1, 292:1, 295:5, 295:6, 297:5
　　population, 289:3
　　woman Prime Minister, 513:4
Indian Ocean, 252:3, 347:2
Indians, American—*see* Civil rights
Individuality/uniqueness, 466:8, 473:5
Indonesia, 295:2
Inflation—*see* Economy
Insurance—*see* Judiciary; Medicine; Transportation—
　　automobiles
Integrity, 470:1
Intellectuals, 464:4
Intelligence—*see* Crime; Foreign affairs
International Bank for Reconstruction and Develop-
　　ment (World Bank), 119:2, 293:6
Iran:
　　foreign affairs/policy, 344:3
　　　　Africa, 256:3
　　oil aspect, 90:4, 96:2
Iraq:
　　foreign affairs/policy:
　　　　Israel, 334:2
　　　　Soviet Union, 341:3
　　　　U.S., 103:4

Iraq *(continued)*
　　press aspect, 361:4
Ireland, 315:1
Isaiah, 140:2
Israel, pp. 324-344
　　Arabs living in, 327:3
　　defense/military aspect, 334:3, 337:4, 338:6
　　existence, right of, 327:1
　　foreign affairs/policy:
　　　　borders/frontiers, 328:1, 328:2, 329:3, 331:1,
　　　　　　332:2, 336:4, 338:2, 339:1, 339:2, 339:4,
　　　　　　342:2
　　　　Britain, 326:3
　　　　Egypt, 329:4, 331:2, 333:3, 339:4, 339:5
　　　　　　Sadat visit—*see* Middle East—Sadat
　　　　guarantees, peace/security, 325:3, 328:1,
　　　　　　331:3, 338:2, 339:4, 341:1
　　　　Iraq, 334:2
　　　　Jordan, 329:4, 331:2, 333:2, 336:1, 337:5,
　　　　　　340:2
　　　　Lebanon, 333:2, 336:1
　　　　occupation of Arab land—*see* Middle East—
　　　　　　Israel
　　　　Palestinians, 324:4, 326:3, 327:2, 331:2,
　　　　　　332:3, 335:5, 336:1, 338:1, 339:1, 341:2
　　　　recognition, 332:1, 339:4
　　　　Romania, 317:3
　　　　settlements/expansionism, 326:4, 334:1,
　　　　　　335:3, 336:1, 341:1, 342:1
　　　　Soviet Union, 341:3
　　　　Syria, 326:5, 329:4, 331:2, 333:2, 336:1
　　　　U.S., 84:1, 105:3, 324:1, 324:5, 326:2, 326:5,
　　　　　　329:4, 329:6, 331:3, 334:5, 335:1, 337:1,
　　　　　　338:6, 339:1, 339:2, 340:3, 341:2, 342:2,
　　　　　　343:2, 343:4, 343:5, 344:1
　　future, 325:6
　　Holocaust, 343:5
　　Jerusalem—*see* Middle East
　　Labor Party, 342:3
　　Likud Party, 335:1, 342:2, 342:3, 343:4
　　self-confidence, 336:2
　　woman Prime Minister, 513:4
Italy:
　　Christian Democratic Party, 302:2, 312:2
　　coalition government, 302:2, 312:2
　　Communism/socialism, 302:2, 307:3, 310:2,
　　　　312:1, 312:2, 315:3, 316:3, 316:4, 317:4,
　　　　321:6, 322:4
　　economic aspect, 310:1, 317:4, 321:6
　　foreign affairs/policy:
　　　　Libya, 312:1
　　　　NATO, 310:1, 312:2
　　　　Soviet Union, 307:3, 315:3
　　　　U.S., 250:4, 317:4
　　gasoline aspect, 91:1

Italy *(continued)*
    motion-pictures aspect, 402:4, 412:3
    railroads, 235:3
    Rome, 303:1
    women's rights, 514:3

J

Jackson, Reggie, 507:6
Jamaica:
    Cuban aspect, 266:5
    foreign dependency, 273:5
    problems, 274:2
    socialism, 274:1
Japan:
    aerospace aspect, 483:1
    baseball, 499:4
    business aspect, 42:2
    defense/military aspect, 290:5, 297:4, 299:3
    democracy in, 295:4
    economic aspect, 295:4
    foreign affairs/policy, 121:3, 297:3, 297:4
        China (mainland), 297:4, 299:3, 300:5, 321:5
        Saudi Arabia, 324:2
        Soviet Union, 297:4, 299:3, 300:5, 321:5
        United Nations (UN), 348:3
        U.S., 288:1, 294:2, 294:5, 297:4, 299:3,
            300:2, 321:5
    housing, 221:2
    Meiji Restoration, 471:3
    population, 289:3
    trade, foreign, 41:2, 45:3, 300:5
        steel exports, 36:2
Jefferson, Thomas, 38:1, 118:1, 132:3, 138:3, 355:1
Jobs—*see* Labor—employment
Johnson, Jack, 487:2
Johnson, Lyndon B., 217:6
Jordan, 336:3
    Israeli aspect, 329:4, 331:2, 333:2, 336:1, 337:5,
        340:2
    Palestinian aspect, 329:5, 335:2
    Syrian aspect, 326:5
    U.S. aspect, 334:5
Journalism/press/news media, pp. 359-372, 465:1
    banking, coverage of, 46:4
    bias/objectivity, 359:1, 363:1, 365:1, 368:1,
        368:5, 369:1, 372:1
    bigness/power of, 359:3, 362:2, 368:3, 369:2,
        371:5
    broadcast, 369:1
        anchor position, 359:2, 361:3, 362:3, 367:2,
            454:3

Journalism/press/news media *(continued)*
    broadcast *(continued)*
        anchor position *(continued)*
            woman, 371:3
        courts aspect, 178:2
        entertainment/show business aspect, 359:2,
            362:4, 370:2
        Fairness Doctrine/equal time, 367:8, 368:2,
            369:2, 450:4
        formality of, 366:6
        local/network aspect, 370:2, 371:5
        newspapers compared with, 362:5
        personalities, 359:5, 367:2, 371:2
        ratings, 362:4, 371:5
        silence aspect, 366:2
        technological aspect, 359:2
    business coverage/aspect, 37:4, 46:4, 49:1
    cartoons/comics, 360:4, 361:1
    catastrophes, coverage of, 364:5
    columns, 365:2
    conflicts of interest, 364:3
    crime, coverage of, 364:1, 364:4, 366:5
    criticism of, 363:7, 369:2
    excesses, 363:4
    foreign systems, 361:4
    freedom of press, 14:1, 122:4, 362:2, 368:3,
        370:1
    giving what customer doesn't want, 365:4
    glamorous aspect, 363:5
    government, coverage of, 14:5, 137:5, 360:2,
        360:3, 361:2, 361:5, 363:2, 364:3, 366:3,
        366:4, 367:6, 368:2, 368:4, 369:2, 369:3,
        370:1
        Congress, TV coverage of, 137:3
        Presidential news conferences (U.S.), 365:5
        Presidential Press Secretary (U.S.), 365:5
        See also politics, below
    independence, 127:4
    informed citizenry, 367:7
    intelligence/spying, foreign, 126:4, 127:4
    investigative, 363:5, 367:5
    judiciary/courts, coverage of, 174:5, 178:2, 180:2
        gag rules, 368:2
    language, abuse of, 374:3
    literature/books compared with, 381:2
    magazines, 376:6, 454:3
        postal rate, 375:5
    meaning of events, finding the, 370:3
    newspapers, 363:1, 363:7, 364:2, 365:3
        broadcast compared with, 362:5
        change, 450:3
        competition, 371:1
        educational aspect, 367:3
        group ownership/chains, 361:5, 363:3, 367:1,
            370:1, 370:4, 371:1

Journalism/press/news media *(continued)*
  newspapers *(continued)*
    personality of, 363:6
    personnel, new breed of, 362:1
    postal rate, 375:5
    quality aspect, 360:1
    readers, 366:1
    rough draft of history, 369:4
    technological aspect, 362:1
  politics, coverage of, 203:5, 207:3, 218:1, 367:8
    Watergate, 363:5
    See also government, above
  repressed aspect, 366:3
  science, coverage of, 486:1
  self-correcting nature, 369:1
  sensationalism, 365:3
  soporific, 365:3
  sources, unnamed, 371:4
  technological aspect, 359:2, 362:1
  newspapers:
    Los Angeles Times, 372:1
    New York Times, The, 359:4, 370:4, 372:1, 375:7
    Tucson Daily Citizen, 371:1
    Wall Street Journal, The, 502:3
    Washington Post, The, 369:4, 372:1
  magazines:
    Collier's, 376:6
    Liberty, 376:6
    Life, 376:6
    Look, 376:6
    New Yorker, The, 373:2
    Saturday Evening Post, The, 373:2, 376:6
    Thoroughbred, 376:4
    TV Guide, 417:5, 455:5
Joyce, James, 378:1, 379:6, 400:7, 460:4
Judaism/Jews—*see* Religion
Judges—*see* Judiciary
Judiciary/courts, pp. 174-180
  bad system, 180:3
  British, 176:1
  caseload/amount of litigation, 174:6, 176:1, 176:4, 180:1
  citizens' courts, 176:5
  civil/criminal aspect, 178:5
  Code of Federal Regulations, U.S., 174:5
  complexity, 175:4
  Constitution, interpretation of, 178:1
  cumbersome aspect, 53:2
  democracy aspect, 175:2, 179:2
  ethics/corruption, 174:5, 178:3
  European, 176:1
  grand jury, 174:5
  insurance, no-fault, 174:3
  judges, 175:4, 176:2, 177:2

Judiciary/courts *(continued)*
  judges *(continued)*
    corrupt, 178:3
    recruitment of, 179:3
  Justice, U.S. Dept. of/Judicial Branch, 135:7, 174:5, 178:5
  lawyers, 174:3, 175:4, 179:3, 180:1
    advertising by, 174:2, 175:1, 177:1, 177:4
    business aspect, 178:4, 179:4
    disassociated, 177:3
    fees, 176:5, 177:1
    public attitude toward, 178:2, 178:3, 180:2
  mechanism, 175:3
  politically moderate, 174:4
  prejudicing of rights, 174:5
  press/TV aspect, 174:5, 178:2, 180:2
    gag rules, 368:2
  prosecutors, 146:4
  public attitude toward, 179:1
    See also lawyers, above
  sentencing, 52:3
  Supreme Court, U.S.:
    function, 176:2
    law-enforcement rulings, 58:1
    secret deliberations, 179:5
  swift/certain justice, 53:2
  tax returns, access to, 178:5
  trial delays, 180:3
  See also Law
Jung, Carl, 515:1

K

Kael, Pauline, 407:6
Keaton, Buster, 401:5, 437:3
Kelley, Clarence M., 53:5
Kennedy, John F., 152:6, 154:5, 201:4, 211:4, 214:2, 275:5, 281:3, 424:5
Khrushchev, Nikita S., 316:2
King, Martin Luther, Jr., 103:2, 199:5
Kissinger, Henry A., 116:3, 212:4, 340:1
Kleindienst, Richard G., 217:6
Kneisel, Franz, 423:6
Knowledge, 464:3
Korea (general):
  Chinese (mainland) aspect, 285:3
  Korean war, 292:4
  uncertain life, 292:4
  U.S. aspect, 285:3
Korea, North, 187:5, 286:2, 288:3, 292:4, 294:3, 295:3, 298:2, 298:5, 300:3, 301:2
Korea, South:
  economic aspect, 286:2, 288:4, 294:3

Korea, South *(continued)*
  foreign affairs:
    China (mainland), 288:3
    Korea, North, 295:3, 298:5
    Romania, 317:3
    Soviet Union, 288:3
    U.S., 290:4, 295:3
      Park, Tongsun, affair—*see* Politics
      troop withdrawal, 187:5, 285:4, 286:1, 286:2, 288:3, 288:5, 292:4, 294:3, 298:2, 298:3, 298:5, 300:3, 300:4, 301:2
      Vietnam, 286:2
  human-rights aspect, 121:1, 289:5, 301:2
  religious aspect, 292:4
Kuhn, Bowie, 494:3

L

Labor:
  aliens, illegal, 153:5, 153:6, 161:4, 162:1, 162:5, 265:4, 267:4, 273:2, 273:3
  big labor, 14:4
  collective bargaining, 162:2, 164:3, 167:2
  Congressional aspect (U.S.), 173:3
  employment/unemployment/jobs, 33:4, 41:1, 48:1, 140:1, 144:3, 150:3, 151:2, 151:3, 152:7, 153:1, 153:5, 153:6, 154:3, 156:2, 156:3, 156:4, 157:3, 158:4, 159:1, 159:6, 160:2, 161:5, 162:3, 163:2, 164:1, 165:5, 166:2, 167:4, 169:1, 169:3, 169:4, 170:3, 170:4, 171:5, 172:1, 172:5, 204:4, 227:4, 465:1
  crime aspect, 159:2, 161:5, 169:1, 226:2
  Europe, 160:2
  placement, 167:3
  public-service jobs, 161:2, 163:3, 163:6, 212:2, 222:3
  schools masking of, 72:4
  subsidies to business for, 160:2
  See also work, below; Civil rights—employment
  International Labor Organization (ILO), 160:5, 163:4
  management aspect, 154:4, 157:5
  retirement, 152:5, 154:1, 157:2, 158:6, 159:4, 163:5, 165:2, 165:4, 166:4, 167:1, 168:4, 221:4, 462:6, 464:2
  safety/health aspect, 151:1, 163:1
  strikes, 150:1, 157:4, 164:3, 182:3
    food stamps/welfare aspect, 158:1, 220:1, 224:2
  time-oriented work, 150:4

Labor *(continued)*
  unions/organized labor, 154:4, 157:4, 158:1, 158:3, 160:4, 162:2, 164:3, 164:4, 165:1
    AFL-CIO, 155:2, 164:1, 172:3, 172:4, 173:3
    conservatism of, 155:3, 164:5
    conventions, 171:2
    militancy, 155:3
    military unions—*see* Defense
    public-employee unions, 172:2
    railroad aspect, 229:1
    right-to-work laws, 164:4
    teacher unions, 70:2
  useless jobs, 473:1
  wage, minimum, 158:5
  work, 159:2, 159:5, 221:4, 222:1, 222:5, 460:2, 465:7, 468:2, 474:2
    See also employment, above
  working at capacity, 470:3
Laetrile—*see* Medicine—cancer
Lancaster, Burt, 416:2
Lance, Bert—*see* Politics
Laos:
  human-rights aspect, 121:1
  press aspect, 361:4
  U.S. aspect, 114:1
Latin America—*see* Americas
Laugerud (Garcia), Kjell, 280:4
Laurel, Stan, 401:5
Law:
  answer, single, 177:2
  aspirations expressed by, 180:4
  fundamental right, 255:2
  teaching/students, 174:1, 176:3
  See also Judiciary
Lawrence, Jacob, 353:5
Lawrence, Steve, 422:3
Lawyers—*see* Judiciary
Lebanon, 116:1, 333:2, 336:1
Lenin, Vladimir I., 98:5, 116:4, 124:6, 292:6, 316:4
Levi, Edward H., 212:4
Liberalism—*see* Politics
Libya:.
  democracy in, 255:4
  foreign affairs/policy:
    Egypt, 248:7
    Ethiopia, 255:6
    Italy, 312:1
    Soviet Union, 341:3
    Sudan, 248:7, 255:6
Life, 459:1, 465:3, 465:4, 466:3, 467:1, 468:2, 469:4, 471:2, 472:3, 473:3, 474:2, 476:5, 478:1, 478:4
Lincoln, Abraham, 132:3, 209:5, 218:1, 281:3
Linowitz, Sol M., 269:4, 280:5
Lippmann, Walter, 35:1

Literature/books, pp. 373-382
  accessibility, 375:1
  anger/seriousness of, 375:3
  best sellers/selling aspect, 376:5, 381:4
  cartoons, 379:3
  critics/reviews, 375:7, 376:4, 376:5, 379:1, 380:7,
    381:3
  dissent aspect, 380:2
  elitist, 375:1
  entertainment aspect, 378:3
  Europe, 377:2
    Britain, 381:3
  freedom of expression, 373:4
  headlines as subject, 381:4
  important issues as subject, 375:6
  Latin America, 381:2
  libraries, 382:3
  motion-pictures aspect, 373:1, 409:4
  novels/fiction, 373:5, 374:5, 375:3, 375:4, 375:6,
    378:5, 380:6, 381:4, 382:2, 435:4
  permanence of, 380:5
  poetry/poets, 355:2, 374:3, 380:6, 382:1, 382:2
  political aspect, 381:2, 466:6
  postal rate, 375:5
  press compared with, 381:2
  publishing, 373:4, 376:2, 380:4
  reading, 375:1
  sex aspect, 378:3, 381:4
  Southern (U.S.) aspect, 374:4
  squalor as subject, 375:2
  stage/theatre compared with, 380:5, 435:4
  success in, 376:1
  television compared with, 378:2
  unhappiness aspect, 381:2
  U.S. aspect, 375:3, 377:2, 381:3, 382:2
  Westerns, 376:3
  writing/writers/authors, 404:6, 463:3
    acting compared with, 380:1
    anonymity, 474:6
    betterment of, 381:3
    cartoonists compared with, 379:3
    central character, writer as, 375:4
    communication, means of, 373:5
    competitive aspect, 374:2
    conceit/the best, 378:4
    confidence, 380:3
    experience, 379:6
    fame, 379:5
    first books, 380:7
    freelance, 376:6
    guidance for readers, 378:1
    importance of, 380:1
    interests of writer, 381:4
    interviews, 374:1
    male/female aspect, 515:1

Literature/books *(continued)*
  writing/writers/authors *(continued)*
    newness aspect, 377:1
    personality as writer, 376:5
    political aspect, 466:6
    publishers, dealing with, 376:2
    readings, 374:1
    recognition, 380:4
    rejections, 373:2
    safety valve, 378:2
    same as other people, 378:5
    singularity aspect, 374:2
    solitude aspect, 375:8
    Southern (U.S.) aspect, 374:4
    talking about, 374:6
    technique, 377:5, 379:2, 381:1
    thinking through fingers, 373:3
    U.S. aspect, 374:4, 377:2
    volume/output, 373:2, 377:3, 377:4, 380:6
  titles:
    Bridges at Toko-Ri, The, 406:6
    Buck Rogers, 379:3
    Crime and Punishment, 375:4
    Dick Tracy, 379:3
    Fan Club, The, 381:4
    Love Story, 379:4
    Man and the Monster Image, 412:4
    Moby Dick, 380:5
    Out Our Way, 379:3
    Peanuts Jubilee, 379:3
    Popeye, 379:3
    Roots, 375:8, 376:1
    Terry and the Pirates, 379:3
    Wash Tubbs, 379:3
Litton Industries, Inc., 518:4
Logic, 471:1
Lombardi, Vince, 470:3
Loner, being a, 458:1
Louis, Joe, 487:2, 508:1
Love, 459:5, 466:7
Loy, Nanni, 402:4
Lubitsch, Ernst, 401:5, 407:5
Lunt, Alfred, 410:2, 434:7

M

Madison, James, 148:5
Magazines—*see* Journalism
Mailer, Norman, 381:3
Malaysia, 105:3
Malcolm X, 469:3
Malta, 315:3, 315:4

Mao Tse-tung, 55:2, 292:6, 348:2
Marine Corps, U.S.—*see* Defense
Marriage, 476:6, 512:4
Marti, Jose, 266:1
Martin, Mary, 433:2
Marx Brothers, 411:5
Marx, Karl, 100:2, 124:6, 173:2, 292:6, 316:4, 481:5
Materialism, 475:5
Mature, Victor, 416:2
Maturity, 471:5
Maugham, Somerset, 196:5
Mauritius, 116:1
Mayer, Louis B., 410:3, 414:1
Mayors—*see* Urban affairs
Mays, Willie, 507:3
Mazursky, Paul, 401:5
McCarthy, Joseph, 204:3
McGovern, George S., 173:3
McQueen, Steve, 401:3
Mead, Margaret, 166:4
Meany, George, 155:2, 172:4
Media, the, 472:5
    See also specific media
Medicine/health, pp. 383-397
    abortion, 387:1, 389:2, 391:3, 394:4, 470:2, 514:3
    advertising, 177:4
    age aspect, 385:3, 391:4
    alcohol, 53:1, 386:3, 388:2, 393:3, 396:3, 473:7
    animal testing, 390:2, 391:2, 394:2, 397:2, 397:3
    cancer, 384:2, 388:4, 388:6, 389:6, 390:2, 391:1, 391:2, 392:3, 392:4, 394:2, 396:3, 397:2, 397:3
        laetrile, 385:2, 386:4, 390:3
    chemicals/additives, 390:2, 390:4, 396:3
        Delaney law, 391:2, 397:3
        saccharin, 389:1, 392:3, 394:2, 397:2, 397:3
    "coldness" of, 395:2
    communicable diseases, 393:3
    costs, 384:4, 385:1, 386:1, 387:2, 391:5, 393:5, 395:2, 395:3, 395:4, 465:1
    developing countries aspect, 393:1
    diet, 383:1
    doctors/physicians, 221:3, 383:2, 384:4, 385:3, 386:2, 387:4, 389:3
        patient relationship, 383:4, 394:3, 395:2
    drug abuse (medical aspect):
        amphetamines, 388:2
        barbiturates, 384:1, 388:2
        heroin, 389:4, 390:1
        LSD, 388:2
        marijuana, 53:1, 388:1, 388:2, 390:1
        stabilization, 388:2
        See also alcohol, above; Crime—drugs
    drugs, approval of, 388:3, 397:1

Medicine *(continued)*
    euthanasia, 391:3
    Food and Drug Administration (FDA), U.S., 387:6, 388:3, 391:2, 394:2, 396:1, 397:1, 397:3
    foreign aspect, 394:3
        Britain, 388:3, 393:2, 394:3
        Canada, 388:3, 393:2, 393:3
        France, 393:2
    future, 383:2, 395:2
    government aspect, 384:4, 385:1, 387:1, 387:6, 388:3, 390:5, 393:2, 393:5, 394:3, 395:2
    handicapped, 383:5, 386:5
    health care, 225:5
    Health, Education and Welfare (HEW), U.S. Dept. of, 131:4, 131:5
    hospitals, 384:4, 387:2, 387:4, 393:5, 395:3
    an industry, 386:2
    insurance, health/medical, 172:3, 226:1, 384:4, 387:2, 388:5, 390:5
        Kennedy-Corman plan, 385:1
    life-style aspect, 387:3, 393:3
    loneliness aspect, 392:1
    malpractice, 394:1
    mental health/psychiatry, 384:3, 392:5, 393:4
        television aspect, 450:5
    pharmacists, 395:1
    prevention, 389:5
    progress in, 387:5
    protein, 383:1
    research, 392:2
    schools, medical, 385:3
    senility, 391:4
    smoking, 53:1, 383:3, 385:4, 388:2, 388:4, 396:3
    socialized, 384:4
    stress, 396:2
    surgery:
        cardiac, 395:3
        unneeded, 387:4, 394:1
    U.S. aspect, 383:1, 387:5, 388:3, 394:3
    Vitamin C, 485:3
    volunteerism, 384:3
Meir, Golda, 324:3, 331:1, 339:5
Merman, Ethel, 433:2
Mexico, 161:4, 265:4, 267:4, 273:2, 273:3
Michener, James A., 406:6
Michigan, 211:6
Middle East, the/Arabs, pp. 324-344
    Balfour Declaration, 327:2
    boycott, 324:2, 337:3
    Communism, 326:5
    demilitarized zone, 325:3
    foreign affairs/policy:
        Africa, 250:5
        Europe, 312:1

Middle East, the/Arabs *(continued)*
  foreign affairs/policy *(continued)*
    Geneva conference, 324:4, 329:1, 329:3, 335:5, 336:3, 338:4, 339:4, 341:3, 343:1
    Soviet Union, 326:5, 328:2, 330:5, 332:5, 336:3, 341:3, 347:2
    United Nations, 325:3, 329:6, 330:5, 332:3, 343:2
    U.S., 324:2, 325:4, 326:2, 328:3, 329:3, 329:4, 330:3, 331:5, 331:6, 336:3, 337:2, 338:6, 339:1, 340:3, 342:2, 342:3
    Gaza, 331:1, 331:2, 335:2
    Golan Heights, 340:2, 340:3
    Israel, Arab advantages over, 325:6, 333:5
    Israeli occupation of Arab land, 324:4, 325:1, 325:3, 328:2, 329:3, 332:1, 332:4, 333:5, 334:3, 335:2, 335:5, 339:4, 341:1, 342:1, 342:2
    Jerusalem, 325:2, 331:1, 334:4
    oil aspect, 81:5, 82:3, 84:1, 91:2, 91:3, 92:5, 94:5, 112:3, 312:1, 333:5, 339:3
    "open diplomacy," 331:5
    Sadat trip to Israel, 324:3, 325:2, 326:1, 327:4, 327:5, 327:6, 329:2, 330:2, 330:3, 332:5, 333:1, 335:3, 335:4, 336:1, 336:5, 340:4, 341:3, 343:3, 344:2
    Sharm el Sheikh, 330:5
    Sinai, 340:2, 340:3
    Suez Canal, 340:2
    war aspect, 326:2, 333:2, 333:3
    West Bank, 326:4, 331:1, 331:2, 332:4, 334:1, 335:1, 335:2, 335:3, 337:5, 340:2, 342:1
    Zionism, 327:2, 334:2, 342:2, 343:2
  See also specific countries; Palestine
Military—*see* Defense
Milton, John, 377:1
Minnelli, Vincent, 411:1
Mitchell, John N., 213:3
Mix, Tom, 434:7
Mobutu Sese Seko, 248:7, 261:2
Modesty, 460:5
Moliere, Jean Baptiste, 439:1
Mondale, Joan, 355:1, 357:5
Mondale, Walter F., 246:1, 259:4
Monetary system—*see* Commerce
Money—*see* Commerce—monetary system; Wealth
Morality, 15:4, 448:1, 470:2, 472:5, 473:7
Mostel, Zero, 439:2
Motion pictures/films/cinema, pp. 398-420, 433:1, 452:1
  art aspect, 419:2
  audience, 398:2, 407:1, 407:6, 409:1, 415:3, 415:5, 416:3, 418:5, 419:4, 449:4, 458:7
    young, 399:1, 405:5
  authenticity/realism, 404:1

Motion pictures/films/cinema *(continued)*
  awards/"Oscar," 403:4, 407:1, 410:5, 420:2
  bad films, 417:2
  Bond, James, films, 417:4
  boring films, 407:6
  British aspect, 417:4
  business/corporate aspect, 402:4, 413:3
  carnival aspect, 399:1
  characters, 398:2
  collaborative aspect, 405:1, 408:3, 419:2
  comedy, 401:4, 401:5, 406:1, 411:5, 413:2, 455:4
  committees involved in, 409:2
  conception, 398:3
  cost aspect, 399:1, 406:5, 412:3, 420:2
  creating a world, 401:1
  crime aspect, 418:6
  critics/reviews, 398:5, 410:2, 412:2, 415:4, 419:2, 441:4
  directing/directors, 398:1, 399:5, 400:1, 400:2, 400:3, 406:5, 411:1, 411:2, 411:4, 413:5, 416:7, 417:3, 417:6, 418:3, 419:2
    auteurs, 405:1, 408:3, 418:2
    comedy, 401:5
  disaster films, 398:2, 402:4
  editing, 401:4, 403:3
  elitism, 407:6
  entertainment aspect, 412:1, 416:1, 419:4, 420:6
  exposition, 416:6
  fashion designing for, 406:2
  "firsts," 400:7
  French aspect, 405:1
  guessing-game aspect, 420:4
  heroes, 416:2
  Hollywood, 401:3, 405:7, 410:3, 410:5, 411:1, 414:1, 416:2, 417:5, 437:5, 447:4, 455:4, 461:3, 462:5
  House Un-American Activities Committee, 414:1
  importance of, 419:2
  influence of, 408:2, 409:6, 418:3, 418:6
  Italian aspect, 402:4, 412:3
  length, 401:4, 403:3
  literature/books aspect, 409:4
  logic aspect, 409:3
  meaning of film, 398:5
  Metro-Goldwyn-Mayer, Inc., 420:3
  moguls, 414:1
  money/box-office aspect, 401:3, 402:4, 408:4, 413:3, 457:3
  morality aspect, 420:6
  Motion Picture Association of America (MPAA), 454:2
  music for, 405:6, 406:6
  National Association of Theatre Owners (NATO), 401:5

Motion pictures/films/cinema *(continued)*
  old days/Golden Years, 403:6, 420:3
  parody, 417:4
  political aspect, 402:4, 414:1, 414:2
  pornography/sex/violence, 400:5, 405:5, 408:2,
    409:5, 409:6, 410:3, 413:4, 415:1, 418:6,
    420:7, 449:3, 465:1, 475:1
  positiveness, 416:2
  preparation, 413:5
  producing/producers, 400:2, 404:4, 419:3
  reality compared with, 418:5
  romantic aspect, 413:3
  schools, 406:4, 418:3
  screenwriting/scripts, 373:1, 398:4, 400:4, 402:5,
    403:6, 404:3, 406:4, 406:6, 407:4, 408:5,
    408:6, 409:4, 410:4, 411:2, 413:5, 415:6,
    417:3, 440:4, 447:4
  silent/sound aspect, 418:1
  small/low-budget films, 402:4, 403:1
  stage/theatre compared with, 401:6, 407:1, 412:6,
    412:7, 413:5, 417:1, 434:7, 435:6, 437:5,
    439:4, 440:4, 440:6, 441:3, 441:5
  story/plot, 400:7, 416:6
  success in, 402:3, 408:4, 409:1, 420:4
  television aspect, 445:4, 449:3, 454:2
  television compared with, 402:1, 410:1, 416:4,
    446:4, 449:4, 451:3, 454:3, 455:4
  television, made for, 399:1, 442:3, 443:5
  television, shown on, 449:3
  treachery aspect, 410:5
  tying society together, 402:6
  U.S. aspect, 405:1, 412:3, 414:4, 417:4, 418:5
  visual aspect, 406:4, 410:4
  women/women's roles, 402:5, 403:5, 403:7,
    407:4, 407:5, 411:2, 417:3
  films:
    Birdman of Alcatraz, 451:3
    Birth of a Nation, 401:5
    Black Sunday, 404:4, 418:5
    Bridges at Toko-Ri, The, 406:6
    Casanova, 398:5
    Chinatown, 404:4
    Citizen Kane, 409:1
    Deep, The, 418:5
    Dog Day Afternoon, 475:1
    Gigi, 411:1
    Godfather, The, 404:2, 415:5
    Gold Rush, The, 401:5
    Gone With the Wind, 505:3
    Great Northfield Minnesota Raid, The, 404:2
    Greed, 401:5
    Jaws, 415:5
    Last Voyage, The, 416:6
    Navigator, The, 401:5
    Network, 448:4

Motion pictures/films/cinema *(continued)*
  films (continued)
    Scenes from a Marriage, 476:2
    Seconds, 446:4
    Star Wars, 409:1, 415:5
    Sunshine Boys, The, 475:1
  See also Acting
Mozambique:
  Communism/Marxism, 259:1
  foreign affairs/policy:
    Cuba, 247:5
    Rhodesia, 246:5
    U.S., 248:7
  press aspect, 361:4
Mozart, Wolfgang Amadeus, 356:5, 429:4
Museums—*see* Arts
Music, pp. 421-430
  acoustics, 428:1
  audience, 421:1, 421:3, 422:1, 422:5, 423:2,
    427:4, 427:5
    See also opera, below
  celebration of life, 466:3
  cello, 427:4
  clarinet, 424:2
  classical, 423:2
  composing/composers/songwriting, 424:3, 425:2,
    425:3, 425:6, 429:2
  concerts, cost of, 422:1
  conducting/conductors, 424:1, 425:2, 425:5,
    426:6, 428:3, 429:1
  contemporary/today, 424:4, 427:2, 427:6
  country music, 422:4, 426:1
  critics/reviews, 381:3, 421:3
  emotion, 427:6
  European aspect, 357:6
  individuality, 423:6
  meaning of, 425:5
  for motion pictures, 405:6, 406:6
  a mystery, 424:1
  opera:
    audience, 422:2, 423:5, 428:2, 429:5
    financial aspect, 421:4, 426:4, 440:5
    greatest art, 425:1
    love of, 428:5
    luxury item, 427:1
    Metropolitan Opera, New York, 421:4, 426:4,
      440:5
    popularity of, 429:5
    singing/singers, 422:2, 423:1, 426:3, 426:5,
      428:2, 429:3, 429:4
    U.S. aspect, 423:5, 433:2
  orchestras, 423:3, 425:2, 426:6, 428:3
  piano, 356:5, 423:4, 424:5, 427:5, 430:2, 462:3
  politicians, playing for, 424:5
  prodigy, 428:4

Music *(continued)*
    radio aspect, 422:3
    records, 422:3, 429:3
    rock-and-roll, 422:3, 423:2, 424:4, 430:3
    routine, becoming, 424:1
    sensible, 430:3
    singing/singers, 421:1, 421:2, 422:5, 424:6, 425:4,
        427:4, 430:1
        See also opera, above
    violin, 423:4, 423:6, 426:2

N

Nabokov, Vladimir, 460:4
Namath, Joe, 490:4
Namibia, 246:4
Nasser, Gamal Abdel, 324:3, 333:3
Natural gas—*see* Energy
Navy, U.S.—*see* Defense
Negroes—*see* Civil rights—blacks
Neto, Agostinho, 252:6
New York (N.Y.), 239:3, 239:4, 239:5, 239:6
    blackout, 95:2, 220:5, 224:5, 226:2
    See also Stage
New Zealand, 295:7
Newman, Paul, 401:3, 414:2
News media—*see* Journalism
Newspapers—*see* Journalism
Nimeiry, Jaafar, 255:6
Nixon, Richard M., 207:4, 211:4, 214:2, 217:6,
    372:1, 376:5, 424:5
    abuses, 16:4
    civil-rights aspect, 23:3, 28:3
    ethics, 266:4
    Korea, 294:3
    Presidential power, 148:4
    press aspect, 368:2
    Watergate aspect, 203:3, 205:5, 207:1, 213:2,
        213:3, 213:4, 213:5, 216:2, 216:3
Northern Ireland, 315:1
Norway, 91:1
Nuclear power—*see* Energy

O

O'Hara, John, 373:4
Ohio State University, 498:1
Oil/energy industry, 81:1, 81:2, 84:1, 84:4, 88:2,
    89:2, 89:5, 95:3

Oil/energy industry *(continued)*
    divestiture, 37:5, 38:1, 40:4, 81:2
    See also Energy—oil
Okinawa, 294:5
Olympic Games—*see* Sports
Opera—*see* Music
Orantes, Manuel, 491:7
Oswald, Lee Harvey, 474:6
Otis, Amos, 505:7

P

Pacific—*see* Asia
Paine, Thomas, 103:2
Painting—*see* Arts
Pakistan:
    democracy in, 301:3
    foreign affairs:
        India, 285:2, 289:2, 292:1
        Soviet Union, 292:1
        U.S., 285:2, 292:1
Palestine/Palestinians, 325:1, 325:3, 328:2, 331:6,
    333:5, 334:2, 334:4, 338:4, 339:2, 347:6
    Israeli aspect, 324:4, 326:3, 327:2, 331:2, 332:3,
        335:5, 336:1, 338:1, 339:1, 341:2
    Jordanian aspect, 329:5, 335:2
    PLO/Yasir Arafat, 326:3, 327:2, 331:2, 332:3,
        336:3, 338:1, 341:3
    state/homeland, 326:5, 329:5, 331:1, 332:4,
        336:3, 337:5, 339:1, 339:4, 340:3, 342:2
    Syrian aspect, 329:5
    U.S. aspect, 341:2
Palmer, Arnold, 492:3
Panama/Panama Canal:
    Communism, 280:3, 281:3
    foreign affairs/policy:
        Belize, 280:4
        Cuba, 269:2, 274:6, 277:3, 279:5, 281:2,
            281:3
        Guatemala, 280:4
        Soviet Union, 269:2, 274:6, 277:2, 277:3,
            279:5, 281:2
        U.S./treaties aspect, 263:4, 263:5, 265:1,
            265:2, 265:3, 267:3, 267:7, 268:1, 268:2,
            269:2, 269:4, 269:5, 270:1, 270:2, 270:4,
            270:5, 272:3, 272:4, 273:1, 274:5, 274:6,
            275:3, 276:1, 276:3, 277:2, 277:3, 277:5,
            278:2, 279:1, 279:5, 280:1, 280:2, 280:3,
            280:5, 281:1, 281:2, 281:3, 281:4, 283:5,
            284:2, 284:4, 518:3
Paris (France), 18:4, 354:4
Park Chung Hee, 292:4, 301:2

Park, Tongsun—*see* Politics
Parties, political—*see* Politics
Pascal, Blaise, 473:1
Patriotism, 182:2, 476:3
Paul VI, Pope—*see* Religion—Catholicism
Pauling, Linus, 485:3
Peace—*see* War/peace
Peace Corps, U.S.—*see* Foreign affairs
Perbisch, Raul, 264:3
Perfection, 458:7, 473:2
Performing arts, the, pp. 398-462
    See also Acting; Dance; Motion pictures; Music;
        Radio; Stage; Television
Personal profiles, pp. 457-463
Peru, 275:1
Philippines:
    martial law, 294:4
    U.S. aspect, 290:4, 294:4, 297:1
Philosophy, pp. 464-477
Photography—*see* Arts
Pinza, Ezio, 430:1
Pippin, Horace, 353:5
Plato, 424:4
Poetry—*see* Literature
Poland, 308:1, 321:3
Police—*see* Crime
Politics/elections, pp. 201–219
    addiction to, 205:4
    advertising aspect, 207:3
    Agnew scandal of 1973, 201:2
    Baptist, election of, 201:4
    business, contributions by, 36:4
    charisma, 211:4
    coalition, 201:5
    conservatism/right, 136:2, 139:2, 206:2, 210:2,
        215:1, 215:2, 217:1, 518:3
    debates, candidate, 367:8
    elder statesman, 206:3
    elections:
        1976- 137:2, 203:1, 213:1
        1984- 212:1
    Electoral College, 201:5, 203:2, 215:3
    ethics/corruption, 204:2
        guilt by accumulation, 204:3
    financing, public, 203:2, 214:3, 218:1, 218:5
    foreign elections, 123:2
    franking privilege, 211:5
    fuzziness aspect, 202:5
    humor aspect, 217:5
    idealism, 201:1
    Lance, Bert, affair, 45:1, 133:3, 203:6, 204:1,
        204:3, 205:2, 205:3, 208:1, 209:5, 215:5,
        216:4, 218:2, 372:1
    League of Women Voters, 367:8
    liberalism/left, 23:5, 136:2, 139:2, 172:3, 203:4,

Politics/elections *(continued)*
    liberalism/left *(continued)*
        206:2, 210:2, 215:1, 216:5
    losing, 213:1
    Park, Tongsun, affair, 209:2, 214:4, 287:3
    parties:
        monopoly of power, 201:5
        opposition party, 14:5
        President, support of, 143:5
        purpose of, 215:4
        third, 215:2
        two-party system, 209:1, 218:3
        See also specific parties and specific countries
    passion in, 307:2, 314:4
    power, 218:4
    press/TV aspect, 203:5, 207:3, 218:1, 367:8
    public-relations imagery, 207:3
    registration, voter, 202:3, 203:2, 210:1
    retirement from, 211:2
    Southern (U.S.) aspect, 208:2, 210:3, 214:1
    ugliness of, 210:4
    uncommitment, climate of, 217:6
    untruth, insensitivity to, 212:3
    Watergate, 16:4, 133:1, 177:3, 203:1, 203:3,
        205:5, 206:6, 207:1, 207:5, 208:6 212:4,
        213:2, 213:4, 213:5, 216:2, 216:3, 217:2,
        218:5, 222:5, 363:5, 472:4
    See also Government
Pollution—*see* Environment
Population—*see* Environment
Porter, Katherine Anne, 382:2
Portugal:
    African aspect, 246:1
        Angola, 261:3
    Communism/socialism, 308:4, 310:2, 320:2
    democracy in, 320:3
Postal Service/mail, U.S., 129:4, 182:3
    book/newspaper/magazine rate, 375:5
Pound, Ezra, 374:3
Poverty/poor—*see* Social welfare
Power, Tyrone, 399:2
Presidency/Executive, U.S., 130:1, 140:4
    appointments by, 130:4, 138:2, 144:1, 205:2
        See also Government—appointments
    budget aspect, 153:4
    Cabinet, 129:3, 132:1, 132:2, 132:4, 133:4,
        147:4, 160:1
    Congressional aspect, 131:3, 134:1, 137:3, 138:3,
        139:4, 140:5, 142:5, 143:5, 148:4, 205:2,
        206:6, 208:2, 208:3, 214:2, 216:1
    detail work, 142:2
    difficulties of, 134:1
    ethics, 135:6
        violations of law, 143:2
    fallibility, 132:3

Presidency/Executive *(continued)*
    Federal Reserve System aspect, 168:3
    foreign-affairs aspect, 108:2, 109:4, 123:5
    leadership aspect, 205:1, 208:5
    openness of, 132:1
    party support of, 143:5
    on pedestal, 143:7
    popularity, 209:3
    power, 137:3, 148:4
    press aspect:
        news conferences, 365:5
        Press Secretary, 365:5
    staff size, 132:4, 135:7
    television aspect, 137:3, 447:1
    term, length of, 133:6
    Vice-Presidential aspect, 142:2, 142:3
    wanting to be President, 217:4
    woman as, 513:2, 514:4
Presley, Elvis, 74:1
Press—*see* Journalism
Prison—*see* Crime
Productivity—*see* Economy
Profits—*see* Commerce
Proust, Marcel, 378:1
Providence (R.I.), 202:3
Puccini, Giacomo, 429:4
Puerto Rico, 263:2, 278:3, 278:4

Q

Qaddafi, Muammar el-, 255:6, 312:1
Quebec—*see* Canada

R

Rabin, Yitzhak, 331:1, 339:5
Racism—*see* Civil rights
Radio, 422:3, 446:5, 450:4, 452:1, 455:1
Railroads—*see* Transportation
Ransom, John Crowe, 382:2
Reagan, Ronald, 217:1
Redford, Robert, 380:1, 401:3, 413:3, 414:2
Reliance, self-, 462:7, 471:2
Religion, 292:4, 355:3, pp. 478-482
    abandonment of, 480:8
    African aspect, 482:1
    Asian aspect, 482:1
    atheism, 480:6
    Bible, the, 478:3, 479:2, 483:6

Religion *(continued)*
    black aspect, 480:2
    Catholicism:
        Pope Paul VI, 480:4, 480:5, 514:3
        the Vatican, 480:4, 514:3
    change/reforms, 480:4, 481:1
    Christianity, 479:1, 479:3, 481:2, 482:1
        Christ, Jesus, 478:3, 480:4, 480:7, 481:5
    diversity, 478:2
    European aspect, 478:2
    freedom of, 122:4, 479:1, 482:1
    God, 466:3, 478:4, 479:2, 479:3, 479:4, 480:1,
        481:2, 483:6
    Judaism/Jews, 336:2, 343:5, 468:5, 481:5
        Zionism—*see* Middle East
    Latin-American aspect, 482:1
    meaning-of-life aspect, 478:1, 478:4
    mission of, 481:4
    organized, 480:1
    origin-of-universe aspect, 483:6
    personal aspect, 479:2
    problems, dealing with one's, 480:3
    religiosity, 481:3
    science/technology aspect, 480:8, 481:2, 483:6
    social activism, 478:3
    Soviet aspect, 480:6
    state, separation of church and, 479:1
    truths, permanent, 479:3
    U.S. aspect, 478:2
    women priests, 480:7
Renoir, Jean, 402:4
Republican Party (U.S.), 204:5, 206:2, 207:1, 211:3,
    215:4, 219:2
    blacks in, 211:6
    broader base, 209:1, 211:6, 214:5, 215:2
    business aspect, 209:1, 219:1
    losses/existence/comeback, 209:1, 211:1, 217:3
    new faces in, 207:4
    social-welfare aspect, 226:1
    soul, party without, 217:3
Restlessness, 469:5
Retirement—*see* Labor
Revenue-sharing—*see* Government
Rhee, Syngman, 292:4
Rhode Island, 202:3
Rhodesia, 253:2, 253:4
    chrome exports, 247:4
    economic aspect, 257:1
    foreign affairs/policy:
        Angola, 256:5
        Botswana, 256:5
        Britain, 253:3, 256:4, 256:5, 257:1, 257:3
        Canada, 282:4
        Mozambique, 256:5
        Romania, 317:3

Rhodesia *(continued)*
    foreign affairs/policy *(continued)*
        sanctions, 249:1, 282:4
        South Africa, 248:6, 253:5, 254:1
        Tanzania, 256:5
        United Nations, 249:1, 282:4
        U.S., 113:4, 246:4, 247:4, 248:6, 250:2,
            253:5, 256:4, 257:3, 258:3
            Young, Andrew, aspect, 250:2
        Zambia, 256:5
    Patriotic Front, 256:5, 259:1
    racial/black aspect, 250:2, 254:1, 256:5, 257:2,
        257:3, 259:2
        majority rule/one-man, one-vote, 246:4, 247:4,
            248:6, 249:6, 251:1, 253:1, 253:3, 253:5,
            254:4, 254:5, 256:4, 257:5, 258:3, 258:6
        whites, 256:5, 257:4
Richardson, Ralph, 401:2
Right and wrong, 466:5
Robbins, Jerome, 460:4
Robinson, Frank, 493:3
Rockefeller, Nelson A., 173:3
Romania, 317:3
Rome (Italy), 303:1
Roosevelt, Franklin D., 18:4, 134:1, 171:5, 214:2,
    270:2, 275:5, 281:3
Rosi, Francesco, 402:4
Russia—*see* Soviet Union

S

Saccharin—*see* Medicine—chemicals
Saudi Arabia, 336:3, 338:5
    foreign affairs/policy:
        France, 324:2
        Germany, West, 324:2
        Japan, 324:2
        Somalia, 248:7
        Soviet Union, 248:7
        U.S., 324:2
    press aspect, 361:4
Scandinavia, 394:3
Schlesinger, James R., 212:4
Schools—*see* Education
Science/technology, 15:1, pp. 483-486
    access aspect, 485:2
    amorality of, 355:3
    computers, 485:1
    disappearing ways of life, 484:3
    educational aspect, 485:5
    environmental aspect, 76:2
    genetics, 483:3

Science/technology *(continued)*
    information explosion, 486:2
    optimists, technological, 486:3
    origin-of-universe aspect, 483:6
    press coverage of, 486:1
    public understanding of, 484:1, 485:5
    religious aspect, 480:8, 481:2, 483:6
    research, 485:1
    scientists, 485:3, 486:2
    Soviet aspect, 304:1, 322:2
    telephone system, 484:2
    women, 485:4
    See also Space
Scofield, Paul, 401:2
Scola, Ettore, 402:4
Seaver, Tom, 494:3
Selznick, David O., 400:2
Senate, U.S.—*see* Congress, U.S.
Sentimentality, 461:3
Seychelles, 252:2, 252:3, 255:5
Sex—*see* Literature; Motion pictures—pornography;
    Television—violence/sex; Stage
Shakespeare, William, 377:1, 380:1, 414:2
Shaw, George Bernard, 166:4, 459:1, 460:4
Sills, Beverly, 460:4
Simon, Neil, 435:1
Simpson, O. J., 403:4, 490:4, 498:4
Sinatra, Frank, 460:2
Singapore, 105:3
Singlaub, John K., 187:5
Sirica, John, 208:6
Skelton, Red, 443:3
Smith, Adam, 35:1, 173:2
Smith, Ian, 249:6, 251:1, 253:2, 253:3, 253:4, 253:5,
    254:4, 254:5, 256:4
Smoking—*see* Medicine
Snead, Sam, 492:3, 509:6
Social Security System, U.S.—*see* Social welfare
Social welfare, pp. 220-227
    Democratic Party (U.S.) aspect, 226:1
    elderly/aged, 221:3, 223:3, 224:6, 385:3, 391:4
    Family Assistance Program, 223:5
    food stamps, 223:4
        for strikers, 158:1, 220:1
        See also welfare, below
    housing, 221:2, 224:6, 225:5
        Federal Housing Administration (FHA), 240:4,
            242:1
        Housing and Urban Development (HUD), U.S.
            Dept. of, 240:4
    income-security system, 221:5
    isolationism, 23:6
    life cycle, distribution of, 221:4
    nursing homes, 223:3
    poverty/poor, 18:2, 23:6, 202:1, 220:5, 222:1,

Social welfare *(continued)*
   poverty/poor *(continued)*
      222:2, 222:4, 224:4, 224:5, 225:8, 226:2,
      226:3, 227:1, 227:4, 470:1, 477:4
   Republican Party (U.S.) aspect, 226:1
   Social Security System, U.S., 166:4, 167:1, 202:1,
      209:3, 213:2, 220:3, 220:4, 221:4, 222:5,
      223:1, 223:2, 224:1, 225:1, 225:2, 226:4,
      227:2
   wealth, redistribution of, 222:4
   welfare, 159:6, 161:2, 163:3, 172:1, 209:3,
      220:2, 222:3, 223:5, 224:1, 225:3, 227:3,
      239:6
      eligibility for, 221:5, 222:1, 224:2
      Federal aspect, 224:3, 225:6, 225:7, 225:8
      for strikers, 224:2
        See also food stamps, above
Socialism, 98:4, 124:6, 160:4, 168:1, 170:2, 182:5,
   304:2, 304:5, 305:4, 465:1
   See also specific countries; Communism
Socrates, 464:3
Somalia:
   Ethiopian aspect, 249:5, 256:3
   Saudi Arabian aspect, 248:7
   Soviet aspect, 248:7, 256:2
   U.S. aspect, 103:4, 256:2
Sondheim, Stephen, 429:2
South (U.S.), 14:2, 32:4, 203:6
   civil-rights aspect, 21:4, 164:4, 246:1
   political aspect, 208:2, 210:3, 214:1
   writers, 374:4
South Africa:
   economic aspect, 261:4
   foreign affairs/policy:
      Angola, 248:2
      Britain, 282:4
      Canada, 250:3, 282:4
      Cuba, 254:1
      France, 254:1
      Rhodesia, 248:6, 253:5, 254:1
      Romania, 317:3
      sanctions/boycott/embargo, 98:1, 246:3,
      249:2, 254:2, 254:3
      United Nations, 246:3
      U.S., 98:1, 113:4, 246:1, 246:2, 248:1, 248:2,
      248:6, 248:7, 249:2, 249:3, 252:7, 253:5,
      254:2, 254:3, 257:6, 258:5, 259:3, 259:4
      Young, Andrew, aspect, 245:5, 250:2
   government, legitimacy of, 261:4
   multinational country, 259:6
   racial/black/apartheid aspect, 245:2, 246:3, 248:1,
      249:2, 250:2, 251:5, 252:7, 254:2, 254:3,
      255:1, 255:2, 257:6, 258:1, 258:2, 258:5,
      259:3, 259:5, 259:6, 347:6
      homelands, 247:2, 259:4

South Africa *(continued)*
   racial/black/apartheid aspect *(continued)*
      majority rule/one-man, one-vote, 245:5, 246:1,
      246:2, 250:3, 259:4
      white aspect, 245:3, 247:1, 249:3, 261:4
   sports aspect, 497:5
   Olympics, 259:5
Soviet Union/Russia/U.S.S.R., 304:5
   arts/culture aspect, 357:3
      dance, 431:5
      stage/theatre, 439:6
   Communism, 314:1, 322:1, 348:1
   Constitution, 305:1
   defense/military aspect, 118:2, 118:4, 185:1,
      191:1, 191:4, 192:2, 303:4, 304:3, 305:3,
      311:2, 311:3, 312:3, 314:1, 314:2, 318:2,
      322:1, 322:2, 323:1, 345:3, 345:4, 346:2
      Air Force: *Backfire* bomber, 198:2
      civil defense, 188:5, 196:4
      Navy, 191:3, 197:1
      test moratorium, 182:5
      U.S. aspect, 97:5, 181:2, 181:3, 183:1, 183:3,
      183:4, 184:2, 185:3, 186:1, 186:2, 186:3,
      186:5, 187:1, 187:3, 189:2, 189:3, 189:4,
      191:3, 191:5, 192:3, 192:4, 192:5, 193:1,
      193:2, 193:3, 194:6, 195:3, 196:1, 196:4,
      197:1, 197:4, 198:2, 198:3, 198:4, 199:2,
      347:3
   democracy in, 318:2
   economic aspect, 312:3, 322:1, 322:2
      employment/work, 304:1, 322:5
   foreign affairs/policy, 116:2, 117:1, 117:3, 118:2,
      312:1
      Africa, 118:2, 245:4, 251:2, 252:6, 252:7,
      255:6, 262:1, 268:5, 312:1, 322:1, 347:2
      Angola, 1'18:2, 251:4, 252:6, 312:1
      Ethiopia, 255:6
      Seychelles, 252:3, 255:5
      Somalia, 248:7, 256:2
      Sudan, 255:6
      Zaire, 251:4, 255:6
      Asia, 299:3
      China (mainland), 285:3, 286:3, 287:2,
      289:1, 289:6, 296:4, 298:4, 300:5,
      301:1, 323:1
      India, 289:1, 289:2, 292:1, 297:5
      Japan, 297:4, 299:3, 300:5, 321:5
      Korea, South, 288:3
      Pakistan, 292:1
      Vietnam, 287:4
      Canada, 271:2, 282:4
      Cuba, 267:2, 268:5, 274:3, 274:6
      detente, 109:2
      domination of world, 113:5, 116:4, 314:2
      Europe, 195:1, 306:1, 311:3, 312:1, 323:1

Soviet Union/Russia/U.S.S.R. *(continued)*
  foreign affairs/policy *(continued)*
    Europe *(continued)*
      Berlin, 319:4
      Czechoslovakia, 312:1
      France, 307:3, 312:2, 315:3
      Greece, 315:3
      Hungary, 312:1
      Italy, 307:3, 315:3
      Malta, 315:3
    immigration, 120:5
    imperialism, 100:2
    Indian Ocean, 252:3, 347:2
    influence, 97:5, 98:4, 105:1
    intelligence/spying, 127:3
    Latin America, 347:2
    loyalty, 100:2
    Middle East, 326:5, 328:2, 330:5, 332:5, 336:3, 341:3, 347:2
      Algeria, 341:3
      Egypt, 255:6, 340:1, 341:3
      Iraq, 341:3
      Israel, 341:3
      Libya, 341:3
      Saudi Arabia, 248:7
      Syria, 330:5, 341:3
      Yemen, South, 341:3, 361:4
    negotiations, 101:2, 123:4
    Panama, 269:2, 274:6, 277:2, 277:3, 279:5, 281:2
    Third World/developing countries, 100:2, 116:2
    U.S., 98:5, 100:4, 104:3, 105:3, 109:2, 109:5, 113:5, 114:1, 115:3, 116:2, 119:4, 120:2, 121:5, 122:2, 252:6, 285:3, 287:2, 292:1, 295:3, 296:4, 298:4, 301:1, 312:3, 314:2, 316:2, 339:4, 345:3, 346:1, 347:2, 347:3
      internal affairs, interference in, 98:3, 100:3, 104:1, 107:4, 302:1, 302:4, 304:3, 307:4, 311:1, 312:4
      trade, 111:1, 106:2, 263:3, 274:4
      See also defense, above
    war/peace, 346:1, 346:3, 348:1, 349:3, 349:4
  freedom of speech in, 464:4
  government turnover, 320:1
  human-rights aspect, 97:1, 100:3, 101:4, 101:5, 104:1, 104:4, 106:2, 115:3, 119:4, 302:1, 304:3, 304:4, 305:1, 307:4, 311:1, 312:4, 318:2, 320:6, 322:5
    dissidents, 107:4, 302:3, 302:4, 304:2, 318:4, 319:1, 515:5
  medicine/health aspect, 394:3
  Presidency of, 305:2
  press aspect, 361:4
  propaganda against, 305:4

Soviet Union/Russia/U.S.S.R. *(continued)*
  religious aspect, 480:6
  technology/science aspect, 304:1, 322:2
Space, 345:2
  budget, 483:1, 483:4
  life, extraterrestrial, 484:4
  NASA, 483:4, 486:4
  safety valve for earth, 483:2
  Spaceship Earth, 483:5
  UFOs, 486:4
Spain, 339:3
  Communism/socialism, 310:3, 315:3, 316:3, 320:5
  democracy/elections/freedom in, 313:4, 316:1, 320:4
  foreign affairs/policy:
    Soviet Union, 315:3
    U.S., 316:1
  terrorism, 320:4
  Union of Democratic Center, 320:5
Speech, freedom of, 14:1, 122:4, 464:4
Sports, 357:6, pp. 487-511
  amateur aspect, 493:4, 498:1
  black aspect, 487:4
  Canadian aspect, 488:3, 493:4
  charisma, player, 488:1
  education/school/college aspect, 61:3, 63:4, 66:5, 498:1
  entertainment aspect, 490:2, 498:4, 505:4
  fans, 501:2, 505:4
  integral part of society, 503:2
  Olympic Games:
    cost, 488:3, 493:4
    International Olympic Committee (IOC), 488:3
    Montreal, 488:3, 493:4
    political aspect, 497:4
    South African aspect, 259:5
  reflects society, 489:1
  salaries, player, 488:1
  South African aspect, 259:5, 497:5
  strife, internal, 505:4
  television aspect, 498:4
  See also specific sports
Sri Lanka, 513:4
Stage/theatre, 407:3, pp. 431-441, 448:4
  Arena Stage, Washington, 438:4
  audience, 407:1, 417:1, 418:1, 431:1, 433:3, 433:4, 434:5, 435:6, 437:1, 438:4, 440:1, 490:2
  awards/"Tony," 433:4, 438:6
  British aspect, 433:2, 436:3, 439:5
  bullfights compared with, 435:6
  consciousness of times, 431:2
  critics/reviews, 433:5, 439:6, 441:4

Stage/theatre *(continued)*
  directing/directors, 417:6, 431:1, 433:3, 438:2, 439:4
  drama, 434:5
  an event, 438:4
  experimentation, 432:1
  fabulous invalid, 441:3
  financial/money/cost aspect, 436:4, 438:4, 438:7
    public investment, 438:5
    subsidies, 432:2, 439:5, 440:5
  government aspect, 432:2, 438:7, 440:5
  "Hey, rube!" aspect, 433:4
  immediacy aspect, 431:1
  institutional/non-profit, 438:7, 439:5, 440:5
  literature/books compared with, 380:5, 435:4
  Long Wharf Theatre, New Haven, 438:4
  mediocrity, 436:3
  mime, 437:2, 437:3
  motion pictures compared with, 401:6, 407:1, 412:6, 412:7, 417:1, 434:7, 435:6, 437:5, 439:4, 440:4, 440:6, 441:3, 441:5
  musicals, 432:1, 433:2, 434:5, 439:2
    rock, 438:1, 439:3, 441:1
  national theatre, 436:3, 439:5
  New York/Broadway, 417:6, 432:1, 432:2, 433:5, 437:5, 438:4, 438:5, 438:6, 438:7, 439:6, 490:2
    Off-Broadway, 431:3
  playwrighting/playwrights, 380:4, 431:1, 435:1, 435:4, 436:3, 440:3, 440:4, 447:4
  producing/producers, 438:3
  proscenium, 436:2
  reflection of lives, 433:1
  rehearsal, 435:1
  repertory, 436:1
  revivals, 437:5, 439:2
  sex, 434:1
  smaller plays, 438:4
  Soviet aspect, 439:6
  style, 439:1
  success, 433:5
  television aspect, 441:3, 449:3, 451:2
  U.S. aspect, 432:2, 433:2, 436:3, 439:5
  plays:
    A Chorus Line, 424:3, 438:1, 441:1
    Annie, 44:1
    Fiddler On the Roof, 431:3
    Gypsy, 429:2
    Hamlet, 441:5
    King and I, The, 431:3
    Music Man, The, 439:2, 439:3
    My Fair Lady, 439:2, 439:3
    Oliver, 441:1
    West Side Story, 432:1
  See also Acting

Stalin, Josef, 100:2, 197:5, 308:4, 310:2
Standard of living—*see* Economy
Stanwyck, Barbara, 403:4
Steel industry:
  Europe, 36:2
  imports/exports, 32:5, 36:2
  Japan, 36:2
  prices, 39:3
Steinbeck, John, 44:1, 373:4
Steinem, Gloria, 514:1
Stevens, Wallace, 380:6
Stock market—*see* Commerce
Stokowski, Leopold, 166:4
Strategic Arms Limitation Talks (SALT)—*see* Defense —arms control
Stravinsky, Igor, 427:6, 431:5
Streisand, Barbra, 405:7, 413:3
Strikes—*see* Labor
Stroheim, Erich von, 402:4
Success, 311:4, 457:1, 459:4, 460:2, 460:4, 460:7, 462:4, 462:8, 465:7, 466:8, 470:6, 474:6, 476:2, 505:6
Sudan:
  Egyptian aspect, 255:6
  Libyan aspect, 248:7, 255:6
  Soviet aspect, 255:6
  U.S. aspect, 248:7
Sullivan, Ed, 443:3
Supreme Court—*see* Judiciary
Swann, Lynn, 490:4
Sweden, 91:1, 417:5
Switzerland, 394:3
Syria, 326:1, 336:3
  Israeli aspect, 326:5, 329:4, 331:2, 333:2, 336:1
  Jordanian aspect, 326:5
  Palestinian aspect, 329:5
    PLO, 341:3
  Soviet aspect, 330:5, 341:3

T

Tanzania, 248:7, 256:5
Tarkenton, Fran, 498:4
Taxes, 136:4, 138:4, 139:1, 144:3, 145:6, 146:1, 149:1, 151:6, 152:3, 157:1, 158:4, 170:4, 172:2, 204:4, 220:4, 223:1, 223:2, 225:2, 226:4, 227:2
  business deductions, 43:2
  capital gains, 155:4, 171:3
  court access to returns, 178:5
  cut/reduction in, 154:5, 167:4, 172:5, 220:3
  energy aspect—*see* Energy
  incentives, 161:3, 165:5

Taxes *(continued)*
    Internal Revenue Service (IRS), U.S., 16:4
    loopholes, 154:2
    rebate—*see* Economy—rebate
    urban/cities aspect, 239:6, 240:1, 242:1
Tchaikovsky, Leopold, 431:5
Technology—*see* Science
Telephone system, 484:2
Television (TV), 357:6, 429:5, pp. 442-456
    addiction/audience-time aspect, 442:6, 447:3, 448:3, 449:5
    American Broadcasting Cos. (ABC), 452:4, 454:2, 498:4
    anthologies, 442:4
    audience, 448:2, 452:4, 452:5, 455:5, 456:1, 456:2
    awards/"Emmy," 444:2
    a babysitter, 449:4
    British aspect, 446:1
    cancellations, 443:2
    censorship, 450:6, 451:1
        pressure groups, 445:2, 447:2, 450:7, 452:5, 453:1, 455:5
        self-regulation, 454:4
    closeness aspect, 442:2, 454:1
    Columbia Broadcasting System (CBS), 442:1, 452:3, 454:2
    comedies, 443:5, 444:3, 451:2, 455:4
    community service/"open time" aspect, 455:2
    Congress (U.S.), coverage of, 137:3
    courts, coverage of, 178:2
    crime aspect, 445:3
        capital punishment, televising of, 57:2
    criticism of, 452:1, 452:4
    cultural aspect, 448:2
    directing/directors, 417:6
    drama, 443:1, 444:3, 445:5
    early years, 443:6
    educational aspect, 485:1
    entertainment aspect, 443:3
    executives, 442:1, 447:5, 480:1
    experimentation/innovation, 453:3, 456:1
    exposure on, 451:3
    family aspect, 446:2, 446:5, 450:6, 452:4
    "family hour," 450:7
    financial/profit aspect, 442:3, 445:2, 448:4, 454:5, 455:2
    future, 443:7, 450:3
    good life, image of, 220:5
    government regulation/control, 444:1, 450:6, 454:4, 455:1
        Federal Communications Commission (FCC), 445:4, 450:4, 455:2, 455:3
    half-step behind viewers, 456:2
    literature/books compared with, 378:2

Television (TV) *(continued)*
    mental-health aspect, 450:5
    monster that eats performers, 448:6
    morality aspect, 448:1
    most-used medium, 449:3
    motion-pictures aspect, 445:4, 449:3, 454:2
    motion pictures compared with, 402:1, 410:1, 416:4, 446:4, 449:4, 451:3, 454:3, 455:4
    motion pictures made for, 399:1, 442:3, 443:5
    motion pictures shown on, 449:3
    National Broadcasting Co. (NBC), 454:2, 498:4
    network control, 445:4, 454:2
    news aspect—*see* Journalism—broadcast
    one-dimensional, 453:4
    perfection aspect, 443:6
    police shows, 445:2
    politics, coverage of, 207:3, 218:1, 367:8
    potential of, 442:4
    Presidential (U.S.) aspect, 137:3, 447:1
    programming aspect, 443:6, 444:1, 445:4, 450:4, 452:3, 452:5, 455:2, 455:3, 454:2
    Public Broadcasting Service (PBS)/Corp. for Public Broadcasting, 444:4, 446:1
    public-interest aspect, 449:2
    quality aspect, 452:4
    ratings, 362:4, 371:5, 447:5, 453:2
    role identification, 453:5
    sameness, 453:3
    series aspect, 442:3, 450:2
    seriousness aspect, 454:3
    soap operas, 365:3
    sports aspect, 498:4
        baseball, 498:7, 503:4
        football, 490:4, 505:3, 506:3
    stage/theatre aspect, 441:3, 449:3, 451:2
    success, 453:2
    talk shows, 443:3, 443:4, 443:5
    technological aspect, 451:5
    test audience, 447:5
    time aspect, 446:4
    U.S. aspect, 446:1
    violence/sex aspect, 370:2, 443:1, 445:1, 445:2, 445:3, 446:3, 447:2, 448:1, 448:2, 449:1, 450:5, 450:6, 450:7, 451:4, 453:1, 453:3, 454:4, 455:3, 455:5, 465:1, 498:4
    visual aspect, 449:5
    Westerns, 445:2
    writing for, 444:5, 447:4, 451:1
    programs:
        Age of Uncertainty, The, 444:5
        Blue Knight, The, 448:2
        Charlie's Angels, 415:5, 453:2
        David Susskind Show, The, 443:3
        Kojak, 451:3, 451:4
        McMillan and Wife, 446:4

Television (TV) *(continued)*
  programs: *(continued)*
    Roots, 453:1
    Saturday Night Live, 450:1
    Through the Night, 445:5
    Tonight Show, The, 410:1, 443:3
    Waltons, The, 453:5
  See also Acting
Temple, Shirley, 409:5
Tennis:
  behavior, player, 502:5
  business aspect, 498:2
  celebrity aspect, 509:3
  inspiration, player, 493:6
  money aspect, 502:4
  opponent as friend, 509:2
  peaks, 509:4
  seedings, 491:7
  tournaments, 492:5, 507:4
  winning/losing, 509:2
  women, 487:1
Terrorism—*see* Crime
Thailand, 294:5, 299:4
Thalberg, Irving, 400:2
Thatcher, Margaret, 513:4
Third World/developing countries, 98:2, 120:4, 124:3, 252:4, 311:3
  aid for, 114:2
  Communism, 100:2
  debts, default on, 51:3
  human-rights aspect, 110:2, 120:3
  medicine/health aspect, 393:1
  multinational-corporations aspect, 39:4, 44:1
  Soviet aspect, 100:2, 116:2
  U.S. aspect, 103:3, 105:1, 108:4, 111:4, 114:2, 116:2, 249:3, 263:5
Thomson, Virgil, 381:3
Time, 477:5
Titian, 356:5
Tolstoy, Leo, 377:3
Torrijos (Herrera), Omar, 274:6
Tracy, Spencer, 408:3
Trade, foreign/imports/exports, 29:3, 30:3, 40:5, 48:3, 51:2, 106:2, 111:1, 150:1, 263:3, 274:4
  balance of payments/deficit, 31:4, 83:2, 92:3, 140:1
  General Agreement on Tariffs and Trade (GATT), 32:2
  protectionism/barriers, 31:3, 31:4, 32:2, 33:4, 36:3, 41:2, 44:5, 45:3, 321:4
  steel, 32:5, 36:2
Transportation, pp. 228-238
  air transportation:
    fares, 229:4, 230:4, 233:2, 233:3, 233:5, 234:2, 234:4, 236:5

Transportation *(continued)*
  air transportation *(continued)*
    government aspect, 46:5
      Civil Aeronautics Board (CAB), U.S., 229:4, 230:4, 233:5, 234:4, 236:5
      politics, 232:3
      regulation, 229:3, 229:4, 230:2, 232:3, 232:4, 233:3, 234:2, 234:4, 236:5
    hijacking, 236:3
    intrastate airlines, 233:5
    overbooking, 233:1
    "Skytrain," 234:2
    subsidies, 231:2, 234:2
    SST/*Concorde,* 110:4, 229:2, 230:1, 232:2, 236:1
  automobile/car, 233:5
    energy aspect—*see* Energy—oil—transportation
    government aspect, 46:5
    insurance, 228:3, 233:4, 234:3
    personalization, 231:5
    prices, 39:3
    safety aspect, 228:4, 230:3, 231:4, 233:4, 235:4, 236:2, 237:3
    size, 231:3, 231:5, 232:1, 233:4, 235:4, 236:2
  bus, 231:2, 233:5, 234:1, 238:2
  energy aspect—*see* Energy—oil
  environmental aspect—*see* Environment
  Interstate Commerce Commission (ICC), U.S., 237:1
  mass transit, 228:2, 237:4
  modes, 228:1, 233:5, 238:3
  railroads, 228:5, 229:1, 233:5, 238:3
    Amtrak, 231:1, 231:2, 234:1, 235:1
    British, 235:3
    French, 235:3
    German, 235:3
    government aspect, 46:5
    Italian, 235:3
    mergers, 235:3, 238:1
    nationalization, 235:3
    subsidies, 231:1, 231:2, 234:1
    unions, 229:1
  subways, 237:4
  trucking, 236:4, 237:1, 237:2, 238:3
  urban/cities aspect, 228:2
Trotsky, Leon, 55:2
Truman, Harry S., 172:3, 207:2, 344:1
Turkey, 306:3, 317:1, 319:5

U

Uganda, 252:4, 254:6, 262:1
Unemployment—*see* Labor—employment

Union of Soviet Socialist Republics (U.S.S.R.)—*see* Soviet Union
Unions—*see* Labor
United Kingdom/Britain/England:
    bureaucracy, 318:1
    Communism/socialism/Marxism, 316:3, 321:2
    Concorde SST, 110:4, 229:2, 230:1, 232:2, 236:1
    Conservative Party, 321:1
    economic aspect, 306:4, 306:5, 313:2, 323:2, 468:5
        Common Market/EEC, 308:3
        middle class, 309:2
    efficiency, 305:5
    elections, 321:1
    excellence, 311:4
    foreign affairs/policy:
        Africa, 246:1, 261:3
            Rhodesia, 253:3, 256:4, 256:5, 257:1, 257:3
            South Africa, 282:4
        Commonwealth/Empire, 309:5
        Europe, Eastern, 321:2
        India, 288:6
        Ireland/Northern Ireland, 315:1
        Israel, 326:3
        Malta, 315:4
        New Zealand, 295:7
        U.S., 105:3, 113:4, 323:2
            Concorde SST aspect, 229:2, 230:1, 232:2, 236:1
    Great Age, 471:3
    history, 468:5
    humor, 309:2, 318:1
    judiciary/courts, 176:1
    Labor Party, 316:3, 321:2
    Liberal Party, 321:1
    literature/books, 381:3
    medicine/health aspect, 388:3, 393:2, 394:3
    monarchy, 318:3
    motion-pictures aspect, 417:4
    North Sea oil, 306:5
    railroads, 235:3
    Silver Jubilee, 308:2
    stage/theatre aspect, 433:2, 436:3, 439:5
    television aspect, 446:1
    woman Prime Minister, 513:4
United Nations (UN), 102:1, 106:5
    agencies of, 349:6
    air-hijacking resolution, 236:3
    Ambassador, position of, 350:2, 350:3, 350:4
    a forum, 347:5
    human-rights aspect, 345:5, 349:2, 349:6
    League of Nations, 308:3
    location of sessions, 347:6
    salaries at, 119:2

United Nations (UN) *(continued)*
    universality, 349:6
    U.S. aspect, 347:7
    See also specific countries and areas
United States (U.S.)—*see* America
Urban affairs/cities, 23:6, 162:3, 169:1, pp. 239-242
    business aspect, 241:5
    crime aspect, 56:4, 58:6
    downtown, 242:4
    exodus from, 239:2, 240:1, 240:3
    families aspect, 242:3
    Federal aspect, 239:2, 239:3, 239:4, 240:1, 240:4, 241:1, 241:4, 241:6, 242:1, 242:2
    fiscal aspect, 239:3, 239:4, 239:5, 239:6
    Mayors, 74:2, 209:3, 241:1, 241:6, 242:3
        black, 19:4
    middle-class aspect, 240:3, 242:3
    neighborhoods, 242:1
    poverty aspect, 224:5
    purpose of, 241:3
    suburbs, 23:6, 239:2, 240:1, 240:4
    tax aspect, 239:6, 240:1, 242:1
    transportation aspect, 228:2
    See also specific cities

V

Valenti, Jack, 445:4
Values, 13:2, 468:3, 475:5
Vance, Cyrus R., 108:3, 114:4, 123:5, 192:5
van Gogh, Vincent, 398:6
Vanity, 476:5
Venezuela, 264:3
    human-rights aspect, 118:1
Verdi, Giuseppe, 429:4
Vice-Presidency, U.S., 142:2, 142:3
Vietnam:
    foreign affairs/policy:
        Asia, 293:5
        Canada, 282:4
        France, 299:2
        Korea, South, 286:2
        Soviet Union, 287:4
        U.S., 99:2, 102:2, 103:4, 106:1, 114:1, 173:3, 287:4, 290:3, 290:4, 293:4, 293:5, 295:3, 296:3, 297:1, 298:2, 299:5, 300:6, 464:4
            pardon for war resisters—*see* Defense— pardon
    independence, 289:4
    peace aspect, 299:2
    redevelopment, 293:6
Volunteers in Service to America (VISTA), 196:2
Vorster, John, 253:5

W

Walker, Deak, 487:5

Wanamaker, John, 49:1

War/peace, 98:4, 107:1, 111:4, 345:1, 345:2, 345:3, 345:4, 346:1, 346:2, 346:3, 346:4, 346:6, 347:1, 347:2, 347:3, 347:4, 348:1, 348:2, 349:1, 349:3, 349:4, 349:5, 350:1
 See also specific wars

Warner, Jack L., 414:1

Warnke, Paul C., 191:4, 192:4

Washington, George, 118:1, 279:2

Watergate—*see* Politics

Wayne, John, 453:2

Wealth/money/affluence, 15:4, 457:3, 457:6, 465:4, 466:4, 473:3, 474:3

Webern, Anton von, 431:5

Welfare—*see* Social welfare

Wells, H.G., 68:2

Wilde, Oscar, 439:1, 442:6

Wilder, Billy, 401:5, 408:1

Williams, J. R., 379:3

Wilson, Woodrow, 98:5, 99:4

Wolfe, Thomas, 411:4

Women/women's rights, 18:2, pp. 512-519
 black aspect, 513:2
 business/careers aspect, 515:6, 516:1, 516:5, 517:4, 517:5, 517:6, 518:1, 518:4
 equal pay, 512:5
 Equal Rights Amendment (ERA), 164:4, 191:2, 512:5, 513:1, 514:2, 515:3, 517:6, 518:3, 519:1
 family/marriage/children aspect, 512:4, 516:4, 516:5, 517:1, 517:4, 517:5
 in Italy, 514:3
 liberation/movement, 512:4, 514:1, 514:3, 514:4, 515:1, 516:1, 516:2, 516:5, 517:5, 518:1, 518:2
 male aspect, 513:3, 513:5, 515:1, 516:3, 516:6, 518:1
 dominance, 512:3
 masculinizing of, 517:1
 in military, 188:1, 191:2, 515:2
 in motion pictures—*see* Motion pictures
 in news media, 371:3
 options, 512:2, 517:6
 parity, 512:3
 potentials/abilities, 517:2, 517:3, 519:2

Women/women's rights *(continued)*
 power aspect, 512:1, 514:4, 516:3
 as President/Prime Minister, 513:2, 513:4, 514:4
 as priests, 480:7
 romantic aspect, 518:2
 in science, 485:4
 separatism, 513:3
 in sports, 487:1
 stereotypes, 513:2, 515:4, 516:4
 successful women, 514:3
 as writers, 515:1

World War I, 347:3

World War II, 36:3, 347:3

World War III, 107:7

Work—*see* Labor

Writing—*see* Literature; Motion pictures—screenwriting; Stage—playwriting; Television

Y

Yemen, South, 341:3, 361:4

Young, Andrew, 107:2, 113:4, 114:4, 114:5, 120:1, 245:4, 250:2, 252:6, 347:5

Youskevitch, Igor, 432:4

Youth—*see* Age

Yugoslavia, 283:2
 Communism, 322:1

Z

Zaire, 249:5
 Communism/Marxism, 259:1
 foreign affairs/policy:
 Angola, 251:4, 252:6, 261:2
 Soviet Union, 251:4, 255:6
 U.S., 113:4, 248:7, 252:6, 261:2
 Katangese aspect, 255:6, 261:2

Zambia, 250:5, 251:3
 Communism/Marxism, 259:1
 Rhodesian aspect, 256:5
 U.S. aspect, 248:7

Zanuck, Darryl F., 400:2

Zola, Emile, 377:3